Handbook of
Family
Measurement
Techniques

Authors

Thomas N. Bradbury, Ph.D., Clinical Intern, Neuropsychiatric Institute, University of California (Los Angeles)

Cheryl Buehler, Ph.D., Associate Professor of Child and Family Studies, University of Tennessee (Knoxville)

Frank D. Fincham, Ph.D., Associate Professor of Psychology, University of Illinois (Urbana-Champaign)

George W. Holden, Ph.D., Assistant Professor of Psychology, University of Texas (Austin)

Gary R. Lee, Ph.D., Professor of Sociology, University of Florida

Barry F. Perlmutter, Ph.D., Assistant Professor of Educational and Counseling Psychology, University of the Pacific

Walter R. Schumm, Ph.D., Associate Professor of Human Development and Family Studies, Kansas State University

Constance L. Shehan, Ph.D., Associate Professor of Sociology, University of Florida

Murray A. Straus, Ph.D., Professor of Sociology, University of New Hampshire

John Touliatos, Ed.D., Professor of Human Development and Family Studies, Texas Christian University

Handbook of
Family
Measurement
Techniques

John Touliatos
Barry F. Perlmutter
Murray A. Straus

Editors

SAGE PUBLICATIONS
The Publishers of Professional Social Science
Newbury Park   London   New Delhi

*To Paula and Kara, to Maryanne and the kids,
and to William Sewell*

For information address:

SAGE Publications, Inc.
2111 West Hillcrest Drive
Newbury Park, California 91320

SAGE Publications Ltd.
28 Banner Street
London EC1Y 8QE
England

SAGE Publications India Pvt. Ltd.
M-32 Market
Greater Kailash I
New Delhi 110 048 India

Printed in the United States of America

Library of Congress Cataloging-in-Publication Data

Touliatos, John.
    Handbook of family measurement techniques / John Touliatos, Barry
F. Perlmutter, Murray A. Straus.
      p. cm.
    Bibliography: p.
    Includes indexes.
    ISBN 0-8039-3121-2
    1. Family—Testing—Abstracts. 2. Psychological tests—Abstracts.
I. Perlmutter, Barry F. II. Straus, Murray Arnold, 1926–
III. Title.
HQ728.T68 1989
306.85—dc20   89-10542
FIRST PRINTING, 1990   CIP

Contents

Preface

The 976 instruments abstracted in this handbook represent the development of measurement within the family field over the past 50-plus years. Of these instruments, more than half have been used in published reports since 1975. These more recently active instruments are afforded relatively detailed treatment. Those for which evidence of recent published activity was not uncovered are also included but in an abbreviated form. Abstracts are grouped according to five general categories (dimensions of interaction, intimacy and family values, parenthood, roles and power, adjustment), with historically detailed chapters introducing each area.

It is anticipated that this book will prove useful for clinicians at all levels as well as for both beginning and sophisticated researchers. Individual abstracts provide general information regarding the content and procedures associated with each instrument, in addition to reliability and validity information and appropriate references. From this perspective, the book is also intended for use in training graduate students enrolled in family-related programs, in general, and family measurement courses, in particular.

We are especially grateful to the over 300 authors of instruments who responded to our request for materials. In addition, we thank the authors who prepared chapters for this book. Also, this handbook would not have been possible without the foundation built by two earlier works by Straus (*Family Measurement Techniques: Abstracts of Published Instruments, 1935–1965,* 1969) and Straus and Brown (*Family Measurement Techniques: Abstracts of Published Instruments, 1935–1974,* 1978). Special thanks are also due to the Texas Christian University Mary Couts Burnett Interlibrary Loan and Acquisitions divisions. Finally, for their conscientious work and editorial guidance, we express our appreciation to Mitch Allen, Executive Editor, Astrid Virding, Senior Production Editor, and Amy Kleiman, Production Editor at Sage Publications, and Janet Brown, Manuscript Editor. Partial support for this project was provided by Texas Christian University and a grant from the TCU Research Fund.

Introduction

The increased sophistication of the family field over the past half century has resulted in a greater awareness of the need for assessment technology. While interest in the family is centuries old, the development of instruments used in understanding family variables has received major attention since only about the mid-1930s. Since that time, researchers and clinicians have used a plethora of instruments of varying types, levels of quality, and foci.

The *Handbook of Family Measurement Techniques* includes abstracts of nearly 1,000 instruments, over 500 of which have been cited in the published literature since 1975. While each instrument is described in some detail, more in-depth treatments including discussions of reliability and validity are presented for these more recent measurement instruments.

Instruments have been organized into five primary (dimensions of interaction, intimacy and family values, parenthood, roles and power, adjustment), and sixteen secondary, areas (see Table I.1). Each primary area is introduced by a chapter designed to summarize the intermingling of conceptual development and measurement concerns (see Chapters 2 through 6). These introductory essays have been written by individuals with particular knowledge and expertise in each of the five areas. These authors have concentrated their efforts on integrating conceptual evaluation with progress in measurement. Within the chapter text that precedes the abstracts for each area, references to abstract numbers appear in italics.

Throughout the organization and writing of this handbook, the primary objective has been to provide a useful compendium, allowing researchers and clinicians alike access to up-to-date information on existing instruments. In keeping with this perspective, three indexes are provided to assist readers in locating desired and/or appropriate instruments: (1) author index, with listings by first, second, and all subsequent authors; (2) title index; (3) classification index, with entries arranged according to the identified subcategories and primary interactants. Within groupings in this third index, instruments are arranged alphabetically by author(s). Further details regarding the classification system are provided later in this chapter.

IDENTIFICATION AND SELECTION OF INSTRUMENTS

Research for this book was conducted to identify instruments used in assessing family-related variables. The literature search, which required approximately three years and included published sources since 1975, involved an exhaustive review of some 60 journals (1975–1986) and a less detailed search involving scores of others. Additionally, a few select journals (e.g., *Family Relations, Journal of Consulting and Clinical Psychology, Journal of Family Psychology,* and *Journal of Marriage and the Family*) were surveyed on into 1988. Several authors also continued to submit post-1986 materials, up until the last possible moment. Abstracts of older instruments (pre-1975) were developed primarily from information in Straus and Brown (1978) and were supplemented by additional materials where necessary.

In order for an instrument to be included, each of the following criteria needed to be met:

(1)   The instrument must either have been described in part or in full in some conveniently available published source (i.e., excluding unpublished manuscripts and documents such as theses and dissertations).

(2)   Instruments that fulfilled all other criteria but did not appear in their entirety in a published work must have been provided to the authors of the handbook with permission to deposit the entire instrument and other relevant information with the National Auxiliary Publications Service (NAPS-3).

(3)   The instrument must have provided a classification or numerical composite based on the sum of the scores from three or more items. (In the case of observational systems or projective techniques, any set of categories that provided a quantitative score was included.)

(4)   The behaviors or characteristics measured must have referred to the subjects' actions or predispositions to act in family-related roles.

(5)   The instrument must have been sufficiently described so as to facilitate replication of results.

Various professional directories were consulted for current addresses of identified instrument authors. Information regarding the project, criteria for inclusion of instruments, and requests for detailed descriptions were mailed to all identified authors for whom addresses were located. Requests included specific concerns to be addressed and the format to be followed when submitting materials for possible inclusion in the handbook.

Of about 625 authors contacted, representing around 750 instruments, slightly less than 50% responded with descriptions from which abstracts could be developed. Additionally, several authors submitted materials on related instruments for which information had not been directly requested. In all, authors provided abstracts and supplemental materials on about 360 instruments in a format approximating that which was requested. Of these instruments, roughly 335 satisfied the five criteria listed above. With few exceptions, where authors provided appropriate information and the instruments were judged to satisfy the listed criteria, final abstracts of those instruments have been included in the handbook. Final abstracts were developed based on all materials, including those submitted by authors and those obtained through other sources.

Where instrument descriptions were not directly provided by authors, further research was conducted to uncover materials from which (1) a judgment could be made regarding the appropriateness of the instrument for inclusion, and (2) a complete abstract could be generated. Information for approximately 275 additional instruments was located in this manner. Restrictions of space and time, however, dictated that only 169 of this latter group be included. Selection of these instruments was based on three considerations: adequacy of representation, at that time, of various subcategories and perspectives within the book; availability of reliability and validity information; and number and quality of references.

FORMAT FOR ABSTRACTS

Each abstract contains the last names and initials of all authors, the full title of the instrument, information regarding availability of the complete instrument, a statement indicating variables measured, an instrument description, and at least one published reference in which use of the instrument is described. The titles and authorships listed are those provided by the instrument authors. Where such information was not directly provided, sequences of authorship and/or titles of instruments were assigned based on interpretations of the literature. For abstracts of instruments that are both pre-1975 and less active, with only a couple of exceptions, only one reference was included. For more recent and/or active instruments, up to four references were included. Where more than four references were identified, attempts were made to include the original, the latest, and at least one on which the instrument author was not listed. In addition, a mix of sources including journals and books from various disciplines was included wherever possible. In some cases, supplemental information was judged to increase the value of the abstract substantially and additional citations were included. Considering limitations of space and the desire to provide as much relevant information as possible, it was decided that references would only be listed for sources in which the instruments were discussed. While theoretical backgrounds and sources of additional information, as well as relevant authors and publication years of references, are noted within some abstracts, complete citations for most of those references have been omitted. It is assumed that investigators desiring further information on these sources will be able to locate the desired citations utilizing the information provided and other library tools such as the *Social Sciences Citation Index* or *Psychological Abstracts.*

Abstracts of these more recent and/or active instruments also received more detailed treatment, including a statement regarding the type of instrument, sample items[1] (except in a few cases where permission was denied), a more complete description of the instrument and procedures, and a comments section including reliability and validity information uncovered during the research and preparation of the volume. Psychometric information presented in the abstracts has been stated objectively. Phrases designed to qualify the merit of instruments or levels of significance (e.g., "significantly different," "very worthwhile," "highly reliable") were avoided. Rather, numbers (e.g., alpha = .68, r = .80) were reported whenever such information was uncovered and appropriate. Validity information, likewise, is presented as objectively as possible. In most cases criteria used by authors in assessing validity are specified. However, conclusions regarding the validity or invalidity of instruments have been omitted.

CLASSIFICATION OF INSTRUMENTS

Instruments were assigned to subcategories based on a Q-sort conducted by the editors. The resulting 16 categories were further combined into five primary areas upon which the handbook is organized. In some instances, the fit between individual instruments and subcategories was necessarily less than ideal. However, in the vast majority of instances, this assignment to subcategories assisted in the development of a coherent and meaningful system for identifying instruments. One further obstacle concerned the means by which subcategories were to be combined into primary areas of emphasis. Readers are urged to view this organization as approximating rather than defining the state of the field.

In addition to organizing instruments by subcategories, an attempt was made to define the primary focus of and interactants assessed by the instruments. Preceding each entry, users of the handbook will note a series of letters and numbers. These symbols were designed to aid in further understanding the purpose and content of the instrument. While developing a familiarity with this system of notation may be less than convenient for the initial or casual user of this volume, more sophisticated or regular users are likely to find this system to be of substantial value. For those readers who desire not to be bothered by this system, the remainder of the book, including author and title indexes and categories of classification, will still prove useful.

Table I.1 describes this classification procedure. Readers should note that the system is used throughout the book in classifying individual instruments as well as for ordering instruments within the third index.

Table I.1 Instrument Codes

Number Codes:

  I. Dimensions of interaction
      1. communication
      2. life-style
      3. networks (kinship, social support)
      4. multidimensional perspectives (overall interaction)

 II. Intimacy and family values
      1. family values
      2. marital relations (marital/family adjustment)
      3. love (liking, affection, trust)
      4. sex
      5. personal/interpersonal perceptions

III. Parenthood
      1. pregnancy, childbearing, and transition to parenthood
      2. parenting

 IV. Roles and power
      1. roles
      2. power

  V. Adjustment
      1. family functioning (overall functioning, adjustment, health)
      2. stress
      3. divorce, including separation and remarriage

Letter Codes:

  Interactants
      a   = husband-wife
      b   = parent-child
      c   = nuclear family
      d   = extended family
      e   = others outside the family
      f   = siblings
      g   = intrapsychic processes

  Focus of Study
      P   = parents
      C   = child
      H   = husband
      W   = wife
      O   = any combination of the above; if there is no capital letter code given, it is under-
            stood to be "O"

Example: III-2/b/g/C measures the child's perception of parent-child interactions. The child
         is the focus of the instrument, even though someone else (e.g., mother) may be
         the informant.
         III-2 = Parenting is the primary variable measured.
         b/g = Primary interactants are parents and their children, with a secondary focus
         on intrapsychic processes (how the child feels about the interaction).
         C = The focus of the study is the child rather than the parent.

JOURNAL ABBREVIATIONS

Names of journals listed in references for individual abstracts have been abbreviated. Abbreviations for journals that are indexed within the *Social Sciences Citation Index* (*SSCI*) are identical to those found in the *SSCI*. Other journals have been assigned abbreviations consistent with the form found in the *SSCI*. Table I.2 contains a complete listing of abbreviations found in the handbook.

ORDERING UNPUBLISHED INSTRUMENTS

A number of the instruments described in this book are not printed in full in a conveniently available published source. In such instances, as a service to readers, a copy of the complete instrument has been obtained from the author(s) and deposited with the National Auxiliary Publications Service (NAPS). A copy of an instrument deposited with NAPS may be secured by directly contacting NAPS and citing the document number indicated in the listing below.

Order from National Auxiliary Publications, c/o Microfiche Publications, P.O. Box 3513, Grand Central Station, New York, NY 10163–3513; telephone: 516/481–2300. Due to possible changes in microfiche and/or copying charges, specific information regarding charges should be obtained prior to ordering.

Because there are multiauthored deposits and it is impossible to split a deposit to print only the needed instrument, an order might contain several measures other than the one being requested. However, instruments deposited as part of this project (i.e., NAPS-3) have been grouped alphabetically by author within the subcategories used in this volume. Therefore, any additional instruments included in a NAPS-3 document will likely be from the same general area. Instruments deposited in conjunction with earlier projects (Straus, 1969; Straus & Brown, 1978) are indicated under the headings NAPS-1 and NAPS-2, respectively. These instruments were grouped into documents by last name of first author only.

If an instrument author him- or herself has deposited a copy of a measure with NAPS or some other depository (e.g., ETS: 609/734–5686; ADI: 202/707–5640; Select Press: 415/924–1612; University Microfilms: 313/761–4700), this information is given in the abstract. Ordering information for author-deposited NAPS instruments is the same as for NAPS instruments deposited as part of this project.

NOTE

1. Sample items were taken verbatim from the original instruments.

Table I.2 Abbreviations of Journal Names

Adolescence (Adolescence)
Altern Lifestyles (Alternative Lifestyles)
Am Acad Chld Adol Psychi (American Academy of Child and Adolescent Psychiatry)
Am Behav Sc (American Behavioral Scientist)
Am Cath Sociol R (American Catholic Sociological Review)
Am J Comm P (American Journal of Community Psychology)
Am J Fam Th (American Journal of Family Therapy)
Am J Ment D (American Journal of Mental Deficiency)
Am J Orthop (American Journal of Orthopsychiatry)
Am J Psychi (American Journal of Psychiatry)
Am J Sociol (American Journal of Sociology)
Am Psychol (American Psychologist)
Am Sociol R (American Sociological Review)
Appl Psyc Meas (Applied Psychological Measurement)
Arch G Psyc (Archives of General Psychiatry)
Arch Psychol (Archives of Psychology)
Arch Sex Be (Archives of Sexual Behavior)
Aus J Educ (Australian Journal of Education)
Aust J Psyc (Australian Journal of Psychology)
Behav Assess (Behavioral Assessment)
Behav Modif (Behavior Modification)
Behav Res T (Behavior Research and Therapy)
Behav Sci (Behavioral Science)
Behav Ther (Behavior Therapy)
Beh Sci Res (Behavior Science Research)
Birth (Birth)
Br J Cl Psy (British Journal of Clinical Psychology)
Br J Ed Psy (British Journal of Educational Psychology)
Br J Med Ps (British Journal of Medical Psychology)
Br J Psych (British Journal of Psychiatry)
Br J Psycho (British Journal of Psychology)
Br J Sex Med (British Journal of Sexual Medicine)
Br J Soc Psych (British Journal of Social Psychology)
Can J Beh S (Canadian Journal of Behavioural Science)
Can J Comm Men Health (Canadian Journal of Community Mental Health)
Can J Psychi (Canadian Journal of Psychiatry)
Child Abuse & Neglect (Child Abuse and Neglect)
Child Dev (Child Development)
Child Fam Beh Ther (Child and Family Behavior Therapy)
Child Psychi Hum Dev (Child Psychiatry and Human Development)
Child St J (Child Study Journal)
Child Welf (Child Welfare)
Comm Monogr (Communication Monographs)
Comm Q (Communication Quarterly)
Cont Ed Fam Phys (Continuing Education for the Family Physician)
Cont Fam Th (Contemporary Family Therapy)
DARCEE Papers and Reports (DARCEE Papers and Reports)
Demography (Demography)
Devel Psyc (Developmental Psychology)
Early Child Dev Care (Early Childhood Development and Care)

Table I.2 continued

Early Child Res Q (Early Childhood Research Quarterly)
Educ Psyc M (Educational and Psychological Measurement)
Educ Psy Res (Educational and Psychological Research)
Educ Res (Educational Research)
Elem Sch J (Elementary School Journal)
Except Chil (Exceptional Children)
Fam (The Family)
Fam Coord (Family Coordinator)
Fam Perspect (Family Perspective)
Fam Process (Family Process)
Fam Relat (Family Relations)
Fam Sys Med (Family Systems Medicine)
Fam Ther (Family Therapy)
Genet Psych Mono (Genetic Psychology Monographs)
Genet Soc Gen Psy Mon (Genetic, Social, and General Psychology Monographs)
Gerontol (Gerontology)
Group Psychoth Psychodrama (Group Psychotherapy and Psychodrama)
Health Psyc (Health Psychology)
Hispan J Beh Sci (Hispanic Journal of Behavioral Sciences)
Home Ec Res J (Home Economics Research Journal)
Human Dev (Human Development)
Hum Comm Res (Human Communication Research)
Infant Ment Health J (Infant Mental Health Journal)
Int J Aging Hum Dev (International Journal of Aging and Human Development)
Int J Comp (International Journal of Comparative Sociology)
Int J Eating Disord (International Journal of Eating Disorders)
Int J Exp Res Educ (International Journal of Experimental Research in Education)
Int J Psycho (International Journal of Psychology)
Int J Sociol Fam (International Journal of Sociology of the Family)
Int J Soc Psychiat (International Journal of Social Psychiatry)
Iowa State J of Research (Iowa State Journal of Research)
Iss Health Care Women (Issues in Health Care of Women)
J Abn C Psy (Journal of Abnormal Child Psychology)
J Abn Psych (Journal of Abnormal Psychology)
J Abn Soc Psy (Journal of Abnormal and Social Psychology)
J Adolescen (Journal of Adolescence)
J Adol Res (Journal of Adolescent Research)
J Aging Stud (Journal of Aging Studies)
J Am Acad Child Adol Psychi (Journal of the American Academy of Child and Adolescent Psychiatry)
J Appl Be A (Journal of Applied Behavior Analysis)
J Appl Beh Sci (Journal of Applied Behavioral Science)
J Appl Comm Res (Journal of Applied Communication Research)
J Appl Devel Psych (Journal of Applied Developmental Psychology)
J Appl Psyc (Journal of Applied Psychology)
J Appl Soc P (Journal of Applied Social Psychology)
J Behav Assess (Journal of Behavioral Assessment)
J Behav Med (Journal of Behavioral Medicine)
J Beh Th Exp Psychi (Journal of Behavior Therapy and Experimental Psychiatry)

(*continued*)

Table I.2 continued

J Child Psychol Psychi (Journal of Child Psychology and Psychiatry and Related Disciplines)
J Clin Child Psych (Journal of Clinical Child Psychology)
J Clin Psyc (Journal of Clinical Psychology)
J Coll Stud Pers (Journal of College Student Personnel)
J Comm (Journal of Communication)
J Comm Psyc (Journal of Community Psychology)
J Comp Fam Studies (Journal of Comparative Family Studies)
J Cons Clin (Journal of Consulting and Clinical Psychology)
J Cons Psych (Journal of Consulting Psychology)
J Cont Psych (Journal of Contemporary Psychology)
J Coun Psyc (Journal of Counseling Psychology)
J Couns Psychother (Journal of Counseling and Psychotherapy)
J Cross-Cul (Journal of Cross-Cultural Psychology)
J Dev Beh Ped (Journal of Developmental and Behavioral Pediatrics)
J Divorce (Journal of Divorce)
J Early Adol (Journal of Early Adolescence)
J Educ Psyc (Journal of Educational Psychology)
J Educ Soc (Journal of Educational Sociology)
J Exp Educ (Journal of Experimental Education)
J Fam Couns (Journal of Family Counseling)
J Fam Iss (Journal of Family Issues)
J Fam Psy (Journal of Family Psychology)
J Fam Ther (Journal of Family Therapy)
J Fam Violence (Journal of Family Violence)
J Genet Psy (Journal of Genetic Psychology)
J Gen Psych (Journal of General Psychology)
J Gerontol (Journal of Gerontology)
J Health So (Journal of Health and Social Behavior)
J Home Ec (Journal of Home Economics)
J Homosexual (Journal of Homosexuality)
J Housing Eld (Journal of Housing for the Elderly)
J Indiv Psy (Journal of Individual Psychology)
J Leisure Res (Journal of Leisure Research)
J Mar Fam (Journal of Marriage and the Family)
J Mar Fam Th (Journal of Marriage and Family Therapy)
J Ment Sci (Journal of Mental Science)
J Nerv Ment (Journal of Nervous and Mental Disease)
J Occup Psy (Journal of Occupational Psychology)
JOGN Nursing (JOGN Nursing)
J Pers Assess (Journal of Personality Assessment)
J Personal (Journal of Personality)
J Pers Soc Psy (Journal of Personality and Social Psychology)
J Polit Mil (Journal of Political and Military Sociology)
J Populat (Journal of Population)
J Projective Tech Pers Assess (Journal of Projective Techniques and Personality Assessment)
J Psychol (Journal of Psychology)
J Psychol Hum Sex (Journal of Psychology and Human Sexuality)
J Psycholin Res (Journal of Psycholinguistic Research)
J Psychopat Beh Assess (Journal of Psychopathology and Behavioral Assessment)

(continued)

Table I.2 continued

J Psychosom (Journal of Psychosomatic Research)
J Res Child Educ (Journal of Research in Childhood Education)
J Res Crime (Journal of Research in Crime and Delinquency)
J Res Pers (Journal of Research in Personality)
J Sex Educ Th (Journal of Sex Education and Therapy)
J Sex Mar Ther (Journal of Sex and Marital Therapy)
J Sex Res (Journal of Sex Research)
J Sci Study of Relig (Journal of the Scientific Study of Religion)
J Soc Behav Pers (Journal of Social Behavior and Personality)
J Soc Clin Psy (Journal of Social and Clinical Psychology)
J Soc Issue (Journal of Social Issues)
J Soc Pers Relat (Journal of Social and Personal Relationships)
J Soc Psych (Journal of Social Psychology)
J Soc Serv Res (Journal of Social Service Research)
J Spec Grp Wk (Journal of Specialists in Group Work)
J Stud Alc (Journal of Studies on Alcohol)
J Vocat Beh (Journal of Vocational Behavior)
J Ado Health Care (Journal of Adolescent Health Care)
J Youth Adoles (Journal of Youth and Adolescence)
Law Human (Law and Human Behavior)
Mar Fam Couns Q (Marriage and Family Counselors Quarterly)
Mar Fam Living (Marriage and Family Living)
Mar Fam Rev (Marriage and Family Review)
Mental Hygiene (Mental Hygiene)
Merrill-Pal (Merrill-Palmer Quarterly)
Mon S Res C (Monographs of the Society for Research in Child Development)
Multi Exp Cl (Multivariate Experimental Clinical Research)
Nurs Res (Nursing Research)
Pac Sociol Rev (Pacific Sociological Review)
Pediat Nurs (Pediatric Nursing)
Pers Indiv Diff (Personality and Individual Differences)
Pers Soc Psy Bul (Personality and Social Psychology Bulletin)
Pert Mot Sk (Perceptual and Motor Skills)
Pop Stud (Population Studies)
Prof Psych (Professional Psychology)
Psych Docs (Psychological Documents)
Psychiat Clin N Amer (Psychiatric Clinics of North America)
Psychiat Q (Psychiatric Quarterly)
Psychiatry (Psychiatry)
Psych Wom Q (Psychology of Women Quarterly)
Psychol B (Psychological Bulletin)
Psychol Mono (Psychological Monographs)
Psychologia (Psychologia)
Psychology (Psychology)
Psychol Rep (Psychological Reports)
Psychol Sch (Psychology in the Schools)
Psychonom Sci (Psychonomic Science)
Psychophysl (Psychophysiology)

(continued)

Table I.2 continued

Psychos Med (Psychosomatic Medicine)
Psychother (Psychotherapy)
Res Aging (Research on Aging)
Res Nurs H (Research in Nursing and Health)
Res Studies St Col of Wash (Research Studies of the State College of Washington)
Rural Socio (Rural Sociology)
Sch Couns (The School Counselor)
Sex Mar Ther (Sexual and Marital Therapy)
Sex Roles (Sex Roles)
Small Gr B (Small Group Behavior)
Soc Beh Per (Social Behavior and Personality)
Social Forc (Social Forces)
Social Ind Res (Social Indicators Research)
Social Inq (Sociological Inquiry)
Social Prob (Social Problems)
Social Psych Q (Social Psychology Quarterly)
Social Sci (Social Science)
Social Sci Info (Social Science Information)
Social Sci Med (Social Science and Medicine)
Social Sci Q (Social Science Quarterly)
Social Serv Rev (Social Service Review)
Social Work (Social Work)
Social Wrk Res Abs (Social Work Research and Abstracts)
Sociol Anal (Sociological Analysis)
Sociol Educ (Sociology of Education)
Sociol Forum (Sociological Forum)
Sociol Q (Sociological Quarterly)
Sociol Soc Res (Sociology and Social Research)
Sociol Spec (Sociological Spectrum)
Sociometry (Sociometry)
South J Educ Res (Southern Journal of Educational Research)
Speech Mono (Speech Monographs)
Theory into Practice (Theory into Practice)
U of Iowa Studies in Child Welfare (University of Iowa Studies in Child Welfare)
U of MN Child Welfare Monographs (University of Minnesota Child Welfare Monographs)
Violence and Victims (Violence and Victims)
Wellness Persp (Wellness Perspectives)
Western J of Black Studies (Western Journal of Black Studies)
Youth Soc (Youth and Society)

REFERENCES

Straus, M. A. (1969) *Family measurement techniques: Abstracts of published instruments, 1935–1965.* Minneapolis: University of Minnesota Press.

Straus, M. A., & Brown, B. W. (1978) *Family measurement techniques: Abstracts of published instruments, 1935–1974.* Minneapolis: University of Minnesota Press.

Table I.3 Ordering from NAPS-1 and NAPS-2

Doc. No.	Pages	Authors' Last Name
NAPS-1:		
00390	60	Adams to Bowerman & Kinch; Nicholson
00391	59	Bronfenbrenner & Devereux to Buerkle & Badgley
00392	62	Chang & Block to Goodrich et al.
00393	60	Harris et al. to Huntington
00394	42	Kirkpatrick & Hobart to Lyle & Levitt
00395	74	Morgan
00396	60	Pikas to Roe & Siegelman
00397	57	Samenfink to Stryker
00398	60	Tyler et al. to Walters
00399	50	Williams to Zuk et al.
NAPS-2:	85	Adamek to Beier-Sternberg
03122		
03123	55	Berardo to Bowerman
03125	65	Bronfenbrenner to Bronson
03126	75	Bruce to Cvetkovich & Lonner
03127	54	Danziger & Greenglass to Driskoll et al.
03128	95	Fink et al.
03129	53	Edwards & Brauburger to Golightly
03130	195	Gottman
03131	83	Hawkins to Holroyd
03132	52	Hurley to Kahn
03133	98	Kieren & Tallman
03134	68	Kando to Khatri
03135	69	Kilpatrick & Smith to Leton
03136	77	Levinger
03137	73	Leventhal & Stollak to Linden & Hackler
03138	72	Lindholm & Touliatos to Lytton
03139	93	Marwell to McDaniel
03140	91	McLeod
03141	26	Meadow & Schlesinger
03142	85	Nakamura to Olson
03143	58	Orlofsky to Pless & Satterwhite
03144	84	Pratt to Reiss
03145	97	Riskin
03146	51	Roman & Bauman to Schultz
03147	82	Schwarzweller & Lyson to Stollack
03148	97	Straus
03149	62	Straus & Cytrynbaum to Szyrynski
03150	96	Tallman et al. to Weiss & Bleckman
03151	67	Wells to Winch & Green
03152	67	Winder & Rau to Zigler et al.

Table I.4 Ordering from NAPS-3

Doc. No.	Pages	Subcategory	Instrument (Abstract) Nos.	Authors
04661	67	I-1 I-2	1, 2, 11, 14, 21, 25, 31	Ahrons & Goldsmith to Schultz
04662	75	I-3	34, 37	Boss et al. to Oliveri & Reiss
04663	90	I-4	40, 42, 53, 56, 61, 64	Armsden & Greensberg to Gilbert et al.
04664	95	I-4	67, 68, 72, 84, 92, 93, 94, 97, 99, 107, 110	Hannum & Casalnuovo to Wachowiak & Bragg
04665	42	II-1 II-2	124 135, 140, 142, 147, 148, 153, 159, 165, 169	Gallagher to Starr & Mann
04666	108	II-3 II-4 II-5	180, 193, 202, 206, 209, 213 222 239, 241	Conger to Hunt & Hunt
04667	95	III-1 III-2	248, 250, 252 259, 261, 262, 274, 275, 276, 280, 282, 283, 285, 286, 289, 290, 295	Englund to Falender & Mehrabian
04668	93	III-2	301, 310, 315, 318, 319, 321, 323, 328, 332, 333, 334, 335, 336	Gjerde et al. to Pumroy
04669	84	III-2	337, 338, 340	Rickard et al. to Roehling & Robin
04670	89	III-2	345, 346, 350, 351, 353	Rothbaum & Schneider-Rosen to Schumm
04671	95	III-2	356, 357, 359, 360, 361, 362, 363, 364	Siegelman & Roe to Smith
04672	81	III-2	366, 369, 371	Stolberg & Ullman to Wasik & Bryant
04673	77	III-2	372, 373	Wolf et al. to Worell & Worell
04674	124	IV-1	381, 382, 384, 385, 387, 388, 391, 395, 399, 407	Coleman et al. to Thomas et al.
04675	68	IV-2	410, 413, 414, 416, 419, 420, 422, 424, 426, 430, 431, 432, 433, 434	Bagarozzi to Stanley
04676	72	V-1	442, 445, 456, 457, 459	Fristad to Skinner et al.
04677	10	V-1	462	van der Veen
04678	99	V-2	471, 477, 479, 480, 481, 482	Koch to Zimmerman
04679	113	V-3	483, 484, 485, 489, 491, 492, 493, 496, 498, 499, 501, 503	Ahrons to Shiller

1 Evolution of the Family Field: Measurement Principles and Techniques

WALTER R. SCHUMM

Prior to the publication of this volume, there were approximately 30 books and 15 review articles dedicated to the review of family measures. Those volumes currently available are listed in Table 1.1, while some of the more notable articles are presented in Table 1.2. The median number of family measures discussed in these books is generally about 60. It is interesting that the more recent volumes (i.e., since 1982) have tended to include fewer measures yet have tended, more often, to discuss issues of reliability and validity. In addition, several of these volumes have presented complete instruments. As might be expected, those texts examining fewer measures have tended to provide more detailed information regarding specific items, norms, reliability, and validity of various instruments. Even review articles have tended to report more information on reliability and validity, while describing a relatively smaller number of measures.

The researcher or clinician is presented with a dilemma. Most sources either provide a large number of instruments with minimal information about each or a far more select representation of the field where each instrument is extensively examined. An additional problem in this latter case, however, is the availability of reviews and/or instruments to individuals with areas of interest that have not been directly addressed. One further area of concern that has received extensive attention in the above-mentioned books and review articles, which was also of great importance in the preparation of this volume, relates to issues of reliability and validity. Investigators frequently require scientifically sound instruments. Yet the tendency, often out of expediency or necessity, has been to use instruments where these issues have not been adequately addressed. One focus of the *Handbook of Family Measurement Techniques* is to provide sufficient information on a large number of measures such that researchers and clinicians can use or modify instruments, yielding results that are as trustworthy as possible.

Straus (1969) commented that, in preparing his first compendium, he found that 80% of the measures had been used only once. Likewise,

Table 1.1 Selected Characteristics of Various Measurement Inventories

Author/Editor	Publication Date	Total Measures	Family Measures	Complete Family Scales	Reliability & Validity Discussed
Bonjean et al.	1967	2,080	188	3	NO
Shaw & Wright	1967	176	24	24	YES
Straus	1969	319	319	0	YES
Johnson	1971	321	71	0	YES
Lake et al.	1973	84	3	0	YES
Chun et al.	1975	3,246	197	0	NO
Johnson	1976	865	118	0	YES
Pfeiffer et al.	1976	92	6	0	NO
Straus & Brown	1978	813	813	0	NO
Woody	1980	96	25	0	NO
Filsinger & Lewis	1981	29	29	0	YES
Olson et al.	1985	9	9	9	YES
Miller	1983	461	27	2	YES
Filsinger	1983	29	29	7	YES
Mitchell	1983	2,672	60	0	NO
Sweetland & Keyser	1983–1984	2,714	106	3	NO
Goldman et al.	1974–1985	2,369	114	0	YES
Mitchell	1985	1,409	43	0	YES
Keyser & Sweetland	1984–1987	619	45	0	YES
O'Leary	1987	38	38	9	NO
Fredman & Sherman	1987	45	34	22	YES
McCubbin & Thompson	1987	17	17	17	YES
Corcoran & Fischer	1987	128	25	25	YES
Beere	1979	235	23	0	YES
Davis et al.	1988	109	19	17	YES
Jacob & Tennenbaum	1988	44	44	0	YES
Grotevant & Carlson	1989	70	70	0	YES
Touliatos et al.	1989	976	976	0	YES
Beere	in press	211	54	0	YES

NOTE: Because some authors/editors did not provide totals, measures were counted. Totals must be considered as estimates because some instruments were cited more than once, while it is likely that others were missed in the counting process.

Bonjean, Hill, and McLemore (1967) reported that only 28% of the measures they reviewed had been used more than once, with only 2.26% having been used more than five times. Lake, Miles, and Earle (1973) noted that most investigators either developed new measures or uncritically adopted available but unproven instruments. They also implied that, while instruments tended to be used based on face validity and availability, criteria that would lend support to the true validity of instruments were frequently paid insufficient attention. Similarly, Chun, Cobb, and French (1975) noted that 63% of the measures they reviewed had been used only once, with only 3% being used 10 or more times.

Table 1.2 Selected Characteristics of Reports/Reviews of Family Measures

Author(s)	Publication Date	Number of Family Measures	Reliability & Validity Discussed
Bodin	1968	17	NO
Cromwell et al.	1976	156	NO
Spanier	1979	18	YES
Schaivi et al.	1979	51	YES
Keck & Sporakowski	1982	13	NO
Snyder	1982	12	YES
Filsinger	1983	5	YES
Forman & Hagan	1983	6	YES
Forman & Hagan	1984	10	YES
Carlson & Grotevant	1987	8	YES
Grotevant & Carlson	1987	13	YES
Margolin	1987	12	YES
Markman & Notarius	1987	12	YES
Skinner	1987	3	YES
Sabatelli	1988	17	YES
Holden & Edwards	1989	50	YES

NOTE: Some reviews were not included, although they discussed the importance of various family concepts, because they did not focus on practical measurement issues (e.g., Fisher, 1976, 1977; Doane, 1978).

Various practical considerations also frequently affect instrumentation decisions. In particular, concerns related to cost with respect to money and time; limitations imposed by age, sophistication, and/or availability of subjects; and constraints imposed by design of the study or clinical setting often influence the development or selection of measures. For example, Jensen, Witcher, and Upton (1987) recently found that several popular family self-report measures required college-level reading ability, which may place them beyond the capacities of many potential subjects or clients. Further, measures must be sensitive enough to assess changes and, in the case of clinical use, they must also allow for diagnostic differentiation. Notably, Spanier (1979) at one point conceded that his own extraordinarily popular Dyadic Adjustment Scale, used extensively in research, is not adequate for diagnostic assessment of therapy clients.

An additional area of concern within the field relates to the cross-acceptance of instruments created by individuals from various disciplines. Straus and Brown (1978) observed that specialists often overlooked measures developed within other fields, even though the various areas might share a need to measure similar concepts. Family issues are often of interest to sociologists, psychologists, physicians, and others with related concerns. As such, measures are frequently developed and published in literature that tends to be read by one group of professionals, frequently to the exclusion of others. One objective of this handbook is to bring measures and techniques from these disciplines together in a single volume. It is hoped that this treatment will facilitate the bridging of many of these gaps.

FOCUS OF THE VOLUME

This handbook was designed with various types and levels of professionals in mind. It is intended for use by clinicians and researchers, ranging from the beginning graduate student to the sophisticated investigator. Throughout the development and preparation of this volume, the needs of users remained of paramount importance. The following list summarizes the primary objectives of the authors:

(1) to allow novice researchers and practitioners to develop rapid familiarity with their area of interest;

(2) to serve as a starting point for persons interested in locating or developing instruments;

(3) to provide the more seasoned researcher or clinician with a comprehensive inventory of instruments and techniques that have shaped the field over the last half century; and

(4) to allow individuals who are already acquainted with the area to assess the state of various subareas with which they might be less familiar.

The combination of the several indexes, abstract chapter essays, detailed abstracts of over 500 recent instruments, and the organization of the book into 16 primary areas also makes this volume especially useful in training graduate students within the family field.

This volume does not cover all family measures and does not attempt to include nonfamily measures. For readers interested in instruments not abstracted within this volume, two additional sources to which they might refer are *Tests in Print* (Mitchell, 1983) and the *Ninth Mental Measurements Yearbook* (Mitchell, 1985). A summary of available compendia and review articles is contained in Tables 1.1 and 1.2.

SELF-REPORT METHODS

Though self-report methods are sometimes vulnerable to social desirability and other response biases, and may be limited by subjects' own-self/ other awareness, they do have many positive characteristics. They often have strong face validity and, because of their low cost and convenience (relative to observational methods), can be used with large groups of subjects or clients (Jacob & Tennenbaum, 1988). Strosahl and Linehan (1986) have developed an intriguing argument that behavioral self-reports may be as, if not more, valid than observational methods if one takes into account situational variability in behaviors.

One area of concern regarding self-report methods has traditionally been their focus on specific situations and the inability to generalize results to other differently structured circumstances. This concern often prompts investigators to use more direct methods (e.g., observational techniques) when assessing attitudes and/or behaviors across environments. While some evidence indicates convergence between the two methods (Snyder, Trull, & Wills, 1987), the general lack of agreement between self-report and observational findings (Keck & Sporakowski, 1982) has often been presumed to reflect more negatively on self-report instruments than on observational methods.

Reliability. There are three different forms of reliability associated with self-report measures: internal consistency, test-retest, and parallel forms. Each type of reliability taps a different source of possible random error that could cause inconsistent measurements of the desired concept. Internal consistency reliability, generally assessed by Cronbach's (1951) coefficient alpha (alpha being a more general form of the Kuder-Richardson or split-half coefficient), assesses how homogeneous the scale's items are. Carmines and Zeller (1979) clearly demonstrated how alpha increased with the average correlation among a scale's items and with the number of items in that scale. A high alpha suggests that random error associated with item wording or changes in subjects' attitudes while responding to the survey are minimal. Various sources (Corcoran & Fischer, 1987; Pfeiffer, Heslin, & Jones, 1976) recommended that alpha be at least .80 before a measure is considered adequately reliable.

A more appropriate decision rule for determining an acceptable level of reliability, however, might be one that considers the interaction between the number of items in a scale and the average correlation between those items in determining alpha. As was mentioned above, an increase in either the number of items or the average interitem correlation will result in an increased alpha. Thus, while an alpha of .80 is achieved for a 20-item scale with an average interitem correlation of .167, the same average interitem correlation for a 10-item scale would result in an alpha of only .67 (Nunnally, 1978). Likewise, raising the number of items to 30, while keeping the average correlation between items at .167, would result in an increase of alpha to .86. And if the number of items increases to 100, given the same average interitem correlation, the resulting alpha would be .95. Table 1.3 illustrates the effect of this interaction where either the number of items or the size of the average correlation between items is varied.

Test-retest reliability is assessed by correlating one measure with itself among the same subjects at two different points in time. It assesses the stability of a measure. Unfortunately, this form of reliability is almost

Table 1.3 Coefficient Alpha: Effects of Varying Average Interitem Correlation
and Number of Items

Number of Items	Average Interitem Correlation			
	.10	.15	.20	.25
10	.53	.64	.71	.77
20	.69	.78	.83	.87
30	.77	.84	.88	.91
50	.85	.90	.93	.94
100	.92	.95	.96	.97

always partly confounded and probably reduced due to authentic changes over time in the concept being measured. Hence, these coefficients can be expected to decrease concomitantly with increases in time between testing sessions. While test-retest reliability of .80 or greater might be acceptable for periods of a week or two between administrations for scales in the 20- to 30-item range, fewer items or longer periods between test sessions may result in somewhat lower correlations being viewed as acceptable.

Equivalent or parallel forms reliability is measured by correlating different versions of the same scale. For most scales, reliability coefficients ranging from .80 (Corcoran & Fischer, 1987) to .85 (Pfeiffer, Heslin, & Jones, 1976) are considered to be acceptable. While each form of reliability testing poses its own set of difficulties, those inherent in this approach to test construction often prove insurmountable for the average researcher or clinician. Investigators frequently find it difficult, if not impossible, to generate a sufficient quantity of items and to administer them to an appropriate number of subjects in order to satisfy the requirements for adequate parallel forms reliability procedures. Thus, although test-retest and alpha coefficients are commonly reported, little attention is usually directed toward equivalent forms reliability testing.

Validity. High levels of reliability indicate that a concept is being measured in a consistent manner. High reliability, however, does not guarantee that the scale being used bears any resemblance to the concept the investigator wishes to assess. For example, investigators who are interested in parents' affections for their children might assess the frequency of corrective statements made by those parents toward their children. Such behaviors could be measured utilizing self-report questionnaires, interviews, and/or observational techniques, with varying approaches to reliability indicating high levels of consistency. However, despite high reliability coefficients, the validity of inferring levels of parental affection based on these results would be seriously in doubt. Validity may be defined as the degree to which an instrument actually assesses what it purports to measure.

Chun, Cobb, and French (1975) discussed various forms of what they refer to as pseudovalidity. One of these, nominal validity, is the assumption that a scale actually does measure what the scale's name implies. Another, validity by fiat, is where an author asserts that a scale has validity but offers no empirical evidence to support that claim. And a third, face validity, is the extent to which the scale's items appear on the surface to be measuring the desired concept. However, face validity boils down to a matter of opinion, opinion over which sharp disagreements are quite possible. As Bagarozzi (1985) has pointed out, some contemporary measures might lack even pseudovalidity.

There are several acceptable ways of measuring true validity. The three most common are content validity, criterion-related validity, and construct validity. Content validity is probably better defined as what Corcoran and Fischer (1987) call logical content validity, where decisions about the apparent relevance of items are made by an independent panel of judges. Criterion-related validity measures how closely related a scale or set of variables is to other relevant external criteria. In particular, criterion-related validity is often assessed in terms of its concurrent validity—Does a score obtained or an instrument correlate with that obtained on another scale or by different groups assessed at the same time as the measure in question?—and predictive validity—Does the variable assessed at one point in time correlate significantly with related concepts assessed at a later time?

The most important, but also the most difficult, form of validity to assess is construct validity. Many authors turn to Campbell and Fiske's (1959) multitrait-multimethod matrix to define construct validity; that is, a scale should correlate with closely related concepts (convergent validity) but not with unrelated concepts (discriminant validity). Construct validity is also sometimes associated with factorial validity—the notion that the subscales of an inventory should, upon factor analysis, reveal the same item groupings as those expected on theoretical grounds. In the final analysis though, construct validity, no matter how it is assessed, is strongest when measurements obtained using instruments are consistent with acceptable theories.

Questionnaires are easy to administer and score but may be plagued by response biases and limitations in types of questions and range of available responses. Interviews, while allowing for a broader range of information to be collected, are often more difficult to quantify. Interviewer bias is an additional problem experienced with this method that cannot be ignored. And projective techniques, while providing the richest array of insightful data, present substantial difficulties related to their consistent interpretation.

In terms of comparing questionnaire and interview studies, an important issue is their relative susceptibility to response bias. Certainly interview studies can control for collusion more easily, preventing spouses from sharing interview data with each other. On the other hand, some evidence suggests that questionnaires afford greater control over socially desirable response sets than do interviews (Dillman, 1978; Schumm, Milliken, Poresky, Bollman, & Jurich, 1983), especially for sensitive areas.

Several scholars have aptly pointed to trade-offs between conceptual richness and empirical specificity (Gilbert & Christensen, 1985). That is, highly concrete variables are easy to measure, but it is often difficult to know what they mean (Pinsof, 1981); apparent technical "goodness" does not guarantee actual validity (Straus, 1964); and irrelevant concepts tend to be easiest to measure (Fredman & Sherman, 1987). Accordingly, current recommendations often lean toward the use of multitrait, multimethod, and multilevel assessments (Cromwell & Peterson, 1981; Filsinger, 1983b; Jacob & Tennenbaum, 1988; Olson, 1981; Pinsof, 1981). *Multitrait* refers to measuring more than one concept, while *multimethod* involves the use of different methods (e.g., self-report versus observational methods) to measure similar concepts. *Multilevel* assessment is an idea more unique to the family area in that it refers to evaluating family life from individual, dyadic, family, and societal perspectives (Filsinger, 1983b; Jacob & Tennenbaum, 1988).

OBSERVATIONAL METHODS

Observational methods are appreciated for their role in directly assessing family interaction processes. Such methods appear to fit the general approach of family systems theories (Filsinger, Lewis, & McAvoy, 1981), while remaining appropriate for both naturalistic (e.g., home observations) and laboratory settings. Observed actions either may have been evoked through ordinary events or games, or decision-making or performance tasks (Jacob & Tennenbaum, 1988), or may be recorded as they naturally occur. Interactions may be evaluated through subjective ratings, either by outsiders or the participants themselves, or by particular coding systems that assess the frequency and timing of specific behaviors. Both verbal and nonverbal behaviors, often using audiotapes or videotapes, may be recorded and subsequently coded. Where mechanical recordings are either not possible or inappropriate, live assessments of behavior may be utilized.

Most family observation studies combine time and/or event sampling. Time sampling involves selecting systematic and repeated intervals or points of time during which preselected behaviors are recorded (e.g., every 30 seconds). Event sampling involves a focus on target behaviors without regard to time intervals during which they can occur. While both methods are popular and economical, particularly where mechanical recording procedures are not available, they each present the investigator with a set of unavoidable sources of invalidity. One problem that must be considered by researchers and clinicians using either method is that of inadequately addressing the contexts within which behaviors occur. Both time and event sampling tend to concentrate on specific events but often ignore precipitating, concomitant, and resulting behaviors. Additionally, time sampling presents the unique risk of failing to record low frequency but important behaviors. Using this technique, such behaviors are only recorded if they occur within the sampling interval.

Reliability. There are a number of ways of assessing reliability for observational data. Haynes (1978) examined and compared six such approaches on the same data set, with resulting reliability coefficients ranging from .22 to .90. The reader is referred to Haynes (1978) for a detailed discussion of some of these differences.

Cohen's (1960) kappa is perhaps the best overall statistic for evaluating reliability of observational measurement systems because it adjusts for chance agreement, a particular problem when assessing frequent behaviors (Gilbert & Christensen, 1985). Data gathered utilizing other types of evaluation procedures, however, typically require alternate approaches. For example, Hartmann (1977) has recommended the use of correlational coefficients to measure agreement on ordinal data. Tinsley and Weiss (1975) have recommended using intraclass correlations to assess interrater reliability. And Pinsof (1981) distinguishes between interrater and intrarater agreement, the latter representing consistency over time for a single observer or rater. When comparing the two, if intrarater reliability is low, then interrater reliability will probably also be low, although the reverse will not necessarily be true. If both interrater and intrarater reliability are low, the measurement system may not have much potential.

There are several threats to interrater reliability. Among the more obvious are the tendency for raters to possibly lose enthusiasm or become better skilled at rating the observed behaviors over time; the accuracy of codings by several raters, thereby allowing observer drift to occur; and incompletely or inconsistently training coders.

One approach to improving interrater reliability, particularly for difficult or complex coding systems, is known as the consensual agreement format (Gilbert & Christensen, 1985). In that approach an odd number of raters are used to individually code data. The data are then finally coded in accordance with the majority opinion, with the objective being the reaching of a consensus.

Validity. Equally, if not more, important to concerns over establishing and maintaining reliable procedures are considerations given to issues of validity. Three major types of validity of interest when collecting observational information are content validity, criterion-related validity, and construct validity. Within the context of observational studies, content validity questions whether a representative sample of behavior is being observed. An examination of criterion-related validity generally includes an assessment of both concurrent and predictive validity. A procedure attending to concerns of concurrent validity allows for evaluation of the relationship of the current measure to other measures for which validity issues have previously been addressed. Such other measurements are typically taken at or about the same time as those of primary interest. Predictive validity relates to the ability to anticipate changes or trends in behavior over time based on the current set of observations. Construct validity within an observational context refers to the ability to relate coding schemes to the desired set of constructs.

There are three primary sources of potential invalidity requiring special attention by the investigator. Two of these sources focus on actions or abilities of observers, while the third is primarily concerned with reactions to the situation of those persons who are observed. Observers can influence the quality of information that is collected, either through the impact of their actions on behaviors of persons being observed, or through their attention to standardized observation and recording techniques. At the same time, subjects may react differently when they know they are being observed, as opposed to when other methods are used or when observations are conducted unobtrusively.

One additional method used in bringing both self-report and observational data into perspective is presented by Olson (1981; Cromwell, Olson, & Fournier, 1976). His four-cell matrix of two types of data (subjective and objective) and two reporters' frames of reference (insider and outsider) are often cited in further classifying both types of measures (Bagarozzi, 1985; Filsinger, 1983a; Markman, Notarius, Stephen, & Smith, 1981). Bagarozzi (1985) further argued that the objective/subjective distinction is less clear than is the insider/outsider distinction. Within Olson's matrix, self-report methods fall into the subjective/insider cell, with behavioral self-reports falling into the objective/insider cell. Likewise, observers' subjective reports fall into the subjective/outsider cell while behavioral methods fall within the objective/outsider cell.

SUMMARY

This volume includes a wide variety of instruments that vary both in concepts assessed and in methodology of assessment. Regardless of the methodology used, one must remain cautious with respect to total acceptance of any single approach. For both self-report and observational measures, it would appear that the field has been more successful in generating large numbers of measures than it has been in adequately validating even a small percentage of those measures (Strosahl & Linehan, 1986). While observational instruments and techniques appear to present a better fit for viewing the family from a systems perspective, their use, due to several practical considerations, has traditionally been less than that of paper-and-pencil measures (Fredman & Sherman, 1987; Strosahl & Linehan, 1986). Furthermore, as has been pointed out before (Schumm, 1982), issues of convergent validity for self-report and observational measures will remain ambiguous until it is clear that both types of instruments are assessing identical concepts in terms of units of analysis, specificity, timing, and so on.

A further consideration relates to uncertainty over the proper selection of dependent variables. With regard to this issue, one concern frequently addressed when developing or modifying an instrument is the unidimensional versus multidimensional nature of the concept being evaluated. Some have argued for more frequent use of unidimensional, shorter scales (Fincham & Bradbury, 1987; Norton, 1983). One problem that often arises when being constrained in this way, however, relates to the selection of an appropriate dependent variable. For example, the use of marital stability as a primary dependent variable is often considered inadequate because many stable marriages are also quite distressed. The question, therefore, arises as to whether a multidimensional perspective that considers both stability and distress might provide a clearer picture of the overall quality of marriage. Thus, while unidimensional systems may be easier to construct and evaluate, conclusions drawn on the basis of interactions between multiple criteria may, in the long run, provide more valuable information.

This book is designed to provide the reader with a substantial number of family measurement instruments and techniques. Care has been taken to provide as much validity and reliability information as was reasonably possible. This collection of instruments is intended to serve both as a beginning point in assisting investigators in developing their own instruments and as an end point in providing instruments that may prove useful in their current forms.

From this volume, it is hoped that readers will recognize not only how the field of family measurement has developed over the last 50 years but also where it is likely to go. It is expected that readers will take advantage of this sourcebook to adopt and/or modify measures, and that the use of these instruments and techniques will contribute to our understanding of the field. From this perspective, this handbook is intended to provide clinicians and researchers alike with a starting point from which they can select and/or construct instruments according to their individual needs.

REFERENCES

Bagarozzi, D. A. (1985). Dimensions of family evaluation. In L. L'Abate (Ed.), *The handbook of family psychology and therapy* (Vol. 2, pp. 989–1005). Homewood, IL: Dorsey.

Beere, C. A. (1979). *Women and women's issues.* San Francisco: Jossey-Bass.

Beere, C. A. (in press). *Gender roles: A handbook of tests and measures.* Westport, CT: Greenwood.

Bonjean, C. M., Hill, R. J., & McLemore, S. D. (1967). *Sociological measurement: An inventory of scales and indices.* San Francisco: Chandler.

Campbell, D. T., & Fiske, D. W. (1959). Convergent and discriminant validation by the multitrait-multimethod matrix. *Psychological Bulletin, 56,* 81–105.

Carmines, E. G., & Zeller, R. A. (1979). *Reliability and validity assessment.* Beverly Hills, CA: Sage.

Chun, K., Cobb, S., & French, J. R. P., Jr. (1975). *Measures for psychological assessment: A guide to 3,000 original sources and their applications.* Ann Arbor: University of Michigan, Survey Research Center of the Institute for Social Research.

Cohen, J. A. (1960). A coefficient of agreement for nominal scales. *Educational and Psychological Measurement, 20,* 37–46.

Corcoran, K., & Fischer, J. (1987). *Measures for clinical practice: A sourcebook.* New York: Free Press.

Cronbach, L. J. (1951). Coefficient alpha and the internal structure of tests. *Psychometrika, 16,* 297–334.

Cromwell, R., Olson, D. H., & Fournier, D. (1976). Tools and techniques for diagnosis and evaluation in marital and family therapy. *Family Process, 15,* 1–49.

Cromwell, R., & Peterson, G. W. (1981). Multisystem-multimethod assessment: A framework. In E. E. Filsinger & R. A. Lewis (Eds.), *Assessing marriage* (pp. 38–54). Beverly Hills, CA: Sage.

Davis, C. M., Yarber, W. L., & Davis, S. L. (Eds.). *Sexuality-related measures: A compendium.* Lake Mills, IA: Graphic.

Dillman, D. A. (1978). *Mail and telephone surveys.* New York: John Wiley.

Filsinger, E. E. (1981). The Dyadic Interaction Scoring Code. In E. E. Filsinger & R. A. Lewis (Eds.), *Assessing marriage* (pp. 148–159). Beverly Hills, CA: Sage.

Filsinger, E. E. (1983a). Assessment: What it is and why it is important. In E. E. Filsinger (Ed.), *Marriage and family assessment: A sourcebook for family therapy* (pp. 11–22). Beverly Hills, CA: Sage.

Filsinger, E. E. (1983b). Choices among marital observation coding systems. *Family Process, 22,* 317–335.

Filsinger, E. E., Lewis, R. A., & McAvoy, P. (1981). Introduction: Trends and prospects for observing marriage. In E. E. Filsinger & R. A. Lewis (Eds.), *Assessing marriage* (pp. 9–20). Beverly Hills, CA: Sage.

Fincham, F. D., & Bradbury, T. N. (1987). The assessment of marital quality: A reevaluation. *Journal of Marriage and the Family, 49,* 797–809.

Forman, B. D., & Hagan, B. J. (1983). A comparative review of total family functioning measures. *American Journal of Family Therapy, 11,* 25–40.

Fredman, N., & Sherman, R. (1987). *Handbook of measurements for marriage and family therapy.* New York: Brunner/Mazel.

Gilbert, R., & Christensen, A. (1985). Observational assessment of marital and family interaction: Methodological considerations. In L. L'Abate (Ed.), *The handbook of family psychology and therapy* (Vol. 2, pp. 961–988). Homewood, IL: Dorsey.

Goldman, B. A., & Busch, J. C. (1978). *Directory of unpublished experimental mental measures* (Vol. 2). New York: Human Sciences.

Goldman, B. A., & Busch, J. C. (1982). *Directory of unpublished experimental mental measures* (Vol. 3). New York: Human Sciences.

Goldman, B. A., & Osborne, W. L. (1985). *Directory of unpublished experimental mental measures* (Vol. 4). New York: Human Sciences.

Goldman, B. A., & Saunders, J. L. (1974). *Directory of unpublished experimental mental measures* (Vol. 1). New York: Behavioral Publications.

Grotevant, H. D., & Carlson, C. I. (1987). Family interaction coding systems: A descriptive review. *Family Process, 26,* 49–74.

Grotevant, H. D., & Carlson, C. I. (1989). *Family assessment: A guide to methods and measures.* New York: Guilford.

Hartmann, D. P. (1977). Considerations in the choice of interobserver reliability estimates. *Journal of Applied Behavior Analysis, 10,* 103–116.

Haynes, S. N. (1978). *Principles of behavioral assessment.* New York: Gardner.

Holden, G. W., & Edwards, L. A. (1989). Parental attitudes toward child rearing: Instruments, issues, and implications. *Psychological Bulletin, 106,* 29:58.

Jacob, T., & Tennenbaum, D. L. (1988). *Family assessment.* New York: Plenum.

Jensen, B. J., Witcher, D. B., & Upton, L. R. (1987). Readability assessment of questionnaires frequently used in sex and marital therapy. *Journal of Sex and Marital Therapy, 13,* 137–141.

Johnson, O. G. (1976). *Tests and measurements in child development: Handbook II* (Vols. 1–2). San Francisco: Jossey-Bass.

Johnson, O. G., & Bommarito, J. W. (1971). *Tests and measurements in child development: A handbook.* San Francisco: Jossey-Bass.

Keck, S. E., & Sporakowski, M. J. (1982). Behavioral diagnosis and assessment in marital therapy. *Journal of Sex and Marital Therapy, 8,* 119–134.

Keyser, D. J., & Sweetland, R. C. (Eds.). (1984). *Test critiques* (Vol. 1). Kansas City: Test Corporation of America.

Keyser, D. J., & Sweetland, R. C. (Eds.). (1985a). *Test critiques* (Vol. 2). Kansas City: Test Corporation of America.

Keyser, D. J., & Sweetland, R. C. (Eds.). (1985b). *Test critiques* (Vol. 3). Kansas City: Test Corporation of America.

Keyser, D. J., & Sweetland, R. C. (Eds.). (1985c). *Test critiques* (Vol. 4). Kansas City: Test Corporation of America.

Keyser, D. J., & Sweetland, R. C. (Eds.). (1986). *Test critiques* (Vol. 5). Kansas City: Test Corporation of America.

Keyser, D. J., & Sweetland, R. C. (Eds.). (1987). *Test critiques* (Vol. 6). Kansas City: Test Corporation of America.

Lake, D. G., Miles, M. B., & Earle, R. B., Jr. (1973). *Measuring human behavior: Tools for the assessment of social functioning.* New York: Teachers College Press.

Markman, H. J., Notarius, C. I., Stephen, T., & Smith, R. J. (1981). Behavioral observation systems for couples: The current status. In E. E. Filsinger & R. A. Lewis (Eds.), *Assessing marriage* (pp. 234–262). Beverly Hills, CA: Sage.

McCubbin, H. I., & Thompson, A. I. (1987). *Family assessment inventories for research and practice.* Madison: University of Wisconsin Press.

Miller, D. C. (1983). *Handbook of research design and social measurement* (4th ed.). New York: Longman.

Mitchell, J. V., Jr. (Ed.). (1983). *Tests in print III.* Lincoln: University of Nebraska Press.

Mitchell, J. V., Jr. (Ed.). (1985). *The ninth mental measurements yearbook* (Vols. 1–2). Lincoln: University of Nebraska Press.

Norton, R. (1983). Measuring marital quality: A critical look at the dependent variable. *Journal of Marriage and the Family, 45,* 141–151.

Nunnally, J. C. (1978). *Psychometric theory* (2nd ed.). New York: McGraw-Hill.

O'Leary, K. D., & Arias, I. (1987). Marital assessment in clinical practice. In K. D. O'Leary (Ed.), *Assessment of marital discord* (pp. 287–312). Hillsdale, NJ: Lawrence Erlbaum.

Olson, D. H. (1981). Family typologies: Bridging family research and family therapy. In E. E. Filsinger & R. A Lewis (Eds.), *Assessing marriage* (pp. 74–89). Beverly Hills, CA: Sage.

Olson, D. H., McCubbin, H. I., Barnes, H., Larsen, A., Muxen, M., & Wilson, M. (1985).

Family inventories (rev. ed.). Minneapolis: University of Minnesota, Family Social Science Department.

Pfeiffer, J. W., Heslin, R., & Jones, J. E. (1976). *Instrumentation in human relations training* (2nd ed.). LaJolla, CA: University Associates, Inc.

Pinsof, W. M. (1981). Family therapy process research. In A. S. Gurman & D. P. Kniskern (Eds.), *Handbook of family therapy*. New York: Brunner/Mazel.

Sabatelli, R. (1988). The assessment of marital relationships: A review and critique of contemporary measures. *Journal of Marriage and the Family, 50,* 891–915.

Schiavi, R. C., Derogatis, L. R., Kuriansky, J., O'Connor, D., & Sharpe, L. (1979). The assessment of sexual function and marital interaction. *Journal of Sex and Marital Therapy, 5,* 169–224.

Schumm, W. R. (1982). Integrating theory, measurement, and data analysis in family studies survey research. *Journal of Marriage and the Family, 44,* 983–998.

Schumm, W. R., Milliken, G. A., Poresky, R. H., Bollman, S. R., & Jurich, A. P. (1983). Issues of measuring marital satisfaction in survey research. *International Journal of Sociology of the Family, 13,* 129–143.

Shaw, M. E., & Wright, J. M. (1967). *Scales for the measurement of attitudes.* New York: McGraw-Hill.

Snyder, D. K. (1982). Advances in marital assessment: Behavioral, communications, and psychometric approaches. In C. D. Spielberger & J. N. Butcher (Eds.), *Advances in personality assessment* (Vol. 1, pp. 169–201). Hillsdale, NJ: Lawrence Erlbaum.

Snyder, D. K., Trull, T. J., & Wills, R. M. (1987). Convergent validity of observational and self-report measures of marital interaction. *Journal of Sex and Marital Therapy, 13,* 224–236.

Spanier, G. B. (1979). The measurement of marital quality. *Journal of Sex and Marital Therapy, 5,* 288–300.

Straus, M. A. (1964). Measuring families. In H. T. Christensen (Ed.), *Handbook of marriage and the family* (pp. 335–400). Chicago: Rand McNally.

Straus, M. A. (1969). *Family measurement techniques.* Minneapolis: University of Minnesota Press.

Straus, M. A., & Brown, B. W. (1978). *Family measurement techniques: Abstracts of published instruments, 1935–1974.* Minneapolis: University of Minnesota Press.

Strosahl, K. D., & Linehan, M. M. (1986). Basic issues in behavioral assessment. In A. R. Ciminero, K. S. Calhoun, & H. E. Adams (Eds.), *Handbook of behavioral assessment* (2nd ed., pp. 12–46). New York: John Wiley.

Sweetland, R. C., & Keyser, D. J. (Eds.). (1983). *Tests.* Kansas City: Test Corporation of America.

Sweetland, R. C., & Keyser, D. J. (Eds.). (1984). *Tests* (Supplement). Kansas City: Test Corporation of America.

Tinsley, H. E. A., & Weiss, D. J. (1975). Interrater reliability and agreement of subjective judgments. *Journal of Counseling Psychology, 22,* 358–376.

2 Dimensions of Marital and Family Interaction

THOMAS N. BRADBURY
FRANK D. FINCHAM

Over the past several decades behavioral scientists from a variety of disciplines have recognized the importance of social interaction, particularly that which occurs in marriages and families. The continuing interest in marital and family interaction holds great promise not only for understanding a significant aspect of daily life but also for devising interventions that will aid in alleviating difficulties that arise in interpersonal settings. These objectives are especially noteworthy in view of the fact that interpersonal problems are cited as the most common reason for seeking counseling in the United States (Veroff, Kulka, & Douvan, 1981).

The importance of understanding social interaction is matched only by the complexity that underlies it. In grappling with this complexity, behavioral scientists are confronted routinely with a wide range of problems, many of which have no obvious resolution: Which parameters of interaction should be attended to and which, if any, can be ignored? Which family members should be observed in interaction, and how might their interactions change with the inclusion of other family members? What reliable patterns or sequences of behaviors emerge from interaction and in what ways might they be important? In what ways are the behaviors exhibited by the interactants related to their thoughts and feelings? How is a given interaction related to prior interactions in the family, and what are its implications for future interactions and outcomes? What is the influence of broader historical and social forces on interaction? In an effort to contend with issues such as these, behavioral scientists have devised a number of tools that allow them to collect in a systematic manner information about particular constructs pertaining to interaction. These tools, which are catalogued in the pages that follow this chapter, vary along several dimensions, including their

AUTHORS' NOTE: Thomas N. Bradbury was supported in the preparation of this chapter by a National Research Service Award from the National Institute of Mental Health and by a grant from the National Science Foundation. The chapter was written while Frank D. Fincham was a Faculty Scholar of the W. T. Grant Foundation.

format (e.g., interviews, questionnaires, observational coding systems), the relationships to which they apply (e.g., husbands and wives, parents and children, couples planning to marry), when they are administered (e.g., before and after counseling, before marriage, after the birth of a child), and the topic with which they are concerned (e.g., quality of the home environment, expectations for marriage, social support networks).

The purpose of this chapter is to provide a context for evaluating the many tools that have been used to study, assess, and treat marital and family interaction. As used here the term *interaction* will refer collectively to the overt behaviors that are exchanged between two or more people, the covert affective and cognitive processes that arise as behaviors are exchanged, and the relatively stable individual difference variables that can influence, and that can be influenced by, overt and covert events. Although this definition may appear overly inclusive, we hope to demonstrate that failure to consider the various facets of interaction and the context in which it occurs has impeded progress in this domain.

Our presentation is guided by two related goals. First, we seek to militate against the many dangers that are inherent in "blind use of instruments" (Straus, 1964, p. 339). Second, we want to encourage readers to become critical consumers of available instruments and active designers of new methods so that their efforts to understand marital and family interaction will be maximally informative. We shall attempt to accomplish these goals by providing a conceptual backdrop against which existing tools can be understood and evaluated. In the first section of the chapter we provide a historical overview of how marital and family interaction evolved to become a viable focus for research and treatment, and we discuss the influence these historical factors have had on measurement practices in this domain. In the second section we discuss several specific implications that the historical analysis has for conducting interaction research on marriages and families. The final section is a summary and discussion of the main points of the chapter.

HISTORICAL OVERVIEW OF CONCEPTUAL DEVELOPMENTS

Although historical analyses can at times be quite divorced from current trends and formulations, it is our impression that elements from the history of marital and family interaction bear a close relationship to contemporary thinking about interaction and that awareness of these elements can be a valuable resource for further development in this domain (see "Implications of Historical Overview," below). Moreover, discussion of the evolution of interactional ideas reflects not only our belief that appreciating and conducting research on interaction requires an understanding of related past efforts but also the belief that more sophisticated research and theory will ensue when attention is given to the far-reaching conceptual shifts that have shaped contemporary thinking about interaction.

Following Christensen (1964) we can identify three important stages in the development of scientific inquiry on marriage and the family. In the preresearch stage, prior to about 1850, little systematic thinking about the family had occurred and prevailing ideas were to a large degree a reflection of "traditional beliefs, religious pronouncements, moralistic exhortations, poetic fantasies, and philosophical speculations" (Christensen, 1964, p. 6). This phase gave way in the second half of the nineteenth century to an era in which Darwin's theory of evolution was applied to a variety of social institutions, including marriage and the family. The all-encompassing theories proffered in this period of social Darwinism were difficult to test and, because it was assumed that the family was best understood in terms of gradual evolutionary changes, direct study of families was eschewed in favor of anecdotal and historical records that were often biased toward proving rather than disproving central tenets.[1]

By the end of the nineteenth century an increasing number of families were subjected to various deleterious economic and social changes. Jacob (1987) notes that for those seeking social reform in this era it became essential to document the conditions confronting the family, and the methods and approaches that were necessary to accomplish this task served to usher in a period of emerging science in family studies. The defining features of this period include an empirical orientation favoring direct study of the family, an emphasis on methodological rigor, and a reduction in value-laden assumptions and preconceptions. An important aspect of this development is the increased attention that has been devoted to interaction in marriages and families. As suggested by our earlier definition, a unique feature of this orientation to marriage and families is its strong emphasis on the relationships that exist between spouses and family members, in addition to the more common focus on either the individuals themselves (e.g., personality) and the external factors that impinge upon them (e.g., social stressors). In the remainder of this section we shift from discussing how the family became a legitimate subject for research to a consideration of how emphasis came to be placed on the interactions among spouses and family members.

There is some consensus that the study of marriages and families evolved from four major intellectual traditions (see Gottman, 1979; Jacob, 1987). These traditions continue to influence the present state of interaction theory and research and they are used to organize the following discussion. The four traditions are symbolic interactionism and family sociology, psychiatry and family therapy, developmental psychology, and learning theory and clinical psychology. Following a discussion of each tradition, we address briefly its influence on measurement in the study of marital and family interaction.[2]

Family Sociology and Symbolic Interactionism

The late 1800s and early 1900s were, as already noted, marked by large-scale social changes and by an attendant need for intervention and reform. Family sociologists were among the first to undertake the task of demonstrating the impact upon the family of such issues as poverty, child labor, divorce, desertion, and women's suffrage. At this time family sociologists tended to view the family as an institution and to examine the interface between the family and the problems of society. Although elements of this perspective are still evident in contemporary family sociology, two important factors brought about a dramatic conceptual shift whereby the family came to be viewed as a context for interaction among its constituent individuals.

The first factor contributing to this shift was the emergence of symbolic interactionism as a school of thought within sociology. Although a detailed discussion of this development is beyond the scope of this chapter, it suffices to note that symbolic interactionism is concerned with the relationship that exists between individuals and society, and particularly with the impact this relationship has on (a) socialization, or the manner by which an individual learns the values, norms, attitudes, and ways of behaving that typify the social groups to which he or she belongs, and on (b) personality organization, or how an individual's personality and behavior patterns develop (see Stryker, 1964). In addition, it bears mention that symbolic interactionism in its early forms placed little emphasis on family functioning. Thus this conceptual framework was concerned with a variety of intraindividual phenomena that were influenced by social interaction.

The second, more proximal factor that served to promote the view of the family as a context for interaction was a 1926 paper by Ernest W. Burgess, "The Family as a Unity of Interacting Personalities." The significance of this paper stems from having extended, in an explicit manner, many of the ideas of symbolic interactionism to the study of the family. Observing that "among all the volumes upon the family . . . there was to be found not a single work that even pretended to study the modern family as behavior or as a social phenomenon" (1926, p. 3), Burgess suggested instead that the family be studied as a "unity of interacting personalities" (p. 5). In a frequently cited passage, Burgess (p. 5) went on to state that

> by a unity of interacting personalities is meant a living, changing, growing thing. I was about to call it a superpersonality. At any rate the actual unity of family life has its existence not in any legal conception, nor in any formal contract, but in the interaction of its members. . . . The family lives as long as interaction is taking place and only dies when it ceases.

This basic idea, which was later discussed more formally by Waller (1938), is viewed by many as having irrevocably transformed the study of the family (e.g., Handel, 1965). What was once thought to be a broad and monolithic entity best examined from an outside perspective was now understood to be a complex and dynamic collection of relationships that was studied more appropriately from an inside perspective with a more microscopic focus.[3]

Consideration of the family as a context for interaction dominated research in family sociology for several decades, and symbolic interactionism continues as a highly visible theoretical perspective in family sociology (Holman & Burr, 1980). Theoretical contributions aside, the fact remains that, despite a clear emphasis on the importance of interpersonal phenomena, actual interactions among family members are rarely observed by symbolic interactionists. Although consistent with the basic theoretical assertion that interaction must be viewed in terms of how the participants define the social situation, this shortcoming appears to be at odds with another assertion, that the basic unit to be observed is the interaction, as it is from interactions that both the individual and society are derived (see Stryker, 1964). Indeed, letters, diaries, autobiographies, and other personal documents were a common source of data collection in the early years of this tradition and, while interest in direct observation has increased in recent years, it is used in only a small proportion of research (Hodgson & Lewis, 1979; Nye, 1988).

To summarize, the first systematic studies of the family were conducted by family sociologists at the turn of the century in an effort to document and change the prevailing economic and social conditions. The theoretical structure afforded by symbolic interactionism, and the extension of this theory by Burgess and others to the study of the family, led to a significant transformation whereby the family came to be treated as a group of interacting individuals rather than as an undifferentiated social institution. Unfortunately, however, the theoretical underpinnings of this tradition appear more pertinent to interaction than do the data derived from those theories.

Influences on measurement. Although interaction research is rare in the family sociology and symbolic interactionism tradition, it is ironic that the few methods developed by sociologists to study overt interaction have come to be widely influential. For example, the observational coding system originated by Bales (1950) to examine problem-solving behavior in groups is a forerunner to the coding systems used by psychiatrists and family therapists (e.g., in *Abstracts 95* and *1089*) and by clinical psychologists (e.g., *91, 115*). Similarly, variations on the revealed differences technique used by Strodtbeck (1951) to engage couples in quasi-naturalistic conflict discussions have been employed frequently in studies of marital interaction (e.g., Gottman, 1979; Raush, Barry, Hertel, & Swain, 1974; see also *89, 1068*).

Rather than addressing overt interaction, however, the measures used more widely within the family sociology and symbolic interactionism tradition were designed to assess perceptions of and beliefs about family interactions and relationships. For example, self-report instruments are available for collecting data on communication (e.g., *5, 17*), interaction in leisure time (e.g., *30, 84*), marital expectations (e.g., *87*), and openness in relationships (e.g., *110*). Thus it can be seen from these measures that the term *interaction* is generally understood to mean perceptions of interaction (and of the relationship more broadly) within this tradition. The development of measures having this orientation follows from the interest in family relationships, but not necessarily in family interaction, that emerged following Burgess's (1926) paper. Attention has also been devoted to measuring cross-generational issues, including attitudes toward nuclear families (e.g., *36*) and relationships involving grandparents (e.g., *35, 55*) and parents and their adult children (e.g., *47*).

Finally, it is interesting to note that, consistent with an earlier emphasis in this tradition, measures have also been designed that provide information on the interface between families and social factors. These include status striving in the family (e.g., *27*), the interplay between work and the family (e.g., *23, 33*), parents' social networks (e.g., *372*), and availability of resources for coping with stressful events (e.g., *473*).[4]

Psychiatry and Family Therapy

A second intellectual tradition that has influenced the study of marital and family interaction can be traced to the work of Sigmund Freud. In particular, Freud's notion that an individual's emotional illness could develop in interactions with others, and that such an illness could be remedied in a therapeutic relationship, represented a qualitatively different way of viewing mental illness (see Kerr, 1981). Despite his radically different stance, Freud nevertheless maintained a clear emphasis on unconscious and intrapsychic conflicts, rather than interactions, as the essential causes of emotional disturbance. It was only after a new generation of psychiatrists realized the limitations of the psychoanalytic perspective that individuals were treated and eventually studied together with their spouses or families.

Movement away from the classic psychoanalytic model occurred on two main fronts, first among marital therapists who sought to treat both husband and wife conjointly (i.e., together in the same session), and later among family therapists who sought to treat individuals diagnosed as schizophrenic with their family members (for detailed histories, see Broderick & Schrader, 1981; Guerin, 1976). Although many analysts defended the need for separate therapies for husbands and wives, several influential theorists (e.g., Ackerman, 1938; Mittelman, 1944) broke with the orthodox practice of psychoanalysis. Ackerman (1954, p. 380) was especially articulate in discussing the rationale for seeing both spouses together, arguing that in

diagnosing marital interaction, "we are not concerned with the autonomous functions and pathology of individual personalities, but rather with
the dynamics of the relationship, that is, with the reciprocal role functions
that define the relations of a husband and wife." Thus between 1930 and
1945 deeply held beliefs about how marital partners should be treated in
therapy underwent a dramatic change, with less emphasis on the individuals themselves and more emphasis on their relationship.

Following recognition of the inadequacy of individually based interventions in the treatment of marital difficulties, it was only a short time before
problems with children, adolescents, and young adults were redefined in
terms of family dynamics and were treated with other family members present. Influenced by such works as Richardson's (1945) *Patients Have Families,* a number of psychiatrists in the 1950s independently initiated treatment
of families, often centered on an individual diagnosed as schizophrenic.
Pioneers in this family therapy movement include, for example, Murray
Bowen, who addressed the emotional bond between a mother and a child in
terms of "mother-patient symbiosis"; Theodore Lidz, who examined interparental distance and hostility (marital "schism") and destructive maternal dominance (marital "skew") in families of schizophrenics; and Lyman
Wynne, who studied schizophrenia and "pseudomutuality," a pattern of
family interaction characterized by feigned and fragile relationships and
avoidance of conflict.

A novel and distinguishing feature of these concepts is that they were
cast at an interpersonal level of analysis and described the interactions of
two or more people. A concept similar in this regard, which would come to
occupy a central position in the family therapy movement, was formalized
as the double bind hypothesis. The product of a collaboration between
Gregory Bateson and Don Jackson, the double bind hypothesis located the
cause of a schizophrenic's deficit in his or her inability to appreciate the
qualifying context of a message (i.e., disordered metacommunication, or
communication about communication). As a consequence, it was reasoned, communication would be misinterpreted and the individual would
be uncertain about how to respond (see Bateson, Jackson, Haley, &
Weakland, 1956).

The double bind hypothesis, together with others deriving from the
family therapy movement, effectively altered the view of schizophrenia as a
disorder within an individual to one that emerges from an individual's
interpersonal exchanges. As Framo (1972, pp. 14–15) observed:

> The family view, in its extreme form, has proposed that the unit of study
> should be the social context of the individual, that symptomatic behavior is
> adaptive to that context, and that if individuals appear to differ from one
> another it is because the situations they are responding to are different. . . .
> From this view, the difference between "normal" people and individuals with

psychiatric problems would be a difference in the current situation (and treatment situation) in which the person is embedded.

This way of thinking has had a lasting impact on how social scientists study and attempt to modify interaction; particularly prominent in this regard has been the formation of several highly developed approaches for treating distressed marriages and families (see Gurman & Kniskern, 1981).

These contributions notwithstanding, a more balanced and critical appraisal of this movement highlights fundamental directions that have yet to be taken. On the one hand, the systems approach to treatment has not been examined empirically in great detail, yet "despite this fact, the approach has flourished and has become the predominant mode of therapy with couples and families. . . family therapy has remained essentially unchanged in a quarter of a century, and hypotheses continue to be accepted by repetition" (Gottman, 1979, p. 256). On the other hand, ideas such as the double bind hypothesis have proven difficult to translate into refutable research propositions and the phenomena implied by these ideas are often difficult to observe reliably (see Jacob, 1975; Olson, 1972; Schuham, 1967). Indeed, as Bateson (1966) himself later acknowledged, the double bind hypothesis may ultimately prove to be untestable.

In summary, by rejecting basic aspects of psychoanalysis, psychiatrists were able to advance a view of marriages and families that underscored the interpersonal setting in which seemingly maladaptive behavior occurred and that discounted the role of intraindividual processes. The complexity that necessarily accompanied this change in perspective was instrumental in facilitating interest in the study of interaction, yet at the same time that complexity has hindered verification of many central concepts. It is difficult to underestimate the impact this tradition has had on present-day thinking about interaction, as many systems-level ideas can be found in modified form in current research. For example, the renewed interest in the relation between psychopathology and family functioning has yielded a number of studies that combine observational data on family interaction with genetic data on an individual's predisposition to various disorders (e.g., Hahlweg & Goldstein, 1987).

Influences on measurement. As might be expected from the foregoing discussion, many of the early measures in the psychiatry and family therapy tradition reflect an interest in families and schizophrenia. These measures include, for example, structured tasks to assess efficiency in communication (e.g., *1013*), procedures for making clinical ratings of families during or after interviews (e.g., *1057, 1067, 1105*), and observational coding systems (e.g., *1089*).

Although the double bind hypothesis and conceptually similar phenomena (e.g., pseudomutuality) are now rarely studied, more recent developments in this tradition perpetuate the earlier emphasis on communication, psychopathology, and systems-level formulations of family and marital interaction. Moreover, there persists a clear tendency to devise measures for examining interaction within the context of therapy. This is evident, for example, in the numerous and varied interaction scales and methods for rating therapy outcome (e.g., *21, 50*), ratings following clinical interviews (e.g., *74*), and methods for assessing different facets of family communication (e.g., *95*) and family alliances exhibited in interactions (e.g., *64*). Alternative methods for the study of interaction, proposed in order to conduct research rather than solely to generate clinically useful data, will be described below in our discussion of the developmental and clinical psychology traditions.

Finally, it bears noting that researchers in the psychiatry and family therapy tradition are broadening their focus. This expansion of research interests includes the investigation of marital and family interaction in families of alcoholics (e.g., *104*) and the impact of expressed emotion (e.g., critical statements) in families on relapse rates in schizophrenic and chronically depressed individuals (see Hahlweg & Goldstein, 1987).

Developmental Psychology

Unlike family sociology and psychiatry, the importance of interaction was recognized very early in the field of developmental psychology. From the 1920s until the 1940s the study of social development via observational methods was common and observational field studies dominated research in this domain in the early 1930s (Cairns, 1979). Despite initial interest in the behavioral exchanges of children with their peers and with their parents (e.g., Symonds, 1937), the study of interaction fell from favor and, as we describe below, nearly three decades passed before major conceptual changes occurred in how interaction was examined and interpreted.

As in family sociology, the forefathers to interactional thought in developmental psychology include George Herbert Mead and James Mark Baldwin, with the latter devoting particular attention to principles of symbolic interactionism in relation to personality development in children. Baldwin's ideas appear to have received little attention before 1951, however, when Robert Sears encouraged investigators to work toward more complex conceptions of social and personality development, especially as this might be achieved via direct study of social interaction. Perhaps because Sears himself did not undertake research on social interaction, his recommendations were not widely heeded and the next several years were characterized by a continuing decline in interactional and observational studies (Parke, 1979). Emphasis was placed instead on the information that interviews and other self-report methods yielded regarding the association between child development and the child-rearing practices of parents. This strategy served to promote a widely received view of the child as a product of parental behavior and attitudes, a unidirectional perspective that would eventuate in the 1950s and early 1960s being known as the heyday of "social mold" theories (see Hartup, 1978).

In the 1960s, an accumulation of results from experimental studies indicated, for example, that infants exhibit a variety of temperaments (see Thomas & Chess, 1977), that mothers respond differently to different children (e.g., Yarrow, 1963), and that infants and children possess a broad range of social skills and capacities (see Parke, 1979). In sharp contrast to the "social mold" view of child development, these findings led in turn to the realization that children played an active role in interaction. This basic sentiment was captured by Bell (1968), who, in highlighting earlier work by Sears, Maccoby, and Levin (1957, p. 82), argued that "the model of a unidirectional effect from parent to child is overdrawn, a fiction of convenience rather than belief." Together with growing concerns over the ecological validity of experimental research and the unreliability of self-report procedures, Bell's paper was seminal in reestablishing interaction as a focus of inquiry in developmental psychology and in highlighting the importance of bidirectional effects in parent-child interaction. Research that immediately followed Bell's (1968) paper was viewed as equally inappropriate for being unidirectional but in the opposite direction (see Lewis & Rosenblum's edited volume, *The Effect of the Infant on Its Caregiver,* 1974). However, later work recognized the middle ground between these two extremes, and the need to study reciprocity and patterns of mutual influence emerged accordingly.

The interest in interaction continues to gain ascendance in developmental psychology, with three trends being particularly evident (see Parke & Asher, 1983). The first trend involves qualification of what is meant by bidirectionality in interaction and acceptance of the notion that bidirectional effects are not necessarily equivalent in strength. Specifically, as Maccoby and Martin (1983, p. 2) note:

> Our current enthusiasm for [the idea of bidirectionality] should not cause us to lose sight of the enormous differential in power and competence that exists between an adult and an infant, and the potential for asymmetry that this implies. Inevitably, the functions of the two parties to a parent-infant interaction sequence are quite unlike, and in certain respects the parent must be the more influential.

The second trend involves consideration of varieties of interaction and the broader context in which it occurs. For example, increasing attention is given to interaction among peers and siblings and to the ways in which parent-child interaction might be moderated by the presence of other family members (e.g., fathers, other children) and by levels of social support. Finally, as Parke and Asher (1983) note in their review of the field of social development, analyses of social interaction are being supplemented with research on the role of affect and cognition; the movement to consider covert processes such as these will be encountered later in our discussion of current trends in clinical psychology.

To summarize, although developmental psychology shares a common heritage of symbolic interactionism with family sociology, the two traditions differ in that developmental psychologists have a long history of direct investigation of interaction. Early interest in interaction waned, however, and many interview studies on socialization were conducted that tended to affirm a tacit model of development in which changes in children were seen as the consequence of parental characteristics. A confluence of factors in the 1960s, most notably experimental research revealing the capabilities of even very young children, led to bidirectional models of child development and increasingly complex theoretical treatments of parent-child interaction. Subsequent investigations reflected this orientation toward reciprocal interactional effects, and recent conceptual and procedural advances have helped to make developmental psychology an active forum for research on interaction.

Influences on measurement. The historical events described above have left their mark on the methods available for the study of interaction in developmental psychology. For example, in a study published before Bell's (1968) seminal paper, Hetherington and Frankie (1967; see *1076*) devised observational measures that allowed them to examine the effects of parental factors (e.g., dominance, warmth) on children's behavior. Thus, consistent with prevailing "social mold" ideas, methods evolved to demonstrate the impact of parents on children (see also *1071*). After Bell's paper, however, procedures emerged that were designed specifically for the study of bidirectional effects in parent-child interaction. Thus, for example, microanalytic coding systems were devised to study synchrony between adult speech and infant behavior (e.g., Condon & Sander, 1974), the sequential structure of mother-infant behavior and the role of infant attention (e.g., Cohn & Tronick, 1987), the processes by which children comply and fail to comply with parental requests in interaction (e.g., Lytton & Zwirner, 1975), and the impact of paternal engagement on mother-infant interaction (e.g., Lamb & Elster, 1985). Thus, whereas research methods previously favored examination of unidirectional effects in interaction, the historical events described earlier promoted the development of methods that would permit investigation of bidirectional effects (see also *69, 98*).

Although the parent-child relationship is a common focus for the study of interaction in the developmental psychology tradition, measures have also been devised to assess interaction among siblings (e.g., Berndt & Bulleit, 1985) and peers (e.g., Walter, 1985), and the impact of the home environment (of which family interaction is one feature) on child development (e.g., *24, 25*). Finally, consistent with the notion that a complete understanding of interaction requires assessment of intrapersonal phenomena, a number of instruments have appeared for measuring perceptions of parent-child relationships (e.g., *3, 7, 40, 61*).

Learning Theory and Clinical Psychology

Research on interaction within clinical psychology traces its lineage to early experimental work on learning. The implications of learning theory and behaviorism for understanding psychological disorders were recognized early, as evidenced by Watson and Rayner's (1920) demonstration of how fears might be classically conditioned in a child, and Jones's (1924) demonstration of how such fears might be eliminated; the latter work was a direct predecessor to Wolpe's (1958) method of treatment via systematic desensitization. Significant changes in behavior were also attained using operant methods. Lindsley and Skinner (1954), for example, showed that the behavior of hospitalized psychotic people could be modified by following their responses with rewarding consequences.

Within this tradition, the study of interaction appears to have emerged as a consequence of seeking to understand and treat a broader range of psychological disorders. Thus observation of interaction occurred as a result of further application of learning principles to disorders that implicated more than one person. One such area where interaction became a focus of study was pioneered by Gerald Patterson (e.g., Patterson, McNeal, Hawkins, & Phelps, 1967) and involves the behavioral exchanges of aggressive children and their families. A central idea in Patterson's work, based upon operant principles, is that family members can reinforce each other's behavior and can, therefore, inadvertently teach each other to engage in dysfunctional behavior. For example, a mother may ask her son to complete a chore and he may respond with noncompliant, aversive behavior; this may lead the mother to decide that it would be easier to withdraw the original request or ask him to do a simpler chore. The son is thus negatively reinforced for his noncompliance and, because her actions terminated the son's aversive behavior, the mother is also negatively reinforced for submitting to his demands (see Patterson & Bank, 1986). Empirical demonstration of such coercive patterns of interaction has led to structured interventions that are designed to reduce antisocial behavior among children by teaching parents more effective ways of responding to aversive acts (see Patterson, 1982).

The research conducted by Patterson and his colleagues is noteworthy not only for its systematic nature but also for its high standards of methodological rigor in collecting reliable and valid observational data. After noting that interventions in families with aggressive children were often hampered when the parents were maritally distressed, Patterson and his colleagues adapted the coding systems devised originally for family interaction so that they could be used to study marital interaction (see Patterson, Reid,

Jones, & Conger, 1975). As a result of this development and of similar attempts to extend behavioral techniques to the treatment of distressed couples (e.g., Liberman, 1970; Stuart, 1969), the study of marriage emerged as the second domain in clinical psychology in which observation of interaction was of primary interest.

Although similar in many ways to Patterson's research on families, early work on treating distressed couples was influenced also by the concept of quid pro quo. Lederer and Jackson (1968, p. 17), who introduced this concept, argued that "close, enduring human relationships depend on an interplay of behavior which signals to each spouse that whatever he received has been forthcoming in response to something given. In other words, a quid pro quo (something for something) agreement is in effect." As a consequence of this view, marital therapists sought to structure the interactions of distressed couples via reciprocity contracting so that patterns of mutual positive reinforcement would be increased (e.g., Azrin, Naster, & Jones, 1973; Stuart, 1969). Quid pro quo contracting is no longer widely used but related interventions designed to improve communication skills and negotiation between spouses are now employed routinely in behavioral marital therapy (see Jacobson & Margolin, 1979). In addition to these attempts to manipulate interaction patterns in therapy, a large number of observational laboratory studies were conducted to identify the behaviors that discriminate distressed and nondistressed couples (e.g., Birchler, Weiss, & Vincent, 1975; see also Raush, Barry, Hertel, & Swain, 1974). Results of these studies indicate, for example, that the interactions of distressed couples are characterized by a higher rate of negative behaviors, greater reciprocity of negative behaviors, and a greater degree of predictability between partner behaviors (see Schaap, 1984).

The clinical and empirical activities described above have been guided loosely by social learning theory. This broadly inclusive framework, offered originally by Rotter (1954) and later elaborated upon by Bandura (e.g., 1977), represents an expansion of earlier learning models in that emphasis is placed on cognitive and social determinants of learning and on the interplay of behavioral, personal, and environmental variables. Although these factors did not go unrecognized in early formulations of marital and family interaction, recent years have witnessed greater interest in expanding the behavioral model, with particular attention being devoted to the cognitive variables (e.g., attributions, beliefs about relationships) that may mediate behavioral exchanges. Efforts to supplement behavioral accounts of interaction by outlining relevant cognitive processes are now evident, for example, in the study of parent-child interaction (e.g., Bugental, 1987), marital interaction (e.g., Bradbury & Fincham, 1989), and behavioral marital therapy (e.g., Baucom & Lester, 1986).

The contribution of learning theory and clinical psychology to the study of interaction is most evident in the methodological sophistication that has developed for the collection and analysis of observational data, in the clear ties that are established between research findings and therapeutic interventions, and in the willingness to subject treatment strategies to rigorous outcome research. Future progress in this tradition is likely to depend on advances in a number of areas. First, not unlike other traditions, the implications of interactions for later family functioning (e.g., child problems, marital discord) have yet to be widely explored. Second, adherents to the social learning perspective have rarely considered the role of individual difference variables in interaction. Third, little attention has yet been devoted to examining the developmental course of family and marital life from this perspective or to the changes that interactions undergo over time (see also Robinson & Jacobson, 1987).

To summarize, as a result of the orientation of early learning theorists, an emphasis on observable phenomena has long been a hallmark of the behavioral perspective in clinical psychology. As part of a natural progression to examine and treat a broader range of problems from this perspective, interest focused on the interactions that characterize families with an aggressive child and distressed marriages. Since the 1960s large bodies of research devoted to these issues have accumulated, and much is now known about the behavioral patterns that relate to family and marital difficulties. Within the framework provided by social learning theory, the current challenge is to expand behavioral models of interaction to include nonobservable phenomena.

Influences on measurement. The movement to extend principles of learning theory in clinical psychology to families and marriages resulted in a variety of procedures for the study of interaction. One such class of procedures, designed for use by outside observers, has been employed to code behaviors exhibited in interaction by parents and children (e.g., *91*) or by spouses (e.g., *15, 65, 115*). A second class of procedures was designed for use by the interactants themselves, to record on a daily basis the interactive events that occur in the home. Again, instruments for parent-child interaction (e.g., *94*) and marital interaction (e.g., *49, 114, 116*) have been developed. Both sorts of procedures are used widely not only for research but also to obtain information on interaction in clinical settings.

Empirical and clinical application of these instruments has been responsible in part for the increasing interest in covert processes in interaction that we described earlier. Specifically, the coding systems used to quantify overt behavior revealed that nonverbal and affective codes were particularly powerful in discriminating distressed and nondistressed couples in problem-solving interactions, so that affect in close relationships has become a popular focus in research and treatment. Similarly, when self-report measures of daily interaction were used, it was determined that spouses did not routinely agree on the events that occurred in their relationship; this had led in turn to research and treatment that emphasizes how spouses perceive and interpret such events (see *11, 60, 85*). In short, there has been a reciprocal relation between historical events in this tradition and the measurement procedures to which it gave rise.

Conclusion

The purpose of the section was to outline the conceptual shifts that resulted in marital and family interaction becoming a topic of scientific interest. In each case it can be seen that a prevailing view of marriages or families was in some way challenged to bring about a clearer focus on the relationships between spouses and family members and the interactions that occurred between them. This is particularly evident, for example, in Burgess's redefinition of the family as a "unity of interacting personalities," the group of psychiatrists that broke with accepted views of marital therapy and schizophrenia, Bell's reconceptualization of parent-child interaction, and Patterson's work on the families of aggressive children. In addition to the general lesson that much can be gained by recognizing and questioning the tacit assumptions that guide research and theory (e.g., that the family is best viewed as an institution), consideration of historical developments can also yield a number of specific recommendations for research on marital and family interaction. We turn next to a discussion of four such recommendations.

IMPLICATIONS OF HISTORICAL OVERVIEW: DESIDERATA FOR RESEARCH ON MARITAL AND FAMILY INTERACTION

In this section we discuss the implications that the foregoing historical analysis has for future research on marital and family interaction. Specifically, we have derived from this analysis four desirable features of interactional research, including testable theory, recognition of the natural context of interaction, adoption of multiple perspectives, and analysis of sequence. In discussing each of these issues we shall show more specifically how they derive from our consideration of the four major research traditions reviewed earlier and how they can guide more meaningful research.

Testable Theory

Our historical review indicates that theory is a necessary, but not sufficient, condition for generating informative interactional research. Specifically, interrelated sets of studies pertaining to interaction have not emerged in family sociology and psychiatry, despite the presence of well-articulated theories and the recognized need for interactional research. As one example, symbolic interactionism makes clear provisions for the study of interaction yet little progress has been made in translating these ideas into a replicable set of interrelated empirical findings. A second example is provided by the double bind hypothesis, which, after more than a decade of research, was deemed untestable in part because the basic phenomenon could not be observed reliably and because it was stated in imprecise terms.

In a discussion of research on interaction within the tradition of developmental psychology, Cairns (1979) suggests that failures of interactional approaches can be attributed in part to inadequate theoretical frameworks, such that the "chasm between concepts and methods" (p. 5) did not permit systematic research to accumulate. Although we agree with the notion that investigators are likely to encounter difficulties in collecting and reducing observational data in the absence of a sound conceptual foundation, our historical overview suggests an important qualification to Cairns's observation. Specifically, while the importance of any guiding theory cannot be denied, we would maintain that *testable* theory is an essential feature of sound research on marital and family interaction, where testable is taken to mean that constructs that constitute the theory can be described unambiguously and hence can be defined operationally and measured reliably.

Recognition of the Natural Context of Interaction

A desirable starting point for developing and refining theory about interaction is suggested by researchers in the psychiatry and family therapy tradition. These researchers emphasized the need to conduct research on interactions that remains faithful to the setting in which they naturally arise, and they warned against the dangers inherent in premature movement away from the natural context of interaction. As Handel noted in discussing research on schizophrenia and the family (in Framo, 1972, p. 95):

> The psychoanalyst sometimes uses the term "flight into reality," and one thing I get, listening to much of the work that has been done, is that there is what I would call a premature flight into coding, a premature concern with how to score and create indexes, and so on. That, it seems to me, is an entirely too limited concept of research. . . . Certainly some of the earlier and more interesting or stimulating work has not been of this character. People were interested in understanding how families function, and they turned their minds loose upon the material. They asked questions, they talked to families, and then they tried to make some sense out of what they found. I think these are the initial studies that have gotten this movement under way.

Thus the shift we highlighted earlier, whereby schizophrenics were thought to be best studied in the context of their families rather than as isolated individuals, was tempered by the need to study the family system in its natural form.

In contrast to the "flight into coding" that Handel warned against, Patterson's work on families with aggressive children routinely involves the collection of data in homes and schools. Similarly, marital research in clinical psychology reflects recognition of the need to study interaction in its natural context, as a number of studies ask couples to record the pleasing and displeasing events that happen in their relationship on a day-to-day basis. Finally, as we noted above, an increasing number of studies in developmental psychology are being conducted with the awareness that environmental conditions can influence the nature of interactions.

The reasons for conducting ecologically informed research on interaction are manifold. First, as implied by the above observations, such an approach can provide a richer appreciation of the interactional phenomena themselves. Second, this approach will provide a view of interaction that is less likely to be a function of laboratory surroundings and that is more generalizable to other real-life settings. Third, observation of phenomena in nonlaboratory settings will make salient the fact that relationships among interactants extend beyond those viewed in the laboratory and can exert important influences on interactional data that are collected. Indeed, it is the historical character of marital and family interactions that distinguish them from the interactions observed in small group research.

Finally, careful observation of interaction in the context in which it typically occurs will have the benefit of yielding observational coding systems that are well matched to the questions of interest; coding systems are less likely to be used for purposes to which they are not suited. An example of using a coding system that was inappropriate for the task at hand is provided by Winter and Ferreira (1967), who worked within the psychiatry and family therapy tradition. These investigators encountered difficulties in using Bales's (1950) interaction process analysis (see "Family Sociology and Symbolic Interactionism," above)—a coding system that was devised for general application to studying problem solving in groups—to study family interaction. They attributed their failure to obtain adequate reliability between coders to "the subtle pattern of nonverbal and verbal communication within a family, and the immensely rich contextual historical background against which a remark by one family member is judged by the others" (Winter & Ferreira, 1967, p. 171). It is reasonable to infer that this difficulty may not have occurred if family interactions were first observed in their natural setting and a coding system had been devised on the basis of those observations.

Multiple Perspectives

At three points in our historical overview we mentioned that researchers are finding it increasingly valuable to combine behavioral data with some other form of data in order to capture and understand the many facets of marital and family interaction. Thus the tradition involving psychiatry and family therapy is now examining genetic as well as interactional variables in research on psychopathology, and, in developmental and clinical psychology, there is growing interest in affective and cognitive processes. We believe that this common pattern across disciplines is important because it highlights the need to include in future research an array of measures to assess interaction along several dimensions.

Using a variety of measures in the study of interaction has an additional advantage insofar as it ensures that the resulting findings are not an artifact of a particular instrument or method. One obvious distinction to draw in this regard is between self-report measures, which tap subjective aspects of interaction, and observational measures, which provide an objective view of behavioral exchange. Although data collected from these perspectives (a) may not converge to a single conclusion (e.g., an interaction coded negative by observers may not be experienced as negative by the participants) and (b) may not be germane to a particular research question, both perspectives are essential to a complete portrayal of interaction in marriages and families. In fact, discrepancies between these two sources of data are often a source of valuable information.[5]

The case for using a variety of measures extends beyond assessing relatively subjective and objective aspects of interaction. That is, the use of different procedures designed to measure similar constructs can be adopted within either self-report or observational approaches. For example, self-report data could be collected via questionnaire or interview methods, and interactions could be coded by observers using two different coding systems. This strategy is particularly important in family research because of the paucity of multitrait, multimethod studies that allow the convergent and divergent validity of constructs to be fully evaluated.

Taking this argument one step further, it is also desirable to examine interaction at various levels of analysis. Thus observation of interaction can entail global ratings of a particular variable (e.g., aggression) as well as fine-grained coding of that variable for each unit of behavior; indeed, multimethod observational strategies can "serve as a protective net against failure to detect interesting patterns which may not appear at the microanalytic level" (Parke & Asher, 1983, p. 492). Self-report measures, in similar fashion, can be designed to assess interactants' global perceptions of the interaction as they watch a replay of it on videotape or their specific reactions to several distinct events in the interaction; alternatively, statelike variables (e.g., level of tension experienced in interaction) and traitlike variables (e.g., neuroticism) can be assessed to tap different levels of analysis.

Analysis of Sequence

Earlier we discussed an important conceptual shift in developmental psychology whereby Bell (1968) recognized the inadequacy of unidirectional models of parent-child interaction, arguing instead for bidirectional models. In retrospect it appears that the failure to consider sequences among behavior promoted the overly simplified unidirectional view of parent-child interaction (i.e., the "social mold" view, based largely on interview data), and, with Bell's delineation of the possible patterns and sequences that might exist between the behaviors (i.e., variance in child behavior could account for variance in subsequent parent behavior), a more powerful, bidirectional class of models could be embraced. Thus the prior tendency to overlook the sequence of behaviors in interaction led to the development of models that neglected basic aspects of the phenomena of interest. Although still not a standard feature of interaction research, consideration of sequences of interactional behavior is increasingly evident in psychiatry and family therapy, developmental psychology, and clinical psychology.

These advances notwithstanding, the trend toward dynamic sequential formulations has not always been followed with statistical analyses that permit the examination of sequences of behaviors.[6] We would argue, however, that because it necessarily involves at least two people behaving over time, interaction cannot be studied adequately without examining sequential relations among behaviors. In addition to providing a much cruder description of interaction process than that available by sequential analyses, analysis of rates of behavior (i.e., nonsequential analysis) is prone to interpretive error: Coded behaviors that arise from interaction are often interpreted as being determined solely by the one individual who exhibits the behaviors. A more appropriate inference is that the behaviors were determined by the larger interactive context in which they occurred.

For example, observation of unhappy couples interacting might reveal that wives are more likely to exhibit defensiveness, and it might be concluded that defensiveness on the part of wives contributes to marital discord. Sequential analysis, in contrast, could reveal that wives tend to be defensive only after husbands accuse them of being inadequate in some way; the previous conclusion, based only on rates of behavior, would then change to address the patterning of behaviors between husbands and wives. Several techniques are now available to analyze sequences of behavior. Although some (such as time-series analysis) require considerable mathematical expertise, others (such as lag sequential analysis) are relatively straightforward and can be applied by most researchers (see Bakeman & Gottman, 1986; Bradbury & Fincham, in press).

CONCLUSION

Behavioral scientists with an interest in marital and family interaction must contend not only with the richness of interactional phenomena but also with the numerous theories, empirical investigations, and methods for data collection and analysis that have been devised to understand them. The purpose of this chapter has been to provide a background for the many measures that have been developed for the study of marital and family interaction, with the intent of enabling those who seek to use these measures to make well-reasoned choices and to collect data that are maximally informative. We have sought to accomplish this goal, first, by adopting a historical perspective to examine factors that, across four separate traditions, facilitated a transition from a noninteractional view to a perspective in which emphasis was placed on the relationships between spouses and family members and on the interactions that occur between them. A general implication of this analysis is that much can be achieved conceptually from critical scrutiny of otherwise implicit notions of how interaction is best approached. In addition, the historical overview allowed us to derive four specific desiderata that should be considered in any study of marital and family interaction, namely, testable theory, recognition of the natural context of interaction, adoption of multiple perspectives, and analysis of sequence.

A risk of setting high standards such as these is that they may actually serve to suppress rather than promote further study of interaction. It is therefore important to emphasize that the desiderata we have specified are perhaps best viewed as criteria to strive for, rather than necessarily attain, in a given investigation. Indeed, these desiderata may be very difficult to address in some situations (e.g., clinical contexts) and may be inconsistent with the goals of some interactional research (e.g., where sequences of behavior are not of immediate interest). Because the recommendations we have offered are unlikely to be met in every instance of data collection, it follows that they can only be achieved fully over the course of several studies on a given topic. Indeed, the importance of programmatic research, which was identified by Berardo (1980) as the first of several "priority needs" for the study of marriages and families in this decade, is especially salient when complex matters such as interaction are under examination.

NOTES

1. A noteworthy exception to the imprecision that characterized data collection in the era of social Darwinism is the work of Frederick LePlay. Although not appreciated at the time, LePlay's (1855) essays were probably the first systematic attempts to obtain valid data on the family, and his methods anticipated the development of modern interview schedules, surveys, and questionnaires.

2. It should be noted that these traditions do not exist in isolation but, for ease of presentation, each will be considered separately. Also, owing to space limitations, our discussion of issues within these traditions will be more illustrative than exhaustive.

3. It bears noting that the work of Thomas and Znaniecki (1918–1920) is an earlier example of how the family can be studied in terms of its internal and subjective elements. This work, to which Burgess alludes in his 1926 paper, has not received the same degree of recognition as has that of Burgess.

4. Some of the interaction instruments catalogued in this volume cannot be attributed directly to any of the four traditions we will be addressing. These instruments were developed instead within other disciplines where interest in interaction is a more recent occurrence. These disciplines include, for example, communication studies (e.g., *13, 51, 109*), social psychology (e.g., *68, 76, 111*), and marital enrichment (e.g., *66, 101, 106, 157*).

5. A third perspective can be obtained by collecting physiological data during interaction. Although not as common as self-report and observational approaches, increasing interest in physiological data is emerging in the clinical psychology tradition as part of the general movement to integrate nonobservable constructs (e.g., affect) with overt behavior.

6. One exception to this observation was discussed earlier and involves the study of interaction in clinical psychology; for example, on the basis of sequential analysis it is known that distressed spouses are more likely than nondistressed spouses to respond to negative partner behaviors with negative behaviors of their own, and that in distressed marriages there is greater stereotypy or predictability between spouses' behaviors.

REFERENCES

Ackerman, N. W. (1938). The unity of the family. *Archives of Pediatrics, 55,* 51–62.

Ackerman, N. W. (1954). The diagnosis of neurotic marital interaction. *Social Casework, 35,* 139–147.

Azrin, N. H., Naster, B. M., & Jones, R. (1973). Reciprocity counseling: A rapid learning-based procedure for marital counseling. *Behaviour Research and Therapy, 11,* 365–382.

Bakeman, R., & Gottman, J. M. (1986). *Observing interaction.* Cambridge: Cambridge University Press.

Bales, R. F. (1950). *Interaction process analysis.* Cambridge, MA: Addison-Wesley.

Bandura, A. (1977). *Social learning theory.* Englewood Cliffs, NJ: Prentice-Hall.

Bateson, G. (1966). Slippery theories. *International Journal of Psychiatry, 2,* 415–417.

Bateson, G., Jackson, D. D., Haley, J., & Weakland, J. (1956). Toward a theory of schizophrenia. *Behavioral Science, 1,* 251–264.

Baucom, D. H., & Lester, G. W. (1986). The usefulness of cognitive restructuring as an adjunct to behavioral marital therapy. *Behavior Therapy, 17,* 385–403.

Bell, R. Q. (1968). A reinterpretation of the direction of effects in studies of socialization. *Psychological Review, 75,* 81–95.

Berardo, F. M. (1980). Decade preview: Some trends for family research and theory in the 1980s. *Journal of Marriage and the Family, 42,* 723–728.

Berndt, T. J., & Bulleit, T. N. (1985). Effects of sibling relationships on preschoolers' behavior at home and at school. *Developmental Psychology, 21,* 761–767.

Birchler, G., Weiss, R., & Vincent, J. (1975). Multimethod analysis of social reinforcement exchange between maritally distressed and nondistressed spouse and stranger dyads. *Journal of Personality and Social Psychology, 31,* 349–360.

Bradbury, T. N., & Fincham, F. D. (1989). Behavior and satisfaction in marriage: Prospective mediating processes. *Review of Personality and Social Psychology, 10,* 119–143.

Bradbury, T. N., & Fincham, F. D. (in press). The analysis of sequence in social interaction. In D. G. Gilbert & J. J. Conley (Eds.), *Personality, social skills, and psychopathology: An individual differences approach.* New York: Plenum.

Broderick, C. B., & Schrader, S. S. (1981). The history of professional marriage and family therapy. In A. S. Gurman & D. P. Kniskern (Eds.), *Handbook of family therapy* (pp. 5–35). New York: Brunner/Mazel.

Bugental, D. B. (1987). Attributions as moderator variables within social interactional systems. *Journal of Social and Clinical Psychology, 5,* 469–484.

Burgess, E. W. (1926). The family as a unity of interacting personalities. *Family, 7,* 3–9.

Cairns, R. B. (1979). Social interactional methods: An introduction. In R. B. Cairns (Ed.), *The analysis of social interaction* (pp. 1–9). Hillsdale, NJ: Lawrence Erlbaum.

Christensen, H. T. (1964). Development of the family field of study. In H. T. Christensen (Ed.), *Handbook of marriage and the family* (pp. 3–32). Chicago: Rand McNally.

Cohn, J. F., & Tronick, E. Z. (1987). Mother-infant face-to-face interaction: The sequence of dyadic states at 3, 6, and 9 months. *Developmental Psychology, 23,* 68–77.

Condon, W. S., & Sander, L. W. (1974). Neonate movement is synchronized with adult speech: Interactional participation and language acquisition. *Science, 183,* 99–101.

Framo, J. L. (1972). *Family interaction.* New York: Springer.

Gottman, J. M. (1979). *Marital interaction: Experimental investigations.* New York: Academic Press.

Guerin, P. J. (Ed.). (1976). *Family therapy: Theory and practice.* New York: Gardener.

Gurman, A. S., & Kniskern, D. P. (1981). *Handbook of family therapy.* New York: Brunner/Mazel.

Hahlweg, K., & Goldstein, M. J. (Eds.). (1987). *Understanding major mental disorder: The contribution of family interaction research.* New York: Family Process Press.

Handel, G. (1965). Psychological study of whole families. *Psychological Bulletin, 63,* 19–41.

Hartup, W. W. (1978). Perspectives on child and family interaction: Past, present, and future. In R. M. Lerner & G. B. Spanier (Eds.), *Child influences on marital and family interaction.* New York: Academic Press.

Hetherington, E. M., & Frankie, G. (1967). Effects of parental dominance, warmth, and conflict on imitation in children. *Journal of Personality and Social Psychology, 6,* 119–125.

Hodgson, J. W., & Lewis, R. A. (1979). Pilgrim's progress III: Trend analysis of family theory and methodology. *Family Process, 18,* 163–173.

Holman, T. B., & Burr, W. R. (1980). Beyond the beyond: The growth of family theories in the 1970s. *Journal of Marriage and the Family, 42,* 729–741.

Jacob, T. (1975). Family interaction in disturbed and normal families: A methodological and substantive review. *Psychological Bulletin, 82,* 33–65.

Jacob, T. (1987). Family interaction and psychopathology: Historical overview. In T. Jacob (Ed.), *Family interaction and psychopathology* (pp. 3–22). New York: Plenum.

Jacobson, N. S., & Margolin, G. (1979). *Marital therapy: Strategies based on social learning and behavior exchange principles.* New York: Brunner/Mazel.

Jones, M. C. (1924). The elimination of children's fears. *Journal of Experimental Psychology, 7,* 383–390.

Kerr, M. E. (1981). Family systems theory and therapy. In A. S. Gurman & D. P. Kniskern (Eds.), *Handbook of family therapy* (pp. 226–264). New York: Brunner/Mazel.

Lamb, M. E., & Elster, A. B. (1985). Adolescent mother-infant-father relationships. *Developmental Psychology, 21,* 768–773.

Lederer, W. J., & Jackson, D. D. (1968). *The mirages of marriage.* New York: Norton.

LePlay, P. G. F. (1855). *Les ouvriers Europeens* [Working-class families of Europe]. Paris: Imprimerie Royale.

Lewis, M., & Rosenblum, L. A. (Eds.). (1974). *The effect of the infant on its caregiver.* New York: John Wiley.

Liberman, R. P. (1970). Behavioral approaches to family and couple therapy. *American Journal of Orthopsychiatry, 40,* 106–118.

Lindsley, O. R., & Skinner, B. F. (1954). A method for the experimental analysis of the behavior of psychotic patients. *American Psychologist, 9,* 419–420.

Lytton, H., & Zwirner, W. (1975). Compliance and its controlling stimuli observed in a natural setting. *Developmental Psychology, 11,* 769–779.

Maccoby, E. E., & Martin, J. A. (1983). Socialization in the context of the family: Parent-child interaction. In E. M. Hetherington (Ed.), *Handbook of child psychology* (Vol. 4, pp. 1–101). New York: John Wiley.

Mittelman, B. (1944). Complementary neurotic reactions in intimate relationships. *Psychoanalytic Quarterly, 13,* 479–491.

Nye, F. I. (1988). Fifty years of family research: 1937–1987. *Journal of Marriage and the Family, 50,* 305–316.

Olson, D. H. (1972). Empirically unbinding the double bind: Review of research and conceptual reformulations. *Family Process, 11,* 69–94.

Parke, R. D. (1979). Interactional designs. In R. B. Cairns (Ed.), *The analysis of social interaction* (pp. 15–35). Hillsdale, NJ: Lawrence Erlbaum.

Parke, R. D., & Asher, S. R. (1983). Social and personality development. *Annual Review of Psychology, 34,* 465–509.

Patterson, G. R. (1982). *Coercive family process.* Eugene, OR: Castalia.

Patterson, G. R., & Bank, L. (1986). Bootstrapping your way in the nomological thicket. *Behavioral Assessment, 8,* 49–73.

Patterson, G. R., McNeal, S., Hawkins, N., & Phelps, R. (1967). Reprogramming the social environment. *Journal of Child Psychology and Psychiatry, 8,* 181–195.

Patterson, G. R., Reid, J. B., Jones, R. R., & Conger, R. E. (1975). *A social learning approach to family intervention* (Vol. 1). Eugene, OR: Castalia.

Raush, H. L., Barry, W. A., Hertel, R. K., & Swain, M. A. (1974). *Communication, conflict, and marriage.* San Francisco: Jossey-Bass.

Richardson, H. B. (1945). *Patients have families.* New York: Commonwealth Fund.

Robinson, E. A., & Jacobson, N. S. (1987). Social learning theory and family psychopathology. In T. Jacob (Ed.), *Family interaction and psychopathology* (pp. 117–162). New York: Plenum.

Rotter, J. B. (1954). *Social psychology and clinical psychology.* Englewood Cliffs, NJ: Prentice-Hall.

Sager, C. J. (1966). The treatment of married couples. In S. Arieti (Ed.), *American handbook of psychiatry* (Vol. 3). New York: Basic Books.

Schaap, C. (1984). A comparison of the interaction of distressed and nondistressed married couples in a laboratory situation: Literature survey, methodological issues, and an empirical investigation. In K. Hahlweg & N. S. Jacobson (Eds.), *Marital interaction: Analysis and modification* (pp. 133–158). New York: Guilford.

Schuham, A. I. (1967). The double-bind hypothesis a decade later. *Psychological Bulletin, 68,* 409–416.

Sears, R. R. (1951). A theoretical framework for personality and social behavior. *American Psychologist, 6,* 476–483.

Sears, R. R., Maccoby, E. E., & Levin, H. (1957). *Patterns of child rearing.* Evanston, IL: Row Peterson.

Straus, M. A. (1964). Measuring families. In H. T. Christensen (Ed.), *Handbook of marriage and the family* (pp. 335–400). Chicago: Rand McNally.

Strodtbeck, F. L. (1951). Husband-wife interaction over revealed differences. *American Sociological Review, 16,* 468–473.

Stryker, S. (1964). The interactional and situational approaches. In H. T. Christensen (Ed.), *Handbook of marriage and the family* (pp. 125–170). Chicago: Rand McNally.

Stuart, R. B. (1969). Operant-interpersonal treatment for marital discord. *Journal of Consulting and Clinical Psychology, 33,* 675–682.

Symonds, P. M. (1937). Some basic concepts in parent-child relations. *American Journal of Psychology, 50,* 195–206.

Thomas, A., & Chess, S. (1977). *Temperament and development.* New York: Brunner/Mazel.

Thomas, W. I., & Znaniecki, F. (1918–1920). *The polish peasant in Europe and America.* Boston: Badger.

Veroff, J., Kulka, R. A., & Douvan, E. (1981). *Mental health in America: Patterns of help-seeking from 1957–1976.* New York: Basic Books.

Waller, W. (1938). *The family: A dynamic interpretation.* New York: Dryden.

Walter, M. D. (1985). Negotiation of responsibility: Judgments of blameworthiness in a natural setting. *Developmental Psychology, 21,* 725–736.

Watson, J. B., & Rayner, R. (1920). Conditioned emotional reactions. *Journal of Experimental Psychology, 3,* 1–14.

Winter, W. D., & Ferreira, A. J. (1967). Interaction process analysis of family decision-making. *Family Process, 6,* 155–172.

Wolpe, J. (1958). *Psychotherapy by reciprocal inhibition.* Stanford, CA: Stanford University Press.

Yarrow, L. J. (1963). Research in dimensions of early maternal care. *Merrill-Palmer Quarterly, 9,* 101–114.

ABSTRACTS OF INSTRUMENTS

NOTE: For additional instruments, see also *Abstracts 1001–1115* in the Abbreviated Abstracts of Instruments (which precedes the Indexes).

Summary of Instrument Codes

Number Codes:

I = Dimensions of interaction—1 = communication; 2 = life-style; 3 = networks; 4 = multidimensional perspectives

II = Intimacy and family values—1 = family values; 2 = marital relations; 3 = love; 4 = sex; 5 = personal/interpersonal perceptions

III = Parenthood—1 = pregnancy, childbearing, and transition to parenthood; 2 = parenting

IV = Roles and power—1 = roles; 2 = power

V = Adjustment—1 = family functioning; 2 = stress; 3 = divorce, separation, and remarriage

Letter Codes:

Interactants—a = husband-wife, b = parent-child, c = nuclear family, d = extended family, e = others outside the family, f = siblings, g = intrapsychic processes

Focus of Study—P = parents, C = child, H = husband, W = wife, O = any combination of the above (if there is no capital letter code given, it is understood to be "O")

I-1/V-3/a/P

1. AHRONS, C. R., & GOLDSMITH, J. Quality of Coparental Communication

Avail: NAPS-3

Variables Measured: Conflict and support in coparental relationships among divorced couples

Type of Instrument: Semistructured interview; may also be adapted using a Likert-type scale

Instrument Description: This instrument consists of two subscales, one addressing conflict (four items) and the other addressing support issues (six items). The scales—which may be used individually, in combination, or as part of a larger interview package—contain five response options ranging from 1 (*always*) to 5 (*never*). Items from the coparental conflict subscale would easily lend themselves to open-ended interview techniques and thus could be used as part of a clinical interview.

Sample Items:

(A) When you and your former spouse discuss parenting issues, how often does an argument result?

(B)   If your former spouse has needed to make a change in visiting arrangements, do you
       go out of your way to accommodate?
(C)   When you need help regarding the children, do you seek it from your former
       spouse?

Comments: Cronbach's alpha is reported in studies with both scales. In studies with approximately 200 subjects equally split between men and women, the author reports alpha
levels for the subscales between .74 and .88.

References:

Ahrons, C. R. (1981). The continuing coparental relationship between divorced spouses. *Am
       J Orthop, 51,* 315–328. Reprinted in D. Olson & B. Miller (Eds.). (1984). *Family
       studies yearbook* (Vol. 2). Beverly Hills, CA: Sage.
Ahrons, C. R. (1983). Predictors of paternal involvement postdivorce: Mothers' and fathers'
       perceptions. *J Divorce, 6*(3), 55–69.
Ahrons, C. R., & Wallisch, L. (1987). Parenting in the binuclear family: Relationships be-
       tween biological and stepparents. In K. Pasley & M. Ihinger-Tallman (Eds.), *Remar-
       riage and stepfamilies: Research and theory.* New York: Guilford.

I-1/c
2. ALEXANDER, J. F. Defensive and Supportive Communication Inter-
action System

Avail: NAPS-3

Variables Measured: Supportive person- and process-enhancing communications, and defensive or person-devaluing communications

Type of Instrument: Rating scale used in assessing live or videotaped interactions

Instrument Description: An observational coding manual describes each category and
subcategory and provides verbal and nonverbal examples. Coders are generally assigned to
one family member or therapist while observing an interaction, or while reading transcripts
and listening to an audiotaped interaction. Behavior is time-sampled in 6-second segments
and coded. If both defensive and supportive behaviors occur during the coding unit, coders
rate the unit as defensive. Coders can also use the manual for molar ratings of larger segments
of interactions by assigning a rating indicating frequency of occurrence for each category
during longer observational periods.

Sample Items: Not applicable.

Comments: Interrater reliability of ratings when behavior has been time-sampled in 6-
second and 1- to 5-minute clusters have averaged .94 for supportiveness, .85 for defensiveness, and .81 for object of communication. Further studies demonstrated Cohen kappa indexes of agreement for bounded speech units in family therapy ranging from .72 to 1.00, and
.76 to .92, for transcriptions of family interaction. Positive correlations among subcategories
and negative correlations between the two major categories reflect convergent and discriminant validity.

References:

Alexander, J. F. (1973). Defensive and supportive communications in normal and deviant
       families. *J Cons Clin, 40,* 223–231.
Alexander, J. F., Barton, C., Schiavo, R. S., & Parsons, B. V. (1976). Behavioral intervention

with families of delinquents: Therapist characteristics and outcome. *J Cons Clin, 44,* 656–664.

Barton, C., Alexander, J. F., Waldron, H., Turner, C. W., & Warburton, J. (1985). Generalizing treatment effects of functional family therapy: Three replications. *Am J Fam Th, 13*(3), 16–26.

I-1/b
3. BARNES, H., & OLSON, D. H. Inventory of Parent-Adolescent Communication

Avail: 1985 Ref.

Variables Measured: Amount of openness, problems or barriers to family communication, and selectivity of family members in their discussions with other family members

Type of Instrument: Self-report questionnaire

Instrument Description: This instrument is a 20-item Likert-type scale designed to measure both positive and negative aspects of communication between teenagers and their parents as well as content and process variables of communication. The scale can be used in questioning the adolescent or either parent. When used with adolescents, it is administered twice, once for each parent. It was derived from an initial item pool of 35 items, with the final scale resulting from a factor analysis on data collected using the overall scale. Two subscales are included. The first, open family communication, is designed to tap positive aspects of communication between parents and their adolescent children. The second, problems in family communication, concentrates on negative aspects of communication. All items on both subscales utilize a 5-point response format ranging from *strongly disagree* to *strongly agree*. Following reversal of scores in the problems subscale, items within subscales are summed to arrive at composite scores.

Sample Items:

(A)   I am very satisfied with how my (mother/father, or adolescent) and I talk together.
(B)   My (mother/father, child) has a tendency to say things to me which would be better left unsaid.
(C)   My (mother/father, child) insults me when s/he is angry with me.

Comments: The 20-item scale was initially believed to contain three factors. The authors report that analyses on this initial scale found Cronbach's alpha to range from .80 to .92 for the subscales. Test-retest correlations after four to five weeks are reported to range from .64 to .78. A second set of studies in which a two-factor solution was used resulted in alpha levels of .78 for the problems in family communication subscale, .87 for open family communication, and .88 for the overall instrument. Factor loadings on the primary factors for the two-factor solution ranged from .48 to .71 for open family communication, and from .26 to .60 for problems in family communication.

Reference:

Olson, D. H., McCubbin, H. I., Barnes, H., Larsen, A., Muxem, M., & Wilson, M. (1985). *Family inventories.* St. Paul, MN: University of Minnesota, Family Social Science.

I-1/c

4. BELL, D. C., BELL, L. G., & CORNWELL, C. Interaction Process Coding Scheme (IPCS)

Avail: ERIC No. ED 248 420

Variables Measured: Communication and interactional styles and processes with marital couples and families

Type of Instrument: Ratings based on audio- or videotaped interactions

Instrument Description: The purpose of the IPCS is to make possible the detailed coding and description of interactional processes. Verbal and paraverbal communication (e.g., laughter, content-free speech) are included. For a 20-minute marital interaction, up to 25 hours can be required for coding all scales. Up to 35 hours may be needed for family transcripts. It has been used to code marital and family interaction processes around a revealed difference task. The instrument was developed for use with audio- or videotaped interactions. To score accurately, a transcription of the interaction process is necessary. The coding manual gives detailed instructions for typing, unitizing (breaking speech into units for coding), and coding each of the various scales. It is possible to use some scales and not others, or to adapt specific scales to better accommodate a particular theoretical interest. Six scales have been identified: (1) floor control measures (who speaks, interruptions, and so on), (2) topic measures (staying on or avoiding task), (3) orientation of speaker (verb tense, use of facts versus opinions, and so on), (4) focus of speech (feelings, attitudes, behaviors), (5) support (positive, negative, neutral tone of voice), (6) acknowledgment of others.

Sample Items:

(A) Floor control: Claiming the floor (Well; Wait a minute).
(B) Focus: Emotions or feelings (You look depressed; He hates her).
(C) Focus: Process of thinking (He took it that way; I must have misinterpreted it).

Comments: The authors report interrater reliabilities ranging from .71 to .97, depending on the scale. Reliabilities for particular scales are reported in the manual. Validity has been assessed using scales from the IPCS to study relationships between family systems and adolescent ego development, and in the study of marital interaction processes in dual-career couples.

References:

Bell, D. C., & Bell, L. G. (1981). *Patterns of verbal communication in strong families.* (ERIC Document Reproduction Service No. ED 216 280)

Bell, D. C., & Bell, L. G. (1983). Parental validation and support in the development of adolescent daughters. In H. D. Grotevant & C. R. Cooper (Eds.), *Adolescent development in the family: New directions for child development.* San Francisco: Jossey-Bass.

Bell, D. C., & Bell, L. G. (1984). Family research project progress report. (ERIC Document Reproduction Service No. ED 248 420)

I-1/a

5. BIENVENU, M. J., Sr. A Marital Communication Inventory (MCI)

Avail: 1983a or 1983b Refs., & Family Life Publications, Inc., P.O. Box 427, Saluda, NC 28773

Variables Measured: Levels of communication between married couples

Type of Instrument: Self-report questionnaire

Instrument Description: The MCI is a 4-point, 46-item Likert-type questionnaire designed to uncover areas of communication difficulty between husbands and wives. Item responses vary from *usually* to *never,* and are scored from 0 to 3. The 46 items refer to the characteristic styles, degrees, and patterns of communication between marriage partners. Elements of communication include the handling of anger and differences, tone of voice, understanding and empathy, self-disclosure, listening habits, nagging, conversational discourtesies, and uncommunicativeness. A second portion of the MCI gives six sentence stems that relate to marital communication, asking respondents to complete each. Separate forms are available for husbands and wives. The inventory was designed for use by counselors as well as by couples in the privacy of their own homes.

Sample Items: The publisher did not grant permission to reproduce items.

Comments: The MCI was originally developed in 1969, and was revised in 1979. The author indicated that split-half reliability of original version was .93. Further evidence of reliability is provided by several others, with Cronbach's alpha generally being reported in the .95 range. Test-retest reliability over five-week (Schumm & Jackson, 1980) and two-month (Rappaport, 1976) periods is reported to be .92 and .94, respectively. Evidence concerning the relationship of MCI scores to several inventories of marital adjustment and communication is also reported in the literature.

References:

Bienvenu, M. J. (1970). Measurement of marital communication. *Fam Coord, 19,* 26–31.

Elliott, M. W. (1982). Communication and empathy in marital adjustment. *Home Ec Res J, 11,* 77–88.

Schumm, W. R., Anderson, S. A., & Griffin, C. L. (1983). The Marital Communication Inventory. In E. E. Filsinger (Ed.), *Marriage and family assessment* (pp. 191–208). Beverly Hills, CA: Sage.

Schumm, W. R., Anderson, S. A., Race, G. S., Morris, J. E., Griffin, C. L., McCutchen, M. B., & Benigas, J. E. (1983). Construct validity of the Marital Communication Inventory. *J Sex Mar Ther, 9,* 153–162.

I-1/a

6. BIENVENU, M. J., Sr. A Premarital Communication Inventory (PCI)

Avail: 1975 Ref., & Family Life Publications, Inc., P.O. Box 427, Saluda, NC 28773

Variables Measured: Areas of communication difficulty between premarital couples

Type of Instrument: Self-report questionnaire

Instrument Description: The PCI is a three-part questionnaire designed to elicit information regarding communication with one's partner and areas of potential difficulty during a pending marriage. Part I consists of 40 three-point items phrased as questions, with response options consisting of *yes, usually; no, seldom;* and *sometimes.* Responses are scored on a 1–3 basis, allowing for summation of scores across items. Scoring varies among items, with individual responses being scored from 0 to 3. Scoring is such that *sometimes* is always scored either 0 or 1, with yes and no responses being scored either 0 or 3. The range of possible scores is from 0 to 120. Higher scores are interpreted as being more favorable. Part II of the PCI contains seven incomplete sentences that can be interpreted as allowing for more open and revealing indications of satisfactory or unsatisfactory communication. Part III requests general information about the respondent. The overall inventory was designed for use by counselors, by ministers, in premarital classes, and for research purposes. Administration time is approximately 10–15 minutes.

Sample Items: The publisher did not grant permission to reproduce items.

Comments: The author reports on a 1971–1973 study during which 530 subjects were administered the PCI. Mean scores for males were reported to be 96.4. Mean scores for females were reported to be 99.0.

References:

Bienvenu, M. J. (1969). Measurement of parent-adolescent communication. *Fam Coord, 18,* 117–121.
Bienvenu, M. J. (1970). Measurement of marital communication. *Fam Coord, 19,* 26–31.
Bienvenu, M. J. (1975). A measurement of premarital communication. *J Comm, 24,* 65–68.
Bienvenu, M. J. (1984). The Sexual Communication Inventory. In *1984 resource guide* (p. 9). Saluda, NC: Family Life.

I-1/b/C
7. BIENVENU, M. J., Sr. Parent-Adolescent Communication Inventory (PACI)

Avail: Family Life Publications, Inc., P.O. Box 427, Saluda, NC 28773

Variables Measured: Interpersonal communication between parent and adolescent

Type of Instrument: Self-report questionnaire

Instrument Description: The PACI is a three-point, 40-item instrument designed to assess levels of communication between parents and their adolescent children. The author indicates that the inventory is best suited for use with adolescents 13 years or older with two parents or parent figures in the home. Alternate forms are available for use with parents and adolescents. Communication is defined as the process of transmitting feelings, attitudes, facts, beliefs, and ideas. The items refer to various styles and characteristics of parent-adolescent communication, such as listening habits, self-expression, understanding, acceptance, criticism, sarcasm, and trust. The instrument is intended for use by counselors, educators, and researchers. When used by counselors, the instrument is intended to highlight areas of communication difficulty within the family. A 9-item sentence-completion inventory is appended to the adolescent form of the questionnaire, and was designed for use along with the multiple-choice portion of the PACI. Response options for the 40-item portion consist of *yes, usually; no, seldom;* and *sometimes.* Responses are scored on a 1–3 basis, allowing for summation of scores across items. Scoring varies among items, with individual responses being scored from 0 to 3. Scoring is such that *sometimes* is always scored either 0 or 1, with *yes* and *no* responses being scored either 0 or 3. The range of possible scores is from 0 to 120. Higher scores are interpreted as being more favorable. Administration time is approximately 20 minutes.

Sample Items: The publisher did not grant permission to reproduce items.

Comments: The PACI was originally developed in 1968 and was revised in 1979. Validity information obtained at that time was based on studies of normal, delinquent, high-achieving, and low-achieving adolescents. The author reports test-retest reliability for three-week (.78) and two-week (.88) periods. LaCoste, Ginter, and Whipple (1987) report on a study in which Cronbach's alpha for the PACI was found to be .93. The PACI was designed for both group and individual administration. Norms and percentile equivalents are presented in the manual.

References:

Bienvenu, M. J. (1969). Measurement of parent-adolescent communication. *Fam Coord, 18,* 117–121.
LaCoste, L. D., Ginter, E. J., & Whipple, G. (1987). Intrafamily communication and familial environment. *Psychol Rep, 61,* 115–118.
Matteson, R. (1974). Adolescent self-esteem, family communication, and marital satisfaction. *J Psychol, 86,* 35–47.
Murphy, D. C., & Mendelson, L. A. (1973). Communication and adjustment in marriage: Investigating the relationship. *Fam Proc, 12,* 317–326.

I-1/II-4/a
8. BIENVENU, M. J., Sr. The Sexual Communication Inventory (SCI)

Avail: Family Life Publications, Inc., P.O. Box 427, Saluda, NC 28773

Variables Measured: Level and type of communication regarding sexual matters among partners

Type of Instrument: Self-report questionnaire

Instrument Description: The SCI is a three-part questionnaire designed to elicit information regarding communication with one's partner regarding sexual issues. Part I consists of 30 three-point items phrased as questions, with response options consisting of *yes, usually; no, seldom;* and *sometimes.* Responses are scored on a 1–3 basis, allowing for summation of scores across items. Possible scores range from 30 to 90. Higher scores are interpreted as being more favorable. Part II of the SCI contains seven incomplete sentences that can be interpreted as allowing for more open and revealing indications of satisfactory or unsatisfactory communication on sexual matters. Part III asks for general information about the respondent. The overall inventory was designed for counseling, classroom, and research use. Administration time is approximately 10–15 minutes.

Sample Items: The publisher did not grant permission to reproduce items.

Comments: The scale was initially constructed using items from the author's other communication scales, clinical experiences, and suggestions from colleagues. The initial item pool was presented to a panel of sex therapists. Feedback from this group resulted in some deletions and additions. The author reports on a pilot study of 19 males and 24 females receiving sex therapy. Mean SCI scores were 64.5 and 65.9 for males and females, respectively. An item analysis resulting from that study resulted in further modifications to the instrument.

References:

Bienvenu, M. J. (1970). Measurement of marital communication. *Fam Coord, 19,* 26–31.
Bienvenu, M. J. (1971). An interpersonal communication inventory. *J Comm, 21,* 381–388.
Bienvenu, M. J. (1976). Dimensions of interpersonal communication. *J Psychol, 93,* 105–111.
Bienvenu, M. J. (1984). The Sexual Communication Inventory. In *1984 resource guide* (p. 4). Saluda, NC: Family Life.

I-1/c

9. BLECHMAN, E. A., McENROE, M. J., RUFF, M., CARR, R., ACHATZKES, A., SHEIBER, F., & DUMAS, J. Blechman Interaction Scoring System (BLISS)

Avail: ASIP, 17 Palmer St. #4, Cos Cob, CT 06807

Variables Measured: Communication and problem-solving behaviors

Type of Instrument: Behavior coding scheme

Instrument Description: The BLISS is a method of observing and coding family interactions in real time, while simultaneously entering the resulting data into a computer for analysis. The INTERACT software system, available with the BLISS, provides the infrastructure of the coding, data-entry, and data-processing system. BLISS was specifically developed to ensure a clear distinction between communication and problem-solving codes. It can be used to code therapist-family as well as intrafamilial interactions. Both a description of interaction units and a fine-grained functional analysis of their impact are derived. Trained observers code live or videotaped interactions involving any number of people. Each interaction giving rise to a "complete thought unit" is coded in a five-part string describing: (1) actor 1; (2) actor 1's behavior; (3) actor 2, who is the object of the behavior; (4) adverbs that modify the behavior; and (5) valence of actor 1's affect. Whenever actor 1's behavior requires a response from actor 2 (e.g., actor 1 seeks attention from actor 2), actor 2's response is coded in the subsequent string. Through sequential analysis of pairs of strings, the BLISS is designed to determine the likelihood of various outcomes of initial behaviors of any given actor. The coding system specifies which strings evidence deficient or skillful communication. Skillful communication is equated with the exclusive use of seven teaching string categories: facilitative listening, self-disclosure, problem solving, request, compliance, descriptive praise, and selective inattention. The INTERACT program allows for analysis of any combination of specific string parts or specific strings, and for clustering of specific strings into all possible categories.

Sample Items: Not applicable.

Comments: The BLISS manual includes various codes and classifications for 22 behaviors, 26 adverbs, 3 levels of affect (negative, neutral, and positive), 8 behavioral responses, 9 interactional settings, and 8 classifications for actors. Several examples of coded interactions are also included.

Reference:

Blechman, E. A., Tryon, A., McEnroe, M. J., & Ruff, M. (in press). Behavioral approaches to psychological assessment: A comprehensive strategy for the measurement of family interaction. In M. M. Katz & S. Wetzler (Eds.), *Contemporary approaches to psychological assessment.* New York: Brunner/Mazel.

I-1/a

10. BORKIN, J., THOMAS, E. J., & WALTER, C. L. The Marital Communication Rating Schedule

Avail: 1980 Ref.

Variables Measured: Verbal behavior pertaining to content of conversations between spouses, vocal characteristics, statements that control or focus the conversation, or referent representations

Type of Instrument: Observational ratings

Instrument Description: The Marital Communication Rating Schedule is an observationally based clinical rating system for assessing verbal behavior in marital communication. It is used by the clinician either immediately following an actual discussion or after reviewing a discussion on audio- or videotape. It is designed to be completed in 5 to 10 minutes by a clinician who is familiar with the categories and the definitions, following his or her listening to a 15- to 30-minute discussion between a married couple. The scale is used to identify specific verbal behaviors that are appropriate targets for modification. Each interactant is rated on each of the 37 categories. The first 20 categories are rated on a 7-point bipolar scale. These are behaviors that may occur too much or too little, where the midpoint indicates appropriateness. The final 17 items are behaviors that are considered dysfunctional and are rated on a 4-point scale from *does not occur* to *occurs frequently*. Although combinations of scores into composite ratings are possible, the author reports that formal scoring has not been used because the instrument is intended to help clinicians identify excessive or deficient behaviors that can be seen by the ratings themselves.

Sample Items:

(A)   Negative Statements (7-point scale).
(B)   Acknowledgments (7-point scale).
(C)   Aversive Tone of Voice (4-point scale).

Comments: The author reports having collected preliminary reliability and validity information. The Marital Communication Rating Schedule is an extension and revision of the Verbal Problem Checklist reported initially by Thomas, Walter, and O'Flaherty (1974). Details and rationale for the revisions and a discussion of other possible uses for the rating schedule appear in Borkin, Thomas, and Walter (1980).

References:

Borkin, J., Thomas, E. J., & Walter, C. L. (1980). The Marital Communication Rating Schedule: An instrument for clinical assessment. *J Behav Assess, 2,* 287–307.

Thomas, E. J. (1977). *Marital communication and decision making.* New York: Free Press.

Thomas, E. J., Walter, C. L., & O'Flaherty, K. (1974). A verbal problem checklist for use in assessing family verbal behavior. *Behav Ther, 5,* 235–246.

I-1/a
11. CHRISTENSEN, A., & SULLAWAY, M. Communication Patterns Questionnaire

Avail: NAPS-3

Variables Measured: Interaction patterns of couples during periods of disagreement

Type of Instrument: Report of behaviors by self and spouse

Instrument Description: The Communication Patterns Questionnaire is a 35-item Likert-type instrument utilizing a 9-point response format. Possible responses range from *very unlikely* to *very likely.* Communication items are classified under three sequential periods: (1) "When some problem in the relationship arises" (4 items ask about discussion or avoidance of the issue); (2) "During a discussion of a relationship problem" (18 items ask about behaviors such as blaming, negotiating, criticizing, defending, demanding, and withdrawing); and (3) "After a discussion of a relationship problem" (13 items ask about behaviors such as withholding and reconciliation, and reactions such as guilt and understanding). Some items assess symmetrical patterns, such as where both members of the couple blame, accuse, and criticize each other. Other items assess asymmetrical patterns, such as where one member of the couple criticizes while the other defends him- or herself. The three subscales of mutual constructive communication, demand-withdraw communication, and demand-withdraw roles have been developed.

Sample Items:

  (A) When some problem in the relationship arises, both members avoid discussing the problem.
  (B) During a discussion of a relationship problem, man criticizes while woman defends herself.
  (C) After a discussion of a relationship problem, both feel each other has understood his or her position.

Comments: The authors report on a study in which responses of 142 couples were evaluated. Correlations between responses of men and women within couples ranged from .73 to .80 for the three subscales. The authors also report that a measure of marital satisfaction correlated .79 with scores obtained on the mutual constructive communication subscale, and -.55 with demand-withdraw communication subscale scores.

Reference:

Christensen, A. (1987). Detection of conflict patterns in couples. In K. Halweg & M. J. Goldstein (Eds.), *Understanding major mental disorder: The contribution of family interaction research.* New York: Family Process.

I-1/a

12. deTURCK, M. A., & MILLER, G. A. Conjugal Understanding Measure

Avail: 1986a Ref.

Variables Measured: Tendency of spouses to engage in stimulus discrimination and generalization when communicating with each other

Type of Instrument: Self-report questionnaire

Instrument Description: This instrument is a 12-item, 5-point Likert-type scale designed to assess marital couples' tendencies to engage in stimulus discrimination when communicating with each other. It is based on a belief that communication within marriages occurs along both marriage-specific and general social dimensions. The scale consists of 8 marriage-specific items and 4 items designed to evaluate more general levels of communication. General levels are those that may occur between friends and acquaintances as well as between spouses. This model is used to evaluate the extent to which couples' relationships are based on marital-specific and interpersonal levels of communication, as opposed to more general levels not usually reserved for spouses.

Sample Items:

  (A) I find it hard to tell my husband (wife) certain things because I am not sure how he (she) will react.
  (B) I often find that my husband (wife) and I make a lot of "small talk" but we rarely if ever discuss intimate personal matters.
  (C) In order to understand why a person feels the way s/he does about things, it is vital to get to know the person as an individual.

Comments: The final version of the scale was developed from an initial pool of 130 items generated by a group of individuals familiar with the authors' two-dimensional model. A panel of three judges reduced this initial pool to 69 items. Factor analysis specifying a two-factor solution with oblique rotation further reduced the scale to 12 items. Although a 13-item version is referred to in deTurck and Miller (1986b), the authors have indicated that the most appropriate version contains 12 items. Correlations reported by the authors between the Conjugal Understanding Measure and measures of dogmatism, empathy, and PCI are -.24, .35, and .46, respectively. Other indications of the instrument's psychometric properties are presented in the references listed below.

References:

deTurck, M. A., & Miller, G. R. (1986a). Conceptualizing and measuring social cognition in marital communication: A validation study. *J Appl Comm Res, 14,* 69–85.
deTurck, M. A., & Miller, G. R. (1986b). The effects of husbands' and wives' social cognition on their marital adjustment, conjugal power, and self-esteem. *J Mar Fam, 48,* 715–724.

I-1/I-4/a
13. FITZPATRICK, M. A. The Relational Dimensions Instrument (RDI)

Avail: 1988 Ref.

Variables Measured: Various dimensions of marital communication and functional style

Type of Instrument: Self-report questionnaire

Instrument Description: The RDI is a 77-item Likert-type questionnaire utilizing a 7-point response format. It measures eight dimensions of marital communication and functional style: sharing (the extent to which individuals share their time and feelings with each other), ideology of traditionalism (belief in conventional family values), ideology of uncertainty (extent to which change and uncertainty in relationships is welcome), temporal regularity (keeping of regular time schedules), autonomy (retaining of private space), assertiveness, undifferentiated space (support for togetherness and lack of privacy), and conflict avoidance (avoidance of conflict and confrontation). The primary use of the RDI is for discriminating between traditional, independent, and separate types of marriage. Administration time is approximately 25 minutes.

Sample Items:

(A)   A woman should take her husband's last name when she marries.
(B)   In marriage/close relationships there should be no constraints or restrictions on individual freedom.
(C)   I feel free to interrupt my spouse/mate when he/she is concentrating on something if he/she is in my presence.

Comments: The author reports that Cronbach's alpha for the RDI is .77. It is further reported that scores on the RDI were compared to a measure of attitudes toward self-disclosure, actual self-disclosing behaviors, attitudes toward appropriate gender-role behaviors, levels of dyadic adjustment and marital happiness, conflict resolution strategies during conversations, power moves in dialogues, and themes used to describe marriage.

Reference:

Fitzpatrick, M. A. (1988). *Between husbands and wives: Communication in marriage.* Newbury Park, CA: Sage.

I-1/a

14. FLOYD, F. J., & MARKMAN, H. J. Communication Skills Test (CST)

Avail: NAPS-3

Variables Measured: Couples' problem-solving skills, facilitative problem-solving behaviors, disruptive communication behaviors, and overall communication proficiency

Type of Instrument: Observational coding system

Instrument Description: The CST is designed to be used by researchers and clinicians in evaluating couples' communication behaviors. Couples are observed during a discussion of a salient relationship problem. Each speech sequence is evaluated in terms of the overall communication proficiency exhibited. Content and affect, both verbal and nonverbal, are rated by a trained coder on a 5-point scale ranging from *very negative* to *very positive*. Criteria for judging categories were derived from research and clinical reports of interactional behaviors that characterize successful marital problem solving. Relative frequency scores are calculated for each category of behavior emitted by each partner during the discussion. The overall mean of ratings is used in determining a communication proficiency rating. Ratings are made of 36 classes of behaviors based on 10-minute-long discussions by the couple.

Sample Items:

(A)   Blaming.
(B)   Negative voice tone.
(C)   Specific plan.

Comments: The authors report that the CST was useful in determining pre- to post-treatment improvements in communication skills for premarital couples engaged in a relationship enhancement intervention. Scores are also reported by the authors to have correlated with measures of marital satisfaction and divorce potential for married couples as well as discriminating distressed and happily married couples. In two studies conducted with the CST, interrater reliabilities were measured at between .71 and .92.

References:

Floyd, F. J. (1988). Couples' cognitive/affective reactions to communication behaviors. *J Mar Fam, 50,* 523–532.

Floyd, F. J., & Markman, H. J. (1984). An economical observational measure of couples' communication skill. *J Cons Clin, 52,* 97–103.

Floyd, F. J., O'Farrell, T. J., & Goldberg, M. (1987). Comparison of marital observational measures: The Marital Interaction Coding System and the Communication Skills Test. *J Cons Clin, 55,* 423–429.

Markman, H. J., Floyd, F. J., Stanley, S. M., & Storaasli, R. D. (1988). Prevention of marital distress: A longitudinal investigation. *J Cons Clin, 56,* 210–217.

I-1/a

15. HAHLWEG, K., REISNER, L., KOHLI, G., VOLLMER, M., SCHINDLER, L., & REVENSTORF, D. Kategoriensystem für Partnerschaftliche Interaktion (KPI)

Avail: 1984a Ref.

Variables Measured: Marital communication and problem-solving skills following behavioral marital therapy

Type of Instrument: Observational coding scheme

Instrument Description: The KPI is a behavioral coding system designed in West Germany primarily for use in evaluating the effects of behavioral marital therapy on interaction styles of couples. The KPI utilizes 12 behavioral content codes in combination with 3 nonverbal codes. The 12 codes are self-disclosure (SO), positive solution (PL), acceptance of other (AK), agreement (ZU), criticize (KR), negative solution (NL), justification (RF), disagreement (NU), problem description (PB), metacommunication (MK), listening (ZH), and rest (RK). The KPI was designed to measure speaker and listener skills, and is based on the notion that such skills serve as the basis for therapeutic approaches. Twenty consecutive 30-second blocks of videotaped interaction are coded, each receiving both behavioral and corresponding nonverbal scores. Coding is accomplished by a minimum of two raters without benefit of a transcript. Defined dimensions are coded along a time line as the videotaped interaction is observed. Nonverbal dimensions of positive, neutral, and negative are also indicated for each coded interaction. A complete description of the instrument and procedures (in English) is available in Hahlweg et al. (1984).

Sample Items: Not applicable.

Comments: The authors report that interrater reliability for the 12 behavioral and 3 nonverbal dimensions ranged from .69 to .94 when six raters were employed, and from .70 to .96 in a study where two raters were utilized. Cronbach's alpha is reported to range from .85 to .99 for the verbal categories, and from .52 to .89 for the nonverbal dimensions. Several differences were noted by the authors between distressed and nondistressed couples. Differences between husbands and wives were also examined.

References:

Hahlweg, K., Reisner, L., Kohli, G., Vollmer, M., Schindler, L., & Revenstorf, D. (1984a). Development and validity of a new system to analyze interpersonal communication: Kategoriensystem für partnerschaftliche Interaktion. In K. Hahlweg & N. S. Jacobson (Eds.), *Marital interaction: Analysis and modification* (pp. 182–198). New York: Guilford.

Hahlweg, K., Revenstorf, D., & Schindler, L. (1984b). Effects of behavioral marital therapy on couples' communication and problem-solving skills. *J Cons Clin, 52,* 553–566.

Hooley, J. M., & Hahlweg, K. (1989). Marital satisfaction and marital communication in German and English couples. *Behav Assess, 11,* 119–133.

Hooley, J. M., Orley, J., & Teasdale, J. D. (1986). Levels of expressed emotion and relapse in depressed patients. *Br J Psychi, 148,* 642–647.

I-1/a

16. JOANNING, H., BREWSTER, J., & KOVAL, J. The Communication Rapid Assessment Scale (CRAS)

Avail: 1984 Ref.

Variables Measured: Maintaining versus destructive qualities of dyadic communication

Type of Instrument: Behavior coding scheme

Instrument Description: The CRAS is a system for classifying dyadic communication according to maintaining and destructive behaviors of partners. Two systems of classification have been developed, one for coding verbal behaviors and the other for coding nonverbal behaviors. The authors indicate that the verbal coding scheme "is decidedly more subjective." The verbal form requires coders to make judgments regarding meanings and intentions by interpreting contexts within which interactions occur. The system for coding nonverbal interactions, on the other hand, is more objective, depending primarily on the presence or absence of behaviors or the distance between interactants. The two systems utilize identical formats and scoring procedures. Discussions lasting 3 to 5 minutes are either recorded or rated live. Coders evaluate the maintaining versus destructive qualities of the interaction with regard to its likely effect on the relationship. Interactions are rated on a 5-point scale, with detailed criteria determining the eventual rating. Use of the nonverbal system involves noting the percentage of time in which eye contact, facial expressions, head nods, posture, distance between partners, hand and leg movements and positions, and nervous behaviors are maintained. Verbal ratings are dependent on topics of discussion, interruptions, ability to remain on one topic of conversation, tone of voice, equality of speaking time, and various qualitative interpretations on the part of the rater.

Sample Items: Not applicable.

Comments: Interrater reliability is reported to be .96 for nonverbal ratings, and to range from .84 to .97 for verbal behavior. Test-retest reliability, based on two 3-minute discussions with 20-minute intervening periods, is reported to be .68 for verbal, and .65 for nonverbal ratings. The CRAS is reported to correlate from .18 to .58 with the Marital Communication Inventory (Bienvenu, 1970), and from .05 to .48 with the Locke-Wallace Marital Adjustment Test (1959).

References:

Joanning, H. (1982). The long-term effects of the Couple Communication Program. *J Mar Fam Th, 8,* 463–468.
Joanning, H., Brewster, J., & Koval, J. (1984). The Communication Rapid Assessment Scale: Development of a behavioral index of communication quality. *J Mar Fam Th, 10,* 409–417.

I-1/a

17. LOCKE, H. J., SABAGH, G., & THOMES, M. M. Primary Communication Inventory (PCI)

Avail: 1967 & 1983 Refs.

Variables Measured: Communication between husbands and wives

Type of Instrument: Self-report questionnaire

Instrument Description: The PCI was originally developed and described, but not published in its entirety, by Locke et al. in a 1956 article. The 26-item scale was modified by Navran (1967) by eliminating one item and revising the original scoring system. The revised scale was included in Navran's article, and has since become the more widely used version of this scale. The PCI was developed for the purpose of measuring communication between spouses. The 25-item version is administered using a 5-point Likert-type response format. Items are in the form of questions in which respondents are asked to indicate (from *very frequently* to *never*) how often certain types of communication take place. Subscores are computed for sections dealing with nonverbal and verbal communication, containing 7 and 18 items, respectively. Navran also indicates that "for the nine items which involve making a judgment about the spouse, the scores were transposed for the two mates, so that the total test scores could more accurately be viewed as a measure of the individual communication behaviors" (Navran, 1967, p. 174). The scale is scored such that higher scores indicate greater frequency of communication.

Sample Items:

(A) How often do you and your spouse talk over pleasant things that happen during the day?

(B) Your spouse wants to visit some close friends or relatives. You don't particularly enjoy their company. Would you tell him (her) this?

(C) Do you understand the meaning of your spouse's facial expressions?

Comments: Navran reports that the revised PCI successfully discriminated between happily and not happily married couples. Differences were not found, however, between the genders within groups. The correlation of the revised PCI with an instrument devised by Navran, the Marital Relationship Inventory, was .82. In the original article, Locke et al. reported correlations ranging from .36 to .72.

References:

Beach, S. R. H., & Arias, I. (1983). Assessment of perceptual discrepancy: Utility of the Primary Communication Inventory. *Fam Proc, 22,* 309–316.

Locke, H. J., Sabagh, G., & Thomas, M. M. (1956). Correlates of primary communication and empathy. *Res Studies St Col of Wash, 24,* 116–124.

Navran, L. (1967). Communication and adjustment in marriage. *Fam Proc, 6,* 173–184.

Yelsma, P. (1986). Marriage versus cohabitation: Couples' communication practices and satisfaction. *J Comm, 36*(4), 94–107.

I-1/a

18. POWERS, W. G., & HUTCHINSON, K. Personal Report of Spouse Communication Apprehension (PRSCA)

Avail: 1979 Ref.

Variables Measured: Apprehension of one spouse toward communicating with other spouse

Type of Instrument: Self-report questionnaire

Instrument Description: This instrument contains 15 Likert-type items with 5 options ranging from *strongly agree* to *strongly disagree*. Items are adjusted for directionality and summed to produce a single score representing one spouse's apprehension toward communicating with the other spouse.

Sample Items:

(A) I don't hesitate to tell my spouse exactly how I feel.
(B) I always avoid speaking when my spouse is tired.
(C) I look forward to telling my spouse my opinion on a subject.

Comments: This instrument is an adaptation of McCroskey's (1970) 20-item Personal Report of Communication Apprehension (PRCA). In developing the instrument, the authors presented subjects with 50 items, including the 20 PRCA items and 30 items adapted to reflect communication apprehension with spouses. A factor analysis of the results yielded 18 items loading at least .50 on the PRCA and 15 items loading at least .50 on the PRSCA, with no items cross-loading. Split-half reliability on the PRSCA is reported at .88. The correlation between the two scales was .16, indicating that the adaptation to reflect communication apprehension with spouses measured a construct independent from the that of the original PRCA. Validity information for the scale can be found in Powers and Hutchinson (1979).

References:

McCroskey, J. C. (1970). Measures of communication-bound anxiety. *Speech Mono, 37,* 269–277.
Powers, W. G., & Hutchinson, K. (1979). The measurement of communication apprehension in the marriage relationship. *J Mar Fam, 41,* 89–95.

I-1/c

19. REISS, D. Pattern Recognition Card Sort for Families

Avail: Outlined in 1968 & 1971 Refs.; details in NAPS-2

Variables Measured: Family problem-solving effectiveness, coordination, and penchant for closure

Type of Instrument: Behavioral rating procedure

Instrument Description: This instrument is a behavioral measure of problem-solving styles employed by families. Three family members are simultaneously seated in separate, sound-proof booths. Communication between family members occurs through the use of head-phones and microphones. Subjects are instructed to work on three pattern recognition tasks. During the first and third tasks they work independently; during the second they are allowed to communicate, and their activities are coordinated. Subjects are each presented with 16 cards with series of letters on them during both the first and the third sets. Instructions indicate the need to separate the cards into no more than 7 categories. During the second, or family, phase of the task subjects are presented with 8 sets of 2 cards each. Identical sets are simultaneously presented to all family members. During this second phase, family members are permitted to communicate with each other regarding categorization techniques for distrib-uting the cards. Evaluations of categorization systems and verbal interactions by participants yield seven measures from which family behavior is inferred: (1) complexity of the sort pattern in the individual and phases, (2) pattern complexity in the family phase, (3) similarity of solutions among family members, (4) synchrony of trial-ending times, (5) average length of the trials, (6) number of changes made by entire family prior to reaching a final solution, (7) family phase trial number after which no more sort changes are made. From these scores are obtained on the variables of closure, configuration, and coordination.

Sample Items: Not applicable.

Comments: The author reported correlations between the three variables listed above and FACES II (Olson, 1982) variables of family cohesion and family adaptability. All correlations were less than .25, with the exception of configuration and family adaptability (-.40). Reiss and Klein (1987) report temporal stability over six to nine months of .72 for configuration, .86 for coordination, and .43 for closure. In addition to the instrument title given above, it is also referred to in the literature as the Card Sort Procedure (CSP).

References:

Reiss, D. (1968). Individual thinking and family interaction. III. An experimental study of categorization performance in families of normals, those with character disorders and schizophrenics. *J Nerv Ment, 146,* 384–403.

Reiss, D. (1971). Varieties of consensual experience. III. Contrast between families of normals, delinquents, and schizophrenics. *J Nerv Ment, 152,* 73–95.

Reiss, D., & Klein, D. (1987). Paradigm and pathogenesis: A family-centered approach to problems of etiology and treatment of psychiatric disorders. In T. Jacob (Ed.), *Family interaction and psychopathology.* New York: Plenum.

Shulman, S., & Klein, M. M. (1983). Distance-sensitive and consensus-sensitive families: The effect on adolescent referral for psychotherapy. *Am J Fam Th, 11*(2), 45–58.

Sigafoos, A., Reiss, D., Rich, J., & Douglas, E. (1985). Pragmatics in the measurement of family functioning: An interpretive framework for methodology. *Fam Proc, 24,* 189–203.

I-1/a
20. STEPHEN, T. D., & HARRISON, T. M. Communication Style Q-Set (CSQS)

Avail: Sort distribution form in 1985 Ref.; item set in 1986 Ref.

Variables Measured: Individual communication style

Type of Instrument: Q-sort

Instrument Description: The CSQS consists of a deck of 100 statements describing aspects of an individual's communication style. The statements are printed on 3 × 5 note cards, which may be sorted by subjects or raters to describe an individual's unique style. In applications where subjects are describing themselves, they are asked to sort each item into nine categories or stacks ranging from least to most characteristic of self. Different frequencies of items are permitted in each stack in such a way that the final arrangement of items forms a quasi-normal distribution. Frequencies for each of the categories are 5, 8, 12, 16, 18, 16, 12, 8, and 5. Administration time is approximately 30–45 minutes. The CSQS overcomes what the authors perceived as two limitations in other measures of communication: (1) that they are context-specific (e.g., only relevant in assessing marital conversation) and, therefore, unable to contribute to a general understanding of communication effects, and (2) that they are often unable to provide sufficiently detailed descriptions of individual actors for application in single-case or clinical studies.

Sample Items:

(A) Avoids talking about emotions.
(B) Laughs frequently.
(C) Uses sarcasm.

Comments: The authors report that five-day test-retest reliability for the CSQS is .77. The results of a factor analysis and other validity information are also reported (Stephen & Harrison, 1986). Of the 100 statements contained in the instrument, 63 form the basis of 13 factors identified by the authors. Taken together, these factors explain 43% of the variance. Factor sizes vary from 2 to 13, with items within factors loading at least .295 on that factor, and less than .295 on all other factors. In addition to the above-named sources of availability, both the item set and the sort distribution are available from Comserve@Rpicicge, the automated information service accessible through Bitnet.

References:

Stephen, T. (1985). Q-methodology in communication science: An introduction. *Comm Q, 33,* 193–208.

Stephen, T., & Harrison, T. (1986). Assessing communication style: A new measure. *Am J Fam Th, 14,* 213–234.

I-1/c

21. TITTLER, B. I., FRIEDMAN, S., & SEEMAN, L. The Tailored Family Interaction Measurement Method

Avail: NAPS-3

Variables Measured: Direction and levels of communication and interaction between family members

Type of Instrument: Observational coding system

Instrument Description: This instrument is an observational method of evaluating family interactions on several levels. Interactions between families presenting for therapy are elicited utilizing a two-part task: Family members are first instructed to attempt to resolve certain differences, and then are each asked to describe a positive family experience. Lengths of interactions on the two-part task vary considerably, but average about 20 minutes. Sixty minutes is used as a cutoff time for all interactions, although the authors report that interactions invariably conclude prior to this point. Interactions are videotaped for later observation. Two independent raters each make eight predictions regarding salient interactional changes expected to result from therapeutic intervention. Discrepancies within the evaluative team are discussed until raters agree regarding expected changes. Each prediction for change involves an interaction measure selected according to a prearranged structure from a pool of such measures. Following several therapy sessions, interactions are evaluated for change according to the predictive criteria. Changes are scored on a 5-point scale ranging from -2 to +2. Changes of 30% to 49% are scored as +1 or -1 (depending on the direction of change). Changes of at least 50% are scored as +2 or -2. Changes of less than 30% are scored "0." Change scores are summed to provide a total change score for the family. What the authors refer to as the "tailoring technique" employed in this instrument was adapted from the goal-attainment scaling approach of Kiresuk (1973).

Sample Items:

(A)   The sibling will talk more.
(B)   Mother and child will talk more to each other.
(C)   There will be more reference to individuals in the family goals.

Comments: The authors report a study in which scores were found to correlate -.57 with mother-child distance and -.65 with Holmes and Rahe's life events measure of stress. A second study is also reported in which scores following six family therapy sessions correlated .84 with therapists' ratings of family change and .67 with families' perceptions of change following 4 months of therapy. Change scores are also reported to have correlated positively with supervisors' ratings of therapist effectiveness (.67), and negatively with the number of therapy sessions (-.77).

References:

Seeman, L., Tittler, B. I., & Friedman, S. (1985). Early interactional change and its relationship to family therapy outcome. *Fam Proc, 24,* 59–68.

Tittler, B. I., Friedman, S., Blotcky, A. D., & Stedrak, J. (1982). The influence of family variables on an ecologically-based treatment program for emotionally disturbed children. *Am J Orthop, 52,* 123–130.

Tittler, B. I., Friedman, S., & Klopper, E. J. (1977). A system for tailoring change measures to the individual family. *Fam Proc, 16,* 119–121.

I-1/III-1/a

22. VINCENT, J. P., COOK, N. I., & BRADY, C. P. Marital Coding System (MCS)

Avail: 1981 Ref.

Variables Measured: Dimensions of spousal communication following the birth of their first child

Type of Instrument: Observational coding system

Instrument Description: The MCS is a system for generating and scoring interactions between spouses during the 30- to 60-day adjustment period following the birth of their first child. The MCS is a modification of the Marital Interaction Coding System (MICS) (Hops, Wills, Patterson, & Weiss, 1973). The major difference between the two systems noted by Vincent et al. is that the MCS does not contain separate categories of nonverbal behavior and that it has "additional categories reflecting emotional expression, supportive and nonsupportive listening, and more subtle distinctions between types of problem-solving behavior" (Vincent et al., 1981, p. 113). Four situations are generated, with each spouse asked to suggest two of the interactional sequences. One situation generated by each spouse is geared toward problem solving, with each partner asked to think of one instance where s/he wished to request a change in some aspect of the spouse's behavior. The other situation generated by each spouse involves an incident where one partner is upset about something that occurred outside the marriage relationship, and wished to discuss the issue with his or her spouse (e.g., problems at work, concerns about relatives). Partners are asked to re-create the situation and to carry on the interaction for five minutes. The entire interaction is videotaped. Coding occurs along 25 dimensions. Ratings of behaviors were factor analyzed and combined to yield nine factors from the emotional, and eight factors from the problem-solving, interactions. Reliability analyses further reduced the number of useful factors to five and seven for emotional and problem-solving discussions, respectively.

Sample Items: Not applicable.

Comments: The authors report Cronbach's alpha for each of the individual factors. Four emotional expression/support factors yielding alphas ranging from .00 to .35 were eliminated from further consideration. Likewise, 1 factor yielding an alpha of .00 was eliminated from the problem-solving group. Remaining alphas are reported to be in the .65 to .99 range.

Reference:

Vincent, J. P., Cook, N. I., & Brady, C. P. (1981). The emerging family: Integration of a developmental perspective and social learning theory. In J. P. Vincent (Ed.) *Advances in family intervention, assessment, and theory* (pp. 89–129). Greenwich, CT: JAI.

I-2/IV-1/c/e
23. BOHEN, H. H., & VIVEROS-LONG, A. Family Management Scale

Avail: 1981 Ref.

Variables Measured: Management of time and activities outside the work setting

Type of Instrument: Self-report questionnaire

Instrument Description: The Family Management Scale is a 5-point, 21-item Likert-type questionnaire intended to assess the management of personal time and interactions with agencies and individuals. The focus of this instrument is the structure of activities such that they have minimal impact on the person's responsibilities to his or her work. Examples of activities frequently requiring juggling include interactions with schools, stores, libraries, and others involved in the social functioning of the individual and his or her family. This instrument was designed to address respondents' feelings regarding the ease or difficulty experienced by virtue of the complex set of situations he or she is forced to negotiate. The Family Management Scale is commonly used as a companion instrument to the Job-Family Role Strain Scale, developed by the same authors concurrent with the current scale. Items were developed along seven dimensions, with from one to five items being constructed for each subarea. Dimensions of interest include (1) health, (2) education and child care, (3) retail services, (4) commuting, (5) family interaction, (6) community interaction, and (7) general overlapping items. All responses are in reaction to the question: "On days when you are working, how easy or difficult is it for you to arrange your time to do each of the following?" Values are assigned to each response option ranging from 1 (*very easy*) to 5 (*very difficult*). An additional option available for selection allows respondents to indicate that the item is not applicable. Values associated with individual items can be summed, both within subscales and across the total instrument.

Sample Items:

(A)   To avoid the rush hour.
(B)   To go on errands (e.g., shoe repair, post office, car service).
(C)   To be home when your children get home from school.

Comments: Content validity was initially assessed by a panel of six judges. Cronbach's alpha was reported by the author to be .93. The scale has been modified and used in multiple forms by various authors. Modifications usually take the form of reducing the number of items.

References:

Bohen, H. H., & Viveros-Long, A. (1981). *Balancing jobs and family life: Do flexible work schedules help?* Philadelphia: Temple University Press.
Burden, D. S. (1986). Single parent and the work setting: The impact of multiple job and home life responsibilities. *Fam Relat, 35,* 37–43.
Katz, M. H., & Piotrkowski, C. S. (1983). Correlates of family role strain among employed Black women. *Fam Relat, 32,* 331–339.

Lewis, S. N. C., & Cooper, C. L. (1987). Stress in two-earner couples and stage in the life-cycle. *J Occup Psy, 60,* 289–303.

I-2/III-2/c/P
24. CALDWELL, B. M., & BRADLEY, R. H. Home Observation for Measurement of the Environment (HOME)

Avail: Center for Research on Teaching and Learning, Education 205, University of Arkansas at Little Rock, 2801 South University Ave., Little Rock, AR 72204

Variables Measured: Quality of children's home environments

Type of Instrument: Observational coding system

Instrument Description: The HOME Inventory is an instrument designed to assess the quality and quantity of support for cognitive, social, and emotional development that is available to a child in or through the home environment. It is intended to be a comprehensive, yet easy-to-use, technique that provides systematic information about objects and events in the home, transactions between parents and children, and the kind of structure provided to children to promote their development. There are currently three versions of the HOME Inventory: (1) infant (ages birth to 3), containing 6 subscales and 45 items; (2) preschool (ages 3 to 6), containing 8 subscales and 55 items; and (3) elementary (ages 6 to 10), consisting of 8 subscales and 59 items. Items differ within each subscale in order to make them appropriate for the differing needs and abilities of children in the three age ranges. This instrument has three primary intended uses: (1) identification of home environments that pose a risk for children's development; (2) evaluation of programs designed to improve parenting skills; and (3) basic research on the relationship between home environments and child's health and development. Information for the binary scoring of the HOME is obtained by observations and hour-long semistructured interviews in homes with the parent and child. A detailed manual (revised in 1984) outlining administration and scoring procedures is available from the above-noted source.

Sample Items (Note: A-B are from the infant, C-D are from the preschool, and E-F are from the elementary versions of the HOME Inventory):

(A) Parent responds to child's verbalizations.
(B) Child is taken to grocery store at least once a week.
(C) Child has at least 10 children's books.
(D) Parent helps child demonstrate some achievement during visit.
(E) Parent encourages child to contribute to the conversation during visit.
(F) Family encourages child to develop and sustain hobbies.

Comments: The authors report that internal consistency for total scores and subscales ranged from .38 to .93 across the 3 versions. Correlations between HOME scores and SES measures ranged from .3 to .6. Multiple correlations with mental test scores are reported to range from .30 to .54 for the 6-month HOME, and .40 to .59 for the 12-month HOME, and were reported to be .72 for the 24-month HOME. Multiple correlations with the Illinois Test of Psycholinguistic Abilities are reported to range from .65 to .71. Multiple correlations between mental test performance and HOME scores ranged from .58 to .67 for preschool children, and from .2 to .4 for elementary-aged youngsters.

References:

Belsky, J., Garduque, L., & Hrncir, E. (1984). Assessing performance, competence and executive capacity in infant play: Relations to home environment and security of attachment. *Devel Psych, 20,* 406–417.

Bradley, R., & Caldwell, B. (1976). Early home environment and changes in mental test performance in children from six to thirty-six months. *Devel Psych, 12,* 93–97.

Bradley, R., & Caldwell, B. (1977). Home observation for measurement of the environment: A validation study of screening efficiency. *Am J Ment D, 81,* 417–420.

Stevens, J., & Bakeman, R. (1985). A factor analytic study of the HOME scale for infants. *Devel Psych, 21,* 1196–1203.

I-2/III-2/b/C

25. HENDERSON, R. W., BERGAN, J. R., & HURT, M., Jr. Henderson Environmental Learning Process Scale (HELPS)

Avail: NAPS-3

Variables Measured: Elements of the home environment that influence intellectual or academic achievement

Type of Instrument: Self-report questionnaire

Instrument Description: The HELPS is a 5-point, 55-item Likert-type instrument designed to assess home environments of children and the extent to which those environments facilitate intellectual and academic achievement. The inventory was designed to be administered during interviews with parents of school-aged children. The interviewer is instructed to sit next to the respondent, reading each question and the available responses, while the participant follows along. Populations investigated with the HELPS are often not well educated. Reading of items is included in order to avoid embarrassing parents whose reading skills are suspect. The scale was designed to be administered by trained research or clinical assistants. Although not indicated by the authors, following slight modification, paper-and-pencil administration should also be possible. Items are in the form of questions, with each response indicated on an appropriate continuum (e.g., *good/poor, excellent/failing, almost every day/very seldom*). Items are scored 1–5, with higher numbers indicating greater experience within that context, contact with learning situations, and so on. The HELPS score is the sum of scores of all items. Areas investigated by this scale include educational aspiration, range of stimuli available within the environment, guidance or teaching provided by parents, variability of adult educational and occupational role models, and the structure of reinforcement within the home to encourage intellectual/academic performance.

Sample Items:

(A)   How often do you take (CHILD) along when you go shopping?
(B)   How often do you talk to (CHILD) about things he/she has seen on TV?
(C)   How often does (CHILD) see you reading something?

Comments: Cronbach's alpha, estimated from use of the HELPS with several samples, is reported to range from .71 to .85. The scale has been modified and used in various forms, with varying numbers of items and identified factors. The senior author indicates that users should modify the instrument according to the age of the sample and intellectual resources that are available within the community (museum, art gallery, zoo, and so on).

References:

Henderson, R. W., Bergan, J. R., & Hurt, M., Jr. (1972). Development and validation of the Henderson Environmental Learning Process Scale. *J Soc Psych, 88*, 185–196.

Mink, I. T., & Nihira, K. (1986). Family lifestyles and child behaviors: A study of direction of effects. *Devel Psych, 22*, 610–616.

Nihira, K., Mink, I. T., & Meyers, C. E. (1985). Home environment and development of slow-learning adolescents: Reciprocal relations. *Devel Psych, 21*, 784–794.

Valencia, R. R., Henderson, R. W., & Rankin, R. J. (1985). Family status, family constellation, and home environment variables as predictors of cognitive performance of Mexican American children. *J Educ Psyc, 77*, 323–331.

I-2/c
26. JENSEN, E. W., JAMES, S. A., BOYCE, W. T., & HARTNETT, S. A. Family Routines Inventory (FRI)

Avail: 1983 Ref.

Variables Measured: Routines involving two or more family members

Type of Instrument: Self-report questionnaire

Instrument Description: The FRI is a two-part, 28-item questionnaire designed to assess the endorsement of routines by the family, the family's adherence to those routines, and the perceived importance of maintaining the routine. For each item, two separate questions are asked: (1) "Is this a routine in your family?" and (2) "How important is this routine for keeping your family strong?" The first question is responded to on a 4-point Likert-type scale with options of *always—every day, 3–5 times a week, 1–2 times a week,* and *almost never.* Response options for the second question include *very important, somewhat important,* and *not at all important.* The authors initially constructed 104 items intended to evaluate 12 domains (workday, weekend and leisure time, children's routines, parent's(s') routines, bedtime, meals, extended family, leaving and homecoming, religious routines, disciplinary routines, household chores, and home entertainment). Pretesting and evaluation of items according to criteria of high perceived importance by judges, generally accepted importance by the sample population, and minimal correlation with race or social class of the judges reduced the item-pool to 28, and the number of domains to 10 (religious and home entertainment routines were eliminated). Four scoring procedures are outlined by the authors. In the first, raw values associated with response options are summed. The second option "is to sum the underlying Thurstone-like scale value (S) of all routines endorsed by a family, again omitting frequency and importance data" (Jensen et al., 1983, p. 205). The authors indicate that this option results in a weighted score ranging from 0 to 255.9. Option 3 is to weight routines by frequency of performance. The fourth option is to weight scores according to the importance placed on the routine by the family.

Sample Items:

(A)   Parent(s) have sometime each day for just talking with the children.
(B)   Family goes someplace special together each week.
(C)   Parents have a certain hobby or sport they do together regularly.

Comments: The authors report 30-day test-retest reliability for scoring options of computing a raw score (.74), a weighted score (.75), and a frequency score (.79). Correlations are also reported between scoring procedures, with raw score and weighted score options reportedly correlated .99, and frequency scores correlated .80 and .81 with raw and weighted scoring options, respectively.

References:

Boyce, W. T., Jensen, E. W., James, S. A., & Peacock, J. L. (1983). The Family Routines Inventory: Theoretical origins. *Social Sci Med, 17,* 193–200.

Jensen, E. W., James, S. A., Boyce, W. T., & Hartnett, S. A. (1983). The Family Routines Inventory: Development and validation. *Social Sci Med, 17,* 201–211.

Sprunger, L. W., Boyce, W. T., & Gaines, J. A. (1985). Family-infant congruence: Routines and rhythmicity in family adaptations to a young infant. *Child Dev, 56,* 564–572.

I-2/e
27. JORGENSEN, S. R., & KLEIN, D. M. Status Striving Index

Avail: 1977 Ref.

Variables Measured: The degree to which a marriage partner values status advancement in the social stratification hierarchy

Type of Instrument: Self-report questionnaire

Instrument Description: The Status Striving Index is a 5-item Likert-style questionnaire utilizing a 4-point response format. Available responses range from *strongly agree* to *strongly disagree*. The instrument was designed to assess the desire of married couples for attaining higher or lower socioeconomic status. Questions relate primarily to status gained through the husband's education and income. Scores for individual items are summed in order to arrive at a total scale score. Administration time is approximately 2–3 minutes.

Sample Items:

(A)   The husband's primary job in marriage is to earn a respectable income so that the wife and children are comfortable.

(B)   It is important to own material things, such as a home, car, furniture, clothes, etc. which compare in value with those of my neighbors, friends, and the people I work with.

(C)   It is important that the husband has a job that lots of people respect.

Comments: Jorgensen (1977) reports on a study in which the Status Striving Index was used to investigate the relationship between degree of status striving, marrying into higher or lower socioeconomic categories, and frequency and intensity of marital conflict. It was concluded that increased levels of marital conflict were experienced only in cases where women married into lower social levels, yet strived to improve their social standing. Similar conclusions were not supported for other groups or combinations of social striving, marrying up or down, and marital conflict.

Reference:

Jorgensen, S. R. (1977). Social class heterogamy, status striving, and perceptions of marital conflict: A partial replication and revision of Pearlin's contingency hypothesis. *J Mar Fam, 39,* 653–661.

I-2/c
28. McCUBBIN, H. I., McCUBBIN, M. A., & THOMPSON, A. I. Family Time and Routines Index (FTRI)

Avail: 1987 Ref.

Variables Measured: The importance of various family routines to keeping the family strong

Type of Instrument: Self-report questionnaire

Instrument Description: The FTRI is a 32-item Likert-type questionnaire designed to assess types of activities and routines families use and maintain, and the value they place upon those practices. Items are in the form of statements describing activities engaged in by family members. Two Likert-type scales are utilized in responding to each item. A 4-point index (*false, mostly false, mostly true, true*), ranging from 0 to 3, is used in combination with a 3-point scale, scored 0–2, with which respondents indicate whether each activity is *not, somewhat,* or *very important to keeping the family together and strong.* Items are grouped within 8 dimensions of interest: (1) parent-child togetherness (5 items), (2) couple togetherness (4 items), (3) child routines (4 items), (4) family togetherness (4 items), (5) family chores routines (2 items), (6) meals together (2 items), (7) relatives connection (4 items), and (8) family management routines (5 items). The FTRI yields two scores, one for the extent to which each of the routines is true for the family, and one for the perceived importance of the routine. Administration time is approximately 20 minutes.

Sample Items:

(A) Parent(s) have some time each day for just talking with the children.
(B) Working parent has a regular play time with the children after coming home from work.
(C) Working parent takes care of the children sometime almost every day.

Comments: The authors report that Cronbach's alpha for the overall FTRI is .88. Correlations are reported between the FTRI and measures of family bonding (.24), family coherence (.34), family celebrations (.30), family satisfaction (.25), and marital satisfaction (.26).

Reference:

McCubbin, H. I., McCubbin, M. A., & Thompson, A. I. (1987). FTRI: Family Time and Routines Index. In H. I. McCubbin & A. I. Thompson (Eds.), *Family assessment inventories for research and practice* (pp. 133–141). Madison, WI: University of Wisconsin-Madison, Family Stress Coping and Health Project.

I-2/d
29. MINDEL, C. H., & WRIGHT, R., Jr. Inconveniences in Living Arrangements

Avail: 1982 Ref.

Variables Measured: Potential areas of inconvenience associated with having an elderly relative live with you

Type of Instrument: Self-report questionnaire

Instrument Description: This instrument is a 5-point, 8-item Likert-type questionnaire designed to assess concerns of adults regarding being inconvenienced by living with their elderly relatives, as well as benefits to the family resulting from these living arrangements. Although not specified by the author, it is presumed that items are in the form of questions, and are responded to on a scale ranging from *very inconvenient* to *very convenient.* The scale was used as part of a larger interview package, and is intended for use with adult relatives who have elderly relatives residing with them.

Sample Items (Note: Exact wording of items was not provided in the reference, thus these sample items must be viewed as reflecting the ideas present in the scale, rather than being exactly reproduced items):

(A) How inconvenient has having an elderly relative live with you been with respect to your social life?

(B) How convenient has having an elderly relative live with you been with respect to child care?

(C) How inconvenient has having an elderly relative live with you been with respect to your privacy?

Comments: The authors report that Inconveniences in Living Arrangements is correlated -.42 with the primary caregiver's level of satisfaction, .29 with level of impairment suffered by the elderly person, -.35 with the number of roles assumed by the relative, and .01 with the race of the family.

Reference:

Mindel, C. H., & Wright, R., Jr. (1982). Satisfaction in multigenerational households. *J Gerontol, 37,* 483–489.

I-2/a
30. ORTHNER, D. K. Leisure Activity-Interaction Index (LAII)

Avail: 1975 & 1976 Refs.

Variables Measured: Participation in joint, parallel, and/or individual leisure activities by husbands and wives

Type of Instrument: Self-report questionnaire

Instrument Description: The LAII was designed to assess the extent to which spouses coparticipate or remain independent in their leisure activities. It provides a measure of the extent of marital companionship as well as the style of companionship. It also is designed to distinguish between highly interactive, or joint, activities and those that require little or no interaction, or parallel activities. It is intended to be independently administered to each member of the couple. Respondents are presented with a list of 96 possible leisure activities. They are asked to indicate the number of hours spent over a limited time period, usually a weekend, in each activity alone, only with their spouse, only with persons other than their spouse, or with their spouse and others. The total number of reported discretionary activity hours are then summed and allocated to each category. The author indicates that, although 96 possible items are included on the LAII, most respondents need only complete the questionnaire for between 10 and 20 of the activities. Administration time is approximately 10 minutes.

Sample Items:

(A) Playing tennis
(B) Walking
(C) Engaging in sexual or affectional activities

Comments: The author indicates that content validity was assessed by four expert raters. It is reported that over 95% of the items were agreed upon by three of four raters. The author further reports that predictive validity was demonstrated by the ability of the scale to distinguish between groups that were theoretically derived. Husbands' and wives' indications of hours spent in shared activities are reported to be correlated .87.

References:

Holman, T. B., & Jacquart, M. (1988). Leisure-activity patterns and marital satisfaction: A further test. *J Mar Fam, 50,* 69–77.

Orthner, D. K. (1975). Leisure activity patterns and marital satisfaction over the marital career. *J Mar Fam, 37,* 91–102.

Orthner, D. K. (1976). Patterns of leisure and marital interaction. *J Leisure Res, 8,* 98–111.

I-2/a
31. SCHULTZ, K. V. The Lifestyle Profile Series

Avail: Psychological Services Press, 18322 Carlwyn Dr. Castro Valley, CA 94546, & NAPS-3

Variables Measured: Satisfaction with and importance of various aspects of one's life-style

Type of Instrument: Series of self-report inventories

Instrument Description: The Lifestyle Profile Series is a series of 16 independent instruments, each focusing on a different aspect of life-styles. The entire series is available from Psychological Services Press. Three of these inventories (marriage, parenting, and intimacy) deal primarily with family-related issues and are also available from NAPS-3. This summary deals only with those three questionnaires. Each instrument contains 10 items addressing a variety of issues within that construct. Individual inventories are divided into two parts: Part A is a 1-item global rating of satisfaction on that construct using an 11-point scale. Part B contains 10 items on which respondents indicate both *how important* and *how satisfying* that area is. Items are answered on an 11-point continuum ranging from *not important* to *very important,* and from *very dissatisfied* to *very satisfied.* The author indicates that the Lifestyle Profile Series has been used as a survey instrument and in educational exercises as well as in clinical assessments and research. The scales are designed for persons of average and above-average intelligence. Average administration time is approximately 3–5 minutes per form.

Sample Items:

Form IV—Marriage

(A)   Who we were—what happened before we were married.
(B)   Health—as it affects our day to day living.
(C)   The place of children in our life.

Form VII—Parenting

(A)   The timing and circumstances surrounding their birth.
(B)   Having the feeling of being loved, cared for and supported.
(C)   Learning how to live with change, uncertainty and stress.

Form VIII—Intimacy

(A) Sharing thoughts, reflections, views, questions about life and living.
(B) Sharing physical closeness—the warm spontaneous body language of intimacy.
(C) Having a committed close relationship with one person, a mate to resonate with at all levels.

Comments: The Lifestyle Profile Series is a modification and expansion of models originally available as the Marriage-Personality Inventory and as the Image Inventory Series. The author reports that reliability values for priorities on Form 0–1 range from .84 to .91. The reliability of health on Form III is reported to be .90.

Reference:

Schultz, K. V. (1978). Life space images: Research model and counseling aid. *J Couns Psychother*, pp. 58–66.

I-2/c
32. SEBALD, H. Family Integration Scale

Avail: 1962 Ref.

Variables Measured: Frequency of joint family or parent-child activities

Type of Instrument: Self-report questionnaire

Instrument Description: The Family Integration Scale is a 4-point, 8-item Likert-type instrument designed to measure the frequency of activities between parents and their children as well as with the family as a whole. Available item responses range from *often* to *never*. The scale is designed to be answered by parents. Activities listed in the instrument frequently deal with participation of the parents in child-oriented events, such as school or hobbies, or with family-oriented activities, such as church and picnics. This instrument is most appropriate when measuring activities of the nuclear family.

Sample Items:

(A) How often do you help your children with their school work and problems?
(B) How often do you attend events like fairs, athletic games, picnics, movies, etc. together as a family?
(C) How often do you work around the home or farm together as a family?

Comments: Split-half reliability, using the Spearman-Brown formula on data from a sample of 303 families, is reported to be .94. The scale was derived from items on the Bardis Familism Scale (1959). The correlation between the Family Integration Scale and the Bardis Familism Scale, using the same sample noted above, is reported to be .95.

References:

Anderson, S. A. (1986). Cohesion, adaptability, and communication: A test on Olson's circumplex model hypothesis. *Fam Relat, 35*, 289–293.
Sebald, H., & Andrews, W. H. (1962). Family integration and related factors in a rural fringe population. *J Mar Fam, 24*, 347–351.

I-2/I-4/a
33. SEKARAN, U. Integration

Avail: 1986 Ref.

Variables Measured: The extent to which spouses' family and work lives are integrated as a total part of their lives

Type of Instrument: Self-report questionnaire

Instrument Description: Integration is a 6-item Likert-type questionnaire utilizing a 5-point response format. Available responses range from *very little* to *very much.* It measures the tendency of spouses to integrate various aspects of their lives, as opposed to segregating and separately treating different parts of the lives. The instrument was designed to assist in assessing both integrated and segregated approaches, particularly in dual-career families. The author indicates that it would be useful in examining whether different personality types would be predisposed to integrate or segregate family and work facets of life.

Sample Items:

(A)   I make it a policy to leave work problems at work and not let them disturb my peace at home.
(B)   My spouse and I discuss our career and family goals and expectations.
(C)   I think my spouse feels that family life should be segregated and kept distinct from work life.

Comments: The author reports that Cronbach's alpha for Integration ranges from .68 for the U.S. samples to .82 for Indian samples. The measure was used in 3 studies in the United States and two studies in India between 1981 and 1987. The correlation between integration and life and job satisfaction have been investigated.

References:

Sekaran, U. (1983). Factors influencing the quality of life in dual-career families. *J Occup Psy, 56,* 161–174.

Sekaran, U. (1985). The paths to mental health: An exploratory study of husbands and wives in dual-career families. *J Occup Psy, 58,* 129–137.

Sekaran, U. (1986). *Dual career families: Contemporary organizational and counseling issues* (p. 218). San Francisco: Jossey-Bass.

I-3/c/d
34. BOSS, P., GREENBERG, J., & PEARCE-McCALL, D. Boundary Ambiguity Scale

Avail: NAPS-3

Variables Measured: Perceptions of family members as to who is and is not a part of their family system

Type of Instrument: A series of self-report questionnaires

Instrument Description: The Boundary Ambiguity Scales is a series of six instruments designed to measure perceptions of various family members as to the content of their family system. These scales, also referred to as the Psychological Presence Scale, are based on the premise that individuals may perceive a person as being psychologically present and affecting the functioning of the family system despite the physical absence of that person. Scales are presented for (1) wives of men declared missing-in-action (18 items), (2) widows (12 items),

(3) parents of adolescents leaving home (11 items), (4) adolescent and adult children of divorce (26 Likert-type perceptual items, plus 9 general information and demographic items), (5) divorced adults (22 items), and (6) caregivers of patients with Alzheimer's disease (22 items). Except as noted above, all items are Likert-type with 5 response options. These instruments are designed to be administered either by mail or in research and/or clinical settings. Administration time for each scale is approximately 5–15 minutes. Scoring is accomplished by reversing appropriate items and summing values associated with responses. Scores are structured such that higher scores are interpreted as indicating greater boundary ambiguity. Complete instructions for scoring and interpreting the scales are contained in the manual.

Sample Items:

(A) (Scale 1) I no longer consider myself an "MIA" wife.
(B) (Scale 2) I feel I have prepared myself for a change in status (to widow).
(C) (Scale 3) I feel that it will be difficult for me now that _____ has left home.
(D) (Scale 4) I hope that my parents' relationship with each other will improve.
(E) (Scale 5) I still consider myself a wife/husband to my former spouse.
(F) (Scale 6) I continue to keep alive my deepest hope that _____ will be like his/her old self again.

Comments: The authors indicate that psychological presence scores for fathers and mothers were correlated .47. Based on reliability and item analyses, 2 items (10 and 11) were deleted from the scale. Cronbach's alpha for the remaining 9-item scale is reported to be .71 for fathers and .77 for mothers. Correlations are reported between psychological presence and somatic symptoms (.16), affect (fathers = .18, mothers = .04), family stress (.03), and feelings about launching the adolescent from the home (fathers = -.44, mothers = -.49).

References:

Boss, P. (1980). The relationship of wife's sex role perceptions, psychological father presence, and functioning in the ambiguous father-absent MIA family. *J Mar Fam, 42,* 541–549.
Boss, P. (1988). *Family stress management.* Newbury Park, CA: Sage.
Boss, P., & Greenberg, J. (1984). Family boundary ambiguity: A new variable in family stress theory. *Fam Proc, 23,* 535–546.
Boss, P., Pearce-McCall, D., & Greenberg, J. (1987). Normative loss in mid-life families: Rural, urban, and gender differences. *Fam Relat, 36,* 437–443.

I-3/d
35. CANTOR, M. H. Family Mutual Aid and Interaction Index

Avail: 1982 Ref.

Variables Measured: Support and assistance given or received between grandparents, their children, and their grandchildren

Type of Instrument: Self-report questionnaire

Instrument Description: This instrument consists of several parts, two of which are of primary consideration for the purposes of this volume: One section contains a 21-item checklist of behaviors that may occur between elderly individuals and their children or grandchildren; the other section consists of a 10-item questionnaire in which elderly respondents are asked from which of seven categories of persons they would seek assistance when a variety of problems occur. The first section of the questionnaire is divided into two parts, with the initial 11 items representing behaviors where the elderly person might render assistance, and the last 10 items consisting of areas that would be of assistance to the elderly person. Seven items are contained within both sections of the questionnaire. Both portions of the questionnaire may be asked of grandparents, their children, and their grandchildren, utilizing a different opening question based on the generational status of the respondent. For grandparents, the initial group of items is preceded by the question: "Do you ever help either your children or grandchildren in any of the following ways?" The question for this section when administered to children or grandchildren is this: "Do your parents or grandparents ever help you in any of the following ways?" The opening question for the second section, detailing assistance delivered to grandparents, is also geared toward the generational status of the respondent ("Do your children or grandchildren ever help you in any of the following ways?" and "Do you ever help your parents or grandparents in any of the following ways?").

Sample Items:

  (A)   Help out when someone is ill.
  (B)   Take care of small children.
  (C)   Give general advice on how to deal with some of life's problems.

Comments: This scale was also used by Louis Harris and Associates in a 1975 study conducted for the National Council on the Aging in which a national population sample was questioned regarding attitudes toward and activities of the elderly. In documents related to this 1975 study, the instrument is referred to as the Exchanges of Support and Assistance Index.

References:

Bengtson, V. L., & Schrader, S. S. (1982). Parent-child relations. In D. J. Mangen & W. A. Peterson (Eds.), *Research instruments in social gerontology: Vol. 2. Social roles and social participation* (pp. 156–160). Minneapolis: University of Minnesota Press.

Cantor, M. H. (1975). Life space and the social support system of the inner city elderly of New York. *Gerontol, 15,* 23–27.

Louis Harris and Associates (1976). *The myth and reality of aging in America.* Washington, DC: National Council on the Aging.

Mitchell, J., & Register, J. C. (1984). An exploration of family interaction with the elderly by race, socioeconomic status, and residence. *Gerontol, 24,* 48–54.

I-3/IV-1/c
36. HELLER, P. L. Nuclear Familism Attitude Scale

Avail: 1976 Ref.

Variables Measured: Attitudes toward two generations of a nuclear family

Type of Instrument: Self-report questionnaire

Instrument Description: This instrument is a 15-item Likert-type questionnaire utilizing a 5-point response format. Response options range from *strongly agree* to *strongly disagree*. The construct of familism often refers to feelings an individual has toward his or her extended family. The Nuclear Familism Attitude Scale modifies this concept somewhat, instead measuring attitudes toward two generations of the nuclear family. Scores on five aspects of familism are obtained: (1) feeling that one belongs primarily to the family group and that other persons are outsiders, (2) integration of individual activities for the achievement of family objectives, (3) feeling that material goods are family property and one is obligated to give assistance when an individual needs it, (4) concern for perpetuation of the family as indicated by helping an adult child begin economic and household activities, and (5) mutual aid and friendly exchange. Each subscale is examined by 3 items. Item scores within subscales are summed and standardized, with sten scores ranging from 0–9 allowing for comparison across content areas. The original scale was derived from item analyses performed on an initial group of 63 items. This first 15-item version was normed on several hundred university undergraduates during 1963. A revision of this original version was constructed and tested in Heller (1976). Six items from the original remained, while 9 items were revised in this latter edition. Revisions were undertaken in order to simplify the wording of the 9 affected items.

Sample Items:

(A)   A married person should be willing to share his home with brothers and sisters of his husband or wife.

(B)   Married children should live close to their parents so that they can help each other.

(C)   If a person finds that his job runs so much against family values that severe conflict develops, he should find a new job.

Comments: In the initial study (Heller, 1970), the author reported that answers to four questions were compared to total scale scores as a validation check. Questions concerned (1) concept of family, (2) recent visits, (3) frequency of gatherings, and (4) willingness to leave the vicinity of parents following graduation. Eta squared, which gives an estimate of explained variation in the dependent variable, was computed for each relationship, and was reported to be .01, .03, .23, and .23, respectively. Goodman and Kruskal's gamma was used to analyze test-retest data, where the initial testing involved originally worded items, and retest data resulted from reworded items. For the 9 altered items, gamma was reported to range from .71 to .98.

References:

Ferraro, K. J., Johnson, J. M., Jorgensen, S. R., & Bolton, F. G., Jr. (1983). Problems of prisoners' families. *J Fam Iss, 4,* 575–591.
Heller, P. L. (1970). Familism scale: A measure of family solidarity. *J Mar Fam, 32,* 73–80.
Heller, P. L. (1976). Familism scale: Revalidation and revision. *J Mar Fam, 38,* 423–429.

I-3/d/e

37. OLIVERI, M. E., & REISS, D. Personal Network Inventory

Avail: NAPS-3

Variables Measured: The existence of friendship and kinship networks

Type of Instrument: Self-report questionnaire

Instrument Description: The Personal Network Inventory is a three-part questionnaire consisting of (1) a listing of up to 12 relatives not living within the household of the nuclear family (the kinship network), as well as up to 18 friends, neighbors, and/or coworkers considered by the respondent to be significant in his or her life (the friendship network); (2) a series of questions exploring the nature of each interpersonal relationship; and (3) indications of the interconnection between persons constituting each individual's network. For both friendship and kinship networks, participants are asked to include those persons they believe to be important to them or play a role of significance within their lives. Questions used to explore the nature of interpersonal relationships examine areas such as the types and frequencies of contact, affective components, and the mutual helping nature of the relationships. Separate indexes are computed for structural, functional, and qualitative aspects of both kinship and friendship networks. Specific measures include (1) the size of the network, (2) density of the network with respect to interconnections, (3) frequency of direct contact, (4) help given, (5) help received, (6) positive sentiment, and (7) feelings of need. Separate forms are provided for adults and adolescents.

Sample Items:

(A)   During the past two years, how often have you *received* the following kind of help from the person listed?

(B)   Again we have listed below four statements. We would like to know the reason why you stay in touch with or regard as important the person you have listed. Please provide this information for each person you have listed.

(C)   Please enter the number that best describes these forms of contact with people you have written on your list (followed by options for telephone conversations and letter writing).

Comments: Test-retest data are provided by the authors regarding the stability of personal network choices and of network size. In a sample of 82 three-member families, an average of 67% of individuals listed by a respondent at the initial administration are reported to have also been listed six to seven months later. Choices within the kin network were reported to contain 79% agreement, while friendship choices were found to be 55% in agreement between testings. Intraclass correlations assessing the stability of the variable of network size was reported to average .65. The authors indicate that, across both kin and friends, size of adolescents' friendship networks showed less stability (r = .49) than did that of mothers (r = .71).

References:

Oliveri, M. E., & Reiss, D. (1981). The structure of families' ties to their kin: The shaping role of social constructions. *J Mar Fam, 43,* 391–407.

Oliveri, M. E., & Reiss, D. (1987). Social networks of family members: Distinctive roles of mothers and fathers. *Sex Roles, 17,* 719–736.

Reiss, D., & Oliveri, M. E. (1983). The family's construction of social reality and its ties to its kin network: An exploration of causal direction. *J Mar Fam, 45,* 81–91.

I-3/c

38. PROCIDANO, M. E., & HELLER, K. Perceived Social Support— Family (PSS-Fa)

Avail: 1983 Ref.

Variables Measured: Individual perceptions of support likely to be received from one's family

Type of Instrument: Self-report questionnaire

Instrument Description: The PSS-Fa is a 3-point (*yes, no, don't know*), 20-item questionnaire designed to assess feelings and experiences related to social support from one's family. It is generally used in conjunction with a parallel instrument, the Perceived Social Support— Friends (PSS-Fr) questionnaire. In constructing the PSS-Fa, item analyses were performed on 84 items generated by the first author and administered to a group of university undergraduates. Initial items were selected based on the author's perception of their relationship to constructs of provision of support, information, feedback, and reciprocity. Item-analyses were used in reducing the number of items, first to 35, and finally to 20. The PSS-Fa is presumed to be unidimensional. The scale is scored such that responses indicative of social support are scored 1, with the remaining 2 options being scored 0. The total number of items scored 1 are then counted, resulting in a possible range of scores from 0 to 20.

Sample Items:

(A)   My family gives me the moral support I need.

(B)   My family enjoys hearing about what I think.

(C)   My family is sensitive to my personal needs.

Comments: In a study by Kurdek and Schmitt (1985–1986), Cronbach's alpha for the PSS-Fa was found to be .87. The authors reports on a study where Cronbach's alpha was found to be .90. Correlations are reported by the authors between the PSS-Fa and PSS-Fr (.24), positive life events (.09), negative life events (-.05), California Personality Inventory (CPI) good impression (.12), CPI social presence (.12), CPI sociability (.13), lack of self-confidence (-.06), and social competence (.35).

References:

Kurdek, L. A., & Sinclair, R. J. (1985–1986). Adolescents' views on issues related to divorce. *J Adol Res, 1,* 373–387.

Procidano, M. E., & Heller, K. (1983). Measures of perceived social support from friends and from family: Three validation studies. *Am J Comm P, 11,* 1–24.

Tute, B., & Hauch, C. (1988). Building on family strength: A study of families with positive adjustment to the birth of a developmentally disabled child. *J Mar Fam Th, 14,* 185–193.

Ward, M., & Lewko, J. H. (1987). Adolescents in families adopting older children: Implications for service. *Child Welf, 66,* 539–547.

I-3/c/d/e

39. TURNER, R. J., FRANKEL, B. G., & LEVIN, D. M. Provision of Social Relations (PSR)

Avail: 1983 Ref.

Variables Measured: Support of family and friends in social relations

Type of Instrument: Self-report questionnaire

Instrument Description: The PSR is a 5-point, 15-item Likert-type questionnaire designed to assess social support networks. The instrument was initially constructed as an 18-item scale, but was reduced by 3 items as a result of a factor analysis. During the development of the scale, items were written based on a five-dimensional conceptualization of support (attachment, social integration, reassurance of worth, reliable alliance, and guidance). The original 18-item version was pretested on a group of 200 university undergraduates. It was subsequently used in another study with a population of physically disabled persons, and in a third with discharged psychiatric patients. It was based on these later two studies that 3 items were dropped from the scale. Of the remaining 15 items, 6 loaded primarily on the "family support" factor, while the remaining 9 loaded primarily on the "friend support" factor. Scores are determined on the family and friend dimensions by summing values associated with responses, with higher scores indicating greater social support. An overall support score can also be obtained by combining the two dimensions. However, when combining these scores a determination should be made as to the relative value of friendship and family support networks. If item scores are summed, the greater weight falls on friendship networks (9 items versus 6 items). This can be equalized, however, by averaging the two dimensional scores rather than summing their scores to arrive at a total.

Sample Items (Note: All sample items listed here are from the Family Support subscale):

(A)   No matter what happens, I know that my family will always be there for me should I need them.
(B)   Sometimes I'm not sure if I can completely rely on my family.
(C)   My family lets me know they think I'm a worthwhile person.

Comments: According to the factor analysis reported by the authors, items in the physical disability study loaded on their primary factors from .39 to .67 and from .52 to .88 for the friend support and family support subscales, respectively. In the study of discharged psychiatric patients, primary loadings ranged from .28 to .75 and from .58 to .90 for friend and family support subscales, respectively. Secondary loadings were all below .33, with all but 1 item loading .20 or less in at least one of the two studies. Cronbach's alpha is reported by the authors to have ranged from .75 to .87 for the two dimensions across studies.

Reference:

Turner, R. J., Frankel, B. G., & Levin, D. M. (1983). Social support: Conceptualization, measurement, and implications for mental health. In J. R. Greenley (Ed.), *Research in community and mental health* (Vol. 3, pp. 67–111). Greenwich, CT: JAI.

I-4/b/e/C

40. ARMSDEN, G. C., & GREENBERG, M. T. Inventory of Parent and Peer Attachment (IPPA)

Avail: 1987 Ref., original inventory, & NAPS-3, revised inventory

Variables Measured: Degree of mutual trust, quality of communication, and extent of anger and alienation in relationships with mother, father, and peers

Type of Instrument: Self-report questionnaire

Instrument Description: The IPPA was developed in order to assess the positive and negative affective and cognitive dimensions of adolescents' relationships with their parents and close friends, particularly how well these figures serve as sources of psychological security. The theoretical framework is attachment theory, originally formulated by Bowlby and recently expanded by others. The IPPA has been used successfully in several studies with adolescents from 12 to 20 years of age. Responses are given on a 5-point Likert-type scale. Negatively worded items are reverse scored, with a total score for each section arrived at by summing the responses. The original version of the IPPA, available in Armsden and Greenberg (1987), had 28 parent and 25 peer items. A revised version, available through NAPS-3, contains 25 items in each of the mother, father, and peer sections.

Sample Items:

(A)   When we discuss things, my parents consider my point of view.
(B)   I can count on my parents when I need to get something off my chest.
(C)   My friends help me to understand myself better.

Comments: Three-week test-retest reliabilities for a sample of 27 18- to 20-year-olds were .93 for parent attachment and .86 for peer attachment. Results from a number of studies indicate that parent attachment scores are related to family and social self scores from the Tennessee Self-Concept Scale as well as to subscales of several other measures of family environment and coping strategies. Peer attachment is positively related to social self-concept on the Tennessee Self-Concept Scale and is negatively associated with loneliness. A number of studies have also assessed the relationship between IPPA scores and various personality variables. Further details are available in Armsden and Greenberg (1987).

References:

Armsden, G. C., & Greenberg, M. T. (1987). The inventory of parent and peer attachment: Individual differences and their relationship to psychological well-being in adolescence. *J Youth Adoles, 16,* 427–454.

Greenberg, M. T., Siegal, J., & Leitch, C. (1984). The nature and importance of attachment relationships to parents and peers during adolescence. *J Youth Adoles, 12,* 373–386.

I-4/c

41. BEARD, D. Questionnaire on Planning Behavior in Families

Avail: 1978 Ref.

Variables Measured: Methods used by families in planning their activities

Type of Instrument: Self-report questionnaire

Instrument Description: This instrument is a 5-point, 86-item Likert-type questionnaire designed to assess planning behaviors of families. An additional demographic section and one general family satisfaction question are also included with the questionnaire. Respondents indicate the extent to which each statement is descriptive of their families on a scale ranging from *not like* to *exactly like*. The scale was designed primarily to assess homemakers' perspectives and planning strategies. The author refers to family systems as being either morphostatic or morphogenic. *Morphostasis* refers to systems in which boundaries are rigid and ones where strategies are inflexible. By contrast, *morphogenic* systems tend to be less rigid and more flexible. The present instrument was intended for use in classifying families within these two categories. A factor analysis reported by the author yielded 8 factors: (1) morphostatic family planning behavior; (2) morphogenic family planning behavior; (3) family coping with demands of random planning behavior; (4) community commitment; (5) individual plan flexibility, morphostatic; (6) resource maximization, morphogenic; (7) family adherence to rules, morphostatic; and (8) individual flexibility, morphogenic, or individual coping with demands. A revised, 57-item, version of this instrument (Buehler & Hogan, 1986) is also in use.

Sample Items:

(A)   Plans are made for buying something only after it is obvious that the time and money are available.

(B)   We often must settle for less than we expect because of emergencies, inflation, and the like.

(C)   Most really important wants can be worked into plans.

Comments: The author indicates that, of 86 items, 75 loaded .30 or above on at least 1 of the 8 factors, with 17 loading .30 or above on at least two factors. Each factor contains at least 1 item loading on more than one factor, with Factor 1 containing 3 items (out of 5), Factor 2 having 8 items (out of 17), and Factor 3 having 6 items (out of 11) that load at least .30 on more than one factor.

References:

Beard, D., & Firebaugh, F. M. (1978). Morphostatic and morphogenic planning behavior in families: Development of a measurement instrument. *Home Ec Res J, 6,* 192–205.

Buehler, C., & Hogan, M. (1986). Planning styles in single-parent families. *Home Ec Res J, 14,* 351–362.

I-4/V-1/c

42. BEAVERS, W. R., HAMPSON, R. B., & HULGUS, Y. F. Self-Report Family Inventory (SFI)

Avail: NAPS-3

Variables Measured: Family members' perceptions of communication and interaction styles, as well as overall health of the family unit

Type of Instrument: Self-report questionnaire

Instrument Description: The SFI is a 5-point, 36-item Likert-type questionnaire designed for use in assessing perceptions of family members with respect to Family Health, Conflict, Family Communication, Family Cohesion, Directive Leadership, and Expressiveness. The SFI is a paper-and-pencil measure that may be completed by all family members, and is intended for use in combination with the BIS-I and BIS-II family rating systems. Abstracts of these instruments appear elsewhere in this volume. Items are in the form of statements regarding family functioning. Each respondent is asked to indicate how well the statement fits his or her family. Good fits are awarded low scores, while poor fits between the item and the family are given high scores. Scores for subscales are computed by summing values for appropriate items and dividing by the number of items within that subscale. Some items are scored on more than one subscale. The current scale represents a modification of an earlier 44-item version (Beavers, Monterro, Heiry, & Mohammed).

Sample Items:

(A) Family members pay attention to each other's feelings.
(B) Our family would rather do things together than with other people.
(C) Grownups in the family compete and fight with each other.

Comments: The authors indicate that Cronbach's alpha for the overall scale is between .84 and .88. Test-retest reliability was assessed for both one- and three-month intervals. Differences between one- and three-month evaluations were slight. Correlations for the six subscales of family health, conflict, communication, cohesion, directive leadership, and expressiveness averaged .85, .54, .39, .60, .44, and .81, respectively. Correlations between the six factors and observational measures of family health and competence were .38, .36, .14, .29, .22, and .40, respectively. Data on several other comparisons are reported in the manual (available from NAPS-3).

References:

Beavers, W. R., Hampson, R. B., & Hulgus, Y. F. (1985). The Beavers systems approach to family assessment. *Fam Proc, 24,* 398–405.
Beavers, W. R., & Voeller, M. N. (1983). Family models: Comparing and contrasting the Olson Circumplex Model with the Beavers Systems Model. *Fam Proc, 22,* 85–98.
Epstein, N. B., Baldwin, L. M., & Bishop, D. S. (1983). The McMaster Family Assessment Device. *J Mar Fam Th, 9,* 171–180.
Lewis, J. M., Beavers, W. R., Gossett, J. T., & Phillips, V. A. (1976). *No single thread: Psychological health in family systems.* New York: Brunner/Mazel.

I-4/c

43. BELL, L. G. Family Paper Sculpture (FPS)

Avail: 1986 Ref.

Variables Measured: Perceived closeness, similarity, and family subsystem boundaries, plus families' relations to the world and aspects of family structure

Type of Instrument: Projective technique with evaluative measures

Instrument Description: The FPS has been used to describe and compare Japanese and American families. It is a semiprojective instrument for measuring various family system characteristics. The original purpose of the measure was to look at experienced closeness and distance among family members. The FPS can be used with individuals, couples, or families. Subjects are asked to make a picture of the family using round disks for individuals, red and black strips to show similarities and differences among individuals, and boundary markers to show individuals who are separate, or pairs, or groups of individuals who belong together. A photograph of the picture is taken. Distance measures and other structural measures of interest are taken from the photograph and from the family explanation of the sculpture. Families take 15 to 45 minutes to complete the exercise. Approximately 30 minutes is required to code items from the photograph.

Sample Items: Not applicable.

Comments: The author reports test-retest reliability of Extremeness of Family Distance of .86. This measure is reported to correlate with several family systems variables associated with family functioning, such as the ability to take responsibility for own thoughts, feelings, and behaviors, depression, degree of warmth and support, and ability to resolve differences.

References:

Bell, D. C., & Bell, L. G. (1984). *Family research project progress report.* (ERIC Document Reproduction Service No. ED 248 420)
Bell, L. G. (1986). Using the Family Paper Sculpture for education, therapy, and research. *Cont Fam Th, 8,* 291–300.
Wedemeyer, N. V., & Grotevant, H. D. (1982). Mapping the family system: A technique for teaching family systems theory concepts. *Fam Relat, 31,* 185–193.

I-4/c
44. BELL, L. G., CORNWELL, C. S., & BELL, D. C. Global Coding Scheme

Avail: ERIC No. ED 248 420

Variables Measured: Marital and family interaction process, including how well family members listen and acknowledge, comfort with disagreement, conflict, affect, and expression of feelings, and family organization and structure

Type of Instrument: Ratings based on audio- or videotaped interactions

Instrument Description: The Global Coding Scheme was developed for macro-analytic coding of marital and family interaction processes. It has been used to describe family system variables in families of adolescents in American and Japanese cultures. Couples and families participate in revealed difference tasks and in constructing a family paper sculpture. The interaction is audio- or videotaped. Coders rate the family on 55 items. Most items are rated on 5 to 6 points from *almost always* to *almost never* or on a scale relevant to the item (e.g., *very unorganized* to *very organized*). Scales can be created by combining relevant items. Family tasks typically last about 1 hour. Coders typically complete ratings in about 2 hours.

Sample Items:

(A)   In general, family members take responsibility for their own actions, feelings, and thoughts, and do not take responsibility for the actions, feelings, or thoughts of others.

(B)   Family members are overly close, stuck, overconcerned with each other.

(C)   Disclosure of thoughts and feelings is clear.

Comments: Reliability varied greatly from item to item. The authors report that scales constructed from coding scheme items (and their reliabilities) include interpersonal boundary (.63), ability to resolve differences (.81), warmth and support (.75), depression (.73), influence of children (.80), and covert conflict (.44). Measures from the Global Coding Scheme have correlated in predictable ways with adolescent ego development, adolescent peer relations, and family members' experience of their own interpersonal distances.

References:

Bell, D. C., & Bell, L. G. (1983). Parental validation and support in the development of adolescent daughters. In H. D. Grotevant & C. R. Cooper (Eds.), *Adolescent development in the family: New directions for child development.* San Francisco: Jossey-Bass.

Bell, L. G. (1986). Using the Family Paper Sculpture for education, therapy, and research. *Cont Fam Th, 8,* 291–300.

Bell, L. G., Cornwell, C. S., & Bell, D. C. (1988). Peer relationships of adolescent daughters as a reflection of family relationship patterns. *Fam Relat, 37,* 171–174.

I-4/c/C

45. BELLAK, L., & BELLAK, S. S. Children's Apperception Test (CAT)

Avail: C.P.S., Inc., Box 83, Larchmont, NY 10538

Variables Measured: Children's individual personalities, levels of adjustment, and perceptions of family relationships

Type of Instrument: Projective technique

Instrument Description: The CAT, originally copyrighted in 1949, consists of 10 cards, each depicting one or more animals in various situations and/or types of interactions. This instrument is intended for use with children from 3 to 10 years of age. Respondents are asked to make up and tell a story related to each picture. In designing the CAT, the authors' objective was to develop an instrument similar to the Thematic Apperception Test (TAT), which was designed for use with adults, but one that would prove useful for children. Thus the use of cards and stories, as well as general administration procedures, were structured to conform to those that the authors had experienced in using the TAT with adults. In selecting scenes for the CAT, an attempt was made to include situations that correspond to those typically experienced by children. Animals, sometimes acting as animals, while at other times being anthropomorphically represented, are depicted in solitary and sibling situations, engaging other animals in play or aggression, and dealing with parental figures. The authors intended the test to be used to investigate what the child sees and thinks, as opposed to how that child sees and thinks, about the world. Prompting by examiners tends to be of the nature: "And what happened next" rather than a more inner-probing "Why did he do that?" Cards are presented in the specified order. Care must be taken to develop proper rapport with the child prior to testing. Along these lines, the authors suggest that children, where appropriate, be led to approach the task as if it were a game rather than a testing situation. Stories and prompts are recorded verbatim so that they may be examined at a later time. Administration of the CAT is estimated to take from 20 to 30 minutes, although individual variation, particularly with respect to the age of the child, should be expected.

Sample Items: Not applicable.

Comments: The CAT may be used as either a method for examining the child's personality or as a means of generating input regarding family interactions and dynamics. Methods of interpretation are flexible, with some methods being detailed in the manual, and may be geared to the needs of the individual examiner. A modified version of the CAT using human figures is also available.

References:

Bellak, L. (1975). *The Thematic Apperception Test, the Children's Apperception Test and the Senior Apperception Technique in clinical use* (3rd ed.). New York: Grune & Stratton.
Bellak, L., & Hurvich, M. (1966). A human modification of the Children's Apperception Test. *J Projective Tech Pers Assess, 30,* 228–242.
Bird, E., & Witherspoon, R. L. (1954). Responses of preschool children to the Children's Apperception Test. *Child Dev, 25,* 35–44.
Passman, R. H., & Lautmann, L. A. (1982), Fathers', mothers', and security blankets' effects on the responsiveness of young children during projective testing. *J Cons Clin, 50,* 310–312.

I-4/c
46. BENE, E., & ANTHONY, J. Family Relations Test

Avail: NFER-Nelson, Darville House, 2 Oxford Rd. East, Windsor, Berkshire SL4 1DF, England

Variables Measured: Children's and adults' feelings about family members

Type of Instrument: Q-sort/semiprojective technique

Instrument Description: The Family Relations Test is a self-report Q-sort inventory that gives the appearance of being a semiprojective technique. Both children's and adults'/married couples' versions of the Family Relations Test are available. Additionally, two children's versions, for use with children ages 3–7 and 7–15 may be purchased from the publisher. All versions specify that respondents select an imaginary family from a set of 21 cutout figures of all ages, shapes, and sizes. Various emotions and attitudes, selected from a set of alternatives printed on cards, are assigned by the respondent to each member of the "family." This instrument is intended for use with clinical populations. It is designed to assess feelings held by respondents toward family members, as well as attitudes and feelings they believe are directed by those family members toward them. The adult and married couple version also allows for evaluation of feelings held that are directed toward the person's spouse and children. When selecting appropriate items to apply to each cutout figure, children are instructed to respond according to current circumstances. Adults, however, are instructed to select figures that represent themselves and others from their families at some point in their childhood. Respondents read statements on 96 cards and assign each to one of the cutout figures. If a statement does not apply to any family member, it is assigned to an additional cutout figure that is set up apart from that of the family. Several dimensions have been identified within each version of the instrument.

Sample Items:

(A)   This person in the family used to hit me a lot.

(B)   This person in the family really understood me.
(C)   This person in the family was very nice to play with.

Comments: Split-half reliability where the number of items assigned to parents was at least 7 is reported to be .80. The test has been used since 1957 to examine diverse populations and circumstances, including children of divorce, families with a homosexual child, psychologically disturbed children, and children in foster homes.

References:

Anderson, J. Z., & White, G. D. (1986). An empirical investigation of interaction and relationship patterns in functional and dysfunctional nuclear families and stepfamilies. *Fam Proc, 25,* 407–422.

Anthony, E. J., & Bene, E. (1957). A technique for the objective assessment of the child's family relationships. *J Ment Sci, 103,* 541–555.

Kauffman, J. M., Hallahad, D. P., & Ball, D. W. (1975). Parents' predictions of their children's perceptions of family relations. *J Pers Assess, 39,* 228–235.

Philipp, R. L., & Orr, R. R. (1978) Family relations as perceived by emotionally disturbed and normal boys. *J Pers Assess, 42,* 121–127.

I-4/I-3/d
47. BENGTSON, V. L. Interaction Index: Associational Solidarity Between Parents and Children

Avail: 1982 Ref.

Variables Measured: Informal and ceremonial activities involving intergenerational interaction

Type of Instrument: Self-report questionnaire

Instrument Description: This instrument is a 8-point, 12-item Likert-type questionnaire designed to assess types and frequencies of interactions between parents and their adult children. It purports to measure associational solidarity, which is defined as objective, rather than subjective, types of interactions. Respondents are asked how often, within a number of situational contexts, they interact with members of their families from other generations. The 12 situations can be categorized within five dimensions: (1) interactions outside the home, (2) visits and conversations, (3) family get-togethers, (4) communicating by writing or telephoning, and (5) exchange of gifts and/or assistance. Responses are indicated on a scale ranging from *almost never* to *almost every day*. The questionnaire was designed as part of a larger instrument to be completed by mail. However, it could also be appropriate for use in an interview format. Two factors, each consisting of 6 items, have been identified within this scale: (1) ceremonial functions and (2) informal interactions. Scores associated with items within factors can be summed to yield factor scores. Two additional items of associational solidarity, an opportunity to list "other" forms of interaction and a question asking the distance the respondent lives from the target individual, are appended to the questionnaire, but are not scored.

Sample Items:

(A)   Recreation outside the home (movies, picnics, swimming, trips, hunting, etc.).
(B)   Brief visits for conversation.
(C)   Family gatherings like reunions or holiday dinners where a lot of family members get together.

Comments: Test-retest reliability over a period of four weeks with a group of 21- to 58-year-old subjects was reported to be .81 for a summation of all 12 item scores. Interitem correlations are reported to range from .05 to .71. Cronbach's alpha for ceremonial and informal Interaction subscales were reported to be .58 and .89, respectively.

References:

Bengtson, V. L., & Lovejoy, M. C. (1973). Values, personality, and social structure: An intergenerational analysis. *Am Behav Sc, 16,* 880–912.
Bengtson, V. L., & Schrader, S. S. (1982). Parent-child relations. In D. J. Mangen & W. A. Peterson (Eds.), *Research instruments in social gerontology: Vol. 2. Social roles and social participation* (p. 155). Minneapolis: University of Minnesota Press.
Bengtson, V. L., Olander, E., & Haddad, A. (1976). The "generation gap" and aging family members. In J. Gubrium (Ed.), *Time, roles and self in old age* (pp. 237–263). New York: Behavioral Publications.
Markides, K. S., & Krause, N. (1985). Intergenerational solidarity and psychological well-being among older Mexican Americans: A three-generations study. *J Gerontol, 40,* 390–392.

I-4/c

48. BLINN, L. M. Family Photo Assessment Process (FPAP)

Avail: 1988 Ref.

Variables Measured: Dimensions of family sociovidistic identity, as measured through analysis of family photographs

Type of Instrument: Method for rating and analyzing family photographs

Instrument Description: The FPAP is a three-step process to be used to assess family identity with respect to cohesiveness, expressiveness, conflict, independence, achievement, intellectualism, activity level, moral or religious emphasis, outdoor orientation, and temporal orientation. In this process family photos are first analyzed for content and structural details. Following this, ratings are made concerning content, picture-taking behavior, and picture exhibition. In this second step, 17 bipolar items are rated on a 5-point continuum according to content of photographs, the person taking the pictures, and care and display of pictures. A third step is then conducted in which families are scored utilizing a 5-point Likert-style scale on 10 dimensions, based on impressions of the photographs. Comprehensive treatment of photographs from a single family is estimated to take approximately three hours. Training is estimated by the author to take approximately six hours.

Sample Items:

(A)   informal behavior 1 2 3 4 5 formal behavior
(B)   candid arrangements 1 2 3 4 5 planned arrangements
(C)   COHESIVENESS or the degree of commitment, help, and support family members provide for one another? How many are group rather than individual pictures? How many show the entire family or members in helping roles?

Comments: The author reports on a study in which 10 coders applied the FPAP to individual photo albums. Correlations between coders' assessments and self-ratings by husbands and wives ranged from -.05 to .72 for husbands and from .18 to .79 for wives. Correlations ranging from -.20 to .46 are also reported for FPAP scores and responses on the Family Environment Scale (Moos, 1974). The author further reports that intercoder reliability ranged from .76 to 1.00 on the 10 dimensions specified in step 3 above.

Reference:

Blinn, L. (1988). The Family Photo Assessment Process (FPAP): A method for validating cross cultural comparisons of family social identities. *J Comp Fam Studies, 19,* 17–35.

I-4/a
49. BRODERICK, J. E., & O'LEARY, K. D. Daily Checklist of Marital Activities (DCMA)

Avail: 1987 Ref.

Variables Measured: Dimensions of behavior engaged in by spouses

Type of Instrument: Spouse observation checklist

Instrument Description: The DCMA is a 109-item checklist of behaviors engaged in by spouses. Individual marital partners are instructed to indicate whether or not each behavior happened on a given day, and, if it did occur, how satisfied or dissatisfied they were with that behavior. Items were derived from the 400-item Spouse Observation Checklist (SOC), developed by Wills, Weiss, and Patterson (1974). Ratings of satisfaction are on a 9-point Likert-type scale ranging from *extremely dissatisfied* to *extremely satisfied*. The indications of satisfaction are collectively referred to as a Daily Satisfaction Rating (DSR). The DCMA is independently filled out by both marital partners. Items are nearly equally divided between describing positive and negative behaviors. Behaviors between spouses are assessed within 12 categories: companionship, affection, consideration, sex, communication process, coupling activities, child care, household management, financial decision making, employment-education, personal habits/appearance, and self-spouse independence. These categories are further combined to yield scores in the areas of appetitive, instrumental, and by-products of marital functioning.

Sample Items:

(A)   Spouse greeted me affectionately.
(B)   Spouse left a chore incomplete.
(C)   Spouse expressed understanding or support of my feelings or mood.

Comments: The authors indicate that DCMA summary scores correlate with the Locke-Wallace Marital Adjustment Test (1959) from .25 to .45. It is also reported that distressed spouses are rated as having fewer positive and a greater number of negative behaviors than couples who are judged to be nondistressed.

References:

Broderick, J. E., & O'Leary, K. D. (1986). Contributions of affect, attitudes, and behavior to marital satisfaction. *J Cons Clin, 54,* 514–517.
O'Leary, K. D. (1987). *Assessment of marital discord.* Hillsdale, NJ: Lawrence Erlbaum.

I-4/a
50. BROWN-STANDRIDGE, M. D. The Brown-Standridge Marital Therapy Interaction Scale

Avail: 1988 Ref.

Variables Measured: Marital behavioral patterns and individual spousal behaviors before and after therapy

Type of Instrument: Observational coding scheme

Instrument Description: This system was designed to evaluate pre- and postintervention communication between spouses, as well as husbands' and wives' interactions with a therapist during the course of marital therapy. Interventions used by the author have taken the form of reflection, or reality confirmation, and reframing, or reality creation. Interventions occur throughout therapy sessions, and have ranged in frequency from 7 to 50 interventions during 50–60 minute therapy sessions. Communications coded are those immediately prior to and immediately following interventions. Sessions are videotaped to facilitate proper identification and coding of sequences of interactions. Areas of interest within this system include symmetrical versus complementary interactions; the open or closed nature of interactions; attentiveness versus nonattentiveness; and agreement, disqualification, ambivalence, confusion, ignoring, or neutrality of the intervention response. Interactions are coded by two independent raters who are blind to the hypotheses.

Sample Items: Not applicable.

Comments: The author reports that interrater reliability for codings was .85 when the intervention variable was included. When the intervention variable was not included, reliability was reported to be .83. It is also reported that coders agreed with each other 91% of the time. Test-retest reliability, or intrarater reliability, as it is referred to by the author, was measured by having coders rate the same interactions twice, separated by three weeks. Intrarater reliability is reported to be .93. The author notes that use of the scale is not limited to those interventions already studied, but is appropriate for any study interested in pre- and postintervention measures related to marital therapy.

References:

Brown-Standridge, M. D., & Piercy, F. P. (1988). Reality creation versus reality confirmation: A process study in marital therapy. *Am J Fam Th, 16,* 195–213.
Piercy, F. P. (1985). Brown-Standridge Marital Therapy Interaction Scale: An introduction. *Am J Fam Th, 13*(4), 77–81.

I-4/a/c

51. BURGOON, J. K., & HALE, J. L. Relational Communication Scale

Avail: 1987 Ref.

Variables Measured: Message themes present in people's relational communication, particularly as it relates to intimacy, composure or arousal, formality, dominance, equality, and task orientation

Type of Instrument: Self-report questionnaire that can also be used to report on perceptions of the behavior of others

Instrument Description: All communication theoretically entails a content level and a relational level. This instrument focuses on the relational level. The scale contains 64 Likert-type items, utilizing a 5-point response format. It measures the themes perceived in people's relational communication, composed of verbal and nonverbal messages that define the nature of the interpersonal relationship. It can be used by participants to report on their own behavior or on perceptions of the behavior of a partner. It is also appropriate for use by observers who are making judgments about interpersonal relationships. Although designed primarily for dyadic relationships, it can be applied to family units. It can be used following several communication episodes, a single episode, or a small segment of an episode. The instrument has frequently been used to measure the effects of changes in gaze, distance, or conversational involvement. It has also been used to assess the relational meanings of nonverbal immediacy behaviors, to determine the relational implications of hostile versus neutral versus pleasant vocal tones, and to measure expected versus actual communication behavior among spouses.

Sample Items:

(A) Person A was intensely involved in the conversation.
(B) A tried to establish rapport with B.
(C) A was more interested in a social conversation than the task at hand.

Comments: Factor analyses indicated the presence of eight factors. The author reports that subscales have been used both separately and in various combinations. Reliability coefficients for the individual subscales are reported to range from .42 to .97 across several studies, with most coefficients in the .70 to .89 range.

References:

Burgoon, J. K., & Hale, J. L. (1984). The fundamental topic of relational communication. *Comm Monogr, 51,* 193–214.
Burgoon, J. K., & Hale, J. L. (1987). Validation and measurement of the fundamental themes of relational communication. *Comm Monogr, 54,* 19–41.

I-4/c/C
52. BURNS, R. C., & KAUFMAN, S. H. Kinetic Family Drawing (K-F-D)

Avail: 1970 Ref.

Variables Measured: Child's perception of family members, including personalities, actions, and styles

Type of Instrument: Projective technique

Instrument Description: The child is asked to "draw a picture of everyone in your family, including you, DOING something. Try to draw whole people, not cartoons or stick people. Remember, make everyone DOING something—some kind of action." The examiner then leaves the room and checks back periodically. The testing is terminated when the child indicates that the task has been completed. Although no time limit is given, average test completion time is approximately 5 minutes. The K-F-D is a modification of the Family Drawing Test (Hulse, 1951). In the original FDT children were asked to draw a picture of their family, but directions to include movement or action was not indicated in the instructions. The K-F-D was developed from the perspective that the child's personality, as well as areas of interest within the family system, are best portrayed when action is included in the drawing. While several objective scoring protocols have been proposed for other projective drawing techniques, the authors did not propose one for the K-F-D. A scoring procedure proposed by O'Brien and Patton (1974) identified 29 "raw drawing variables" and 15 "transformed drawing variables." From these, scoring criteria have been developed for rating drawings according to interpersonal orientation, figure facing, and figure activity level. An additional scoring technique for the K-F-D has been proposed by Mostkoff and Lazarus (1983). These authors objectified 20 criteria by which drawings can be quantified and interpreted.

Sample Items: Not applicable.

Comments: Test-retest reliabilities reported for the 20 variables in the Mostkoff and Lazarus scoring procedures are reported to range from .46 to .90. Interrater reliability for the 20 variables ranged from .86 to 1.00, with a mean of .97.

References:

Burns, R. C., & Kaufman, S. H. (1970). *Kinetic Family Drawings (K-F-D): An introduction to understanding children through kinetic drawings.* New York: Brunner/Mazel.

Knoff, H. M., & Prout, H. T. (1985). The kinetic drawing system: A review and integration of the Kinetic Family and School Drawing techniques. *Psychol Sch, 22,* 50–59.

Mostkoff, D. L., & Lazarus, P. J. (1983). The Kinetic Family Drawing: The reliability of an objective scoring system. *Psychol Sch, 20,* 16–20.

O'Brien, R. P., & Patton, W. F. (1974). Development of an objective scoring method for the Kinetic Family Drawing. *J Pers Assess, 38,* 156–164.

I-4/a

53. BUUNK, B. Relational Interaction Satisfaction Scale

Avail: NAPS-3

Variables Measured: Satisfaction with the interaction with your partner in an intimate relationship

Type of Instrument: Self-report questionnaire

Instrument Description: The development of the scale was guided by reinforcement theory. Rather than measuring a global evaluation of the relationship, or assessing diverse aspects and determinants of marital adjustment, this scale measures the frequency with which interactions with a partner in an intimate relationship are experienced as rewarding and not as punishing. There are 8 items, each answered using a 5-response Likert-type scale. Response options range from *never* to *very often.* Item scores are summed, with scores from 3 items being reverse coded. The scale is designed for use with married, dating, and cohabiting couples. It has been used primarily in evaluating relationships of couples in the Netherlands.

Sample Items:

(A)   I feel happy when I'm with my partner.
(B)   We have quarrels.
(C)   I regret being married/living together/being involved in this relationship.

Comments: The author reports that Cronbach's alpha has been measured at from .83 to .88 for various samples. Test-retest reliability over a three-month period was .83. Over a five-year period test-retest reliability was measured at .45. Correlations between husbands' and wives' scores is reported to be .62. Correlations with other scales have been negative for exchange orientation and conflict styles, and positive with communication skills in marriage. A further study reports that the scale accurately discriminated between couples who broke up and those who did not as a consequence of extradyadic relationships.

References:

Buunk, B. (1987). Conditions that promote break-ups as a consequence of extradyadic involvements. *J Soc Clin Psy, 5,* 237–250.

Buunk, B., & Bosman, J. (1985). Attitude similarity and attraction in marital relationships. *J Soc Psych, 126,* 133–134.

Buunk, B., & Nijskens, J. (1980). Communicatie en satisfactie in intieme relaties [Communication and satisfaction in intimate relationships]. *Gedrag, Tijdschrift voor Psychologie, 8*, 240–260.

I-4/a
54. CHARNY, I. W. Existential/Dialectical Profile of Marital Functioning and Interaction

Avail: 1986a Ref.

Variables Measured: Relationship values and marital functioning

Type of Instrument: Observational coding system

Instrument Description: This model is used as a framework for scoring marital interactions. Scores may be based on therapists' observations, discussions with the couple regarding key areas of functioning, or an exercise with the couple scored for consensual discussion. There are no specific questions to be answered. However, in two studies reported by the author, specific questions have been formulated in order to guide the exploration of various content areas. These two studies also utilized a standardized structure for recording the data in the spouse's own words. Husbands' and wives' self-reports and reports of each other were utilized in generating data for the ratings. The model calls for the observation of five areas of marital functioning (family management, companionship, relationship and communication, attraction and sexuality, and parenthood), plus five dimensions of relationship values (competence, commitment, respect, control, and closeness). Scores are given to each spouse so that a pattern or system-picture of their interactions is developed. Ratings are not assigned to the interaction of the couple together. A total of 50 scores are created, 25 for each spouse. The existential assumption of the model is that all couples will fall short of ideal functioning in some areas, because it is characteristic of virtually all couples to be less than wholly competent in all functional areas of marriage. Anticipated time for use of this model by experienced raters in scoring interactions is approximately 10 minutes. Inexperienced raters can expect to take up to 30 minutes. Ratings are generally based on interviews lasting 45 to 90 minutes.

Sample Items: Not applicable.

Comments: The author reports that interrater reliability with three raters has been measured in one study at .89, and in another at .90. A quantitative scoring system has been developed that may be used to compare pre- and postintervention (therapy) behaviors. The system has been used to evaluate interactions among couples where one member has had a stroke and for changes in couple interactions following therapy of midlife "empty nest" crises. Further studies currently under way include evaluating marital interactions of children of Holocaust survivors as well as interactions within extramarital affairs.

References:

Charny, I. W. (1986a). An existential/dialectical model for analyzing marital functioning and interaction. *Fam Proc, 25*, 571–590.
Charny, I. W. (1986b). "Marital trap analysis"—incompetence, complementarity, and success traps: Identifying potential future dysfunctions based on a couple's current collusive agreements. *Cont Fam Th, 9*, 163–180.

I-4/III-2/d

55. CHERLIN, A. J., & FURSTENBERG, F. F., Jr. Grandparent Study Interview Schedule

Avail: 1986 Ref.

Variables Measured: Knowledge of, involvement in, and attitudes toward the raising of one's own grandchildren

Type of Instrument: Interview questionnaire

Instrument Description: This instrument, untitled by the authors, is a 132-item protocol for conducting telephone interviews with grandparents regarding their attitudes and relationships with their grandchildren. Questions cover several areas, including (but not limited to) geographical distance between grandparent and grandchildren, frequency of contact, financial support, parentlike behavior, exchange of services, traditional versus modern family values, and other areas concerned with attitudes toward family life. Items are of various forms, including Likert-type, multiple-choice, *yes-no*, direct information, and open-ended questions. In addition, the interviewer is asked to rate respondents on an 8-item combination Likert-type (6 items) and open-ended (2 items) questionnaire immediately following administration of the interview. These 8 items ask for ratings of intelligence, hesitation in responses, interest or enthusiasm of respondent, attentiveness, truthfulness, and whether or not respondents were tired at the conclusion of interviews. Not all items are asked of all subjects. Rather, some questions are only appropriate depending on the answer to prior items (e.g., "How many great-grandchildren, if any, do you have?" followed by "What difference, if any, is there between being a grandparent and a great-grandparent?").

Sample Items:

(A)   Is your relationship with (CHILD)'s (natural) mother: (a) extremely close; (b) quite close; (c) fairly close; or (d) not very close? (f) Mother deceased; (g) No relationship.

(B)   In what way, if any, are (CHILD)'s parents bringing (him/her) up differently from how you brought up your children?

(C)   When there is important family news, are you: (a) one of the first to hear it; (b) one of the last; or (c) somewhere in between?

Comments: The authors report Cronbach's alpha for several small subscales contained within the overall instrument, with coefficients generally in the .70s. A factor analysis of data collected as a result of a portion of this survey revealed five primary factors: distance, frequency of contact, financial support, parentlike behavior, and exchange of services. Multiple regression analysis was used to further examine variables and trends identified as a part of this study. Additional details are available in the reference listed below.

Reference:

Cherlin, A. J., & Furstenberg, F. F., Jr. (1986). *The new American grandparent: A place in the family, a life apart.* New York: Basic Books.

I-4/a

56. CHRISTIANO, D. J. The Marital Decision Survey (MDS)

Avail: NAPS-3

Variables Measured: Dependence on spouse's behavior for satisfaction and rewards, and ability to affect partner's behavior by making changes in one's own behavior

Type of Instrument: Self-report questionnaire

Instrument Description: The MDS is an 85-item Likert-style questionnaire utilizing a 5-point response option format. Administration time is estimated to be less than 30 minutes. Scores are provided for each of four variables (marital independence, dependence, interdependence, and satisfaction). It is based on social exchange theory and is designed to be used by both practitioners and researchers. The author indicates that researchers may find the instrument useful in operationalizing power and satisfaction in marital relationships. Practitioners may find it to be of use in identifying specific tension areas within a couple's relationship. Respondents are asked to evaluate their own best possible outcome given particular sets of alternatives. Items were selected because of their relevance to both dual-career and traditional marriages.

Sample Items:

(A)   How would you feel if your spouse works part-time and you work full-time?

(B)   How would you feel if you and your spouse both bring home a few hours of work during the weekend?

(C)   How would you feel if your spouse does housework and you do not do housework?

Comments: The author reports that the MDS differentiated between one- versus two-career marriages. It was not able to discriminate between male and female respondents or between high versus low levels of marital adjustment.

Reference:

Christiano, D., & Fong, M. (1980). Strategies for reduction of conflict and tension in two-career families. *Fam Persp, 14,* 73–81.

I-4/c/C

57. CONDON, S. M., COOPER, C. R., & GROTEVANT, H. D. Family Discourse Code

Avail: Select Press, P.O. Box 9838, San Rafael, CA 94912

Variables Measured: Relationship of adolescent individuality and connectedness within the family system

Type of Instrument: Linguistic coding scheme

Instrument Description: The Family Discourse Code is a system for identifying the construct of individuation in families with adolescents. Families, sitting at home in their own kitchens, are instructed to spend 20 minutes planning the day-to-day activities of a two-week vacation, assuming the availability of unlimited funds. Observers are not present during the family's discussion, but the entire process is audiotaped and subsequently transcribed for later analysis. The first 300 speech units are sufficient to serve as the basis for analysis. Each utterance is coded in terms of "move" and "response." Utterances are thought to move the conversation when they provide direction for the interaction. Response refers to the observation that speech units appear to be in response to those utterances immediately preceding them. The authors note that speech tends to encompass both move and response. In addition to coding utterances on these two criteria, both the source and the object of each message are noted. Fourteen specific communication behaviors are coded. These behaviors have been grouped into four-factor analytically determined dimensions: self-assertion, permeability, mutuality, and separateness.

Sample Items: Not applicable.

Comments: The authors' four-factor model was examined with respect to individual communicative behaviors. Intercorrelations of frequencies of utterances served as input for the factor analysis, with the four chosen factors accounting for 51.3% of the total variance. Factors contain from one to five types of behavior, with primary factor loadings ranging from .28 to .92.

References:

Condon, S. M., Cooper, C. R., & Grotevant, H. D. (1984). Manual for the analysis of family discourse. *Psych Docs, 14*(8; Manuscript No. 2616).

Cooper, C. R., Grotevant, H. D., & Condon, S. M. (1983). Individuality and connectedness in the family as a context for adolescent identity formation and role taking skill. In H. D. Grotevant & C. R. Cooper (Eds.), *Adolescent development in the family: New directions for child development* (Vol. 22). San Francisco: Jossey-Bass.

Grotevant, H. D., & Cooper, C. R. (1985). Patterns of interaction in family relationships and the development of identity exploration. *Child Dev, 56,* 415–428.

Grotevant, H. D., & Cooper, C. R. (1986). Individuation in family relationships: A perspective on individual differences in the development of identity and role-taking skill in adolescence. *Human Dev, 29,* 82–100.

I-4/c

58. CROMWELL, R., FOURNIER, D., & KVEBAEK, D. The Kvebaek Family Sculpture Technique (KFST)

Avail: 1980 Ref.

Variables Measured: Cohesiveness of real and ideal family relationships

Type of Instrument: See below

Instrument Description: The KFST is a procedure designed for use in assessing family members' perceptions of real versus ideal family relationships. The instrument was originally developed, but not published, by Kvebaek (1973) as a diagnostic device for use in family therapy in Norway. It was modified and expanded for use as a research instrument in the United States, as described by Cromwell, Fournier, and Kvebaek (1980). The KFST consists of a square board, one meter on all sides, divided into 10 rows and 10 columns. It is designed to be used on a table approximately the same size as the board. The board's appearance is much the same as a chess or checkerboard, with the exception of the number of squares (100 versus 64). Family members are first instructed individually and then as a group to arrange a set of wooden sculptures depicting family members in such a way that relationships within their family are properly represented. Figures available for use include four grandparents, two parents, four children, two persons from outside the family, and one family pet. Thus the clinician or researcher is able to structure the task to include either the nuclear family or a somewhat extended family. No other instructions regarding the placement of specific figures are given. Sculptures are assessed by measurement of distances between placements of various figures. Clients or subjects are instructed to complete the task both as they realistically view their families and as they would like their families to be under ideal conditions. Once each member of the family has sculpted both real and ideal conditions, the entire family is asked to develop real and ideal sculptures based on a consensus of opinion regarding familial relationships. Total administration takes approximately 30 minutes.

Sample Items: Not applicable.

Comments: The KFST was originally developed as a therapeutic technique. As such, exact measurements were not considered to be necessary. Rather, it was seen as a means for therapists to gain insight into the inner workings of families, and to begin to set the course of therapy. Since its introduction to the United States in 1974, various scoring techniques have been developed and modified. The instrument is now used in both research and clinical settings. An extensive description and scoring system is presented in Cromwell, Fournier, and Kvebaek (1980). A self-administered, paper-and-pencil version of the KFST has also been developed (Schmid, Rosenthal, & Brown, 1988).

References:

Cromwell, R. E., Fournier, D., & Kvebaek, D. (1980). *The Kvebaek Family Sculpture Technique: A diagnostic and research tool in family therapy.* Jonesboro, TN: Pilgrimage.

Cromwell, R. E., & Peterson, G. W. (1981). Multisystem-multimethod assessment: A framework. In E. E. Filsinger & R. A. Lewis (Eds.), *Assessing marriage.* Beverly Hills, CA: Sage.

Schmid, K. D., Rosenthal, S. L., & Brown, E. D. (1988). A comparison of self-report measures of two family dimensions: Control and cohesion. *Am J Fam Th, 16,* 73–77.

Weber, J. A., & Fournier, D. G. (1986). Death in the family. *J Fam Iss, 7,* 277–296.

I-4/III-1/f/C
59. DelGIUDICE, G. T. Sibling Jealousy Questionnaire

Avail: 1986 Ref.

Variables Measured: Negative effects of birth of a new baby on the behavior of siblings; personal difficulties of siblings, plus interactions with baby and with parents

Type of Instrument: Questionnaire format with parental ratings of their children

Instrument Description: The Sibling Jealousy Questionnaire was developed to measure the frequency of certain behaviors that are indicative of jealousy observed in children following the birth of a sibling. A questionnaire format was used, with parents rating the behavior of their older children. A 5-point Likert-style scale was utilized. Parents indicated how often, from *always* to *never*, their older children behaved in each of eight ways (regressive behavior, temper tantrums, harsh physical interaction with the baby, takes toys for self, verbalizes dislike for baby, nightmares, sleeping problems, and harsh physical interaction with one or both parents). Two additional open-ended questions are also asked of parents. The scale is intended for populations of 2- to 16-year-old children who have experienced the birth of a sibling within the past one to two years.

Sample Items:

(A)   Throws temper tantrums *always . . . never.*
(B)   Has nightmares *always . . . never.*
(C)   Takes toys or objects *always . . . never* from baby to have for self.

Comments: The author reports that the scale was developed for a study in which parental ratings of jealousy of siblings present during the birth of the new baby were compared with those of children not present for the birth of the baby. No significant differences were detected in the behaviors of the two groups.

Reference:

DelGiudice, G. T. (1986). The relationship between sibling jealousy and presence at a sibling's birth. *Birth, 13*, 250–254.

I-4/a
60. FILSINGER, E. E. Dyadic Interaction Scoring Code (DISC)

Avail: 1981 Ref.

Variables Measured: 23 behavioral codes usually grouped into categories of positive, negative, and task-oriented behaviors

Type of Instrument: Observational coding system

Instrument Description: The DISC is intended to be used in recording of marital and other dyadic interaction by trained observers. The system was originally used with the Datamyte 900 Data Collector, a portable event recorder for entering data in naturalistic or experimental settings. Using the hand-held system, the coder enters coded numbers into the memory bank by depressing keys on the numbered keypad. The coded number is stored in memory along with the time of occurrence of the behavior. If two coders are used, one observes the male and the other the female. Because the units are synchronized it is possible to analyze reciprocal dyadic behaviors in addition to individual behaviors. Base rates as well as conditional probabilities and lag sequences can be examined.

Sample Items:

(A)   Interruption
(B)   Problem description
(C)   Compromise

Comments: While the instrument is designed to be used with any length of observed behavior, the authors have found that coders typically need to rest after 15–20 minutes of observations. Training coders may take up to four weeks. Intercoder agreement (reliability) ratings are reported to be above .70. Cohen's kappa is also reported to be above .70. The DISC has been factor analyzed along with paper-and-pencil measures of marital functioning and loads on the same factor with marital adjustment. It has also been correlated with relevant measures from the FES and IMC session satisfaction (Filsinger, 1983a). In longitudinal studies, the DISC is reported to have predicted relationship adjustment and stability over a period of five years.

References:

Filsinger, E. E. (1981). The dyadic interaction scoring code. In E. E. Filsinger (Ed.), *Assessing marriage: New behavioral approaches* (pp. 148–159). Beverly Hills, CA: Sage.
Filsinger, E. E. (1983a). A machine-aided marital observation coding system: The dyadic interaction scoring code. *J Mar Fam, 45*, 623–632.
Filsinger, E. E. (1983b). Choices among marital observation coding systems. *Fam Proc, 22*, 317–335.

I-4/b/e/C
61. FLOYD, H. H., & SOUTH, D. R. Parent-Peer Orientation Scale

Avail: NAPS-3

Variables Measured: The relative influence of parents and peers on the orientation of youth in the areas of dress, recreation, identification, and companionship

Type of Instrument: Self-report questionnaire

Instrument Description: The scale consists of 20 single-sentence statements related to the parent versus peer orientation of youth from middle childhood through adolescence. Items are rated using a 5-point Likert-type format with response options ranging from *strongly agree* to *strongly disagree.*

Sample Items:

(A) It is more rewarding for me to work with friends and schoolmates than with my parents.
(B) I prefer to grow up to be more like my friends rather than my parents.
(C) It is more enjoyable for me to spend the evenings or weekends with friends.

Comments: The Parent-Peer Orientation Scale has been used in assessing racial and cultural differences in adolescent orientation.

References:

DiCindio, L. A., Floyd, H. H., Wilcox, J., & McSeveney, D. R. (1983). Race effects in a model of parent-peer orientation. *Adolescence, 18,* 369–379.
Floyd, H., & South, D. (1972). Dilemma of youth: A choice of parents or peers as a source of orientations. *J Mar Fam, 34,* 627–634.
Zumami, M., & Floyd, H. (1980). Parent orientation: A comparison of Okinawan and non-Okinawan youth. *Youth Soc, 12,* 33–50.

I-4/IV-2/c
62. GEHRING, T. M. Family System Test (FAST)

Avail: 1986 Ref.

Variables Measured: Individual and group perceptions of cohesion and power within the family in typical, ideal, and conflict situations

Type of Instrument: Combination of figure placement and observational rating techniques

Instrument Description: The FAST is a clinically derived figure placement technique that can be used with anyone over the age of 6. Test materials consist of a monochromatic square board divided into 81 (5 cm. × 5 cm.) squares, male and female schematic wooden figures (8 cm.) to represent family members, and cylindric blocks of three different heights (1.5 cm., 3 cm., 4.5 cm.). Cohesion is represented by the closeness between figures on the squares of the board. Power is represented by the elevation of figures on the blocks. Subjects construct representations of their families as they perceive them typically, ideally, and in conflict situations. Each representation is followed by a semistructured interview. After the individual procedure is completed, the family as a group is asked to portray their relationships together. They are encouraged to discuss their perceptions of cohesion and power in the family and to reach a consensus. SPRINT (systemic performance roles in interaction) ratings are made during these family interactions. Criteria for observation are chosen with respect to specific clinical and research purposes. Individual administration time is approximately 5 minutes per representation. Family interactions last from 10 to 30 minutes. A schematic representation of the FAST as well as details of specific scoring criteria are contained in Gehring and Wyler (1986), and in the manual available through NAPS-3. The manual is written entirely in German.

Sample Items: Test instructions for the individual conflict representation: "In every family there are conflicts and disagreements. Think first of an important conflict in your family and then arrange the figures and blocks according to this conflict." The subsequent interview consists of five questions. Samples from this list are as follows:

(A)   What is the conflict about?
(B)   Which family members are involved in the conflict?
(C)   What roles do the family members play in the conflict?

Comments: The author reports that studies with a nonclinical population of parents and adolescents demonstrated correlations for cohesion and power ranging from .04 to -.17. Test-retest reliability for adolescents averaged .78 for cohesion and .70 for power over one week, and .54 and .69, respectively, over a four-month period. Convergent and discriminant validity were also evaluated.

References:

Feldman, S. S., & Gehring, T. M. (1988). Changing perceptions of cohesion and power across adolescence. *Child Dev, 59,* 1034–1045.
Gehring, T. M., & Feldman, S. S. (1988). Adolescents' perceptions of family cohesion and power: A methodological study of the Family System Test. *J Adol Res, 3,* 33–52.
Gehring, T. M., & Schultheiss, R. B. (1987). Spatial representation and assessment of family relationships. *Am J Fam Th, 15,* 261–264.
Gehring, T. M., & Wyler, I. L. (1986). Family System Test (FAST): A three-dimensional approach to investigate family relationships. *Child Psychi Hum Dev, 16,* 235–248.

I-4/c
63. GERBER, G. L., & KASWAN, J. W. Family Distance Doll Placement Technique

Avail: 1971 Ref.

Variables Measured: Psychological distance in the family

Type of Instrument: Projective interview technique

Instrument Description: The Family Distance Doll Placement Technique was developed to assess the degree to which family members feel close and related to one another while at the same time maintaining their own boundaries as separate and distinct individuals. Respondents are read a series of five stories covering themes of "happy family," "worried family," "sad family," and "angry family." Participants are asked to tell stories in response to each, and to place a family of four dolls on a board to represent the story themes. The dolls were 3.5 to 5 inches tall, and were attached to bar magnets so that they could be placed in standing positions on the metal board. Psychological distance within the family is assessed by the types of groupings or subgroupings into which the dolls are arranged. Doll arrangements are categorized into eight "family grouping schemata." Psychological distance between dyads is measured in two ways: (1) the physical distance between members of the dyad, and (2) the way each member of the dyad is oriented in relation to the other, as measured by four "focus categories." The technique was designed for use with children and adults, both individually and as families. Administration time is approximately 15–30 minutes.

Sample Item: Think of a story about a happy family. Place the dolls on the board to show what is happening in your story, and then tell me the story you have made up.

Comments: Judging of doll placements and accompanying stories are accomplished by a combination of objective measurement and clinical judgment. The authors report that interjudge agreement for assignment to eight agreed-upon categories ranged from .84 to .88. It is reported (Gerber & Kaswan, 1971) that use of the Family Distance Doll Placement Technique led to the conclusion that the family unit was more connected for positive than for negative emotions.

References:

Gerber, G. L. (1973). Psychological distance in the family as schematized by families of normal, disturbed, and learning-problem children. *J Cons Clin, 40,* 139–147.

Gerber, G. L. (1977). Family schemata in families of symptomatic and normal children. *J Clin Psyc, 33,* 43–48.

Gerber, G. L., & Kaswan, J. W. (1971). Expression of emotion through family grouping schemata, distance, and interpersonal focus. *J Cons Clin, 36,* 370–377.

I-4/c

64. GILBERT, R., SALTAR, K., DESKIN, J., KARAGOZIAN, A., SEVERANCE, G., & CHRISTENSEN, A. The Family Alliances Coding System (FACS)

Avail: NAPS-3

Variables Measured: Positive and negative alliances within families

Type of Instrument: Behavior coding scheme

Instrument Description: The FACS is a system for classifying the positive and negative content of interactions between family members. In using the FACS, tape recordings and transcripts of two structured interactions, each lasting 10 minutes, are coded for affective quality (positive, negative, or neutral) and for six positive and eight negative types of comments. Each event, defined as spoken content from one person to another, is coded. A new event occurs with each change in either of the interactants. Coders note who is speaking, to whom the speech is directed, and the affective quality of the speech. In addition, when family members speak about another member, this too is noted. Codes for content areas are each assigned scores based on prior ratings of these dimensions by a group of 20 graduate students. In determining scores, the clinical psychology graduate students were presented with the list of 17 content areas, and were asked to rate each in terms of its indication of a positive or negative alliance. Ratings were on a -10 to +10 scale. Final scores assigned to each code were determined by averaging ratings by these judges. Codes (and their ratings) are as follows: affection (+9.0), agree-approve (+6.2), positive affect (+5.8), paraphrase or clarify or reflect (+5.1), defend/protect (+4.8), positive coalition (+3.0), positive appeal (+1.5), guiding question (+0.4), structure (+0.4), neutral affect (+0.2), personal statement (0.0), behavior control statement (-1.8), negative appeal (-1.8), negative coalition (-3.0), disagree-disapprove (-5.4), threat (-5.4), negative affect (-5.8), opposing question (-6.3), disaffiliate/sarcasm (-6.8), and attack (-9.3). Thus, for example, if one family member attacks another, the attack earns a rating of -9.3, whereas an act of defending or protecting another would be rated +4.8. Overall scores are computed for each alliance by summing scores from codes across the interaction.

Sample Items: Not applicable.

Comments: The author indicates that interrater reliability was determined by comparing coding of interactions by three independent coders. At least two of the three coders are reported to have agreed on sequences and scores for 97% of the speech events.

References:

Gilbert, R., & Christensen, A. (1988). The assessment of family alliances. In R. J. Prinz (Ed.), *Advances in behavior assessment of children and families* (Vol. 4, pp. 221–254). Greenwich, CT: JAI.
Gilbert, R., Christensen, A., & Margolin, G. (1984). Patterns of alliances in nondistressed and multiproblem families. *Fam Proc, 23,* 75–87.

I-4/a
65. GOTTMAN, J. M., NOTARIUS, C. I., & MARKMAN, H. J. Couples Interaction Scoring System (CISS)

Avail: 1979 Ref.

Variables Measured: Communication and problem-solving skills of marital partners

Type of Instrument: Behavioral coding scheme

Instrument Description: The CISS (pronounced "kiss") is a system for coding verbal and nonverbal content present in discussions by marital couples. The authors describe this instrument as having two distinct foci, each coded by different observers. One focus is on verbal behavior and is referred to as a "content" system. Each utterance is coded in terms of this system. The other focus is on nonverbal behavior, both that of the speaker and of the listener. Behavior is coded in terms of each "thought unit," defined as the smallest intelligible unit of speech. For each thought unit, the speaker receives both a content and a nonverbal code, and the listener receives a nonverbal code. It is possible for several thought units to occur within the same sentence. The authors have experimented with at least three types of staged but unstructured interactions: (1) discussion of a problem area volunteered by the couple, (2) discussion of problems not focused on by the couple, and (3) general discussion of the couple's daily activities. Interactions are 10 to 15 minutes in length and are videotaped for later coding. Codes are assigned based on 28 content and 3 nonverbal areas. Nonverbal behaviors are rated as one of the following: positive, negative, or neutral, based on facial expression, tone of voice, and body position or movement. The authors emphasize that only those nonverbal behaviors believed to be reflective of the interaction, and not those indicative of the inner state of the interactants (e.g., "I feel rotten, but I enjoy talking with you"), are coded. The 28 content areas are combined into eight primary summary codes (problem talk, mind reading, proposing solution, communication talk, agreement, disagreement, summarizing other, summarizing self). This system of coding allows for examinations of both the process and content of communication. Recent modifications of the CISS have concentrated on coding of behavior at the nonverbal level. Having found that affective content is often more properly coded at this level, the authors have refined and further developed the nonverbal portion of the CISS into an independent instrument, the Specific Affect Coding System (SPAFF; Gottman & Levenson, 1986).

Sample Items: Not applicable.

Comments: Coding is accomplished by pairs of observers, each concentrating on either verbal or nonverbal levels of the interaction. This allows coders to concentrate on specific levels and types of communication, while facilitating appropriate checks on interrater reliability. The authors indicate that Cohen's kappa averages .91 for content codes and .715 for nonverbal codes. The instrument has been primarily used in comparisons of distressed and nondistressed couples.

References:

Gottman, J. M. (1979). *Marital interaction: Experimental investigations.* New York: Academic Press.

Gottman, J. M., & Levenson, R. W. (1986). Assessing the role of emotion in marriage. *Behav Asses, 8,* 31–48.

Miller, P. C., Lefcourt, H. M., Holmes, J. C., Ware, E. E., & Saleh, W. E. (1986). Marital locus of control and marital problem solving. *J Pers Soc Psy, 51,* 161–169.

Notarius, C. I., Markman, H. J., & Gottman, J. M. (1983). Couples Interaction Scoring System: Clinical implications. In E. E. Filsinger (Ed.), *Marriage and family assessment: A sourcebook for family therapy* (pp. 117–136). Beverly Hills, CA: Sage.

I-4/a
66. GUERNEY, B. G., Jr., & CAVANAUGH, J. The View Sharing Inventory (VSI)

Avail: 1985 Ref.

Variables Measured: Own views, partner's views, and areas of conflict

Type of Instrument: Self-report questionnaire

Instrument Description: The VSI is a 4-point, 66-item Likert-type scale. The scale is divided into two parts, with Part A (50 items) measuring views in 10 areas upon which couples commonly base much of their relationship. These areas are leisure and vacations, job and community, financial considerations, friends and relatives, sex, children, housekeeping and grooming, religion, communication, and roles and division of labor. Part B (16 items) assesses the strength of their desire to see changes in a variety of areas such as use of alcohol and drugs, and gambling. The VSI was designed for use by mental health professionals, clergy, and others who attempt to aid couples in marital preparation or problem prevention programs. The objective of the VSI is to provide clients with a rationale for discussing certain areas of agreement or disagreement, and to identify areas where changes are desired. This instrument was designed to be scored quickly, with couples tabulating the results themselves. Each member of the couple indicates his or her responses to items on the same questionnaire form. The couple's score is the difference between scores obtained by the two respondents. Administration and scoring is estimated to take less than 30 minutes.

Sample Items:

(A) If you have deep roots in a good community, it would usually be better to turn down an offer of a promotion or better job for you or your partner than to move away.

(B) Staying with an organization that offers only average pay with strong job security is a better idea than seeking a new job with much better pay but very little long-range security.

(C) To live in an area good for cultural or recreational activity or educational opportunities for children is just as important as the type of job one gets.

Comments: The authors report that validity of the VSI was examined through several methods. A group of 20 experts in the field were asked to assess the importance of both the 10 areas in Part A and the items themselves. Ratings for the 10 areas averaged 3.8 on a 4-point scale. Ratings on individual items averaged 3.2, with the exception of the job and community subscale (mean rating 2.6). Items from this subscale were later replaced or revised. It is also reported that 10-day test-retest reliability with a group of 50 undergraduates was .90 for Part A and .79 for Part B.

References:

Cavanaugh, J., & Guerney, B. G., Jr. (1985). The View Sharing Inventory. In P. A. Keller & L. G. Ritt (Eds.), *Innovations in clinical practice: A source book* (Vol 4). Sarasota, FL: Professional Resource Exchange.

Most, R. K., & Guerney, B. G., Jr. (1983). An empirical evaluation for training leaders for premarital Relationship Enhancement. *Fam Relat, 32,* 239–251.

I-4/c

67. HANNUM, J. W., & CASALNUOVO, J. Family Interaction Coding System (FICS)

Avail: NAPS-3

Variables Measured: Family styles of interaction

Type of Instrument: Behavior coding system

Instrument Description: The FICS is a system for coding family interactions in 13 behavioral categories: agreement (AG), disagreement (DI), support (SU), nonsupport (NS), constructive problem solving (CP), nonconstructive problem solving (NP), noninvolvement (NI), democratic process control (DC), authoritarian process control (AC), passive process control (PC), neutral (NU), compliance (CM), and noncompliance (NC). The system was designed along the lines of the Marital Interaction Coding System (Hops, Wills, Patterson, & Weiss, 1971). The FICS is used to code audio- or videotaped family interactions. Situations may be structured or unstructured. Each statement made by a member of the family during the interaction is coded. In the situation used by the authors (1984), families were asked to discuss an area of unresolved conflict. However, the authors note that this task failed to generate sufficient negative behavior, and that other instructions for interactions might prove more worthwhile. A total of 13 categories were classified in Hannum and Mayer (1984). However, 23 categories are fully described in the 1980 manual deposited with NAPS-3. It is suggested that users interested in the FICS obtain the manual, using its detailed examples in developing definitions for the categories mentioned in the article referenced below.

Sample Items: Not applicable.

Comments: The authors indicate that interrater reliability across all variables was .97 for three university undergraduate coders. Perfect agreement between the three raters was reported for 42% of the observations. According to Hannum and Mayer (1984, p. 743): "The discrepancy between the two methods of assessing reliability is due partly to the wide range in frequency of occurrence of the coded behaviors across categories."

Reference:

Hannum, J. W., & Mayer, J. M. (1984). Validation of two family assessment approaches. *J Mar Fam, 46,* 741–748.

I-4/II-2/a

68. HATFIELD, E., TRAUPMANN-PILLEMER, J., & O'BRIEN, M. U. Global and Detailed Measures of Equity/Inequity

Avail: NAPS-3

Variables Measured: Men's and women's perceptions of how fair and equitable their dating and marital relationships are

Type of Instrument: Self-report questionnaire

Instrument Description: The instrument comprises two separate scales. The first, the global measure of equity/inequity, contains only one item. This item asks respondents to consider what each partner puts into and receives from the relationship, and to indicate how their relationships "stack up." The second scale, the detailed measure of equity/inequity, consists of 25 items and takes approximately 15 minutes to complete. Items from both scales are evaluated using a 7-point response format ranging from +3 (*I am getting a much better deal than my partner*) to -3 (*my partner is getting a much better deal than I am*). This second scale evaluates the areas of personal, emotional, and day-to-day concern, as well as opportunities gained or lost. The 25 items from the detailed measure scale are averaged in order to arrive at a total index score. Respondents receiving an average score of +3 to +1.50 are classified as overbenefited; those scoring -1.49 to +1.49, as equitably treated; and those scoring -3 to -1.50, as underbenefited.

Sample Items:

(A) Social Grace: Some people are sociable, friendly, relaxed in social settings. Others are not.
(B) Understanding and Concern: Some people know their partner's personal concerns and emotional needs and respond to them.
(C) Day-to-Day Maintenance: Some people contribute time and effort to household responsibilities such as grocery shopping, making dinner, cleaning, and car maintenance. Others do not.

Comments: Detailed information on the construction of the scales, as well as reliability and validity information, can be found in the 1981 reference listed below. The authors report that reliability and validity were assessed in two studies. Cronbach's alpha is reported to vary from .87 to .90 for the detailed measure scale. Validity was assessed by evaluating the relationship of these scales to overall affect, as measured by Austin's Mood Scale (see 1975 reference for a description of the Mood Scale).

References:

Austin, W. G., Hatfield, E., & Walster, G. W. (1975). Equity with the world: An investigation of the trans-relational effects of equity and inequity. *Sociometry, 38,* 474–496.
Traupmann, J., Petersen, R., Utne, M., & Hatfield, E. (1981). Measuring equity in intimate relations. *Appl Psyc Meas, 5,* 467–480.

I-4/b
69. HOLDEN, G. W. Parent-Child Observation Form for Public Settings

Avail: 1983 Ref.

Variables Measured: Elements of interactions between parents and their children in public settings

Type of Instrument: Coding of observed behaviors

Instrument Description: This instrument provides a system for recording ongoing dyadic interactions between parents and their children in public settings such as supermarkets and malls. Equipment consists of a clipboard with a sweep second hand stopwatch attached, observation forms, and a pencil. Observation forms are divided into seven rows and six columns. Each row represents 1 minute and each column represents 10 seconds. Each observation form can be used for 7 minutes of observations. The seven rows are subdivided into two halves so that parental behavior can be recorded on the top, with the child's behavior recorded on the bottom half of the row. This procedure can also be used to code tape-recorded and/or transcribed interactions. Behaviors to be coded include the child's motor behaviors (e.g., reaches for things, hold objects, points), elicitors (e.g., requests, demands), and compliant and noncompliant behavior. Parental behaviors that are noted are initiation of talking, showing affection, providing food or objects, taking objects, teaching, and responding to the child's behavior. The length of the observation period depends on the needs of the investigator. Frequency tabulations, rates of behavior, and sequential analyses can be computed from data gathered during observations.

Sample Items: Not applicable.

Comments: The author reports one study in which two judges were found to agree in an average of 81% of their behavioral ratings. A subsequent study found an average kappa of .73 for two raters.

Reference:

Holden, G. W. (1983). Avoiding conflict: Mothers as tacticians in the supermarket. *Child Dev, 54,* 233–240.

I-4/c
70. HOWELLS, J. G., & LICKORISH, J. R. Family Relations Indicator (FRI)

Avail: Family Relations Indicator 1985, International Universities Press, Inc., P.O. Box 1524, 59 Boston Post Rd., Madison, CT 06443–1524

Variables Measured: Family members' perceptions of each other and the family unit

Type of Instrument: Projective technique

Instrument Description: The current Family Relations Indicator is a revision of an earlier (1963) version by the same authors. The complete instrument consists of 40 pictures printed on laminated cards. Of these, 16 are for use with families having boys or girls only, while 8 are used with both types of families. Thus a set of 24 pictures are normally used for presenting to the parents and children of any particular family. If a family contains both boys and girls, the parents should be presented with the full set of 40 pictures. This will normally require two half-hour sessions. The pictures were designed with the intent of making all presentations as neutral as possible. Children in the pictures appear to be from 7 to 12 years of age. All scenes were designed to be familiar to children of school age. The FRI is administered using an interview format. Family members are shown cards and are asked to tell what they believe is going on in the picture. Responses are recorded. Those that are personality descriptions or a "directed component" are analyzed. Each directed component and each personality description is entered on a rectangular relationships grid, divided into rows and columns, one for each member of the family. The column represents doer of the action, while rows represent the subject. Personality descriptions are entered in the diagonal cells. Directed components are entered in the remaining cells to show direction of the action.

Sample Items: Not applicable.

Comments: The pictures and scoring procedures have been developed by the authors through clinical use and experience. The authors report that the current version is the result of six years of experience with the original FRI. The present set of pictures contains many revisions from the original instrument. German and Italian versions are also available.

References:

Howells, J. G., & Lickorish, J. R. (1963). The Family Relations Indicator: A projective technique for investigating intra-family relationships: Designed for use with emotionally disturbed children. *Br J Ed Psy, 33,* 286–296.

Howells, J. G., & Lickorish, J. R. (1973). *The Family Relations Indicator.* New York: Brunner/ Mazel.

Howells, J. G., & Lickorish, J. R. (1985). *The Family Relations Indicator.* Madison, CT: International Universities Press.

I-4/a/b/c
71. HUDSON, W. W. Clinical Assessment System (CAS)

Avail: Dorsey Press, 224 S. Michigan Avenue, Suite 440, Chicago, IL 60604; also available in 1982a reference

Individual Scales and Variables Measured: (1) index of marital satisfaction (IMS)—discord between married couples or others engaged in romantic relationships; (2) child's attitude toward mother (CAM)—the degree or magnitude of problems children have in their relationships with their mothers; (3) child's attitude toward father (CAF)—the degree or magnitude of problems children have in their relationships with their fathers; (4) index of family relations (IFR)—perceptions of problems in family relationships; and (5) index of parental attitudes (IPA)—parental perceptions of problems in parent-child relationship with a specific child

Type of Instrument: A series of self-report questionnaires

Instrument Description: The five instruments noted above are contained within the Clinical Assessment System. Each is suitable for use with clients aged 12 years or older and produces scores from 0 to 100, with higher scores indicating more serious problems. Each scale contains 25 Likert-type items utilizing 5-point response option formats. Administration time is approximately 5–7 minutes for each scale. Hand scoring generally requires 3–5 minutes per scale. Scoring formulas are described in Hudson (1982a). The combined package of scales is available for use with the Clinical Assessment System, a computerized program which administers any or all scales to clients, scores the scales, stores obtained results, and produces graphic reports of client progress over time. Several other scales are also developed or being developed for use with the CAS. Included among these are measures of relationships with brothers and sisters, and partner or spouse abuse scales (both physical and nonphysical abuse). The CAS currently comes complete with 20 different scales grouped among three general areas: personal adjustment problems, problems with your spouse or partner, problems with family relationships. The CAS can also be adapted by the user to include other scales written or obtained by the user, and to expand or modify scales added to the system by the user. An examination copy of the complete CAS, including detailed instructions, can be obtained by sending three formatted diskettes and a stamped, self-addressed return mailer to the WALMYR Publishing Co., P.O. Box 3554 Leon Station, Tallahassee, FL 32315. The author notes that diskettes will not be returned unless adequate postage is enclosed. The CAS program is designed for use on any IBM PC, XT, AT, or compatible computer having 256K or more memory and using DOS 2.1 or higher.

Sample Items:

Scale #1 (IMS)	(A)	I feel that my partner is affectionate enough.	_____
	(B)	I feel that my partner treats me badly.	_____
	(C)	I feel that my partner really cares for me.	_____
Scale #2 (CAM)	(A)	My mother gets on my nerves.	_____
	(B)	I get along well with my mother.	_____
	(C)	I feel that I can really trust my mother.	_____
Scale #3 (CAF)	(A)	My father gets on my nerves.	_____
	(B)	I get along well with my father.	_____
	(C)	I feel that I can really trust my father.	_____
Scale #4 (IFR)	(A)	The members of my family really care about each other.	_____
	(B)	I think my family is terrific.	_____
	(C)	My family gets on my nerves.	_____
Scale #5 (IPA)	(A)	My child gets on my nerves.	_____
	(B)	I get along well with my child.	_____
	(C)	I feel that I can really trust my child.	_____

Comments: The author reports that Cronbach's alpha for each of the above scales is consistently greater than .90 and typically falls close to .95. Known groups validity, estimated using the point biserial correlation, is reported to nearly always exceed .60. Additional psychometric details are reported in the references. Presumptive evidence is reported on content, construct, and factorial validity. The scales are each copyrighted by the author. He indicates permission for them to be reproduced in any quantity provided the format and content of each is not changed, copyright notations are maintained on all copies, and the scales are not produced for sale or other commercial applications. Permission is also granted to store the scales in a computer or electronic environment solely for purposes of producing hard copies or reproduction masters. Permission is specifically *not* granted to store or use these scales in any kind of automated equipment or software that is designed to administer the scale to respondents, except when used with the complete Clinical Assessment System.

References:

Hudson, W. W. (1982a). *The Clinical Measurement Package: A field manual.* Chicago: Dorsey.

Hudson, W. W. (1982b). A measurement package for clinical workers. *J Appl Beh Sci, 17,* 229–238.

Hudson, W. W., & Acklin, J. D. (1980). Assessing discord in family relationships. *Social Wrk Res Abs, 16,* 21–29.

Hudson, W. W., & Glisson, D. F. (1976). Assessment of marital discord in social work practice. *Social Serv Rev, 50,* 293–311.

I-4/a

72. IMIG, D. R. Family Relations Effectiveness Scale (FRES)

Avail: NAPS-3

Variables Measured: Perceptions of family effectiveness, managerial efficacy, family support, sense of worth, mutual understanding, and cohesion

Type of Instrument: Self-report questionnaire

Instrument Description: This scale is used in assessing individual perceptions of family functioning as reflected by the dimensions of control, regard, and involvement. A questionnaire format with a 5-point (*strongly agree* to *strongly disagree*) Likert-type response scale is used. The FRES is designed for use in both research and therapeutic settings. It has been used to assess both normal and clinical populations. Respondents are asked to check one of the five choices for each of 16 test items. Each choice is assigned a numerical value, with the total FRES score being a summation of all item scores. Scores on the family managerial efficacy, family regard, and family involvement subscales are similarly calculated. Administration time is estimated to be less than 2 minutes.

Sample Items:

(A)   Accomplishing what we want to do seems to be difficult.
(B)   We encourage each other to develop in his or her own individual way.
(C)   Usually each of us goes his own separate way.

Comments: The FRES was adapted from a 48-item Family Adjustment (later renamed Family Effectiveness) measure derived from the original 80-item Family Concept Inventory (van der Veen & Novak, 1974; van der Veen et al., 1964). The author of the FRES initially developed a 20-item instrument based upon these original 48 items. The author reports that a subsequent factor analysis resulted in the elimination of 4 items, leaving the 16 items currently incorporated into the FRES. The author reports that Cronbach's alpha for the FRES ranges from .81 to .90 for a sample of husbands and wives, with test-retest correlations over a two-year period of .54 for husbands and .70 for wives.

References:

Imig, D. R. (1981). Accumulated stress of life changes and interpersonal effectiveness in the family. *Fam Relat, 30*, 367–371.
Imig, D. R., & Imig, G. L. (1986). Influences of family management and spousal perceptions on stressor pile-up. *Fam Relat, 34*, 227–232.
van der Veen, F., & Novak, A. L. (1974). A family concept of the disturbed child. *Am J Orthop, 44*, 763–772.

I-4/a
73. IPAT Staff. The Marriage Counseling Report (MCR)

Avail: Institute for Personality and Ability Testing, P.O. Box 188, Champaign, IL 61820

Variables Measured: Compatibility of marital and premarital couples

Type of Instrument: Interpretive procedure

Instrument Description: The MCR is a format for interpreting 16-PF (Cattell & Eber, 1962) protocols of men and women engaged in romantic relationships. The 16-PF is a 187-item general personality inventory used both as a diagnostic aid in therapy and as a tool for defining personality structures within research populations. Administration time for the 16-PF is approximately 1 hour. The MCR is a seven-page computer-generated interpretation of paired personality profiles of the two individuals involved in the relationship. It examines both individual personalities of respondents and likely issues of concern for the couple. The report highlights areas in which personalities of partners are likely to complement each other, as well as those areas where combinations of specific personality types might be associated with marital difficulties. This interpretive procedure may be utilized both with married couples and with persons exploring their relationship prior to marriage. The instrument was developed for use by psychologists, counselors, ministers, and other mental health professionals. It is intended for use as a starting point for discussing relevant issues with the couple, and not as an indication as to which couples should or should not remain together. Support materials, including a user's guide and Marriage Counseling Worksheets, are also available from the publisher.

Sample Items: While sample items could be listed for the 16-PF, the MCR is an interpretive procedure for the 16-PF, and not the questionnaire itself. Therefore, listing sample items for the MCR was judged to be inappropriate.

Comments: Several studies have been published examining validity and reliability of the 16-PF. While specific information was not available for MCR interpretative procedures, the overall test is presumed by the authors to share many of the qualities that have been established for other uses of the 16-PF.

Reference:

IPAT Staff. (1988). The Marriage Counseling Report (MCR). In *IPAT, 1987–88 catalog of psychological assessment instruments, computer interpretive services, and books* (pp. 6–7). Champaign, IL: Institute for Personality and Ability Testing.

I-4/c
74. KINSTON, W., LOADER, P., & STRATFORD, J. Current Family State Assessment (CFSA)

Avail: Family Research Programme, B.I.O.S.S., Brunel University, Uxbridge, Middlesex UB8 3PH, England

Variables Measured: Several levels of interaction within families

Type of Instrument: Observational rating scale

Instrument Description: The purpose of the CFSA is to provide systematic data on observed family interaction at a particular point in time. It was designed for use by family therapists and consists of 30 categories of family interaction, each of which has its own 5-point ordinal rating scale. Ratings are based on observations of family behavior and are recorded immediately following a clinical interview with the family. The rating schedule incorporates a glossary, which consists of definitions of categories. Anchor descriptions are provided for the first, third, and fifth points of the rating scale for each category. This rating system is designed to permit a reduction and summary of family interactional data and to allow comparison both between and within families over time. While designed specifically for use in clinical settings, the CFSA may also prove useful in other situations where direct observation of family interactions is desirable. Use of the rating system by an experienced rater takes approximately 10 to 20 minutes.

Sample Items: Category—Interruptions

Description: One person speaks before another is finished; includes simultaneous speech, laughter, actions (e.g., leaving room) and children showing their drawings or calling attention to themselves during play.
Anchor Points:
    5: Many interruptions—very disruptive either by intensity, timing, frequency, or duration.

3: Some interruptions—within normal limits: interruptions are not disturbing in amount or their nature.

1: No/few interruptions—would reflect marked passivity, inhibition, control, isolation.

Comments: The authors report that interrater reliability has been investigated, but that intrarater reliability and validity of the CFSA have not been established.

Reference:

Kinston, W., Loader, P., & Stratford, J. (1979). Clinical assessment of family interaction: A reliability study. *J Fam Ther, 1*, 291–312.

I-4/e

75. LEVENSON, R. W., & GOTTMAN, J. M. Dating and Assertion Questionnaire (DAQ)

Avail: 1978 Ref.

Variables Measured: Social competence and social skills related to dating and to assertive behaviors

Type of Instrument: Self-report questionnaire

Instrument Description: The DAQ is an 18-item Likert-type questionnaire. Two 9-item subcategories related to dating and assertion behaviors are individually measured. The focus of both areas is on social skills. The questionnaire is designed primarily for use with college student populations. It may be used as a pre- or posttest device for measuring change that occurs due to social skills training. Half the items use a 4-point and half use a 5-point response format. Items using a 4-point format examine frequency of specified behaviors. Items using a 5-point scale measure the relative comfort of subjects in those situations. Scores associated with individual item responses are summed for each of the two subscales yielding total scores on dating and assertion behaviors.

Sample Items:

. . . next to each of the items on the following list, place the number which best indicates the likelihood of your behaving in that way. Be as objective as possible.

(A) Maintain a long conversation with a member of the opposite sex.
(B) Be confident in your ability to succeed in a situation in which you have to demonstrate your competence.

After each situation circle one of the numbers from 1 to 5 which best describes you using the following scale:

1 = . . . so uncomfortable . . . avoid it if possible.
2 = . . . very uncomfortable . . . lot of difficulty handling this situation.
3 = . . . somewhat uncomfortable . . . some difficulty . . .
4 = . . . quite comfortable . . . able to handle . . .
5 = . . . very comfortable . . . handle this situation very well.
(C) You have enjoyed this date and would like to see your date again. The evening is coming to a close and you decide to say something.

Comments: Cronbach's alpha for the dating and assertive subscales is reported to be .92 and .85, respectively. Test-retest reliability over a two-week period is reported to be .71. Validity of the scales was evaluated through examination of differences in scores of clinical and nonclinical college student samples.

Reference:

Levenson, R. W., & Gottman, J. M. (1978). Toward the assessment of social competence. *J Con Clin, 46,* 453–462.

I-4/IV-2/a
76. LUND, M. Lund Investment Scale

Avail: 1985 Ref.

Variables Measured: Investment made in a romantic relationship

Type of Instrument: Self-report questionnaire

Instrument Description: This instrument is a 26-item Likert-type questionnaire designed to measure the investment made by individuals in their romantic relationships. Subjects are asked to respond to each item in terms of the investment they have made with respect to that area of their romantic relationship. Items were developed from open-ended responses by 30 undergraduates to questions about their romantic relationships and about romantic relationships in general. Specifically, subjects were asked "to give concrete examples of effort, sacrifice, resources, and demonstrations of intention to continue a relationship" (Lund, 1985, p. 8). Specific items were generated covering 26 areas identified through these student responses. The items were then administered to a second sample of 111 undergraduates. Factor analyses performed by the author on this and three other scales resulted in all 26 items being retained in the final version of the scale. An overall investment score is obtained by summing values associated with responses to individual items.

Sample Items:

- (A)   Spending your free time with your partner rather than doing other things or seeing other people.
- (B)   Buying gifts for your partner or paying for entertainment (considering both amount and expense).
- (C)   Integrating your partner into your family (such as introducing them, arranged shared social activities, or revealing your feelings and plans).

Comments: A factor analysis reported in Lund (1985) found that approximately 40% of the scale variance was explained by a single factor. The author, therefore, elected to treat the scale as being unitary. Cronbach's alpha is reported by the author to range from .93 to .96. Additionally, high Investment Scale scores were reported to be correlated with length of time the couple has been together .26 and, in a longitudinal study, .74 with the individual's commitment to the relationship.

Reference:

Lund, M. (1985). The development of investment and commitment scales for predicting continuity of personal relationships. *J Soc Pers Relat, 2,* 3–23.

I-4/a

77. MANSON, M. P. California Marriage Readiness Evaluation (CMRE)

Avail: Western Psychological Services, 12031 Wilshire Blvd., Los Angeles, CA 90025

Variables Measured: Strength and weakness in three aspects of marriage readiness: personality, preparation, and interpersonal compatibility

Type of Instrument: Self-report questionnaire

Instrument Description: This instrument is a 110-item *true/false* and 5-item projective completion questionnaire designed to assess readiness for marriage among individuals and couples. Scores are derived indicating strengths and weaknesses along three key dimensions (denoted by 1–3) and eight areas (denoted by a-h): (1) Personality: (a) character structure, (b) emotional maturity, (c) marriage readiness; (2) Preparation for Marriage: (d) family experiences, (e) dealing with money, (f) planning ability; (3) Interpersonal Compatibility: (g) marriage motivation and (h) compatibility. In addition to scores for each of the eight areas measured, a total score indicating overall readiness for marriage is computed. The questionnaire is designed for use with couples approaching marriage, whether problems have been noted or not. For those with problems, areas of concern can be further recognized, developed, and dealt with by a qualified clinician. For those without problems, the California Marriage Readiness Evaluation can serve to heighten awareness of individual differences between potential spouses, as well as provide a vehicle for developing greater insight into the attitudes, beliefs, and personality of one's potential spouse. The greater the number of items that are marked true about the respondent, the higher his or her level of marriage readiness. Administration time is approximately 15–30 minutes.

Sample Items:

(A) I have been gainfully employed for the last two years or more.
(B) After I marry I plan to participate in community affairs.
(C) Children are a nuisance. (Copyright 1965 by Western Psychological Services. Reprinted by permission of the publisher, Western Psychological Services, 12031 Wilshire Boulevard, Los Angeles, California 90025)

Comments: The eight subscales in use with this instrument are not intended to be orthogonal. Rather, items are generally scored on multiple scales, with individual items being included in scores for between one and five subscales.

References:

Knox, D., & Knox, F. (1974). Preparation for marriage: Beyond the classroom. *J Fam Couns, 2*, 16–22.

Manson, M. P. (1965). *California Marriage Readiness Evaluation: Manual.* Los Angeles: Western Psychological Services.

Manson, M. P. (1988). California Marriage Readiness Evaluation. In *Western Psychological Services 1988–89 catalog* (p. 159). Los Angeles: Western Psychological Services.

Reiner, B. S., & Edwards, R. L. (1974). Adolescent marriage: Social or therapeutic problem? *Fam Coord, 23*, 383–390.

I-4/g
78. MARTIN, D. V., & MARTIN, M. The Marriage and Family Attitude Survey

Avail: Psychologists and Educators, Inc., Sales Division, P.O. Box 513, Chesterfield, MO 63017

Variables Measured: Attitudes of adolescents and nonmarried adults toward marriage and intimate relationships

Type of Instrument: Self-report questionnaire

Instrument Description: This instrument is a 58-item Likert-type questionnaire designed to stimulate discussion about marriage and family life. Items are answered according to a 5-point scale, with options ranging from *strongly agree* to *strongly disagree*. The questionnaire is appropriate for use with all ages of adolescents and young, unmarried adults. It would be appropriate for use in junior and senior high classrooms, as well as group workshops, churches, and so on. It may also be appropriate for use with individuals presenting for counseling on relationship issues. Ten separate topical areas are covered in the questionnaire: (1) premarital sex, (2) marriage and divorce, (3) childhood and child rearing, (4) division of household labor and professional employment, (5) marital and extramarital sexual relationships, (6) privacy rights and social needs, (7) religion, (8) communication expectations, (9) parental relationships, and (10) professional counseling services. While it appears that individual topic area scores may be derived by summing values assigned to specific responses for items within that area, this procedure is not discussed in the manual. The manual indicates that individual item scores that are in agreement with those listed in the scoring key receive 1 point. Profiles for persons scoring in various ranges are listed in the manual.

Sample Items:

(A) I believe it is wrong to engage in sexual intercourse before marriage.
(B) If both my spouse and I work, I would leave my child with a relative or friend while at work.
(C) I have trouble expressing what I feel towards the other person in an intimate relationship.

Comments: This instrument was developed for use in a study of 5,000 students attending one of six secondary schools, colleges, and universities. Items were selected by a panel of nine marriage and family therapists and one psychologist. Items included in the final version of the questionnaire were approved by at least seven panel members.

References:

Martin, D. V. (1982). Premarital group counseling. *J Spec Grp Wk, 2,* 96–105.
Martin, D. V., & Martin, M. (1984). Selected attitudes toward marriage and family life among college students. *Fam Relat, 33,* 293–300.

I-4/c
79. McCUBBIN, H. I., & THOMPSON, A. I. Family Celebrations Index (FCELEBI)

Avail: 1987 Ref.

Variables Measured: Families' celebrations of special events throughout the year

Type of Instrument: Self-report questionnaire

Instrument Description: The FCELEBI is a 4-point, 9-item Likert-type questionnaire designed to assess the extent of family involvement in celebrations throughout the year. Items are in the form of short statements describing situations typically celebrated by families. Respondents indicate the extent to which the family practices each type of celebration (*never, seldom, often, always*) listed. Two factors are identified: (1) unique celebrations, focusing on those events not specific to family members; and (2) intrafamily celebrations, emphasizing events more specifically affecting members of the immediate family. The authors indicate that the FCELEBI is useful in tracking types of activities in which families participate across the life span. Family interests, as well as participation in joint activities, tend to change as both the children and the marriage mature.

Sample Items:

(A) Special changes and events (e.g., graduation, promotion)
(B) Yearly major holidays (4th of July, New Year's)
(C) Occasions (e.g., Valentine's Day, Mother's Day)

Comments: The authors indicate that Cronbach's alpha for the overall scale is .69. Factor loadings are reported to be from .29 to .67 for the first factor (unique) and from .40 to .75 for the second factor (intrafamily). However, if the item "Religious occasions (holy days, etc.)" is removed from Factor 1, reported loadings are from .60 to .67. The authors indicate that families with children living in the home tend to report greater family-type celebrations of events. FCELEBI scores are reported to correlate with measures of flexibility (.22), coherence (.24), family time and routines (.30), family satisfaction (.20), and family traditions (.29).

Reference:

McCubbin, H. I., & Thompson, A. I. (1987). FCELEBI: Family Celebrations Index. In H. I. McCubbin & A. I. Thompson (Eds.), *Family assessment inventories for research and practice* (pp. 169–172). Madison: University of Wisconsin-Madison, Family Stress Coping and Health Project.

I-4/II-1/c
80. McCUBBIN, H. I., & THOMPSON, A. I. Family Traditions Scale (FTS)

Avail: 1987 Ref.

Variables Measured: Activities and practices in which families continue to engage based on values and/or respect

Type of Instrument: Self-report questionnaire

Instrument Description: The FTS is a 20-item questionnaire, utilizing a *yes-no* response format, designed to assess the extent to which families maintain joint activities out of a sense of tradition. According to instructions listed at the top of the questionnaire: "Traditions are those things we do as a family . . . things . . . which we always do, which we have done in the past, which we are likely to continue to do, and which we value and/or respect." Respondents indicate whether or not each activity is a tradition with their families. The authors have grouped traditions within four broad classifications: (1) traditions around holidays; (2) traditions around changes (e.g., marriage, death); (3) religious occasions; and (4) family special events (e.g., reunions). A score is derived for each subsection by counting the number of activities to which respondents have indicated a *yes* response. An overall FTS score is obtained by adding scores from the subscales.

Sample Items:

(A)   (Holidays) Gift giving and sharing.
(B)   (Changes) Special rituals (i.e., choose names, planting of a tree, having special flowers, and so on).
(C)   (Religious) How children participate in service.

Comments: The authors indicate that Cronbach's alpha for the overall scale is .85. Means and percentile rankings for scores ranging from 19 to 38 are presented in the reference listed below.

Reference:

McCubbin, H. I., & Thompson, A. I. (1987). FTS: Family Traditions Scale. In H. I. McCubbin & A. I. Thompson (Eds.), *Family assessment inventories for research and practice* (pp. 163–165). Madison: University of Wisconsin-Madison, Family Stress Coping and Health Project.

I-4/c
81. McENROE, M. J. Evaluation of the Process and Impact of Communication (EPIC)

Avail: ASIP, 17 Palmer St. #4, Cos Cob, CT 06807

Variables Measured: Satisfaction of family members with a specific intrafamilial discussion

Type of Instrument: Self-report questionnaire

Instrument Description: EPIC is a 5-point, 30-item questionnaire designed to assess family members' perceptions of a recently completed discussion. It is intended as an instrument to distinguish between state and trait reports of satisfaction within interpersonal relations. The questionnaire is administered immediately following either a structured or an unstructured interaction, usually under the direction of a family therapist. Respondents indicate their perceptions of the frequency of various occurrences during the interaction, ranging from *never* (scored 0) to *always* (scored (4). Sixteen items are reverse-scored. Overall scale scores can range from 0 to 120. Items were constructed to assess individual and group perceptions of empathy, understanding, trust, attractiveness, and power within the particular interaction. Measures are not taken regarding overall levels of satisfaction with the relationship. Rather, they are situation-specific, allowing for an analysis of immediate behaviors and perceptions of family members, and their antecedent events. Scores of family dyads may be compared, with the purpose of understanding and remediating behavioral sequences occurring during preceding interactions. The author notes that the EPIC may be used either by itself or in combination with systems for coding behavior during the interaction.

Sample Items:

(A)   I enjoyed this conversation.
(B)   Others rejected or insulted me.
(C)   No one listened to what I was saying.

Comments: The author reports that split-half reliability of the EPIC was found to be .96 among 26 families attending a child psychiatry outpatient clinic. A correlation of .50 is reported between EPIC and the Marital Adjustment Test.

Reference:

Blechman, E. A., Tryon, A., McEnroe, M. J., & Ruff, M. (in press). Behavioral approaches to psychological assessment: A comprehensive strategy for the measurement of family interaction. In M. M. Katz & S. Wetzler (Eds.), *Contemporary approaches to psychological assessment.* New York: Brunner/Mazel.

I-4/a
82. McHUGH, G. A Courtship Analysis

Avail: Family Life Publications, P.O. Box 427, Saluda, NC 28773

Variables Measured: Characteristics of one's courtship partner

Type of Instrument: Partner-rating inventory

Instrument Description: A Courtship Analysis is a 150-item questionnaire on which respondents indicate the presence or absence of a series of characteristics in their courtship partner. The scale is a revision of a 1961 questionnaire developed by the same author. This instrument was designed for use in counseling and classroom situations with premarital couples. The author indicates that it may also prove useful with married couples engaged in marriage counseling. Items are grouped into 12 primary areas: (1) habits, (2) religion, (3) health, (4) common interests, (5) sex attitudes, (6) adaptability, (7) background, (8) sense of humor, (9) ambition, (10) money, (11) relationship, and (12) marriage. Respondents are asked to read each item, and to indicate whether the item is *true* (+), or *not true* (-) about their partners. Two other response options are a *question mark (?),* indicating that they do not know if the item is true, and an X, indicating that the item does not apply to their relationship (e.g., items about brothers and sisters when the partner is an only child). All items are presumed to use the stem: "My courtship partner . . . " The scale is intended to be completed by both partners in the relationship. Administration time is estimated to be 15–30 minutes.

Sample Items: The publisher did not grant permission to reproduce items.

Comments: The author indicates that the test is not intended to be scored. However, scores could be derived if desired by individual users of the instrument by counting the number of + and − scores within each subsection. The instrument is intended as a means of assisting couples to examine their relationships. However, it is not intended as a measure of prediction regarding the success or failure of a relationship.

Reference:

McHugh, G. (1979). *Teacher's and counselor's manual for A Courtship Analysis and a Dating Problems Checklist.* Saluda, NC: Family Life.

I-4/c
83. MICHAELSON, R., & BASCOM, H. L. Family Relationship Inventory (FRI)

Avail: Psychological Publications, 5300 Hollywood Blvd., Los Angeles, CA 90027

Variables Measured: Family relationships (e.g., most esteemed family member, least esteemed family member, strongest relationship, most distant relationship)

Type of Instrument: Interview questionnaire, and procedure

Instrument Description: The FRI consists of 50 items printed on cards 3 × 2 inches. Twenty-five items have positive valence (trusts me), and 25 have negative valence (talks too much). The sum of the response valences (either +1 or 1 constitutes a score). The manual gives suggested procedures for administering the FRI to young children, older children, adolescents, adults, and large families. As each item is read, the respondent must decide whether it best describes him- or herself, some member of the family constellation, including pets, or no one. If the item fails to describe a member of the family constellation, it is placed in the wastebasket. Family scores are entered on a scoring form. Boxes at the bottom of the form show most and least esteemed family member, closest relationship, and most distant relationship. A diagonal line on the upper portion of the scoring form is designed to allow the test administrator to pick out self-esteem scores for individual respondents. Individual relationships are indicated on an Individual Relationship Wheel and these relationships are combined on the Family Gram.

Sample Items:

(A)   Loves me.
(B)   Tries to act fair.
(C)   Trusts me.

Comments: The FRI, originally published in 1973, was revised and republished in 1982. While items are intended for classification of one family member or another, an additional format allowing for multiple classifications is also detailed in the manual. Test-retest reliability over a 2-week period for a group of 16 female and 1 male high school students enrolled in a child development class is reported in the manual. Reliability coefficients for scores on self, mother, father, and sibling are reported to be .77, .82, .88, and .90, respectively.

Reference:

Nash, L., Morrison, W. L., & Taylor, R. M. (1982). *Family Relationship Inventory* (rev. ed.). Los Angeles: Psychological Publications.

I-4/a
84. MILLER, B. C. Companionate Activities Measure

Avail: NAPS-3

Variables Measured: Amount of companionship in marriage or marriagelike relationship

Type of Instrument: Self-report questionnaire

Instrument Description: In the study (Miller, 1976) for which this 8-item scale was created, it was reasoned that an individual's perception of how frequently companionate activities were shared with a partner would be positively related to satisfaction with the relationship, but that satisfaction and activities were distinct and separate concepts. Therefore, the Companionate Activities Measure was created to assess the respondent's estimate of how frequently eight different activities were experienced together in the past month. Activities were taken from previous work by Orden and Bradburn (1968), but were revised and scored differently (0 to 7 in the last month) to increase the variability of scores. The questions were designed to be asked by an interviewer, but could easily be self-administered.

Sample Items: In the past month, how often have you and your (husband/wife/partner):

(A)   visited friends together?
(B)   spent an evening just visiting with each other?
(C)   had a good laugh together or shared a joke?

Comments: The author reports Cronbach's alpha for the scale to be .75. It is also reported that construct validity was assessed by comparisons of scores on the Companionate Activities Measure with indexes of number of children, social class, and satisfaction with marriage.

References:

Miller, B. C. (1976). A multivariate developmental model of marital satisfaction. *J Mar Fam,* *38,* 643–657.
Orden, S. R., & Bradburn, N. M. (1968). Dimensions of marriage happiness. *Am J Sociol, 73,* 715–731.

I-4/II-2/IV-2/g/a
85. MILLER, P. C., LEFCOURT, H. M., & WARE, E. E. Marital Locus of Control Scale

Avail: 1983 Ref.

Variables Measured: Internal versus external locus of control for marital outcomes

Type of Instrument: Self-report questionnaire

Instrument Description: The Marital Locus of Control Scale is a 44-item Likert-type questionnaire utilizing a 10-point response format. The instrument is intended for use primarily with married couples. It was designed to assess beliefs about the causes of marital outcomes. Possible item responses range from *disagree very much* to *agree very much*. The four subscales of ability, effort, context, and luck are measured. The first two subscales assess internal, and the latter two assess external, attributes. The total externality score consists of the external less the internal attributes, or luck and context attribution scores less ability and effort scores. Administration time is approximately 15 minutes.

Sample Items:

(A) When we have unpleasant experiences in our marriage I can always see how I have helped to bring them about.
(B) Putting effort into the relationship will practically guarantee a successful marriage.
(C) Sexual compatibility is something of a mystery to me, it is something that just happens.

Comments: The authors report that a factor analysis with varimax rotation resulted in a two-factor solution, with items loading either as internal or external. Cronbach's alpha is reported to be .82 for the combined scale. Externality scores on the Marital Locus of Control Scale were compared with those obtained on Rotter's Locus of Control Scale and Lefcourt's Multidimensional Multiattributional Causality Scale. Internality scores were compared to degree of intimacy in marriage, as measured with the Miller Social Intimacy Scale. Additionally, internals were reported to be more actively engaged in problem-solving activities than were externals under laboratory conditions.

References:

Miller, P. C., Lefcourt, H. M., Holmes, J. G., Ware, E. E., & Saleh, W. G. (1986). Marital locus of control and marital problem solving. *J Pers Soc Psy, 51,* 161–169.
Miller, P. C., Lefcourt, H. M., & Ware, E. E. (1983). The construction and development of the Miller Marital Locus of Control Scale. *Can J Beh S, 15,* 266–279.

Smolen, R. C., & Spiegel, D. A. (1987). Marital locus of control as a modifier of the relationship between the frequency of provocation by spouse and marital satisfaction. *J Res Pers, 21,* 70–80.

I-4/c
86. MURRAY, H. A. Thematic Apperception Test (TAT)

Avail: Psychological Corporation, 304 East 45th St., New York, NY 10017

Variables Measured: An abundance of individual and family-related personality traits and styles of interaction

Type of Instrument: Projective technique

Instrument Description: The TAT is a series of pictures that are individually presented to the respondent(s). The subject tells or writes a story about what the characters in the picture are doing, how they feel, what will happen next, and so forth. There are many variations of presentation. One variation of particular interest to family theorists involves having a family view each card and jointly develop the story. It is common to use only a portion of the 20 pictures, with many investigators electing to present either 6 or 10 of the total. Stories can be scored in terms of underlying personality needs or in terms of manifest content. A variety of scoring techniques have been developed. Several adaptations of the TAT have also been developed specifically to assess family or family-related variables. Included among this group are the following: Minuchin, Montalvo, Guerney, Rosman, and Schumer (1967); Murstein (1976); and Kadushin, Waxenberg, and Sager (1971). The adaptation by Minuchin et al. examined variables such as nurturance, behavior control, guidance, family harmony, and acceptance of responsibility. Murstein's instrument, known as the Marriage Apperceptive Thematic Examination, expressly focused on heterosexual situations. The instrument by Kadushin et al. was named the Family Story Technique (FST), and consisted of the 10 original TAT cards thought most likely to elicit stories of family functioning.

Sample Items: Not applicable.

Comments: Since its development in 1938 (copyright 1943), the TAT has become one of the most widely used clinical instruments. Administration, interpretation, and scoring procedures have become abundant, resulting largely from the ever-present need for dissertation topics relevant to graduate students' fields of study. Included among these are a number of variations appropriate for use with couples and families. Thus, an instrument and a methodology initially developed to assist in understanding individuals has become a popular tool in the evaluation of couples and families.

References:

Breit, M. (1982). Separation anxiety in mothers of latency-age fearful children. *J Abn C Psy, 10,* 135–144.

Murray, H. A. (1943). *Thematic Apperception Test manual.* Cambridge, MA: Harvard University Press.

Murstein, B. I. (1976). *Who will marry whom?* New York: Springer. Richardson, V., & Partridge, S. (1982). Construct validation of imaginative assessment of family orientation and status perception: Theoretical and methodological implications for the Thematic Apperception Test. *Educ Psyc M, 42,* 1243–1251.

I-4/a/e
87. MURSTEIN, B. I. Marital Expectation Test (MET)

Avail: 1976a Ref.

Variables Measured: Expectations regarding characteristics desired or perceived in partners contemplating marriage

Type of Instrument: Self-report questionnaire

Instrument Description: The MET is a 130- to 135-item Likert-type questionnaire used to examine perceptions and expectations of behavior held by partners in romantic relationships. The 130-item version is administered to men, while the 135-item inventory is given to women. The two forms share an initial 76 items, with remaining items differing for the two versions. All items are in the form of statements and are responded to on a 5-point scale according to how accurate the statement is in its description. Subjects are asked to respond to each item up to 10 times, with each administration focusing on a different perceptual set. Responses from various sets are then compared, with scores generated by summing the absolute differences of individual items across administrations. The 10 perceptual sets are (1) importance of item for self, (2) ideal-self, (3) self, (4) ideal-spouse, (5) perception of girlfriend or boyfriend, (6) importance of items about partner, (7) prediction of how girlfriend or boyfriend sees ideal-spouse, (8) prediction of how girlfriend or boyfriend sees ideal-self, (9) prediction of how girlfriend or boyfriend sees her- or himself, and (10) prediction of how girlfriend or boyfriend sees you. Final forms of the questionnaire were derived from factor analytic studies on an initial pool of 262 and 263 items for men and women, respectively. Some items were taken from similar instruments, while others were specifically constructed for the MET.

Sample Items (Note: All sample items are from the shared 76 items):

(A)   I am a good listener.
(B)   My entire family is liked by my boyfriend (girlfriend).
(C)   I think that only in emergencies should the wife contribute to the financial support of the family.

Comments: The author reports that test-retest correlations over three weeks ranged from .71 to .91 for women and from .62 to .79 for men. Each sample contained nine respondents, and each completed the MET from three perceptual sets. A factor analysis conducted by the author resulted in 42 factors with eigenvalues greater than 1.0, of which nine were given further consideration. Separate analyses were conducted for men and for women. Details of the factor analysis and comparisons in the factor structure for American and French samples are contained in Murstein (1976b).

References:

Murstein, B. I. (1971). Self-ideal-self discrepancy and the choice of marital partner. *J Cons Clin, 37,* 47–52.

Murstein, B. I. (1972). Person perception and courtship progress among premarital couples. *J Mar Fam, 34,* 621–627.

Murstein, B. I. (1976a). *Who will marry whom? Theories and research in marital choice.* New York: Springer.

Murstein, B. I. (1976b). Qualities of desired spouse: A cross-cultural comparison between French and American college students. *J Comp Fam Studies, 7,* 455–469.

I-4/c/e

88. MURSTEIN, B. I., WADLIN, R., & BOND, C. F. The Revised Exchange-Orientation Scale (EOS)

Avail: 1987 Ref.

Variables Measured: Individual need to reciprocate for personal favors or good deeds; awareness of value assigned to individual efforts versus efforts of others

Type of Instrument: Self-report questionnaire

Instrument Description: The Revised EOS is a 5-point, 21-item Likert-type questionnaire designed to assess individual awareness of one's own efforts. The EOS was first applied to married couples in 1977 and has undergone several revisions since. The version presented in this abstract is the latest available at this time. The scale was designed for use with any population where the relative value of services rendered would be of interest. These might include the workplace, friendships, dating couples, family environments, and marital relationships. It is based on the theory that people are constantly aware of their own motivation and behavior, but are much less aware of the intentions and thoughts of others. Thus, it is believed, they are likely to be more accurate in assigning value to their own behavior than they are to that of another person. In examining this construct with married couples, it has been discovered that happily married couples, and those generally engaged in closer relationships, tend to be less concerned about maintaining a proper exchange of effort. The current revision of what is commonly referred to as the E scale was derived from an initial pool of 56 items, some of which were drawn from earlier versions of the scale, while others were newly constructed. Pilot testing was conducted on a group of university undergraduates. Based on results from this sample, items with the highest means and lowest standard deviations were selected for final inclusion.

Sample Items:

(A) I usually remember if I owe someone money or if someone owes me money.
(B) When buying a present for someone I often try to remember the value of what they have given me in the past.
(C) If my spouse feels entitled to an evening out with friends of either sex, then I feel entitled to do the same.

Comments: The authors report that Cronbach's alpha, in a study utilizing university undergraduates, was .82 for males and .89 for females. Utilizing an additional sample of 16 married couples, the authors found a correlation of .53 between scores obtained by husbands and those of their wives. Murstein et al. (1987) also report details of item-total correlations for husbands and wives, as well as comparisons within and between items for men and women.

References:

Broderick, J. E., & O'Leary, K. D. (1986). Contributions of affect, attitudes, and behavior to marital satisfaction. *J Cons Clin, 54,* 514–517.

Murstein, B. I., Cerreto, M., & MacDonald, M. (1977). A theory and investigation of the effect of exchange-orientation on marriage and friendship. *J Mar Fam, 39,* 543–548.

Murstein, B., & MacDonald, M. G. (1983). The relationship of "exchange-orientation" and "commitment" scales to marriage adjustment. *Int J Psycho, 18,* 297–311.

Murstein, B., Wadlin, R., & Bond, C. F., Jr. (1987). The Revised Exchange-Orientation Scale. *Small Gr B, 18,* 212–223.

I-4/c
89. OLSON, D. H. Inventories of Premarital, Marital, Parent-Child, and Parent-Adolescent Conflict

Avail: 1983 Ref.

Variables Measured: Interaction processes of decision making, problem solving, and conflict resolution in couples and families

Type of Instrument: Self-report questionnaires and observer-rated interactions

Instrument Description: This set of four inventories all utilize the same basic format and examine similar variables. The format of the instruments is similar to that of the Revealed Difference Technique (RDT) developed by Strodtbeck (1951). This involves having the individuals read and respond on individual forms, and then jointly discuss and resolve any differences they have on the issues presented. The discussions are video- or audiotaped, and are later coded for content using a standardized coding system developed from the Inventory of Marital Conflict (IMC), referred to as the Marital and Family Interaction Coding System. The vignettes present different points of view to the husband and the wife, thereby increasing the chance that there will be conflict. The number of vignettes presented ranges from 18 to 40, but varies with each inventory.

Sample Items (Note: Sample item is from the Inventory of Premarital Conflict):

(A) Joel likes to spend his money on material possessions. Recently he bought a new sports car that Suzie thought was too expensive. Joel felt that the car fit his personality and could not understand why Suzie was so upset. Who is most responsible? What should they do?
   a) Joel should consider Suzie's point of view before making such large purchases.
   b) Suzie should not be so critical of how Joel spends his money.

Comments: The coding of the interactional material is accomplished using the MFICS coding system (described in Olson, 1985). Interrater reliability is reported by the author to have averaged between .80 and .90, with the split-half reliability reported to average about .70 when infrequent codes are eliminated.

References:

Norem, R. H., & Olson, D. H. (1983). Interaction patterns of premarital couples: Typological assessment over time. *Am J Fam Th, 11*(2), 25–37.

Olson, D. H. (1983). *Inventories of premarital, marital, parent-child, and parent-adolescent conflict.* St. Paul: University of Minnesota, Family Social Science.

Olson, D. H., McCubbin, H. I., Barnes, H., Larsen, A., Muxen, M., & Wilson, M. (1985). *Family inventories.* St. Paul: University of Minnesota, Family Social Science.

Olson, D. H., & Ryder, R. G. (1970). Inventory of Marital Conflicts: An experimental interaction procedure. *J Mar Fam, 32,* 443–448.

I-4/c
90. OLSON, D. H. Clinical Rating Scale (CRS) for the Circumplex Model of Marital and Family Systems

Avail: Family Social Science, University of Minnesota, 290 McNeal Hall, St. Paul, MN 55108

Variables Measured: Cohesion, adaptability, and communication within family systems

Type of Instrument: Behavior rating system

Instrument Description: The Circumplex Model defines 3 general and 16 specific types of marital and family systems. The CRS is used in conjunction with the Circumplex Model in order to rate the behavior of family systems. Ratings are based on a semistructured interview with an individual family member or with several family members. Raters indicate their perceptions of families along 26 categories within the three dimensions of family cohesion, family change or adaptability, and family communication. Each specific category contains examples of appropriately scored behaviors. One format used to generate information and dynamics about relevant dimensions is to ask the family members to describe and discuss how they handle daily routines, what a typical weekend is like, what they do separately and together, and how they make decisions. Family members are rated on cohesion by assessing such components as emotional bonding and parent-child coalitions. Adaptability is rated on components such as leadership and rules. Communication is rated on such components as continuity tracking and clarity. Administration and scoring time requirements vary according to interview length.

Sample Items:

(A)   Emotional bonding
(B)   Negotiation
(C)   Respect and regard

Comments: The author reports on a study with 64 families in which interrater reliability has been found to range from .84 to .88.

References:

Olson, D. H. (1986). Circumplex Model VII: Validation studies and FACES III. *Fam Proc,* *25,* 337–351.
Olson, D. H., McCubbin, H. I., Barnes, H., Larsen, A., Muxem, M., & Wilson, M. (1985). *Family inventories.* St. Paul, MN: Family Social Science, University of Minnesota.
Olson, D. H., Russell, C. S., & Sprenkle, D. H. (1980). Circumplex Model of Marital and Family Systems II: Empirical studies and clinical intervention. In J. P. Vincent (Ed.), *Advances in family intervention, assessment and theory.* Greenwich, CT: JAI.
Olson, D. H., Russell, C. S., & Sprenkle, D. H. (1983). Circumplex Model VI: Theoretical update. *Fam Proc, 22,* 69–83.

I-4/c/C
91. PATTERSON, G. R., RAY, R. S., SHAW, D. A., & COBB, J. A.
Family Interaction Coding System (FICS)

Avail: 1978 & 1982 Refs.

Variables Measured: Home conditions and interactions related to children's desirable and undesirable behaviors

Type of Instrument: Behavior coding scheme

Instrument Description: The FICS is an observational coding system based on social learning theory. It was designed for use in identifying interactional styles in homes of problem children. Trained observers code live interactions every 6 seconds for a minimum of 70 minutes according to 29 criteria. Observations take place in subjects' homes at times when all family members are present. The observational session is structured according to 8 criteria in order to maximize the variability of interactions. Rules such as no television, no outgoing telephone calls, and only briefly answering incoming calls serve to increase the likelihood that meaningful interactions will occur. Observers focus on one member of the family at a time, recording which of 14 aversive and 15 prosocial behaviors occur during each 6-second interval, referred to as a "frame." Coding sheets are set up with five frames per line. Thus 30 seconds of behavior is recorded on each line. Automatic timing devices are used to alert the coder when each new frame and line is to begin. Coders record both the behavior of the target and the behaviors of other family members in response to that of the target. Following 5 minutes of observation, a new target is randomly selected and the process is repeated. The system is used with both clinical and research populations in order to identify contingencies that maintain undesirable behavioral patterns in families.

Sample Items: Not applicable.

Comments: The FICS was originally developed in the mid-1960s using longhand accounts of behavior. Subsequent revisions experimented with various methods of recording interactions, including use of microphones for the observer to speak into. Test-retest coefficients for the current version of the FICS are reported to average .80. Interrater reliability, based on agreement within 30-second lines, is reported to be .72.

References:

Hoffman, D. A., Fagot, B. A., Reid, J. B., & Patterson, G. F. (1987). Parents rate the Family Interaction Coding System comparisons of problem and nonproblem boys using parent-derived behavior composites. *Behav Asses, 9,* 131–140.
Patterson, G. R. (1982). *A social learning approach: Vol 3. Coercive family process.* Eugene, OR: Castalia.
Reid, J. B. (Ed.). (1978). *A social learning approach: Vol 2. Observation in home settings.* Eugene, OR: Castalia.
Weinrott, M. R., & Jones, R. R. (1984). Overt versus covert assessment of observer reliability. *Child Dev, 55,* 1125–1137.

I-4/c
92. PEROSA, L. M., & PEROSA, S. L. Structural Family Interaction Scale (SFIS)

Avail: NAPS-3

Variables Measured: Family interaction patterns as evidenced by conflicts and conflict resolution, relationships, and interactional style

Type of Instrument: Self-report questionnaire

Instrument Description: The SFIS is a 4-point, 85-item Likert-type scale designed to measure family interactions defined in accordance with Minuchin's (1974) structural model of family functioning. Items are in the form of statements, with responses ranging from *very true* to *very false.* The scale was designed for completion by all family members aged 12 years or older. A total of 13 primary and 10 secondary scales are defined. Primary scales include enmeshment, disengagement, overprotection, neglect, flexibility, rigidity, conflict avoidance, conflict resolution, conflict expression without resolution, parent management, triangulation, parent-child coalition, and detouring. Ten secondary scales of 2 items each were developed to portray more accurately specific patterns of interactions within families. Scores can be derived for both individuals and families. Individual responses are assigned weights from 1 from 4, with responses to items within scales being summed. Where more than one family member is administered the test, scores from all family members are averaged within each subscale. A family incongruency score is then computed by subtracting all dyad scores from the average score, and dividing the sum by the number of subtractions.

Sample Items:

(A) At home we go out of our way to constantly do things for each other.

(B) When one family member tries to bring up an issue the other member puts off discussing it by saying "let's talk about it later."

(C) Family members seem to "pair off" in the same way around issues in discussions or fights.

Comments: Cronbach's alpha is reported by the author based on a study with 50 families, half of which had a learning disabled child. Alpha is reported to be at or above .50 for nine primary subscales. Alpha for the four remaining primary subscales is reported to be .49, .47, .44, and .25. Item subscale correlations ranged from .50 to .70 for primary subscales, and from .70 to .83 for secondary subscales. Interjudge reliability for assigning items to subscales was reported to be .95 for six family therapists. The authors indicate that studies examining revisions of the 85-item SFIS are currently under way.

References:

Perosa, L., Hansen, J., & Perosa, S. (1981). Development of the Structural Family Interaction Scale. *Fam Ther, 8,* 77–90.

Perosa, L., & Perosa, S. (1982). Structural interaction patterns in families with a learning disabled child. *Fam Ther, 9,* 175–187.

I-4/II-2/c

93. PERSHING, B. Family Policy Inventory

Avail: NAPS-3

Variables Measured: General family policies covering several diverse areas

Type of Instrument: Self-report questionnaire

Instrument Description: This instrument contains a list of 108 possible general family policy problem situations dealing with selection of goals; acquisition, protection, and use of resources; and general living conditions concerned with family structure and functions. The author lists 11 specific variables that are measured: (1) family use of social and physical space; (2) instrumental activities; (3) expressive activities; (4) goals; (5) use of community resources; (6) money management; (7) household activities and production; (8) use of consumer information; (9) use of time; (10) communication; (11) guidance, discipline, allowances, and activities of children. The instrument is intended for use with adult men and women. However, the author indicates that it could easily be adapted for use with adolescents. Respondents score each item on a scale from 1 to 99. Low scores indicate that there is *no established policy* for the given activity. High scores indicate that there is an *established policy*. A score of 50 indicates that the item *does not apply* to the subject's family. All items use the stem: "'To what extent has your family established a general policy regarding the following . . . "

Sample Items:

(A) Controlling the amount of time children are allowed to watch TV.

(B) Spending time together as a family group.

(C) Accumulating funds for use during retirement.

Comments: The author indicates that content validity was judged by a panel of home management experts. Subscales were determined by factor analysis. The author reports that the overall measure of sampling adequacy (MSA) was .85 and that the index of factorial simplicity was .61.

Reference:

Pershing, B. (1979). Family policies: A component of management in the home and family setting. *J Mar Fam, 41,* 573–581.

I-4/III-2/b
94. PRINZ, R. J. The Conflict Behavior Questionnaire (CBQ)

Avail: NAPS-3

Variables Measured: Parents' and adolescents' perceptions of communication and conflict

Type of Instrument: Self-report questionnaire

Instrument Description: The CBQ is a 44-item, forced-choice, true/false questionnaire designed to assess the extent of conflict and negative communication that exists between adolescents and their parents. Separate versions are available for administration to parents and to adolescents. The instrument is titled "Interaction Behavior Questionnaire" on respondents' forms. Parallel forms interchanging "Mom" and "Dad" are available for use with adolescents. Respondents are asked to indicate whether each statement has been *true* or *false* over the past four weeks in their interactions at home. Adolescent forms request responses to items primarily indicating positive and negative behaviors by the parent toward the respondent. Parent forms request information primarily indicative of behaviors of the son or daughter. Additionally, each form contains some items geared toward parent-child interactions (e.g., "We joke around often") rather than specifically in terms of behaviors or attitudes of one person toward the other. In families with two parents, adolescents complete forms for both the mother and the father. While the majority of items use a negative response set, there are also several items that must be reverse-scored. The scale is considered to be unidimensional, with the number of negative responses serving as the overall CBQ score. Items generally reflect areas of misunderstandings, arguments, and communication deficits. The current version of the CBQ is a revision of the original 75-item scale. A 20-item version is also available (Roehling & Robin, 1986). Both scales were constructed based on item analyses of the original 75 items, and both are reported to correlate in the high .90s with the original.

Sample Items:

(A) At least three times a week, we get angry at each other.
   (Parent version)
(B) My mom understands me.
   (Adolescent/Mom)
(C) My dad seems to be always complaining about me.
   (Adolescent/Dad)

Comments: There is some confusion in the literature regarding authorship of this instrument. However, it appears that the CBQ was first developed by Prinz for use in his dissertation (1977). Cronbach's alpha for the CBQ is reported to be at least .90 for mothers and adolescents. Test-retest correlations over periods of six to eight weeks are reported to range from .57 to .61 for mothers, and from .84 to .85 for fathers. Agreement between parents and adolescents for the 22 items that are identical for all forms is reported to be 67% for distressed dyads and 84% for nondistressed dyads.

References:

Foster, S. L., Prinz, R. J., & O'Leary, K. D. (1983). Impact of problem-solving communication training and generalization procedures on family conflict. *Child Fam Beh Ther, 5,* 1–23.

Prinz, R. J., Foster, S. L., Kent, R. N., & O'Leary, K. D. (1979). Multivariate assessment of conflict in distressed and nondistressed mother-adolescent dyads. *J Appl Be A, 12,* 691–700.

Robin, A. L. (1981). A controlled evaluation of problem-solving communication training with parent-adolescent conflict. *Behav Ther, 12,* 593–609.

Roehling, P. V., & Robin, A. L. (1986). Development and validation of the Family Beliefs Inventory: A measure of unrealistic beliefs among parents and adolescents. *J Cons Clin, 54,* 693–697.

I-4/c
95. RISKIN, J. Family Interaction Scales (FIS)

Avail: 1982 Ref.

Variables Measured: Dimensions of family interactions

Type of Instrument: Observational rating scale

Instrument Description: The FIS was developed to aid in quantifying and understanding dimensions of family interactions. The current version of the instrument is described by the author as "macroanalytic," or global in nature. The initial micro-analytic coding scheme was designed around ratings of 152 speeches, divided into two equal sections of 76 speeches, each lasting 2–3 minutes (Riskin, 1964). The more recent version relies upon ratings of behavior during an overall family interview. Using this system, general ratings of the entire family are generated on each of 17 dimensions. Dimensions include clarity, topic continuity, appropriate topic change, commitment, request for commitment, information exchange, agreement, disagreement, support, attack, intensity, humor, interruptions, laughter, who speaks, intrusiveness, and mind reading. Raters are instructed to score the family on each dimension on a 5-point Likert-type scale, with end points dependent on the nature of the dimension being used. All ratings are of the family as a whole and are to be based on impressions formed by the entire interview. Along these lines, instructions to raters also indicate that family ratings should not be overly influenced by any one individual within the family system. Interviews typically involve several hours of interaction and often center on the family's evening meal. Scoring time is estimated to be approximately 10 minutes. Detailed instructions are provided in Riskin (1982).

Sample Items: Not appropriate.

Comments: The FIS appears to have undergone an evolution from the original 1964 procedure. References are available indicating differing versions in 1968, 1974, and 1982, sometimes with the author listed as Riskin, other times as Riskin and Faunce. The version described in this abstract is from Riskin (1982). Reliability and validity information is not detailed in the literature. However, comparisons of ratings on the 17 dimensions are contained in Riskin (1982).

References:

Faunce, E. E., & Riskin, J. (1970). Family Interaction Scales: II. Data analysis and findings. *Arch G Psyc, 22,* 513–526.

Riskin, J. (1964). Family Interaction Scales. *Arch G Psyc, 11,* 484–494.

Riskin, J. (1982). Research on "nonlabeled" families: A longitudinal study. In F. Walsh (Ed.), *Normal family processes* (pp. 67–93). New York: Guilford.

Riskin, J., & Faunce, E. E. (1972). An evaluative review of family interaction research. *Fam Proc, 11,* 365–455.

I-4/b

96. ROBERTS, G. E., & McARTHUR, D. S. Roberts Apperception Test for Children (RATC)

Avail: Western Psychological Services, 12031 Wilshire Blvd., Los Angeles, CA 90025

Variables Measured: Profiles of anxiety, aggression, depression, rejection, and unresolved outcome; adaptive issues, including reliance on others, support-other, support-child, limit setting, problem identification, and levels of resolution

Type of Instrument: Projective technique

Instrument Description: The RATC is a projective test consisting of 16 cards that is designed for children ages 6 to 15. The cards present everyday interpersonal situations drawn with simple line drawings. The 16 situations include at least one child in every picture with eight adult females and five adult males. The range of situations includes family interaction, parent-child relationships, peer interaction, nudity, school attitude, and emotional responses of anxiety, aggression, and depression. Stories resulting from the pictures are scored by an objective scoring system in which the scorer marks the presence of the profile scales and clinical indicators. The raw score for each scale is converted to a T-score according to four age groupings. Norms for the scales were developed on well-adjusted children. The test is appropriate for clinical diagnosis, as well as for assessing treatment outcome and situational crises in normal children. Administration time is approximately 30 minutes. Scoring is usually accomplished in 30–60 minutes.

Sample Items: Not applicable.

Comments: References in the RATC Manual indicate that both interrater and split-half reliability studies have been conducted. Interrater reliability on various subscales is reported to range from .55 to .98. Split-half reliability for the subscales is reported to range from .44 to .86. Validity, also detailed in the manual, has been assessed through investigations of intercorrelations among various RATC measures, thematic content elicited by various cards, and comparisons of test responses by well-adjusted and problem children.

References:

Brassard, M. (1986). Family assessment approaches and procedures. In M. M. Knoff (Ed.), *The assessment of child and adolescent personality* (pp. 399–449). New York: Guilford.

Friedrich, W. (1984). Roberts Apperception Test for Children. In D. Keyser & R. Sweetland (Eds.), *Test critiques* (Vol 1., pp. 543–548). St. Louis: Test Corporation of America.

Obrzut, J., & Boliek, C. (1986). Thematic approaches to personality assessment with children and adolescents. In M. M. Knoff (Ed.), *The assessment of child and adolescent personality* (pp. 173–198). New York: Guilford.

I-4/c

97. RORSCHACH, H. The Family Rorschach

Avail: Carter et al. version from NAPS-3 (note that when ordering the Family Rorschach instrument from NAPS-3, the document number is listed under Carter et al. and not under Rorschach); others available in references listed below

Variables Measured: Family relationships and functional capacity

Type of Instrument: Projective technique

Instrument Description: The Rorschach is a series of 10 cards used with clinical populations to elicit information about underlying personality characteristics and conflicts. Several authors have developed coding schemes and perspectives specific to issues of family dynamics and relationships. One such system was developed by Loveland et al. (1963). These authors used two variations of a combined individual and family administration. In both systems, individual family members are first administered the Rorschach in the traditional fashion. Following this procedure, family members are brought together in a room and directed to spend 5 minutes with each card discovering similarities between their responses. One system ends there, while the other continues with family members comparing responses during the family session to their individual protocols. Another procedure, developed by Levy and Epstein (1964), is similar to that of Loveland et al. with the exception that individual administration of the Rorschach occurs a week or more prior to the family administration. Shapiro and Wild (1976) devised a system by which families were asked to come to a consensus on only one item per card, rather than being forced to agree on as many responses as possible. These investigators, in differentiating clinical from normal families, focused exclusively on the final response given by each family, rather than on family processes or earlier responses. Wynne et al. (1977) scored individual protocols in evaluating differences in communication styles between families with disturbed members and normal families. More recently, Liaboe and Guy (1985), among others, have referred to cards IV and VII as the father and mother cards, respectively. These cards have been used to elicit responses presumed to be indicative of family or parental relationships. Various coding schemes have been developed for interpreting responses from these cards. A similar family-related procedure was developed by Carter et al. (1987). These investigators used responses to the Rorschach to distinguish families with schizophrenic offspring from those with more normal-functioning children. In this version of the Family Rorschach, family members are first tested individually and then together as a family. Only cards I, II, and VIII are used, and families are instructed to come to an agreement regarding the content of each card during the joint portion of the task. Scoring procedures are specified according to the degree and quality of agreements between family members.

Sample Items: Not applicable.

Comments: Several other versions of the Family Rorschach are also available. The above list is intended to illustrate procedures in use and is not meant to be exhaustive.

References:

Carter, L., Robertson, S. R., Ladd, J., & Alpert, M. (1987). The Family Rorschach with families of schizophrenics: Replication and extension. *Fam Proc, 26*, 461–474.

Levy, J., & Epstein, N. B. (1964). An application of the Rorschach test in family investigation. *Fam Proc, 3*, 344–376.

Liaboe, G. P., & Guy, J. D. (1985). The Rorschach "father" and "mother" cards: An evaluation of the research. *J Pers Assess, 49*, 2–5.

Loveland, N. T., Wynne, L. C., & Singer, M. T. (1963). The Family Rorschach: A new method for studying family interaction. *Fam Proc, 2*, 187–215.

Shapiro, L., & Wild, C. The product of the Consensus Rorschach in families of male schizophrenics. *Fam Proc, 15,* 211–224.

Wynne, L. C., Singer, M. T., Bartko, J. J., & Toohey, M. L. (1977). Schizophrenics and their families: Research on parental communication. In J. M. Tanner (Ed.), *Developments in psychiatric research.* London: Hodder & Stoughton.

I-4/b

98. SANTROCK, J. W., & WARSHAK, R. A. Parent-Child Interaction Coding System

Avail: 1979 Ref.

Variables Measured: Interaction styles of parents and their children

Type of Instrument: Observational coding scheme

Instrument Description: This observational coding system was designed to allow for quantification of levels of interaction between parents and their children. The authors videotaped two 10-minute interactions between a parent and his or her child. During the first session, subjects were asked to discuss plans for spending the weekend together. The second interaction was a discussion of the main problems of the family. Parent and child behaviors were rated separately on 9-point scales following observation of each session. The authors report that many of the categories were modified or derived from those developed by Baumrind (1971), reflecting authoritarian, authoritative, and laissez-faire parenting styles. Following correlation analyses, eight parent and seven child items were retained. The parent items include control (firm versus lax), encourages independence, engages in intellectually meaningful verbal interaction, attentive to child, authoritarian, authoritative, permissive, and maturity. Child items retained in the final version were warmth, self-esteem, anxiety, demandingness, maturity, sociability, and independence.

Sample Items: Not applicable.

Comments: The authors indicate that interrater reliability of parent behavior ratings was assessed by comparing ratings by two psychology graduate students. One student scored all tapes, while the other rated only 25% of the respondents. Neither rater was told that reliability checks would be conducted. Correlations for subcategories reported by the authors range from .83 to .90. Interrater reliability for child behaviors, utilizing the same procedure as noted above, are reported to range from .69 to .92.

Reference:

Santrock, J. W., & Warshak, R. A. (1979). Father custody and social development in boys and girls. *J Soc Issue, 35*(4), 112–125.

I-4/a/e/W

99. SAUNDERS, D. G., LYNCH, A. B., GRAYSON, M., & LINZ, D. Inventory of Beliefs About Wife Beating (IBWB)

Avail: English version in 1987 Ref.; Spanish & Hebrew versions from NAPS-3

Variables Measured: Desire for punishment of wife beaters, responsibility for wife abuse, and sympathy for women who are battered

Type of Instrument: Self-report questionnaire

Instrument Description: The IBWB is a measure of beliefs and attitudes about wife beating. *Beating* is defined on the questionnaire as "repeated hitting, intending to inflict pain." It is a 31-item Likert-style scale (note that the Spanish version contains only 24 items), utilizing a 7-point response format. Response options range from *strongly agree* to *strongly disagree*. Items are divided into five dimensions, including wife beating is justified, wives gain from beatings, help should be given, offender should be punished, and offender is responsible. Items from the first three dimensions may be combined into an index of "sympathy for battered women." The instrument is intended to measure the attitudes of the public, professionals, abusers, victims, and other populations. It is also expected to be sensitive to changes due to treatment, professional education, and other interventions. The authors report that some treatment programs have substituted the term *hitting* for *beating*. Pilot data indicate that greater variance can be achieved on some items with this substitution.

Sample Items:

(A) Sometimes it is OK for a man to beat his wife.
(B) If a wife is beaten by her husband, she should divorce him immediately.
(C) Husbands who batter are responsible for the abuse because they intended to do it.

Comments: The authors report that Cronbach's alpha for the five subscales range from .61 to .86, and that alpha for the sympathy scale (combination of the first three dimensions) is .89. Correlations with the Rape Myth Acceptance Scale are reported, with the highest correlations being with "justified" (.56) and "wives gain" (.62) subscales. Scores on the IBWB were also compared with several other measures of attitudes toward women, gender-role stereotyping, hostility toward women, and various self-reports of abuse and violence potential. In a test of divergent validity, IBWB and personality scores from three different instruments were compared, generally evidencing low correlations. The results of a factor analysis, as well as specific validity and reliability information, are contained in the reference listed below. Also, while the instrument appears in the reference listed below, instructions to respondents are not presented in the article. Instructions are contained in the version deposited with NAPS-3.

Reference:

Saunders, D. G., Lynch, A. B., Grayson, M., & Linz, D. (1987). The Inventory of Beliefs About Wife Beating: The construction and initial validation of a measure of beliefs and attitudes. *Violence and Victims, 2,* 39–57.

I-4/a

100. SCHLEIN, S., & GUERNEY, B. G., Jr. The Relationship Change Scale (RCS)

Avail: 1977 Ref., & IDEALS (Institute for the Development of Emotional and Life Skills), P.O. Box 391, State College, PA 16804

Variables Measured: Change in the quality of a relationship

Type of Instrument: Self-report questionnaire

Instrument Description: The RCS is a 5-point, 37-item Likert-type scale designed to measure changes in the quality of various types of close relationships over time. Response options for individual items range from *much less* to *much greater*. Quality of the relationship is assessed in terms of a variety of areas in relationships such as satisfaction, communication, trust, intimacy, sensitivity, openness, and understanding. The RCS was designed to assess change occurring as a result of therapy or some other intervention. The wording of items can be altered in order to request information appropriate to the time frame of interest to the investigator or therapist.

Sample Items:

(A)   In comparison with 3 months ago, my ability to express positive feelings toward my partner is:

(B)   In comparison with 3 months ago, my ability to constructively express negative feelings toward my partner is:

(C)   In comparison with 3 months ago, my willingness to share my personal concerns with my partner is:

Comments: The authors indicate that the RCS correlated with two measures designed to assess specific components of relationship change. In a study of 96 dating couples, the correlation between the RCS and the handling problems change scale is reported by the authors to be .29, while the correlation with the satisfaction change scale is reported as .49.

References:

Guerney, B. G., Jr. (1977). *Relationship Enhancement: Skill-training programs for therapy, problem prevention, and enrichment.* San Francisco: Jossey-Bass.

Guerney, B. G., Jr., Coufal, J., & Vogelsong, E. (1981). Relationship Enhancement versus a traditional approach to therapeutic/preventative/enrichment parent-adolescent programs. *J Cons Clin, 49,* 927–929.

Rankin, E. A., & Campbell, N. D. (1983). Perception of relationship changes during the third trimester of pregnancy. *Iss Health Care Women, 6,* 351–359.

Ridley, C. A., Jorgensen, S. R., Morgan, A. C., & Avery, A. W. (1982). Relationship Enhancement with premarital couples: An assessment of effects on relationship quality. *Am J Fam Th, 10*(3), 41–48.

I-4/IV-1/a

101. SCHUMM, W. R., EGGEMAN, K., & MOXLEY, V. Kansas Marital Goals Orientation Scale

Avail: 1985 Ref.

Variables Measured: Degree of intentionality in a couple's marital relationship; the extent to which they are working to improve their relationships now and for the future

Type of Instrument: Self-report questionnaire

Instrument Description: This 7-item questionnaire was designed to assess one goal of marital enrichment programs, which is to facilitate couples' taking a more active role in improving and developing their relationship now and in the future. It can be used with both questionnaire and interview surveys. The authors indicate that, for couples who are not familiar with marriage enrichment goals or experiences, some of the items may seem far-fetched.

Sample Items:

(A)   How often do you and your husband discuss the way you would like your marriage to be five years from now?

(B)   To what extent do you think you and your husband agree on long-term goals for your marriage?

(C)   How often does your husband consider specific ways in which he can change in order to improve your relationship?

Comments: The authors report that test-retest reliability for this instrument has ranged from .89 to .91. Cronbach's alpha is reported to range from .86 to .95. Correlations between scores achieved by husbands and wives in one study in which there was an intervention were .87 for a pretest and .76 for a posttest.

References:

Eggeman, K. W., Moxley, V., & Schumm, W. R. (1985). Assessing spouses' perceptions of Gottman's temporal form in marital conflict. *Psychol Rep, 57,* 171–181.
Eggeman, K. W., Smith-Eggeman, B., Moxley, V., & Schumm, W. R. (1986). A marriage enrichment program for newlywed couples. *Wellness Persp, 3,* 32–36.

I-4/c/g
102. SCHUTZ, W. Schutz ELEMENTS of Awareness

Avail: WSA, Box 259, Muir Beach, CA 94965

Variables Measured: Intra- and interpersonal behaviors, feelings, and perceptions

Type of Instrument: Self-report questionnaire

Instrument Description: The Schutz ELEMENTS is a series of instruments, based on the 1984 revision of the FIRO theory, that are designed to measure inclusion, control, and openness within a number of settings. Individual scales contained within the ELEMENTS package include self-concept (ELEMENT S), self-esteem (ELEMENT E), interpersonal behavior (ELEMENT B), interpersonal feelings (ELEMENT F), close relations (ELEMENT C), family relations (ELEMENT P), work relations (ELEMENT W), Job and career fit (ELEMENT J), team compatibility (team compatibility index), and decision making (concordance). The two instruments that deal primarily with family measurement issues are ELEMENT C (the successor to MATE from the FIRO series) and ELEMENT P. ELEMENT C was designed as a parallel instrument to ELEMENT P, and is to be completed by any two people in a close relationship. Such relationships include couples, lovers, friends, or family members. The instrument may be administered to either one or both persons in the relationship. Subcategories evaluated by these two instruments include inclusion, control, openness, significance, competence, loveability, presence, self-control, and self-awareness. ELEMENT C contains 24 items, and takes approximately 10 minutes to complete. Calculation of indexes takes an additional 15 minutes. If both persons complete ELEMENT C, direct discussion of each item is utilized to clarify differences in perceptions and feelings about the issue. This discussion typically takes approximately 60 to 90 minutes. ELEMENT P was designed to evaluate any dyadic family relationship from the past. Items are responded to with a particular period of time in mind. As with ELEMENT C, ELEMENT P may be administered to one or both persons in the relationship. The number of items, administration, and scoring procedures for ELEMENT P are identical to those used with ELEMENT C.

Sample Items:

(A)   You feel I am competent.
(B)   I loved you.
(C)   I am aware of myself.

Comments: All instruments contained in the Schutz ELEMENTS are based on the revised FIRO theory (Schutz, 1984) and earlier FIRO instruments (Schutz, 1967), published by Consulting Psychologists Press. Many of these ELEMENTS are updates of original FIRO scales. All may be self-scored.

References:

Schutz, W. (1967). *The FIRO scales.* Palo Alto, CA: Consulting Psychologists Press.
Schutz, W. (1984). *The truth option.* Berkeley, CA: Ten Speed.
Schutz, W. (1987a). *Guide to ELEMENT B.* Muir Beach, CA: WSA.
Schutz, W. (1987b). *Guide to ELEMENT C.* Muir Beach, CA: WSA.

I-4/III-2/b/e/C
103. SEBALD, H. Adolescents' Parental/Peer Reference Group

Avail: 1986 Ref.

Variables Measured: Orientation of teenagers toward parents and peers when seeking advice

Type of Instrument: Self-report questionnaire

Instrument Description: This instrument asks teenagers to indicate which reference group they use in making a series of 18 decisions regarding their hobbies, habits, and social preferences. Subjects are asked to respond to the following question for each item: "If you had to decide between your friends' and your parents' opinions and feelings in the following situations, whose opinion would you consider more important?" Three response options are available: *parents, friends,* or *undecided.* The author has used this instrument in sociological and social psychological studies of attitudes held by groups of high school students. Scoring is accomplished by determining the average percentage of responses in which either parents or peers are indicated as being the primary reference group. Average scores across group members on individual items may also be examined.

Sample Items:

(A) On what to spend money.
(B) Which courses to take at school.
(C) Participating in drinking parties.

Comments: The author has used this instrument in a study comparing reference groups of White, middle-class high school boys from 1963 with those of White, middle-class high school boys and girls in 1976 and 1982. He reports a decline of parent orientation from 1963 to 1976, and a partial recovery by 1982.

Reference:

Sebald, H. (1986). Adolescents' shifting orientation toward parents and peers: A curvilinear trend over recent decades. *J Mar Fam, 48,* 5–13.

I-4/c
104. STEINGLASS, P. Home Observation Assessment Method (HOAM)

Avail: 1979 Ref.

Variables Measured: Frequency and variability of behaviors employed by families in their use of time and space within the home

Type of Instrument: Observation system for quantifying home-based family behavior

Instrument Description: The HOAM is a structured on-line behavioral observation coding system designed to generate frequency counts of selective aspects of interactional behavior. Although originally designed for use in studies of alcoholic families, it is potentially broadly applicable, with minor modifications, for use with both traditional and nontraditional families. Seven aspects of home behavior are recorded: (1) physical location in the home, (2) identity of other people in the room with subject, (3) physical distance between subject and others while talking, (4) basic physical and verbal interaction rates, (5) content of decision-making verbal exchanges, (6) affective level of verbal exchanges, and (7) outcome of verbal exchanges. Coding is performed by a two-person team of observers, with each observer assigned to one family member. Observers move about the home with subjects, recording interactional behavior on coding sheets. Coding may continue for up to four hours per session. Data generated are used to construct a series of indexes of couple-level interactional behavior. Thus far, 25 such indexes have been developed, created by asking two questions, related to frequency and variability of behaviors, related to each of the seven dimensions.

Sample Items: Not applicable.

Comments: Factor analyses performed on the 25 behavioral variables resulted in the identification of an underlying structure composed of five dimensions (intrafamily engagement, distance regulation, extrafamily engagement, structural variability, and content variability). The author reports that observer agreement for various HOAM codes range from .63 to .96. Kappa was used to determine observer reliability. The author reports that the majority of such statistics were greater than .40. When used to analyze interactions within alcoholic families, it is reported that HOAM discriminates between three subclassifications of alcoholic families. The author also indicates that the HOAM factor of intrafamily engagement predicts long-term marital stability.

References:

Steinglass, P. (1979). The Home Observation Assessment Method (HOAM): Realtime naturalistic observation of families in their homes. *Fam Proc, 18,* 337–354.
Steinglass, P. (1980). Assessing families in their own homes. *Am J Psychi, 137,* 1523–1529.
Steinglass, P. (1981). The alcoholic family at home: Patterns of interactions in dry, wet, and transitional stages of alcoholism. *Arch G Psyc, 38,* 578–584.
Steinglass, P., Tislenko, L., & Reiss, D. (1985). Stability/instability in the alcoholic marriage: The inter-relationships between course of alcoholism, family process and marital outcome. *Fam Proc, 24,* 365–376.

I-4/a

105. STEPHEN, T. D., & MARKMAN, H. Relationship World Index— Version 2 (RWI-2)

Avail: 1983 Ref.

Variables Measured: Symbolic interdependence, defined as the extent to which relationship members have constructed a shared view of reality

Type of Instrument: Q-sort

Instrument Description: The RWI-2 is a 60-item Q-sort that is administered to both members of an intimate relationship. The items, individually printed on 3 × 5 index cards, consist of belief statements regarding intimate relationships. Respondents sort cards into 15 piles along a continuum of agreement ranging from *strongly disagree* to *strongly agree*. Different frequencies of items are allowed in each pile: 2, 2, 3, 3, 4, 4, 7, 10, 7, 4, 4, 3, 3, 2, and 2. A score on symbolic interdependence is derived by correlating the two sets of ratings produced by the members of the couple. In this way, the RWI-2 is designed to provide a supraindividual, or relationship, level of measurement. The procedure also may be used to assess an individual's beliefs about relationships. In this alternative application, rankings for each item become the subject of the analysis. Administration time is approximately 30–50 minutes.

Sample Items:

(A) A relationship is a place to escape chaos and strife in life.
(B) Sometimes it is necessary to bend the truth a little bit in order to maintain a good relationship.
(C) Jealousy does not enter into a good relationship.

Comments: The authors report that test-retest reliability is .73. It is also reported that correlations were examined between symbolic interdependence and commitment and adjustment/happiness over a six-month period, as well as between symbolic interdependence and time spent talking in long- versus short-distance couples and breakups. More detailed reliability and validity information can be found in the references listed below. In addition to the above-named source of availability, the item set is also available from Comserve@Rpicicge, the Bitnet electronic information service.

References:

Stephen, T. (1984). Symbolic interdependence and post-break-up distress: A reformulation of the attachment construct. *J Divorce, 8*(1), 1–16.
Stephen, T. (1985). Fixed-sequence and circular-causal models of relationship development: Divergent views on the role of communication in intimacy. *J Mar Fam, 47*, 955–963.
Stephen, T. (1986). Communication and interdependence in geographically separated relationships. *Hum Comm Res, 13*, 191–210.
Stephen, T., & Markman, H. (1983). Assessing the development of relationships: A new measure. *Fam Proc, 22*, 15–25.

I-4/a

106. STUART, R. B., & JACOBSON, B. Couple's Pre-Counseling Inventory (CPCI)

Avail: Research Press, 2612 N. Mattis Ave., Champaign, IL 61821

Variables Measured: Interactions, communication, and willingness to work together in order to maintain an intimate relationship

Type of Instrument: Self-report questionnaire

Instrument Description: The CPCI was originally published in 1973, was revised in 1983, and was further restructured in 1987. The current version includes the option of a computer scoring service. According to the manual: "The CPCI is intended to collect data for planning and evaluating relationship enhancement therapy based upon the principles of social learning theory." The inventory contains 16 pages and 347 bits of information for each member of the couple, covering 12 key areas of relationships: (1) general and specific happiness; (2) caring behaviors; (3) conflict management; (4) communication assessment; (5) sexual interaction; (6) moods and management of personal life; (7) decision making; (8) division of home, child care, and work responsibilities; (9) child management; (10) goals of counseling; (11) previous marriages and/or relationships; and (12) additional information. A separate general information and background section is also included. Items are presented in various formats, including Likert-type, direct informational questions (e.g., "Approximately how many times . . . "), and open-ended items. The CPCI is geared toward examining both the need for change and the commitment of the couple to undergo needed change. It is intended for use with cohabiting couples, whether married or not, and for both heterosexual and homosexual partnerships. The CPCI is not necessarily used in finding means for salvaging relationships. Rather, it was designed to be useful in examining needs and motivations and determining necessary avenues of treatment if the relationship is to survive. Information generated through use of this instrument is intended to be used in a therapeutic environment.

Sample Items:

(A)   Please list ten positive things that your partner does that please you.
(B)   We fight over small differences rather than negotiate.
(C)   My partner enjoys just sitting and talking with me.

Comments: The CPCI is intended for use where therapy utilizing social learning theory is considered. Cronbach's alpha, based on a sample of 43 couples seeking marriage therapy and 12 couples participating in a marriage enrichment program, ranged from .85 to .91 for various scales. Correlational data comparing the CPCI with numerous other instruments are presented in the manual.

Reference:

Stuart, R. B., & Jacobson, B. (in press). Couple's Pre-Counseling Inventory: Psychometric properties and norms. *Am J Fam Th.*

I-4/a
107. SURRA, C. A. Activities Checklist (AC)

Avail: NAPS-3

Variables Measured: Behavioral interdependence between partners and between partners and members of the social network

Type of Instrument: Self-report questionnaire

Instrument Description: The AC was designed to measure behavioral interdependence between partners. Its purpose is to assess the extent to which dating partners become interdependent and involved with each other relative to social networks. The instrument was developed with the idea of measuring developmental change in interdependence from the casual dating stage through early marriage. Respondents indicate the frequency with which they performed each activity over a specified time period. Alternately, they may indicate the number of days of a given month on which specified activities were performed. Frequency is recorded for affectional activities done with the partner; for instrumental activities done alone and with the partner; and for leisure activities done with the partner, with the partner and family members or friends, and with family members or friends without the partner. Instrumental activities are subclassified as typically done by men or women. To score the AC, both the total frequency of affectional activities and the proportion of activities in each subcategory are calculated. The instrument contains a total of 31 items.

Sample Items:

(A)   Talked about personal or family problems.
(B)   Hugged and kissed.
(C)   Did repairs on the house or apartment.

Comments: Premarital activities used in the AC were developed from diaries of daily activities done by dating partners. Marital activities were selected from the Spouse Observation Checklist (Weiss & Margolin, 1977). Independent judges categorized the activities into one of the three domains, and subcategorized instrumental activities as traditionally male or female.

References:

Surra, C. A. (1985). Courtship types: Variations in interdependence between partners and social networks. *J Pers Soc Psy, 49,* 357–375.

Surra, C. A., Chandler, M., & Asmussen, L. (1987). Effects of premarital pregnancy on the development of interdependence in relationships. *J Soc Clin Psy, 5,* 123–139.

I-4/c
108. TAYLOR, J. Taylor's Affiliation Inventory

Avail: 1988 Ref.

Variables Measured: Levels of rewards and costs associated with relations within the family

Type of Instrument: Self-report questionnaire

Instrument Description: This instrument contains 16 items, half related to costs and half related to rewards associated with intrafamilial relations. Each item is rated (0–8) on a scale ranging from *never* to *always*. Items contrasting costs and rewards are included for each of eight domains (acceptance, pleasurableness, resourcefulness, regard, pridefulness, focal supportiveness, global supportiveness, and cooperativeness). Scores for items within domains are summed, giving a possible range of 0 to 64 for each domain. Reversing the polarity of the cost subscale gives a total affiliation score (AF = R + [64-C]) with a range of 0 to 128. Various names or titles are filled in to designate the relation of interest (e.g., "I speak positively about my wife's personality" or "I point out my child's faults"). While the instrument would likely prove applicable to families of all races, the author has found it particularly useful in assessing characteristics of Black families.

Sample Items:

(A) _____ speaks positively about _____'s personality.
(B) _____ boasts about _____'s behavior.
(C) _____ points out _____'s faults.

Comments: The author reports mean scores on the Reward, Cost, and Total AF indexes to be 44.6, 21.3, and 87.3, respectively. Split-half reliabilities for the two subscales are each reported to be .78. Split-half reliability for Total AF is reported to be .87. The author indicates that the two subscales correlate -.51. Scores on Taylor's Affiliation Inventory have been compared with those obtained on indexes of parental control and to socioemotional development of children, patterns of child maltreatment, and styles of managing the home environment. Quality of social support to the mother, estimated by the author from this inventory, has been compared with maternal self-esteem and with maternal behaviors toward persons inside and outside the immediate household.

Reference:

Taylor, J., & McMillian, M. (1988). Taylor's Affiliation and Control Inventories. In R. L. Jones (Ed.), *Tests and measurements for Black populations*. Berkeley, CA: Cobb & Henry.

I-4/a
109. TING-TOOMEY, S. The Intimate Negotiation Coding System (INCS)

Avail: 1983a & 1983b Refs.

Variables Measured: Verbal behaviors and strategies for negotiating within marital relationships

Type of Instrument: Behavior coding system

Instrument Description: The INCS is a system for coding verbal sequential behaviors geared toward the discussion or resolution of differences between married couples. The INCS includes 12 dimensions, or types of acts, combined into three categories of behaviors: integrative, descriptive, and disintegrative. Integrative and disintegrative behaviors contain further descriptions of three additional forms that the act may take. Descriptive behaviors each contain only one primary definition. The coding system is used to quantify and analyze videotaped interactions based on responses to two instruments. Couples first complete the Dyadic Adjustment Scale (DAS) (Spanier, 1976). They are then presented with a series of themes and improvisations related to areas often related to marital conflict (Gottman, 1979). The DAS item on which couples most disagree, together with the conflict situation with which they indicate they most closely identify, are selected for active discussion. Codings are based on these discussions, with each utterance being coded. Coders receive approximately 24 hours of training prior to using the INCS.

Sample Items:

(A)　Coaxing: mutual-oriented act which attempts to make the partner feel good about himself/herself before making explicit any other motivation behind the act.

(B)　Socio-Emotional Description: descriptive statements concerning one's feelings upon various issues, ideas, or persons in a leveling manner.

(C)　Confronting: individual-oriented act which directly attacks, criticizes, or negatively evaluates the partner's feelings/ideas.

Comments: The author indicates using two primary and two secondary coders. Cohen's kappa was used to determine intercoder reliability on 20% of the verbal interactions. Kappa is reported to have ranged from .86 to .95.

References:

Ting-Toomey, S. (1983a). An analysis of verbal communication patterns in high and low marital adjustment groups. *Hum Comm Res, 9,* 306–319.
Ting-Toomey, S. (1983b). Coding conversation between intimates: A validation study of the Intimate Negotiation Coding System (INCS). *Comm Q, 31,* 68–77.

I-4/a
110. WACHOWIAK, D. G., & BRAGG, H. K. Marital Contract Assessment Blank (MCAB)

Avail: NAPS-3

Variables Measured: Openness of communication in a marriage

Type of Instrument: Self-report instrument

Instrument Description: This instrument was designed as a measure of the amount of openness present in marital relationships. It assesses marriages along eight dimensions outlined by O'Neill and O'Neill (1972) as critical to marital openness. These are (1) here-and-now living and realistic expectations, (2) privacy, (3) open and honest communication, (4) role flexibility, (5) open companionship, (6) equality, (7) identity, and (8) trust. The MCAB is a 56-item forced-choice questionnaire and is intended for use with married couples of all ages. It is also adaptable for use with premarrieds. It has been specifically tailored to be used by clinicians involved in the assessment of couples entering counseling with relationship concerns. To meet this end, it allows the opportunity for written amplification on choices made. Scores may be placed on a profile sheet that allows the couple and their counselor to compare answers to particular items as well as to assess areas of potential conflict. It may also be used in research investigating communication issues within intimate and romantic relations. Administration time is approximately 20 minutes.

Sample Items:

(A) 1. It is hard for me to be frank and open with my spouse.
    2. I'm comfortable being frank and open with my spouse.
(B) 1. Our marital roles are separate and distinct.
    2. Our marital roles are quite flexible.
(C) 1. My spouse and I don't believe in separate vacations.
    2. My spouse and I feel that it is important to spend some of our vacation time apart.

Comments: The authors report that six-week test-retest reliability for the MCAB is .89. KR-20 coefficients for the eight subscales are reported to range from .32 to .70, with a total scale coefficient of .79. Correlations are reported between the MCAB and church attendance (-.48), number of children (-.42), and age of respondent (-.23). Correlations are also reported between individual subscales and Locke-Wallace Marital Adjustment scores, with frequent differences in correlations for men and women. Differences in correlations are reported for scores on trust (.24 for men, .73 for women), role flexibility (-.01 for men, -.32 for women), open companionship (.18 for men, .38 for women), and for the total MCAB (.07 for men, .36 for women).

Reference:

Wachowiak, D., & Bragg, H. (1980). Open marriage and marital adjustment. *J Mar Fam, 43,* 57–62.

I-4/a
111. WALSTER, E., UTNE, M. K., & TRAUPMANN, J. Global Measures of Participants' Inputs, Outcomes, and Equity/Inequity

Avail: 1978 & 1988 Refs.

Variables Measured: Equity versus inequity in romantic relationships

Type of Instrument: Self-report questionnaire

Instrument Description: This instrument is an 8-point, 4-item Likert-type questionnaire designed to assess the level of equity in a relationship. Items are in the form of questions, asking respondents to describe their and their partners' contributions and outcomes within the confines of their romantic relationships. Each item is rated on a scale ranging from +4 (*extremely positive*) to -4 (*extremely negative*). Scoring is accomplished by comparing each partners' relative contributions and outcomes. Scores approaching zero are interpreted as indicative of equitable relationships. The higher or lower the score, the less equitable the relationship is presumed to be. An individual's status within a relationship is evaluated as "greatly underbenefitted," "slightly underbenefitted," "equitably treated," "slightly overbenefitted," or "greatly overbenefitted." The authors have used this scale largely as an adjunct to assessments of sexual relationships. Their purpose has generally been to assess the relationship between overall equitability and double standards within sexual dimensions of relationships. Others have used the scale to examine equitability as it relates to dating and/or marital relationships.

Sample Items:

(A)   All things considered, how would you describe your partner's contributions to your relationship?

(B)   All things considered, how would you describe your outcomes from your relationship?

(C)   All things considered, how would you describe your partner's outcomes from your relationship?

Comments: The authors found that respondents who perceived themselves to be involved in equitable relationships also felt more content, happy, less angry, and less guilty than did those who perceived themselves to be either underbenefited or overbenefited.

References:

Cate, R. M., Lloyd, S. A., & Long, E. (1988). The role of rewards and fairness in developing premarital relationships. *J Mar Fam, 50,* 443–452.

Davidson, B. (1984). A test of equity theory for marital adjustment. *Social Psych Q, 47,* 36–42.

Martin, M. W. (1985). Satisfaction with intimate exchange: Gender-role differences and the impact of equity, equality and rewards. *Sex Roles, 13,* 597–605.

Walster, E., Walster, G. W., & Traupmann, J. (1978). Equity and premarital sex. *J Pers Soc Psy, 36,* 82–92.

I-4/II-4/a
112. WEIS, D. L. Attitudes Toward Marital Exclusivity Scale

Avail: 1981 & 1987 Refs.

Variables Measured: Attitudes toward exclusive relationships within marriage

Type of Instrument: Self-report questionnaire

Instrument Description: This instrument is a 5-point, 7-item Likert-type questionnaire designed to assess perceptions regarding the acceptability of both sexual and nonsexual extramarital relationships with friends of the opposite gender. Instructions for the questionnaire describe a scenario where the respondent's spouse and the spouse of an opposite-gender friend have each left town on extended trips. The respondent is asked to indicate the acceptability of a range of behaviors, arranged in ascending order of presumed sexual intent, from spending an evening together to sexual involvement.

Sample Items:

(A)   Going to a movie or the theater.
(B)   Dancing to the stereo.
(C)   Spending a few days at a secluded cabin.

Comments: Cronbach's alpha is reported to vary from .85 to .88 for the combined scale. The author notes that nearly 85% of both male and female undergraduate respondents approved of at least one behavior listed in the inventory. However, acceptability of activities represented by items with sexually explicit content were reported to be low. Of 379 females, only 2.2% said that sexual involvement would be acceptable.

References:

Weis, D. L., & Felton, J. R. (1987). Marital exclusivity and the potential for future marital conflict. *Social Work, 32,* 45–49.

Weis, D. L., & Slosnerick, M. (1981). Attitudes toward sexual and nonsexual extramarital involvements among a sample of college students. *J Mar Fam, 38,* 349–358.

Weis, D. L., Slosnerick, M., Cate, R., & Sollie, D. L. (1986). A survey instrument for assessing the cognitive association of sex, love, and marriage. *J Sex Res, 22,* 206–220.

I-4/a

113. WEISS, R. L., & BIRCHLER, G. R. Areas of Change Questionnaire (AC)

Avail: 1983 Ref.

Variables Measured: Changes in the marital relationship that are desired by either the husband or the wife

Type of Instrument: Self-report questionnaire

Instrument Description: The AC is a 7-point, 34-item Likert-type questionnaire designed to assess the extent to which marital partners would like their spouses to increase or decrease each of several behaviors. Each item receives a rating ranging from +3, indicating that the behavior should occur *much more often,* to -3, indicating a desire to have the behavior occur *much less frequently.* In addition to rating changes desired in one's mate, the respondent is also instructed to complete the AC with respect to how desirable changes in his or her behavior would be viewed by the spouse. Each item on the first form uses the stem: "I want my partner to . . . " Items for the second form each begin with: "It would please my partner if I . . . " Scores from the dual administration are combined in order to determine both the extent of change that is desired and the agreement or disagreement among spouses regarding which behaviors require change. In addition to changes desired, both levels of agreement and disagreement are noted. It is expected that a greater desire for change will be inversely related to the level of satisfaction with the current state of the relationship. The AC may be used in both research and clinical settings. Computerized scoring and interpretation services are available from Multi-Health Systems, Inc. (P.O. Box 87, Lynbrook, NY 11563).

Sample Items:

(A) . . .   participate in decisions about spending money.
(B) . . .   prepare interesting meals.
(C) . . .   have sexual relations with me.

Comments: The authors report a split-half reliability of .88 for the AC, and a correlation with the Locke-Wallace Marital Adjustment Test (1959) of -.68. Average scores reported from a study comparing distressed and nondistressed couples were 28.0 and 6.9, respectively. An adaptation of the AC for children, the Parent-Child Areas of Change Questionnaire (Jacob & Seilhamer, 1985) is also available.

References:

Belsky, J., Perry-Jenkins, M., & Crouterr, A. C. (1985). The work-family interface and marital change across the transition to parenthood. *J Fam Iss, 6,* 205–220.

Jacob, T., & Seilhamer, R. A. (1985). Adaptation of the Areas of Change Questionnaire for parent-child relationship assessment. *Am J Fam Th, 13*(2), 28–38.

Margolin, G., Talovic, S., & Weinstein, C. D. (1983). Areas of Change Questionnaire: A practical approach to marital assessment. *J Cons Clin, 51,* 920–931.

Noller, P. (1981). Gender and marital adjustment level differences in decoding messages from spouses and strangers. *J Pers Soc Psy, 41,* 272–278.

I-4/a

114. WEISS, R. L., PATTERSON, G. R., HOPS, H., & WILLS, T. A. The Spouse Observation Checklist (SOC)

Avail: 1979 Ref.

Variables Measured: Pleasing and displeasing activities engaged in by marital couples, as well as costs and benefits associated with pleasing one's mate

Type of Instrument: Self-report questionnaire

Instrument Description: Two related instruments will be described. The SOC is a 400-item questionnaire designed to assess satisfaction with joint activities of husbands and wives; The Cost-Benefit Exchange Sheet (Weiss & Perry, 1979), formerly referred to as the Pleases and Displeases (P & D) Benefit Exchange scale, is composed of the positive items from the SOC, and is designed to assess both costs and benefits associated with pleasing one's spouse. Items on the SOC are in the form of behavioral statements, to which respondents indicate the number of times the activity occurred that day, and whether they found it to be pleasing or displeasing. Appropriate notations can also be made where activities are pleasing at times and displeasing at others. Items are contained within 12 categories: (1) affection, (2) companionship, (3) consideration, (4) sex, (5) communication process, (6) coupling activities, (7) child care and parenting, (8) household management, (9) financial decision making, (10) employment-education, (11) personal habits and appearance, and (12) self and spouse independence. The instrument is intended to be completed by both marital partners on a daily basis for two weeks. Daily scores are computed for each category in terms of both pleases and displeases. The Cost-Benefit Exchange index is a 5-point Likert-type rating system for evaluating costs and benefits of pleasing behaviors. Each respondent indicates the extent to which he or she benefited from activities of their spouse, as well as a rating of costs incurred for each activity in which the spouse claims to have benefited. By comparing costs and benefits for both spouses, areas in which husbands or wives perceive the relationship to be unequal can be highlighted.

Sample Items:

(A)   We listened to music on the radio or stereo.
(B)   Spouse listened sympathetically to my problems.
(C)   We invited a couple of our friends over to visit.

Comments: The SOC and the Cost-Benefit Exchange Sheet can be used either individually or in combination. Computerized scoring is available for both instruments. Validity information on the SOC comes from a number of studies. One popular area of study has been comparisons of distressed and nondistressed marital couples. Distressed couples have been consistently found to exhibit proportionately fewer pleasing behaviors than nondistressed couples (4:1 pleasing:displeasing ratios versus reports of from 12:1 to 30:1 for nondistressed partners).

References:

McHale, S. M., & Huston, T. (1985). The effect of the transition to parenthood on the marriage relationship. *J Fam Iss, 6,* 409–433.

Weiss, R. L., Hops, H., & Patterson, G. R. (1973). A framework for conceptualizing marital conflict: A technology for altering it, some data for evaluating it. In F. W. Clark & L. A. Hamerlynek (Eds.), *Critical issues in research and practice: Proceedings of the Fourth Banff International Conference on Behavior Modification.* Champaign, IL: Research Press.

Weiss, R. L., & Perry, B. A. (1979). P & D Benefit Exchange. In R. L. Weiss & B. A. Perry (Eds.), *Assessment and treatment of marital dysfunction.* Eugene: University of Oregon, Oregon Marital Studies Program.

Weiss, R. L., & Perry, B. A. (1983). The Spouse Observation Checklist: Development and clinical applications. In E. E. Filsinger (Ed.), *Marriage and family assessment: A sourcebook for family therapy* (pp. 65–84). Beverly Hills, CA: Sage.

I-4/a

115. WEISS, R. L., SUMMERS, K. J., & FENN, D. Marital Interaction Coding System-III (MICS-III)

Avail: 1979 Ref.

Variables Measured: Interactions engaged in by spouses while attempting to negotiate marital conflicts

Type of Instrument: Behavioral coding system

Instrument Description: The MICS-III is a system for assessing strategies by which marital partners discuss and negotiate areas of concern. Interactions may be generated through suggestions by the examiner, or by couples themselves, and may represent real or imagined conflicts. The focus lies in interaction strategies and not with the actual content of the disagreement. Interactions, lasting approximately 10 minutes, occur without the examiner in the room, and are recorded (either audiotaped or videotaped) for later coding. The authors define 32 codes, 2 of which are new to the MICS-III. Codes are contained within three behavioral (modifier, nonverbal affect carrier, and state) and seven functional (problem description, blame, proposal for change, validation, invalidation, facilitation, and irrelevant) categories used to classify activity. Eight codes are referred to as dual-status, and may function as either modifier or nonverbal affect carrier codes. In using the MICS-III, observers record behavior within 30-second sequences. Each behavioral category is listed on coding sheets by a two-letter abbreviation. By using these codes, observers are capable of recording relatively large volumes of activity. Following each 30-second sequence, raters move to the next line and once again begin coding behaviors from within the interaction. This instrument is designed for use by two coders working independently. However, raters are expected to compare codings, and to resolve any differences such that a consensus is developed. Coders falling below a level of 70% agreement receive further training prior to coding further observations.

Sample Items: Not applicable.

Comments: Development of this instrument was guided by theoretical and methodological considerations initially presented in the Family Interaction Coding System (Patterson, Ray, Shaw, & Cobb, 1969). The MICS was originally developed by Hops, Wills, Patterson, and Weiss (1972), and has since been revised on three occasions (MICS, MICS-revised, MICS-II, MICS-III). The authors indicate two methods for interpreting coded responses: First, a base-rate for individual behavioral categories may be calculated. This allows for identification of deficits and excesses in behavioral strategies; second, sequential analyses may be employed to track behavioral patterns. The authors recommend a combined approach whereby both methods are utilized.

References:

Clingempeel, W. G., & Brand, E. (1985). Quasi-kin relationships, structural complexity, and marital quality in stepfamilies: A replication, extension, and clinical implications. *Fam Relat, 34,* 401–409.

Jacobson, N. S. (1977). Problem solving and contingency contracting in the treatment of marital discord. *J Cons Clin, 45,* 92–100.

Weider, G. B., & Weiss, R. L. (1980). Generalizability theory and the coding of marital interaction. *J Cons Clin, 48,* 469–477.

Weiss, R. L., & Perry, B. A. (1979). P & D Benefit Exchange. In R. L. Weiss & B. A. Perry (Eds.), *Assessment and treatment of marital dysfunction.* Eugene: University of Oregon, Oregon Marital Studies Program.

Weiss, R. L., & Summers, K. J. (1983). Marital Interaction Coding System-III. In E. E. Filsinger (Ed.), *Marriage and family assessment: A sourcebook for family therapy* (pp. 85–115). Beverly Hills, CA: Sage.

I-4/a
116. WEISS, R. L., VINCENT, J. P., & BIRCHLER, G. R. Inventory of Rewarding Activities (IRA)

Avail: 1979 Ref.

Variables Measured: Actual and desired activities in which one has recently been engaged

Type of Instrument: Self-report questionnaire

Instrument Description: The IRA is a 5-point, 100-item multiple choice questionnaire designed to assess whether and with whom an individual has engaged in various activities in the recent past. Each item details a different activity, to which respondents indicate whether they have *not done* (indicated by leaving the item blank), *done alone, with spouse and family members, with spouse and other adults, with others (nonfamily),* or *with spouse only*. In addition to not marking a response when the activity was not done, respondents are instructed to enter a check mark if they have done the activity within the past four weeks, a check mark and a plus (+) sign if they have done this and would like to do it more often, or just a plus sign if they have not done this within the past four weeks, but would like to engage in this activity more frequently. The instrument is designed to be completed by both marital partners. Several scoring options are indicated: (1) Answer sheets are designed such that a measure of spouse agreement, both with respect to activities in which the couple has engaged and with respect to the pleasure each takes in engaging in that activity, can be easily obtained; (2) comparison of activity totals, both with regard to actual and desired activities; and (3) the proportion of activities engaged in with one's partner, family, friends, and alone. Computerized scoring is also available.

Sample Items:

(A)   Practicing singing or playing an instrument.
(B)   Conversations about local, regional, or world events.
(C)   Go to meetings of a club or an organization.

Comments: Birchler and Webb (1977) report that distressed couples engaged in 46% of their activities together and 39% alone, while nondistressed couples indicated rates for joint and solitary activities at 56% and 28%, respectively. Nondistressed couples also reported more frequent sexual intercourse during the previous month (11.6 versus 6.5) than did distressed couples. Note: The IRA is also referred to in the literature as the Marital Activities Inventory (MAI).

References:

Birchler, G. R., & Webb, L. J. (1977). Discriminating interaction behaviors in happy and unhappy marriages. *J Cons Clin, 45,* 494–495.

Birchler, G. R., Weiss, R. L., & Vincent, J. P. (1975). Multimethod analysis of social reinforcement exchange between maritally distressed and nondistressed spouse and stranger dyads. *J Pers Soc Psy, 31,* 349–360.

Smith, G. T., Snyder, D. K., Trull, T. J., & Monsma, B. R. (1988). Predicting relationship satisfaction from couples' use of leisure time. *Am J Fam Th, 16,* 3–13.

Weiss, R. L., Hops, H., & Patterson, G. R. (1973). A framework for conceptualizing marital conflict: A technology for altering it, some data for evaluating it. In F. W. Clark & L. A. Hamerlynek (Eds.), *Critical issues in research and practice: Proceedings of the Fourth Banff International Conference on Behavior Modification.* Champaign, IL: Research Press.

Weiss, R. L., & Perry, B. A. (1979). P & D Benefit Exchange. In R. L. Weiss & B. A. Perry (Eds.), *Assessment and treatment of marital dysfunction.* Eugene: University of Oregon, Oregon Marital Studies Program.

I-4/a
117. WHITE, L., JOHNSON, D. R., BOOTH, A., & EDWARDS, J. N.
Nebraska Scale of Marital Interaction

Avail: 1983 Ref.

Variables Measured: Marital interaction in day-to-day activities

Type of Instrument: Self-report questionnaire

Instrument Description: This 5-item Likert-type questionnaire was designed to assess joint participation among married couples in common, everyday activities. Items are answered according to four response options that indicate the frequency of joint participation (*almost always, usually, occasionally,* or *never*) in various activities. The scale was developed for use with telephone or personal interviews as well as with paper-and-pencil administration to a general population of married persons.

Sample Items:

(A)   How often do you eat your main meal together?
(B)   How often do you visit friends together?
(C)   When you go out—say to play cards, bowling, or a movie—how often do you do this together?

Comments: The authors indicate that Cronbach's alpha for this 5-item scale is .91, based on data obtained from a national probability sample of 2,033 married men and women under 55 years of age. It is also reported that the scale correlates in expected directions with other indicators of marital quality such as marital happiness (.46), marital problems (-.28), marital disagreement (-.26), and marital instability (-.32).

References:

Booth, A., Johnson, D., White, L., & Edwards, J. (1985). Predicting divorce and permanent separation. *J Fam Iss, 6,* 331–346.

Johnson, D., White, L., Edwards, J., & Booth, A. (1986). Dimensions of marital quality: Toward methodological and conceptual refinement. *J Fam Iss, 7,* 31–49.

White, L. (1983). Determinants of spousal interaction: Marital structure or marital happiness? *J Mar Fam, 44,* 511–519.

White, L., & Booth, A. (1985). The quality and stability of remarriages: The role of stepchildren. *Am Sociol R, 50,* 689–698.

I-4/V-2/g/a
118. ZARIT, S. H., REEVER, K. E., & BACH-PETERSON, J. Caregiver Burden Scale

Avail: 1980 Ref.

Variables Measured: Feelings associated with caring for a spouse afflicted with senile dementia

Type of Instrument: Self-report questionnaire

Instrument Description: The Caregiver Burden Scale is a 3-point, 29-item instrument designed to assess feelings of husbands and wives who serve as primary caregivers to the elderly and senile spouses. Items take the form of statements related to feelings, fears, and frustrations associated with caregiving. Response options range from *not at all* to *extremely.* The questionnaire can be self-administered as a paper-and-pencil instrument, but is typically given orally as part of an extended interview covering various aspects of coping with senile spouses. The scale may be appropriate for both clinical and research purposes. Items were selected based on clinical experiences of the authors, as well as a review of research conducted with this population. The instrument was designed to assess burdens in the areas of the caregiver's health, psychological well-being, finances, social life, and the caregiver's relationship with the spouse in need of care. The instrument, with slight modifications, would also be appropriate for use with primary caregivers other than spouses. Total burden scores are computed by summing response values across items for the entire instrument. Subscales were not identified by the authors.

Sample Items:

(A)   I feel resentful of other relatives who could but who do not do things for my spouse.
(B)   I feel that my spouse makes requests which I perceive to be over and above what s/he needs.
(C)   Because of my involvement with my spouse, I don't have enough time for myself.

Comments: Cronbach's alpha for the Caregiver Burden Scale is reported to be .79. A somewhat altered version of the scale was apparently used by Pratt, Schmall, Wright, and Cleland (1985). These authors report the Caregiver Burden Scale to be a 22-item instrument. Zarit et al. report correlations between burden scores and measures of mental status (-.06), duration of illness (.02), memory problems (.16), behavior problems (-.07), physical activity of daily living (physical ADL; Lawton, 1971) (-.06), instrumental ADL (-.20), and family visits (-.048).

References:

Barber, C. E. (1988). Correlates of subjective burden among adult sons and daughters caring for aged parents. *J Aging Stud, 2,* 133–144.

Pratt, C. C., Schmall, V. L., Wright, S., & Cleland, M. (1985). Burden and coping strategies of caregivers to Alzheimer's patients. *Fam Relat, 34,* 27–33.

Zarit, S. H., Reever, K. E., & Bach-Peterson, J. (1980). Relatives of the impaired elderly: Correlates of feelings of burden. *Gerontol, 20,* 649–655.

NOTE: For additional instruments, see also *Abstracts 1001–1115* in the Abbreviated Abstracts of Instruments (which precedes the Indexes).

3 Intimacy and Family Values

WALTER R. SCHUMM

The vast majority of scales in this chapter are self-report questionnaires, largely a consequence of the nature of the concepts being measured—values, perceptions of subjects, satisfaction, feelings of love. Of the two dozen or so measures that are not self-report questionnaires, most are coding or rating schemes for assessing various aspects of a love relationship, and most are relatively recent: Approximately two-thirds of the non-self-report measures have been published since 1974. While most scholars now consider self-report and observational measures to be complementary rather than contradictory in the information they provide (Baucom & Adams, 1987; Filsinger, 1983; Mederer & Hill, 1983), observational measures represent a small minority of the total number of measures discussed within this chapter; therefore, this chapter's review will focus on self-report measures.

Most therapists or researchers who are reviewing this chapter probably will have three primary considerations in mind:

(1) measuring a certain concept important to them (has someone already measured the concept or do I need to start from scratch?);

(2) the length (and/or difficulty) of the measure (will it fit in my overall assessment package or survey?); and

(3) the validity of the measure (will it really measure what I want to measure?).

With respect to the first question, concepts are identified within each of five sets of measures considered in Chapter 3. The objective of listing or tabling measures in terms of their apparent concepts is to assist readers in finding a set of measures that approximates the concept the reader is interested in assessing. In listing the concepts, it became apparent that, in some cases, measures could be labeled differently from the way their authors had identified them. For example, the concept that Barrett-Lennard conceptualized quite clearly in 1962 as positive regard has been remeasured under a variety of new names, including love, acceptance, caring, rejection, and positive affect. Therefore, some measures are listed under concepts different from their original labels.

The second consideration—length of the measure—may seem a rather mundane concern, but the measures ranged from 1 item to nearly 300 items. Obviously, such differences are substantial. In general, shorter measures are unidimensional, more recent in construction, and designed more for basic than applied or clinical research. Even though a family studies researcher and a family therapist might want to measure the same concept, they might very well choose measures of different lengths to suit their particular needs. Therefore, measures have been categorized not only by concept but by length when several lengths were available. In particular, measures have been classified in five categories of length: 3 to 6, 7 to 15, 16 to 40, 41 to 99, and 100 or more items. Scales with fewer than 7 items can normally fit onto one-half page of a survey or assessment device. Scales with between 7 and 15 items may take up to a full page. Scales with 16 to 40 items will normally require two to three pages to complete. Scales of 41 to 99 items may require as many as ten pages to complete, though use of small print might reduce their length to as few as two pages (e.g., Bienvenu's, 1970, 46-item Marital Communication Inventory, *Abstract 5*), minus instructions, fits into two pages with its small print). Scales of 100 to 300 items are often complete assessment packages in themselves and may normally be suitable in their entirety only for clinical assessment, assuming that Dillman's (1978, p. 55) assertion that 11 pages or 125 items represents the maximum length of a survey (beyond that length, response rates begin to decrease sharply). Of course, the longer inventories often include briefer subscales that may be extracted for a variety of uses. In some cases, the concepts measured by such subscales are most appropriate for chapters in this handbook other than Chapter 3.

The third consideration is the validity of the measure. Assuming that the reader has found measures of suitable length that claim to measure what is wanted, how does one decide which measure is the best for the intended application? Of course, one may find that no such measure exists or that the present ones are not suitable; however, everything else being equal, it is usually better to build upon previous research and established measures rather than to reinvent them. Straus and Brown (1978, p. 4) noted a decade ago that measures become more valuable with each use, a situation that favors—when possible—use of established measures over the creation of new, similar ones. In selecting from among established measures of a given length, one should consider several criteria, as discussed in more detail in Chapter 1, including reliability, validity, the suitability of the scale to the type of subjects you intend to work with, the extent to which the scale has been used in other research or has been widely recognized, and the ease of administration. Ultimately, you may have to consider the measures on an item-by-item basis to decide which one is most likely to assess the concept you want to measure. While reviewing individual items may seem unnecessary, it often is important, as certain items may lose their relevance over time and scales often weight some items more than others (which you may

Table 3.1 Classification of Marital Relations Measures by Concept and Item Length

Concept		4–6 Items	7–15 Items	16–40 Items	41–99 Items	100+ Items
				Length		
Marital quality						
A. composite scales (1156)	1929–1971	1131	149, 1137, 1151, 1153, 1154	149, 1147, 1148, 1157	149, 1132, 1134, 1143, 1158	136, 150, 1149
	1972–1979			68		
	1980–1987	148	132, 141	163, 164		
B. inventories with subscales (1138)	1939–1971		158	1135		1134
	1972–1979		139	168		167, 1130
	1980–1987			135, 162, 169		157
C. unidimensional scales (marital satisfaction) (1139, 1144)	1939–1971	1141				
	1972–1979	133, 151, 168		167	161	
	1980–1987	135, 155, 166	144, 157, 162			
Marital stability	1939–1971		1134			
	1972–1979				137	
	1980–1987	140, 142	134, 147, 152, 169, 171, 172, 192	153		
Marital social desirability	1939–1971		138		138	
	1972–1979					
	1980–1987		157	167		
Family satisfaction or functioning	1939–1971					
	1972–1979			159		
	1980–1987	167				
Marital problems or conflicts	1939–1971	158, 1150		1152		
	1972–1979	139			170	
	1980–1987	173		143, 433	143	

Concept		4–6 Items	7–15 Items	Length 16–40 Items	41–99 Items	100+ Items
Cohesion, positive interaction, companionship	1937–1971	158, 1133, 1134, 1135, 1146, 1155		1134	1140	
	1972–1979	139, 168		167		
	1980–1987	135	157		388	
Friends or in-laws	1939–1971		150			
	1972–1979		170			
	1980–1987		157			
Roles (239)	1939–1971	1135				
	1972–1979			167		
	1980–1987		157			
Children	1939–1971	1135				
	1972–1979	154, 1142		167		
	1980–1987		157			
Personality or personal habits	1939–1971		150			
	1972–1979		170			
	1980–1987		157			

(continued)

Table 3.1 continued

Concept		4–6 Items	7–15 Items	Length 16–40 Items	41–99 Items	100+ Items
Financial	1939–1971	1135	150			
management	1972–1979		170	167		
	1980–1987	142				
Communication	1939–1971					
	1972–1979					
	1980–1987	135, 142	157, 169			
Conflict	1939–1971					
resolution	1972–1979		170	167		
(160, 1145)	1980–1987		156, 157			
Affective	1939–1971	1135	150			
expression/	1972–1979	168		167		
sexual relations	1980–1987	135	169			
Consensus	1937–1971		1134, 1136			
	1972–1979		133, 168			
	1980–1987	135, 162				

NOTE: All measures cited are self-report instruments except those listed under concept in parentheses.

Table 3.2 Classification of Love Measures by Concept and Item Length

Concept		4–6 Items	7–15 Items	16–40 Items	41–99 Items	100+ Items
				Length		
Positive affect (*180, 306, 351,* 427, 477, 1160, 1168, 1172, 1174)	1939–1971	*264, 1169*	*308, 1167, 1170, 177, 1162, 1163, 1173*	1175, 1177, 1178	*336, 344, 1176*	*339*
	1972–1979			327		
	1980–1987		*416*	191, 195, 210, 259, 281, 289, 298	*265, 295, 342, 358*	*320*
Positive regard (*205, 307, 341*)	1939–1971			176		
	1972–1979		*202*	198	*343*	
	1980–1987	176	*361*	213		
Feelings of love, romantic love	1939–1971			186		
	1972–1979	*1164*	184	184, 197, 203, 207		
	1980–1987	183	183	193, 185		
Intimacy and trust (*187, 196, 1166*)	1939–1971		1165			
	1972–1979				*200*	
	1980–1987		188	194, 211	*199, 208*	
Premarital relationship development	1939–1971			1161		
	1972–1979	1171		178, 212	*189*	*204*
	1980–1987			179, 206		

NOTE: All measures cited are self-report instruments except those listed under concepts in parentheses; items with italicized numbers focus on parent-child relationships more than marital or premarital dyadic relationships.

or may not agree with). On some occasions, items may be irrelevant due to cultural differences. An example is item 23 in Spanier's (1976) Dyadic Adjustment Scale (*168*), "Do you kiss your mate?" Kissing is more relevant to marital adjustment in some cultures than others as it is not a key aspect of physical affection in some societies.

VALUES/BELIEFS ABOUT FAMILY LIFE

The first area, that of values or beliefs about family life is somewhat unusual in its characteristics. Most of the scales have been developed since 1974 with only four developed prior to 1970. Those early scales include the Traditional Family Ideology Scale (1955; *126*), the Hardy Divorce Scale (1967; *494*), the Familism Scale (1959; *119*), and the Index of Consensus (1957; *121*). More recent scales have attempted to improve upon the older measures, but unfortunately the reader has little choice of length because several concepts have only one measure and, even where more than one exists, the lengths of the scales are often similar. One exception is for values regarding children, with one measure in each of the five length categories (*122, 348, 271, 123, 120,* from shortest to longest, respectively). Quite a few measures are available to assess traditionalism (*124, 125, 126, 1119, 1121, 1124*) and familism (*119, 1117, 1128, 1129*). Measures are also available to assess parent-child relationship values (*126, 385*), marital roles (*126*), attitudes toward divorce (*494, 496*), attitudes about grandparenting (*129*), socialization values (*316*), locus of control in relationships (*85, 130, 154*), family planning attitudes (*127, 1120, 1122*), relationship beliefs (*182*), value of one's own home/residence (*128*), family traditions (*81*), and premarital attitudes or values regarding marriage (*147, 1118, 1123, 1127*), as well as composite value measures (*121, 126, 1116, 1125, 1126*). One concern with values as independent variables is that the implicit model is often too simplistic—that is, values per se or differences in values should predict relationship development or relationship functioning. By contrast, well-established psychological models such as Rotter's reinforcement expectancies model (Rotter, 1966, 1975) and Fishbein's (1967) reasoned action theory are more complex in their use of values as well as having been moderately successful in explaining human behavior. Future research on family values could be improved greatly by careful borrowing from such already established theories, not to mention extension or improvement of those theories. In particular, future research should explore the role of variables intervening between values and standard dependent variables.

MARITAL RELATIONS

Of the five topic areas within this chapter, the area with the longest history and best selection of measures is that of marital relations. The oldest measures cited are Hamilton's (1929) interview rating instrument (*1139*), Kirkpatrick's (1937) Family Interests Scale (*1146*), Terman's (1939) Marital Happiness Index (*1157*), and Burgess's (1939) Marriage Adjustment Form (*136*) and Marriage Prediction Schedule (*137*). There appear to be five overall concepts in this area, with at least 15 concepts that often are part of the longer inventories, if not subconcepts of the five overall concepts. Two of the overall concepts fit Lewis and Spanier's (1979) views of marital quality and marital stability. Under marital quality—the first major subconcept under the area of marital relations—there have been three basic approaches to measurement. First, several scales, particularly those originating before 1975, consist of a variety of items that may be measuring different concepts though the scales are almost exclusively used as total score measures: Here such scales are called "composite" measures of marital quality. Perhaps the best known such measure is the Locke-Wallace (1959) Marital Adjustment Test (*149*). A second approach, more popular in the 1970s and early 1980s, has been to assess marital quality by assessing several clearly defined subconcepts. The best known instrument using the second approach is Spanier's (1976) Dyadic Adjustment Scale (*168*), which includes subscales of satisfaction, consensus, cohesion, and affectional expression. Another scale designed with more than one dimension is the Orden-Bradburn (1968) Marriage Adjustment Balance Scale (*158*), which measures both happiness and tensions. However, there is some possibility that its two factors may simply be opposite sides of the same coin (concept), as has been shown by Zeller and Carmines (1980) to be the case with the Rosenberg Self-Esteem Scale. A third approach, recommended recently by Fincham and Bradbury (1987) and Sabatelli (1988) is to assess global perception of marital quality, often as a dependent variable, using related, more specific concepts as predictor variables of the global perception. In particular, Fincham and Bradbury (1987) and Sabatelli (1988) have both cited Norton's (1983) Quality Marriage Index (*155*) and Schumm, Jurich, and Bollman's (1986) Kansas Marital Satisfaction Scale (*166*) as examples of measures of global evaluations of marriage. Measures following this third approach appear to be more recent in origin and are often briefer in length than some of the longer inventories developed in the late 1970s (though those inventories often include similar, shorter scales that are in themselves global evaluations, such as the dyadic satisfaction subscale of the Dyadic Adjustment Scale). In general, the composite measures very greatly in length, while the subscale measures are of intermediate length and the global evaluation measures tend to be shorter. Overall, while there are few marital quality scales of fewer than seven items, there are many longer scales to choose from at present.

With respect to the second major subconcept under marital relations— marital stability—there appears to have been a surge of interest since the early 1970s, not merely measuring the concept as the presence or absence of divorce, but in terms of perceived likelihood of divorce, perceived alternatives to current marriage, and strength of commitment to current marriage. In fact, in terms of sophisticated measurement, this area seems to have improved substantially within the past 20 years. However, there seems to be a need for research that compares the different approaches to measuring stability—for example, under what conditions does a high score on perceived marital alternatives actually represent a greater chance of divorce? Some individuals might envision an array of potential alternatives if their spouses were to die or leave but yet remain highly committed to their present marriages. For others, a large number of attractive alternatives might readily weaken their current commitments. On the other hand, perceptions of minimal alternatives might enhance commitment to stability but not growth in marriage. Future research should go further in evaluating the concurrent and discriminant validity of the various approaches to measuring marital commitment.

The third subconcept under marital relations—marital social desirability—is remarkable for the combination of its alleged importance and the paucity of measures available for measuring it. Probably Edmonds's (1967) Marital Conventionalization Scale (138)—or abbreviated versions of it— has been the most widely used instrument for measuring marital social desirability. It is interesting that some of both the primary social desirability items and the filler items used in the Edmonds's scale are adopted directly or with some modification from previous marital adjustment measures (e.g., 1134). However, relatively little is known about its construct validity though it has yielded marginal to fair levels of internal consistency reliability in some studies. Truly understanding the causes of social desirability may require further qualitative work before quantitative research can make much more progress. In any event, the area of marital social desirability deserves much more attention in future research, particularly in terms of construct validation. Furthermore, in such research it will be critical to keep in mind that, while individual and marital social desirability may be correlated concepts, they are not identical, despite the fact that previous research has often treated them as if they were equivalent concepts, equally valid for controlling social desirability response bias in marital quality research.

The fourth primary topic under marital relations is similar to the marital quality concept except that it is expanded to include family, as well as marital, quality. While most such scales are included in the first section in Chapter 6, those pertaining to family satisfaction or adjustment are included here. Notably, there are few measures available in this area, which is one reason behind the development of at least one of those available, the Kansas Family Life Satisfaction Scale. One cause of the limited number of family quality scales may be the relatively low number of families who meet criteria for a family scale that assesses sibling relationships. In some of our research at Kansas State, we have found that as few as 10% of households, even in rural areas, at any point in time actually meet the criteria for application of such a family scale (at least two children and both parents living at home). Future research might focus on improvement of the few scales presently available.

A fifth topic area that is associated with a variety of measures could be addressed as "sore points" in marriage, matters of conflicts or problems, sharp disagreements, negative interaction, unmet needs, transgressions, or upsetting sorts of relationship problems. Most of these measures have been developed fairly recently and their lengths vary considerably. However, it is likely that more research needs to be done with such measures to establish discriminant validity between them and more clearly defined concepts such as cohesion or consensus. The importance of such measures hinges in part on one's theory about what makes relationships work—the absence of annoying differences, the ability to tolerate them, or the ability to resolve them satisfactorily. If the latter two relationship skills are more important, then a high volume of problems would be more a symptom than a root cause of dysfunction.

The remaining concepts are in many cases only part of larger inventories, although some are addressed by individual instruments. Because many of the measures are subscales within larger inventories, their lengths are often relatively short. Some of the subscales address issues considered in more detail in other chapters (e.g., roles and power, dimensions of interaction). The historical development of many of the scales has been relatively even, with no surge of new scales within the past decade. On the other hand, some concepts have only one measure from inventories within this chapter, which may force readers to develop their own measures in many situations. For example, not shown in Table 3.1 are measures for history of family distress in one's family of origin (*167*), decision making/ goal setting (*170*)—although there is a marital goals orientation scale available that is not abstracted in this volume (Eggeman, Moxley, & Schumm, 1985)—family anomie or alienation (*154*), and marital equity (*68*).

LOVE

The second large body of measures within this chapter includes those associated with love, liking, affection, or trust. Both prior to and after 1975 about two-thirds of the measures have dealt with the marital dyad and another third with parent-child relationships; however, since 1975 a bit more attention has been paid to extramarital and family concepts. The largest number of items deals with positive affect, scales that usually have positive regard at their center but also include items or subscales that appear to include a broader range of affective concepts. Before 1973 most such scales dealt with parent-child relations. One of the oldest scales is

Miller's (1940) Perceived Closeness-to-the-Mother Scale (*1167*). Other older scales include Utton's (1949) Childhood Experience Rating Scales (*1174*), Stryker's (1955) Married Offspring Parent Adjustment Checklist (*1173*), Roth's (1961) Mother-Child Relationship Evaluation (*344*), Bowerman and Irish's (1962) Closeness to Parent Questionnaire (*264*), Roe and Siegelman's (1963) Parent Child Relations Questionnaire (*339*), Heilbrun's (1964) Parent-Child Interaction Rating Scales (*308*), and Pumroy's (1966) Maryland Parent Attitude Survey (*336*). However, increasingly scales are focusing on marriage, although the number of recent parent-child scales is larger than the number of recent marital scales. Some of the measures are relatively long, although there is a good range of lengths, excepting the category of six or fewer items. There are also scales that deal with positive regard or acceptance/rejection more purely, without including other, although related, concepts. Whether the more recent scales have actually made substantial improvements over the positive and unconditional regard scales in Barrett-Lennard's (1962) Relationship Inventory (*176*) remains an open question.

A large number of measures deal with feelings of love, especially romantic love. Romantic love measures seem to have had their heyday in the 1970s, although some were created in the 1980s. Because the issue of whether romantic love is a constructive or destructive factor in relationship development and maintenance remains to be resolved, the usefulness of such measures remains somewhat controversial, although they are probably always going to evoke interest.

More recently, scales have also been created for measuring intimacy and trust. However, when evaluating scales within this category, one has to be rather careful. Some of the scales include items that reflect variables, such as regard or honesty, that are assumed to be factors underlying or predictive of trust or intimacy. However, it may be better to ask subjects directly about intimacy or trust and determine if indeed their perceptions are actually predicted by positive regard or openness. On other occasions, measures of intimacy seem almost identical to other measures of empathy. Perhaps such confusion reflects a lack of consensus about the definition of *intimacy* or *trust*. Of course, if one were to define *intimacy* as a condition of high regard, congruence, and empathy, then one would probably use measures of regard, congruence, and empathy to measure intimacy. However, *intimacy* might be defined differently, such that relationships high on regard, congruence, and empathy might not always be high in intimacy. For example, spouses might hold each other in high regard and be empathic and open but spend too little time together with a resulting loss in intimacy. In other words, some factors may be necessary but not sufficient conditions for intimacy.

There are also measures of intimacy or love feelings, keyed specifically to the premarital period, that focus on presumed indicators of courtship progress or readiness for marriage. It appears that many of these measures were developed in the 1970s and that most are of at least medium length. A danger here is that older measures may lose their predictive power over time as styles of relationship development change; for example, if the frequency of premarital cohabitation increases over time, will that change the content needed to assess relationship development currently? In other words, there may remain a lot of room for future instrument development in this particular area, especially in terms of the development of brief (but still valid) measures.

An area that overlaps closely with the topic of the next section of this chapter (sex) is sexual jealousy, assessed by three measures (*219, 218, 444*); here an important question is the extent to which the measures developed outside the United States (some developed in Europe) are as valid in application in North America. There are also a small number of scales for the concepts of cohesion, bonding, and attachment (*209, 175, 386*), partner idealization (*190*), interpersonal need assessment (*201*), and communication factors such as congruence or self-disclosure (*176, 181*) and empathy (*176*). Unfortunately, when one has few measures to select from, one must consider the need to develop alternative measures if the current measures are not deemed adequate. In general, there appears to be more need for further instrument development in the "love" area than in the marital adjustment area.

The fourth topic area is sexuality, which is obviously related at least indirectly to the other areas of love, intimacy, satisfaction, and values. The historical development of these measures reflects a major surge of activity since 1974, although a few measures (*230, 232*) were developed quite early. However, the number of measures available for assessing individual concepts is relatively small, offering few choices in length. Measures are available for assessing sex knowledge (*230, 233*), associations between love and sex (*234*), premarital sexual standards and decision making (*221, 232*), attitudes toward sexual interest shown by children (*374*), the impact of or beliefs about vasectomy (*229, 1180*), herpes knowledge and attitudes (*216, 217*), sex education (*1179*), physiological measures (*214, 225*), attitudes toward extramarital sex (*112, 220, 231*), sexual jealousy (*218, 219*), abortion attitudes (*224*), sexual communication (*8*), as well as global sexual attitudes (*226*) and sexual satisfaction/functioning (*127, 215, 222, 223, 227, 228, 233, 251*). The combination of breadth but lack of depth in terms of multiple measures for similar concepts offers good prospects for future instrument development in the area of sexuality. Recently, of course, a notable compendium has appeared that provides complete copies of many sex measures and examples of items from other measures (Davis, Yarber, & Davis, 1988). Readers who wish a more detailed treatment of sexuality measures than can be provided in this volume may do well to consult the Davis, Yarber, and Davis (1988) compendium.

However promising research with sexuality measures may be, several precautions are in order. Due to the sensitivity of the topic and requirements for confidential treatment of data, such research may involve higher costs in order to meet standard human subjects requirements. When such requirements are not met, the consequences can be disturbing and adversely affect subsequent research. In one case, a poorly conducted survey drew intense community criticism and led to refusals to other, non-sex-related surveys for up to four years after the offending study (some citizens refused to participate in any research conducted by other researchers in the same university department). Another problem involves dissemination of results. In one study, the media interviewed a researcher and sensationalized the results while overlooking the important psychosocial implications of the research. Because the community agency that had sponsored the study and had provided subjects had not agreed to the sensationalization, the credibility of the researchers and their ability to use the same subjects (and agency) again were adversely affected.

From a clinical perspective, assessment of sexual attitudes and functioning must be handled with particular skill; clients can easily be alienated if overwhelmed with unfamiliar questions or material in preliminary interviews (Malatesta & Adams, 1986, p. 500). Other important concerns include medical assessment to rule out organic problems, the potential effects of drugs on sexual performance and deviancy, limitations of physiological measures, and a lack of rigorous evaluation among some sex therapists, as discussed in detail in Malatesta and Adams (1986).

Thus both researchers and clinicians need to pay special attention to their use of sex measures or else risk a variety of adverse effects upon their subjects/clients, themselves, and their present and possible future research.

PERSONAL/INTERPERSONAL PERCEPTIONS

Turning to the last area within Chapter 3, the reader will find a much smaller number of measures than in the four previous areas. However, development of measures in this area has been relatively even over time, with no apparent surges or slumps. Some scales pertain to personality traits (242, 243, 245, 1191), premarital perceptions (237), perceptions of self as parent (283), perceptions of siblings (280), and perceptions of ideal spouse (236) and actual partner (241, 1183). Some of the instruments that are older or have not been cited in subsequent research very often include perceptions of parents by children (1181, 1182, 1184, 1186, 1193, 1194, 1195), perceptions of children by parents (1182, 1186, 1195, 1196), as well as perceptions of marriage (1185, 1189) and of family life (1192, 1197). Many of the measures involve relatively large numbers of items, making them less useful for basic research, although still suitable for some clinical work. A problem that further complicates matters is theory that is often implicit in the study of perceptions among family members. In many situations, the eventual, if not immediate, goal of the research is to compare perceptions—for example, husband's versus wife's, father's versus adolescent's, ideal versus actual role. The intuitively reasonable approach with such measures is to predict a dependent variable such as marital satisfaction from each perception and a difference score between the two perceptions. The problems of difference scores have been debated extensively in the literature (Schumm & Kirn, 1982). However, Glenn (in press) has clearly pointed out that one cannot predict anything from two perceptions and their raw difference score because the raw difference score is a linear combination of the two perceptions. As Glenn (in press) notes, many scholars have tried various "tricks" to solve such problems. What it seems has been overlooked in the controversy is that predicting a dependent variable from two perceptions is a three-dimensional geometric problem. Two perceptions predicting a dependent variable actually define a (flat) plane in three-dimensional space. Adding a raw difference score to the model shifts only the angle of the plane, leaving the basic flat shape the same. In fact, sound theory may predict something other than a (flat) plane shape. For example, equity theory would predict a rooftop or gable shape with points of equity to be associated with highest satisfaction and points away from that "rooftop" edge to be associated with lower satisfaction, on both sides of the "rooftop." One equation, perhaps the simplest equation, that can predict such a model involves the absolute value of a difference score between the two perceptions, although complex polynomial functions can also approximate the same shape. Once the characteristics of such three-dimensional problems are fully explored, analysis of family member perceptions may proceed much more fruitfully. If so, there may be a brighter future for perceptual measures than one might expect at the present time, given the analytical problems observed to date (Schumm, 1982, 1983).

CONCLUSIONS

At the present time, the areas of marital relations and love provide the reader with the richest source of relatively valid, reliable measures. In the case of several important concepts, the reader can even select from among a wide range of instrument lengths, depending on the measurement situation. The area of perceptions and the area of values provide some important measures but theoretical or methodological limitations will hamper the effective application of many instruments—theory being perhaps a greater problem for values research, and methodology being a greater problem for perception research. Ethical considerations may predominate in the sexual area, with important methodological implications (maintaining a high percentage of valid responses in current and future research, particularly).

Nevertheless, when one adopts the approach used in this chapter—to classify measures by general concept and by length—it becomes apparent that there are a lot of "gaps" in the measurement grid. Some concepts are not particularly reliable or valid, further reducing the effective number of desirable measures and creating even more "gaps." Where possible, readers should try to use existing measures that are of suitable length and validity; however, in many situations, new measures may have to be designed. Hopefully, though, such new measures will undergo thorough evaluation in several studies so as to not others of the many measures used once and forgotten.

REFERENCES

Barrett-Lennard, G. T. (1962). Dimensions of therapist response as causal factors in therapeutic change. *Psychological Monographs, 76*(43; Whole No. 562).

Baucom, D. H., & Adams, A. N. (1987). Assessing communication in marital interaction. In K. D. O'Leary (Ed.), *Assessment of marital discord* (pp. 139–181). Hillsdale, NJ: Lawrence Erlbaum.

Bienvenu, M. J., Sr. (1970). Measurement of marital communication. *Family Coordinator, 19,* 26–31.

Burgess, E. W., & Wallin, P. (1953). *Engagement and marriage.* New York: Lippincott.

Davis, C. M., Yarber, W. L., & Davis, S. L. (Eds.). (1988). *Sexuality-related measures: A compendium.* Lake Mills, IA: Graphic.

Dillman, D. A. (1978). *Mail and telephone surveys: The total design method.* New York: John Wiley.

Edmonds, V. H. (1967). Marital conventionalization: Definition and measurement. *Journal of Marriage and the Family, 29,* 681–688.

Eggeman, K., Moxley, V., & Schumm, W. R. (1985). Assessing spouses' perceptions of Gottman's temporal form in marital conflict. *Psychological Reports, 57,* 171–181.

Filsinger, E. E. (1983). Assessment: What it is and why it is important. In E. E. Filsinger (Ed.), *Marriage and family assessment: A sourcebook for family therapy* (pp. 11–22). Beverly Hills, CA: Sage.

Fincham, F. D., & Bradbury, T. N. (1987). The assessment of marital quality: A reevaluation. *Journal of Marriage and the Family, 49,* 797–809.

Fishbein, M. (1967). Attitude and the prediction of behavior. In M. Fishbein (Ed.), *Readings in attitude theory and measurement* (pp. 477–492). New York: John Wiley.

Glenn, N. D. (in press). A flawed approach to solving the identification problem in the estimation of mobility effect models: A comment on Brody and McRae. *Social Forces.*

Lewis, R. A., & Spanier, G. B. (1979). Theorizing about the quality and stability of marriage. In W. R. Burr, R. Hill, F. I. Nye, & I. L. Reiss (Eds.), *Contemporary theories about the family: Research-based theories* (Vol. 1). New York: Free Press.

Locke, H. J., & Wallace, K. M. (1959). Short marital adjustment and prediction tests. *Marriage and Family Living, 21,* 251–255.

Malatesta, V. J., & Adams, H. E. (1986). Assessment of sexual behavior. In A. R. Ciminero,

K. S. Calhoun, & H. E. Adams (Eds.), *Handbook of behavioral assessment* (pp. 496–525; 2nd ed.). New York: John Wiley.

Mederer, H., & Hill, R. (1983). Critical transitions over the family life span: Theory and research. *Marriage and Family Review, 6,* 39–60.

Norton, R. (1983). Measuring marital quality: A critical look at the dependent variable. *Journal of Marriage and the Family, 45,* 141–151.

Rotter, J. B. (1966). Generalized expectancies for internal versus external control of reinforcement. *Psychological Monographs, 80*(1; Whole No. 609).

Rotter, J. B. (1975). Some problems and misconceptions related to the construct of internal versus external control of reinforcement. *Journal of Consulting and Clinical Psychology, 43,* 56–67.

Sabatelli, R. M. (1988). Measurement issues in marital research: A review and critique of contemporary survey instruments. *Journal of Marriage and the Family, 50,* 891–915.

Schumm, W. R. (1982). Integrating theory, measurement, and statistical analysis in family studies survey research. *Journal of Marriage and the Family, 44,* 983–998.

Schumm, W. R. (1983). Theory and measurement in marital communication training programs. *Family Relations, 32,* 3–11.

Schumm, W. R., & Kirn, J. E. (1982). Evaluating equity in the marital relationship: An alternative approach. *Psychological Reports, 51,* 759–762.

Schumm, W. R., Paff-Bergen, L. A., Hatch, R. C., Obiorah, F. C., Copeland, J. M., Meens, L. F., & Bugaighis, M. A. (1986). Concurrent and discriminant validity of the Kansas Marital Satisfaction Scale. *Journal of Marriage and the Family, 48,* 381–387.

Spanier, G. B. (1976). Measuring dyadic adjustment: New scales for assessing the quality of marriage and similar dyads. *Journal of Marriage and the Family, 38,* 15–28.

Straus, M. A., & Brown, B. W. (1978). *Family measurement techniques: Abstracts of published instruments, 1935–1974* (rev. ed.). Minneapolis: University of Minnesota.

Zeller, R. A., & Carmines, E. G. (1980). *Measurement in the social sciences.* Cambridge: Cambridge University Press.

ABSTRACTS OF INSTRUMENTS

NOTE: For additional instruments, see also *Abstracts 1116–1195* in the Abbreviated Abstracts of Instruments (which precedes the Indexes).

Summary of Instrument Codes

Number Codes:

I = Dimensions of interaction—1 = communication; 2 = life-style; 3 = networks; 4 = multidimensional perspectives

II = Intimacy and family values—1 = family values; 2 = marital relations; 3 = love; 4 = sex; 5 = personal/interpersonal perceptions

III = Parenthood—1 = pregnancy, childbearing, and transition to parenthood; 2 = parenting

IV = Roles and power—1 = roles; 2 = power

V = Adjustment—1 = family functioning; 2 = stress; 3 = divorce, separation, and remarriage

Letter Codes:

Interactants—a = husband-wife, b = parent-child, c = nuclear family, d = extended family, e = others outside the family, f = siblings, g = intrapsychic processes

Focus of Study—P = parents, C = child, H = husband, W = wife, O = any combination of the above (if there is no capital letter code given, it is understood to be "O")

II-1/d

119. BARDIS, P. D. Familism Scale

Avail: 1959, 1979, & 1988 Refs.

Variables Measured: Attitudes and responsibilities toward the nuclear and extended family

Type of Instrument: Self-report questionnaire

Instrument Description: This scale is a 5-point, 16-item Likert-style questionnaire. There are currently three versions of the scale (A Familism Scale, A Familism Scale: Extended Family Integration, and A Familism Scale: Nuclear Family Integration), all of which are reproduced in Bardis (1988). The Familism Scale was designed to measure attitudes and values directed toward the family as a social entity. Questions relate to support for, and loyalty toward, members of the extended family, including parents, brothers and sisters, in-laws, aunts, uncles, and cousins. Respondents are instructed to indicate their level of agreement, from *strongly disagree* (coded 0) to *strongly agree* (coded 4), with each statement as it relates to families in general. This perspective differs from most other instruments in that responses are not made from a consideration of one's own family, but rather from the perspective of an overall impression of familial relations in general. An overall familism score is obtained by summing responses to each of the items. No items are reversed-scored. Scores can range from 0 to 64, with higher scores indicating more familistic attitudes. The

Familism Scale has been translated into various languages and has been used cross-culturally to investigate this construct.

Sample Items:

(A)   A person should always support his uncles and aunts if they are in need.
(B)   The family should consult close relatives (uncles, aunts, first cousins) concerning its important decisions.
(C)   The family should have the right to control the behavior of each of its members completely.

Comments: Split-half reliability has been reported to range from .77 to .84. One-month test-retest reliability is reported to be .90. A factor analysis of the scale (Rao & Rao, 1979) indicates the presence of two factors measuring nuclear familism and extended familism.

References:

Bardis, P. D. (1959). A familism scale. *Mar Fam Living, 21,* 340–341.
Bardis, P. D. (1988). *Marriage and family: Continuity, change and adjustment.* Dubuque, IA: Kendall-Hunt.
Blair, M. J. (1972). An evaluation of the Bardis Familism Scale. *J Mar Fam, 34,* 265–268.
Rao, V. V. P., & Rao, V. N. (1979). An evaluation of the Bardis Familism Scale in India. *J Mar Fam, 41,* 417–421.

II-1/IV-1/g/W
120. BECKMAN, L. J. The Motivations for Children and Work Questionnaire

Avail: 1979a & 1979b Refs.

Variables Measured: Women's rewards and costs associated with having children and working

Type of Instrument: Self-report questionnaire

Instrument Description: This instrument is a 7-point, 112-item questionnaire. Response options are scored from 1 to 7, and range from *of no importance* to *extremely important.* Items are designed to be asked in an interview format, but the questionnaire could also be paper-and-pencil administered. An earlier 60-item version examined costs and rewards of having additional children and of working. The current version examines three constructs: satisfactions and costs associated with parenthood in general, employment, and costs and rewards of having an additional child. Items related to costs and rewards associated with an additional child are not available in the published sources. The other portions of the scale, however, are available. The scale has been used primarily in studies examining roles and levels of satisfaction of women. Interviews in which the total scale was used lasted an average of 70 minutes.

Sample Items:

(A)   (Reward of parenthood) Contribution to society by raising a good person.
(B)   (Cost of employment) Problems and strain in marital relationship.
(C)   (Reward of employment) Sense of fulfillment.

Comments: The author reports that satisfaction with parenthood is correlated .45 with motivation for parenthood, and that rewards of parenthood is correlated .48 with rewards of additional children. Additional correlations were computed for costs of parenthood and costs of additional children (.60), and between satisfaction with employment and satisfaction with parenthood (-.05) and motivation for parenthood (-.02).

References:

Beckman, L. J. (1977). Exchange theory and fertility-related decision-making. *J Soc Psych, 103*, 265–276.

Beckman, L. J. (1978). The relative rewards and costs of parenthood and employment for employed women. *Psych Wom Q, 2*, 215–234.

Beckman, L. J. (1979). Fertility preferences and social exchange theory. *J Appl So P, 9*, 147–169.

Beckman, L. J., & Houser, B. B. (1979). Perceived satisfactions and costs of motherhood and employment among married women. *J Populat, 2*, 306–327.

II-1/c
121. FARBER, B. Index of Consensus

Avail: 1957 Ref.

Variables Measured: Values taken into account by the family in making decisions

Type of Instrument: Rank-ordering

Instrument Description: The Index of Consensus consists of 10 values, which, for all but one item, are accompanied by definitions that are rank-ordered by family members. Statements are presented in random order. Respondents are asked to indicate the relative importance of each value by placing the number "1" by the item believed to be most important in judging the success of families, followed by the number "2" by the next most important, and so on, until all 10 items are numbered. The author indicates four aims in developing the specific items: (1) to stress values relevant to family decision making, (2) to permit designation of specific hierarchies of values, (3) to use general definitions that would be applicable to a wide audience, and (4) to cover as many basic issues related to family values as possible with a limited number of items. The instrument was designed to be simultaneously, but independently, administered to both marital partners. While the items were intended to be read by the respondent, the author indicated that it was occasionally necessary to read items aloud to participants. Rank-ordering of husbands and their wives are then compared utilizing correlational techniques.

Sample Items:

(A)   A place in the community. The ability of a family to give its members a respected place in the community and to make them good citizens (not criminals or undesirable people).

(B)   Healthy and happy children.

(C)   Satisfaction in affection shown. Satisfaction of family members with amount of affection shown and of the husband and wife in their sex life.

Comments: The Index of Consensus is also referred to in the literature as the Farber Index of Consensus, and as the Value Consensus Index. At one time, it was combined with another instrument by Farber, the Role Tension Index (1956), with the combined instrument referred to as the Marital Integration Index. Rho values for the Index of Consensus are reported to range from -.64 to +.88.

References:

Craddock, A. E. (1977). Relationships between authoritarianism, marital power expectations, and marital value systems. *Aust J Psyc, 29,* 211–221.

Craddock, A. E. (1980). Marital problem-solving as a function of couples' marital power expectations and marital value systems. *J Mar Fam, 42,* 185–196.

Farber, B. (1957). An index of marital integration. *Sociometry, 20,* 117–134.

Hoffman, S. R., & Levant, R. F. (1985). A comparison of childfree and child-anticipated married couples. *Fam Relat, 34,* 197–203.

II-1/c
122. FAVER, C. A. Family Values Scale

Avail: 1981, 1982a, & 1982b Refs.

Variables Measured: Value assigned by an individual to forming and rearing a family

Type of Instrument: Self-report questionnaire

Instrument Description: The purpose of the scale is to measure the value or importance assigned by an individual to the attainment and experiences of family formation and family interaction. The scale consists of three statements, each of which has five response alternatives ranging from *agree* to *disagree*. Each item is scored from 1 to 5, with high scores representing high family values. The final score for the scale is obtained by averaging the scores on the individual items. The three items were developed by Jean D. Manis of the University of Michigan's Center for Continuing Education of Women and were included in a mailed questionnaire survey conducted by the center.

Sample Items:

(A) The rewards and satisfactions of raising a family are more important to me than anything else.

(B) I would not take a job that would interfere with the things I like to do with my family.

(C) I can't imagine having a fully satisfying life without having children.

Comments: The author reports that analyses of one study population utilizing the Family Values Scale revealed that a dichotomous variable derived from the scale was related to age, marital status, life cycle stage, and employment status. It is also reported that in the 45- to 64-year-old cohort, level of family values interacted with marital status in predicting life satisfaction.

References:

Faver, C. A. (1981). Women, careers, and family: Generational and life-cycle effects on achievement orientation. *J Fam Iss, 2,* 91–112.

Faver, C. A. (1982a). Achievement orientation, attainment values, and women's employment. *J Vocat Beh, 20,* 67–80.

Faver, C. A. (1982b). Life satisfaction and the life-cycle: The effects of values and roles on women's well-being. *Sociol Soc Res, 66,* 435–451.

II-1/III-1/b/P

123. FAWCETT, J. T. Value of Children (VOC)

Avail: 1975 Ref.

Variables Measured: Beliefs regarding the functions of children and childbearing

Type of Instrument: Self-report questionnaire

Instrument Description: The VOC scale is a 45-item Likert-style questionnaire designed to elicit beliefs and values associated with having children. The scale was one portion (question 42) of an extensive cross-cultural interview questionnaire utilized in a study of attitudes toward children (Arnold et al., 1975). The complete interview lasted an average of 77 minutes and covered over 400 items. Interviews were completed with subjects from six countries, each with its own unique culture and customs regarding child rearing. The VOC portion of the questionnaire is described as utilizing an unusual 7-point response format. Respondents are initially asked to decide whether they primarily *agree* or *disagree* with each item, followed by further questioning regarding the level of their agreement or disagreement. This format was used due to the author's beliefs that opposite-pole continuum scales yielded little meaningful information in some cultures, particularly those where respondents had little formal education. Items for which subjects failed to respond were coded "4" on the scale, with disagreement responses being coded 1–3, and agreement responses coded 5–7. The 45-item final version resulted from experimentation with earlier, and larger, versions. The final version was designed such that constructs of interest were each measured by at least two items. The author indicates that the scale was not constructed with psychometric considerations of validity and reliability in mind, but that statistical criteria were utilized in refining the scale at various points. Nine subscales of the VOC were identified and served as the basis for analyses: (1) continuity, tradition, security; (2) parenthood satisfactions; (3) role motivations; (4) happiness and affection; (5) goals and incentives; (6) social status; (7) external control; (8) costs of children; and (9) decision-mindedness.

Sample Items:

(A)   Caring for children is a tedious and boring job.

(B)   A good reason for having children is that they can help when parents are too old to work.

(C)   It is only with a child that a person can feel completely free to express his love and affection.

Comments: The VOC was used by the Arnold et al. (1975) to compare attitudes toward children among urban and rural samples in Korea, Taiwan, Japan, Hawaii, Philippines, and Thailand. Data on this as well as other portions of the study are presented in that reference.

References:

Arnold, F., Bulatao, R. A., Buripakdi, C., Chung, B. J., Fawcett, J. T., Iritani, T., Lee, S. J., & Wu, T. S. (1975). *The value of children: A cross-national study: Vol. 1. Introduction and comparative analysis.* Honolulu, HI: East-West Center, East-West Population Institute.

Heltsley, M. E., Warren, R. D., & Lu, H. H. M. (1981). Determinants of family size for low-income families: Sex role orientation and value of children. *Home Ec Res J, 9,* 284–296.

Leavy, R. L., & Hough, O. B. (1983). The value and cost of children: Cross-generational and sex differences in perceptions among parents. *Home Ec Res J, 12,* 57–62.

Miller, J. A., Jacobsen, R. B., & Bigner, J. J. (1981). Liberal arts versus vocational college students and the value of children: A comparative analysis. *J Coll Stud Pers, 22,* 436–440.

II-1/d/b
124. GALLAGHER, B. J., III. The Generationalism Scale

Avail: NAPS-3

Variables Measured: Modern versus traditional attitudes

Type of Instrument: Self-report questionnaire

Instrument Description: The Generationalism Scale is a 23-item scale originally designed to measure differences in modern and traditional values and attitudes of persons from different generations. However, the author reports that it is equally valuable in examining differences between any two groups of respondents. Questions posed in the questionnaire are answered according to a 5-point Likert-style response format ranging from *definitely yes* to *definitely no.* The author defines modernity as a set of attitudes, beliefs, behaviors, and so on especially characterizing persons in highly urbanized, highly industrialized, and highly educated social settings. Modern and traditional items are presented in a mixed order throughout the questionnaire. Scores are determined for seven subscales, including child rearing, religion, political activism, the role of women in society, sexual freedom, prerequisites for marriage, and social mobility.

Sample Items:

(A)   Do you think physical punishment should be a significant part of parental discipline?
(B)   Do you believe that churches have a strong obligation to upgrade the general morality?
(C)   Should a person get involved in a public issue involving him?

Comments: The author reports that items were selected based on personal interviews with students, peers, members of older generations, and experts in the field of the family as well as on newspaper questionnaires on computer dating. Validity testing was conducted by having undergraduate college students during the spring and fall of 1970 rate the items along a conservative-liberal continuum. These evaluations were utilized in changing, adding, and deleting items from the original instrument. Split-half reliability is reported by the author to be .77.

References:

Gallagher, B. J., III (1974). An empirical analysis of attitude differences between three kin-related generations. *Youth Soc, 5,* 327–349.

Gallagher, B. J., III (1976). Ascribed and self-reported attitude differences between generations. *Pac Sociol Rev, 19,* 317–332.

Gallagher, B. J., III (1979). Attitude differences across three generations: Class and sex components. *Adolescence, 14,* 503–516.

II-1/g
125. GLEZER, H. Traditional Family Values

Avail: 1988 Ref.

Variables Measured: Support for traditional family values

Type of Instrument: Self-report questionnaire

Instrument Description: Traditional Family Values is a 5-point, Likert-type questionnaire designed to assess support for traditional values of marriage as a worthwhile institution, the importance to a marriage of having children, sexual fidelity among marital partners, and the maintenance of traditional gender roles among married couples. Items are in the form of statements to which respondents indicate the extent of their agreement or disagreement. Responses are scored 1–5, and range from *strongly disagree* to *strongly agree*. Scores are computed by summing values associated with each response. Some items are reverse-scored, such that higher scores indicate greater levels of traditionalism. Subscales for this instrument were not established by the author. The scale was developed for, and to date has been used only with, Australian families. However, it is appropriate for use with any national or cultural population. The version of the scale available in Amato (1988) includes two items that have been altered due to the specific aims of the study reported on in that article. Amato did not indicate the original content of the two altered items.

Sample Items:

(A)   You need two parents to bring up a child.
(B)   Married people are happier.
(C)   A woman is only fulfilled when she becomes a mother.

Comments: Cronbach's alpha for the Traditional Family Values scale is reported in Amato (1988) to be .83.

Reference:

Amato, P. R. (1988). Parental divorce and attitudes toward marriage and family life. *J Mar Fam, 50,* 453–461.

II-1/IV-1/c
126. LEVINSON, D. J., & HUFFMAN, P. E. Traditional Family Ideology Scale (TFI)

Avail: 1955 Ref.

Variables Measured: Traditional values, roles, and relationships within the family

Type of Instrument: Self-report questionnaire

Instrument Description: The TFI is a 7-point, 40-item Likert-type questionnaire developed in 1950 to examine traditional values and styles of relationships within families. Items are in the form of statements and measure attitudes within four dimensions: (1) parent-child relationships and child-rearing techniques (15 items), (2) husband-wife roles and relationships (8 items), (3) general male-female relationships and concepts of masculinity and femininity (13 items), and (4) general values and aims for the family (4 items). Response options range from *strong agreement* to *strong disagreement,* and are scored on a scale ranging from +3 to -3. Six items are intended to identify a democratic orientation within the family. The remaining items are divided between five overlapping dimensions of authoritarian or autocratic orientation. These five dimensions are not considered to be independent, with some items being scored on more than one subscale. Subscales (and the number of items within that scale) are conventionalism (13), authoritarian submission (15), exaggerated masculinity and femininity (20), extreme emphasis on discipline (8), and moralistic rejection of impulse life (12). The only scoring procedure suggested by the authors is the computation of an overall score, derived by summing response values from each item.

Sample Items:

(A)   A man who does not provide well for his family ought to consider himself pretty much a failure as husband and father.

(B)   A child should not be allowed to talk back to his parents, or else he will lose respect for them.

(C)   Some equality in marriage is a good thing, but by and large the husband ought to have the main say-so in family matters.

Comments: Split-half reliability of the TFI is reported to be .84. The author reports on the construction of a 12-item short form of the TFI that reportedly correlated .67 with authoritarianism, .64 with ethnocentrism, and .46 with religious conventionalism. Test-retest reliability of the short form over a period of six weeks was reported by the authors to be .93.

References:

Alper, T. G. (1974). Achievement motivation in college women: A now-you-see-it-now-you-don't phenomenon. *Am Psychol, 29,* 194–203.

Levinson, D. J., & Huffman, P. E. (1955). Traditional family ideology and its relation to personality. *J Personal, 23,* 251–273.

Richmond-Abbott, M. (1984). Sex-role attitudes of mothers and children in divorced, single-parent families. *J Divorce, 8*(1), 61–81.

Strong, L. D. (1978). Alternative marital and family forms: Their relative attractiveness to college students and correlates of willingness to participate in nontraditional forms. *J Mar Fam, 40,* 493–503.

II-1/II-4/c

127. MERCIER, J. M. Attitudes Towards Family Planning Education Scale

Avail: 1980 Ref.

Variables Measured: Attitudes related to several practical and moral issues of family planning education

Type of Instrument: Self-report questionnaire

Instrument Description: This instrument is composed of 66 Likert-style items intended for assessing attitudes of individuals toward family planning education and for providing information about adolescent sexuality. It was designed for use in developing curriculum in family planning education. Eight separate dimensions are measured: community effect, educational setting, family integration, family size and spacing, goals, premarital sex, religious and moral issues, and responsibility. Subjects indicate their level of agreement or disagreement with each item on a 12-point scale. Responses are scored such that intervals between response options are greatest at the extremes. Thus, indicating *extreme disagreement* with a statement is scored "0," while *extreme agreement* is scored "16." Responses near the middle of the continuum (*simple agreement or disagreement*) are scored 1 point apart from each other, while those at the extremes differ from their nearest neighbors by 3 points. The instrument takes less than one half hour to administer and is appropriate for use with all age groups from junior high on up.

Sample Items:

(A)   Family planning can help couples to improve their relationship.

(B)   Family planning needs to be taught so that parents can decide timing and spacing of their children.

(C)   Abortion is an unacceptable method of birth control.

Comments: The instrument was developed according to theoretical conceptualization. Dimensions and items related to each dimension were evaluated by a panel of four specialists in family planning. Data relative to the refinement of the scale were analyzed using interitem correlations, alpha estimates of reliability, and factor analysis. The author reports that Cronbach's alpha for the final dimensions ranged from .56 to .87 in a study of secondary students, and from .69 to .88 with a sample of adults. Further reliability information is available in Mercier (1980).

References:

Mercier, J. M. (1980). Development of an instrument to measure attitudes toward family planning education. *Iowa State J of Research, 55,* 99–118.

Mercier, J. M. (1984). Family planning education: How do adults feel about it? *Fam Relat, 33,* 523–530.

Mercier, J. M., & Hughes, R. P. (1981). Attitudes of selected secondary students toward family planning education. *Home Ec Res J, 10,* 127–136.

II-1/g
128. O'BRYANT, S. L. Subjective Value of Home Scale

Avail: O'Bryant & Wolf, 1983

Variables Measured: Attachment to the home as measured by traditional family orientation, competence in a familiar environment, cost versus comfort trade-off, and status value of home ownership

Type of Instrument: Self-report questionnaire

Instrument Description: The Subjective Value of Home Scale is a 24-item Likert-style instrument developed to assist in understanding and measuring the subjective meaning of home. It was developed primarily for use with elderly persons, but could be used in evaluations of home with subjects of any age. The overall instrument contains from 5 to 7 randomly ordered items from each of the four subscales listed above. All items are scored using a 6-response option format ranging from *strongly disagree* to *strongly agree*. Administration time is approximately 15 minutes.

Sample Items:

(A)   I would not want to give up my home because it's our family home.
(B)   I can walk around my place in the dark because I know where everything is.
(C)   My residence is costing me more than it's worth.

Comments: The original scale contained 52 items. The current 24-item version resulted from a factor analysis with varimax rotation on data utilizing all original items. The author reports that items with structure loadings of at least .37 only were retained in the final version. Subsequent research by the author has investigated the relationship of subscale scores to housing satisfaction, intention to move, and actual relocation. Cronbach's alpha for the subscales is reported to be .81 (traditional family orientation), .72 (competence in a familiar environment), .74 (cost versus comfort trade-off), and .85 (status value of home ownership).

References:

O'Bryant, S. L. (1983). The subjective value of "home" to older homeowners. *J Housing Eld, 1,* 29–44.

O'Bryant, S. L., & McGloshen, T. H. (1987). Older widow's intentions to stay or move from their homes. *Home Ec Res J, 15,* 177–183.

O'Bryant, S. L., & Nocera, D. (1985). The psychological significance of homeownership to older women. *Psych Wom Q, 9,* 107–115.

O'Bryant, S. L., & Wolf, S. (1983). Explanations of housing satisfaction of older homeowners and renters. *Res Aging, 5,* 217–233.

II-1/d
129. ROBERTSON, J. F. Meaning of Grandparenthood

Avail: 1982 Ref.

Variables Measured: Values associated with being a grandparent

Type of Instrument: Self-report questionnaire

Instrument Description: This instrument is a 5-point, 29-item Likert-style questionnaire designed to assess feelings, beliefs, values, and attitudes toward being a grandparent. Items are in the form of statements, and are responded to according to a 5-point format ranging from 1 = *strongly agree* to 5 = *strongly disagree.* The scale is based on interaction theory (Mead, 1934), which states that role concepts are different from behaviors associated with those roles, and that concepts precede behaviors. Thus this instrument was designed to examine the concepts, or role definitions and expectations, associated with being a grandparent. The construct of the grandparent role is examined in the current scale through two dimensions, labeled personal dimension and social dimension. Scores on the two dimensions are interpreted as classifying grandparents into one of four types: (1) high scorers on both dimensions are classified as apportioned role meaning type; (2) low scorers on both dimensions are classified as remote type; (3) persons classified as high on the personal but low on the social dimensions are classified as individualized; and (4) respondents scoring low on personal and high on social dimensions are classified as symbolic types.

Sample Items:

(A)   I would tell my grandchildren to always remember that love and companionship are more important to a successful marriage than money.

(B)   Going to visit a friend for Christmas is more enjoyable than having Christmas with one's family.

(C)   Life would be very lonely for me without my grandchildren.

Comments: The author indicated that, in developing a pure system of classification, several items were removed. This resulted in only 12 items that were substantially related to the two dimensions. Data on these 12 items, along with the rationale for keeping only this relatively small group, are contained in Robertson (1977). The complete 29-item scale appears in the source of availability noted above.

References:

Mindel, C. H. (1982). Kinship relations. In D. J. Mangen & W. A. Peterson (Eds.), *Research instruments in social gerontology: Vol. 2. Social roles and social participation* (pp. 187–229). Minneapolis: University of Minnesota Press.

Robertson, J. F. (1975). Interaction in three-generation families, parents as mediators: Towards a theoretical perspective. *Int J Aging Hum Dev, 6,* 103–110.

Robertson, J. F. (1977). Grandmotherhood: A study of role conceptions. *J Mar Fam, 39,* 165–174.

II-1/c

130. SOURANI, T., & ANTONOVSKY, A. Family Sense of Coherence Scale (FSOC)

Avail: 1988 Ref.

Variables Measured: Ability of families to comprehend and manage meaningful stimuli presented by various outside forces

Type of Instrument: Self-report questionnaire

Instrument Description: The FSOC is a 7-point, 26-item semantic differential scale. Thus specific response options differ with each item. It was designed to measure the extent to which the family, as perceived by the original respondent, is confident that the stimuli impinging upon it in the realm of family life are comprehensible, that it has resources to manage demands posed by these stimuli, and that these demands are challenges worthy of engagement. The scale was designed such that scores reflect how the family perceives family life, as opposed to perceptions of the individual respondent. The questionnaire was developed for use in either interview or self-completion form. The original scale was written in Hebrew and used in Israel. An English translation is available in the source indicated above. Item scores are summed, with various methods of assessing overall family scores discussed in Antonovsky and Sourani (1988). Administration time is approximately 10–15 minutes.

Sample Items:

(A) When you have to get things done which depend on cooperation among all members of the family, your feeling is: (there's almost no chance that the things will get done . . . the things will always get done).

(B) Let's assume that unexpected guests are about to arrive and the house isn't set up to receive them. Does it seem to you that: (the job will fall on one person . . . all the members of the family will pitch in to get the house ready).

(C) Family life seems to you (full of interest . . . totally routine).

Comments: The authors report that Cronbach's alpha for the FSOC is approximately .92. Correlations between scores obtained by husbands and wives averaged .71 to .77.

References:

Antonovsky, A. (1987). *Unraveling the mystery of health.* San Francisco: Jossey-Bass.
Antonovsky, A., & Sourani, T. (1988). Family sense of coherence and family adaptation. *J Mar Fam, 50,* 79–92.

II-2/a

131. AZRIN, N. H., NASTER, B. J., & JONES, R. Marital Happiness Scale

Avail: 1973 Ref.

Variables Measured: Marital happiness with regard to household responsibilities, child rearing, social activities, money, communication, sex, academic or vocational progress, personal independence, and personal habits

Type of Instrument: Self-report questionnaire

Instrument Description: The Marital Happiness Scale is a one-page, 10-item questionnaire for evaluating marital happiness in therapy settings. The scale is designed to provide a rapid measure of happiness at the start of each therapy session. The instrument identifies specific areas of marital distress and happiness, thereby allowing the therapist to work with the couple more efficiently and effectively. Little or no scoring time is needed. Respondents circle their percentage of happiness, listed from 0% to 100% in increments of 10, for each item. The therapist can either average the scores or use only the final item to gauge overall happiness.

Sample Items:

- (A) Household responsibilities
- (B) Rearing of children
- (C) Social activities

Comments: Although specific reliability and validity information was not available, the authors report that average scores have been found to remain constant when readministered daily or weekly over a period of three weeks in the absence of directive therapy. They report that scores generally increase within one week when behavioral marital therapy is used as an intervention.

References:

Azrin, N. H., Besalel, V. A., Bechtel, R., Michalicek, A., Mancera, M., Carroll, D., Shuford, D., & Cox, J. (1980). Comparison of reciprocity and discussion-type counseling for marital problems. *Am J Fam Th, 8*(4), 21–28.

Azrin, N. H., Naster, B. J., & Jones, R. (1973). Reciprocity counseling: A rapid learning-based procedure for marital counseling. *Behav Res T, 11,* 365–382.

II-2/a
132. BAHR, S. J., CHAPPELL, C. B., & LEIGH, G. K. Marital Satisfaction

Avail: 1983 Ref.

Variables Measured: Quality of and satisfaction with marriage

Type of Instrument: Self-report questionnaire

Instrument Description: This 10-item, 5-point Likert-style questionnaire is designed to measure the extent to which an individual is satisfied with his or her current marriage. Item scores within factors are summed.

Sample Items:

- (A) If you were to marry again, would you want to marry the same person? (There are five possible responses ranging from *yes, certainly* to *no, certainly.*)
- (B) In relation to the marriages of my friends and associates, I would say my marriage is: (There are five possible responses ranging from *much more satisfying* to *much less satisfying.*)

Comments: The 10 items were chosen after a review of existing studies and scales of marital satisfaction. For both husbands and wives, a factor analysis revealed a single factor. This factor was found to account for over 50% of the variance for each sample. All item loadings on this factor were in excess of .60. Theta was reported by the authors to be .89 for husbands and .91 for wives.

Reference:

Bahr, S. J., Chappell, C. B., & Leigh, G. K. (1983). Age at marriage, role enactment, role consensus, and marital satisfaction. *J Mar Fam, 45,* 795–803.

II-2/a

133. BEIER, E. G., & STERNBERG, D. P. Beier-Sternberg Discord Questionnaire (DQ)

Avail: 1987 Ref.

Variables Measured: Marital discord, conflict, and happiness related to typical marital issues and concerns among newlywed couples

Type of Instrument: Self-report questionnaire

Instrument Description: The DQ is a 10-topic questionnaire requiring 5 to 10 minutes to complete. It is self-administered and completed independently by each spouse. It was designed for use by couples in their first marriage who have been married from three to six months. The purpose of the questionnaire is to obtain data about degree of conflict over topics described as major problems in marriage, and the degree of unhappiness attached to such disagreements. Each topic is first rated on a 7-point Likert-style scale for degree of agreement between spouses regarding the topic. For each topic the respondent is then asked to indicate the level of happiness or unhappiness (again on a 7-point Likert scale) disagreements in each area cause him or her. Ratings from each scale are averaged. Individual topical ratings are also compared.

Sample Items:

(A)   Money.
(B)   Doing things together in spare time.
(C)   Religion.

Comments: The authors report that the DQ was found to have some relationship with nonverbal behaviors such as eye contact, self- and other-touching, and open or closed postural positions. They also report that the subscales are significantly correlated with each other, indicating that conflict is related to unhappiness.

References:

Beier, E. G., & Sternberg, D. P. (1977). Subtle cues between newlyweds. *J Comm, 27,* 92–97.
Beier, E. G., & Sternberg, D. P. (1987). Beier-Sternberg Discord Questionnaire. In K. Corcoran & J. Fischer, *Measures for clinical practice* (pp. 419–420). New York: Free Press.
Sternberg, D. P., & Beier, E. G. (1977). Changing patterns of conflict. *J Comm, 27,* 97–100.

II-2/V-3/a

134. BOOTH, A., JOHNSON, D. R., EDWARDS, J. N., & WHITE, L. Nebraska Scale of Marital Instability

Avail: 1983 & 1987 Refs.

Variables Measured: Marital instability and the propensity to divorce

Type of Instrument: Self-report questionnaire. May be used as a paper-and-pencil measure or in an interview format

Instrument Description: This 13-item scale includes both a cognitive component (thinking the marriage is in trouble or considering the idea of getting a divorce) and actions (discussing the possibility with spouse, friends, clergy, and so on). The scale taps both frequency and timing of indicators. Behavior or views held within the last three years or currently were assigned more weight than those held earlier. A clinical version of the scale is also available.

Sample Items:

(A)   Even people who get along quite well with their spouse sometimes wonder whether their marriage is working out. Have you ever thought your marriage might be in trouble? Have you thought this within the last three years? Do you feel this way now?

(B)   As far as you know has the thought of getting a divorce ever crossed your (husband's/wife's) mind in the last three years? Is (he/she) thinking about it now?

(C)   Because of problems people are having with their marriage, they sometimes leave home either for a short time or as a trial separation. Has this ever happened to you? Has this happened within the last three years?

Comments: The scale was administered to a national sample of 2,033 married men and women under 55 years of age in 1980 and again in 1983. Cronbach's alpha is reported to be .91. Validity was assessed in a number of ways. A panel of 36 experts ranked the items according to potential for predicting dissolution. The correlation between judges' ratings on items and scale scores by participants is reported to be .80. Scale scores were also correlated with the incidence of divorce reported in a reinterview of the original sample in 1983. Among those reporting no signs of instability in 1980, 3% were divorced or permanently separated three years later. Of those scoring high in 1980, 27% were divorced by 1983.

References:

Booth, A., Johnson, D., & Edwards, J. (1983). Measuring marital instability. *J Mar Fam, 45,* 387–394.

Booth, A., Johnson, D., White, L., & Edwards, J. (1984). Women, outside employment, and marital instability. *Am J Sociol, 90,* 567–583.

Edwards, J., Johnson, D., & Booth, A. (1987). Coming apart: A prognostic instrument of marital breakup. *Fam Relat, 36,* 168–170.

II-2/a
135. BOWEN, G. L. Marital Quality Scale (MQS)

Avail: NAPS-3

Variables Measured: Affectional expression, marital leisure agreement, general marital consensus, marital satisfaction, and communication apprehension

Type of Instrument: Self-report questionnaire. May be used as a paper-and-pencil measure or in an interview format

Instrument Description: The MQS is a 27-item Likert-style scale divided into the five theoretically and empirically derived subscales listed above. It was designed to assess the quality of the couple's relationship as a functioning dyad. Although originally constructed for use in personal interview surveys, it may also be administered by telephone or mail. To calculate a score on the MQS, all survey items are first recoded to range from 0 to 4. Items are coded so that low scores indicate high marital quality. Items within subscales are summed and averaged in order to determine the overall level of marital quality.

Sample Items: Most persons have disagreements in the relationships. Please indicate the letter that best corresponds to the degree of agreement or disagreement you and your partner have in the following areas:

(A)   Handling family finances.
(B)   Ways of dealing with parents and in-laws.
(C)   How do you feel about the companionship that you and your spouse have in doing

things together during leisure or non-work time? Do you feel the companionship is very good, okay, or not so good?

Comments: The MQS is a factor analyzed adaptation of the Dyadic Adjustment Scale by Spanier and from the measure of Communication Apprehension by Powers and Hutchinson. The author reports Cronbach's alpha ranged from .73 for the affectional expression subscale to .91 for the combined MQS score.

Reference:

Bowen, G. L., & Orthner, D. K. (1983). Sex-role congruency and marital quality. *J Mar Fam, 45,* 223–230.

II-2/a
136. BURGESS, E. W. A Marriage Adjustment Form

Avail: 1939 & 1953 Refs., & from Family Life Publications, P.O. Box 427, Saluda, NC 28773

Variables Measured: Marital adjustment or success

Type of Instrument: Self-report questionnaire

Instrument Description: The Marriage Adjustment Form is a three-part questionnaire intended to assess husbands' and wives' adjustment to marriage. The scale was first published in 1939 (Burgess & Cottrell, 1939), and was reprinted 14 years later (Burgess & Locke, 1953). It is also currently available through Family Life Publications. Items are stated and answered in various formats, with two sections containing Likert-type items and the third being composed of a checklist. Some items contain several parts. The three primary groups of items were designed to assess: (1) personal levels of satisfaction with various aspects of marriage such as affection, confiding, methods of settling disagreements, and loneliness; (2) frequency of disagreement over family life matters; and (3) sources of unhappiness in the marriage. Husbands and wives are asked to fill out the inventory independently, with scores being derived for each. Items are scored according to a system of predetermined weights. Estimated administration time for the Marriage Adjustment Form is 30–50 minutes.

Sample Items: The publisher did not grant permission to reproduce items.

Comments: The Marriage Adjustment Form will probably be of greatest use as an aid in premarital counseling. Scoring procedures are available, with high scores indicative of greater adjustment. While this instrument does not offer a direct prediction of success or failure in marriage, it does allow for ratings of the couple ranging from extremely well adjusted to extremely maladjusted.

References:

Burgess, E. W. (1984). The Marriage Prediction Schedule. In *1984 resource guide* (p. 4). Saluda, NC: Family Life Publications.
Burgess, E. W., & Cottrell, L. S. (1939). *Predicting success or failure in marriage.* New York: Prentice-Hall.
Burgess, E. W., & Locke, H. J. (1953). *The family: From institution to companionship.* New York: American Book Company.
Burgess, E. W., & Wallin, P. (1953). *Engagement and marriage.* New York: Lippincott.

II-2/a
137. BURGESS, E. W. A Marriage Prediction Schedule

Avail: 1939 & 1953 Refs., & from Family Life Publications, P.O. Box 427, Saluda, NC 28773

Variables Measured: Variables associated with successful marriages

Type of Instrument: Self-report questionnaire

Instrument Description: The Marriage Prediction Schedule is a five-part questionnaire designed to assess the likely success or failure of a pending marriage. It was first published (Burgess & Cottrell, 1939) as the Burgess-Cottrell Marriage Prediction Schedule, and was later included in another source (Burgess & Locke, 1953) with a note that it was reproduced by permission of Ernest W. Burgess, Leonard S. Cottrell, Paul Wallin, and Harvey J. Locke. It is also currently available under the title noted above, with only Burgess listed as the author. The five sections contained in the instrument were designed to cover: (1) social position and elements of the respondent's relationship with his or her parents; (2) personality characteristics of the respondent, the prospective spouse, and the respondent's mother and father; (3) social relationships; (4) activities participated in with prospective mate; and (5) plans for living arrangements and life-style with mate following marriage. A factor analysis of items answered from the male perspective indicated the presence of five factors: psychogenic, cultural impress, SES, economic role, and affectional or response patterns. Items, both within and between subsections, carry various response options but are generally Likert-type in format. The scale is a total of 84 items in length, with an estimated administration time of 30–50 minutes.

Sample Items: The publisher did not grant permission to reproduce items.

Comments: The Marriage Prediction Schedule will probably be of greatest use as an aid in premarital counseling. Scoring procedures are available, with high scores indicative of greater adjustment. This instrument does not offer direct predictions of adjustment in marriage. However, the manual does indicate the percentage of persons with various ranges of scores who will have successful or unsuccessful marriages.

References:

Burgess, E. W. (1984). The Marriage Prediction Schedule. In *1984 resource guide* (p. 4). Saluda, NC: Family Life Publications.
Burgess, E. W., & Cottrell, L. S. (1939). *Predicting success or failure in marriage.* New York: Prentice-Hall.
Burgess, E. W., & Locke, H. J. (1953). *The family: From institution to companionship.* New York: American Book Company.
Burgess, E. W., & Wallin, P. (1953). *Engagement and marriage.* New York: Lippincott.

II-2/II-5/a
138. EDMONDS, V. H. Marital Conventionalization (MC) Scale

Avail: 1967 Ref.

Variables Measured: The extent to which a person distorts the appraisal of his marriage in the direction of social desirability

Type of Instrument: Self-report questionnaire

Instrument Description: This instrument is a 50-item scale designed to be the equivalent of a social desirability, or lie, scale for situations involving marital interactions and stability. The scale contains 34 *true/false* items developed to measure the stated construct, with an additional 16 items examining traditional areas of concern within marriages taken from the Burgess-Wallin Marital Happiness Scale. This latter group of 16 items was added in order to disguise the true purpose of the MC Scale. Only the 34 social desirability items are scored, with higher scores indicating a greater desire to display a socially desirable marital profile. An alternate form of the MC Scale, developed through item analyses of the original instrument, contains only 15 items.

Sample Items:

(A)   There are some things about my marriage that do not entirely please me.
(B)   There is never a moment that I do not feel "head over heels" in love with my mate.
(C)   I have never regretted my marriage, not even for a moment.

Comments: The author reports that the long and short forms of the MC Scale are correlated .99. The mean long-form score reported for a sample of 100 persons in the original validation study conducted in 1965 was 11.8 (SD = 8.3). The author also reports that MC Scale scores correlate .63 with the Locke-Wallace Short Scale of Marital Adjustment, indicating that there may be a conventionalization component to this other instrument. The percentage of respondents answering each item in a socially desirable direction, as well as item-total correlations, are listed in Edmonds (1967).

References:

Edmonds, V. H. (1967). Marital conventionalization: Definition and measurement. *J Mar Fam, 29,* 681–688.
Miller, P. C., Lefcourt, H. M., Holmes, J. G., Ware, E. E., & Saleh, W. E. (1986). Marital locus of control and marital problem solving. *J Pers Soc Psy, 51,* 161–169.
Schumm, W. R., Bollman, S. R., & Jurich, A. P. (1981). The validity of Edmonds' Marital Conventionalization Scale. *Psychol Rep, 109,* 65–71.
Wilson, M. R., & Filsinger, E. E. (1986). Religiosity and marital adjustment: Multidimensional interrelationships. *J Mar Fam, 48,* 147–151.

II-2/a
139. GILFORD, R., & BENGTSON, V. Two-Factor Marital Satisfaction Scale

Avail: 1979 & 1982 Refs.

Variables Measured: Spouses' evaluations of their relationship regarding positive marital interaction and negative sentiment

Type of Instrument: Self-report questionnaire

Instrument Description: This instrument is a 10-item Likert-style questionnaire utilizing a 5-point response format. Respondents are asked to read a list of "some things husbands and wives do when they are together" and to indicate "how often it happens between you and your spouse." Half of the items refer to positive interaction and half to negative sentiment. Possible responses range from *hardly ever* to *always*. It was designed to measure independent positive and negative factors underlying self-reported marital satisfaction. This conceptualization is based on Homan's (1974) exchange theory, which views human behavior in a relationship as maintained by actors' perceptions of rewards over costs in interaction and sentiment. Each factor is assessed through an examination of responses to 5 items. Item scores within factors are summed, yielding a positive interaction and a negative sentiment score, each ranging from 5 to 25.

Sample Items:

(A)   You calmly discuss something together.
(B)   One of you is sarcastic.
(C)   You laugh together.

Comments: The authors report two studies in which the scale has been used. In the first (1971), three generations of married respondents (n = 1,056), ages 17 to 93, were questioned using several instruments, including the Two-Factor Marital Satisfaction Scale. A factor analysis using a varimax rotation was conducted, from which the authors derived a two-factor solution. In the second study (1985), 832 persons from three generations were assessed. Data from each generational group were analyzed separately. The original factor structure was confirmed, with loadings on primary factors ranging from .46 to .86. Loadings on the secondary factor ranged from -.06 to -.48. Cronbach's alpha for this second administration ranged from .80 to .89. Average interitem correlations within the two factors ranged from .34 to .75 for various generational groups.

References:

Gilford, R., & Bengtson, V. (1979). Measuring marital satisfaction in three generations: Positive and negative dimensions. *J Mar Fam, 41,* 387–398.

Mangen, D. (1982). Dyadic relations. In D. Mangen & W. Peterson (Eds.), *Research instruments in social gerontology* (Vol. 2, pp. 62–64, 96–97). Minneapolis: University of Minnesota Press.

Markides, K., & Hoppe, S. (1985). Marital satisfaction in three generations of Mexican Americans. *Social Sci Q, 66,* 147–154.

II-2/a
140. GREEN, R. G. Inventory of Alternative Attractions (IAA)

Avail: NAPS-3

Variables Measured: The strength of a marital partner's attractions to alternative relationships, statuses, or benefits that would be available to them if they were not married to their present spouse

Type of Instrument: Self-report questionnaire

Instrument Description: The IAA is a 6-item questionnaire constructed to assess marital partners' perceptions of their degree of attraction to relationship alternatives. It also has been used retrospectively to assess divorced and separated persons' perceptions of the attractions they perceived during a previous relationship. The instrument asks respondents to consider particular time periods (e.g., the last six months) and to evaluate the frequency with which they were attracted to relationship benefits or statuses that would be available to them if they were not married to their present spouse. All items are questions tagged onto the stem "How often (during a designated time period) were you attracted to: . . . " These benefits and statuses include personal freedom, sexual relations, spending money, enjoyment from friends, respect from other people, and relationships with parents. Responses are made using a 5-point Likert-style format, with response options ranging from *never* to *always*. A total score, representing the strength of attractions to relationship alternatives, is obtained by summing all items.

Sample Items:

(A)   The spending money you might have if you were single or married to someone else?

(B)   The personal freedom you might have if you were single or married to someone else?
(C)   Having sexual relations with someone other than your spouse?

Comments: The author reports Cronbach's alpha to be .88. Concurrent criterion validity was evaluated by comparing IAA scores for divorced persons (16.9) with those of married persons (10.4). IAA scores were also found to correlate -.57 with scores on the Dyadic Adjustment Scale. The author also indicates that separate analyses revealed that reliability and validity coefficients did not differ by gender.

References:

Green, R. G. (1983). The influence of divorce prediction variables on divorce adjustment: An expansion and test of Lewis' and Spanier's theory of marital quality and marital stability. *J Divorce, 7*(1), 67–82.
Green, R. G., & Sporakowski, M. S. (1983). The dynamics of divorce: Marital quality, alternative attractions and external pressures. *J Divorce, 7*(2), 77–88.

II-2/a
141. HENDRICK, S. S. Relationship Assessment Scale

Avail: 1988 Ref.

Variables Measured: Satisfaction with a romantic or marital relationship

Type of Instrument: Self-report questionnaire

Instrument Description: The Relationship Assessment is a 5-point, 7-item Likert-style scale. It was developed as a generic measure of relationship satisfaction. This instrument was based on, and replaced, an earlier version of Hendrick's Marital Assessment Questionnaire. The author indicates that the Relationship Assessment Scale should be used for all future purposes, and that the Marital Assessment Questionnaire should no longer be used. Items are scored such that higher scores indicate greater relationship satisfaction. Items 4 and 7 are reverse-scored. The scale was designed for both clinical and research use. It is appropriate for married couples, couples who are living together, dating couples, gay couples, and, with minimal changes, even for friendships.

Sample Items:

(A)   How well does your partner meet your needs?
(B)   In general, how satisfied are you with your relationship?
(C)   How often do you wish you hadn't gotten into this relationship?

Comments: The author reports that Cronbach's alpha is .86. It is also indicated that the Relationship Assessment Scale correlated .80 with Spanier's Dyadic Adjustment Scale. Correlations have also been examined between this instrument and passionate love, altruistic love, self-disclosure to a lover, commitment, investment in the relationship, and game-playing love. In a discriminant analysis of couples staying together versus breaking up, the Relationship Assessment Scale correctly assigned 91% of the "together" couples and 86% of the "apart" couples.

References:

Hendrick, S. S. (1981). Self-disclosure and marital satisfaction. *J Pers Soc Psy, 40,* 1150–1159.

Hendrick, S. S. (1988). A generic measure of relationship satisfaction. *J Mar Fam, 50,* 93–98.

II-2/a
142. HONEYCUTT, J. M. Satisfaction with Marital Issues and Topics (SMI)

Avail: NAPS-3

Variables Measured: Couples' satisfaction with marital dimensions of interpersonal sharing, financial management, sexual enjoyment, and the issues of fidelity and drug use

Type of Instrument: Self-report questionnaire

Instrument Description: The SMI is designed to measure 21 different topics related to marital satisfaction. The author makes a distinction between marital *satisfaction* and marital *adjustment*, claiming that this instrument is meant only to measure the former. It is a 21-item Likert-style scale with seven response options for each item. Subjects circle the appropriate number depending on their level of satisfaction with that facet of the marital relationship, ranging from *extremely dissatisfied* (1) to *extremely satisfied* (7). Administration time is approximately 3–5 minutes.

Sample Items:

(A) Moral and religious beliefs and practices.
(B) My partner's job.
(C) How we communicate.

Comments: The SMI is an expanded version of the Problem Inventory (Gottman, Notarius, Gonso, & Markman, 1976). It also contains items originally found in Spanier's (1976) dyadic consensus measure. The author reports that Cronbach's alpha for the instrument is .92. Factor analyses have resulted in identification of the four factors mentioned in the "Variables Measured" section above. Reliabilities of the four factors range from .55 to .90. The author also reports that the overall scale correlates .80 with Norton's (1983) Quality Marriage Index (QMI) Scale, indicating that, the more spouses are satisfied with relational issues, the happier the marriage. The individual subscales of the SMI correlate from .38 to .74 with the QMI.

References:

Gottman, J. M., Notarius, L., Gonso, J., & Markman, H. (1976). *A couple's guide to communication.* Champaign, IL: Research Press.
Honeycutt, J. M. (1986). A model of marital functioning based on an attraction paradigm and social-penetration dimensions. *J Mar Fam, 48,* 651–659.
Norton, R. (1983). Measuring marital quality: A critical look at the dependent variable. *J Mar Fam, 45,* 141–151.
Spanier, G. B. (1976). Measuring dyadic adjustment: New scales for assessing the quality of marriage and similar dyads. *J Mar Fam, 38,* 15–28.

II-2/a
143. HOSKINS, C. N. The Partner Relationship Inventory (PRI)

Avail: Consulting Psychologists Press, Inc., 577 College Ave., Palo Alto, CA 94306

Variables Measured: Interactional, emotional, and sexual needs in relationships, and areas of conflict when needs are perceived as being unmet by one or both partners

Type of Instrument: Self-report questionnaire

Instrument Description: The PRI Long Form (80 items) and Forms IA and IB (40 items each) contain interactional and emotional needs scales. PRI Form II (33 items) has six alternate forms and includes a sexual needs scale along with a combined interactional/emotional needs scale. The test can be used either with one partner or with a couple in counseling. All forms consist of declarative statements with four response options (*definitely feel, feel slightly, cannot decide,* and *definitely do not feel*). The scales are offset from each other on the scoring key, with totals obtained by adding the appropriate columns. The higher the score on any one of the scales, the greater the perceived lack of fulfillment of those needs.

Sample Items:

(A) We do not think alike on many things.
(B) I long for more warmth and love from my partner.
(C) I feel my partner cares as much about my sexual satisfaction as his (her) own.

Comments: The author reports that correlations between various PRI scores and the Locke-Wallace Marital Adjustment Scale (Locke & Wallace, 1959) ranged from -.46 to -.73. The reliability of the PRI Long Form was evaluated by correlating morning and evening forms for each category. Reported correlations ranged from .84 to .95. Correlations between partner's scores on the interactional and emotional needs scales are reported between .50 and .59. Correlations between alternate forms IA and IB (40 items) for the interactional needs and emotional needs scales are reported to be .94 and .93, respectively. The author further reports that Cronbach's alpha on the six alternate forms (30 items) ranged from .64 to .91.

References:

Bowen, M. (1976). Theory in the practice of psychotherapy. In P. Guerin (Ed.), *Family therapy: Theory and practice.* New York: Gardner.

Hoskins, C. N. (1987). *The Partner Relationship Inventory.* Palo Alto, CA: Consulting Psychologists Press.

II-2/a
144. JOHNSON, D. R., BOOTH, A., WHITE, L., & EDWARDS, J. N. Nebraska Scale of Marital Happiness

Avail: 1986 Ref.

Variables Measured: Personal satisfaction or happiness with marriage

Type of Instrument: Self-report questionnaire

Instrument Description: This instrument comprises 11 items designed to assess the degree of personal satisfaction or happiness felt by an individual about his or her marriage. Item response formats vary, with individual items utilizing either 3- or 5-point response formats. The scale taps global feelings about the marriage, as well as the individual's evaluation of specific aspects of the relationship. It has been used in both telephone and personal interviews, as well as being administered in more traditional written questionnaire form.

Sample Items:

(A) I am going to mention some different aspects of married life. For each one, I would like you to tell me whether you are very happy, pretty happy, or not too happy with this aspect of your marriage. How happy are you with the amount of understanding you receive from your husband/wife?

(B) Would you say your feelings of love for your husband/wife are extremely strong, very strong, pretty strong, not too strong, or not strong at all?

(C) Compared to other marriages you know about, do you think your marriage is better than most, about the same as most, or not as good as most?

Comments: The authors report that the scale was administered to a national probability sample of 2,033 married men and women under 55 years of age in 1980 and again in 1983. Cronbach's alpha is reported by the authors to be .86. The scale is reported to correlate negatively with marital problems (-.47), marital disagreement (-.47), marital instability (-.54), and positively with marital interaction (.46).

References:

Booth, A., Johnson, D., White, L., & Edwards, J. (1985). Predicting divorce and permanent separation. *J Fam Iss, 6,* 331–346.

Johnson, D., White, L., Edwards, J., & Booth, A. (1986). Dimensions of marital quality: Toward methodological and conceptual refinement. *J Fam Iss, 7,* 31–49.

White, L., & Booth, A. (1985). The quality and stability of remarriages: The role of stepchildren. *Am Sociol Rev, 50,* 689–698.

II-2/a
145. JOHNSON, D. R., BOOTH, A., WHITE, L., & EDWARDS, J. N.
Nebraska Scale of Marital Problems

Avail: 1986 Ref.

Variables Measured: Personal traits and behaviors that may have led to problems in the marriage

Type of Instrument: Self-report questionnaire

Instrument Description: This instrument contains 13 items, drawn from several sources, that indicate the extent to which personal traits and behaviors of either spouse have led to problems in the marriage. Although items may be answered through simple *yes-no* responses, no set response format was used with this questionnaire. The measure taps only one spouse's perception that problems exist; however, it is believed by the authors to be indicative of the nature of the marital relationship. The scale is designed to be used in personal and telephone interviews as well as in more conventional paper-and-pencil administration.

Sample Items: I'd like to mention a number of problem areas. Have you had a problem in your marriage because one of you:

(A) Gets angry easily? Which one of you?
(B) Has feelings that are easily hurt?
(C) Is domineering?

Comments: The authors report that the scale was administered to a national probability sample of 2,033 married men and women under 55 years of age in 1980 and again in 1983. Cronbach's alpha is reported by the authors to be .76. The scale is reported to correlate negatively with marital happiness (-.47) and interaction (-.28) and positively with marital disagreement (.54) and instability (.54).

References:

Booth, A., Johnson, D., White, L., & Edwards, J. (1985). Predicting divorce and permanent separation. *J Fam Iss, 6,* 331–346.
Johnson, D., White, L., Edwards, J., & Booth, A. (1986). Dimensions of marital quality: Toward methodological and conceptual refinement. *J Fam Iss, 7,* 31–49.
White, L., & Booth, A. (1985). The quality and stability of remarriages: The role of stepchildren. *Am Sociol Rev, 50,* 689–698.

II-2/a
146. KELSO, J., STEWART, M. A., BULLERS, L., & EGINTON, R.
Measure of Marital Satisfaction (MMS)

Avail: 1984 Ref.

Variables Measured: Areas of marital conflict

Type of Instrument: Self-report questionnaire

Instrument Description: The MMS is a 13-item questionnaire designed as a screening device for couples that might be experiencing marital difficulties. Response formats differ among items and include *yes-no* and multiple option (3–5 options per item) formats. Several items contain multiple parts, with each part receiving an independent score. The instrument was designed to be given to parents of children attending a psychiatric clinic, and is intended for use with both parents. The instructions somewhat mask the true intent of the questionnaire, stating that, in addition to influencing his or her own mental health, the child's behavior affects the outlook and behavior of the parent as well. In fact, the MMS is intended to allow therapists to recognize and intervene in stressful home environments and marriages. Details of scoring are provided in the reference listed below. Scores can range from 26 to 72, with higher scores evidencing greater levels of marital dissatisfaction.

Sample Items:

(A)   In the past six months, how often have you and your spouse agreed on ways of handling situations involving your children? (This question is followed by four activities, rated *always, usually,* or *sometimes.*)

(B)   Over the last six months, have you been getting on each other's nerves around the house?

(C)   In the past two years, have any of your quarrels led to physical violence and injury to each other? (This question is answered either *yes* or *no,* and followed by two questions inquiring about seeking medical treatment and police involvement.)

Comments: The authors report Cronbach's alpha for the entire instrument to be .95. Test-retest reliability over a two- to six-month period was assessed using a nonclinic population, and was found to be .81. The authors also used the MMS to compare samples of clinic parents with married and divorced control groups. They report that both divorced men and women controls had greater dissatisfaction than did married controls, and that married parents of clinic patients achieved scores lower than divorced couples but higher than married controls.

Reference:

Kelso, J., Stewart, M. A., Bullers, L., & Eginton, R. (1984). The Measure of Marital Satisfaction: A questionnaire to screen parents for marital problems. *Child Psychi Hum Dev, 15*, 86–103.

II-2/II-1/a
147. KINNAIRD, K. L., & GERRARD, M. Attitudes Toward Marriage
Scale

Avail: NAPS-3

Variables Measured: Attitudes toward marriage

Type of Instrument: Self-report questionnaire

Instrument Description: The Attitudes Toward Marriage Scale is a 14-item measure based on one published by Wallin (1954) and later used by Rubin (1977) and Greenberg and Nay (1982). It requires individuals to rate on a 5-point Likert-style scale their attitudes toward marriage. Of the 14 items on this scale, 9 were taken directly from the scale proposed by Wallin (1954), with some changes in wording. The remaining 5 items are reported by the authors to be original. The items include questions and statements about marriage. The responses are summed for an attitudes toward marriage score, such that higher scores indicate a positive attitude toward marriage and lower scores indicate a negative attitude toward marriage. This measure was designed as part of a research effort to assess differences among college-age women from various family backgrounds in their attitudes toward marriage and divorce. The authors indicate that the instrument can also be used as a tool to promote self-awareness and discussion among high school and college students.

Sample Items:

(A) Do you ever have doubts about whether you would enjoy living exclusively with one person after marriage?
(B) Do you ever worry that the person you marry wouldn't fulfill his responsibilities in the marriage?
(C) A bad marriage is better than no marriage at all.

Comments: The authors report that Cronbach's alpha was measured at .88, and that test-retest reliability was found to be .87. It was also found that college-age women from intact families had higher scores, and thus more positive attitudes toward marriage, than did those from father-absent families.

References:

Greenberg, E. F., & Nay, W. R. (1982). The intergenerational transmission of marital instability reconsidered. *J Mar Fam, 44*, 335–347.
Kinnaird, K. L., & Gerrard, M. (1986). Premarital sexual behavior and attitudes toward marriage and divorce among young women as a function of their mothers' marital status. *J Mar Fam, 48*, 757–765.
Rubin, R. H. (1977). *Family structure and peer group affiliation as related to attitudes about male-female relations among Black youth.* San Francisco: R & E Research Associates.
Wallin, P. (1954). Marital happiness of parents and their children's attitude to marriage. *Am Sociol Rev, 19*, 20–23.

II-2/c

148. KINNAIRD, K. L., & GERRARD, M. Family Atmosphere Questionnaire

Avail: NAPS-3

Variables Measured: Perceptions of family harmony and conflict

Type of Instrument: Self-report questionnaire

Instrument Description: The Family Atmosphere Questionnaire is a 5-item measure that was condensed from a questionnaire developed by Landis (1960). It uses a 5-point Likert-style response format to solicit an individual's perception of family unity, security, general happiness, and the amount of conflict in his or her family. This derived measure has two forms that are identical with the exception of the instructions. Form A instructs the respondents to describe their families as they were during their childhoods. Form B asks for current descriptions of their families. In the original study, the three family harmony items and two family conflict items from each form were summed and averaged to create a family harmony index and a family conflict index for each subject. The instrument is intended as a research instrument to be used with adolescent and adult subjects.

Sample Items:

(A)   Sense of family unity.
(B)   Relationship between parents.
(C)   Relationship between my parents and me.

Comments: The authors report Cronbach's alpha and test-retest reliability to be .87 and .92, respectively. They also report on a study of differences among college-age women where individuals from intact families indicated a higher level of harmony than did those from divorced and reconstituted families. Subjects in this study also indicated less family conflict than did individuals from divorced and reconstituted families.

References:

Kinnaird, K. L., & Gerrard, M. (1986). Premarital sexual behavior and attitudes toward marriage and divorce among young women as a function of their mothers' marital status. *J Mar Fam, 48,* 757–765.

Landis, J. T. (1960). The trauma of children when parents divorce. *Mar Fam Living, 22,* 7–13.

II-2/a

149. LOCKE, H. J., & WALLACE, K. M. Locke-Wallace Marital Adjustment Test (MAT)

Avail: 1959 Ref.

Variables Measured: Areas of satisfaction, agreement, and cooperation with one's spouse

Type of Instrument: Self-report questionnaire

Instrument Description: The MAT is a 15-item questionnaire designed to assess levels of satisfaction and accommodation of husbands and wives to each other. Items vary somewhat in both form and scoring. Item 1 asks marital partners to indicate the overall happiness in their marriage on a 7-point scale. However, scoring is weighted such that increasingly happier responses receive disproportionately high ratings. Overall scores on this item range from 0 to

35. Items 2–9 ask respondents to indicate the extent of agreement or disagreement between partners in eight key areas of marital interaction and perspective. With the exception of sexual relations and demonstrations of affection, where positive responses received higher weightings, all items in this section are scored on a 5 (*always agree*) to 0 (*always disagree*) basis. Other items utilize 2-, 3-, and 4-point weighted scales. The overall range of possible scores is 2 to 158. A cutoff score of 100 is generally used, with higher scores being interpreted as indicating better marital adjustment. The MAT is one of the most widely used and adapted scales in the family literature. Through the years, it has served as the standard by which authors of new instruments have tended to validate their work.

Sample Items: For items 2–9, respondents are asked to indicate the level of agreement or disagreement between themselves and their spouses in each area.

(A)   Handling family finances.
(B)   Matters of recreation.
(C)   When disagreements arise, they usually result in: husband giving in (0 points), wife giving in (2 points), agreement by mutual give and take (10 points).

Comments: Authorship and proper citation of the Locke-Wallace MAT is often confused in the literature. The following chronology is an attempt to clear up questions related to this issue. The original Locke Marital Questionnaire contained 50 items and was published in 1951. From this original pool of items, Locke and Williamson (1958) later factor analyzed what they considered to be the best 19 items. The resulting 8-factor solution became known as a short form of the original Marital Questionnaire. In 1959, Locke and Wallace published an article containing 15 items, which they called the Locke-Wallace Marital Adjustment Test. This is the instrument commonly referred to as the Locke-Wallace MAT. In that same article, these authors also published a 35-item instrument, which they named the Marital Prediction Test. In 1974, Kimmel and van der Veen published another factor analysis of the original 1951 instrument. Like the analysis of Locke and Williamson (1958), these authors used only select items from the original 50-item version. However, unlike the previous study, Kimmel and van der Veen used 23 of the original items (the 19 items used by Locke and Williamson, plus an additional 4 items they reported were significant from the original pool). This resulted in a 2-factor solution, with separate loadings indicated for husbands, wives, and a combination of all respondents. Thus the proper citation for the original 50-item questionnaire is Locke (1951); for the 19-item version it is Locke and Williamson (1958); for the 23-item, 2-factor solution the proper citation is Kimmel and van der Veen (1974); and for the 15-item MAT and the 35-item Marital Prediction Test the most appropriate citation remains Locke and Wallace (1959).

References:

Broderick, J. E., & O'Leary, K. D. (1986). Contributions of affect, attitudes, and behavior to marital satisfaction. *J Cons Clin, 54,* 514–517.

Cross, D. G., & Sharpley, C. F. (1981). The Locke-Wallace Marital Adjustment Test reconsidered: Some psychometric findings as regards its reliability and factorial validity. *Educ Psyc M, 41,* 1303–1306.

Kimmel, D., & van der Veen, F. (1974). Factors of marital adjustment in Locke's Marital Adjustment Test. *J Mar Fam, 36,* 57–63.

Locke, H. J. (1951). *Predicting adjustment in marriage: A comparison of a divorced and a happily married group.* New York: Holt.

Locke, H. J., & Wallace, K. M. (1959). Short marital adjustment and prediction tests: Their reliability and validity. *Mar Fam Living, 21,* 251–255.

Locke, H. J., & Williamson, R. C. (1958). Marital adjustment: A factor analysis study. *Am Sociol Rev, 23,* 562–569.

Meeks, S., Arnkoff, D. B., Glass, C. R., & Notarius, C. I. (1986). Wives' employment status, hassles, communication, and relational efficacy: Intra- versus extra-relationship factors and marital adjustment. *Fam Relat, 34,* 249–255.

II-2/a
150. MANSON, M. P., & LERNER, A. Marriage Adjustment Inventory (MAI)

Avail: Western Psychological Services, 12031 Wilshire Blvd., Los Angeles, CA 90025

Variables Measured: Degree of adjustment to common areas of marital concern and/or conflict

Type of Instrument: Self-report questionnaire

Instrument Description: The MAI is a 157-item questionnaire designed to highlight those areas of good and poor adjustment to marriage. Each item states a problem that occurs in some marriages. Respondents are presented with a booklet containing all 157 negatively worded items detailing undesirable characteristics or behaviors. Persons completing the MAI are given four options in responding to items: For each item perceived to apply to the wife, the circle containing the letter "W" is blackened; for each item perceived to apply to the husband, the circle containing the letter "H" is blackened; items pertaining to neither spouse are left unmarked; items that apply to both partners are responded to by blackening both the "H" and the "W" circles. Evaluations are scored according to 12 variables: (1) family relationships (liking for immediate and extended family), (2) dominance, (3) immaturity, (4) neurotic traits, (5) sociopathic traits, (6) money management, (7) children, (8) interests, (9) physical, (10) abilities, (11) sex, and (12) incompatibility. The total number of items marked is counted to obtain the score for husband, wife, and the couple. These three scores are then added for a total evaluation score. Low scores indicate few problems.

Sample Items:

(A)   Is chiefly interested in money.
(B)   Is unfair in many ways.
(C)   Feels lonely most of the time. (Copyright 1962 by Western Psychological Services. Reprinted by permission of the publisher, Western Psychological Services, 12031 Wilshire Boulevard, Los Angeles, California 90025)

Comments: The MAI is structured such that each item is scored on only one subscale. The instrument was designed for use in clinical settings with couples where adjustment is an issue (e.g., marriage counseling, marriage enhancement seminars). For each of the 12 categories noted above a score, indicating that the individual is "happy," "average," or "unhappy," is obtained. Norms are provided in the manual, which is available through the publisher.

References:

Manson, M. P., & Lerner, A. (1962). *The Marriage Adjustment Inventory: Manual.* Los Angeles: Western Psychological Services.
Manson, M. P., & Lerner, A. (1988). The Marriage Adjustment Inventory: Manual. In *Western Psychological Services 1988–89 catalog* (p. 159). Los Angeles: Western Psychological Services.

II-2/a
151. MILLER, B. C. Marital Satisfaction Scale

Avail: 1982 Ref.

Variables Measured: Satisfaction with marriage

Type of Instrument: Self-report questionnaire

Instrument Description: In contrast to longer and more complex measures of marital adjustment, this 8-item scale was developed to measure how satisfied people are with their marriages. It is a spouse's subjective rating of current satisfaction with specific dimensions of his or her marriage. Response choices range from *very dissatisfied* (scored "1") to *perfectly satisfied* (scored "5"). Individual item scores are summed over eight different dimensions to create a composite measure of marital satisfaction that could range from 8 to 40. One of the items implies that children are or were present in the marriage and is not applicable for childless couples. The item could be dropped from the scale for all respondents, or, if total scores were computed as an item mean, this particular item could be dropped selectively for those without children. The lead-in was written for an interview format, but could easily be adapted for a questionnaire.

Sample Items:

(A) How satisfied are you *currently* with the way *money* is handled in your marriage?

(B) How satisfied are you *currently* with the amount of *affection* in your marriage?

(C) How satisfied are you *currently* with the way you and your (husband/wife) deal with *inlaws* in your marriage?

Comments: The author reports on one study involving 140 subjects where Cronbach's alpha was found to be .81. Construct validity was assessed by correlating scores on the Marital Satisfaction Scale with those obtained by other measures. The author reports a correlation of .37 between this scale and the frequency of activities in which couples were jointly engaged.

References:

Mangen, D. J. (1982). Dyadic relations. In D. J. Mangen & W. A. Peterson (Eds.), *Research instruments in social gerontology: Vol 2. Social roles and social participation* (p. 98). Minneapolis: University of Minnesota Press.

Miller, B. C. (1975). Child density, marital satisfaction, and conventionalization: A research note. *J Mar Fam, 37,* 11–12.

Miller, B. C. (1976). A multivariate developmental model of marital satisfaction. *J Mar Fam, 38,* 643–657.

II-2/a
152. MORGAN, M. Y., & SCANZONI, J. Scale of Permanence/Pragmatism in Close Relationships (PPCR)

Avail: 1987 Ref.

Variables Measured: Commitment to needs of a romantic relationship versus individual concerns and needs

Type of Instrument: Self-report questionnaire

Instrument Description: The PPCR is a 5-point, 7-item Likert-style scale designed to measure balance or favor in personal interests at the expense of the stability of a romantic relationship. Item responses range from *very often* to *never.* The final version of the PPCR was derived from a factor analysis of never-married university undergraduates' responses to an initial 16-item questionnaire. Twelve of these initial items were developed following a review of the literature. The remaining 4 items were originally proposed by Scanzoni (1968).

Sample Items:

(A)   Divorce is wrong except when one partner commits adultery.
(B)   Under certain conditions, sexual intercourse between single persons may be permissible.
(C)   It is proper for a couple to feel that if their marriage does not work out, they can obtain a divorce.

Comments: The factor analysis performed by the authors resulted in the elimination of 9 out of 16 of the original items. The authors indicate that the analysis revealed a 5-factor solution. However, only 3 factors contained at least 3 items each, and only 1 of those was judged by the authors to be psychometrically appropriate. Of the 7 items remaining as the PPCR, 3 were constructed specifically for this scale. The remaining 4 items originated in Scanzoni (1968). Cronbach's alpha for the remaining scale is reported to be .83. Alpha for the second- and third-best factors was reported to be .43 and .34, respectively. Factor 1 was found to explain 27% of the total variance of the scale.

Reference:

Morgan, M. Y., & Scanzoni, J. (1987). Assessing variation in permanence/pragmatism orientations: Implications for marital stability. *J Divorce, 11*(1), 1–24.

II-2/a
153. MURSTEIN, B. I., & MacDONALD, M. G. Commitment Attitude Questionnaire

Avail: NAPS-3

Variables Measured: Attitudes of permanency and attachment in marital relationships

Type of Instrument: Self-report questionnaire

Instrument Description: This instrument, alternately referred to as the Commitment Attitude Questionnaire, the Commitment Scale, and the Attitude Questionnaire, is a 5-point, 19-item Likert-type questionnaire. The scale was designed to assess commitment to a marriage relationship along the dimensions of permanency and attachment. The Commitment Attitude Questionnaire was derived from an initial pool of 44 items. A factor analysis revealed six factors, which the authors labeled exchange, commitment, paranoia, expectation of others, obligation, and permanency. They indicate that the only factors of direct interest for their purposes were permanency and commitment. The commitment subscale was subsequently renamed "attachment," with 5 items being drawn from each of these two factors. An additional 9 items were constructed and added to the 10 items selected from the factor analysis, yielding an overall 19-item scale. Items are in the form of statements, and are rated according to a 5-point response format ranging from *strongly agree* to *strongly disagree*. Several items are reversed-scored, with high scores indicating a stronger sense of attachment or commitment.

Sample Items:

(A)   I feel obliged to have sex with my spouse if he/she wants to because sometimes he/she will engage in it when I want to and he/she doesn't.
(B)   Marriage contracts should be renewable every three years.
(C)   My caring for my spouse means even more than my caring for myself.

Comments: The authors indicate that Cronbach's alpha for the overall scale is .92. Comparison of husband and wife scores revealed higher commitment scores for wives. Correlations of individual items with the Marriage Adjustment Scale (Burgess, Locke, & Thomes, 1971) ranged from .03 to .56 with a median of .37. The overall correlation between the Commitment Attitude Questionnaire and the Marriage Adjustment Scale was reported to be .62 for husbands and .69 for wives.

Reference:

Murstein, B. I., & MacDonald, M. G. (1983). The relationship of "exchange-orientation" and "commitment" scales to marriage adjustment. *Int J Psycho, 18,* 297–311.

II-2/a
154. NEAL, A. G., IVOSKA, W. J., & GROAT, H. T. Family Alienation

Avail: 1976 Ref.

Variables Measured: Dimensions of alienation between husbands and wives

Type of Instrument: Self-report questionnaire

Instrument Description: This instrument is a 25-item forced-choice inventory designed to assess dimensions of marital alienation among husbands and wives. Five dimensions were identified: (1) couple estrangements, (2) generation gap, (3) loneliness of wife and mother role, (4) family meaninglessness, and (5) uncontrollability of family life. Items were constructed with one positive and one negative choice for each. In constructing the scale, 12 items were generated and pretested for each of four alienation variables: meaninglessness, or the extent to which respondents perceived events within the family as *chaotic, lacking in coherence,* and as *overwhelmingly complex* (Neal et al., 1976, p. 397); normlessness, defined as the perception that behaviors that are generally socially disapproved of are necessary in attaining goals; social isolation, or the extent to which the individual finds him- or herself isolated from others; and powerlessness, or a low expectation of being able to control the outcome of events. Criteria for scalogram analysis were applied to the results in order both to reduce the size of the final scale and to provide for a more psychometrically balanced instrument.

Sample Items:

(A1) Sometimes it seems that most married couples have almost nothing in common.
(A2) The majority of married couples share many common interests.
(B1) At times, family problems seem so complex that it just confuses a person to think about them.
(B2) Family life is seldom as complicated as many people make it out to be.
(C1) Most women can achieve the kind of family life they want.
(C2) The kind of family life most women dream about is difficult for them to attain.

Comments: The authors report correlations between the four alienation variables within scores by each gender as well as comparisons of men's and women's scores. Correlations of scores within gender ranged from .38 to .53 for women and from .24 to .52 for men. Correlations between men and women ranged from .01 to .19. Correlations between men's and women's scores for the four variables were .18, .05, .10, and .12 for meaninglessness, normlessness, social isolation, and powerlessness, respectively.

Reference:

Neal, A. G., Ivoska, W. J., & Groat, H. T. (1976). Dimensions of family alienation in the marital dyad. *Sociometry, 39,* 396–405.

II-2/a
155. NORTON, R. Quality Marriage Index (QMI)

Avail: 1983 Ref.

Variables Measured: Perceived quality of the marital relationship

Type of Instrument: Self-report questionnaire

Instrument Description: The QMI is a 6-item Likert-type questionnaire designed to assess variables that determine the quality of a marital relationship. All items are in the form of statements and are phrased in terms of a positive aspect of the marriage. Of the 6 items, 5 require that respondents indicate their level of agreement or disagreement with each item on a 7-point scale ranging from *very strong disagreement* to *very strong agreement.* The remaining item is rated on a 10-point scale ranging from *very unhappy* to *perfectly happy.* The author indicates that this happiness item was adapted from Kimmel and van der Veen (1974). Items were selected based on factor and item analyses of data from a 20-item version of the instrument. Eight items loaded primarily on the factor that eventually became the QMI. The two items phrased in terms of negative constructs, dealing with consideration of and discussions regarding the dissolution of the marriage, loaded negatively on the factor and were eliminated. The instrument was initially administered to a sample of 430 married persons as part of a 261-item instrument, 122 items of which focused on communication issues within the marriage. The QMI may be useful in both research and clinical settings and with both individuals and marital partners. Overall QMI scores are computed by summing standardized scores for each item.

Sample Items:

(A)   We have a good marriage.
(B)   My relationship with my partner is very stable.
(C)   Our marriage is strong.

Comments: The author reports that interitem correlations range from .68 to .85. Factor loadings on the primary factor, based on the 20-item factor analysis, for the 6 items are reported to range from .68 to .83, with secondary loadings ranging from .21 to .39.

References:

Grover, K. J., Paff-Bergen, L. A., Russell, C. S., & Schumm, W. R. (1984). The Kansas Marital Satisfaction Scale: A further brief report. *Psychol Rep, 54,* 629–630.
Norton, R. (1983). Measuring marital quality: A critical look at the dependent variable. *J Mar Fam, 45,* 141–151.
Schumm, W. R., Paff-Bergen, L. A., Hatch, R. C., Obiorah, F. C., Copeland, J. M., Meens, L. D., & Bugaihis, M. A. (1986). Concurrent and discriminant validity of the Kansas Marital Satisfaction Scale. *J Mar Fam, 48,* 381–387.

II-2/a
156. NOTARIUS, C. I., & VANZETTI, N. A. Marital Agendas Protocol (MAP)

Avail: 1983 Ref.

Variables Measured: Relational efficacy and problem areas among married couples

Type of Instrument: Self-report questionnaire

Instrument Description: The MAP is a 4-item scale primarily designed to assess relational efficacy among husbands and wives. Spouses first rate the perceived severity of 10 common marital problem areas currently facing the relationship (money, communication, in-laws, sex, religion, recreation, friends, alcohol or drugs, children, and jealousy). In addition to the 10 listed problem areas, space is provided for respondents to add other areas that are problematic within their marital relationship. Each problem area is rated on a scale from 0 to 100, with low scores indicating that the area is *not at all a problem* and high scores indicating that the area is *a very severe problem.* Relational efficacy is assessed by having the respondent indicate his or her expectancy for being able to reach a mutually satisfactory resolution to disagreements arising within each problem area using a scale from 0 (*We can resolve 0 out of 10 disagreements that may arise in this area*) to 10 (*We can resolve 10 out of 10 disagreements that may arise in this area*). An overall measure of relational efficacy is then obtained by averaging the ratings given to each of the problem areas. Respondents also indicate the extent to which they hold themselves, their partner, or both equally responsible for unresolved disagreements in each problem area. Administration time is approximately 15 minutes.

Sample Items:

(A) Consider the list below of marital issues that all marriages must face. Please rate how much of a problem each area currently is in your relationship by writing in a number from 0 to 100.

(B) How do you predict your spouse will respond to question 1?

(C) Out of every 10 disagreements in each marital area below, how many do you believe you and your spouse resolve to your mutual satisfaction?

Comments: The author reports that test-retest reliability over a period averaging two weeks was .81. It is also reported that relational efficacy correlates .57 with the Locke-Wallace Marital Adjustment Test, -.43 with husbands' report of *displeases* on the Spouse Observation Checklist (Weiss & Perry, 1983), and -.36 and .32 with wives' report of *displeases* and *pleases,* respectively (Meeks, Arnkoff, Glass, & Notarius, 1986).

References:

Meeks, S., Arnkoff, D., Glass, C., & Notarius, C. (1986). Wives' employment status, hassles, communication and relational efficacy: Intra- versus extra-relationship factors and marital adjustment. *Fam Relat, 35,* 249–255.

Notarius, C., & Vanzetti, N. (1983). The Marital Agendas Protocol. In E. E. Filsinger (Ed.), *A sourcebook of marital and family assessment* (pp. 209–227). Beverly Hills, CA: Sage.

II-2/I-1/a
157. OLSON, D. H., FOURNIER, D. G., & DRUCKMAN, J. M. Enriching and Nurturing Relationship Issues, Communication and Happiness
(ENRICH), and Premarital Personal and Relationship Evaluation (PRE-
PARE)

Avail: Prepare/Enrich Office, P.O. Box 190, Minneapolis, MN 55440

Variables Measured: Major problems related to personal, interpersonal, and external issues in relationships among marital (ENRICH) and premarital (PREPARE) couples

Type of Instrument: Self-report questionnaire

Instrument Description: Both PREPARE and ENRICH contain 115 Likert-style items and
utilize a 5-point response format ranging from *strongly disagree* to *strongly agree.* The questionnaires are conceptually similar, with each designed to serve as a diagnostic tool in assessing relationship problems. PREPARE was developed first and was designed for use with
premarital couples. ENRICH is used to assess relationship difficulties among married couples. Categories evaluated by ENRICH are idealistic distortion, marital satisfaction, personality issues, communication, conflict resolution, financial management, leisure activities, sexual
relationship, children and marriage, family and friends, equalitarian roles, and religious orientation. Of these 12 categories, 11 are also measured by PREPARE. The only category not
shared by the two instruments is marital satisfaction. A set of questions assessing realistic
expectations is substituted in its place for use with PREPARE. Although the two instruments
evaluate similar relationship issues, many PREPARE items needed to be rewritten in order to
be appropriate for use in the marital instrument. Approximately 40% of the items on the two
instruments are identical. The remainder have changes ranging from minor rewording to
complete revisions. Items within each subscale are summed, with individual subscales being
separately evaluated.

Sample Items (Note: All items are taken from the ENRICH questionnaire):

(A)   My partner and I understand each other completely.
(B)   I am not pleased with the personality characteristics and personal habits of my
       partner.
(C)   My partner is too critical or often has a negative outlook.

Comments: The authors report Cronbach's alpha, based on a study of 672 couples (1,344
individuals), as averaging .74 with a range of .48 to .92 for the 12 ENRICH scales. Test-retest
reliability over a four-week period, based on a study of 115 individuals, is reported to have
ranged from .77 to .92, with a mean of .87.

References:

Fournier, D. G., Olson, D. H., & Druckman, J. M. (1983). Assessing marital and premarital
    relationships: The PREPARE-ENRICH inventories. In E. E. Filsinger (Ed.), *Mar-
    riage and family assessment.* Beverly Hills, CA: Sage.
Fowers, B. J., & Olson, D. H. (1986). Predicting marital success with PREPARE: A predic-
    tive validity study. *J Mar Fam Th, 12,* 403–413.
Fowers, B. J., & Olson, D. H. (1989). Enrich Marital Inventory: A discriminant validity and
    cross-validation assessment. *J Mar Fam Th, 15,* 65–89.
Olson, D. H., McCubbin, H. I., Barnes, H., Larsen, A., Muxem, M., & Wilson, M. (1985).
    Family inventories. St. Paul: University of Minnesota, Family Social Science.

II-2/a
158. ORDEN, S. R., & BRADBURN, N. M. Marriage Adjustment Balance Scale (MABS)

Avail: 1968 Ref.

Variables Measured: Marriage satisfaction with regard to companionship and sociability, marriage tensions, and marriage adjustment

Type of Instrument: Self-report questionnaire

Instrument Description: The MABS represents a combined treatment of three separate indexes: satisfaction with companionship, satisfaction with sociability, and tensions. For each index, subjects indicate which behaviors they have engaged in. Responses to companionship and sociability items are on a 4-point scale, while items on the tension checklist are given using a *yes-no* format. The author reports that scoring is accomplished in the following manner:

Scores for 0, 1, and 2 on the companionship index and scores for 0 and 1 on sociability were collapsed into a "zero" category. This reduced both indexes to 4-point scales ranging from 0 to 3. Then the sociability and companionship indexes were combined into a total satisfactions scale ranging from 0 to 6. On the tensions index, categories 4 through 8 were collapsed, giving a tensions scale ranging from 0 to 4. The difference between total satisfactions and tensions thus runs from a possible score of +6 to -4. For ease in computation, these scores were converted to an 11-point scale ranging from 10 to 0. The scores for 0, 1, 2, and 3 are negative scores in which tensions exceed satisfactions, a score of 4 is the zero or balance score, and the scores from 5 to 10 are the positive scores where satisfactions exceed tensions.

Sample Items:

(A) I'm going to read you some things that married couples often do together. Tell me which ones you and your (husband/wife) have done together in the past few weeks.
(a) Had a good laugh together or shared a joke.
(b) Been affectionate toward each other.
(B) . . . tell me which ones caused differences of opinions or were problems in your marriage during the past few weeks.
(a) Being tired.
(b) Irritating personal habits.

Comments: The authors report that construct validity was assessed by comparing MABS scores to self-reports of marriage happiness. The companionship index was found to be more strongly related to marriage happiness than was the sociability index.

References:

Burke, R. J., Weir, T., & DuWors, R. E. (1979). Type A behavior of administrators and wives' reports of marital satisfaction and well being. *J Appl Psyc, 64,* 57–65.
Orden, S. R., & Bradburn, N. M. (1968). Dimensions of marriage happiness. *Am J Sociol, 73,* 715–731.

II-2/c

159. PLESS, I. B., & SATTERWHITE, B. Family Functioning Index (FFI)

Avail: NAPS-3

Variables Measured: Marital satisfaction, disagreements, happiness, communication, weekends together, and problem solving

Type of Instrument: Self-report questionnaire

Instrument Description: This instrument is a 19-item questionnaire designed to measure areas of family functioning. Individual items use differing response formats, including 3-point and 5-point Likert-type, *yes-no,* multipart questions. It was developed for use in both research and clinical settings with families that contain children. It has been used primarily in evaluations of families with chronically ill children. The FFI was intended for use as a predictive or intervening measure, rather than as an outcome measure. Parallel forms are available for husbands and wives. Scores range from 0 to 35, with higher scores indicating better functioning. Administration time is approximately 10 minutes.

Sample Items:

(A) Do you find your husband an easy person to talk to when something is troubling you?

(B) Would you say disagreements in your household come up more often, about the same, or less often than in other families you know?

(C) Do the children find it easy to talk to you about their problems?

Comments: The FFI has been used to distinguish between well-functioning families and those who caseworkers from family counseling agencies indicate do not function well. The correlation between FFI scores of husbands and wives is reported by the authors to be .72, with smaller correlations reported in what the authors refer to as "troubled families."

References:

Brown, J. S., Rawlinson, M. E., & Hardin, D. M. (1982). Family functioning and health status. *J Fam Iss, 3,* 91–110.

Forman, B. D., & Hagan, B. J. (1984). Measures for evaluating total family functioning. *Fam Ther, 11,* 1–36.

Pless, I. B., & Satterwhite, B. B. (1973). A measure of family functioning and its application. *Social Sci Med, 7,* 613–621.

Satterwhite, B. B., & Pless, I. B. (1976). The Family Functioning Index: Five-year test-retest reliability and implications for use. *J Comp Fam Studies, 7,* 111–116.

II-2/IV-2/a

160. RAUSH, H. L., BARRY, W. A., HERTEL, R. K., & SWAIN, M. A. A Coding Scheme for Interpersonal Conflict (CSIC)

Avail: 1974 Ref.

Variables Measured: Dimensions and levels of conflict in intimate dyadic relationships

Type of Instrument: Behavioral coding scheme

Instrument Description: Interactions of couples based on improvisational conflict scenes are tape-recorded, transcribed, and analyzed. Recordings are listened to with the assistance of transcripts. Transcripts are edited and expanded based on utterances understood by raters that were initially undecipherable by transcribers. Each act, with the exception of the first and last acts defined as any statement or meaningful action (e.g., prolonged silences) sandwiched between two acts of the dyadic partner, was assigned to an action category. Acts ranged from single words to lengthy statements. The authors initially assigned acts to 36 such categories, later reducing that number to 12 and finally to 6. The 6 action categories used in the final version suggested by the authors are cognitive, resolving, reconciling, appealing, rejecting, and coercive acts. Double coding of acts is kept to a minimum, and triple coding is never used. In addition to being assigned to one action category, each act was also coded for phase, defined as the phase of the conflict situation in which it occurs. Three phases identified by the authors are introductory, conflict, and resolution or postresolution. Coding may be accomplished with raters working independently, with codings compared for reliability, or together with the intention of coming to a consensus regarding the coding of each act.

Sample Items: Not applicable.

Comments: The authors report that early studies with a 40-category system resulted in three-rater reliability of .36, with two out of three raters agreeing 40% of the time. However, total disagreement, with each rater selecting a different category, occurred 24% of the time. When the categories were reduced to 6, total agreement increased to 50%, with total disagreement dropping to 10%. An analysis of variance on codings for all couples utilizing the 40-category system revealed that, although individual acts were often not consistently coded, overall ratings of behavior by coders did not differ within dyads. Interrater reliability reported by others has been as high as .95 (Billings, 1979) for the 6-category system.

References:

Billings, A. (1979). Conflict resolution in distressed and nondistressed married couples. *J Cons Clin, 47*, 368–376.

Craddock, A. E. (1980). Marital problem-solving as a function of couples' marital power expectations and marital value systems. *J Mar Fam, 42*, 185–196.

Raush, H. L., Barry, W. A., Hertel, R. K., & Swain, M. A. (1974). *Communications, conflict, and marriage.* San Francisco: Jossey-Bass.

II-2/a
161. ROACH, A. J. Marital Satisfaction Scale (MSS): Form B

Avail: 1981 Ref.

Variables Measured: Level of satisfaction within one's own marriage

Type of Instrument: Self-report questionnaire

Instrument Description: The MSS is a 5-point, 48-item questionnaire designed to assess what the author views as a unidimensional construct of marital satisfaction. Items are in the form of statements and are intended to measure the respondent's attitudes toward his or her own marital relationship, as opposed to facts regarding that relationship. Responses to individual items are on a 5-point scale ranging from *strongly agree* to *strongly disagree*. Items were constructed such that scores could reasonably be expected to change as an individual's attitude and level of satisfaction with the marriage evolve. The MSS was developed in 1975 from an initial pool of 73 items, originally referred to as the Marital Satisfaction Inventory (MSI). A factor analysis of the MSI resulted in the elimination of 3 items. Based on further examination of item-total correlations, the author subsequently reduced the scale to 48 items (Roach, Frazier, & Bowden, 1981). Each of the 48 items contained in the final version was found to correlate greater than .50 with the original 73-item questionnaire (actual range of correlations was .51 to .82). A total MSS score is computed by summing values associated with individual responses to each item.

Sample Items:

(A)   The future of my marriage looks promising to me.
(B)   I am definitely satisfied with my marriage.
(C)   I get along well with my spouse.

Comments: The 3 sample items listed above have the highest item-total correlations of any in the scale (.82, .79, and .77, respectively). The author reports that Cronbach's alpha for the 70-item MSI was in the neighborhood of .98 for various studies. Test-retest reliability for the MSI, with retest results obtained ranging from three weeks to seven months following initial testing, was found to be .76. Correlations are also reported with the Locke-Wallace (1959) Marriage Adjustment Test (.63), as well as with measures of social desirability (.33) and the Marriage Problem Checklist (Roach, 1977) (-.73). Further reliability and validity information is available in the references listed below. The author notes that the title of the instrument was changed to the MSS in order to avoid confusion when another scale (Marital Satisfaction Inventory) was developed and published by Snyder (1979). (See abstract 167.)

References:

Kurdek, L. A., & Schmitt, J. P. (1986a). Interaction of sex role self-concept with relationship quality and relationship beliefs in married, heterosexual cohabiting, gay, and lesbian couples. *J Pers Soc Psy, 51*, 365–370.
Kurdek, L. A., & Schmitt, J. P. (1986b). Relationship quality of partners in heterosexual married, heterosexual cohabiting, and gay and lesbian relationships. *J Pers Soc Psy, 51*, 711–720.
Kurdek, L. A., & Schmitt, J. P. (1987). Partner homogamy in married, heterosexual cohabiting, gay, and lesbian couples. *J Sex Res, 23*, 212–232.
Roach, A. J., Frazier, L. P., & Bowden, S. R. (1981). The Marital Satisfaction Scale: Development of a measure for intervention research. *J Mar Fam, 43*, 537–546.

II-2/a
162. ROFE, Y. Marital Happiness Scale

Avail: 1988 Ref.

Variables Measured: Satisfaction and happiness within marital relationships

Type of Instrument: Self-report questionnaire

Instrument Description: This 20-item scale was designed to measure dimensions of marital satisfaction among Israeli women. It is a modification of a 22-item marital happiness scale used in Rofe (1985), originally developed for examining both male and female perceptions of marital satisfaction. The current scale could easily be modified for use with husbands in addition to wives. A factor analysis of questionnaire responses yielded four dimensions of marital happiness: (1) 13 items loaded primarily on an index of overall marital satisfaction and feelings of love; (2) 3 items are principally concerned with marital disagreements; (3) sexual satisfaction is examined by 2 items; and (4) 2 items load primarily on a physical appearance factor. All items are in the form of questions, with answers provided utilizing a 3-point response format. Sample items listed below reflect areas examined by 3 items, but not the exact wording of questions used in examining those areas.

Sample Items:

(A)   Satisfaction from marriage.
(B)   Disagreement about housekeeping.
(C)   Husband's sexual satisfaction.

Comments: The factor analysis reported in Rofe (1988) indicates that 44.1% of the scale variance was explained by the first factor. All items loaded at least .51 on their primary factor, and no more than .40 on any of the other factors. The scale was used to examine differences between levels of satisfaction expressed by women of Asian or African and Western descent. The author reports that, when the effects of education and number of children were partialed out, no significant differences between these groups of women were detected. It is also reported that level of education had the greatest impact on overall marital satisfaction of all variables studied.

References:

Rofe, Y. (1985). The assessment of marital happiness. In J. N. Butcher & C. D. Spielberger (Eds.), *Advances in personality assessment* (Vol. 4, pp. 55–82). Hillsdale, NJ: Lawrence Erlbaum.

Rofe, Y. (1988). Marital happiness among mixed and homogeneous marriages in Israel. *J Mar Fam, 50*, 245–254.

II-2/a
163. RUST, J., BENNUN, I., CROWE, M., & GOLOMBOK, S. The Golombok Rust Inventory of Marital State (GRIMS)

Avail: NFER Nelson, Darville House, 2 Oxford Road East, Windsor, Berks SL4 1DE, England

Variables Measured: Satisfaction with one's marital relationship

Type of Instrument: Self-report questionnaire

Instrument Description: The GRIMS has been developed for use in marriage guidance, for marital and family therapy, and for research in these areas. It is a 28-item Likert-style questionnaire, with four response options ranging from *strongly disagree* to *strongly agree*. Items ask respondents to evaluate their marital relationship with regard to their own and their spouse's personality traits and behavior characteristics. Other items inquire about activities of the couple or perceptions of marriage in general. The GRIMS is a companion scale to the Golombok Rust Inventory of Sexual Satisfaction (GRISS), also published by NFER. Administration time is approximately 6 minutes.

Sample Items:

(A)   Marriage is really more about security and money than about love.
(B)   I really appreciate my partner's sense of humour.
(C)   It is useless carrying on with a marriage beyond a certain point.

Comments: The GRIMS was developed from 180 items generated by a group of marriage guidance counselors and therapists. Item and factor analyses resulted in a reduction of the scale to its current length. The authors report that split-half reliability for the scale is .92 for men and .90 for women. Samples used in validating the GRIMS included couples presenting themselves for marriage guidance and normal controls. The authors also report the correlation between change scores following therapy and therapists' ratings of improvement to be .52. Further information regarding item analyses, validity, and reliability can be found in the references listed below.

Reference:

Rust, J., Bennun, I., Crowe, M., & Golombok, S. (1986). The Golombok Rust Inventory of Marital State (GRIMS). *J Sex Mar Ther, 1,* 55–60.
Rust, J., Golombok, S., & Collier, J. (1988). Marital problems and sexual dysfunction: How are they related? *Br J Psychi, 152,* 629–631.
Rust, J., Golombok, S., & Pickard, C. (1987). Marital problems in general practice. *Sex Mar Ther, 2,* 127–130.

II-2/a
164. SABATELLI, R. M. The Marital Comparison Level Index (MCLI)

Avail: 1984 Ref.

Variables Measured: Marital experiences, expectations, and complaints

Type of Instrument: Self-report questionnaire

Instrument Description: The MCLI is a 7-point, 32-item Likert-type questionnaire. It was designed to provide researchers with a measure of marital complaints by focusing on the contrast between marital experiences and expectations. The goal in the development of the MCLI was to construct an internally consistent, unidimensional construct reflecting spouses' perceptions of the degree to which their marital relationship measures up to their unique impressions of, or opinions about, acceptable marital behavior. Respondents are instructed that these expectations are derived from observations of, and personal experiences in, relationships and are not necessarily the same as ideals. Items were derived from Lewis and Spanier's (1979) inductive theory of marital quality and stability. For each item, respondents are asked how their experiences within their relationships compare with their expectations. Item responses range from *worse than I expect* to *better than I expect,* and are scored from -3 to +3.

Sample Items:

(A)   The amount of companionship you experience.
(B)   The amount of the responsibility for household tasks shared.
(C)   The amount of conflict over the use of leisure time that you experience.

Comments: The author reports that the final 32-item version contains those items loading on a single factor and scored as being highly important to a marriage by a sample of 301 married respondents. Factor loadings are reported to range from .38 to .77. Cronbach's alpha is reported to be .93. The author also reports that lower complaint levels were associated with relatively higher commitment levels and the greater likelihood of perceiving the marriages as being equitable and fair.

References:

Sabatelli, R. M. (1984). The marital comparison level index: A measure for assessing outcomes relative to expectations. *J Mar Fam, 46,* 651–662.
Sabatelli, R. M., & Cecil-Pigo, E. F. (1985). Relational interdependence and commitment in marriage. *J Mar Fam, 47,* 931–937.

II-2/c

165. SCHUMM, W. R., JURICH, A. P., & BOLLMAN, S. R. Kansas Family Life Satisfaction (KFLS) Scale

Avail: NAPS-3

Variables Measured: Satisfaction with family relationships

Type of Instrument: Self-report questionnaire

Instrument Description: This 4-item Likert-style scale was designed to assess satisfaction with three key types of family relationships and with family life as a whole. The design was parallel to the Kansas Marital Satisfaction Scale (and uses one item from the KMSS) in format and general principle. One item each is used to assess satisfaction with the marriage, with children or with parents (depending on the subject), the parent-child relationship, and sibling relationships. It is designed for use in interview or questionnaire surveys, and has been used with 7- and 5-point response formats. The scale is intended for use with families containing a mother, father, and preferably at least two children. Individual item scores are summed to arrive at a composite scale score. Higher scores indicate greater satisfaction with family life.

Sample Items:

(A) Your family life.
(B) Your relationship with your spouse.
(C) Your relationship with your child(ren).

Comments: The authors report on a study of 620 families. Cronbach's alpha was calculated as .83 for fathers, .79 for mothers, and .82 for adolescents. Adolescents are reported to have been found to be least satisfied with family life relative to their parents. The authors also report that a Korean translation of the KFLS Scale has been found to have an alpha of .89. Correlations are also reported between scale scores and satisfaction with quality of life, locus of control, religiosity, income, total number of family members, and age of adolescent. Exact correlations and further reliability information are reported in the references listed below.

References:

Jeong, G. J., & Schumm, W. R. (in press). Family satisfaction in Korean/American marriages: An exploratory study of the perceptions of Korean wives. *J Comp Fam Studies*.

McCollum, E. E., Schumm, W. R., & Russell, C. S. (1988). Reliability and validity of the Kansas Family Life Satisfaction Scale in a predominately middle-aged sample. *Psychol Rep, 62*, 95–98.

Schumm, W. R., McCollum, E. E., Bugaighis, M. A., Jurich, A. P., & Bollman, S. R. (1986). Characteristics of the Kansas Family Life Satisfaction Scale in a regional sample. *Psychol Rep, 58*, 975–980.

Schumm, W. R., McCollum, E. E., Bugaighis, M. A., Jurich, A. P., Bollman, S. R., & Reitz, J. (1988). Differences between Anglo and Mexican-American family members on satisfaction with family life. *Hispan J Beh Sci, 10*, 39–53.

II-2/a

166. SCHUMM, W. R., JURICH, A. P., & BOLLMAN, S. R. Kansas Marital Satisfaction Scale

Avail: 1986 Ref.

Variables Measured: Perceived marital satisfaction

Type of Instrument: Self-report questionnaire or interview

Instrument Description: This 3-item Likert-type questionnaire was designed initially to assess three different aspects of satisfaction with marriage: marriage as an institution, the marital relationship, and the character of one's spouse. However, in practice, the authors report that the three items proved to have adequate reliability to be treated as a scale. It can be used in interview or questionnaire surveys, and has been used with 4-, 5-, and 7-point response formats. The most popular treatment is as a 7-point scale, with possible responses ranging from *extremely dissatisfied* to *extremely satisfied*. It is intended to be used with almost all married populations. Scoring is accomplished by summing scores for individual items.

Sample Items:

(A)   How satisfied are you with your marriage?
(B)   How satisfied are you with your relationship with your husband?
(C)   How satisfied are you with your husband as a spouse?

Comments: The Kansas Marital Satisfaction Scale has been used in numerous studies. Cronbach's alpha is reported by the authors to range from .81 to .98, with most studies reporting alphas in the .90 and above range. It has been correlated with marital social desirability (.42 to .54), positive regard (.42 to .70), individual social desirability (.05 to .39), locus of control (.18 to .31), church attendance (.22 to .24), total family income (.30), personal depression (.33), and several other constructs. The scale has also been used to differentiate couples in therapy from nontherapy couples while controlling for marital social desirability, income, age, education, duration of marriage, and number of children. Test-retest reliability is reported to have been .71 over a 10-week period and to have ranged from .62 to .72 over six months. The authors also indicate that a Korean translation of the KMS scale featured an alpha of .93 and a normal distribution, and was correlated with income (.42) and with wife's English proficiency (.36).

References:

Fincham, F. D., & Bradbury, T. N. (1987). The assessment of marital quality: A reevaluation. *J Mar Fam, 49,* 797–809.
Mitchell, S. L., Newell, G. K., & Schumm, W. R. (1983). Test-retest reliability of the Kansas Marital Satisfaction Scale. *Psychol Rep, 53,* 545–546.
Schumm, W. R., Bollman, S. R., & Jurich, A. P. (1981). The validity of Edmonds' Marital Conventionalization Scale. *J Psychol, 109,* 65–71.
Schumm, W. R., Paff-Bergen, L. A., Hatch, R. C., Obiorah, F. C., Copeland, J. M., Meens, L. D., & Bugaighis, M. A. (1986). Concurrent and discriminant validity of the Kansas Marital Satisfaction Scale. *J Mar Fam, 48,* 381–387.

II-2/a
167. SNYDER, D. K. Marital Satisfaction Inventory (MSI)

Avail: Western Psychological Services, 12031 Wilshire Blvd., Los Angeles, CA 90025

Variables Measured: Satisfaction with marriage and dimensions of interaction between spouses

Type of Instrument: Self-report questionnaire

Instrument Description: The MSI is a 280-item *true-false* inventory including one validity scale, one global satisfaction scale, and nine additional scales assessing specific dimensions of spousal interaction (affective communication, problem-solving communication, time together, disagreement about finances, sexual dissatisfaction, role orientation, family history of distress, dissatisfaction with children, and conflict over child rearing). It is intended primarily for clinical use with distressed couples and for research with both distressed and nondistressed samples. Items from the first nine scales are presented in random order, followed by items from the two child-rearing scales. Couples without children skip these last two scales, thus completing only 239 items. The MSI is administered to spouses separately, requiring approximately 30 minutes to complete. Hand-scoring takes about 5 minutes. Alternatively, optically scannable answer sheets can be mailed to the publisher for computer scoring and return of a computer-based interpretive report. A third option allows computer administration, with generation of an interpretive report on the clinician's own computer.

Sample Items:

(A)   I have important needs in my marriage that are not being met.
(B)   Our marriage has never been in difficulty because of financial concerns.
(C)   My spouse sometimes shows too little enthusiasm for sex. (Copyright 1979 by Western Psychological Services. Reprinted by permission of the publisher, Western Psychological Services, 12031 Wilshire Boulevard, Los Angeles, California 90025)

Comments: The author reports on a substantial body of research in which reliability and validity of the MSI have been investigated. Test-retest reliability over a six-week period is reported to range from .84 to .94. Cronbach's alpha is reported to range from .80 to .97. Studies of discriminant validity reported by the author have found that the MSI distinguishes between couples in therapy and controls, and between couples in marital therapy and those treated in a clinic specializing in sexual dysfunctions. Additional research has focused on combinations of convergent and discriminant validity. Further detailed information regarding validity and reliability can be found in the references listed below.

References:

Scheer, N. S., & Snyder, D. K. (1984). Empirical validation of the Marital Satisfaction Inventory in a nonclinical sample. *J Cons Clin, 52,* 88–96.
Snyder, D. K. (1979). Multidimensional assessment of marital satisfaction. *J Mar Fam, 41,* 813–823.
Snyder, D. K. (1983). Clinical and research applications of the Marital Satisfaction Inventory. In E. E. Filsinger (Ed.), *Marriage and family assessment: A sourcebook for family therapy* (pp. 169–189). Beverly Hills, CA: Sage.
Snyder, D. K., Wills, R. M., & Kaiser, T. W. (1981). Empirical validation of the Marital Satisfaction Inventory: An actuarial approach. *J Cons Clin, 49,* 262–268.

II-2/a
168. SPANIER, G. B. Dyadic Adjustment Scale (DAS)

Avail: 1976 Ref.

Variables Measured: Marital or dyadic adjustment

Type of Instrument: Self-report instrument

Instrument Description: The DAS is a 32-item, primarily Likert-style questionnaire utilizing 5-, 6-, and 7-point response formats. There are also two items that are answered either *yes* or *no*. The majority of items use a 6-point format, with options scored from 0 to 5, and ranging from either *always agree* to *always disagree* or *all the time* to *never*. The scale was designed to assess the quality of dyadic relationships. Although the author indicates it can be utilized in assessing various types of committed couple relationships, including unmarried cohabitation, over 90% of the more than 1,000 reported studies using the DAS have involved married couples. The DAS has been translated into several languages for use with various nationalities and cultural groups. In the initial, primary portion of the instrument, respondents are asked to indicate the extent of agreement or disagreement between themselves and their partners on each of 22 issues. Other items relate to specific shared behaviors between partners (e.g., "Do you kiss your mate?") and attitudes. Factor analysis resulted in the identification of four factors: dyadic satisfaction, dyadic cohesion, dyadic consensus, and affectional expression. In addition to the reference listed above, the DAS is also available in paper-and-pencil and computer versions from Multi-Health Systems, Inc., 95 Thorncliffe Park Dr., Suite 100, Toronto, Ontario, Canada M4H 1L7.

Sample Items:

(A) Please indicate below the approximate extent of agreement or disagreement between you and your partner for . . . handling family finances.
(B) How often do you discuss or have you considered divorce, separation, or terminating your relationship?
(C) Do you and your mate engage in outside interests together?

Comments: Cronbach's alpha is reported to be .96 for the overall DAS, and to range from .73 to .94 for the four subscales. Each of its items are also reported to discriminate between married and divorced couples. Mean scale scores reported by the author for married and divorced samples were 114.8 and 70.7, respectively. The correlation between the DAS and the Locke-Wallace Marital Adjustment Scale (1959) is reported by the author to be .86 among marital couples and .88 among divorced respondents. Items were initially evaluated by three judges for content validity. All items in the final version were judged appropriate by these judges.

References:

Kazak, A. E., Jarmas, A., & Snitzer, L. (1988). The assessment of marital satisfaction: An evaluation of the Dyadic Adjustment Scale. *J Fam Psy, 2,* 82–91.

Schumm, W. R., Paff-Bergen, L. A., Hatch, R. C., Obiorah, F. C., Copeland, J. M., Meens, L. D., & Bugaighis, M. A. (1986). Concurrent and discriminant validity of the Kansas Marital Satisfaction Scale. *J Mar Fam, 48,* 381–387.

Spanier, G. B. (1976). Measuring dyadic adjustment: New scales for assessing the quality of marriage and similar dyads. *J Mar Fam, 38,* 15–28.

Spanier, G. B., & Filsinger, E. E. (1983). The Dyadic Adjustment Scale. In E. E. Filsinger (Ed.), *Marriage and family assessment: A sourcebook for family therapy.* Beverly Hills, CA: Sage.

II-2/a
169. STARR, S., & MANN, J. Marriage Satisfaction Survey

Avail: NAPS-3

Variables Measured: Couple's perceived satisfaction within the marital relationship with regard to openness of communication and self-disclosure, management functions, sexuality, and investment or commitment to the relationship

Type of Instrument: Self-report questionnaire

Instrument Description: This instrument requires that couples rate themselves and their spouses on their satisfaction in a variety of areas of marital function deemed amenable to change in therapy. The survey was developed for clinical use with couples engaged in marital therapy. The questionnaire contains 32 Likert-style items in which subjects indicate their own satisfaction as well as their spouse's performance within the marital relationship. In addition, 11 items are included dealing with levels of satisfaction with how each spouse perceives his or her work as a partner with the spouse. All items are rated on a 6-point scale, with response options ranging from *very low satisfaction* to *very high satisfaction*. Administration time is approximately 15 minutes.

Sample Items:

(A)   Willingness to work on family problems.
(B)   Respecting your spouse's views and opinions.
(C)   Ability to provide emotional support for your spouse.

Comments: The author reports that test-retest reliability for satisfaction with self and satisfaction with spouse was .57 and .69, respectively. It is also reported that the scale success-fully discriminated between couples referred for treatment and controls from the community. It is further reported that the Marriage Satisfaction Survey correlates .61 with the Marital Adjustment Test (Locke & Wallace, 1959).

Reference:

Cowan, C. P., Cowan, P. A., Heming, G., Garrett, E., Coysh, W. S., Curtis-Boles, H., & Boles, A. J., III (1985). Transitions to parenthood. *J Fam Iss, 6,* 451–481.

II-2/a
170. SWENSEN, C. H., & FIORE, A. Scale of Marriage Problems

Avail: 1975 Ref.

Variables Measured: Marriage problems as they relate to several common areas of diffi-culty for married couples

Type of Instrument: Self-report questionnaire

Instrument Description: The Scale of Marriage Problems is a 43-item Likert-style instru-ment utilizing a 3-point response format. Response options include whether the item in question represents an area that is *never a problem, occasionally a problem,* or *a serious or constant problem.* Seven scores are obtained, including a total marriage problems index and six subscales (problem solving, decision making, and goal setting; child rearing and home labor; relatives and in-laws; personal care and appearance; money management; and expres-sion of affection and relationships with people outside the marriage). The questionnaire is intended for use with married couples of all ages and lengths of marriage. Administration time is approximately 10–15 minutes.

Sample Items:

(A)   Husband and wife seem to want different things out of marriage.
(B)   Disagreement on what children should be allowed to do and what they should not be allowed to do.
(C)   Disagreement on how to raise children that one of you brought to this marriage from a previous marriage.

Comments: The scale was composed of problems couples seeking marriage counseling presented to five different counseling centers. These problems were presented to a sample of married couples. Subscales were derived from a factor analysis of these data. The authors report Cronbach's alpha for the subscales in the range of .32 to .85. Results of research reported by the authors indicated that couples seeking marriage counseling scored signifi-cantly higher than happily married couples. It was also reported that marriage problems, as measured by the Scale of Marriage Problems, were lower for couples who had been married longer, and that such problems declined for couples who increased their commitment to each other. The authors indicate that the most recent summary of research results using this instrument are contained in Swensen and Fiore (1982).

References:

Brody, G. H., Pillegrini, A. D., & Sigel, I. E. (1986). Marital quality and mother-child and father-child interactions with school-aged children. *Devel Psych, 22,* 291–296.

Swensen, C. H., & Fiore, A. (1975). A factored measure of the primary dimension in marriage. In J. W. Pfeiffer & J. E. Jones (Eds.), *The 1975 handbook for group facilitators.* San Diego, CA: University Associates.

Swensen, C. H., & Fiore, A. (1982). A scale of marriage problems. In P. A. Keller (Ed.), *Innovations in clinical practice: A sourcebook.* Sarasota, FL: Professional Resource Exchange.

Swensen, C. H., & Trahaug, G. (1985). Commitment and the long term marriage relationship. *J Mar Fam, 47,* 939–945.

II-2/a
171. UDRY, J. R. Marital Alternatives Scale

Avail: 1981 Ref.

Variables Measured: Perception of how much better or worse off a person would be without his or her current marital partner

Type of Instrument: Self-report questionnaire

Instrument Description: The Marital Alternatives Scale is an 11-item Likert-style questionnaire. A 4-point response format, ranging from *impossible* to *certain,* is used to have married individuals indicate (1) how much better or worse off they would be without their current spouses, and (2) their perceptions of the ease or difficulty with which they could attract a new mate. The scale is based on the premise that persons contemplating leaving their current marriage partner first consider their resources and options, generally being more likely to act when their possibilities are favorable. In answering the items, respondents are instructed to assume that their spouse is going to leave them this year. Two factors are identified by the author: (1) spouse replacement and (2) economic maintenance. Each item is in the form of a question, with all using the stem "How likely is it that: . . . " Items are worded as if to be asked of wives, but could easily be adapted for use with husbands as well.

Sample Items:

(A) You could get another man better than he is?
(B) You would be able to live as well as you do now?
(C) Your prospects of a happy future would be bleak?

Comments: The author reports that the split-half reliability for the 11-item scale is approximately .70 for both husbands and wives. It is further reported that all items correlate from .20 to .80 with the total score, computed by summing values associated with responses to individual items. Validity information reported includes the following: (1) 10% of couples with high scale scores were divorced or separated one year subsequent to testing, with 18% separated or divorced after two years, and (2) divorce rates for low-scoring couples were 1% after one year and 3% after two years.

References:

Udry, J. R. (1981). Marital alternatives and marital disruption. *J Mar Fam, 43,* 889–897.
Udry, J. R. (1983). The marital happiness/disruption relationship by level of marital alternative. *J Mar Fam, 45,* 221–222.

II-2/a
172. WEISS, R. L., & CERRETO, M. C. The Marital Status Inventory (MSI)

Avail: 1980 Ref.

Variables Measured: Likelihood that the marriage will fail to survive

Type of Instrument: Self-report questionnaire

Instrument Description: The MSI is a 14-item questionnaire designed to assess the likelihood that the marriage will soon end in divorce. Items are in the form of statements to which
respondents indicate either *true* or *false,* and are ordered from least to most serious. Items
were designed to fall along a 6-point continuum of dissatisfaction with one's marriage. Points
included in this continuum were (1) thinking about separation or divorce; (2) discussions with
and inquiries to trusted friends without spouse's knowledge; (3) planning the content of active
discussion with spouse; (4) establishing financial independence from spouse; (5) serious planning for initiating legal action; and, finally, (6) filing for divorce. Following pilot testing, one
item was dropped from the initial 15-item pool, and the order of the remaining set was
adjusted to reflect frequencies of responses. The authors indicate that both a total summated
score and the seriousness of specific *true* responses should be considered.

Sample Items:

(A)   I have occasionally thought of divorce or wished that we were separated, usually
after an argument or other incident.

(B)   I have considered divorce or separation a few times other than during or shortly
after a fight, although only in vague terms.

(C)   I have thought specifically about separation or divorce. I have considered who
would get the kids, how things would be divided, pros and cons of such actions, etc.

Comments: The authors report that the coefficient of reproducibility (CR), the minimum
marginal reproducibility (MMR), and the coefficient of scalability (CS) for the MSI are .90,
.21, and .87, respectively. Others (Crane & Mead, 1980; Crane, Newfield, & Armstrong,
1984) report split-half reliability for the MSI to be approximately .86.

References:

Arias, I., & Beach, S. R. H. (1987). Validity of self-reports of marital violence. *J Fam
Violence, 2,* 139–149.
Crane, D. R., Newfield, N. C., & Armstrong, D. (1984). Predicting divorce at marital therapy
intake: Wives' distress and the Marital Status Inventory. *J Mar Fam Th, 10,* 305–312.
Forehand, R., Brody, G., Long, N., Slotkin, J., & Fauber, R. (1986). Divorce/divorce potential and inter parental conflict: The relationship to early adolescent social and cognitive
functioning. *J Adol Res, 1,* 389–397.
Weiss, R. L., & Cerreto, M. C. (1980). The Marital Status Inventory: Development of a
measure of dissolution potential. *Am J Fam Th, 8*(2), 80–85.

II-2/a
173. WHITE, L., BOOTH, A., JOHNSON, D. R., & EDWARDS, J. N.
Nebraska Scale of Marital Disagreement

Avail: 1986 Ref.

Variables Measured: Marital disagreement

Type of Instrument: Self-report questionnaire

Instrument Description: This scale consists of four summable items, each asking how often a particular level of disagreement between the respondent and his or her spouse occurs. The items are drawn from several sources. Response options are *never, rarely, sometimes, often,* and *very often.* The questionnaire was developed for use in telephone or personal interviews as well as for paper-and-pencil administration to the general population of married persons.

Sample Items:

(A)   How many serious quarrels have you had with your spouse in the last two months?
(B)   In many households bad feelings and arguments occur from time to time. In some cases people get so angry that they slap, hit, punch, kick, or throw things at one another. Has this ever happened between you and your (husband/wife)?

Comments: The authors indicate that Cronbach's alpha for this 4-item scale is .54, based on data obtained from a national probability sample of 2,033 married men and women under 55 years of age. It is also reported that the scale correlates in expected directions with other indicators of marital quality such as marital happiness (-.47), marital problems (.54), marital interaction (-.27), and marital instability (.54).

References:

Booth, A., Johnson, D., White, L., & Edwards, J. (1985). Predicting divorce and permanent separation. *J Fam Iss, 6,* 331–346.
Johnson, D., White, L., Edwards, J., & Booth, A. (1986). Dimensions of marital quality: Toward methodological and conceptual refinement. *J Fam Iss, 7,* 31–49.
White, L., & Booth, A. (1985a). The quality and stability of remarriages: The role of stepchildren. *Am Sociol R, 50,* 689–698.
White, L., & Booth, A. (1985b). Transition to parenthood and marital quality. *J Fam Iss, 6,* 435–449.

II-2/a
174. WILLIAMS, A. M. Marital Satisfaction Time Lines (MSTL)

Avail: 1979 Ref.

Variables Measured: Level of satisfaction with marital interactions

Type of Instrument: Self-report questionnaire

Instrument Description: The MSTL contains essentially one item: Respondents (husbands and wives) are asked to indicate the extent to which their interactions were pleasant, neutral, or unpleasant during each 15-minute segment of their waking hours spent together over a period of time. The index is designed to be filled out four times per hour by each member of the couple every day for two weeks. Respondents are presented with a time-line grid with the hours of the day going across, and five lines going down. Beside the lines are the symbols + +, +, 0, -, and − −, representing five levels of satisfaction ranging from *very pleasant* to *very unpleasant.* The author indicates that these five points may be reduced to three to ease data analysis. Appropriate markings are written on the grid for each individual 15-minute period through the two-week period. In addition, respondents are also asked three questions, requesting information on the most and least pleasant behaviors, and behaviors that could have improved the neutral time spent together. These questions are answered several times over the course of keeping the interactional record. The instrument may be used in research with both normal and stressed couples, and with couples undergoing marriage therapy from an applied behavioral analysis perspective.

Sample Items: Not applicable.

Comments: The author indicates that husband-wife agreement on the MSTL averaged .73 for couples rated as "happy," and .44 for a sample of couples undergoing therapy. Several differences between response patterns of happily married and distressed couples are reported by the author. A more complete description and comparison of the two sample groups is available in Williams (1979).

Reference:

Williams, A. M. (1979). The quantity and quality of marital interaction related to marital satisfaction: A behavioral analysis. *J Appl Be A, 12,* 665–678.

II-3/c
175. BARDIS, P. D. Borromean Family Index

Avail: 1975 Ref.

Variables Measured: Feelings and attitudes toward the family

Type of Instrument: Self-report questionnaire

Instrument Description: This instrument is a 5-point, 18-item questionnaire designed to assess both forces that pull an individual away from his or her family and forces that keep him or her attracted to the family. The name of the instrument comes from the coat of arms of the Borromeo family during the Renaissance. It consisted of three rings, no two of which were linked. However, if any of the rings was removed from the group, the remaining rings would no longer be connected. The conceptualization of the Borromean Family Index was that families can be pulled and pushed, but remain strong so long as none of the family members deserts the common cause. The scale is available in two forms: one for single persons and another for those who are married. Each contains two parts: (1) forces that attract you to your family, and (2) forces that pull you away from your family. Each subscale contains nine items and utilizes a 5-point response format (scored 0–4) ranging from *absent* to *very strong.* Items are in the form of single words (e.g., companionship) or short phrases. The instructions request respondents to consider all items with respect to their attitudes and feelings about "your own family (father, mother, brothers, sisters)," in the case of single persons, or "your own family (spouse and children, if any)" when being administered the married version. Scores for subscales are arrived at by summing responses to individual items within that section. The author indicates that the first subscale measures internal attraction, while the second is to be considered an external attraction score. High internal and low external scores are interpreted as indicating a profamily orientation.

Sample Items:

(A)   Family love.
(B)   Friends outside my family.
(C)   Common interests.

Comments: The author indicates that split-half reliabilities of the married persons' internal and external subscales are .87 and .91, respectively, and that test-retest reliability was determined to be .83. For the single persons' index split-half, reliabilities for the two subscales are reported to be .92 and .80, respectively, with test-retest reliability of .90.

References:

Bardis, P. D. (1975). The Borromean family. *Social Sci, 50,* 144–158.
Bardis, P. D. (1988). *Marriage and family: Continuity, change, and adjustment.* Dubuque, IA: Kendall-Hunt.

II-3/a
176. BARRETT-LENNARD, G. T. The (Barrett-Lennard) Relationship Inventory

Avail: 1978 Ref.

Variables Measured: Empathy, level of regard, congruence, and unconditionality among participants in dyadic relationships

Type of Instrument: Self-report questionnaire

Instrument Description: The Relationship Inventory (RI or BLRI) is a questionnaire research instrument usually answered by one or both participants in a dyadic relationship. The principal forms contain 64-items worded to describe the response of another person to oneself or one's own response to the other. For each item subjects select one of six possible answers. Nonoverlapping but interspersed groups of 16 items, 8 worded positively and 8 negatively, yield measures of the variables listed above. Adaptations of the instrument include forms for an observer to answer, either to describe one person's response to another or to rate qualities of a relationship dyad as a unit. Additional forms are designed for dyad members to portray qualities of their relationship, for group or family members to describe their group's or family's response to them, and for participants in a relationship to predict each other's responses. Further research on the Relationship Inventory with married couples (Schumm et al., 1983; Eggeman, Moxley, & Schumm, 1985) examined the factor structure of a 15-item version. These authors have identified three primary factors: positive regard, empathy, and congruence of one's spouse toward oneself as perceived by the subject.

Sample Items:

(A)   He respects me as a person.
(B)   How much he likes or dislikes me isn't changed by anything I tell him about myself.
(C)   His response to me is so automatic that I don't get through to him.

Comments: The RI was first developed in the late 1950s, initially for use in studying therapy or helping relationships and has been employed since in at least 500 studies of widely varied aim, method, and focus. The author reports that the four component scales have been evaluated for reliability (test-retest and internal) and that there is a broad spectrum of evidence supporting the validity of the instrument. Cronbach's alpha for factors identified in the revised and shortened version (Eggeman, Moxley, & Schumm, 1985) are reported to range from .76 to .96 (regard), .83 to .92 (empathy), and .77 to .96 (congruence). Test-retest reliabilities over a six-month period for factors within the 15-item version are reported to range from .65 to .86 (regard), .73 to .83 (empathy), and .73 to .76 (congruence).

References:

Barrett-Lennard, G. T. (1962). Dimensions of therapist response as causal factors in therapeutic change. *Psych Mon, 76*(43, Whole No. 562).

Barrett-Lennard, G. T. (1978). The Relationship Inventory: Later development and adaptations. *JSAS Catalog of Selected Documents in Psychology, 868* (Ms. No. 1732, 55 pages).

Barrett-Lennard, G. T. (1986). The Relationship Inventory now: Issues and advances in theory, method and use. In L. S. Greenberg & W. M. Pinsof (Eds.), *The psychotherapeutic process: A research handbook* (pp. 439–476). New York: Guilford.

Eggeman, K., Moxley, V., & Schumm, W. R. (1985). Assessing spouses' perceptions of Gottman's temporal form in marital conflict. *Psychol Rep, 57,* 171–181.

Schumm, W. R., Anderson, S. A., Race, G. S., Morris, J. E., Griffin, C. L., McCutchen, M. B., & Benigas, J. E. (1983). Construct validity of the Marital Communication Inventory. *J Sex Mar Th, 9,* 153–162.

Wampler, I. S., & Powell, G. S. (1982). The Barrett-Lennard Relationship Inventory as a measure of marital satisfaction. *Fam Relat, 31,* 139–145.

II-3/b/P

177. BENGTSON, V. L. Positive Affect Index: Subjective Solidarity Between Parents and Children

Avail: 1982 Ref.

Variables Measured: Perceived levels of positive affect among parents and their adult children

Type of Instrument: Self-report questionnaire

Instrument Description: This instrument is a 6-point, 10-item Likert-type questionnaire designed to assess the extent of positive feelings between parents and their adult children. The instrument is intended for use in evaluating feelings within multigenerational families. Items are asked of parents regarding perceptions of their children, and their beliefs as to their children's attitudes toward them. The questionnaire is actually two 5-item scales with nearly identical items. The feelings of understanding, trust, fairness, respect, and affection are repeated within both halves of the instrument, first with respect to respondents' perceptions as to how their children view them, followed by questions inquiring as to how they feel about their children. Response options range from 1 = *not well* to 6 = *extremely well*. Scores within the two subscales may be summed. Alternately, an overall score may be obtained by summing values from all responses.

Sample Items:

(A)   How well do you feel this child understands you?
(B)   How much do you trust this child?
(C)   How much respect do you feel from this child?

Comments: The instrument was administered by mail to a sample of 2,044 members of three-generation families, with a 64% response rate. Test-retest reliability over a period of four weeks with an additional sample of 21- to 58-year-old subjects is reported to be .89. Interitem correlations from samples averaging 67 and 43 years of age are reported to range from .41 to .73. Cronbach's alpha is listed as being .92.

References:

Bengtson, V. L., & Lovejoy, M. C. (1973). Values, personality, and social structure: An intergenerational analysis. *Am Behav Sc, 16,* 880–912.

Bengtson, V. L., Olander, E., & Haddad, A. (1976). The "generation gap" and aging family members. In J. Gubrium (Ed.), *Time, roles and self in old age* (pp. 237–263). New York: Behavioral Publications.

Bengtson, V. L., & Schrader, S. S. (1982). Parent-child relations. In D. J. Mangen & W. A. Peterson (Eds.), *Research instruments in social gerontology: Vol. 2. Social roles and social participation* (p. 154). Minneapolis: University of Minnesota Press.

Markides, K. S., & Krause, N. (1985). Intergenerational solidarity and psychological well-being among older Mexican Americans: A three-generations study. *J Gerontol, 40,* 390–392.

II-3/a

178. BRAIKER, H. B., & KELLEY, H. H. Development of Intimate Relationships

Avail: 1979 Ref.

Variables Measured: Developmental stages in the progression of feelings of intimacy in a relationship

Type of Instrument: Self-report questionnaire

Instrument Description: This instrument, left untitled by the authors, is a 9-point, 25-item Likert-type questionnaire designed to assess the development of intimacy in relationships. Items are in the form of questions to which respondents indicate how much of a feeling they had (e.g., "How committed did you feel . . . ") or in which activity they engaged (e.g., "How much did you tell . . . ") at a particular stage in the development of their relationship. The questionnaire can also be used to chart the progress of a relationship by having respondents indicate their attitudes at various points along the courtship continuum. Responses, both within subjects and between partners, can then be examined at specific stages of development. Another use might be to assess the extent of mutual versus unilateral progression in depth of commitment. Responses are on a 9-point continuum ranging from *very little or not at all* to *very much or extremely.* This instrument is appropriate for evaluating people involved in varying levels of relationships, from dating to married to divorced. Items are combined into four subscales, determined by factor and cluster analyses: (1) love, (2) ambivalence, (3) maintenance of the relationship, and (4) conflict within the relationship. The instrument seeks to tap the interpersonal nature of the relationship in order to assess effort put forth by partners toward enrichment, improvement, and maintenance. Values associated with individual items within subscales are summed to arrive at scores for subscales.

Sample Items:

(A)　To what extent did you have a sense of "belonging" with (＿＿＿＿＿＿)?

(B)　How often did you and (＿＿＿＿＿＿) argue with each other?

(C)　To what extent did you reveal or disclose very intimate things about yourself or personal feelings to (＿＿＿＿＿＿)?

Comments: Some of the items in this instrument were derived from Rubin's (1970) measure of romantic love. Internal consistency of the four subscales is reported by Isabella and Belsky (1985) to range from .61 to .90, with a mean of .76.

References:

Belsky, J., Perry-Jenkins, M., & Crouter, A. C. (1985). The work-family interface and marital change across the transition to parenthood. *J Fam Iss, 6,* 205–220.

Braiker, H. B., & Kelley, H. H. (1979). Conflict in the development of close relationships. In R. L. Burgess & T. L. Huston (Eds.), *Social exchange in developing relationships* (pp. 135–168). New York: Academic Press.

Isabella, R. A., & Belsky, J. (1985). Marital change during the transition to parenthood and security of infant-parent attachment. *J Fam Iss, 6,* 505–522.

McHale, S. M., & Huston, T. L. (1985). The effect of the transition to parenthood on the marriage relationship. *J Fam Iss, 6,* 409–433.

II-3/a

179. CHRISTENSEN, A., & KING, C. E. The Relationship Events Scale

Avail: 1983 Ref.

Variables Measured: Progress in courtship

Type of Instrument: Self-report questionnaire

Instrument Description: This instrument contains 19 *true/false* items that reflect increasing levels of intimacy, interdependence, and commitment in dating relationships. The items mark specific events that frequently occur in dating relationships with varying levels of commitment between the dating partners. Items are grouped in six levels, with directions indicating how the relationship may be classified based on the number of items from each level that are responded to as being true.

Sample Items:

(A) My partner has called me an affectionate name (sweetheart, darling, etc.).
(B) We have received an invitation for the two of us as a couple.
(C) My partner has said "I love you" to me.

Comments: The authors report on a study with 55 couples in which the responses of male and female members of the couples were correlated .81. It was also found that couples ranking higher on the Relationship Events Scale were more likely to remain together at follow-up five months later. The relationship between this scale and length of the dating relationship, degree of emotional attachment, expectancy that the relationship will be permanent, and subject's classification of the relationship as casually dating, going steady, and so on were also investigated.

Reference:

King, C. E., & Christensen, A. (1983). The Relationship Events Scale. *J Mar Fam, 44,* 671–677.

II-3/IV-2/c

180. CONGER, R. D. Social Interaction Scoring System (SISS)

Avail: NAPS-3

Variables Measured: Affective content of interactions between family members

Type of Instrument: Behavior coding scheme

Instrument Description: The SISS is a series of behavioral coding systems used to quantify videotaped interactions between family members. The two portions of this instrument of particular interest to family investigations are SISS-1 and SISS-2. The first of these focuses on the type of communication (verbal, physical, or gestural) and the quality of the emotional affect reflected (positive, negative, or neutral). SISS-2 is concerned primarily with attempts by members of the family to influence the behavior of other family members through various command and compliance statements. Use of both systems requires the selection of a focal individual within the family. Families are videotaped during three 15-minute focused interactions. The author has used the SISS with interactions involving parents assisting their child with a difficult task, all three family members playing a game together, and interactions between the parents that excluded their child. With SISS-1, ratings of interactions are coded according to the interaction type, level of emotional affect, and the other person to whom the statement is directed. In addition to the three types of communication, statements are coded with respect to whether the focal person was on the giving or receiving end of each interchange. Thus six interaction types are generated. Affect is classified as either positive or negative, and either personal, self-related, or general. A neutral classification is also included. Using SISS-2, events are coded in terms of interaction direction, command or comply status, emotional affect, and the identity of the other person. Six levels of command/comply interchanges are coded: (1) prescriptive, (2) interrogative or ambiguous, (3) proscriptive, (4) requests permission, (5) comply, and (6) refuse. Specific coding instructions and definitions are contained in the manual (available from NAPS-3).

Sample Items: Not applicable.

Comments: The author reports that agreement between raters ranged from 46% to 82% for various categories of behavior. Observer agreements of assessments based on individual family members were reported to be in the same range as those generated through codings of behavior exhibited by the entire family.

References:

Conger, R. D., Brainerd, D. W., Birch, L. L., Friedberg, P. J., & Navarro, L. A. (1986). Assessing the quality of family observations: A comparative analysis. *J Mar Fam, 48,* 361–373.

Conger, R. D., McCarty, J. A., Yang, R. K., Lahey, B. B., & Burgess, R. L. (1984). Mother's age as a predictor of observed maternal behavior in three independent samples of families. *J Mar Fam, 46,* 411–424.

Conger, R. D., McCarty, J. A., Yang, R. K., Lahey, B. B., & Kropp, J. P. (1984). Perception of child, child-rearing values, and emotional distress as mediating links between environmental stressors and observed maternal behavior. *Child Dev, 55,* 2234–2247.

II-3/a

181. DAVIDSON, B., & BALSWICK, J. The Affective Self-Disclosure Scale for Couples (ASDC)

Avail: 1988 Ref.

Variables Measured: Expressions of various types of emotion to one's spouse

Type of Instrument: Self-report questionnaire

Instrument Description: The ASDC is a 4-point, 32-item Likert-type questionnaire designed to assess both people's willingness to express positive and negative emotions to their marital partners and their beliefs regarding the willingness of their spouses to express such affective states to them. Respondents are presented with 16 statements regarding affective self-disclosure in 16 different areas. For each, spouses indicate whether they would *never, seldom, often,* or *very often* tell their partners how they feel. They are then asked to indicate how likely they believe it to be that their spouses would directly communicate such feeling to them. The ability to tell one's spouse is referred to as "output," and the belief that the spouse would communicate his or her feelings is referred to as "input." The 16 affective statements are grouped within four broad categories of emotion: love, happiness, sadness, and anger. Each subscale contains four items. Scores can be computed for input and output indexes within subscales, and for input and output summed across the four subscales. Scores are also computed for differences between perceptions of output and input. Spouses with relatively high input scores are said to be overbenefiting, while those with higher output scores are classified as underbenefiting. Administration time is estimated to be 8 minutes.

Sample Items:

(A)   When I do feel resentment toward my wife I tell her.
(B)   When my wife does feel resentment toward me she tells me.

Comments: The ASDC is a direct extension of Balswick's Expression of Emotion Scale, first presented in 1975. The authors indicate that husbands who received more emotional content than they gave tended to have lower levels of marital adjustment ($r = -.20$). Relationships between marital adjustment and underbenefiting in husbands, overbenefiting in wives, and underbenefiting in wives were reported to be $-.01$, $.04$, and $.07$, respectively. Correlations between marital adjustment and perceived underbenefiting and overbenefiting are reported to be $-.20$ and $.40$, respectively.

References:

Balswick, J. (1988). *The inexpressive male.* Lexington, MA: Lexington Books.
Davidson, B., Balswick, J., & Halverson, C. (1983a). Affective self-disclosure and marital adjustment: A test of equity theory. *J Mar Fam, 45,* 93–102.
Davidson, B., Balswick, J., & Halverson, C. (1983b). The relation between spousal affective self-disclosure and marital adjustment. *Home Ec Res J, 11,* 381–391.

II-3/II-2/a
182. EIDELSON, R. J., & EPSTEIN, N. Relationship Belief Inventory (RBI)

Avail: 1987 Ref.

Variables Measured: Irrational or unrealistic beliefs regarding romantic relationships

Type of Instrument: Self-report questionnaire

Instrument Description: The RBI is a 6-point, 40-item questionnaire designed to assess irrational beliefs related to romantic relationships. Items take the form of statements, worded either in realistic or unrealistic directions. Response options are scored 0–5, and range from *I strongly believe that the statement is false* to *I strongly believe that the statement is true.* The RBI was developed from an initial list of 128 items generated through input from 20 marital therapists. Item analyses, following administration of the scale to a sample of 47 couples beginning marital therapy, resulted in a reduction of the instrument to 12 items for each of the five clinically identified factors. Further testing with a nonclinical sample resulted in the elimination of four additional items from each subscale, leaving only the 40 items present in the current version. The five subscales are (1) disagreement is destructive, (2) mind reading is expected, (3) partners cannot change, (4) sexual perfectionism, and (5) the sexes are differ-ent. Following reversal of appropriate items, subscale scores are obtained by summing values associated with the 8 subscale items. The RBI is designed to measure belief systems about relationships, rather than beliefs necessarily regarding a relationship the respondent might be involved with at the time of testing. Thus administration instructions are prefaced with the statement: "The statements below describe ways in which a person might feel about a relation-ship with another person."

Sample Items:

(A)   If your partner expresses disagreement with your ideas, s/he probably does not think highly of you.

(B)   I do not expect my partner to sense all my moods.

(C)   Damages done early in a relationship probably cannot be reversed.

Comments: Eidelson and Epstein (1982) report that intercorrelations among the 5 sub-scales range from .17 to .44. Cronbach's alpha is reported to range from .72 to .81. Correla-tions between subscales and the Irrational Beliefs Test (Jones, 1968) ranged from .11 to .31. Correlations with the Locke-Wallace Marital Adjustment Scale (Locke & Wallace, 1959) were reported to range from -.26 to -.53 for the clinical sample and from .00 to -.43 for the nonclinical sample.

References:

Eidelson, R. J., & Epstein, N. (1982). Cognition and relationship maladjustment: Develop-ment of a measure of dysfunctional relationship beliefs. *J Cons Clin, 50,* 715–720.

Eidelson, R. J., & Epstein, N. (1987). Relationship Belief Inventory. In K. D. O'Leary (Ed.), *Assessment of marital discord: An integration for research and clinical practice* (pp. 330–333). Hillsdale, NJ: Lawrence Erlbaum.

Epstein, N., & Eidelson, R. J. (1981). Unrealistic beliefs of clinical couples: Their relationship to expectations, goals, and satisfaction. *Am J Fam Th, 9*(4), 13–22.

Kurdek, L. A., & Schmitt, J. P. (1986). Early development of relationship quality in heterosex-ual married, heterosexual cohabiting, gay and lesbian couples. *Devel Psych, 22,* 305–309.

II-3/e/C

183. HATFIELD, E., & EASTON, M. The Juvenile Love Scale (JLS) (A Child's Version of the Passionate Love Scale)

Avail: 1988 Ref.

Variables Measured: Passionate love in children

Type of Instrument: Self-report questionnaire

Instrument Description: The JLS is designed to be an exact equivalent of Hatfield and Sprecher's Passionate Love Scale (PLS), which measures passionate love in adolescents and adults. The JLS taps cognitive, emotional, and behavioral indicators of a "desire for union." The standard form contains 30 items, each responded to on a 9-point scale ranging from *agree very little* to *agree very much*. A 15-item version is also available. Different administration procedures are utilized with younger (3 to 7 years of age) and older children. With very young children a script is provided. Respondents indicate their answers on a large "ruler," placing stacks of checkers at appropriate points on the ruler. With older children, identical procedures to those employed in the PLS are used. Children simply circle the number indicating how true each statement is for them. Individual item scores are summed to produce a total index. The scale is designed to be given either individually or in large groups. Administration time is approximately 20 minutes for the short version and 35 minutes for the full-length JLS.

Sample Items:

(A) I feel like things would always be sad and gloomy if I had to live without _____ forever.

(B) Did you ever keep thinking about _____ when you wanted to stop and couldn't?

(C) I want _____ to know me, what I am thinking, what scares me, what I am wishing for.

Comments: The authors report that the short and long versions of the JLS are correlated .98. Cronbach's alpha has been reported in the .94 to .98 range. Factor analyses reported by the authors have found that 38% to 53% of the variance was accounted for by the first factor, leading the authors to the conclusion that only one factor is present.

References:

Hatfield, E., Schmitz, E., Cornelius, J., & Rapson, R. L. (1988). Passionate love: How early does it begin? *J Psychol Hum Sex, 1,* 77–88.

Hatfield E., & Sprecher, S. (1986). Measuring passionate love in intimate relations. *J Adolescen, 9,* 383–410.

Hatfield E., & Walster, G. W. (1978). *A new look at love.* Latham, MA: University Press of America.

II-3/a
184. HATFIELD, E., & SPRECHER, S. The Passionate Love Scale (PLS)

Avail: 1986 Ref.

Variables Measured: Passionate love, indicated by cognitive, emotional, and behavioral indicants of "longing for union"

Type of Instrument: Self-report questionnaire

Instrument Description: The PLS comes in both a short (15-item) and a long (30-item) version. Items are responded to according to a 9-point scale with *not at all true* appearing under the "1," *moderately true* appearing under the "4" and "5," and *definitely true* appearing under the "9" response options. Respondents circle the number that best indicates how true each statement is for them. Individual item scores are summed to produce a total score. The PLS is designed to be given either individually or in large groups, and to be used with anyone over the age of 10. It has been used by the authors to evaluate men and women of various ethnic groups. Administration time is approximately 15 minutes for the short version and 30 minutes for the full-length version of the PLS.

Sample Items:

(A) I would feel despair if _____ left me.

(B) Sometimes I feel I can't control my thoughts; they are obsessively on _____.

(C) I would rather be with _____ than anyone else.

Comments: The authors report that the short and long forms are correlated .98. Cronbach's alpha for the long version is reported to be .94. For the 15-item version, coefficient alpha is reported to be .91. It is further reported that the scale is unidimensional, with a factor analysis revealing one major factor accounting for 70% of the variance. The validity of the scale was assessed by comparing scores with a social desirability scale (r = .09) and with other measures of love and intimacy. Details of these analyses can be found in the references listed below.

References:

Hatfield, E., Schmitz, E., Cornelius, J., & Rapson, R. L. (1988). Passionate love: How early does it begin? *J Psychol Hum Sex, 1,* 77–88.

Hatfield E., & Sprecher, S. (1986). Measuring passionate love in intimate relations. *J Adolescen, 9,* 383–410.

Hatfield, E., & Walster, G. W. (1978). *A new look at love.* Latham, MA: University Press of America.

II-3/a
185. HENDRICK, C., & HENDRICK, S. S. Love Attitudes Scale

Avail: 1986 Ref.

Variables Measured: Attitudes toward passionate, game-playing, friendship-based, practical, possessive or dependent, and altruistic love

Type of Instrument: Self-report questionnaire

Instrument Description: The Love Attitudes Scale was developed based on the typology of love styles created by Lee (1973). The scale is a 5-point, 42-item Likert-style questionnaire, and is scored so that lower scores indicate a greater extent of the love style being expressed. The scale measures a multidimensional perspective of love. Thus six subscales (eros, ludus, storge, pragma, mania, agape), defined according to the variables listed above, are individually scored. Each subscale contains 7 items. A total score is not derived. The scale has been used largely with college students, although a slightly reworded version can be used with married couples. The scale is designed to explore various dimensions of attitudes toward or "styles" of loving a romantic partner.

Sample Items:

(A)   My lover and I have the right physical "chemistry" between us.
(B)   I enjoy playing the "game of love" with a number of different partners.
(C)   One consideration in choosing a partner is how he/she will reflect on my career.

Comments: Subscales were determined by factor analyses with varimax rotations conducted on data from two studies. The authors report that loadings on primary factors were generally above .50. Interitem correlations within subscales ranged from .19 (storge) to .43 (agape). Subscale intercorrelations in the two-factor analytic studies are all .25 or below, with the exception of correlations of agape with eros (.27 to .32), ludus (-.28 to -.42), and mania (.23 to .30). The authors report that Cronbach's alpha and test-retest reliability, respectively, for the six subscales are as follows: eros (.70, .60), ludus (.76, .72), storge (.62, .72), pragma (.81, .78), mania (.73, .75), and agape (.84, .73). The authors further report that validity of the scales has been examined in conjunction with numerous demographic, personality, and attitude variables.

References:

Adler, N. L., Hendrick, S. S., & Hendrick, C. (1987). Male sexual preference and attitudes toward love and sexuality. *J Sex Educ Th, 12,* 27–30.

Hendrick, C., & Hendrick, S. S. (1986). A theory and method of love. *J Pers Soc Psy, 50,* 392–402.

Hendrick, C., & Hendrick, S. S. (1988). Lovers wear rose colored glasses. *J Soc Pers Relat, 2,* 161–183.

Richardson, D. R., Medvin, N., & Hammock, G. (1988). Love styles, relationship experience, and sensation seeking: A test of validity. *Pers Indiv Diff, 9,* 645–651.

II-3/a
186. KNOX, D. Love Attitudes Inventory

Avail: Family Life Publications, Inc., P.O. Box 427, Saluda, NC 28773

Variables Measured: Romantic versus conjugal love

Type of Instrument: Self-report questionnaire

Instrument Description: The Love Attitudes Inventory is a 30-item Likert-style scale utilizing a 5-point response format. Respondents indicate their level of agreement, ranging from *strongly agree* (or *definitely yes*) to *strongly disagree* (or *definitely not*) for each item. Items are scored such that a value of 1 indicates the most romantic attitude, and a value of 5 indicates the most conjugal response. The instrument assesses views of love ranging on a continuum from extreme romanticism to extreme realism. The latter is referred to as conjugal love. Administration time is approximately 15 minutes.

Sample Items: The publisher did not grant permission to reproduce items.

Comments: The inventory was constructed from an initial pool of 200 items based on a literature review by the author. The items were submitted to 10 professionals in the field of marriage and family; 85 items were retained, based on 70% or greater agreement per item when asked to classify them as "romantic" or "conjugal" in nature. An item analysis resulted in the author's selecting 30 items for the final scale.

References:

Knox, D. (1970). Conceptions of love at three developmental levels. *Fam Coord, 19,* 151–157.

Knox, D. (1988). *Choices in relationships* (2nd ed.). St. Paul, MN: West.

Knox, D., & Sporakowski, M. J. (1968). Attitudes of college students toward love. *J Mar Fam, 30,* 638–642.

Simmons, C. H., Kolke, A. V., & Shimizu, H. (1986). Attitudes toward romantic love among American, German, and Japanese students. *J Soc Psych, 126,* 327–336.

II-3/c
187. KUETHE, J. L. Kuethe's Symbolic Figure Placement Technique (SFPT)

Avail: 1962 Ref.

Variables Measured: Individual perception of emotional support and closeness in interpersonal relationships

Type of Instrument: See instrument description.

Instrument Description: Kuethe's SFPT was the first published attempt to establish a system for quantifying the subjective placement of dolls or similar figures as a means of understanding the nature of social schemas. Since his initial article in 1962, several additional systems, geared toward more specific social situations, have also been developed. Kuethe's SFPT was designed to evaluate the emotional closeness felt by respondents to members of their families. Subjects were presented with a piece of blue felt mounted on a wall and nine sets of felt objects. The felt objects adhered to the blue piece, yet could be removed without leaving evidence as to their placement. The nine sets of objects, presented in random order, were (1) woman and child; (2) man and child; (3) three rectangles, each of different height; (4) man, woman, and child; (5) man, woman, and dog; (6) square, circle, and triangle; (7) man, woman, and two rectangles; (8) two women and two rectangles; (9) three men and three rectangles. Relative placement of objects was noted. Others (see references listed below) have further developed this technique by measuring the distance between objects.

Sample Items: Not applicable.

Comments: In addition to Kuethe's use of felt, SFPTs developed by various authors have used media such as wooden objects, paper cutouts, and dolls. There is often notice taken of the relative placement of objects, as well as orientation of objects toward or away from each other, and distances between placed objects. The measure is usually taken to be a projective assessment of interpersonal relationships, quite often those between family members. The technique is used with individuals, couples, and entire families.

References:

Kanoy, K. W., Cunningham, J. L., White, P., & Adams, S. J. (1984). Is family structure that critical? Family relationships of children with divorced and married parents. *J Divorce, 8*(2), 97–105.
Klopper, E. J., Tittler, B. I., Friedman, S., & Hughes, S. J. (1978) A multi-method investigation of two family constructs. *Fam Proc, 17,* 83–93.
Kuethe, J. (1962). Social schemas. *J Abn Soc Psy, 64,* 31–38.

II-3/a
188. LARZELERE, R. E., & HUSTON, T. L. Dyadic Trust Scale

Avail: 1980 Ref.

Variables Measured: Trust toward dating or marriage partner

Type of Instrument: Self-report questionnaire

Instrument Description: The Dyadic Trust Scale is an 8-item, 7-point Likert-style questionnaire. Response options for each item range from *very strongly agree* to *very strongly disagree.* The instrument is designed to measure interpersonal trust toward a partner in a close relationship. It is most suitable for dating and married couples, or for people in similar close relationships. The total dyadic trust score is the sum of the individual scores on the 8 items.

Sample Items:

(A) My partner is primarily interested in his/her own welfare.
(B) There are times when my partner cannot be trusted.
(C) I feel that my partner can be counted on to help me.

Comments: The authors report Cronbach's alpha to be .93 for a heterogeneous sample of dating, married, and divorced partners (Larzelere & Huston, 1980), and from .85 to .88 on homogeneous samples of married couples (Hansen, 1985; Schumm et al., 1985). Construct validity was assessed by comparing Dyadic Trust scores with indexes of love, intimacy of self-disclosure, and relationship status. Discriminant validity was assessed by comparing test scores with those obtained on two measures of trust toward people in general (Rotter's Interpersonal Trust Scale and Wrightsman's Trustworthiness subscale).

References:

Hansen, G. L. (1985). Perceived threats and marital jealousy. *Social Psych Q, 48,* 262–268.

Larzelere, R. E., & Huston, T. L. (1980). The Dyadic Trust Scale: Toward understanding interpersonal trust in close relationships. *J Mar Fam, 42,* 595–604.

Schumm, W. R., Bugaighis, M. A., Buckler, D. L., Green, D. N., & Scanlon, E. D. (1985). Construct validity of the Dyadic Trust Scale. *Psychol Rep, 56,* 1001–1002.

II-3/a
189. LEWIS, R. A. The Dyadic Formation Inventory (DFI)

Avail: NAPS-2

Variables Measured: The development of dyadic identities and relationships

Type of Instrument: Self-report questionnaire

Instrument Description: The DFI is a 5-point, 74-item questionnaire, developed in 1968 and designed to assess dimensions within which dyadic relationships, particularly those of a romantic nature, form and develop. Items are in the form of questions, with response options ranging from *never* to *very often*. Items are contained within seven factors: (1) dyadic crystallization, or "the degree to which two interacting personalities have formed a discernible pair system"; (2) dyadic inclusiveness, defined as "the extent to which pair members prefer each other to parents, siblings and friends of both sexes"; (3) dyadic exclusiveness, considered to be "the extent to which pair members exclude third persons from their two-person relationship"; (4) pair commitment, or "the degree to which two persons determine to continue their relationship"; (5) couple identity, defined as "the extent to which a couple has achieved a sense of 'we-ness' "; (6) identification as a pair, or "the degree to which the couple's significant others identify the couple as a viable pair"; and (7) dyadic interaction, or "the degree to which two persons interact or function together rather than autonomously." Most of the individual indexes are formed by summing an individual's responses on each of the items, multiplied by their factor loadings.

Sample Items:

(A)   How often are you given an invitation to a social function by friends who just assume that you would bring along the other person?

(B)   Have you two ever broken off your relationship completely and then gotten back together again?

(C)   When you have leisure time on evenings and weekends, to what extent have you done the following things together (followed by a list of 12 activities)?

Comments: Intercorrelations among the factors are reported to range from .02 to .83, with a median of .39 (Lewis, 1973). Results from longitudinal evaluations reported by the author are interpreted as indicating that all subscales, with the exception of the pair identity scale, discriminate between groups of couples who are likely to continue, versus dissolve, their relationships within three months.

References:

Filsinger, E. E., McAuoy, P., & Lewis, R. A. (1982). An empirical typology of dyadic formation. *Fam Proc, 21,* 321–335.

Lewis, R. A. (1972). A developmental framework for the analysis of premarital dyadic formation. *Fam Proc, 11,* 17–48.

Lewis, R. A. (1973). The Dyadic Formation Inventory: An instrument for measuring heterosexual couple development. *Int J Soc Fam, 3,* 207–216.

Stephen, T. D. (1984). Symbolic interdependence and post-break-up distress: A reformulation of the attachment construct. *J Divorce, 8*(1), 1–16.

II-3/a/H
190. LOPATA, H. Z. Sanctification of Husband

Avail: 1981 Ref.

Variables Measured: Tendency of a widow to idealize her former husband

Type of Instrument: Self-report questionnaire

Instrument Description: The Sanctification of Husband scale is composed of 14 items, half of which are bipolar (semantic differential/SD). The other seven items (life together/LT) are directed toward an evaluation of the deceased former spouse and utilize a 4-point response format ranging from *strongly agree* to *strongly disagree.* These latter items ask the widow to indicate her attitudes regarding how her life was with her former husband. Scores on both portions of the scale tend to be heavily weighted toward sanctification of the deceased former husband. The instrument has been used in studies examining the social roles of widows. It is appropriate for all adult ages, although in practice the author reports that 60% of subjects have been over the age of 65. The SD and LT portions of the scale are scored separately. Total scores for both sections are computed by summing values associated with individual responses within each subscale.

Sample Items:

(A)　My husband was an unusually good man.
(B)　My husband and I felt the same way about almost everything.
(C)　Honest-Dishonest.

Comments: The author reports that gamma associations range from .60 to .90, with an average of .80, for the SD items, and from .62 to .91, with an average of .78, for LT items. Between-scale gamma associations are reported to average .71, with a range from .54 to .89.

References:

Lopata, H. Z. (1973). *Widowhood in an American city.* Cambridge, MA: Schenkman.

Lopata, H. Z. (1979). *Women as widows.* New York: Elsevier.

Lopata, H. Z. (1981). Widowhood and husband sanctification. *J Mar Fam, 43,* 439–450.

II-3/c
191. LOWMAN, J. Inventory of Family Feelings (IFF)

Avail: 1987 Ref.

Variables Measured: Positive and negative feelings of family members for each other

Type of Instrument: Self-report questionnaire

Instrument Description: This instrument is a 3-point, 38-item questionnaire designed to assess feelings held by family members for each other. The final scale was developed from an initial pool of 101 items. This number was reduced to the current level through use of a factor analysis. Items are presented in the form of statements, and are responded to for each member of the family. The IFF is set up with items going down and space for up to six family members going across. For each item, respondents are asked to circle either "A" (*agree*), "N" (*neutral*), or "D" (*disagree*) under each family member's name. Administration of this instrument allows for the generation of five types of scores: individual scores, defined as ratings given to one member from another; dyad scores, which are represented by the average of two family members' scores for each other; response scores, which are the average of all scores produced by one person across members of his or her family; reception scores, which represent scores given to one family member by the rest; and family unit scores, or the average of all scores produced by the entire family. The Inventory of Family Feelings can also be used to develop a graphic representation of a family sociogram, the procedure for which is fully described in Lowman (1981). The IFF is a unidimensional scale, with total scores produced by summing appropriate values for each item.

Sample Items:

(A) I feel close to this family member.
(B) This family member doesn't show a lot of consideration toward me.
(C) I feel very warm toward this member.

Comments: The author reports test-retest reliability over a two-week period of .96. Correlations are reported between scores obtained on the IFF and the MMPI psychopathology scale (-.33), with the Locke-Wallace Marital Adjustment Test (.49), and with observational ratings of the affective component of family behavior (.49).

References:

Coleman, M., & Ganong, L. (1987). Marital conflict in stepfamilies: Effects on children. *Youth Soc, 19,* 151–172.

Fredman, N., & Sherman, R. (1987). *Handbook of measurements for marriage and family therapy.* New York: Brunner/Mazel.

Lowman, J. C. (1980). Measurement of family affective structure. *J Pers Assess, 44,* 130–141.

Lowman, J. C. (1981). Love, hate, and the family: Measures of emotion. In E. Filsinger & R. Lewis (Eds.), *Assessing marriage: New behavioral approaches* (pp. 55–73). Beverly Hills, CA: Sage.

II-3/a
192. LUND, M. The Lund Commitment Scale

Avail: 1985 Ref.

Variables Measured: Commitment of an individual to his or her current romantic relationship

Type of Instrument: Self-report questionnaire

Instrument Description: This instrument is a 9-item Likert-type scale designed to measure the extent of a person's commitment to and sense of permanence in a romantic relationship. Items were developed from open-ended responses by 30 undergraduates to questions about their romantic relationships, and about romantic relationships in general. Specifically, they were asked about their understanding of what commitment means in a relationship, and the difference between a relationship where there is and is not commitment. Student responses resulted in 18 items, which were then administered to a second sample of undergraduates. The current 9-item scale was derived from the item analysis on this initial pool. An overall commitment score is obtained by summing values associated with responses to individual items.

Sample Items:

(A)   How likely is it that your relationship will be permanent?
(B)   How much trouble would ending your relationship be to you personally?
(C)   In your opinion, how committed is your partner to this relationship?

Comments: A factor analysis reported by the author examining a combination of items from the Lund Commitment Scale and Rubin's Love Scale (1970) found factor loadings in the .29 to .81 range for the 9 commitment items. With the exception of 1 item, the 9 statements from the love scale loaded from .28 to .48 on this same factor. The remaining love scale item loaded .10. Cronbach's alpha for the commitment scale is reported to be .82. Validity assessments, also presented in Lund (1985), indicate that the commitment scale was correlated .36 with the length of the person's relationship.

Reference:

Lund, M. (1985). The development of investment and commitment scales for predicting continuity of personal relationships. *J Soc Pers Relat, 2,* 3–23.

II-3/a
193. MATHES, E. W. Romantic Love Symptom Checklist

Avail: NAPS-3

Variables Measured: Romantic feelings

Type of Instrument: Self-report questionnaire

Instrument Description: The Romantic Love Symptom Checklist is composed of 76 feelings that an individual may have when thinking of a romantic partner. The instrument was designed to measure romantic passion. Respondents are instructed to mark *true* by those feelings elicited by the thought of a loved one, and *false* by those feelings not elicited in this manner. The number of *true* responses is counted and serves as the respondent's score on the checklist. The scale was designed for use with all ages of persons involved in romantic relationships.

Sample Items:

(A)   As if each day is special.
(B)   Wow!
(C)   Preoccupied with thoughts of her or him.

Comments: The author reports that a measure of internal reliability (not specified) was .95 for both men and women. Correlations are reported between the checklist and the Peak Experience Scale (.45 for men, .36 for women), the Absorption Scale (.28 for men, .23 for women), and Rubin's Romantic Love Scale (.37 for men, .48 for women).

References:

Mathes, E. W. (1982). Mystical experiences, romantic love, and hypnotic susceptibility. *Psychol Rep, 50,* 701–702.

Mathes, E. W., & Wise, P. S. (1983). Romantic love and the ravages of time. *Psychol Rep, 53,* 839–864.

II-3/a
194. MILLER, R. S., & LEFCOURT, H. M. Miller Social Intimacy Scale

Avail: 1982 Ref.

Variables Measured: Degree of closeness felt to person with whom subject feels closest

Type of Instrument: Self-report questionnaire

Instrument Description: The Miller Social Intimacy Scale is a 17-item Likert-style scale utilizing a 10-point response format. Available responses range from *very rarely* to *almost always*. Six items concern frequency of events, while the remainder inquire about intensity of feelings. It was designed to investigate closeness with intimate others. Subjects are asked to indicate how they would describe their current relationship with their closest friend. An additional question asks whether the friend being described is the respondent's spouse. An initial 30-item pool was developed through interviews with university undergraduates. Item analyses reduced the scale to the 17 current questions. Administration time is approximately 5–10 minutes.

Sample Items:

(A) How often do you show him/her affection?
(B) How much do you like to spend time alone with him/her?
(C) How important is it to you that he/she understands your feelings?

Comments: Cronbach's alpha is reported by the authors to be in the range of .86 to .91. Test-retest reliability is reported to be .96. Convergent validity has been evaluated in studies comparing scores with other measures of trust, intimacy, and loneliness. Discriminate validity has been investigated in research comparing scores of closest friend and acquaintance and between distraught married couples and those securely attached to their mates. The authors report that subjects with less intimate relationships have been found to be more distressed following stressful events than those with closer intimate relationships.

References:

Miller, R. S., & Lefcourt, H. M. (1982). The assessment of social intimacy. *J Pers Assess, 46,* 514–518.
Miller, R. S., & Lefcourt, H. M. (1983). Social intimacy: An important moderator of stressful life events. *Am J Comm P, 11,* 127–139.

II-3/a
195. O'LEARY, K. D., FINCHAM, F., & TURKEWITZ, H. Positive Feelings Questionnaire (PFQ)

Avail: 1987 Ref.

Variables Measured: Positive affect toward spouse

Type of Instrument: Self-report questionnaire

Instrument Description: The PFQ is a 17-item Likert-type inventory utilizing a 7-point response format. Available responses range from *extremely negative* to *extremely positive*. It was designed to assesses the overall affect an individual feels toward his or her spouse. The questionnaire was initially developed in order to predict outcome in marital therapy. PFQ scores are calculated by summing scores from each individual item.

Sample Items:

(A)   How do you feel about having married your spouse?
(B)   Touching my spouse makes me feel . . .
(C)   Having sex with my spouse makes me feel . . .

Comments: The authors report that all items in the scale meet a homogeneity coefficient of > .50. Studies where the PFQ has been correlated with other instruments are also reported: Marital Adjustment Test (.70), Navran Communication Scale (.40), and Beck Depression Inventory (-.16). It is also reported that the PFQ has been found to predict change in marital therapy for women but not for men, and that women's experiences with physical aggression in a dating relationship as both victims and aggressors were associated with lowered levels of positive affect toward a partner, as measured by the PFQ.

References:

Broderick, J., & O'Leary, K. D. (1986). Contributions of affect, attitudes, and behavior to marital satisfaction. *J Cons Clin, 54,* 514–517.
O'Leary, K. D. (Ed.). (1987). *Assessment of marital discord: An integration for research and clinical practice.* Hillsdale, NJ: Lawrence Erlbaum.
O'Leary, K. D., Fincham, F., & Turkewitz, H. (1983). Assessment of positive feelings toward spouse. *J Cons Clin, 51,* 949–951.
Turkewitz, H., & O'Leary, K. D. (1981). A comparative outcome study of behavioral marital therapy and communication therapy. *J Mar Fam Th, 7,* 159–169.

II-3/a
196. OLSON, D. H., & SCHAEFER, M. T. Personal Assessment of Intimacy in Relationships (PAIR) Inventory

Avail: 1981 Ref.

Variables Measured: Emotional, social, sexual, intellectual, and recreational intimacy, as well as conventionality

Type of Instrument: Self-report questionnaire

Instrument Description: The PAIR is a 60-item Likert-style questionnaire utilizing a 5-point response format. Each item is responded to from both perceived and ideal perspectives. It was developed as a tool for educators, researchers, and therapists, and is appropriate for use in evaluating and working with couples in marital therapy and enrichment groups. Individuals, married or unmarried, describe their relationships in terms of how they currently perceive them and how they would like them to be. Subjects indicate the extent of their *agreement* or *disagreement* with 10 items for each of six subscales. Individual items within subscales are summed to arrive at total scores for each area. These totals are then translated into scores resembling percentiles, with a range of 0 to 96.

Sample Items:

(A)   We have very few friends in common.
(B)   I sometimes feel lonely when we are together.
(C)   My partner seems disinterested in sex.

Comments: The final 60-item PAIR Inventory was culled from an original pool of 75 items. The original scale was administered to a sample of 192 married couples ranging in age from 21 to 60 years as part of a large battery of instruments. The authors report that the results were subjected to both factor and item analyses. The 10 items judged best on a number of criteria were retained in the final scale. Loadings of items on their primary factors ranged from .21 to .78. The authors further report that, with the exception of the spiritual subscale, correlations between PAIR subscales and the Locke-Wallace Marital Adjustment Scale all exceeded .30. Cronbach's alpha for each of the six subscales is reported to be at least .70.

References:

Hatch, R. C., James, D. L., & Schumm, W. R. (1986). Spiritual intimacy and marital satisfaction. *Fam Relat, 10,* 241–261.
Johnson, S. M., & Greenberg, L. S. (1985). Emotionally focused couples therapy: An outcome study. *J Mar Fam Th, 11,* 313–317.
Schaefer, M. T., & Olson, D. H. (1981). Assessing intimacy: The Pair Inventory. *J Mar Fam Th, 7,* 47–60.

II-3/a
197. ORLOFSKY, J. L., & LEVITZ-JONES, E. M. Intimacy Status Interview and Rating Manual

Avail: NAPS-2

Variables Measured: Intimacy maturity in young adulthood (i.e., the propensity and capacity of the individual for developing and maintaining mutually satisfying close friendships and love relationships)

Type of Instrument: Semistructured interview protocol

Instrument Description: A semistructured interview is used to assess intimacy in relationships with close friends and lover(s). Four criteria are used to determine intimacy status: (1) involvement with friends, (2) commitment to an enduring love or other such primary relationship, (3) depth of communication and caring in close relationships, and (4) degree of dependence or autonomy in close relationships. These criteria combine to define seven intimacy statuses, clustered into four types of relationship styles: intimate and preintimate, pseudo-intimate and stereotyped, merger committed and uncommitted, and isolated. The interview consists of two sections. The first part inquires about closest friendships, particularly with same-gender friends. The second part emphasizes romantic relationships. A manual, including illustrative sketches of characters fitting each category, is available. Administration time is 30–40 minutes.

Sample Items:

(A) How would you describe your feelings for her/him?
(B) Can you describe some of the experiences in which you've felt closest to her/him?
(C) What kinds of things do the two of you talk about? . . . Do you share your worries and problems with her/him? (Can you give me some examples?)

Comments: Validity for the intimacy statuses have been examined in several studies. The authors report that statuses differ in the accurate prediction of partners' attitudes and self-concepts, in the depth of self-disclosure to partners, and in their ability to express and articulate affective experience. Differences are also reported regarding degree of identity resolution, resolution of previous psychosocial crises, and in security of interpersonal attachment and separation-individuation. Interrater reliability is reported to average .81. A revised manual is currently in preparation and is expected to be published in *Ego Identity: A Handbook for Psychosocial Research* (Marcia, Matteson, Waterman, Archer, & Orlofsky).

References:

Levitz-Jones, E. M., & Orlofsky, J. L. (1985). Separation-individuation and intimacy capacity in college women. *J Pers Soc Psy, 49,* 156–169.

Orlofsky, J. L., & Ginsburg, S. D. (1981). Intimacy status: Relationship to affect cognition. *Adolescence, 61,* 92–100.

Orlofsky, J., Marcia, J., and Lesser, I. (1973). Ego identity status and the intimacy versus isolation crisis of young adulthood. *J Pers Soc Psy, 27,* 211–219.

Prager, K. J. (1986). Intimacy status: Its relationship to locus of control, self-disclosure, and anxiety in adults. *Pers Soc Psy Bul, 12,* 91–109.

II-3/a
198. RUBIN, Z. Romantic Love Scale

Avail: 1973 Ref.

Variables Measured: Feeling of love toward a specified individual

Type of Instrument: Self-report questionnaire

Instrument Description: The Romantic Love Scale is a 9-item questionnaire designed to measure feelings of romantic attachment to another individual. Responses are made along a continuum with three defined points listed as *not at all true, disagree completely; moderately true, agree to some extent;* and *definitely true, agree completely.* However, the author indicates that measurements with a ruler are made in order to convert responses to a 9-point scoring system. The scale was originally written in 1969 and published in 1970 as a 13-item scale. Four items judged by the author to be less appropriate were dropped beginning with the 1973 reference. This reference lists the original scale, while noting which items are no longer in use. The Romantic Love Scale is often utilized as a companion instrument to the Liking Scale, also available in Rubin (1973). Overall scale scores are derived by summing values associated with each response.

Sample Items:

(A)   I feel that I can confide in _____ about virtually everything.
(B)   I would do almost anything for _____.
(C)   If I were lonely, my first thought would be to seek _____ out.

Comments: The author initially utilized the questionnaire to examine loving and liking relationships between dating partners on a university campus. Loving and liking scores were found to correlate .56 for males and .36 for females. It is also indicated that men and women reported nearly identical love scores for each other, but that women reported significantly higher levels of liking their partners than did men. A validity check asked respondents to indicate whether they were in love with their partners. Subjects answered the question by circling either *yes, no,* or *uncertain.* The correlation between this simplistic index and the Romantic Love Scale was reported to be .61 for women and .53 for men. Correlations between the Liking Scale and this index of love were .29 for women and .36 for men.

References:

Berman, W. H. (1985). Continued attachment after legal divorce. *J Fam Iss, 6,* 375–392.
King, C. E., & Christensen, A. (1983). The Relationship Event Scale: A Guttman scaling of progress in courtship. *J Mar Fam, 45,* 671–677.
Richardson, D. R., Medvin, N., & Hammock, G. (1988). Love styles, relationship experience, and sensation seeking: A test of validity. *Pers Indiv Diff, 9,* 645–651.
Rubin, Z. (1973). *Liking and loving: An invitation to social psychology.* New York: Holt.

II-3/a
199. RYDER, R. G. Lovesickness (LS) Scale

Avail: NAPS-2

Variables Measured: The degree to which a person reports wanting more attention or caring from his or her spouse

Type of Instrument: Self-report questionnaire

Instrument Description: The LS Scale is a 32-item questionnaire developed to assess the extent to which a person is satisfied with the attention and concern received from his or her spouse. Items are scored *true, partly true,* or *false.* Half the items are worded in each direction, with values from negatively worded items being reversed prior to scoring. The LS Scale would be appropriate for use in varied contexts where attention from the spouse is of interest. The author initially developed this instrument to aid in assessing feelings of lovesickness in husbands where there was a newborn child in the family. The measure is equally appropriate for use with husbands and wives.

Sample Items:

(A)   I know my spouse loves me but I wish he/she would show it more.
(B)   I wish my spouse paid more attention to me.
(C)   My spouse always pays careful attention to how I feel about matters.

Comments: While Ryder did not report reliability information on the LS Scale, others (Doherty, 1981; Sabatelli, Buck, & Dreyer, 1982) report Cronbach's alpha to be in the .82 to .91 range. Ryder examined change scores from four months postmarriage to one to two years later for three groups: childless couples, couples with at least one child, and couples pregnant with their first child. Results indicated that, while scores of both husbands and wives tended to increase for all groups, LS scores of wives tended to increase more than those of husbands, with particularly large differences when the wife was pregnant during the second test administration. Sabatelli, Buck, and Dreyer reported correlations of .49 to .58 between the LS Scale and the Locke-Wallace Marriage Adjustment Test (1959).

References:

Doherty, W. J. (1981). Locus of control differences and marital dissatisfaction. *J Mar Fam, 43,* 369–377.
Ryder, R. G. (1973). Longitudinal data relating marriage satisfaction and having a child. *J Mar Fam, 35,* 604–606.
Sabatelli, R. M., Buck, R., & Dreyer, A. (1982). Nonverbal communication accuracy in married couples: Relationship with marital complaints. *J Pers Soc Psy, 43,* 1088–1097.

II-3/a

200. SCHLEIN, S., GUERNEY, B. G., Jr., & STOVER, L. The Interpersonal Relationship Scale (IRS)

Avail: 1977 Ref., & IDEALS (Institute for the Development of Emotional and Life Skills), P.O. Box 391, State College, PA 16804

Variables Measured: The quality of interpersonal relationships, particularly trust and intimacy

Type of Instrument: Self-report questionnaire

Instrument Description: An initial pool of 106 5-point, Likert-type items was constructed by the authors and their colleagues. These were presented to eight judges whose field of study emphasized interpersonal relationships. They were asked to estimate the value of the item as a measure of trust, intimacy, or both. An item was retained when at least six judges rated it as suitable. This process and further minor pruning by the authors eliminated all but 52 items. Most of the research utilizing this instrument has been with families.

Sample Items:

(A) I share and discuss my problems with my partner.
(B) I listen carefully to my partner and help him/her solve problems.
(C) My partner would tell a lie if he/she could gain by it.

Comments: The authors indicate that two-month test-retest reliability with 20 married couples, reported by Rappaport (1976), was .92. Investigations into the validity of the IRS have examined correlations with the Premarital Communication Inventory (.69), the (modified) Primary Communication Inventory (.55), the Relationship Scale-Self (.79), and the Relationship Scale-Partner (.70). Further details regarding reliability and validity information are provided in the references listed below.

References:

Guerney, B. G., Jr. (1977). *Relationship Enhancement: Skill-training programs for therapy, problem prevention, and enrichment.* San Francisco: Jossey-Bass.

Miller, R. S., & Lefcourt, H. M. (1982). The assessment of social intimacy. *J Pers Assess, 46,* 514–518.

Rappaport, A. F. (1976). Conjugal relationship enhancement program. In D. H. L. Olson (Ed.), *Treating relationships* (pp. 41–66). Lake Mills, IA: Graphic.

Ross, E. R., Baker, S. B., & Guerney, B. G., Jr. (1985). Effectiveness of Relationship Enhancement therapy versus therapist's preferred therapy. *Am J Fam Th, 13*(1), 11–21.

II-3/IV-2/a

201. SCHUTZ, W. C. Fundamental Interpersonal Relations Orientation (FIRO) Scales

Avail: Consulting Psychologists Press, 577 College Ave., Palo Alto, CA 94306

Variables Measured: Feelings and behaviors relative to interpersonal needs for inclusion, control, and affection

Type of Instrument: Self-report questionnaire

Instrument Description: The FIRO Scales are a series of instruments, based on the original (1958) FIRO theory, that are designed to measure the areas of inclusion, control, and affection. The series consists of different scales for evaluating behaviors toward other people (FIRO-B), feelings (FIRO-F), relationships between marital couples or other closely related individuals (marital attitude evaluation, or MATE), adults' parents prior to the age of 6 (life interpersonal history enquiry, or LIPHE), and relationships in educational settings (educational values, or VAL-ED). In addition, a form of the FIRO for use in measuring behaviors of children (FIRO-BC), developed with the assistance of Marilyn Wood, and a version for measuring defensive or coping mechanisms (coping operations preference enquiry, or COPE) are also available. Most versions consist of at least six individual Guttman-type scales, each containing 9 items. The tests are easily scored, with FIRO-B norms provided. Complete instructions for interpreting results are provided in the manual. The instruments have been used with a wide variety of populations. An updated version of the FIRO Scales, Schutz ELEMENTS of Awareness (Schutz, 1987) is available through WSA publishers.

Sample Items:

(A)   When I was a child, I wanted my mother to allow me more freedom.
(B)   I want you (Mate) to spend more time with me.
(C)   I get close to people.

Comments: Reproducibility coefficients, that is, being able to predict responses on individual items from scale scores, are reported to be at least .88 for all scales, with most values exceeding .90. Test-retest reliability for FIRO-B subscales is reported to range from .71 to .82. The scales were originally published in 1958.

References:

Akin, G. (1982). Interpersonal correlates of Fromm's character types. *Soc Beh Per, 10,* 77–81.

O'Leary, M. R., Donovan, D. M., Chaney, E. F., & Speltz, M. L. (1979). Correlates of clinicians' perceptions of patients in alcoholism treatment. *J Clin Psych, 40,* 344–347.

Ryan, L. F. (1977). *Clinical interpretation of the FIRO-B.* Palo Alto, CA: Consulting Psychologists Press.

Schutz, W. C. (1958). *FIRO-A: Three-dimensional theory of interpersonal behavior.* New York: Rinehart.

Vickers, R. R., Jr., & Hervig, L. K. (1981). Comparison of three psychological defense mechanism questionnaires. *J Pers Assess, 45,* 630–638.

II-3/III-2/b/P
202. SCHWARZ, J. C. Schwarz-Zuroff Love Inconsistency Scale (LI)

Avail: NAPS-3

Variables Measured: Inconsistency in mother's love and affection toward the subject, and inconsistency in father's love and affection toward the subject

Type of Instrument: Questionnaire rating perceptions of family behaviors

Instrument Description: The LI is a 4-point, 13-item Likert-style scale concerned with the consistency of parental love and affection. Positively keyed items describe the parent as sometimes loving and sometimes hating, negatively keyed items impute consistent love to the parent. Each item is rated on a scale ranging from *not true* to *very true.* Forms of the questionnaire and norms are available for separate ratings of both mother and father by four family members: mother, father, college-age child, and sibling. The total LI score is the mean of responses to all items. Multiple rater aggregate scores are obtained by standardizing scores for individual raters and then taking the mean of these standard scores.

Sample Items:

(A)   If something got my father angry, the whole family would suffer.
(B)   My brother/sister could always depend on our mother to be kind and considerate toward him/her.
(C)   My spouse could be warm and affectionate, but sometimes he/she said cold, cuttings things to our son/daughter.

Comments: The LI was developed specifically to test the hypothesis that unstable parental affection, especially on the part of the opposite-gender parent, and in combination with other factors, would be associated with depression-proneness. The initial pool contained 25 items, all worded in the first person. According to the authors, factor analyses on two samples revealed similar factor structures, with the 13 items retained in the final version loading above .52 on the first factor. Cronbach's alpha for the final scale is reported to be approximately .90. Normative data were then collected as a part of the same study described in the abstract of the Schwarz Inter-Parental Conflict Scale (IPC), detailed elsewhere in this volume. Pairwise correlations between the four rater types are reported to have ranged from .33 to .65. Both the mother's and father's four-rater aggregate LI scores were correlated negatively with warmth (-.50 and -.56, respectively), discipline (-.35 and -.30, respectively), and positively with self-assertion (.36 and .33, respectively).

References:

McCranie, E. W., & Bass, J. D. (1984). Childhood family antecedents of dependency and self criticism: Implications for depression. *J Abn Psych, 93*, 3–8.

Schwarz, J. C., & Zuroff, D. C. (1979). Family structure and depression in female college students: Effects of parental conflict, decision-making power, and inconsistency of love. *J Abn Psych, 88*, 398–406.

Southworth, S., & Schwarz, J. C. (1987). Post-divorce contact, relationship with father, and heterosexual trust in female college students. *Am J Orthop, 57*, 371–382.

II-3/a
203. SHOSTROM, E. L. Caring Relationship Inventory (CRI)

Avail: Educational and Industrial Testing Service, P.O. Box 7234, San Diego, CA 92107

Variables Measured: Feelings and attitudes of members of romantically inclined dyads toward each other

Type of Instrument: Paper-and-pencil questionnaire

Instrument Description: The CRI is an 83-item true/false questionnaire designed to evaluate the essential elements of love or caring in romantic relationships. Five elements of love are assessed (affection—agape, friendship, eros, empathy, and self-love), with two additional scales clustered according to Maslow's concepts of "being love" and "deficiency love." The questionnaire is responded to twice: first as it applies to the other member of the pair, and second as it applies to an ideal mate. Separate forms are used for male and female respondents. The CRI is intended for use in counseling and therapeutic settings as well as a means of facilitating discussion in marriage and family courses.

Sample Items:

(A)   I have the feeling that we are "buddies" together.
(B)   It is easy to turn a blind eye to her faults.
(C)   My feeling for him is based on his accomplishments.

Comments: The author reports that split-half reliability for the five CRI elements of love range from .74 to .87 with a median of .80. For the two subscales of being love and deficiency love, the split-half reliability is reported to be .82 and .66, respectively. CRI scores have been compared to those on the Pair Attraction Inventory (Shostrom, 1971) and the Personal Orientation Inventory (Shostrom, 1974). Further reliability and validity information is provided in the CRI manual.

References:

Shostrom, E. L., Knapp, L. F., & Knapp, R. R. (1975). *Actualizing therapy: Foundation for a scientific ethic.* San Diego: EdITS.

Zuckerman, M., Neeb, M., Ficher, M., Fishkin, R. E., Goldman, A., Fink, P. J., Cohen, S. N., Jacobs, J. A., & Weisberg, M. (1985). Nocturnal penile tumescence and penile responses in the waking state in diabetic and nondiabetic sexual dysfunctionals. *Arch Sex Be, 14,* 109–129.

II-3/a
204. SHOSTROM, E. L. Pair Attraction Inventory (PAI)

Avail: Educational and Industrial Testing Service, P.O. Box 7234, San Diego, CA 92107

Variables Measured: Conscious and unconscious factors involved in the selection of a mate or a friend of the opposite gender

Type of Instrument: Self-report instrument

Instrument Description: The PAI is a 224-item *true/false* questionnaire designed to measure elements underlying opposite-gender attractions. It is designed to measure both complementarity and symmetry in pair relationships. The complementarity construct contains four subscales: (1) mother-son, the nurturing relationship; (2) father-daughter, the supporting relationship; (3) shrew-nice guy, the challenging relationship; and (4) tyrant-nice gal, the educating relationship. Two subscales are designed to measure symmetry: (1) hawks, the confronting relationship, and (2) doves, the accommodating relationship. One additional subscale, rhythmic score, the actualizing relationship is also used. The questionnaire is designed to be independently administered to partners in dyadic relationships. Items are presented in contrasting pairs. One statement of each pair describes the respondent's feelings toward the other person, while the other statement refers to the other person's feeling toward the respondent. Separate booklets are provided for males and females along with special answer profile sheets. Inventory booklets are reusable. The intended population is adult couples. Scoring procedures are described in the manual. Administration time is approximately 10–30 minutes.

Sample Items:

(A) 1. He likes me to lean on him for support.
2. I value his strength and his ability to be helpful.
(B) 1. I am constantly trying to prove that I am his equal or better.
2. I often attack him in an attempt to prove my superiority.

Comments: The author reports that test-retest reliability estimates for the PAI scales range from .78 to .93, with a median of .89. PAI scores have been compared to those obtained on the Personal Orientation Inventory (Shostrom, 1963) and the Caring Relationship Inventory (Shostrom, 1966). Further details regarding reliability and validity are contained in the PAI manual.

References:

Kellerman, H. (1977). Shostrom's mate selection model, the Pair Attraction Inventory, and the Emotions Profile Index. *J Psychol, 95,* 37–43.

Miaoulis, C. N., & Gutsch, K. U. (1979). A study of the innovative use of time and planned short term treatment in conjoint counseling. *South J Educ Res, 13,* 135–143.

Shostrom, F. L., & Knapp, R. R. (1977). Relationship between clinical ratings and inventory measures of intrapersonal styles: Validity of the Pair Attraction Inventory. *Educ Psyc M, 37,* 541–543.

Tan, G., & Lawlis, G. F. (1976). Correlational study of children's school achievement and parental interactional perception. *Psychol Rep, 38,* 578.

II-3/c

205. STOVER, L., GUERNEY, B. G., Jr., GINSBERG, B., & SCHLEIN, S. The Acceptance of Other Scale (AOS)

Avail: 1977 Ref., & IDEALS (Institute for the Development of Emotional and Life Skills), P.O. Box 391, State College, PA 16804

Variables Measured: Understanding and acceptance conveyed by one person in his or her verbal responses to communication from another person

Type of Instrument: Behavior rating system

Instrument Description: The AOS gives primary weight to empathy as a form of acceptance, and to those responses that encourage others to follow their own line of thought. It assesses sensitivity to an interactant's phenomenological field, willingness to stay within boundaries defined by the other's field, and sensitivity to feelings, needs, and motivations of the other as expressed by both words and manner. The guiding question in its development was this: "What would be the best and worst responses that could be made to another's statement by a Rogerian psychotherapist?" An 8-point scale is used, with the lowest level of responses being argumentative and accusative, midlevel responses being typical of ordinary conversation, and high-level responses being ones that convey complete empathic acceptance of the other person. The scale can be used to rate communication, defining the response unit either as an arbitrary unit of time (the authors recommend 1 minute) or as a statement by the person being rated that is sandwiched between two statements made by another person. The authors report that the latter method is preferred for most applications. When used to analyze dyadic interactions, the AOS has been used in conjunction with the Verbal Interaction Task (VIT). A more complete explanation of the VIT appears in the description of the Self-Feeling Awareness Scale located elsewhere in this volume.

Sample Items: Not applicable.

Comments: Interrater reliability of the AOS system is reported by the authors to range from .89 to .96. Correlations are reported between the AOS and the Self-Feeling Awareness Scale (.30 to .32), the Family Life Questionnaire—Father, Son (.26 to .39), and the Premarital Communication Inventory (.23). The authors report that correlations between the AOS and several other paper-and-pencil measures of interpersonal behavior or adjustment were not significant.

References:

Guerney, B. G., Jr. (1977). *Relationship Enhancement: Skill-training programs for therapy, problem prevention, and enrichment.* San Francisco: Jossey-Bass.

Guerney, B. G., Jr., Coufal, J., & Vogelsong, E. (1981). Relationship Enhancement versus a traditional approach to therapeutic/preventative/enrichment parent-adolescent programs. *J Cons Clin, 49,* 927–929.

Guerney, B. G., Jr., Vogelsong, E. L., & Coufal, J. (1983). Relationship Enhancement versus a traditional treatment: Follow-up and booster effects. In D. Olson & B. Miller (Eds.), *Family studies review yearbook* (Vol. 1, pp. 738–756). Beverly Hills, CA: Sage.

Most, R. K., & Guerney, B. G., Jr. (1983). An empirical evaluation for training leaders for premarital Relationship Enhancement. *Fam Relat, 32,* 239–251.

II-3/g
206. SURRA, C. A. Turning Point Code I

Avail: NAPS-3

Variables Measured: Frequency or proportion of occurrence of subjective reasons for changes in interpersonal or romantic commitment

Type of Instrument: System for rating self-reports of reasons for behavior

Instrument Description: The Turning Point Code is designed to assess partners' subjective reasons for becoming more or less committed. The instrument is typically used in conjunction with retrospective interviews of newlyweds, or in prospective interviews of dating partners. Respondents are asked to plot changes over time in the "chance of marriage" (CM) to their partners. CM is a measure of commitment ranging from 0% to 100%. Each time the CM changes, respondents are asked to tell why the change occurred. These explanations are categorized according to their content using the Turning Point Code. This system of classification contains four categories of reasons: intrapersonal/normative (or individual), dyadic, social network, and circumstantial. The author indicates that a revised and expanded version of this system, Turning Point Code II, has also been used in completed but unpublished studies.

Sample Items: Not applicable.

Comments: The four categories were developed from content analysis of reasons given by 50 newlywed couples. The author reports that agreement using the four-category scheme was measured at 93%. A manual for use of this system is available through NAPS-3.

References:

Lloyd, S. A., & Cate, R. M. (1985). Attributions associated with significant turning points in premarital relationship development and dissolution. *J Soc Pers Relat, 2,* 419–436.

Surra, C. A. (1987). Reasons for changes in commitment: Variations by courtship type. *J Soc Pers Relat, 4,* 17–33.

Surra, C. A., Arizzi, P., & Asmussen, L. (1988). The association between reasons for commitment and the development and outcome of marital relationships. *J Soc Pers Relat, 5,* 47–63.

Surra, C. A., & Huston, T. L. (1987). Mate selection as a social transition. In D. Perlman & S. Duck (Eds.), *Intimate relationships: Development, dynamics, and deterioration* (pp. 88–120). Newbury Park, CA: Sage.

II-3/a
207. SWENSEN, C. H., & GILNER, F. Scale of Feelings and Behavior of Love (Love Scale)

Avail: 1973 Ref.

Variables Measured: Feelings, behaviors, and beliefs associated with being in love

Type of Instrument: Self-report questionnaire

Instrument Description: The Love Scale is a 120-item Likert-type scale utilizing a 3-point response format ranging from *never* to *frequently* true of the relationship. Seven scores are obtained, including the overall Love Scale and six subscales (verbal expression of affection; self-disclosure of intimate facts about oneself; toleration of the less pleasant aspects of the loved person; nonmaterial evidence of love such as moral support, encouragement, and interest; unexpressed feelings; and material evidence, such as money, gifts, and chores). The scale was designed to be used by adolescents and adults of all ages in the description of all types of love relationships. The authors report that administration time is dependent upon the reading ability of the subject, but that the questionnaire is usually completed within 20–30 minutes.

Sample Items:

(A)   The loved one tells you that he (she) trusts you completely.
(B)   You pray for the loved one.
(C)   The loved one helps you with tasks such as homework, household tasks, etc.

Comments: The scale was based upon statements obtained during interviews in which subjects were asked to describe what characterized their relationships with people they loved. These statements were given to samples of varying ages and completed for different relationships, then factor analyzed. The authors report two-week test-retest reliabilities ranging from .77 to .96. It is also reported that married couples seeking marriage counseling score significantly lower than happily married couples. The authors indicate that couples at more complex levels of ego development express significantly more love to each other than couples at less complex stages, and that expression of love declines the longer people are married.

References:

Swensen, C. H. (1973). Scale of the feelings and behavior of love. In J. W. Pfeiffer & J. E. Jones (Eds.), *The 1973 handbook for group facilitators.* San Diego: University Associates.

Swensen, C. H., Eskew, R., & Kohlhepp, K. (1981). Stage of family life cycle, ego development, and the marriage relationship. *J Mar Fam, 43,* 841–853.

Swensen, C. H., & Gilner, F. (1964). Factor analysis of statements of love relationships. *J Indiv Psy, 20,* 186–188.

Swensen, C. H., & Trahaug, G. (1985). Commitment and the long term marriage relationship. *J Mar Fam, 47,* 939–945.

II-3/a
208. TESCH, S. A. Psychosocial Intimacy Questionnaire (PIQ)

Avail: 1985 Ref.

Variables Measured: Level of psychosocial intimacy in a relationship

Type of Instrument: Self-report questionnaire

Instrument Description: The PIQ is a 60-item Likert-style instrument designed to measure psychosocial intimacy in a specific relationship, either friendship, courtship, or marriage. Items are statements that refer to a relationship with a specific individual. That individual's name or title (e.g., "my mother," "John," and so on) is filled in where blanks occur within questions. Respondents indicate their level of agreement or disagreement according to six response options. Negatively worded items are reverse-scored, with response values from individual items summed to yield a composite score. Total scores can range from 60 to 360.

Sample Items:

(A) I talk to _____ about anything and everything.
(B) _____ doesn't take our relationship very seriously.
(C) I would change jobs or schools in order to be near _____.

Comments: The author reports on two studies in which Cronbach's alpha was .97 and .98. Test-retest reliability over a three-week period is reported to be between .69 and .84. Positive correlations are reported between the PIQ and trust (.73), love (.65), and an intimacy versus isolation scale (.49 to .61). The correlation between scores on this instrument and a social desirability scale is reported by the author to be .01. A factor analysis is also reported by the author in which the factors of romantic love, supportiveness, and communication ease were identified. However, the factor structures were less than pure, with several items obtaining high loadings on more than one factor. Thus the author has indicated a single-factor treatment for the questionnaire.

Reference:

Tesch, S. A. (1985). The Psychosocial Intimacy Questionnaire: Validational studies and an investigation of sex roles. *J Soc Pers Relat, 2,* 471–488.

II-3/a
209. THOMPSON, L., & WALKER, A. J. Attachment Scale

Avail: NAPS-3

Variables Measured: Perceived attachment

Type of Instrument: Self-report questionnaire

Instrument Description: The Attachment Scale is a 5-point, 9-item Likert-style scale designed to assess attachment or emotional dependence in interpersonal relationships. The questionnaire has been administered both in interview and in paper-and-pencil formats. Response options range from *not true* to *always true,* and are coded 1–5. Item scores are summed and divided by 9 in order to arrive at a mean scale score. Administration time is approximately 2–4 minutes.

Sample Items:

(A) We're emotionally dependent on each other.
(B) When we anticipate being apart, our relationship intensifies.
(C) Our best times are with each other.

Comments: The authors report that Cronbach's alpha for the Attachment Scale has ranged from .86 to .91. The 9 items contained in this scale were derived from a factor analysis conducted on 50 original items developed to reflect various aspects of intimacy. The factor analysis resulted in the creation of five separate scales, including attachment, intimacy, disclosure, tension, and worry. The authors report that items contained within each scale loaded at least .5 on that scale, with loadings on nonprimary factors of less than .25. The Attachment Scale has been used to distinguish among relationships according to generation, aid exchange patterns, and marital status of young adult women.

References:

Townsend, J. K., & Worobey, J. (1987). Mother and daughter perceptions of their relation-
ships: The influence of adolescent pregnancy status. *Adolescence, 22,* 487–496.
Walker, A. J., & Thompson, L. (1984). Mothers and daughters: Aid patterns and attachment.
J Mar Fam, 47, 313–322.
Walker, A. J., Thompson, L., & Morgan, C. S. (1987). Two generations of mothers and
daughters: Role position and interdependence. *Psych Wom Q, 11,* 195–208.

II-3/II-5/c/e
210. VAUX, A. Social Support Appraisals Scale (SS-A)

Avail: 1986, & Vaux & Athanassopulou, 1987, Refs.

Variables Measured: Perceived level of love, esteem, and involvement received from family and friends

Type of Instrument: Self-report questionnaire

Instrument Description: The SS-A is a 4-point, 23-item Likert-type questionnaire designed
to assess social support received by an individual through interactions with family, friends, and
others. The questionnaire is based on Cobb's (1976) conception of social support. Items are in
the form of statements, to which respondents indicate their level of agreement. Response
options are given values from 1 to 4, and range from *strongly agree* to *strongly disagree.* The
instrument can be administered either as a paper-and-pencil measure or utilizing an interview
format. The author used the SS-A as one of a battery of instruments during telephone
interviews examining various dimensions and correlates of support. Of the 23 items contained
in the overall SS-A, 8 are directly related to interactions with or support received from one's
family. In addition, Vaux and Athanassopulou (1987) included an additional 5 items appropriate for married respondents that relate to treatment from one's spouse. Scores for the three
subscales of family, friends, and others are computed separately by summing values for items
within each subscale. An overall measure of support is arrived at by combining scores from
the three dimensions.

Sample Items (Note: All items listed here are taken from the family subscale):

(A)   My family cares for me very much.
(B)   My family holds me in high esteem.
(C)   Members of my family rely on me.

Comments: In keeping with the theme of this volume, information presented here relates
only to the family subscale of the SS-A. Reliability and validity information on the SS-A is
presented in Vaux et al. (1986). Cronbach's alpha is reported to be .80. These authors also
indicate correlations between the SS-A and several other instruments, including Perceived
Social Support (Procidano & Heller, 1979) (.56), Network Satisfaction (Vaux, 1982) (.32 to
.45), and the Family Relations Index (Holahan & Moos, 1982)—cohesion (.29), expressiveness (.12), and conflict (-.24) subscales. Additional correlations are presented for several
other scales.

References:

Vaux, A. (1987). Appraisals of social support: Love, respect, and involvement. *J Comm Psyc,
15,* 493–502.
Vaux, A., & Athanassopulou, M. (1987). Social support appraisals and network resources. *J
Comm Psyc, 15,* 537–556.

Vaux, A., Phillips, J., Holly, L., Thomson, B., Williams, D., & Stewart, D. (1986). The Social Support Appraisals (SS-A) Scale: Studies of reliability and validity. *Am J Comm P, 14,* 195–219.

II-3/a
211. WALKER, A. J., & THOMPSON, L. Intimacy Scale

Avail: 1983 Ref.

Variables Measured: Perceived intimacy

Type of Instrument: Self-report questionnaire

Instrument Description: The Intimacy Scale is a 7-point, 17-item Likert-style scale designed to assess emotional closeness in interpersonal relationships. The questionnaire has been administered in both interview and paper-and-pencil formats. Response options range from *not true* to *always true,* and are coded 1–7. Item scores are summed and divided by 17 in order to arrive at a mean scale score. Administration time is approximately 3–5 minutes.

Sample Items:

(A)   We want to spend time together.
(B)   S/he is important to me.
(C)   I'm sure of this relationship.

Comments: The authors report that Cronbach's alpha for the Intimacy Scale has ranged from .91 to .97. The 17 items contained in this scale were derived from a factor analysis conducted on 50 original items, developed to reflect various aspects of intimacy. The factor analysis resulted in the creation of five separate scales, including attachment, intimacy, disclosure, tension, and worry. The authors report that items contained within each scale loaded at least .5 on that scale, with loadings on nonprimary factors of less than .25. The Intimacy Scale has been used to distinguish among relationships according to amount of contact between participants in the relationship.

References:

Thompson, L., & Walker, A. J. (1987). Mothers as mediators of intimacy between grandmothers and their young adult granddaughters. *Fam Relat, 36,* 72–77.
Townsend, J. K., & Worobey, J. (1987). Mother and daughter perceptions of their relationships: The influence of adolescent pregnancy status. *Adolescence, 22,* 487–496.
Walker, A. J., & Thompson, L. (1983). Intimacy and intergenerational aid and contact among mother and daughters. *J Mar Fam, 46,* 841–849.

II-3/a
212. WHITE, J. G. Marriage Scale

Avail: Psychologists and Educators, P.O. Box 513, Chesterfield, MO 63006

Variables Measured: Compatibility of interests among romantically involved couples

Type of Instrument: Self-report questionnaire

Instrument Description: The Marriage Scale is a 21-item questionnaire designed to identify areas in which couples who are married, engaged, or going steady are likely to experience success or difficulty. The questionnaire was originally copyrighted in 1973. Items are in the form of questions, asking information regarding the importance of various perspectives and attitudes for a happy marriage. Responses are on a 10-point continuum with varying end points depending on the requirements of each specific question. A second section requesting demographic information and responses to items related to current life circumstances is also completed. The Marriage Scale is designed to be completed independently by both members of the couple. Completed questionnaires are then compared and used as the basis for discussion in clinical practice or relationship seminars. The publisher indicates that the questionnaire is intended for persons with at least a high school reading level and that it is not appropriate for individuals with below-average reading skills. Administration time is approximately 10–15 minutes.

Sample Items:

(A) Should a couple be sympathetically understanding and tolerant with each other?
(B) How necessary is it for a couple to have a similar outlook on life? This includes aspirations and goals, the purpose of living and the place of the family in the whole scheme of things?
(C) How necessary is parental approval of my marriage?

Comments: The instrument is intended for use in clinical practice where couples' responses to each item can be compared. Thus norms are presented for each item individually. All norms relate to happily married persons. Procedures for developing composite scores are not specified. Separate norms are presented for husbands and wives with 1–9, 10–19, 20–29, 30–39, 40–49, and 50+ years of marriage.

Reference:

White, J. G. (1987). Marriage Scale. In *Education-psychology catalog* (p. 1). Chesterfield, MO: Psychologists and Educators, Inc.

II-3/a

213. WORELL, J., & LANGE, S. The Dyadic Support Scale (DSS)

Avail: NAPS-3

Variables Measured: Social and emotional support between intimates

Type of Instrument: Self-report questionnaire

Instrument Description: The DSS is a 7-point, 30-item Likert-type scale designed to assess two styles of emotional support in a close relationship. The two styles are referred to as agentic and communal support. Agentic support, assessed with 15 items, consists of behaviors characterized by dominance, orientation toward self-interest, and a cognitive problem-solving approach. Communal support, also assessed by 15 items, is characterized by nondominance, focus on the friend, and a feeling or empathic approach. The scales are used to examine the relationship between types of interpersonal support and satisfaction, commitment, and other relevant variables within close friendships, between dating partners, and in intimate partner pairs. Respondents indicate the extent to which each listed behavior is characteristic of her- or himself, from *not at all* to *almost always,* with respect to a specific friend or partner relationship. Three alternate forms of the DSS are available, evaluating support between friends and between partners, and a reverse-order stem in which the respondent reports on which of these behaviors the friend or partner uses. In this manner, reciprocal scores can be obtained, measuring both perceived support behaviors given, as well as received, in a close relationship. The DSS was designed for use with persons from early adolescence through adulthood. Administration time is approximately 15 minutes.

Sample Items:

(A)   I tell my friend/partner how to solve a problem.

(B)   When my friend/partner is upset, I try to distract him/her by suggesting that we do some activity together (go to a movie, have a drink).

(C)   I give encouragement and praise to my friend/partner when I know s/he is attempting something difficult.

Comments: The authors report that Cronbach's alpha for the agentic and communal support subscales are .87 and .91, respectively. It is also reported that communal support correlates .45 with relationship satisfaction among males and .69 among females. The authors have also explored the relationship of the DSS to gender-role measures, with findings that communal scores for "feminine" respondents are higher than for "masculine" subjects. The authors have also found that females tend to score higher on the communal scale, while males tend to score higher on the agentic scale. The DSS is adapted from the Nurturance Behavior Scale (Moeschl, 1983).

Reference:

Worell, J. (1985). Emotional support in adolescent relationships. *Social Sci, 70,* 156–158.

II-4/g/H
214. BARLOW, D. H., BECKER, R., LEITENBERG, H., & AGRAS, W. S. Psychophysiological Measures of Male Sexual Arousal

Variables Measured: Changes in penile volume or circumference in response to sexual arousal

Type of Instrument: Physiological measures

Instrument Description: There are two types of instruments that are primarily used to measure male physiological responses to sexual arousal: (1) volumetric devices and (2) circumferential devices. A volumetric instrument was first developed by Freund (1963). This device consists of a glass cylinder into which the penis is inserted. An inflatable cuff is used to form an air-tight seal around the penis. Measurements of the displacement of either air or water, depending on the construction of the device, are used to infer changes in penile size. Due to the involved nature of these devices, their use is generally limited to laboratory environments with subjects who remain awake through the procedure. In contrast to volumetric instruments, circumferential devices, also referred to as strain gauges, may be used to measure changes in penile size during various waking and sleeping states. While strain gauges come in several varieties, including mercury-filled (developed by Shapiro and Cohen; described by Fisher, Gross, & Zuch, 1965) and graphite-filled (Jovanovic, 1967) tubing, the most widely used variety consists of arcs of surgical spring material connected by paired mechanical gauges (Barlow, Becker, Leitenberg, & Agras, 1970). Types of strain gauges are reported to vary in size, ease of use, and shelf life. All are commercially available through several sources. For further information, please refer to the references listed below.

Sample Items: Not applicable.

Comments: While volumetric devices are reported to indicate changes in penile size more accurately, their bulk and obtrusiveness tend to limit their usefulness. Circumferential devices, while somewhat less accurate, can often be individually fitted by the subject or patient, are frequently worn under one's clothing, and are comfortable enough to be useful in measuring changes during sleeping as well as waking states.

References:

Abel, G. G., Blanchard, E. B., Murphy, W. D., Becker, J. V., & Djenderedjian, A. (1981). Two methods of measuring penile response. *Behav Ther, 12,* 320–328.

Barlow, D. H., Becker, R., Leitenberg, H., & Agras, W. S. (1970). A mechanical strain gauge for recording penile circumference change. *J Appl Be A, 3,* 73–76.

Fisher, C., Gross, J., & Zuch, J. (1965). Cycle of penile erection synchronous with dreaming (REM) sleep. *Arch G Psyc, 12,* 29–45.

Freund, K., Langevin, R., & Barlow, D. (1974). Comparison of two penile measures of erotic arousal. *Behav Res T, 12,* 335–340.

Geer, J. H. (1980). Measurement of genital arousal in human males and females. In I. Martin & P. H. Venables (Eds.), *Techniques in psychophysiology* (pp. 431–458). New York: John Wiley.

Hatch, J. P. (1981). Psychophysiological aspects of sexual dysfunction. *Arch Sex B, 10,* 49–64.

II-4/III-2/b/C

215. BENNETT, S. M., & DICKINSON, W. B. Sex Education Inventory (SEI)

Avail: 1988 Ref.

Variables Measured: Sources of sexual education, family environment for obtaining sexual information, and recent sexual experiences

Type of Instrument: Self-report questionnaire

Instrument Description: The SEI is a 57-item questionnaire designed to assess college students' preferred and actual sources of sexual information, satisfaction with sex education that is provided, and various aspects of the students' family environments that might have facilitated sex education in the home. The level of recent sexual activity is also assessed with this instrument. The SEI is a revision of the Student Sex Education Survey (SESS; Bennett & Dickinson, 1980). Portions of the SEI were based on or inspired by instruments by Sorensen (1973), Spanier (1977), and Reiss (1967). Item formats include Likert-type checklists and *true-false* questions. Scores are reported individually for several subscales. Administration time is approximately 25 minutes.

Sample Items:

(A)   My father probably would stand by me if I had a serious problem related to sex.

(B)   Circle the letters next to all the factors which have discouraged you from discussing sex-related topics with your father (12 options, labeled "a" through "l" are given).

(C)   Which parent should take a more active role in the sex education of children?

Comments: The authors report coefficients of stability over periods ranging from one to four weeks to be from .58 to .95 for various subscales. Correlations are reported between the number of aspects of sex education for which students indicate their parents should be responsible and those for which parents took responsibility to range from .32 to .47. Correlations are also reported between the SEI and the Allgeier Sexual Knowledge Scale (Allgeier, 1978) (.44), and with Eysenck's Inventory of Attitudes to Sex (1970) (ranging from .23 to .45).

References:

Bennett, S. M. (1984). Family environment for sexual learning as a function of fathers' involvement in family work and discipline. *Adolescence, 19,* 609–627.

Bennett, S. M., & Dickinson, W. B. (1980). Student-parent rapport and parent involvement in sex, birth control, and venereal disease education. *J Sex Res, 16,* 114–130.

Bennett, S. M., & Dickinson, W. B. (1988). Sex Education Inventory: Preferred and actual sources. In C. M. Davis, W. L. Yarber, & S. L. Davis (Eds.), *Sexuality-related measures: A compendium* (pp. 73–77). Lake Mills, IA: Graphic.

II-4/e

216. BRUCE, K. E. M. Herpes Attitudes Scale (HAS)

Avail: 1986 Ref.

Variables Measured: Students' attitudes about genital herpes, including attitudes toward oneself if one had genital herpes, attitudes toward herpes sufferers, communication about herpes, effects on intimate and friendship relationships, and myths about herpes

Type of Instrument: Self-report questionnaire

Instrument Description: The HAS was designed to measure undergraduate students' attitudes about genital herpes, but could be revised easily for administration to other groups of people. It is a 40-item Likert-style scale, with five response options ranging from *strongly disagree* to *strongly agree*. Administration time is approximately 15–20 minutes. Half of the items reflect tolerant and half reflect intolerant attitudes. The intolerant items are reverse-scored. Total scores are computed by adding the scores of the individual items and standardizing the scores to a 1 to 100 scoring system, such that higher scores reflect more tolerant attitudes. The following formula is used in computing this score: HAS Score = 25 (the sum of all $X \times N$)/N, where X is the scored value of each item and N is the number of items properly completed.

Sample Items:

(A)   I would be embarrassed to tell anyone if I had genital herpes.
(B)   If I had genital herpes, I would tell a potential sex partner.
(C)   If I got genital herpes, I would not want to have children.

Comments: The author reports that factor analyses have indicated the presence of four factors, accounting for 43% of the variance. Research indicates that undergraduates who personally know someone with genital herpes show more tolerant attitudes. No sex differences are apparent, although attitudes of older students tend to be more tolerant. The correlation between attitudes and knowledge about genital herpes is .19. Cronbach's alpha for the total scale is reported to be .91. Content validity of the items was assessed by a medical doctor, three health educators, and a graduate student with genital herpes.

Reference:

Bruce, K. E. M., & McLaughlin, J. (1986). The development of scales to assess knowledge and attitudes about genital herpes. *J Sex Res, 22,* 73–84.

II-4/e

217. BRUCE, K. E. M. Herpes Knowledge Scale (HKS)

Avail: 1986 Ref.

Variables Measured: Students' knowledge about genital herpes, including cause, symptoms, and treatment, recurrences, prevalence, contagion, complications, relationship of oral and genital herpes, and myths about herpes

Type of Instrument: Paper-and-pencil test of knowledge

Instrument Description: The HKS was designed to measure undergraduate students' knowledge about genital herpes, but could be revised easily for administration to other groups of people. The HKS is a 54-item *true/false* test, including a response option *don't know*. A response of *don't know* is scored as an incorrect response. The scale contains half true and half false items. The total score is obtained by scoring the response to each item as correct or incorrect, adding the number of correct responses, and expressing the sum as the percentage of items scored correctly out of the total number of items. Completion time is approximately 15–20 minutes.

Sample Items:

(A)   Several hundred people are expected to catch genital herpes from toilet seats this year.
(B)   If both parents have genital herpes, their children will be born with herpes.
(C)   A genital herpes infection usually leads to syphilis.

Comments: Studies with the HKS have found that students who personally know someone who has genital herpes score significantly higher on this scale. Males and females score similarly, but knowledge is generally higher for older students. The correlation between knowledge and attitudes about genital herpes is reported by the author as .19. The correlation between HKS scores and self-rated knowledge is .46. Cronbach's alpha is reported by the author as .88 for the overall scale. Content validity was assessed by a medical doctor, three health educators, and a graduate student with genital herpes.

Reference:

Bruce, K. E. M., & McLaughlin, J. (1986). The development of scales to assess knowledge and attitudes about genital herpes. *J Sex Res, 22,* 73–84.

II-4/II-3/a
218. BUUNK, B. Actual Sexual Jealousy Scale

Avail: 1981 Ref.

Variables Measured: Jealousy experienced in the past as a response to a partner's actual sexual involvement with someone of the opposite gender

Type of Instrument: Self-report questionnaire

Instrument Description: This scale has been used primarily in the Netherlands, and it is designed to measure the extent to which an actual sexual attraction in the past evoked a negative emotional response and to assess the way the partner's behavior in that situation was perceived. Fifteen perceptions and five emotions are included in the scale. There are two versions, one measuring reactions to a partner's specific behavior from the past, and the other evaluating responses to more or less frequently occurring behaviors (e.g., flirting). A Likert-style response format with five possible responses for each item was used. A composite score is obtained by summing the responses. Four items are intended to be reverse-scored.

Sample Items:

(A)   I could hardly stand my partner's paying me less attention than formerly.

(B) I found it unpleasant that my partner enjoyed certain things more with the other person than with me.

(C) I was pleased for my partner that he/she had an enjoyable experience.

Comments: The author reports reliability of the scale (Cronbach's alpha) to be .93. Few variables have been found to correlate significantly with the general version of the scale, although what are reported as moderate correlations have been found with neuroticism and relational satisfaction. The specific version is reported to correlate with aggression and marital deprivation as attributions for the extramarital behavior and neuroticism, and with aggression-pushing as a way of handling conflicts regarding extramarital sex. The author further reports that women tend to score higher than men.

References:

Bringle, R. G., & Buunk, B. (1986). Examining the causes and consequences of jealousy. In R. Gilmour & S. Duck (Eds.), *The emerging field of personal relationships* (pp. 225–240). Hillsdale, NJ: Lawrence Erlbaum.

Buunk, B. (1981). Jealousy in sexually open marriages. *Altern Lifestyles, 4,* 357–372.

Buunk, B. (1986). Husband's jealousy. In R. A. Lewis & R. Salt (Eds.), *Men in families* (pp. 97–114). Beverly Hills, CA: Sage.

II-4/II-3/a
219. BUUNK, B. Anticipated Sexual Jealousy Scale

Avail: 1988 Ref.

Variables Measured: Anticipated jealousy with regard to a partner's potential sexual and erotic involvement with someone of the opposite gender

Type of Instrument: Self-report questionnaire

Instrument Description: Sexual jealousy is defined as an aversive emotional reaction that occurs as the result of a partner's actual or imagined sexual attraction to a third person. The Anticipated Sexual Jealousy Scale measures the extent to which the idea of such a sexual attraction evokes a negative emotional response. Subjects indicate their likely reaction were their partners to engage in each of five behaviors, ranging from flirting to engagement in a long-term sexual relationship with a member of the opposite gender other than themselves. Considering the possible negative reaction to the word *jealousy,* however, subjects are instead asked to indicate how bothered they would be by each behavior, on a 9-point scale ranging from *extremely bothered* to *extremely pleased.* A composite score is arrived at by summing the responses to individual items. The Anticipated Sexual Jealousy Scale has been used primarily in evaluating attitudes of couples in the Netherlands.

Sample Items:

(A) How would you feel if the partner were to engage in light petting with another person of the opposite sex?

(B) How would you feel if the partner were to fall in love with another person of the opposite sex?

(C) How would you feel if the partner were to engage in sexual intercourse with another person of the opposite sex?

Comments: The author reports Cronbach's alpha ranged from .90 and .94 for various samples. The test-retest correlation over three months was .76. However, test-retest over five years was .00. The scale is reported to correlate positively with jealousy as perceived by the spouse. The scale has been found to discriminate between individuals scoring low and high in sexual permissiveness, and is positively correlated with moral disapproval of extramarital sex. The author further reports that high and positive correlations have been demonstrated between this scale and others also designed to measure jealousy.

References:

Bringle, R. G., & Buunk, B. (1986). Examining the causes and consequences of jealousy. In R. Gilmour & S. Duck (Eds.), *The emerging field of personal relationships* (pp. 225–240). Hillsdale, NJ: Lawrence Erlbaum.

Buunk, B. (1982). Anticipated sexual jealousy: Its relationship to self-esteem, dependency and reciprocity. *J Pers Soc Bul, 8,* 310–316.

Buunk, B. (1988). The anticipated sexual jealousy scale. In C. M. Davis, W. L. Yarber, & S. L. Davis (Eds.), *Sexuality related measures: A compendium.* Lake Mills, Iowa: Graphic.

II-4/e
220. BUUNK, B. Extramarital Behavioral Intentions Scale

Avail: 1988 Ref.

Variables Measured: Intention to engage in a variety of extramarital sexual and erotic behaviors

Type of Instrument: Self-report questionnaire

Instrument Description: This scale comprises five Likert-style questions, each with seven response options ranging from *certainly not* to *certainly yes.* Each question asks whether or not the respondent would engage in a specific extramarital activity, ranging from flirting to carrying on a long-term sexual relationship, if the opportunity were to present itself. The scale is based on the assumption that specific extramarital behavioral intentions correlate highly with actual future behavior. It has been used primarily in evaluating the extramarital intentions of married persons in the Netherlands. Administration time is 1–2 minutes.

Sample Items: Would you engage in the following behavior with another man/woman if the opportunity were to present itself?

(A)   Light petting.
(B)   Falling in love.
(C)   Sexual intercourse.

Comments: The author reports that Cronbach's alpha varied from .73 to .91 in various samples. Over a three-month time period, test-retest reliability was measured at .70. However, over a five-year period, the test-retest correlation was .00. The author reports that high correlations were found between scores on the scale and extramarital involvement during the previous year. It is also reported to correlate highly with various indicators of sexual permissiveness of the subject and his or her reference group. The author also reports that a high correlation was found between scores on the scale and extramarital intentions as perceived by the subject's spouse.

References:

Buunk, B. (1980). Extramarital sex in the Netherlands: Motivations in social and marital context. *Altern Lifestyles, 3,* 11–39.

Buunk, B. (1982). Anticipated sexual jealousy: Its relationship to self-esteem, dependency and reciprocity. *Pers Soc Psy Bul, 8,* 310–316.

Buunk, B. (1988). The extramarital behavioral intentions scale. In C. M. Davis, W. L. Yarber,

& Davis, S. L. (Eds.), *Sexuality related measures: A compendium.* Lake Mills, IA: Graphic.

II-4/e
221. CHRISTOPHER, F. S., & CATE, R. M. Inventory of Sexual Decision-Making Factors

Avail: 1984 Ref.

Variables Measured: Influence of positive affect and communication, arousal and receptivity, obligation and pressure, and circumstance on initial decision to engage in sexual intercourse in a new relationship

Type of Instrument: Self-report questionnaire

Instrument Description: The Inventory of Sexual Decision-Making Factors is a survey instrument designed to tap into salient factors that influence individuals when they first engage in intercourse in a new relationship. Its 34 items use a 7-point Likert format with a 1 indicating the particular item was *not at all important* as an influence and a 7 indicating that it was a *very important* influence. The scale measures four areas of influence, as determined by a factor analysis: positive affect/communication (14 items), arousal/receptivity (9 items), obligation/pressure (6 items), and circumstance (5 items). Scoring consists of summing the responses for each of the items in the subscales. The inventory was developed using an undergraduate college population.

Sample Items:

(A)   How much your partner liked you.
(B)   How much you pressured your partner to engage in intercourse.
(C)   How much alcohol/drugs you had.

Comments: The authors report that Cronbach's alpha for the four scales ranged from .67 to .86. They also report gender differences for the positive affect/communication and for the obligation/pressure subscales. Differences are also indicated for the saliency of the arousal/receptivity and for the positive affect/communication subscales for individuals of different levels of lifetime sexual experience.

Reference:

Christopher, F. S., & Cate, R. M. (1984). Factors involved in premarital sexual decision making. *J Sex Res, 20,* 363–376.

II-4/a
222. DAVIDSON, J. K., Sr., & DARLING, C. A. Desired Changes in Sex Life Checklist

Avail: NAPS-3

Variables Measured: Desired changes in sex life

Type of Instrument: Self-report checklist of desired changes

Instrument Description: The purpose of this subscale is to provide a self-assessment of satisfaction with men's and women's current sex lives. Respondents are presented with a one-page questionnaire with the following instructions: "Which of the following changes, if any, would you like to have in your current sex life? (Check All Applicable Categories)." The 42-item checklist is part of a comprehensive survey instrument measuring several aspects of sexual expression and satisfaction. One additional item contained at the bottom of the checklist enables subjects to indicate other desired changes in their sex lives not specified on the checklist. Items are arranged in a checklist format for ease of response. The instrument is intended for utilization with men and women over the age of 18 who have one or more years of college. The checklist may be scored either on the basis of the total number of desired changes in a person's current sex life or by calculating group means regarding desired changes in sex life.

Sample Items:

(A)   More foreplay.
(B)   More frequent orgasms.
(C)   Ability to have multiple orgasms.

Comments: The subscale has been employed in research projects evaluating sexual knowledge, attitudes, and practices among college students; self-perceptions of female sexuality; and perceptions of the female sexual response.

References:

Darling, C. A., & Davidson, J. K., Sr. (1986a). Coitally active university students: Sexual behaviors, concerns, and challenges. *Adolescence, 21,* 403–419.
Darling, C. A., & Davidson, J. K., Sr. (1986b). Enhancing relationships: Understanding the feminine mystique of pretending orgasm. *J Sex Mar Ther, 12,* 182–196.
Davidson, J. K., Sr., & Darling, C. A. (1988). Changing autoerotic attitudes and practices among college females: A two year follow-up study. *Adolescence, 23,* 773–792.

II-4/I-4/a
223. DEROGATIS, L. R. Derogatis Sexual Functioning Inventory (DSFI)

Avail: Clinical Psychometric Research, P.O. Box 619, Riderwood, MD 21139

Variables Measured: Attitude toward, frequency, and quality of sexual activities

Type of Instrument: Self-report questionnaire

Instrument Description: The DSFI is a 258-item questionnaire designed to measure several aspects of sexual attitudes and satisfaction. Items are organized along 10 dimensions, referred to in the questionnaire as "sections." Section names (and descriptions) are as follows: (1) information (general sexual knowledge), (2) experience (sexual experiences), (3) drive (frequency of sexual activities), (4) attitudes (regarding sexual behavior), (5) psychological symptoms (problems and complaints), (6) affects (general emotional state), (7) gender role definition (personality traits), (8) fantasy (sexual fantasies), (9) body image (perceptions of attractiveness), and (10) sexual satisfaction. Items are phrased as statements but use response formats particular to the needs of each individual section. Scores are computed for each dimension, with scaled scores from each dimension combined to derive an overall sexual functioning score. Separate norms, and in places separate questions, are provided for men and women. The DSFI is frequently used in assessing sexual dysfunction among husbands and wives. Administration time is approximately 30–40 minutes.

Sample Items:

(A)   Premarital intercourse is beneficial to later marital adjustment (indicate level of *agreement* or *disagreement*).

(B)   Masturbation by either partner is an indicator of poor marital adjustment (*true or false*).

(C)   Usually, my partner and I have good communication about sex (*true or false*).

Comments: The author (Derogatis, 1980) reports that test-retest correlations over a period of two weeks among 8 of the 10 sections ranged from .61 to .96, with only one dimension (information) reportedly below .70. Internal consistency coefficients are reported to range from .56 to .97.

References:

Derogatis, L. R. (1980). Psychological assessment of psychosexual functioning. *Psychiat Clin N Amer, 3*, 113–131.

Derogatis, L. R., & Melisaratos, N. (1979). The DSFI: A multidimensional measure of sexual functioning. *J Sex Mar Ther, 5*, 244–281.

Derogatis, L. R., & Meyer, J. K. (1979). A psychological profile of the sexual dysfunctions. *Arch Sex Be, 8*, 201–223.

LoPiccolo, J., & Steger, J. C. (1974). The Sexual Interaction Inventory: A new instrument for assessment of sexual dysfunction. *Arch Sex Be, 3*, 585–595.

II-4/g
224. FINLAY, B. Scale of Favorability Toward Abortion

Avail: 1981 Ref.

Variables Measured: Attitude toward abortion under various circumstances

Type of Instrument: Self-report questionnaire

Instrument Description: This 8-item questionnaire is designed to assess attitudes toward abortion under less than ideal maternal circumstances. Respondents are presented with a series of statements, each indicating a different set of circumstances. They are asked to circle the number next to each where they believe a woman would be justified in seeking an abortion. The scale is designed to be used as a written instrument, but the author indicates that it may also be utilized as an interview questionnaire. The number of positive responses to items is noted, with higher scores indicating that abortion is acceptable across a wider range of circumstances.

Sample Items:

(A)   The pregnancy is the result of rape.

(B)   The woman is an unmarried 14-year-old.

(C)   The woman feels that she cannot afford another baby.

Comments: The author reports that scores on this instrument correlate from .47 (females) to .55 (males) with a measure of sexual conventionality (Finlay, 1981). Additionally, the correlation between scores on this scale and a 5-point, 1-item measure of attitude toward abortion was .767. Guttman scalogram analysis was reported, with a coefficient of reproducibility of .922, and a coefficient of scalability of .735.

Reference:

Finlay, B. A. (1981). Sex differences in correlates of abortion attitudes among college students. *J Mar Fam, 43*, 571–583.

Finlay, B. A. (1985). Correlates of abortion attitudes and implications for change. In P. Sachdev (Ed.), *Perspectives on abortion* (pp. 178–190). Metuchen, NJ: Scarecrow.

II-4/g/W

225. GEER, J. H., MOROKOFF, P., & GREENWOOD, P. Psychophysiological Measures of Female Sexual Arousal

Variables Measured: Vaginal blood volume and labial temperature fluctuations

Type of Instrument: Physiological measures

Instrument Description: Use of psychophysiological measures of female sexual responsiveness was first reported by Geer, Morokoff, and Greenwood (1974). Currently, two primary
types of instruments are in use: (1) the vaginal photoplethysmograph, which measures vaginal
blood volume, and (2) the labial thermistor-clip, used to assess changes in temperature. The
vaginal photoplethysmograph, reported by Geer et al., is based on work by Masters and
Johnson (1966). This instrument, resembling a clear plastic tampon, consists of a light source
and sensor attached to a small cylinder, which is inserted approximately 1.5 inches into the
vagina. This instrument allows for measurements of changes in blood pressure and volume
within the vagina in the presence of various types of sexual stimuli, and during most forms of
direct sexual stimulation other than intercourse. The second type of physiological measure,
the thermistor-clip (reported by Henson, Rubin, Henson, & Williams, 1979), is a small gauge
used to objectively measure variations in temperature resulting from vasocongestion of the
labia. This instrument is often used in combination with other devices to compare changes in
temperature of the labia and those of other parts of the body (e.g., the chest). Both the
vaginal photoplethysmograph and the thermistor-clip operate on the premise that genital
vasocongestion is one principal physiologic change occurring during female sexual arousal
(Masters & Johnson, 1966).

Sample Items: Not applicable.

Comments: Both the vaginal photoplethysmograph and the labial thermistor-clip have
been shown to detect physiological changes during sexual arousal under varying conditions.

References:

Geer, J. H. (1980). Measurement of genital arousal in human males and females. In I. Martin
    & P. H. Venables (Eds.), *Techniques in psychophysiology* (pp. 431–458). New York:
    John Wiley.
Geer, J. H., Morokoff, P., & Greenwood, P. (1974). Sexual arousal in women: The develop-
    ment of a measurement device for vaginal blood volume. *Arch Sex Be, 3,* 559–564.
Henson, D. E., Rubin, H. B., & Henson, C. (1978). Consistency of the labial temperature
    change measure of human female eroticism. *Behav Res T, 16,* 125–129.
Henson, D. E., Rubin, H. B., & Henson, C. (1982). Labial and vaginal blood volume
    responses to visual and tactile stimuli. *Arch Sex Be, 11,* 23–31.
Hoon, P. W., Wincze, J. P., & Hoon, E. F. (1976). Physiological assessment of sexual arousal
    in women. *Psychophysl, 13,* 196–204.

II-4/g

226. HENDRICK, S. S., & HENDRICK, C. Sexual Attitudes Scale

Avail: 1987a Ref.

Variables Measured: Attitudes toward sexuality, specifically with regard to permissiveness,
sexual practices, communion or idealistic sexuality, and instrumentality or mechanistic and
biological sexuality

Type of Instrument: Self-report questionnaire

Instrument Description: The Sexual Attitudes Scale is a 5-point, 43-item Likert-style scale designed to use a multidimensional, multitopic approach to the measurement of sexual attitudes. Respondents are asked to indicate the extent to which they agree or disagree with each statement. Four subscales are identified: (1) permissiveness, defined as permitting casual, open sexuality; (2) sexual practices, emphasizing a responsible and tolerant attitude toward sexuality; (3) communion, defined as idealistic attitudes toward sexuality; and (4) instrumentality, indicating mechanistic or biological attitudes toward sexuality. Items are scored such that lower scores indicate that more of a particular sexual attitude is being expressed. The subscales are scored separately. A total composite score is not derived. The scale has been used largely with college students in examinations of their attitudes toward sexuality.

Sample Items:

(A) I do not need to be committed to a person to have sex with him/her.
(B) Birth control is part of responsible sexuality.
(C) Sex is best when you let yourself go and focus on your own pleasure.

Comments: The authors report that Cronbach's alpha and test-retest reliability, respectively, for the four subscales are as follows: permissiveness (.94, .88), sexual practices (.69, .80), communion (.79, .67), and instrumentality (.80, .66). Studies examining construct validity of the scales have examined them in conjunction with numerous demographic, personality, and attitude variables. Criterion validity has been examined through examinations of relationships with the Sexual Attitudes Scale and the Sexual Opinion Survey, the Reiss Male and Female Premarital Sexual Permissiveness Scales, and the Revised Mosher Guilt Inventory. These relationships are discussed in detail in Hendrick and Hendrick (1987a).

References:

Adler, N. L., Hendrick, S. S., & Hendrick, C. (1987). Male sexual preference and attitudes toward love and sexuality. *J Sex Educ Th, 12,* 27–30.

Hendrick, S. S., & Hendrick, C. (1987a). Multidimensionality of sexual attitudes. *J Sex Res, 23,* 502–526.

Hendrick, S. S., & Hendrick, C. (1987b). Love and sexual attitudes, self-disclosure, and sensation seeking. *J Soc Pers Relat, 4,* 281–297.

Hendrick, S. S., Hendrick, C., Slapion-Foote, M. J., & Foote, F. H. (1985). Gender differences in sexual attitudes. *J Pers Soc Psy, 48,* 1630–1642.

II-4/a
227. HUDSON, W. W. The Index of Sexual Satisfaction (ISS)

Avail: 1981 Ref.

Variables Measured: Perception of the magnitude of a sexual problem in a dyadic relationship

Type of Instrument: Self-report questionnaire

Instrument Description: The ISS is a 5-point, 25-item Likert-type questionnaire designed to assess the degree or magnitude of problems clients have in the sexual component of their relationship. Items are in the form of statements, with response options ranging from *rarely or none of the time* to *most or all of the time.* The scale was designed for use with clients aged 12 years or older. The scale is unidimensional, producing scores ranging from 0 to 100. Higher scores are presumed to indicate more serious problems. The clinical cutting score for this instrument is 30. Administration time is approximately 5–7 minutes.

Sample Items:

(A)   I feel that sex is dirty and disgusting.
(B)   Sex with my partner has become a chore for me.
(C)   Sex is fun for my partner and me.

Comments: The author indicates that Cronbach's alpha for the ISS has consistently been measured at above .90, with typical readings in the .95 range. Known groups validity estimated using the point biserial correlation is reported nearly always to be greater than .60.

References:

Cheung, P. P. L., & Hudson, W. W. (1982). Assessing marital discord in clinical practice: A revalidation of the Index of Marital Satisfaction. *J Soc Serv Res, 5,* 101–118.

Hudson, W. W. (1982). A measurement package for clinical workers. *J Appl Beh Sci, 17,* 229–238.

Hudson, W. W., Harrison, D. F., & Crosscup, P. C. (1981). A short-form scale to measure sexual discord in dyadic relationships. *J Sex Res, 17,* 157–174.

Hudson, W. W., Murphy, G. J., & Cheung, P. P. L. (1980). Marital and sexual discord among older couples. *Social Wrk Res Abs, 16,* 11–16.

II-4/a

228. LoPICCOLO, J., & STEGER, J. C. The Sexual Interaction Inventory (SII)

Avail: 1974 Ref.

Variables Measured: Sexual activities, levels of sexual satisfaction, and dysfunctions among heterosexual couples

Type of Instrument: Self-report questionnaire

Instrument Description: The SII is a 6-point, 102-item Likert-type questionnaire designed to assess levels of sexual activity, satisfaction, and dysfunction. It consists of an identical list of 6 items that are asked for each of 17 behaviors developed from a list originally published by Bentler (1968). Two items from this list inquire as to the frequency of activity (1, *never*; 2, *rarely*—10% of the time; 3, *occasionally*—25% of the time; 4, *fairly often*—50% of the time; 5, *usually*—75% of the time; 6, *always*), while the other items ask the respondent to indicate levels of satisfaction, both real and ideal, regarding both one's self and the mate. Response options for these items range from *extremely unpleasant* to *extremely pleasant*. The 17 behaviors to which subjects respond cover a range of sexual expression from seeing one's partner while nude to intercourse in which both partners experience orgasm. Seven items deal with female actions toward the male, seven items deal with male actions toward the female, and three items examine the mutual actions of kissing, intercourse, and intercourse involving mutual orgasm. Scoring procedures call for the derivation of scores for 11 scales (frequency dissatisfaction, male; self-acceptance, male; pleasure mean, male; perceptual accuracy, male of female; mate acceptance, male of female; total disagreement; frequency dissatisfaction, female; self-acceptance, female; pleasure mean, female; perceptual accuracy, female of male; and mate acceptance, female of male). Administration time is approximately 15–30 minutes. Scoring is estimated to take 10–15 minutes.

Sample Items:

(A)   The male giving the female a body massage, not touching her breasts or genitals.
(B)   The female caressing the male's genitals with her hands until he ejaculates.
(C)   The male caressing the female's genitals with his mouth until she reaches orgasm.

Comments: The authors report that Cronbach's alpha for the 11 scales ranged from .79 to .93. Two-week test-retest reliability reportedly ranges from .53 to .90 for the 11 scales.

References:

LoPiccolo, J., & Steger, J. C. (1974). The Sexual Interaction Inventory: A new instrument for assessment of sexual dysfunction. *Arch Sex Be, 3,* 585–595.

Nowinski, J. K., & LoPiccolo, J. (1979). Assessing sexual behavior in couples. *J Sex Mar T, 5,* 225–243.

II-4/I-4/a/H
229. MASCHHOFF, T. A., FANSHIER, W. E., & HANSEN, D. J. Sexual and Marital Impact of Vasectomy

Avail: 1976 Ref.

Variables Measured: Effect of having a vasectomy on marital and sexual satisfaction

Type of Instrument: Self-report questionnaire

Instrument Description: This instrument, untitled by the authors, is an 11-item questionnaire designed to assess pre- and postsurgical attitudes toward both sexual and other types of communication among married men and women. Four additional items are added to the postsurgical assessment requesting information about the surgery itself. Items are in the form of questions and are designed to be answered by both husbands and wives on a before and after basis. Response formats vary, with questions answered using *yes-no, husband/wife,* 3-point, and 6-point options. Space is also generally provided for respondents to leave written comments.

Sample Items:

(A)   Does your spouse show you the affection you want?

(B)   Do you feel satisfied with your present sexual relationship?

(C)   What was the major motivating factor for your seeking a vasectomy?

Comments: The authors utilized this instrument in a study of 50 couples presenting at a health department family planning clinic for vasectomies. They indicate that couples seeking vasectomies tended to be in their mid- to late 20s, and that only seven of the males and eight of the females had previously been married. Percentages of participants indicating specific responses to each item are listed in the reference noted below. Responses are indicated for men versus women, and for pre- and postsurgical administrations.

Reference:

Maschhoff, T. A., Fanshier, W. E., & Hansen, D. J. (1976). Vasectomy: Its effect upon marital stability. *J Sex Res, 12,* 295–314.

II-4/g
230. McHUGH, G. Sex Knowledge Inventory

Avail: Family Life Publications, P.O. Box 427, Saluda, NC 28773

Variables Measured: Knowledge of sexual anatomy, sex technique, and contraception

Type of Instrument: Self-report questionnaire

Instrument Description: The Sex Knowledge Inventory is a two-part questionnaire examining sexual and anatomical knowledge. Form X contains 80 5-point items examining 13 areas of overall sexual knowledge. Areas assessed include (1) general; (2) sex act techniques; (3) the hymen; (4) possible causes of poor sexual adjustment; (5) sex dreams; (6) birth control; (7) sterilization and circumcision; (8) menstruation; (9) conception, pregnancy, childbirth; (10) superstitions, misconceptions, misinformation; (11) masturbation; (12) venereal disease; and (13) effects of menopause on sex life. Individual sections contain from 2 to 15 items. Form Y contains 106 items that assess anatomical knowledge and knowledge of male and female sexual and reproductive systems, and physiological understanding of the processes of sexual arousal and intercourse. Responses to items from Form Y are made from lists of possible correct answers that are supplied to respondents. Both forms come with extensive instructions for use by marriage counselors. The instrument was initially constructed in 1950. Portions were revised in 1955, 1968, 1977, and 1979, in order to include language and knowledge more in keeping with the times.

Sample Items: The publisher did not grant permission to reproduce items.

Comments: The Sex Knowledge Inventory is designed for use primarily in teaching, birth control education and counseling, marriage counseling, and marriage enrichment programs. The instrument comes with an extensive manual that describes likely avenues of discussion for many items.

References:

Abramowitz, N. R. (1971). Human sexuality in the social work curriculum. *Fam Coord, 20,* 349–354.
Bardis, P. D. (1963). Influence of family life education on sex knowledge. *Mar Fam Living, 25,* 85–88.
Digran, M., & Anspaugh, D. (1978). Permissiveness and premarital sexual activity: Behavioral correlates of attitudinal differences. *Adolescence, 13,* 703–711.

II-4/a/e
231. REISS, I. L. Reiss Extramarital Sexual Permissiveness Scales

Avail: 1988 Ref.

Variables Measured: Acceptance of extramarital sexual intercourse, both on a personal and a societal basis, for husbands and wives

Type of Instrument: Self-report questionnaire

Instrument Description: Subjects are asked to respond to a series of Guttman-type questions, utilizing a forced-choice *yes-no* response format, related to their views on extramarital coitus. There are four 4-item general permissiveness subscales, and three 4-item subscales examining views related to personal permissiveness. Questions are asked based on the premise of a happy or unhappy marriage, whether it is the husband or the wife who is having the affair, and according to four specific dimensions of the extramarital relationship: (1) love relationship, (2) primarily a physical relationship, (3) the spouse is in agreement that the affair may occur, (4) the affair is not consensual. Administration time is approximately 10 minutes.

Sample Items:

(A) A husband is in a happy marriage. In the extramarital relationship love is emphasized and this type of relation is approved by his mate. Do you find this extramarital relationship acceptable?

(B) If you were in a happy marriage would you make an agreement with your mate to permit each other extramarital sexual relationships focused on physical pleasure?

(C) If you were in a happy marriage would the idea of your having an extramarital love relationship, but without agreement from your mate, be acceptable to you?

Comments: The author reports that Guttman criteria concerning the coefficient of reproducibility and coefficient of scalability have been examined. It is also reported that claims to construct validity for the instrument were strengthened by finding expected differences between religiously devout and nondevout groups of subjects.

References:

Reiss, I. L. (1988). Reiss Extramarital Sexual Permissiveness Scales. In C. M. Davis, W. L. Yarber, & S. L. Davis (Eds.), *Sexuality-related measures: A compendium.* Lake Mills, IA: Graphic.

Reiss, I. L., Anderson, R., & Sponaugle, G. C. (1980). A multivariate model of the determinants of extramarital sexual permissiveness. *J Mar Fam, 42,* 395–411.

II-4/e
232. REISS, I. L. Reiss Male and Female Premarital Sexual Permissiveness Scales

Avail: 1988 Ref.

Variables Measured: Acceptance of premarital sexual permissiveness

Type of Instrument: Self-report questionnaire

Instrument Description: This instrument was designed to evaluate general acceptance of differing levels of premarital sexual activity. Twelve identical questions, utilizing a 6-point response format, are asked regarding acceptance of specific activities for males and females. Respondents indicate their acceptability of three specific behaviors (kissing, petting, and coitus) under each of four sets of circumstances. The circumstances include couples who "do not feel particularly affectionate" and those who feel "strong affection," "love," and "engagement." Administration time for the 24 items contained in the combination male-female version is approximately 10 minutes.

Sample Items:

(A) I believe that kissing is acceptable for the male before marriage when he is engaged to be married.

(B) I believe that petting is acceptable for the female before marriage even if she does not feel particularly affectionate toward her partner.

(C) I believe that full sexual relations are acceptable for the male before marriage when he is engaged to be married.

Comments: The author reports that the coefficient of reproducibility for the scale was above 90%, and that the coefficient of scalability was above 65%. Construct validity was investigated by comparing scores of parents and college students, Whites and Blacks, and males and females. Further information regarding validity and reliability is available in Reiss (1964, 1967).

References:

Reiss, I. L. (1964). The scaling of premarital sexual permissiveness. *J Mar Fam, 26,* 188–198.
Reiss, I. L. (1967). *The social context of premarital sexual permissiveness.* New York: Holt.

Reiss, I. L. (1988). Reiss Premarital Sexual Permissiveness Scales. In C. M. Davis, W. L. Yarber, & S. L. Davis (Eds.), *Sexuality-related measures: A compendium*. Lake Mills, IA: Graphic.

II-4/a
233. RUST, J., & GOLOMBOK, S. Golombok Rust Inventory of Sexual Satisfaction (GRISS)

Avail: NFER Nelson, Darville House, 2 Oxford Road East, Windsor, Berks SL4 1DE, England

Variables Measured: Male and female perspectives on quality of their sexual relationship

Type of Instrument: Self-report questionnaire

Instrument Description: The GRISS is printed on a single sheet and is carbon-backed with an attached scoring sheet giving transformations and a profile. It is for use in sexual dysfunction clinics and research. It is a 28-item Likert-style scale measuring an overall male scale, an overall female scale, and 12 subscales: impotence, premature ejaculation, male avoidance, male nonsensuality, male dissatisfaction, infrequency, noncommunication, female dissatisfaction, female nonsensuality, female avoidance, vaginismus, and anorgasmia. Items are answered on a 5-point scale ranging from *always* to *never applies*. Separate questionnaires are provided for men and women. The scoring sheet provides for an overall couple profile as well as one for individuals. The GRISS is a companion scale to the Golombok Rust Inventory of Marital State (GRIMS), also published by NFER. Administration time is approximately 10 minutes.

Sample Items:

(A)   Do you find it hard to tell your partner what you like and dislike about your sexual relationship?
(B)   Does your vagina become moist during lovemaking?
(C)   Are you able to delay ejaculation during intercourse if you think you may be "coming" too quickly?

Comments: The current version of the GRISS was developed from an initial pool of 96 items. The authors report that the 28-item version is a result of psychometric considerations and individual item analyses. Particular attention was paid to replacement of items that were found to be offensive by clients. Split-half reliabilities for the overall instrument of .94 for women and .87 for men are reported. Split-half reliabilities of the subscales are reported to range from .61 to .83, with an average of .74. The authors report on validity studies in which the GRISS was used to discriminate between sex therapy clients and controls, where GRISS profiles were compared with diagnoses assigned by therapists, and by correlating change scores with therapists' ratings of improvement (.53). Further information is available in the references listed below.

References:

Golombok, S., Rust, J., & Pickard, C. (1984). Sexual problems encountered in general practice. *Br J Sex Med, 11*, 171–175.
Rust, J., & Golombok, S. (1985). The Golombok Rust Inventory of Sexual Satisfaction (GRISS). *Br J Cl Psy, 24*, 63–64.
Rust, J., & Golombok, S. (1986). The GRISS: A psychometric instrument for the assessment of sexual dysfunction. *Arch Sex Be, 15*, 153–161.

II-4/II-3/a
234. WEIS, D. L. The Sex-Love-Marriage Association (SLM) Scale

Avail: 1981 Ref.

Variables Measured: Cognitive associations between sex, love, and marriage

Type of Instrument: Self-report questionnaire

Instrument Description: The SLM Scale is a 5-point, 8-item Likert-type questionnaire designed to assess an individual's belief that love and/or marriage either enhance or are necessary for a satisfactory sexual relationship. Items on the SLM Scale were originally constructed as part of the Sex Attitudes Survey (McHugh & McHugh, 1976). Respondents are asked to indicate the extent of their agreement or disagreement with each statement on a 1–5 scale. Scores associated with each response are summed to arrive at an overall SLM score.

Sample Items:

(A) A man can't have a satisfactory and satisfying sex life without being in love with his partner.

(B) A successful and satisfying sex partnership cannot be established unless the sex partners are quite willing to limit all the sexual intercourse they have to each other.

(C) Sexual intercourse is better—more enjoyable, intense, and satisfying—if the sex partners are married to each other.

Comments: Norms and psychometric properties are reported based on two studies with a combined sample of 1,156 university undergraduates. Cronbach's alpha for the combined scale is reported to range from .75 to .80. A factor analysis reported by the author indicated that 75% of the variance was accounted for by a single-factor solution.

References:

Weis, D. L., & Slosnerick, M. (1981). Attitudes toward sexual and nonsexual extramarital involvements among a sample of college students. *J Mar Fam, 38,* 349–358.

Weis, D. L., Slosnerick, M., Cate, R., & Sollie, D. L. (1986). A survey instrument for assessing the cognitive association of sex, love, and marriage. *J Sex Res, 22,* 206–220.

II-5/g/e
235. ALLEN, B. P., & POTKAY, C. R. Adjective Generation Technique (AGT)

Avail: 1983 & 1988 Refs.

Variables Measured: Favorability, anxiety, and femininity as they relate to descriptions of self and others

Type of Instrument: Spontaneously generated adjectives

Instrument Description: The AGT is a self-report method used primarily for describing self and others. It is similar to an open-ended adjective checklist, except that subjects or clients spontaneously produce whatever adjectives they want. Individuals are asked to record adjectives (usually five) that best describe themselves or some target person, group, or social institution (e.g., family, marriage). While a set number of adjectives is typically requested, the AGT has also been used where the number of adjectives to be named was not specified. In one such study, the mean number of adjectives generated was about 11. Each adjective is given a value from 0 to 600 on favorability (FAV), anxiety (ANX), and femininity (FEM). The

AGT values list currently contains 2,200 words, each normed by 50 males and 50 females on each dimension.

Sample Items:

(A)   Happy = (Female subjects) 413 FAV, 370 ANX, 195 FEM.
(B)   Playful = (Female subjects) 315 FAV, 398 ANX, 414 FEM.
(C)   Demanding = (Female subjects) 207 FAV, 452 ANX, 450 FEM.

Comments: Intraindividual variability is greater for unstructured measurement modes such as the AGT than for structured modes. Studies examining multiple administrations over time have yielded correlations of .41 and .74. The authors also report that AGT FAV values correlated significantly with the self-regard scale of the Personal Orientation Inventory (.53). Additional reliability and validity information is available in the references.

References:

Allen, B. P., & Potkay, C. R. (1983). *Adjective Generation Technique (AGT): Research and applications.* New York: Irvington.
Potkay, C. R., & Allen, B. P. (1988). The Adjective Generation Technique (AGT): Assessment via word descriptions of self and others. In C. Spielberger & J. N. Butcher (Eds.), *Advances in personality assessment* (Vol. 7, pp. 127–159). Hillsdale, NJ: Lawrence Erlbaum.

II-5/a
236. ANDERSON, S. A., BAGAROZZI, D. A., & GIDDINGS, C. W. IMAGES

Avail: 1986 Ref.

Variables Measured: Qualities associated with the ideal spouse

Type of Instrument: Self-report questionnaire

Instrument Description: IMAGES is a 35-item, 7-point, Likert-style questionnaire designed to assess both conscious and unconscious visions of the ideal spouse. Initial development of the scale included modifications of items previously used to measure mate selection, marital satisfaction, marital quality, and marital adjustment. The authors attempted to create a scale that would measure several aspects of the above construct. A total of 47 behaviorally worded items were initially generated and administered to a university undergraduate sample. Factor and item analyses resulted in a 7-factor, 35-item solution. The number of items per factor vary from three to eight. Identified factors are emotional gratification and support, sex role orientation and physical attraction, spousal satisfaction, parent-sibling identification, emotional maturity, intelligence, and homogamy. Subscale scores are obtained by summing response values within factors.

Sample Items:

(A)   My spouse confides in me.
(B)   My spouse acts like a husband/wife should act.
(C)   My spouse is very much like my mother.

Comments: The authors indicate that subscale items retained from the initial item pool each loaded at least .40 on their primary scale. Loadings on secondary factors were generally reported to be less than .30, although two items were retained that loaded .40 and .45 on secondary factors. Item-to-subscale correlations for the final version range from .36 to .76. Cronbach's alpha for the seven subscales is reported to range from .70 to .87.

Reference:

Anderson, S. A., Bagarozzi, D. A., & Giddings, C. W. (1986). IMAGES: Preliminary scale construction. *Am J Fam Th, 14,* 357–363.

II-5/II-2/a
237. CALLAN, V. J. A Partner Selection Scale

Avail: 1983 Ref.

Variables Measured: Influence on partner selection of females' perceptions of male academic success, economic success, and willingness to allow an open and trusting relationship

Type of Instrument: Self-report instrument

Instrument Description: The measure taps what emerge as two critical issues in the choice of a marriage partner by educated single females: judgments of his potential academic and economic success, and his willingness to allow a relationship characterized by commitment, open and honest communication, and trust. The measure consists of 11 items tapping two scales determined by factor analysis. Items are rated on a Likert-style scale from 1 (*not important*) to 4 (*very important*). The original populations used in developing this scale were Australian college-educated women who intended to be childless and Australian single women who intended to become mothers someday. Scoring involves the summation of responses to the 6 items in the academic and economic success of partner subscale, and the 5 items in the open and trusting relationship subscale. The author reports that the two subscales seem to differentiate between women in terms of different intentions about wanting a family and their choice of a partner.

Sample Items:

(A) He wants to move ahead and improve our economic status.
(B) He wants total commitment to our relationship.
(C) He will provide a deep and companionable relationship.

Comments: The author reports that the composition of the two subscales was determined by a factor analysis utilizing a varimax rotation. Items on the first subscale each loaded at least .48 on that factor. Items on the second subscale each loaded at least .46 on that subscale.

Reference:

Callan, V. J. (1983). Childlessness and partner selection. *J Mar Fam, 45,* 181–186.

II-5/III-2/g/b/C
238. CHANG, J., & BLOCK, J. H. Parent Identification Adjective Checklist

Avail: NAPS-1

Variables Measured: Conceptualization of self, ideal self, mother, father, identification with each parent, and self-acceptance

Type of Instrument: Adjective checklist

Instrument Description: This instrument is a 79-item adjective checklist designed to yield a comprehensive personality description. Respondents are administered the checklist at least four times: once each to measure self, ideal self, perceptions of mother, and perceptions of father. Participants are instructed to place an "X" next to the 30 items from the list that are most characteristic of self, ideal self, mother, or father, and an "O" next to the 30 items perceived to be least characteristic. No marking is placed next to the remaining 19 items. Identification with each parent is scored by the number of correspondences between the ideal self and the parent in question, while self-acceptance is evaluated by comparing responses detailing self and ideal self. The checklist may be appropriate for use in both research programs and clinical evaluations. The instrument was developed in 1960, but has remained in active use in recent years.

Sample Items:

(A)   Dependent
(B)   Determined
(C)   Personally charming

Comments: While Chang and Block (1960) initially utilized this instrument in evaluations of homosexuals, various other investigators have used it primarily in assessments of perceived parental power and identification (Acock & Yang, 1984; McDonald, 1977, 1980). McDonald (1977) reports that indicators of paternal power are correlated with paternal identification, based on the Parent Identification Adjective Checklist, .36 for males and .38 for females. Maternal power is reported to be correlated .45 for males and .26 for females.

References:

Acock, A. C., & Yang, W. S. (1984). Parental power and adolescents' parental identification. *J Mar Fam, 46,* 487–495.
Chang, J., & Block, J. (1960). A study of identification in male homosexuals. *J Cons Psych, 24,* 307–310.
McDonald, G. W. (1977). Parental identification by the adolescent: A social power approach. *J Mar Fam, 39,* 705–719.
McDonald, G. W. (1980). Parental power and adolescents' parental identification: A reexamination. *J Mar Fam, 42,* 289–296.

II-5/IV-1/g
239. COWAN, C. P., & COWAN, P. A. The Pie

Avail: NAPS-3

Variables Measured: Sense of self in one's major life roles and relationships

Type of Instrument: See description below.

Instrument Description: The Pie was designed to serve as an indicator of an individual's sense of the relational self, or the sense of self in one's major life roles and relationships. Given a page with a circle four inches in diameter, each respondent is asked to list the major roles in his or her life and to divide the circle or "pie" so that each section reflects the salience of each role. This does not necessarily reflect the time spent in each role. Respondents fill in two circles: one pie for "Me as I am" and another for "Me as I'd like to be." The authors have identified four major categories of roles: (1) family roles, such as partner, parent, son/daughter, and sibling; (2) work and student roles; (3) social and leisure roles; and (4) self-descriptive statements. The authors derive three scores from the Pie: (1) the actual size of each piece of the pie is used to indicate salience of each role; (2) satisfaction with the salience of any role is calculated by examining the difference in relative size of pie portions for actual and ideal roles; (3) complexity of roles is measured by the number of roles that constitute the "now pie."

Sample Items: Not applicable.

Comments: The authors indicate that one-year test-retest reliability for the family-related roles of sibling, son or daughter, houseperson, parent, and partner were .49, .62, .70, .92, and .94, respectively. They also found that size of the parent role endorsed by new mothers and fathers yielded a cross-time correlation at 6 and 18 months postpartum of .58. Additional findings indicated that the combined size of partner and lover pieces of the pie for nonparents grew significantly larger over a one-year period, while those of new parents decreased in size. Concomitantly, parent roles are reported to have increased from 20.3% (males) and 39.1% (females) of the pie during the initial 18 months following the birth of the couple's first child.

References:

Cowan, C. P., & Cowan, P. A. (1988). Who does what when partners become parents: Implications for men, women, and marriage. *Mar Fam Rev, 12*(3/4), 105–124.

Cowan, C. P., Cowan, P. A., Coie, L., & Coie, J. (1978). Becoming a family: The impact of a first child's birth on the couple's relationship. In W. B. Miller & L. F. Newman (Eds.), *The first child and family formation* (pp. 296–324). Chapel Hill, NC: Carolina Population Center.

Cowan, C. P., Cowan, P. A., Heming, G., Garrett, E., Coysh, W. S., Curtis-Boles, H., & Boles, A. J., III (1985). Transitions to parenthood: His, hers and theirs. *J Fam Iss, 6,* 451–481.

Wilkie, C. F., & Ames, E. W. (1986). The relationship of infant crying to parental stress in the transition to parenthood. *J Mar Fam, 48,* 545–550.

II-5/f/g/C

240. DANIELS, D., & PLOMIN, R. The Sibling Inventory of Differential Experience (SIDE)

Avail: Test Collection, Educational Testing Service, Princeton, NJ 08541 (Accession No. 014603)

Variables Measured: Adolescents' and young adults' perceptions of differences between themselves and their siblings with regard to personality, parental treatment, peer characteristics, and events specific to the individual

Type of Instrument: Self-report questionnaire

Instrument Description: The SIDE is a 5-point, 73-item Likert-type questionnaire designed to assess perceptions of adolescents and young adults as to differences between themselves and their siblings. Perceived differences are examined with respect to 11 subscales: (1) sibling antagonism, (2) sibling caretaking, (3) sibling jealousy, (4) sibling closeness, (5) maternal affection, (6) maternal control, (7) paternal affection, (8) paternal control, (9) peer college orientation, (10) peer delinquency, and (11) peer popularity. The SIDE is constructed such that all sibling interaction scales appear in items 1–25, followed by parental treatment scales (items 26–33), followed by peer group characteristic scales (items 34–59), with events specific to you or your sibling being measured by items 60–73. Items take various forms, including questions, statements, and phrases. Response formats also vary from one section to another, but always ask the respondent to compare self experiences with those of a sibling. Additionally, items 66–73 allow for both Likert-type and open-ended responses by following the rating with instructions to "Explain." Formulas for combining items within the Events section are not specified. The questionnaire was designed for administration to junior and senior high school students (ages 12 to 18), but can also be adapted for use with either parents or young adults. Specific instructions for adapting the scale are contained in the manual.

Sample Items:

(A)　In general, who has started fights more often?

(B)　(Asked separately for both mother and father) Has shown interest in things we like to do.

(C)　Who has been more likely to have a psychological problem? . . . Explain.

Comments: The authors report that two-week test-retest reliabilities for subscales range from .77 to .93, with a mean of .84. Correlations between average scores obtained from siblings were all negative, ranging from -.23 to -.73. Only 7 of the 55 interscale correlations are reported to exceed .30. Results of a factor analysis are reported in the manual.

References:

Daniels, D. (1986). Differential experiences of siblings in the same family as predictors of adolescent sibling personality differences. *J Pers Soc Psy, 51,* 339–346.

Daniels, D., Dunn, J., Furstenberg, F. F., Jr., & Plomin, R. (1985). Environmental differences within the family and adjustment differences within pairs of adolescent siblings. *Child Dev, 56,* 764–774.

Daniels, D., & Plomin, R. (1985). Differential experience of siblings in the same family. *Devel Psych, 21,* 747–760.

II-5/a

241. HUNT, J. A., & HUNT, R. A. MIRROR—Couple Relationship Inventory

Avail: NAPS-3

Variables Measured: Perceptions of self and partner regarding various dimensions of their relationship

Type of Instrument: Self-report questionnaire

Instrument Description: The 16-page MIRROR inventory booklet contains 336 items plus eight demographic and self-rating questions. Each partner answers 168 items about self and the same 168 items rephrased with reference to the partner. The MIRROR is designed for use with couples who are dating, engaged, married, or otherwise living together. Couples answer the questionnaire independently. The answer format provides a choice from two alternatives for each question. Administration time is approximately 45 minutes. The 168 items in each portion of the instrument cover 24 subscales or variables. These variables are clustered into two dimensions (content and process) plus an attitude scale to measure overly positive or negative approaches to the MIRROR for either self or the partner. Each subscale consists of 6 to 10 items, with fewer than 10% of the 168 items scored on more than one scale. A detailed administration and scoring manual is available. The MIRROR may be computer-scored. It is also available in an interactive computer format. Results are expressed in a 1–10 numerical score for each subscale. The resulting MIRROR Guide is designed for couples to use as a discussion and exploration aid.

Sample Items:

(A)　I am usually more:
    (a)　Changeable and impulsive or
    (b)　Stable and disciplined.

(B)　I worry a lot about what will happen in the future.
    (a)　True or
    (b)　False

Assume that your partner has made the statement by each number. Even if you might not make either response, please choose the one that is closer to what you would say:

(C) I'm not getting anywhere in life.
   (a) I wish you would not worry or
   (b) You sound discouraged.

Comments: The authors report that MIRROR is based on statistical analyses of two previous editions with the 168 items refined out of an original item pool of 450 items.

Reference:

Hunt, J. A., & Hunt, R. A. (1988). *Manual and handbook: MIRROR—Couple Relationship Inventory.* Pasadena, CA: DATASCAN, Inc.

II-5/c
242. LaFORGE, R., & SUCZEK, R. S. Interpersonal Checklist (ICL)

Avail: 1955 Ref.; manual (using the ICL, 1976) available through Educational Testing Service Test Collection, Princeton, NJ 08540; also available in the University Associates Instrumentation Kit, published by University Associates, Inc., 8517 Production Ave., San Diego, CA 92121

Variables Measured: Structured descriptions of self or descriptions of others with regard to various interpersonal categories and levels of intensity

Type of Instrument: Checklist

Instrument Description: The ICL is a 134-item checklist, listed alphabetically, of which 128 items are scored. Each of 16 interpersonal categories are represented by 8 items of varying levels of intensity. Interpersonal categories included are dominant, independent, competitive, punitive, hostile, rebellious, distrustful, self-effacing, submissive, docile, dependent, cooperative, affiliative, supportive, nurturant, and mentoring. Levels of intensity range from minimal to extreme. The ICL is used for obtaining structured descriptions of self or descriptions by others (e.g., self, mother, father, spouse, each child in the family, and ideal self). It was designed for use in research on families, small groups, and assessment or diagnosis. Each interpersonal category is represented by 8 items: one at Intensity level 1, three at Intensity 2, three at Intensity 3, and one at Intensity 4. Thus the Intensity classification is designed to be orthogonal to the Interpersonal classification. Administration time is approximately 15 minutes.

Sample Items:

(A)   Able to give orders.
(B)   Resentful.
(C)   Trusting and eager to please.

Comments: The author reports that test-retest reliability over a three-month period ranged from .64 to .77 for the various subscales. Communalities are reported to range from .51 to above .90. The ICL has been used in hundreds of reported studies. Thus information regarding the validity of the ICL is extensive. A summary of information regarding validity and reliability is provided in the manual.

References:

LaForge, R., Leary, T. F., Naboisek, H., Hoffey, H. S., & Freedman, M. B. (1954). The interpersonal dimension of personality: II. An objective study of repression. *J Personal, 23,* 129–153.

LaForge, R., & Suczek, R. F. (1955). The interpersonal dimension of personality: III. An interpersonal check list. *J Personal, 24,* 94–112.

Leary, T. F. (1957). *Interpersonal diagnosis of personality.* New York: Ronald.

Lewis, R. A., Freneau, P. J., & Roberts, C. L. (1979). Fathers and the postparental transition. *Fam Coord, 28,* 514–528.

Paddock, J. R., & Nowicki, S., Jr. (1986). An examination of the Leary Circumplex through the Interpersonal Checklist. *J Res Pers, 20,* 107–144.

II-5/III-2/b/g/C
243. OFFER, D., OSTROV, E., & HOWARD, K. I. The Offer Parent-Adolescent Questionnaire (OPAQ)

Avail: Center for the Study of Adolescence, Michael Reese Hospital and Medical Center, 31st and Lake Shore Drive, Chicago, IL 60616

Variables Measured: Relationship of adolescent self-image and parental perceptions of the adolescent

Type of Instrument: Self-report questionnaire

Instrument Description: The OPAQ is a 6-point, 50-item questionnaire designed to examine the relationship between adolescent self-image and perceptions of the adolescent held by the parent. Questions are divided along 11 dimensions consisting of (1) impulse control, (2) emotional tone, (3) body image, (4) social relationships, (5) sexual attitudes, (6) family relationships, (7) mastery, (8) vocational/educational goals, (9) emotional health, (10) superior adjustment, and (11) idealism. Usually, the Offer Self-Image Questionnaire (OSIQ) is administered to adolescents in order to assess their self-image, and the OPAQ is administered to their parents in order to determine how they view their adolescents. Through the use of these two tests and their 11 common scales, congruence and dissimilarity of perceptions between parent and adolescent can be measured. In this way, investigators are able to examine problematic self-image perceptions in the adolescent, as well as difficulties between parents and their adolescent children. Both the OPAQ and the OSIQ can be administered as paper-and-pencil questionnaires. Administration time for the OPAQ is approximately 20 minutes. The OSIQ contains 130 items and has an administration time of approximately 45 minutes. The questionnaires can be scored either by hand or by computer. A commercial computerized scoring service is also available. In scoring, items on each scale are averaged to yield 11 raw scale scores. These raw scores are then transformed in order to yield 11 standard scale scores. Norms are available based on age and gender of the adolescent and gender of the parent.

Sample Items:

(A)   My son feels tense most of the time.
(B)   My son "loses his head" easily.
(C)   Having a girlfriend is important to my son.

Comments: The authors provide information on Cronbach's alpha for ratings by parents of 13- to 15-year-old males and females. Alpha coefficients are presented separately for mothers' and fathers' ratings. For the 11 subscales, the authors indicate that alpha for fathers' ratings ranged from .24 to .82 (median = .52) for their sons, and from .51 to .82 (median = .67) for daughters. For ratings by mothers, alpha is reported to have ranged from .12 to .82 for sons, and from .46 to .86 (median = .59) for daughters.

Reference:

Offer, D., Ostrov, E., & Howard, K. I. (1982). Family perceptions of adolescent self-image. *J Youth Adoles, 11,* 281–292.

II-5/g
244. STOVER, L., GUERNEY, B. G., Jr., GINSBERG, B., & SCHLEIN, S. The Self-Feeling Awareness Scale (SFAS)

Avail: 1977 Ref., & IDEALS (Institute for the Development of Emotional and Life Skills), P.O. Box 391, State College, PA 16804

Variables Measured: Speaker's feeling awareness, stated in subjective terms

Type of Instrument: Behavior rating system

Instrument Description: The SFAS is an 8-point scale on which comments related to oneself are rated according to their likelihood of leading another person to respond to the speaker's phenomenology, as opposed to some other aspect of his or her statement. Most research with this instrument has been conducted with families. When analyzing dyadic interactions, the scale has been used in conjunction with the Verbal Interaction Task (VIT) (Guerney, 1977) in which two interaction tasks are accomplished in each of two ways. With the VIT, pairs of family members are instructed to discuss something they would like to see changed in themselves and their partner, while either openly expressing feelings or helping the other person to express feelings. Interactions are analyzed based on 4 minutes of tape-recorded speech for each of four types of interactions. If the SFAS is utilized in a group context, separate scores are generated for each person spoken to directly. Communications are scored such that high-level statements include important feelings put in subjective terms, mid-level statements emphasize ordinary social conversation, and low-level statements deal primarily with deficiencies of oneself or another without acknowledging one's feelings or the subjective nature of the perceptions.

Sample Items: Not applicable.

Comments: Interrater reliability of the SFAS is reported by the authors to range from .88 to .97. Correlations are reported between the SFAS and the Acceptance of Other Scale (.30 to .32). The authors report that no significant relationships were discovered between the SFAS and paper-and-pencil measures used to access general communication or the quality of relationships.

References:

Guerney, B. G., Jr. (1977). *Relationship Enhancement: Skill-training programs for therapy, problem prevention, and enrichment.* San Francisco: Jossey-Bass.

Guerney, B. G., Jr., Coufal, J., & Vogelsong, E. (1981). Relationship Enhancement versus a traditional approach to therapeutic/preventative/enrichment parent-adolescent programs. *J Cons Clin, 49,* 927–929.

Guerney, B. G., Jr., Vogelsong, E. L., & Coufal, J. (1983). Relationship Enhancement versus a traditional treatment: Follow-up and booster effects. In D. Olson & B. Miller (Eds.), *Family studies review yearbook* (Vol. 1, pp. 738–756). Beverly Hills, CA: Sage.

Most, R. K., & Guerney, B. G., Jr. (1983). An empirical evaluation for training leaders for premarital Relationship Enhancement. *Fam Relat, 32,* 239–251.

II-5/a/g
245. TAYLOR, R. M., & MORRISON, L. P. The Taylor-Johnson Temperament Analysis (T-JTA)

Avail: Psychological Publications, Inc., 5300 Hollywood Blvd., Los Angeles, CA 90027

Variables Measured: Personality traits influential in personal functioning and interpersonal relationships

Type of Instrument: Self-report instrument

Instrument Description: The T-JTA is a 180-item paper-and-pencil test used to measure nine bipolar personality traits (nervous/composed, depressive/light-hearted, active social/quiet, expressive responsive/inhibited, sympathetic/indifferent, subjective/objective, hostile/tolerant, and self-disciplined/impulsive) presumed to influence personal functioning and interpersonal relationships. The scale is designed as both a diagnostic device and as a counseling tool in working with individuals, couples, and families. With couples and families, test questions can be answered first as they apply to oneself, and again as they apply to a spouse or other family member. The authors refer to this method of comparison as "criss-cross" scoring. This method is geared to elicit similarities, differences, and areas of misunderstanding between individuals involved in intimate relationships. Test profiles and an extensive manual containing norms (including crisscross norms), scoring procedures, and reliability and validity information are available from the publisher. Hand-scoring stencils are furnished together with the manual. Alternatively, computer scoring is available. Administration time is approximately 20–40 minutes.

Sample Items:

(A) Is . . . quick to know when someone needs encouragement or a kind word?
(B) If called upon, would . . . be fair and impartial in helping others to settle their differences?
(C) Is . . . able to express affection without embarrassment?

Comments: Extensive reliability and validity information is reported in the test manual. In one study, test-retest reliability for the nine subscales over a one- to three-week interval was reported to range from .74 to .90. Split-half reliability for the subscales is reported to range from .71 to .86. Scores on the T-JTA have been compared with those of several other personality inventories, including the 16 PF and the MMPI.

References:

Cromwell, R. E., Olson, D. H. L., & Fournier, D. G. (1976). Diagnosis and evaluation in marital and family counseling. In D. H. L. Olson (Ed.), *Treating relationships* (chap. 22). Lake Mills, IA: Graphic.

Phillips, C. E. (1973). Some useful tests for marriage counselors. *Fam Coord, 22,* 43–44.

Roffe, M. W., & Britt, B. C. (1981). A typology of marital interaction for sexually dysfunctional couples. *J Sex Mar Ther, 7,* 207–222.

Sampel, D. D., & Seymour, W. R. (1980). A comparative analysis of the effectiveness of conciliation counseling on certain personality variables. *J Mar Fam Th, 6,* 3.

NOTE: For additional instruments, see also *Abstracts 1116–1195* in the Abbreviated Abstracts of Instruments (which precedes the Indexes).

4 Parenthood

GEORGE W. HOLDEN

The study of parenthood has long occupied a central place in research into child and family development. For it is the family—and the intrafamily processes—that are generally acknowledged to play a major role in ontogeny. Parents, at least for the first few years of a child's life, have been considered to be principal causal agents in behavioral, emotional, personality, and cognitive development. These effects are accomplished through a variety of active and passive, reactive and proactive, processes (see Baumrind, 1980; Holden, 1985; Maccoby & Martin, 1983; Radke-Yarrow & Zahn-Waxler, 1986; Sears, Maccoby, & Levin, 1957).

Since the 1930s, investigators have developed, at a prolific rate, questionnaires, interviews, and observational instruments to assess characteristics and processes of the family. Because these instruments are the vehicles for executing research, they provide a historical record of the ways in which psychological phenomena have been studied. The instruments as a corpus reveal assumptions, approaches, and biases about the topic matter. Of particular importance here are the assumptions about those aspects of a family environment that influence the developing organism, what processes contribute to that influence, how those processes can be assessed, and what factors mediate those influences.

The instruments also document the wide range of concepts and variables that have been and are being studied under the rubric of parenthood. One of the earliest topics studied—parental attitudes toward child rearing—has of late seen a resurgence of interest under the more general label of parental social cognition. Other topics, including parents' views on their adjustment to parenthood, the quality of their relationship with their children, their home environment, and satisfaction with parenting have histories of varying length, and continue to be studied vigorously. In addition to parental self-report instruments, children's views of their parents have also received considerable attention, as will be seen.

This chapter has four goals. The first objective is to introduce the instruments in this section by providing a brief historical background. A second goal is to provide a conceptual framework for this extensive body of research by organizing the instruments into discrete categories. The third objective is to critically evaluate the quality of the instruments on parent-hood and discuss methodological issues inherent in the topic. A final objective is directed to the future, with a discussion of how instruments can be improved and areas of parenthood that can be explored further.

RESEARCH INTO PARENTHOOD

Given the prominent position in psychological research occupied by research into the family and parent-child relations, a comprehensive historical review would require several volumes. More general histories, such as the history of developmental psychological research, are already available and the reader is referred elsewhere for more detail and greater depth (e.g., Cairns, 1983).

Historical Overview

If not the origin of the species, one of the first parenthood instruments was published in 1899 by Charles Sears. Under the guidance of G. Stanley Hall at Clark University, Sears developed a survey to assess adults' attitudes toward the punishment of children. Although a few instruments appeared in the intervening years, it was not until the 1930s that researchers began to churn out a variety of instruments designed to assess a wide range of constructs and variables related to parenthood.

As is well recognized, Sigmund Freud's work provided a major stimulus for understanding the role of parents in the development of children's personalities (e.g., Freud, 1936). His theory of psychosexual stage development and the potential for fixations opened the door to inquiries about the role that parents play in their children's development. In actuality, Freud did not spell out the impact of parents, as

> the references to the significance of parent-child relationships occur relatively infrequently in Freud's writings. . . . Freud's contribution consists in outlining some of the main dynamic factors which operate in the human economy, and he has left it to his successors to discover how these apply in the varieties of human relationships. (Symonds, 1949, p. 174)

Individuals such as Ernst Jones (1923) and Karen Horney (1933) helped to fill in Freud's outline.

Despite the lack of detail, Freud's work was very influential in prompting physicians and clinicians to turn their attention to parents and the child-rearing environment. For example, David Levy (1943) studied mothers whose psychological problems were manifested in an "overprotective" parenting style and how this maternal behavior resulted in children's behavior problems. Researchers in child development, such as those at the Universities of Iowa and Minnesota, instigated studies exploring how the environment, as represented by parents, affects children. John B. Watson, the father of behaviorism, also provided a strong impetus for the study of the family environment with his provocative statements about the impact of classical conditioning on children and his extremist views on child rearing (e.g., Watson, 1928).

How was this interest in parental influence translated into research? Most of the early efforts to study parental influence relied on the new social psychological construct of attitudes (Allport, 1935). It was believed that if parental attitudes could be assessed, those would then reflect the family atmosphere to which the child was exposed. Hence, the origin of the parental child-rearing attitude questionnaires. With little more evidence than the intuitive appeal that the approach offered, the use of parental attitude surveys blossomed into a major research paradigm. Without doubt, the popularity of this approach was highly correlated with its ease of administration and scoring.

The underlying model of parents and parent-child relations inherent in the early attitude questionnaires was refreshingly simple—and inaccurate. Parental behavior was conceived as being a direct reflection of global attitudes of warmth, control, or punitiveness, for example. Therefore, to determine parental behavior in a variety of circumstances and thus the child-rearing environment, all that was needed was to assess the underlying parental attitudes. Parental behavior, as determined by the attitudes, would then result in the children's developmental outcome.

To be fair, some early parenthood investigators did not subscribe to such assumptions and did recognize some problems in accurately accessing parental attitudes. For example, Helen Koch and her colleagues in 1934 expressed doubts about the quality and validity of their own parental self-report attitude scales (see *Abstract 1288*). Other researchers recognized that children's perceptions of their parents' behavior were important as well as the parents' views of their attitudes, and by the end of the 1930s a number of instruments assessing children's perceptions of their parents were available (Stogdill, 1937). Although the study of parental attitudes did not wane, there was a proliferation in the type and scope of constructs and variables being studied in relation to the family during the 1930s and 1940s.

It is clear that the early model of global attitudes guiding parental behavior and resulting in child outcome is currently untenable. Such unidirectional and deterministic views would receive little support today. The bidirection of parent-child relations is now well acknowledged (Bell & Harper, 1977). Furthermore, more complex conceptualizations of parents and children, including transactional and systems theories, are now appreciated (Sameroff, 1983). For example, rather than viewing parental behavior as being guided by only one variable, Belsky (1984) has proposed that parenting is influenced by a complex interplay among the individual's developmental history, marital relations, work status, social network, and child characteristics, in addition to the parent's attitudes and personality.

Such current views of parents and parent-child relations have not appeared out of the blue, but rather they have been built upon the fruitful efforts of previous researchers. It is only thanks to the pioneers and explorers of research into the family—and those who have developed instruments to assess particular characteristics—that current researchers have been able to reach our current level of understanding about parenthood. Some of those many researchers and their pioneering ideas are described next.

Evolution of Parenthood Concepts

The instruments that appear in this handbook, in combination with those detailed in Straus (1969) and Straus and Brown (1978), provide an almost exhaustive catalog of the measures developed to assess variables related to parenthood. In order to review the parenthood instruments found in this volume, which also includes abstracts of the majority of instruments described in the two previous volumes, the instruments were organized into conceptual categories based on the primary focus of the instrument. For the purposes of this chapter, seven categories were formed: (a) parental social cognition and behavior; (b) parent-child relationships; (c) home environment; (d) marital issues and the transition to parenthood; (e) parental self-perceptions; (f) particular target groups; and (g) miscellaneous instruments. Each category was then divided into two—depending on whether the parent or the child was the respondent.

Subcategories were also created to differentiate related but distinct concepts. For example, semantic and conceptual confusion has frequently characterized descriptions of parental self-report questionnaires: Some "attitude" surveys assess parental behavior, and some behavioral surveys consist mostly of attitude and beliefs statements. Definitions will be provided to clarify some of the related concepts.

1936–1974

A total of 204 parenthood instruments, developed from 1936 through 1974, were abstracted in Straus (1969) and Straus and Brown (1978). That translates to an average of more than five new parenthood instruments identified per year. Out of those instruments, only eighteen continue to be actively used and are included in the current volume along with the recently developed instruments. Thus the vast majority of instruments developed from 1936 through 1974 have been retired from active research. Yet these instruments continue to provide a useful archival record. The instru-

Table 4.1 A Conceptual Typology of Abstracted Parenthood Instruments, 1936–1974

Primary Focus:	Respondent	
	Parent	*Child*
Parental social cognition and behavior		
attitudes	34	8
practices	38	21
beliefs	12	1
subtotal	84	30
Parent-child relationships		
interactions	13	2
quality of relationship	16	11
parental involvement	2	3
decision making	3	7
subtotal	34	23
Home environment		
environment	4	1
Marital issues and transition to parenthood		
marital relations	1	0
adjustment to parenthood	10	0
subtotal	11	0
Parental self-perceptions		
satisfaction/self-esteem	2	1
Target groups		
adolescent issues	1	6
Miscellaneous		
other instruments	11	0
Totals	147	61

NOTE: Numbers indicate the frequency of instruments that fall in each category out of a total of 204 instruments. In some cases, instruments used both parent and child as respondents.

ments depict a gradual expansion of the concepts studied regarding the role parents play in the development of their children. Table 4.1 lists the number of instruments occupying each category and subcategory.

Parental social cognition and behavior. As can be seen in Table 4.1, the category with the greatest number of instruments concerns parents' thinking and child-rearing practices: 57% of the instruments that use parents, versus 49% in which children served as respondents, were developed to assess parental attitudes, beliefs, or behavior.

As discussed above, the earliest parenthood instruments were questionnaires designed to assess global attitudes toward child rearing. Attitudes are commonly defined as an individual's predisposition, reaction to, or affective evaluation of the supposed facts about an object or situation (e.g., Oskamp, 1977). Thus items eliciting parental agreement or disagreement with statements about children and child-rearing practices were created in an effort to identify the parent's attitude. In the 1930s, some of the first attitude surveys were developed by individuals such as Lois Ackerley, Ralph Stogdill, and Helen Koch.

The prototypic attitude survey consisted of a set of statements about children. The parents then decided how much they agreed or disagreed with the item and responded on a rating scale in the approach advocated by Rensis Likert (1932). The first two attitude surveys were designed to assess parental attitudes toward children's freedom ("A preschool child should never be allowed to have his own way"; *1291*), and attitudes toward control ("Parents should not try to control the behavior of their children"; *1213*). These two examples are representative of the majority of items on attitude surveys. The items were written in the third person and were context-free statements. It was believed that, by posing generalized statements, the resulting data would be more predictive of a large class of parental behavior than would situation-specific items.

The majority of the 34 instruments in this subcategory were designed to measure parental attitudes toward democratic control, discipline, or acceptance of the child. In addition, instruments assessed attitudes toward overprotection, the use of fear, sex roles, independence, and traditionality. A few instruments that would have been classified in this category attained prominence and continue to be used, and so are included in the next section. These include the surveys developed by Earl Schaefer and Richard Bell in 1958 (PARI—Parent Attitude Research Instrument; *347*), Jeanne Block in 1965 (CRPR—Child Rearing Practices Report; *263*), Donald Pumroy in 1966 (MPAS—Maryland Parent Attitude Survey; *336*), and Bertram Cohler and his colleagues in 1970 (MAS—Maternal Attitude Survey; *279*). It is interesting that the instrument developed by Edward Shoben in 1949 (PAS—Parent Attitude Survey, *1341*), which influenced the development of many subsequent surveys, is no longer used.

Almost since their inception, attitude surveys have faced periodic criticism. Indeed, a large number of concerns have been identified—there are both methodological (Becker & Krug, 1965) and conceptual problems inherent in that approach for assessing parental social cognition or behavior (Holden & Edwards, 1989). An alternative to global attitude surveys came in the form of instruments to assess parental child-rearing practices. These were pioneered by such individuals as Robert Sears and his colleagues (*1336*) in the 1950s and Martin Hoffman (*1276*), Walter Emmerich (*1243*), and Leonard Eron and his colleagues (*1253*) in the early 1960s. The 38 instruments in this subcategory focused on parental practices concerning areas such as control, acceptance, nurturance, and, most frequently, reactions to child behavior. About half of the instruments involved parental interviews; others were either surveys or observations.

The items on many of the instruments were intended to assess parental practices, but it would be more accurate to describe them as assessing parental behavioral intentions. Reports of practices can be captured best by questions such as "Yesterday, how many times did you hug your child?" Instead, a number of the parental practices surveys presented hypothetical situations and asked the parents to project how they think they would react or behave in that situation. Thus the items are more accurately described as parental reports of their presumed behavior rather than their actual practices. Data revealing the relations between these parental behavior intentions and actual behavior have yet to be collected.

Contrasting those instruments directed at global attitudes or behavioral intentions, 12 instruments were designed to collect information about parental beliefs or knowledge about children. Beliefs are defined as those ideas about facts or expectancies that could be, in principle, proved or disproved (see Sigel, 1985). Child-rearing attitudes, then, are a function of child-rearing beliefs. The study of parental beliefs began with Ralph Ojemann's 1934 survey (*1312*) of beliefs about the age in which particular self-reliant behaviors should emerge. Parents were asked to write down the age at which they thought a child could perform various acts (e.g., "I believe that a child should be able to wash, scald, and dry the dishes after a family meal by the age of ___ "). No other instruments focused exclusively on beliefs until the late 1960s. At that time, new questionnaires were created to reveal parental beliefs about the appropriateness of various sex-role-typed behavior (*1292*), means-ends relations in child rearing (*1248*), and knowledge of developmental issues (*1269, 1362*).

In conjunction with instruments designed to collect data from parents, it was recognized in the 1930s that children's perceptions of parents also were important—and in some cases may even be more important than the actual parental behavior. For example, if a child believes she is rejected by her father, that perception may be more meaningful or predictive than the father's views of his own behavior. Thus, since 1894, children's views of their parents have been studied (see reviews by Goldin, 1969; Stogdill, 1937). A total of 30 instruments have been identified that determined how offspring viewed their parents' attitudes, behavior, or beliefs. Of these instruments, 53% were designed for adolescents, 30% were designed for younger children, and the rest were created for adults to report retrospectively on how their parents had reared them when they were younger.

Parent-child relationships. Instruments directed at the parent-child relationship are qualitatively different from the first category because, rather than assessing parental behavior or thinking, the instruments focus on the dyadic nature of the parent-child relationship: 23% of the instruments with parents as respondents fit this category, as do 38% of the child instruments. Four subcategories were developed to reflect the instruments designed to assess (a) parent-child interactions, (b) the quality of the parent-child relationship, (c) the level of parental involvement with the child, and (d) parent-child decision making.

In contrast to the self-report measures that characterize the first category, investigations into parent-child interactions relied mostly on a new approach—observations. Barbara Merrill Bishop (*1217*) pioneered this method of recording parent-child interactions in 1951. In that instrument, she used a time-sampling approach to observe the frequencies of certain behaviors and then made ratings of those behaviors. Data collected from the Fels Longitudinal study were coded in a similar fashion by other investigators (*1236*). A total of 13 instruments developed from 1936 through 1974 were identified with a primary emphasis on rating the frequency with which certain child-rearing behaviors occurred. The most commonly rated behaviors were disciplinary responses, but other parental behaviors such as nurturant acts were also sometimes coded. The data were based on observations lasting from 16 minutes on one occasion (*1311*) to eight hours over a period of two days (*1328*).

Closely related to instruments assessing the frequencies of interactions were instruments designed to assess the quality of parent-child interactions. For example, instead of focusing on variables such as the types of maternal punishments used or ratings of child compliance, researchers' interests shifted to communicative ease or family cohesion as dependent variables. This set of instruments also differed from those assessing interactions because they relied far more frequently upon self-report measures. Investigations aimed explicitly at understanding the quality of fathers' relationships with their children first appeared with the development of two such instruments in 1964 and 1965 (*1304, 1330*).

One key index of a parent-child relationship concerns the level of parental involvement. Five instruments were created to assess this basic characteristic; four of them first appeared around 1970. Two of the surveys assessed parents' reports of their own involvement (e.g., *1361*), and three instruments collected that data from the offspring (e.g., *1301*).

The final subcategory of the parent-child relationship category is noteworthy because it represents a new approach. Ten instruments were identified that were developed from 1946 through 1971 to assess the intrafamily process of decision making between parents and children. These instruments were designed to reveal the quality of how decisions were arrived at in the family, with the goal of determining how democratic or autocratic the parents were. Previously, this type of information had been inferred by responses to attitude scales. All but two of the family decision making instruments were questionnaires (*1237, 1246*); seven utilized children as respondents (e.g., *1272, 1343*).

The home environment. Parental behavior or parent-child interaction could not cover all aspects of the home environment. Thus, beginning in 1941, five instruments were developed that assessed a new family characteristic—the quality of the home environment. Four of these instruments (*1222, 1264, 1324, 1376*) were designed to assess, through parental interviews, aspects of physical (e.g., books, educational toys and materials) as well as social environments (educational activities) provided for children. The fifth instrument (*1376*) used child interviews to supplement those from parents.

Marital relations and the transition to parenthood. Human ecologists such as Urie Bronfenbrenner (1979) have long advocated the position that human development occurs within multiple contexts and multiple relationships. The first relationship outside the parent-child relationship to receive systematic attention was marital relations before and during the transition to parenthood. Of the eleven identified instruments that fit this category, one concerns mothers' perceptions of their husbands (*1312*) and the others assess reactions to the transition to parenthood (e.g., *1200, 1205*). The instruments, mostly developed in the early 1970s, focused on decisions or motivations underlying childbearing (*1201, 1208*), the adjustment or lack of adjustment to the newborn (*1200*), and/or father involvement (*1202, 1205*).

Parental self-perceptions. Data on parents' perceptions about themselves and their roles as parents were first collected in 1963. This approach represented a marked shift from previous work in which attitudes and/or beliefs about children were of primary concern. Only with the development of these instruments were parental thoughts and feelings formally recognized as significant variables. However, up through 1974, only two instruments were developed to explore this new construct; both focused on parental dissatisfaction with the role of parent. One instrument (*1361*) used an interview format, while the second, a questionnaire, assessed both the parents' and their children's views of parental dissatisfaction (*1259*). Implicit in the study of parental satisfaction or dissatisfaction is the importance of parental emotions and affect. Therefore, these instruments represent another milestone in the study of parenthood as they expanded the domain of parental research to include parental affect.

Particular target groups. Seven instruments were aimed at addressing the unique issues associated with one particular developmental stage: adolescence. The instruments were mostly developed in the early 1970s, although they first appeared in 1937 (*1221*). All of these instruments were questionnaires and focused on the nature of parent-child conflicts, independence from parents, dating, and adjustment to adolescence (e.g., *1242, 1227, 1352*).

Miscellaneous. Eleven instruments developed from 1936 through 1974 defied classification into one of the categories above. These miscellaneous instruments ranged from assessing parents' contraceptive knowledge (*1203*) to children's preferences for rewards and punishments from their parents (*1232*).

Recent Developments

There are 128 primary and 26 secondary instruments included in this handbook that have been identified as having been developed or used since 1975. Taken together, these instruments show indications of both continuity and change with the instruments developed before 1975. Continuity is demonstrated by the large number of new instruments that are similar to old ones in format and design, although they may expand upon the subject matter. Change is illustrated in the frequency of publication of new instruments; the rate has increased to approximately 10 new instruments per year. Change is also apparent in the expansion of the parenthood topics under investigation. Although the parental behavior and parent-child relations categories continue to be the categories that attract the most attention, the development of instruments in the other four categories has increased. More subtle changes concerning concepts and variables can also be seen, as is discussed below.

Parental social cognition and behavior. The relative number of instruments assessing parents' behaviors, attitudes, or beliefs has decreased, as this category now accounts for only 40% of the parenthood instruments designed with parents as respondents, a decrease of 30% (see Table 4.2). However, the majority of the instruments using children as respondents (45%) are accounted for by this category. Surveys assessing parental attitudes toward child rearing have continued to be a prominent research paradigm; they now represent the single most popular subcategory. The new attitude surveys closely resemble their predecessors from the 1930s and 1940s. The major exception is that some of the instruments have expanded into new domains of parent-child relations. Surveys now include assessments of attitudes toward educating children (*368*) and attitudes regarding the emotional climate in the family, as revealed by variables such as anger, frustration, and pleasure caused by children (*286, 295, 320*).

A total of 25 new instruments have been identified that assess parental practices; 11 are responded to by parents (e.g., *257, 281, 342*) while others use children as respondents (e.g., *266, 307, 346*). Most of the recent instruments are similar to those developed previously: they are predominately Likert-type questionnaires (only two are interviews) and assess frequently investigated topics like parental disciplinary responses, responsiveness, and acceptance. A few new variables have been introduced though, such as consistency of parental love and frequency of affection (*259*). One change that has occurred with some of the instruments is a move toward greater situational specificity in the items. For example, the Iowa Parent Behavior Inventory (*281*) includes relatively detailed and concrete behavior-based items to assess the frequency of parental behavior (e.g., "Require your child to remain seated in the car while you are driving").

The most noticeable change in the category of parental social cognition

TABLE 4.2 A Conceptual Typology of Abstracted Parenthood Instruments, 1975–1988

Primary Focus:	Respondent	
	Parent	*Child*
Parental social cognition and behavior		
attitudes	22	1
practices	11	14
beliefs	16	2
subtotal	49	17
Parent-child relationship		
interaction	13	0
quality of relationship	8	2
parental involvement	3	2
decision making	4	4
subtotal	28	8
Home environment		
environment	5	2
Marital issues and transition to parenthood		
marital relations	2	0
adjustment to parenthood	13	0
subtotal	15	0
Parental self-perceptions		
satisfaction/self-esteem	3	1
anxiety/stress/support	8	0
subtotal	11	1
Target groups		
adolescent issues	6	8
those at risk for parenting problems	3	0
subtotal	8	2
Miscellaneous		
other instruments	6	2
Totals	123	38

NOTE: Numbers indicate the frequency of instruments that fall in each category out of a total of 154 instruments. In some cases, instruments used both parents and children as respondents.

and behavior is the dramatic increase in instruments assessing parental beliefs. Sixteen instruments are included that document various aspects of parental beliefs or knowledge about their children (e.g., *285, 290*). Beliefs about breast-feeding (*258*), how much control parents have over their children's development (*273*), and parental knowledge about behavioral principles (*275*) are representative of the efforts designed to uncover the belief structure held by parents. In addition, two instruments have been identified that assess children's views of their own or their parents' beliefs (*247, 238*).

Parent-child relationships. The relative number of instruments identified as assessing parent-child interactions and relationships has remained approximately equal to that found in Straus (1969) and Straus and Brown (1978). However, the type of instrument has changed. All but one of the instruments are now observational techniques involving the coding of parent-child dyadic interactions, and 10 of these 13 instruments assess parental and/or children's behavioral frequencies (e.g., *270, 299, 324*). In contrast to this approach, previous observational instruments were characterized by the practice of reducing the data into ratings.

Relatively few new instruments have been developed with the purpose of identifying the quality of the parent-child relationship; the subcategory that constituted one-half of the category with the earlier scales now makes up only one-quarter of the category. Again, the trend is toward observational instruments rather than self-report instruments, as found with five of the eight instruments that focus on the parents (e.g., *272, 345*). Variables such as acceptance, anxiety, dominance, closeness, and desire for change in the relationship are sampled by these instruments.

Five instruments in this section offer new assessments of parental involvement. Two of the surveys are directed either at particular individuals such as fathers (*261*) or, in the case of divorce, the nonresidential parent (*485*). The other three instruments provide assessments of children's perceptions of their parents' involvement with them (e.g., *323*).

Instruments directed at parent-child decision making form the final subcategory in parent-child relations. All but one of the eight identified instruments are questionnaires concerning how parents and/or their children arrive at decisions (e.g., *292, 363, 371*). The new instruments, as a group, provide a more thorough probing of different areas of parent-child decision making than the earlier set of decision-making instruments.

Home environment. Seven new instruments assessing home environments have been identified as appearing since 1974. Three utilize both an interview and an observation approach for collecting detailed information about such things as the number of intellectually stimulating objects in the environment, the quality of parenting, the quality of the housing, and the frequency in which the child goes out of the home for educational experiences (*302, 331, 325*). Caldwell and Bradley's Home Observation for Measurement of the Environment (HOME, *24*) is the best known and most popular instrument for assessing the quality of the home environment; it has been shown to be especially useful in differentiating the home environments of lower- and middle-socioeconomic-status families.

Marital relations and transition to parenthood. The only instruments included in this section that directly deal with marital relations and parenthood are two questionnaires that focus on discrepancies between the mother's and father's expectations or disciplinary practices (*352, 428*). In contrast, a number of instruments have been created to further explore issues related to the transition to parenthood. The 13 instruments address questions such as motivations for having—or not having—children, parents' and siblings' adjustment, and changes that have occurred in the family as a consequence of the birth (e.g., *246, 250, 255*).

Parental self-perceptions. The category that has experienced the greatest growth in the number of instruments developed for parents as respondents is that of parental self-perceptions. Eleven new instruments have been included that assess a variety of parents' thoughts about themselves. Three surveys were designed to determine the level of parental satisfaction or self-esteem related to parenting (*304, 305, 353*), and eight surveys measured the negative side of parental self-perceptions, including concerns, anxieties, stressors, and the presence or absence of a social support network (*274, 362, 372*).

Particular target groups. Adolescent issues have received increasing attention in recent years as reflected by the 14 new instruments identified that address questions particular to children of that age group. In addition to parent-child conflict and adjustment, two instruments now address dating issues (*318, 319*). These instruments differ from earlier ones directed at this age group in that almost half of the instruments now include parents of adolescents as respondents, either alone or along with the adolescents. A new target group has also attracted the attention of those who develop instruments. Three instruments that attempt to identify parents who will experience difficulties in their role as parents and consequently may be at risk for child abuse or neglect are also included. These questionnaires are in the tradition of the parent attitude instruments, but were explicitly designed to reveal those who may experience problems in parenting or have tendencies to abuse their children (*260, 309, 423*).

Miscellaneous instruments. The miscellaneous category includes eight instruments. Among those, one is designed to reveal the extent and types of involvement of grandparents of children (*55*), a second instrument deals with parental perceptions and relations toward their children's school (*291*), and a third focuses on college students' views about their parents' role in their sex education (*215*).

METHODOLOGICAL ISSUES

The study of the family presents a methodological challenge to the researcher. The primary phenomena of interest, those naturally occurring parent-child interactions in the home, are not readily accessible to investigators due to ethical and practical considerations. Consequently, most investigators rely on self-reports to collect data. With the exception of the observational instruments, which compose only 8% of the parenthood instruments in this handbook, almost all of the instruments were designed to collect self-reports from parents or children. Indeed, self-report data are indispensable and provide the only reasonable way to access certain types of information. However, as has been periodically acknowledged, a number of potential problems exist with self-report data in general and with parental interviews or surveys in particular (e.g., Yarrow, 1963). Some of those problems will be discussed below.

The decision to use a self-report device, an observational approach, or some other type of instrument involves multiple considerations, including the types of questions being addressed, the time and resources available, and the expertise of the investigator. Another key consideration should lie in evaluating the quality of the instrument. The major evidence for the quality of an instrument is its reliability and validity. However, across the 154 primary and secondary instruments fully abstracted in this volume, reliability data are provided for only 68% of the instruments, while a mere 32% of the abstracts mention any validity data.

It is of crucial importance to know how reliable an instrument is because that information provides an index of how well the instrument can measure a psychological construct and whether it is free from random errors. For instance, we know a yardstick provides an excellent measurement of short distances just as a quartz watch provides a highly accurate assessment of the passage of relatively small amounts of time. If we use either instrument repeatedly, we are confident that we will get the same result. Or, if we choose to use only a part of the yardstick, we are still assured of an accurate measurement. But are we equally confident about the use of a psychological measuring stick or just one subscale from a questionnaire?

Validity is a more complex question as there are a large number of ways to demonstrate validity (e.g., Messick, 1980). The fundamental issue with validity is whether the instrument measures the psychological construct that it was intended to measure. Again, we are confident based on previous experience and widespread use that a yardstick is a good tool with which to quantify short distances or that a wristwatch is an effective way to document the passage of time from one day to the next. But can one be equally confident that parental reactions to a series of statements provide an accurate reflection of an underlying, subjective psychological construct? Both reliability and validity are continua but they are also related; the less reliable an instrument is, the less valid it can be.

Because the type of instrument raises unique problems and necessitates evaluation using different forms of reliability, a discussion of reliability, validity, and other methodological issues will be divided according to the three categories of instruments: questionnaires, interviews, and observations. Of the instruments receiving full treatment in this section, the questionnaire format was utilized in 125 of the instruments; interviews, in 14; observations, in 11; and a combination of interviews and observations, in 4.

Questionnaires

If researchers' gold is good ideas, then their silver is time. And no method is as easy to use, fast, and economical as paper-and-pencil surveys. It has been no coincidence that over two-thirds of the parenthood instruments have utilized this format. It only takes from 2 to 45 minutes to fill out the questionnaires, with a median time of 30 minutes. Those surveys represent a variety of styles and formats, as illustrated by the number of items. One instrument has as few as 3 items and another as many as 233 items; the median number of items is 35. These items generally consist of a single sentence but, depending on the instrument, are responded to in a variety of ways including Likert-type ratings, multiple choice, Q-sorts, and true-false responses. However, 85% of the surveys utilized a Likert-type rating, most commonly in the form of a 5-point agree/disagree scale.

The obvious cost of collecting data so quickly is that complex family experiences must be abstracted into a few words. As such, the approach is the most removed from actual behavior of the three methods (Lytton, 1971). Data on reliability and validity provide an indication of the extent of those costs.

Reliability. There are two major types of reliability information computed on questionnaires: test-retest and internal consistency. Test-retest reliability provides an assessment of how similarly the same subject responds to the same questions on different occasions. An interval of one to four weeks usually occurs before the second assessment, so recall memory does not dominate performance. The second major type of reliability, internal consistency, concerns how well items within a scale or across the instrument as a whole hang together to measure the same psychological construct. Both types of reliability should be provided in order to reveal more fully the quality of an instrument.

Only 8% of the questionnaires are supported with both types of reliability data. Test-retest data were available for only 10% of the surveys, whereas internal consistency data alone were provided for 44% of the questionnaires. No reliability data were provided for over one-third of the surveys. Of 24 instruments for which test-retest data were available, the median correlation was .73 (range .40 to .98). As would be expected on theoretical grounds, internal consistency coefficients tended to exceed those reported for test-retest. A total of 65 instruments provide such data. There are a few different ways to compute internal consistency; the most common approach is either split-half reliability or Cronbach's coefficient alpha. The latter approach is preferred as it is not affected by the particular order of items. The median internal consistency reported across the 65 instruments is in the low .80s, with a range of .32 to .97. A reliability coefficient of at least .80 is considered appropriate for research (Nunnally, 1978).

Although a few surveys or subscales do attain high levels of reliability with either test-retest correlations or alpha coefficients above .90 (e.g., *269, 282, 298*), most of the questionnaires have reliability coefficients in the range of .61 to .82. They are better characterized as having only marginally acceptable levels. Why is this so? A variety of concerns have been expressed, including problems with construction of the items, response sets, and conceptual difficulties. Likert, a founding father of questionnaires, advised in 1932 that those who developed questionnaires must avoid every kind of vagueness or ambiguity. That advice continues to be given today (Converse & Presser, 1986). A few examples of ambiguity will help to highlight this problem. Some ambiguity arises with items worded in the third-person format ("A parent should . . . ") where respondents do not know whether to answer in terms of "cultural norms, professional opinion, empirical facts, or beliefs about what is best for others, none of which may have anything to do with what the parent actually does with his own child" (Becker & Krug, 1965, p. 361). In responding to items, many surveys rely on response scales defined by vague probability terms such as "strongly disagree," "slightly agree," "frequent," or "often." Such vague terms can be interpreted by two individuals quite differently; in addition, such terms may not provide meaningful distinctions to some items but a mismatch of item and response scale (see Holden & Edwards, 1989).

Aside from ambiguity in items or response scales, another class of problems concerns the propensity of some respondents to use "response sets" when filling out questionnaires. These sets include the acquiescence set (agreeing with oppositely worded statements); the opposition set (disagreeing with all statements); the extreme set (selecting extreme responses); and social desirability, or selecting the response that the respondent believes to be the most socially accepted response. Strategies devised to combat these problems include presenting paired items (*336*), using Q-sort responses (*263*), or reversing the direction of certain items on preexisting scales as Schludermann and Schludermann (1977) did on Schaefer and Bell's PARI (*347*).

Validity. Only 25% of the questionnaires are supported with validity data in the abstracts or refer to validity data in other sources. Of these, the most common type of evidence is convergent validity, by correlating the scale with another instrument. A second form is criterion group validity, or testing how well an instrument discriminates two or more groups of individuals of known differences. The major limitation of the validity evidence has been the failure to examine the relations between responses on questionnaires and actual parental behavior. Although a handful of studies have addressed this question (reviewed in Holden & Edwards, 1989), and at least one study found some significant relations between survey responses and behavioral observations (Tulkin & Cohler, 1973), the topic has received inadequate attention. Clearly, more effort devoted to establishing the validity of surveys is warranted.

Other issues. Ten questionnaires given full treatment in this volume were designed to assess adults' recollections of their parents' child-rearing behavior. However, parental retrospective memory is notoriously faulty (e.g., McGraw & Molloy, 1941; Wenar & Coulter, 1962) and data based on memories of past events should be interpreted cautiously and considered generally reconstructive rather than veridical. The type of response provided on questionnaires has been shown to be related to the educational level of the respondent (e.g., Becker & Krug, 1965). Thus it is imperative that the educational level of individuals be controlled for to avoid this confound. A final issue in the use of surveys to assess parenthood variables concerns the subtle problem of the creation—as an artifact—of a parental attitude when there never was one in the first place. Social psychologists call this problem the assessment of "nonattitudes" (e.g., Smith, 1984). For a more detailed discussion of these and other problems related to questionnaire use, some of which are particular to parents and children, see Holden and Edwards (1989).

Interview Instruments

Fourteen of the instruments rely solely on interviews; another four combine interview and observation. Although interviews are also self-report devices, the flexibility afforded by the presence of the interviewer avoids some of the problems inherent with questionnaires. Sensitive interviewers can omit inappropriate questions, rephrase other questions, or probe responses to maximize the quality of the respondent's answers. The costs of the flexibility and open-ended responses come when it is time to reduce the data. In comparison to analyzing questionnaire data, it is considerably more difficult and time-consuming to transcribe tapes and then reliably code the responses.

In addition to data reduction problems, a second set of considerations involves possible bias introduced by the interview method. Given that an interview is a social interaction, a number of subtle and complex forces can be operating—on both sides of the microphone. Physical characteristics of the interviewer and respondent (e.g., gender, attractiveness, age, race), as well as the social competence of the individuals as they interact, can influence the quality of the data elicited (Warwick & Lininger, 1975). Response sets are also a likely consequence of the social situation. It is reasonable to suspect that many parents may be susceptible to a social desirability bias, either consciously or otherwise, during an interview. In addition, the parent's responses may also be influenced by a "courtesy" bias (maintaining a pleasant atmosphere) or an "ingratiation" bias (distorting responses to win the approval of the interviewer). The fact that parents are ego-invested in both their children and their own parenting also should not be ignored (Yarrow, 1963).

Reliability. In addition to the two types of reliability that can be coded with the questionnaire, a third type can be used with interviews—that of interrater reliability. If ratings are made from interviews, as they were with about half of the interviews, then interrater reliability should be assessed. Of the 18 instruments in this section utilizing interviews, three abstracts present no reliability data, two provide test-retest data, nine report internal consistency, and five assess interrater reliability. Although the average retest correlation was low (.61), the median alpha coefficient attained a marginally acceptable level at .78 (range .39-.94). More success was achieved in establishing reliable interrater agreement; the median reliability coefficient was .90 (range .28-.95).

Validity. Five of the interview instruments have validity information provided. Two instruments use criterion groups to demonstrate the utility of the instrument (*255, 307*). Another correlates the data with the predicted variable (*331*), and a fourth compares the results of the interview with independent judges' assessments, finding that in 47 of 50 cases the outcomes were the same (*265*). The validity data for the fifth instrument, while not detailed in the abstract, is reported to be available elsewhere (*322*).

Observational Instruments

Observational instruments represent an alternative to self-report instruments and thereby avoid many of the problems associated with them. However, observational instruments continue to be rare; only 16 instruments or 10% of the parenthood instruments in this volume were developed in that format. Although observations cannot be used for collecting certain types of data, such as those dealing with questions about social cognition or past events, there are many questions related to parental behavior and parent-child interactions where observational instruments are the preferred method (Lytton, 1971).

A variety of reasons account for the limited development of this methodology. One reason is that the approach requires more knowledge than the other two methods (see Bakeman & Gottman, 1986, for an excellent primer on observational methodology). Observational data also require a considerable investment of time for training observers and coders, and for collecting the data. One instrument developer reported that it took five months just to train a coder (*277*). If the observations are videotaped (e.g., *345*), then there is the added expense of procuring the equipment.

Although some types of bias can be avoided with observations, other types can be introduced. Two types of bias are the most likely: self-presentation bias on the part of the subjects—or reacting to the awareness that they are being observed (see Zegiob, Arnold, & Forehand, 1975)—and experimenter bias. Ritter and Langlois (1988) have recently demonstrated an example of experimenter bias. They found that subjects' physical attractiveness influenced the global—but not molecular—ratings of those coding the videotapes.

Another potential problem with observational data concerns the stability and instability of observed behavior. How reliable is a sample of behavior from one occasion to the next? It is commonly assumed that any behavioral observation provides a representative sample of behavior. However, depending on the type of behavior examined and the eliciting conditions, the sample of behavior may not be representative. Parent-child dyadic behavior sampled with the recently developed instruments varies from three minutes to two hours, with a median of 40 minutes. There is little doubt that, in general, the larger the sample of behavior, the more representative and accurate the sample of behavior becomes. In a systematic study of observational data on parent-infant interaction, Wachs (1987) found that stability of behavior increased as more observations were combined, but that data from a single 45-minute observation period did not provide a stable or reliable assessment of behavior.

Reliability. Of the 16 observational instruments, 5 have no reliability information provided. One instrument is supported by internal consistency data (*22*), and the 10 others are supported by some form of interrater reliability. Across the instruments, the median coefficient of the interrater agreement is in the .80s, a figure generally accepted as adequate. However, the average percentage of agreement does not control for chance agreements. The preferred estimate of interrater reliability is found by using Cohen's Kappa (see Bakeman & Gottman, 1986), yet only one instrument (*306*) is supported by such data.

Validity. Two observational instruments have some type of validity data reported in the abstracts (*324, 334*); two others indicate that the information can be located elsewhere (*306, 345*). Both instruments that have the information in the abstracts were evaluated using the criterion group approach and indicate that the observational instrument was effective at discriminating between two groups of individuals. For example, Mash and his colleagues (*324*) found that their observational instrument could reliably discriminate the interactions of normal and disturbed samples of parents and children.

Summary of Methodological Issues

The 154 instruments detailed in this section of the handbook represent a wide range of approaches to addressing variables related to the family. Each type of instrument has particular strengths and weaknesses. The major methodological problem is a fundamental one: There is inadequate attention devoted by the authors of instruments to reporting psychometric properties. The burden of proof should be on instrument developers to show that their instruments are of high quality, as indicated by reliability and validity data. Although some well-constructed instruments do indeed have good psychometric properties, many do not. Consumers need to shop carefully.

Given the incomplete psychometric data reported in the literature for most of the instruments, and the variability due to the characteristics of particular samples of participants, it should become standard practice for investigators to analyze and report the internal consistency of the instrument or subscales. Cronbach's coefficient alpha is the appropriate statistic to use and can easily be computed with a number of statistical packages— programs that are inexpensive and easy to use on personal computers.

FUTURE DIRECTIONS AND CONCLUSIONS

The evolution of the scientific enterprise occurs through the transmission of concepts, approaches, and instruments. Although the parenthood instruments described in this handbook and in Straus (1969) and Straus and Brown (1978) have assessed a large number of variables and concepts related to parenthood, it can be argued that they represent a skewed evolutionary tree. The great majority of instruments have focused on static variables or constructs such as parental attitudes, beliefs, or behavioral intentions, or children's perceptions of the quality of the parent-child relationship. These approaches are useful and important, but one type of family characteristic has been largely neglected: processes in parenthood. With the notable exception of the decision-making instruments, intrafamily processes have been ignored.

Family processes such as parental problem solving, decision making, monitoring, limit setting, balancing the competing needs of spouse and child, resolving conflicts, and modifying behavior under different circumstances are examples of common psychological processes that have received little attention in parenthood research. Similarly, how parents or the family change over time has not been studied developmentally (Maccoby, 1984). But, as Bell has pointed out, if parents are to be effective, they must be affected by the products of their tutelage and they must change (Bell & Harper, 1977). What it takes to be an effective parent of an infant is quite different from what it takes to an effective parent of a preschooler. Although there have been a few studies of continuity and change in parental attitudes (e.g., Roberts, Block, & Block, 1984), studies incorporating a developmental and process approach to parenthood are all too rare and long overdue.

A second area ripe for future work concerns more comprehensive assessments of the environment. The instrument developed by Caldwell and Bradley (24) to assess the home environment was designed to identify disadvantaged homes but is limited in its ability to differentiate middle-class homes. Furthermore, certain areas of parental influence, such as the motivational atmosphere created by parents for their children, have gone essentially unexplored.

Another area needing more extensive work is parental and child social cognition. Close relationships are sometimes characterized by conflicting thoughts and feelings, but the multidimensional nature of parents' thoughts have yet to be systematically documented. The instruments that assess the discrepancies in parents' actual and ideal behavior (e.g., *317*) provide a first step in this area. Another area of social cognition that needs more work lies in children's perceptions of their parents. Given the large number of instruments assessing children's views of adults, it is surprising that so few studies have explored the accuracy of children's perceptions (e.g., Michaels, Messe, & Stollak, 1983). How children's ages, as indicative of cognitive development, influence their perceptions also needs to be studied more systematically.

A final area that is currently ripe for additional work is the relationship between social cognition and behavior. Renewed attention should be devoted to understanding how attitudes, beliefs, current perceptions, or situational circumstances influence parental or child behavior. With the borrowing of theories and findings from social psychology (e.g., Ajzen & Fishbein, 1980), one can anticipate considerable advances.

Along with these proposed areas for substantive work, there are some methodological directions that need attention. The continued development of observational instruments to provide a better foundation of parental behavior is imperative. A second area of methodological work that merits investigation is a more comprehensive inquiry into the nature of self-report data. Self-reports will never be completely replaced: their ease, utility, portability, convenience, and economy are second to none. But a concerted effort is needed to understand the interaction between respondents and self-report instruments. There are two basic directions for systematic methodological inquiry. The first direction lies in developing the science of instrument construction. Understanding the properties of instruments, such as order of presentation effects or effects of different response scales on responses, is needed. The second direction is understanding the interaction between characteristics of the respondents and questionnaires. What type of individual will provide more veridical data? What personality, educational, or socioeconomic characteristics of parents are associated with more accurate self-reports of their own behavior?

In addition to systematic methodological studies, alternative approaches to questionnaires, interviews, or observations are needed to capture and examine the dynamic quality of dyadic and triadic relations. Technology can assist in developing video or microcomputer approaches. For example, Holden (1988) explored adult problem-solving behavior by developing interactive computer software to examine how parents and nonparents solve a common child-rearing problem—that of diagnosing why an infant was crying. The processes of searching for information and hypothesis selection were then revealed as subjects confidentially solved the problem on the computer. The use of computers and videotapes to explore and model interactive qualities represents an exciting area of methodological advancement yet to be tapped.

These suggestions await future research. For the present, the parenthood instruments found in this handbook stand as testimony to the pioneering and sustained efforts to understand the role of parenthood in human development. Collectively, the instruments have been erected upon the findings and assumptions of the past and will provide a foundation for the development of a new generation of methodologically and conceptually sophisticated instruments. It is hoped that the next generation of instruments will reflect a transformation from their current status as the outputs of a cottage industry into products from a leading scientific business.

REFERENCES

Ajzen, I., & Fishbein, M. (1980). *Understanding attitudes and predicting social behavior.* Englewood Cliffs, NJ: Prentice-Hall.

Allport, G. (1935). Attitudes. In C. Murchison (Ed.), *The handbook of social psychology* (pp. 798–844). Worcester, MA: Clark University Press.

Bakeman, R., & Gottman, J. M. (1986). *Observing interaction: An introduction to sequential analysis.* New York: Cambridge University.

Baumrind, D. (1980). New directions in socialization research. *American Psychologist, 35,* 639–652.

Becker, W. C., & Krug, R. S. (1965). The parent attitude research instrument—A research review. *Child Development, 36,* 329–365.

Bell, R. Q., & Harper, L. V. (1977). *Child effects on adults.* Hillsdale, NJ: Lawrence Erlbaum.

Belsky, J. (1984). The determinants of parenting: A process model. *Child Development, 55,* 83–96.

Bronfenbrenner, U. (1979). *The ecology of human development.* Cambridge: Cambridge University Press.

Cairns, R. B. (1983). The emergence of developmental psychology. In W. Kessen (Ed.) & P. H. Mussen (Series Ed.), *Handbook of child psychology: Vol. 1. History, theory, and methods* (pp. 41–102). New York: John Wiley.

Converse, J. M., & Presser, S. (1986). *Survey questions: Handcrafting the standardized questionnaire.* Beverly Hills, CA: Sage.

Freud, S. (1936). *The problem of anxiety.* New York: Norton.

Goldin, P. C. (1969). A review of children's reports of parent behaviors. *Psychological Bulletin, 71,* 222–236.

Holden, G. W. (1985). How parents create a social environment via proactive behavior. In T. Garling & J. Valsiner (Eds.), *Children within environments: Towards a psychology of accident prevention* (pp. 193–215). New York: Plenum.

Holden, G. W. (1988). Adults' thinking about a child-rearing problem: Effects of experience, parental status, and gender. *Child Development, 59,* 1623–1632.

Holden, G. W., & Edwards, L. (1989). Parental attitudes toward child rearing: Instruments, issues, and implications. *Psychological Bulletin 106*, 29–58.

Horney, K. (1933). Maternal conflicts. *American Journal of Orthopsychiatry, 3*, 455–463.

Jones, E. (1923). The phantasy of the reversal of generations. In *Papers on psycho-analysis* (pp. 674–679). New York: Wood.

Levy, D. M. (1943). *Maternal overprotection.* New York: Columbia University Press.

Likert, R. (1932). A technique for the measurement of attitudes. *Archives of Psychology, 22*, 5–55.

Lytton, H. (1971). Observation studies of parent-child interaction: A methodological review. *Child Development, 42*, 651–684.

Maccoby, E. E. (1984). Socialization and developmental change. *Child Development, 55*, 317–328.

Maccoby, E. E., & Martin, J. (1983). Socialization in the context of the family: Parent-child interaction. In E. M. Hetherington (Ed.) & P. H. Mussen (Series Ed.), *Handbook of child psychology: Vol. 4. Socialization, personality, and social development* (pp. 1–101). New York: John Wiley.

McGraw, M. B., & Molloy, L. B. (1941). The pediatric anamnesis: Inaccuracies in eliciting developmental data. *Child Development, 12*, 255–265.

Messick, S. (1980). Test validity and the ethics of assessment. *American Psychologist, 11*, 1012–1027.

Michaels, G. Y., Messe, L. A., & Stollak, G. E. (1983). Seeing parental behavior through different eyes: Exploring the importance of person perception processes in parents and children. *Genetic Psychology Monographs, 107*, 3–60.

Nunnally, J. C. (1978). *Psychometric theory* (2nd ed.). New York: McGraw-Hill.

Oskamp, S. (1977). *Attitudes and opinions.* Englewood Cliffs, NJ: Prentice-Hall.

Radke-Yarrow, M., & Zahn-Waxler, C. (1986). The role of familial factors in the development of prosocial behavior: Research findings and questions. In D. Olweus, J. Block, & M. Radke-Yarrow (Eds.), *Development of antisocial and prosocial behavior* (pp. 207–233). New York: Academic Press.

Ritter, J. M., & Langlois, J. H. (1988). The role of physical attractiveness in the observation of parent-child interactions: Eye of the beholder or behavioral reality? *Developmental Psychology, 24*, 254–263.

Roberts, G. C., Block, J. H., & Block, J. (1984). Continuity and change in parents' child-rearing practices. *Child Development, 55*, 586–597.

Sameroff, A. J. (1983). Developmental systems: Contexts and evolution. In W. Kessen (Ed.) & P. H. Mussen (Series Ed.), *Handbook of child psychology: Vol. 1. History, theory, and methods* (pp. 239–294). New York: John Wiley.

Schludermann, S., & Schludermann, E. (1977). A methodological study of a revised maternal attitude research instrument: Mother's PARI Q4. *Journal of Psychology, 95*, 77–86.

Sears, R. R., Maccoby, E. E., & Levin, H. (1957). *Patterns of child rearing.* Evanston, IL: Harper & Row.

Sigel, I. E. (1985). A conceptual analysis of beliefs. In I. E. Sigel (Ed.), *Parental belief systems: The psychological consequences for children* (pp. 345–371). Hillsdale, NJ: Lawrence Erlbaum.

Smith, J. W. (1984). Nonattitudes: A review and evaluation. In C. F. Turner & E. Martin (Eds.), *Surveying subjective phenomena* (Vol. 2, pp. 215–255). New York: Russell Sage.

Straus, M. A. (1969). *Family measurement techniques: Abstracts of published instruments, 1935–1965.* Minneapolis: University of Minnesota Press.

Straus, M. A., & Brown, B. W. (1978). *Family measurement techniques: Abstracts of published instruments, 1935–1974* (rev. ed.). Minneapolis: University of Minnesota Press.

Stogdill, R. M. (1937). Survey of experiments of children's attitudes toward parents: 1894–1936. *Journal of Genetic Psychology, 51*, 293–304.

Symonds, P. M. (1949). *The dynamics of parent-child relationships.* New York: Columbia University Press.

Tulkin, S. R., & Cohler, B. J. (1973). Childrearing attitudes and mother-child interaction in the first year of life. *Merrill-Palmer Quarterly, 19,* 95–106.

Wachs, T. (1987). Short-term stability of aggregated and nonaggregated measures of parental behavior. *Child Development, 58,* 796–797.

Watson, J. B. (1928). *Psychological care of the infant and child.* New York: Norton.

Warwick, D. P., & Lininger, C. A. (1975). *The sample survey: Theory and practice* (pp. 182–219). New York: McGraw-Hill.

Wenar, C., & Coulter, J. B. (1962). A reliability study of developmental histories. *Child Development, 33,* 453–462.

Yarrow, M. R. (1963). Problems of methods in parent-child research. *Child Development, 34,* 215–226.

Zegiob, L. E., Arnold, S., & Forehand, R. (1975). An examination of observer effects in parent-child interactions. *Child Development, 46,* 509–512.

ABSTRACTS OF INSTRUMENTS

NOTE: For additional instruments, see also *Abstracts 1196–1375* in the Abbreviated Abstracts of Instruments (which precedes the Indexes).

Summary of Instrument Codes

Number Codes:

I = Dimensions of interaction—1 = communication; 2 = life-style; 3 = networks; 4 = multidimensional perspectives

II = Intimacy and family values—1 = family values; 2 = marital relations; 3 = love; 4 = sex; 5 = personal/interpersonal perceptions

III = Parenthood—1 = pregnancy, childbearing, and transition to parenthood; 2 = parenting

IV = Roles and power—1 = roles; 2 = power

V = Adjustment—1 = family functioning; 2 = stress; 3 = divorce, separation, and remarriage

Letter Codes:

Interactants—a = husband-wife, b = parent-child, c = nuclear family, d = extended family, e = others outside the family, f = siblings, g = intrapsychic processes

Focus of Study—P = parents, C = child, H = husband, W = wife, O = any combination of the above (if there is no capital letter code given, it is understood to be "O")

III-1/g/P
246. BLAKE, J. Attitudes Toward Childlessness

Avail: 1979 Ref.

Variables Measured: Attitudes toward common reasons given for remaining childless

Type of Instrument: Self-report questionnaire

Instrument Description: This instrument is a 5-point, 7-item Likert-type questionnaire designed to assess popular conceptions of satisfaction with childlessness. Items are in the form of statements and are responded to on a 5-point scale ranging from *strongly agree* to *strongly disagree*. For scoring purposes, responses are assigned values from 1 to 5. The questionnaire was originally developed for use in a national Gallup survey of 1,600 adults regarding attitudes toward childlessness and reasons for having children. In constructing the questionnaire, the author surveyed the available literature on childlessness, including letters written to various publications detailing pressures felt by childless couples, as well as correspondence detailing reasons for remaining childless. Ideas expressed or discussed by newspaper advice columnists and women's magazines were also surveyed for relevant concepts. The resulting questionnaire contains 5 items detailing possible disadvantages and 2 items related to possible advantages of remaining childless. Items are scored such that high scores indicate attitudes in disagreement with remaining childless. The author refers to the two extreme positions as antinatalist, or prochildlessness, and pronatalist, or antichildlessness. Two scores are derived from responses to this instrument: (1) attitudes toward childlessness based on disadvantages, and (2) attitudes toward childlessness based on advantages.

Sample Items:

(A) Having a child gets in the way of the closeness and intimacy of a couple's relationship.

(B) People who are childless are more likely to be lonely in their older years than persons who have had children.

(C) It seems to me that childless couples are the ones who are having the best time in life.

Comments: The author reports that interitem correlations for items evaluating disadvantages range from .08 to .40, and that item-total correlations range from .20 to .35. However, if results from one weak item measuring financial aspects of childlessness are removed, item-total correlations for this subscale are reported to range from .27 to .39. The two positive items are reported to correlate .30 with each other, and from -.09 to .15 with items dealing with disadvantages of childlessness. Further information is provided in Blake (1979) regarding responses according to age, gender, race, religion, marital status, income level, community size, region of the country, and education of respondents.

Reference:

Blake, J. (1979). Is zero preferred? American attitudes toward childlessness in the 1970's. *J Mar Fam, 41,* 245–257.

III-1/g/C
247. BRODZINSKY, D. M., SINGER, L. M., & BRAFF, A. M. Adoption Motivation Q-Sort

Avail: 1984 Ref.

Variables Measured: Children's beliefs regarding appropriate reasons for adopting

Type of Instrument: Q-sort

Instrument Description: The Adoption Motivation Q-sort contains 25 statements of reasons sometimes given by adults for adopting children. It was designed for use with children ages 4 to 13. Administration occurs subsequent to a general interview in which the level of understanding regarding concepts related to adoption are discussed. Only those children demonstrating at least a basic level of understanding regarding adoption are administered the Q-sort. Respondents are presented with a series of cards and are, in turn, read the statements on each card. They are asked whether the statement represents a *good reason; could be a reason, but not a good one;* or *not a good reason* for adults to adopt a child. No limit is placed on the number of statements that may be placed in any one group. Where concepts appear to be difficult for children to comprehend, brief explanations are permitted. Following placement of the final card, those included in the good reason stack are spread out in front of the child. A request is then made for the child to pick the best reason for adopting. This request is repeated until the child has selected his or her option as to the three best reasons an adult can give for adopting a child.

Sample Items:

(A) Parents want to give love to a child.

(B) Parents want someone to help with chores around the house.

(C) Because they can't make their own baby.

Comments: The authors used this instrument in assessing differing types of motivation indicated by children at various ages regarding adoption. They found that younger children, and in particular very young children, attributed less motivation to parental needs and desires for the future, reasons of infertility, and being motivated to provide for the child's welfare.

References:

Brodzinsky, D. M., Schechter, D., & Brodzinsky, A. B. (1986). Children's knowledge of adoption: Developmental changes and implications for adjustment. In R. D. Ashmore & D. M. Brodzinsky (Eds.), *Thinking about the family: Views of parents and children* (pp. 205–232). Hillsdale, NJ: Lawrence Erlbaum.
Brodzinsky, D. M., Singer, L. M., & Braff, A. M. (1984). Children's understanding of adoption. *Child Dev, 55,* 869–878.

III-1/g/P
248. ENGLUND, C. L. Perceived Importance of Children

Avail: NAPS-3

Variables Measured: Adults' perceptions regarding the importance of children

Type of Instrument: Card sort

Instrument Description: This instrument consists of 30 statements printed on 2 × 3 inch cards. Cards are sorted into seven piles representing varying levels of importance, preferably with no more than five cards per pile. The cards can be sorted according to various sets of conditions or instructions (e.g., how one feels prior to having children, following the decision or realization that one would have no additional children). The instrument was designed as a means of ascertaining which clusters of items are important to different groups under varying conditions. Analysis consists of considering which statements are placed in early versus late piles, with early piles presumed to be more important to the respondent. Items were developed from stated advantages to having children, as reported by a cross-national study of persons under 40 years of age (Hoffman & Manis, 1979). Individual items were designed around eight central issues: primary group ties, source of stimulation and fun, expanding self by adding meaning and purpose to life, providing a source of immortality, adult status or social identity, adding to a sense of achievement and creativity, economic utility, and morality. The author indicates that three additional items did not fit within the structure of the above listed categories. Administration time is approximately 5–20 minutes.

Sample Items:

(A)   Able to teach them.
(B)   Gives husband an incentive for working.
(C)   Love and companionship in old age.

Comments: The author reports that the relationship between this instrument and that developed by Hoffman and Manis was evaluated. Similar rankings of priority items were noted. Differences in patterns of marital couples with differing family composition patterns were also reported.

References:

Englund, C. L. (1983). Parenting and parentage: Distinct aspects of children's importance. *Fam Relat, 32,* 21–28.
Hoffman, L. W., & Manis, J. D. (1979). The value of children in the United States: A new approach to the study of fertility. *J Mar Fam, 41,* 583–596.

III-1/V-2/g/P
249. FIELD, T. Perinatal Anxieties and Attitudes Scale (PAAS)

Avail: 1980 Ref.

Variables Measured: Mother's anxieties and attitudes related to her pregnancy and the pending birth of her baby

Type of Instrument: Self-report questionnaire

Instrument Description: The PAAS is a 52-item questionnaire designed as a post hoc inventory for assessing areas of maternal anxiety during pregnancy. Items are in the form of questions, with respondents indicating whether or not each area was a concern for them during their recent pregnancy. Questions are answered either *yes* or *no.* The scale is divided into six categories of concern: (1) attitudes toward self during pregnancy (10 items), (2) anxieties and attitudes regarding the fetus during pregnancy (6 items), (3) anxieties and attitudes toward labor and birth (17 items), (4) anxieties and attitudes following the birth (9 items), (5) anxieties and attitudes toward the baby during the postpartum period (10 items), and (6) anxieties and attitudes regarding the early weeks after finding out that she was pregnant (7 items). Individual totals are computed for the six areas, with a grand total derived by summing scores from the individual subscales. The scale is most appropriate for use with teenage mothers, particularly those who may be expected to experience additional anxiety over having been pregnant or in dealing with their newborn infants.

Sample Items:

(A)   Did you plan to have this baby?
(B)   Were you afraid your baby might be born deformed?
(C)   Did you want to take care of your baby yourself?

Comments: The author developed the PAAS for a study utilizing several measures that compared teenage and older mothers. Several comparisons of data on these measures are contained in the reference listed below.

Reference:

Field, T. (1980). Early development of infants born to teenage mothers. In K. Scott, T. Field, & E. Robertson (Eds.), *Teenage parents and their offspring* (pp. 145–175). New York: Grune & Stratton.

III-1/e/a/P
250. HARRIMAN, L. C. Parenthood Adjustment Questionnaire

Avail: NAPS-3

Variables Measured: Potential areas of adjustment or change in personal and marital life accompanying parenthood

Type of Instrument: Self-report questionnaire

Instrument Description: The parenthood adjustment questionnaire is a 42-item scale designed to measure marital adjustment issues related to parenthood. The intended population is parents of young children. The scale is composed of two factors, one measuring personal life (26 items) and the other measuring marital life (16 items). Each item is responded to on four separate criteria: (1) the extent of change (no change, less now, more now) and (2) whether the change was positive or negative, (3) major or minor, and (4) easy or difficult. Separate forms are provided for husbands and wives.

Sample Items:

(A)   Have contact with friends.
(B)   Have privacy.
(C)   Have time for your husband/wife.

Comments: The author reports that split-half reliability was measured at .64. The final 42 items, and the two factors used to represent them, resulted from a review of the original 56 items by a panel of specialists working in the field. The original items were generated through an examination of relevant areas of the literature by the author.

References:

Harriman, L. C. (1983). Personal and marital changes accompanying parenthood. *Fam Relat, 32*, 387–394.
Harriman, L. C. (1985). Marital adjustment as related to personal and marital changes accompanying parenthood. *Fam Relat, 34*, 233–239.

III-1/II-4/a
251. HETHERINGTON, S. E. Intimate Relationship Scale

Avail: 1988 Ref.

Variables Measured: Perceptions of changes in intimacy and sexuality in couples following the birth of a child

Type of Instrument: Self-report questionnaire

Instrument Description: The Intimate Relationship Scale is a 12-item questionnaire primarily designed to assess sexual satisfaction following the birth of a baby. In addition to these, another 12 items are included that assess the number of children in the home, current contraceptive behavior, and various questions related to the delivery and postpartum period. The final 6 items are intended to be answered only by women and deal with the delivery, physical strength, discomfort with intercourse, and perceived physical appearance. Items related to intimacy and sexuality are answered utilizing a 5-point Likert-type response format ranging from *much less* to *much more*. Other items use various response formats. The scale is intended to measure changes in intimacy and sexuality along three dimensions: physical, cognitive or intellectual, and personal or emotional. Values associated with scores from specific responses are summed within the three dimensions.

Sample Items:

(A)   Since the birth of the baby, the frequency that my spouse and I are having sex is:
(B)   Since the birth of the baby, my spouse and I find time for quiet conversation:
(C)   Since the birth of the baby, my desire to touch and hold is being satisfied.

Comments: The scale was originally referred to as being authored by S. E. Fischman. Hetherington is the name this author currently is using. The author indicates that all items had corrected item-total correlations in excess of .25. Cronbach's alpha is reported to be .86 for fathers and .87 for mothers. Interitem correlations are reported to average .34 for fathers, with the only negative correlation being between items 2 (feelings of fatigue interfere with making love) and 11 (comfort in talking with spouse about sex). Interitem correlations for women are reported to average .36, with all items correlating in a positive direction.

References:

Davis, C. M., Yarber, W. L., & Davis, S. L. (Eds.). (1988). *Sexuality-related measures: A compendium.* Lake Mills, IA: Graphic.

Fischman, S. H., Rankin, E. A., Soeken, K. L., & Lenz, E. R. (1986). Changes in sexual relationships in postpartum couples. *JOGN Nursing, 15,* 58–63.

III-1/g/c/e/d/P
252. HOBBS, D. F., Jr. Difficulty Index for First-Time Parents

Avail: NAPS-3

Variables Measured: Potential difficulties faced during the transition to parenthood

Type of Instrument: Self-report questionnaire

Instrument Description: This instrument is a 23-item Likert-type questionnaire designed to identify those areas causing difficulty for recent first-time parents. Respondents indicate the degree of difficulty caused by each area, with responses on a 3-point scale (0–2) ranging from *none* to *very much.* Possible scores range from 0 to 46, with higher scores indicating greater difficulty. Some items were constructed from clinicians' reports, with others selected from LeMasters's indication of difficulties reported by new parents (1957). In addition to the original version, a recent 37-item revision of the scale (Difficulty Index for First-Time Parents—Revised) is available from NAPS-3.

Sample Items:

(A)   Interference from in-laws.
(B)   Decreased sexual responsiveness of self.
(C)   Physical tiredness and fatigue.

Comments: In the original study utilizing this scale, the author indicated that 86.8% of couples were classified as experiencing slight crises, with no couples found to experience extensive or severe crises. Women in this study were found to have higher scale scores (mean = 9.1) than did men (mean = 6.3). However, there are questions as to the generalizability of these findings, considering that 96% of the couples in this sample reported that the pregnancy was desired. In a replication (Hobbs & Cole, 1976), mean scores for fathers and mothers were found to be 5.9 and 9.7, respectively.

References:

Hobbs, D. F., Jr. (1965). Parenthood as crisis: A third study. *J Mar Fam, 27,* 367–372.

Hobbs, D. F., Jr. (1968). Transition to parenthood: A replication and extension. *J Mar Fam, 30,* 413–417.

Hobbs, D. F., Jr., & Cole, S. P. (1976). Transition to parenthood: A decade replication. *J Mar Fam, 38,* 723–731.

Hobbs, D. F., Jr., & Patterson, S. B. (1980). Transition to parenthood: The "baby honeymoon" hypothesis. *Fam Perspect, 14,* 47–51.

III-1/e/P
253. HOUSEKNECHT, S. K. Concern for Pressures and Sanctions That Accompany Nonparenthood

Avail: 1977 Ref.

Variables Measured: Concern for pressures and sanctions that accompany voluntary childlessness

Type of Instrument: Self-report questionnaire

Instrument Description: This instrument is designed to measure personal awareness of negative societal pressures and sanctions that often accompany the decision to remain childless. Respondents are presented with a picture of a 10-rung ladder. Above and below each rung is a number, from 0 to 10. The following statement is then read aloud to subjects: "Now I am going to ask you some questions which you can answer by looking at this drawing of a ladder. Suppose we say that the top of the ladder represents that which would bother you most while the bottom of the ladder represents that which would bother you least. After I read each statement, just point to the place on the ladder that you feel indicates how much each situation would bother you if it did, in fact, occur." An alternate form for women with children replaces the last portion of the statement ("it did, in fact, occur") with "you had been married for quite a while and had no children." Scores on individual items are summed for an overall scale score that can range from 0 (low concern) to 60 (high concern).

Sample Items:

(A)   Parents urging you to have a child.
(B)   People saying you are being selfish.
(C)   Married women with children giving hints that they think you should have children.

Comments: The author reports on research in which this instrument was used. It was found that women desiring not to have children had mean scores of 24.67, while women desiring children scored an average of 32.37. Reliability and validity information for this instrument are not reported.

Reference:

Houseknecht, S. K. (1977). Reference group support for voluntary childlessness: Evidence for conformity. *J Mar Fam, 39,* 285–292.

III-1/g/P
254. RABIN, A. I., & GREENE, R. J. The Child Study Inventory (CSI)

Avail: NAPS-2

Variables Measured: Men's and women's motivation for becoming parents

Type of Instrument: Self-report questionnaire

Instrument Description: The CSI is a 4-point, 18-item questionnaire designed to assess types of motivation for becoming a parent. Fourteen items are scored, with the remaining four items considered as fillers. Four dimensions of motivation are examined: (1) altruistic, indicating motivation to care for and nurture children; (2) fatalistic, indicated by expressions of predestination, or that men and women were created for the purpose of procreating; (3) narcissistic, or motivation to have children reflect positively on the parents; and (4) instrumental, or indications that children are useful to their parents in various ways. Items are in the form of sentence stems, with four options for completing each sentence. Each of the four response options corresponds to one of the types of motivation described above. Respondents are instructed to rank-order the four options, with values being assigned on the basis of ranking. Thus each type of motivation receives a score from 1 to 4 for each of 14 items. Total scores for each type can range from 14 to 56.

Sample Items:

(A)   Women want children because . . .
      ( ) Children hold the marriage together.
      ( ) It is a function of the mature adult.
      ( ) They like to care and provide for children.
      ( ) They want to perpetuate themselves.
(B)   Parents expect their children . . .
      ( ) To fulfill the purpose of life.
      ( ) To strengthen the family.
      ( ) To be healthy and happy.
      ( ) To follow in their footsteps.

Comments: The authors indicate that, in the course of developing the CSI, response options were presented to five judges for coding. All but one judge correctly coded all options for each item into the proper motivation categories. Following revisions to problem items, agreement was achieved by all five judges. Test-retest correlations over two and a half weeks are reported to be .79, .54, .68, and .53, respectively, for the four dimensions of motivation. Correlations are also reported between the four dimensions and parenting styles for both mothers and fathers. Details of these investigations are presented in Rabin and Greene (1968).

References:

Rabin, A. I. (1965). Motivation for parenthood. *J Projective Tech Pers Asses, 29,* 405–411.
Rabin, A. I., & Greene, R. J. (1968). Assessing motivation for parenthood. *J Psychol, 69,* 39–46.
Reading, J., & Amatea, E. S. (1986). Role deviance or role diversification: Reassessing the psychosocial factors affecting the parenthood choice of career-oriented women. *J Mar Fam, 48,* 255–260.

III-1/g/P
255. STEFFENSMEIER, R. H. Transition Difficulty

Avail: 1982 Ref.

Variables Measured: Degree of difficulty in the transition to parenthood

Type of Instrument: Structured, forced-response interview

Instrument Description: This 25-item questionnaire is intended to measure the level of difficulty during the transition to parenthood experienced during the initial three to six months following the birth of the first child. The items concern subjective assessments of problems, changes, worries, gratifications, and self-definitions of parenting experienced since the baby's birth. Items are divided into three subscales based on dimensions of parental responsibilities and restrictions, parental gratifications, and marital intimacy and stability. The instrument was initially designed to be administered during separate home interviews with mothers and fathers, but is adaptable to a self-administered questionnaire format.

Sample Items:

(A) How much have you experienced worry about being a good parent?
(B) How much have you been bothered by being interrupted by the baby in the middle of doing something?
(C) To what extent do you feel more or less happy since the baby was born?

Comments: The author reports that Cronbach's alpha for the three subscales range from .75 to .82. Comparisons between the Transition Difficulty questionnaire and Hobbs's (1965) Difficulty Index for First-Time Parents are also reported. The author found that the parental responsibilities and restrictions subscale of the current instrument discriminated between parents experiencing normal transitions and those experiencing extensive or severe crises. The present instrument was an attempt to build upon procedures reported by Hobbs (1965) and Russell (1974). The Transition Difficulty questionnaire has since been modified by Pistrang (1984).

References:

Myers-Walls, J. A. (1984). Balancing multiple role responsibilities during the transition of parenthood. *Fam Relat, 33,* 267–271.
Pistrang, N. (1984). Women's work involvement and experience of new motherhood. *J Mar Fam, 46,* 433–447.
Steffensmeier, R. H. (1982). A role model of the transition to parenthood. *J Mar Fam, 44,* 319–334.

III-1/c/P
256. WENTE, A. S., & CROCKENBERG, S. B. Changes in Routine

Avail: 1976 Ref.

Variables Measured: Parental perceptions of changes brought on by the birth of a first child

Type of Instrument: Self-report questionnaire

Instrument Description: Changes in Routine is a 7-point, 18-item Likert-type questionnaire designed to assess fathers' adjustment considerations during the initial three months following the birth of the first child. The questionnaire consists of one general question asking fathers to estimate the overall amount of change to their routines experienced during the initial three months. This item is followed by 17 specific areas of possible change or adjustment. The authors indicate that four of these items failed to correlate sufficiently with the item on which overall change is indicated, and so were not included in scoring or further analyses. Response formats for all items range from 1 = *no change* to 7 = *severe change*. The scale has been modified by Goldberg and Easterbrooks (1984) for use in assessing husbands' and wives' perceptions of change. Goldberg and Easterbrooks refer to their instrument, containing 14 items, as the Bother Scale. It has also been modified (16 items) for use with both parents by Goldberg, Michaels, and Lamb (1985).

Sample Items:

(A) Baby's crying.
(B) Missing sleep.
(C) Not enough time for family.

Comments: The original authors report correlations ranging from .37 to .68 between individual items and overall adjustment. Goldberg and Easterbrooks report Cronbach's alpha for their version of .81 for all items, and from .72 to .83 for two subscales.

References:

Goldberg, W. A., & Easterbrooks, M. A. (1984). Role of marital quality in toddler development. *Devel Psych, 20,* 504–514.
Goldberg, W. A., Michaels, G. Y., & Lamb, M. E. (1985). Husbands' and wives' adjustment to pregnancy and first parenthood. *J Fam Iss, 6,* 483–503.
Wente, A. S., & Crockenberg, S. B. (1976). Transition to fatherhood: Lamaze preparation, adjustment difficulty and the husband-wife relationship. *Fam Coord, 25,* 351–357.

III-2/IV-2/b/P
257. ABELMAN, R. Parental Disciplinary Orientations

Avail: 1986 Ref.

Variables Measured: Parental disciplinary strategies and orientations

Type of Instrument: Self-report questionnaire

Instrument Description: This instrument comprises a series of eight hypothetical situations and nine possible responses common to each situation. Parents are presented with each situation, following which they indicate which of the nine responses they would be likely to use. Each response option receives a rating of 0 (*no*), 1 (*maybe*), or 2 (*yes*). The same set of possible responses is utilized for each hypothetical situation. Situations are equally divided between those with positive and negative themes. Responses include both positive and negative options, as well as categories of induction and sensitization within both the positive and the negative dimensions. Induction methods are characterized by "reasoning, explanation, and appeals to the child's pride and achievement, and they exert little external power over the child" (Abelman, 1986, p. 54). Sensitization techniques refer to those involving either physical punishment or force, or depriving the child of objects or privileges. These categories, as well as Abelman's basis for the current instrument, can be found in Hoffman and Saltzstein (1967) and Hoffman (1970). Abelman also credits Korzenny, Greenberg, and Atkin (1979) for their contribution to the development of this instrument. Scoring is accomplished by summing values associated with each response. Scores are obtained for each of the four categories defined by positive-negative and induction-sensitization dimensions.

Sample Items:

(Situations)

(A) Suppose (Name of child) does something really nice for you to show that (he/she) loves you. What would you do?
(B) Suppose (Name of child) hits a child in the neighborhood after an argument, and you find out. What would you do?

(Responses)
(A) Say you are proud of (him/her).
(B) Don't talk to (him/her) for a while.

Comments: The author reports on a factor analysis in which 10 responses loaded from .36 to .85 on inductive orientation, while the other 8 items loaded primarily on sensitizing orienta-

tion (.13 to .73). Secondary loadings ranged from .01 to .27, and from .02 to .27, for the inductive and sensitizing orientations, respectively.

Reference:

Abelman, R. (1986). Children's awareness of television's prosocial fare. *J Fam Iss, 7,* 51–66.

III-2/b/P
258. BARANOWSKI, T., RASSIN, D. K., RICHARDSON, C. J., BROWN, J. P., & BEE, D. E. Attitudes and Beliefs About Breastfeeding

Avail: 1986 Ref.

Variables Measured: Benefits for infants, and social, personal, and physical inconveniences of breast-feeding

Type of Instrument: Self-report questionnaire

Instrument Description: This 26-item instrument was designed to specify the beliefs of mothers in regard to methods for feeding their infants. Differences in beliefs regarding breast-feeding and formula-feeding mothers are examined. Items were developed from a review of the literature and from comments by mothers during field-testing. Mothers are requested to state their level of agreement or disagreement with each item using a 5-point Likert-style scale.

Sample Items:

(A)   Breastfeeding is best for my baby.
(B)   Breastfeeding causes people to have sex less.
(C)   Breastfeeding can be very annoying.

Comments: In a study with 358 White, Black, and Mexican-American subjects, each of four factor scores correlated significantly and in the expected direction with whether mothers breast-fed. The pattern of correlations varied by ethnicity of the mother.

Reference:

Baranowski, T., Rassin, D. K., Richardson, C. J., Brown, J. P., & Bee, D. E. (1986). Attitudes toward breastfeeding. *J Dev Beh Ped, 7,* 367–372.

III-2/II-3/b/C
259. BARBER, B. K., & THOMAS, D. L. Parental Support Inventory (PSI)

Avail: NAPS-3

Variables Measured: Parental supportive behavior with respect to general support, physical affection, companionship, and sustained contact

Type of Instrument: Children's ratings of parental behaviors

Instrument Description: The PSI is a 20-item Likert-style questionnaire, with subjects asked to respond to each item separately for both their mothers and their fathers. The initial 13 items rely on a 5-point response format with response options ranging from *never* to *very often*. The remaining seven items ask whether specific behaviors are *not, somewhat,* or *very much like* the parent (rated 1, 2, or 3). The PSI was designed to examine the multidimensional nature of parental support. Items from three child-report parent behavior instruments (Heilbrun, 1964; Hollender, 1973; Schaefer, 1965) were combined, administered, and factor analyzed in the development of the current instrument. The scale is designed for use primarily with children and adolescents. It can also be used with parents who are asked to describe their perceptions of their relationships with their children.

Sample Items:

(A)   Whenever I had any kind of problem I could count on this parent to help me out.
(B)   This parent hugs and kisses me often.
(C)   This parent shares many activities with me.

Comments: The authors report that a factor analysis on the PSI resulted in the discovery of four primary factors: general support, physical affection, companionship, and sustained contact. Cronbach's alpha for these factors is reported to range from .85 to .90 for fathers, and from .79 to .87 for mothers.

Reference:

Barber, B. K., & Thomas, D. L. (1986). Multiple dimensions of parental supportive behavior: The case for physical affection. *J Mar Fam, 48,* 783–794.

III-2/IV-2/b/P
260. BAVOLEK, S. J. Adult-Adolescent Parenting Inventory (AAPI)

Avail: Family Development Resources, Inc., 767 Second Ave, Eau Claire, WI 54703

Variables Measured: Parenting and child-rearing attitudes that are high risk for child abuse and neglect; subscales examine inappropriate expectations of children, empathic awareness of children's needs, belief in the use of corporal punishment, and reversing family roles

Type of Instrument: Self-report questionnaire

Instrument Description: The AAPI is an inventory designed to assess the parenting and child-rearing attitudes of adults and adolescents. Developed as a 32-item, 5-point Likert-type scale with responses ranging from *strongly agree* to *strongly disagree,* responses provide an index of risk for practicing abusive and neglecting parenting and child-rearing behaviors. Two equivalent forms are available. A stencil is provided for scoring. The AAPI worksheet and table of norms located in the handbook allow for the conversion of raw scores to standard scores for plotting on the profile sheet. A respondent's attitudes in each of the four subscales can be compared with the parenting and child-rearing attitudes of abusive or nonabusive parents or abused and nonabused adolescents. Norm tables are provided for variables of race (Black and White), status (abusive or nonabusive and abused or nonabused), gender, and age.

Sample Items:

(A)   Young children should be expected to comfort their mother when she is feeling blue.
(B)   Children should be expected to verbally express themselves before the age of one year.
(C)   Children should always be spanked when they misbehave.

Comments: The AAPI is supported by a wide body of research, largely master's theses and dissertations, conducted since 1978. Studies have examined the predictive validity of AAPI subscales, as well as the general relationship of family experiences to parenting values and attitudes. The author reports internal reliability equal to or greater than .70 for each of the four subscales. Test-retest reliability of the entire test is reported to be .76. Factor loadings for items within scales are reported to be at least .20.

References:

Bavolek, S. J. (1986). *The Adult-Adolescent Parenting Inventory.* Schaumburg, IL: Family Development Associates.

Bavolek, S. J., Kline, D., & McLaughlin, J. (1979). Primary prevention of child abuse: Identification of high risk adolescents. *Child Abuse Neglect, 3,* 1071–1080.

III-2/b/P

261. BIGNER, J. J. Attitudes Toward Fathering Scale

Avail: NAPS-3

Variables Measured: Fathers' traditional or developmental orientation to their paternal roles

Type of Instrument: Self-report questionnaire

Instrument Description: The Attitudes Toward Fathering Scale was developed to empirically assess the traditional versus developmental role orientation of men to their fathering roles. It is intended for use with all social and ethnic groups. The 36 items in the scale utilize a Likert-type question format based on a 5-point rating system ranging from *strongly agree* to *strongly disagree.* There are an equal number of items measuring developmental and traditional orientations. Scoring of items features a weighting of responses for developmental items that range from a weight of 5 points for *strongly agree* to 1 point for *strongly disagree.* Scoring is reversed on those items measuring developmental orientation. Thus the higher the summed score of all items, the more the subject is likely to have a developmental orientation to his fathering role. The lower the score, the more likely he is to have a traditional orientation.

Sample Items:

(A) Child should not be expected to obey rules and commands without being given reasons for them.

(B) Discipline of children should be mainly the father's responsibility.

(C) Firm and strict discipline in childhood creates a strong character later in life.

Comments: Content validity of the Attitudes Toward Fathering Scale is reported by the author to be .84, with test-retest reliability of .82. The scale is based on earlier (1946) work by Elder.

Reference:

Bigner, J. J. (1977). Attitudes toward fathering and father-child activity. *Home Ec Res J, 6,* 98–106.

III-2/b/P

262. BIGNER, J. J. Father-Child Activity Scale

Avail: NAPS-3

Variables Measured: Degree of active involvement in parenting or caregiving activities of a father with his preschool-aged child

Type of Instrument: Self-report questionnaire

Instrument Description: The Father-Child Activity Scale was developed to empirically assess father's involvement in parenting or caregiving activities with his preschool-aged child.

It is a 26-item Likert-style questionnaire with response options ranging from *always* to *never*. Scores range from 26 to 130, with responses of *always, often, sometimes, seldom,* and *never* weighted with 5, 4, 3, 2, and 1 points, respectively. Responses are summed for a total score. The higher the score, the higher the level of involvement by the father in the raising of his son or daughter.

Sample Items:

(A)   I put my child to bed at night.
(B)   If my child cried or called at night I would take care of him.
(C)   I babysit when my wife is busy or away from home.

Comments: The author reports that content validity of the Father-Child Activity scale has been measured at .86 and that test-retest reliability of the instrument was found to be .82.

Reference:

Bigner, J. J. (1977). Attitudes toward fathering and father-child activity. *Home Ec Res J, 6,* 98–106.

III-2/b/P
263. BLOCK, J. H. The Child-Rearing Practices Report (CRPR)

Avail: NAPS-2

Variables Measured: Parental child-rearing orientations and values

Type of Instrument: Q-sort

Instrument Description: The CRPR is a 91-item Q-sort examining parental child-rearing attitudes and values. Items are presented as statements, and are designed to be relevant to children's socialization. Parents are instructed to sort the statements into seven piles of 13 items each, with piles ranging from *most descriptive* to *most undescriptive*. In administering this instrument, parents are asked to focus on a specific child in the family. Individual items emphasize parental behaviors directed toward that child. Alternate forms of the test are available, with one form being appropriate for use by mothers and fathers (Form I) and the other designed for administration to adolescents and young adults (Form II). When using Form II, respondents are asked to describe the child-rearing practices and values of their parents. All items on Form II are worded in the third person and relate to the respondent's mother or father. The items were constructed utilizing a combination of mother-child observations, discussions with colleagues from several countries, and a search of the available literature. The author indicates that, since its development in 1965, the CRPR has been used with over 6,000 subjects from a variety of cultures and countries, and has been translated into at least eight foreign languages. Administration time is approximately 30–45 minutes.

Sample Items (Note: All sample items are from Form I):

(A)   I encourage my child always to do (his/her) best.
(B)   I don't think young children of different sexes should be allowed to see each other naked.
(C)   I believe physical punishment to be the best way of disciplining.

Comments: The author reports that test-retest reliability of the CRPR has been assessed in two independent studies. However, in both studies an intervention occurring between the two test administrations may have lowered correlations. Still, in the first study reliability over eight months was reported to average .71, and in the second study retesting three years later revealed group reliability coefficients ranging from .61 to .69. Extensive validity information is presented in over 25 published studies and numerous theses and dissertations. A sampling of these references is presented below.

References:

Block, J. H. (1972). Generational continuity and discontinuity in the understanding of societal rejection. *J Pers Soc Psy, 22,* 333–345.

Block, J. H., Block, J., & Morrison, A. (1981). Parental agreement-disagreement on child-rearing orientations and gender-related personality correlates in children. *Child Dev, 52,* 965–974.

Costos, D. (1986). Sex role identity in young adults: Its parental antecedents and relation to ego development. *J Pers Soc Psy, 50,* 602–611.

Gjerde, P. F. (1988). Parental concordance on child rearing and the interactive emphases of parents: Sex-differentiated relationships during the preschool years. *Devel Psych, 24,* 700–706.

III-2/II-3/b/C

264. BOWERMAN, C. E., & IRISH, D. P. Closeness to Parent

Avail: 1962, 1984, & 1987 Refs.

Variables Measured: A child's perceived closeness to a parent or parent-substitute

Type of Instrument: Self-report questionnaire

Instrument Description: The Closeness to Parent scale is a 5-item questionnaire used in assessing feelings held by children for their parents. The scale was first developed by Bowerman and Irish (1962), who used it as part of a battery of instruments. Others (Coleman & Ganong, 1984; Ganong & Coleman, 1987) have adapted these 5 items from the original scale, dropped the remaining items and scales, and added additional items of their own. The core of the instrument, however, has remained the original 5-item scale. The questions may be asked regarding any number of parents or parent-figures (e.g., stepmother, stepfather, grandmother, grandfather). Responses to four of the items are made according to a 3-point scale on which respondents indicate how frequently each activity occurs (*most of the time, about half of the time,* or *hardly ever*). The fifth question, which asks about the closeness of their relationship with that person, is answered on a 3-point scale ranging from *very close* to *not very close.* Scores for each parent or parent-figure are summed.

Sample Items:

(A)   Do you talk over your personal matters with your mother (father)?

(B)   Do you ever feel that your mother (father) neglects you and your wishes?

(C)   In general, how well do you get along with your mother (father)?

Comments: Items in the original paper are listed in footnotes contained within the article. Reliability data are not provided, but a comparison of mean scores for males versus females, various ages of adolescents, and differing geographical regions are presented. The two later articles (Coleman & Ganong, 1984; Ganong & Coleman, 1987) both embedded the Closeness to Parent questionnaire within a larger group of items. Both articles give credit for the original instrument, however, to Bowerman and Irish.

References:

Bowerman, C. E., & Irish, D. P. (1962). Some relationships of stepchildren to their parents. *Mar Fam Living, 24,* 113–121.

Coleman, M., & Ganong, L. H. (1984). Effect of family structure on family attitudes and expectations. *Fam Relat, 33,* 425–432.

Ganong, L. H., & Coleman, M. (1987). Stepchildren's perceptions of their parents. *J Genet Psy, 148,* 5–17.

III-2/II-3/b/C

265. BRICKLIN, B. Bricklin Perceptual Scales: Child-Perception-of-Parents-Series (BPS)

Avail: Village Publishing, Village Barn Center Furlong, PA 18925

Variables Measured: Child's perceptions of parents' competency and ability to be a role model for learning skills of competency, warmth and empathy, consistency, and possession of admirable traits

Type of Instrument: Self-report, interview-based questionnaire

Instrument Description: The BPS is a nonverbal clinical tool that measures children's attitudes toward and perceptions of each parent. An 8-inch long card with *not so well* at one end and *very well* at the other is used to code responses to verbally presented items. The two response extremes are connected by a thick black line. Children indicate their response to each item by punching a hole at an appropriate place along the line. The examiner's side of the card has the line broken down into 60 incremental spaces. Responses are coded according to the number of the space that corresponds to the area punched by the child. The child responds to 64 questions, half of which pertain to each parent. Questions for each parent are exactly the same but are presented at widely different points in the examination. Items have been combined to form subscales of competency, empathy, consistency, and positive influence. The BPS has been found to be particularly useful in custody decisions.

Sample Items:

(A)   If you were having a problem with a school subject, how well would Mom do at helping you to understand and deal with what it is that's troubling you?
(B)   How well does Dad do at making you feel really loved?
(C)   If you tried to stay up real late, way past your regular bedtime, how often would Mom make sure you got to bed at regular bedtime?

Comments: Validity information provided by the author includes two studies, both of which involved using the BPS to determine the parent most fitting to be granted custody where custody was in dispute. In the first, two persons unfamiliar with the case histories involved were asked to review large quantities of information on 21 children and their parents, and to determine which parent should be awarded custody. Judges came to similar conclusions in all but one instance. In each case, the BPS came to the same conclusion as the two judges. In the second study, the BPS was used in 29 cases that eventually went to trial. In all but two of these cases, BPS conclusions were the same as those of the trial judges.

Reference:

Bricklin, B. (1984). *Bricklin Perceptual Scales: Child-Perception-of-Parents-Series.* Furlong, PA: Village.

III-2/b/C
266. BRONFENBRENNER, U., & DEVEREUX, E. C., Jr. Cornell Parent Behavior Inventory

Avail: NAPS-1

Variables Measured: Parental role performance related to interactions with an adolescent child

Type of Instrument: Self-report questionnaire

Instrument Description: The original form of this instrument is a 100-item Likert-style questionnaire examining 20 levels of adolescents' perceptions of their parents' role performances. Other versions have included 45 items examining 15 variables (Siegelman, 1965); 30 items, with a 10-item short form (Devereux, Bronfenbrenner, & Rodgers, 1966); and 40 items, comprising the combined 30-item and 10-item versions mentioned above (Rodgers, 1966). Questions are answered using a 5-point scale, with various anchors and value ranges associated with different versions. The scale was designed to be group-administered to adolescents. Children respond to each item with respect to each parent, resulting in each item being responded to twice. In the original 100-item version, 20 variables (5 items for each) divided into the two broad categories of expressive functions and instrumental functions were examined. Each broad category contains 10 variables and 50 items. Subjects are asked to indicate the extent to which each item "applies to each parent's treatment of you as you were growing up." The scale has been translated into at least one other language (German), and has been used extensively with several populations since its original development. Various modifications to the scale have facilitated its use with teachers, peer groups, and other socializing agents, in addition to parents, for whom the scale was originally designed.

Sample Items:

(A) Punished me by sending me out of the room.
(B) I can count on her to help me out if I have some kind of problem.
(C) He lets me off easy when I do something he doesn't like.

Comments: Various authors have conducted factor analyses on the Cornell Parent Behavior Inventory, resulting in varying solutions and numbers of acceptable items. Reliability estimates for various subscales have generally been reported at or above .50.

References:

Abraham, K. G., & Christopherson, V. A. (1984). Perceived competence among rural middle school children: Parental antecedents and relation to locus of control. *J Early Adol, 4,* 343–351.

Bronfenbrenner, U. (1961). Some familial antecedents of responsibility and leadership in adolescents. In L. Petrullo & B. L. Bass (Eds.), *Leadership and interpersonal behavior* (pp. 239–271). New York: Holt.

Devereux, E. C., Jr., Bronfenbrenner, U., & Rodgers, R. R. (1970). Child-rearing in England and the United States: A cross-national comparison. *J Mar Fam, 31,* 257–270.

Rodgers, R. R. (1971). Changes in parental behavior reported by children in West Germany and the United States. *Human Dev, 14,* 208–224.

Siegelman, M. (1965). Evaluation of Bronfenbrenner's questionnaire for children concerning parental behavior. *Child Dev, 36,* 163–174.

III-2/b/C

267. BRONFENBRENNER, U., DEVEREUX, E. C., Jr., & RODGERS, R. R. Cornell Socialization Inventory (PPT)

Avail: 1974 & 1977 Refs.

Variables Measured: Socialization practices of parents, peers, and teachers

Type of Instrument: Self-report group-administered questionnaire

Instrument Description: The PPT measures behaviors of persons considered to be socializing agents for the subject. Socializing agents are those, such as parents, peers, and teachers, who significantly influence the behavior and development of children. Subjects are generally 10- to 14-year-old children. Both 11- and 12-item versions of the PPT have been used. Devereux et al. (1974) contains the original 12-item scale. The 11-item version contained in Avgar, Bronfenbrenner, and Henderson (1977) was developed by deleting one item from the original scale. The PPT is a Likert-style scale with five possible responses for each item, ranging from *never* to *very often*. Various dimensions of behavior, such as expression of affection, modes of discipline, expectations, and demands, are examined. Children are asked how often during the past year each socializing agent about whom he or she is being questioned engaged in the behavior described by the item. Items are summed to give composite scores indicating the frequency of support, disciplinary, and in some cases controlling behaviors are exercised by others.

Sample Items:

(A)   I can count on her to help me out if I have some kind of problem.
(B)   She acts cold and unfriendly when I do something she doesn't like.
(C)   He worries that I cannot take care of myself.

Comments: The PPT is a shortened version of Cornell Parent Behavior Inventory. Studies using the PPT have been conducted in at least seven countries. Reliabilities for the combined 11-item scale, derived from separate studies in several different countries, have ranged from .58 to .82 for samples where the socializing agent was either mother, father, peer, or teacher. Separate reliability ranges have also been calculated for the support (.46 to .77) and discipline (.45 to .84) subscales. In societies where control was deemed a separate factor, reliability analyses indicated a range of .43 to .49 for mothers and .43 to .72 for fathers as socializing agents. The control factor was not found for actions of peers or teachers.

References:

Avgar, A., Bronfenbrenner, U., & Henderson, C. R., Jr. (1977). Socialization practices of parents, teachers, and peers in Israel: Kibbutz, moshav, and city. *Child Dev, 48,* 1219–1227.

Devereux, E. C., Jr., Shouval, R., Bronfenbrenner, U., Rodgers, R. R., Kav-Venaki, S., Kiely, E., & Karson, E. (1974). Socialization practices of parents, teachers, and peers in Israel: The kibbutz versus the city. *Child Dev, 45,* 269–281.

Smart, R., & Smart, M. (1973). New Zealand preadolescents' parent-peer orientation: Parent perceptions compared with English and American. *J Mar Fam, 35,* 142–149.

III-2/b/P

268. BROUSSARD, E. R. Neonatal Perception Inventories (NPI)

Avail: 1978 Ref.

Variables Measured: Maternal expectations and perceptions regarding infants' behaviors

Type of Instrument: Self-report questionnaire

Instrument Description: The NPI was developed in 1963 as a 5-point, 6-item Likert-type questionnaire designed to assess mothers' perceptions and beliefs regarding both normal infant behavior and the behavior of their own neonate. The questionnaire is intended as a method for screening newborn infants for possible abnormal psychosocial development. It is based on the theory that the mother's perception of her infant is likely to foretell later psychosocial difficulties for the child. The NPI is intended as a diagnostic tool allowing additional parent-child services to be focused where they are most needed and can best be expected to achieve positive results. Items are in the form of questions regarding normal infant behaviors. Respondents are asked to indicate, within a range from *a great deal* to *none,* the frequency of each behavior. The NPI is administered twice: once within the first two postpartum days, and the other time approximately one month after delivery. Mothers answer each item from two distinct perspectives during each administration: (1) behaviors of the average child and (2) behaviors of her own child. Both summation and comparison scores can be computed.

Sample Items:

(A) How much crying do you think your baby will do?
(B) How much trouble do you think your baby will have feeding?
(C) How much trouble do you think that your baby will have settling down to a predict-able pattern of eating and sleeping?

Comments: The author reports that predictive validity was assessed by comparing evaluations of children at 4, 10 to 11, 15, and 19 years of age with earlier NPI scores. Ratings at one month postpartum were found to be predictive of psychopathology at these later ages.

References:

Broussard, E. R. (1978). Psychosocial disorders in children: Early assessment of infants at risk. *Cont Ed Fam Phys, 8*(2), 44–57.
Broussard, E. R. (1979). Assessment of the adaptive potential of the mother-infant system: The Neonatal Perception Inventories. In P. M. Taylor (Ed.), *Parent-infant relationships* (pp. 249–268). New York: Grune & Stratton.
Broussard, E. R. (1984). The Pittsburgh first-borns at age 19 years. In R. Tyson, J. Call, & E. Galenson (Eds.), *Frontiers of infant psychiatry* (Vol 2, pp. 522–530). New York: Basic Books.
Harper, J. J., Smith, P., Dickey, D., & Broussard, E. R. (1982). Screening and assessment of psychosocial dysfunction in a private pediatric practice. *Infant Ment Health J, 3,* 199–208.

III-2/b/P
269. BURGE, P. L. Child-Rearing Sex Role Attitude Scale

Avail: 1981 Ref.

Variables Measured: Parental attitudes regarding societal gender roles and child-rearing practices

Type of Instrument: Self-report questionnaire

Instrument Description: The Child-Rearing Sex Role Attitude Scale is a 28-item Likert-style questionnaire, with respondents indicating how often (from *always* to *never*) each statement is true for them. The scale explores the extent to which traditional versus nontraditional gender-role attitudes influence child-rearing practices of the parents.

Sample Items:

(A)   Both boys and girls need to develop social skills.
(B)   Only male children should be guided toward leadership positions.
(C)   My daughter should expect to be taken care of throughout her life.

Comments: The author reports reliability analyses indicating that Cronbach's alpha for the scale was .92, with an average interitem correlation of approximately .30. Further, the standard error of measurement is reported to be 3.5.

Reference:

Burge, P. L. (1981). Parental child-rearing sex role attitudes related to social issue sex role attitudes and selected demographic variables. *Home Ec Res J, 9,* 193–199.

III-2/b
270. CALDWELL, B. M., & HONIG, A. S. APPROACH: A Procedure for Patterning Responses of Adults and Children

Avail: Syracuse University, Center for Instructional Development, 111 Waverly Ave, Syracuse, NY 13244

Variables Measured: Interactions between parents and their children

Type of Instrument: Behavior coding scheme

Instrument Description: APPROACH is a system for recording and classifying behavior between caretakers and children. Observations may occur in any environment, but typically are recorded in the homes of participants. An observer is stationed in the home for the duration of the coding session, ranging from 5 minutes up to as long as is deemed necessary by the investigator. Virtually all behaviors and interactions are recorded by the observer. Observers speak into a microphone, detailing specific behaviors of all participants (usually a mother and child) every 5 seconds. In instances where behaviors change within the span of 5 seconds, each change in behavior is also noted. Specific behaviors are then coded according to a specific and predetermined system. Emitted behaviors are coded by breaking up the narrative description into behavioral clauses, each of which contains four basic components: the subject of the clause, the predicate, the object, and some qualifier. Each component is translated into a numerical code and grouped into a five-digit statement summarizing the behavior. Various formats for recording behavior have been experimented with, including videotaping of behaviors without a live observer being present, having the observer videotape interactions, utilizing shorthand codings without the benefit of a recording device, and audio-recording of interactions with the intent of later coding the behaviors or using the tape recordings to fill in gaps left by note-taking on the part of the live observer. The APPROACH system of coding has been adapted by others, depending on their own particular needs. One adaptation of note is the PACIC (Lytton, 1973, 1977, 1980), which expanded the coding system used in the original APPROACH.

Sample Items: Not applicable.

Comments: The authors indicate that extensive training, on the order of 60 hours, is required prior to utilizing the APPROACH in a clinical or research setting. Interrater reliability is reported to range from .42 to .99, depending on the type of behavior being coded and the number of extra codes being used.

References:

Caldwell, B. M. (1969). A new "approach" to behavioral ecology. In J. P. Hill (Ed.), *Minnesota symposium on child psychology* (Vol. 2, pp. 74–109). Minneapolis: University of Minnesota Press.

Lytton, H. (1980). *Parent-child interaction.* New York: Plenum.

Slatter, M. A. (1986). Modification of mother-child interaction processes in families with children at risk for mental retardation. *Am J Ment D, 91,* 257–267.

Wittmer, D. S., & Honig, A. S. (1988). Teacher re-creation of negative interactions with toddlers. *Early Child Dev Care, 33,* 77–88.

III-2/II-1/a/P

271. CALLAN, V. J. Attitudes to Having Children

Avail: 1986 Ref.

Variables Measured: Attitudes about having children, including benefits and costs involved for individuals and the couple

Type of Instrument: Self-report questionnaire, administered either as a paper-and-pencil measure or as an interview

Instrument Description: This Likert-style scale contains five subscales and a total of 29 items. Responses are entered using a 7-option format ranging from *never happens* to *always happens* for each item. The five subscales are restrictions and disruptions (7 items), emotional satisfaction and fulfillment (11 items), effects on the marital relationship (2 items), marital costs (4 items), and life-style costs (5 items). Studies utilizing the Attitudes to Having Children scale have compared attitudes of samples from Australian, Greek, and Italian cultural groups. Subscale scores are arrived at by summing the scores from items within that subscale. General norms have not been established. However, the scale could be used in comparing attitudes of different groups.

Sample Items:

(A)   Having a child has made me more mature and settled.
(B)   When you have children there are few stimulating exchanges of ideas.
(C)   There is no spontaneity in our life any longer.

Comments: The author reports that subscales were determined by the results of a factor analysis utilizing a varimax rotation. It is reported that only items loading highly on various subscales were used in constructing the final version of the scale. It is also reported that studies using the scales found considerable cross-cultural similarities in dimensions that emerged.

References:

Callan, V. J. (1980). The value and cost of children: Australian, Greek and Italian couples in Sydney, Australia. *J Cross-Cul, 11,* 482–497.

Callan, V. J. (1986). The impact of the first birth: Married and single women preferring childlessness, one child, or two children. *J Mar Fam, 48,* 261–269.

Callan V. J., & Gallois, C. (1983). Perceptions about having children: Are daughters different from their mothers? *J Mar Fam, 45,* 607–612.

III-2/b

272. CALLAN, V. J., & NOLLER, P. Indexes of the Parent-Child Relationship

Avail: 1986 Ref.

Variables Measured: Extent to which interactions between family members, and particularly between parents and their children, are marked by anxiety, involved behavior, strength, dominance, and friendliness

Type of Instrument: Ratings scale to be used either by participants or by expert coders in evaluating interactions

Instrument Description: The scale is composed of four bipolar dimensions, each with six response options. Responses are time-sampled ratings of videotaped interactions. Family members viewing tapes use the four dimensions, making ratings every 15 seconds. The scale is designed to have ratings continue for 3 to 5 minutes, generating 12–20 ratings for each dimension. These ratings are then summed or averaged for each dimension. The scale and rating procedures are designed to be used primarily in evaluating families with adolescent children. The purpose of the scale is to tap differences in perceptions of family interactions.

Sample Items: Not applicable.

Comments: The authors state that the items are theoretically based. Where family members are asked to rate each other, the reliability of ratings may be of less clinical interest than differences between ratings by various members. However, if expert raters are utilized, training should be conducted to ensure similar rating procedures, and interrater reliabilities should be evaluated.

References:

Callan, V. J., & Noller, P. (1986). Perceptions of communicative relationships in families with adolescents. *J Mar Fam, 48,* 813–820.

Noller, P., & Callan, V. J. (1988). Understanding parent-adolescent interactions: The perceptions of family members and outsiders. *Devel Psych, 24,* 707–714.

III-2/IV-2/b/P

273. CAMPIS, L. K., LYMAN, R. D., & PRENTICE-DUNN, S. The Parental Locus of Control Scale (PLOC)

Avail: 1986 Ref.

Variables Measured: Parental locus of control

Type of Instrument: Self-report questionnaire

Instrument Description: The PLOC is a 5-point, 47-item Likert-type questionnaire designed to assess parental locus of control for parent-child situations. An initial pool of 200 items was generated by modifying items from several previously developed locus of control scales (James, 1957; Lewis, Dawes, & Cheyney, 1974; Nowicki & Strickland, 1973; Reid & Ware, 1974; Rotter, 1966) so that all items applied to parent-child relationships and circumstances. Original items developed by the authors were also included in this initial item pool. Item analyses based on testing, first with faculty and graduate students, and then with parents of elementary school-age children, resulted in the final 47-item version. Five factors identified by the authors are labeled parental efficacy, parental responsibility, child control of parents' life, parental belief in fate/chance, and parental control of child's behavior. Each subscale, with the exception of the child control of parents' life (7 items) subscale, contains 10 items. Scoring of some items is reversed. Individual factor scores are obtained by summing values associated with responses to items within subscales.

Sample Items:

(A) When something goes wrong between me and my child, there is little I can do to correct it.
(B) Parents who can't get their children to listen to them don't understand how to get along with their children.
(C) My life is chiefly controlled by my child.

Comments: The authors report that Cronbach's alpha for the five subscales ranges from .65 to .77 in one study, and from .44 to .79 in another. However, they report that the elimination of one item from the parental efficacy subscale raised the alpha levels from .62 to .79. Alpha for the total scale is reported to be .92. Correlations between the subscales and several other personality measures are reported in the reference given below. Correlations generally ranged from near .00 to .50. Further validity information is contained in the reference.

Reference:

Campis, L. K., Lyman, R. D., & Prentice-Dunn, S. (1986). The Parental Locus of Control Scale: Development and validation. *J Clin Child Psych, 15,* 260–267.

III-2/b/P
274. CHRISTENSEN, A., PHILLIPS, S. B., GLASGOW, R. E., & JOHNSON, S. M. Child Development Scale

Avail: NAPS-3

Variables Measured: Parental expectations of child development

Type of Instrument: Questionnaire for examining knowledge

Instrument Description: The scale consists of 26 items adapted from the Vineland Social Maturity Scale (Doll, 1947). Each item describes a behavior typical of children at a certain level of development (e.g., goes to bathroom unassisted). Parents indicate the age (within half-year levels) at which the average child would be able to perform the stated activity. Each item is scored in terms of its departure from the norms from the Vineland Social Maturity Scale and the Washington Child Development Guide (Barnad & Powell, 1972). Two total scores are then created: the extent of high expectations (the degree to which parents expected children to perform behaviors earlier than they should) and the absolute discrepancy from established norms.

Sample Items:

(A) Can button and unbutton _____
(B) Bathes self unaided _____
(C) Does routine household chores _____

Comments: The authors report that validity and reliability of the Child Development Scale have not been investigated.

Reference:

Christensen, A., Phillips, S., Glasgow, R. E., & Johnson, S. M. (1983). Parental characteristics and interactional dysfunction in families with child behavior problems: A preliminary investigation. *J Abn C Psy, 11,* 153–166.

III-2/b/P

275. CHRISTENSEN, A., PHILLIPS, S. B., GLASGOW, R. E., & JOHNSON, S. M. The Problem Situations Scale

Avail: NAPS-3

Variables Measured: Parental knowledge of behavioral principles

Type of Instrument: Self-report questionnaire

Instrument Description: This scale consists of 12 short descriptions of common behavior problems with children. For each situation, the parent chooses one of eight possible options, equally divided into positive solutions (e.g., *feeling expression, positive consequences for appropriate behavior*) and negative solutions (e.g., *threat, punishment*). Examples of possible solutions include (1) praise or reward your child whenever he does what you would like him to do, (2) sit down and talk to your child about his feelings, and (3) ignore your child and continue with what you were doing. Each parent receives a summary score reflecting the frequency of his or her choice of positive and behavioral solutions.

Sample Items:

(A)   Your son habitually will not eat his dinner. What would you decide to do?

(B)   Your five-year-old child still wets the bed at night. In addition to having him go to the bathroom before bed, what else would you do?

(C)   Your child embarrasses you when you go shopping by throwing a tantrum if he cannot have a treat. How would you deal with this?

Comments: The authors report that validity and reliability of the Problem Situations Scale have not been investigated.

Reference:

Christensen, A., Phillips, S., Glasgow, R. E., & Johnson, S. M. (1983). Parental characteristics and interactional dysfunction in families with child behavior problems: A preliminary investigation. *J Abn C Psy, 11,* 153–166.

III-2/IV-2/b/P

276. CHRISTENSEN, A., PHILLIPS, S. B., GLASGOW, R. E., & JOHNSON, S. M. Upsetting Behavior Questionnaire

Avail: NAPS-3

Variables Measured: Parental tolerance of child deviant behavior

Type of Instrument: Self-report questionnaire

Instrument Description: This instrument is a 9-point, 9-item questionnaire designed to assess parents' reactions to various annoying behaviors sometimes exhibited by children. Each item begins with an underlined one- or two-word descriptor, followed by a definition of the behavior. An example of the upsetting behavior is also included with some items. The response format allows items to be rated from 1 to 9. Scores of "1," "5," and "9" are categorized as *not upsetting, moderately upsetting,* and *extremely upsetting,* respectively. Other possible scores are not directly defined. Item scores are summed for an overall indication of how upsetting the parent finds such behaviors.

Sample Items:

(A) *Threat:* The child explicitly or implicitly warns that a negative consequence will occur if his desires are not met. For example, the child says, "If you don't let me go out and play now, I won't do my chores tonight." Or, the child says to his sibling, "If you don't give me back my truck, I'll hit you."
(B) *Yell:* The child shouts or talks loudly.
(C) *Disapproving Tone:* The child says something with a tone of disapproval. The manner in which the child speaks, not the content, is the defining feature of disapproving tone.

Comments: The author indicates that reliability and validity information regarding the Upsetting Behavior Questionnaire are not available.

Reference:

Christensen, A., Phillips, S., Glasgow, R. E., & Johnson, S. M. (1983). Parental characteristics and interactional dysfunction in families with child behavior problems: A preliminary investigation. *J Abn C Psy, 11,* 153–166.

III-2/b/P
277. CLARKE-STEWART, K. A. Mother-Child Interaction Scales

Avail: 1973 Ref.

Variables Measured: Relationship of mothers' behaviors to behaviors of their very young children

Type of Instrument: Behavior coding system

Instrument Description: The Mother-Child Interaction Scales is a system for the longitudinal analysis of maternal and child behavior. There are 26 coded maternal variables, including areas such as holding the infant, being affectionate, physical stimulation, leaving the room, and restraining behavior. Child behaviors are coded along 23 dimensions, many of which involve direct interaction with the mother. This instrument was designed to assist in understanding repeated interactions observed over a nine-month period. Observations occurred both in the home and in more structured laboratory settings, with the author preferring a total of 12 observational sessions—7 of which occurred in the mother's home—over a nine-month period. Live (as opposed to videotaped) maternal and child behavior is continuously recorded and coded. The coding procedure for home visits consists of having an observer (same gender, race, and approximate age) follow the infant around for three consecutive 30-minute sessions, making notations regarding the infant's behaviors and the child's mother's attempts to influence the infant's behavior. Throughout each session the observer records behaviors during each 10-second interval. A recording playing through earphones lets the observer know when each 10-second observation period begins and ends. Only those behaviors within the predetermined categories are coded, although time is allowed following each 30-minute session for editorial comments by the observer.

Sample Items: Not applicable.

Comments: The author indicates that interrater reliability, following five months of training, ranged from .70 to .80, with a mean of .75. Details regarding measures used in conjunction with the Mother-Child Interaction Scales, exact procedures for laboratory observations,
and samples of observational situations are provided in Clarke-Stewart (1973). The method
has been adapted slightly by others (see references below), but retains the flavor of multiple
categories of maternal and child observations conducted over time.

References:

Clarke-Stewart, K. A. (1973). Interactions between mothers and their young children: Charac-
    teristics and consequences. *Mon S Res C, 38*(6–7, Serial No. 153).
Crawford, J. W. (1982). Mother-infant interaction in premature and full-term infants. *Child
    Dev, 53,* 957–962.
Dunn, J., & Munn, P. (1985). Sibling quarrels and maternal intervention: Individual differ-
    ences in understanding and aggression. *J Child Psychol Psychi, 27,* 583–595.
Hegland, S. M. (1983). Social initiation and responsiveness in parent-infant interaction.
    Home Ec Res J, 12, 71–75.

III-2/b/P
278. COHEN, D. J., & DIBBLE, E. Parent's Report (PR)

Avail: 1974 Ref.

Variables Measured: Parents' behavior toward their children

Type of Instrument: Self-report questionnaire

Instrument Description: The PR is a 7-point, 48-item Likert-type questionnaire designed to
assess parents' behaviors toward their children on five dimensions: (1) respect for autonomy,
(2) control through guilt and anxiety, (3) consistency, (4) child-centeredness, and (5) parental
temper and detachment. Items were developed along conceptual lines proposed by Schaefer
and Bell (1958), but for which Schaefer and Bell credit earlier studies by Stogdill, Read,
Radke, and Wiley. The scale was designed for use with parents of children ages 2 through
early adolescence. Items take the form of statements of children's or parents' behaviors.
Parents are asked to indicate the frequency of each behavior, with response options ranging
from *never* = 0 to *always* = 6. Parallel columns are provided for ratings of actual and ideal
responses. In developing the PR, 3 behaviorally descriptive items were generated for each of
16 categories of parenting style. Categories were equally divided between those considered by
the authors to be socially desirable and socially undesirable. Three different scoring systems
are suggested by the authors: (1) Items may be considered separately; (2) items within the 16
behavioral categories may be considered together; (3) values associated with all 48 items may
be summed in order to arrive at a total score.

Sample Items:

(A)   I see both the child's good points and his faults.
(B)   I forget things he has told me.
(C)   I let him express his feelings about being punished or restricted.

Comments: The authors indicate that PR scores are correlated from .34 to .53 with parental perceptions of the effects of day care on relationships with their children. The 5 factors
were defined by a factor analysis, with all items loading at least .30 on their primary factors.
Of the 48 items, 15 loaded greater than .30 on multiple factors. Additional information
regarding the factor analysis and validity of the scale is contained in Cohen, Dibble, and
Grawe (1977a, 1977b).

References:

Cohen, D. J., Dibble, E., & Grawe, J. M. (1977a). Parental style. *Arch G Psyc, 34,* 445–451.
Cohen, D. J., Dibble, E., & Grawe, J. M. (1977b). Fathers' and mothers' perceptions of children's personality. *Arch G Psyc, 34,* 480–487.
Dibble, E., & Cohen, D. J. (1974). Companion instruments for measuring children's competence and parental style. *Arch G Psyc, 30,* 805–815.
Roopnarine, J. L., Mounts, N. S., & Casto, G. (1986). Mothers' perceptions of their children's supplemental care experience: Correlation with spousal relationship. *Am J Orthop, 56,* 581–588.

III-2/b/P
279. COHLER, B. J., WEISS, J. L., & GRUNEBAUM, H. Maternal Attitude Scale (MAS)

Avail: NAPS-1

Variables Measured: Maternal attitudes toward the resolution of relationship issues between mothers and their preschool children

Type of Instrument: Self-report questionnaire

Instrument Description: The MAS is a 6-point, 233-item Likert-style questionnaire designed for use with mothers of preschool children. Items are in the form of statements, with response options ranging from *strongly agree* to *strongly disagree.* The 233 items are combined within five second-order factors: (1) appropriate control of the child's aggressive impulses, (2) encouragement versus discouragement of reciprocity between mother and child, (3) appropriate versus inappropriate closeness, (4) acceptance versus denial of emotional complexity in child rearing, and (5) comfort versus discomfort in perceiving and meeting the baby's physical needs. These factors were designed to tap key considerations in mothers' effectiveness and satisfaction with their mother-child relationships. The impetus for the development of the MAS was provided through work by Sander (1962), which discussed issues in mother-young child relationships.

Sample Items:

(A)   When the baby is born he (she) already has a personality of his (her) own.
(B)   A mother and her 5-month-old child should be able to understand each other fairly well.
(C)   Bodily changes in pregnancy make a woman feel very unattractive.

Comments: Cronbach's alpha for the five second-order factors is reported to range from .81 to .96, with one-month test-retest reported to range from .62 to .78. Validity information for the MAS comes partially from research comparing hospitalized mentally ill and normal mothers of young children. Mentally ill mothers believe less in developing reciprocity, more in denying child care concerns, and less in fostering appropriate closeness with their children.

References:

Cohler, B. J., Grunebaum, H., Weiss, J. L., Hartman, C., & Gallant, D. (1976). Child care attitudes and adaptation to the maternal role among mentally ill and well mothers. *Am J Orthop, 46,* 123–134.
Cohler, B. J., Weiss, J. L., & Grunebaum, H. (1970). Child care attitudes and emotional disturbance among mothers of young children. *Genet Psych Mono, 82,* 3–47.
Fry, P. S., & Thiessen, I. (1981). Single mothers and single fathers and their children: Percep-

tions of their children's needs, their own needs and career needs. *Br J Soc Psych, 20,* 97–100.

Hock, E. (1980). Working and nonworking mothers and their infants: A comparative study of maternal caregiving characteristics and infant social behavior. *Merrill-Pal, 26,* 79–101.

III-2/e/b/P

280. CONE, J. D., WOLFE, V. V., & DeLAWYER, D. D. Parent/Family Involvement Index (P/FII)

Avail: NAPS-3

Variables Measured: Parental participation in children's special education programs

Type of Instrument: Behavior checklist

Instrument Description: The P/FII is a 63-item behavior checklist intended to be completed by teachers, teaching aides, or others familiar with the parent's(s') participation in school-related activities. It is specifically designed to evaluate participation and cooperation with the school by parents of special education children. Items are in the form of statements, to which respondents indicate *yes, no, not applicable,* or *don't know.* Educators are instructed to indicate whether or not each parent has participated in the stated manner. Where the child lives with both parents, behaviors are checked for both the mother and the father. Items are grouped into 12 categories, with from 3 to 7 items per category: (1) contact with teacher, (2) participation in special education process, (3) transportation, (4) observations at school, (5) educational activities at home, (6) attending parent education/consultation meetings, (7) classroom volunteering, (8) parent-parent contact and support, (9) involvement with administration, (10) involvement in fund-raising activities, (11) involvement in advocacy groups, and (12) disseminating information. One additional 6-point item asks educators to rate the overall involvement of each parent. Scores are independently determined for each of the 12 categories. Administration time is estimated to be 12–15 minutes when ratings are obtained for both mothers and fathers.

Sample Items:

(A)   Parent has attended individual or family counseling sessions conducted by a psychologist, psychiatrist, or other mental health professional to assist in adjusting to the child's handicap.

(B)   Parent has volunteered at least once to assist in the classroom.

(C)   Parent performs informal home activities specifically designed to reinforce and maintain skills learned in school or suggested by the teacher.

Comments: Means and standard deviations for ratings of mothers and fathers within each category are presented in Cone, DeLawyer, and Wolfe (1985). Percentile rankings are provided in the manual (available through NAPS-3). KR-21 reliability coefficients are reported to range from .48 to .92, with all categories except fathers' observations at school and involvement in fund-raising, and mothers' contact with teacher, achieving KR-21 reliabilities of at least .72. Correlations between P/FII ratings and total involvement ratings, as well as several demographic variables, are reported in the reference noted below.

Reference:

Cone, J. D., DeLawyer, D. D., & Wolfe, V. V. (1985). Assessing parent participation: The Parent/Family Involvement Index. *Except Chil, 51,* 417–424.

III-2/IV-2/II-3/b/P

281. CRASE, S. J., CLARK, S. G., & PEASE, D. The Iowa Parent Behavior Inventory (IPBI)

Avail: Iowa State University Research Foundation, Inc., 315 Beardshear Hall, Iowa State University, Ames, IA 50011

Variables Measured: Parental behaviors in relation to a child

Type of Instrument: Self-report questionnaire

Instrument Description: The IPBI is a self-rating scale designed to assess parental behavior in relation to a child. Parents respond to one of two 5-point, 36-item Likert-type questionnaire forms (mother or father forms). The current version of the IPBI resulted from a factor analysis conducted on the original 67-item version. The current version of the test was designed to be self-administered. Ratings are based on each parent's perceptions of his or her own behavior. Each item represents an actual behavioral situation. Responses range from 1 to 5, with low scores indicating the parent almost never behaves in the manner indicated, and high scores being indicative of frequent behaviors. Individual factors are scored independently. The mother form contains six factors (parental involvement, limit setting, responsiveness, reasoning guidance, free expression, and intimacy), while the father form contains five factors (parental involvement, limit setting, responsiveness, reasoning guidance, and intimacy).

Sample Items:

(A) Excuse yourself from invited guests when your child asks for help with such things as pasting, sewing, or model building.

(B) Require your child to remain seated in the car while you are driving.

(C) Give your child things he or she especially likes when he or she is ill.

Comments: Factor intercorrelations reported by the authors range from .04 to .50 for mothers, and from .26 to .61 for fathers. It is further reported that reliability coefficients for the individual factors range from .62 to .81 for mothers, and from .64 to .84 for fathers. Several theses and dissertations have examined the relationship of the IPBI to children's self-concept, parental behavior and age, child's age, maternal employment status, and children's social competencies.

References:

Crase, S. J., Clark, S., & Pease, D. (1980). Assessment of child-rearing behaviors of midwestern rural parents. *Home Ec Res J, 9,* 163–172.

Elrod, M. M., & Crase, S. J. (1980). Sex differences in self-esteem and parental behavior. *Psychol Rep, 46,* 719–727.

Mullis, R. L., Smith, D. W., & Vollmers, K. E. (1982). Parental guidance and prosocial behaviors in young children. *Fam Perspect, 16,* 83–89.

III-2/IV-2/b/P

282. DE MAN, A. F. The Autonomy-Control Scale (A-C Scale)

Avail: NAPS-3

Variables Measured: Adults' perceptions of level of control exercised by their parents during respondents' childhood and adolescent years

Type of Instrument: Self-report questionnaire

Instrument Description: The A-C Scale is a 30-item Likert-type questionnaire designed to examine adults' memories of childhood interactions with their parents. Items are geared toward an assessment of parental control, reflecting variations in restrictions placed by parents on the behavior of their children. The author indicates that adult children's responses on this variable tend to be both easier to obtain and more accurate than those of their parents. The A-C Scale consists of two subscales: (1) 14 items applicable to childhood before the age of 12 and (2) 16 items applicable to the adolescent years. Factor analysis by the author revealed three factors: (1) freedom of personal choice and responsibility, (2) presence of family rules, and (3) freedom to assert self vis-á-vis parents. All items utilize a 5-point response format ranging from *always* to *never*. A total score is obtained by summing values associated with the selected responses. Low scores indicate that parents exercised high levels of control, while high scores indicate that the child was permitted high levels of autonomy. Administration time is approximately 10 minutes.

Sample Items:

(A)   (Childhood item) Did your parents require you to tell them where you were going and what you were about to do?

(B)   (Childhood item) Did your parents insist that you go to bed at a particular set time?

(C)   (Adolescence item) Were you allowed to stay out at night as late as you wished?

Comments: Items were selected by a panel of five judges, and were based largely on previously published instruments (Itkin, 1952; Koch, Dentler, Dysart, & Streit, 1934; Stott, 1940). These judges also developed new items to supplement those selected from other instruments. The author reports eight-week test-retest reliability for the A-C Scale of .91. Research is also reported in which age of respondent was associated with perceptions of parental control, with younger adults remembering their parents as being more permissive. Additionally, it was found that respondents from backgrounds judged to be controlling tended to report lower self-esteem and greater adjustment, alienation, anomie, trait anxiety, and conservatism than did those from backgrounds classified as more permissive.

References:

De Man, A. F. (1982a). Autonomy-control variation and self-esteem: Additional findings. *J Psychol, 111,* 9–13.

De Man, A. F. (1982b). Autonomy-control variation in child rearing and self-image disparity in young adults. *Psychol Rep, 51,* 1039–1044.

De Man, A. F. (1986). Parental control in child rearing and trait anxiety in young adults. *Psychol Rep, 59,* 477–478.

De Man, A. F. (1987). Parental control in child rearing and adjustment in young adults. *Perc Mot Sk, 65,* 917–918.

III-2/II-5/b/P

283. DeSALVO, F. J., Jr., & ZURCHER, L. A. Parenting Discrepancy Scale (PDS)

Avail: NAPS-3

Variables Measured: Discrepancy between parent's ideal self and current perception of self

Type of Instrument: Self-report questionnaire

Instrument Description: The Parenting Discrepancy Scale is a 20-item questionnaire designed to measure the difference between the way a parent would like to be (ideal parenting skills, attitudes, and behavior) and the way that parent perceives him- or herself at present (real parenting skills, attitudes, and behavior). The questions are set in Likert-style format with six response options for each item. Possible responses range from *all the time* to *never* for each item. The difference between real and ideal ratings are calculated for each item. Thus, if the parent indicates that he or she *occasionally* behaves in a particular fashion (scored a "4"), but that the ideal situation would be to behave in that way *most of the time* (scored a "2"), the score for that item would be a "2" (4 − 2 = 2). In this way, each item is scored from 0 to 5, with a possible range of scale scores of 0 to 100.

Sample Items:

(A)   I have to yell to show my child I mean business.
(B)   I wish my child would show more respect for me.
(C)   I think my child often has good ideas.

Comments: Cronbach's alpha is reported by the authors to be .76 for the entire scale. The issue of validity was addressed in two ways. First, the authors attempted to ensure content validity by having five judges evaluate items on the scale. Items were included if judges considered them to be relevant statements about parenting skills, attitudes, or behaviors, and clearly worded to indicate typical high or low discrepancy statements. Construct validity was assessed by comparing scores on the Parenting Discrepancy Scale with measures taken on the Rosenberg Self-Image Scale. Correlations were -.22 for fathers and -.21 for mothers. The authors report that this result was unexpected and may demonstrate a difference between how adults evaluate themselves as parents and how they perceive their self-image.

Reference:

DeSalvo, F. J., Jr., & Zurcher, L. A. (1984). Defensive and supportive communication in a discipline situation. *J Psychol, 117,* 7–17.

III-2/b/P
284. DIELMAN, T. E., & BARTON, K. Child-Rearing Practices Questionnaire (CRPQ)

Avail: Institute for Personality and Ability Testing, P.O. Box 188, Champaign, IL 61820

Variables Measured: Structure of child-rearing practices of parents

Type of Instrument: Self-report questionnaire

Instrument Description: The CRPQ is a commercially available 143-item Likert-style questionnaire designed to measure 15 factors for mothers and 11 factors for fathers related to child-rearing practices. Response options for individual options vary according to the nature of the item. Some items include responses indicating frequency of occurrence, while others give options for behaviors of respondents. Additional factor analytic solutions have yielded varying numbers of subscales. The instrument is a result of research initially conducted by Sears, Maccoby, and Levin (1957), and later expanded by Dielman, Barton, Cattell, and others during the 1970s. It has been used in several studies since that time to investigate various aspects of child-rearing practices.

Sample Items:

(A)   How important is it to you that your child(ren) do exactly those things that you tell them to do?
(B)   How often does a young (3- to 6-year-old) child's behavior require a spanking?
(C)   Would you rather help a third grader make something or teach a 1-year-old to talk?

Comments: The CRPQ is widely used in studies investigating relationships between child-rearing practices and personality structures of children, school achievement, behavior problems, early school child personality factors, and family relationships. The structure of the instrument is the result of extensive factor analyses. Barton (1981) found that six factors measured by the CRPQ are common between mothers and fathers. These factors were labeled punishment versus reason, promotion of dependence-independence, rules and regulations, spouse involvement, high use of rewards, and preference for younger children.

References:

Barton, K. (1981). Six child rearing dimensions common to both fathers and mothers. *Mult Exp Cl, 5,* 91–97.

Barton, K., Dielman, T. E., & Cattell, R. B. (1977). Child-rearing practices related to child personality. *J Soc Psych, 101,* 75–85.

Barton, K., Dielman, T. E., & Cattell, R. B. (1986). Prediction of objective child motivation test scores from parents' reports of child-rearing practices. *Psychol Rep, 59,* 343–352.

Dielman, T. E., Barton, K., & Cattell, R. B. (1977). Relationships among family attitudes and child rearing practices. *J Genet Psy, 130,* 105–112.

III-2/b/C
285. DREGER, R. M. Characterization of Parent

Avail: NAPS-3

Variables Measured: Adults' childhood memories of their parents. Also, adults' present attitudes toward their parents as remembered from their childhood

Type of Instrument: Series of paper-and-pencil ratings made by adult children of the parents

Instrument Description: The Characterization of Parent scale consists of two sets of 14 items each, suitable for use with nonclinical as well as clinical populations. Ratings are made in a bipolar response format using brief phrases or single adjectives to anchor each item. The response scheme utilizes a line drawn between the two extremes, with eight dashed lines at equal intervals along a continuum. Respondents check anywhere along the line between the extremes, with their markings not being limited to the dashes on the line. Raw scores are expressed in tenths of a point (4.3, 5.6, and so on). Raw scores are multiplied by factor weights for items on the individual subscales. The first set of items pertains to the subject's mother and the second to his or her father. The scale is not intended as an objective measure of childhood attitudes toward one's parents. Rather, it is designed to assess current memories of attitudes that were held long ago. It is recognized that these memories may or may not coincide with actual parental behavior when the respondent was a child. In clinical practice, it has been found that many respondents answer items in terms of their current attitudes toward their parents based on early memories. The author cautions that clinicians need to be aware of the different response perspectives of subjects. The Characterization of Parent scale is used primarily in private clinic settings to assess the realistic or unrealistic nature of present attitudes. Together with other information, this scale is designed to give information on reality-testing.

Sample Items:

(A)   Just . . . . Unjust
(B)   Controlled . . . . Nervous
(C)   Drunk . . . . Sober

Comments: Items from the Characterization of Parent scale were derived from scales provided by the Psychological Service Center of the University of Southern California. Subsequent research by Dreger resulted in standardization and the current factor structure reported for this instrument. Factor analyses were conducted on three occasions (1960, 1961, and 1972) utilizing comparable but different samples of college undergraduates. The author reports that the latest analysis resulted in the recognition of two factors for both mothers and fathers. The first factor highlights attitudes toward parents that reflect an ideal but strict religious fatherhood or motherhood, while the second factor relates to an ideal but more lenient secular fatherhood or motherhood. The author reports similarity coefficients for the factors ranging from .82 to .99. Correlations between factors are reported to range from .13 to .52.

Reference:

Dreger, R. M., & Sweetland, A. (1960). Traits of fatherhood as revealed by the factor-analysis of a parent-attitude scale. *J Gen Psych, 96,* 115–122.

III-2/b/P
286. EASTERBROOKS, M. A., & GOLDBERG, W. A. Parental Attitudes toward Childrearing (PACR)

Avail: NAPS-3

Variables Measured: Parental attitudes toward the expression of affection, children's autonomous behavior, discipline and self-control, and feelings of being annoyed or upset by their children's behavior

Type of Instrument: Self-report questionnaire

Instrument Description: The PACR is a 51-item Likert-style scale that addresses issues salient for mothers and fathers of young children. The questionnaire examines four dimensions of child rearing, referred to as warmth (10 items), independence (9 items), strictness (13 items), and aggravation (19 items). Parents indicate the extent of their agreement with each item according to a 6-point response format. Possible responses range from *strongly disagree* to *strongly agree.* All statements are phrased in the first person. For each subscale, negatively worded items are reverse-scored, inclusive item scores are summed, and averages are calculated to yield mean scores. Administration time is approximately 15 minutes.

Sample Items:

(A)   I express affection by hugging, kissing, and holding my child.
(B)   I make sure I know where my child is and what s/he is doing.
(C)   I find that taking care of a young child is much more work than pleasure.

Comments: The authors report that responses from 76 mothers and 74 fathers of toddler-aged children were used in a confirmatory cluster analysis of the theoretically based subscales. Cronbach's alpha for subscales is reported by the authors to range from .58 to .78, with a mean of .69. The authors report that many of the PACR items were adapted from Block's (1965) Childrearing Practices Report. A number of other items are reported to be adapted from Cohler's (1977) Maternal Attitudes Scale. Items from these scales were modified to fit the authors' Likert format, to be phrased in the first person, to be appropriate for fathers as well as mothers, and to suit parents of young children. The remaining items, as well as subscales of the PACR, are reported to have been created by the authors.

References:

Easterbrooks, M. A., & Goldberg, W. A. (1984). Toddler development in the family: Impact of father involvement and parenting characteristics. *Child Dev, 55,* 740–752.
Easterbrooks, M. A., & Goldberg, W. A. (1985). Effects of maternal employment on toddlers, mothers, and fathers. *Devel Psych, 21,* 774–783.
Goldberg, W. A., & Easterbrooks, M. A. (1985). Role of marital quality in toddler development. *Devel Psych, 20,* 504–514.
Holden, G. W., & Edwards, L. (1989). Parental attitudes toward child rearing: Instruments, issues, and implications. *Psychol B, 106,* 29–58.

III-2/IV-2/b/P
287. ELDER, G. H. Index of Parental Socialization Styles. Mother and Father Versions

Avail: 1980 Ref.

Variables Measured: Socialization for independence during the adolescent years

Type of Instrument: Questionnaire on which adolescents rate parental behavior

Instrument Description: This 5-item questionnaire was developed from survey data on approximately 12,000 adolescents during 1960. Adolescent subjects are asked to respond to each item twice, once with regard to interactions with each parent. The scale was designed to serve as a global measure of independence training. The first item contains seven response options. All other items contain five options. Individual response options are scored either zero or one, with responses indicating conditions presumed to be conducive to independence training assigned values of one. Total scale scores thus range from zero to five. Parents are assigned to low, intermediate, or high categories of independence training based on total scores from ratings by their adolescent child.

Sample Items:

(A)   In general, how are most decisions made between you and your mother/father?
(B)   Does your (mother/father) let you have more freedom to make your own decisions and to do what you want than (she/he) did two or three years ago?
(C)   When you don't know why your (mother/father) makes a particular decision or has certain rules for you to follow, will (she/he) explain the reason?

Comments: The author states that low-scoring parents tend to be autocratic and seldom explain their reasons to their children. It is also reported that fathers are more likely to score low. In the initial 1960 study, 15.6% of fathers and 8.3% of mothers had total scores of either zero or one.

References:

Anderson, J. G., & Evans, F. B. (1976). Family socialization and educational achievement in two cultures: Mexican-American and Anglo-American. *Sociometry, 39,* 209–222.
Elder, G. H., Jr. (1980). *Family structure and socialization.* New York: Arno.
Streitmatter, J., & Jones, R. (1982). Perceived parent and teacher socialization styles on self-esteem in early adolescence. *J Early Adol, 2,* 151–161.

III-2/b
288. ELIAS, G. The Family Adjustment Test (FAT)

Avail: Psychometric Affiliates, Box 807 Murfreesboro, TN 37133

Variables Measured: Intrafamily homeyness versus homelessness (acceptance versus rejection), and 10 subscores: attitude toward mother, attitude toward father, father-mother attitude quotient, oedipal, struggle for independence, parent-child friction and harmony, interparental friction and harmony, family inferiority or superiority, rejection of child, and parental qualities

Type of Instrument: Questionnaire in which attitudes and opinions are surveyed

Instrument Description: A detailed questionnaire measuring what people think about families in general. The FAT contains 114 Likert-style items utilizing a 5-point scoring format with response options ranging from *always* to *never*. Research from which the FAT was first developed was initiated in 1944. The research was originally intended to distinguish between soldiers who would fail to make adequate adjustments to army life during the World War II. The original pool of statements from which the scale was developed contained 524 items. The current version carries a 1954 copyright. A detailed instruction and scoring manual is available from the publishers. The final version has been used in assessing the adjustment of thousands of individuals. Administration time is estimated to be approximately 35 minutes. The test may be administered individually or to large groups. Oral individual administration is also possible.

Sample Items:

(A)   Children _____ feel their parents are better to other people than to them.
(B)   A child _____ hears his parents say bad things behind each other's back.
(C)   Mothers _____ scold their children unjustly.

Comments: Extensive validity research from the 1940s and early 1950s is reported by the author and is detailed in the test manual. Split-half reliability, established in these early studies, is reported to be .97.

References:

Campbell, D. T. (1950). The indirect assessment of social attitudes. *Psychol B, 47,* 15–38.
Crosby, J. F. (1971). The effect of family life education on the values and attitude of adolescents. *Fam Coord, 20,* 137–140.
Elias, G. (1951). Self-evaluative questionnaires as projective measures of personality. *J Cons Psych, 15,* 496–500.

III-2/II-3/c/C
289. EMERY, R. E. Children's Perception Questionnaire (CPQ)

Avail: NAPS-3

Variables Measured: Children's perceptions of acceptance by parents and of marital discord

Type of Instrument: Self-report questionnaire

Instrument Description: The CPQ is a 3-point, 38-item questionnaire. It was designed to measure perceptions of 8- to 17-year-old children regarding the level of acceptance they receive from their parents, and the extent of any difficulties currently being encountered by the child's parents. Twelve items were constructed specifically to assess level of parental discord, and 7 items intended to measure felt acceptance were taken from Schaefer's (1965) Children's Report of Parental Behavior Inventory. The remaining 19 items relate to interactions with family and friends, and are used to mask the intent of the scale. A factor analysis resulted in two parental discord items and one felt acceptance item being eliminated from their respective subscales. The 19 filler items, as well as the 3 items eliminated based on the factor analysis, are not scored. Response options are *true, somewhat true,* and *not true* (scored 1–3). Scores are computed for the two identified subscales by summing values associated with items within each factor and dividing by the number of items in that factor (10 and 6).

Sample Items:

(A) My parents like to talk to me and be with me much of the time.
(B) I don't see my parents fight often, but I think they do fight a lot.
(C) You wouldn't know it by the way they act in front of me, but I know my parents are not too happy.

Comments: The author reports that Cronbach's alpha for parental discord, also referred to as the marital perception scale, was .90, and was .87 for the felt acceptance scale. Items retained based on the factor analysis are reported to load at least .42 for the marital discord subscale, and .62 for the felt acceptance dimension.

References:

Emery, R. E., & O'Leary, D. K. (1982). Children's perceptions of marital discord and behavior problems of boys and girls. *J Abn C Psy, 10,* 11–24.

Kurdek, L. A., & Sinclair, R. J. (1986). Adolescents' views on issues related to divorce. *J Adol Res, 1,* 373–387.

Kurdek, L. A., & Sinclair, R. J. (1988). Adjustment of young adolescents in two-parent nuclear, stepfather, and mother-custody families. *J Cons Clin, 56,* 91–96.

III-2/b/P
290. EPSTEIN, A. S. High/Scope Knowledge Scale

Avail: NAPS-3

Variables Measured: Knowledge of infant and child development during the first two years of life

Type of Instrument: Card sort with cards placed into piles indicating developmental age of the child

Instrument Description: The Knowledge Scale uses a card-sorting technique to assess expectations about children's early development. Respondents sort a series of statements describing the needs and abilities of infants and toddlers according to the age category they think each behavior would first appear. Sorting categories are as follows: Birth to 1 month, 1 to 4 months, 4 to 8 months, 8 to 12 months, 12 to 18 months, and 18 to 24 months or older. The instrument can be administered orally, with the interviewer reading each statement from a card and asking the respondent to sort the cards into piles by age. Alternatively, respondents can read and sort the cards themselves. Interviewers then circle the respondent's choices on a score sheet. The scale asks 73 items and takes approximately 20–30 minutes to administer. Scores indicate correct, early, and late expectations for the instrument as a whole. In addition, scores can be computed for three subscales: basic care; physical, perceptual, and motor development; and cognitive, language, and social development.

Sample Items:

(A)   Explore things that an adult gives them by putting them into their mouths?
(B)   Sit without any support?
(C)   Take out small objects and put them back into a bigger container?

Comments: Knowledge Scale scores are reported by the author to predict parenting styles among pregnant and parenting adolescents, and with older mothers. According to the author, correct expectations correlate with supportive mother-child interactions observed during the baby's first year of life, early expectations correlate with demanding or controlling styles of interaction, and late expectations are related to a lack of stimulation by young parents. Additional studies are also reported to have found that 12- to 15-year-old mothers had generally inappropriate expectations for their infants, and that Knowledge Scale scores correlate positively with experience in older mothers.

References:

Epstein, A. S. (1980). *Assessing the child development information needed by adolescent parents with very young children* (Final report, Grant No. 90-C-1341, U.S. Dept. HHS). Ypsilanti, MI: High/Scope.

Stevens, J. H., Jr. (1984). Child development knowledge and parenting skills. *Fam Relat, 33,* 237–244.

III-2/e/b/C
291. EPSTEIN, J. L., & BECKER, H. J. Hopkins Surveys of School and Family Connections

Avail: Center for Research on Elementary & Middle Schools, Johns Hopkins University, 3505 N. Charles Street, Baltimore, MD 21218

Variables Measured: Nature and extent of teachers' contacts with parents, teachers' attitudes regarding interactions with families, and parents' perceptions of communications with and attitudes toward schools

Type of Instrument: Series of self-report questionnaires

Instrument Description: The Hopkins Surveys of School and Family Connections is a set of four instruments assessing various aspects of the parent-teacher relationship. The four surveys are designed to be used concomitantly in the development of an overall picture of parental and teacher attitudes and actions toward both each other and the educational process. Form 1-T, Survey of Teachers, was developed in 1980 to assess the nature and extent of teachers' contacts with parents, topics teachers discuss with parents, the use of 14 techniques for involving parents in learning activities at home, estimates of parents' effectiveness, and teachers' attitudes about parent involvement. It covers 36 questions, over 150 items of information, and 13 pages. Form 2-T is a 1987 revision of the Survey of Teachers. This form includes items on teacher attitudes regarding parent involvement, communication with families, use of parent-volunteers, effectiveness of parent involvement programs, and parental educational responsibilities. It includes 10 questions, over 100 items of information, and six pages. Form 1-P (1981) and 2-P (1987) parallel the teacher forms in areas of inquiry, but are geared toward an examination of parental perceptions of their involvement in the education of their children. Primary areas of concern examined in the parent forms include school support for parental involvement, quality of homework assignments, ratings of teacher skills, and overall effectiveness of the educational system. Form 1-P includes 33 questions, and over 70 items of information. Form 2-P includes 6 questions, over 50 items of information, and five pages. The complete group of surveys include hundreds of items, written in various formats and from differing perspectives. The questionnaires can be used in full, in part, or adapted for use as research instruments or as tools for self-assessments by schools. The authors indicate that the 1987 surveys can be scaled to assess the strength of five major types of parent involvement for building a comprehensive educational program: (1) basic obligations of parents, such as home conditions for learning; (2) basic obligations of schools; (3) volunteers at the school building; (4) involvement in learning activities and homework at home; and (5) governance, decision making, and advisory roles for parents. Administration time for individual forms varies from approximately 15–40 minutes.

Sample Items:

Form 1-T, 1980—Techniques: How often used it this year?

(A)   Ask parents to watch a specific television program with their child and to discuss the show afterward.
(B)   Give an assignment that requires the children to ask their parents questions—for example, that the children write about their parents' experiences.

Form 2-T, 1987—Type of Involvement

(A)   Workshops for parents to build skills in parenting and understanding their children at each grade level.
(B)   Communications about report cards so that parents understand students' progress and needs.

Form 1-P, 1981—Indicate level of agreement

(A)   I understand more this year than I did last year about what my child is being taught in school.
(B)   I don't feel I've had enough training to help my child with reading or math problems.

Form 2-P, 1987—Indicate frequency of activity

(A)   Talk with the child about school work.
(B)   Listen to a story the child wrote.

Comments: The author reports that reliability coefficients for the surveys have not been calculated. However, the instruments have been utilized in several studies examining city and statewide educational systems. They report that the earlier surveys have been used in full and adapted forms, and have been translated by other researchers for use in the United States and elsewhere.

References:

Becker, H. J., & Epstein, J. L. (1982). Parent involvement: A survey of teacher practices. *Elem Sch J, 83*, 85–102.

Epstein, J. L. (1985a). Parents' reactions to teacher practices of parent involvement. *Elem Sch J, 86*, 277–294.

Epstein, J. L. (1985b). A question of merit: Principals' and parents' evaluations of teachers. *Educ Res, 14*, 3–10.

Epstein, J. L. (in press). Effects on student achievement of teachers' practices of parent involvement. In S. Silvern (Ed.), *Literacy through family, community, and school interaction*. Greenwich, CT: JAI.

III-2/IV-1/c/C
292. EPSTEIN, J. L., & McPARTLAND, J. M. Family Decision-Making Style Scale

Avail: 1984 Ref.

Variables Measured: Nature and extent of child's participation in family decisions

Type of Instrument: Self-report questionnaire

Instrument Description: This scale is a 12-item questionnaire consisting of 9 *true-false* and 3 multiple choice items. *True-false* responses are scored as either 1 or 0. Multiple choice items each contain two response options scored as 1 and two scored as 0. The scale was designed for students in grades 4–12, and for cross-sectional or longitudinal studies of family environments and change in family practices as the child matures. The scale measures students' reports of their parents' practices that include or exclude the child from participating in family decisions, how much the parents trust the child to make good decisions, and how accepting or encouraging the parents are of the child's participation. The general theme is the design of the family authority structure, and specific practices that illustrate how decision-making responsibilities are shared at home. The scale was designed for use in two-parent households, but can easily be adapted for use with single-parent families. A second, alternative format asks each question twice, pertaining once to the respondent's mother and the other time to his or her father. Administration time is approximately 5–10 minutes.

Sample Items:

(A)   (*true or false*) I often do not know why I am supposed to do what my parents tell me to do.
(B)   How are most decisions about you made in your family?
      0 = My parents *tell me* just what to do.
      0 = My parents ask me how I feel and then *they* decide.
      1 = My parents tell me how they feel and then *I* decide.
      1 = My parents *let me* decide.
(C)   How much do you take part in making family decisions about yourself?
      1 = *Very much;* 1 = *Much;* 0 = *Some;* 0 = *None at all*

Comments: The authors indicate that internal reliability (KR-8) for the Family Decision-Making Style Scale is .71. The results of multivariate regression analyses indicated that high scores were related to greater independence, more positive attitudes toward school, and getting higher grades. The authors indicate that this instrument can be used in combination with the Rules in the Home Checklist (Epstein & McPartland, 1984) to assess two dimensions of family authority structure.

References:

Epstein, J. L. (1981). Patterns of classroom participation, student attitudes, and achievements. In J. L. Epstein (Ed.), *The quality of school life.* Lexington, MA: Lexington.

Epstein, J. L. (1983). Longitudinal effects of person-family-school interactions on student outcomes. In A. Kerckhoff (Ed.), *Research in sociology of education and socialization* (Vol. 4). Greenwich, CT: JAI.

Epstein, J. L. (1984). A longitudinal study of school and family effects on student development. In S. A. Mednick, M. Harway, & K. Finello (Eds.), *Handbook of longitudinal research* (Vol. 1). New York: Praeger.

Epstein, J. L., & McPartland, J. M. (1979). Authority structures. In H. Walberg (Ed.), *Educational environments and effects.* Berkeley, CA: McCutchan.

III-2/IV-2/b/P
293. EPSTEIN, J. L., & McPARTLAND, J. M. Rules in the Home Checklist

Avail: 1984 Ref.

Variables Measured: Number of rules parents set for child

Type of Instrument: Checklist

Instrument Description: This instrument is an 18-item checklist of the rules that control children's behavior at home, including rules for curfews, chores, clothing, hair styles, restrictions about friends, social life, and other behaviors. Subjects are children, who are asked to check *yes* or *no* in response to each listed rule. The scale is appropriate for middle school through senior high school students, but can be shortened to 14 items for students in the elementary grades by removing items that refer to behaviors of older children. Scoring is accomplished by counting the number of *yes* versus *no* responses. Administration time is approximately 5–10 minutes.

Sample Items:

(A) Time to be in at night on weekends.
(B) Clothes you may wear.
(C) Going to church or temple.

Comments: The authors report KR-8 reliability of .75. Regression analyses reported by the authors also indicate that students with few rules at home have less positive attitudes about school. An additional finding was that more decision-making opportunities but not fewer rules seemed to work to the advantage of the student in building positive attitudes and school-related behaviors. The authors noted that the Rules in the Home Checklist can be used in combination with the Family Decision-Making Style Scale (Epstein & McPartland, 1984) to assess two dimensions of family authority structure.

References:

Epstein, J. L. (1981). Patterns of classroom participation, student attitudes, and achievements. In J. L. Epstein (Ed.), *The quality of school life.* Lexington, MA: Lexington.
Epstein, J. L. (1983). Longitudinal effects of person-family-school interactions on student outcomes. In A. Kerckhoff (Ed.), *Research in sociology of education and socialization* (Vol. 4). Greenwich, CT: JAI.
Epstein, J. L. (1984). A longitudinal study of school and family effects on student development. In S. A. Mednick, M. Harway, & K. Finello (Eds.), *Handbook of longitudinal research* (Vol. 1). New York: Praeger.
Epstein, J. L., & McPartland, J. M. (1979). Authority structures. In H. Walberg (Ed.), *Educational environments and effects.* Berkeley, CA: McCutchan.

III-2/b
294. EYBERG, S. M., & ROBINSON, E. A. Dyadic Parent-Child Interaction Coding System (DPICS)

Avail: Select Press, P.O. Box 9838, San Rafael, CA 94912

Variables Measured: Content and style of interactions between parents and their young children

Type of Instrument: Observational behavior-coding system

Instrument Description: The DPICS is a behavior coding system for quantifying and classifying styles of interaction between parents and their young children in laboratory or clinical settings. It was designed for use in evaluating family functioning, and for monitoring progress made by parents in parent-training programs. Ratings are based on observations made during three 5-minute semistructured parent-child interactions. Interactions vary in amount of parental control elicited, child-directed play, parent-directed play, and cleanup. The DPICS assesses 29 categories of behavior, combined and classified into 10 mother and 2 child variables. Behaviors of parents that are directed toward their children are noted in terms of descriptive statements, reflective statements, descriptive/reflective questions, acknowledgment, physical positive, physical negative, labeled praise, unlabeled praise, critical statements, and direct and indirect commands. Children's behaviors are noted in terms of compliance, whining, crying, yelling, smart talk, being physically negative or destructive, and whether the child changes the activity. The system was designed for use with one family at a time, and is presumed not to be appropriate for group use.

Sample Items: Not applicable.

Comments: The authors indicate that use of the DPICS with families containing normal or conduct-problem children resulted in correct classification for 94% of the families. They also report that 61% of the variance in parental reports of behavior problems at home was related to DPICS scores. Interrater reliability for 244 5-minute observations was reported to be .91 and .92 for parent and child behaviors, respectively. Specific criteria for rating behaviors are provided in the manual.

References:

Eyberg, S. M., & Robinson, E. A. (1982). Parent-child interaction training: Effects on family functioning. *J Clin Child Psych, 11,* 130–137.

Robinson, E. A., & Eyberg, S. M. (1981). The Dyadic Parent-Child Interaction Coding System: Standardization and validation. *J Cons Clin, 49,* 245–250.

Webster-Stratton, C. (1984). Randomized trial of two parent-training programs for families with conduct-disordered children. *J Cons Clin, 52,* 666–678.

Webster-Stratton, C., & Hammond, M. (1988). Maternal depression and its relationship to life stress, perceptions of child behavior problems, parenting behaviors, and child conduct problems. *J Abn C Psy, 16,* 299–315.

III-2/II-3/b/P

295. FALENDER, C. A., & MEHRABIAN, A. Emotional Impact of Parental Attitudes

Avail: NAPS-3

Variables Measured: Attitudes of parents that induce pleasure, arousal, and dominant emotional reactions in their children

Type of Instrument: Self-report questionnaire

Instrument Description: The instrument is a 46-item scale utilizing a 9-point response format. Response options range from very strong agreement to very strong disagreement, and are coded from +4 to -4. The overall scale is composed of three subscales. These are designed to measure parental attitudes that induce emotional states of pleasure (18 items), arousal (12 items), and dominance (16 items) in children. The authors emphasize that scores obtained from parental responses on the three subtests represent pleasure, arousal, and dominance levels experienced by the child and not those experienced directly by the parent. Norms and scoring procedures are provided for each subscale. The items are designed to tap areas of parental attitudes that influence the emotional climate and state of mind of the child. The scale is intended for use with parents who have children up to the age of 15.

Sample Items:

(A)   Taking a few minutes to just be with my child helps me relax.
(B)   Children become too excited if they watch horror shows.
(C)   My child must try every food I serve.

Comments: The authors report that studies have been conducted to assess discriminant validity between the subscales, but that further research is required to fully establish convergent validity. KR-20 reliability coefficients of .79, .62, and .77 for the pleasure, arousal, and dominance scales, respectively, are reported.

Reference:

Falender, C. A., & Mehrabian, A. (1980). The emotional climate for children as inferred from parental attitudes. *Educ Psyc M, 40,* 1033–1044.

III-2/b/P
296. FIELD, T. Interaction Rating Scales (IRS)

Avail: Field, 1980, Ref.

Variables Measured: Behaviors exhibited by mothers and their infants during face-to-face interactions and during feeding

Type of Instrument: Behavior rating scale

Instrument Description: The IRS is a 2-part, 31-item multiple choice instrument for use in rating behaviors of mothers and their 4-month-old infants. Ratings are made on the basis of videotaped mother-child interactions. The two primary categories of interactions assessed with the IRS are face-to-face interactions between mother and child, and behaviors present during feeding. Each category contains separate items for assessing behaviors of infants and those of mothers. All items on which behaviors of infants are assessed are also used in the assessment of mothers, although scorable options differ between the two groups. Additional items were constructed for rating maternal behaviors to supplement the set used in assessing infants. Items take the form of descriptive phrases, with three options available for each item. Options are assigned values ranging from one to three. Scores within the four subsections are summed to arrive at totals for infants and mothers within each category.

Sample Items:

(A)   State rating
    1. predominantly drowsy
    2. somewhat drowsy
    3. predominantly alert
(B)   Physical activity
    1. frequent squirming/arching of back
    2. occasional squirming/arching of back
    3. relaxed body with cycling of limbs toward mother

Comments: The author reports interrater reliability coefficients for each item. Correlations range from .82 to .98. Means for individual items, as well as further detail regarding other instruments used in conjunction with the IRS, are contained in Field (1980).

References:

Field, T. (1980). Interactions of preterm and term infants with their lower and middle class teenage and adult mothers. In T. Field, S. Goldberg, D. Stern, & A. M. Sostek (Eds.), *High-risk infants and children: Adult and peer interactions* (pp. 113–132). New York: Academic Press.

Field, T., Sandberg, D., Garcia, R., Vega-Lahr, N., Goldstein, S., & Guy, L. (1985). Pregnancy problems, postpartum depression, and early mother-infant interactions. *Devel Psych, 21,* 1152–1156.

Field, T. M., Wildmayer, S. M., Stringer, S., & Ignatoff, E. (1980). Teenager, lower class, Black mothers and their preterm infants: An intervention and development follow-up. *Child Dev, 51,* 426–436.

Reis, J., Barbera-Stein, L., & Bennett, S. (1986). Ecological determinants of parenting. *Fam Relat, 35,* 547–554.

III-2/b/P
297. FIELD, T. Maternal Developmental Expectations and Childrearing Attitudes Survey (MDECAS)

Avail: 1980 Ref.

Variables Measured: Mothers' knowledge of appropriate ages for the achievement of various developmental milestones in children

Type of Instrument: Examination of knowledge

Instrument Description: The MDECAS is a 2-part, 21-item questionnaire examining mothers' knowledge of appropriate ages for a series of infant behaviors, and responses to difficult behaviors exhibited by the infant (crying, feeding, and so on). Part I, the Developmental Milestones Survey, consists of 8 items. Part II, the Childrearing Survey, contains 13 items designed to determine mothers' typical reactions to various situations and behaviors. Each item in the Developmental Milestones Survey is in the form of a question, beginning with one of two stems: "At what age do you think your baby . . . " or "At what age should your baby . . . " Behaviors listed in the instrument are appropriate for infants to exhibit initially at from one month to two years of age. Behaviors included in the MDECAS (and the appropriate age listed by the author for each activity) are smile (4 weeks), crawl (32 weeks), sit without support (32 weeks), pull self up using furniture (40 weeks), first independent steps (52 weeks), first real words (52 weeks), potty trained (2 years), and obey the word "no" (2 years). The questionnaire was designed for use in comparisons of teenage and older mothers. Administration is possible using either paper-and-pencil or interview formats.

Sample Items (Note: Sample items are from the Childrearing Survey):

(A) Let's say your baby is fed and dry. How much crying can you expect from that baby?
1) no crying at all
2) it depends on the baby

(B) A baby should be fed:
1) on a strict schedule
2) every few hours unless he's complaining of hunger

(C) What kind of punishment might you use:
1) scolding
2) shaking or spanking

Comments: The author developed the PAAS for a study utilizing several measures that compared teenage and older mothers. Several comparisons of data on these measures are contained in the references listed below.

References:

Field, T. (1980). Early development of infants born to teenage mothers. In K. Scott, T. Field, & E. Robertson (Eds.), *Teenage parents and their offspring* (pp. 145–175). New York: Grune & Stratton.

Field, T., Sandberg, D., Garcia, R., Vega-Lahr, N., Goldstein, S., & Guy, L. (1985). Pregnancy problems, postpartum depression, and early mother-infant interactions. *Devel Psych, 21,* 1152–1156.

Reis, J. (1988). Child-rearing expectations and developmental knowledge according to maternal age and parity. *Infant Ment Health J, 9,* 287–304.

III-2/II-3/b/C
298. FINE, M. A., MORELAND, J. R., & SCHWEBEL, A. I. Parent-Child Relationship Survey (PCRS)

Avail: 1983 Ref.

Variables Measured: Adults' perception of their parent-child relationships with regard to trust, communication, closeness, acceptance of the parent, anger at the parent, and respect, admiration, and value of the parent

Type of Instrument: Self-report questionnaire

Instrument Description: The Parent-Child Relationship Survey is designed to assess adults' perceptions of the quality of their relationships with their mothers and fathers. Separate scales are provided for assessing the current status of the relationship with each parent. The scale has also been used in assessing perceptions of relations with stepparents. Respondents are asked to rate the quality of their relationships on 24-items utilizing a 7-point Likert-style format. It is intended to be used with adults over the age of 18. However, applications with minors are possible. Scoring is accomplished by summing the values assigned to responses to each item. Scores for negatively worded items are reversed. Administration time is estimated to be approximately 15 minutes.

Sample Items:

(A)   How much time do you feel you spend with your father (mother)?
(B)   How easily do you accept the weaknesses in your mother (father)?
(C)   How close do you feel to your father (mother)?

Comments: The authors report that the PCRS has been used in discriminating between persons from divorced and intact families, as well as between intact and stepparent families. Separate factor analyses are reported by the authors for ratings of relationships with mothers and fathers. Each resulted in four-factor solutions with positive affect as the primary factor. Additional factors on the father scale were father involvement, communication, and anger. Additional factors on the mother scale were resentment/role confusion, identification, and communication. Cronbach's alpha for the total scales are reported by the authors to be .96 and .94 for the father and mother scales, respectively.

References:

Fine, M. A., Moreland, J. R., & Schwebel, A. I. (1983). Long-term effects of divorce on parent-child relationships. *Devel Psych, 19,* 703–713.
Fine, M. A., Worley, S., & Schwebel, A. I. (1985). The Parent-Child Relationship Survey: An examination of its psychometric properties. *Psychol Rep, 57,* 155–161.
Sauer, L., & Fine, M. A. (1988). Parent-child relationships in stepparent families. *J Fam Psy, 1,* 434–451.

III-2/IV-2/b
299. FOREHAND, R. L., PEED, S., ROBERTS, M., McMAHON, R. J., GRIEST, D. L., & HUMPHREYS, L. Behavioral Coding System

Avail: 1981 Ref.

Variables Measured: Parent's and child's behavior in a situation where noncompliance is expected

Type of Instrument: Behavior observation coding scheme

Instrument Description: This instrument, untitled by the authors, is a system for recording interactions between a parent and his or her child. While behaviors of either parent may be recorded, the system only allows for recordings related to one parent at a time. This system is used as part of a behavioral assessment package in order to develop proper clinical strategies for remediating problem behavior by the child. Participants have generally presented either their child, their family, or themselves for treatment regarding a specific problem with the child's behavior. The primary objective of this coding system is to develop an adequate understanding of all events that might influence the maintenance of the problem behavior. Observations are made in both clinic and home settings. A series of 10 × 3 grids are set up for recording observations. Six dimensions of parental behavior are recorded: (1) rewards; (2) attends, defined as parental phrases objectively describing the behavior of the child (e.g., standing in the center of the room); (3) questions; (4) commands, scored as alpha (orders and so on, where it is reasonable for the child to respond) or beta (commands where the child does not have a reasonable opportunity to respond), (5) warnings regarding noncompliance; and (6) time-out. Children's behaviors are recorded in terms of compliance, noncompliance, and whether or not the behavior was appropriate. Behavior is recorded over the course of 40 minutes, with groups of interactions noted on a continuous basis for 30 seconds at a time. Up to 10 interactions are documented during each 30-second segment.

Sample Items: Not applicable.

Comments: According to the authors, 25% of the home interactions are recorded by two coders. Interrater reliability, computed on the basis of these observations, is reported to be .75. It is also reported that behavior in the home and in the clinic are equally appropriate when developing intervention strategies.

References:

Forehand, R. L., King, H. E., Peed, S., & Yoder, P. (1975). Mother-child interactions: Comparisons of a non-compliant clinic group and a non-clinic group. *Behav Res T, 13,* 79–84.
Forehand, R. L., & McMahon, R. J. (1981). *Helping the noncompliant child: A clinician's guide to parent training.* New York: Guilford.
Humphreys, L., Forehand, R., McMahon, R., & Roberts, M. (1978). Parent behavioral

training to modify child noncompliance: Effects on untreated siblings. *J Beh Th Exp Psychi, 9,* 235–238.

Peed, S., Roberts, M., & Forehand, R. (1977). Evaluation of the effectiveness of a standardized parent training program in altering the interaction of mothers and their noncompliant children. *Behav Modif, 1,* 323–350.

III-2/b/C

300. GILBERT, L. A., & HANSON, G. R. Perceptions of Parental Role Scales (PPRS)

Avail: Marathon Consulting and Press, P.O. Box 09189, Columbus, OH 43209

Variables Measured: Parents' teaching of skills related to cognitive, emotional, and social growth, values, health- and hygiene-related issues, and basic needs of the child; parental interfacing between the child and social institutions and between the child and the family

Type of Instrument: Self-report questionnaire

Instrument Description: The PPRS is designed to measure perceived parental role responsibilities. It consists of 78 items assessing 13 parental responsibilities in three major domains: teaching the child, meeting the child's basic needs, and interfacing between the child and the family and other social institutions. Each scale contains from 5 to 7 items. Completion time is approximately 15 minutes. Respondents are asked to indicate how important they believe each item to be as a parental responsibility during the various stages of raising a child under normal conditions. Each item is rated on a 5-point Likert-style scale with response options ranging from *not at all important as a parental responsibility* to *very important as a parental responsibility.* Higher scores on each scale reflect greater perceived parental role responsibility.

Sample Items:

(A)   Teach child to be sensitive to the feelings of others.
(B)   Made child feel important.
(C)   Consult with teachers and child care providers about child's development.

Comments: Cronbach's alpha, as well as test-retest reliability information, was reported by the author. Alphas ranged from .81 to .91, with a median of .86 for the 5–7 item subscales. Test-retest coefficients ranged from .69 to .91, with a median of .82. Subscales were identified using a rational or intuitive model rather than through psychometric evaluations. The author reports that, due to the nature of the model, the scales should be related, and that factor analyses to reduce the number of subscales were thus deemed to be inappropriate. The PPRS has been utilized by the authors and their colleagues in several studies examining differences in role perceptions and activities among various populations. The scale is reproduced in Gilbert and Hanson (1983). It is also available, together with the manual, from Marathon Consulting (see above).

References:

Gilbert, L. A. (1985). *Men in dual-career families: Current realities and future prospects.* Hillsdale, NJ: Lawrence Erlbaum.

Gilbert, L. A., & Hanson, G. R. (1983). Perceptions of parental role responsibilities among working people: Development of a comprehensive measure. *J Mar Fam, 45,* 203–212.

III-2/b/a

301. GJERDE, P. F., BLOCK, J., & BLOCK, J. H. Family Interaction Q-Sort (FIQ)

Avail: NAPS-3

Variables Measured: Dimensions of interactions in parent-child and parent-parent relationships

Type of Instrument: Behaviors are rated using a Q-sort procedure

Instrument Description: The FIQ consists of 33 widely ranging statements about the interactive behavior of parents. It is a macroscopic instrument designed to assess parent-child (school-age and adolescent children) and parent-parent relationships in clinically unselected families in both dyadic and triadic family settings. Interactional sequences are observed and ratings of behaviors from those sequences are made by two judges acting independently. Statements, representing specific parental behaviors, are sorted into nine piles, ranging from most to least characteristic. The author indicates that the items do not stem from any single theoretical framework. Rather, an attempt was made to include important interactional dimensions from a variety of frameworks. Several items are reported to require high degrees of inferences.

Sample Items:

(A) Parent appears to be responsive to child's needs, opinions, and feelings.
(B) Parent seems at ease and relaxed in the situation, relates to child in an active secure manner.
(C) Parent tends to withdraw from participation with other family member(s), becomes inaccessible to others.

Comments: The author reports on one study where 18 judges were used to assess 44 family sessions. Judges were randomly assigned and paired, with two judges rating each set of interactions. Extensive training and monitoring of judges' ratings were utilized in an attempt to enforce reliable rating procedures. The average Spearman-Brown adjusted item reliability coefficients ranged from .40 to .74 for the 33 items, with an average item reliability of .59. Additionally, the authors report that reliabilities of scales based upon subsets of items are generally greater, ranging from .85 to .95.

References:

Block, J., Block, J. H., & Gjerde, P. F. (1988). Parental functioning and the home environment in families of divorce: Prospective and concurrent analyses. *J Am Acad Child Adol Psychi, 27*, 207–213.
Gjerde, P. F. (1986). The interpersonal structure of family interaction settings: Parent-adolescent relations in dyads and triads. *Devel Psych, 22*, 297–304.

III-2/b/C

302. GLEZER, H. Positive Attitudes Toward Living at Home

Avail: 1988 Ref.

Variables Measured: Adults' and adolescents' positive and negative evaluations of their families of origin

Type of Instrument: Self-report questionnaire

Instrument Description: This instrument is a 5-point, 6-item Likert-style questionnaire designed to assess perceptions held by adolescents and adults regarding the environment in their families of origin. Items are in the form of statements to which respondents indicate their level of agreement or disagreement. Response options range from *strongly disagree* to *strongly agree* and are coded from 1 to 5. Items deal with the following constructs: pleasantness of the living situation, ability to discuss matters, perception of acceptance, comfort, frequency of arguments, and overall quality of the environment. Item scores are summed to yield a total attitudes score. This instrument is probably most appropriate for use in investigations of family environments. It may also be useful as part of a larger battery of instruments evaluating families of origin with clinical samples. The scale was developed for use with Australian families and to date has only been used with that group. However, it is appropriate for use with any national or cultural population.

Sample Items:

(A) It is/was pleasant living with my parents and family.
(B) I can/could always discuss things that are/were important to me.
(C) Generally, there is/was nothing good about living at home.

Comments: Cronbach's alpha for the Positive Attitudes Toward Living at Home scale is reported in Amato (1988) to be .83.

Reference:

Amato, P. R. (1988). Parental divorce and attitudes toward marriage and family life. *J Mar Fam, 50,* 453–461.

III-2/b/C
303. GREENBERGER, E., GOLDBERG, W. A., & CRAWFORD, T. J.
Beliefs about the Consequences of Maternal Employment for Children (BACMEC)

Avail: 1988 Ref.

Variables Measured: Beliefs regarding positive and negative consequences related to the well-being of children resulting from maternal employment

Type of Instrument: Self-report questionnaire

Instrument Description: The BACMEC is a 24-item questionnaire designed to measure beliefs about the consequences for children of mothers' paid work outside the home. All items are in Likert format and are phrased as statements to which respondents are asked to *agree* or *disagree* along a 6-point continuum. Beliefs about both costs (11 items) and benefits (13 items) are included. Higher subscale scores indicate stronger beliefs in both potential costs and benefits of maternal employment. The 24 items taken together yield a total scale score that is scored in the direction of agreement with costs statements and disagreement with benefits statements. Either a sum or a mean score can be used. The authors report use of the BACMEC with college-age and adult populations.

Sample Items:

(A) Children are less likely to form a warm and secure relationship with a mother who is working full time.
(B) Children of working mothers are more likely than other children to experiment with drugs, alcohol and sex at an early age.

(C)   Children whose mothers work are more independent and able to do things for themselves.

Comments: The authors report that over two-thirds of the items correlate with the total score at least .50, and more than three-fourths of the items correlate at least .60 with their respective subscale totals. Cronbach's alpha is reported to be between .89 and .94 for total scores, from .88 to .94 for costs, and from .83 to .91 for benefits. Convergent, divergent, and concurrent validity analyses have been conducted by the authors. They report correlations of at least .55 between the BACMEC and scores on an attitude scale measuring opposition to maternal employment. Correlations with a measure of social desirability are reported to be less than .10 for the total score, as well as for scores obtained on subscales.

Reference:

Greenberger, E., Goldberg, W. A., Crawford, T. J., & Granger, J. (1988). Beliefs about the consequences of maternal employment for children. *Psych Wom Q, 12,* 35–59.

III-2/V-3/b/a/P

304. GUIDUBALDI, J., & CLEMINSHAW, H. K. Cleminshaw Guidubaldi Parent Satisfaction Scale

Avail: Original scale in 1985 Ref.; revised scale in 1988 Ref.

Variables Measured: Satisfaction in parental role with regard to support from spouse or ex-spouse, your relationship with the child, and your performance in the role of parent

Type of Instrument: Self-report questionnaire

Instrument Description: The original scale contained 50 items spread across five factors. The most recent version of this instrument, however, is a 45-item, three-factor questionnaire utilizing a Likert-style format with four response options per item. It is designed to assess parental satisfaction within the above-listed areas. Parents are asked to respond to each statement by circling a number from 1 to 4, representing options ranging from *strongly agree* to *strongly disagree.* Negative items are reverse-scored, after which items from subsections are combined to yield both total and subscale scores. Total administration time is approximately 10 minutes.

Sample Items:

(A)   I am happy with the amount of interest that my spouse/ex-spouse has shown in my children.
(B)   My children are usually a joy and fun to be with.
(C)   I am upset with the amount of yelling I direct toward the children.

Comments: The authors report that the current 45-item, three-factor solution resulted from factor analyses conducted on data obtained from a nationwide sample of 699 families randomly selected from 38 states in a study of the impact of divorce on children. Construct validity was assessed through comparisons of scores on this scale with those on three other measures of adjustment, satisfaction, and marital satisfaction. The authors report correlations with these three instruments in the .46 to .56 range. Cronbach's alpha is reported to have ranged from .82 to .96 for the three subscales. Two-year test-retest reliability is reported to range from .59 to .81.

References:

Cleminshaw, H. K., & Guidubaldi, J. (1981). *Assessing parent satisfaction*. Beverly Hills, CA: Sage.

Guidubaldi, J., & Cleminshaw, H. K. (1985). The development of the Cleminshaw Guidubaldi Parent Satisfaction Scale. *J Clin Child Psych, 14*, 293–298.

Guidubaldi, J., & Cleminshaw, H. K. (1988). Development and validation of the Cleminshaw Guidubaldi Parent Satisfaction Scale. In M. J. Fine (Ed.), *The second handbook on parent education: Contemporary perspectives*. San Diego, CA: Academic Press.

Guidubaldi, J., Cleminshaw, H. K., Perry, J. D., Nastasi, B. K., & Lightel, J. (1986). The role of selected family environment factors in children's post-divorce adjustment. *Fam Relat, 35*, 141–151.

III-2/e/P
305. HARRELL, J. E., & RIDLEY, C. A. Parent Satisfaction with Child Care Scale

Avail: 1975 Ref.

Variables Measured: Overall parental satisfaction with available child care services

Type of Instrument: Self-report questionnaire

Instrument Description: This instrument is a 5-point, 12-item questionnaire designed to assess perceptions regarding the quality of available substitute child care as well as the overall level of satisfaction with that care. While the scale was developed for use with mothers, slight modifications would also make it appropriate for administration to fathers and other primary caretakers. Items were constructed based on interactions with day-care center personnel, interviews with mothers using day-care facilities, and a study of what was termed "mother substitutes" by Perry (1961). Items are in the form of questions, and ask respondents to indicate the level of convenience, dependability, and so on they have experienced with specific types of substitute child care. The 5-point rating scale ranges from *extremely* to *not at all*. Scores are assigned such that high levels of the given construct result in high scores. An overall satisfaction score is generated by summing values associated with responses to each item.

Sample Items:

(A) In terms of convenience, would you say that (form of child care being used) is extremely convenient, very convenient, somewhat convenient, very inconvenient, or not at all convenient?

(B) In terms of having a good price, would you say that . . .

(C) In terms of being positively viewed by your child, would you say that . . .

Comments: The authors used this questionnaire as part of a larger package of instruments administered during 45-minute interviews with mothers. However, paper-and-pencil administration of the Parent Satisfaction with Child Care Scale would also be appropriate. Correlations are reported between maternal satisfaction with child care and maternal work satisfaction (.27), and with the quality of mother-child interactions (.07). It is further reported that 68.6% of employed mothers interviewed for their study indicated that satisfactory substitute child care positively influenced their work, with the remainder reporting no such influence.

References:

Anderson-Kulman, R. E., & Paludi, M. A. (1986). Working mothers and the family context: Predicting positive coping. *J Vocat Beh, 28,* 241–253.

Harrell, J. E., & Ridley, C. A. (1975). Substitute child care, maternal employment and the quality of mother-child interaction. *J Mar Fam, 37,* 556–564.

III-2/II-3/b

306. HAUSER, S. T., POWERS, S. I., WEISS-PERRY, B., FOLLANSBEE, D., RAJAPARK, D. C., & GREENE, W. M. Family Constraining and Enabling Coding System (CECS)

Avail: "Under contract" Ref.

Variables Measured: Interactions in which parents and adolescents actively resist differentiation or encourage and support expression of independent thoughts and perceptions by one another

Type of Instrument: Interaction coding system

Instrument Description: The CECS is a micro-analytic scheme for coding family communication. Parent and adolescent speeches are coded for affective and cognitive constraining categories and for affective and cognitive enabling categories. It is based on the psychoanalytically oriented theoretical work of Stierlin (1974), who addressed how family members respond to adolescents who are attempting to individuate from the family. Two parents and the target adolescent engage in a revealed differences task, using members' responses to the Kohlberg Moral Judgment Interview as the material to discuss. Differences are presented to the family so that the following order of coalitions is standardized: mother and child versus father, father and child versus mother, and mother and father versus child. Family members are given 10 minutes for each set of differences and are asked to defend their individual positions and then come to a consensus. This discussion is audiotaped and the transcription then becomes the basis for coding. Coding permits frequency analysis of communication events and sequences. Communication is coded according to 18 scales, each with conceptual and operational definitions. One primary—but not the sole—purpose of the coding system is to enable the researcher to characterize family patterns that are predictive of adolescent ego development and of progressions or regressions in ego development.

Sample Items: Not applicable.

Comments: The authors report that reliabilities for the constraining and enabling codes have been calculated both in terms of percentage of exact agreement (range: 84% to 99%) and Cohen's kappa (range: .42 to .93). Reliabilities for discourse change codes are reported to range from 95% to 98% agreement, and kappa, from .45 to .73. Several studies are reported in which construct validity of the CECS has been investigated (see references below).

References:

Hauser, S. T., Houlihan, J., Powers, S. I., Jacobson, A. M., Noam, G. G., Weiss-Perry, B., & Follansbee, D. (1987). Interaction sequences in families of psychiatrically hospitalized and nonpatient adolescents. *Psychiatry, 50,* 308–319.

Hauser, S. T., Jacobson, A. M., Wertlieb, D., Weiss-Perry, B., Follansbee, D., Wolfsdorf, J. I., Herskowitz, R. D., Houlihan, J., & Rajapark, D. C. (1986). Children with recently diagnosed diabetes: Interactions within their families. *Health Psyc, 5,* 273–296.

Hauser, S. T., with Powers, S. I., & Noam, G. G. (in press). *Separating and connecting: Teenage paths of development in families.* New York: Free Press.

Hauser, S. T., Powers, S. I., Noam, G. G., Jacobson, A. M., Weiss, B., & Follansbee, D. J. (1984). Familial contexts of adolescent ego development. *Child Dev, 55,* 195–213.

III-2/II-3/IV-2/b/P

307. HAZZARD, A., CHRISTENSEN, A., & MARGOLIN, G. Parent Perception Inventory (PPI)

Avail: 1983 Ref.

Variables Measured: Children's positive and negative perceptions of their mothers and fathers

Type of Instrument: Orally administered self-report questionnaire

Instrument Description: The PPI is a structured interview and self-report rating scale designed to tap children's and adolescents' perceptions of parental behaviors. For each parent, the child rates how often the parent engages in nine positive and nine negative behavior classes. Items are read aloud to the child, who responds by rating the parent's behavior on a 5-point scale ranging from *never* to *a lot.* The positive behavior classes are positive reinforcement, comfort, talk time, involvement in decision making, time together, positive evaluation, allowing independence, assistance, and nonverbal affection. Negative classes are privilege removal, criticism, command, physical punishment, yelling, threatening, time-out, nagging, and ignoring. The child rates the mother's behaviors and then the father's behaviors. After each item is read, a list of examples are given until the child is thought to understand the question. The answer sheet contains columns of response options, each with a picture of a flask-shaped object at the top. The flasks range from clear to completely darkened in. The extent to which the flask is darkened corresponds to the response option. In this way, small children are able to comprehend the options available to them in rating the behaviors of their parents. Values assigned to specific item responses are summed on each of the four subscales (mother positive, mother negative, father positive, father negative) in order to arrive at total subscale scores. Administration time is approximately 10–15 minutes.

Sample Items:

(A) How often does your mom (dad) take away things when you misbehave (like not letting you watch TV or ride your bike or stay up late or eat dessert)?

(B) How often does your mom (dad) thank you for doing things (tell you when she likes what you did, give you something, let you do something special when you're good)?

(C) How often does your mom (dad) talk to you (listen to you, have a good conversation with you)?

Comments:; The authors report that internal consistency coefficients for the four subscales are .84 (mother positive), .78 (mother negative), .88 (father positive), and .80 (father negative). Children's self-concept scores correlated positively with mother's and father's positive PPI scores, and negatively with negative PPI scores. Research conducted by the authors also found that, as compared to control children, children from distressed clinic families rated both parents lower in positive and higher in negative behavior.

Reference:

Hazzard, A., Christensen, A., & Margolin, G. (1983). Children's perceptions of parental behaviors. *J Abn C Psy, 11,* 49–60.

III-2/II-3/b/g/C

308. HEILBRUN, A. B., Jr. Parent-Child Interaction Rating Scales

Avail: 1964 & 1976 Refs.

Variables Measured: Adolescents' perceptions of their parents' behaviors toward and feelings for them

Type of Instrument: Self-report questionnaire

Instrument Description: This instrument is an 5-point, 8-item Likert-type questionnaire designed to assess adolescents' perceptions of their parents' nurturing attitudes, feelings, and behaviors toward them. Response options range from 1 to 5, with each point anchored by a descriptive phrase. Respondents are instructed to indicate their perceptions of each of their parents with regard to every item. The eight modes of nurturing examined by this instrument include (1) affection I (felt affection), (2) affection II (expressed affection), (3) approval of adolescent's behavior, (4) sharing feelings and experiences, (5) concrete giving, (6) encouragement, (7) trust placed in adolescent by parent, and (8) sense of security with parents. Scores are summed across all items for ratings of each parent. Higher scores are indicative of greater perceived nurturance. While the exact wording of items, as well as the 5-point scale anchors, are not presented in either reference, sufficient descriptive information is contained such that reasonably close items could be constructed.

Sample Items:

(A) My mother/father trusts me as a family member.
(B) My mother/father shares his/her personal feelings and experiences with me.
(C) I feel secure in my relationship with my mother/father.

Comments: The author found that mothers received a greater proportion of high nurturance scores than did fathers. It was also noted that mothers tended to be rated higher by their sons, while fathers were given higher nurturance ratings by their daughters. Scores obtained in ratings of fathers and mothers were reported to correlate .68 for males and .41 for females.

References:

Ellis, G. J., Thomas, D. L., & Rollins, B. C. (1976). Measuring parental support: The interrelationship of three measures. *J Mar Fam, 38*, 713–722.

Heilbrun, A. B., Jr. (1964). Parental model attributes, nurturant reinforcement, and consistency of behaviors in adolescents. *Child Dev, 35*, 151–167.

Heilbrun, A. B., Jr., Bateman, C. P., Heilbrun, K. L., & Herson, A. M. (1981). Retrospections of mother: The effect of time interval upon perception. *J Genet Psy, 138*, 133–142.

Nowicki, S., Jr., & Segal, W. (1974). Perceived parental characteristics, locus of control orientation and behavioral correlates of locus of control. *Devel Psych, 10*, 33–37.

III-2/d/e/P

309. HELFER, R. E., HOFFMEISTER, J. K., & SCHNEIDER, C. Michigan Screening Profile of Parenting (MSPP)

Avail: Test Analysis and Development Corp., 2400 Park Lake Dr., Boulder, CO 80301

Variables Measured: Parents' perceptions of childhood experiences, appropriate behavior for their children, and current interactions with family and friends

Type of Instrument: Self-report questionnaire

Instrument Description: The MSPP is a four-part questionnaire designed to provide mental health professionals with assistance in determining parenting beliefs and childhood perceptions of parents (or prospective parents). This information may then be used in discussing and/ or remediating parenting strategies. Section A of the questionnaire asks for varying types of demographic information. Responses to items on Section B (30 items) generate four scale scores: emotional needs met (ENM), relationship with parents (RWP), expectations of children (EOC), and coping (COP). ENM was developed to evaluate whether the childhood environment of the adult was physically, developmentally, and/or emotionally punitive. RWP items evaluate levels of love and affection with one's parents. The EOC subscale is used to examine respondents' beliefs that young children should adhere to their parents' wishes. COP examines the appropriateness of current coping strategies for family-related crises. Sections C (18 items) and D (9 items) are geared toward adults with and without children, respectively. With the exception of 1 item in Section C, all items contained within Sections B, C, and D are answered according to a 7-point Likert-type format according to the level of agreement or disagreement with each statement. In scoring the MSPP, where responses are generally consistent, those specific responses that fail to converge with overall response indications are discarded. In this way, the authors hope to control for person-item interactions, carelessness, and misunderstanding. Where responses are inconsistent on specific subscales, scores for those subscales are not computed. An overall inconsistent response set, however, is clinically interpreted. Computerized scoring is available only through the publisher. Scoring keys are not available.

Sample Items:

(A)   No one has ever really listened to me.
(B)   When I am very upset, my partner understands and tries to be helpful.
(C)   Children should know, even before the age of 2 years, what parents want them to do.

Comments: Correlations between the four Section B measures are reported to range from .05 to .43. The authors report on studies investigating the ability of MSPP scores to discriminate parents known to have difficulty interacting with their children from those with no reported difficulties. Known problem parents were correctly identified in 83% of 215 cases. Nonproblem parents were correctly identified in 77% of 186 cases.

References:

Avison, W. R., Turner, R. J., & Noh, S. (1986). Screening for problem parenting: Preliminary evidence on a promising instrument. *Child Abuse & Neglect, 10,* 157–170.
Helfer, R., Hoffmeister, J. K., & Schneider, C. (1978). *Report on the research using the Michigan Screening Profile of Parenting (MSPP).* Boulder, CO: Test Analysis and Development Corporation.

III-2/II-5/a/P

310. HEMING, G., COWAN, P. A., & COWAN, C. P. Ideas About Parenting

Avail: NAPS-3

Variables Measured: Parenting ideologies and marital partners' agreement related to child rearing

Type of Instrument: Self-report questionnaire

Instrument Description: This instrument was designed to examine child-rearing attitudes of marital couples. Two versions are available: a 56-item questionnaire intended for use by parents of children 0 to 18 months and an 80-item questionnaire with separate forms for use with parents of 3- to 4- or 3- to 5-year-old children. Both versions contain a 10-item subset designed to measure parents' expectations regarding maturity levels of their children. This subscale asks respondents to indicate the age at which they believe a number of behaviors should occur (e.g., "stop sucking thumb," "go to neighbors without supervision"). For the remainder of the questionnaire, respondents are asked to indicate their level of agreement or disagreement with various statements. These remaining items utilize a 9-point Likert-type response format. In addition to indicating their own beliefs, parents are also asked to indicate the likely responses of their spouses. This allows for scoring according to individual beliefs, as well as perceived and actual discrepancies between parents. The authors indicate that many of the items for this instrument were drawn directly from previously developed measures of child-rearing ideologies (e.g., Baumrind, 1974; Cohler, Weiss, & Grunebaum, 1970).

Sample Items:

(A) When a child is called, he or she should come immediately.
(B) A six month old baby can tell you exactly what he or she wants if you watch and listen.
(C) I encourage my child always to do his or her best.

Comments: The authors indicate that preliminary factor analyses have identified three factors: (1) authoritarian control, (2) child-centeredness, and (3) permissive-protectiveness. Split-half and alpha reliabilities for these factors are reported in the .60 to .72 range. The child-centeredness subscale is reported to be useful in predicting fathers' involvement in child care. The authors also indicate that perceived agreement in parenting ideologies is useful in predicting adaptation during the transition to parenthood.

Reference:

Cowan, C. P., Cowan, P. A., Heming, G., Garrett, E., Coysh, W. S., Curtis-Boles, H., & Boles, A. J., III (1985). Transitions to parenthood: His, hers and theirs. *J Fam Iss, 6,* 451–481.

III-2/IV-1/b/P
311. HEREFORD, C. F. Parental Attitude Survey Scales

Avail: 1963 Ref.

Variables Measured: Parental attitudes regarding own role, parent-child interactions, and child's behaviors

Type of Instrument: Self-report questionnaire

Instrument Description: This instrument is a 5-point, 75-item Likert-type questionnaire designed to measure parental attitudes in five areas: confidence in the parental role, causation of the child's behavior, acceptance of the child's behavior and feelings, mutual understanding, and mutual trust. An original pool of over 200 items was generated through an examination of the available literature, supplemented where needed by original items written by the project staff. Judges' ratings reduced this number to 125, with the final 75 items being selected based on psychometric considerations following administration to a sample of parents. All but 23 of the final 75 items appeared in previous instruments. A total of 52 items were taken from the Parental Attitude Research Instrument (Schaefer & Bell, 1958; 39 items), Methods for Community Mental Health Research (Glidewell, Mensh, Domke, Gildea, & Buchmueller, 1957; 5 items), Family Problems Scale (Loevinger & Sweet, unpublished; 4 items), Parent Attitude Survey (Pierce-Jones, unpublished; 3 items), and Parent Attitude Questionnaire (Shapiro, unpublished; 1 item). Items are scored according to level of agreement or disagreement, ranging from *strongly agree* (+2) to *strongly disagree* (-2). Item values within subscales are summed to arrive at composite scores.

Sample Items:

(A)   I feel I am faced with more problems than most parents.
(B)   Some children are so naturally headstrong that a parent can't really do much about them.
(C)   The earlier a child is weaned from its emotional ties to its parents the better it will handle its own problems.

Comments: Split-half reliabilities for the five subscales are reported in the original reference and range from .68 to .86 with a mean of .80. Interscale correlations are reported to be in the .33 to .62 range. Cronbach's alpha for the subscales is reported by Roosa and Vaughan (1984) to be in the .71 to .86 range.

References:

Hampson, R. B., Schulte, M. A., & Ricks, C. C. (1983). Individual versus group training for foster parents: Efficiency/effectiveness evaluations. *Fam Relat, 32,* 191–201.
Hereford, C. F. (1963). *Changing parental attitudes through group discussion.* Austin: University of Texas Press.
Roosa, M. W., & Vaughan, L. (1984). A comparison of teenage and older mothers with preschool age children. *Fam Relat, 33,* 259–265.
Summerlin, M. L., & Ward, G. R. (1978). The effect of parental participation in a parent group on a child's self-concept. *J Psychol, 100,* 227–232.

III-2/IV-2/b/P
312. HONIG, A. S., & CALDWELL, B. M. Implicit Parental Learning Theory Interview (IPLET)

Avail: Syracuse University, Center for Instructional Development, 111 Waverly Ave., Syracuse, NY 13244

Variables Measured: Methods used by parents to encourage and discourage typical behaviors of preschool-aged children

Type of Instrument: Behavior observation scale

Instrument Description: The IPLET is a 45-item inventory utilized during structured interviews of parents and their preschool-aged children. Five forms of the IPLET are available, one each for ages 1, 2, 3, 4, and 5–6. The form appropriate for use with parents of 5- to 6-year-old children contains 20 items rather than the usual 45 items. The inventory is administered as a structured interview designed to assess (1) the array of behaviors that a parent would either encourage or discourage and (2) the type of teaching technique that would be employed to produce either response stabilization or change. Areas are assessed via verbal reports of the caretaker. The instrument is designed such that data from (1), above, will indicate parental values for developmental achievements, while also providing an index of indifference about the child's performance. Responses are coded in terms of "what child does" and "what mother does." Data from (2), above, are intended to reflect types of teaching techniques likely to be used by the parent. Inferences are drawn from this latter purpose regarding the parent's theory about how children learn. Coding of responses involves a determination of whether a parent tends to rely on direct manipulation of the environment (e.g., provide or deprive of privileges, physical punishment), symbolic manipulations (e.g., promises or threats, and commands), or absence of response. Scoring results in a profile of the frequency with which different types of teaching techniques are employed. Administration time is approximately 45 minutes.

Sample Items:

(A)　(Age 1 year) Climbs out of bed after being put to bed.
(B)　(Age 3 years) Says "please" when he asks for things.
(C)　(Age 5–6 years) Finishes puzzles or games he tries out on his own.

Comments: The IPLET was first developed in the mid-1960s. It may be appropriate for both research use and clinical evaluation. The authors report that intercoder reliability of maternal responses quickly reaches the level of .90 or above.

References:

Gunn, P., & Berry, P. (1985). Down's Syndrome temperament and maternal response to descriptions of child behavior. *Devel Psych, 21,* 842–847.

Honig, A. S., Caldwell, B. M., & Tannenbaum, J. (1970). Patterns of information processing used by and with young children in a nursery school setting. *Child Dev, 41,* 1045–1065.

Honig, A. S., Tannenbaum, J., & Caldwell, B. M. (1973). Maternal behavior in verbal report and in laboratory observation: A methodological study. *Child Psychi Hum Dev, 3,* 216–230.

III-2/IV-2/b/C

313. INAZU, J. K., & FOX, G. L. MDREL: Mother-Daughter Relationship

Avail: 1980 Ref.

Variables Measured: Daughter's assessment of overall quality of the mother-daughter relationship

Type of Instrument: Self-report questionnaire

Instrument Description: MDREL is a 9-item, Likert-type scale designed to measure the mother's role as a source of socioemotional support. The index represents the daughter's assessment of the overall quality of one dimension of her relationship with her mother. Areas evaluated include the daughter's perception of the levels of open communication, uncertainty, and ambiguity in defining the mother-daughter relationship. High overall scores indicate more positive relationships. Administration time is approximately 1–5 minutes.

Sample Items:

(A)　My mother doesn't seem to trust me.
(B)　I tell my mother only those things I think she can handle without getting upset.
(C)　I never know whether my mother really loves me or not.

Comments: The authors report that MDREL was derived from a factor analysis of 23 initial statements. It has been used in investigations of mother-daughter communication about sexuality and the daughter's sexual status, as well as daughter's desired age at marriage and intended family size.

References:

Fox, G. L., Fox, B. R., & Frohardt-Lane, K. (1982). Socialization for fertility. In G. L. Fox (Ed.), *The childbearing decision: Fertility attitudes and behavior* (pp. 81–102). Beverly Hills, CA: Sage.

Fox, G. L., & Inazu, J. K. (1980). Patterns and outcomes of mother-daughter communication about sexuality. *J Soc Issue, 36,* 7–29.

Inazu, J. K., & Fox, G. L. (1980). Maternal influence on the sexual behavior of teen-age daughters: Direct and indirect sources. *J Fam Iss, 1,* 81–102.

III-2/IV-2/b/P

314. ITKIN, W. Intra-Family Attitude Scales

Avail: 1967 Ref.

Variables Measured: Acceptance-rejection of children, dominance-submissiveness of parental control, and favorable attitude of parents and children for each other

Type of Instrument: Self-report questionnaire

Instrument Description: The Intra-Family Attitude Scales are a series of five questionnaires designed for measuring attitudes of family members toward each other. The five instruments assess (1) opinions regarding the bringing up of children, (2) opinions regarding the disciplining of children, (3) attitudes toward discipline exercised by parents, (4) parental judgment regarding a particular child, and (5) children's attitudes toward their parents. Individual scales vary in length from 30 to 37 items, with most utilizing 3-point or 5-point response formats. Statements are generally responded to in terms of intensity of agreement. Some scales, however, also rely on *true/false* and multiple-choice items. Scale scores are derived by summing values associated with individual responses within scales. Scales are scored such that higher totals indicate more favorable attitudes. The scales were constructed in 1949, with language appropriate to the times. Thus, while the scales have been in use within the past decade, individual investigators have, at times, elected to make changes in the ways in which certain items are stated.

Sample Items (Note: All sample items are from opinions regarding the bringing up of children):

(A)　A parent should look after his (or her) young child both at school and at play.

(B)　If parents can afford to do so, they should send a child to a military or boarding school, where he (or she) could obtain the proper training with the least inconvenience to the parents.

(C)　A family should move out of an unwholesome neighborhood for the sake of the children even if such a move would make it necessary for the father to travel farther to work.

Comments: Split-half reliability for the various instruments is reported to range from .68 to .95. Available information regarding validity of the scales indicates that self-ratings correlated from -.70 to -.80 with attitudes toward parents, -.62 with attitude scores of parents, -.26 with attitudes regarding disciplining of children and from .63 to .67 with attitudes toward discipline exercised by parents.

References:

Drill, R. L. (1986). Young adult children of divorced parents: Depression and the perception of loss. *J Divorce, 10*(1/2), 169–187.

Itkin, W. (1952). Some relationships between intra-family attitudes and premarital attitudes toward children. *J Genet Psy, 80,* 221–252.

Shaw, M. E., & Wright, J. M. (1967). *Scales for the measurement of attitudes.* New York: McGraw-Hill.

Smith, R. M., & Walters, J. (1978). Delinquent and non-delinquent males' perceptions of their fathers. *Adolescence, 13,* 21–28.

III-2/b

315. JACOB, T., & SEILHAMER, R. A. Parent-Child Areas of Change Questionnaire (PC-ACQ)

Avail: NAPS-3

Variables Measured: Degree to which the responding parent or child desires change in a range of relationship-relevant behaviors

Type of Instrument: Self-report questionnaire

Instrument Description: The PC-ACQ was developed for the purpose of evaluating parent-child relationships and identifying problem areas. It is adapted from the Areas of Change Questionnaire (Weiss, Hops, & Patterson, 1973). Respondents rate items that are assumed to be behavioral indicators of parent-adolescent conflict. The 32 items in the child form are geared toward preadolescents and adolescents, and are written at the fifth-grade reading level. Respondents indicate their desire for change on a 7-point Likert-style scale ranging from *much less* (-3) to *no change* (0), to *much more* (+3). A total score is obtained by summing the absolute values of responses. The parent version of the scale uses the same format and contains 34 items. The PC-ACQ is designed to provide normative data on parent-child relationship satisfaction and information about problem areas, to serve as a criterion measure for the selection and classification of distressed and nondistressed families, and as a method for stimulating laboratory discussions of family-relevant issues. In clinical settings the questionnaire is intended to provide a quantitative measure of distress, target problem areas for intervention, and provide a pre- and postintervention measure for evaluating therapeutic effects. Administration time is approximately 10–15 minutes.

Sample Items:

(A)   I want my child to keep his/her room clean and neat.
(B)   I want my child to spend time at home with the family.
(C)   I want my father/mother to let me dress the way I like.

Comments: The authors report on a study in which families with alcoholic, depressed, or normal fathers were compared. They indicate that desire for change (DC) scores for father-child relationships differed among children of distressed (alcoholic or depressed) and nondistressed families. Scores for mother-child relationships differentiated mothers in the group with alcoholic fathers from others. Mothers in depressed and normal groups were reported not to differ significantly. The relationship of PC-ACQ scores to those on the Child Behavior Checklist (Achenbach, 1978) and the Dyadic Adjustment Scale (Spanier, 1976) were also investigated. Cronbach's alpha for various dyadic pairings is reported to range from .91 to .94.

Reference:

Jacob, T., & Seilhamer, R. A. (1985). Adaptation of the Areas of Change Questionnaire for parent-child relationship assessment. *Am J Fam Th, 13*(2), 28–38.

III-2/II-1/b/C
316. KOHN, M. L. Index of Parental Values

Avail: 1977 Ref.

Variables Measured: Parents' valuation of characteristics more or less desirable for a child the same age and gender as one of their own

Type of Instrument: Structured interview

Instrument Description: Parents are presented with a series of 13 behaviors and personality characteristics. Each parent is instructed to respond to each of four questions regarding the desirability of these items for children the same age and gender as one of their own children. The 13 items refer to good manners, effort at succeeding, honesty, being neat and clean, exercising good sense and sound judgment, self-control, acting like a boy or girl should, getting along with peers, obeying parents, responsibility, consideration, being interested in how and why things happen, and being a good student. The four questions ask parents to indicate the most, and then the three most, desirable, and least, and then the three least important, characteristics from the list. Following parental ratings, scores are assigned to items according to the following criteria: 5 = *the most valued of all;* 4 = *one of the three most valued, but not the most valued;* 3 = *not valued or devalued;* 2 = *one of the three least important, but not the least important;* and 1 = *the least important of all items.* Factor scores for self-direction/conformity and maturity/immaturity are assigned on the basis of individual item scores.

Sample Items:

(A) Which three qualities listed on this card would you say are the most desirable for a (boy, girl) of (child's) age to have?
(B) Which one of these three is the most desirable of all?
(C) All of these may be desirable, but could you tell me which three you consider least important?

Comments: The studies upon which this instrument is based were initiated during the late 1950s. The scale was originally published in 1969 by Dorsey in the first edition of Kohn's 1977 book. It has since been translated into several languages, contained as part of several studies related to parental values, factorially and longitudinally studied and modified (Schaefer & Edgerton, 1985). It appears as item 128 in both the 1969 and the 1977 editions of *Class and Conformity.* The author reports that scoring of the index has evolved from percentage distributions, to ordinary factor analyses, to confirmatory factor analyses, and from models for one family member to models that include data from both parents and one child.

References:

Kohn, M. L. (1977). *Class and conformity: A study in values* (2nd ed.). Chicago: University of Chicago Press.

Kohn, M. L., & Schooler, C. (1983). *Work and personality: An inquiry into the impact of social stratification.* Norwood, NJ: Ablex.

Kohn, M. L., Slomczynski, K. M., & Schoenbach, C. (1986). Social stratification and the transmission of values in the family: A cross-national assessment. *Sociol Forum, 1,* 73–102.

Schaefer, E. S., & Edgerton, M. (1985). Parent and child correlates of parental modernity. In I. E. Sigel (Ed.), *Parental belief systems* (pp. 287–318). Hillsdale, NJ: Lawrence Erlbaum.

III-2/b/P
317. LAWTON, J. T., COLEMAN, M., BOGER, R., GALEJS, I., PEASE, D., PORESKY, R., & LOONEY, E. NC-158 Q-Sort Inventory of Parenting Behaviors

Avail: Institute for Family and Child Study, Michigan State University, East Lansing, MI 48824

Variables Measured: Parents' actual and ideal beliefs about child rearing

Type of Instrument: Q-sort

Instrument Description: The instrument is composed of 72 statements of parenting behaviors with 18 statements in each of four domains of children's development: physical, intellectual, social, and emotional. The entire procedure is completed twice: first as a measure of actual, and then as a measure of ideal, development. Administration time for each perspective (actual and ideal) is approximately 15–20 minutes. Each item expresses a particular parenting behavior related to one of the four domains. Items are written in what is designed as a theoretically neutral form. Respondents are asked to prioritize the collection of statements about characteristics of parenting behaviors into a designated number of categories on a specified dimension from most to least like how I raise my child. A detailed manual for the instrument is available through the above-listed source.

Sample Items:

(A)   I encourage my child to use his or her hands skillfully (e.g., reach for a rattle or color or cut with scissors).
(B)   I talk to my child about how things look or how things happen.
(C)   I encourage my child to share toys.

Comments: The current set of items was developed from content analyses conducted on an initial pool of 158 items. The initial items were examined by a group of nine experts in the area of child development and family studies. Items included in the final version of the instrument were judged to exhibit clarity and singularity in describing an important characteristic of child development in the domain to which they belonged. Test-retest reliability is reported by the authors to be .72.

References:

Galejs, I., & Pease, D. (1986). Parenting beliefs and locus of control orientation. *J Psychol, 120,* 501–510.

Lawton, J. T., & Coleman, M. (1984). Parents' perceptions of parenting. *Infant Ment Health J, 4,* 352–361.

Lawton, J. T., Coleman, M., Boger, R., Pease, D., Galejs, I., Poresky, R., & Looney, E. (1983). A Q-sort assessment of parents' beliefs about parenting in six midwestern states. *Infant Ment Health J, 4,* 344–351.

Schuler, S. G., Lawton, J. T., Fowell, N., & Madsen, M. K. (1984). A study of parents' perceptions of actual and ideal child-rearing practices. *J Genet Psy, 145,* 77–87.

III-2/IV-2/b/P
318. LESLIE, L. A. Attempt to Influence Parental Reaction to Dating Relationship Scale (AIPRDR)

Avail: NAPS-3

Variables Measured: Young adults' attempts to influence their parents' impressions of their dating relationships

Type of Instrument: Self-report questionnaire

Instrument Description: The AIPRDR consists of 24 items assessing behaviors children have engaged in to manage parents' impressions of a current dating relationship. It is designed to be used as a companion instrument to the Parental Reaction to Dating Relationship Scale (PRDR) (Leslie, Huston, & Johnson, 1986). Both instruments can be used with parents and their children. An alternate means of evaluation would be for the PRDR to be administered to parents and for the AIPRDR to be used with their dating children. Four categories of behaviors are assessed by the AIPRDR: verbal statements, increasing the amount of time spent together by the partner and parent(s), suggesting ways to the partner that he or she might impress parent(s), and engaging in behaviors designed to please parent(s). The scale is designed to provide an index of behaviors engaged in by a child to influence his or her parents' perceptions of the dating relationship. Respondents are asked separately to indicate which behaviors have been engaged in by the child toward each parent. Instructions can be specified to indicate whether the behaviors have occurred within a specified time period. A score of 1 is given if a parent has engaged in a behavior and 0 if the behavior has not occurred. Scores for each of the four specific types of behaviors, as well as the total scale, can be summed to arrive at composite scores.

Sample Items:

(A)   Have partner visit with my parent before or after our dates.
(B)   Talk about my partner's family life and background with my parent.
(C)   Ask partner to do special things for my parent (e.g., send birthday card).

Comments: Items were generated by 106 undergraduate students who were asked to identify things they have done or would do if they wanted their parents to have a good impression of a relationship or a partner.

Reference:

Leslie, L. A., Huston, T. L., & Johnson, M. P. (1986). Parental reaction to dating relation-
    ships: Do they make a difference? *J Mar Fam, 48,* 57–66.

III-2/IV-2/b/C
319. LESLIE, L. A. Parental Reaction to Dating Relationship Scale (PRDR)

Avail: NAPS-3

Variables Measured: Ways in which parents attempt to influence dating relationships of their children

Type of Instrument: Self-report questionnaire

Instrument Description: The PRDR consists of two scales measuring approving (39 items) and disapproving (33 items) parental behaviors relative to a child's dating relationships. It was designed to be used as a companion instrument to the Attempt to Influence Parental Reaction to Dating Relationship Scale (AIPRDR) (Leslie, Huston, & Johnson, 1986). Each scale assesses six categories of behaviors: verbal statements, inclusion or exclusion in group activities, facilitation or interference with opportunities for interaction, promises or threats regarding resources, development or avoidance of a personal relationship, and showing respect or lack of respect for the child. The scale is designed to provide an index of behaviors engaged in

by a parent to influence the dating relationships of their children. The PRDR can be administered to parents, children, or both. Parents are asked to indicate if they have engaged in each
of the 72 behaviors relative to a particular dating partner. Where children serve as respondents, they are asked to indicate which behaviors have been engaged in by their parents. The
questionnaire is answered separately for each parent. Instructions can be specified to indicate
whether the behaviors have occurred within a specified time period. A score of 1 is given if a
parent has engaged in a behavior and 0 if the behavior has not occurred. The scores for
approving and disapproving behaviors, as well as the six specific types of behaviors, can be
summed to arrive at composite scores.

Sample Items:

(A)   Invite my partner to share in activities such as fishing, tennis, shopping (with or
      without me).
(B)   Talk about other people I could date.
(C)   Relay phone messages to me from my partner.

Comments: Items were generated by 106 undergraduate students who were asked to
identify things done by their parents to indicate approval or disapproval of a dating relationship or a dating partner. The resulting items were administered to a second undergraduate
sample. Correlations were computed between each of the six subscales and total approval or
disapproval scores minus the scores from that subscale. Correlations for approving behavior
ranged from .60 to .86, and from .18 to .53 for disapproving scores. The correlation between
approval and disapproval scores was .00 for mothers and .10 for fathers.

Reference:

Leslie, L. A., Huston, T. L., & Johnson, M. P. (1986). Parental reaction to dating relationships: Do they make a difference? *J Mar Fam, 48,* 57–66.

III-2/II-3/b
320. LINEHAN, M. M., PAUL, E., & EGAN, K. J. Parent Affect Test
(PAT)

Avail: 1983 Ref.

Variables Measured: Dimensions of parental anger and pleasure toward their children

Type of Instrument: Self-report questionnaire

Instrument Description: The PAT is a 40-item questionnaire designed to assess areas in
which parents are likely to feel positively or negatively toward one of their children. The
instrument is equally divided between positive and negative circumstances, with parents asked
to respond to each in terms of six bipolar scales. The scales include (1) *feel angry . . . feel
pleased;* (2) *feel bad . . . feel good;* (3) *feel tense . . . feel relaxed;* (4) *want to hit/spank . . .
want to hug/kiss;* (5) *want to yell . . . want to praise;* and (6) *want to send child to room . . .
want to be with child.* The PAT was originally envisioned as a test of anger-eliciting situations.
Responses of parents, however, resulted in the construction of an additional positive set of
items. In developing the test, a sample of 244 fathers and 323 mothers were asked to list all
situations they could remember in which one of their children did something either upsetting
or positive. Over 1,000 situations were generated, from which 164 were retained. The final
selection of 20 positive and 20 negative items, referred to as PATp (pleased) and PATa (anger)
resulted from further pilot testing of the remaining situations, followed by item analyses.
Scores are determined by averaging responses on an 8-point continuum to the six bipolar

scales, and then summing these averages across the 20 PATa and 20 PATp items. Thus scores could range from 20 to 160 for each of the two PAT scales.

Sample Items:

(A)   My child gets into some things that don't belong to him/her.
(B)   I repeat more than once what I want my child to do, and he/she still doesn't do it.
(C)   My child shares a favorite possession with a friend.

Comments: The authors indicate that Cronbach's alpha for the PATa and PATp was found to be .92 and .96, respectively. It is also reported that mothers scored higher than did fathers on the PATp, but that no significant differences were detected on the PATa. Correlations are reported between PATa scores and self-reports of anger (.76, mothers; .27, fathers), self-reported intense or frequent pleasure (-.51, mothers; -.50, fathers), and between PATp scores and social desirability (-.24, mothers; .41, fathers), self-reported anger (.30, mothers; -.51, fathers), and self-reports of intense or frequent pleasure (.02, mothers; .50, fathers).

Reference:

Linehan, M. M., Paul, E., & Egan, K. J. (1983). The Parent Affect Test: Development, validity, and reliability. *J Clin Child Psych, 12,* 161–166.

III-2/b/e
321. LITTLE, L. F. Little Parental Valuing Styles Scale (LPVSS)

Avail: NAPS-3

Variables Measured: Parental perceptions of their problematic children

Type of Instrument: Self-report questionnaire

Instrument Description: The LPVSS is a 6-point, 56-item Likert-style questionnaire designed to assess parents' attitudes, values, and perceptions of their problematic children. Five dimensions and two subdimensions of parenting style are identified: (1) rejecting, defined by negative attitudes toward their children; (2) ignoring, defined as when little attention is given to the child by his or her parent regardless of the situation; (3) overvaluing, consisting of (3a) overprotective styles, or fears regarding the ability of the child to protect him- or herself, and (3b) overindulgent styles, where parents fail to prescribe limits for their children's behaviors; (4) extrinsic, defined by parental indications that the child is valued according to the needs of the parent that are met by the child; and (5) intrinsic, indicating that parents accept their children as growing and learning individuals deserving of positive attention. Items are in the form of statements, and are scored on a 0–5 scale ranging from *hardly ever* to *almost always.* Subscale scores are derived by summing values associated with responses within each and dividing by the number of items used to evaluate that dimension. The result is a parent profile designed to render an overall picture of parenting style. High scores are intended to indicate greater degrees of a specific style. The author recommends administering the questionnaire to both parents so that styles can be compared and dealt with, particularly where remediation of the child's difficulties is desired. The LPVSS may be used for both clinical and research purposes.

Sample Items:

(A)   When _____ acts up in front of others, I am embarrassed.
(B)   _____ just doesn't do anything right.
(C)   _____ accepts discipline that protects his/her health and safety.

Comments: The author indicates that split-half reliabilities of the subscales range from .32 to .76. A validity study comparing parents of truant and nontruant children is also reported by the author. Parents of truant children scored higher on measures of over-protection and overindulgence, and lower on intrinsic parenting styles, than did parents of nontruant youngsters.

References:

Little, L. F. (1986). Gestalt therapy with parents when a child is presented as the problem. *Fam Relat, 35,* 489–496.
Little, L. F., & Thompson, R. (1983). Truancy: How parents and teachers contribute. *Sch Couns, 30,* 285–291.

III-2/b
322. MARJORIBANKS, K. Marjoribanks Family Learning Environment Schedule

Avail: 1979 & 1980 Refs.

Variables Measured: Parents' aspirations for their children and themselves, reinforcement of aspirations, parental knowledge of child's education progress, and press for independence

Type of Instrument: Interview questionnaire

Instrument Description: This instrument is used during semistructured home interviews of parents. A total of 78 questions, many of which have subsections, are asked of both parents. Questions are open-ended but generally require only a few words or sentences to answer. Issues examined by this scale focus on family knowledge of and involvement in children's academic and independent development. The scale was originally developed for use by the author on Australian populations.

Sample Items:

(A)   What kind of job would you like your child to have after leaving school?
(B)   What grades do you expect your child to receive in examinations at school?
(C)   How often would you help your child with her/his English grammar?

Comments: The author reports that reliability and validity information is available in the 1979 reference listed below.

References:

Marjoribanks, K. (1979). *Families and their learning environments.* London: Routledge & Kegan Paul.
Marjoribanks, K. (1980). *Ethnic families and children's achievements.* London: Allen & Unwin.
Marjoribanks, K. (1987). Ability and attitude correlates of academic achievement: Family-group differences. *J Educ Psyc, 78,* 171–178.

III-2/b/P
323. MARJORIBANKS, K. Perceived Family Environment Scale

Avail: NAPS-3

Variables Measured: Adolescents' perceptions of their parents' interest and encouragement in educational and occupational goals for the adolescent

Type of Instrument: Self-report questionnaire

Instrument Description: This instrument is an 8-item, primarily Likert-type questionnaire. The scale is designed to measure three dimensions of the family environment: (1) adolescents' perceptions of their parents' educational and occupational aspirations for them; (2) encouragement adolescents perceive they received from their parents in relation to schooling; (3) perceptions of parents' general interest in education. The initial six items are in the form of statements and are measured with a 5-point response format ranging from *strongly agree* to *strongly disagree*. The final two items are questions containing instructions to "Provide appropriate checklist of alternatives . . . " and "Provide either appropriate categories or leave as an open alternative for rating." The questionnaire was developed in Australia, and was designed for use with secondary school students.

Sample Items:

(A)   When I was in high school my father/mother was *very interested* in my school work.
(B)   My father/mother *often praised* me for things I did while I was in high school.
(C)   When you were in high school what job did your father/mother want you to have after leaving school?

Comments: The author indicates that the theta reliability estimate for each item was greater than .75. The results of a multiple regression analysis with several variables related to family environment are contained in Marjoribanks (1986, 1987).

References:

Marjoribanks, K. (1985). Families, schools, and aspirations: Ethnic group differences. *J Exp Educ, 53,* 141–147.
Marjoribanks, K. (1986). Cognitive and environmental correlates of aspirations: Attitude group differences. *J Res Child Educ, 1,* 95–103.
Marjoribanks, K. (1987). Gender-social class, family environments and adolescents' aspirations. *Aus J Educ, 31,* 43–54.

III-2/IV-2/b
324. MASH, E. J., TERDAL, L. G., & ANDERSON, K. A. Response-Class Matrix (RCM)

Avail: 1981 Ref.

Variables Measured: Parent-child interactional styles, including categories of behavior such as compliance, independence, questioning, and commands

Type of Instrument: Observational recording system

Instrument Description: Parent and child behaviors are time-sampled and rated during hour-long interactions according to criteria detailed on structured coding sheets. The RCM is designed for the behavioral assessment of dyadic social interaction in structured clinic, laboratory playroom, or home settings. Developed originally to evaluate mother-child interactions in populations of young developmentally delayed and handicapped children, its use has since been extended to several other populations. The measure was designed for use with preschool and elementary-school-age children. The RCM protocol consists of two coding sheets. The Child's Consequent Behavior Record includes six child behaviors that could occur in response to seven possible behaviors of the parent. The Parental Consequent Behavior Record includes seven parental behaviors that could occur in response to the six child behaviors. The instrument has been used in formulating treatment programs, in describing interaction patterns in families, and as a treatment outcome measure.

Sample Items: Not applicable.

Comments: Behaviors are typically rated by two observers. The authors estimate that approximately 10–15 hours of training using semistandardized training protocols are necessary for adequate interrater reliability to develop. It is reported that the RCM has been used to discriminate between parent-child interactions of disturbed and normal populations. The authors report that it has also been correlated with other family measures related to parental reports of stress, perceived child behavior problems, and parenting self-esteem.

References:

Mash, E. J., & Barkley, R. A. (1986). Assessment of family interaction with the Response-Class Matrix. In R. J. Prinz (Ed.), *Advances in behavioral assessment of children and families* (Vol. 2, pp. 29–67). Greenwich, CT: JAI.

Mash, E. J., Terdal, L., & Anderson, K. (1973). The Response-Class Matrix: A procedure for recording parent-child interactions. *J Cons Clin, 40,* 163–164.

Mash, E. J., Terdal, L., & Anderson, K. (1981). The Response-Class Matrix: A procedure for recording parent-child interactions. In R. A. Barkley (Ed.), *Hyperactive children* (pp. 419–436). New York: Guilford.

III-2/b/P

325. MEYERS, C. E., MINK, I. T., & NIHIRA, K. Home Quality Rating Scale (HQRS)

Avail: Neuropsychiatric Institute, Lanterman State Hospital Research Group, UCLA, Los Angeles, CA 90024

Variables Measured: Characteristics of parents and the home environment that relate to the development of mentally retarded children

Type of Instrument: Observational rating scale

Instrument Description: The HQRS is a 32-item questionnaire designed to be filled out by an interviewer immediately following completion of a structured, two-hour long, interview with parents of a mentally retarded child. Interviews take place with the parents in their home, with the child generally present for at least a part of the interview. Several questionnaires are completed by the parents, all of which are geared toward gaining a greater understanding of the child, his or her parents, and the home environment. Items on the HQRS, completed by the interviewer, are generally Likert-type, utilizing a 5-point response format. Other formats used include 3- and 4-point items, checklists, and *yes-no* and open-ended questions. The HQRS is intended to assess some of the more subtle aspects of the environment (e.g., love, guilt, concern) that might not be adequately tapped directly through parent-answered questionnaires. It is completed following the two-hour interview so that impressions formed on the basis of interactions and observations can be documented. In completing this questionnaire, the interviewer is encouraged to go over parents' responses to other questions, notes taken during the interview, and recollections of observations made. It is thus a subjective representation of parental characteristics and the home environment. The questionnaire assesses five primary areas: harmony of the home and quality of parenting, concordance in support of care for the child, openness and awareness of the respondent, safety of the dwelling and the quality of the structure and furnishing with regard to child rearing, and quality of the residential area.

Sample Items:

(A)   Extent to which the parent/caretaker exhibits control over the child in various ways versus indulging the child, letting the child have his/her way.

(B)   Is there overprotection (where parent/caregiver's attachment represents a potentially unwholesome interdependence)?

(C)   Rate the respondent's ability to cope with the retarded child and the problems brought about by the child's condition. Was the respondent successfully coping with the child and the care required? Or was the respondent overwhelmed by the child and the care required?

Comments: A manual is available that provides means and standard deviations for all items. The complete factor analysis, including loadings for every item on each of five factors for each of two samples (trainable mentally retarded and educable mentally retarded), is also provided in the manual. Correlations between factors are reported to range from .02 to .62.

References:

Blacher, J., Nihira, K., & Meyers, C. E. (1987). Characteristics of home environment of families with mentally retarded children: Comparison across levels of retardation. *Am J Ment D, 91,* 313–320.

Bristol, M. M., Gallagher, J. J., & Schopler, E. (1988). Mothers and fathers of young developmentally disabled and nondisabled boys: Adaptation and spousal support. *Devel Psych, 24,* 441–451.

Nihira, K., Mink, I. T., & Meyers, C. E. (1985). Home environment and development of slow-learning adolescents: Reciprocal relations. *Devel Psych, 21,* 784–794.

Nihira, K., Tomiyasu, Y., & Oshio, C. (1987). Homes of TMR children: Comparison between American and Japanese families. *Am J Ment D, 91,* 486–495.

III-2/b/P

326. MOERK, E. L. Psycholinguistic Classification System for Analyzing Mother-Child Interactions

Avail: 1983 Ref.

Variables Measured: Mothers' displaying of linguistic information for their children during verbal interactions with those children

Type of Instrument: Classification and methodological system for chronicling observed interactions

Instrument Description: A methodology was developed to study verbal interactions between mothers and young preschool children that are conducive to the acquisition and development of language skills. The main goal was to capture interactional contingencies within behavioral episodes. Two major aspects of these interactions were differentiated: the illocutionary force of the utterances, captured in 23 categories, and the informative aspects of the utterances. The latter are differentiated into 39 categories of maternal teaching techniques and 37 categories of filial learning strategies. The categories are defined relationally and are intended to capture information arising from the relationships between utterances. Sequential dependencies between the diverse teaching techniques and learning strategies are ascertained by means of Markov chain analyses. Structures of interactions are described based upon these conditional probabilities and their comparison with chance probabilities. Because the analysis is interactional and structural, the teaching and learning of a wide range of linguistic items can be studied with this method.

Sample Items: Not applicable.

Comments: Recent investigative domains in which the author reports using the above-mentioned categories include training and learning of past and future tense, present progressive, prepositional phrases, and the major syntactic structures, such as the equational sentence and the S-V-O sentence.

References:

Moerk, E. L. (1976). Processes of language teaching and training in the interactions of mother-child dyads. *Child Dev, 47,* 1064–1078.

Moerk, E. L. (1983). *The mother of Eve—as a first language teacher.* Norwood, NJ: Ablex.

Moerk, E. L. (1985). Analytic, synthetic, abstracting, and word-class-defining aspects of verbal mother-child interactions. *J Psycholin Res, 14,* 263–287.

III-2/II-3/b/P
327. PARKER, G., TUPLING, H., & BROWN, L. Parental Bonding Instrument

Avail: 1979 Ref.

Variables Measured: Parental care and protection of children as dimensions of parent-child bonding

Type of Instrument: Self-report questionnaire

Instrument Description: The Parental Bonding Instrument is a 4-point, 25-item Likert-style scale used to measure dimensions of parent-child bonding. Adult respondents are asked to answer each question as it relates to their biological parents or parent figures as they are remembered from the subject's first 16 years. Respondents are asked to indicate whether each statement is *very like, moderately like, moderately unlike,* or *very unlike* their parent. Of the 25 items, 12 items relate to care and 13 relate to protection of the child by the parent. Administration time is approximately 2–5 minutes.

Sample Items:

(A) Spoke to me with a warm and friendly voice.
(B) Liked me to make my own decisions.
(C) Could make me feel better when I was upset.

Comments: The scale was developed from an initial pool of 114 items generated from literature reviews and clinical experience. Pilot studies and factor analyses eventually reduced the scale to its current 25 items. The author reports that test-retest reliability for the full current version is in excess of .90. Validity has been assessed in several studies including investigations with siblings, comparisons of scores given by adult children with those obtained on self-ratings by their parents, and corroborative interviews.

References:

Palmer, R. L., Oppenheimer, R. & Marshall, P. D. (1988). Eating-disordered patients remember their parents: A study using the Parental Bonding Instrument. *Int J Eating Disord, 7,* 101–106.

Parker, G. (1983). *Parental overprotection: A risk factor in psychosocial development.* New York: Grune & Stratton.

Parker, G., & Barr, R. (1982). Parental representations of transsexuals. *Arch Sex Be, 11,* 221–230.

Parker, G., Tupling, H., & Brown, L. B. (1979). A parental bonding instrument. *Br J Med Ps, 52,* 1–10.

III-2/b/P
328. PARKS, P. L., & SMERIGLIO, V. L. Infant Caregiving Inventory (ICI)—Revised

Avail: NAPS-3

Variables Measured: Parental perceptions about the influences of infant caregiving practices on infant and maternal well-being

Type of Instrument: Self-report questionnaire

Instrument Description: The ICI is designed to test perceptions and the level of knowledge of parents regarding influences on infant and maternal well-being. It is a 38-item questionnaire, of which only 34 items are scored. The remaining items are treated as fillers. For each item, respondents indicate whether a particular event or type of interaction has *no, slight, moderate,* or *strong* influence on some aspect of infant development. Six areas of concern are measured: personality at school age, physical growth, intelligence at school age, physical health, baby's level of happiness, and mother's level of happiness. Individual item scores within subscales are summed. The ICI was designed to have programmatic, clinical, and research utility. The instrument is intended for use with parents but may also prove useful with other caregivers. It has been used by the authors with adolescent and adult mothers. Administration time is approximately 10 minutes.

Sample Items:

(A)   I think that the amount of time babies see their relatives has _____ influence on their intelligence when they reach school-age.

(B)   I think that taking babies for recommended physical check-ups has _____ influence on their physical growth.

(C)   I think that the age when babies are started on solid foods has _____ influence on their personality when they reach school-age.

Comments: The authors report that Cronbach's alpha for the revised ICI was .94, .90, and .91, respectively, for mothers from low, middle, and high socioeconomic groups. In a separate analysis, the authors found that alpha was .94 for 48 mothers of infants with physical and developmental disabilities. Validity was assessed by comparing scores of single-child mothers, those with more than one child, and public health nurses and aides. Nurses and aides had the highest scores, followed by mothers with multiple children and mothers with one child. Other validity and reliability information for the original (25-item) ICI is available in the references listed below. The authors also report current work on the development of a shortened (10-item) version of the ICI.

References:

Parks, P. L., & Smeriglio, V. L. (1983). Parenting knowledge among adolescent mothers. *J Youth Ado Health Care, 4,* 163–167.

Parks, P. L., & Smeriglio, V. L. (1986). Relationships among parenting knowledge, quality of stimulation in the home and infant development. *Fam Relat, 35,* 411–416.

Smeriglio, V. L., & Parks, P. (1983). Measuring mothers' perceptions about the influences of infant caregiving practices. *Child Psychi Hum Dev, 13,* 189–200.

III-2/V-2/g/P
329. PEARLIN, L. I. Parental Stress

Avail: 1978 Ref.

Variables Measured: Emotions associated with perceptions of parental stress

Type of Instrument: Self-report questionnaire

Instrument Description: This instrument is a 4-point, 7-item Likert-type questionnaire designed to evaluate stressors specific to functioning within the role of parent. The author's perspective is that strains and stresses within one role may be insulated from those of other areas of the person's life. Thus it is necessary to evaluate stress specifically as it affects the person within each individual role. The Parental Stress questionnaire was administered as part of a large battery of instruments designed to evaluate strains, stresses, and coping skills in many areas of life. The instrument was designed to be administered during personal interviews. Examiners were instructed to hand respondents a list of seven adjectives and to read the question: "When you think of your experiences as a parent, how _____ do you feel?" The question was reread seven times, each time with a different adjective used in place of _____. An overall parental stress score can be computed by summing values associated with various response options.

Sample Items:

(A)   When you think of your experiences as a parent, how frustrated do you feel?
(B)   When you think of your experiences as a parent, how tense do you feel?
(C)   When you think of your experiences as a parent, how contented do you feel?

Comments: The author reports that the results of a factor analysis indicated the presence of one factor, with items loading on that factor from .69 to .84.

References:

Menaghan, E. (1983). Marital stress and family transitions: A panel analysis. *J Mar Fam, 45,* 371–386.

Pearlin, L. I., & Lieberman, M. A. (1979). Social sources of emotional distress. In R. G. Simmons (Ed.), *Research in community and mental health* (pp. 217–248). Greenwich, CT: JAI.

Pearlin, L. I., Menaghan, E. G., Lieberman, M. A., & Mullan, J. T. (1981). The stress process. *J Health So, 22,* 337–356.

Pearlin, L. I., & Schooler, C. (1978). The structure of coping. *J Health So, 19,* 2–21.

III-2/b/C

330. PERRIS, C., JACOBSSON, L., LINDSTROM, H., VON KNOR-RING, L., & PERRIS, H. EMBU (Egna Minnen Betraffande Uppfostran): An Inventory for Assessing Memories of Parental Rearing Behaviour

Avail: 1984 Ref.

Variables Measured: Adults' memories of various aspects of their parents' child-rearing behaviors

Type of Instrument: Questionnaire rating parental behaviors

Instrument Description: The EMBU is an 81-item inventory comprising 14 a priori aspects of parental rearing behavior: abusive, depriving, punitive, shaming, rejecting, overprotective, overinvolved, tolerant, affectionate, performance oriented, guilt engendering, stimulating, favoring siblings, and favoring self. The question format of the EMBU is a 4-point Likert-style scale to be scored separateiy for the two parents. In addition, two questions concerning the strictness and consistency of parental child-rearing strategies have been added to the instrument. Administration time is estimated to be approximately 30 minutes. The instrument was originally written in Swedish and was used in the Netherlands. It has since been translated into at least 16 languages. The EMBU has been used with a variety of clinical samples, including depressives, phobics, addicts, epileptics, suicide attempters, alcoholics, and obsessive-compulsive neurotics.

Sample Items:

(A)   Did it happen that your parents gave you more corporal punishment than you deserved?
(B)   Did your parents show with words and gestures that they liked you?
(C)   Did it happen that you wished your parents would worry less about what you were doing?

Comments: The authors indicate that Cronbach's alpha is .80. They also report correlations between consistency and strictness of .43 for fathers and .27 for mothers. Correlations between 14 factor analytically identified subscales are reported to vary widely, ranging from .00 to .74 for mothers, and from .00 to .79 for fathers.

References:

Arrindell, W. A., Emmelkamp, P. M. G., Monsma, A., & Brilman, E. (1983). The role of perceived parental rearing practices in the aetiology of phobic disorders: A controlled study. *Br J Psychi, 143,* 183–187.
Arrindell, W. A., Perris, C., Perris, H., Eisemann, M., van der Ende, J., & von Knorring, L. (1986). Cross-national invariance of dimensions of parental rearing behaviour: Comparison of psychometric data of Swedish depressives and healthy subjects with Dutch target rating on the EMBU. *Br J Psychi, 148,* 305–309.
Arrindell, W. A., & van der Ende, J. (1984). Replicability and invariance of dimensions of parental rearing behaviour: Further Dutch experiences with the EMBU. *Pers Indiv Diff, 5,* 671–682.
Perris, C., Arrindell, W. A., Perris, H., Eisemann, M., van der Ende, J., & von Knorring, L. (1986). Perceived depriving parental rearing and depression. *Br J Psychi, 148,* 170–175.

III-2/b/P
331. PORESKY, R. H. Environmental Assessment Index

Avail: 1987 Ref.

Variables Measured: Developmental and educational support provided to children through qualities of the home environment

Type of Instrument: Interview schedule/observational technique

Instrument Description: The Environmental Assessment Index was designed as a measure of the developmental and educational support provided to children as a result of the quality of their physical and social home environments. The instrument is intended for use with families of children between 3 and 11 years old. The intent in developing the index was to provide a basis for predicting children's future cognitive and social development. The complete 44-item instrument is administered during a home visit. A 24-item short form is also available. Each item is scored according to a *yes-no* format. On the long form, 26 items are appropriate for scoring either as a result of responses to interview inquiries or through direct observation. The additional 18 items are always rated based on direct observation. A total score is obtained by counting the number of items answered *yes.* Home interviews from which scores are derived last approximately 60 minutes. This index is a revision of the STIM (Caldwell, 1967) and HOME (Bradley & Caldwell, 1976), which were developed for children under 3 years of age. The NC-124 Technical Committee assisted in the refinement of this instrument for assessing the quality of children's homes.

Sample Items:

(A)   Three or more puzzles.
(B)   Child is encouraged to learn to use numbers or mathematics.
(C)   Ten or more children's books are present and visible in the home.

Comments: The author reports that Cronbach's alpha for the long and short form are .74 and .82, respectively. The part-whole correlation of the short and long forms was found to be .93. Test-retest reliability over two years was reported to be .66 and .72 for the long and short forms, respectively. It was also found that correlations with measures of intellectual functioning (PPVT and WISC) were .42 and .47, respectively, for the long form, and .35 and .46 for the short form.

Reference:

Poresky, R. H. (1987). Environmental Assessment Index: Reliability, stability, and validity of the long and short forms. *Educ Psyc M, 47,* 969–975.

III-2/IV-2/b/C
332. PORTER, B. Porter Parental Behavior and Feelings Inventory

Avail: NAPS-3

Variables Measured: Parental predictions of probable behavior toward their children following specific incidents

Type of Instrument: Self-report questionnaire

Instrument Description: This instrument is a 19-item Likert-type questionnaire. Each item is answered from each of three perspectives: (1) parents indicate their likely behavioral response to the child, according to an 8-point response format. Possible responses range from hitting the child with force to hugging and enthusiastically praising the child. (2) Parents indicate the feeling they believe they would have toward the child at that moment, according to a 6-point response format ranging from *extremely negative* to *extremely positive*. (3) Parents indicate how likely they think their child would be to display the behavior that was described, according to a 6-point response format ranging from *not at all likely* to *extremely likely*.

Sample Items:

(A)   You have been angrily reprimanding your child for being disobedient. He (she) looks at you, screams "I hate you," and runs out of the room.

(B)   Your child has worked hard in school and proudly hands you a report card with all A's. He (she) tells you he (she) is confident he (she) can continue to get report cards like this if he (she) works hard.

(C)   Your child's essay has not been a winner in the school essay contest and he (she) is very disappointed. You are aware of how hard he (she) tried and of the fact that he (she) stayed home from a birthday party to finish it on time.

Comments: The author reports that pilot data with 20 couples revealed test-retest correlations for fathers over a three- to four-week period to be .81 on the negative scale (behavioral responses 1–4), and .90 on the positive scale (behavioral responses 5–8). For mothers involved in the same study, test-retest correlations are reported to be .89 on the negative scale and .72 on the positive scale. Cronbach's alpha is reported to be .71 for the positive scale and .70 for the negative scale.

Reference:

Hershorn, M., & Rosenbaum, A. (1985). Children of marital violence: A closer look at unintended victims. *Am J Orthop, 55,* 260–266.

III-2/b/C
333. PRINZ, R. J. Daily Home Report (DHR)

Avail: NAPS-3

Variables Measured: Distressing or pleasant interactions between adolescents and their parent(s)

Type of Instrument: Self-report questionnaire

Instrument Description: The DHR is a combination *yes-no* and Likert-type questionnaire designed to allow parents and their adolescent children to keep daily records of areas of conflict between them. Both parent and adolescent forms are available. The two forms are parallel, with statements reflecting either the parent's or the child's perspective (e.g., "My adolescent yelled at me" versus "I yelled at my mom"). The initial 11 items are answered on a *yes-no basis*. This is followed by three 5-point items and one 4-point item asking how the adolescent got along with the respondent, with the respondent's spouse, how angry the adolescent or the parent (depending on who was responding) was that day, and a general measure of how nice or argumentative their interactions were on that day. Participants are instructed to fill out the questionnaire on a daily basis for one week, and to mail each questionnaire back to the examiner as it was completed. Thus both parent and child are to mail one completed questionnaire each day for seven days. While the author intended the DHR for use in analyzing interactions between mothers and their children, it might also prove appropriate for use with fathers and their adolescents, or as a measure of both parents' interactions with their teenager. Scoring is accomplished by combining response-values for items 2–10. Items 1 and 11 each indicate that, for one reason or another, there was not much interaction on that day. Separate scores are computed for each day that the inventory is completed.

Sample Items:

(A)   My mom and I had a disagreement that was upsetting to me.
(B)   My adolescent was generally pleasant to me today.
(C)   I made one or more unfair, unkind, or insulting comments to my adolescent.

Comments: The author indicates that the DHR was successful in discriminating distressed from nondistressed families. Distressed families, according to both adolescents and their mothers, were found to have a greater ratio of arguments to other behaviors, and more frequent conflicts.

References:

Foster, S. L., Prinz, R. J., & O'Leary, K. D. (1983). Impact of problem-solving communication training and generalization procedures on family conflict. *Child Fam Beh Ther, 5*,
1–23.
Prinz, R. J., Foster, S. L., Kent, R. N., & O'Leary, K. D. (1979). Multivariate assessment of
conflict in distressed and nondistressed mother-adolescent dyads. *J Appl Be A, 12*,
691–700.

III-2/b/C
334. PRINZ, R. J. Interaction Behavior Code (IBC)

Avail: NAPS-3

Variables Measured: Positive and negative interactions between adolescents and their parents

Type of Instrument: Behavior coding and rating scheme

Instrument Description: The IBC is a behavioral index for use in coding and rating behaviors present in tape-recorded interactions between adolescents and their parents. Adolescents are instructed to initiate discussion with their parent(s) regarding an issue in which they would like to see changes. Interactions last for 10 minutes with only the adolescent and his or her parent(s) in the room, and are recorded with the participants' knowledge. Participants are instructed to determine some course of action that can be implemented at home. The author reported using this procedure exclusively in evaluating mother-child interactions. However, it might also prove appropriate for father-child dialogues, as well as for interactions between both parents and the adolescent. Four raters are assigned to listen to each recording twice, and then to rate them according to criteria specified on the code sheet. Raters first indicate the presence or absence of each of 22 positive or negative behaviors, with presence scored "1" and absence scored "0." Following this, ratings are made on a 3-point scale as to the presence of nine types of interaction ($0 = no$; $.5 = a little$; $1 = a lot$). Finally, two constructs are rated on 4-point scales, and two others are rated on 5-point scales. Scores are computed on the basis of average ratings by the four independent judges. Eight scores are generated: (1) positive parent behavior, (2) positive adolescent behavior, (3) negative parent behavior, (4) negative adolescent behavior, (5) resolution, (6) insult, (7) friendliness, and (8) problem solving.

Sample Items (Note: All sample items are from the first part of the rating form):

(A)   Negative exaggeration—putting excessive emphasis on the other person's negative qualities.

(B)   Yelling—raising the volume of one's voice in an angry manner.

(C)   Ridicule, make fun of—to tease, mock, or belittle the other.

Comments: Interrater reliability among the four judges is reported to range from .82 to .93 for the eight categories of scores. The author indicates that scores successfully discriminated between distressed and nondistressed families.

References:

Foster, S. L., Prinz, R. J., & O'Leary, K. D. (1983). Impact of problem-solving communication training and generalization procedures on family conflict. *Child Fam Beh Ther, 5,* 1–23.

Prinz, R. J., Foster, S. L., Kent, R. N., & O'Leary, K. D. (1979). Multivariate assessment of conflict in distressed and nondistressed mother-adolescent dyads. *J Appl Be A, 12,* 691–700.

Prinz, R. J., & Kent, R. N. (1978). Recording parent-adolescent interactions without the use of frequency or interval-by-interval coding. *Behav Ther, 9,* 602–604.

III-2/b/C

335. PRINZ, R. J. Issues Checklist (IC)

Avail: NAPS-3

Variables Measured: Areas of conflict between adolescents and their parents

Type of Instrument: Self-report questionnaire

Instrument Description: The IC is a combination *yes-no* and 5-point, 44-item questionnaire designed to determine those issues that typically cause conflict in parent-adolescent relationships. The questionnaire is generally administered to both parents and their teenage children, with responses examined both individually and in comparison to each other. Adolescents with both parents involved in their upbringing complete the questionnaire once with regard to disputes with each parent. Respondents are asked to circle either *yes* or *no* to indicate whether or not the issue has been a topic of conversation during the past four weeks. For those issues that have been discussed, the respondent first indicates the number of times the topic has come up, and then rates how "hot" the discussions were regarding this topic. Ratings are on a 5-point, Likert-type scale ranging from 1 = *calm* to 5 = *angry*. Three scores are generated through use of the IC: (1) A count of the number of issues discussed is referred to as a quality of issues score; (2) an intensity rating is derived by computing the mean response on the Likert-type questionnaire; and (3) intensity by frequency is "computed by multiplying each frequency estimate by its corresponding intensity rating, summing the products, and dividing by the sum of the frequency estimates."

Sample Items:

(A)   Telephone calls.

(B)   How neat clothing looks.

(C)   Going places without parents (shopping, movies, etc.)

Comments: There is some confusion in the literature regarding authorship of this instrument. However, it appears that the IC was first developed by Prinz for use in his dissertation (1977). Test-retest reliability over a period of six to eight weeks for a sample of adolescents is reported to range from .49 to .87 for quality of issues, from .37 to .49 for intensity, and from .15 to .24 for the intensity by frequency scores. Test-retest correlations for parents are reported to be .55 to .65, .66 to .81, and .40 to .90 for quality of issues, intensity, and intensity by frequency, respectively. Adolescent-parent correlations for the IC are reported to range from .10 to .64 for various items, with an average of .28.

References:

Forehand, R., Long, N., Brody, G. H., & Fauber, R. (1986). Home predictors of young adolescents' school behavior and academic performance. *Child Dev, 57,* 1528–1533.

Foster, S. L., Prinz, R. J., & O'Leary, K. D. (1983). Impact of problem-solving communication training and generalization procedures on family conflict. *Child Fam Beh Ther, 5,* 1–23.

Prinz, R. J., Foster, S. L., Kent, R. N., & O'Leary, K. D. (1979). Multivariate assessment of conflict in distressed and nondistressed mother-adolescent dyads. *J Appl Be A, 12,* 691–700.

Roehling, P. V., & Robin, A. L. (1986). Development and validation of the Family Beliefs Inventory: A measure of unrealistic beliefs among parents and adolescents. *J Cons Clin Psy, 54,* 693–697.

III-2/IV-2/II-3/b/P
336. PUMROY, D. K. Maryland Parent Attitude Survey

Avail: NAPS-3

Variables Measured: Disciplinarian, protective, indulgent, and rejecting parenting styles

Type of Instrument: Self-report questionnaire

Instrument Description: This instrument presents subjects with 95 pairs of items related to child-rearing practices. Respondents are instructed to select the one option from each pair that best represents his or her attitudes toward raising children. An attempt was made to pair items such that the social desirability of each is approximately equal. The questionnaire was designed to distinguish between disciplinarian, protective, indulgent, and rejecting parents. Administration time is approximately 30–40 minutes.

Sample Items:

(A) 1. Children should learn to keep their place.
     2. Children should be required to consult their parents before making any important decisions.
(B) 1. Parents should insist that everyone of their commands be obeyed.
     2. Children should be protected from upsetting experiences.
(C) 1. Parents know what is good for their children.
     2. A good leather strap makes children respect parents.

Comments: The author reports both test-retest (.62 to .73) and split-half (.67 to .84) reliability. The following validity information is also reported by the author: Males score higher on the disciplinarian scale while females score higher on the indulgent scale; older subjects average lower scores on the disciplinarian scale and higher on the rejecting scale than do younger subjects; mothers who scored higher on the disciplinarian scale were observed to be more directing and restricting in their interactions with their children than were those who scored lower; parents scoring higher on the disciplinarian scale averaged more sessions in parent discussion groups than did other parents; and parents scoring highest on the rejecting scale tended to attend fewer parent discussion meetings than did other parents.

References:

Gordon, M., & Tegtmyer, P. F. (1983). Oral-dependent content in children Rorschach protocols. *Perc Mot Sk, 57,* 1163–1168.

Pumroy, D. K. (1966). Maryland Parent Attitude Survey: A research instrument with social desirability controlled. *J Psychol, 64,* 73–78.

Slough, N. M., Kogan, K. L., & Tyler, N. B. (1978). Derivation of parent norms for the Maryland Parent Attitude Survey. *Psychol Rep, 42,* 183–189.

Tolar, A. (1967). An evaluation of the Maryland Parent Attitude Survey. *J Psychol, 67,* 69–74.

III-2/b/P

337. RICKARD, K., GRAZIANO, W., & FOREHAND, R. Maternal Expectations, Attitudes, and Belief Inventory (MEABI)

Avail: NAPS-3

Variables Measured: Mothers' expectations and beliefs regarding the behavior and development of their young children

Type of Instrument: Self-report questionnaire

Instrument Description: The MEABI is a 7-point, 67-item inventory designed to assess maternal knowledge and attitudes with regard to their preschool-aged children. Items are in the form of phrases, statements, and questions. Response options, scored 1–7, range from *strongly disagree* to *strongly agree.* The MEABI consists of five subscales: (1) parent knowledge of child development norms, referred to as PKCDN (20 items); (2) need to be liked, or NBL (7 items), which assesses mothers' need for approval for their child-rearing practices; (3) maternal reactions to a child's deviant behavior, or MRCDB, which assesses parental use of praise and discipline (23 items); (4) should-should not, or SSN (12 items), used to assess maternal beliefs regarding unacceptable behavior by her child; and (5) belief in child monitoring and guidance, or BCMG (5 items), used to determine what the mother believes is the optimal level of intervention by a parent in order to promote the development of a child. The third subscale, MRCDB, is further divided into five dimensions: (a) use of praise, (b) allowing a behavior, (c) spanking, (d) ignore the behavior or utilize "time-out" procedures, and (e) reasoning with the child. Separate scores are computed for each subscale and dimension, yielding a total of nine scores obtained through use of the MEABI. The authors indicate that several items from the PKCDN subscale were selected from a number of earlier instruments.

Sample Items:

(A) A 4 or 5 year old should be able to correctly carry out the following: (followed by 20 items including:) Copy a square.

(B) If a child has behavior problems, other people usually perceive this as the parents' fault.

(C) If your child was jumping up and down on the furniture, would you try to reason with him/her about it?

Comments: The authors report reliability and validity information with respect to nine subscales. They indicate that test-retest reliability over a period of three weeks ranged from .44 to .78, with a median of .70. Cronbach's alpha for the nine subscales is reported to have ranged from .35 to .83, with a median of .67. Correlations are also reported between each subscale and various demographic variables, and with each other. Further details are contained in Rickard, Graziano, and Forehand (1984).

Reference:

Rickard, K. M., Graziano, W., & Forehand, R. (1984). Parental expectations and childhood deviance in clinic-referred and non-clinic children. *J Clin Child Psych, 13,* 179–186.

III-2/b/C
338. ROBIN, A. L., & FOX, M. Parent-Adolescent Interaction Coding System (PAICS)

Avail: NAPS-3

Variables Measured: Positive, negative, and neutral interactions between parents and their adolescent children

Type of Instrument: Behavior coding scheme

Instrument Description: The PAICS is a system for classifying behaviors present in verbal interactions between adolescents and their parents. Fifteen classifications of behavior are coded, of which seven are positive (agree-assent, appraisal, consequential statements, facilitation, humor, problem solution, and specification of the problem), five are negative (command, complaint, defensive behavior, interruption, and put-down), and three are neutral (no response, problem description, and talk). Behaviors are classified on the basis of audiorecordings, with individual behaviors noted within 30-second time intervals. No limits are set as to the number of behaviors that may be coded within each interval. Behaviors are defined as statements that are "both homogeneous in content and bound by the statements of other family members." Scores may be computed based on either the frequency of individual behavioral categories or ratios of behaviors within positive, negative, and neutral dimensions. The PAICS is intended for use by both researchers and clinicians, although the authors note that the instrument may not be appropriate for use by the average clinician. The PAICS is based on the Marital Interaction Coding System (MICS; Weiss & Summers, 1973). The authors indicate that the original MICS categories were revised to reflect the nature of parent-adolescent interactions, and to be more appropriate for use with audiotapes. The MICS was designed for use with videotaped interactions. Training of PAICS raters is reported to take 25–30 hours.

Sample Items: Not applicable.

Comments: The authors indicate that, following 25–30 hours of training, raters can be expected to achieve agreement ratings of no higher than 70% to 80%. In actual practice, interrater agreement ranged from 58% to 86%, with a mean of 64%.

References:

Robin, A. L. (1981). A controlled evaluation of problem-solving communication training with parent-adolescent conflict. *Behav Ther, 12,* 593–609.

Robin, A. L., & Canter, W. (1984). A comparison of the Marital Interaction Coding System and community ratings for assessing mother-adolescent problem solving. *Behav Assess, 6,* 303–313.

Robin, A. L., & Weiss, J. (1980). Criterion-related validity of behavioral and self-report measures of problem-solving communication skills in distressed and non-distressed parent-adolescent dyads. *Behav Asses, 2,* 339–352.

III-2/II-3/IV-2/b/C
339. ROE, A., & SIEGELMAN, M. Parent-Child Relations Questionnaire (PCR)

Avail: NAPS-1

Variables Measured: Adolescents' and grown children's memories of rewards, punishments, and affectional styles during their childhood years that were used by their parents

Type of Instrument: Self-report questionnaire

Instrument Description: The PCR is a 5-point, 130-item Likert-type questionnaire designed to assess several dimensions of parent-child interaction. Scores are generated for a total of 10 subscales, six affectional behaviors (loving, protecting, demanding, rejecting, neglecting, and casual) and four rewarding or punishing types of behaviors (symbolic love reward, direct object reward, symbolic love punishment, and direct object punishment). Each reward-punishment subscale contains 10 items, while the six affectional dimensions are each evaluated with 15 items. Items are in the form of statements to which respondents indicate their level of agreement, ranging from *very untrue* to *very true* (scored 1–5). Each item is answered twice, with responses solicited from adults regarding their memories of behaviors of both their mothers and their fathers. Respondents are instructed to answer each item as they remember interactions with their parents at age 12. A factor analysis of the entire questionnaire revealed three factors: loving-rejecting, casual-demanding, and overt concern. Administration time is approximately 20 minutes.

Sample Items:

(A)   My mother objected when I was late for meals.
(B)   My mother was generally interested in my affairs.
(C)   My mother let me off easy when I did something wrong.

Comments: The original 1963 article in which this instrument was described details the original model upon which the PCR was developed, as well as extensive reliability and validity checks. Reliability of the various subscales is reported to range from .69 to .90. The PCR has remained popular, with several authors having developed shortened versions and/or additional factor analyses based on the original PCR. A 50-item, five-dimensional version (PCRII), developed in 1979 by the original authors (authorship is reversed from the original version), is available through NAPS-3 (see *Abstract 356*).

References:

Colangelo, N., Rosenthal, D., & Dettman, D. (1984). Maternal employment and job satisfaction and their relationship to children's perception and behaviors. *Sex Roles, 10,* 693–702.

Philliber, S. G., & Graham, E. H. (1981). The impact of age of mother on mother-child interaction patterns. *J Mar Fam, 43,* 109–115.

Roe, A., & Siegelman, M. (1963). A Parent Child-Relations Questionnaire. *Child Dev, 34,* 355–369.

Scheck, D. C., & Emerick, R. (1976). The young male adolescent's perception of early child-rearing behavior: The differential effects of socioeconomic status and family size. *Sociometry, 39,* 39–52.

III-2/IV-2/b
340. ROEHLING, P. V., & ROBIN, A. L. Family Beliefs Inventory (FBI)

Avail: NAPS-3

Variables Measured: Unrealistic beliefs regarding communication between parents and their adolescent children

Type of Instrument: Self-report questionnaire

Instrument Description: The FBI is a 7-point Likert-type questionnaire designed to assess the level of unrealistic expectations held by adolescents and their parents regarding each other's behaviors. Parents and adolescents respond to different forms of the instrument, with items rated by adolescents geared toward behaviors of their parents, and those responded to by parents geared toward behaviors of their adolescent children. All behaviors deal with some level of interaction between parent and adolescent, either with actions that should be volunteered by adolescents (parent version) or not demanded by their parents (adolescent version). Responses are on a 7-point scale ranging from (1) *do not agree at all* to (7) *totally agree*. Items are divided into 10 categories: (1) who should youth's friends be, (2) how money is spent, (3) being nice to teen's friends, (4) spending time away from home, (5) using the telephone, (6) staying out past curfew, (7) cleaning one's room, (8) talking back to parents, (9) earning money away from home, and (10) helping out around the house. Parents respond to 8, and adolescents respond to 6, items within each category. Thus parents indicate ratings for 80 items, while adolescents respond to a total of 60 items. Parental responses are scored along six dimensions: (1) ruination, or the belief that adolescents will ruin their future prospects if given too much freedom; (2) obedience, defined as the belief that parents deserve absolute respect and obedience; (3) perfectionism, meaning that teenage behavior should be flawless; (4) malicious intent; (5) self-blame, defined as a belief in the parents' being to blame for undesirable adolescent behavior; and (6) approval, the belief that their child-rearing tactics must have the approval of their children. Adolescent responses are categorized along four similarly defined dimensions: (1) ruination, (2) unfairness, (3) autonomy, and (4) approval.

Sample Items (Note: Sample items are from the adolescent inventory):

(A)   Parents might occasionally offer advice about an adolescent's choice of friends.
(B)   It is unfair for parents to put limits on telephone time.
(C)   Teenagers should be able to come home as late as they wish.

Comments: The authors report that Cronbach's alpha for the various dimensions ranged from .46 to .84. Correlations are reported between fathers' ratings of obedience and ruination (.56), perfectionism (.68), and approval (-.45). Mothers' obedience ratings correlated .64 and .46 with ruination and perfectionism, respectively. Adolescents' ratings of ruination were correlated .58 with unfairness and .61 with autonomy.

Reference:

Roehling, P. V., & Robin, A. L. (1986). Development and validation of the Family Beliefs Inventory: A measure of unrealistic beliefs among parents and adolescents. *J Cons Clin Psy, 5,* 693–697.

III-2/II-3/b
341. ROHNER, R. P. Parental Acceptance-Rejection Behavior Observation Procedures

Avail: 1984 Ref.

Variables Measured: Parental acceptance-rejection and children's behavioral dispositions

Type of Instrument: Behavior observation

Instrument Description: Observations are made of children's interactions with their care-taker(s) and peers during behavioral sessions. Where only one caretaker is involved, parent-child observations take place for 20 minutes on each of three separate occasions. Where both parents serve as caretakers, two 20-minute observation sessions are scheduled with each caretaker. In addition to these, it is recommended that observation sessions be conducted in free-play settings where the subject is interacting with a peer. It is recommended that sessions with siblings not be conducted. Child-peer sessions last at least 20 minutes and should be repeated at least once. Sessions with parents are to focus on parental warmth, aggression, neglect, and undifferentiated rejection, and child behaviors indicating aggression, dependence, self-esteem, self-adequacy, emotional responsiveness, emotional stability, and world-view. Several behavioral manifestations of these dispositions are listed in the manual. Observers are instructed to record as much of the verbal and physical interaction as possible. Coding of observations is conducted subsequent to the session. It is recommended that at least two coders are used, with behaviors being evaluated one variable at a time, according to the format of the instrument's coding sheet (provided in the manual).

Sample Items: Not applicable.

Comments: The author notes the importance of observations taking place during a time that is as normal as possible for the child. Unusual situations and times of particular stress are to be avoided when selecting appropriate settings for behavioral observations.

Reference:

Rohner, R. (1984). *Handbook for the study of parental acceptance and rejection.* Storrs, CT: Center for the Study of Parental Acceptance and Rejection.

III-2/II-3/b/C
342. ROHNER, R. P. Parental Acceptance-Rejection Interview Schedule (PARIS)

Avail: 1984 Ref.

Variables Measured: Warmth, control, and acceptance-rejection dimensions of parent-child interactions

Type of Instrument: Interview questionnaire

Instrument Description: Two versions of the PARIS are available: the adult PARIS and the child PARIS. The adult version is designed for interviews with the primary caretaker. The standard form of the questions presume that the primary caretaker is the child's mother. Items require slight modification when used with other caretakers. The child version is designed for use in interviews with children from age 7 on up. The child PARIS contains 76 items, while the adult versions comprises 61 items. Each version is conceptually divided into four sections. In the adult PARIS, these sections deal with identification of the child's primary caretaker, perceptions of maternal and paternal warmth or acceptance-rejection, perceptions of maternal and paternal control or permissiveness-strictness, and identification of the child's coping strategies. Sections examined in the child PARIS are perceptions of maternal and paternal warmth and control, and the child's ability to cope with perceived acceptance or rejection, and control, by his or her parents. Response formats and coding schemes are provided in the manual (Rohner, 1984).

Sample Items: Adult PARIS

(A)   How much time on a typical day during the week does P spend with you?

(B)   Do you make P do jobs around the house, like emptying the trash or cleaning his/ her room or not?

(C)   What else do you do when P doesn't follow your rules?

Child PARIS

(A)   Does your mother have any other rules that you can think of? Are there any other things you're supposed to do or not supposed to do? (List them)

(B)   How do you feel when your mother punishes you?

(C)   Does your father ever try to explain to you what you've done wrong, and why it's wrong?

Comments: Some items on the PARIS require specific response formats, while others allow for more of an open response format. When open formats are used, responses are sometimes written down verbatim. At other times only the number of responses given is noted.

Reference:

Rohner, R. (1984). *Handbook for the study of parental acceptance and rejection.* Storrs, CT: Center for the Study of Parental Acceptance and Rejection.

III-2/II-3/b/C
343. ROHNER, R. P. Parental Acceptance-Rejection Questionnaire (PARQ)

Avail: 1984 Ref.

Variables Measured: Perceptions of acceptance or rejection by one's mother or other caretaker

Type of Instrument: Self-report questionnaire

Instrument Description: The PARQ is a 60-item Likert-type scale utilizing a 4-point response format. Respondents indicate whether each item is *almost always true, sometimes true, rarely true,* or *almost never true.* It was designed to measure perceptions of maternal acceptance along four dimensions of acceptance-rejection: warmth or affection (20 items), aggression or hostility (15 items), neglect or indifference (15 items), and undifferentiated rejection (10 items). Three separate versions of the PARQ are available for use with adults (adult PARQ), mothers (mother PARQ), and children (child PARQ). The adult version asks respondents to answer all items in terms of their perceptions of how they were treated by their mothers when they were 7 through 12 years old. The mother PARQ requests that respondents (mothers) assess their current treatment of their children. The child PARQ may be used with children as young as 7 years, and may continue to be used for as long after that (e.g., to age 18) as the youth is able to respond in the present tense to questions about perceived parental treatment. All three versions are constructed in like manner, with the exception that all items on the adult PARQ are worded in the past tense, while wording of the other two versions are in present tense. Administration time for the child version is approximately 15–20 minutes, but is partially dependent on the child's reading skill. The other two versions each require approximately 10–15 minutes to complete.

Sample Items:

(A) I hug and kiss my child when he/she is good.
(B) I am concerned with who my child's friends are.
(C) When my child misbehaves, I compare him/her unfavorably with other children.

Comments: The authors report that Cronbach's alpha for subscales of the adult version range from .86 to .95 and from .72 to .90 for the child PARQ. Validation studies are reported in which various PARQ versions were compared to scores obtained on Schaefer's (1964) Child's Report of Parent Behavior Inventory (CRPBI) and to Bronfenbrenner's Parental Behavior Questionnaire (BPB) (Siegelman, 1965). Correlations between the various scales are reported as follows: warmth/affection and CRPBI acceptance, .83 (child) to .90 (adult); aggression/hostility and BPB physical punishment, .55 (child) to .43 (adult); neglect/indifference and CRPBI hostile detachment, .64 (child) to .86 (adult); and undifferentiated rejection and CRPBI rejection, .74 (child) to .81 (adult).

References:

Rohner, R. (1984). *Handbook for the study of parental acceptance and rejection.* Storrs, CT: Center for the Study of Parental Acceptance and Rejection.
Rohner, R. P. (1986). *The warmth dimension.* Beverly Hills, CA: Sage.
Rohner, R. P., & Pettengill, S. M. (1985). Perceived parental acceptance-rejection and parental control among Korean adolescents. *Child Dev, 56,* 524–528.
Rohner, R. P., & Rohner, E. C. (Eds.). (1980). Worldwide tests of parental acceptance-rejection theory [Special Issue]. *Beh Sci Res, 15.*

III-2/II-3/b/P
344. ROTH, R. M. The Mother-Child Relationship Evaluation (MCRE)

Avail: Western Psychological Services, 12031 Wilshire Blvd., Los Angeles, CA 90025

Variables Measured: Presence of maternal attitudes by which mothers often relate to their children

Type of Instrument: Self-report questionnaire

Instrument Description: The MCRE is a 5-point, 48-item Likert-style questionnaire designed to be completed by mothers to measure levels of attitudes held by mothers toward their children. Items take the form of statements indicating either attitudes held or behaviors directed toward children. Both positive and negative, as well as neutral, attitudes and behaviors are detailed in the items. Respondents indicate their level of agreement, from *strongly agree* to *strongly disagree*, with each item. The questionnaire was designed to be of use in clinical practice and in research on "relationships between maternal attitudes and children's behavior, self-perceptions, and attitudes; relationships between maternal attitudes and maternal self-perceptions; social status identity" (Roth, 1980). The author cautions that the MCRE is intended to be "primarily exploratory and experimental, rather than a refined clinical measurement" (Roth, 1980). Scores are derived on four primary dimensions: acceptance, overprotection, overindulgence, and rejection. Within each of these areas, however, several concerns and variables are also addressed.

Sample Items:

(A) My child cannot get along without me.
(B) A mother should be resigned to the fate of her child.
(C) Child have rights of their own. (Copyright 1961, 1980 by Western Psychological

Services. Reprinted by permission of the publisher, Western Psychological Services, 12031 Wilshire Boulevard, Los Angeles, California 90025)

Comments: The original copyright date on the MCRE was 1961. The manual was revised and republished in 1980. Correlations ranging from .41 to .57 between items for acceptance, overprotection, overindulgence, and rejection were calculated and reported in the manual. However, the authors caution that each category is explained by only 6 items, and that these reliability data should be considered lower bounds of true reliability. It is also reported that scales are intercorrelated from .28 to .68, with all but one correlation being at least .40. Norms and instructions for interpreting results are contained in the manual.

Reference:

Roth, R. M. (1980). *The Mother-Child Relationship Evaluation: Manual* (2nd ed.). Los Angeles: Western Psychological Services.

III-2/II-3/IV-2/b/P
345. ROTHBAUM, F., & SCHNEIDER-ROSEN, K. Parental Acceptance Coding Scheme

Avail: NAPS-3

Variables Measured: Parental evaluation of the child, availability to the child, and structure provided for the child

Type of Instrument: Scheme for coding of videotaped parental behavior

Instrument Description: The Parental Acceptance Coding Scheme was designed as a system for scoring observations of videotaped parental interactions with 18- to 30-month-old children. There are 13 criteria for scoring Parental Acceptance, each of which has two or three subcriteria. Each criterion is rated on a 5-point scale. Behavioral descriptions of the end points and the midpoint of these scales are provided. The 13 primary criteria are as follows: evaluative affect, individualized content, encouraging effort, emphasizing child's acceptable behavior, physical presence, acknowledging, participation, standing back, quality of assistance, explanations, mood and motivation setting, consistency, and regulating options. Acceptance is defined as integration of the child's needs with parent's needs and reality constraints. It is mainly concerned with needs for control. High acceptance is presumed to indicate harmony and compatibility of needs for control. Low acceptance indicates adversity and incompatibility. Midlevel acceptance is indicative of bargaining over needs for control. Raters, following 60 hours of training, score 1-minute episodes, selecting the most relevant criteria, and averaging the score for those criteria. Final scores are computed by averaging the scores from 18 minutes of interaction involving five situations. The 18-minute observation period takes about three hours to score.

Sample Items: Not applicable.

Comments: The current version of this instrument was derived from an earlier edition used to score parents of 6- to 9-year old children. The author reports that reliability and validity information comes from this earlier version, but that the current version is heavily based on the earlier one. Ratings of maternal acceptance derived from videotaped observations were found to be correlated from .65 to .92 with ratings of maternal acceptance based on interview data. It is also reported that ratings resulting from 6-minute observation periods correlated .82 with ratings based on full-length observations. Interrater reliability is reported to range from .80 to .86. Validity studies have examined the relationship of former and current versions of the Parental Acceptance Coding Scheme to several other parent-child interaction scales. Details are provided in the references listed below.

References:

Rothbaum, F. (1986). Patterns of parental acceptance. *Genet Soc Gen Psy Mon, 112,* 435–458.
Rothbaum, F. (1988). Maternal acceptance and child functioning. *Merrill-Pal, 34,* 163–184.

III-2/b/C

346. SCHAEFER, E. S. Child's Report of Parental Behavior Inventory (CRPBI)

Avail: NAPS-3

Variables Measured: Children's perceptions of parental behavior

Type of Instrument: Self-report questionnaire

Instrument Description: The CRPBI is a 3-point Likert-type questionnaire designed to assess children's perceptions with respect to parental acceptance, permitted psychological autonomy, and level of parental control. Nearly identical forms are available for indicating behaviors of mothers and fathers. Several versions of this instrument have been developed and are currently in use. The original instrument (Schaefer, 1965a) contained 260 items organized into 26 subscales of 10 items each. Later that same year (Schaefer, 1965b), a factor analysis of the instrument resulted in a 192-item, 18-factor version. These 18 scales were combined into three primary dimensions of acceptance versus rejection, psychological autonomy versus psychological control, and firm versus lax control. This revision is considered by the author to be the standard form of the instrument. Additional revisions encompassing three dimensions have included 64 items and 8 of the original subscales (Cross, 1969), 108 items and 18 subscales (Schludermann & Schludermann, 1970), and 56 items and 6 subscales (Burger, Armentrout, & Rapfogel, 1973). In the Schludermann and Schludermann revision, original item analyses provided by Schaefer (1965a) were examined, resulting in six 8-item scales and twelve 5-item scales. As in both versions reported by Schaefer, a three-dimensional solution was found to explain the data most completely. Additional modifications effected by Schludermann and Schludermann (available through NAPS, document number 01182) included the elimination of items they viewed as inappropriate for certain ethnic and/or cultural groups. A later factor analysis of this 108-item form utilizing an oblique rotation uncovered five primary factors (Kawash & Clewes, 1988).

Sample Items:

(A) Makes me feel better after talking over my worries with him.
(B) Wants to know exactly where I am and what I am doing.
(C) Feels hurt when I don't follow advice.

Comments: Information presented for the original 260-item version indicated KR-20 reliabilities for a sample of the subscales ranging from .66 to .84. Technical information regarding various versions is generally presented in the references listed below.

References:

Burger, G. K., Armentrout, J. A., & Rapfogel, R. G. (1973). Estimating factor scores for children's reports of parental child-rearing behaviors. *J Genet Psy, 123,* 107–113.

Cross, H. J. (1969). College students' memories of the parents: A factor analysis of the CRPBI. *J Cons Clin, 33,* 275–278.

Kawash, G. F., & Clewes, J. L. (1988). A factor analysis of a short form of the CRPBI: Are children's perceptions of control and discipline multidimensional? *J Psych, 122,* 57–67.

Schaefer, E. S. (1965a). Children's Reports of Parental Behavior: An inventory. *Child Dev, 36,* 413–424.

Schaefer, E. S. (1965b). A configurational analysis of children's reports of parent behavior. *J Cons Psych, 29,* 552–557.

Schludermann, S., & Schludermann, E. (1970). Replicability of factors in Children's Report of Parent Behavior (CRPBI). *J Psychol, 76,* 239–249.

Schludermann, S., & Schludermann, E. (1983). Sociocultural change and adolescents' perceptions of parent behavior. *Devel Psych, 19,* 674–685.

Teleki, J. K., Powell, J. A., & Claypool, P. L. (1984). Parental child-rearing behavior perceived by parents and school-age children in divorced and married families. *Home Ec Res J, 13,* 41–51.

III-2/V-1/c

347. SCHAEFER, E. S., & BELL, R. Q. Parental Attitude Research Instrument (PARI)

Avail: 1958 Ref.

Variables Measured: Multiple areas related to child rearing, family attitudes, and family functioning

Type of Instrument: Self-report questionnaire

Instrument Description: This scale comprises 115 Likert-type items, and utilizes a 4-point response format ranging from *strongly agree* to *strongly disagree.* In all, 23 subscales are measured, each being evaluated by virtue of five items. The subscales cover the areas of encouraging verbalization, fostering dependency, seclusion of the mother, breaking the will, martyrdom, fear of harming the baby, marital conflict, strictness, irritability, excluding outside influences, deification, suppression of aggression, rejection of the homemaking role, equalitarianism, approval of activity, avoidance of communication, inconsiderateness of the husband, suppression of sexuality, ascendancy of the mother, intrusiveness, comradeship and sharing, acceleration of development, and dependency of the mother. The PARI has been adapted by several authors, often resulting in shorter versions, independent factor analyses, and varying factor structures. Two major factors of democratic and authoritarian attitudes have been replicated in several studies (Schaefer, 1961; Zuckerman et al., 1961). Separate forms are available for use with mothers and fathers.

Sample Items:

(A) Children should be allowed to disagree with their parents if they feel their own ideas are better.

(B) All young mothers are afraid of their awkwardness in handling and holding the baby.

(C) Children need some of the natural meanness taken out of them.

Comments: The authors (1958) report KR-20 reliabilities for the 23 subscales. For first mothers, reliabilities ranged from .34 to .77, with a median of .65. For new, but not first-time, mothers, KR-20s were reported to range from .40 to .77, with a median of .68. Several studies have examined other psychometric properties of the scale.

References:

Becker, W. C., & Krug, R. S. (1965). The Parent Attitude Research Instrument—A research review. *Child Dev, 36*, 329–365.

Perry, J. C., Jensen, L., & Adams, G. R. (1985). The relationship between parents' attitudes toward child rearing and the sociometric status of their preschool children. *J Psychol, 119*, 567–574.

Schaefer, E. S., & Bell, R. Q. (1958). Development of a parental attitude research instrument. *Child Dev, 29*, 339–361.

Zuckerman, M., Ribback, B. B., Monashkin, I., & Norton, J. A., Jr. (1958). Normative data and factor analysis on the Parent Attitude Research Instrument. *J Cons Psych, 22*, 165–171.

III-2/II-1/b/C

348. SCHAEFER, E. S., & EDGERTON, M. Schaefer and Edgerton Revision of M. L. Kohn's (1977) Rank Order of Parental Values

Avail: 1985 Ref.

Variables Measured: Parental values for behaviors and characteristics of their children

Type of Instrument: Rank-order questionnaire

Instrument Description: Parents are handed three sets of cards, one at a time. Each set contains five cards, with each card having a behavior, attitude, or characteristic printed on it. Respondents are asked to rank-order the five cards in terms of how important each characteristic is to them for their child. Cards are ordered from that which parents wish their child to learn first to that which they find least important. Card sets are both handed to parents and read aloud by the experimenter. Individual items are scored according to their rank-ordering. Three composite scores (conformity, self-directing, and social) are derived by summing individual scores from appropriate items. Details regarding scoring procedures are provided in the source listed below.

Sample Items (First set of cards):

(A)   to think for him/herself
(B)   to keep him/herself and his/her clothes clean
(C)   to be curious about many things
(D)   to be polite to adults
(E)   to be kind to other children

Comments: This instrument is a revision of the 13-item Index of Parental Values (Kohn, 1977). The original instrument was developed during the late 1950s and initially published in 1969. This revision departs from the original in that all items in each of the three sets are rank-ordered, whereas, in the original, parents were asked to indicate their top and bottom choices from a single group of behaviors and other characteristics.

References:

Kohn, M. L. (1977). *Class and conformity: A study in values* (2nd ed.). Chicago: University of Chicago Press.

Schaefer, E. S., & Edgerton, M. (1985). Parent and child correlates of parental modernity. In I. E. Sigel (Ed.), *Parental belief systems* (pp. 287–318). Hillsdale, NJ: Lawrence Erlbaum.

III-2/b/C

349. SCHAEFER, E. S., & EDGERTON, M. The Parental Modernity Inventory (PM)

Avail: 1985 Ref.

Variables Measured: Attitudes toward child rearing and education that are predictive of intellectual competence of the child

Type of Instrument: Self-report questionnaire

Instrument Description: The PM is a 5-point, 30-item Likert-type questionnaire. Response options range from *strongly disagree* to *strongly agree*. Items were designed for use with parents. However, the questionnaire may be adapted for use with teachers or other inter-actants by eliminating or rewording 5 items containing the phrase "my child." The questionnaire can be administered either orally or in written form. The scale is designed to measure two variables related to parental modernity: PM progressive, measuring modern progressive attitudes, and PM authoritarian, which evaluates authoritarian and conformist attitudes. The PM progressive attitudes score is derived from summing response values from 8 items. The remaining 22 item scores are summed in order to arrive at the PM authoritarian score. A single index of modernity is derived by subtracting authoritarian from progressive scores. A previous version of the PM was titled the Childrearing and Education Research Instrument (CERI).

Sample Items:

(A) Since parents lack special training in education, they should not question the teacher's teaching methods.

(B) Children will not do the right thing unless they must.

(C) Children's learning results mainly from being presented basic information again and again.

Comments: The authors report that split-half reliabilities for the PM range from .88 to .94. Test-retest reliability is reported to be .89. Separate reliability analyses performed on data from Black and White samples are reported to have yielded internal consistency and test-retest reliabilities ranging from .84 to .94. Correlations of PM scales with teacher ratings of child intelligence have been reported to range from .29 to .72.

Reference:

Schaefer, E. S., & Edgerton, M. (1985). Parent and child correlates of parental modernity. In I. E. Sigel (Ed.), *Parental belief systems* (pp. 287–318). Hillsdale, NJ: Lawrence Erlbaum.

III-2/b/C

350. SCHAEFER, E. S., & FINKELSTEIN, N. W. Child Behavior Toward Parent Inventory

Avail: NAPS-3

Variables Measured: Parental reports of child's behavior toward the parent

Type of Instrument: Behavior rating inventory

Instrument Description: This instrument is a 4-point, 155-item questionnaire consisting of 31 subscales containing five items each. Respondents indicate the extent to which each behavior is descriptive of their child, with response options ranging from *very much like* to *not at all like*. Individual subscales assess various types of behavior exhibited by children toward their parents. A factor analysis identified three major factors: (1) resists control and attempts to control parent, (2) positive involvement versus avoidance of affection and shared activity, and (3) independence versus dependence in deciding and doing things. The scale was developed to complement the Children's Reports of Parental Behavior Inventory (Schaefer, 1965). The subscales are often used individually and in various combinations rather than as a cohesive unit by investigators interested in different aspects of parent-child interactions. A short form of the instrument by Schaefer and Edgerton, containing five 5-item scales (instrumental independence, positive involvement, compliance and obedience, resisting and controlling, and detachment and distance), is also available from NAPS-3. An additional short form (Clingempeel & Segal, 1986) has been developed for use in assessing reports of stepparents.

Sample Items:

(A)   Tells me about his/her friends or activities.
(B)   Tries to do things for himself/herself.
(C)   Pushes me away when I get close.

Comments: The inventory was originally developed in 1975 but has never been published in its entirety. The original factor and reliability analyses reported by the author indicate KR-20 values ranging from .69 to .95 (median .88) for the 31 5-item scales. The factor analysis examined groupings of subscales rather than items, with subscales loading at least .55 on their primary factors.

References:

Brook, J. S., Whitman, M., & Gordon, A. S. (1981). Maternal and personality determinants of adolescent smoking behavior. *J Genet Psy, 139,* 185–193.

Brook, J. S., Whitman, M., Gordon, A. S., & Brook, D. W. (1984). Paternal determinants of female adolescents' marijuana use. *Devel Psych, 20,* 1032–1043.

Clingempeel, W. G., & Segal, S. (1986). Stepparent-stepchild relationships and the psychological adjustment of children in stepmother and stepfather families. *Child Dev, 57,* 474–484.

Savin-Williams, R. C., & Small, S. A. (1986). The timing of puberty and its relationship to adolescent and parent perceptions of family interactions. *Devel Psych, 22,* 342–347.

III-2/II-3/b/P

351. SCHAEFER, E. S., INGRAM, D. D., BAUMAN, K. E., SIEGEL, E., & SAUNDERS, M. M. Attachment Inventory

Avail: NAPS-3

Variables Measured: Maternal acceptance, rejection, involvement, and level of interaction with her infant

Type of Instrument: Behavior-observation rating system

Instrument Description: The Attachment Inventory is a 75-item rating scale on which mothers' levels of acceptance versus rejection, and involvement with their infants, are assessed. Observations are made at 4 and 12 months, with ratings assigned following an interview during which a series of additional instruments is administered. Scores are assigned on a 5-point Likert-type scale, ranging from *very much like her* to *not at all like her*. In addition, raters indicate whether or not they had an opportunity to observe each maternal behavior. Ratings on individual items are combined within two factors: positive interaction and irritable/

punitive. The instrument, originally constructed in 1978, was designed to be simultaneously filled out by multiple raters.

Sample Items:

(A)   Mother praises baby's new responses or responses to new events.
(B)   Mother looks at baby without a trace of tenderness.
(C)   Mother stimulates baby frequently (e.g., lots of talking, handling, playing).

Comments: The authors report reliabilities for interaction/stimulation of .82 and .84. Reliabilities for punitiveness/irritability are reported to be .28 and .46 for 4 and 12 months, respectively. Stability of factor scores between 4 and 12 months was reported to be .55 for interaction/stimulation, and .33 for punitiveness/irritability. Factor loadings were reported for 11 interaction/stimulation and for 7 punitiveness/irritability items (a total of 18 of 75 items). Primary factor loadings ranged from .65 to .82 for the interaction factor and from .65 to .72 for the punitive factor. Cross-loadings ranged from .00 to .48 for Factor I and from .01 to .32 for Factor II. In all, 5 of 11 and 1 of 7 items on the two factors, for which data were provided, loaded .30 or greater on the secondary factor at 4 months, 12 months, or both.

References:

Flick, L. H., & McSweeney, M. (1987). Measures of mother-child interaction: A comparison of three methods. *Res Nurs H, 10,* 129–137.
Schaefer, E. S., Hunter, W. M., & Edgerton, M. (1986). Maternal prenatal, infancy and concurrent predictors of maternal reports of child psychopathology. *Psychiatry, 50,* 320–331.

III-2/IV-2/b/P
352. SCHECK, D. C. Inconsistent Parental Discipline Scale (IPD)

Avail: 1979 Ref.

Variables Measured: Consistency of disciplinary actions by both parents

Type of Instrument: Self-report questionnaire

Instrument Description: The IPD is a 5-point, 7-item questionnaire designed to assess adults' perceptions of the consistency of their parents' disciplinary strategies when the respondent was about 12 years old. Items are scored on a 1–5 basis, with response options ranging from *very untrue* to *very true.* Respondents are asked to answer each item with regard to each parent. Thus each item is given two responses. The author recommends that the questionnaire be combined with items from other scales so that the nature of the task might be disguised. A companion instrument to the IPD by the same author, the Parental Disagreement on Expectations of the Child Scale, is also available in the source noted above. Scoring of the IPD is accomplished by summing values associated with responses to each of the 7 items. Overall scores can range from 5 to 35.

Sample Items:

(A) My mother (father) sometimes carried out threatened punishment and sometimes did not.

(B) My mother (father) sometimes gave a warning before punishing me and sometimes did not.

(C) My mother (father) often punished me for things which she (he) had previously told were right.

Comments: The author indicated that IPD items were adapted from scales previously constructed by Andry (1960), Distler (1965), and Itkin (1952). Spearman-Brown split-half reliability for the IPD is reported to be .71 for ratings of fathers' disciplinary consistency, and .62 for maternal ratings. Correlations are reported between the IPD and Rotter's Locus of Control Scale (.12 for fathers, .15 for mothers), family size (.11 for fathers, .15 for mothers), and social class (.10 for fathers, .14 for mothers).

References:

Scheck, D. C. (1978). An exploratory investigation of the interaction effects of three child-rearing dimensions upon the development of internal-external control orientation in adolescent females. *Psychology, 15,* 8–13.

Scheck, D. C. (1979). Two measures of parental consistency. *Psychology, 16,* 37–39.

Scheck, D. C., & Emerick, R. (1976). The young male adolescent's perception of early child-rearing behavior: The differential effects of socioeconomic status and family size. *Sociometry, 39,* 39–52.

Scheck, D. C., Emerick, R., & El-Assal, M. M. (1973). Adolescents' perceptions of parent-child relations and the development of internal-external control orientation. *J Mar Fam, 35,* 643–654.

III-2/b/P
353. SCHUMM, W. R. Kansas Parental Satisfaction Scale

Avail: NAPS-3

Variables Measured: Perceived satisfaction with parenting

Type of Instrument: Self-report questionnaire

Instrument Description: This 3-item Likert-type scale was designed as a parallel instrument to the Kansas Marital Satisfaction Scale. Satisfaction is assessed with respect to oneself as a parent, behavior of children, and relationship with children. It has been used with both 7- and 5-point response formats, with response options ranging from *strongly agree* to *strongly disagree.* The author reports a preference for the 7-point option. It is intended to be used with married or unmarried parents of one or more children. A composite score, using the summed scores from the individual items, is used. Total scores range from 3 to 21 points.

Sample Items:

(A) How satisfied are you with your children's behavior?

(B) How satisfied are you with yourself as a parent?

(C) How satisfied are you with your relationship(s) with your children?

Comments: The author notes that the first item originally read: "How satisfied are you with your children?" This was later changed to " . . . with your children's behavior?" Cronbach's alpha for the scale is reported by the author to range from .78 to .85. Correlations are reported between this instrument and frequency of job/family conflicts (-.25), severity of job/family conflicts (-.47), self-esteem (.23 to .55), internal locus of control (.18), and marital satisfaction (.23). The author reports that the lowest score of the 3 items was on satisfaction with self as a parent, followed by satisfaction with the relationship with children. Alpha for a Korean language translation is reported to be .92.

References:

James, D. E., Kennedy, C. E., & Schumm, W. R. (1986). Changes in parental attitudes and practices following a religiously oriented parent education program. *Fam Perspect, 20,* 45–59.

James, D. E., Schumm, W. R., Kennedy, C. E., Grigsby, C. C., & Shectman, K. L. (1985). Characteristics of the Kansas Parental Satisfaction Scale among two samples of married parents. *Psychol Rep, 57,* 163–169.

Jeong, G. J., & Schumm, W. R. (in press). Family satisfaction in Korean/American marriages: An exploratory study of the perceptions of Korean wives. *J Comp Fam Studies.*

Schumm, W. R., Nichols, C. W., Shectman, K. L., & Grigsby, C. C. (1983). Characteristics of responses to the Kansas Marital Satisfaction Scale by a sample of 84 married mothers. *Psychol Rep, 53,* 567–572.

III-2/b/P
354. SEARS, R. R., MACCOBY, E. E., & LEVIN, H. Patterns of Child-Rearing Interview

Avail: 1957 Ref.

Variables Measured: A wide range of child-rearing practices, a sampling of which includes those related to feeding, toilet training, dependency, gender, aggression, restrictions, and demands

Type of Instrument: Interview schedule

Instrument Description: The Patterns of Child-Rearing Interview protocol was developed for a 1951–1952 study of child-rearing practices of 379 mothers of kindergarten children from two New England communities, one described in the original study as "middle class" and the other as "working class." The interview schedule consisted of 72 open-ended questions, with many items containing instructions for interviewers to follow up answers with further probes. Questions were designed to elicit a comprehensive picture of prenatal and child-rearing practices up until that point. A group of scales containing a total of 143 item were used to quantify information obtained during the interview. The scales were developed according to the degrees of difference that could be distinguished by a panel of 10 graduate students. The interview protocol, since its original publication in 1957, has been used in part by many investigators, but tends not to be used in its entirety. It has recently been translated and used to examine child-rearing practices among the Chinese (Ho & Kang, 1984). It was also used, 25 years later, to examine second-generation child-rearing practices of the original Sears, Maccoby, and Levin sample (McClelland & Pilon, 1983).

Sample Items (Note: These items are from the list of those asked of mothers):

(A) All babies cry, of course. Some mothers feel that if you pick up a baby every time it cries, you will spoil it. Others think you should never let a baby cry for very long. How do you feel about this?

(B) . . . the question of being neat and orderly and keeping things clean. What do you expect of (your child) as far as neatness is concerned? How do you go about getting him to do this?

(C) . . . when (your child) is playing with one of the other children in the neighborhood and there is a quarrel or a fight—how do you handle this?

Comments: The original reference contains interrater correlations for each item with respect to judges' interpretation of open-ended questionnaire items. Correlations for the 143 items range from .47 to .99, with most items in the .60 to .80 range. Other information regarding validity issues is contained in the references listed below.

References:

Barsch, R. T. (1968). *The parent of the handicapped child: The study of childrearing practices.* Springfield, IL: Charles C Thomas.

Ho, D. Y. F., & Kang, T. K. (1984). Intergenerational comparisons of child-rearing attitudes and practices in Hong Kong. *Devel Psych, 20,* 1004–1016.

McClelland, D. C., & Pilon, D. A. (1983). Sources of adult motives in patterns of parent behavior in early childhood. *J Pers Soc Psy, 44,* 564–574.

Sears, R. R., Maccoby, E. E., & Levin, H. (1957). *Patterns of child rearing.* New York: Harper & Row.

III-2/IV-2/b/C
355. SEBES, J. M. Adolescent Abuse Inventory (AAI)

Avail: 1986 Ref.

Variables Measured: Adolescents' normal and acting out behaviors, parental attitudes toward possible actions taken in response to such behavior, and parental likelihood of behaving in such a fashion

Type of Instrument: Self-report questionnaire

Instrument Description: The AAI was developed to assess the possible risk for maltreatment in families with adolescents aged 11 to 15 who have been identified as "troubled." The questionnaire is composed of 26 hypothetical situations that include a specific adolescent behavior (from typical adolescent assertion for independence through delinquency) to which a parent is responding (from appropriate responses through physical abuse). Two separate forms, one for males and one for females, are available. After each situation, parents are asked to respond to the three 7-point Likert-type items and one open-ended question. The 3 items following each scenario address (a) the frequency of adolescent behaviors, (b) parental attitudes toward maltreatment, and (c) the parent's likelihood of acting abusively or appropriately. Total administration time is approximately 30 minutes.

Sample Items:

(A) Jeff came home sobbing from a date one night. His sister came in and woke her parents up and asked them to come in and talk to Jeff to see what was wrong. The parent said, "Jeff will forget about it quicker if we don't pay any attention to it."

(B) Sam came in drunk one night and began to argue with his mother. His father came in just as Sam yelled an obscene remark at his mother, and his father then punched him.

(C) Jeff came home and plopped his very bad report card in front of his parent. While reading the paper his parent said, "With parents like you have, I don't know how you turned out so stupid."

Comments: The AAI has been used in different ways to define high risk. The method used by the authors sums scores across the b and c scales (above) for each parent, excluding the appropriate parenting items (due to a reported reliability of .12 for this subscale). This leaves a total of 44 items. Reports of reliability of various subcategories of the remaining items range from .24 to .88, with an average reported reliability for the 26-item scale of .71 for both mothers and fathers.

References:

Garbarino, J., Schellenbach, C., & Sebes, J. (1986). *Troubled youth, troubled families*. New York: Aldine.
Garbarino, J., Sebes, J., & Schellenbach, C. (1984). Families at risk for destructive parent-child relations in adolescence. *Child Dev, 55,* 174–183.

III-2/b/P

356. SIEGELMAN, M., & ROE, A. The Parent-Child Relations Questionnaire II (PCRII)

Avail: NAPS-3

Variables Measured: Adult children's memories of parental actions toward them when they were about 12 years old

Type of Instrument: Self-report questionnaire

Instrument Description: The PCRII is a 4-point, 50-item Likert-type questionnaire designed to assess previous behavior of parents toward their now adult children. This instrument, developed in 1973 but copyrighted 1979, is a short form of the 10-factor, 130-item Parent-Child Relations Questionnaire (PCR; Roe & Siegelman, 1963). In the PCRII, adults serve as respondents, indicating whether each statement represents a behavior of their mothers or fathers during the time when the respondent was growing up, particularly prior to the time of their twelfth birthday. The authors indicate that items are specifically targeted toward behaviors, and not to attitudes or feelings. The vocabulary is geared to persons with fourth-grade reading skills. Separate forms are provided for rating mother-daughter, father-daughter, mother-son, and father-son relationships. While there is substantial overlap, items differ between forms but always fall within the dimensions of loving, rejecting, casual, demanding, and attention. Ten items are scored within each dimension on each form. Items are in the form of statements, to which respondents indicate whether each is *very true, tended to be true, tended to be untrue,* or *very untrue.* Scoring is on a 1–4 basis, with scores assigned to individual responses summed within factors.

Sample Items:

(A) Did not bother much about enforcing rules.
(B) Said nice things about me.
(C) Gave me new things as a reward, such as toys.

Comments: The authors indicate that KR-20 reliabilities ranged from .63 to .97 for the five subscales across various samples. A factor analysis resulted in the interpretation of three primary factors, with items from loving and rejecting loading on one factor, casual and demanding items loading on another, and attention items loading on the third factor.

References:

Jackson, L. A., Ialongo, N., & Stollak, G. E. (1986). Parental correlates of gender role: The relations between parents' masculinity, femininity, and child-rearing behaviors and their children's gender roles. *J Soc Clin Psy, 4,* 204–224.

Siegelman, M. (1981). Parental backgrounds of homosexual and heterosexual women: A cross-national replication. *Arch Sex Be, 10,* 371–378.

McCrae, R. R., & Costa, P. T., Jr. (1988). Recalled parent-child relations and adult personality. *J Personal, 56,* 417–434.

Tzuriel, D., & Haywood, H. C. (1985). Locus of control and child-rearing practices in intrinsically motivated and extrinsically motivated children. *Psychol Rep, 57,* 887–894.

III-2/b/P

357. SIGEL, I. E., FLAUHGER, J., REDMAN, M., SANDER, J., & STINSON, E. Parent Belief Strategy Interview

Avail: NAPS-3

Variables Measured: Parents' understanding of normal child development

Type of Instrument: Interview coding scheme

Instrument Description: This instrument consists of three primary elements: (1) a set of 12 written vignettes representing situations within physical, social, moral, and intrapersonal domains that parents typically encounter in child rearing; (2) a structured interview with parents asking a series of seven open-ended questions for each vignette; and (3) a series of 25 definitions that serve as the basis for coding parental responses. Vignettes were designed to elicit parents' beliefs about how children learn, as well as specific teaching strategies parents employ to facilitate the learning process. Interviews are tape-recorded for later coding. Vignettes deal with the areas of emotional control, sharing, measurement, cheating, unfairness, fear, written instructions, being truthful, failure, hitting, property rights, and time. For each, parents are first asked what they would do to help their child deal effectively with the situation, such as "What would you do or say to help (child) learn to control his/her emotions, what words would you use?" The technique stated by the parent is labeled "Strategy I." Following the parent's statement of Strategy I, he or she is asked how this strategy will help his or her child. The response to this question is termed "Construct I." Interviewers request two specific strategies (i.e., "If what you tried didn't work . . . ") and accompanying constructs, followed by an inquiry as to other possible strategies, and questions dealing with whether or not the parent believes his or her child, as well as most children, will ever master the behavior. Evaluation of the data is accomplished by examining frequencies for each behavioral strategy employed by parents across the 12 situations. Specific vignettes, questions, and definitions are contained in the manual (available through NAPS-3).

Sample Items:

(A)   (Child's name) is trying to put together a model, and after much effort, it falls apart. He/she is upset and acts distressed. You want to help (child) learn to control his/her emotions.

(B)   (Child's name) won't share the use of the TV with his/her brother or sister. The two kids are arguing. You want to help him/her learn to share.

(C)   (Child's name) comes to you with a yardstick and asks you how many cubic meters of water your bathtub could hold. You want to help him/her learn about measurement.

Comments: The authors indicate that a factor analysis revealed factors related to physical knowledge, intrapsychic concerns, and moral/social situations. Mean interrater agreement across 20% of 164 interview conducted by the authors is reported to have been .94.

References:

McGillicuddy-Delisi, A. V. (1982). The relationship between parents' beliefs about development and family constellation, socioeconomic status, and parents' teaching strategies. In L. M. Laosa & I. E. Sigel (Eds.), *Families as learning environments for children* (pp. 261–299). New York: Plenum.

McGillicuddy-Delisi, A. V. (1985). The relationship between parental beliefs and children's cognitive level. In I. E. Sigel (Ed.), *Parental belief systems* (pp. 7–24). Hillsdale, NJ: Lawrence Erlbaum.

Sigel, I. E. (1982). Reflections on the belief-behavior connection: Lessons learned from a research program on parental belief systems and teaching strategies. In R. D. Ashmore & D. M. Brodzinsky (Eds.), *Thinking about the family: Views of parents and children* (pp. 35–65). Hillsdale, NJ: Lawrence Erlbaum.

Skinner, E. A. (1985). Determinants of mother sensitive and contingent-response behavior: The role of childrearing beliefs and socioeconomic status. In I. E. Sigel (Ed.), *Parental belief systems* (pp. 51–82). Hillsdale, NJ: Lawrence Erlbaum.

III-2/IV-2/II-3/b/P

358. SLATER, M. A., POWER, T. G., & VINCENT, J. P. Parenting Dimensions Inventory (PDI)

Avail: 1987 Ref.

Variables Measured: Parental support, control, and structure

Type of Instrument: Self-report questionnaire

Instrument Description: The PDI is a 54-item Likert-type scale created to assess nine parenting dimensions (nurturance, sensitivity to child's input, nonrestrictive attitude, type of control strategy, amount of control, maturity demands, involvement, consistency, and organization). Various portions of the PDI utilize forced-choice "a" or "b" formats, and 4-point, 5-point, and 6-point response formats. Items were adapted from several existing instruments, including the Parent Attitude Research Instrument (Schaefer & Bell, 1958), the Block Childrearing Practices Report (Block, 1965), the Parent Attitude Inquiry (Baumrind, 1971), the Childrearing Practices Questionnaire (Dielman & Barton, 1981), and others. The instrument was designed to assess parenting attitudes and behaviors for parents of elementary-school-aged children. Administration time is approximately 15–20 minutes.

Sample Items:

(A) I think a child should be encouraged to do things better than others.

(B) Select either (1) or (2) below:

(1) Nowadays too much emphasis is placed on obedience for children.

(2) Nowadays parents are too concerned about letting children do what they want.

(C) Please indicate . . . how often you did the following activities with your child in the past month.

1. Visit friends or relatives with child.

Comments: The author reports that the PDI was developed and revised to its present form on a sample of 112 parents of 6- to 11-year-old children. It was cross-validated on an independent sample of 140 parents. Finally, the PDI was used to investigate differential parenting in single- (n = 102) versus two-parent (n = 140) families. Validity of the PDI was examined in comparison with scores of children's behavior problems and social competence, as measured by the Child Behavior Checklist. Cronbach's alpha for the nine subscales is reported to range from .54 to .79. Further information regarding reliability and validity is available in the reference listed below.

Reference:

Slater, M. A., & Power, T. G. (1987). Multidimensional assessment of parenting in single-parent families. In J. P. Vincent (Ed.), *Advances in family intervention, assessment, and theory* (Vol. 4, pp. 197–228). Greenwich, CT: JAI.

III-2/b/C

359. SMALL, S. A. Adolescent's Participation in Activities with Parents Scale

Avail: NAPS-3

Variables Measured: Time spent with parents in recreational or leisure activities

Type of Instrument: Self-report questionnaire

Instrument Description: This instrument is a 6-point, 6-item Likert-type questionnaire designed to examine the amount of time the preadolescent or adolescent spends with his or her parent in educational and recreational activities (e.g., watching television, playing games, attending movies or events). The six response categories range from *a few times a day* to *never*. An overall composite score is obtained by summing the scores across items. Questionnaire respondents are children, with separate forms being used for participation in events with mothers versus fathers.

Sample Items:

(A)   How often do you watch television with your mother/father?
(B)   How often do you go to movies or events with your mother/father?
(C)   How often do you have friendly talks with your mother/father?

Comments: The author reports that Cronbach's alpha has been measured at .68. Individual item-total correlations range from .39 to .52, with a mean of .45.

References:

Demo, D. H., Small, S. A., & Savin-Williams, R. C. (1987). Family relations and the self-esteem of adolescents and their parents. *J Mar Fam, 49*, 705–715.
Small, S. A. (1988). Parental self-esteem and its relationship to childrearing practices, parent-adolescent interaction and adolescent behavior. *J Mar Fam, 50*, 1063–1072.

III-2/IV-2/b/C

360. SMALL, S. A. Child's Non-Adherence to Parental Advice Scale

Avail: NAPS-3

Variables Measured: Children's following of advice of parents on a variety of issues

Type of Instrument: Self-report questionnaire

Instrument Description: This 10-item instrument was developed for use with preadolescents and adolescents. There are four response categories ranging from *strong yes* to *strong no*. An overall composite score is obtained by summing the scores across items. The measure asks the children whether they follow the advice of their parents on a variety of issues (e.g., physical appearance, time spent studying, choice of friends, drug use). Separate forms of the scale, substituting "mother" for "father," assess the child's tendency to follow advice of his or her mother and father.

Sample Items:

(A)   I usually follow my mother's/father's advice about the clothes I wear.
(B)   I usually follow my mother's/father's advice in matters that concern friends of the opposite sex or dating.
(C)   I usually follow my mother's/father's advice about which clubs or social groups I should join.

Comments: The author reports that Cronbach's alpha has been measured at .89. Individual item-total correlations range from .43 to .70, with a mean of .57.

References:

Savin-Williams, R. C., & Small, S. A. (1986). The timing of puberty and its relationship to adolescent and parent perceptions of family interactions. *Devel Psych, 22,* 343–347.
Small, S. A. (1988). Parental self-esteem and its relationship to childrearing practices, parent-adolescent interaction and adolescent behavior. *J Mar Fam, 50,* 1063–1072.

III-2/II-3/b/P
361. SMALL, S. A. Parental Affection to the Child Scale

Avail: NAPS-3

Variables Measured: A parent's affection to a specific child

Type of Instrument: Self-report questionnaire

Instrument Description: This instrument is a 7-item Likert-style questionnaire designed to assess how frequently a parent displays affectionate behaviors to a child. It was developed for use with preadolescents and adolescents. There are six response categories, ranging from *a few times a day* to *never*. An overall composite score is obtained by summing the scores across items.

Sample Items:

(A)   How often do you kiss your child?
(B)   How often do you tell your child that you love him/her?
(C)   How often do you hug or embrace your child?

Comments: The author indicates that Cronbach's alpha for this instrument is .89. The correlation between this scale and the parent support subscale from the Cornell Behavior Inventory—which assesses the child's report of the parent's support, affection, and positive sentiment for the child—is reported to be .31. Item-total correlations are reported to range from .55 to .85.

References:

Demo, D. H., Small, S. A., & Savin-Williams, R. C. (1987). Family relations and the self-esteem of adolescents and their parents. *J Mar Fam, 49,* 705–715.
Savin-Williams, R. C., & Small, S. A. (1986). The timing of puberty and its relationship to adolescent and parent perceptions of family interactions. *Devel Psych, 22,* 343–347.

III-2/IV-2/b/C

362. SMALL, S. A. Parental Concern About Child's Behavior Scale

Avail: NAPS-3

Variables Measured: Parental concern and worry about a preadolescent or adolescent child's behavior

Type of Instrument: Self-report questionnaire

Instrument Description: This 4-point, 26-item Likert-style questionnaire was developed for use with parents of preadolescents and adolescents. An overall composite score is obtained by summing scores across items. This instrument was designed to measure issues and concerns that most adults encounter in their role as parents. Most items involve issues related to the child's autonomy. This measure was modeled after Pearlin and Schooler's Strain Scale (1978). The parental concerns included in the current scale were identified from issues that were repeatedly cited in a pilot study of parents of preadolescent and adolescent children. Parents had been asked to identify issues they were most concerned about, difficulties they encountered rearing a child this age, and issues that evoked the most parent-child conflict.

Sample Items:

(A)　How often do you wonder if your child might be using too much alcohol?
(B)　How often does it happen that your advice and guidance concerning who your child chooses as friends is ignored by your child?
(C)　How often does it happen that you are treated without proper respect by your child?

Comments: The author indicates that Cronbach's alpha for this instrument is .91. The correlation between this scale and the Parental Stress Scale is reported to be .62. Item-total correlations are reported to range from .17 to .69.

References:

Savin-Williams, R. C., & Small, S. A. (1986). The timing of puberty and its relationship to adolescent and parent perceptions of family interactions. *Devel Psych, 22,* 343–347.
Small, S. A. (1988). Parental self-esteem and its relationship to childrearing practices, parent-adolescent interaction and adolescent behavior. *J Mar Fam, 50,* 1063–1072.

III-2/IV-2/b/P

363. SMALL, S. A. Parental Control over Decisions Involving the Child Scale

Avail: NAPS-3

Variables Measured: Decision making between parent and child

Type of Instrument: Self-report questionnaire

Instrument Description: This instrument is a 5-point, 15-item Likert-type questionnaire designed for use in assessing parent-child control over common decision areas. Parents are asked how decisions are made on a variety of issues commonly discussed in families with preadolescent and adolescent children. The five response options fall along a continuum from high parental domination (*the parent[s] decide*) to high parental permissiveness (*the child decides*). An overall composite score is obtained by summing the scores across items. Items can also be looked at individually to examine on which issues parents are most and least permissive or controlling. The measure is modeled after the single-item Independence Training Index (Elder, 1963; Kandel & Lessor, 1972).

Sample Items:

(A)   In your family, who decides what time your child goes to bed at night?
(B)   In your family, who decides where your child is allowed to go with his or her friends?
(C)   In your family, who decides whether or not your child is allowed to drink or smoke?

Comments: The author reports that Cronbach's alpha has been measured at .88. Individual item-total correlations range from .38 to .72, with a mean of .54.

References:

Demo, D. H., Small, S. A., & Savin-Williams, R. C. (1987). Family relations and the self-esteem of adolescents and their parents. *J Mar Fam, 49,* 705–715.
Savin-Williams, R. C., & Small, S. A. (1986). The timing of puberty and its relationship to adolescent and parent perceptions of family interactions. *Devel Psych, 22,* 343–347.
Small, S. A. (1988). Parental self-esteem and its relationship to childrearing practices, parent-adolescent interaction and adolescent behavior. *J Mar Fam, 50,* 1063–1072.

III-2/b/g/C
364. SMITH, T. E. Youth Information and Opinion Form

Avail: NAPS-3

Variables Measured: What adolescents think about themselves, their parents, and other matters

Type of Instrument: Self-report questionnaire

Instrument Description: This instrument contains 102 items requesting information from adolescents regarding controls exercised over them by their parents, advice and structure provided by parents, and the subject's own behaviors and perceptions regarding advice offered by parents and teachers. There are 28 items asking directly about self-perceptions, and 37 items requesting information regarding behaviors of each of the subject's parents. Parental items are identical for mothers and fathers. Item scores are combined in order to examine 38 variables. Questions appear on an optical scanning sheet with seven response options available for each item. Responses are entered as T, 1, 2, 3, 4, 5, or F, with T indicating that the item is entirely true, F indicating that it is entirely false, and the numbers 1–5 indicating that the item falls somewhere in between the two extremes. For scoring purposes, items are coded from 1 to 7 with T being equal to 1 and F being scored as 7. An additional 33 items request demographic and behavioral information. The test booklet is six pages long. Scoring instructions are contained in an accompanying three-page instruction packet.

Sample Items:

(A)   My father should never deliberately let anything hurt me.
(B)   My mother has taught me to question my parent's orders when I have a reason to do so.
(C)   I myself believe most teachers are unfair.

Comments: The author reports use of this instrument with a group of several thousand sixth- to twelfth-grade public school students (Smith, 1977). In this study, it is reported that 15 of the 38 variables were measured by four items each: two positive items and two negative items. Omega is used to measure internal consistency and is reported for the sets of four items to have a mean of .66 and a median of .68.

References:

Smith, T. E. (1976). Push versus pull: Intra-family versus peer-group variables as possible determinants of adolescent orientations toward parents. *Youth Soc, 8,* 5–26.
Smith, T. E. (1977). An empirical comparison of potential determinants of parental authority. *J Mar Fam, 39,* 153–164.
Smith, T. E. (1983). Parental influence: A review of the evidence of influence and a theoretical model of the parental influence process. In A. C. Kerckhoff (Ed.), *Research in sociology of education and socialization* (Vol. 4, pp. 13–45). Greenwich, CT: JAI.

III-2/b/C
365. SPENCE, J. T., & HELMREICH, R. L. Parental Attitudes Questionnaire

Avail: 1978 Ref.

Variables Measured: Children's perceptions of their parents' attitudes and actions, and the family atmosphere

Type of Instrument: Self-report questionnaire

Instrument Description: This instrument is a 5-point, 63-item Likert-type questionnaire designed to measure adolescents' views of their parents and the family atmosphere. Respondents were instructed to include stepparents, foster parents, or any other adult guardian with primary responsibility within the definition of "parent." The questionnaire consists of two sections, with the first section divided into three parts. Section I contains 58 items and assesses parental attitudes and behaviors, as well as the family atmosphere. The initial 8 items of this section are designed to measure aspects of both parents or the family as a whole. The remaining two parts are parallel 25-item sets inquiring specifically about the mother and father, respectively. Each item in Section I is rated on a 5-point scale ranging from *very characteristic* to *very uncharacteristic.* Section II consists of 4 items designed to assess with which parent the adolescent most closely identifies, and a single item inquiring about the level of parental agreement regarding child rearing. These final 5 items are rated on 5-point scales designed to be applicable to each specific item. The authors report that development of the Parental Attitudes Questionnaire was particularly influenced by Baumrind (1971), Coopersmith (1967), and Heilbrun (1973).

Sample Items:

(A)   Members of my family are very close and get along amazingly well.
(B)   My mother believed there was no reason why she should have her own way all the time any more than I should have mine.
(C)   My father didn't want me to bother him with unimportant little problems.

Comments: The authors indicate that factor analyses of Section I with high school students from homes that had been intact since birth yielded 9 factors, with 7 of the factors common to both boys and girls. The structures of the remaining 2 factors differed by gender. Factors varied from 3 to 11 items. Cronbach's alpha for the 11 factors was reported to range from .53 to .89. Intercorrelations among factors reportedly ranged from .00 to .89.

References:

Hill, J., Holmbeck, G., Marlow, L., Green, T., & Lynch, M. (1985). Pubertal status and parent-child relations in families of seventh-grade boys. *J Early Adol, 5,* 31–44.

Spence, J. T., & Helmreich, R. L. (1978). *Masculinity & femininity: Their psychological dimensions, correlates, and antecedents.* Austin: University of Texas Press.

III-2/b

366. STOLBERG, A. L., & ULLMAN, A. J. Single Parenting Questionnaire (SPQ)

Avail: NAPS-3

Variables Measured: Dimensions of single-parent/child interaction

Type of Instrument: Self-report questionnaire

Instrument Description: The SPQ is a 4-point, 88-item primarily Likert-type questionnaire designed to assess aspects of single parents' interactions with their children. The scale was developed for use with divorced custodial parents. Item formats include both questions and statements, each containing four response options. Possible responses differ from one item to the next, with specific options geared to the requirements of each individual item. Response options are designed to provide a *most-to-least* or *least-to-most* listing. Six dimensions are measured by the SPQ: (1) problem-solving skills, (2) parental warmth, (3) discipline procedures, (4) parent rules, (5) enthusiasm for parenting, and (6) parent support systems. Responses are scored 1–4, with values within dimensions summed to arrive at subscale scores. Higher scores are interpreted as reflecting better parenting skills. An overall SPQ score is also generated. A revised 100-item version of the questionnaire is currently undergoing validation studies by the authors.

Sample Items:

(A) How often does your child come and talk to you about a problem?
   a. I think my child talks to me whenever he/she has a problem.
   b. I think my child usually talks to me whenever he/she has a problem.
   c. I think my child keeps most of his/her problems to him/herself, but sometimes talks to me.
   d. My child rarely discusses his/her problems with me.

(B) When I am not at home, my child knows how I can be reached
   a. At all times.
   b. About three quarters of the time.
   c. About half the time.
   d. About a quarter of the time.

Comments: The authors indicate that Cronbach's alpha for the subscales ranges from .63 to .77, with an alpha for the combined scale of .86. Two-week test-retest correlations are reported to range from .40 to .67. The SPQ is reported to correlate .44 with Fisher's Divorce Adjustment Scale.

References:

Stolberg, A. L., Camplair, C., Currier, K., & Wells, M. J. (1987). Individual, familial and environmental determinants of children's post-divorce adjustment and maladjustment. *J Divorce, 11*(1), 51–70.

Stolberg, A. L., & Garrison, K. M. (1985). Evaluating a primary prevention program for children of divorce. *Am J Comm P, 13,* 111–124.

Stolberg, A. L., & Ullman, A. J. (1985). Assessing dimensions of single parenting: The single parenting questionnaire. *J Divorce, 8*(2), 31–45.

III-2/b/P

367. STOLLAK, G. E. Sensitivity to Children Questionnaire

Avail: NAPS-2

Variables Measured: Adults' interactional styles with children

Type of Instrument: Projective content rating scale

Instrument Description: The Sensitivity to Children Questionnaire is a projective technique and behavior rating instrument for use in examining adult communications with children in problem situations. The following variables are scored based on ratings of adults' indications of their likely actions: (1) lecturing-directing, (2) power assertion-control, (3) adult expression of child's influence upon them, (4) empathy, (5) ridicule-interrogation, and (6) instrumental control. In generating data to be rated, subjects are asked to respond to projective items by writing their likely responses, but not their reasons, to a 6-year-old child in each of 8 to 16 situations. The instructions request that respondents pretend they are a parent of the child described in each situation. Each writing sample is scored according to the variables listed above. Category scores across items can be summed. An update of the Sensitivity to Children Questionnaire, the Parent-Child Interaction Projective Tape (PCIPT; Teyber, Messe, & Stollak, 1977), utilized the same six factors, but incorporated 25 categories on which ratings were made. In using the PCIPT, subjects are asked to respond verbally to audio-recordings of four male child's communications, pretending that they are the parent of the child.

Sample Items (Note: sample items listed are categories upon which adult responses to the PCIPT are rated):

(A)   Lecturing, arguing.
(B)   Warning, admonishing, threatening.
(C)   Statement of child feelings.

Comments: Of the 25 categories on the PCIPT, 20 are reported to load at least .30 on identified factors. The remaining 5 categories have factor loadings ranging from .20 to .24. Mean interrater reliability for two sets of three raters each on the 25 categories is reported to be .91.

References:

Stollak, G. E. (1973). An integrated graduate-undergraduate program in the assessment, treatment, and prevention of child psychopathology. *Prof Psych, 4,* 158–169.

Stollak, G. E., Green, L., Scholom, A., Schrieber, J., & Messe, L. A. (1975). The process and outcome of play encounters between undergraduates and clinic-referred children: Preliminary findings. *Psychother, 12,* 327–331.

Stollak, G. E., Scholom, A., Kallman, J. R., & Saturansky, C. (1973). Insensitivity to children: Responses of undergraduates to children in problem situations. *J Abn C Psy, 4,* 158–169.

Teyber, E. C., Messe, L. A., & Stollak, G. E. (1977). Adult responses to child communications. *Child Dev, 48,* 1577–1582.

III-2/b/C
368. STROM, R. D. Parent as a Teacher Inventory (PAAT)

Avail: Scholastic Testing Service, 480 Meyer Rd., P.O. Box 1056, Bensenville, IL 60106–8056

Variables Measured: Child-rearing expectations regarding the child's creativity, parental frustration and control, play, and parental perception of their ability to facilitate the teaching/learning process for their child

Type of Instrument: Self-report questionnaire

Instrument Description: The PAAT is intended as a means of assessing parental strengths, needs, and attitudes related to rearing 3- to 9-year-old children. This instrument was designed to yield information relevant for diagnosis, guidance, and curriculum planning. Ten items, designed to assess each of five variables (creativity, frustration, control, play, and teaching/learning), make a composite instrument of 50 items. Items are patterned so that each variable occurs once in every 5 items. Items are rated on a 4-point scale, with options ranging from *strong yes* to *strong no.* Responses are coded such that desired responses receive maximum scores. A total score is obtained by summing all 50 scores, with subtotals derived for each subscale. Response values for each item are entered on parents' personal profiles. The profile is intended to accompany the inventory as a guide for feedback to respondents as well as for program planning. Administration time is approximately 15 minutes.

Sample Items: The publisher did not grant permission to reproduce items.

Comments: The author reports on several studies with a combined subject population of over 3,000 families. Cronbach's alpha is reported to be above .75. Validity has been assessed through relating expressed behavior on the inventory with observed behavior in the home. In a study of 30 intact Mexican American families, behaviors were observed related to 38 of the 50 PAAT items. Observed and self-reported behaviors were reported to be consistent 66% of the time. Other uses of this instrument have stressed measuring the effect of various clinical interventions geared toward developing parenting skills in families from various cultural and socioeconomic backgrounds. The instrument is available from the source listed above, in both English and Spanish.

References:

Strom, R., Graf, P., Betz, A., & Wurster, S. (1985). A comparison of West German and guestworker parents' childrearing attitudes and expectations. *J Comp Fam Studies, 15,* 427–440.

Strom, R., Hathaway, C., & Slaughter, H. (1981). The correlation of maternal attitudes and preschool children's performance on the McCarthy scales of children's abilities. *J Instruc Psy, 8,* 139–145.

Strom, R., & Johnson, A. (1978). Assessment for parent education. *J Exp Educ, 47,* 9–16.

Strom, R., Rees, R., Slaughter, H., & Wurster, S. (1981). Childrearing expectations of families with atypical children. *Am J Orthop, 51,* 285–296.

III-2/b/P
369. STROM, R. D., & COOLEDGE, N. J. Parental Strength and Needs Inventory (PSNI)

Avail: NAPS-3

Variables Measured: Personal strengths and concerns regarding parental roles and obligations

Type of Instrument: Self-report questionnaire

Instrument Description: The PSNI is a series of four 4-point, 60-item Likert-type questionnaires designed to assess parental satisfaction, expectations, roles, and areas of difficulty. Separate forms of the inventory are available for administration to parents of children (ages 7–11) and adolescents (ages 12–18), as well as forms designed for direct administration with both children and adolescents. Each form contains six subareas measuring parent satisfaction, parent success, home teaching, parent difficulty, parent frustration, and information needs. Response options range from *always* to *never,* and are assigned values from one to four. Higher values are assigned to responses most indicative of parental strength. Each subarea is measured by 10 items. A score of 25 on any subset can serve as a point of overall differentiation between strength and need. Parent satisfaction, success, and home teaching scores are combined to yield a single measure of parent potentials. The remaining subsets of parent difficulty, frustration, and information needs are combined into a measure of parent concerns. An individual parent profile is developed, allowing for comparisons of adult and child responses within the family. Directions for parents describe the PSNI as an inventory of personal feelings about one's relationship to a particular son or daughter. Child participants are told the inventory purpose is to find out how boys and girls of their age feel about how they are being brought up. Administration time is approximately 15–20 minutes.

Sample Items (Note: All sample items are from the teenage child version):

(A)   My parents like to discuss feelings and ideas with me.
(B)   It's hard for my parents to accept my values.
(C)   My parents need to know more about helping me handle problems with other kids.

Comments: The PSNI was originally administered as an open-ended interview, with responses coded according to categories as defined in the current version. Interrater reliability for coded responses is reported by the author to have been .95. In a study of construct validity, 30 graduate students were asked to match 30 randomly selected responses from the open-ended instrument with 25 items on the Likert-type form. The degree of agreement is reported to have exceeded 91%. Cronbach's alpha for the six subsets is reported to range from .80 to .91, with alpha for second-order subsets of concerns and potentials ranging from .88 to .95.

References:

Strom, R. (1985). Developing a curriculum for parent education. *Fam Relat, 34,* 161–167.
Strom, R. (1988). Home and school assessment of exceptional families. *Int J Exp Res Educ,* 25, 96–111.
Strom, R., & Cooledge, N. (1984). Parental success as perceived by parents, teachers, and children. *Child St J, 14,* 339–347.
Strom, R., Jones, E., & Daniels, S. (1988). Parent education for the deaf. *Educ Psy Res, 8,* 117–128.

III-2/b/g/C
370. SWANSON, G. E. Child-Parent Relationship Scale (CPRS)

Avail: 1950 Ref.

Variables Measured: Children's feelings of happiness and satisfaction resulting from the parent-child relationship

Type of Instrument: Self-report questionnaire

Instrument Description: The CPRS is a 50-item questionnaire, developed in 1945 and first published in 1950, designed to assess adolescents' views as to areas of satisfaction and dissatisfaction in their parent-child relationships. Respondents indicate whether they agree, disagree, or are uncertain about each statement by answering either *Y* (yes), *N* (no), or *?* (uncertain). The final form of the questionnaire was derived from an initial 92-item pool. Items were generated from the Minnesota Scale for the Survey of Opinion (Rundquist & Sletto, 1936), elementary and secondary forms of the California Test of Personality (Tiegs, Clark, & Thorpe, 1939), the Family Relationships Questionnaire (Havinghurst & Taba, 1949), an untitled list published by Healy and Bronner (1936), and others developed by the author. Pilot testing and item analyses with a group of 200 delinquent boys resulted in final selection of the 50-item version. Additional validity studies were conducted with various populations.

Sample Items:

(A) It is hard for me to feel pleasant at home.
(B) I find more understanding at home than elsewhere.
(C) My parents tell other people things about me that I think they should not mention.

Comments: The initial pool of 92 items was subjected to an item analysis whereby answers from respondents in the top quartile were compared to those in the bottom quartile. Items retained in the final form were those that discriminated best between these two groups. Split-half reliability based on the pilot sample of 200 delinquents was reported by the author to be .96. Further testing with normal high school students, also presented in the original article, resulted in a reliability coefficient of .93. Validity information was obtained by the author by comparing judges' ratings and CPRS scores for 100 boys matched for IQ, religious affiliation, and other factors, half of whom were delinquent. Correlations between ratings and test scores averaged .95.

References:

Durrett, D. D., & Kelly, P. A. (1974). Can you really talk with your child? A parental training program in communication skills toward the improvement of parent-child interaction. *Group Psychoth Psychodrama, 27,* 98–109.

Serot, N. M., & Teevan, R. C. (1961). Perception of the parent-child relationship and its relation to child development. *Child Dev, 32,* 373–378.

Swanson, G. E. (1950). The development of an instrument for rating child-parent relationships. *Social Forc, 29,* 84–90.

Ternay, M. R., Wilborn, B., & Day, H. D. (1985). Perceived child-parent relationships and child adjustment in families with both adopted and natural children. *J Genet Psy, 146,* 261–272.

III-2/b/P
371. WASIK, B. H., & BRYANT, D. The Parent Means-End Problem Solving Instrument (PMEPS)

Avail: NAPS-3

Variables Measured: Parental means-end thinking with respect to child rearing and interpersonal issues

Type of Instrument: Interview and rating system

Instrument Description: The PMEPS was designed to measure parent means-end thinking, presumed to be a problem-solving process, through what is termed an "open-middle" format. Each individual is provided with the beginning and the ending of a story, and is asked to make up a story that connects the beginning with the end. The stories in this instrument have been developed specifically for parents, and cover topics on child care, developmental and interpersonal issues, and child management. Scoring is done by raters who make a determination on whether the responses should be classified as (1) relevant to the story, (2) irrelevant to the story, (3) an enumeration of a previously given response, or (4) responses based on revision to the presented story. Responses across the 10 stories are summed for each category. Responses are also categorized into one of seven solutions that are common across many problem situations (e.g., cooperate or compromise) and for story-specific relevant means. A 5-item version of the PMEPS is also available. Administration time for the 10-item version is approximately 20 minutes.

Sample Items:

(A)　Sara's older boy, a 2-year-old, was picking on the younger one. He took the baby's toys away, pushed him over, and made him cry. The story ends with both boys calmed down and playing nicely together. Start with Sara seeing the older one pick on the baby.

(B)　Martha is going back to work soon after her baby is born. Begin the story with Martha worried about what arrangements to make for her baby. End it with her finding a good place for him during the day.

(C)　Every time Paula sees a particular friend who has 2 older children, her friend offers unwanted advice about how Paula should raise her baby. Paula is angry at her friend. The story ends with Paula no longer angry at her friend because she is no longer advising Paula without being asked. Begin the story with Paula being angry with her friend.

Comments: The instrument is based on a previously developed, but unpublished, format by Platt and Spivack (1975). The authors indicate that the PMEPS has been used to distinguish between maltreating and nonmaltreating parents, and between low- and middle-income mothers. Test-retest reliabilities over a four- to six-week period for the main response category and the revisions category were reported to be .62 and .44, respectively.

Reference:

Azar, S. T., Robinson, D. R., Hekimian, E., & Twentyman, G. T. (1984). Unrealistic expectations and problem-solving ability in maltreating and comparison mothers. *J Cons Clin,* *52,* 687–691.

III-2/I-3/e
372. WOLF, B., WEINRAUB, M., & HAIMO, S. Social Network Form (SNF)

Avail: NAPS-3

Variables Measured: Characteristics of parents' social and support networks

Type of Instrument: Self-report questionnaire

Instrument Description: The SNF is a 23-item questionnaire concerning the nature and extent of social supports available to a parent. The questionnaire covers six basic areas: social contact, emotional support, support for parenting concerns, practical support received, and coping ability. The SNF asks respondents to list the four friends and relatives they see most frequently. The respondent is then asked to rate or comment upon the extent to which relationships with these four people are intimate, supportive, and helpful. Questions involve both ratings and open-ended questions. While many of the items request information regarding relationships with the four listed individuals, several questions allow for referral to other people from within the social network. Information on scoring is provided with the testing form. Administration of the SNF takes approximately 30 minutes.

Sample Items:

(A) How many times in the last month have you had some type of contact with each person? Please indicate the type of contact (in person, singly; in person, with a group; telephone or letter) and times per month.

(B) How much emotional support do you feel you get from each of these people? Use a scale from 1 to 10, where 1 = no emotional support and 10 = total emotional support.

(C) Do you feel you're getting the support and help you need as a parent (A 1–9 scale, from *never* to *always* is used for this item.)?

Comments: The authors report that Cronbach's alpha, computed on items making up the summary scores of total social contacts, emotional support, parent support, child care help, and household help ranged from .65 to .95, with a median of .78. Test-retest reliability over a two- to three-week period is also reported. Test-retest reliability was .67 for total social contacts, .89 for emotional support, .98 for household help, .91 for child care, .87 for household coping, .51 for child care responsibilities, .67 for coping with finances, .61 for emotional coping, and .67 for overall coping. Validity studies have examined use of the SNF with mothers in single-parent and two-parent households, and employed versus unemployed mothers. Detailed information on the SNF is available in Weinraub and Wolf (1983).

References:

Weinraub, M., Jaeger, E., & Hoffman, L. W. (1988). Predicting infant outcome in families of employed and non-employed mothers. *Early Child Res Q, 3,* 361–378.

Weinraub, M., & Wolf, B. (1983). Effects of stress and social supports on mother-child interactions in single- and two-parent families. *Child Dev, 54,* 1297–1311.

Weinraub, M., & Wolf, B. (1987). Stressful life events, social supports and parent child interaction: Similarities and differences in single parent and two parent families. In C. F. Boukydis (Ed.), *Research on support for parents and infants in the postnatal period.* Norwood, NJ: Ablex.

III-2/b/C

373. WORELL, J., & WORELL, L. The Parent Behavior Form (PBF)

Avail: NAPS-3

Variables Measured: Parental warmth, control, and cognitive mediation for both mothers and fathers

Type of Instrument: Self-report questionnaire

Instrument Description: The three factors of parental warmth, parental control, and parental cognitive mediation are assessed by means of 13 empirically derived scales containing 9 items each. All items on the PBF are answered twice, once for each parent. The 13 content scales were developed by means of cluster analysis, with the 9 items loading highest on each cluster constituting each separate scale. The 13 scales are supplemented by two additional response-control scales designed to assess inconsistency and social desirability. The 15 scales are as follows: (1) acceptance (a), (2) active involvement (AI), (3) egalitarianism (E), (4) cognitive independence (CI), (5) cognitive understanding (CU), (6) cognitive competence (CC), (7) lax control (LC), (8) conformity (C), (9) achievement (a), (10) strict control (SC),

(11) punitive control (PC), (12) hostile control (HC), (13) rejection (R), (14) inconsistent responding (IR), and (15) social desirability (SD). The inventory consists of short behavioral statements, to which respondents answer on a three-choice objective format (*like, somewhat like, unlike*). The PBF was designed for use with adolescents, and for adults recalling the earlier behavior of their parents during their own middle adolescence (when they were "about age 16"). The format is also suitable for describing behaviors of caretakers other than parents. Additional forms of the PBF are designed for use with younger children (ages 8–12) and with parents. A somewhat shortened version of the children's version, containing 10 scales, is also available. The PBF can be used to compare parent and child perceptions, as well as those of both parents. Scores for each 9-item scale are summed and recorded on a grid to provide a profile across scales. Administration time is approximately 30 minutes.

Sample Items:

(A)   Allows discussion of right and wrong.
(B)   Likes to discuss current events with me.
(C)   Wants me to have the same religious beliefs as s/he does.

Comments: The authors report on several studies in which the PBF has been utilized. Average subscale reliabilities (Cronbach's alpha) reported range from .49 to .89. Scales reportedly as correlating from .46 to .81 with W are AI, E, CC, CU, and CI. Scales reported to correlate negatively (-.35 to -.85) with W are AC, SC, HC, and R. The authors also report that the factor structure of the PBF includes three primary factors: warmth, control, and cognitive mediation.

References:

Kelly, J. A., & Worell, L. (1976). Parent behaviors related to masculine, feminine, and androgynous sex-role orientation. *J Cons Clin, 44,* 843–851.

Kelly, J. A., & Worell, L. (1977). The joint and differential perceived contribution of parents to adolescents' cognitive functioning. *Devel Psych, 13,* 282–283.

McCraine, E. W., & Bass, J. D. (1984). Childhood family antecedents of dependency and self-criticism: Implications for depression. *J Abn Psych, 93,* 3–8.

Wilbert, L. A., & Hanson, G. R. (1983). Perceptions of parental role responsibilities among working people: Development of a comprehensive measure. *J Mar Fam, 45,* 203–212.

III-2/II-4/b/P

374. ZUCKERMAN, M. Parental Attitudes Scale

Avail: 1988 Ref.

Variables Measured: Attitudes of parents toward sexual interest and curiosity among their children

Type of Instrument: Self-report questionnaire

Instrument Description: This instrument is a 4-point, 12-item questionnaire designed to assess attitudes of parents regarding their children's sexual activities, comments, and exposure. The Parental Attitudes Scale is part of a larger battery of attitude scales known as the Human Sexuality Questionnaire. Items are in the form of statements, to which parents indicate whether they *strongly* or *mildly agree or disagree*. Scores from the 12 items are summed, yielding a response range from 12 to 48. Of the 12 items, 5 were first constructed for use in the suppression of sex scale from the Parental Attitude Research Instrument (Schaefer & Bell, 1958), 5 came from the PARI (Zuckerman, 1959), and 2 were constructed specifically for inclusion in this instrument.

Sample Items:

(A) A young child should be protected from hearing about sex.
(B) Sex play is a normal thing in children.
(C) It is very important that young boys and girls not be allowed to see each other completely undressed.

Comments: The author reports that test-retest reliability for this questionnaire over periods of 15 weeks ranged from .63 to .76 for males and from .77 to .90 among females.

References:

Davis, C. M., Yarber, W. L., & Davis, S. L. (1988). *Sexuality-related measures: A compendium.* Syracuse, NY: Graphic.

Zuckerman, M. (1973). Scales for sex experience for males and females. *J Cons Clin, 41,* 27–29.

Zuckerman, M., & Myers, P. L. (1983). Sensation seeking in homosexual and heterosexual males. *Arch Sex Be, 12,* 347–356.

Zuckerman, M., Tushup, R., & Finner, S. (1976). Sexual attitudes and experience: Attitude and personality correlates and changes produced by a course in sexuality. *J Cons Clin, 44,* 7–19.

NOTE: For additional instruments, see also *Abstracts 1196–1375* in the Abbreviated Abstracts of Instruments (which precedes the Indexes).

5 Roles and Power

CONSTANCE L. SHEHAN
GARY R. LEE

This chapter, as well as instruments described in this section of the *Handbook of Family Measurement Techniques*, is divided into two parts: (1) issues related to family roles and (2) those concerned with the exercise of power within families. However, while the two concepts are related enough that they appear here under the same heading, the histories of their respective fields have tended to take different paths and to emphasize different conceptual courses of development. For this reason, these two fields will be examined separately within this chapter.

ROLES

Historical Overview

"Role" is one of the most frequently used concepts in sociology and the other social sciences. In spite of the utility of the concept—or perhaps because of it—no consensus about its meaning or measurement has been reached, even after five decades of study. There are two distinct traditions regarding the concept of role, both of which originated in the 1930s. The *structural* tradition, which emphasizes the normative aspects of status, can be traced back to Ralph Linton (1936, 1945), who defined role as "the attitudes, values, and behavior ascribed by the society to any and all persons occupying the status" (1945, pp. 77). The *interactionist* tradition emerged from the work of George Herbert Mead (1934) and emphasizes the behavioral regularities that spring from social interaction (Nye, 1976).

Research on family roles generally reflects this distinction between the normative or attitudinal and behavioral emphases. A large body of research focuses on family role expectations—for spouses (e.g., Abstracts *155, 218, 360*), parents, (e.g., *297*), grandparents (e.g., *373, 374, 457*), and adult children's filial responsibilities to elderly parents (e.g., *290, 437*). The proliferation of studies on gender-role beliefs reflects this tradition. A growing number of studies, on the other hand, examine actual performance of family roles. The developing emphasis on the assignment of domestic work roles to family members represents the behavioral dimension.

The first major sociological study of the division of household labor was Blood and Wolfe's (1960) *Husbands and Wives*. The research topic did not receive much further attention from family sociologists until the mid-1970s when data from "newly discovered" time use studies conducted by home economists provided undeniable evidence that husbands of employed wives spent no more time in household labor than did husbands of full-time homemakers. Feminist scholars incorporated these findings into their critiques of traditional family life, and provided the impetus for a new interest in research and theory about the division of labor. Home economists, incidentally, had been collecting detailed information about the amount of time allocated to housework by household members since the 1920s. The time use measures they developed in the late 1960s have given a new direction to social science research on household labor in the past decade.

Finally, the publication of Nye's volume *Role Structure and Analysis of the Family* in 1976 addressed the conceptual confusion that had surrounded the role concept. It provided a cogent discussion of the two broad approaches to roles (e.g., the structural and the interactionist) along with suggestions for measurement strategies.

Conceptual Development from 1934 to 1975

An important stage in the development of research and theory on marital role relations occurred in the mid-1950s, with the publication of Parsons and Bales's (1955) book *Family, Socialization and Interaction Process*. In this volume, Bales and Slater (1955) published their study of group interaction processes that is a bench mark in the differentiation of "instrumental" and "expressive" roles.

Bales and Slater observed interaction in small problem-solving groups in a laboratory setting. At the conclusion of each session, the members of each group were asked to identify (1) the person who had the best ideas with respect to solving the group's problem and (2) the person who was best liked by the other members of the group. In the vast majority of cases, different persons were named in response to the two questions. Bales and Slater concluded that small groups tend to develop internal structures reflecting a specialization of leadership, resulting in the emergence of task (instrumental) and socioemotional (expressive) leaders who are different persons.

Although all subjects in Bales and Slater's research were males, Zelditch (1955) extended these authors' ideas to families via cross-cultural research. Leik (1963) has shown that, while males and females frequently interact with one another according to stereotypical role patterns if they are strangers, these distinctions tend to break down in actual families where spouses are intimately acquainted with one another. Others (e.g., Reiss & Lee, 1988) have argued that the intensity and complexity of contemporary family life do not facilitate strict segregation of marital roles along instrumental/expressive lines. The cross-cultural regularity of this pattern has subsequently been questioned by Aronoff and Crano (1975; Crano & Aronoff, 1978). Their research, however, employed data on task accomplishment rather than leadership, and is thus not entirely germane to Zelditch's theory.

The utility of the instrumental/expressive dichotomy for contemporary families therefore has been seriously questioned. Studies such as that of Zelditch discovered that, within nuclear families, husbands tend to assume leadership for instrumental tasks and wives for socioemotional tasks, and that this division of responsibilities is highly consistent across nonindustrial cultures. The increasing participation of married women in the labor force further blurs this distinction. The traditional instrumental/expressive dichotomy is rarely employed in contemporary research and theory.

A second major research tradition regarding marital roles also began in the 1950s with the publication of Elizabeth Bott's (1957) study, *Family and Social Network*. Bott was concerned with the extent to which the role behaviors of husbands and wives are "joint" versus "segregated." Segregated marital roles exist when spouses do different things in terms of both domestic labor and leisure activities. Joint roles involve sharing of responsibilities and activities and working together. Bott's thesis was that the degree of segregation of conjugal roles is a function of the connectedness of each spouse's social network. Those who are embedded in a close-knit network of intimate associates, all of whom know one another, are more likely to establish and maintain segregated marital role patterns. Such close-knit networks exert pressure on the spouses as individuals to maintain behavior patterns established prior to marriage and to continue with premarital associations as if the marriage had not occurred. Spouses with more loose-knit networks are not subjected to the same kinds of pressure from their nonmarital associates, and thus are more likely to establish companionate, cooperative relations with their spouses.

Subsequent research and theory (see Lee, 1979, for a review) has suggested that the connectedness of social networks is not a primary causal factor here, contrary to Bott. However, the concepts of joint and segregated marital roles have considerable currency, and have been used to shed light on a variety of issues in the study of role relations (see Rainwater, 1965; Rubin, 1976, for studies of marital role segregation in the lower socioeconomic segments of society).

The division of family work by spouses became a major research focus with the publication of *Husbands and Wives* (Blood & Wolfe, 1960). Blood and Wolfe found that husbands of employed wives were more involved in performing tasks considered to be "feminine" (e.g., preparing breakfast, doing dishes, picking up the living room) than were husbands of full-time homemakers. Blood and Wolfe proposed two alternative explanations for their findings: resource theory and ideology theory. In essence, resource theory held that the distribution of relevant resources (e.g., skills, muscular strength, time) determines who is primarily responsible for performance of domestic tasks. The alternative explanation holds that the division of household labor is determined by traditional family ideology. Blood and Wolfe concluded that their findings supported resource theory.

Resource theory juxtaposed role differentiation theory and exchange theory (Pleck, 1985). The first theory, formulated by Parsons and Bales (1955), proposed that the assignment of "instrumental" roles to husbands and the "expressive" roles to wives was a universal feature of families and other social groups. Men's limited participation in family work is a reflection of gender-role differentiation in which men specialize in wage earning and women specialize in housework and child care. Applications of exchange theory held that husbands' successful performance of the wage-earning role was provided to wives in exchange for love, companionship, and household services (Scanzoni, 1972).

Conceptual Development from 1975 to the Present

In 1976, Nye and his associates published an edited volume titled *Role Structure and Analysis of the Family*, which assisted in the clarification of the role concept. The Nye volume follows a structural approach. It gives considerable attention to the further refinement of the structural concept of role. Its elaboration of the concept centers on the identification of family roles. Two fundamental issues are discussed—the degree of specificity necessary in identifying family roles and the focal points used in identifying roles. As they point out, a fundamental source of confusion regarding the role concept is that it has been conceptualized as both a singular set of behaviors associated with a given social position (status) and as multiple sets of behavioral expectations associated with a given position. Some scholars use the other positions that are occupied by the incumbent of the position of interest as the focal point for role identification (Merton, 1957). Others subdivide the role concept on the basis of tasks that are performed rather than categories of persons who are served (Bates, 1956).

A major development in the conceptualization of family roles occurred when social scientists "discovered"—in the late 1970s—the time use data that had been provided by large-scale surveys conducted in the 1960s and early 1970s (Pleck, 1985). These data clearly revealed an inequitable division of household labor in dual-earner couples. They consistently indicated that—contrary to Blood and Wolfe's findings—husbands of employed wives did not perform more housework and child care than did husbands of housewives. The patterns revealed by time use studies became the focus of one major criticism of "the" family by feminist scholars, who saw the inequitable allocation of family work as domestic exploitation of women (Hartmann, 1981; Mainardi, 1970; Polatnick, 1973–1974). And the division of family labor moved into the center of the debate about gender roles and the family (Pleck, 1985).

Throughout the 1960s, the number of articles devoted to gender roles had been small and the study of gender roles was considered a minor one in family studies (Scanzoni & Fox, 1980). But beginning in the 1970s, considerable research was conducted to determine individuals' normative beliefs about gender-role behavior. The data reveal a trend toward more egalitarian preferences for women's roles (see Thornton, Alwin, & Camburn, 1983).

Several new or revised theories about the division of household labor have emerged in the past five years. Geerken and Gove (1983) have modified the new home economics idea of maximizing household utility in domestic labor as well as in market labor. Huber and Spitze (1983) have presented a theory of gender stratification that explains the division of domestic labor in terms of women's degree of labor force participation. Finally, Pleck (1985) has developed a role overload theory, which holds that the inequitable division of labor in two-earner couples can be attributed to traditional gender-role ideology and husbands' low psychological involvement in families.

Methodological Issues

Measurement of marital and familial roles has proven to be highly problematic in terms of both the prescriptive and the behavioral dimensions, although issues involved in the behavioral domain appear to be somewhat more intractable. Measurement of the domestic division of labor, in particular, has been characterized by inconsistency. Researchers have typically operationalized the division of household labor in "proportional" or relative rather than absolute terms. The most widely used measure of this type has been the eight-item index developed by Blood and Wolfe (1960). In this measure, respondents are presented with eight household tasks: (1) Who repairs things around the house? (2) Who mows the lawn? (3) Who shovels the sidewalk? (4) Who keeps track of the money and the bills? (5) Who does the grocery shopping? (6) Who gets the husband's breakfast on workdays? (7) Who straightens up the living room when company is coming? (8) Who does the evening dishes? Possible responses include husband always, husband more than wife, husband and wife exactly the same, wife more than husband, wife always (examples of similar measures include *1379*, *1416*, and *1435*). The number of tasks listed on derivatives of the Blood and Wolf scale varies from 8 to 100 (e.g., *1424*).

The advantage of this type of measure is that it is relatively easy for individuals to answer (Pleck, 1985). However, two problems emerge from this sort of measurement procedure. One is that variation across couples or families in the absolute amount of housework or child care is ignored. This is critical, because families' overall domestic work loads may vary substantially according to factors such as numbers and ages of children, housing type (single-family home versus apartment or condominium), and the families' standards or preferences for domestic order.

Second, they do not provide data on how much family work either spouse performs alone. Moreover, estimates of each spouse's contribution to domestic labor are confounded by the contribution of the other spouse. For example, Barnett and Baruch (1987) found that wife's employment increases the husband's proportional share of housework and child care, but not his absolute contribution to these activities. The apparently greater domestic efforts of husbands of employed wives are due not to increased contributions by husbands, but instead to decreased involvement on the part of employed wives. Wives' employment may mean that less total work gets done, but this will appear as increased efforts by husbands if role enactment is measured in proportional terms.

Until recently, these proportional measures similar to Blood and Wolfe's dominated research on couples' performance of domestic labor. However, in the mid-1970s, social scientists became aware of time use measures developed years before in home economics. The U.S. Department of Agriculture has been funding studies of housework since the 1920s. Two of the earliest studies were done by Wilson (1929) and Warren (1938). Wilson's study compared the use of time by farm, village, and city homemakers. It was the first real attempt to describe the household work load (Walker & Woods, 1976). A few additional studies of time used in household labor in rural areas were conducted at land grant colleges during the 1940s and 1950s. In 1961, a major study of the use of time in household labor by all household workers was begun at Purdue University (Manning, 1968). In that study, approximately 100 wives kept time use records for one week in each of four seasons. In the late 1960s, Walker and Woods (1976) conducted a study of household production in nearly 1,300 households in Syracuse, New York. Data were collected by personal interviews with wives and by means of a one-day time record. In the former, wives were asked to recall the amount of time spent on domestic labor by all workers in the family (e.g., husbands and children as well as wives) during the previous day. The time record, on the other hand, consisted of a grid that listed different types of household work on the vertical axis and time periods (in 10-minute intervals) on the horizontal axis (see Walker & Woods, 1976, for detailed information and for a list of 150 published and unpublished research reports on time spent in household labor). This research continued a series of projects on household labor begun at Cornell in the 1920s. Walker and Woods's measurement of household work represented a major achievement in this line of scholarly inquiry.

A number of recent studies, such as the Panel Study of Income Dynamics and the 1977 Quality of Employment Survey, have employed estimates of the actual or absolute amount of time invested by each spouse in the performance of selected tasks (see Berardo, Shehan, & Leslie, 1987; Rexroat & Shehan, 1987). This strategy avoids the mutual confounding problem inherent in proportional measures, but allows subsequent reconstruction of proportional estimates if desired (e.g., *1386*). One problem here involves ensuring that a representative selection of tasks normatively assigned to each gender is included. Second, results may be affected by both the time period chosen (day, week, month, and so on) and by respondents' selective recall. Because persons have a known tendency to overestimate their own efforts and underestimate their spouses' (Condran & Bode, 1982), perhaps because they are unaware of some of the things their spouses do, it is important to obtain independent estimates from each spouse rather than to rely on only one.

Warner (1986) compared four methods of assessing the domestic division of labor: relative distribution, weighted relative distribution (where tasks are weighted by their frequency of performance), absolute time reconstruction, and activity logs. She found differences in average total estimates across methods to be relatively small, especially for wives. However, this does not ensure that the variable will behave consistently in relation to other variables regardless of measurement strategy, as our earlier discussion of wives' employment and husbands' domestic labor demonstrates. Researchers need to be aware that differences in measurement techniques may produce substantial differences in results.

Future Directions

The study of roles, particularly gender and marital roles, is likely to become even more significant in the near future. The primary reason for this resides in the two ways of defining the role concept noted earlier, prescriptive and behavioral, and the relation between them.

While it is common to think of normative and behavioral definitions of roles as alternative conceptualizations, each actually refers to an independent aspect of reality. Individuals have ideas about the ways in which domestic responsibilities should be divided, both in general and in their own families, and they also have actual divisions of labor. We know that attitudes and expectations have changed dramatically in recent decades in the direction of greater egalitarianism (Mirowsky & Ross, 1987; Thornton, Alwin, & Camburn, 1983). However, except for the rapid increase in married women's participation in the labor force, behavioral changes have not kept pace (Coverman & Sheley, 1986; Rexroat & Shehan, 1987). As Condran and Bode (1982, p. 425) have succinctly noted: "Attitudes and sympathies may have changed, but husbands still don't wash the dishes very often."

Several recent studies have shown that marital quality is adversely affected by spousal discrepancies in role expectations, particularly when the wife's expectations are more egalitarian than the husband's (Bowen & Orthner, 1983; Li & Caldwell, 1987). Scanzoni and Arnett (1987) provide evidence that egalitarian expectations themselves are negatively related to marital commitment. They attribute this to an association of traditional role expectations with an emphasis on the value of marital permanence for its own sake. However, it is equally likely that egalitarian expectations are more difficult to achieve in reality, and more susceptible to violation by continuing patterns of domestic behavior. This may produce feelings of frustration and inequity, which in turn diminish marital quality and stability.

Recent changes in the nature of family relations and the expected and actual roles of husbands and wives are likely to have far-reaching consequences. Many of the consequences have to do with the increasing likelihood of disjunctions between the role expectations of spouses, and between these expectations and the domestic realities confronted by contemporary couples. Theoretically based research on family roles is vital to the understanding of recent and future changes in family structures and dynamics.

POWER

Historical Overview

Built into the traditional husband and parent roles is legitimate authority—the right and responsibility to exercise control over wives and children, respectively. "Historically, men have been given the right to control women through abusive means, if necessary, because women and children have often been seen as chattel along with farm animals and property" (Steinmetz, 1987, p. 727). Early studies of family power addressed the issue of control through examinations of the final outcomes of decision making. Little or no attention was given to the processes through which final decisions were made. Predominant measures of family power provided no indication of the conflict that ensued or the resistance that had to be overcome in arriving at final decisions. Consistent with the paradigm that was preeminent in social science in the 1950s and early 1960s—structural functionalism—early studies of family power appeared to operate under the assumption of consensus. As conflict theory gained advocates in the mid- to late 1960s, family scholars began to recognize that conflict in intimate groups is inevitable and that attention should be given to conflict resolution techniques. The legitimacy of this academic concern was substantiated with the "discovery" of family violence that occurred with labeling of the "battered child syndrome" in the early 1960s and the subsequent media coverage. Family violence became established as a primary research topic in the family sciences in the early 1970s. The research on family power, then, has followed a bifurcated path, emphasizing decision-making outcomes, primarily, and family conflict and violence to a lesser extent.

Blood and Wolfe (1960) are generally identified as the first scholars to launch a major study of decision-making power. Their research set the standard for the three decades of work that followed. Many of the conceptual and methodological issues that have been addressed in subsequent research emerged from Blood and Wolfe's study. Blood and Wolfe were actually influenced by the earlier work of Herbst (1952), who developed a typology of marital power. The fundamental principles of power and dependence in close relationships, however, emerged from even earlier work, most notably, from Waller's study of courtship on college campuses, which gave rise to his principle of least interest. Waller (1938) argued that the partner with the least interest in the relationship has the higher probability of exploiting the other partner.

In spite of the publication of *Husbands and Wives* in 1960, the concept of family power did not gain prominence in the family sociological literature until the middle and late 1960s. Scanzoni (1979) observes that the term *power* was absent from such influential scholarly volumes in family studies as Christensen's (1964) *Handbook of Marriage and the Family* and Nye and Berardo's (1966) *Emerging Conceptual Frameworks in Family Analysis*. Because of a paradigm shift in sociology, family power began to receive more research attention, so that, by 1970, Safilios-Rothschild, in her decade review of research conducted during the 1960s, was able to comment about the "abundance of research studies" on family power structure and decision-making patterns. As Safilios-Rothschild observed, however, this body of research was marked by conceptual and methodological problems. These limitations have proved to be so persistent and difficult to overcome that some researchers are now arguing for the abandonment of the concept of power (Szinovacz, 1987).

As noted above, the study of family violence did not become established as a major topic of research until the early 1970s. A special issue of the *Journal of Marriage and the Family* in 1971 that was devoted to the topic is identified as the starting point of this body of literature (Steinmetz, 1987). Straus (1979) and his colleagues have articulated the conceptual links between power, conflict, and violence in families, largely in response to the considerable confusion that has existed. Scholars have defined conflict in widely divergent ways. Some (e.g., Dahrendorf, 1959) use the term *conflict* to refer to differences of opinion and the term *conflict management* to refer to steps taken to advance one's own interests. Coser (1956), on the other hand, uses the term *conflict* to refer to overt actions that constitute responses to differences of opinion. Straus (1979), following Coser's usage, developed a Conflict Tactics Scale to measure the use of reasoning, verbal aggression, and violence as a response to differences of opinion within families. Straus's conceptualization and operationalization of conflict have generated considerable research on family conflict and violence since the early 1970s.

Conceptual Development from 1934 to 1975

Explanation of marital power in the years between 1934 and 1975 was dominated by resource theory and its various revisions. In this section, we briefly discuss the emergence of resource theory as it developed from Herbst's initial formulation of marital power, through Wolfe's adaptation and integration with the concept of authority, and Blood and Wolfe's application in *Husbands and Wives* (1960). We then discuss Rodman's (1972) reconciliation of resources and normative prescriptions as bases of marital power in the theoretical statement known as resources in cultural context and Burr's (1973) further elaboration of Rodman's work in a theoretical statement referred to as normative resource theory.

Herbst's (1952, 1954) work represented the beginning of formal theoretical models of family power. Herbst drew on classic social psychological theories, most notably Lewin's field theory. Herbst argued that marital interaction consists of two dimensions—an activity dimension (e.g., actual division of family labor) and a decision dimension (e.g., who decides about the allocation of time to family labor and the assignment of tasks). Power was defined as the ability to control the decision-making dimension. Herbst developed a typology of interaction patterns consisting of four classifications: husband is dominant, wife is dominant, spouses operate independently, and spouses operate jointly. From this typology emerged his identification of family power structures: autocratic, where decisions are made by one spouse only (either wife dominant or husband dominant); autonomic; and syncratic.

Blood and Wolfe's heuristic study, *Husbands and Wives,* owes Herbst an intellectual debt, insofar as it reflects an adoption of his emphasis on control of decision making. Blood and Wolfe's collaboration was preceded by Wolfe's development of a model of power and authority in families that, like Herbst, borrowed from Lewin's field theory. *Power* was defined by Wolfe as differential control of resources of value to others for need fulfillment. *Resources* were defined as any "property of a person or group that can be made available to others as instrumental to the satisfaction of their needs or the attainment of their goals" (Wolfe, 1959, p. 100). Wolfe's other central concept, authority, can be traced back to Dubin's (1951) work on administrative relations. *Authority* was defined as legitimate power and was viewed as an aspect of role prescriptions and group norms.

Wolfe's work was the basis for the development of two theoretical frameworks that came to dominate the study of marital power: resource theory and ideological theory. Resource theory asserts that the balance of power (in terms of control over decision making) is on the side of the partner who contributes the greatest resources to the marriage. Resource theory is a form of exchange theory centered on three major assumptions of exchange: First, individuals continually attempt to satisfy their needs. Second, most individual needs are met through social interaction, which involves a continual exchange of resources. Third, to the extent that one's spouse (or interaction partner) is the best source of valued resources, then he or she can wield power over the dependent spouse. Either spouse can be more powerful, depending on the distribution of resources, but in our society, husbands tend to have greater control over such valued resources as income, education, and occupational status.

Blood and Wolfe adopted the resource theory as a way of accounting for the long-term movement away from patriarchal marriages, in which husbands' power was normatively prescribed, to modern marriages, in which husbands' greater power is derived from their greater success in bargaining in those areas open to negotiation. These authors posed resource theory as an alternative to ideological theory, which held that cultural ideas about who should have power or control over decisions influences actual control over decisions. Blood and Wolfe's empirical tests of ideological theory did not support that hypothesis. Their findings were used as evidence that normative definitions of legitimate power did not have an effect on marital power.

In a significant development in the conceptualization of marital power, Rodman (1972) offered a reconciliation of the resource and ideological theories. Rodman's synthesis, known as the theory of resources in cultural context, developed out of his insightful reexamination of conflicting findings regarding resources and power from studies of 11 different cultures. In some studies (e.g., those conducted in Denmark, Greece, Yugoslavia, and Turkey), husbands' socioeconomic resources did not increase their power relative to their wives—they either decreased it or had no effect on it—and in other societies, wives' employment had no impact on their power (e.g., two studies in the United States and one in Greece). Rodman proposed that norms about authority operate as an intervening or contingency variable moderating the effect that resources have on power. In modernizing societies (e.g., those changing from patriarchy to egalitarianism), it is the families in the middle and upper classes that first accept the norms of marital egalitarianism. As a result, even though higher-status husbands have more resources than lower-status husbands, they are more likely to believe that they should share control over decision making with their wives.

The theory of resources in cultural context was further specified by Burr (1973), who argued that this particular interaction effect of resources and ideology on marital power holds only in transitional societies. Once egalitarian norms have fully permeated a society, the relationship between resources and marital power becomes positive. Burr's refinement of the normative-resource theory more fully accentuates its link to exchange theory. Exchange processes occur in a normative context; norms about reciprocity and distributive justice affect family exchanges (Cromwell & Olson, 1975).

The theoretical approaches developed during this period (e.g., resource theory, ideological theory, resources in cultural context, and normative resource theory) have dominated the study of marital/family decision making in the ensuing decades. They are multidisciplinary perspectives representing a juxtaposition of social psychological approaches, such as field theory, with sociological concepts, such as norms and roles (see Cromwell & Olson, 1975, chap. 2; Scanzoni, 1979b, for a more detailed discussion of the epistemological roots of the early conceptualizations of marital and family power).

Conceptual Development from 1975 to the Present

The major conceptual developments during this period include the identification of multiple domains of power, by Cromwell and Olson (1975), and the systematic application of conflict theory and social exchange theory to the explanation of marital power processes. Additionally, scholars have attempted to refine the concept of resources (emphasizing the subjective process involved in evaluating resources as rewarding or costly) and to explicate more fully the role of ideology in shaping power relations, by examining the nature of norms (including gender roles) defining legitimate authority.

Just as Blood and Wolfe's resource theory dominated the earlier period of scholarship on family power, the work of Cromwell and Olson moved the research in a new direction in the period that followed. A major legacy of Cromwell and Olson's work has been their identification of three conceptual domains of family power: bases, processes, and outcomes. This delineation of power domains was essential in reducing the conceptual confusion that had characterized the family power literature in the preceding decades.

The bases of family power consist primarily of the resources an individual possesses that may increase her or his ability to exercise control over a particular situation (Olson & Cromwell, 1975). Cromwell and Olson drew on the earlier work of French and Raven (1959) in their specification of the six bases of family power (e.g., normative authority or legitimacy, identification, superior knowledge, persuasive ability, ability to reward, and ability to punish). This reliance on scholarship outside the family area, reflected in Cromwell and Olson's use of French and Raven's work, is characteristic of the continuing interplay between family scholarship and the broader social scientific literature that has been so profitable in the study of family power. As Cromwell and Olson (1975) note, these bases of power are clearly related to the general resources often considered by sociologists (e.g., income, education, and occupational status). Violence or physical force can also be used as a resource to gain one's wishes in a manner similar to money, status, and personal attributes. All too often, violence is used as a resource when all else fails or is perceived to have failed (Steinmetz, 1987).

The second domain of family power, labeled power processes, emerges from the recognition that decision making or problem solving involves more than final outcomes. Individuals go through a series of stages of information exchange, persuasion, consideration of alternatives, and negotiation before arriving at a final decision or solution. Thus the term *power processes* refers to the ongoing interactional strategies individuals use to maximize the impact of their resources in their attempts to take control of family decision making. The empirical identification of the processes of power utilization is exceedingly difficult and the research literature on this domain of power is weaker than research on the other two domains as a result (Scanzoni, 1979). Olson and Cromwell offered a suggestion for increasing the empirical accessibility of this domain, however, in their delineation of two important dimensions of power processes. The first aspect of power processes that can be assessed directly is the number of attempts an individual makes to change the behavior of another, which Olson and Cromwell refer to as "assertiveness." The second aspect of power processes that can be observed directly is the number of effective attempts that an individual makes that actually change another's behavior, which they refer to as "control."

In some earlier work, Sprey (1972, p. 236) also argued for concepts that would encourage the examination of power processes, or "powering," which he described as "the ongoing confrontation in which the power inputs of all participants are reciprocally put to the test." His concept of powering rests on the explicit recognition that each person's inventory of resources changes over the course of family life and that his or her bargaining power also changes as a result. Sprey argued that, while individuals might have great difficulty relating to the abstract concept of power, they would be able to describe the "moves and countermoves, threats, and promises, aggression and appeasement" that take place during family bargaining sessions (Sprey, 1972, p. 237). Increasingly, measures are being developed that tap the processual aspects of conflicted interactions, including control strategies (e.g., *419* and *435*), and/or that indicate that a particular family relationship may have the potential for violence (e.g., *423*).

The final domain of power identified by Cromwell and Olson is "outcomes," which essentially involves the identification of the family member who makes the final decision or who "wins" in negotiations. As Scanzoni (1979, p. 302) notes, this domain has received more research attention than the other two but should be "relegated to a much less central position" in future research. Outcomes are only one stage of the bargaining or powering process, rather than its entirety—as was assumed in the previous period of scholarship on family power.

In summary, one of the major contributions of Cromwell and Olson's (1975) reconceptualization of family power, which set the stage for subsequent research, is their recognition that resources and outcomes, the emphases of the research conducted during the previous period, were only two of the many dimensions of power that should be studied. In the earlier period of research, power was conceptualized as the ability to influence another person's behavior but was operationalized in static terms, as the final outcome of some decision-making process. Resources, which were conceptualized as the primary determinants of this ability to control outcomes, were also conceptualized in static terms. In the multidimensional approach to power, which views power as an ongoing process of interaction, manipulation of resources is a central aspect of negotiation.

Another major development in the family power literature since the late 1960s has been the attempt to integrate the concepts and assumptions of conflict theory. This theory assumes that conflict is inevitable in all dyads or groups in which members are differentiated by status and possess divergent goals. Families are likely to be such groups (Sprey, 1969). Conflict theories of family violence articulate the links between authority and power and identify violence as a likely outcome when the two phenomena are discordant. Authority involves voluntary compliance to another person's wishes whereas power involves the ability to carry out one's own will in spite of resistance (discussed in Scanzoni, 1979). Conflict in families often occurs when one person has the authority (i.e., the normatively prescribed right) to demand certain behavior from others but not the power to do so in the face of resistance. Steinmetz (1987) offers the example of parents of teenagers. Built into the parental role is the right and responsibility to control children's behavior, yet parents of teenagers may not have the ability to enforce their authority. In such cases of incongruity, family violence can erupt (Steinmetz, 1971, 1974; Straus, 1971).

A similar conclusion is reached by both Blau (1964) and Homans (1974), whose concepts "fair exchange" and "distributive justice" reflect the normatively defined legitimacy of power relations. As Homans (1974) argued, when the rule of distributive justice is violated—that is, when the costs of an intimate exchange are perceived by one individual as exceeding the rewards—conflict may erupt as participants in the exchange challenge the existing power structure.

Another major issue that has been addressed during this period of scholarship on family power—in addition to the multidimensionality of the concept and the role of conflict in power relations—is the articulation between exchange and power relations. Consideration of this issue has involved a more comprehensive integration of exchange concepts and principles than was found in the earlier period of scholarship. Several scholars have made valuable contributions in the systematic application of exchange to power relations. Safilios-Rothschild's (1976) theory of relative love and need, for instance, incorporates the exchange ideas of dependence and perceived alternatives. Application of the principles of social exchange to the examination of marital power relations should prove to be quite valuable, in that it will require researchers to focus more explicitly on power dynamics, particularly on bargaining and negotiation processes (McDonald, 1980). Scanzoni's (1979a, 1979b) efforts to reconceptualize power, from a focus on decision-making outcomes to decision making as composed of several parallel processes (e.g., attraction, negotiation, and communication as well as exchange) is particularly insightful in this regard.

Methodological Issues

Measurement problems have characterized the marital power literature for three decades (see McDonald, 1980; Safilios-Rothschild, 1970; Szinovacz, 1987, for detailed discussions of these issues). Blood and Wolfe's "final say" measure of the outcome of decision making, and others modeled after it, continues to be the most widely used self-report measure in family power research, even though it has been criticized on several grounds (Szinovacz, 1987).

Blood and Wolfe's original measure is composed of a "lead-in statement" and a list of eight decision areas. Respondents are presented with the following. "In every family somebody has to decide such things as where the family will live and so on. Many couples talk such things over first, but the final decision often has to be made by the husband or wife. For instance, who usually makes the final decision about . . . ?" The following issues are then presented: what job the husband should take, what car to get, whether or not to buy life insurance, where to go on a vacation, what house or apartment to take, whether or not the wife should go to work or quit work, what doctor to have when someone is sick, and how much money the family can afford to spend per week on food. Respondents are given a choice of the following response categories: husband always, husband more than the wife, husband and wife exactly the same, wife more than husband, and wife always (Blood & Wolfe, 1960). (Herbst's original decision-making outcome measure appears in *Abstract 417* in this volume.)

One of the fundamental problems with Blood and Wolfe's measure, and others that have been modeled after it (e.g., *425* and *431*), is that it gives a rather static picture of family power relations. It is incapable of tapping the dynamic nature of family power processes. Instead, it focuses entirely on one stage of the power process—the outcome.

A second criticism of Blood and Wolfe's measure is that its particular selection of decision areas may be biased. Blood and Wolfe (1960) selected these eight items because they are all relatively important and represent situations faced by nearly all couples. Additionally, they attempted to include a range of items in terms of gender type. Some scholars have argued that their selection of items is more heavily weighted toward decisions that are typically made by men. Moreover, all decisions are weighted equally, as though they are equal in their implications for family life and in the frequency with which they are made. When Centers, Raven, and Rodriguez (1971) added six decisions to Blood and Wolfe's original list, they found that the balance of power shifted somewhat toward wives.

A third criticism of the "final say" self-report measures is that they artificially restrict their focus to the marital dyad, ignoring other family members who may play a central role in decision making. In fact, Blood and Wolfe only included wives in their study, which has raised serious questions concerning congruence between spouses' perceptions of marital power (see *Abstract 177*, which measures conflict but focuses on wives only). Scholars have asked not only about the extent of congruence but what to do about incongruence. Some have argued that incongruence is, in itself, a valuable indicator of power imbalances (Szinovacz, 1987).

Another concern about self-report measures of decision-making power is that they may actually tap perceptions of legitimate authority rather than actual power. Studies have found that individuals can report about what decisions have been made but have difficulty determining who made them (McDonald, 1980) (see *Abstracts 207* and *209* for measures that attempt to uncover attitudes toward legitimate authority directly). The study of family conflict and violence also engenders major measurement difficulties. First, whenever researchers attempt to inquire about sensitive topics, they run the risk of obtaining socially desirable responses. Second, most studies of family conflict and violence are retrospective in nature and are subject to biases that result from inaccurate recall of details. Third, inconsistencies in the definition of neglect and abuse make comparability of findings across studies difficult. And fourth, the tendency of family scholars in general to obtain data from only one family member has characterized early research on family violence (other methodological problems are discussed in detail in Steinmetz, 1987).

One prototypic measurement strategy in the study of family violence is the Conflict Tactics Scale (Straus, 1979, *435*) in which respondents are presented with a list of 19 behavioral items representing possible responses to conflicts of interests among family members. Respondents are asked to indicate how frequently they and other family members involved in the conflict exhibited each of the 19 behaviors during the previous 12 months. The items can be repeated for any family role relationship. Items represent three different conflict management strategies: discussion or reasoning, verbal aggression, and physical aggression or violence. Various adaptations of this instrument have been developed to tap additional responses to family conflict. For instance, Alford (1982) added seven items to the inventory of responses to family conflict, to allow for avoidance attempts and to distinguish more finely among various types of arguments (see *410*).

Although the CTS (and others modeled after it) is susceptible to recall error, it appears to be fairly effective in avoiding high refusal rates and/or socially desirable responses (Straus, 1979). This success can be attributed to the fact that violent and aggressive acts are presented in the context of more legitimate responses to family conflict. Verbal and physical abuse appear on the questionnaire only after such conflict management strategies as discussion or reasoning are mentioned. This placement lends the air of "conflict as a last resort" that serves to legitimize the reporting of the use of violence. Additionally, the use of physical force by parents on children or the use of physical force between children, which are generally perceived by Americans as more common or more expected types of family violence, are presented before the use of physical violence with spouses. Straus (1979) argues that these contextual features reduce the risk of refusal and social desirability bias.

Observational or behavioral measures of family power dynamics have also been criticized by family power scholars. First, these techniques often take place in a laboratory setting and involve trivial tasks that may not give an accurate picture of family decision making about important issues that occurs in the home over a longer period of time. Second, the coding of behavioral sequences that is at the core of observational techniques is complex and time-consuming. It may also be unreliable. Finally, because of the nature of laboratory tasks, only a static picture of family power is provided (Szinovacz, 1987).

Directions for Future Research

During the past decade, significant advances have been made in the conceptualization of family power processes, most notably in the delineation of multiple domains of power and the systematic application of social exchange theories. There is now an increased sensitivity to measurement problems and an awareness of the complexities of family power relationships (Szinovacz, 1987). Measurement techniques, however, still lag behind the level of conceptual sophistication. Research continues to focus on decision-making outcomes and most measures involve only minor changes in the final say questions developed by Blood and Wolfe (McDonald,

1980). The literature is bereft of serious attempts to obtain information about the actual exercising of power by family members. A lack of resources, for instance, might be offset by the use of highly effective persuasion strategies (see Szinovacz, 1987). Additionally, the literature has failed to examine the attempts of family members to resist power exertion (Szinovacz, 1987). The "silent" exercise of power in nonconflictual situations that operates to prevent overt conflict and the perceptions that give rise to acquiescence to the will of others need to be studied closely (see *Abstracts 413* and *412* for observational measures that tap the processual aspects of family power). This suggests that increased use of observational techniques and multitrait, multimethod approaches must occur.

As Szinovacz (1987) suggests, old measures do not need to be abandoned in order to make progress in measurement. Existing measures can also be refined. For instance, instead of simply asking respondents about the "final say" in their family decisions, researchers can ask for respondents estimates of the likelihood that they will get their own way in certain situations and what they would have to do to ensure that they were successful. (Several measures included in this handbook ask respondents to identify conflict resolution and/or conflict management strategies. See, for instance, *422, 437,* and *409.*) Behavioral methods could be improved if the observations involved more "natural" interactions, specifically, if they were longer, less structured, and carried out in naturalistic, everyday settings. Family members could be asked to resolve issues that are important to their families (as indicated in prior self-report instruments) and allowed to create their own solutions to problem situations rather than being forced to respond to researchers' solutions. And, finally, respondents could be asked to elaborate on the answers they provide to self-report instruments and to discuss their behavior after participating in observational techniques.

McDonald (1980) also argued for a broader conceptualization of the exchanges underlying the exercise of power, one that recognizes the cooperative aspects of family interaction rather than focusing only on the competitive. Additionally, the concepts of trust, commitment, and reciprocity need to be more fully incorporated into the study of power. Commitment, McDonald argues, may replace dependency in marriage as spouses' access to economic resources becomes more balanced. Additional variables that need to be included are personality characteristics and interpersonal orientations (Szinovacz, 1987).

Another major consideration for the future of research on family power is the application of additional theoretical frameworks. While the adoption of social exchange has been profitable, the use of only one theoretical perspective may limit explanatory potential (McDonald, 1980).

Finally, if the study of power processes in families is to progress beyond the marital dyad, other family members need to be included in research (see *Abstract 414* for a measure that focuses on sibling power relations and

432 for a measure that focuses on parent-child power relations). Power relationships between parents and children, between siblings, and between the nuclear and extended families must receive more attention. This would enable the examination of coalition formation in family groups.

REFERENCES

Alford, R. (1982). Intimacy and disputing styles within kin and nonkin relationships. *Journal of Family Issues, 3,* 361–374.

Aronoff, J., & Crano, W. (1975). A re-examination of the cross-cultural principles of task segregation and sex role differentiation in the family. *American Sociological Review, 40,* 12–20.

Bales, R. F., & Slater, P. (1955). Role differentiation in small decision-making groups. In T. Parsons & R. F. Bales (Eds.), *Family, socialization and interaction process* (pp. 259–306). New York: Free Press.

Banton, M. (1965). *Roles.* New York: Basic Books.

Barnett, R. L., & Baruch, G. K. (1987). Determinants of fathers' participation in family work. *Journal of Marriage and the Family, 49,* 29–40.

Bates, F. (1956). Position, role, and status: A reformulation of concepts. *Social Forces, 34,* 313–321.

Berardo, D., Shehan, C., & Leslie, G. (1987). A residue of tradition: Jobs, careers, and spouses' time in housework. *Journal of Marriage and the Family, 49,* 381–390.

Biddle, B., & Thomas, E. (1966). *Role theory: Concepts and research.* New York: John Wiley.

Blau, P. M. (1964). *Exchange and power in social life.* New York: John Wiley.

Blood, R. O., & Wolfe, D. M. (1960). *Husbands and wives: The dynamics of married living.* New York: Free Press.

Bott, E. (1957). *Family and social network.* London: Tavistock.

Bowen, G. L., & Orthner, D. K. (1983). Sex-role congruency and marital quality. *Journal of Marriage and the Family, 45,* 223–230.

Buckley, W. (1967). *Sociology and modern systems theory.* Englewood Cliffs, NJ: Prentice-Hall.

Burr, W. R. (1973). *Theory construction and the sociology of the family.* New York: John Wiley.

Centers, R., Raven, B. H., & Rodriguez, A. (1971). Conjugal power structure: A reexamination. *American Sociological Review, 36,* 264–278.

Christensen, H. T. (Ed.). (1964). *Handbook of marriage and the family.* Chicago: Rand McNally.

Condran, J. G., & Bode, J. G. (1982). Rashomon, working wives, and family division of labor: Middletown, 1980. *Journal of Marriage and the Family, 44,* 421–426.

Coser, L. (1956). *The functions of social conflict.* New York: Free Press.

Coverman, S., & Sheley, J. F. (1986). Changes in men's housework and child-care time, 1965–1975. *Journal of Marriage and the Family, 48,* 413–422.

Crano, W. D., & Aronoff, J. (1978). A cross-cultural study of expressive and instrumental role complementarity in the family. *American Sociological Review, 43,* 463–471.

Cromwell, R. E., & Olson, D. H. (1975). *Power in families.* New York: Halstead.

Dahrendorf, R. (1959). *Class and class conflict in industrial society.* London: Routledge & Kegan Paul.

Dubin, R. (1951). *Human relations in administration.* Englewood Cliffs, NJ: Prentice-Hall.

French, J. R. P., & Raven, B. (1959). The bases of social power. In D. Cartwright (Ed.), *Studies in social power* (pp. 607–623). Ann Arbor: University of Michigan Press.

Geerken, M., & Gove, W. (1983). *At home and at work: The family's allocation of labor.* Beverly Hills, CA: Sage.

Gelles, R., & Straus, M. (1979). Determinants of violence in the family: Toward a theoretical integration. In W. Burr, R. Hill, F. I. Nye, & I. Reiss (Eds.), *Contemporary theories about the family* (pp. 549–581). New York: Free Press.

Gross, N., Mason, W., & McEachern, A. (1958). *Explorations in role analysis.* New York: John Wiley.

Hartmann, H. (1981). The family as the locus of gender, class, and political struggle: The example of housework. *Signs: Journal of Women in Culture and Society, 6,* 366–394.

Heiss, J. (1968). *Family roles and interaction.* Chicago: Rand McNally.

Herbst, P. G. (1952). The measurement of family relationships. *Human Relations, 5,* 3–35.

Herbst, P. G. (1954). Conceptual framework for studying the family. In O. A. Oeser & S. B. Hammond (Eds.), *Social structure and personality in a city.* New York: Macmillan.

Homans, G. C. (1974). *Social behavior: Its elementary forms.* New York: Harcourt Brace Jovanovich.

Huber, J., & Spitze, G. (1983). *Sex stratification: Children, housework, and jobs.* New York: Academic Press.

Jackson, J. (1972). *Role.* London: Cambridge University Press.

Lee, G. R. (1979). The effects of social networks on the family. In W. R. Burr, R. Hill, F. I. Nye, & I. L. Reiss (Eds.), *Contemporary theories about the family: Vol. 1. Research-based theories* (pp. 27–56). New York: Free Press.

Leik, R. K. (1963). Instrumentality and emotionality in family interaction. *Sociometry, 26,* 131–145.

Lewin, K. (1951). *Field theory in social sciences.* New York: Harper & Row.

Li, J. T., & Caldwell, R. A. (1987). Magnitude and directional effects of marital sex-role incongruence on marital adjustment. *Journal of Family Issues, 8,* 97–110.

Linton, R. (1936). *The study of man.* New York: Appleton-Century-Crofts.

Linton, R. (1945). *The cultural background of personality.* New York: Appleton-Century-Crofts.

Mainardi, P. (1970). The politics of housework. In R. Morgan (Ed.), *Sisterhood is powerful.* New York: Vintage.

Manning, S. (1968). Time use in household tasks by Indiana families. *Purdue University Agricultural Experiment Station Research Bulletin,* no. 837.

McDonald, G. (1980). Family power: The assessment of a decade of theory and research, 1970–1979. *Journal of Marriage and the Family, 38,* 355–362.

Mead, G. H. (1934). *Mind, self, and society.* Chicago: University of Chicago Press.

Merton, R. (1957). *Social theory and social structure.* New York: Free Press.

Mirowsky, J., & Ross, C. E. (1987). Belief in innate sex roles: Sex stratification versus interpersonal influence in marriage. *Journal of Marriage and the Family, 49,* 527–540.

Nye, F. I. (1976). *Role structure and analysis of the family.* Beverly Hills, CA: Sage.

Nye, F. I., & Berardo, F. M. (1966). *Emerging conceptual frameworks in family analysis.* New York: Macmillan.

Nye, F. I., & Gecas, V. (1976). The role concept: Review and delineation. In F. I. Nye (Ed.), *Role structure and analysis of the family* (pp. 3–14). Beverly Hills, CA: Sage.

Olson, D. H., & Cromwell, R. E. (1975). Methodological issues in family power. In R. E. Cromwell & D. H. Olson (Eds.), *Power in families* (pp. 131–150). New York: Halstead.

Parsons, T., & Bales, R. (Eds.). (1955). *Family, socialization and interaction process.* New York: Free Press.

Pleck, J. (1985). *Working wives, working husbands.* Beverly Hills, CA: Sage.

Polatnick, M. (1973–1974). Why men don't rear children: A power analysis. *Berkeley Journal of Sociology, 18,* 45–86.

Rainwater, L. (1965). *Family design.* Chicago: Aldine.

Reiss, I. L., & Lee, G. R. (1988). *Family systems in America* (4th ed.). New York: Holt, Rinehart & Winston.

Rexroat, C., & Shehan, C. (1987). The family life cycle and spouses' time in housework. *Journal of Marriage and the Family, 49,* 737–750.

Rodman, H. (1972). Marital power and the theory of resources in cultural context. *Journal of Comparative Family Studies, 3,* 50–69.

Rollins, B. C., & Bahr, S. J. (1976). A theory of power relationships in marriage. *Journal of Marriage and the Family, 38,* 619–628.

Rubin, L. (1976). *Worlds of pain: Life in the working-class family.* New York: Basic Books.

Safilios-Rothschild, C. (1970). The study of family power structure: A review of 1960–69. *Journal of Marriage and the Family, 32,* 539–552.

Safilios-Rothschild, C. (1976). A macro- and micro-examination of family power and love: An exchange model. *Journal of Marriage and the Family, 38,* 355–362.

Scanzoni, J. (1970). *Opportunity and the family.* New York: Free Press.

Scanzoni, J. (1972). *Sexual bargaining: Power politics in American marriage.* Englewood Cliffs, NJ: Prentice-Hall.

Scanzoni, J. (1979a). Social exchange and behavioral interdependence. In R. Burgess & T. Huston (Eds.), *Social exchange in developing relationships* (pp. 61–98). New York: Academic Press.

Scanzoni, J. (1979b). Social processes and power in families. In W. Burr, R. Hill, F. I. Nye, & I. Reiss (Eds.), *Contemporary theories about the family* (Vol. 1). New York: Free Press.

Scanzoni, J., & C. Arnett. (1987). Enlarging the understanding of marital commitment via religious devoutness, gender-role preferences, and locus of marital control. *Journal of Family Issues, 8,* 136–156.

Scanzoni, J., & Fox, G. L. (1980). Sex roles, family, and society: The seventies and beyond. *Journal of Marriage and the Family, 42,* 743–758.

Sprey, J. (1969). The family as a system in conflict. *Journal of Marriage and the Family, 31,* 699–706.

Sprey, J. (1972). Family power structure: A critical comment. *Journal of Marriage and the Family, 34,* 235–238.

Steinmetz, S. (1971). Occupation and physical punishment: A response to Straus. *Journal of Marriage and the Family, 33,* 664–666.

Steinmetz, S. (1974). Occupational environment in relation to physical punishment and dogmatism. In S. K. Steinmetz & M. A. Straus (Eds.), *Violence in the family.* New York: Harper & Row.

Steinmetz, S. (1987). Family violence: Past, present, and future. In M. Sussman & S. K. Steinmetz (Eds.), *Handbook of marriage and the family* (pp. 725–766). New York: Plenum.

Straus, M. (1971). Some social antecedents of physical punishment: A linkage theory interpretation. *Journal of Marriage and the Family, 33,* 658–663.

Straus, M. (1979). Measuring intrafamily conflict and violence: The Conflict Tactics (CT) Scales. *Journal of Marriage and the Family, 41,* 75–88.

Straus, M., Gelles, R., & Steinmetz, S. (1980). *Behind closed doors: Violence in the American family.* Garden City, NY: Anchor/Doubleday.

Szinovacz, M. (1987). Family power. In M. Sussman & S. Steinmetz (Eds.), *Handbook of marriage and the family* (pp. 651–694). New York: Plenum.

Thornton, A., Alwin, D., & Camburn, D. (1983). Sex role attitudes and attitude change. *American Sociological Review, 48,* 211–227.

Walker, K., & Woods, M. (1976). *Time use: A measure of household production of family goods and services.* Washington, DC: American Home Economics Association.

Waller, W. (1938). *The family: A dynamic interpretation.* New York: Cordon.

Warner, R. L. (1986). Alternative strategies for measuring household division of labor. *Journal of Family Issues, 7,* 179–195.

Warren, J. (1938). *Use of time in its relation to home management.* Unpublished doctoral dissertation, Cornell University.

Wilson, M. (1929). Use of time by Roegon farm homemakers. *Oregon Agricultural Experiment Station Bulletin*, no. 256.

Wolfe, D. N. (1959). Power and authority in the family. In D. Cartwright (Ed.), *Studies in social power* (pp. 99–117). Ann Arbor: University of Michigan, Institute for Social Research.

Zelditch, M., Jr. (1955). Role differentiation in the nuclear family: A comparative study. In T. Parsons & R. F. Bales (Eds.), *Family, socialization and interaction process* (pp. 307–352). New York: Free Press.

Znaniecki, F. (1965). *Social relations and social roles.* San Francisco: Chandler.

ABSTRACTS OF INSTRUMENTS

NOTE: For additional instruments, see also *Abstracts 1376–1458* in the Abbreviated Abstracts of Instruments (which precedes the Indexes).

Summary of Instrument Codes

Number Codes:

  I = **Dimensions of interaction**—1 = communication; 2 = life-style; 3 = networks; 4 = multidimensional perspectives

 II = **Intimacy and family values**—1 = family values; 2 = marital relations; 3 = love; 4 = sex; 5 = personal/interpersonal perceptions

III = **Parenthood**—1 = pregnancy, childbearing, and transition to parenthood; 2 = parenting

 IV = **Roles and power**—1 = roles; 2 = power

  V = **Adjustment**—1 = family functioning; 2 = stress; 3 = divorce, separation, and remarriage

Letter Codes:

Interactants—a = husband-wife, b = parent-child, c = nuclear family, d = extended family, e = others outside the family, f = siblings, g = intrapsychic processes

Focus of Study—P = parents, C = child, H = husband, W = wife, O = any combination of the above (if there is no capital letter code given, it is understood to be "O")

IV-1/a
375. AMATEA, E., & CROSS, G. Life Role Salience Scale (LRSS)

Avail: Reading & Amatea, 1986, Ref.

Variables Measured: Attitudes regarding the value and style of commitment to the life roles of occupation, marriage, parenting, and home care

Type of Instrument: Self-report questionnaire

Instrument Description: The LRSS was designed to assess attitudes toward personal role expectations. It is a 40-item Likert-style scale covering the four life roles listed above. Respondents indicate the extent of their agreement with each item. For each major life role there are two scales indicating personal value attributed to the role and the level of commitment felt with regard to performance of the role. Each scale contains five statements, each suggesting either the value attributed to a particular role status or the level of commitment to performing that role. The LRSS evaluates eight separate dimensions composed of each of the four life roles examined from both a value and a commitment perspective.

Sample Items:

(A)   Having work/a career that is interesting and exciting to me is my most important life goal.

442

(B)   I value being involved in a career and expect to devote the time and effort needed to develop it.

(C)   I expect to work hard to build a good marriage relationship even if it means limiting my opportunities to pursue other personal goals.

Comments: The number of factors was selected by use of a principal components factor analysis using the eigenvalue greater than 1.0 rule, with oblique and varimax rotations on two different data sets. The authors report that item loadings on their primary factors range from .58 to .82. Of the 32 possible combinations of factors, correlations of at least .40 are reported twice. Cronbach's alpha is reported to range from .79 to .94 for the various scales. Test-retest correlations over a two-week period are reported to be at least .71 for each of the eight scales. Positive correlations are also reported between the scales and behavioral career and family role involvement.

References:

Amatea, E., & Clark, J. (1984). A dual career workshop for college couples: Effects of an intervention program. *J Coll Stud Pers, 25,* 271–272.

Amatea, E., Cross, G., Clark, J., & Bobby, C. (1986). Assessing the work and family role expectations of career-oriented men and women: The life role salience scales. *J Mar Fam, 48,* 831–838.

Reading, J., & Amatea, E. S. (1986). Role deviance or role diversification: Reassessing the psychological factors affecting the parenthood choice of career-oriented women. *J Mar Fam, 48,* 255–260.

IV-1/a

376. BAHR, S. J., CHAPPELL, C. B., & LEIGH, G. K. Quality of Role Enactment

Avail: 1983 Ref.

Variables Measured: Quality of self-role enactment and quality of spouse-role enactment

Type of Instrument: Self-report questionnaire

Instrument Description: This is an 18-item questionnaire, with 9 items measuring self-role enactment and 9 measuring spouse-role enactment. Six possible responses are provided for each item. The items ask about how well people enact typical household tasks such as house-keeping, yard work, child care, helping each other with problems, and expressing physical affection. The instrument is designed to be completed by married couples. The items within each factor were standardized, multiplied by the factor score coefficient, and summed to form the composite score.

Sample Items: People vary a good deal on how well they do different things. Please give your best estimate of how well you (and your spouse if married) do each of the following things:

(A)   Housekeeping of yourself.

(B)   Housekeeping of your spouse.

Comments: Factor analysis resulted in four scales. Theta for each scale is reported by the authors to be .71 for husbands' self-role enactment, .69 for husbands' spouse-role enactment, .76 for wives' self-role enactment, and .71 for wives' spouse-role enactment.

Reference:

Bahr, S. J., Chappell, C. B., & Leigh, G. K. (1983). Age at marriage, role enactment, role consensus, and marital satisfaction. *J Mar Fam, 45,* 795–803.

IV-1/a
377. BAHR, S. J., CHAPPELL, C. B., & LEIGH, G. K. Role Consensus

Avail: 1983 Ref.

Variables Measured: Perceived disagreement between spouses regarding marital roles and responsibilities

Type of Instrument: Self-report questionnaire

Instrument Description: This 9-item questionnaire was designed to be given to married couples. Each item has five responses ranging from *never disagree* to *almost always disagree.* Item scores within factors are summed.

Sample Item:

(A)   How often have you and your spouse disagreed about housekeeping?
(B)   . . . about earning a living?
(C)   . . . about keeping in touch with relatives?

Comments: Among both husbands and wives, factor analysis revealed a single factor. In both cases, this factor accounted for over 40% of the variance, and the authors report that all items loaded at .48 or above. The composite scale constructed from these items yielded a theta of .81 for wives and .80 for husbands.

Reference:

Bahr, S. J., Chappell, C. B., & Leigh, G. K. (1983). Age at marriage, role enactment, role consensus, and marital satisfaction. *J Mar Fam, 45,* 795–803.

IV-1/a
378. BIRD, G. W., & BIRD, G. A. Family Task Sharing Scale

Avail: 1984 Ref.

Variables Measured: Extent of shared household responsibilities between marital couples

Type of Instrument: Self-report questionnaire

Instrument Description: The Family Task Sharing Scale is a 6-point, 22-item Likert-style questionnaire designed to assess the extent to which common household responsibilities are shared between husbands and wives. For each item, respondents indicate how family tasks are divided by circling the appropriate response (*wife only, wife more than husband, wife and husband about same, husband more than wife, husband only,* or *neither husband nor wife*). Because the purpose of the scale is to identify the degree of task-sharing rather than which spouse has major responsibility for each task, the responses are coded to reflect amount of sharing: 1 = *tasks not shared;* 2 = *tasks partly shared;* 3 = *tasks equally shared.* Mean scores for each of seven subareas (meal preparation, child care, maintenance, family management, financial management, cleaning, and gardening) are computed.

Sample Items:

(A)   Shopping for food.
(B)   Chauffeuring children.
(C)   Coordinating day-to-day family activities.

Comments: The seven subareas were arrived at by use of a factor analysis with varimax rotation. The authors report that all items loaded on their primary factors at .48 or above. Scale scores have been compared to gender-role orientation, family and community role salience for husbands, and level of income and extent of employment for wives.

Reference:

Bird, G. W., Bird, G. A., & Scruggs, M. (1984). Determinants of family task sharing: A study of husbands and wives. *J Mar Fam, 46,* 345–355.

IV-1/a
379. BJORKQUIST, P. A. Family Responsibility Index (FRI)

Avail: 1984 Ref.

Variables Measured: Division of family role responsibilities between spouses

Type of Instrument: Self-administered questionnaire

Instrument Description: The FRI is designed to assess each spouse's degree of behavioral participation in 54 specific tasks distributed among 10 separate areas of typical responsibilities for families. Respondents are asked to rate on a 5-point summated rating scale the extent of their responsibility for each task during a typical workweek. Responses are coded from 5 (*husband/wife always*) to 1 (*wife/husband always*), with a zero listed for items that do not apply. The FRI is hand-scored by summing the amounts circled for each category. The total of the 10 category scores is used to come up with the final FRI summed score. Because husbands and wives complete different versions, a differential score may be obtained to indicate the relative balance of responsibility within a couple.

Sample Items:

(A)   Mow lawn.
(B)   Put dishes in dishwasher/wash dishes.
(C)   Make major financial decisions (e.g., buy insurance, select financial investments).

Comments: The author reports on one study in which both members of 10 dual-career couples were administered the FRI twice, 7 to 10 days apart. Between-spouse correlations on the initial administration are reported to have ranged from .64 to .89, with a mean of .82. Second administration correlations reportedly ranged from .00 to .82, with a mean of .36. A validity check relating FRI scores to information obtained during interviews indicated correlations ranging from .46 to .96, with means of .88 for husbands and .86 for wives.

Reference:

Alley, P. M. (1984). The Family Responsibility Index: A behavioral measure of marital work allocation. *J Pers Assess, 48,* 3–5.

IV-1/a
380. BLOOD, R. O., Jr., & WOLFE, D. M. Task Participation Index and Role Specialization Index

Avail: 1960 Refs.

Variables Measured: Relative extent of performance and the division of labor in household task performance by husband and wife

Type of Instrument: Self-report questionnaire

Instrument Description: The Task Participation Index and the Role Specialization Index are each derived from responses to the identical 5-point, 8-item Likert-type questionnaire. For each index, respondents are asked to indicate which marital partner most often does each of eight common household tasks. Response options range from *husband always* (1) to *wife always* (5). The Task Participation Index consists of the sum of the response values to these items. The Role Specialization Index score is the number of tasks performed exclusively by one partner or the other. Instructions for the questionnaire ask respondents to indicate how they and their spouses "divide up family jobs." The original questionnaire has been modified and used in many ways. Some investigators have added, deleted, or modified questions in order to examine the constructs of marital participation and role specialization within more specific contexts (Aldous, 1969; Beckman & Houser, 1975; Brubaker, 1985). Others have expanded the original framework to include subscales indicating which spouse ought to and actually performed each task, as well as individual levels of satisfaction with the current division of labor among marital partners (Brinkerhoff & White, 1978). Several other revisions are also found in the literature on marital roles and power. The base of the original questionnaire, however, has generally been maintained.

Sample Items:

(A)   Who does the evening dishes?
(B)   Who keeps track of the money and the bills?
(C)   Who mows the lawn?

Comments: Due to the number of variations of the original scale that have been constructed according to the individual needs of various researchers, little validity or reliability information in studies containing only the eight items written by Blood and Wolfe is reported. The correlation of scores obtained by marital couples has been reported to be .61 (Granbois & Willett, 1970).

References:

Blood, R. O., Jr., & Wolfe, D. M. (1960). *Husbands and wives: The dynamics of married living.* Glencoe, IL: Free Press.

Brinkerhoff, D. B., & White, L. K. (1978). Marital satisfaction in an economically marginal population. *J Mar Fam, 40,* 259–267.

Nicola, J. S., & Hawkes, G. R. (1986). Marital satisfaction of dual-career couples: Does sharing increase happiness? *J Soc Behav Pers, 1,* 47–60.

Quarm, D. (1981). Random measurement error as a source of discrepancies between the reports of wives and husbands concerning marital power and task allocation. *J Mar Fam, 43,* 521–535.

Warner, R. L. (1986). Alternative strategies for measuring household division of labor. *J Fam Iss, 7,* 179–195.

IV-1/c
381. COLEMAN, M., GANONG, L. H., & BRYAN, L. First Impressions Questionnaire (FIQ)

Avail: NAPS-3

Variables Measured: Perceptions of families or family roles

Type of Instrument: Semantic differential questionnaire for rating families

Instrument Description: The FIQ is a 40-item scale designed to measure perceptions of stimulus families or family members along six dimensions: evaluative, potency, activity, satisfaction/security, personal character, and stability. It was originally developed for use in a study of college students' attitudes toward family structure. Families are rated on the FIQ's 40 bipolar items using a 7-point continuum. Subjects place an "X" at the appropriate place on the continuum in order to indicate their perceptions of the stimulus family described in a vignette. Items are randomly ordered, with half the positive adjectives appearing on the left and half on the right. Items are scored such that high scores represent positive attitudes. Administration time is approximately 15 minutes.

Sample Items:

(A) sensitive/insensitive
(B) affectionate/hateful
(C) predictable/unpredictable

Comments: Items included on the FIQ were derived from a factor analysis conducted on an initial pool of 60 items. The authors report results indicating a solution of 40 items and six factors. These 40 items were readministered by the authors to a second sample, resulting in confirmation of the general factorial solution. Individual factors contain from 2 to 19 items. The authors report that Cronbach's alpha for the six factors ranges from .43 to 94.

References:

Bryan, L. R., Coleman, M., Ganong, L. H., & Bryan, S. H. (1986). Person perception: Family structure as a cue for stereotyping. *J Mar Fam, 48,* 169–174.

Coleman, M., & Ganong, L. H. (1987). The cultural stereotyping of stepfamilies. In K. Pasley & M. Ihinger-Tallman (Eds.), *Remarriage and stepparenting: Current research and theory.* New York: Guilford.

IV-1/a
382. COWAN, C. P., & COWAN, P. A. The "Who Does What?"

Avail: NAPS-3

Variables Measured: Spouses' perceptions of gender roles for family responsibilities and household tasks

Type of Instrument: Self-report questionnaire

Instrument Description: The "Who Does What?" was designed to assess spouses' perceptions of the relative responsibilities along three dimensions: (1) household tasks, (2) family decision making, and (3) the caring for and rearing of children. It also examines each partner's satisfaction with the current arrangements. For each item, individuals indicate who does what on a 9-point scale ranging from *she does it all* to *he does it all.* Ratings are also collected regarding how the respondent would prefer responsibilities to be divided. Six versions of the scale are currently available: (1) couples without children, (2) expectant couples, (3) couples with 6-month-old children, (4) couples with 18-month-old children, (5) couples with children aged 3 to 4 years, and (6) couples with 5- to 6-year-old children. In all versions, the 12 household task and 12 decision-making items are identical. However, the wording of responses to child care items differ, with childless and expectant couples indicating "how I think it would be" and "how I would like it to be." Child care items also contain slight differences in wording to reflect the circumstances of couples with children of various ages. An additional set of eight items and one additional dimension reflecting perceived parental competence are also added for parents of the older groups of children. Scores are calculated by summing values assigned to responses within the three dimensions for each set of items. Two additional scores, task sharing and role satisfaction, are also computed. Task sharing is calculated by computing the average absolute difference between "how it is now" scores and 5. An even division yields a score of 0. The higher the score, the greater the role differentiation. Role satisfaction is computed by calculating the average difference between scores for "how it is now" and "how I'd like it to be."

Sample Items:

(A)   Planning and preparing meals.
(B)   How we spend time at home.
(C)   Deciding about the baby's feeding schedule.

Comments: The authors report both Cronbach's alpha and Spearman-Brown's split-half reliabilities for all subscales in the .92 to .99 range. Correlations between husband and wife "as it is now" scores for various dimensions are reported to range from .31 to .66. Additional validity information is presented in the references listed below.

References:

Cowan, C. P., & Cowan, P. A. (1988). Who does what when partners become parents: Implications for men, women, and marriage. *Mar Fam Rev, 12*(3/4), 105–124.
Cowan, C. P., Cowan, P. A., Coie, L., & Coie, J. (1978). Becoming a family: The impact of a first child's birth on the couple's relationship. In W. B. Miller & L. F. Newman (Eds.), *The first child and family formation* (pp. 296–324). Chapel Hill, NC: Carolina Population Center.
Cowan, C. P., Cowan, P. A., Heming, G., Garrett, E., Coysh, W. S., Curtis-Boles, H., & Boles, A. J., III (1985). Transitions to parenthood: His, hers and theirs. *J Fam Iss, 6*, 451–481.

IV-1/a
383. DUNN, M. S. Marriage Role Expectation Inventory (MREI)

Avail: Family Life Publications, P.O. Box 427, Saluda, NC 28773

Variables Measured: Individual expectations within areas relevant to establishing relationships and interpersonal commitments

Type of Instrument: Self-report questionnaire

Instrument Description: The MREI is a 5-point, 71-item Likert-type questionnaire designed to assist respondents in preparing for marriage and family life. The instrument is a revised version of a 1960 instrument (available in Dunn, 1960) based on the distinction between traditional and companionship expectations. The MREI consists of two primary subscales and eight areas of concern related to expectations and interactions among married couples. The first primary subscale contains 34 items and assesses attitudes regarding a companionship-equalitarian relationship. The remaining 37-item section evaluates attitudes toward a traditional or patriarchal relationship between spouses. The eight areas of concern are authority, homemaking, children, personality, social participation, sexual relations, education, and employment and support. Items take the form of statements, each presumed to begin with the stem "In my marriage I expect . . . " Responses are scored from 1 to 5, and range from *strongly agree* to *strongly disagree*. Scores for the eight subareas are derived by summing across items. The inventory was designed as an aid to examining values and perspectives rather than determining readiness for marriage. It can be used as a teaching aid, in premarriage or marriage awareness seminars by ministers and therapists, and by researchers interested in exploring interpersonal expectations. Separate forms are available for use with men and women.

Sample Items: The publisher did not grant permission to reproduce items.

Comments: Norms included in the manual are based on responses to the MREI by over 500 high school students. Individual responses are plotted on a profile sheet. The MREI has also been adapted by Weeks and Thornburg (1977) for use with children.

References:

Andress, E. L., & Maxwell, J. W. (1982). Marriage role expectations of divorced men and women. *J Divorce, 5*(4), 55–66.

Dunn, M. (1960). Marriage role expectations of adolescents. *Mar Fam Living, 22*, 55–66.

Nickols, S. A., Fournier, D. G., & Nickols, S. Y. (1986). Evaluation of a preparation for marriage workshop. *Fam Relat, 35*, 563–571.

Tarson, J. H. (1984). The effects of husband's unemployment on marital and family relations in blue-collar families. *Fam Relat, 33*, 503–511.

IV-1/a

384. GOLDBERG, W. A. Allocation of Household Tasks Checklist (AHTC)

Avail: NAPS-3

Variables Measured: Comparison of husband and wife with regard to division of labor, responsibility for ensuring that household tasks are completed, and interest in having such tasks completed

Type of Instrument: Self-report questionnaire

Instrument Description: The AHTC is designed to measure several issues that emerge in the study of couples' division of household labor. In addition to asking (1) who does which tasks, the AHTC measures (2) who assumes primary responsibility for the task, and (3) who cares most about the task being completed. It is intended for use with men and women who are married or live with another adult. Each of the three areas mentioned above is assessed through a series of five feminine-typed major household tasks, four masculine-typed tasked, and four feminine-typed minor household chores. In the "who usually does" section, the respondent supplies the percentage of time each of the 13 tasks is usually done by self and spouse. For the "responsibility" and "cares" sections, the respondent checks *self* or *spouse* by each item to indicate which person either has major responsibility for the task or cares more if it gets done. Scores are computed for these sections by counting the number of times each member of the couple was indicated as having greater responsibility or as caring more about whether the task gets done.

Sample Items:

(A)   Food shopping.
(B)   Car repairs.
(C)   Setting the table.

Comments: The masculine-feminine gender-typing of task items was determined by 34 independent raters. Agreement among raters exceeded 97% for 11 of the 13 items, and was 82% and 94% for the remaining two items. Reliability information is reported by the author from a study in which 39 couples responded to the AHTC three times during a single year. Cronbach's alpha for *who usually does* responses to the three scales is reported to range from .78 to .88 for feminine major household tasks, from .88 to .92 for masculine house tasks, and from .75 to .87 for feminine chores. Most of the individual task items are reported to be slight modifications of tasks compiled by J. Leite and M. Weinraub. However, the author claims responsibility for subscale formation and, with feedback from M. Lamb, for creation of the three sections (*usually does*, *responsibility*, and *cares*).

Reference:

Goldberg, W. A., Michaels, G. Y., & Lamb, M. E. (1985). Husbands' and wives' adjustment to pregnancy and first parenthood. *J Fam Iss, 6,* 483–503.

IV-1/II-1/g/P
385. HARE-MUSTIN, R. T., & BRODERICK, P. C. Motherhood Inventory (MI)

Avail: NAPS-3

Variables Measured: Attitudes toward women's roles, beliefs, and behaviors as they apply to a broad range of variables associated with motherhood

Type of Instrument: Self-report questionnaire

Instrument Description: The MI is a 4-point, 40-item Likert-type questionnaire designed to assess attitudes toward motherhood and feminist perspectives. Items are in the form of statements to which respondents indicate the extent of their agreement or disagreement. Items are assigned to six categories: (1) women's control over reproduction, (2) adoption, (3) punitive aspects of motherhood, (4) caring for men, (5) women's identity and motherhood, and (6) the myth of motherhood. Descriptions of these classifications can be found in Hare-Mustin and Broderick (1979). Development of the MI was based on a review of the literature, as well as sentence completions of motherhood stems. The final version of the instrument was reviewed by a panel of 12 judges and was balanced for positive and negative direction. Scoring procedures whereby items within categories are combined appear to be possible, but are not specified. Rather, the authors report on differences between target groups based on responses to individual items. The MI is available from NAPS-3 in both Spanish and English.

Sample Items:

(A)   Women should give up their children for adoption if they don't want to raise a child.
(B)   The love and altruism of mothers is what has made men's achievements possible.
(C)   Breastfeeding in public should be acceptable even in front of strangers.

Comments: Hare-Mustin and Broderick (1979) report on differences between men and women, younger (17–23 years) versus older (24–69 years) respondents, persons with college degrees versus those without degrees, Catholics and non-Catholics, and never-married versus married or formerly married respondents. Correlations are also reported for individual MI items and scores from the Attitudes Toward Women Scale (AWS, Spence, Helmreich, & Stapp, 1973). MI idealization of motherhood items are reported to correlate greater than .50 with the AWS profeminist score. Various factor analytic comparisons examining differences between groups on the MI are contained in Hare-Mustin, Bennett, and Broderick (1983).

References:

Hare-Mustin, R. T., Bennett, S. K., & Broderick, P. C. (1983). Attitude toward motherhood: Gender, generational, and religious comparisons. *Sex Roles, 9,* 643–661.

Hare-Mustin, R. T., & Broderick, P. C. (1979). The myth of motherhood: A study of attitudes toward motherhood. *Psych Wom Q, 4,* 114–128.

Hare-Mustin, R. T., & Lamb, S. (1984). Family counselors' attitudes toward women and motherhood: A new cohort. *J Mar Fam Th, 10,* 419–421.

IV-1/II-3/d
386. HARTSHORNE, T. S., & MANASTER, G. J. Grandchild Role Conception Scale

Avail: 1982 Ref.

Variables Measured: Grandchildren's perceptions of social and personal dimensions of their relationships with their grandparents

Type of Instrument: Self-report questionnaire

Instrument Description: This instrument is a 10-item Likert-type questionnaire designed to assess role conceptions of grandchildren regarding their grandparents. The scale was specifically designed for assessing roles of grandmothers, but could be used with equal ease in evaluating role conceptions related to either grandparent. The pool of items was based on a 12-item scale by Robertson (1976), also designed to measure personal and social role conceptions. These 12 items were rewritten, added to 4 original items, and pilot tested. An item analysis resulted in 6 items being discarded. The socialized dimension is defined as the belief that grandparental roles are a function of social forces and/or societal needs. The personal dimension is characterized by the recognition of individual needs and a desire for personal fulfillment. On the basis of responses, grandchildren are classified as having one of four orientations: (1) apportioned, or having both high social and personal conceptions; (2) individualized, or having low social and high personal conceptions; (3) symbolic, or high social but low personal conceptions; or (4) remote, characterized by persons with both low social and personal conceptions of grandparents.

Sample Items:

(A) It is very important that my grandparents be involved with family activities.

(B) My grandparent has brought a very important sense of perspective to my life.

(C) It is important that grandchildren spend a part of their holidays visiting their grandparent.

Comments: The social dimension and the personal dimension each have half of the items in the Grandchild Role Conception Scale geared toward it. The authors report that Cronbach's alpha was found to be .68, .86, and .86 for the social and personal dimensions and the combined 10-item questionnaire, respectively.

Reference:

Hartshorne, T. S., & Manaster, G. J. (1982). The relationship with grandparents: Contact, importance, role conception. *Int J Aging Hum Dev, 15,* 233–245.

IV-1/d/b

387. HILDRETH, G. J., & RETHERFORD, P. Measurements of Participation and Enjoyment of Older Women in Family Maintenance Activities

Avail: NAPS-3

Variables Measured: Degree of participation by older women in family and house maintenance activities of their adult children and grandchildren

Type of Instrument: Interview questionnaire

Instrument Description: The instrument was designed to gather data through interviews with elderly women who interact on a regular basis with their adult children and grandchildren. Elderly women respond to 35 items dealing primarily with participation and enjoyment of participation in household activities. Response options for each question range from 0 (*never*) to 4 (*all of the time*). Additional demographic information is also requested. Administration time is approximately 45 minutes. Responses from all items are scored and summed in order to obtain an overall index of participation.

Sample Items:

(A)   Do you do the laundry for yourself or for your relatives? How much do you enjoy this activity?

(B)   Do you make contributions to the family income by means of lawn upkeep, redecorating, etc.? How much enjoyment do you receive?

(C)   Do you spend time just visiting your grandchildren or young relatives? What level of enjoyment do you receive from this activity?

Comments: Items used for this instrument were adapted from three other measures developed by Streib (1965), Streib and Schneider (1971), and Sussman (1959). All items were assessed by a panel of judges with experience in research methods and family relations of older women. The authors report that the instrument was pilot tested using 15 elderly women who indicated that they understood the questions and had no difficulty supplying answers.

References:

Hildreth, G. J., Van Laanen, G., Kelley, E., & Durant, T. (1980). Participation in and enjoyment of family maintenance activities by elderly women. *Fam Relat, 29,* 386–390.
Streib, G. F. (1965). Intergenerational relations: Perspectives of the two generations of the older parent. *J Mar Fam, 27,* 469–476.
Streib, G. F., & Schneider, J. (1971). *Retirement in American society.* Ithaca, NY: Cornell University Press.
Sussman, M. B. (1959). *Sourcebook in marriage and the family.* Boston: Houghton Mifflin.

IV-1/II-2/a

388. HUSTON-HOBURG, L., & STRANGE, C. Spouse Support Questionnaire

Avail: NAPS-3

Variables Measured: Married students' perceptions of the support they receive from their spouses

Type of Instrument: Self-report questionnaire

Instrument Description: This instrument is a six-page questionnaire designed to assess attitudes held and behaviors exhibited by married students who have returned to college and their spouses. The items are primarily Likert-type in format, generally with five or six response options. The questionnaire consists of a section requesting demographic information, six sections containing multiple Likert-type items, and two multiple-choice items. While most items refer to support rendered by one's spouse, some items inquire about personal needs of the individual respondent (e.g., need for tutoring in a subject, help in dealing with stress, help in beginning to look for a job). The instrument was used by the authors with subjects solicited by mail; however, it would also be appropriate for use with an interview format. It was designed to assess students' perceptions of the support they receive from their spouses in three primary areas: attitudinal, emotional, and functional. Many of the items refer to male/female roles and role expectations. Respondents are asked to indicate both their own and their spouse's views in this area. Only one member of the marital partnership is asked to fill out the questionnaire, with that person being a student. The authors analyzed data from the questionnaire on an item-by-item basis. However, the combination of scores to form composite indexes also appears to be a reasonable method for assessing the construct of spousal support.

Sample Items:

(A) Being a parent is as important for a man as it is for a woman.

(B) I find I have more conflicts with my spouse when I am enrolled in school.

(C) What childcare arrangements do you rely on most so that you are able to study and attend classes?

Comments: The author indicates several differences between men's and women's perceptions of support, as well as differences in cross-role behaviors. Differences are reported on an item-by-item basis and are detailed in the reference listed below.

Reference:

Huston-Hoburg, L., & Strange, C. (1986). Spouse support among male and female returning adult students. *J Coll Stud Pers, 27,* 388–394.

IV-1/e/W

389. LOPATA, H. Z. Relations-Restrictive Attitude Scale

Avail: 1973 Ref.

Variables Measured: Extent to which social relations of widows are restricted by perceptions of others as to their roles and appropriate behaviors

Type of Instrument: Self-report questionnaire

Instrument Description: This instrument is composed of two subscales. Item Set A is a Likert-style scale containing 15 statements with which widows are asked either to agree or to disagree on a 4-point scale. Item Set B contains 21 statements that subjects indicate are either true or false. All items refer to attitudes concerning relationships with children and friends, sexual relations, status, decision making, and independence. A total score is derived by summing individual item values for all 36 items of the combined scale. Scores can range from 0 to 19, with higher scores indicating more restrictive attitudes.

Sample Items:

(A) One problem with adult children is that they always want you to do favors for them—babysit, or sew, or things like that.

(B)   Sons are more help to a widow than daughters.
(C)   I did not know anything about our finances when my husband died.

Comments: Reports of research conducted utilizing the Relations-Restrictive Attitude Scale have indicated that the scale has primarily been used with elderly populations. In one study, 87% of the sample (301 subjects) were over the age of 55, and 50% were at least 65 years old. The average length of time since the death of the previous husband was reported to be 11.45 years.

References:

Lopata, H. Z. (1973). *Widowhood in an American city.* Cambridge, MA: Schenkman.
Lopata, H. Z. (1979). *Women as widows.* New York: Elsevier.
Lopata, H. Z. (1981). Widowhood and husband sanctification. *J Mar Fam, 43,* 439–450.

IV-1/c/C
390. McCUBBIN, H. I., & PATTERSON, J. M. Adolescent-Family Inventory of Life Events and Changes (A-FILE)

Avail: 1987 Ref.

Variables Measured: Major changes in the lives of adolescents within the context of roles and responsibilities within the family

Type of Instrument: Self-report questionnaire

Instrument Description: This instrument is a 50-item questionnaire utilizing a *yes-no* response format, designed to record life events and changes an adolescent perceives his or her family has experienced during the past 12 months. A-FILE also records the occurrence of 27 events presumed to take longer to adapt to or that, by their nature, have chronic effects and hence generate a prolonged residue of strain and possible distress. Events are divided into six general categories: (1) transitions—related to role or status transitions of family members, the addition of family members, or geographical mobility of family members; (2) sexuality—focusing on pregnancy, childbearing, and the onset of sexual activity; (3) losses—such as those related to the death of family members, relatives, or friends or to loss of property or income; (4) responsibilities and strains—focusing on interpersonal tension and strains related to health care and finances; (5) substance use—concentrating on the use of alcohol or other drugs, conflict about substance use, or a premature exit from school; and (6) legal conflict—with items indicating arrest or assault of a family member. Adolescents are instructed to indicate which events have occurred, first within the previous 12 months, and then prior to the previous 12-month period. A score is derived for each subsection by counting the number of events to which respondents have indicated a *yes* response. Overall recent and past life A-FILE scores are obtained by adding scores from the subscales. A separate 77-item questionnaire for use with young adults (YA-FILE; Grochowski & McCubbin, 1987) is also available. The identical six factors are examined with both versions. Administration time is approximately 10 minutes for A-FILE and 15 minutes for YA-FILE.

Sample Items:

(A)   Parent quit or lost a job.
(B)   Increased arguments about getting the jobs done at home.
(C)   Family member was robbed or attacked (physically or sexually).

Comments: The authors indicate that Cronbach's alpha for total recent life changes is .69. Wide variability in frequency of occurrence for many items (i.e., death of a parent) is reported to have resulted in low alpha coefficients for many of the subscales. Two subscales with levels reported by the authors are responsibilities and strains (.67) and legal conflicts (.89). Test-retest reliability over a period of two weeks for the overall scale is reported to be .82. Overall A-FILE scores were correlated with use, during the past year, of cigarettes (.18), alcohol (.27), and marijuana (.21). Both Cronbach's alpha and test-retest reliability for YA-FILE are reported to be .85.

References:

Grochowski, J., & McCubbin, H. I. (1987). YA-FILE: Young Adult-Family Inventory of Life Events and Changes. In H. I. McCubbin & A. I. Thompson (Eds.), *Family assessment inventories for research and practice* (pp. 113–122). Madison: University of Wisconsin-Madison, Family Stress Coping and Health Project.

McCubbin, H. I., Needle, R., & Wilson, M. (1985). Adolescent health risk behaviors: Family stress and adolescent coping as critical factors. *Fam Relat, 34,* 51–62.

McCubbin, H. I., & Patterson, J. (1987). A-FILE: Adolescent-Family Inventory of Life Events and Changes. In H. I. McCubbin & A. I. Thompson (Eds.), *Family assessment inventories for research and practice* (pp. 101–110). Madison: University of Wisconsin-Madison, Family Stress Coping and Health Project.

IV-1/a
391. MELTON, W. Mate Selection Value Emphasis Index

Avail: NAPS-3

Variables Measured: The desirability of expressive and instrumental family role characteristics for a prospective spouse

Type of Instrument: Self-report questionnaire

Instrument Description: This instrument is composed of 22 Likert-style items utilizing a 5-point response option format. It is designed to assess the extent to which young adults emphasize expressive and instrumental role characteristics for a prospective spouse. Respondents indicate the relative importance of characteristics of a potential marriage partner on a scale ranging from *extremely important* to *not important.* Among the 22 items, 6 are identified as indicators of expressive and 6 as instrumental role preferences for a mate. These item scores are summed to determine composite scores. The remaining items are treated as fillers and are not used with either index. Administration time is approximately 20 minutes.

Sample Items:

(A) Do you rate mutual affection (love) between you and your mate as . . .
(B) Do you rate your mate's being kind and considerate of you as . . .
(C) Do you rate your mate's desire to work and save for future needs as . . .

Comments: The author reports that Cronbach's alpha is .82 for the expressive and .99 for the instrumental indexes.

References:

Melton, W., & Thomas, D. L. (1976). Instrumental and expressive values in mate selection of Black and White college students. *J Mar Fam, 38,* 509–517.

Rao, V. V. P., & Rao, V. N. (1980). Instrumental and expressive values in mate selection among Black students. *Western J Black Studies, 4,* 50–56.

IV-1/e
392. MILLER, B. C. Anticipatory Role Socialization Measure

Avail: 1982 Ref.

Variables Measured: Amount of learning about a role prior to occupying that role

Type of Instrument: Self-report questionnaire

Instrument Description: This measure was created to operationalize a concept in the role theory literature that suggested there are ways of learning about and preparing for social roles before actually occupying them, and that such "anticipatory socialization" is related to the ease of transition into any given role. It has been used by the author primarily to measure anticipation of roles and role satisfaction within marriage. Five questions assess the extent to which respondents learn about a new role through observing and talking with others, reading, taking formal classes, and having experiences that are similar to what the new role would require. The questions were designed to be asked by an interviewer, but could easily be modified to fit a self-administered questionnaire format. The amount of learning about a given role before having to perform it is indicated with four response alternatives ranging from *none* (scored "1") to *a lot* (scored "4"). Item scores are summed to arrive at a composite measure.

Sample Items:

(A) How much did you learn about what to expect by *observing* friends or relatives going through the same thing?
(B) How much prior *experience* did you have with situations similar to what (the new role) would require?
(C) How much preparation did you get by *reading* about what (the new role) would be like?

Comments: The author reports that Cronbach's alpha for the Anticipatory Role Socialization Measure was .74 in a study of marital satisfaction with 140 subjects. It is also reported that conceptual bases of the measure were suggested in Burr (1972).

References:

Burr, W. R. (1972). Role transitions: A reformulation of theory. *J Mar Fam, 34,* 407–416.
Mangen, D. J. (1982). Dyadic relations. In D. J. Mangen & W. A. Peterson (Eds.), *Research instruments in social gerontology: Vol 2. Social roles and social participation* (p. 106). Minneapolis: University of Minnesota Press.
Miller, B. C. (1976). A multivariate developmental model of marital satisfaction. *J Mar Fam, 38,* 643–657.

IV-1/g
393. MILLER, B. C. Ease of Role Transitions Measure

Avail: 1982 Ref.

Variables Measured: Ease of entering and leaving social roles

Type of Instrument: Self-report questionnaire

Instrument Description: This scale was an attempt to operationalize a concept, the ease of role transition, that had been developed theoretically (Burr, 1972) but for which no previous measure could be found. It was designed to evaluate difficulty experienced in transitions into and out of major roles. Specifically, this measure was used in a study investigating subjects' most recent major family role change. Roles were identified (such as getting married, becoming a parent) and ease of role transition questions were asked regarding experiences related to that role change. Respondents were asked each of the five questions, using a 4-point response format for their answers. Available responses ranged from *strongly agree* to *strongly disagree*. Scores from individual items were summed in order to arrive at a composite score.

Sample Items:

(A)   After (name the event), I was surprised that I had to change so many of the ways I was doing things.

(B)   For a while after the change I was anxious about how things would turn out.

(C)   I wasn't affected too much and my life stayed about the same.

Comments: The author reports that Cronbach's alpha for the scale, based on a sample of 140 married adults, has been measured at .75. Construct validity was assessed by comparisons of scale scores with the amount of anticipatory socialization and satisfaction with marriage.

References:

Burr, W. R. (1972). Role transitions: A reformulation of theory. *J Mar Fam, 34,* 407–416.

Mangen, D. J. (1982). Dyadic relations. In D. J. Mangen & W. A. Peterson (Eds.), *Research instruments in social gerontology: Vol 2. Social roles and social participation* (p. 49). Minneapolis: University of Minnesota Press.

Miller, B. C. (1976). A multivariate developmental model of marital satisfaction. *J Mar Fam, 38,* 643–657.

IV-1/b

394. MINDEL, C. H. Attitudes Toward Multigenerational Households

Avail: Mindel, 1982, Ref.

Variables Measured: Attitudes and obligations of adults toward assisting their elderly parents

Type of Instrument: Self-report questionnaire

Instrument Description: The Attitudes Toward Multigenerational Households questionnaire was developed in 1977 as a 5-point, 8-item instrument designed to assess the level of responsibility and obligation felt by adult children for the care and well-being of their elderly parents. Items are in the form of statements and are rated according to the respondent's level of agreement or disagreement (1 = *strongly disagree;* 5 = *strongly agree*). The scale was initially designed for use as part of a larger interview on multigenerational families. However, it may also be administered in a paper-and-pencil format. It is intended for administration to elderly persons and their adult children.

Sample Items:

(A)   If children have enough room in their homes it is only proper for them to ask their elderly relative to live with them.

(B)   People who cannot live independently should live with their children rather than
      live in a boarding home (i.e., a residence where room and board is provided).
(C)   When parents get older and need help they should be asked to move in with their
      married children.

Comments: The author indicates that Cronbach's alpha for this instrument is .85. Reliability with a younger population was reported to be .78. The scale is reported to correlate .33
with the question: "Do you think it is a good idea for elderly to live with their adult children?"
Item-total correlations are reported to range from .40 to .78. The author also indicates that
persons from younger and older generations tend to have different perceptions regarding the
role of adult children in providing for their elderly parents.

References:

Mindel, C. H. (1982). Kinship relations. In D. J. Mangen & W. A. Peterson (Eds.), *Research
    instruments in social gerontology: Vol. 2. Social roles and social participation* (pp. 187–
    229). Minneapolis: University of Minnesota Press.
Mindel, C. H., & Wright, R., Jr. (1982). Satisfaction in multigenerational households. *J
    Gerontol, 37,* 483–489.

IV-1/c
395. NYE, F. I., & GECAS, V. The Washington Family Role Inventory

Avail: NAPS-3

Variables Measured: Family roles related to housekeeping, child care, child socialization,
kinship, sex, provider, therapy, and recreation

Type of Instrument: Self-report questionnaire

Instrument Description: This instrument was created to measure the normative structure
and actual functioning of American families. Respondents are asked to indicate which member of the couple makes, or used to make, most of the decisions with respect to a list of 74
activities. The dimensions of role concept measured by the inventory are (1) normative (who
should perform the task), (2) preference (who would they like to have performed the task),
(3) behavior (who actually performs the task), (4) power (who makes the decisions with
respect to the task), (5) conflict (how much conflict results from performing the task), and (6)
competence (how well does each individual perform the task). A 5-point response format
(*husband entirely, husband more, husband and wife equally, wife more, wife entirely*) is utilized. The inventory is designed for couples who have or have had children, but some of the
subscales can be employed with unmarried or childless couples. It has been utilized primarily
as a written questionnaire, but could also be used with an interview format. Administration
time is approximately 20–30 minutes.

Sample Items:

(A)   Earning the family income.
(B)   Housekeeping.
(C)   Relations with relatives.

Comments: The authors report that scores from the Washington Family Role Inventory
have correlated over .60 with independent measures such as marital satisfaction. They further
report that the instrument has been used in two large surveys, one of which served as the data
base for the 1976 reference listed below.

References:

Bahr, S. J., Chappell, C. B., & Leigh, G. K. (1983). Age at marriage, role enactment, role consensus, and marital satisfaction. *J Mar Fam, 45,* 795–803.
Nye, F. I. (1974). Emerging and declining family roles. *J Mar Fam, 36,* 238–245.
Nye, F. I. (1976). *Role structure and analysis of the family.* Beverly Hills, CA: Sage.

IV-1/V-2/c/g/W
396. PARRY, G., & WARR, P. Home and Employment Role (HER) Scales

Avail: 1980 Ref.

Variables Measured: Mothers' attitudes toward domestic roles, paid employment, and the strain generated by their interaction

Type of Instrument: Self-report questionnaire

Instrument Description: The HER Scales are composed of three separate indexes measuring home role attitude (HRA), employment role attitude (ERA), and interaction strain (IS). An initial pool of items was generated through unstructured interviews with mothers, both those employed outside the home and those who were not so employed, as well as a search of the literature. Pilot testing with 27 respondents facilitated reduction of the initial pool (size unknown) to a group of 48 items. The final 36 items of the instrument were selected based on psychometric considerations following testing with 185 women. Each of the three final scales contains 12 items, scored as *yes, true, no, untrue,* and *don't know.* Scale scores, ranging from 12 to 36, are computed by summing values associated with individual responses. The instrument was designed for use in Great Britain in research examining attitudes of employed mothers who have dependent children.

Sample Items:

(A) My family really shows that they appreciate all I do for them.
(B) People where I work are very friendly.
(C) The hours I work make it very difficult to look after the children.

Comments: The authors report that correlations between the HRA, ERA, and IS subscales range from .25 to .47. Cronbach's alpha is reported to be .71, .78, and .75 for the HRA, ERA, and IS scales, respectively. Correlations between IS and social supports were reported to be .22 for women employed part-time and .36 for mothers employed outside the home on a full-time basis. Correlations reported between a measure of life satisfaction and HRA and ERA were .48 and .32, respectively. It was also reported that positive affect tended to be associated with ERA, while negative affect was more closely associated with HRA scores.

Reference:

Parry, G., & Warr, P. (1980). The measurement of mothers' work attitudes. *J Occup Psy, 53,* 245–252.

IV-1/c
397. PENDLETON, B. F., POLOMA, M. M., & GARLAND, T. N. Dual-Career Family Scales

Avail: 1980 Ref.

Variables Measured: Marriage type, domestic responsibility, satisfaction, self-image, career salience, and career line

Type of Instrument: Self-report questionnaire

Instrument Description: The Dual-Career Family Scales is a 31-item questionnaire designed to measure six dual-career family dimensions. The six dimensions are listed above. Each of the 31 items is measured first on a 5-point (*strongly agree* to *strongly disagree*) Likert scale used for reliability and multivariate analyses, and then is recoded to a dichotomous classification for Guttman scaling. The six scales were deductively formed and tested for use in research and dual-career family policy formulation and for counseling purposes. The original instrument was based upon mailed questionnaires sent to wives who were employed in professional-level occupations. However, the questions were designed so that they could also be used in either telephone surveys or face-to-face interviews. Administration time is approximately 5 minutes.

Sample Items:

(A)   If a child were ill and needed to remain home from school, I would be (have been) more likely to stay home with him/her than my husband.

(B)   Although my husband may assist me, the responsibility for homemaking tasks is primarily mine.

(C)   I would be a less fulfilled person without my family life.

Comments: The author reports that Cronbach's alpha for the six subscales are as follows: marriage type (.67), domestic responsibility (.42), satisfaction (.50), self-image (.73), career salience (.57), and career line (.76). The author notes the following corrections with regard to the reference listed below: (1) p. 272, under "Career Salience," V19 should read "My career is as important to my husband as it is to me"; (2) p. 274, right-hand column under "Career Salience" paragraph, the eighth line down in this paragraph should read "the wife perceives her husband to be as interested in her career as she is (V19), the wife's . . . "

Reference:

Pendleton, B. F., Poloma, M. M., & Garland, T. N. (1980). Scales for investigation of the dual-career family. *J Mar Fam, 42,* 269–276.

IV-1/IV-2/a
398. PRATT, L. Conjugal Organization Index

Avail: 1976 Ref.

Variables Measured: Husband-wife companionship, conjugal power, and gender-role differentiation

Type of Instrument: Self-report questionnaire

Instrument Description: This index is composed of a listing of 24 tasks commonly undertaken by married couples. Tasks are divided into four categories involving conjugal division of tasks (3 items), conjugal division of tasks—child's health (7 items), conjugal division of tasks—wife's health (7 items), and conjugal power (7 items). For each item in all but the wife's health category, respondents are asked to indicate whether primary responsibility for that task is assumed by the husband, by the wife, or if responsibility is shared between the husband and wife. In the wife's health category, respondents indicate whether or not the woman's husband performs any of a series of tasks when the wife is ill and bedridden. The questionnaire is designed for use in personal interviews or paper-and-pencil questionnaires. Coded responses are summed for each dimension of conjugal organization.

Sample Items:

(A)   (Child's Health) Teaching the child the proper foods to eat.
(B)   (Wife's Health) Calls from work to find out how you are.
(C)   (Power) Deciding upon the size of your family.

Comments: Reliability and validity information on the Conjugal Organization Index was not available.

References:

Pratt, L. (1972). Conjugal organization and health. *J Mar Fam, 34,* 85–95.
Pratt, L. (1976). *Family structure and effective health behavior: The energized family.* Boston: Houghton Mifflin.

IV-1/V-1/c
399. RETTIG, K. D., & BUBOLZ, M. M. Perceptual Indicators of Family Well-Being: Resource Exchange Theory

Avail: NAPS-3

Variables Measured: Family members as resources for love, status, services, information, goods, and money

Type of Instrument: Self-report questionnaire

Instrument Description: The instrument is a Likert-style questionnaire with 21 items covering affective components and 46 items dealing with frequency of occurrences related to a series of personal needs. These needs are met by interpersonal resource exchanges of the above-listed variables. Of the frequency items, 27 relate to the respondent's mate, 11 to the oldest child, and 8 to the family as a whole. The respondent is presumed to be the receiver of these resources. The affective evaluation scale consists of both cognitive and affective dimensions ranging from 1 (*terrible*) to 7 (*delighted*). Frequency of receiving resources is scored on an 8-point scale ranging from *never* to *2–3 times each day.* Each score is converted to a decimal by including the score in the numerator and 365 (days in a year) in the denominator. For example: *about once each week* = 52/365 = .14.

Sample Items:

(A)   How would you feel about your own family life if you considered only the love and affection you experience?
(B)   How often does your mate spend several minutes just talking with you?
(C)   How often does your oldest child who lives with you tell or show you that he/she admires and respects you?

Comments: The authors report that the instrument is based on the Resource Exchange Theory of Foa and Foa, but was developed entirely by themselves. Hierarchical complete-linkage cluster analyses were used to evaluate the validity of love, status, services, information, goods, and money resource classes. The authors report that affective evaluation measures are positively related to Rosenberg's Self-Esteem Scale. Modifications of the instrument, based on 1987 and 1988 data, are currently under way.

References:

Rettig, K. D., & Bubolz, M. M. (1983a). Interpersonal resource exchanges as indicators of quality of marriage. *J Mar Fam, 45,* 497–509.

Rettig, K. D., & Bubolz, M. M. (1983b). Perceptual indicators of family well-being. *Social Ind Res, 12,* 417–438.

IV-1/a

400. RICHARDSON, M. S., & ALPERT, J. L. Role Perception Scale

Avail: 1980 Ref.

Variables Measured: Perceptions of roles of work, marriage, parent, and combined roles of work-marriage and work-parent

Type of Instrument: Questionnaire for describing a character created in a projective story

Instrument Description: The Role Perceptions Scale is a combination projective methodology and objective scale used to assess role perceptions. Respondents initially write a story according to each of three sets of circumstances ("Joe is sitting with his young child"; "Frank and his wife, Anne, are sitting in their living room"; "Tom is sitting at the desk in his office.") Instructions given to subjects indicate that "this is a test of imagination, one form of intelligence." The story is to include what led up to the event, what is occurring at that moment, the character's thoughts and feelings, and the story outcome. Five minutes is allowed for writing each story. Following the construction of each story, the subject is asked to complete a 40-item *true/false* questionnaire regarding the main character of that story. Role perceptions are assessed according to innovativeness, affectivity, involvement, and competition.

Sample Items:

(A)   She (he) is expected to follow set roles.
(B)   She (he) feels discouraged.
(C)   She (he) doesn't really care.

Comments: The authors report that a factor analysis indicated that three subscales (innovativeness, affectivity, and involvement) loaded predominantly on a single factor, subsequently labeled role engagement. The fourth subscale, competition, is reported to have loaded on a separate factor. The authors also report patterns of gender differences for factor scores.

Reference:

Richardson, M. S., & Alpert, J. L. (1980). Role perceptions: Variations by sex and roles. *Sex Roles, 6,* 783–793.

IV-1/d

401. ROBERTSON, J. F. Perceptions of Appropriate and/or Expected Grandparent Behavior

Avail: 1976 Ref.

Variables Measured: Adults' expectations regarding appropriate roles and behaviors of their grandparents

Type of Instrument: Self-report questionnaire

Instrument Description: This instrument is a 10-item list of role-appropriate behaviors. The instrument was designed for administration to adults regarding expectations they have about their grandparents' behaviors. Available response options are *yes, no,* and *NA* (nonapplicable). The instrument was designed as one in a series, described in Robertson (1976), geared toward understanding the nature of the relationship between grandparents and their grandchildren. The author treats each item individually, reporting the frequency of *Yes, No,* and *NA* responses for each. However, the scale might also lend itself to an overall score by assigning values to responses and summing across items. The overall score could be used to evaluate the strength of role definition held by both children and adults regarding their grandparents. The author also suggests that differences between actual perceptions of grandparents and ideal concepts of the grandparent role could be derived by administering the questionnaire twice and comparing responses.

Sample Items:

(A)   Somebody who gave you gifts of money or took you places.
(B)   Somebody who kept you informed of family heritage, rituals, news, folklore, etc.
(C)   Somebody who you could rely on for emotional comfort.

Comments: The author indicates that 4 items from the questionnaire received positive responses from at least 40% of respondents. All but 1 item received positive indications from at least 23% of the sample. The remaining item (somebody who aids in financial support) received positive indications from only 8.1%.

References:

Robertson, J. F. (1975). Interaction in three-generation families, parents as mediators: Towards a theoretical perspective. *Int J Aging Hum Dev, 6,* 103–110.
Robertson, J. F. (1976). Significance of grandparents: Perceptions of young adult grandchildren. *Gerontol, 16,* 137–140.

IV-1/d
402. ROBERTSON, J. F. Role Behaviors with Grandchildren

Avail: 1977 Ref.

Variables Measured: Behaviors engaged in by grandparents with their grandchildren

Type of Instrument: Self-report questionnaire

Instrument Description: This instrument is a 14-item list of role-appropriate behaviors often thought to be engaged in by grandparents. The instrument was designed for administration to grandparents regarding their actual behavior with their grandchildren. Thus, rather than examining perceptions of roles, it was designed to assess actual behaviors in which grandparents engaged. It includes items related to providing services, advice, values, and information. The instrument was designed to be administered to grandparents and asks whether or not each activity is engaged in by the grandparent (*yes, no,* or *inappropriate*), the frequency with which each behavior is engaged (three options: (1) *high frequency* equals once a month or more, (2) *low frequency* equals a few times per year or less, (3) *inappropriate* and who was the initiator of the activity (*grandparent, grandchild, child,* or *inappropriate*). Items to which responses would be inappropriate for all three questions are those where the age, gender, distance from grandchild, health, and so on make performance of the behavior unlikely or impossible. The author examined data collected with this questionnaire on an item-by-item basis. It appears, however, that values could be summed across items to arrive at a composite indication of the clarity of role definitions for grandparents.

Sample Items:

(A)   Provide gifts.
(B)   Babysit with grandchildren.
(C)   Home recreation.

Comments: The author indicates percentages of grandparents engaging in each activity. While many grandparents reported engaging in several of the behaviors, the percentage also indicating a high level of activity in each area ranged from a low of 0.0 to a high of 55.2%. Of the 14 behaviors, 8 were reportedly engaged in with a high frequency by fewer than 10% of the respondents. Only 1 behavior (baby-sit with grandchildren) was reported at a high frequency by at least half the respondents. And even with this behavior, only slightly over one-third (35.2%) indicated that they initiated the activity.

References:

Robertson, J. F. (1975). Interaction in three-generation families, parents as mediators: To-wards a theoretical perspective. *Int J Aging Hum Dev, 6,* 103–110.
Robertson, J. F. (1977). Grandmotherhood: A study of role conceptions. *J Mar Fam, 39,* 165–174.

IV-1/a
403. SCANZONI, J. Role of Wife, Husband, Father, and Mother Scales

Avail: 1980 Ref.

Variables Measured: Preferences for interchangeability of men and women in paid work and domestic work or child care

Type of Instrument: Self-report questionnaire

Instrument Description: The purpose of these questionnaires is to assess the degree to which persons seek rewards or costs in domestic versus occupational spheres. The questionnaires are often treated as measuring independent constructs and may be used together or separately. All four questionnaires (role of wife, role of husband, role of father, and role of mother) utilize Likert-style items and a 5-point response format. The combined questionnaires have a length of 24 items.

Sample Items:

(A)   A married woman's most important task in life should be taking care of her husband.
(B)   The father has more of a responsibility than the mother to punish the children.
(C)   A mother of preschool children should work only if the family really needs the money a whole lot.

Comments: The author reports that Cronbach's alpha for the individual scales has been found to be at or above .80 on repeated usages. Covariance has been examined between these instruments and several variables including fertility control variables, occupational behaviors, and religious devoutness.

References:

Scanzoni, J., & Arnett, C. (1987). Enlarging the understanding of marital commitment via religious devoutness, gender role preferences, and locus of marital control. *J Fam Iss, 8*, 136–156.
Scanzoni, J., & Szinovacz, M. (1980). *Family decision making: A developmental sex role model.* Beverly Hills, CA: Sage.

IV-1/b/C
404. SEELBACH, W. C. Filial Responsibility Expectancy Scale

Avail: 1978 Ref.

Variables Measured: Responsibility of children for their aged parents

Type of Instrument: Self-report questionnaire

Instrument Description: This instrument is a 5-point, 6-item Likert-type questionnaire designed to measure beliefs regarding adult children's duties and responsibilities toward their elderly parents. Individual items evaluate beliefs regarding expected geographic proximity, care during illness, financial obligations, visitations, writing, and general responsibility. A total scale score is derived by summing values associated with responses to individual items. Scores above the median (24–30) are referred to as indicating extended or high expectations. Scores from 6–23 are referred to as nucleated or exhibiting low expectations. A second 11-item scale (Seelbach, 1978) was used in conjunction with the Filial Responsibility Expectancy Scale to evaluate specific areas in which adult children assisted their elderly parents.

Sample Items:

(A)   Married children should live close to parents.
(B)   Children should give their parents financial help.
(C)   Children who live at a distance should write to their parents at least once a week.

Comments: The author utilized the scale in evaluating beliefs of elderly respondents regarding duties and responsibilities of their adult children. The scale would also be appropriate, however, for evaluating beliefs of adult children. Results reported by the author indicate that older respondents tended to score higher on filial responsibility. It was also found that extended expectations were associated with marital status, with widowed and divorced persons having higher expectations of their children than did those still residing with their spouses. Respondents in poor health were also reported to have greater expectations of their children.

References:

Cicirelli, V. G. (1984). Adult children's helping behavior to elderly parents: The influence of divorce. *J Fam Iss, 5*, 419–440.
Seelbach, W. C. (1978). Correlates of aged parents' filial responsibility expectations and realizations. *Fam Coord, 27*, 341–350.
Seelbach, W., & Sauer, W. (1977). Filial responsibility expectations and morale among aged persons. *Gerontol, 17*, 492–499.

IV-1/a
405. SEKARAN, U. Enabling

Avail: 1986 Ref.

Variables Measured: The extent to which spouses are helpful to and supportive of each other

Type of Instrument: Self-report questionnaire

Instrument Description: Enabling is an 8-item Likert-style questionnaire utilizing a 5-point response format. Available responses range from *strongly agree* to *strongly disagree*. It was designed to measure how supportive emotionally and in sharing of household responsibilities spouses are of each other. The focus is on enabling each member of the couple to pursue personal and career goals. The instrument is particularly relevant to research in the area of dual-earner families. A total score is derived by summing scores associated with responses for individual items.

Sample Items:

(A)   The principle of give and take is the golden rule we follow in our house.
(B)   I seem to be taking on far more responsibility for home and family obligations than my spouse does.
(C)   If my spouse were a little more understanding and supportive, my life would be much easier to handle.

Comments: The author reports that Cronbach's alpha ranged from .68 for U.S. samples to .79 for Indian samples. The measure was used in three studies in the United States and two studies in India between 1981 and 1987. Correlations were examined between enabling and satisfaction with the marriage, family, and career.

References:

Sekaran, U. (1983). Factors influencing the quality of life in dual-career families. *J Occup Psy, 56,* 161–174.
Sekaran, U. (1985). The paths to mental health: An exploratory study of husbands and wives in dual-career families. *J Occup Psy, 58,* 129–137.
Sekaran, U. (1986). *Dual career families: Contemporary organizational and counseling issues* (p. 219). San Francisco: Jossey-Bass.

IV-1/a
406. SEKARAN, U. Multiple Role Stresses

Avail: 1986 Ref.

Variables Measured: Stresses and strains experienced by spouses due to their continually taking on multiple roles

Type of Instrument: Self-report questionnaire

Instrument Description: This 5-point, 20-item Likert-type scale measures the extent to which spouses experience stress due to the pressure of having to maintain several roles. Roles are listed, and respondents are asked to indicate their level of stress as it relates to each activity or role. Roles that are examined are those that deal with common marital and family problems. Issues relate to individual needs and the accompanying roles and responsibilities, as well as to roles necessitated by needs of the respondent's spouse and children. The scale is particularly useful in evaluating pressures incurred by persons engaged in dual-career marriages.

Sample Items:

(A)   Helping children in their activities.

(B)   Care of older family members.

(C)   Handling unforeseen or new situations.

Comments: The author reports that Cronbach's alpha for the Multiple Role Stresses questionnaire range from .82 for U.S. samples to .93 for Indian samples. The measure was used in three studies in the United States and two studies in India between 1981 and 1987.

References:

Sekaran, U. (1983). Factors influencing the quality of life in dual-career families. *J Occup Psy, 56*, 161–174.

Sekaran, U. (1985). The paths to mental health: An exploratory study of husbands and wives in dual-career families. *J Occup Psy, 58*, 129–137.

Sekaran, U. (1986). *Dual career families: Contemporary organizational and counseling issues* (pp. 217–218). San Francisco: Jossey-Bass.

IV-1/V-2/a/W

407. THOMAS, S., SHOUN, S., & ALBRECHT, K. Career/Marital Stress of Women Inventory (CMSWI)

Avail: NAPS-3

Variables Measured: Women's career goals, plus stress factors related to marriage, family, and work

Type of Instrument: Self-report questionnaire

Instrument Description: The CMSWI is a 46-item questionnaire designed for use with dual-career couples engaged in professions demanding high levels of commitment and academic preparation. It was developed for assessing perceptions of both spouses regarding the developmental progress of the wife's career, her marital/family and work-related stressors, coping strategies, current career status, and future career goals and plans. Subscales of marital/family stress are dyadic interaction, resource management, and family crises. Subscales for work-related stress include career adjustment and work environment. Separate forms are provided for husbands and wives, with the husband's form asking for his perceptions of his wife's satisfaction and levels of stress. Response formats are varied, but structured, throughout the instrument. Four-point Likert-style scale response options are used in the stress factor sections, with multiple-choice options predominating throughout most of the remainder of the questionnaire. Stress scale and subscale scores are obtained by summing responses to items. Some open-ended items are included in order to allow narrative descriptions of coping strategies and future goals. The final items are semiprojective in nature, asking respondents what advice they would give their daughters about career planning. Administration time is estimated to be 45 minutes.

Sample Items:

(A)   (for wives) In general, how satisfied are you in your current work situation?

(B)   (for husbands) In general, how satisfied is your wife in her current work situation?

(C)   (for both) What was your *initial* career goal or ambition?

Comments: The entire instrument was reviewed by three university faculty members who conduct research on stress, women's issues, and family problems. Additionally, 20 graduate students in child and family studies were solicited for their comments regarding specific items. The questionnaire was then pilot tested on, and discussed with, 10 couples, resulting in further modifications. Cronbach's alpha for the various subscales is reported by the authors to be .77

(career adjustment), .67 (work environment), .77 (resource management), .64 (dyadic interaction), and .35 (family crises).

References:

Thomas, S., Albrecht, K., & White, P. (1984). Determinants of marital quality in dual-career couples. *Fam Relat, 33,* 513–521.

White, P., Mascalo, A., Thomas, S., & Shoun, S. (1986). Husbands' and wives' perceptions of marital intimacy and wives' stresses in dual-career marriages. *Fam Perspect, 20,* 27–35.

IV-1/c

408. YOGEV, S., & BRETT, J. M. Family Involvement Scale

Avail: 1985 Ref.

Variables Measured: Psychological involvement in the roles of spouse and parent

Type of Instrument: Self-report questionnaire

Instrument Description: The Family Involvement Scale is a 5-point, 11-item Likert-type instrument, with response options ranging from *strongly disagree* to *strongly agree.* It is designed to measure the degree of psychological identification with the roles of spouse and parent, the importance of family roles to self-image and self-concept, and the individual's commitment to family roles. The scale was designed on the premise that a person highly involved in his or her family differs from a person with low involvement with respect to participation in housework and child care activities, as well as with respect to marital satisfaction and role overload. The scale was designed for use with married persons who have children and a spouse living at home. Those without children should be administered a shortened 6-item version. Administration time is approximately 5–10 minutes. Family Involvement Scale items are modeled after a job involvement instrument by Lodahl and Kejner (1965).

Sample Items:

(A)   A great satisfaction in my life comes from being a parent.
(B)   Nothing in life is as important as being a spouse.
(C)   The most important things that happen to me are related to my family roles.

Comments: The authors report that Cronbach's alpha for this instrument ranges from .80 to .84. The relationship of Family Involvement Scale scores to age of children, participation in child care activities, and marital satisfaction have been examined.

Reference:

Yogev, S., & Brett, J. M. (1985). Patterns of work and family involvement among single and dual-earner couples. *J Appl Psyc, 70,* 754–768.

IV-2/c/d/e

409. ALFORD, R. D. Intimacy and Disputing Styles

Avail: 1982 Ref.

Variables Measured: Relationship between levels of intimacy and violence in interpersonal interactions

Type of Instrument: Self-report questionnaire

Instrument Description: This instrument, untitled by the author, is a 6-point, 26-item Likert-type questionnaire designed to assess the relationship between levels of intimacy and violence involved in conflict resolution. Each item details a different type of relationship, with 14 items dealing with kinship relationships and 12 dealing with relationships with nonfamily members. Respondents are asked: "When you have a conflict or disagreement with this person [the 26 categories of people], how do you most often respond to that conflict?" (Alford, 1982, pp. 365–366). Response options include *avoidance, discussion, argument, fight by raising voices or similar tactics, fight by yelling and screaming or insulting,* and *fighting by yelling, screaming, insulting, pushing, shoving, hitting,* and so on. Each response option is defined for participants. In addition to indicating techniques for conflict resolution, respondents are also asked to indicate the level of intimacy they feel with the person described by the item, and the frequency of contact they have with that person. These latter ratings are accomplished using 5- and 6-point Likert-type scales, respectively. The author indicates that areas covered by the Conflict Tactics Scale (Straus, 1979) served as the base for the development of this scale.

Sample Items (Note: All sample items given here relate to ratings of family members):

(A) Mother's Father
(B) Younger Sister
(C) Husband

Comments: The author (Alford, 1982) presents means, standard deviations, and frequency data for all 26 items. Correlations between extreme disputing styles and intimacy, frequency of contact, gender, and age of respondents are also presented in the article. Although some exceptions are noted, the general finding presented by the author was that greater intimacy was associated with greater violence in dispute resolution.

Reference:

Alford, R. D. (1982). Intimacy and disputing styles within kin and nonkin relationships. *J Fam Iss, 3,* 361–374.

IV-2/V-3/a
410. BAGAROZZI, D. A. Spousal Inventory of Desired Changes and Relationship Barriers (SIDCARB)

Avail: NAPS-3

Variables Measured: Desired level of behavior change by spouse, willingness to separate or divorce, and barriers to separation or divorce

Type of Instrument: Self-report questionnaire

Instrument Description: The SIDCARB is a 24-item Likert-style questionnaire utilizing a 7-point response format. Specific response options vary according to the nature of each item. The scale was designed to gain the spouse's perception of what the author terms "the conjugal exchange process." The behaviors and attitudes of partners are assessed along the three dimensions mentioned above. The first 10 items in Factor 1 assess spouses' perceptions of fairness in the exchange process within areas of marital exchange such as household chores, finances, sexual relations, and children. Questions 11–15 deal with satisfaction and commitment. Questions 18–25 assess the strength of internal and external barriers to terminating the relationship. Husbands' scores are compared with those obtained by their wives in order to examine relative power and influence within the relationship with respect to the ability to call an end to the marriage.

Sample Items: Evaluate whether your husband/wife is doing his/her fair share to contribute to the overall satisfaction of the marriage and the degree to which you would like to see changes in his/her behavior.

(A)   Household Chores: cooking, cleaning, repairs around the house, gardening, shopping, taking out the trash, care of the automobile, pets, etc.

(B)   In general, how satisfied are you with your marriage? If your marriage were not satisfying, would any of the following circumstances prevent you from leaving your spouse? How important would each one be?

(C)   Obligations to children.

Comments: The author reports on two separate studies in which psychometric properties of the SIDCARB were assessed. In the first, correlations between the three factors ranged from -.19 to +.24. Cronbach's alpha for the factors ranged from .74 to .86 in the initial study and from .74 to .90 in the replication study. It is also reported that t-tests were conducted in order to determine if significant differences existed in how husbands and wives responded to the three subscales. No significant differences are reported.

References:

Bagarozzi, D. A. (1983). Methodological developments in measuring social exchange perceptions in marital dyads: SIDCARB. A new tool for clinical intervention. In D. A. Bagarozzi, A. P. Jurich, & R. W. Jackson (Eds.), *Marital and family therapy: New perspectives in theory, research and practice* (pp. 79–104). New York: Human Sciences.

Bagarozzi, D. A., & Atilano, R. B. (1982). SIDCARB: A clinical tool for rapid assessment of social exchange inequities and relationship barriers. *J Sex Mar T, 8,* 325–334.

Bagarozzi, D. A., & Pollane, L. (1983). A replication and validation of the Spousal Inventory of Desired Changes and Relationship Barriers (SIDCARB): Elaborations on diagnostic and clinical utilization. *J Sex Mar T, 9,* 303–315.

IV-2/a

411. BLOOD, R. O., Jr., & WOLFE, D. M. Decision Power Index

Avail: 1959 & 1960 Refs.

Variables Measured: Relative power of husband and wife regarding decisions affecting both spouses

Type of Instrument: Self-report questionnaire

Instrument Description: The Decision Power Index is a 5-point, 8-item Likert-type questionnaire designed to assess the extent to which marital partners exercise power in decision making. The respondent is asked to indicate "who has the final say" with respect to each of eight common decisions. Possible responses range from *husband always* (5) to *wife always* (1). Instructions for the questionnaire indicate that couples often talk over such areas, but that the final decision is often made by one spouse or the other. Respondents are asked to indicate which of them is more likely to make the final (italicized in the instructions) decision with regard to each area. Responses are used to classify couples as maintaining one of four marital power structures: (1) husband-dominant, (2) wife-dominant, (3) autonomic, or (4) syncratic. Syncratic couples are those in which half or more of the decisions are reported as being equally shared between husband and wife. Husband-dominant couples are those with fewer than four equally shared decisions, whose overall Decision Power Index scores are greater than 28. Wife-dominant couples also indicate fewer than four equally shared decisions, but the overall score is below 20. Autonomic couples are those in which decisions are generally not shared, and where an equal number of decisions are left to each partner. There have been many revisions and modifications of the basic procedure of this instrument. In various versions, items have been added, deleted, or modified; response formats have been altered; and new scoring systems have been created. Still, the basic structure, as established in the original scale, has generally been maintained.

Sample Items:

(A) . . . who makes the final decision about what car to get?
(B) . . . about whether or not to buy some life insurance?
(C) . . . about what doctor to have when someone is sick?

Comments: Several studies have been conducted using the Decision Power Index. Among findings reported in the literature, coefficient alpha has been reported to be .62, coefficients of reproducibility for husbands and wives have been reported to be .86 and .88, respectively, and the correlation of responses by spouses has been reported to be .35.

References:

Blood, R. O., Jr., & Wolfe, D. M. (1960). *Husbands and wives: The dynamics of married living.* Glencoe, IL: Free Press.

Cooney, R. S., Rogler, L. H., Murrell, R. M., & Ortiz, V. (1982). Decision making in intergenerational Puerto Rican families. *J Mar Fam, 44,* 621–631.

Lundgren, D. C., Jergens, V. H., & Gibson, J. L. (1982). Marital power, roles, and solidarity and husbands' and wives' appraisals of self and other. *Sociol Inq, 52,* 33–52.

Quarm, D. (1981). Random measurement error as a source of discrepancies between the reports of wives and husbands concerning marital power and task allocation. *J Mar Fam, 43,* 521–535.

Wolfe, D. M. (1959). Power and authority in the family. In D. Cartwright (Ed.), *Studies in social power* (pp. 99–117). Ann Arbor, MI: Institute for Social Research.

IV-2/a

412. ERICSON, P. M., & ROGERS, L. E. Relational Communication Coding System (RELCOM)

Avail: 1973 & 1979 Refs.

Variables Measured: Control and domination in husband-wife transactions

Type of Instrument: Behavior coding scheme

Instrument Description: RELCOM is a system for coding and classifying interactions between any two persons. The authors have used this system primarily in the classification of interaction patterns of husbands and wives. Conversations between spouses are elicited through use of structured interactional tasks. These interactions are recorded and later transcribed. Coders work from a combination of transcripts and tape recordings in rating interactions. Use of RELCOM involves a three-step process. First, messages within interactions are assigned three-digit codes to indicate the speaker, a grammatical code, and a response code that relates each message to the previously coded message. Five grammatical codes (*assertion, question, talk-over, noncomplete, and other*) and 10 response codes (*support, nonsupport, extension, answer, instruction, order, disconfirmation, topic change, initiation-termination,* and *other*) are utilized. The second step in the process is the translation of these numerical codes into one of three control directions: (1) assertion of one's own definition regarding an aspect of the relationship (coded with an arrow pointing up); (2) acceptance of the spouse's definition (arrow pointing down); or (3) nondemanding, nonaccepting interactions (coded by an arrow pointing sideways). The third step in the process involves combining pairs of interactions, with final classification of the interactions being in one of nine transactional types: (1) one-up, one-down; (2) one-down, one-up; (3) competitive; (4) submissive; (5) neutralized symmetry; (6) one-up, transitory; (7) transitory, one-up; (8) one-down transitory; and (9) transitory, one-down. Examples of interactions, arrow directions, and specific scoring procedures are contained in the two references noted above. For the most detailed description of the procedure, the reader is referred to Ericson and Rogers (1973).

Sample Items: Not applicable.

Comments: Development of the RELCOM was based on earlier systems reported by Sluczki and Beavin (1965) and Mark (1971). The authors report that intercoder reliability averaged .86 for all variables and over several interactional topics. Several measures and correlations resulting from the use of RELCOM are reported in Courtright, Millar, and Rogers-Millar (1979). These authors were particularly interested in the constructs of dominance and domineering behavior on the part of spouses.

References:

Courtright, J. A., Millar, F. E., & Rogers-Millar, L. E. (1979). Domineeringness and dominance: Replication and expansion. *Comm Monogr, 46,* 179–192.
Ericson, P. M., & Rogers, L. E. (1973). New procedures for analyzing relational communication. *Fam Proc, 12,* 245–267.
Mark, R. A. (1971). Coding communication at the relationship level. *J Comm, 21,* 221–232.
Rogers, L. E., & Bagarozzi, D. A. (1983). An overview of relational communication and implications for therapy. In D. A. Bagarozzi, A. P. Jurich, & R. W. Jackson (Eds.), *Marital and family therapy: New perspectives in theory, research and practice.* New York: Human Sciences.

IV-2/a

413. FITZPATRICK, M. A., & WITTEMAN, H. Verbal Interaction Compliance-Gaining Coding Scheme (VICS)

Avail: NAPS-3

Variables Measured: Techniques used during interactions that are designed to gain compliance from the other person

Type of Instrument: Ratings scheme for use with transcribed conversations

Instrument Description: The coding scheme measures several types of compliance-gaining messages: force to comply comes from characteristics of the speaker; force to comply comes from characteristics of the listener; force to comply comes from the relationship between interactants; force to comply comes from the positive or negative nature of a specific activity; force to comply comes from a specific enabling or disabling agent outside the relationship; speaker uses evaluatively neutral questions to find information on which to build persuasive case; force to comply comes from the exertion of control; force to comply comes from a direct request or emerges from the situation, and where the focus is on mutually satisfactory outcome.

Sample Items: Not applicable.

Comments: The VICS is a hierarchical, sieve communication coding scheme. That is, every communication act is not assumed to serve a persuasive function. Transcribed dialogue is divided into psychological thought units. Each unit is categorized as being either agreement, refutation, discounts, other, or compliance. The author reports that the VICS has been used in evaluating various types of marriages and persuasive outcomes.

Reference:

Witteman, H., & Fitzpatrick, M. A. (1986). Compliance-gaining in marital interaction: Power bases, processes and outcomes. *Comm Monogr, 53,* 130–143.

IV-2/II-3/f/C
414. FURMAN, W., & BUHRMESTER, D. Sibling Relationship Questionnaire (SRQ)

Avail: NAPS-3

Variables Measured: Sibling relationships with respect to warmth or closeness, relative status or power, conflict, and rivalry

Type of Instrument: Self-report questionnaire

Instrument Description: The SRQ is a 5-point, 48-item questionnaire designed to assess perceptions of relationships between siblings. Parallel forms are available for administration to children 9 years of age or older, parents of children in this age range, and parents of younger children. The form of the test on deposit with NAPS-3 is appropriate for administration to parents of children age 9 and older. Scoring procedures are also deposited for a 38-item version of the instrument. Subscales are constructed along 16 dimensions, each measured by 3 items. An earlier version of the SRQ (in Furman & Buhrmester, 1985) used 51 items. The current version eliminated use of two "general relationship evaluation" indexes labeled satisfaction and importance, plus the 3-item parental partiality, and added two subscales evaluating maternal partiality and paternal partiality. In addition to maternal and paternal partiality, the current version contains subscales of intimacy, prosocial behavior, companionship, similarity, nurturance by and of the sibling, admiration of and by the sibling, affection, dominance of and by the sibling, quarreling, antagonism, and competition. Items are in the form of questions, with responses for nearly all items ranging from 1 = *hardly at all,* to *EXTREMELY much.* Subscales combine to measure four primary constructs: (1) warmth/closeness, (2) relative status/power, (3) conflict, and (4) rivalry. Administration time is approximately 20 minutes for children and 15 minutes for adults.

Sample Items:

(A) Some siblings do nice things for each other a lot, while other siblings do nice things for each other a little. How much do both _____ and this sibling do nice things for each other?

(B) How much does _____ tell this sibling what to do?

(C) Who gets more attention from mother, _____ or this sibling?

Comments: The author indicates that Cronbach's alpha for the subscales averaged .80, with no subscale receiving an alpha of less than .63. Test-retest reliability over a period of 10 days is reported to average .71. Perceptions of family members are all reported to correlate at least .57.

References:

Furman, W., & Buhrmester, D. (1985). Children's perceptions of the qualities of sibling relationships. *Child Dev, 56,* 448–461.

Furman, W., Jones, L., Buhrmester, D., & Adler, T. (1989). Children's, parents', and observers perspective on sibling relationships. In P. G. Zukow (Ed.), *Sibling interactions across cultures.* New York: Springer-Verlag.

IV-2/c

415. GARRISON, J. P., & PATE, L. E. Measure of Interpersonal Power (MIP)

Avail: 1977 Ref.

Variables Measured: Interpersonal power within families

Type of Instrument: Self-report questionnaire

Instrument Description: The MIP is a 34-item Likert-style questionnaire utilizing a 7-point response format. Possible responses range from *strongly agree* to *strongly disagree.* It was developed to measure and compare dimensions of power within the four interpersonal contexts of acquaintance, friend, coworker, and family member. Family was defined as "someone you are genetically or legally related to through marriage." Items are randomly ordered, with some positively and others negatively worded. Three factors are evaluated: positive personal power, negative personal power, and reward power. Item scores within factors are summed in order to arrive at composite scores for each factor.

Sample Items:

(A)   This person has a great deal of influence over my behavior.
(B)   I don't do what this person says because I don't believe in what they say or do.
(C)   This person is able to delegate responsibility to others.

Comments: The authors report that the MIP has been analyzed for dimensionality, factor reliability, and construct validity. A factor analysis utilizing an oblique rotation was conducted on the 34-item scale. Several factor solutions were examined, with final reliance on the three factors mentioned above. Of the original 34 items, 12 had primary loadings on one of these three factors. The remaining 22 items have been retained as part of the scale, but do not load highly on any of the three factors. A detailed explanation of the factor analysis can be found in Garrison and Pate (1977).

References:

Garrison, J. P., & Pate, L. E. (1977). Toward development and measurement of the interpersonal power construct. *J Psychol, 97,* 95–106.

Garrison, J. P., Pate, L. E., & Sullivan, D. L. (1981). An extension of source valence research using multiple discriminant analysis. *J Soc Psych, 115,* 259–269.

IV-2/II-3/c

416. HENGGELER, S. W. Family Relationship Questionnaire (FRQ)

Avail: NAPS-3

Variables Measured: Dyadic (mother-father, mother-child, father-child) warmth, conflict, and dominance

Type of Instrument: Self-report questionnaire

Instrument Description: The FRQ has 11, 5-point, Likert-type items that assess each family member's perception of affect, conflict, and dominance with each of the three family dyads mentioned above. The first three questions require respondents to indicate who (mother or father) *always* or *usually* gets their own way. The remaining questions require responses ranging from *never* to *always*. These qualitative items are based on those developed by Hetherington and Frankie (1965). In father-absent families, only items that pertain to the mother-child dyad are used. The FRQ was designed as a straightforward instrument for use with families of varying socioeconomic and cultural backgrounds. The author indicates that ratings of the entire family may be excluded, resulting in a 9-item questionnaire. Administration time is approximately 5 minutes.

Sample Items:

(A)   When mother and father disagree with each other _____.

(B)   Mother and son/daughter _____ have arguments with each other.

(C)   Our family is _____ warm and affectionate toward each other.

Comments: The author reports that mean test-retest reliability across items was .67. Several additional findings are cited by the author as indicators of validity, including the following: (1) Father ratings of father-son affect significantly predicted familial arrest history; (2) mother ratings of mother-son affect predicted son's delinquency status; (3) ratings of dyadic affect, conflict, and dominance were not influenced by multisystemic therapy, in contrast with numerous observational measures that were influenced; (4) parental ratings of dyadic conflict were associated with social desirability; and (5) family disturbance was not associated with intrafamily agreement. Further details can be found in the references listed below.

References:

Borduin, C. M., & Henggeler, S. W. (1987). Post-divorce mother-son relations of delinquent and well-adjusted adolescents. *J Appl Devel Psych, 8,* 273–288.

Hanson, C. L., Henggeler, S. W., Haefele, W. F., & Rodick, J. D. (1984). Demographic, individual, and family relationship correlates of serious and repeated crime among adolescents and their siblings. *J Cons Clin, 52,* 528–538.

Henggeler, S. W., Rodick, J. D., Borduin, C. M., Hanson, C. L., Watson, S. M., & Urey, J. R. (1986). Multisystemic treatment of juvenile offenders: Effects on adolescent behavior and family interaction. *Devel Psych, 22,* 132–141.

Henggeler, S. W., & Tavormina, J. B. (1980). Social class and race differences in family interaction: Pathological, normative, or confounding methodological factors? *J Genet Psy, 137,* 211–222.

IV-2/c
417. HERBST, P. G. Day at Home

Avail: 1952 & 1954 Refs.

Variables Measured: Maternal versus paternal decision-making power within the family

Type of Instrument: Behavioral-report questionnaire

Instrument Description: Day at Home is a 33-item questionnaire designed to assess relative power held by parents with respect to interpersonal and household activities. Two questions are asked for each item: (1) "Who decides . . . "; and (2) "Do your parents disagree . . . " The first question is answered by selecting from options including *mother, father, other adults, the subject, brothers* (older or younger), and *sisters* (older or younger). Most items, however, are most appropriately answered by indicating that responsibility is carried by one or the other of the parents. In fact, while data are collected regarding decisions made by siblings and others, only those in which respondents indicate that primary responsibility was assumed by a parent are scored. The second question is answered on a 3-point scale, with points defined by *often, sometimes,* and *never.* Day at Home is used to evaluate four dimensions of family living: (1) family activity, including household duties, child care, social, and economic concerns; (2) tension within the family, measured through an examination of areas of disagreement; (3) family interaction patterns with respect to dominance styles; and (4) family structure patterns, assigned on the basis of the relative frequency of family interaction patterns. All questions relate to activities that could conceivably be performed by either parent. The instrument was designed for administration to school-aged children. The questionnaire was originally part of a 1948–1950 study of Australian communities.

Sample Items:

(A1) Who decides at what time you have to get out of bed?
(A2) How often do your parents disagree as to what time you ought to be up?
(B1) Who decides what groceries to buy?
(B2) Do your parents disagree as to what groceries should be bought?

Comments: Coding instructions for determining family structure are contained within Herbst (1952). In addition to determining dominance within the family, the Day at Home has also been used to examine parental behaviors and gender-role identification among children. Some items are obviously products of the generation and culture for which the instrument was originally developed (e.g., chopping wood, having tea, listening to a program on the wireless, putting out the milk bottles). However, with some minor modification, the scale could be used within the current cultural climate.

References:

Dietrich, K. T. (1975). A reexamination of the myth of Black matriarchy. *J Mar Fam, 37,* 367–374.
Herbst, P. G. (1952). The measurement of family relationships. *Human Relat, 5,* 3–35.
Herbst, P. G. (1954). Conceptual framework for studying the family. In O. A. Oeser & S. B. Hammond (Eds.), *Social structure and personality in a city.* New York: Macmillan.
Hillenbrand, E. D. (1976). Father absence in military families. *Fam Coord, 25,* 451–458.

IV-2/a
418. HOSKINS, C. N. The Dominance-Accommodation Scale (DAC)

Avail: 1986 Ref.

Variables Measured: Dominant and accommodating behaviors in an interactive relationship between partners, either married or living together

Type of Instrument: Self-report questionnaire

Instrument Description: The DAC is 48-item Likert-style scale with five response options for each item. It consists of a series of declarative statements with subjects indicating the extent to which they agree or disagree with each statement. The content is reflective of sexual relations, relationships with friends, how to spend leisure time, demonstration of affection, conventionality, what and when to eat, sleeping and waking patterns, allocation of responsibilities for household tasks, finances, and philosophy of life. The scale has been used primarily with middle-aged professionals with at least some college education.

Sample Items:

(A) If we disagree on what the most important things in life are, it is better in the long run if I go along with my partner's opinions.

(B) Even though I can tell when my partner wants sex, I don't feel I have to accommodate him (her).

(C) If my partner objects to my telling a waitress that she charged too little, I don't do it.

Comments: The author reports two separate factor analyses on the DAC. Each analysis resulted in a two-factor solution. However, there are substantial differences between the two solutions, with many items crossing factors or substantially loading on both in one study or the other. This implies that treating the DAC as a single-factor scale may be a more appropriate solution. The author reports that a further study designed to clarify the factor structure of the DAC is currently under way.

Reference:

Hoskins, C. N. (1986). Measuring perceived dominance-accommodation: Development of a scale. *Psychol Rep, 58,* 627–642.

IV-2/a
419. LANER, M. R. Competitiveness Scale

Avail: NAPS-3

Variables Measured: Perceived use of pleasant, unpleasant, and aggressive or abusive forms of competitive behavior in interpersonal relationships

Type of Instrument: Questionnaire for rating one's partner in a relationship

Instrument Description: The Competitiveness Scale is a 50-item Likert-style questionnaire utilizing a 3-point response format. According to the author, the scale was developed from a typology originally presented by Harvey Ruben (1980). Respondents are asked to indicate whether the behavior mentioned in the item is *quite typical, used occasionally,* or *never used* by their relationship partner. For scoring purposes, both *typical* and *occasional* responses are scored 1 point. The scale is divided into three subcategories, with a maximum of 20 points on the pleasant subscale, 22 on the unpleasant subscale, and 8 on the aggressive/abusive subscale. Administration time is approximately 15 minutes.

Sample Items:

(A) Uses charm (Pleasant)
(B) Cheats (Unpleasant)
(C) Displays anger (Aggressive/Abusive)

Comments: The scale has been used by the author to evaluate competitiveness in courting relationships, gender differences in the rating of partners as being competitive, and the relationship of pleasant versus unpleasant competitiveness and combativeness.

References:

Laner, M. R. (1986). Competition in courtship. *Fam Relat, 35,* 275–279.

Laner, M. R. (1989a). Competition and combatitiveness in courtship: Reports from men. *J Fam Violence, 4,* 47–62.

Laner, M. R. (1989b). Competitive versus noncompetitive styles: Which is most valued in courtship. *Sex Roles, 20,* 163–170.

Laner, M. R. (1989). Competition and combatitiveness in courtship: Reports from women. *J Fam Violence, 4,* 181–195.

IV-2/a

420. LEDERHAUS, M. A. Intradyad Purchasing Agreement Scale

Avail: NAPS-3

Variables Measured: Husband/wife agreement on decisions related to selecting vacation arrangements; also, influence of education, employment status, and economic well-being on which spouse serves as the primary decision maker for the couple

Type of Instrument: Self-report questionnaire

Instrument Description: This instrument is a 16-item scale with item formats including *yes-no*; two-option forced choice, fill in the blank; and five- and six-option Likert-style items. Six additional items request demographic information in various formats. A worksheet is also provided for determining net financial worth. Identical questionnaires are completed by both members of the dyad. Respondents are asked to report comparative influences of specific actions and decisions related to problem recognition, search for information, and final phases of decision making. Responses of the couple are averaged, with the person receiving primary credit for decisions on 60% of the items being considered the more instrumental half of the dyad. Joint decision making is presumed when 60% or more of the responses indicate that *both equally decide* various issues. The scale was designed for use with married couples over the age of 65, although the author states that it can be used with any age group.

Sample Items:

(A) Who, do you feel, *first recognized the idea* of taking a family vacation?
(B) Who gathered information necessary to make decisions about the destination(s) first considered?
(C) How much total elapsed time in days, weeks, or months did it take to gather information about the destination(s) first considered?

Comments: The author reports that an analysis of instrumentality performed using husbands' responses only, wives' responses only, and the mean of the two responses were similar.

References:

Lederhaus, M. A., & King, R. L. (1981). Decision-making influence of husbands and wives within older family dyads: A study of the decision to purchase vacation travel. In *Developments in marketing science proceedings* (Vol. 4, pp. 37–41). Muncie, IN: Ball State University and the Academy of Marketing Science.
Lederhaus, M. A., & Paulson, S. K. (1986) An analysis of dyadic dominance in family decision-making among older adults. *Sociol Spec, 6,* 161–177.

IV-2/I-4/c

421. MADANES, C., DUKES, J., & HARBIN, H. T. Family Hierarchy Test (FHT)

Avail: 1978 Ref.

Variables Measured: Structure of power and importance in familial relationships

Type of Instrument: See instrument description

Instrument Description: The FHT, also referred to as the Family Structure Task (FST), utilizes a series of eight diagrams, each depicting a family of four stick figures. Figures are arranged in varying orders, levels, and patterns within the diagrams. Family members are asked, both individually and as a group, to choose the one most closely resembling the relationship within their family. Subjects indicate which member of the family is represented by each stick figure by writing the name of each person represented by the respective drawing. They then are asked to move the figures to indicate the relative distance of each family member from each of the others. The respondent indicates the relationships between family members by verbally explaining the placement of figures. Diagrams are examined for hierarchies, comparing immediate family members as well as those of one generation versus the other. Projective assessments are made of individual choices, consensus choices selected by families, and interactions taking place during the interaction and placement of figures by the entire family.

Sample Items: Not applicable.

Comments: Quantitative information may be generated through use of this test by comparing the relative distance between various individuals and generations on the diagrams. Thus the FHT may be used in research on family structure and hierarchies. It will probably prove more useful, however, as a clinical device for evaluating and working with family relationships. Results of the FHT are assessed for appropriate versus inappropriate hierarchical relationships within families. The author has used the instrument to examine heroin addicts, schizophrenics, and nonclinical families, reporting that families of heroin addicts evidenced the weakest generational boundaries, while normal families were found to have boundaries marked by closeness and strong generational hierarchies.

References:

Madanes, C. (1978). Predicting behavior in an addict's family: A communicational approach. In L. Wurmser (Ed.), *The hidden dimension* (pp. 368–380). New York: Jason Aronson.

Madanes, C., Dukes, J., & Harbin, H. T. (1980). Family ties of heroine addicts. *Arch G Psyc, 37*, 889–894.

Madanes, C., & Harbin, H. T. (1983). Family structure of assaultive adolescents. *J Mar Fam Th, 9*, 311–316.

Simon, J., Wilkerson, J., & Keller, J. F. (1982). Marriage dilemma and an assessment device. *Fam Ther, 9*, 127–132.

IV-2/a/W

422. MADDEN, M. E., & JANOFF-BULMAN, R. Attributions Regarding Conflict

Avail: NAPS-3

Variables Measured: Attributions of blame and control for marital conflict

Type of Instrument: Self-report questionnaire

Instrument Description: This instrument is a 14-item questionnaire examining women's blame and control issues within marital conflict situations. Response options and formats vary for individual items but generally follow a 5-point Likert-style design. Respondents react to two hypothetical conflict scenarios in which jealousy and a financial argument are central themes, and to two actual conflicts they have recently experienced. They are asked to rate how serious and important the conflicts are; to divide blame among themselves, their husbands, other people, and the impersonal world; and to rate other aspects of conflict situations. The scale is independently responded to for each conflict situation.

Sample Items:

(A)   How serious do you think this problem is?

(B)   Who or what do you think is most to blame for the situation that you just described?
(C)   Do you think that you could have avoided this conflict before it occurred?

Comments: The authors report that specific open-ended interview questions are asked of subjects following their answers to several of the items in the scale (e.g., "Why do you assign blame that way?" "Describe the ideal and actual resolutions for this conflict"). Reliability and validity information on this instrument is not available.

Reference:

Madden, M. E., & Janoff-Bulman, R. (1981). Blame, control, and marital satisfaction: Wives' attributions for conflict in marriage. *J Mar Fam, 43,* 663–674.

IV-2/III-2/b/P
423. MILNER, J. S. The Child Abuse Potential (CAP) Inventory

Avail: Psytec Inc., P.O. Box 564, Dekalb, IL 60115

Variables Measured: Potential for physical child abuse

Type of Instrument: Self-report questionnaire

Instrument Description: The CAP Inventory is a 160-item, self-administered questionnaire that is answered in forced-choice, *agree/disagree* format. Of the total, 77 items relate to abuse while others are included as portions of various validity checks and experimental scales. Abuse potential is evaluated along six primary dimensions, determined by a factor analysis with promax rotation: (1) distress, (2) rigidity, (3) unhappiness, (4) problems with child and self, (5) problems with family, (6) problems from others. The CAP also contains faking good, faking bad, and random response indexes. It was designed primarily as a screening tool for the detection of physical child abuse. It was developed specifically to be used by protective services workers in their investigations of reported physical child abuse cases. It may also be used in evaluations of program interventions. Hand-scoring templates and a computer scoring program are available. Administration time is approximately 12–20 minutes.

Sample Items:

(A)   I always try to check on my child when it's crying.
(B)   Things have usually gone against me in life.
(C)   Spanking is the best punishment.

Comments: More than 100 publications and papers describing the development, reliability, and validity of the CAP Inventory have been generated. The CAP Inventory Manual (1986) contains an extensive review of the research literature on the inventory. According to the manual, loadings on the six factors detailed above, listed in order, range from .27 to .81 (36 items), .17 to .74 (14 items), .13 to .60 (11 items), .21 to .56 (6 items), .26 to .68 (4 items), and .29 to .67 (6 items). Split-half reliabilities are reported as generally in the .90s for the entire scale, and ranging from approximately .60 to .95 for individual subscales.

References:

Milner, J. S. (1986). *The Child Abuse Potential Inventory: Manual* (2nd ed.). Webster, NC: Psytec Corporation.
Milner, J. S., Gold, R. G., Ayoub, C., & Jacewitz, M. M. (1984). Predictive validity of the Child Abuse Potential Inventory. *J Cons Clin, 52,* 879–884.
Milner, J. S., Gold, R. G., & Wimberley, R. C. (1986). Prediction and explanation of child

abuse: Cross-validation of the Child Abuse Potential Inventory. *J Cons Clin, 54,* 865–866.

IV-2/a/C
424. O'LEARY, K. D., & PORTER, B. O'Leary-Porter Overt Hostility Scale

Avail: NAPS-3

Variables Measured: Spouses' perceptions of the frequency of positive and negative interactions displayed toward each other in the presence of their child

Type of Instrument: Self-report questionnaire

Instrument Description: This instrument is a 5-point, 10-item Likert-style questionnaire designed to assess the amount that parents openly argue in the presence of their child. Items assess differences over areas such as discipline, complaints about each other, physical or verbal abuse, and displays of affection. Item response options range from *never* to *very often.* The original format of the questions requested information about disagreements between spouses. However, the current version has been modified, with each item now asking how often the individual respondent's child has heard him or her arguing about a series of issues. The scale was originally designed to assess how this specific aspect of a marriage might predict child conduct problems.

Sample Items:

(A)   How often has *this* child heard you argue about the wife's role in the family? (Housewife, working wife, etc.)
(B)   How often do you complain to your spouse about his/her personal habits in front of *this* child?
(C)   Husbands and wives often disagree on the subject of discipline. How often do you and your spouse argue over disciplinary problems in the child's presence?

Comments: The author reports that Cronbach's alpha for an earlier version of this scale was measured at .86, and that two-week test-retest reliability was .96. Correlations are reported between this instrument and the Locke-Wallace Marital Adjustment Scale among clinic (.63) and nonclinic (.43) samples as well as with maternal reports of girls' conduct disorders (.30). Correlations are also reported with conduct problems of young boys (.40) and pathology for boys (.43 to .45).

References:

Emery, R. E., & O'Leary, K. D. (1982). Children's perceptions of marital discord and behavior problems of boys and girls. *J Abn C Psy, 10,* 11–24.
Emery, R. E., & O'Leary, K. D. (1984). Marital discord and child behavior problems in a nonclinic sample. *J Abn C Psy, 12,* 411–420.
Johnson, P. L., & O'Leary, K. D. (1987). Parental behavior patterns and conduct problems in girls. *J Abn C Psy, 15,* 573–581.
Porter, B., & O'Leary, K. D. (1980). Marital discord and childhood behavior problems. *J Abn C Psy, 8,* 287–295.

IV-2/a
425. PRICE, S. J. Price Decision-Making Scale

Avail: 1976 Ref.

Variables Measured: Marital decision making

Type of Instrument: Self-report questionnaire

Instrument Description: This instrument is a 5-point, 10-item Likert-style scale examining decisions that all married couples make. Each respondent indicates which spouse makes each of 10 decisions (pays bills, home decorated, to have children, money spent on food, money spent on clothes, wife's work, husband's work, guests in home, extra money, where couple lives). Scores from individual items are summed. Possible scores range from 10 to 50, with higher scores indicating that the husband, and lower scores indicating that the wife, made more of the decisions. Administration time is approximately 5 minutes.

Sample Items:

(A)   Who pays the bills?
(B)   How much money is spent on food?
(C)   Who you invite to your home?

Comments: The author reports that half of the original respondents were contacted and readministered the questionnaire approximately one year after data were collected. Test-retest correlations are reported to be .91 for husbands and .88 for wives.

Reference:

Price-Bonham, S. (1976). A comparison of weighted and unweighted decision-making scores. *J Mar Fam, 38,* 629–640.

IV-2/a
426. SANFORD, D. G. Spouse Interaction Test (SIT)

Avail: NAPS-3

Variables Measured: Situational self-esteem related to marital interactions

Type of Instrument: Self-report questionnaire

Instrument Description: The SIT comprises 15 hypothetical situations representing common marital conflicts in five areas (e.g., sex, finance, leisure time, children, and household responsibilities). Three hypothetical vignettes are presented for each of the five areas: one in which the wife "intentionally" acted in opposition to her husband, one in which the wife "accidentally" acted in opposition to her husband, and one in which they simply had a difference of opinion. Each vignette is followed by three Likert-style questions assessing the probability that the respondent would feel hurt and insulted if that situation had occurred between himself and his wife, the probability that the respondent would engage in an argument if this situation occurred, and the probability that the respondent would become violent with his wife if this situation occurred. Questions are responded to utilizing a 4-point response format ranging from *very likely* to *very unlikely* A total of 45 questions are asked (for 15 hypothetical situations with 3 questions for each situation). Respondents are assigned scores between 1 and 15 reflecting the number of situations they would see as damaging to their self-esteem. Administration time is approximately 10–15 minutes.

Sample Items:

(A)   Your partner refuses to make love with you, claiming that all you're ever interested in is sex.

(B)   You have just received a raise. Your partner wants to use the money to redecorate the house and you want to put it towards buying a new car.

(C)   One of your children has been misbehaving. Your wife didn't know that you told him to stay in the house and she lets him go out.

Comments: The authors report that the SIT has been found to discriminate maritally violent men from satisfactorily married men and from nonviolent, maritally discordant men. They report that the SIT correlates .23 with the Rosenberg Self-Esteem Scale (Rosenberg, 1965), which measures global self-esteem.

Reference:

Goldstein, D., & Rosenbaum, A. (1985). An evaluation of the self-esteem of maritally violent men. *Fam Relat, 34,* 425–428.

IV-2/II-3/a/e
427. SCHAEFER, E. S., & EDGERTON, M. Autonomy and Relatedness Inventory (ARI)

Avail: 1987 Ref.

Variables Measured: Several aspects of relationships between two people

Type of Instrument: Behavior-rating questionnaire

Instrument Description: The ARI consists of 24 Likert-style items intended for measuring various dimensions of dyadic relationships involving husbands and wives, relatives, or friends. Six subareas of such relationships are evaluated by four items each. The subareas are relatedness, hostile control, acceptance, hostile detachment, control, and autonomy. The inventory may be administered either orally or utilizing a written format. Respondents are asked to indicate how closely each item describes the person being rated, ranging from *not at all like* to *very much like.*

Sample Items:

(A)   Talks over his/her problems with me.
(B)   Won't take no for an answer when he/she wants something.
(C)   Lets me do anything I want to do.

Comments: The authors indicate that the current version of the ARI is descended from item, scale, and factor analyses of an earlier unpublished version known as the Marital Autonomy and Relatedness Inventory. Other previous versions evaluated eight subscales and consisted of either 30 or 32 items. The authors report that correlations between the ARI and Spanier's (1976) index of marital adjustment have been used to evaluate concurrent validity of the ARI as a measure of the quality of marital relationships. The authors report on a study in which ARI scores were first compared to those obtained on a scale of demoralization among parents of kindergarten children and were again compared three years later when the children were in the third grade. The correlation between autonomy and relatedness subscales was reported to be .38 and .56 at kindergarten and third grade, respectively. Test-retest reliability over the three-year period was reported to be .63 for both subscales. In this same study, acceptance was found to correlate from .75 to .80 with autonomy and from .69 to .75 with relatedness. Further reliability and validity information can be found in the reference noted below.

Reference:

Schaefer, E. S., & Burnett, C. K. (1987). Stability and predictability of quality of women's marital relationships and demoralization. *J Pers Soc Psy, 53*, 1129–1136.

IV-2/III-2/b/P
428. SCHECK, D. C. Parental Disagreement on Expectations of the Child Scale (PDEC)

Avail: 1979 Ref.

Variables Measured: Consistency of expectations for the child shared by both parents

Type of Instrument: Self-report questionnaire

Instrument Description: The PDEC is a 5-point, 6-item questionnaire designed to assess adults' perceptions of the consistency of their parents' behavior when the respondent was about 12 years old. Items are scored on a 1–5 basis, with response options ranging from *very untrue* to *very true*. Respondents are asked to answer each item with regard to each parent. Thus each item is given two responses. The author recommends that the questionnaire be combined with items from other scales so that the nature of the task might be disguised. A companion instrument to the PDEC by the same author, the Inconsistent Parental Discipline Scale (IPD), is also available in the source noted above. Scoring of the PDEC is accomplished by summing values associated with responses to each of the 6 items. Overall scores can range from 5 to 30.

Sample Items:

(A) My mother (father) was almost never able to agree with my father (mother) on what I should be punished for.

(B) My mother (father) was usually unable to agree with my father (mother) about things they expected me to do.

(C) My mother (father) occasionally told me things which were just opposite of what my father (mother) told me.

Comments: The author indicated that two of the items contained in this instrument were adapted from a global measure of inconsistency developed by Distler (1965). Split-half reliabilities for the PDEC were reported to be .78 for the father scale and .72 for perceptions of mothers' behaviors. Correlations are reported between the PDEC and Rotter's Locus of Control Scale (.16 for fathers, .10 for mothers), family size (.15 for fathers, .10 for mothers), and social class (.14 for fathers, .09 for mothers).

References:

Scheck, D. C. (1978). An exploratory investigation of the interaction effects of three child-rearing dimensions upon the development of internal-external control orientation in adolescent females. *Psychology, 15*, 8–13.

Scheck, D. C. (1979). Two measures of parental consistency. *Psychology, 16*, 37–39.

Scheck, D. C., & Emerick, R. (1976). The young male adolescent's perception of early child-rearing behavior: The differential effects of socioeconomic status and family size. *Sociometry, 39*, 39–52.

Scheck, D. C., Emerick, R., & El-Assal, M. M. (1973). Adolescents' perceptions of parent-child relations and the development of internal-external control orientation. *J Mar Fam, 35*, 643–654.

IV-2/a
429. SCHUMM, W. R. Kansas Marital Conflict Scales

Avail: 1985 Ref.

Variables Measured: Husband or wife's perceptions of their stages of marital conflict in accordance with Gottman's three stages of agenda-building, arguing, and negotiation

Type of Instrument: Self-report questionnaire

Instrument Description: This 37-item scale is designed to measure wives' perceptions of the behaviors mentioned above. It is divided into three subscales with 11, 15, and 11 items. The three sections relate a series of behaviors (different for each subscale) to a particular stem. The stem for the agenda-building section reads: "When you and your husband are beginning to discuss a disagreement over an important issue, how often." The stem for the arguing section reads: "After you and your husband have been discussing a disagreement over an important issue for a while, how often." The third stem, designed for the negotiation section of the questionnaire, reads: "About the time you and your husband feel you are close to a solution to your disagreement over an important issue, how often." The instrument was designed as an alternative means of collecting information desired by Gottman, without the expense of observations necessitated by Gottman's system of data collection. Estimated administration time is 15–20 minutes.

Sample Items:

(A) When you and your husband are beginning to discuss a disagreement over an important issue, how often do you both begin to understand each other's feelings reasonably quickly?

(B) After you and your husband have been discussing a disagreement over an important issue for a while, how often are you able to clearly identify the specific things about which you disagree?

(C) About the time you and your husband feel you are close to a solution to your disagreement over an important issue, how often are you able to completely resolve it with some sort of compromise that is OK with both of you?

Comments: The author reports that Cronbach's alpha for each scale ranges from .83 to .96. Test-retest correlations over six months are reported to range from .64 to .96. Correlations were also examined between scores on the Kansas Marital Conflict Scales and various aspects of marital quality and social desirability. However, the author reports that sample sizes were too small to place significant confidence in the reported correlations.

References:

Eggeman, K. W., Moxley, V., & Schumm, W. R. (1985). Assessing spouses' perceptions of Gottman's temporal form in marital conflict. *Psychol Rep, 57,* 171–181.
Eggeman, K. W., Smith-Eggeman, B., Moxley, V., & Schumm, W. R. (1986). A marriage enrichment program for newlywed couples. *Wellness Persp, 3,* 32–36.

IV-2/a
430. SCHWARZ, J. C. Schwarz Inter-Parental Conflict Scale (IPC)

Avail: NAPS-3

Variables Measured: The frequency of arguments between parents

Type of Instrument: Self and spouse or parent-rating scale

Instrument Description: The IPC is a 7-point, 37-item Likert-style scale on which respondents indicate the frequency of arguments between parents. Arguments are grouped under four broad categories: finance and spouse's responsibilities, spouse's personal characteristics, child-rearing practices, and joint family activities. Responses range from *never* to *at least once a week,* and are scored on a 0 to 6 scale. Separate forms for children and spouses are provided. Two scores are derived through use of the IPC: a score representing overall conflict and a subscale score representing conflict over child-rearing methods. Higher scores indicate increasing conflict. The overall score is obtained by taking the mean of all 37 items. Subscale scores are determined by the mean of items from that section. Multiple rater aggregate scores for the IPC are obtained by standardizing scores for individual raters and then taking the mean of these standard scores.

Sample Items:

(A)   Budgeting
(B)   Mutuality of recreational interests
(C)   Organizing leisure-time activities

Comments: The IPC originated as a 77-item scale. An item validation study, including item and factor analyses, reduced this to the current 37 items. According to the author, data from this study indicated that the IPC correlates .07 with social class, .10 with fathers' education, .04 with mothers' education, -.03 with students' gender, and -.22 with a scale of defensiveness. Normative data for the final version of the IPC were derived from a subsample of 214 families from among 360 who participated in a larger study of family dynamics. About 1,800 individuals associated with the 360 families participated in the overall study, which employed multiple measures of the parents' marital relationship, child-rearing behavior, personality, social behavior, and adjustment. Each family unit consisted of a college freshman and the student's roommate, mother, father, and one sibling within three years of the student's age. Half of the families were selected because of elevated student ratings of parental conflict scores. The author reports that internal consistency ratings for college students averaged .90, and that one-week test-retest reliability was .86. Additional research utilizing the IPC (Kurdek, in press) has been reported in which Cronbach's alpha was measured at .95.

References:

Hindy, C. G., Schwarz, J. C., & Brodsky, A. (1989). *If this is love, why do I feel so insecure?* New York: Atlantic Monthly.

Kurdek, L. A., & Sinclair, R. J. (1986). Adolescents' views on issues related to divorce. *J Adol Res, 1,* 373–387.

Kurdek, L. A., & Sinclair, R. J. (1988). Adjustment of young adolescents in two-parent nuclear, stepfather, and mother-custody families. *J Cons Clin, 56,* 91–96.

Schwarz, J. C., & Zuroff, D. C. (1979). Family structure and depression in female college students: Effects of parental conflict, decision-making power, and inconsistency of love. *J Abn Psych, 88,* 398–406.

IV-2/III-2/a/P

431. SCHWARZ, J. C. Schwarz Inter-Parental Influence Scale (IPI)

Avail: NAPS-3

Variables Measured: The relative influence of the mother versus the father in family decision making, both in general and in regard to children's behavior

Type of Instrument: Self and spouse or parent-rating scale

Instrument Description: The IPI is a 5-point, 13-item Likert-style scale. It provides two scores: a total score representing overall influence and a subscale score representing influence over children's behavior. Individual item scores range from 1 to 5. The overall score is obtained by taking the mean of all 13 items. The minimum score of 1 indicates *extreme maternal influence in family decision making.* The maximum of 5 indicates *extreme paternal influence.* A score of 3 indicates equal influence. The subscale score for influence over children's behavior is obtained by taking the mean for items 3, 5, 7, and 9. Multiple rater aggregate scores for the IPI are obtained by standardizing scores for individual raters and then taking the mean of these standard scores.

Sample Items:

(A)   How much money to spend on recreation.
(B)   Children's duties and household responsibilities.
(C)   Which doctor or dentist to consult.

Comments: The IPI was developed from an initial pool of 22 items. Some of the items are reported by the author to have been original, while others were adapted from inventories by Blood and Wolf (1960), Safilios-Rothschild (1969), and Burchinal (1965). The original version of the instrument was administered to a group of introductory psychology students and their parents. Parents were sent questionnaires and were asked to return them by mail after having completed them. The final version of the scale was determined following item and scale analyses. The author reports that items retained in the final version each generated reliable agreement between the student and one or both parents. A second sample of students and their parents were then surveyed. Results reported from this study indicate correlations of .49 between student and father ratings, .45 between student and mother ratings, and .57 between student ratings and a composite of mother and father ratings. Test-retest reliability for students is reported to be .91. Normative data were then collected as part of the same study described in the abstract of the Schwarz Inter-Parental Conflict Scale (IPC), detailed in *Abstract 430.*

References:

Hindy, C. G., Schwarz, J. C., & Brodsky, A. (1989). *If this is love, why do I feel so insecure?* New York: Atlantic Monthly.

Schwarz, J. C., & Getter, H. (1980). Parental conflict and dominance in late adolescent maladjustment: A triple-interaction model. *J Abn Psych, 89,* 573–580.

Schwarz, J. C., & Zuroff, D. C. (1979). Family structure and depression in female college students: Effects of parental conflict, decision-making power, and inconsistency of love. *J Abn Psych, 88,* 398–406.

IV-2/III-2/b/C

432. SMALL, S. A. Desire for Greater Autonomy from Parents Scale

Avail: NAPS-3

Variables Measured: Child's satisfaction with the amount of decision-making freedom he or she is given by parents

Type of Instrument: Self-report questionnaire

Instrument Description: This instrument is a 6-point, 15-item Likert-style questionnaire developed for use with preadolescents and adolescents. Response options range from *my parent should give me much more say* to *I have too much say.* An overall composite score is obtained by summing the scores across items. This instrument was designed to assess the child's desire for greater self-regulation or autonomy across a range of decisions commonly encountered by preadolescents and adolescents.

Sample Items:

(A)   How do you feel about how much say you have about what time you must come in at night?

(B)   How do you feel about how much say you have about who you are allowed to have as friends?

(C)   How do you feel about how much say you have about the clothes you wear or how you wear your hair?

Comments: The author indicates that Cronbach's alpha for this instrument is .76. The correlation between this scale and the child's perception of parental control, as assessed by the control-autonomy subscale from Schaefer's (1965) Child Report of Parent Behavior Inventory, is reported to be .32. This instrument is also reported to correlate with the child's report of parent-child conflict (.37). The author found item-total correlations to range from .11 to .55.

References:

Savin-Williams, R. C., & Small, S. A. (1986). The timing of puberty and its relationship to adolescent and parent perceptions of family interactions. *Devel Psych, 22,* 343–347.
Small, S. A. (1988). Parental self-esteem and its relationship to childrearing practices, parent-adolescent interaction and adolescent behavior. *J Mar Fam, 50,* 1063–1072.

IV-2/II-2/a
433. SMOLEN, R. C., SPIEGEL, D. A., & MARTIN, C. J. The Marital Transgression Scale (MTS)

Avail: NAPS-3

Variables Measured: Spouse's perception of the frequency of provocative marital behavior demonstrated by his/her mate

Type of Instrument: Self-report questionnaire

Instrument Description: The MTS is a 5-point, 18-item Likert-style questionnaire designed to assess perceptions related to frequently occurring, anger-arousing marital situations. The response format allows for ratings ranging from *never* to *very often.* Items were initially developed by a group of married persons, not selected for marital stress, instructed to generate examples of provocative marital situations. Situations were then presented to a second group for frequency ratings. The 18 items rated as being both frequently occurring and anger-arousing were selected for inclusion. The scale is intended for use with both distressed and nondistressed couples.

Sample Items:

(A)   Your spouse has agreed to do some task that is important to you, but keeps putting it off.

(B)   Your spouse makes a major purchase without consulting you first.

(C)   Your spouse criticizes you in public.

Comments: The authors report that Cronbach's alpha for a sample not selected for marital distress was .81. Item-test correlations are reported to average .43. Correlations are reported between husbands' MTS scores and marital satisfaction as measured by Spanier's Dyadic Adjustment Scale (-.42), the Zung Self-Rating Depression Scale (.29), and the Miller Marital Locus of Control Scale (-.41). Correlations between wives' MTS scores and marital satisfaction and internal locus of control were reported to be -.72 and -.27, respectively. Correlations among clinic samples of couples treated for sexual dysfunctions were also reported. MTS scores were found to correlate with scores on the Dyadic Adjustment Scale (-.34, male; -.66, female) and with depression (.40, females only).

References:

Smolen, R. C., & Spiegel, D. A. (1987). Marital locus of control as a modifier of the relationship between the frequency of provocation by spouse and marital satisfaction. *J Res Pers, 21,* 70–80.

Smolen, R. C., Spiegel, D. A., & Martin, C. J. (1986). Patterns of marital interaction associated with marital dissatisfaction and depression. *J Beh Th Exp Psychi, 17,* 261–266.

IV-2/c
434. STANLEY, S. F. Family Decision-Making Attitude Scale (FDMAS)

Avail: NAPS-3

Variables Measured: Equalitarian attitudes toward family decision making

Type of Instrument: Self-report questionnaire

Instrument Description: The FDMAS is a 12-item Likert-type questionnaire utilizing a 4-point response option format. Available responses indicate varying levels of agreement and disagreement. It was developed to measure attitudes concerning how rules and decisions over conflicts should be made in families. It is appropriate for administration to adolescents and adults. Approximate administration time is 5–10 minutes.

Sample Items:

(A) In resolving family conflicts, a young child's feelings are not as important as those of a parent.

(B) Most often when a parent and adolescent disagree, the parent should make the decision as to what ought to be done.

(C) If you gave kids a say in deciding family responsibilities, they'd never agree to do any work.

Comments: The author reports that three-month test-retest reliability on a sample of 15 adolescents and their parents was .89. Construct validity was assessed through an examination of the items by five professionals in the field of family therapy and family research. This examination resulted in the elimination of two items and the rewording of two other. The author further reports an average correlation, for 32 parents, between the FDMAS and the nonauthoritarian subscale of the Parent Attitude Research Instrument of .67.

Reference:

Stanley, S. (1978). Family education to enhance the moral atmosphere of the family and the moral development of adolescents. *J Cons Psyc, 25,* 110–118.

IV-2/c

435. STRAUS, M. A. Conflict Tactics Scales (CTS)

Avail: Forms A and N are in Straus, 1979; Form N is in the appendix to Straus, Gelles, & Steinmetz, 1980; the most recent version, Form R, is in Gelles & Straus, 1988, and in Straus & Gelles, 1989

Variables Measured: Reasoning, verbal aggression, and physical violence in response to a conflict with, or anger at, other members of the family

Type of Instrument: Self-report questionnaire

Instrument Description: The CTS is a 7-point, 19-item Likert-type questionnaire designed to assess individual responses to situations within the family involving conflict. The introduction asks the subject to think of the times "when they disagree, get annoyed with the other person, or just have spats or fights because they're in a bad mood or tired or for some other reason." Respondents are then asked to indicate how often they did each of the CTS items in the past 12 months. The response categories are *once, twice, 3–5 times, 11–20 times, more than 20 times,* and *never.* Each item is asked both for what the respondent did and for what the other family member did. These pairs of questions can be repeated for any family role relationship, such as spousal, parent-child, and sibling. The CTS can be administered either as a questionnaire or as part of a more extensive personal interview. Each of three scales (reasoning, verbal aggression, and physical aggression or violence) is scored by summing the values for the response categories or by summing weighted response categories. An incidence rate is often computed for use in conjunction with the violence scale.

Sample Items:

(A)   Discussed an issue calmly.
(B)   Insulted or swore at him/her.
(C)   Slapped him/her.

Comments: The author reports that Cronbach's alpha has been found to range from .42 to .88 for the three scales. The author indicates that eight studies have been conducted examining the CTS factor structure, with six of the eight reportedly confirming the original structure. Concurrent validity has been examined by comparing reports obtained separately from husbands and wives and from parents and their children. Correlations are reported to range from .19 to .80, with a mean of about .4.

References:

Gelles, R. J., & Straus, M. A. (1988). *Intimate violence.* New York: Simon & Schuster.
Straus, M. A. (1979). Measuring intrafamily conflict and violence: The Conflict Tactics (CT) Scales. *J Mar Fam, 41,* 75–88.
Straus, M. A., & Gelles, R. J. (1989). *Physical violence in American families: Risk factors and adaptations to violence in 8,145 families.* New Brunswick, NJ: Transaction.
Straus, M. A., Gelles, R. J., & Steinmetz, S. K. (1980). *Behind closed doors: Violence in the American family.* New York: Doubleday/Anchor.

IV-2/I-4/c

436. STRAUS, M. A., & TALLMAN, I. Simulated Family Activity Measurement (SIMFAM)

Avail: 1971 Ref.

Variables Measured: Power, support, communication, creativity, and problem-solving ability of both the individuals and the family as a group

Type of Instrument: Combination objective and observational rating scale

Instrument Description: SIMFAM is a set of experimental tasks designed to elicit a sample of family interaction as well as a set of observational categories and other procedures necessary for measuring the variables of (1) power exercised by each family member; (2) support extended and received by each family member; (3) communication frequency, channels, and ability; (4) creativity; and (5) problem-solving ability of both the family group and each individual member. The tasks are also designed to provide a framework for experimentally varying such factors as frustration, volume and channels of communication, and problem-solving ability of each family member. One task makes use of colored balls and pushers and is restricted to specially equipped rooms, whereas the other task, using beanbags thrown onto a target on the floor, may be given in the home. In both tasks family members are instructed to determine the rules of the game by inferring the correct actions from green lights flashed for correct responses and red lights for incorrect responses. These lights are also connected to electrical counters that provide the score for problem-solving ability. Other variables are measured by direct observation or by coding from a tape recording. Each score, with the exception of the creativity index, is recorded in terms of both the initiating and the recipient actor.

Sample Items: Not applicable.

Comments: The authors report interrater reliability coefficients from studies conducted in Bombay, Minneapolis, and San Juan ranging from .43 to .98. SIMFAM creativity scores are reported to correlate from .17 to .33 with results from the Minnesota Test of Creative Thinking.

References:

Foss, D. C., & Straus, M. A. (1976). Culture, crisis, creativity of families in Bombay, San Juan, and Minneapolis. In L. Lenero-Otero (Ed.), *Beyond the nuclear family model: Contemporary family sociology in cross-cultural perspective.* London: Sage/International Sociological Association.

Straus, M. A. (1988). Exchange and power in marriage in cultural context: Bombay and Minneapolis comparisons. In S. K. Steinmetz (Ed.), *Family and support systems across the life span* (pp. 135–154). New York: Plenum.

Straus, M. A., & Tallman, I. (1971). SIMFAM: A technique for observational measurement and experimental study of families. In J. Aldous (Ed.), *Family problem solving* (pp. 380–438). Hinsdale, IL: Dryden.

Tallman, I., Marotz-Baden, R., & Pindas, P. (1983). *Adolescent socialization in cross-cultural perspective: Planning for social change.* New York: Academic Press.

IV-2/c
437. TAYLOR, J. Taylor's Control Inventory

Avail: 1988 Ref.

Variables Measured: Levels of induction and coercion associated with relations within the family

Type of Instrument: Self-report questionnaire

Instrument Description: This instrument contains 16 items, half related to coercion and half related to induction associated with intrafamilial relations. Each item is rated (0–8) on a scale ranging from *never* to *always*. Items contrasting coercion and induction are included for each of eight domains (insistence, demandingness, forcefulness, guardedness, impatience, irrationality, entropy, and regimentation). The Control Inventory was designed as a parallel instrument to Taylor's Affiliation Inventory. Rating and scoring procedures are identical to the Affiliation Inventory, except here the polarity of induction items is reversed and added to the straight sum of coercion items. The higher the total score, the more controlling the relationship is presumed to be. While the instrument would likely prove applicable to families of all races, the author has found it particularly useful in assessing characteristics of Black families.

Sample Items:

(A) ＿＿＿＿＿＿ insists on ＿＿＿＿＿＿'s own way with ＿＿＿＿＿＿.
(B) ＿＿＿＿＿＿ uses threats to get ＿＿＿＿＿＿ to do things.
(C) ＿＿＿＿＿＿ tries to see ＿＿＿＿＿＿'s side when we (they) disagree.

Comments: The author reports mean scores on the induction, coercion, and total indexes to be 45.6, 18.5, and 36.9, respectively. Split-half reliabilities for the two subscales are reported to be .80 and .84. Split-half reliability for the total score is reported to be .86. The author indicates that the two subscales correlate -.37. Scores on Taylor's Control Inventory have been compared with those obtained on indexes of parental affiliation and with socioemotional development of children, patterns of child maltreatment, and styles of managing the home environment.

Reference:

Taylor, J., & McMillian, M. (1988). Taylor's Affiliation and Control Inventories. In R. L. Jones (Ed.), *Tests and measurements for Black populations.* Berkeley, CA: Cobb & Henry.

NOTE: For additional instruments, see also *Abstracts 1376–1458* in the Abbreviated Abstracts of Instruments (which precedes the Indexes).

6 Adjustment

CHERYL BUEHLER

The purpose of this chapter is to discuss the conceptual evolution of "family adjustment" by examining assessment devices in the substantive areas of family functioning, family stress, and divorce. This concurrent analysis of conceptualization and assessment is important because "what we know about any concept is based on the information that is contained within its measure" (Sabatelli, 1988, p. 891). In turn, clear conceptualization helps organize theoretical formulations and empirical findings. In other words, "What we know and how we know it are inextricably linked" (Miller, Rollins, & Thomas, 1982, p. 852).

This examination of family adjustment was conducted as follows. The abstracts of the measures in this section were reviewed for conceptual and operational definitions, as well as for indicators of construct dimensionality, reliability, and validity. Next, some of the references cited for each measure were reviewed to identify important information that was not included in the abstract. The conclusions about psychometric properties of the measures are based on these two reviews, rather than information provided solely in the abstracts. Finally, observations concerning changes in the conceptualization of family adjustment have been gleaned from theoretical and empirical reports as well as research reviews in the areas of family functioning, stress, and divorce.

FAMILY ADJUSTMENT

What is adjustment? Webster (1965) defines "to adjust" as to settle; resolve; adapt; regulate; to bring to a more satisfactory state; and to conform oneself. "Adjustment" is defined as the act or process of adjusting; the state of being adjusted; and a means by which things are adjusted one to another. In reference to the marital relationship, Sabatelli (1988)

AUTHOR'S NOTE: I would like to thank Dr. Jan Allen for her helpful comments on this chapter.

has defined adjustment as "those processes that are presumed to be necessary to achieve a harmonious and functional marital relationship."

It is clear from these definitions, and from an examination of the literature on family functioning, stress, and divorce, that the concept of adjustment has been used in a variety of ways to mean a variety of things. Until
recently, when the concepts have been more clearly distinguished, *adjustment, adaptation,* and *redefinition* have been used synonymously. Four
definitional issues are particularly interesting and influential. The first issue
centers on adjustment conceptualized as a current level of functioning as
well as a response to change. The "current level of functioning" definition
seems to derive from a wellness/illness model of functioning, such that
"being adjusted" means doing well and being in a healthy state. "Unad-
justed," from this perspective, means doing poorly and being in some sort
of pathological state. This conceptualization of adjustment has been used
most often by scholars who have identified important dimensions of family
functioning. The identified dimensions have served as the criteria for family wellness and illness (e.g., Bloom, 1985; *Abstracts 438, 440, 447, 451,
453*).

The "adjustment as a response (or set of responses) to change(s)" definition has been used frequently in the area of family stress. Early conceptualizations within this perspective centered on the regulation and calibration
aspect of adjustment, that is, well-adjusted families returned to a steady
state of functioning after the changes occurred. More recent conceptualizations have moved away from the homeostatic model of stability and change
toward a model that acknowledges the complexities of families' responses
to stress and that recognizes that some families grow as a response to
change (rather than maintain or calibrate) (Antonovsky & Sourani, 1988;
McCubbin & Patterson, 1983b).

McCubbin and Patterson (1983b, p. 25) have distinguished conceptually
between adjustment and adaptation based on the depth of systemic response and the response time frame. They have defined adjustment as a
short-term response that is characterized by first-order change. Family
rules, roles, and relationships are slightly modified but not redefined. They
have defined adaptation as a long-term response that involves more significant second-order change.

McCubbin and McCubbin (1988) also have distinguished between adjustment and adaptation based on the type of initial change and strain within
the family. They have proposed that adjustment is most relevant as a
response to normative change, whereas adaptation is a response to nonnormative change.

A second important issue is that adjustment has been defined as both a
process and an outcome (or a state). However, even when conceptualized as
a process, the measures of adjustment often have assessed the current behavioral, cognitive, and affective manifestations of the process because the

assessments have been based on self-reports and the research designs employed have been cross-sectional rather than longitudinal.

A third important issue that influences the definition of adjustment is the recommendation that assessments should be made at the individual, dyadic, and family levels (Cromwell & Peterson, 1981; Walker, 1985). In some instances, the same measure may be used for each level (*443, 459*). However, we cannot assume that the concepts of individual, dyadic, and family adjustment are isomorphic. Great care must be taken to conceptualize adjustment clearly at each level of the system and to use appropriate, valid measures that correspond with the formulated conceptualizations.

A final important issue is the recent trend toward defining adaptation (and thus adjustment by inference) as system-environment fit (Antonovsky & Sourani, 1988; McCubbin & Patterson, 1983a; Melson, 1980; Menaghan, 1983; *441, 449, 450, 460*). This definition is based on an ecological view of family functioning in which the system's demands and resources are matched with environmental demands and resources. A well-adjusted family would be defined by a good fit with its environment, whereas a poorly adjusted family would be defined by a significant lack of fit.

Although it is evident that the concept of adjustment does not have one clear definition, recent conceptualizations have added increased precision to the various definitions. However, because of the multiple uses of the concept, it is important that researchers and clinicians clearly specify for their readers and clients their particular definition of adjustment. It also will be helpful to keep these various definitions and issues in mind as you review the rest of this chapter and the set of measurement abstracts that follow.

The measures in this chapter have been divided into three areas: family functioning, stress, and divorce. A major purpose of this chapter is to discuss the evolution of concepts in these areas by examining the abstracted measures. In established areas of scholarly inquiry (such as parenting), this has been accomplished by comparing the measures published from 1936 to 1974 that are abstracted in the volume by Straus and Brown (1978) with the measures published from 1975 to 1986 abstracted in this volume (Holden, Chapter 4). However, this type of analysis is limited in this chapter because there were so few measures published between 1936 and 1974 in the areas of family functioning, stress, and divorce. Specifically, this volume includes 9 abstracts of older family functioning measures (using the primary code for classification) and 28 abstracts of more recent measures. It includes 3 older measures of stress and 22 measures published in more recent years. Finally, only 1 older divorce measure is included, compared with 22 more recent ones. It is also important to note that family functioning, stress, and divorce were not included as major categories of measures in the Straus and Brown volume.

Thus the first specific observation to offer is that the conceptualization and measurement of adjustment-related constructs have increased dramatically in the last few decades. These data support Bloom's (1985) conclusion that the conceptual and empirical literature on family functioning has increased substantially since 1965. This recent increase in holistic measures of family functioning and adjustment to change indicates a growing interest in examining families as unique structural and interactional systems. It seems reasonable to speculate that this assessment trend has resulted, to a great degree, from the increased understanding and acceptance of family systems and ecosystems theoretical perspectives.

The specific conceptual and methodological issues generated by examining the measures of family functioning (438–463) will be discussed first, followed by issues related to stress (464–482) and divorce (483–504). These specific issues will be summarized by identifying common themes and implications for the overall concept of family adjustment.

FAMILY FUNCTIONING

Nine issues emerged from the analysis of the 28 recent and 9 older measures of family functioning included in this book. These issues are (a) the type of measure, (b) the level of analysis, (c) the dimensions of family functioning, (d) the focus of the measure, (e) the source of data within the family, (f) family structural and sociodemographic variations, (g) the development of family types, (h) reliability, and (i) validity.

Type of Measure

Of the older measures, 2 use observational methods and 7 use self-report methods (3 interviews and 4 questionnaires). Of the more recent measures, 3 are observational and 25 are self-report. Of the self-report measures, there are 22 questionnaires, 1 interview, and 2 Q-sorts (462 has both a questionnaire and Q-sort version). Thus there has been a dramatic increase in the use of self-report questionnaires to assess family functioning. Compared with most observational techniques, questionnaires are relatively easy to administer and score. In addition, they are used most appropriately when one is interested in an "insider's perspective" (Olson, 1977) of family functioning and when the subjective, perceptual component of experience is important.

Level of Analysis

Of the older measures, 6 focus on the entire family system, 2 on outside relationships, and 1 on the marital dyad. Of the more recent measures, 24 focus on the entire family, 2 on the marital dyad, and 1 on the sibling dyad.

At least 2 of the measures designed to assess family functioning at the family level also can be used to assess the functioning of various dyads within the family (*443, 459*).

These data indicate that much of the growth in the assessment of family functioning has centered on attempts to measure individual family members' perceptions of how the family *as a whole* functions on a variety of different dimensions. Because the focus of most of these measures is the family system, the dimensions of functioning assessed differ somewhat from dimensions assessed when the focus is dyadic or individual adjustment (e.g., the use of induction may be assessed in the parent-child relationship; depression may be assessed as an indicator of individual adjustment).

Salient Dimensions of Family Functioning

The most frequently assessed dimensions of family functioning include cohesion, the ability to grow, adaptation, communication, affective involvement, and control (conceptualized by some as the type of authority patterns in the family and by others as the amount of control the family feels over its fate) (see Table 6.1). An examination of measures published from 1936 to 1986 indicates that the more recent measures of family functioning are much more comprehensive than were earlier measures. This is one indication of more sophisticated conceptualizations of family dynamics. Although this greater comprehensiveness provides a more valid representation of the complexities of family life, it also has led to a proliferation of identified dimensions. As can be seen in Table 6.1, many of the concepts identified and measured by various scholars seem synonymous.

One obvious task for those interested in identifying important dimensions of family functioning is to condense this list of dimensions. I am not suggesting that it be reduced to only two or three salient dimensions, but that it be systematically and carefully culled down to a more manageable and meaningful number (i.e., 5 to 10).

As represented by the current work of several scholars, this reduction can be accomplished by several different methods (e.g., Bloom, 1985; *451, 453, 462*). Olson and his colleagues (*453*) extensively reviewed the family process literature for indications of major dimensions of family functioning and identified over 50 concepts. After examining the uses and definitions of these various concepts, these scholars concluded that most represented some aspect of either family cohesion or adaptability. Thus they derived two major dimensions of family functioning using an inductive classification schema.

Others have used various empirical techniques to reduce the number of salient dimensions. Van der Veen (*462*) factor analyzed eight first-order factors and derived two second-order ones, labeled family integra-

Table 6.1 Identified Dimensions of Family Functioning

Dimension	Abstract Number
growth	438, 448, 463
competence	447
health	453
family stress	439, 461
cohesion	438, 439, 451, 453, 455, 462, 463
family stress	439, 461
family satisfaction	439, 443
family support	439
family adaptation	439, 447, 453, 462, 463
role conflict	439
role overload	439
role ambiguity	439
role nonparticipation	439
psychosomatic symptoms	439
life satisfaction	439
role preparedness	439
problem solving	440
communication	440, 447, 459, 461, 463
roles	440
affective responsiveness	440, 459
affective involvement	440, 447, 459, 461
behavior control	440
family relationship with environment	441
social desirability in families	442, 449
family harmony	443
marital jealousy	444
sibling bereavement	445
family origin intimacy	446
family origin autonomy	446
alliances	447
boundaries	447
esteem and communication	449
mastery and health	449
extended family social support	449
financial well-being	449
financial support	449
financial commitment	450
financial confidence	450
challenge	450
control	450, 451, 455, 459
expressiveness	451, 455
conflict	451, 455, 461
independence	451, 455
achievement	451, 455
intellectual	451, 455
active-recreational	451, 455
moral religious	451, 455
organization	451, 455

Table 6.1 continued

tion and adaptive coping. Using two different methods of dimension reduction, both Olson and Van der Veen have identified family cohesion/integration and adaptability as the major (second-order) dimensions of family functioning.

Bloom's (1985) recent empirical work does not support this much reduction. He systematically compared the Family Environment Scale (*451*), The Family Concept measure (*462*), FACES (*453*), and the Family Assessment Measure (*459*) by administering the instruments to several different samples. Through systematic item reduction, he reduced the items from the four self-report measures to 85 items that form 15 related, but nonredundant first-order factors. Bloom conceptually grouped these 15 factors into three second-order dimensions using Moos's original framework. The Relationship Dimension includes family cohesion, expressiveness, conflict, sociability, idealization, and disengagement (see Bloom's paper for conceptual definitions of each of these factors). According to his findings, cohesion is the most salient first-order factor in this dimension. The Personal Growth Dimension includes intellectual/cultural, active/recreational, and religious factors. Bloom's suggestion that this dimension be renamed Family Values corresponds with Reiss's (1981) conceptualization of family paradigms or belief systems. Very few of the existing measures in the assessment of family functioning include an assessment of family values, and Bloom's work indicates that this is an important, but neglected, area in the assessment of family functioning. The System Maintenance dimension includes democratic style of authority, laissez-faire style, authoritarian style, locus of control, enmeshment, and organization. Locus of control is the central factor of this dimension in his samples. Through this systematic procedure, 26 first-order dimensions were meaningfully reduced to 15. This type of critical examination needs to continue to facilitate conceptual clarification and refinement.

Although, conceptually, social desirability is not a dimension of family functioning, the influence of socially desirable responses on the validity of the family functioning measures is a concern. Skinner et al. (*459*) have incorporated a measure of social desirability into the Family Assessment

Measure so that the influence can be assessed concurrently. Others have correlated their measures with one of social desirability (typically the Crowne-Marlow scale) and have reported relatively low correlations (less than .35) (*440, 453, 462*).

Focus of the Measure

One of the important trends in the assessment of family functioning is the development of different "versions" of specific measures. Instruments that include this feature have respondents read each item and respond based on how they perceive their current, *actual* family. On another version, respondents are asked to read the same set of questions and respond based on their *ideals* (see *441, 451, 453, 462*). The actual and ideal scores then can be compared to measure satisfaction (*441, 453*). This method of measuring satisfaction may be less biased by social desirability than direct, Likert-type satisfaction measures. Finally, scores across various family members can be compared by creating a congruence score (*462*). The conceptualization and assessment of dimensions of family functioning have been improved by the development of these different versions of measures.

Source of Data

An important issue with survey measures is the source of information. Possible informants include parents, spouses, children, teachers, and mental health professionals. Only one of the seven older self-report measures uses a child informant. Adult family members are informants for the other six measures. Of the more recent measures, children are informants for three measures, both children and adults for six measures, and adults only for the rest. Although the finding that one-third of the measures use child informants provides evidence that children's perspectives on their families are considered important, this issue needs further attention.

One of the barriers to obtaining data from multiple family members has been the dilemma of how to treat the different scores statistically in a conceptually meaningful manner. Summing or averaging the scores has been done when members are asked to report on shared family behavior (e.g., Lavee, McCubbin, & Olson, 1987). An alternative is to use each individual family member's scores as manifest variables indicating a latent construct in LISREL analysis (Barber, 1987; Lavee, McCubbin, & Olson, 1987). This latter technique is particularly promising because the contribution of each family member's score is empirically estimated based on the patterns of covariation among the variables in the proposed model. Thus the assumption of equal weighting that is made when scores are averaged does not have to be accepted arbitrarily. For example, if the child's perception is a better indicator of the latent construct "family control" than the parents' perceptions, the LISREL estimate will indicate this. The assumption of equal importance or weighting is no longer necessary because of recent technological and statistical innovations.

Structural and Cultural Variations

Most of the research on the major dimensions of family functioning has been conducted using White, middle-class, two-parent, first-married families, and should be generalized only to families with those characteristics. Although limited in scope, a few of the measures have been tested using other samples. The comparisons between single- and two-parent families have revealed few differences (*440, 447, 451*), whereas comparisons between first-married and remarried families have shown both differences and similarities (Peek, Bell, Waldren, & Sorell, 1988; Zucker-Anderson & White, 1986; *440, 451, 453, 462*).

Only two reports were given in which the family scores were correlated with indicators of socioeconomic status (*440, 447*). Racial comparisons were made with three of the measures (*438, 446, 451*). Thus researchers and clinicians should cautiously interpret most of the family functioning measures in terms of application with low-SES families, single-parent and stepfamilies, and families of color. It is evident that much more research is needed in this area.

Family Types

In 1982, Epstein, Bishop, and Baldwin argued that typologizing families was premature and that a better approach at the time was to continue attempts to identify important dimensions. For the most part, scholars have directed their efforts toward the identification of dimensions rather than the development of family typologies. Four notable exceptions include the typologies developed by Olson and his colleagues (1979), McCubbin and McCubbin (1988), Kantor and Lehr (1975), and Reiss (1981). The first two are based on self-report, questionnaire data (*450, 453*), and the latter two, on observational data (the assessment devices are not included in this collection).

Epstein et al.'s preference for dimensions rather than types was based on the concern with the loss of variance and the extreme data reduction that often occurs when types are created. In addition, interval-level data are converted to nominal-level data, creating statistical difficulties.

These limitations, however, need to be considered in conjunction with the strengths of typologies. Practically speaking, typologies are easily conveyed to clients and students because they usually make clear, intuitive sense. In addition, there is new evidence indicating that family types may be important intervening variables in the relationship between stressors and family well-being (Malia, Norem, & Garrison, 1988). Thus the "stress process" may differ for different types of families, and current measures of family functioning seem to be able to identify these various types validly. Therefore, it seems important that scholars continue to condense and refine the major dimensions of family functioning, as well as to develop valid family typologies.

Reliability

Information on the reliability of the older measures was not provided in the Straus and Brown (1978) collection, and because few of these measures are used currently, there is very little information available. Of the 24 more recent family functioning measures with scaled items, 19 (79%) have been assessed for interitem consistency (usually by Cronbach's alpha), and 10 (42%), for test-retest stability. The interitem consistency reliabilities are much better for total scales than for individual subscales. Fourteen of the total scales have interitem reliabilities above .80 (*438–440, 443, 445, 446, 448–450, 452, 457–460*). Five of the scales have reliabilities lower than .70. None of the measures has interitem reliabilities of .80 for each of the subscales contained in the total measure. Three have reliabilities between .70 and .80 (*440, 452, 458*). Thus many of the total scales have adequate interitem consistency reliability, but inadequate reliabilities for the subscales.

The time period between assessments for test-retest reliability ranged from one week to two months. Seven of the ten measures have scores above .80 for the total measure (*439, 441, 446, 447, 453, 455, 462*). The other three have scores that range between .70 and .80 (*443, 452, 461*). Although fewer than half of the measures have been assessed for stability across time, the ones tested have demonstrated adequate stability. There were very few assessments of test-retest reliability for the subscales.

The three observational measures have been assessed for interrater reliability. Two range from .70 to .80 (*438, 463*) and one is above .80 (*447*). Extensive training has been required to obtain these levels of reliability, and thus tends to discourage the use of the measures by untrained personnel and by scholars who cannot afford the training.

Validity

The abstracts and attached references were examined for evidence of content, criterion, and construct validity. There seems to be some confusion in the assessment literature concerning the appropriate evidence for criterion and construct validity. A common indicator of validity is a high correlation between the measure of question and an established measure of the same concept. Some scholars use this correlation as evidence of concurrent, criterion validity (e.g., Forman & Hagan, 1983), whereas others use the correlation as evidence of convergent, construct validity (e.g., Grotevant & Carlson, 1987). In this discussion, this correlation was used as evidence of criterion validity, regardless of how it was labeled by the author.

Of the 27 measures, 9 have evidence of content validity (*440, 441, 445–447, 453, 455, 462, 463*). Because adequate content validity is necessary for other types of validity, researchers may have assessed but not reported content validity.

Thirteen of the measures have evidence of criterion validity (*438–441, 446–448, 451, 453, 454, 456, 461, 463*). Concurrent rather than predictive validity has been assessed most often. Some measures evidence several types of concurrent validity (e.g., *448, 461*).

Eighteen of the measures have some evidence of construct validity (*440, 441, 443, 444, 446–453, 457, 458, 460–463*). For most of these measures, construct validity has been assessed by correlating the scales with measures of theoretically connected concepts. Very few have been validated by the use of multitrait, multimethod analyses. Most of the measures need further evidence of both criterion and construct validity using a greater variety of samples or larger, more representative ones.

The dimensionality of family functioning and the issue of differentially weighting the various dimensions (subscales) are related to construct validity. The evidence of dimensionality (i.e., the number of factors and the pattern of loadings) is minimal for most of the measures and often sample-specific. Therefore, the dimensionality and patterns of items need to be assessed in *every* study in which a measure is used. They cannot be assumed. This recommendation also includes a test for unidimensionality when expected. Confirmatory factor analysis is the method of choice for this type of examination.

Most scholars have chosen not to differentially weight the major dimensions of family functioning. It is possible, however, that different dimensions may be more important than others at certain stages of the life cycle and may correlate differentially with various indicators of individual well-being. Efforts to weight seem premature at this time given the current state of conceptualization and measurement, but the issue of weighting may be an important research concern in the future.

STRESS

There are 4 older and 22 more recent measures of stress included in this volume (three of the abstracts include two measures each *471, 476, 479*). The older measures include very few items and are focused on distress and problems. They do not reflect recent conceptualizations of the variables important in the stress process. The notable exception is Hill's measure

(*1463*). Data collected with this measure contributed to the conceptualization of the ABC-X model of family stress, which has served as the foundation for most of the recent conceptualization and research in the area of
family stress.

There are 21 self-report measures included in this section (20 questionnaires and one interview schedule) and one observational measure (*477*).
The focus of these measures is varied. Six address the entire family system;
three, the parent-child relationship; one, the marital dyad; five, kin relationships; and seven, the individual family member. Adult family members
are the informants for 20 of the measures. Both children and adults are the
informants for two (*469, 471*). None of the measures was developed for
sole use by children.

Most of the measures in this chapter were developed for use with specific populations and/or problems. Seven of the measures focus on issues
related to the care of handicapped or chronically ill family members or
elderly care (*467, 469, 471, 475, 476, 478, 482*). Other topics include parents with young children (*464*), work and family (*465*), dating (*466*), parenthood (*468, 479, 480*), separation of family members (*472*), and married
college women (*481*). Four of the measures are generic assessments of
stress-related concepts (*470, 473, 474, 477*).

In addition, most of these measures assess concept(s) in the stress process, not the concept of stress, per se. The following concepts are measured: distress (*464, 466, 468, 476–481*), relationship strain (*464, 467, 469,
471, 480*), role strain (*465, 481*), daily hassles (*470*), life events (*474, 482*),
change (*471, 474, 476, 482*), coping (*472, 473, 475, 482*), and resources
(*482*). These concepts will be discussed within the context of current conceptualizations of stress-related concepts. In contrast to the section on
family functioning, this discussion of stress-related concepts and measures
is organized by concept rather than by issue, because some of the issues are
concept-specific.

Crisis and Stressors

One of the basic tenets of most models of family stress is that families
who experience various stressors are more likely, over time, to experience
crisis (Hill, 1949; McCubbin & Patterson, 1983a). Burr (1973, p. 200) has
defined *crisis* as the "variation in the amount of disruptiveness, incapaci-
tatedness, or disorganization of the family system." It seems that Burr is
referring to disruption created from second-order rather than first-order
change, such that major changes in family rules, roles, and relationships
have occurred. There are no measures of family crisis in this section of
instruments.

The concept of *stressor* is multidimensional and is defined by several
important characteristics. Stressors include discrete life events, series of

events (transitions), chronic life strains, and daily hassles (Pearlin & Schooler, 1978; *470*). These experiences have the potential of producing change in the family system (McCubbin et al., 1980) and can be normative or nonnormative. Because a major component of stressors is the set of changes experienced by family members, it is important to identify salient dimensions of change. These include the amount of change (Holmes & Rahe, 1967; Sarason, Johnson, & Siegal, 1978; *474, 476*), the perceived difficulty of the change (Harriman, 1986), the perceived positiveness or negativeness of the change (Buehler & Langenbrunner, 1987; Chiriboga, 1978; Sarason, Johnson, & Siegal, 1978; Suls, Gastorf, & Witenberg, 1979; *476*), the degree of intrusiveness (Chiriboga & Dean, 1978), perceived control over the change (Paykel, 1983; Suls, Gastorf, & Witenberg, 1979), and expectedness of the change (Suls, Gastorf, & Witenberg, 1979).

The amount of change and the perceived valence (i.e., positiveness, negativeness) have received the greatest attention in the family stress literature. The amount of change often is measured by summing the number of changes that have occurred during a specified time period (Buehler & Langenbrunner, 1987; Lavee, McCubbin, & Olson, 1987; *474*). This dimension has been labeled frequency or occurrence.

These changes also can be divided by life areas such as parent-child, marital, kin, employment, finances, housing (Buehler & Langenbrunner, 1987) and by the type of stressor (Lavee, McCubbin, & Olson, 1987). Although not currently done, the assessment of the occurrence of life change could include indicators of the "depth" and "breadth" of change in the family system. Depth of change is defined as the overall number of changes experienced by family members during the time period, whereas breadth is defined as the number of life domains in which change has occurred.

One of the major concerns related to the assessment of stressors is the importance of separating the external, objective aspects of stressors from the internal, subjective response (e.g., distress) (Dohrenwend & Shrout, 1985; Reiss & Oliveri, 1980; *470, 476*). This problem can be alleviated by obtaining separate occurrence and severity scores (Reich, Parrella, & Filstead, 1988). Empirically, stressor occurrence and severity scores are only weakly correlated (Buehler & Langenbrunner, 1987; Reich, Parrella, & Filstead, 1988). The occurrence score represents the objective component of the stressor, whereas the severity score represents the subjective, perceptual component. The use of this assessment technique is facilitated by including a response category for changes that have occurred but were not perceived as disruptive or bothersome (Buehler & Langenbrunner, 1987).

Another important issue is the assessment of family rather than individual stressors. Most of the measures adopted from the psychological literature have focused on individuals (Holmes & Rahe, 1967; *470*). The Family Inventory of Life Events (*474*) is the only measure in this chapter that adequately addresses this issue. Respondents can check items based solely on their own experiences or they can respond based on the experiences of any family member. This latter technique assesses stressors at the family system level rather than at the individual level of experience.

Resources

Resources facilitate the family's ability to prevent change from creating a crisis in the family system (Burr, 1973; McCubbin & Patterson, 1983b). Resources are distinguished from coping in that resources are what the family is or has, whereas coping is what it does (adapted from Pearlin & Schooler, 1978).

Resources include individual family members' personal resources, the family system's internal resources, and social support. Specific resources are only potentially available to family members during stressful situations. Family members select and choose to use resources that are available to them based on their perceptions of availability and utility. Thus it is important to recognize that resources are often person-/family- and situation-specific (Gross, Crandall, & Knoll, 1980). In addition, a resource may be useful in dealing with certain changes yet serve as a constraint when dealing with others. For example, some divorcing individuals would consider social support from relatives very effective for coping with changes during the divorce transition, whereas others would not define help from their relatives as effective. Social support from relatives would be a resource in the former scenario, but not in the latter. Therefore, it is important to assess both resource availability and efficacy. For example, the availability of family system resources can be measured by most of the current measures of family functioning. Efficacy can be assessed by subjects' self-reports, as well as by correlating the use of various resources with a variety of outcome measures (adapted from Menaghan, 1983).

Family system resources have been a major focus in the research on family stress (Moos, 1984). Specifically, the resources of family cohesion and adaptability have been highlighted in the research on families' differential vulnerabilities to stressors (Olson & McCubbin, 1982; Walker, 1985). A recent trend is the use of family typologies based on family system resources (conceptualized as dimensions of family functioning in the previous section). In 1980, McCubbin and his associates (p. 162) stated that "the 16 family types derived from the Circumplex Model may be useful in explaining the variability among families in their response to stress." These 16 types they referred to are based on cohesion and adaptability scores. This prediction was supported recently, but the researchers used the three, second-order types of the Circumplex Model of family functioning, rather than the 16, first-order types (Malia, Norem, & Garrison, 1988). The conceptualization of family types as indicators of family resources has been a significant advance in the family stress literature.

Recently, the concept of family coherence has received attention. Coherence is defined as a pervasive, enduring, dynamic feeling of confidence that the internal and external environments are predictable, manageable, and meaningful (Antonovsky, 1987). Empirically, the family's sense of coherence is related strongly to family adaptation (Antonovsky & Sourani, 1988).

Although the focus of this chapter is on individual concepts and not specific model building with those concepts, an important issue is the functional form of resources in the stress processes. Do resources directly influence outcome measures, or do they indirectly influence the outcomes by buffering or exacerbating the effects of the stressors? This is an issue that requires future empirical attention.

Perception

In the stress literature, *perception* has been defined as the family's assessments of whether the stressors are challenging or threatening (Hill, 1958), are serious (Burr, 1973), or are manageable (Imig & Imig, 1986; Walker, 1985).

Lazarus (1966) has preferred the concept of appraisal to perception. Primary appraisal refers to the perception of the situation in terms of the degree of threat. Secondary appraisal refers to the perception and evaluation of coping resources. The effects of primary and secondary appraisals seem to depend on the type of stressful conditions involved (Meeks, Arnkoff, Glass, & Notarius, 1986).

Family members' perceptions of the situation itself and of their abilities to manage the changes have correlated strongly with various measures of well-being (Imig & Imig, 1986; Lavee, McCubbin, & Patterson, 1985; Lazarus & Folkman, 1984; Meeks, Arnkoff, Glass, & Notarius, 1986). Although empirical evidence supports the importance of the perception factor in family members' coping with stressful changes, definitionally, the concept is ambiguous and imprecise. As a result of this ambiguity, measures of family members' perceptions have overlapped substantially with some measures of resources (e.g., personal efficacy, sense of coherence), well-being, adaptation, and the severity of change (particularly primary appraisal) (Antonovsky & Sourani, 1988; McKenry & Price, 1984).

Regardless of the ambiguous nature of some of the stress constructs, it is important to recognize that a valid model of family stress is primarily an "insiders'" rather than "outsiders'" model of functioning (Olson, 1977). Family members' assessments of the key concepts are critical for explaining and predicting crisis and adaptation. One of the assessment problems associated with this research is that correlations among various self-report measures of the concepts may reflect both true and method variance. The solution to this problem, however, is not to convert to an "outsiders'"

model because family members perceptions are so important and, therefore, the external validity of the model would be threatened (Lazarus,
DeLongis, Folkman, & Gruen, 1985). The problem can be minimized (but
not eliminated) by clarifying the conceptual definitions of the constructs,
by carefully selecting measures, and by using statistical techniques that
control for correlated error variances (see Antonovsky & Sourani, 1988,
for an excellent discussion and example of this issue).

Coping

Coping is a multidimensional concept that includes cognitive, behavioral, and emotional attempts to prevent, alleviate, or respond to stressors/
demands (McCubbin & Patterson, 1983b; Moos, 1984). Drawing heavily
on Pearlin and Schooler's (1978) conceptualization of coping, Moos (1984)
has clarified these three domains of coping. Cognitive or appraisal-focused
coping is using cognitive attempts to define (and to redefine) the meaning
of the situation. Problem solving or behavioral coping is action that attempts to modify or eliminate the source of stress or to deal with the
tangible consequences of an unavoidable problem. Emotion-focused coping includes attempts to manage the affect aroused by stressful situations.
Although resources are used in the coping process, they are conceptually
distinct from coping responses (Pearlin & Schooler, 1978) and must be
distinctly operationalized.

The efficacy of coping attempts from these different domains is
situation- and stressor-specific (Lazarus & Folkman, 1984; McCubbin,
1979). Coping efficacy or effectiveness can be measured by subjects' self-
reports of perceived effectiveness and by changes in outcomes variables,
such as adaptation and well-being (Menaghan, 1983). In addition, according to Menaghan (1983), the usage and effectiveness of coping variables
need to be assessed separately. Theoretically, coping can affect adaptation
(or well-being) directly and/or indirectly, by buffering or exacerbating the
effects of stressors/demands on outcome variables (Voydanoff & Donnelly,
1985).

Several scholars have forwarded the idea of levels of coping, but have
conceptualized the levels differently. Walker (1985) has suggested that coping behaviors are very specific responses, whereas coping patterns and,
ultimately, strategies are more global. McCubbin (1979) conceptualized
two levels—behaviors and patterns. Menaghan (1983) defined coping efforts as specific actions in specific situations and coping styles as generalized strategies. The measures of coping in this volume include both behaviors and patterns/strategies (372, 473, 475, 482). The patterns are based on
factor analytic results from a few specific samples of families and, therefore, need to be reexamined with each use of the measure to assess the
stability of the patterns.

Adaptation

Adaptation, as defined in the literature on family stress, is an outcome concept and should not be confused with the concept of adaptability discussed in the section on family functioning. It has been conceptualized as the major dependent construct in the Double ABC-X and Family Adjustment and Adaptation Response models of family stress and ranges from "bonadaptation" to "maladaptation" (McCubbin & Patterson, 1983a, 1983b). Adaptation has been defined as "a fit at two levels—between the family members and the family unit and between the family unit and the community" (Lavee & McCubbin, 1985, p. 1, cited in Antonovsky & Sourani, 1988). With the exception of the measure of family adaptation developed by Sourani and Antonovsky (*460*), most scholars have operationalized adaptation as well-being rather than system-environment fit (Buehler, Hogan, Robinson, Levy, 1985–1986; Lavee, McCubbin, & Olson, 1987; Lavee, McCubbin, & Patterson, 1985; Voydanoff & Donnelly, 1985).

Antonovsky and Sourani (1988) have discussed the tautological problems that have been created by certain operational definitions of adaptation. Their points will not be reiterated here, except to reinforce the suggestion that measures of adaptation and predictor variables should be carefully examined for conceptual and operational redundancy.

Reliability

Of the 20 more recent stress measures with scaled items, 18 have been assessed for interitem consistency and 6 for test-retest stability. As with the family functioning measures, consistency reliabilities for the total scales are more acceptable than those for the individual subscales. Twelve (60%) of the total scales have reliabilities above .80 (*464, 466, 467, 469, 470, 473, 476, 478–481*). Four of the total scales have reliabilities between .70 and .80 (*465, 468, 471, 474*). One measure has interitem reliabilities of .80 and above for each of the subscales contained in the total measures (*466*), and one has reliabilities above .70 (*472*). Three of the measures have test-retest coefficients above .80 (*464, 471, 473*) and two have coefficients above .70 (*470, 468*).

Thus most of the self-report measures of stress concepts have adequate interitem consistency reliability when used in their entirety. As highlighted by Lavee, McCubbin, and Olson (1987), the assessment of this type of reliability is not appropriate for measures of life events and need not be calculated as evidence of reliability. Where appropriate, scholars need to gather data more consistently on test-retest stability.

Both the interview and the observational measure have been assessed for interrater reliability. The coefficient for *Abstract 471* was above .90 and for *Abstract 477* was above .70 (using a more stringent criterion). These data indicate adequate levels of interrater reliability.

Validity

Of the 22 measures, 2 have evidence of content validity (*464, 465*); 6 have evidence of concurrent, criterion validity (*464, 467, 468, 474, 475, 477*). The evidence of construct validity has come primarily from factor analyses that assess dimensionality and from correlations between theoretically linked concepts. In all, 15 of the measures have some evidence of construct validity (*464, 466–478, 481*). One of the most significant contributions to the assessment of validity has been the use of LISREL to assess the adequacy of the various measures of the stress concepts (Lavee, McCubbin, & Olson, 1987; Lavee, McCubbin, & Patterson, 1985; Malia, Norem, & Garrison, 1988; Pearlin, Menaghan, Lieberman, & Mullan, 1981). Stress researchers need to continue and increase these efforts to establish construct validity.

DIVORCE

There are 22 recent divorce-related measures in this volume, compared with 1 older measure. This dramatic increase in assessment devices reflects the growing scholarly interest in divorce and remarriage. Of the more recent measures, 20 are self-report questionnaires and 2 are self-report interviews. (Three of the measures were developed in an interview format but have been used subsequently in questionnaires—*483–485*.) Four of these measures are used with children (*486, 499, 502, 503*) and one with teachers (*493*). There are no observational measures. Again, there is an obvious emphasis on the assessment of "insiders' " subjective responses. Four issues will be addressed in this section: (a) level of analysis, (b) content of the measure, (c) reliability, and (d) validity.

Level of Analysis

Most of the measures in this section assess individual feelings and/or adjustment (*486, 487, 490, 493, 494, 496, 497, 500–502, 504*). Three of the measures assess the entire remarried family system (*488, 498, 499*); five, the former spouse relationship (*483, 484, 489, 491, 492*); and four, the parent-child relationship (*483, 485, 495, 503*).

Thus the levels of analysis for the measures of divorce-related concepts differ substantially from the levels assessed by the measures of family functioning. Although the number of measures has increased during the last three decades, the focus has remained on individual and dyadic adjustment. Despite Ahrons's (1980) identification of the binuclear family system, divorce adjustment continues to be conceptualized and measured primarily as an individual or dyadic phenomenon. The three measures that assessed the entire family system were developed for use with remarried families. It seems as though "family" is only addressed when there is a marriage present (either first or subsequent). We need to recognize that in our culture families exist without marriages and that family functioning is an important issue in single-parent families, as well as in first- and remarried families.

Content of Measures

A very diverse set of divorce-related concepts is included in this volume. Each of the family-level measures assess integration or cohesion in remarried families (*488, 498, 499*). At the dyadic level, both former spouse and parent-child relations are addressed. Communication (*483, 484*) and conflict (*489*) between former spouses has received attention. In terms of parent-child relations, parental involvement (*485*), perceived relationship quality (*495*), and children's loyalty conflicts between parents (*503*) are assessed. Several concepts at the individual level are measured: adult's adjustment or well-being (*490, 501*), children's beliefs about the divorce (*486*), children's life events (*502*), former spouse attachment (*487, 497, 504*), role expectations for former spouses (*491*), general attitudes about divorce (*493, 494, 496*), and perceived barriers to divorce (*492*).

In contrast to many of the other measures on "adjustment," the divorce-related measures typically address a unidimensional, specific aspect of functioning postdivorce or remarriage. Generally, the selected concepts have not been extracted from a comprehensive model of family functioning postdivorce.

These measures also indicate that researchers have chosen to develop divorce-specific measures of dyadic and family functioning rather than use more established general measures of family functioning. This is necessary in some cases because of the unique characteristics of single-parent and remarried families and because the measures of family functioning typically have been developed for intact, first-married families. However, it is important to consider using valid and reliable general measures of functioning with single-parent, binuclear, and remarried families, in addition to structure-specific measures (Peek, Bell, Waldren, & Sorell, 1988; Zucker-Anderson & White, 1986).

Reliability

Of the 19 divorce-related measures with scaled items, 14 (74%) have been assessed for interitem consistency and 4 (21%) for test-retest reliability. (*Abstract 502* is a life events measures and should not be assessed for consistency.) The consistency reliabilities of those assessed have been good. Twelve of the total scales have coefficients above .80 (*483, 485–487, 489–491, 493, 494, 496, 497, 504*), and two have coefficients between .70 and .80 (*492, 496*). Only two of the eight multidimensional measures have adequate subscale reliabilities (*483, 490*). In terms of test-retest reliability, two of the four measures have coefficients above .80 (*489, 496*). None falls into the .70 to .80 range.

Validity

Most of the efforts at validation of the divorce-related measures have centered on construct validity. Only two measures have evidence of content validity (*502, 491*) and of concurrent, criterion validity (*492, 486*). None has evidence of predictive validity. Twelve have some evidence of construct validity (*486, 487, 489, 490, 496–498, 500–504*). Most of this evidence is based on correlations with theoretically relevant measures.

Some of the assessments of construct validation have helped clarify certain divorce-related concepts. For example, there is recent evidence that the concept of attachment to the former spouse is unidimensional rather than multidimensional (*487, 504*). In addition, the concept of attachment is related to, but conceptually distinct from, the overall quality of the former spouse relationship (Wright & Price, 1986).

Although over half of the measures have some evidence of validity, the assessments have been very limited. In most cases, validation has been conducted with only one or two samples. As part of the continued efforts to assess validity, it would be helpful to examine concurrent validity by correlating the divorce-specific measures with appropriate general measures. In addition, the effect of time since the separation needs to be assessed for each measure of adjustment. Although tests to date have found very low correlations (*486, 487, 497*), time is conceptually such an important factor in the adjustment process that its effects need to be considered as the measures are validated.

CONCLUSION

In this chapter, over 70 measures of family functioning, stress, and divorce-related concepts were reviewed in order to examine changes in the conceptualizations of family adjustment during the past few decades. It seems that the concept of adjustment is best conceived of as a broad, general description rather than a specific concept with a singular definition and measure.

It also was clear from this review that scholars tend to conceptualize adjustment and its various components as "insider" phenomena. Most of the measures in this section were self-report questionnaires that assessed subjective perceptions of thoughts, beliefs, feelings, behaviors, and interaction processes. This choice of assessment methods is very appropriate for thoughts, beliefs, and feelings because observational methods would necessitate too much inference from behavior. Scholars who use these self-report measures need to continue their efforts toward accounting and controlling for various response sets, such as social desirability.

The assessment of behavior and family interaction processes is less clear-cut. Although self-report assessments prevail, the use of valid and reliable observational devices is important, particularly in the area of family functioning. Self-report and observational methodologies offer different, but equally relevant, information about family adjustment.

The reliability and validity of the measures in this chapter need continued attention. The interitem consistency reliabilities for most total scales were good. The reliabilities were not adequate for most subscales and could be improved by adding additional items and validating the factor structures across samples. There need to be more assessments of test-retest reliability. This is particularly important because many of these measures could be used to assess changes in family patterns over time. Inadequate stability of the measures limits the longitudinal assessment of family functioning.

It was clear from this review that most of the measures in this section need additional validation. Most of the evidence of construct validity was provided from one or two studies. This process of validation could be accomplished if scholars who use these measures would include validation objectives in their research designs. This also needs to include the systematic assessment of dimensionality.

With these suggestions in mind, it is important to highlight the progress that has been made in the conceptualization and measurement of adjustment-related concepts. We are beginning to understand how families function during times of stability and change. Currently, there is more research being conducted with the entire family system as the focus. This research has been facilitated greatly by recent statistical and technological advances. Although much more research is needed, we are beginning to expand our vision beyond the middle-class, intact, first-married family. It is our continuing challenge to better understand the complexities of various family structures and patterns of functioning, as well as the reciprocal effects between family and individual well-being.

REFERENCES

Ahrons, C. (1980). Divorce: A crisis of family transition and change. *Family Relations, 29,* 533–540.

Antonovsky, A. (1987). *Unraveling the mystery of health: How people manage stress and stay well*. London: Jossey-Bass.

Antonovsky, A., & Sourani, T. (1988). Family sense of coherence and family adaptation. *Journal of Marriage and the Family, 50*, 79–92.

Barber, B. K. (1987). Marital quality, parental behaviors and adolescent self-esteem. *Family Perspective, 21*(4), 244–368.

Bloom, B. B. (1985). A factor analysis of self-report measures of family functioning. *Family Process, 24*, 225–240.

Buehler, C., Hogan, M. J., Robinson, B., & Levy, R. (1985–1986). The parental divorce transition: Divorce-related stressors and well-being. *Journal of Divorce, 92*(2), 61–81.

Buehler, C., & Langenbrunner, M. (1987). Divorce-related stressors: Occurrence, disruptiveness, and area of life change. *Journal of Divorce, 11*(1), 25–50.

Burr, W. (1973). *Theory construction and the sociology of the family*. New York: John Wiley.

Chiriboga, D. (1978). Life event weighting systems: A comparative analysis. *Journal of Psychosomatic Research, 21*, 415–422.

Chiriboga, D., & Dean, H. (1978). Dimensions of stress: Perspectives from a longitudinal study. *Journal of Psychosomatic Research, 22*, 47–55.

Cromwell, R. E., & Peterson, G. W. (1981). Multisystem-multimethod assessment: A framework. In E. E. Filsinger & R. A. Lewis (Eds.), *Assessing marriage: New behavioral approaches*. Beverly Hills, CA: Sage.

Dohrenwend, B. P., & Shrout, P. (1985). "Hassles" in the conceptualization and measurement of life stress variables. *American Psychologist, 40*, 780–785.

Epstein, N. B., Bishop, D. S., & Baldwin, L. M. (1982). McMaster model of family functioning: A view of the normal family. In F. Walsh (Ed.), *Normal family processes* (pp. 115–141). New York: Guilford.

Forman, B. D., & Hagan, B. J. (1983). A comparative review of total family functioning measures. *American Journal of Family Therapy, 11*(4), 25–40.

Gross, I., Crandall, E., & Knoll, M. (1980). *Management for modern families*. Englewood Cliffs, NJ: Prentice-Hall.

Grotevant, H. D., & Carlson, C. I. (1987). Family interaction coding systems: A descriptive review. *Family Process, 26*, 49–74.

Harriman, L. C. (1986). Marital adjustment as related to personal and marital changes accompanying parenthood. *Family Relations, 34*, 233–239.

Hill, R. (1949). *Families under stress*. Westport, CT: Greenwood.

Hill, R. (1958). Generic features of families under stress. *Social Casework, 49*, 139–150.

Holmes, T., & Rahe, R. (1967). The social readjustment rating scale. *Journal of Psychosomatic Research, 11*, 213–218.

Imig, D., & Imig, G. (1986). Influences of family management and spousal perceptions on stressor pile-up. *Family Relations, 34*, 227–232.

Kantor, D., & Lehr, W. (1975). *Inside the family*. San Francisco: Jossey-Bass.

Lavee, Y., McCubbin, H. I., & Olson, D. H. (1987). The effect of stressful life events and transitions on family functioning and well-being. *Journal of Marriage and the Family, 49*, 857–873.

Lavee, Y., McCubbin, H., & Patterson, J. (1985). The double ABCX model of family stress and adaptation: An empirical test by analysis of structural equations with latent variables. *Journal of Marriage and the Family, 47*, 811–825.

Lazarus, R. S. (1966). *Psychological stress and the coping process*. New York: McGraw-Hill.

Lazarus, R., DeLongis, A., Folkman, S., & Gruen, R. (1985). Stress and adaptational outcomes. *American Psychologist, 40*, 770–779.

Lazarus, R., & Folkman, S. (1984). *Stress, appraisal, and coping*. New York: Springer.

Malia, J. A., Norem, R. H., & Garrison, M. E. (1988, November). *An examination of differences in the stress process in balanced, midrange, and extreme families using multi-sample LISREL analysis*. Paper presented at the 50th Annual Conference of the National Council on Family Relations, Philadelphia, PA.

McCubbin, H. (1979). Integrating coping behavior in family stress theory. *Journal of Marriage and the Family, 41,* 237–244.

McCubbin, H. I., Joy, C., Cauble, A. E., Comeau, J., Patterson, J., & Needle, R. (1980). Family stress and coping: A decade review. *Journal of Marriage and the Family, 42,* 855–871.

McCubbin, H. I., & McCubbin, M. A. (1988). Typologies of resilient families: Emerging roles of social class and ethnicity. *Family Relations, 37,* 247–259.

McCubbin, H. I., & Patterson, J. M. (1981). *Systematic assessment of family stress, resources, and coping*. St. Paul: University of Minnesota.

McCubbin, H., & Patterson, J. (1983a). Family adaptation to crises. In H. McCubbin, A. E. Cauble, & J. Patterson (Eds.), *Family stress, coping and social support* (pp. 26–47). Springfield, IL: Charles C Thomas.

McCubbin, H., & Patterson, J. (1983b). Family transitions: Adaptation to stress. In H. I. McCubbin & C. R. Figley (Eds.), *Stress and the family: Vol. 1. Coping with normative transitions* (pp. 5–25). New York: Brunner/Mazel.

McKenry, P. C., & Price, S. (1984). The present state of family relations research. *Home Economics Research Journal, 12,* 381–401.

Meeks, S., Arnkoff, D., Glass, C., & Notarius, C. (1986). Wives' employment status, hassles, communication, and relational efficacy: Intra- versus extra-relationship factors and marital adjustment. *Family Relations, 34,* 249–255.

Melson, G. (1980). *Family and environment: An ecosystem perspective*. Minneapolis: Burgess.

Menaghan, E. G. (1983). Individual coping efforts and family studies: Conceptual and methodological issues. In H. I. McCubbin, M. B. Sussman, & J. M. Patterson (Eds.), *Social stress and the family: Advances and developments in family stress theory and research*. New York: Haworth.

Miller, B. C., Rollins, B. C., & Thomas, D. L. (1982). On methods of studying marriages and families. *Journal of Marriage and the Family, 44,* 851–873.

Moos, R. H. (1984). Context and coping: Toward a unifying conceptual framework. *Division 27 Distinguished Contributions Awards*, pp. 5–25.

Olson, D. H. (1977). Insiders' and outsiders' view of relationships: Research strategies. In G. Levinger & H. Raush (Eds.), *Close relationships*. Amherst: University of Massachusetts Press.

Olson, D. H., & McCubbin, H. I. (1982). Circumplex model of marital and family systems V: Application to family stress and crisis intervention. In H. I. McCubbin, A. E. Cauble, & J. M. Patterson (Eds.), *Family stress, coping and social support* (pp. 48–72). Springfield, IL: Charles C Thomas.

Olson, D. H., Sprenkle, D., & Russell, C. (1979). Circumplex model of marital and family systems I: Cohesion and adaptability dimensions, family types and clinical applications. *Family Process, 14,* 1–35.

Paykel, E. (1983). Methodological aspects of life events research. *Journal of Psychosomatic Research, 27,* 341–352.

Pearlin, L. I., Menaghan, E. G., Lieberman, M. A., & Mullan, J. T. (1981). The stress process. *Journal of Health and Social Behavior, 22,* 337–356.

Pearlin, L. I., & Schooler, C. (1978). The structure of coping. *Journal of Health and Social Behavior, 19,* 2–21.

Peek, C. W., Bell, N. J., Waldren, T., & Sorell, G. T. (1988). Patterns of functioning in families of remarried and first-married couples. *Journal of Marriage and the Family, 50,* 699–708.

Reich, W. P., Parrella, D. P., & Filstead, W. J. (1988). Unconfounding the Hassles Scale: External sources versus internal responses to stress. *Journal of Behavioral Medicine, 11*(3), 239–249.

Reiss, D. (1981). *The family's construction of reality.* Cambridge, MA: Harvard University Press.

Reiss, D., & Oliveri, M. E. (1980). Family paradigm and family coping: A proposal for linking the family's intrinsic adaptive capacities to its responses to stress. *Family Relations, 29,* 431–444.

Sabatelli, R. M. (1988). Measurement issues in marital research: A review and critique of contemporary survey instruments. *Journal of Marriage and the Family, 50,* 891–915.

Sarason, I., Johnson, J., & Siegel, J. (1978). Assessing the impact of life changes: Development of the life experiences survey. *Journal of Consulting and Clinical Psychology, 46,* 932–946.

Straus, M. A., & Brown, B. W. (1978). *Family measurement techniques: Abstracts of published instruments, 1935–1974* (rev. ed.). Minneapolis: University of Minnesota Press.

Suls, J., Gastorf, J., & Witenberg, S. (1979). Life events, psychological distress and the Type A coronary-prone behavior pattern. *Journal of Psychosomatic Research, 23,* 315–319.

Voydanoff, P., & Donnelly, B. W. (1985, October). *Economic distress, coping, and quality of family life.* Paper presented at the symposium, "Economic Distress and Families: Coping Strategies and Social Policy," University of Dayton, Dayton, Ohio.

Walker, A. J. (1985). Reconceptualizing family stress. *Journal of Marriage and the Family, 47,* 827–837.

Webster's Seventh New Collegiate Dictionary. (1965). Springfield, MA: G. & C. Merriam.

Wright, D. W., & Price, S. J. (1986). Court-ordered child support payment: The effect of the former-spouse relationship on compliance. *Journal of Marriage and the Family, 48,* 869–874.

Zucker-Anderson, J., & White G. D. (1986). An empirical investigation of interaction and relationship patterns in functional and dysfunctional nuclear families and stepfamilies. *Family Process, 25,* 407–422.

ABSTRACTS OF INSTRUMENTS

NOTE: For additional instruments, see also *Abstracts 1459–1472* in the Abbreviated Abstracts of Instruments (which precedes the Indexes).

Summary of Instrument Codes

Number Codes:

  I = Dimensions of interaction—1 = communication; 2 = life-style; 3 = networks; 4 = multidimensional perspectives

  II = Intimacy and family values—1 = family values; 2 = marital relations; 3 = love; 4 = sex; 5 = personal/interpersonal perceptions

  III = Parenthood—1 = pregnancy, childbearing, and transition to parenthood; 2 = parenting

  IV = Roles and power—1 = roles; 2 = power

  V = Adjustment—1 = family functioning; 2 = stress; 3 = divorce, separation, and remarriage

Letter Codes:

Interactants—a = husband-wife, b = parent-child, c = nuclear family, d = extended family, e = others outside the family, f = siblings, g = intrapsychic processes

Focus of Study—P = parents, C = child, H = husband, W = wife, O = any combination of the above (if there is no capital letter code given, it is understood to be "O")

V-1/c

438. BEAVERS, W. R., GOSSETT, J., & KELSEY-SMITH, M. Beavers Interactional Scales

Avail: NAPS-3 (The Beavers Interactional Scales and the Beavers Self-Report Family Inventory are each part of "The Beavers Systems Model of Family Assessment: Reliability, Validity, and Norms" by Y. F. Hulgus, R. H. Hampson, & W. R. Beavers; for availability information, please refer to *Abstract 42*, the Beavers Self-Report Family Inventory)

Variables Measured: Health, competence, and styles of families

Type of Instrument: Observational rating scales

Instrument Description: The Beavers Interactional Scales are two of three instruments designed to be used in conjunction with each other and are included within the Beavers Systems Model of Family Assessment (BSM). These two scales are referred to as (1) the Beavers Interactional Scale I: Family Competence (BIS-I) (formerly known as the Beavers-Timberlawn Family Evaluation Scale), authored by W. R. Beavers and J. Gossett; and (2) the Beavers Interactional Scale II: Family Style (BIS-II) (formerly known as the Centripetal/Centrifugal Family Style Scale), authored by M. Kelsey-Smith and W. R. Beavers. The third component of the model, reported separately in this handbook, is the Self-Report Family Inventory (SFI; W. R. Beavers, R. B. Hampson, & Y. F. Hulgus), a 36-item self-report questionnaire. Both the BIS-I and the BIS-II are questionnaires for use in rating the behavior of families. The BIS-I consists of 13 items examining various components of competence, plus 1 general item referred to as a Global Health-Pathology Scale. This final item is rated on a 10-point continuum ranging from "Healthiest" to "Most Pathological." The remaining 13 items allow for ratings of families based on 9-point Likert-type scales containing half-point increments ranging from 1 to 5. End points vary from one item to the next and are dependent upon the exact nature of each item. The BIS-II is a 5-point, 9-item Likert-type scale used to evaluate the overall style of the family when viewed together as a systemic unit. Each of items 1 to 8 assesses different aspects of family functioning and style. The final item, as with BIS-I, solicits a global rating used to assess the overall functional style of the family unit. With both the BIS-I and the BIS-II, the final items are also compared with average ratings across other items within the scale. This score serves as a check on the reliability of ratings within that scale. Ratings for both the BIS-I and the BIS-II are based on observations of 10-minute videotaped interactions of families. Four discussion topics are used by the authors in generating interactions: (1) plan a family outing, (2) what closeness means in the family, (3) what is currently the most troubling difficulty in the family, and (4) family strengths. Ratings are made on all items following observation of the complete videotaped interaction.

Sample Items:

(A) Rate this family's overall efficiency in negotiating problem solutions.
(B) Rate the degree to which the members speak for one another, or make "mind reading" statements.
(C) Adults in all families have conflicts. In this family, adult conflicts are . . . (1 = quite open; 5 = indirect, covert, hidden)

Comments: The authors report that extensive training is necessary to ensure the highest possible levels of reliability between raters. Workshops and training sessions are periodically held for persons interested in fully understanding the Beavers Systems Model of Family Assessment. Various training materials (videotaped instructions and so on) are being developed for future use in training raters. Previous reports indicated that interrater reliability on 12 BIS-I items ranged from .58 to .79, with 8 of those items demonstrating reliability coefficients below .70. More recent indications by the authors are that interrater reliability among trained raters for these items range from .72 to .89, with an average of .94 for a combined total of these 12 items. One item (invasiveness) is reported to have interrater reliability in the .49 range and has been dropped by the authors from all research studies. Cronbach's alpha for the BIS-I is reported to be .94. Alpha for the BIS-II is reported to be .84.

References:

Beavers, W. R., Hampson, R. B., & Hulgus, Y. F. (1985). The Beavers systems approach to family assessment. *Fam Proc, 24,* 398–405.

Green, R. G., Kolevzon, M. S., & Vosler, N. R. (1985). The Beavers-Timberlawn Model of family competence and the Circumplex Model of family adaptability and cohesion: Separate but equal? *Fam Proc, 24,* 385–398.

Hampson, R. B., Beavers, W. R., & Hulgus, Y. F. (1988). Commentary: Comparing the Beavers and Circumplex models of family functioning. *Fam Proc, 27,* 85–92.

Lewis, J. M., Beavers, W. R., Gossett, J. T., & Phillips, V. A. (1976). *No single thread: Psychological health in family systems.* New York: Brunner/Mazel.

V-1/V-2/c

439. CALDWELL, S. M. Family Well-Being Assessment (FWA)

Avail: 1988 Ref.

Variables Measured: Levels of well-being and stress within the family unit

Type of Instrument: Self-report questionnaire

Instrument Description: The FWA is a 6-point Likert-type instrument designed to measure various dimensions of children's and adults' perceptions of family life. The FWA is intended to evaluate the family as an interactional system. Separate forms are provided for 9- to 18-year-old children (66 items) and for their parents (74 items). Items are in the form of statements to which respondents are instructed to indicate their level of agreement or disagreement. Response headings include *STRONG agreement, moderate agreement, slight agreement, slight disagreement, moderate disagreement,* and *STRONG disagreement.* Response options under each heading are *YES, Yes, yes, no, No,* and *NO.* Capital letters and underlining are used in to indicate the emphatic nature of each response. The child FWA was designed to assess well-being along 11 dimensions: (1) family stress, (2) family satisfaction, (3) family support, (4) family cohesion, (5) family adaptation, (6) role conflict, (7) role overload, (8) role ambiguity, (9) role nonparticipation, (10) psychosomatic symptoms, and (11) life satisfaction. The adult scale includes the identical grouping of subscales, with the addition of 4 items designed to evaluate role preparedness. Scores for responses, coded 1–6, are summed and averaged within subscales to arrive at mean scores for each dimension. Low scores are interpreted as evidence of lower levels of stress and greater perceptions of well-being. Administration time is estimated to be 15–20 minutes.

Sample Items:

(Child version)

(A)   I am asked to do things around my home without enough time or help to do them.
(B)   My family regularly takes time to discuss family matters.

(Adult version)

(A)   My spouse disagrees with the way the housework is done.
(B)   In general, I like being a member of my family.

Comments: The author reports that Cronbach's alpha for the combined scale was .89 for the children's and .90 for the parents' versions. Alpha for individual subscales ranged from .22 to .89 for children and from .38 to .90 for adults. Subscales varied in size from 3 to 8 items. Test-retest reliability over one to three weeks was reported to be .88. Correlations between subscales range from .12 to .66, with most around .35 to .55. Construct validity was assessed by comparing scores from families with chronically ill children with those of control families. Results of these and other measures of validity are presented in Caldwell (1988).

Reference:

Caldwell, S. M. (1988). Measuring family well-being: Conceptual model, reliability, validity, and use. In C. F. Waltz & O. L. Strickland (Eds.), *Measurement of clinical and educational nursing outcomes: Vol 1. Client-centered outcomes.* New York: Springer.

V-1/c
440. EPSTEIN, N. B., BALDWIN, L. M., & BISHOP, D. S. McMaster Family Assessment Device (FAD)

Avail: 1983 Ref.

Variables Measured: Dimensions of family functioning

Type of Instrument: Self-report questionnaire

Instrument Description: The FAD is a 4-point, 60-item Likert-type questionnaire designed to assess family functioning along six dimensions: (1) problem solving, (2) communication, (3) roles, (4) affective responsiveness, (5) affective involvement, and (6) behavior control. A seventh subscale, with the purpose of yielding an overall rating of family functioning (general functioning), is also used. Items are in the form of statements to which respondents indicate their level of agreement or disagreement in terms of how closely the statement describes their family (*strongly agree, agree, strongly disagree,* or *disagree*). The FAD was constructed on the basis of the McMaster Model of Family Functioning. This model postulates that family functioning is based on the six dimensions noted above. In developing this instrument, the authors wrote 40 items for each of the six dimensions. The resulting 240-item questionnaire was administered to a sample of 294 persons from 112 families—93 of which had one psychiatrically hospitalized member—and 209 university undergraduates enrolled in an introductory psychology class (total sample = 503). On the basis of factor and item analyses, the scale was reduced to 41 items measuring the six stated dimensions, plus an additional 12 items for use as the general functioning subscale. Subscales were later slightly expanded, resulting in a 60-item, seven-dimensional index. The FAD is intended for administration to adults and high school-aged adolescents. Administration time is estimated to be 15–20 minutes.

Sample Items:

(A) Planning family activities is difficult because we misunderstand each other.
(B) You can't tell how a person is feeling from what they are saying.
(C) Some of us just don't respond emotionally.

Comments: Cronbach's alpha is reported to be .92 for general functioning and to range from .72 to .83 for the six original dimensions. Test-retest over a period of one week is reported to range from .66 to .76. The correlation between the FAD and the Locke-Wallace Marital Adjustment Test (1959) is reported to be .53. Correlations between subscales and a measure of social desirability reportedly range from -.06 to -.19.

References:

Byles, J., Byrne, C., Boyle, M. H., & Offord, D. R. (1988). Ontario child health study: Reliability and validity of the general functioning subscale of the McMaster Family Assessment Device. *Fam Proc, 27,* 97–104.

Epstein, N. B., Baldwin, L. M., & Bishop, D. S. (1983). The McMaster Family Assessment Device. *J Mar Fam Th, 9,* 171–180.

Forman, B. D., & Hagan, B. J. (1984). Measures for evaluating family functioning. *Fam Ther, 11,* 1–36.

Miller, E. W., Epstein, N. B., Bishop, D. S., & Keitner, G. I. (1986). The McMaster Family Assessment Device: Reliability and validity. *J Mar Fam Th, 11,* 345–356.

V-1/IV-1/e/c
441. FEETHAM, S. L. Feetham Family Functioning Survey (FFFS)

Avail: 1982 Ref.

Variables Measured: Relationships between the family and external social units, functional task-oriented subsystems of the family, and intrafamilial relationships

Type of Instrument: Self-report questionnaire

Instrument Description: The FFFS is a 7-point, 21-item Likert-type questionnaire designed to assess the abilities of families to function, both as units within the community and within their own internal and interrelated systems. Although the FFFS may be administered to any family, it was specifically developed with families containing handicapped infants in mind. Items are intended to cover three key constructs: (1) family interactions with the broader community; (2) relationship of the family to various subsystems, such as division of labor and assignment of other internally generated responsibilities; and (3) reciprocal relationships within the structure of the family. The instrument consists of 21 items derived from a review of the family functioning literature as well as from clinical observations of handicapped infants. For each item, respondents indicate answers to "How much is there now?" "How much should there be?" "How important is this to me?" Thus responses are generated to a total of 3 × 21, or 63 items. Each response is on a 7-point continuum ranging from *little* (scored 1) to *much* (scored 7). Four measures are computed, including one for each of the three direct measures noted above and a discrepancy score computed by subtracting how much there should be from how much there is.

Sample Items:

(A)   Disagreement with spouse.
(B)   Problems with other children.
(C)   Time with health professionals.

Comments: Information regarding item means and standard deviations, validity, reliability, and a factor analysis are presented in Roberts and Feetham (1982). Cronbach's alpha for the four measures is reported to range from .66 to .84. Two-week test-retest reliability is reported to be .93. Five-year test-retest reliability was found to be .83. Scores obtained by husbands and wives were reported to correlate .72.

References:

Roberts, C. S., & Feetham, S. L. (1982). Assessing family functioning across three areas of relationships. *Nurs Res, 3,* 231–235.
Schilling, R. F., Kirkham, M. A., Snow, W. H., & Schinke, S. P. (1986). Single mothers with handicapped children: Different from their married counterparts? *Fam Relat, 35,* 69–77.

V-1/c
442. FRISTAD, M. A. Family Assessment Scale (FAS)

Avail: NAPS-3

Variables Measured: Family health and pathology

Type of Instrument: Self-report questionnaire

Instrument Description: The FAS is a 4-point, 20-item Likert-type scale initially designed to assess social desirability in the self-report of family functioning among clinical populations. It was adapted from Jemail and LoPiccolo's Marital Defensiveness Scale (1983), which purportedly measures the tendency to endorse socially desirable items that are unlikely to occur and to deny socially undesirable items that characterize many honest responses. The following four modifications were made to the Marital Defensiveness Scale during the development of the FAS: (1) The words "mate," "spouse," marriage," and "couple" were replaced with "family" or "family member" on each item; (2) response options ranging from 1 to 4, with high scores indicative of increased social desirability, were constructed to replace the original dichotomous (0–1) scale; (3) the original scale was altered in order to make it more appropriate for use with either gender; and (4) the scale was abbreviated to 20 items. A factor analysis of the new scale resulted in a five-factor solution. Identified dimensions were family bliss (6 items), family satisfaction (5 items), negative feelings or actions (3 items), communication or understanding (4 items), and negative verbal behavior (2 items). Specific items loading on the various factors are detailed in Fristad (1988).

Sample Items:

(A)   I have never regretted being a member of my family, not even for a moment.
(B)   I never say anything bad about family members; not even to my close friends.
(C)   I sometimes try to get even with family members, rather than forgive and forget.

Comments: Items were assigned to factors based on primary loadings, with five factors having loadings of .35 or more on more than one factor. All items are assigned only to those factors on which they had the greatest loading. The author indicates that item-total correlations for the combined scale ranged from .39 to .71, with a mean of .56.

Reference:

Fristad, M. A. (1988). Assessing social desirability in family self-report. *Perc Mot Sk, 66,* 131–137.

V-1/c
443. GUERNEY, B. G., Jr. The Family Life Questionnaire (FLQ)

Avail: 1977 Ref., & IDEALS (Institute for the Development of Emotional and Life Skills), P.O. Box 391, State College, PA 16804

Variables Measured: Harmony and satisfaction in family life

Type of Instrument: Self-report questionnaire

Instrument Description: The FLQ is a 24-item Likert-style scale designed as a measure of harmony and satisfaction that could be completed by all literate members of families. Scores on the FLQ range from 24 to 96, with higher scores indicating more harmony and satisfaction in family or dyadic relationships. The instrument allows comparable assessments for all family members. Adapted forms are available for married couples, fathers and sons, and mothers and daughters. These three forms, respectively, are known as the Family Life Questionnaire—Conjugal (FLQ-C); Family Life Questionnaire—Father, Son (FLQ-FS); and the Family Life Questionnaire—Mother, Daughter (FLQ-MD). The latter two are identical except for changing father and son to mother and daughter wherever appropriate. The scale is appropriate for research or clinical assessment in which an overall measure of family harmony and satisfaction is desired, including changes resulting from enrichment or therapeutic interventions.

Sample Items:

(A)   It's easy to laugh and have fun when we are together.
(B)   At least one of us gets angry about very unimportant things.
(C)   At least one of us gets things his or her own way too much.

Comments: The author reports that test-retest reliability over a two-month period has been measured at .61 to .84. Cronbach's alpha is reported to range from .84 to .91. Construct validity has been assessed in studies examining the relationship of various forms of the FLQ to improvement as a result of therapy or enrichment interventions. Correlations are also reported between the FLQ-C and the Marital Adjustment Test (.78), the Marital Communication Inventory (.78), and the Primary Communication Inventory (.69). Correlations between the FLQ-FS and Acceptance of Others (.39) and Unobtrusively Observed Acceptance of Others (.26) are also reported.

References:

Guerney, B. G., Jr. (1977). *Relationship Enhancement: Skill-training programs for therapy, problem prevention, and enrichment.* San Francisco: Jossey-Bass.

Guerney, B. G., Jr., Coufal, J., & Vogelsong, E. (1981). Relationship Enhancement versus a traditional approach to therapeutic/preventative/enrichment parent-adolescent programs. *J Cons Clin, 49,* 927–929.

Guerney, B. G., Jr., Vogelsong, E. L., & Coufal, J. (1983). Relationship Enhancement versus a traditional treatment: Follow-up and booster effects. In D. Olson & B. Miller (Eds.), *Family studies review yearbook* (Vol. 1, pp. 738–756). Beverly Hills, CA: Sage.

Harrell, J., & Guerney, B. G., Jr. (1976). Training married couples in conflict negotiation skills. In D. Olson (Ed.), *Treating relationships.* Lake Mills, IA: Graphic.

V-1/II-3/g/a

444. HANSEN, G. L. Hansen's Hypothetical, Jealousy Producing Events

Avail: 1982 Ref.

Variables Measured: Marital jealousy

Type of Instrument: Self-report questionnaire

Instrument Description: This instrument is designed to measure marital jealousy using hypothetical, jealousy-producing events. Subjects are asked to indicate how they would feel about their mate's behavior in each of eight situations on a scale from 1 (*be extremely pleased*) to 11 (*be extremely disturbed or bothered*). Each situation is described so that the subject's mate is freely choosing to engage in the behavior described, enjoying it, and not directly affecting the welfare of the subject. Reports of subjects being disturbed by events are interpreted as indicating that he or she views the mate's behavior as contrary to his or her definition of the marriage or as being threatening to the marriage. Items may be treated and responses interpreted individually, or item scores may be summed in order to come up with an overall jealousy score. The measure is intended for married subjects but can also be used with unmarried persons, particularly if they are asked to indicate how they would feel if they were married. Administration time is approximately 5–10 minutes.

Sample Items:

(A) Your mate has a job which requires him/her to work a normal 40 hours per week. In addition to working these 40 hours per week, your mate feels very committed to his/her job and devotes, on the average, an additional 10 hours per week to work-related activities which require him/her to go back to the office in the evenings and on weekends. Your mate does not receive extra pay for these activities.

(B) Your mate has become good friends with a co-worker of the opposite sex who you do not know very well. Your mate and his/her friend enjoy having lunch together, discussing their respective lives, and providing each other emotional support. (Their relationship does not have a sexual component.)

Comments: The author reports that Cronbach's alpha for the 8-item scale was found to be .65. It is also reported that total jealousy scores have been found to correlate .24 for males and .25 for females with gender-role traditionalism, from -.19 (female) to -.20 (male) with marital alternatives, and -.23 with self-esteem in females.

References:

Hansen, G. L. (1982). Reactions to hypothetical, jealousy producing events. *Fam Relat, 31*, 513–518.

Hansen, G. L. (1983). Marital satisfaction and jealousy among men. *Psychol Rep, 52*, 363–366.

Hansen, G. L. (1985). Perceived threats and marital jealousy. *Social Psych Q, 48*, 262–268.

V-1/f/C
445. HOGAN, N. S. Hogan Sibling Inventory of Bereavement (HSIB)

Avail: NAPS-3

Variables Measured: Coping and adaptation characteristics of adolescent sibling bereavement

Type of Instrument: Self-report questionnaire

Instrument Description: The HSIB is a 109-item self-report survey instrument designed to measure the sibling bereavement process, including the respondent's level of coping and adaptation. It is appropriate for persons aged 10 through young adulthood. Items sample information about personal bereavement as well as bereavement of the mother, father, and surviving sibling and the effects of friends, religion, and school upon the grieving process. The scale is scored using a 5-point Likert format, with response options ranging from *almost always true* to *hardly ever true*. A stem ("Since my brother/sister died I feel . . . ") was used to focus respondents on the time period subsequent to the death of their siblings. Administration time is approximately 30–45 minutes.

Sample Items:

(A)   I miss sharing with my dead brother/sister.
(B)   I should have died and my dead brother/sister should have lived.
(C)   I believe I will see my dead brother/sister again in heaven.

Comments: This instrument was piloted with 40 bereaved siblings, aged 13 to 18, who had experienced the death of a sibling within three years of testing. Subscales of the HSIB are not indicated. Cronbach's alpha for the entire instrument is reported by the author to be .883, indicating that the average interitem correlation is approximately .065. Content validity was assessed using a panel of 10 bereaved adolescents, 10 bereaved parents, and five professionals who work with bereaved siblings.

Reference:

Hogan, N. S. (1988). The effects of time on the adolescent sibling bereavement process. *Pediat Nurs, 14*, 333–335.

V-1/c/d
446. HOVESTADT, A. J., ANDERSON, W. T., PIERCY, F. P., COCHRAN, S. W., & FINE, M. Family of Origin Scale (FOS)

Avail: 1985 Ref.

Variables Measured: Level of perceived health in one's family of origin

Type of Instrument: Self-report questionnaire

Instrument Description: The FOS is a 5-point, 40-item Likert-style questionnaire. The scale takes approximately 10 minutes to complete. Subjects apply each statement to their family of origin as they remember it. Scores can range from 40 to 200, with higher scores indicating higher levels of perceived health. Half of the items are designed to reflect autonomy and half to reflect intimacy. Health is viewed as the ability to be close to and to be separate from significant others at the same time. The FOS is used as an instrument in intergenerational research. It is also intended for subjects who are prepared for family of origin therapy. Simple scoring procedures are fully explained in the 1985 reference listed below.

Sample Items:

(A) In my family, it was normal to show both positive and negative feelings.
(B) People in my family often made excuses for their mistakes.
(C) My family was receptive to the different ways various family members viewed life.

Comments: Test-retest reliability is reported by the authors to have been .97 in a study with 41 psychology graduate students.

References:

Hovestadt, A. J., Anderson, W. T., Piercy, F. P., Cochran, S. W., & Fine, M. (1985). A family-of-origin scale. *J Mar Fam Th, 11,* 287–297.
Lee, R. E., Gordon, N. G., & O'Dell, J. W. (1989). The validity and use of the Family-of-Origin Scale. *Am J Fam Th, 15,* 19–27.

V-1/c
447. KINSTON, W., LOADER, P., & MILLER, L. The Family Health Scale (FHS)

Avail: Family Research Programme, B.I.O.S.S., Brunel University, Uxbridge, Middlesex UB8 3PH, England

Variables Measured: Quality of overall family functioning

Type of Instrument: Observational rating scale

Instrument Description: The FHS is designed to quantify the quality of overall family functioning from the perspective of an external observer. It consists of 26 rating scales grouped under six headings, each of which refers to a major dimension of family functioning. The six headings are affective status, alliances, communication, adaptability and stability, boundaries, and family competence. The main scales and subscales were clinically derived, and the rating procedure was designed to conform as closely as possible to clinical logic. Rating is performed on a seven-point continuum from "breakdown of functioning" to "optimal functioning," and it requires the exercise of clinical judgment. Ratings may be based on whatever information is available on the family but, according to the authors, should be based on a valid, standardized method for directly observing family interaction. The FHS is designed to be acceptable to a wide range of clinicians and to be applicable to both clinic and nonclinic families. The scoring procedure allows weighting of subscale and main scale scores using clinical judgment. The average of scored main scales provides a single score ranging from 1 to 7, which is designed to represent overall family health. Experience in family therapy is required for effective use of this instrument. An experienced rater completes the FHS in about 15 minutes.

Sample Items: Not applicable.

Comments: The authors report that the FHS has been used to discriminate between groups of families where different levels of family functioning would be expected, and within them where it appears sensitive to the expected wide variation in family functioning.

References:

Kinston, W., & Loader, P. (1988). The Family Task Interview: A tool for clinical research in family interaction. *J Mar Fam Th, 14,* 67–87.

Kinston, W., Loader, P., & Miller, L. (1987a). Emotional health of families and their members where a child is obese. *J Psychosom, 31,* 583–599.

Kinston, W., Loader, P., & Miller, L. (1987b). Quantifying the clinical assessment of family health. *J Mar Fam Th, 13,* 49–67.

Stratford, J., Burck, C., & Kinston, W. (1982). Influence of context on the assessment of family interaction: A clinical study. *J Fam Ther, 4,* 359–371.

V-1/c
448. KOLEVZON, M. S., & GREEN, R. G. Family Awareness Scales (FAS)

Avail: Kolevzon & Green, in Corcoran & Fischer, 1987 Ref., & Green, 1987a Ref.

Variables Measured: Family members' perceptions of the competence of their family units

Type of Instrument: Self-report questionnaire

Instrument Description: The FAS is a 14-item questionnaire utilizing a Likert-style format with five response options per item. It is based on the Beavers-Timberlawn Model of family competence. The items were developed to provide a self-report alternative to the Beavers Timberlawn Family Evaluation Scales (BTFES), an observational rating scale. The language used in the BTFES items was replaced by words and phrases that the FAS authors maintain are more easily comprehended by family members. The items are designed to tap aspects of family structure, goal-directed negotiation, autonomy of family members, and the nature of family expression. A total score, representing a family member's perception of the competence of his or her family unit, is obtained by reverse-scoring appropriate items and then summing all items.

Sample Items:

(A) How often are family members open and willing to listen to the statements of other family members?

(B) How frequently do the members of your family say or admit that they are responsible for their own past and present behavior?

(C) How many emotional problems does your family have compared to most families?

Comments: Studies utilizing the FAS have been conducted on several diverse populations of adolescents and their families. The authors report that Cronbach's alpha across these studies has ranged from .84 to .89. It is also reported that the FAS correlates .33 with the BTFES and from .70 to .90 with the Self-Report Family Inventory. The FAS has also been used to differentiate clinical from nonclinical families. Note: There appears to be some confusion in the literature regarding the order of authorship for this instrument; the sequence listed in this abstract is not intended as an endorsement of the order given.

References:

Beavers, W. R., Hampson, R., & Hulgus, Y. (1985). Commentary: The Beavers systems approach to family assessment. *Fam Proc, 24,* 398–405.

Green, R. G. (1987a). Measuring family member's assessments of the functioning of their family units: The family awareness scales. In N. Gottleib (Ed.), *Perspectives on direct practice evaluation.* Seattle, WA: Center for Social Welfare Research.

Green, R. G. (1987b). Self-report measures of family competence. *Am J Fam Th, 15,* 163–168.

Kolevzon, M. S., & Green, R. G. (1987). Family Awareness Scale. In K. Corcoran & J. Fischer (Eds.), *Measures for clinical practice: A sourcebook* (pp. 436–439). New York: Free Press.

V-1/c

449. McCUBBIN, H. I., & COMEAU, J. K. Family Inventory of Resources for Management (FIRM)

Avail: 1987 Ref.

Variables Measured: Description and predictions regarding a family's adaptation to stress

Type of Instrument: Self-report questionnaire

Instrument Description: The FIRM is a 4-point, 69-item Likert-type questionnaire designed to assess the ability of the family to deal effectively with stressors. The instrument seeks to evaluate which resources families have, lack, or have depleted. It is hypothesized that families possessing a larger repertoire of resources will manage more effectively and will be able to adapt better to stressful situations. The selection of items for FIRM was influenced by literature and typology theory of family adjustment and adaptation in three primary areas: (1) personal resources, (2) family system internal resources, and (3) established social support systems. Items are in the form of statements, with respondents indicating how well they describe the family (*not at all* = 0 to *very well* = 3). Items on the FIRM are divided among six factors: (1) family strengths I (esteem and communication), which assess the presence of a combination of personal, family system, and social support resources along the dimensions of family esteem, communication, mutual assistance, optimism, problem-solving ability, and encouragement of autonomy among family members; (2) family strengths II (mastery and health), assessing resources in the areas of a sense of mastery over family events and outcomes, family mutuality, and physical and emotional health; (3) extended family social support, indicated by the mutual help and support given to and received from relatives; (4) financial well-being; (5) financial support; and (6) social desirability. These last two factors were added to the original scale in order to obtain additional information, but are not considered major dimensions or subscales of the instrument. Scoring is accomplished by summing values associated with response options within subscales. Administration time is approximately 35 minutes.

Sample Items:

(A) We have money coming in from our investments (such as rental property, stocks, bonds, etc.).

(B) Being physically tired much of the time is a problem in our family.

(C) We do not plan too far ahead because many things turn out to be a matter of good or bad luck anyway.

Comments: The authors indicate that Cronbach's alpha for the FIRM is .89. Alpha for the first four subscales is reported to be .62 for extended family support and .85 for each of family strengths I, family strengths II, and financial well-being. The four primary subscales are reportedly intercorrelated in the .19 to .37 range. Correlations are also reported between overall FIRM scores and measures of family cohesion (.46), expressiveness (.27), conflict (-.30), and organization (.25).

Reference:

McCubbin, H. I., & Comeau, J. (1987). FIRM: Family Inventory of Resources for Management. In H. I. McCubbin & A. I. Thompson (Eds.), *Family assessment inventories for research and practice* (pp. 145–160). Madison: University of Wisconsin-Madison, Family Stress Coping and Health Project.

V-1/c

450. McCUBBIN, M. A., McCUBBIN, H. I., & THOMPSON, A. I.
Family Hardiness Index (FHI)

Avail: 1987 Ref.

Variables Measured: The ability of the family to resist stress and to adapt to new situations

Type of Instrument: Self-report questionnaire

Instrument Description: The FHI is a 4-point, 20-item Likert-type questionnaire designed to assess the ability of families to adapt to and effectively deal with stressors. "Family hardiness" specifically refers to the internal strengths and durability of the family unit and is characterized by a sense of control over the outcomes of life events and hardships. It is represented by a view of change as being beneficial and growth-producing, and by an active rather than passive orientation in adjusting to and managing stressful situations. The FHI measures four key variables: (1) cooriented commitment (8 items), indicating the family's sense of internal strengths, dependability, and an ability to work together; (2) confidence (4 items), indicated by the family's sense of being able to plan ahead, being appreciated for efforts, and their ability to endure hardships and experience life with interest and meaningfulness; (3) challenge (5 items), measured by assessing the family's efforts to be innovative, active, to experience new things, and to learn; and (4) control (3 items), reflected by a family's sense of being in control of family life rather than it being shaped by outside events and circumstances. Respondents are presented with a series of statements regarding family activities and attitudes, and are asked to indicate whether each is *false* (0), *mostly false* (1), *mostly true* (2), *true* (3), or *not applicable* (0). Totals within subscales are derived by summing values associated with responses within that factor. High scores are presumed to indicate greater levels of hardiness.

Sample Items:

(A)   Trouble results from mistakes we make.
(B)   It is not wise to plan ahead and hope because things do not turn out anyway.
(C)   Our work and efforts are not appreciated no matter how hard we try and work.

Comments: The authors indicate that Cronbach's alpha for the FHI is .82. Factor loadings are reported to be in the range of .52 to .85. Correlations are reported between overall FHI scores and family flexibility (.22), family time and routines (.23), and family satisfaction (.20).

Reference:

McCubbin, M. A., McCubbin, H. I., & Thompson, A. I. (1987). FHI: Family Hardiness Index. In H. I. McCubbin & A. I. Thompson (Eds.), *Family assessment inventories for research and practice* (pp. 125–130). Madison: University of Wisconsin-Madison, Family Stress Coping and Health Project.

V-1/c
451. MOOS, R. H., & MOOS, B. S. Family Environment Scale (FES)

Avail: Consulting Psychologists Press, 577 College Ave., Palo Alto, CA 94306

Variables Measured: Relationship, personal growth, and system maintenance dimensions of family environments

Type of Instrument: Self-report questionnaire

Instrument Description: The FES was designed to measure social climates of all types of families. It is composed of 90 true-false items scored on 10 subscales. Subscales evaluated with the FES are cohesion, expressiveness, conflict, independence, achievement orientation, intellectual-cultural orientation, active-recreational orientation, moral-religious emphasis, organization, and control. There are three forms: (1) the "real form" measures people's perceptions of their current family environments, (2) the "ideal form" measures people's conceptions of ideal family environments, (3) the "expectations form" measures people's expectations about new family settings (such as a couple's expectations about what their family will be like after the birth of a child). Administration time is approximately 15 minutes.

Sample Items:

(A)   Family members really help and support one another.
(B)   Family members often keep their feelings to themselves.
(C)   We fight a lot in our family.

Comments: The FES has been used widely in many research projects. There are approximately 200 publications describing its applications. The authors report that evidence on construct validity comes from studies investigating the ability of the FES to discriminate among families, associations between family climate and life transitions and crises, and several other types of investigations. Details are provided in the second edition of the FES manual. The authors report that normative samples have been obtained on 1,125 normal and 500 distress families. Internal consistency for the 10 subscales is reported by the authors to range from .61 to .78. Test-retest correlations for the individual subscales are reported to range from .68 to .86 after 2 months, .54 to .91 at 4 months, and .52 to .89 in a 12-month follow-up study.

References:

Moos, R. (1984). Context and coping: Toward a unifying conceptual framework. *Am J Comm P, 12,* 5–25.

Moos, R. (1985). Evaluating social resources in community and health care contexts. In P. Karoly (Ed.), *Measurement strategies in health psychology* (pp. 433–459). New York: John Wiley.

Moos, R., & Moos, B. (1984). The process of recovery from alcoholism. III. Comparing functioning in families of alcoholic and matched control families. *J Stud Alc, 45,* 111–118.

V-1/c

452. OLSON, D. H., LARSEN, A. S., & McCUBBIN, H. I. Family Strengths Scale

Avail: 1985 Ref.

Variables Measured: Family strengths of pride and accord

Type of Instrument: Self-report questionnaire

Instrument Description: The Family Strengths Scale is a 12-item Likert-style instrument utilizing a 5-point response format. It was designed to measure positive qualities of families that aid in their abilities to effectively negotiate social and familial environmental influences. Items for this instrument were developed following a literature review to determine those attributes that allow some families to successfully negotiate their circumstances. Initially, 25 items were designed to evaluate families in terms of their pride, positive values and beliefs, and accord. Following factor and test-retest analyses, the scale was shortened, first to 14 and later to 12 items. The final 12-item scale evaluates factors of pride and accord. A balance of positively and negatively worded items were included in order to prevent response sets and to decrease the influence of social desirability. Scores for the two subscales are determined by summing responses on all appropriate items.

Sample Items:

(A)   Family members respect one another.
(B)   Family members feel loyal to the family.
(C)   Accomplishing what we want to do seems difficult for us.

Comments: Analyses of internal properties of the scale reported by the authors were conducted using a sample of 2,740 husbands, wives, and adolescents. This sample was split into two groups, with data from 1,330 subjects used in developing properties of the scales, and data from the remaining 1,410 subjects used for replication purposes. A factor analysis using a varimax rotation was conducted, resulting in loadings ranging from .59 to .76 for the 7-item pride subscale, and from .47 to .64 for the 5-item accord factor. Cronbach's alpha for the pride and accord subscales are reported to be .87 and .73, respectively, and .83 for the combined 12-item scale. Test-retest correlations for 116 subjects are reported to be .73 for pride, .79 for accord, and .58 for the combined scale.

References:

McCubbin, H. I., Joy, C., Cauble, A., Comeau, J., Patterson, J., & Needle, R. (1980). Family stress and coping: A decade review. *J Mar Fam, 42,* 855–871.
McCubbin, H. I., & Patterson, J. M. (1981). *Systematic assessment of family stress resources and coping: Tools for research, education, and clinical intervention.* St. Paul, MN: Family Social Science.
Olson, D. H., McCubbin, H. I., Barnes, H., Larsen, A., Muxem, M., & Wilson, M. (1985). *Family inventories.* St. Paul, MN: University of Minnesota, Family Social Science.

V-1/c

453. OLSON, D. H., PORTNER, J., & LAVEE, Y. FACES III (Family Adaptability and Cohesion Evaluation Scales)

Avail: 1985 Ref.

Variables Measured: Family cohesion and adaptability

Type of Instrument: Self-rating questionnaire

Instrument Description: This instrument is designed to classify families into 3 general and 16 specific types on adaptability and cohesion dimensions. FACES III was developed to improve the reliability, validity, and clinical utility of FACES I and II. The instrument can be administered on an individual basis, with couples, or with families. Four forms are available, each containing 20 Likert-style items. The separate forms contain items examining perceived and ideal families, and perceived and ideal couples. Forms are constructed along similar dimensions. On all forms the odd items are summed to arrive at a cohesion score, and even items are summed to arrive at a measure of adaptability. Each item asks the frequency of a specific behavior using a 5-point response format, with possible responses ranging from *almost never* to *almost always*.

Sample Items:

(A)   Family members like to spend free time with each other.
(B)   Rules change in our family.
(C)   It is hard to tell who does which household chores.

Comments: Scores between family members tend to vary considerably, with correlations reported by the author to be generally in the .30 to .40 range. The author cites these figures in arguing for obtaining independent ratings from multiple family members. It is reported that the cohesion and adaptability portions of the scale, which were intended to be orthogonal, correlate .03. Cronbach's alpha is reported to be .77 for cohesion, .62 for adaptability, and .68 for the total scale.

References:

Olson, D. H. (1986). Circumplex model VII: Validation studies and FACES III. *Fam Proc, 25,* 337–351.
Olson, D. H., McCubbin, H. I., Barnes, H., Larsen, A., Muxem, M., & Wilson, M. (1985). *Family inventories.* St. Paul, MN: University of Minnesota, Family Social Science.

V-1/V-2/c/e
454. PATTERSON, G. R. Oregon Social Learning Center (OSLC) Family Crisis List

Avail: 1982 Ref.

Variables Measured: Areas in which families are experiencing immediate difficulty

Type of Instrument: Checklist of incidents

Instrument Description: This instrument consists of a list of 71 specific incidents, divided among seven categories, that might be considered crises by families. One additional item appended to each category allows respondents to indicate crises within that category that are not listed. Incidents range from mildly stressful (e.g., "Someone returned from a long trip of over a day") to those that could be expected to result in significant turmoil within the family (e.g., "Someone in the family learned they have a chronic illness, e.g., cancer, TB, muscular dystrophy, etc."). The instrument is generally administered to either therapy patients or families of therapy patients. Respondents are administered the OSLC Family Crisis List daily, weekly, or monthly, according to the format of the investigation, and are asked to circle each event that has occurred within the last day, week, and so on. Scoring is accomplished by counting the number of circled statements within each group. Categories of crises (and the number of items within that group) are family (18), household and transportation (19), economic (7), health (8), school (9), social interchange (4), and legal (6). The authors have typically used this instrument in examinations of environmental stressors, behavior of children within families, and coping strategies of these families.

Sample Items:

(A)   Adults had a serious disagreement with a neighbor or friend.
(B)   Someone in the family went to see a lawyer.
(C)   School complained about child's academic progress (doing poorly).

Comments: The author, reporting on data from a small sample, noted that mothers identified based on family problems reported an average of from 1.60 to 5.55 crises per day, or approximately 11 to 39 crises per week. Eight nonclinic families reported only an average of 4.75 crises per week. The author's focus in using this instrument appears to be a greater understanding of both the need for coping strategies and the appropriate use of resources available to the family when attempting to deal with both inconveniences and crises.

References:

Patterson, G. R. (1982). *A social learning approach: Vol. 3. Coercive family process.* Eugene, OR: Castalia.
Patterson, G. R. (1983). A change agent for family process. In N. Garmezy & M. Rutter (Eds.), *Stress, coping, and development in children.* New York: McGraw-Hill.

V-1/c

455. PINO, C. J., SIMONS, N., & SLAWINOWSKI, M. J. Children's Version Family Environment Scale (CFES)

Avail: Slosson Educational Press, P.O. Box 280, East Aurora, NY 14050

Variables Measured: Family environment with regard to achievement, intellectual, and recreational orientation; cohesion; expressiveness; conflict; independence; moral-religious emphasis; organization; and control

Type of Instrument: Interview and picture interpretation instrument for children

Instrument Description: Children are presented with a series of 30 items. Each item consists of three identical pictures, labeled "A," "B," and "C." Each picture is a cartoon-type drawing of a child interacting with one or more adults. Bubbled captions indicate comments of the interactants in the drawings. For each item the child is instructed to select the interaction best answering the question: "Which picture looks like your family?" The CFES was designed as a downward extension of the Family Environment Scale (FES) (Moos & Moos, 1974). The Children's Version Family Environment Scale was developed for use in conjunction with the original FES. The CFES is compatible with the FES profile. The author indicates that family scores can be compared across the two instruments for clinical utilization.

Sample Items:

(A)   Girl is on her two-wheel bicycle with parents watching.
      a. (Father) "We'll help you."; (Daughter) "I want to do it myself!"
      b. (Father) "If you need help, we'll help you!"; (Daughter) "I want to do it my-self!"
      c. (Father) "Do it and we'll help you."; (Daughter) "I want to do it myself!"
(B)   Mother is holding a report card and talking with her daughter.
      a. (Mother) "Grades don't matter!"
      b. (Mother) "You tried. That is important!"
      c. (Mother) "You need to get all "A" 's!"

Comments: The authors report on a study in which content validity was investigated. Correct identification with scale meanings for children was assessed. They also report that test-retest reliability was computed to be .80.

References:

Pino, C. J. (1984). Family diagnosis and treatment planning in multi-module family therapy and personalized family enrichment. *Fam Ther, 11,* 175–184.

Pino, C. J. (1985). A content validity study of the Children's Version Family Environment Scale. *Child St J, 15,* 311–316.

Pino, C. J. (1989). *Imagery in family diagnosis and therapy: CFES sourcebook.* East Aurora, NY: United Educational.

V-1/a
456. PRETZER, J., EPSTEIN, N., & FLEMING, B. Marital Attitude Survey (MAS)

Avail: NAPS-3

Variables Measured: Expectancies and attributions that play important roles in marital interaction

Type of Instrument: Self-report questionnaire

Instrument Description: The MAS consists of a series of 74 statements expressing expectations and attributions regarding the respondent's own marital relationship. Respondents are asked to rate their endorsement of each statement on a 5-point scale ranging from *strongly agree* to *strongly disagree.* Scores are obtained on the eight subscales of perceived ability of couple to change relationship, expectancy of improvement in relationship, attribution of causality (for problems) to spouse's behavior, attribution of causality to spouse's personality, attribution of causality to own behavior, attribution of causality to own personality, attribution of malicious intent to spouse, and attribution of lack of love to spouse. The scale was designed for use with both therapy-seeking and non-therapy-seeking couples.

Sample Items:

(A)   There's no way for us to change this relationship.
(B)   My personality would have to change for my partner and me to get along better.
(C)   I doubt if my partner deliberately does things to irritate me.

Comments: The author reports that Cronbach's alpha for the MAS has been measured from .66 to .89 for seven of the eight subscales, with only attribution of causality to own behavior (.58) falling below this standard. Further reports indicate it has been used as a measure of dysfunctional cognitions associated with marital distress. An additional study examined relationships between MAS subscales and measures of marital distress, communication, depression, and beliefs regarding relationships. A discriminant function analysis based on MAS subscales is reported to have correctly classified 81% of study subjects.

Reference:

Epstein, N., Pretzer, J. L., & Fleming, B. (1987). The role of cognitive appraisal in self-reports of marital communication. *Behav Ther, 18,* 51–69.

V-1/c/C

457. ROELOFSE, R., & MIDDLETON, M. R. Family Functioning in Adolescence Questionnaire (FFAQ)

Avail: NAPS-3

Variables Measured: Overall family health plus structural, affective, communication, behavior control, value transmission, and external systems dimensions of family functioning

Type of Instrument: Self-report questionnaire

Instrument Description: The FFAQ is a 42-item self-report measure developed to assess family functioning as perceived by adolescent children within the family. It is available with a manual containing instructions for administration and scoring. The measure is based on a model integrating family systems theory and developmental tasks of adolescence. It is designed to be particularly appropriate for use with adolescents in the final two or three years of secondary school. Responses are checked on a 4-point scale ranging from *almost always true* to *hardly ever true*. Individual item scores are summed to yield a total score and subscale scores on each of the six dimensions listed above. Each subscale contains 7 items. The scale was developed in Australia and has been used in studies in both Australia and South Africa.

Sample Items:

(A)   In our family, everyone helps with the chores.
(B)   I wonder if my parents really love me.
(C)   If you say something in our family, people ignore you.

Comments: The author reports that validity and reliability information is based on a sample of 413 Australian adolescents with a mean age of 15.7. The mean correlation between subscale totals and the items that compose them was .53, with a range of .34 to .76. However, a factor analysis reported by the author resulted in a single-factor solution. Correlations between subscales range from .76 to .89. Criterion validity was assessed by correlating scores on the FFAQ with those on the Erikson Psychosocial Stage Inventory (.46) and a second measure of adequacy of means-ends problem solving by adolescents in real-life situations (.33). Cronbach's alpha for the total scale is reported to be .90. Alpha for the individual subscales ranged from .40 to .79.

Reference:

Roelofse, R., & Middleton, M. R. (1985). The Family Functioning in Adolescence Questionnaire: A measure of psychosocial family health during adolescence. *J Adolescen, 8,* 33–45.

V-1/V-2/c

458. SKINNER, D. A., & McCUBBIN, H. I. Dual Employed Coping Scales (DECS)

Avail: 1987 Ref.

Variables Measured: Family coping behaviors when both spouses are employed

Type of Instrument: Self-report questionnaire

Instrument Description: The DECS is a 5-point, 58-item Likert-style questionnaire designed to identify and assess coping behaviors spouses find helpful in managing work and family roles when both partners are employed outside the home. Items are in the form of phrases indicating strategies used by the couple in dealing with the pressures of their situation.

Respondents indicate their level of agreement, from 1 = *strongly disagree* to 5 = *strongly agree*. Items were developed within five identified coping strategies: (1) maintaining, strengthening, and restructuring the family system—this focuses on coping behaviors utilized within the family system that are aimed at restructuring roles, family-related decision making, and maintaining the family system; (2) modifying conditions of work-family interface, defined as coping behaviors that attempt to accommodate work and family to each other; (3) managing psychological tensions and strains, which relates to individual behaviors that attend to personal needs and focus on reducing the perceived stress and demands of the present situation; (4) perceptually controlling the meaning of the life-style, which refers to maintained optimism and belief in the life-style; and (5) developing interpersonal relationships and procurement of support outside the family. Administration time is approximately 30 minutes.

Sample Items:

(A)   Becoming more efficient; making better use of my time "at home."
(B)   Believing that we have much to gain financially by our both working.
(C)   Working out a "fair" schedule of household tasks for all family members.

Comments: A factor analysis conducted by the authors resulted in the identification of four primary factors. Those factors (and their reported alpha coefficients) are (1) maintaining, strengthening and restructuring the family system (.72); (2) procurement of support (.74); (3) modifying roles and standards (.78); and (4) maintaining perspective, reducing tension (.76). The authors report that Cronbach's alpha for the overall DECS is .86. Intercorrelations between the factors ranged from .21 to .41. Husband-wife differences reported by the authors indicate that wives tend to have greater coping skills under dual-employment conditions than do their husbands. This difference was noted for each of the four identified factors.

Reference:

Skinner, D. A., & McCubbin, H. I. (1987). DECS: Dual Employed Coping Scales. In H. I. McCubbin & A. I. Thompson (Eds.), *Family assessment inventories for research and practice* (pp. 259–270). Madison: University of Wisconsin-Madison, Family Stress Coping and Health Project.

V-1/c
459. SKINNER, H. A., STEINHAUER, P. D., & SANTA-BARBARA, J. The Family Assessment Measure (FAM-III)

Avail: NAPS-3

Variables Measured: Family strengths and weaknesses

Type of Instrument: Self-report questionnaire

Instrument Description: The FAM-III is a 4-point Likert-style questionnaire composed of three separate rating scales, all of which assess various dimensions of family strengths and weaknesses. Each of the three scales, referred to as a general scale (50 items), a self-rating scale (42 items), and a dyadic relationship scale (42 items), examine seven specific areas of family functioning: task accomplishment, role performance, communication, affective expression, involvement, control, and values and norms. In addition, two response-style subscales, social desirability and denial, are included as part of the general scale. Each scale serves a distinct function: The general scale focuses on the family as a system; the dyadic relationship scale examines relationships between specific pairs; the self-rating scale taps the individual's perception of his or her functioning in the family. FAM is based on a process model of family functioning that integrates different approaches to family therapy and research. The instrument may be used as a clinical diagnostic tool, as a measure of therapy outcome, or as an instrument for basic research on family processes. Administration time is approximately 20–30 minutes.

Sample Items:

(A)   (From the General Scale) We spend too much time arguing what our problems are.

(B)   (From the Self-Rating Scale) I often don't understand what other family members are saying.

(C)   (From Dyadic Scale) This person worries too much about me.

Comments: The authors report reliability data (Cronbach's alpha) for each of the three scales for both adults and children: general scale (adults = .93, children = .94), dyadic relationship scale (adults = .95, children = .94), and self-rating scale (adults = .89, children = .86). Intercorrelations between the scales are reported to range from .25 to .82. Additional validity information on a total of 475 families is contained in the references listed below.

References:

Blackman, M., Pitcher, S., & Rauch, F. (1986). A preliminary outcome study of a community group treatment programme for emotionally disturbed adolescents. *Can J Psychi, 31,* 112–118.

Skinner, H. A., Santa-Barbara, J., & Steinhauer, P. D. (1983). The Family Assessment Measure. *Can J Comm Men Health, 2,* 91–105.

Steinhauer, P. D., Santa-Barbara, J., & Skinner, H. A. (1984a). Clinical applications of the process model of family functioning. *Can J Psychi, 29,* 98–111.

Steinhauer, P. D., Santa-Barbara, J., & Skinner, H. A. (1984b). The process model of family functioning. *Can J Psychi, 29,* 77–88.

V-1/c

460. SOURANI, T., & ANTONOVSKY, A. Family Adaptation Scale (FAS)

Avail: 1988 Ref.

Variables Measured: Satisfaction with the fit between family members and the family unit, and between the family unit and the community

Type of Instrument: Self-report questionnaire

Instrument Description: The FAS is a 7-point, 11-item semantic differential questionnaire. Two response extremes, corresponding to scores of 1 (*I'm not satisfied*) and 7 (*I'm completely satisfied*), were used for the first 10 items. Item 11 asks about overall adaptation and uses response anchors of *ideally adjusted family* and *a family which is not at all adjusted.* This scale was designed to measure the extent to which the individual expresses satisfaction with the way family members fit with each other and the family fits with its community. The questionnaire was developed for use in either interview or self-completion form. The original scale was written in Hebrew and used in Israel. An English translation is available in the source indicated above. Item scores are summed, with various methods of assessing overall family scores discussed in Antonovsky and Sourani (1988). Administration time is approximately 10–15 minutes.

Sample Items:

(A)   Are you satisfied in belonging to your family?

(B)   Are you satisfied with the family's way of life?

(C) Are you satisfied with the way the family relates to the wishes of all the family members.

Comments: The authors report that Cronbach's alpha for the FAS is approximately .87. Correlations between scores obtained by husbands and wives and ratings by a social worker are reported to be in the range of .51 to .55.

References:

Antonovsky, A. (1987). *Unraveling the mystery of health.* San Francisco: Jossey-Bass.
Antonovsky, A., & Sourani, T. (1988). Family sense of coherence and family adaptation. *J Mar Fam, 50,* 79–92.

V-1/c
461. TAVITIAN, M. L., LUBINER, J., GREEN, L. A., GREBSTGEIN, L. C., & VELICER, W. F. Family Functioning Scale (FFS)

Avail: 1987 Ref.

Variables Measured: Perceptions of one's family, including positive family affect, family communication, family conflicts, family worries, and family rituals

Type of Instrument: Self-report questionnaire

Instrument Description: The FFS is a five-dimensional scale designed to measure perceived family functioning. The currently available version contains 32 items. However, an expanded 42-item version is presently undergoing reliability and validity testing, and is expected to be available soon. The instrument provides a series of statements regarding family life and asks the individual to rate each statement as it applies to his or her family on a 7-point Likert-type scale ranging from *never* to *always.* The scale is intended for use with both clinical and nonclinical populations, and can be used as an initial screening device for dysfunctional families. Its initial development emphasized internal validation using typically nonclinical samples (e.g., college students), while recent studies have concentrated on external validation utilizing clinical groups (e.g., schizophrenics, alcohol-troubled individuals). Scoring is based on an additive sum of the items for each subscale, yielding independently derived scores for each of the above-named subscales. Administration time is approximately 10–15 minutes.

Sample Items:

(A) My family is proud of me.
(B) I tell people in my family when I am angry with them.
(C) People in my family argue about doing household chores.

Comments: Items were assigned to subscales based on a principal components factor analysis. Test-retest reliability of the FFS subscales over a four-week interval on 150 undergraduates is reported to range from .46 to .63. The authors further report that canonical correlation analysis indicated that 60% of the variance of the test can be predicted upon retest. Cronbach's alpha across several studies is reported to range from .72 to .93. Validity studies reported by the authors have included confirmatory factor analysis of the FFS with the Family Assessment Device (FAD) and the Family Adaptability and Cohesion Scales (FACES III). The FFS is also reported to have discriminated between two clinical groups (schizophrenics and alcohol-troubled individuals) and a nonclinical comparison group.

Reference:

Tavitian, M. L., Lubiner, J., Green, L., Grebstein, L. C., & Velicer, W. F. (1987). Dimensions of family functioning. *J Soc Behav Pers, 2,* 191–204.

V-1/c
462. VAN DER VEEN, F. Family Concept Test

Avail: NAPS-3

Variables Measured: Social and emotional aspects of the entire family unit

Type of Instrument: Q-sort or self-report instrument (two forms)

Instrument Description: The Family Concept Test is an 80-item inventory developed in the early 1960s and designed to assess socioemotional aspects of the family unit. Each item is descriptive of the entire family unit and not individual relationships within the family. The instrument exists in two forms: a Q-sort format and a 9-point Likert-type scale. The Q-sort presents the 80 items describing families on separate cards in random order. Respondents arrange the cards into nine piles ranging from *least like my family* to *most like my family,* with a specified number of cards in each pile. In the alternate form of the test, respondents are provided with a booklet containing all items and are asked to rate each item from 0 (*least like my family*) to 8 (*most like my family*). Respondents may also be asked to complete the test twice: once with respect to the real family and once with respect to the person's conception of the ideal family. Use of the Family Concept Test allows for the generation of several global measures, including family effectiveness, measuring overall adjustment; family satisfaction, calculated by correlating real and ideal family scores; and family congruence, represented by the extent of agreement between two family members. Additionally, factor analyses have yielded two underlying second-order factors labeled family integration and adaptive coping, and eight first-order factors (consideration versus conflict, family actualization or inadequacy, open communication, community sociability, family ambition, locus of control, togetherness/separateness, and family loyalty). One additional item set represented on several different factors is referred to as closeness versus estrangement.

Sample Items:

(A) We get along very well in the community.
(B) We are an affectionate family.
(C) We just cannot tell each other our real feelings.

Comments: The author reports test-retest reliability from several studies. For a clinic waiting list group of 50 parents administered the Q-sort, test-retest over three and a half months was reported to be .56 for real and .66 for ideal family concepts. Correlations among nonclinic parents over a 17-month span, and those of college students over a four-week period, were found to be .67 and .71, and .80 and .87 for real and ideal family concepts, respectively. Q-sort and inventory administrations are reported to correlate .95 for family effectiveness and .90 for family satisfaction. Further evidence of reliability, as well as considerable information regarding validity of the scale, are presented in the manual.

References:

Anderson, J. Z., & White, G. D. (1986). An empirical investigation of interaction and relationship patterns in functional and dysfunctional nuclear families and stepfamilies. *Fam Proc, 25,* 407–422.

Forman, B. D., & Hagan, B. J. (1984). Measures for evaluating total family functioning. *Fam Ther, 11,* 1–36.

Levant, R. F., & Doyle, G. F. (1983). An evaluation of a parent education program for fathers of school-aged children. *Fam Relat, 32,* 29–37.

van der Veen, F., & Novak, A. L. (1971). Perceived parental attitudes and family concepts of disturbed adolescents, normal siblings, and normal controls. *Fam Proc, 10,* 327–343.

V-1/c

463. WAMPLER, K. S., & HALVERSON, C. F., Jr. Georgia Family Q-Sort

Avail: 1989 Ref.

Variables Measured: Family cohesion, adaptability, communication, and competence and source of leadership within the family

Type of Instrument: Q-sort

Instrument Description: The Georgia Family Q-Sort is an observational measure of family functioning. It was designed to describe the interaction of a family in any setting doing any task. The Q-sort can be used to describe a brief interaction or patterns occurring over a longer period of time. Though designed for use by outside observers, family members could also use the Q-sort to describe their own perceptions of the family process. An optimal family proto-type is available for use in comparing a given family to the optimal prototype. The procedure consists of 43 items on cards that are sorted by an observer into nine stacks representing points along a dimension of salience. Items are forced into a seminormal distribution ranging from *least-like family* (three cards), *not-like the family much at all* (four cards), *not-like the family* (five cards), *a-little-not-like the family* (six cards), *neutral or not salient for this family* (seven cards), *a-little-like the family* (six cards), *like the family* (five cards), *very-much-like the family* (four cards), and *most-like the family* (three cards). The Q-sort procedure is accomplished in approximately 20 minutes following observation.

Sample Items:

(A)   Enjoy being together.
(B)   Child is not given autonomy.
(C)   Can't agree on how to accomplish task.

Comments: Using data from the first two years of a longitudinal study of intact families with a preschool child, the authors report interrater reliabilities ranging from .56 (year 1) to .77 (year 2). Mean internal consistency across both years for the subscales is reported to range from .54 to .84. Stabilities from year 1 to year 2 are reported to have ranged from -.01 for the chaotic subscale to .47 for negative affect and .50 for reserved.

Reference:

Wampler, K. S., Halverson, C. F., Moore, J. J., & Walters, L. H. (1989). The Georgia Family Q-Sort: An observational measure of family functioning. *Fam Proc, 28,* 1–16

V-2/III-2/b/P
464. ABIDIN, R. Parenting Stress Index (PSI)

Avail: Pediatric Psychology Press, 320 Terrell Road West, Charlottesville, VA 22901

Variables Measured: Stress experienced by parents as a result of their child's behavioral characteristics, parental personality characteristics, and stresses within the family environment; ability of the parent-child system to withstand stress; dysfunctional nature of the parent-child system

Type of Instrument: Self-report questionnaire

Instrument Description: The PSI was developed as a screening and diagnostic instrument for use with parents of children age 10 and below, with the primary focus being on the preschool child. It is a 101-item questionnaire to which parents respond on a 5-point Likert-type continuum ranging from *strongly agree* to *strongly disagree*. There is an additional optional 19-item Life Stress Scale that may also be administered. Administration time is 20–25 minutes. The scale helps clinicians identify components of the parent-child system that are dysfunctional or that represent stresses with which the parent is having difficulty coping. The PSI is scored by use of self-scoring answer sheets. The examiner adds the item weights to obtain a subscale score, and subsequently adds the subscale scores to obtain the domain and total scores.

Sample Items:

(A)   My child is so active that it exhausts me.
(B)   My child gets upset easily over the smallest thing.
(C)   Most of my life is spent doing things for my child.

Comments: The PSI comes with a comprehensive testing manual complete with validity and reliability information. To date over 50 research studies have been completed using the PSI. Factor analyses were used to support subscales and the division of the test into child and parent characteristic domains. Alpha and test-retest reliability scores are well within acceptable levels.

References:

Lafiosca, T., & Loyd, B. (1986). Defensiveness and the assessment of parental stress and anxiety. *J Clin Child Psych, 15,* 254–259.
Loyd, B. H., & Abidin, R. R. (1985). Revision of the parenting stress index. *J Ped Psych, 10,* 169–177.
Mash, E. J., & Johnston, C. (1983). The prediction of mother's behavior with their hyperactive children during play and task situations. *Child Fam Beh Ther, 5,* 1–14.
Webster-Stratton, C., & Hammond, M. (1988). Maternal depression and its relationship to life stress, perceptions of child behavior problems, parenting behaviors, and child conduct problems. *J Abn C Psy, 16,* 299–315.

V-2/IV-1/c
465. BOHEN, H. H., & VIVEROS-LONG, A. Job-Family Role Strain Scale

Avail: 1981 Ref.

Variables Measured: General concerns regarding the pressures of fulfilling both family and work roles

Type of Instrument: Self-report questionnaire

Instrument Description: The Job-Family Role Strain Scale is a 5-point, 19-item Likert-type questionnaire designed to assess role strain resulting from attempting to fulfill the demands of two sometimes competing roles: family person and worker. The scale was developed concurrently and as a companion instrument to the Job-Family Management Scale. Concepts at the foundation of the scale were developed from work by Komarovsky (1977), who postulated six modes or dimensions in which role conflicts cause tension or discomfort. Five of these modes served as the basis for the current instrument: (1) ambiguity about norms, (2) socially structured insufficiency of resources for role fulfillment, (3) low rewards for role conformity, (4) conflict between normative phenomena, and (5) overload of role obligations. From 3 to 6 items, each in the form of a statement, were developed for each mode. The items, both positive and stressful, are geared toward internalized values and emotions. Examples of such emotions include contentment, fulfillment, self-doubt, and worry. The response format is structured such that high scores indicate greater levels of role strain, with values for each mode and for the overall scale arrived at by summing the appropriate values from individual items.

Sample Items:

(A) My job keeps me away from my family too much.
(B) I worry that other people at work think my family interferes with my job.
(C) I feel more respected than I would if I didn't have a job.

Comments: Content validity was initially assessed by a panel of six judges. Cronbach's alpha was reported by the author to be .72. The scale has been modified and used in multiple forms by various authors. Modifications usually take the form of reducing the number of items.

References:

Bohen, H. H., & Viveros-Long, A. (1981). *Balancing jobs and family life: Do flexible work schedules help?* Philadelphia: Temple University Press.

Burden, D. S. (1986). Single parent and the work setting: The impact of multiple job and home life responsibilities. *Fam Relat, 35,* 37–43.

Katz, M. H., & Piotrkowski, C. S. (1983). Correlates of family role strain among employed Black women. *Fam Relat, 32,* 331–339.

Lewis, S. N. C., & Cooper, C. L. (1987). Stress in two-earner couples and stage in the life-cycle. *J Occup Psy, 60,* 289–303.

V-2/I-4/e

466. CALVERT, J. D., MOORE, D., & JENSEN, B. J. Dating Anxiety Survey (DAS)

Avail: 1987 Ref.

Variables Measured: Male and female dating anxiety as measured by passive contact, active intentions, and dating interactions

Type of Instrument: Self-report questionnaire

Instrument Description: The DAS contains separate forms for males and females. Each form contains 23 Likert-style items and utilizes a 7-point response option format. Available responses range from no anxiety to extreme anxiety. Three subareas are measured by this instrument: passive contact (7 items), active intentions for dating (8 items), and dating interactions (8 items). The passive contact subscale includes items dealing with heterosocial contact that is initiated by someone other than the respondent. The active intentions for dating subscale deals with situations initiated by the respondent. The dating interactions subscale deals with common situations encountered on dates. The scale was designed for use with college populations. Individual item responses within subscales are summed in order to arrive at three composite scores.

Sample Items:

(A)   Just being around a particularly good looking guy (girl).
(B)   Calling up a guy (girl) just to talk.
(C)   Kissing goodnight at the end of the date.

Comments: Division of the scale into three subscales resulted from a factor analysis of the total instrument. The author reports Cronbach's alpha for the three scales to range from .87 to .93 for males and from .90 to .92 for females. Correlations with dating history and measures of general social anxiety and heterosocial skills are reported by the authors to range from .30 to .50.

Reference:

Calvert, J. D., Moore, D., & Jensen, B. J. (1987). Psychometric evaluation of the Dating Anxiety Survey: A self-report questionnaire for the assessment of dating anxiety in males and females. *J Psychopat Beh Assess, 9,* 341–350.

V-2/III-2/c
467. FRIEDRICH, W. N., GREENBERG, M. T., & CRNIC, K. Questionnaire on Resources and Stress—Short Form (QRS-F)

Avail: 1983 Ref.

Variables Measured: Stress in families that care for developmentally delayed or mentally retarded children

Type of Instrument: Self-report questionnaire

Instrument Description: The QRS-F is a 52-item psychometrically determined version of the 285-item Questionnaire on Resources and Stress (QRS; Holroyd, 1974). Both scales are intended for use with families of handicapped children. In addition, a 66-item version of the scale, as reported by Holroyd, is also available. While the QRS-F is intended primarily for use in assessing families with handicapped children, Holroyd maintained that the original long and short versions of the QRS were also appropriate for use with families where one member was ill, presumably on a chronic basis. The QRS-F was developed following item analyses of 289 QRSs. Items found to be most reliable were factor analyzed, resulting in four factors: parent and family problems, pessimism, child characteristics, and physical incapacitation. As in the original instrument, items are responded to according to a *true/false* format.

Sample Items:

(A)   _____ doesn't communicate with others of his/her age group.
(B)   Other members of the family have to do without things because of _____.
(C)   Our family agrees on important matters.

Comments: The authors report that items for the QRS-F were selected in the following manner: Item-total correlations and KR-20 reliabilities were calculated for all content and lie items from the original scale (222 items); items that were retained each correlated at least .40 with total scores; when retained items were removed, scale means had to drop from .2 to .7;

and item responses had to successfully differentiate between parents of handicapped and nonhandicapped children. Following removal of unacceptable items, item-total correlations for the short form were found to range from .15 to .63. QRS-F and QRS scores were found to correlate .997. Interitem correlations were reported to range from .00 to .78, with a mean value of .26.

References:

Friedrich, W. N., Cohen, D. S., & Wilturner, L. S. (1987). Family relations and marital quality when a mentally handicapped child is present. *Psychol Rep, 61,* 911–919.

Friedrich, W. N., Greenberg, M. T., & Crnic, K. (1983). A short-form of the Questionnaire on Resources and Stress. *Am J Ment D, 88,* 41–48.

Friedrich, W. N., Wilturner, L. T., & Cohen, D. (1985). Coping resources and parenting mentally retarded children. *Am J Ment D, 90,* 130–139.

Holroyd, J. (1974). The Questionnaire on Resources and Stress: An instrument to measure family response to a handicapped family member. *J Comm Psyc, 2,* 92–94.

V-2/III-2/g/P

468. HOCK, E., GNEZDA, T., & McBRIDE, S. The Maternal Separation Anxiety Scale (MSAS)

Avail: 1989 Ref.

Variables Measured: Maternal attitudes, feelings, and beliefs regarding routine and brief separations from their young children

Type of Instrument: Self-report questionnaire

Instrument Description: The MSAS is a 5-point, 35-item Likert-style questionnaire designed to assess mothers' reactions to brief and routine separations from their children. Items are in the form of statements, with response options (scored 1–5) ranging from *strongly disagree* to *strongly agree.* The instrument is composed of three subscales, determined through use of factor analysis. The subscales, consisting of 21, 7, and 7 items, respectively, are intended to measure: (1) maternal separation anxiety, reflecting aspects of maternal anxiety and feelings of guilt resulting from or in anticipation of leaving the child, as well as anxiety expressed regarding the importance of exclusive maternal care; (2) separation promotes sociability and independence, including items related to the child's ability to adapt to and profit from nonmaternal care; and (3) employment-related separation, with items asking mothers to indicate their level of concern regarding leaving their children, plus their concerns with the maternal role and interests they have in pursuing a work-related identity. Scoring is accomplished by summing values associated with responses within subscales. In order to ensure that subscale scores are comparable, when scoring the 21-item first factor, the sum of item scores is divided by three. An overall separation anxiety score can be derived by summing subscale scores and dividing by three.

Sample Items:

(A) I miss holding or cuddling my child when I am away from him/her.
(B) My life wouldn't be complete without a career.
(C) If a child is independent and outgoing, he/she will make friends easily without his/her mother's help.

Comments: The authors indicate that Cronbach's alpha for the three subscales was .90, .71, and .79, respectively. In addition, stability coefficients for the summed items of each factor and the total MSAS were reported to be .73, .58, and .72, respectively, for the three factors, and .75 for the total MSAS. Validity was examined by comparing the MSAS with the Emotional Status Index and with the Maternal Separation Interview.

References:

DeMeis, D. K., Hock, E., & McBride, S. L. (1986). The balance of employment and mother-hood: Longitudinal study of mothers' feelings about separation from their first-born infants. *Devel Psych, 22,* 627–632.

Hock, E., McBride, S., & Gnezda, M. T. (1989). Maternal separation anxiety: Mother-infant separation from the maternal perspective. *Child Dev, 60,* 793–802.

V-2/d
469. HOLROYD, J. Questionnaire on Resources and Stress for Families with Chronically Ill or Handicapped Members (QRS)

Avail: Clinical Psychology Publishing Co., Inc., 4 Conant Square, Brandon VT 05733

Variables Measured: Stress in families that care for relatives who are ill or disabled

Type of Instrument: Self-report questionnaire

Instrument Description: The QRS is a 285-item *true-false* questionnaire requiring approximately one hour to complete. It comes with a manual, test booklets, answer and profile sheets, and scoring templates. A short form (66 items) is also commercially available. The scale is designed to measure stress in families who are caring for chronically ill or handicapped family members. The scale is administered to any member of the family other than the identified patient. There are 15 subscales covering three domains: personal problems for the respondent, family problems, and problems for the index case. The short form contains 11 subscales and is based on a factor analysis of the long version of the test. Computer scoring is available.

Sample Items:

(A) _____ demands that others do things for him/her more than is necessary.
(B) _____ can get around the neighborhood quite easily.
(C) I have given up things I have really wanted to do in order to care for _____.

Comments: The author reports that extensive validity and reliability information is available in the test manual. Nearly all validation research has examined child and adolescent patient populations. A few studies are reported in which the QRS has been used to evaluate family stress before and after various treatments. KR-20 reliability is reported by the author to be .96 for the overall 285-item scale, yielding an average interitem correlation of .078. KR-20 for the short version is reported to be between .79 and .85.

References:

Friedrich, W. N., Greenberg, M. T., & Crnic, K. (1983). A short-form of the Questionnaire on Resources and Stress. *Am J Ment D, 88,* 41–48.

Holroyd, J. (1974). The Questionnaire on Resources and Stress: An instrument to measure family response to a handicapped family member. *J Comm Psyc, 2,* 92–94.

Holroyd, J. (1988). A review of criterion validation research on the Questionnaire on Resources and Stress for Families with Chronically Ill or Handicapped Members. *J Clin Psy, 44,* 335–354.

Holroyd, J., & Guthrie, D. (1986). Family stress with chronic childhood illness: Cystic fibro-sis, neuromuscular disease, and renal disease. *J Clin Psy, 42,* 552–561.

V-2/c
470. KANNER, A. D., COYNE, J. C., SCHAEFER, C., & LAZARUS, R. S. Hassles Scale

Avail: 1981 Ref.

Variables Measured: Frequency and intensity of hassles with regard to family, work, economic, practical, health, and environmental settings

Type of Instrument: Self-report questionnaire

Instrument Description: The Hassles Scale is a 117-item self-report index of daily stress in people's lives. Administration time is approximately 10–15 minutes. The instrument contains subscales assessing hassles in each of the above-listed areas. Respondents are presented with a list of hassles from which they indicate which hassles have occurred in their lives within the past month. Hassles that have occurred are rated on a 3-point scale according to their level of severity (*somewhat, moderately,* or *extremely*). Two scores are generated: A frequency measure is generated by counting the number of items receiving responses. An intensity measure is calculated by summing the scores assigned and dividing by the frequency measure. The scale is intended for adults. Scores for each subscale are calculated independently. Therefore, the level of family stress can be assessed separately from the other subscales.

Sample Items:

(A)   Problems with your children.
(B)   Problems with your lover.
(C)   Overloaded with family responsibilities.

Comments: The entire 117-item scale is contained in the 1981 reference listed below. The 10 items used to form the family subscale are listed as numbers 7, 20, 55, 58, 73, 74, 76, 78, 87, and 104. (Note: There is no indication in that article as to which items form the family subscale.) The authors report that Cronbach's alpha for the entire scale is approximately .90, indicating an average interitem correlation of approximately .074. A study conducted by the authors is reported in which 100 adults aged 45 to 64 were administered the Hassles Scale monthly for nine months. The average test-retest reliability was reported as .79 for the frequency score and .48 for intensity.

References:

DeLongis, A., Coyne, J. C., Dakof, G., Folkman, S., & Lazarus, R. S. (1982). Relationship of daily hassles, uplifts, and major life events to health status. *Health Psyc, 1,* 119–136.
Kanner, A. D., Coyne, J. C., Schaefer, C., & Lazarus, R. S. (1981). Comparison of two modes of stress management: Daily hassles versus major life events. *J Behav Med, 4,* 1–39.
Reich, W. P., Parrella, D. P., & Filstead, W. J. (1988). Unconfounding the Hassles Scale: External sources versus internal responses to stress. *J Behav Med, 11,* 239–249.
Zarski, J. J. (1984). Hassles and health: A replication. *Health Psyc, 3,* 243–251.

V-2/c
471. KOCH, A. Family Adaptation to Medical Stressors (FAMS)

Avail: NAPS-3

Variables Measured: Impact of stress associated with illness on the family members, interactions, and the family system

Type of Instrument: Questionnaire and interview protocol

Instrument Description: The FAMS is a 158-item interview schedule designed to assess families' reactions to medically related stress. Items vary in format and include checklists, Likert-type and *yes-no* items, direct response (e.g., "At which hospital is the patient in treatment?"), and open-ended questions. A total of six subscale scores are computed from 47 of the items, including (1) increased negative emotions, (2) illness anxiety, (3) depression, (4) trust, (5) rules prohibiting emotional expression, and (6) role flexibility. Scores from subscales 1–4 and 5–6 are summed to arrive at second-order FAMS scores, labeled "resources" (FAMS-R) and "outcomes" (FAM-O). Interviews are conducted with the entire family, with family members asked to come to a consensus on many items. Interviews last approximately 45–60 minutes. An alternate 47-item form of the FAMS may be administered as a paper-and-pencil instrument. The same constructs are assessed with either form.

Sample Items:

(A)   Has support or comfort family members give one another changed?
(B)   Do family members believe they can trust most people to do what they say they will do?
(C)   Has anyone's eating habits changed?

Comments: The author reports that interrater reliability for interview responses to the 47 items from which subscores are derived was .99. Test-retest reliability for 10 families over four weeks was found to be .85. Test-retest reliability for one family from this sample that experienced severe medically related stress was calculated to be .69. Cronbach's alpha for the entire FAMS is reported to be .75. Results of a factor analysis reported by the author indicate that items load from .41 to .69 on their primary factors. Secondary factor loadings are not reported. A total of 30 of the 47 FAMS items were determined to belong to one of the identified factors. The correlations between total recent stressors and the six identified factors are reported to be -.07 (trust), .28 (role flexibility), .34 (depression), .39 (illness anxiety), .39 (rules prohibiting emoting), and .41 (increased emotion).

References:

Koch, A. Y. (1983). Family adaptation to medical stressors. *Fam Sys Med, 1,* 78–87.
Koch, A. (1985). A strategy for prevention: Role flexibility and affective reactivity as factors in family coping. *Fam Sys Med, 3,* 70–81.
Koch-Hattem, A., Hattem, D. M., & Plummer, L. P. (1987). The role of mental-health resources in explaining family adaptation to stress: A preliminary analysis. *Fam Sys Med, 5,* 206–219.
Plummer, L. P., & Koch-Hattem, A. (1986). Family stress and adjustment to divorce. *Fam Relat, 35,* 523–529.

V-2/c/e
472. McCUBBIN, H. I. Family Coping Inventory (FCI)

Avail: 1987 Ref.

Variables Measured: Spouses' strategies for coping with permanent, extended, or repeated family separations

Type of Instrument: Self-report questionnaire

Instrument Description: The FCI is a 4-point, 70-item Likert-type questionnaire designed to assess behaviors by which spouses cope when faced with separation from their marriage partners. Items are in the form of phrases, to which respondents indicate how much each strategy helps in coping with the separation. Responses range from *not helpful* (scored 0) to *very helpful* (scored 3). Scoring instructions differ depending on the type of separation experienced by the respondent. Long-term separations are scored according to five dimensions, each containing from 4 to 6 items: (1) maintaining family integrity, (2) developing interpersonal relationships and social support, (3) managing psychological tension and strain, (4) believing in the value of spouse's profession and maintaining an optimistic definition of the situation, and (5) developing self-reliance and self-esteem. Short-term but recurring separations are classified within three categories, each containing 3 items: (1) fitting into corporate life-style, (2) developing self and interpersonal relationships, and (3) establishing independence and self-sufficiency. Coping strategies for the final type of separation, divorce, are assessed along five dimensions, containing from 5 to 18 items each: (1) developing self and self-esteem and establishing independence; (2) involvement in tension-releasing social and routine activities and contacts with relatives; (3) investing in children and maintaining family stability; (4) maintaining social support through religious and social activities; and (5) expressing feelings and seeking understanding through personal and professional relationships.

Sample Items:

(A) Talking with other individuals in my same situation.
(B) Believing that the institutions that my spouse and I work for have my family's best interest in mind.
(C) Going shopping with the children or by myself.

Comments: The author reports that Cronbach's alpha for various subscales within the three primary dimensions ranges from .71 to .86. Various coping strategies are reported to correlate from .16 to .28 with a measure of androgynous gender-role orientation. An adaptation of the FCI, the Coping Strategies and Resources Inventory (Berman & Turk, 1981), has been developed for use with divorced individuals.

References:

Berman, W. H., & Turk, D. (1981). Adaptation to divorce: Problems and coping strategies. *J Mar Fam, 43,* 179–189.
Lowenstein, A. (1986). Temporary single parenthood: The case of prisoner's families. *Fam Relat, 35,* 79–85.
McCubbin, H. I. (1987). FCI: Family Coping Inventory. In H. I. McCubbin & A. I. Thompson (Eds.), *Family assessment inventories for research and practice* (pp. 211–224). Madison: University of Wisconsin-Madison, Family Stress Coping and Health Project.
McCubbin, H. I., Dahl, B. B., Lester, G. R., Benson, D., & Robertson, M. L. (1976). Coping repertoires of families adapting to prolonged war-induced separation. *J Mar Fam, 38,* 461–471.

V-2/I-3/c/e
473. McCUBBIN, H. I., OLSON, D. H., & LARSEN, A. S. Family Crisis Orientated Personal Evaluation Scales (F-COPES)

Avail: 1987 Ref.

Variables Measured: Use of family versus other resources in coping with crises within the family

Type of Instrument: Self-report questionnaire

Instrument Description: The F-COPES inventory is a 5-point, 30-item Likert-type questionnaire designed to identify problem-solving and behavioral strategies utilized by families in difficult or problematic situations. Coping strategies are examined in terms of reliance both on resources available within and on those external to the immediate family. Items are in the form of phrases describing behavioral strategies. Response options range from *strongly disagree* to *strongly agree,* and are scored 1–5. The item pool was reduced from 49 to 30 items based on results of a preliminary factor analysis. Items are grouped into three internal and five external coping strategies. Internal coping patterns are identified as (1) confidence in problem solving, (2) reframing family problems, and (3) family passivity. External strategies include (1) church or religious resources, (2) extended family, (3) friends, (4) neighbors, and (5) community resources. Each factor contains either three or four items. A second factor analysis resulted in the identification of five primary factors, each containing from 4 to 9 items. This second factor analysis also resulted in the elimination of one additional item. Details regarding the factor studies are presented in McCubbin, Olson, and Larsen (1987). Summed scores are obtained within each category and for the instrument as a whole. Administration time is estimated to be 20 minutes.

Sample Items:

(A)   Sharing our difficulties with relatives.
(B)   Seeking encouragement and support from friends.
(C)   Seeking information and advice from persons in other families who have faced the same or similar problems.

Comments: Cronbach's alpha is reported to range from .64 to .84 for factors within the five-factor solution, with an overall F-COPES alpha of approximately .86. Test-retest reliability over a period of four weeks is reported to be .81 for the combined scale and to range from .61 to .95 for individual factors.

References:

Marotz-Baden, R., & Colvin, P. L. (1986). Coping strategies: A rural-urban comparison. *Fam Relat, 35,* 281–288.
McCubbin, H. I., Olson, D. H., & Larsen, A. S. (1987). F-COPES: Family Crisis Oriented Personal Evaluation Scales. In H. I. McCubbin & A. I. Thompson (Eds.), *Family assessment inventories for research and practice* (pp. 259–270). Madison: University of Wisconsin-Madison, Family Stress Coping and Health Project.
Patterson, J. M., & McCubbin, H. I. (1984). Gender roles and coping. *J Mar Fam, 46,* 95–104.
Ventura, J. N., & Boss, P. G. (1983). The Family Coping Inventory applied to parents with new babies. *J Mar Fam, 45,* 867–875.

V-2/V-1/c/e
474. McCUBBIN, H. I., & PATTERSON, J. M. Family Inventory of Life Events and Changes (FILE)

Avail: 1987 Ref.

Variables Measured: Stresses and strains experienced by the family with respect to traumatic events, changing circumstances, and role identities

Type of Instrument: Self-report questionnaire

Instrument Description: This instrument is a 71-item questionnaire, utilizing a *yes-no* response format, designed to record life events and changes encountered by the family during the past 12 months. Each item is worded to reflect a change of sufficient magnitude to require some adjustment in the regular pattern of interaction of family members. The emphasis is on change, which may be either positive or negative. FILE may be scored in five ways, depending upon the purpose and ultimate use of the statistical information in research and/or counseling: (1) family life events score, (2) family-couple life events score, (3) family-couple discrepancy scores, (4) family readjustment score, and (5) family-couple readjustment score. In each scoring procedure, the instrument may be completed by adult family members, either independently or together. Standardized family weights have been assigned to each item for the two readjustment scores. Weights indicate the relative "stressfulness" of items, that is, the degree of social readjustment an average family will make in its usual pattern of life as a result of experiencing each event or strain. Events are contained within nine general categories: (1) intrafamily strains, (2) marital strains, (3) pregnancy and childbearing strains, (4) financial and business strains, (5) work-family transitions and strains, (6) illness and family "care" strains, (7) losses, (8) transitions "in and out," and (9) legal. Several categories have subareas contained within them. Administration time is approximately 40 minutes.

Sample Items:

(A)   Increase of husband/father's time away from family.
(B)   Took out a loan or refinanced a loan to cover increased expenses.
(C)   Parent/spouse became seriously ill or injured.

Comments: The authors report that Cronbach's alpha for the overall scale ranges from .72 to .81. Test-retest reliability for the individual subscales, as well as the overall instrument, is reported to range from .66 to .84. Percentage agreement for individual items between the two test administrations ranged from .72 to .77. Total FILE scores were correlated with the Family Environment Scales (Moos, 1974): dimensions of cohesion (-.24), independence (-.16), organization (-.14), and conflict (.23).

References:

McCubbin, H. I., & Patterson, J. M. (1987). FILE: Family Inventory of Life Events and Changes. In H. I. McCubbin & A. I. Thompson (Eds.), *Family assessment inventories for research and practice* (pp. 81–98). Madison: University of Wisconsin-Madison, Family Stress Coping and Health Project.
Patterson, J. M. (1985). Critical factors affecting family compliance with home treatment for children with cystic fibrosis. *Fam Relat, 34,* 79–89.
Patterson, J. M., & McCubbin, H. I. (1983). The impact of family life events and changes on the health of a chronically ill child. *Fam Relat, 32,* 255–264.
Plummer, L. P., & Koch-Hattem, A. (1986). Family stress and adjustment to divorce. *Fam Relat, 35,* 523–529.

V-2/b/P
475. McCUBBIN, M. A. Coping Health Inventory for Parents (CHIP)

Avail: 1987 Ref.

Variables Measured: Methods used by parents in attempting to cope with a serious illness afflicting one of their children

Type of Instrument: Self-report questionnaire

Instrument Description: The CHIP is a 4-point, 45-item Likert-type questionnaire designed to assess coping strategies employed by parents when serious or chronic illness strikes one of their children. Items are in the form of phrases describing behavioral or emotional strategies and are responded to in terms of how helpful respondents have found each to be (from 3 = *extremely helpful* to 0 = *not helpful*). Two additional options are presented as explanations for those coping strategies that have not been employed: *chose not to* and *not possible*. Three factors, referred to as coping patterns, have been identified within this instrument: (1) family integration, cooperation, and an optimistic definition of the situation (FAM), which focuses on strengthening family life and relationships, as well as the parent's outlook on life with a chronically ill child; (2) maintaining social support, self-esteem, and psychological stability (SUP), which involves parental efforts to develop relationships with others, to engage in activities that enhance feelings of individual identity and self-worth, and behaviors where the intention is to manage psychological tensions and pressures; and (3) understanding the health care situation through communication with other parents and consultation with the health care team (MED), which reflects parental relationships with both health care professionals and other parents of chronically ill children. These behaviors include developing a further knowledge and understanding of the illness and mastering any home care treatments and prescribed medical regimens. Only coping strategies utilized by parents are included in subscale scores. Scores are derived by summing values associated with response options for items within subscales. Thus each subscale score is a summation determined by all positive responses rather than an average of those positive responses given.

Sample Items:

(A)   Trying to maintain family stability.
(B)   Trusting my spouse (or former spouse) to help support me and my child(ren).
(C)   Working outside employment.

Comments: The author indicates that loadings of items on their primary factors ranged from .48 to .74. It is also reported that both mothers and fathers tend to have higher scores for all three coping strategies when they belong to what is termed "high conflict" rather than "low conflict" families. In a study reported by the author and her colleagues involving families with a child suffering from cystic fibrosis, it was found that maternal FAM scores were correlated .20 with children's height/weight indexes, that maternal SUP scores correlated .23 with changes in pulmonary functioning, and that fathers' SUP scores were correlated .22 with height/weight and .31 with pulmonary functioning.

References:

McCubbin, M. A. (1987). CHIP: Coping Health Inventory for Parents. In H. I. McCubbin & A. I. Thompson (Eds.), *Family assessment inventories for research and practice* (pp. 175–192). Madison, WI: University of Wisconsin-Madison, Family Stress Coping and Health Project.
McCubbin, H. I., McCubbin, M. A., Patterson, J. M., Cauble, E., Wilson, L. R., & Warwick, W. (1983). CHIP—Coping Health Inventory for Parents: An assessment of parental coping patterns in the care of the chronically ill child. *J Mar Fam, 45,* 359–370.
Patterson, J. M. (1985). Critical factors affecting family compliance with home treatment for children with cystic fibrosis. *Fam Relat, 34,* 79–89.
Powers, G. M., Gaudet, L. M., & Powers, S. (1986). Coping patterns of parents of chronically ill children. *Psychol Rep, 59,* 519–522.

V-2/g/d
476. MONTGOMERY, R. J. V., GONYEA, J. G., & HOOYMAN, N. R.
Measurement of Burden

Avail: 1985 Ref.

Variables Measured: Relationship between caring for an elderly relative and subjective and objective burden

Type of Instrument: Self-report questionnaire

Instrument Description: The Measurement of Burden is a two-part questionnaire designed to measure (1) perceptions of decreased time, personal freedom, and other objective indexes of expenses associated with caring for an elderly relative, and (2) feelings recognized by respondents as a result of the burden of caring for an elderly relative. The first index is referred to as the measurement of objective burden, while the second is called the measurement of subjective burden. Both scales are Likert-type and utilize 5-point rating scales. Both scales can be used as paper-and-pencil measures but were utilized as questionnaires by the authors during the course of a 45-minute interview. The objective scale asks respondents to indicate, relatively, how much of each resource they currently have compared with the time prior to caring for the elderly relative. Rating options include *a lot more (better), a little more (better), the same, a little less (worse),* and *a lot less (worse).* Options on the subjective questionnaire ask respondents to indicate how often they experience each feeling, ranging from *rarely or never* to *most of the time.* Scores on the two scales are computed and evaluated independently. Items used to assess objective burden were derived from studies of the effects that caring for others generally has on caregivers' lives. The subjective burden questionnaire was derived from an earlier 29-item instrument by Zarit, Reever, and Bach-Peterson (1980).

Sample Items:

(Objective burden)

(A)   Amount of time you have to yourself.
(B)   Amount of privacy you have.
(C)   Your relationships with other family members.

(Subjective burden)

(A)   I feel it is painful to watch my (relative) age.
(B)   I feel useful in my relationship with my (relative).
(C)   I feel afraid for what the future holds for my (relative).

Comments: The authors report that Cronbach's alpha for the objective and subjective scales was found to be .85 and .86, respectively. Objective and subjective burden were reported to be correlated .34. Multiple regression analysis was used to exam the relationship of burden to various demographic variables and caregiving tasks. Subjective burden was found to be related to income ($r = .35$, Beta $= .31$) and age ($r = -.32$, Beta $= -.28$). Objective burden was most related to Type 7 tasks (walking, providing transportation, and running errands) ($r = .42$, Beta $= .35$), Type 2 tasks (providing nursing care, bathing, and dressing) ($r = .42$, Beta $= .34$), and number of others who assist ($r = -.19$, Beta $= -.24$).

Reference:

Montgomery, R. J. V., Gonyea, J. G., & Hooyman, N. R. (1985). Caregiving and the experience of subjective and objective burden. *Fam Relat, 34,* 19–26.

V-2/II-3/a
477. PETERSON, D. R. Interaction Records

Avail: NAPS-3

Variables Measured: Conflict, stress, support, and enjoyment dimensions of significant interactions between marital couples

Type of Instrument: Coding scheme for interpreting narrative accounts of interactions

Instrument Description: Participants are asked to provide immediate, independent, narrative accounts of interactions that occur in their daily lives. They are asked to indicate the conditions under which each interaction took place, how it started, what happened then, and how it came out. Each episode is independently coded according to expressions of affection, anger, distress, and calm. The author reports that accounts are diverse in content and subtlety but typically appear authentic and revealing. Writing time per episode ranges from a few minutes to an hour. Complex coding requires about 30 minutes per episode. Simplified coding procedures are available and generally shorten coding time to about 5 minutes for most episodes. Although the coding scheme is described in the references below, specific coding procedures are detailed in the manual (available through NAPS-3).

Sample Items:

(A) *The conditions under which the exchange took place.* Where and when did it happen? Were there any special conditions that influenced what happened between you?

(B) *How the interaction started.* Who made the first move? What did that person say or do?

(C) *What happened then.* Please write a fairly detailed description of the exchange from start to finish. Who did and said what to whom? What were you thinking and feeling as the action went on? What ideas and emotions did your partner seem to have? How did it all come out? Begin the account here and continue on the other side as necessary.

Comments: The author reports that interjudge agreements for major categories of affect show kappa values in the .70s. Studies have investigated the ability of the instrument to discriminate between disturbed, average, and satisfied married couples. Patterns of expression and reciprocity in constructive and destructive marital conflicts have also been investigated.

References:

Peterson, D. R. (1979a). Assessing interpersonal relationships by means of interaction records. *Behav Assess, 1,* 221–236.

Peterson, D. R. (1979b). Assessing interpersonal relationships in natural settings. *New Directions for Methodology of Behavioral Science, 2,* 33–54.

Peterson, D. R. (1982). Functional analysis of interpersonal behavior. In J. C. Anchin & D. J. Kiesler (Eds.), *Handbook of interpersonal psychotherapy.* New York: Pergamon.

V-2/d
478. ROBINSON, B. C. Caregiver Strain Index (CSI)

Avail: 1983 Ref.

Variables Measured: Areas of difficulty faced by caretakers of the elderly following hospitalization for hip surgery

Type of Instrument: Self-report questionnaire

Instrument Description: The CSI is a 13-item questionnaire designed to evaluate levels of stress faced by caregivers of temporarily incapacitated elderly family members, friends, or neighbors. Responses are given in a *yes-no* and follow-up format. Items are administered as part of an interview, with respondents requested to give examples of incidents fitting each category where they indicate that there has been a problem. Thus both a quantitative measure (*yes* = 1; *no* = 0) and qualitative information regarding areas of stress are recorded. For all but one item (financial strain), examples are given along with the simple statement of the type of difficulty. Items were generated from earlier interviews with adult children in which questions were asked regarding difficulties experienced in the care of elderly parents. Ten stressors present in the current questionnaire resulted from an examination of these interview data. A review of the literature generated an additional 3 items. One additional open-ended item was initially included in which respondents were asked to indicate if there were any "other" stressors. This item was dropped from the questionnaire when it was discovered that positive responses to it were of too low a frequency to justify its continued inclusion. The questionnaire is intended to yield an overall index of strain determined by counting the number of items to which the respondent answers *yes*.

Sample Items:

(A) Sleep is disturbed (e.g., because _____ is in and out of bed or wanders around at night).

(B) It is inconvenient (e.g., because helping takes so much time or it's a long drive over to help).

(C) It is a physical strain (e.g., because of lifting in and out of a chair; effort or concentration is required).

Comments: The author reports that Cronbach's alpha for the 13-item scale is .86. The relationship of caregiver strain and several patient characteristics were examined. Correlations with the CSI reported by the author include anxiety of the elderly person (.31), performance of daily living activities by the elderly person (-.46), mental impairment of the elderly person (.39), and satisfaction with one's medical progress (-.28).

Reference:

Robinson, B. C. (1983). Validation of a caregiver strain index. *J Gerontol, 38,* 344–348.

V-2/III-2/II-5/b/g/P
479. SCHAEFER, E. S., & MANHEIMER, H. Dimensions of Perinatal Adjustment

Avail: NAPS-3

Variables Measured: Maternal attitudes and adjustment, and pre- and postnatal infant health issues

Type of Instrument: Self-report questionnaire

Instrument Description: The Dimensions of Perinatal Adjustment is a group of several questionnaires that may be used either independently or in combination. Various portions of the overall inventory measure maternal and infant health, psychosomatic reactions to pregnancy, and psychological stressors resulting from the pregnancy. The inventory was first reported in 1960 and has been used extensively since. The combined instrument uses *true/false,* Likert-type, and *yes-no* options, with individual response formats often tailored to the requirements of the question. Research using the inventory has rarely included all scales. Instead, individual portions have been used independently, as dictated by research questions and needs. The scales are available as a group and are organized as follows:

Postnatal Research Inventory:
A. The mother's health inventory since delivery
B. The baby's health inventory
C. Postpartum research inventory (20 subscales)

           Pregnancy Research Questionnaire (also referred to as Pregnancy Research Inventory)

1.   Psychosomatic reactions to pregnancy
   A. demographics
   B. health problems during this pregnancy
   C. health problems before this pregnancy
   D. problems of menstruation
   E. reactions to anxiety and interpersonal conflict
2.   Psychological reactions to pregnancy (contains 7 scales: maternal feeling, dependency, irritability and tension, depression and withdrawal, fears for baby, lack of desire for pregnancy, and fears for self)

Sample Items:

(A)   (Mother's Health) Has the experience of childbirth limited the amount of work you can do?
(B)   (Baby's Health) Wants to eat very often.
(C)   (Postpartum Research Inventory) The experience of having a baby has made me a happier person.
(D)   (Health Problems During Pregnancy) Do you have trouble getting to sleep or staying asleep?
(E)   (Health Problems Before Pregnancy) Were you troubled by headaches?
(F)   (Problems of Menstruation) Did you feel tired?
(G)   (Reactions to Anxiety) Count number of symptoms underlined.
(H)   (Psychological Reactions) Before pregnancy, I had been looking forward to having a baby.

Comments: In their initial report of the inventory, the authors indicated that Cronbach's alpha for six dimensions of psychological reactions to pregnancy (all but maternal feeling) ranged from .67 to .94. They also indicated reliability coefficients for psychosomatic anxiety symptoms before (.87) and during (.88) pregnancy and for symptoms at menstruation (.88). Other authors have reported reliability and validity information on various portions of the overall instrument. Details can be found in the references listed below.

References:

Egeland, B., & Farber, E. A. (1984). Infant-mother attachment: Factors related to its development and changes over time. *Child Dev, 55*, 753–771.

Erickson, M. T. (1976). The influence of health factors on psychological variables predicting complications of pregnancy, labor and delivery. *J Psychosom, 20*, 21–24.

Klusman, L. E. (1975). Reduction of pain in childbirth by the alleviation of anxiety during pregnancy. *J Cons Clin, 43*, 162–165.

Wright, B. M., & Zucker, R. A. (1980). Parental responses to competence and trauma in infants with reproductive casualty. *J Abn C Psy, 8*, 385–395.

Yang, R. K., Zweig, A. R., Douthitt, T. C., & Federman, E. (1976). Successive relationships between maternal attitudes during pregnancy, analgesic medication during labor and delivery, and newborn behavior. *Devel Psych, 12*, 6–14.

V-2/III-2/b/P

480. SMALL, S. Parental Stress Scale

Avail: NAPS-3

Variables Measured: Stress in one's role as a parent of a specific child

Type of Instrument: Self-report questionnaire

Instrument Description: This 9-item instrument was developed for use with parents of preadolescents and adolescents. There are four response categories ranging from *very* to *not at all*. An overall composite score is obtained by summing the scores across items. This instrument was designed to tap the psychological stress or emotional upset that an individual experiences in his or her role as a parent of a specific child. The measure was modeled after the parental stress measure developed by Pearlin and Schooler (1978).

Sample Items:

(A) When you think of your current experiences as the parent of this child, do you feel bothered or upset?
(B) When you think of your current experiences as the parent of this child, do you feel frustrated?
(C) When you think of your current experiences as the parent of this child, do you feel successful?

Comments: The author indicates that Cronbach's alpha for this instrument is .89. The correlation between the Parental Stress Scale and a measure of parental worry and concern about the child's behavior is reported to be .62. Item-total correlations for 8 of the items are reported to range from .60 to .75. The final item (" . . . unsure of yourself?") is reported to correlate .49 with the total scale.

Reference:

Savin-Williams, R. C., & Small, S. A. (1986). The timing of puberty and its relationship to adolescent and parent perceptions of family interactions. *Devel Psych, 22,* 343–347.

V-2/IV-1/g/W
481. VAN METER, M. J. S. Role Strain Scale

Avail: NAPS-3

Variables Measured: Potential stress areas and conscious use of coping techniques for the alleviation of stress among married college women

Type of Instrument: Self-report instrument

Instrument Description: The Role Strain Scale is a 6-point, 20-item Likert-style instrument developed to assess married college women in the potentially conflictual roles of family and school. Items measure attitudes as well as behavioral coping strategies. The measure was designed to be self-administered as part of a mailed questionnaire. Respondents indicate their level of agreement with each item along a continuum from *strongly disagree* to *strongly agree.* Eight items are reverse-scored. Item scores are summed and averaged with higher scores indicative of greater levels of role strain. Administration time is estimated to be less than 10 minutes.

Sample Items:

(A) I felt under pressure in my other roles.
(B) I felt no guilt about pursuing my education and interests.
(C) The amount of work I had to do interfered with how well it got done.

Comments: The author reports that Cronbach's alpha for the Role Strain Scale is .82. According to the author, this instrument has also been related to health (r = -.41) and management skills (r = -.27) among married college women.

Reference:

Van Meter, J. J. S., & Agronow, S. J. (1982). The stress of multiple roles: The case for role strain among married college women. *Fam Relat, 31,* 131–138.

V-2/d
482. ZIMMERMAN, S. L. Adult Day Care: Its Coping Effects for Families of Primary Caregivers of Elderly Disabled Persons

Avail: NAPS-3

Variables Measured: Family stress and coping mechanisms when the family serves as primary caregiver of an elderly disabled person

Type of Instrument: Self-report questionnaire

Instrument Description: This instrument is a precoded, structured questionnaire containing 167 forced-choice and demographic items and six open-ended questions. Nearly all forced-choice items adhere to a Likert-type format allowing for answers on a 1 to 5 scale. Specific response options vary according to the nature of the item. Seven general areas are measured, including (1) family stress; (2) stress pileup or accumulation; (3) family resources, both community and family; (4) coping effects of adult day care as a resource; (5) change in families' capacity to cope with care of the older person; (6) perceptions and evaluations of resources; and (7) plans for the future, including placement of the elderly person out of the home. An overall index for family stress, coping, resources, and perception is obtained by summing and averaging the items composing each scale. Plans regarding placement of the elderly person out of the home in the future consists of a single item scaled 0 for *no* and 1 for *yes.* The questionnaire is intended to determine those factors contributing to the coping effects of adult day care for families of caregivers of elderly disabled persons and influences on their long-term care plans for these persons. The questionnaire is intended to be used in a telephone interview format. Administration time is approximately 30 minutes.

Sample Items:

(A)   To what extent has adult day care helped you and your family to keep up with household chores?

(B)   Before the elderly disabled member was in adult day care, to what extent were you able to attend to needs of other family members?

(C)   How has adult day care affected the way you feel about the older disabled person?

Comments: The author reports that scores of coping effects correlate .43 with evaluation scores of adult day care. This instrument represents an expansion of one developed at an earlier time by the author to assess the coping effects of a family subsidy program for families of severely mentally handicapped children. It is generally based on the Social Readjustment Rating Scale (Holmes & Rahe, 1967) and another scale developed by McCubbin and Patterson (1981) designed to evaluate family resources for coping with stress.

References:

Zimmerman, S. L. (1986). Adult day care: Correlates of its coping effects for family of an elderly disabled member. *Fam Relat, 35,* 305–311.

Zimmerman, S. L. (1988). Containing the cost of care for elderly disabled family members as a case of implicit family policy: From a family stress perspective. In S. L. Zimmerman, *Understanding family policy.* Newbury Park, CA: Sage.

V-3/III-2/b/P

483. AHRONS, C. R., & GOLDSMITH, J. Content of Coparental Interaction

Avail: NAPS-3

Variables Measured: Relationship and interactions between divorced couples, related both to parenting and to interpersonal issues

Type of Instrument: Semistructured interview; may also be adapted using a Likert-style scale

Instrument Description: The Content of Coparental Interaction scale is composed of two subscales. The nonparental dimension is a 13-item, 6-point subscale with response options ranging from 1 = *once a week or more* to 6 = *never*. The parental dimension is a 10-item, 5-point subscale with options ranging from *always* to *never*. Each subscale can be used separately, in coordination with the other, or as part of a larger package examining several areas of interaction between divorced couples. The nonparental dimension subscale asks subjects how often during the past few months they and their former spouses have engaged each other in a number of activities and topics of conversation. The parental dimension subscale asks which of a series of activities and topics of conversation have been jointly approached that relate to parenting the couple's children.

Sample Items:

(A) Over the past few months, how often have you and your former spouse talked about new experiences you are having in your present lives?

(B) Over the past few months, how often have you and your former spouse had physical contact (e.g. hugging, kissing) without sexual intercourse?

(C) Which of the following have been shared between you and your former spouse? (a) Making major decisions regarding your children's lives?

Comments: Cronbach's alpha is reported by the author to range from .90 to .95.

References:

Ahrons, C. R. (1981). The continuing coparental relationship between divorced spouses. *Am J Orthop, 51*, 315–328. Reprinted in D. Olson & B. Miller (Eds.). (1984). *Family studies yearbook* (Vol. 2). Beverly Hills, CA: Sage.

Ahrons, C. R. (1983). Predictors of paternal involvement postdivorce: Mothers' and fathers' perceptions. *J Divorce, 6*(3), 55–69.

Ahrons, C. R., & Wallisch, L. (1987). Parenting in the binuclear family: Relationships between biological and stepparents. In K. Pasley & M. Ihinger-Tallman (Eds.), *Remarriage and stepfamilies: Research and theory*. New York: Guilford.

V-3/a

484. AHRONS, C. R., & GOLDSMITH, J. Feelings and Attitudes Toward Former Spouse

Avail: NAPS-3

Variables Measured: Feelings and attitudes toward former spouse with regard to guilt, anger, compassion, parenting skills, and psychological distance

Type of Instrument: Likert-style items are Q-sorted into categories

Instrument Description: Subjects are given 25 randomly ordered cards, each containing a statement from one of five categories. Respondents are instructed to indicate how often the statement is true of their feelings and attitudes toward their former spouses. Responses range from 1 = *always* to 5 = *never*. Following responses, cards are stacked according to the number of the response given to the item. This scale can be used alone or in combination with a series of other scales and as part of an extended interview.

Sample Items:

(A)   I wish I had tried harder to make the marriage work.
(B)   I want to get back at him/her for what's been done to me.
(C)   My former spouse is a good parent to the children.

Comments: Cronbach's alpha is reported individually for each of the five subscales and ranges from .51 to .93.

References:

Ahrons, C. R. (1981). The continuing coparental relationship between divorced spouses. *Am J Orthop, 51,* 315–328. Reprinted in D. Olson & B. Miller (Eds.). (1984). *Family studies yearbook* (Vol. 2). Beverly Hills, CA: Sage.
Ahrons, C. R. (1983). Predictors of paternal involvement postdivorce: Mothers' and fathers' perceptions. *J Divorce, 6*(3), 55–69.
Ahrons, C. R., & Wallisch, L. (1987). Parenting in the binuclear family: Relationships between biological and stepparents. In K. Pasley & M. Ihinger-Tallman (Eds.), *Remarriage and stepfamilies: Research and theory.* New York: Guilford.

V-3/III-2/b/P
485. AHRONS, C. R., & GOLDSMITH, J. Nonresidential Parent-Child Involvement Scale

Avail: NAPS-3

Variables Measured: Involvement of divorced, noncustodial, nonresidential parents in the raising of children who were products of the former marriage

Type of Instrument: Self-report based on a semistructured interview

Instrument Description: This is a 5-point, 8-item scale asking in which activities the nonresidential parent is involved. The initial question—"Are you involved with the children in the following areas?"—is followed by a series of activities to which respondents indicate levels of involvement ranging from 1 = *very much* to 5 = *not at all*. Interactions that are asked about relate to both discussions a parent might have with his or her children and more active engagement, such as celebrations and vacations.

Sample Items:

(A)   Disciplining the children.
(B)   Religious or moral training (if any).
(C)   Taking the children for recreational activities (e.g. sports).

Comments: The author reports Cronbach's alpha for the 10-item scale to be in the range of .92 to .95.

References:

Ahrons, C. R. (1981). The continuing coparental relationship between divorced spouses. *Am J Orthop, 51,* 315–328. Reprinted in D. Olson & B. Miller (Eds.). (1984). *Family studies yearbook* (Vol. 2). Beverly Hills, CA: Sage.

Ahrons, C. R. (1983). Predictors of paternal involvement postdivorce: Mothers' and fathers' perceptions. *J Divorce, 6*(3), 55–69.

Ahrons, C. R., & Wallisch, L. (1987). Parenting in the binuclear family: Relationships between biological and stepparents. In K. Pasley & M. Ihinger-Tallman (Eds.), *Remarriage and stepfamilies: Research and theory.* New York: Guilford.

V-3/b/C

486. BERG, B., & KURDEK, L. A. Children's Beliefs About Parental Divorce Scales

Avail: 1987 Ref.

Variables Measured: Peer ridicule and avoidance, paternal or maternal blame, fear of abandonment, hope of reunification, and self-blame in children of divorced parents

Type of Instrument: Self-report questionnaire

Instrument Description: This 36-item self-report instrument is intended to identify children's problematic attitudes associated with their parents' divorce and to permit the planning of therapeutic intervention. Reading difficulty is at approximately the fourth-grade level, and items are in a *yes-no* format. Scoring is accomplished by tabulating the number of items endorsed in the problem attitude direction. Scores of the six scales and the total can be derived separately.

Sample Items:

(A) It would upset me if other kids asked a lot of questions about my parents.

(B) It was usually my father's fault when my parents had a fight.

(C) I sometimes worry that both my parents will want to live without me.

Comments: The authors report correlations between the total score from this scale and anxiety (.50) and peer relations (.49). Various scale scores are also reported to correlate with these and other measures of concurrent validity. Cronbach's alpha for the six scales range from .54 to .78, with .80 for the total. Test-retest correlations over a nine-week period ranged from .41 to .72 for the six scales and .65 for the total. The scale is a revision of the Family Story Test (Kelly & Berg, 1978).

References:

Kelly, R., & Berg, B. (1978). Measuring children's reactions to divorce. *J Clin Psyc, 34,* 215–221.

Kurdek, L. A., & Berg, B. (1987). Children's Beliefs About Parental Divorce Scale: Psychometric characteristics and concurrent validity. *J Cons Clin, 55,* 712–718.

V-3/a

487. BERMAN, W. H. Ex-Spouse Preoccupation Scale

Avail: 1988b Ref.

Variables Measured: Preoccupation with thoughts of an ex-spouse

Type of Instrument: Self-report questionnaire

Instrument Description: The Ex-Spouse Preoccupation Scale is a 7-point, 7-item Likert-type questionnaire designed to measure the extent to which an ex-spouse remains on one's mind in the months following a divorce. The instrument is unidimensional, with response values summed to arrive at an overall scale score. Each item is in the form of a question. The instrument has been used as part of a larger battery in the investigation of postdivorce adjustment. The scale appears in 3- and 7-item versions, with both 5-point and 7-point response options being used. The scale appears both under the current title and as "Spouse-Related Thoughts." The author has indicated (in personal communication) that he prefers the current title, 7 items, and a 7-point scale. Items for the scale are based on variables described by Weiss (1975) and Parkes (1972).

Sample Items:

(A)   In the past two weeks, how often have you thought about your ex-husband?

(B)   How often in the past couple of weeks have things reminded you of him, triggered thoughts about him?

(C)   How much have you thought about what happened in your marriage in the past few weeks?

Comments: The author reports on a factor analysis in which all items had primary loadings (range of loadings was .51 to .82) on a single factor, accounting for 55% of the variance. Cronbach's alpha is reported to be .84.

References:

Berman, W. H. (1985). Continued attachment after legal divorce. *J Fam Iss, 6,* 375–392.

Berman, W. H. (1988a). The relationship of ex-spouse attachment to adjustment following divorce. *J Fam Psy, 1,* 312–328.

Berman, W. H. (1988b). The role of attachment in the post-divorce experience. *J Pers Soc Psy, 54,* 496–503.

V-3/I-1/c

488. DUBERMAN, L. Reconstituted Family Integration Scale

Avail: 1975 Ref.

Variables Measured: Integration of reconstituted families, that is, consisting of a husband and wife, at least one of whom has been previously married and at least one of whom has a child from that previous marriage; subscores are derived for each of three categories: husband/wife relationship score (HWRS), stepparent/stepchild relationship score (PCRS), and stepsibling relationship score (SSRS); an overall family integration score (FIS) is also computed

Type of Instrument: Three-part instrument including closed-ended written questions, open-ended taped oral interview, and ratings based on observations

Instrument Description: Subjects are husbands and wives in reconstituted families. Children are excluded. Excluding demographic questions, each interview lasts approximately two hours and contains approximately 25 questions. Interviews are broken into two parts. The couple initially is interviewed together in order to obtain demographic information. One partner then exits to another room to fill out the written questionnaire. The remaining spouse undergoes the open-ended interview. Upon completion of the interview, husband and wife trade places in order to complete the interview/questionnaire process.

Sample Items:

(A)   Discuss the topic of visitation.

(B)   How do children from different marriages get along together?

(C)   Write the name of the child on the short line to the left and then place an X on the line between *very close* and *very distant* to indicate how you feel about this child. Draw more lines if needed.

Comments: Interest is centered on the reconstituted family as a unit. Did the members have an image of themselves as one entity? What process had they gone through to attain or not attain this solidarity? The primary focus was on integration of the members into one unit. "Integration" is defined as the linkages and relationships within the reconstituted family as a whole.

Reference:

Duberman, L. (1975). *The reconstituted family: A study of remarried couples and their children.* Chicago: Nelson-Hall.

V-3/a/P
489. EMERY, R. E. Acrimony Scale (AS)

Avail: NAPS-3

Variables Measured: Areas of potential conflict between parents who have either divorced or separated

Type of Instrument: Self-report questionnaire

Instrument Description: The AS is a 4-point, 25-item Likert-style questionnaire designed to assess the present or potential level of conflict between former spouses. Items are in the form of questions and are answered according to the frequency with which the person experiences the problem indicated in the item. Response options range from *almost never* to *almost always,* and are scored on a 1–4 basis. Reverse-scoring is necessary on 11 items. Although the author recognizes only a total AS score, items within the questionnaire reflect problems related to children, money, visitation with children, interactions with the former spouse, and overall adjustment to divorce or separation.

Sample Items:

(A)   Do you feel friendly toward your former spouse?

(B)   Are gifts to the children a problem between you and your former spouse?

(C)   Has your former spouse adjusted to being divorced from you?

Comments: The author indicates that internal consistency is in the .83 to .86 range and that test-retest reliability is .88. Correlations are reported between the AS and maternal depression (.42), children's perceived cognitive competence (.49), and children's WISC-R scores (-.32).

References:

Emery, R. E., & Wyer, M. M. (1987). Child custody mediation and litigation: An experimental evaluation of the experience of parents. *J Cons Clin, 55,* 179–186.

Shaw, D. S., & Emery, R. E. (1987). Parental conflict and other correlates of the adjustment of school-age children whose parents have separated. *J Abn C Psy, 15,* 269–281.

Shaw, D. S., & Emery, R. E. (1988). Chronic family adversity and school-age children's adjustment. *Am Acad Child Adol Psychi, 27,* 200–206.

V-3/a

490. FISHER, B. F. Fisher Divorce Adjustment Scale (FDAS)

Avail: The Family Relations Learning Center, 450 Ord Dr., Boulder, CO 80303

Variables Measured: Adjustment to the termination of a romantic relationship

Type of Instrument: Self-report questionnaire

Instrument Description: The FDAS is a 5-point, 100-item Likert-type questionnaire de-signed to assess levels of adjustment when a love relationship has been terminated. In addition to a total composite score, six subscales are identified: (1) self-worth, (2) disentanglement, (3) anger, (4) grief, (5) trust and intimacy, and (6) social self-worth. Respondents are instructed to indicate their present feelings and attitudes with respect to each statement. Response options range from *almost always* to *almost never.* The author indicates that, while the scale is intended for measuring adjustment, it is not designed to measure emotional illness. While many types of love relationships can serve as the basis for responses, it is thought to be difficult for a widowed person to complete and to be most appropriately utilized as a pre- and posttherapy or class measure of change and increased adjustment. The FDAS is most often utilized by clinicians conducting divorce or personal growth seminars.

Sample Items:

(A)   I am constantly thinking of my former love-partner.
(B)   It is easy for me to accept my becoming a single person.
(C)   I blame my former love-partner for the failure of our love-relationship.

Comments: The author indicates that Cronbach's alpha for the total scale score is .98, and that alpha for subscales ranges from .87 to .95. Preliminary data utilizing the FDAS indicate that pretherapy scores increase as the length of time since being actively engaged in the love relationship increases.

References:

Plummer, L. P., & Koch-Hattem, A. (1986). Family stress and adjustment to divorce. *Fam Relat, 35,* 523–529.
Saul, S. C., & Scherman, A. (1984). Divorce grief and personal adjustment in divorced persons who remarry or remain single. *J Divorce, 7*(3), 75–85.
Stolberg, A. L., & Ullman, A. J. (1984). Assessing dimensions of single parenting: The Single Parenting Questionnaire. *J Divorce, 8*(2), 31–45.

V-3/a

491. GOETTING, A. Divorce Chain Questionnaire

Avail: NAPS-3

Variables Measured: Beliefs about appropriate behavioral expectations for divorced cou-ples regarding their continuing relationship, the relationship between their former and current spouses, and their relationship with the former spouse upon the spouse's remarriage

Type of Instrument: Self-report questionnaire

Instrument Description: The Divorce Chain Questionnaire is a 74-item, 18-page Likert-style questionnaire taking approximately one hour to complete. Items are divided into eight groups according to the relationship being examined (divorced couple, current husband with former husband, current wife with former wife, self with remarried former spouse) and the gender of the person whose behavior is being examined. Each section begins with a 5–6 line description of the situation, followed by several items expanding on the specifics of the situation and posing questions regarding possible actions and complications. Wherever appropriate, items are paired such that, for each situation described, expectations are measured for both members of the relationship. Five response options, ranging from *absolutely must* to *absolutely must not*, are provided for each item. The questionnaire is not necessarily intended for use with divorced couples. Rather, it enables the user to examine attitudes toward behavioral expectations for divorced couples in general. Although no scoring procedures are specified by the author, specific investigators may elect to combine items, either according to the eight subgroups or the results of factor analytic studies.

Sample Items (Section 1 description): *John* and *Tina* are divorced and have three small children. Both are married to someone else now, and neither have children by these present marriages. *John* and *Tina* live in the same town, and their children live with *Tina* and her present husband. What do you think *Tina* should do in the following situations with *John*?

(A) Since the divorce *John* has never been late in paying *Tina* all of the money that he has owed her, and *Tina* has always handled that money responsibly so that their children have had everything that they need. This month school will begin, and *Tina* needs extra money to buy clothes and school supplies for their children. If *John* seems to have enough money, should *Tina* ask *John* for some extra money?

(B) If instead of needing clothes and school supplies for their children, *Tina* needs that extra money for unexpected car and house repairs, should she ask *John* for the money?

Comments: The author reports a mean item reliability for paired items of .68. Split-half reliability of the total scale is reported to be .97.

References:

Goetting, A. (1979). The normative integration of the former spouse relationship. *J Divorce, 2*(4), 395–414.

Goetting, A. (1980). Former spouse-current spouse relationships: Behavioral expectations. *J Fam Iss, 1,* 58–80.

Goetting, A. (1983). The relative strength of the husband-wife and parent-child dyads in remarriage: A test of the Hsu model. *J Comp Fam Studies, 14,* 117–128.

V-3/V-2/a
492. GREEN, R. G. Inventory of External Pressures to Remain Married (IEP)

Avail: NAPS-3

Variables Measured: The perceived strength of marital partners' environmental pressures to remain in their present marriage

Type of Instrument: Self-report questionnaire

Instrument Description: The IEP is a 9-item questionnaire constructed to assess marital partners' perceptions of external pressures to remain married. It also has been used to retrospectively assess divorced and separated persons' perceptions of the pressures they perceived prior to the breakup of the previous relationship. The instrument asks respondents to consider particular time periods (e.g., the last six months) and to rate the amount of pressure experienced to remain married. These pressures include obligations to marital vows and to dependent children, religious beliefs, financial costs of divorce, and pressures from social networks of neighbors, work mates, people in the spouses' church, relatives, and friends. All questions use 5-point Likert-style response formats. Response options for social network questions range from *never opposed* to *always opposed*. Options for the other questions also range from 1 to 5 and include (in order from 1 to 5) *a great deal, quite a bit, a fair amount, little,* and *none*. A total score, representing the amount of perceived pressure to remain married, is obtained by summing all items.

Sample Items: Please check the space below which best describes the amount of pressure to remain married you might feel from each source if you wanted to get a divorce:

(A)   Obligations to marital vows . . .
(B)   Obligations to your children . . .
(C)   Obligations to religious beliefs . . .

Comments: The author reports Cronbach's alpha to be .79. Concurrent criterion validity was evaluated by comparing IEP scores for divorced persons (19.3) with those of married persons (23.1). IEP scores were also found to correlate .28 with scores on the Dyadic Adjustment Scale.

References:

Green, R. G. (1983). The influence of divorce prediction variables on divorce adjustment: An expansion and test of Lewis' and Spanier's theory of marital quality and marital stability. *J Divorce, 7*(1), 67–82.
Green, R. G., & Sporakowski, M. S. (1983). The dynamics of divorce: Marital quality, alternative attractions and external pressures. *J Divorce, 7*(2), 77–88.

V-3/e/C
493. GREEN, V. P. Teacher Attitude Toward Divorce and the Role of the School

Avail: NAPS-3

Variables Measured: Teachers' opinions and knowledge about children of divorced families; teachers' attitudes toward the role and responsibilities of schools to these children

Type of Instrument: Self-report questionnaire

Instrument Description: The instrument is a 37-item questionnaire designed to assess opinions and knowledge of teachers regarding divorce as it might relate to their students. An additional 15-item biographical section requesting information on the teacher's marital status, parents' marital status, age, gender, geographic location, and grade level taught is also administered. Total administration time is approximately 20 minutes. The questionnaire has both a 31-item Likert-style and a 6-item *true/false/no information* section. The Likert-style items utilize a 5-point answer format, with response options ranging from *strongly agree* to *strongly disagree*. The scale is designed to be used with classroom teachers, K-12. Negative items are reversed-scored, after which items from subsections are combined to yield overall scores for knowledge, opinion, role of the school, and attitudes and knowledge about home environment during the process of divorce.

Sample Items:

(A)   Teachers should not be expected to give special help to children of divorce.
(B)   Poor families seem to have a greater divorce rate.
(C)   Divorce is not related to children's behavior in the classroom.

Comments: The author reports that Cronbach's alpha for the 37-item scale is .87.

Reference:

Green, V. P., & Schaefer, L. (1984). The effects of personal divorce experience on teacher perceptions of children of divorce. *J Divorce, 8*(2), 107–110.

V-3/II-1/a
494. HARDY, K. R. Hardy Divorce Scale

Avail: 1967 Ref.

Variables Measured: Attitudes toward divorce

Type of Instrument: Self-report questionnaire

Instrument Description: The Hardy Divorce Scale is a 12-item Likert-style scale with five response options ranging from *strongly agree* to *strongly disagree*. It was originally employed in 1954 with college students but is equally appropriate for use with adolescents and adults. The original intent of the instrument was to assess attitudes toward divorce so that persuasive arguments could later be used in challenging those attitudes. The original study in which this scale was used investigated group conformity and attitude change. Most items relate to general conditions under which the granting of a divorce would be appropriate. More recent uses of the scale have included investigating liberal versus conservative views of divorce (Jorgensen & Johnson, 1980) and general attitudes toward divorce (Coleman & Ganong, 1984).

Sample Items:

(A) I feel that divorce is a sensible solution to many unhappy marriages.
(B) Marriage is a sacred covenant which should be broken only under the most drastic circumstances.
(C) Children are better off living with one parent rather than with two who cannot get along well together.

Comments: Split-half reliability using the Spearman-Brown formula is reported to be .85.

References:

Coleman, M., & Ganong, L. H. (1984). Effect of family structure on family attitudes and expectations. *Fam Relat, 33*, 425–432.
Jorgensen, S. R., & Johnson, A. C. (1980). Correlates of divorce liberality. *J Mar Fam, 42*, 617–626.
Shaw, M. E., & Wright, J. M. (1967). *Scales for the measurement of attitudes.* New York: McGraw-Hill.

V-3/b
495. HOBART, C. Semantic Index of Relationships (SIR)

Avail: 1987 Ref.

Variables Measured: Relationship between parents, their children, and their stepchildren

Type of Instrument: Self-report questionnaire

Instrument Description: The SIR is a 7-point, 13-item semantic differential questionnaire designed to evaluate (step)parent-child relationships within remarried families. The questionnaire is intended to be filled out by parents and stepparents. Each respondent completes the

SIR three times for each child: once each for his or her own perceptions, once for the presumed perceptions of the spouse, and once for the respondent's perceptions of how the child views their relationship. Items are formed by opposite-pole adjectives separated by seven blanks. Respondents are instructed to place an "X" in the appropriate blank to indicate how the relationship is perceived. The author indicates that administration of the inventory can be a lengthy process for persons with large stepfamilies. Therefore, the number of children for whom the SIR is completed is often limited, either by total number or by number within each of five categories: (1) his in-living children; (2) his out-living children; (3) her in-living children; (4) her out-living children; (5) their children. "In-living" refers to children in the custody of the respondent or his/her spouse. "Out-living" refers to children living with the other parent from the divorce. Depending on the number of children involved and the nature of the interview, the author reports that administration time often runs between one and two hours. Scoring of the SIR is accomplished by summing values associated with responses across the scale.

Sample Items:

(A) ONESIDED . . . . MUTUAL
(B) QUARRELSOME . . . . AGREEABLE
(C) EXPRESSIVE . . . . GUARDED

Comments: The author reports that the SIR was originally developed as a 26-item instrument, but that pretesting and analysis resulted in a reduction to 13 items in the current version. Detailed information is contained in Hobart (1987) regarding relationships between parents and stepparents and their children and stepchildren. Results are presented both by living arrangements and by age of the child.

References:

Hobart, C. (1987). Parent-child relations in remarried families. *J Fam Iss, 8,* 259–277.
Hobart, C., & Brown, D. (1988). Effects of prior marriage children on adjustment in remarriage: A Canadian study. *J Comp Fam Studies, 19,* 381–396.

V-3/II-1/a
496. KINNAIRD, K. L., & GERRARD, M. Attitudes Toward Divorce Scale

Avail: NAPS-3

Variables Measured: Attitudes toward the acceptability of divorce

Type of Instrument: Self-report questionnaire

Instrument Description: The Attitudes Toward Divorce Scale is an original measure based on a questionnaire described by Hardy (1957) and later used by Ganong et al. (1981). The instrument is a Likert-style scale utilizing a 5-point response format. Individuals are asked to indicate the extent of their agreement with 12 statements about the acceptability of divorce. Half the items are positive and half are negative statements. Scores assigned to responses are summed (negatively worded items are reverse-scored) in order to arrive at a total attitude toward divorce score. This measure was designed as part of a research effort to assess differences among college-age women from various family backgrounds in their attitudes toward divorce. The authors also indicate that the instrument may be used as a tool to promote self-awareness and discussion in high school and college students.

Sample Items:

(A) The marriage vow "till death do us part" represents a sacred commitment to another person and should not be taken lightly.

(B) These days, the marriage vow "till death do us part" is just a formality. It doesn't really mean that people should stay in an unsatisfactory marriage.

(C) Most people who get divorced do so as a last resort—only after trying other solutions to the problems in their marriage.

Comments: The authors report that Cronbach's alpha for the Attitudes Toward Divorce Scale is .77 and that test-retest reliability was found to be .86. It was also found that individuals from reconstituted families had higher test scores, indicating more positive attitudes toward divorce, than did those from divorced or intact families.

References:

Ganong, L., Coleman, M., & Brown, G. (1981). Effect of family structure on marital attitudes of adolescents. *Adolescence, 16,* 281–288.

Hardy, K. R. (1957). Determinants of conformity and attitude change. *J Abn Soc Psy, 54,* 289–294.

Kinnaird, K. L., & Gerrard, M. (1986). Premarital sexual behavior and attitudes toward marriage and divorce among young women as a function of their mothers' marital status. *J Mar Fam, 48,* 757–765.

V-3/II-3/a

497. KITSON, G. C. Dimensions of Attachment to the Spouse in Divorce

Avail: 1982 Ref.

Variables Measured: Sustained or lingering attachment, relief, guilt, reluctance, and pressure associated with divorce

Type of Instrument: Self-report questionnaire

Instrument Description: This instrument is a 12-item Likert-type questionnaire designed to measure feelings associated with divorce. It consists of three 4-item subscales, each intended to assess a different dimension of attachment: (1) lingering attachment to the former spouse (referred to by the author as "attachment"), (2) relief and guilt, and (3) reluctance and pressure. Each subscale is measured using a 5-point scale (scored 1–5) ranging from *not at all my feelings* to *very much my feelings.* Values associated with item responses within subscales are summed to arrive at overall scores. The first subscale was derived from a factor analysis on an initial pool of 9 items. The other subscales were originally constructed in their current forms. The scale was designed to measure continuing bonds to the ex-spouse following separation and divorce. The instrument was developed for use as part of a broader interview but can also be used in a paper-and-pencil format. The scale has been modified and adapted as a unidimensional scale by Thompson and Spanier (1983).

Sample Items:

(A) I feel I will never get over the divorce.

(B) This has been coming for a long time, and I'm glad we've finally made the break.

(C) I'm going ahead with the divorce only because it's what my husband (wife) wants.

Comments: The author reports that factor score coefficients for the 4 lingering attachment subscale items are .11, .12, .26, and .51. Cronbach's alpha for lingering attachment is reported to be .80. Alphas for relief and guilt, and for reluctance and pressure, are reported to be .64

and .79, respectively. Correlations are reported between lingering attachment and a measure of distress (.43), between being the person who suggested the divorce and relief and guilt (-.36), and between having the spouse suggest the divorce and feelings of reluctance and pressure (.44).

References:

Kiecolt-Glasser, J. K., Fisher, L. D., Ogrocki, P., Stout, J. C., Speicher, C. E., & Glaser, R. (1987). Marital quality, marital disruption, and immune function. *Psychos Med, 49,* 13–33.

Kitson, G. C. (1982). Attachment to spouse in divorce: A scale and its application. *J Mar Fam, 44,* 379–393.

Thompson, L., & Spanier, G. B. (1983). The end of marriage and acceptance of marital termination. *J Mar Fam, 45,* 103–113.

Wright, D. W., & Price, S. J. (1986). Court-ordered child support payment: The effect of the former-spouse relationship on compliance. *J Mar Fam, 48,* 869–874.

V-3/I-4/c
498. KNAUB, P. K., & HANNA, S. L. Remarried Family Inventory

Avail: NAPS-3

Variables Measured: Perceptions of family strength in divorced families

Type of Instrument: Self-report questionnaire

Instrument Description: This instrument is a 44-item Likert-style scale utilizing a 5-point response format. It measures three dimensions used to determine the success of the remarried family: (1) a family strengths score, (2) a marital satisfaction score, and (3) the subject's own perception of his or her adjustment. The Remarried Family Inventory is intended for use with husbands and wives in the remarried family. The family strengths subscale contains 19 items and measures eight components of family strength. Respondents indicate their perceptions concerning their partner, their own children, the stepchildren in the home, any children born to the remarried couple, and their overall feeling toward all the children in the home. Marital satisfaction is measured by the Marital Need Satisfaction Scale (Stinnett, Collins, & Montgomery, 1970).

Sample Items:

(A)   Rate the closeness of your relationship with the children in the home.
(B)   How often do you experience conflict with the children?
(C)   How well, generally, do you think you handle conflict situations?

Comments: The authors report the correlations between the three indexes to be .82 for marital satisfaction and family strength, .69 for family perception of adjustment and family strength, and .58 for perception of adjustment and marital satisfaction.

References:

Hanna, S. L., & Knaub, P. K. (1981). Cohabitation before remarriage: Its relationship to family strengths. *J Alternative Lifestyles, 4,* 507–522.

Knaub, P. K., & Hanna, S. L. (1984). Children of remarriage: Perceptions of family strengths. *J Divorce, 7*(3), 73–90.

Stinnett, N., Collins, J., & Montgomery, J. E. (1970). Marital need satisfaction of older husbands and wives. *J Mar Fam, 32,* 428–434.

V-3/I-4/c/C
499. KNAUB, P. K., & HANNA, S. L. Remarried Family Inventory for Children

Avail: NAPS-3

Variables Measured: Perceptions of family strength by children in divorced families

Type of Instrument: Self-report questionnaire

Instrument Description: The instrument is a child-oriented adaptation of the Remarried Family Inventory (Hanna & Knaub, 1981). It contains a variety of item formats, ranging from demographic and open-ended questions to 40 Likert-style items utilizing a 5-point response format. All information is gathered using a written questionnaire format. Administration time is approximately 30 minutes. The Likert-style portion of the inventory is referred to as the family strength scale. The overall inventory is designed to measure eight aspects of family strength (perception of happiness, closeness, and self-worth, communication satisfaction, doing things together, perception of appreciation received and shown, and effectiveness in handling conflict). Additional purposes of the inventory include gathering of demographic information, insight as to the perceptions of children regarding their stepfamily's adjustment, and the nature of their relationships with natural- and stepparents. The family strength scale focuses on children's perceptions of the natural parents, stepparent, and the stepfamily as a whole.

Sample Items:

(A)   How happy are you with your stepfamily?

(B)   How often do you have conflict ("fights" or arguments) with your natural parent?

(C)   How would you rate the relationship between you and your natural parent who doesn't live with you?

Comments: The scale contains items written in a variety of formats. Several questions are designed to be answered with a *yes* or *no* response. Others ask subjects to list information. Open-ended items are set up to elicit written responses ranging in length from a short sentence to a complete paragraph. In addition, the 40-item family strength scale utilizes a Likert-style format.

References:

Hanna, S. L., & Knaub, P. K. (1981). Cohabitation before remarriage: Its relationship to family strengths. *J Alternative Lifestyles, 4,* 507–522.

Knaub, P. K., & Hanna, S. L. (1984). Children of remarriage: Perceptions of family strengths. *J Divorce, 7*(3), 73–90.

V-3/III-2/c/P
500. LOWERY, C. R. Custody Decision Form (CDF)

Avail: 1985 Ref.

Variables Measured: Criteria used by parents in making custody decisions following divorce

Type of Instrument: Self-report questionnaire

Instrument Description: The CDF is an 11-point, 20-item questionnaire designed to assess factors determining parental qualifications to receive custody of children when the couple divorces. In constructing the questionnaire, divorcing parents were identified through court records and contacted regarding their participation in the study. Audiotaped interviews were conducted in which parents were asked to indicate those factors influencing their decisions regarding custody, with those responses used in the development and refinement of the CDF. Questionnaire items are responded to on an 11-point continuum ranging from *of little importance* to *highly important*. This scoring procedure allows for both the evaluation of qualifications of individual parents for custody and a qualitative assessment of the relative consideration given to each of the 20 criteria. Thus, in addition to indicating the relative importance of each item, respondents could also be asked which parent best satisfies each criterion. The questionnaire could be used in divorce mediation cases, in counseling where both parents are involved, and in research investigating variables related to custody attitudes and decisions.

Sample Items:

(A)   The parent's ability to provide for the child financially.

(B)   The parent's sense of responsibility to the child (making sure the child is eating properly, is dressed properly, gets medical attention when needed).

(C)   The emotional quality of the relationship between the child and parent (e.g., trust, warmth, and interests that are mutual).

Comments: A factor analysis performed by the author revealed three primary factors. The first factor, containing 8 items and accounting for 50% of the variance, was concerned with selecting a parent who was both able and interested in providing for the child. The second and third factors concern maintenance of the child's social network and cultural values, respectively. Of the 20 items, 16 are represented on one of the factors.

References:

Lowery, C. R. (1981). Child custody decisions in divorce proceedings: A survey of judges. *Prof Psych, 12,* 492–498.

Lowery, C. R. (1984). The wisdom of Solomon: Criteria for child custody from the legal and clinical points of view. *Law Human, 8,* 371–380.

Lowery, C. R. (1985). Child custody in divorce: Parents' decisions and perceptions. *Fam Relat, 34,* 241–249.

Settle, S. A., & Lowery, C. R. (1982). Child custody decisions: Content analysis of a judicial survey. *J Divorce, 6*(1/2), 125–138.

V-3/V-2/g
501. RASCHKE, H. J. Postdivorce Problems and Stress Scale (PPSS)

Avail: NAPS-3

Variables Measured: Problems and stresses faced by newly divorced persons

Type of Instrument: Self-report questionnaire

Instrument Description: This instrument is a 4-point, 52-item Likert-style questionnaire designed to assess feelings, attitudes, and difficulties encountered by persons in the months and years following a divorce. In all, 3 primary and 17 subdimensions of problems and stress are categorized. The primary scales (and their subdimensions) are (1) perceived, unpleasant, unfavorable emotional states (depression, emotional turmoil, loneliness, guilt, and trauma); (2) perceived satisfaction with new roles (as a single parent, as a friend, as a worker on a job, as a date, as a former spouse, and as a club or organization member); and (3) perceived ability to fulfill or deal with new roles (as a single parent, as a friend, as a worker on a job, as a date, as a former spouse, and as a club or organization member). This instrument was originally administered as part of a 273-item scale constructed for the author's dissertation. Different forms of the scale, including 68-item (Raschke, 1977) and 60-item (Salts & Zongker, 1983) versions, have also appeared in the literature.

Sample Items:

(A)   As compared to before the separation, in general how would you say you feel most of the time now—in higher or lower spirits?
(B)   Compared to before your separation, do you feel you have more or less ability to get along with people on your job?
(C)   Do you blame yourself for your separation and/or divorce?

Comments: The author reports that a factor analysis of responses to the PPSS revealed 10 factors. The primary factor of perceived unpleasant emotional states contains 21 items and is reported to account for 41.3% of the variance. Remaining factors each account for between 3.9% and 10.8% of the variance. The primary correlation reported for the PPSS was with level of social participation (.38).

References:

Raschke, H. J. (1977). The role of social participation in postseparation and postdivorce adjustment. *J Divorce, 1*(2), 129–140.
Raschke, H. J., & Barringer, K. D. (1977). Postdivorce adjustment among persons participating in Parents-Without-Partners organizations. *Fam Perspect, 11,* 23–34.
Salts, C. J., & Zongker, C. E. (1983). Effects of divorce counseling groups on adjustment and self concept. *J Divorce, 6*(4), 55–67.

V-3/V-2/b/g/C
502. SANDLER, I. N., WOLCHIK, S. A., BRAVER, S. L., & FOGAS, B. S. Divorce Events Schedule for Children (DES-C)

Avail: 1985, 1986, & 1987 Refs.

Variables Measured: Children's perceptions of positive and negative qualities of events surrounding the divorce of their parents

Type of Instrument: Self-report questionnaire

Instrument Description: The DES-C is a 15-point, 62-item Likert-type questionnaire designed to evaluate the impact of a divorce on children. Respondents read a list of events or perceptions regarding behaviors in which they have engaged, attitudes of their parents toward either the child or each other, and interactions that have occurred between their parents. For each item, children indicate whether or not the event has occurred within the past three months, and, if so, how positive or negative they found that event to be. All responses are on a 15-point continuum, with seven negative and seven positive options, plus a middle point for indicating neutral events. Events that have occurred in the past, but not within the previous three months, are also scored on a 15-point scale. Response scores thus range from -7 to +7. The initial pool of 210 events was generated in a two-step process through (1) nominations by a group of 40 children, 40 parents, and 20 lawyers and psychologists who were asked to list events believed to significantly affect children of divorce and (2) a request to these persons to expand on this list by considering five areas: (a) parent-child relationships, (b) relationships with friends and relatives, (c) changes in parents' lives, (d) economic changes, and (e) legal concerns. Following reduction of the pool by the authors and pilot testing of the questionnaire, a final 62-item version was formed. The authors report having administered the DES-C to children from 8 to 15 years of age.

Sample Items:

(A) Mom and Dad differ in how they want you to be.
(B) Mom gets mad at you or tells you that you are bad.
(C) Your friends tease you or are mean to you.

Comments: The authors report that test-retest reliability for individual items over a period of two weeks ranged from -.07 to 1.00, with a median of .61. They point out, however, that this figure should be thought of as a low estimate of reliability due to the fact that the instrument asks for events that have occurred over the past three months and not merely affective levels of the child. Additional events may have occurred between test administrations, as well as other events no longer being within the three-month timeframe. The relationship of DES-C scores to variables such as age, gender, and income are reported in the references listed below.

References:

Sandler, I. N., Wolchik, S. A., & Braver, S. L. (1987). The stressors of children's post-divorce environments. In S. A. Wolchik & P. Karoly (Eds.), *Children of divorce: Empirical perspectives on adjustment.* New York: Gardner.

Sandler, I. N., Wolchik, S. A., Braver, S. L., & Fogas, B. S. (1986). Significant events of children of divorce: Toward the assessment of risky situations. In S. M. Auerbach & A. Stolberg (Eds.), *Crisis intervention with children and families* (pp. 65–83). New York: Hemisphere.

Wolchik, S. A., Sandler, I. N., Braver, S. L., & Fogas, B. S. (1985). Events of parental divorce: Stressfulness ratings by children, parents, and clinicians. *Am J Comm P, 14,* 59–74.

V-3/b/C

503. SHILLER, V. M. Loyalty Conflict Assessment Test

Avail: NAPS-3

Variables Measured: Divorce-related loyalty conflict in children

Type of Instrument: Interview-coding scheme

Instrument Description: This 15-item test presents children in divorced or separated families with hypothetical situations in which they must choose between doing an activity with their mother or father. Ten test items present children with situations in which one parent or the other unexpectedly offers an attractive opportunity at a time when the other parent is scheduled to have the child. In each of the other five situations, the child has the freedom to choose to do an activity with either parent. After being presented with each dilemma, the child is asked the following questions: (1) What would you do? (Latency to respond is measured, in addition to noting which parent is selected.) (2) Why would you choose to do (activity chosen)? (Rationale for the child's decision is scored according to a coding system included with the scale. Major scoring categories are attractiveness of activity determinant, desire to be with mother or with father, external factors determinant, ethical issues determinant, and conflict response.) (3) How much would you worry that you did the right thing (scored 1–7)? (4) How badly would you think (the parent not chosen) would feel (scored 1–7)? Administration time is approximately one hour.

Sample Items:

(A) You are spending the day with your dad, and you're supposed to be back at your mom's house at 5:00. Your dad decides it would be fun for the two of you to go out to McDonald's for supper and to a movie, and says you could get back to your mom's by bedtime. He asks you whether you want to go.

(B) You're supposed to go over to your dad's tomorrow, and your dad said something about helping him wash the car. Your best friend's mother calls up and suggests that you and your mom could go with them to the new Star Trek movie tomorrow; they won free tickets. You've been dying to see the movie. However, you think your dad's sort of been counting on you to help.

(C) Your class is going on a trip and your teacher asks you if one of your parents could come along. Both your mom and dad say they could go. Who would you ask to go?

Comments: The author reports on a study in which correlations between latency to respond, sum of *don't know* responses, and conflict response ratings were obtained for samples in two types of custody arrangements. In samples of boys in joint physical custody and boys in maternal physical custody, correlations ranged from .62 to .77 and from .65 to .79, respectively. In the joint custody sample, children's worry ratings correlated from .63 to .80 with these measures. In the maternal custody sample, however, correlations between these three measures and self-reported worry were reported to range from -.15 to .11.

Reference:

Shiller, V. M. (1986). Loyalty conflicts and family relationships in latency age boys: A comparison of joint and maternal custody. *J Divorce, 9*(4), 17–38.

V-3/II-3/a

504. THOMPSON, L., & SPANIER, G. B. Acceptance of Marital Termination: The Thompson and Spanier Revision of Kitson's Dimensions of Attachment to the Spouse in Divorce

Avail: 1983 Ref.

Variables Measured: Spouse's acceptance of separation and divorce

Type of Instrument: Self-report questionnaire

Instrument Description: This instrument, untitled by the authors, is a 4-point, 11-item questionnaire designed to assess feelings related to the termination of one's marriage. Respondents are asked to indicate the extent to which items reflect their current feelings. Items are in the form of statements, largely affective in nature, with response options (scored 1–4) ranging from *not at all* to *very much.* High scores are interpreted as indicating positive feelings and greater levels of acceptance. The final instrument is the result of a factor analysis on an initial pool of 15 items. The item pool was established from a group of 17 items originally available in an unpublished manuscript (Kitson & Sussman, 1974). The entire set of items, in a slightly different form, was published in Kitson (1982).

Sample Items:

(A) Sometimes I just can't believe that we got a divorce (separation).

(B) This has been coming for a long time, and I'm glad we've finally made the break.

(C) Divorce is one of the most tragic things that can happen to a person.

Comments: The authors indicate that 4 items from the 15-item factor analysis were discarded due to their not adequately reflecting the primary acceptance factor. Cronbach's alpha for the remaining 11-item scale is reported to be .90. Regression analysis results are reported in which several marital-history variables were regressed on acceptance of marital termination. Areas with the highest reported correlations were spouse-suggested divorce (-.50 males, -.31 females);

personal commitment (-.42 males, -.42 females); marital harmony (-.42 males, -.29 females), and affectional expression (-.14 males, -.42 females). Further details are provided in Thompson and Spanier (1983).

References:

Emery, R. E., & Wyer, M. M. (1987). Child custody mediation and litigation: An experimental evaluation of the experience of parents. *J Cons Clin, 55,* 179–186.
Kitson, G. C. (1982). Attachment to spouse in divorce: A scale and its application. *J Mar Fam, 44,* 379–393.
Thompson, L., & Spanier, G. B. (1983). The end of marriage and acceptance of marital termination. *J Mar Fam, 45,* 103–113.

NOTE: For additional instruments, see also *Abstracts 1376–1458* in the Abbreviated Abstracts of Instruments (which precedes the Indexes).

Abbreviated Abstracts of Instruments

I-1/a
1001. ALDOUS, J. Husband's and Wife's Communication Index

Avail: 1969 Ref.

Variables Measured: Frequency of husband and wife discussions on various subjects

Instrument Description: Husband is asked five items and wife is asked six items related to marital communication as part of an in-depth interview with each.

Reference:

Aldous, J. (1969). Wives' employment status and lower-class men as husband-fathers: Support for the Moynihan thesis. *J Mar Fam, 31,* 469–476.

I-1/c
1002. ALKIRE, A. A. Parent-Child Communication Assessment

Avail: NAPS-2

Variables Measured: Ability of family members to communicate information to each other

Instrument Description: Family members take turns describing 16 designs to each other. Receivers of descriptions must pick out described designs. Success of each person in communicating needed information is noted.

Reference:

Alkire, A. A. (1969). Social power and communication within families of disturbed and nondisturbed preadolescents. *J Pers Soc Psy, 13,* 335–349.

I-1/III-2/b
1003. BRIM, O. G., Jr., GLASS, D. C., & LAVIN, D. E. Parent Decision Process Test

Avail: 1962 Ref.

Variables Measured: Process used by couple in arriving at decisions

Instrument Description: Procedure includes from 84 to 228 items, taking 90–120 minutes to complete, depending on whether it is being filled out by one or both partners. It takes subjects through a number of problem situations and examines solution strategies.

Reference:

Brim, O. G., Jr., Glass, D. C., & Lavin, D. E. (1962). *Personality and decision process: Studies in the social psychology of thinking.* Stanford, CA: Stanford University.

I-1/b
1004. BUGENTAL, D. B. Measure of Conflicting Communication

Avail: 1971 Ref.

Variables Measured: Consistency of verbal content and vocal intonation of messages between parents and their children

Instrument Description: Ratings are made of verbal content and vocal intonation on a number of dimensions. Scores are compared to determine consistency of messages.

Reference:

Bugental, D. B., Love, L. R., & Kaswan, J. W. (1971). Verbal-nonverbal conflict in parental messages to normal and disturbed children. *J Abn Psych, 77,* 6–10.

I-1/b
1005. DANZIGER, K., & GREENGLASS, E. R. Verbal Exchange Analysis

Avail: NAPS-2

Variables Measured: Speech with the purpose of conveying information, pleasing others, making demands, and defending oneself

Instrument Description: A series of utterances is classified according to 29 coding categories. Coder determines classification based on a series of binary decisions regarding fit of utterance with various subcategories.

Reference:

Greenglass, E. (1971). A cross-cultural comparison of the child's communication with his mother. *Devel Psych, 5,* 494–499.

C/I-1/III-2/b
1006. ELDER, G. H., Jr. Index of Maternal Explanations

Avail: 1971 Ref.

Variables Measured: Child's perceptions of frequency of mother's explanations for her behavior toward the child

Instrument Description: Children indicate the frequency of explanations given to them for each of three maternal behaviors.

Reference:

Elder, G. H., Jr. (1971). Racial conflict and learning. *Sociometry, 34,* 151–173.

I-1/a
1007. GOODMAN, N., & OFSHE, R. Communication Efficiency Test

Avail: 1968 Ref.

Variables Measured: Efficiency of communication strategies between husband and wife

Instrument Description: Couples play the game of *Password* in an attempt to communicate each of 12 goal words to each other. Communication efficiency is assessed as a function of incorrect responses to cue words.

Reference:

Goodman, N., & Ofshe, R. (1968). Empathy, communication efficiency, and marital status. *J Mar Fam, 30,* 597–603.

P/I-1/III-2/b
1008. GORDON, T. Listening for Feelings of Children

Avail: 1970 Ref.

Variables Measured: Parents' affective recognition of typical children's messages

Instrument Description: For each of 20 statements read by parents, the emotion believed to be expressed by a child making the statement is indicated.

Reference:

Gordon, T. (1970). *Parent effectiveness training.* New York: Peter H. Wyden.

I-1/a
1009. HILL, R. L., STYCOS, J. M., & BACK, K. W. Marital Communication and Agreement Test

Avail: 1970 Ref.

Variables Measured: Topics on which husband and wife report communication

Instrument Description: Couples separately fill out a 13-item questionnaire indicating how often they discuss a series of topics and how close their views are on those topics.

Reference:

Hill, R. L. (1970). *Family development in three generations.* Cambridge, MA: Schenkman.

I-1/a
1010. KAHN, M. Marital Communication Scale

Avail: NAPS-2

Variables Measured: Nonverbal communication skills between husband and wife

Instrument Description: Husband and wife are given different sets of eight sentences they are to speak to the other. Each sentence is designed to convey one of three meanings, which the partner is to identify by nonverbal behaviors of the communicator.

Reference:

Kahn, M. (1970). Nonverbal communication and marital satisfaction. *Fam Process, 9,* 449–456.

I-1/a
1011. KARLSSON, G. Spousal Communication Indexes

Avail: 1951 Ref.

Variables Measured: Accuracy at understanding spouse's wishes

Instrument Description: There are two indexes: (1) multiple-choice items asking frequency and accuracy of communications, and (2) checklist for frequency of actual and desired behaviors. There are 38 items total.

Reference:

Karlsson, G. (1951). *Adaptability and communication in marriage: A Swedish predictive study of marital satisfaction.* Uppsala: Almquist and Wiksells.

I-1/III-2/b
1012. LOEFFLER, D., BERDIE, R., & ROTH, J. Intergeneration Communication Questionnaire

Avail: NAPS-2

Variables Measured: Comfort of college-aged subject and same-sex parent at discussing various topics and sharing information

Instrument Description: The questionnaire is meant to be used with college freshmen and their same-sex parents. Part one, containing 50 items, asks general questions about the subject. Part two asks with which person from among seven possibilities the student would be likely to discuss several matters.

Reference:

Loeffler, D., Berdie, R., & Roth, J. (1969). Content and process of inter-generation communication. *Fam Coord, 18,* 345–352.

I-1/c
1013. REISS, D. Lattice Language Communication Task

Avail: 1969 Ref.

Variables Measured: Ability to communicate efficiently with family members in a contrived situation in order to share information

Instrument Description: Four family members are seated so that they can pass notes but cannot see the others. Each has a series of numbers and blank spaces. Each family member begins with different numbers showing and is to fill in the blanks so that all members show the same sequence. Members sequentially take turns and pass notes.

Reference:

Reiss, D. (1969). Individual thinking and family interaction. #IV. A study of information exchange in families of normals, those with character disorders and schizophrenics. *J Nerv Ment, 149,* 473–490.

I-2/a
1014. BALSWICK, J. Spouse Participation Support Scale

Avail: 1970 Ref.

Variables Measured: Spouse participation support

Instrument Description: This is a 3-item Likert-type scale examining frequency of attending events, relaxational activities, and meals eaten with one's spouse.

Reference:

Balswick, J. (1970). The effect of spouse companionship support on employment success. *J Mar Fam, 32,* 212–215.

I-2/c/e/C
1015. DENTLER, R. A., & MONROE, L. J. Home Centered Activity Scale

Avail: 1961 Ref.

Variables Measured: Adolescent activities engaged in at home versus away from home

Instrument Description: Subjects indicate how much of their time is spent on each of five activities, some of which are home oriented and some of which are not home oriented.

Reference:

Dentler, R. A., & Monroe, L. J. (1961). The family and early adolescent conformity and deviance. *J Mar Fam, 23,* 241–247.

I-2/II-2/c
1016. DYER, E. D. Democratic Companionship Conception of the Family

Avail: 1970 Ref.

Variables Measured: Roles of companionship and democratic decision making in development of the ideal home environment

Instrument Description: Six multiple-choice interview questions examining the importance of the above variables are asked of subjects.

Reference:

Dyer, E. D. (1970). Upward social mobility and nuclear family integration as perceived by the wife in Swedish urban families. *J Mar Fam, 32,* 341–350.

I-2/c
1017. DYER, E. D. Leisure Time Index

Avail: 1970 Ref.

Variables Measured: Extent to which leisure time activities are shared family activities

Instrument Description: Respondent lists all leisure time activities and is asked whether and how often each activity is shared with another family member.

Reference:

Dyer, E. D. (1970). Upward social mobility and nuclear family integration as perceived by the wife in Swedish families. *J Mar Fam, 32,* 341–350.

I-2/g
1018. HILL, R. J. Favorableness of Attitude to Marriage Scale

Avail: 1954 Ref.

Variables Measured: Attitudes toward marriage and remaining single

Instrument Description: Nine items are asked concerning favorableness toward being married.

Reference:

Wallin, P. (1954). Marital happiness of parents and their children's attitude to marriage. *Am Sociol R, 19,* 20–23.

I-2/g/W
1019. HILL, R. L. Wife's Self-Sufficiency Score

Avail: 1949 Ref.

Variables Measured: Self-sufficiency of wife while husband was away at war

Instrument Description: Six open-ended questions are asked about life during separation due to World War II.

Reference:

Hill, R. L. (1949). *Families under stress: Adjustment to the crises of war separation and reunion.* New York: Harper.

I-2/I-3/g/d
1020. INKELES, A., & MILLER, K. A. Comparative Family Modernism-1 Scale

Avail: 1974 Ref.

Variables Measured: Opinions toward family size limitation, autonomy from family elders, equal rights of women, and the family as a source of prestige in society

Instrument Description: Respondents are asked 8 items designed to be comparable across diverse cultures at different levels of development.

Reference:

Inkeles, A., & Miller, K. A. (1974). Construction and validation of a cross-national scale of family modernism. *Int J Sociol Fam, 4,* 127–147.

I-2/c
1021. KLAPP, O. E. Family Ritual Index

Avail: 1959 Ref.

Variables Measured: Ritual behavior, defined as "symbolic behavior that develops in groups and is repeated for its own sake because of the meaning and satisfaction that participants get out of it"

Instrument Description: Subject indicates presence or absence of 26 family rituals and the degree of importance placed on each by his or her family.

Reference:

Klapp, O. E. (1959). Ritual and family solidarity. *Social Forc, 37,* 212–214.

I-2/I-4/b/g/C
1022. LeCOMTE, W. F., & LeCOMTE, G. K. Family Traditionalism Scales

Avail: 1973 Ref.

Variables Measured: Approval of traditional values regarding career choice, dating, religion, woman's role, father's authority, respect for elders, and marriage

Instrument Description: This is a 35-item questionnaire (five items for each of the seven values listed above) using a 7-point Likert-type scale measuring approval/disapproval of each set of traditional values.

Reference:

LeComte, W. F., & LeComte, G. K. (1973). Generational attribution in Turkish and American youth. *J Cross-Cul, 4,* 175–186.

I-2/g
1023. MURSTEIN, B. I. Expediency Scale (Scale E)

Avail: 1976 Ref.

Variables Measured: The desire to be married or to marry at some point in the future

Instrument Description: Respondents are asked 22 questions related to the desire to marry. All but 4 items are answered either *yes* or *no.*

Reference:

Murstein, B. I. (1976). *Who will marry whom? Theories and research in marital choice.* New York: Springer.

I-2/c/C
1024. STROUP, A. L., & ROBINS, L. N. Conforming Family Life-Style Scale

Avail: 1972 Ref.

Variables Measured: Conformity and concern of parents

Instrument Description: Subject indicates which of 10 criteria are met by their parents.

Reference:

Stroup, A. L., & Robins, L. N. (1972). Elementary school predictors of high school dropout among Black males. *Sociol Educ, 45,* 212–222.

I-2/c/C
1025. STROUP, A. L., & ROBINS, L. N. Disorganized Family Life-Style Scale

Avail: 1972 Ref.

Variables Measured: Disorganization or illegitimacy of a child's home environment

Instrument Description: Subjects indicate which of 12 criteria are met by their parents. Scores are interpreted as indicating the degree of disorganization of the home environment.

Reference:

Stroup, A. L., & Robins, L. N. (1972). Elementary school predictors of high school dropout among Black males. *Sociol Educ, 45,* 212–222.

I-2/c/C
1026. STROUP, A. L., & ROBINS, L. N. High Status Childhood Home Scale

Avail: 1972 Ref.

Variables Measured: Status of the child's home environment

Instrument Description: Subjects indicate which of seven criteria are met by their home environment.

Reference:

Stroup, A. L., & Robins, L. N. (1972). Elementary school predictors of high school dropout among Black males. *Sociol Educ, 45,* 212–222.

I-2/III-2/c/C
1027. TULKIN, S. R. Family Participation Scale

Avail: NAPS-2

Variables Measured: Child's perception of frequency of interactions with parents

Instrument Description: Children indicate which activities they participate in with their parents as well as the amount of time spent in joint activities.

Reference:

Tulkin, S. R. (1968). Race, class, family and school achievement. *J Pers Soc Psy, 9,* 31–37.

I-2/g
1028. VEROFF, J., & FELD, S. Marriage Restrictiveness Index

Avail: 1970 Ref.

Variables Measured: Perception of marriage as restrictive and burdensome compared with the single life

Instrument Description: Questions are asked regarding life-style changes that resulted from getting married.

Reference:

Veroff, J., & Feld, S. (1970). *Marriage and work in America.* New York: Van Nostrand Reinhold.

I-3/d
1029. ABRAHAMSON, M. Pervasiveness of Kinship Organization Index

Avail: 1969 Ref.

Variables Measured: Working, living, and interacting with extended families

Instrument Description: Four items examine the impact of extended families on daily living.

Reference:

Abrahamson, M. (1969). Correlates of political complexity. *Am Sociol R, 34,* 690–701.

I-3/IV-1/d
1030. ALDOUS, J. Intergenerational Continuity Index

Avail: 1965 Ref.

Variables Measured: Continuity across generations in religious affiliation, education, and marital role factors

Instrument Description: This instrument examines differences between three generations of a family on the above-listed variables.

Reference:

Aldous, J. (1965). The consequences of intergenerational continuity. *J Mar Fam, 27,* 462–468.

I-3/d
1031. BERARDO, F. M. Kinship Interaction

Avail: NAPS-2

Variables Measured: Frequency of visiting relatives

Instrument Description: Subjects are asked how often they see each of a series of close relatives.

Reference:

Berardo, F. M. (1966). Kinship interaction and migrant adaptation in an aerospace-related community. *J Mar Fam, 28,* 296–304.

I-3/d
1032. BULTENA, G. L. Familial Interaction Index

Avail: 1969 Ref.

Variables Measured: Frequency of interaction between the elderly and their families

Instrument Description: The elderly person is asked how often he or she sees each sibling and each adult child.

Reference:

Bultena, G. L. (1969). Rural-urban differences in the familial interaction of the aged. *Rural Socio, 34,* 5–15.

I-3/c/e/C
1033. KANDEL, D. B., & LESSER, G. S. Index of Reliance

Avail: 1972 Ref.

Variables Measured: Person a child would rely on for personal advice

Instrument Description: Ten situations are presented with a choice of seven people to go to for advice, and child indicates the person he or she would approach.

Reference:

Kandel, D. B., & Lesser, G. S. (1972). *Youth in two worlds.* San Francisco: Jossey-Bass.

I-3/d
1034. KEY, W. H. Family Participation Scale

Avail: 1961 Ref.

Variables Measured: Frequency of visits with both the immediate and the extended families

Instrument Description: Subject is asked 11 questions examining interactions with family members.

Reference:

Key, W. H. (1961). Rural-urban differences and the family. *Sociol Q, 2,* 49–56.

I-3/II-2/d
1035. LITWAK, E. Extended Family Orientation Scale

Avail: 1960 Ref.

Variables Measured: Like or dislike of extended family

Instrument Description: Four items are asked examining familial interaction preferences.

Reference:

Litwak, E. (1960). Occupational mobility and extended family cohesion. *Am Sociol R, 25,* 9–21.

I-3/d
1036. ROGERS, E. M., SEBALD, H., & ANDREWS, W. H. Family Integration and Kinship Orientation Scales

Avail: 1962 Ref.

Variables Measured: Family integration and kinship orientation

Instrument Description: A series of 27 items are used to assess the involvement of the family in the activities and lives of other family members.

Reference:

Rogers, E. M., & Sebald, H. (1962). Familism, family integration and kinship orientation. *Mar Fam Living, 24,* 25–30.

I-3/c
1037. ROSEN, B. C. Familistic-Individualistic Value Orientation

Avail: 1956 Ref.

Variables Measured: Independent orientation versus reliance on family

Instrument Description: Nine items examine specific areas of family versus independent orientation.

Reference:

Rosen, B. C. (1956). The achievement syndrome: A psychocultural dimension of social stratification. *Am Sociol R, 21,* 203–211.

I-3/d
1038. SCHNAIBERG, A. Extended Family Ties Index

Avail: 1970 Ref.

Variables Measured: Adult relationships with their parents and other adult relatives; the extent to which the extended family plays an important part in their lives

Instrument Description: Seven items are asked about family relationships.

Reference:

Schnaiberg, A. (1970). Measuring modernism: Theoretical and empirical explorations. *Am J Sociol, 76,* 399–425.

I-3/d
1039. SCHWARZWELLER, H. K. Kinship Involvement Measures

Avail: 1971 Ref.

Variables Measured: Frequency of visits with relatives living within 50 miles

Instrument Description: This measure, which can be used as a short interview or question-naire, asks about family visits.

Reference:

Schwarzweller, H. K., Brown, J. S., & Mangalam, J. J. (1971). *Mountain families in transition.* University Park: Pennsylvania State University Press.

I-3/d
1040. STRAUS, M. A. Kinship Integration and Network Connectedness Indexes

Avail: NAPS-2

Variables Measured: Proportion of social life involving relatives and extent to which friends are friends of each other

Instrument Description: Subjects are asked to indicate the eight people they most often visit socially and whether each person named is a relative.

Reference:

Straus, M. A. (1969). Social class and farm-city differences in interaction with kin in relation to societal modernization. *Rural Socio, 34,* 476–495.

I-3/II-2/d
1041. STRAUS, M. A. Kinship Solidarity Indexes

Avail: NAPS-2

Variables Measured: Liking for and frequency of visiting relatives

Instrument Description: Subjects indicate how often they visit and how much they like each of their brothers, sisters, aunts, and uncles.

Reference:

Hutter, M. (1970). Transformation of identity, social mobility, and kinship solidarity. *J Mar Fam, 32,* 133–137.

I-3/f/C
1042. SWEETSER, D. A. Communication Scale

Avail: 1970 Ref.

Variables Measured: Frequency of interaction between adult siblings

Instrument Description: Subject is asked about frequency of uninvited and invited visits and phone conversations with siblings.

Reference:

Sweetser, D. A. (1970). The structure of sibling relationships. *Am J Sociol, 76,* 47–58.

I-3/a/e
1043. UDRY, J. R., & HALL, M. Interconnectedness of Social Networks Index

Avail: 1965 Ref.

Variables Measured: Interconnectedness of spouses' social networks

Instrument Description: Interviews are conducted with the four people named by each spouse as being frequent contacts. Questions revolve around their knowledge of others also named.

Reference:

Udry, J. R., & Hall, M. (1965). Marital role segregation and social networks in middle-class middle-aged couples. *J Mar Fam, 27,* 392–395.

I-3/d
1044. WINCH, R. F., & GREER, S. A. Extended Familism Scale

Avail: NAPS-2

Variables Measured: Presence of, interaction with, and support (through trading services) of kin in the community

Instrument Description: This is an interview procedure in which questions focus on relations and mutually advantageous activities carried out with area kin.

Reference:

Winch, R. F., & Greer, S. A. (1968). Urbanism, ethnicity, and extended familism. *J Mar Fam, 30,* 40–45.

I-3/f/C
1045. YOURGLICH, A., & SCHIESSL, D. Sibling Systems Scale

Avail: NAPS-2

Variables Measured: Actions and behavioral expectations between siblings

Instrument Description: Subjects are administered a 62-item scale asking frequency with which they contact siblings, and the reliance upon the sibling for various types of interactions.

Reference:

Yourglich, A. (1966). Constructing a sibling systems measurement device. *Fam Coord, 15,* 107–111.

I-4/c
1046. BEHRENS, M. L., MEYERS, D. I., GOLDFARB, W., GOLDFARB, N., & FIELDSTEEL, N. D. Henry Ittleson Center Family Interaction Scales

Avail: 1969 Ref.

Variables Measured: Seven aspects of family life, including parent-child, spousal, and sibling interactions

Instrument Description: Ratings are made of families on each of the scales according to observations made during a three-hour home visit that includes mealtime. Focus is on evaluating the family as a dynamic unit and on interactions of family members.

Reference:

Behrens, M. L., Meyers, D. I., Goldfarb, W., Goldfarb, N., & Fieldsteel, N. D. (1969). The Henry Ittleson family interaction scales. *Genet Psych Mon, 80,* 203–295.

I-4/b/C
1047. BERG, I. Self-Administered Dependency Questionnaire (SADQ)

Avail: 1974 Ref.

Variables Measured: Child dependence on mother for affection, communication, assistance, and travel

Instrument Description: This 21-item questionnaire, completed by mothers, asks questions about behavior during a typical school week of the past three months.

Reference:

Berg, I. (1974). A self-administered dependency questionnaire for use with the mothers of school children. *Br J Psychi, 124,* 1–9.

I-4/c
1048. BORKE, H. A Method for Systematically Observing Family Interaction

Avail: 1967 Ref.

Variables Measured: Social interaction within the family

Instrument Description: Taped family interactions are used to classify interactional styles between individual family members as generally going toward, against, or away from each other, according to Horney's classifications. Eight primary categories and 20 subcategories are used.

Reference:

Borke, H. (1967). The communication of intent: A systematic approach to the observation of family interaction. *Human Relat, 20,* 13–28.

I-4/c
1049. BORKE, H. A Procedure for Analyzing Family Interaction from Video Tapes

Avail: 1969 Ref.

Variables Measured: Verbal and nonverbal family interactions. Seeking and giving information, support, and guidance, as well as other related behaviors

Instrument Description: Videotapes of family interactions are evaluated for 12 content areas. All areas deal with types and quality of interactions.

Reference:

Borke, H. (1969). The communication of intent: A revised procedure for analyzing family interaction from video tapes. *J Mar Fam, 31,* 541–544.

I-4/c/e/C
1050. BOWERMAN, C. E., & KINCH, J. W. Family-Peer Group Orientation Questionnaire

Avail: NAPS-1

Variables Measured: Influence of family versus friends on children

Instrument Description: Subjects indicate whether family or friends exert greater influence on a number of criteria.

Reference:

Bowerman, C. E., & Kinch, J. W. (1959). Changes in family and peer orientation of children between the fourth and tenth grades. *Social Forc, 37,* 206–211.

I-4/c
1051. BRIM, O. G., Jr., FAIRCHILD, R. W., & BORGATTA, E. F. Family Problems Index

Avail: 1961 Ref.

Variables Measured: Child rearing, husband-wife relations, style of life, community involvement, and religion

Instrument Description: Subjects check which of 25 items related to family life during the past year they see as problems needing solutions.

Reference:

Brim, O. G., Jr., Fairchild, R. W., & Borgatta, E. F. (1961). Relations between family problems. *Mar Fam Living, 23,* 219–226.

I-4/III-2/b/e/C
1052. BRITTAIN, C. V. Cross-Pressures Test (CPT)

Avail: 1963 Ref.

Variables Measured: Peer versus parental influences on adolescent decisions

Instrument Description: Twelve forced-choice items are included where one choice would be approved of by parents and the other by friends. Scale is meant to be answered by adolescents.

Reference:

Brittain, C. V. (1963). Adolescent choices and parent-peer cross pressures. *Am Sociol R, 28,* 385–391.

I-4/a
1053. BURGESS, E. W., & WALLIN, P. Engagement Success Inventory

Avail; 1954 Ref.

Variables Measured: Likelihood of success of an engagement

Instrument Description: This 25-item questionnaire, administered to engaged couples, examines areas of agreement/disagreement and satisfaction in demonstration of affection, confiding, common interests, and areas of complaints.

Reference:

Burgess, E. W., Wallin, P., & Shultz, G. D. (1954). *Courtship, engagement and marriage* (pp. 236–241, 429–430). Philadelphia: Lippincott.

I-4/a
1054. CARLAN, R. W., REYNOLDS, R., GREEN, L. W., & KHAN, N. I. Interspousal Agreement Index

Avail: 1971 Ref.

Variables Measured: Extent to which husband and wife agree in areas related to decision making, finances, religion, moving, and desired qualities of daughter-in-law

Instrument Description: An 8-item questionnaire is given separately to husband and wife. Interspousal agreement score is derived from level of agreement on all items.

Reference:

Carlan, R. W., Reynolds, R., Green, L. W., & Khan, N. I. (1971). Underlying sources of agreement and communication between husbands and wives in Dacca, East Pakistan. *J Mar Fam, 33,* 571–583.

I-4/c
1055. CATTELL, R. B., & CABOT, P. S. Family Attitude Scales

Avail: 1948 Ref.

Variables Measured: Emotional relations, including affection, hostility, domination, overprotection, and jealousy among family members

Instrument Description: Ten scales of 24 items each are used in rating the strength of attitudes held by family members. Instrument is meant to be used by a social worker following direct observation of the family.

Reference:

Cattell, K. B. (1948). *A guide to mental testing* (pp. 302–325). London: University of London Press.

I-4/c
1056. CAVAN, R. Rating Scales for Family Integration and Adaptability

Avail: 1945 Ref.

Variables Measured: Degree of affection, cooperation, shared activities, tension, economic interdependence, materialistic orientation, and responsibility in families

Instrument Description: Scale measures 17 factors related to family integration and adaptability. Ratings are made by caseworkers from case reports.

Reference:

Burgess, E. W., & Locke, H. J. (1945). *The family.* Chicago: University of Chicago Press.

I-4/IV-2/c
1057. CHANCE, E. Family Interaction Scoring System

Avail: 1955 Ref.

Variables Measured: Interpersonal relations along dimensions of positive versus negative and controlling versus submissive behavior, conflicts, and defense mechanisms

Instrument Description: Ratings are made following interviews with families. Twenty items from four categories are used in evaluating family members. A parallel Q-sort with 20 items is also used to have subjects evaluate themselves and other family members.

Reference:

Chance, E. (1955). Measuring the potential interplay of forces within the family during treatment. *Child Dev, 26,* 241–265.

I-4/c/C
1058. COBB, H. V. Sentence-Completion Wish Test

Avail: 1954 Ref.

Variables Measured: Child's wishes concerning parents' and siblings' behaviors and characteristics

Instrument Description: Subjects are asked to complete 24 sentence stems related to their wishes for parental and sibling behaviors and characteristics.

Reference:

Cobb, H. V. (1954). Role-wishes and general wishes of children and adolescents. *Child Dev, 25*, 161–171.

I-4/c/W
1059. COUGHENOUR, M. C. Family Functions of Activities in Food Consumption

Avail: NAPS-2

Variables Measured: Homemaker satisfaction with activities related to family food consumption (shopping, cooking, eating, and so on)

Instrument Description: The scale consists of 16 items that ask for frequency of events and satisfaction with those events.

Reference:

Coughenour, C. M. (1972). Functional aspects of food consumption activity and family life cycle stages. *J Mar Fam, 34*, 656–664.

I-4/c
1060. CRAWFORD, C. O. Attachment to Family of Orientation Index

Avail: 1966 Ref.

Variables Measured: Shared activities with family members

Instrument Description: Four questions ask about subject's willingness to interact with his or her family in various common situations.

Reference:

Crawford, C. O. (1966). Family attachment, family support for migration and migration plans of young people. *Rural Socio, 31*, 293–300.

I-4/a
1061. CROUSE, B., KARLINS, M., & SCHRODER, H. M. Integrative Complexity in Marriage Index

Avail: 1968 Ref.

Variables Measured: Ability of each partner to be adaptive and flexible

Instrument Description: This 3-item sentence-completion test examines adaptive and flexible behavior of husband and wife.

Reference:

Crouse, B., Karlins, M., & Schroder, H. M. (1968). Conceptual complexity and marital happiness. *J Mar Fam, 30*, 643–646.

I-4/f/g/C
1062. DALES, R. J. Developmental Tasks Scale for Sibling Relations

Avail: NAPS-1

Variables Measured: Sibling relations

Instrument Description: A checklist is used to enable children to indicate whether problems exist in each of five areas.

Reference:

Dales, R. J. (1955). A method for measuring developmental tasks: Scales for selected tasks at the beginning of adolescence. *Child Dev, 26*, 111–122.

I-4/c
1063. ERON, L. D., WALDER, L. O., & LEFKOWITZ, M. M. Parental Disharmony Scale

Avail: 1971 Ref.

Variables Measured: Disagreement about matters of importance to the family

Instrument Description: This is a structured interview with 13 questions on family disharmony. Item scores (0–3) are summed to arrive at an overall disharmony score.

Reference:

Eron, L. D., Walder, L. O., & Lefkowitz, M. M. (1971). *Learning of aggression in children.* Boston: Little, Brown.

I-4/II-4/c/C
1064. EVANS, R. B. Family Background Questionnaire

Avail: NAPS-2

Variables Measured: Growing-up variables related to later male homosexuality

Instrument Description: A total of 27 items asking about family background are answered using a scale from *often* to *never*.

Reference:

Evans, R. B. (1969). Childhood parental relationships of homosexual men. *J Cons Clin, 33*, 129–135.

I-4/a
1065. FELDMAN, H., & RAND, M. E. Egocentrism-Altercentrism Rating Scale for Husband-Wife Interaction

Avail: 1965 Ref.

Variables Measured: Concern for self, partner, or self and partner combination

Instrument Description: Partners are given conflicting instructions preceding participation in a six-minute tape-recorded role-play situation. Each is unaware of the other's instructions. Interactions are observed for egocentric and altercentric behaviors.

Reference:

Feldman, H., & Rand, M. E. (1965). Egocentrism-altercentrism in the husband-wife relationship. *J Mar Fam, 27,* 386–391.

I-4/c/g/C
1066. FERDINAND, T. N., & LUCHTERHAND, E. G. Family Background Scores

Avail: 1970 Ref.

Variables Measured: Child's estrangement from family, parental advice-seeking, permissiveness, and family discord

Instrument Description: Children are asked 16 questions or are asked to respond to 16 statements related to the above variables. Scores are combined to come up with the four indexes.

Reference:

Ferdinand, T. N., & Luchterhand, E. G. (1970). Inner-city youth, the police, the juvenile court, and justice. *Social Prob, 17,* 510–527.

I-4/c
1067. GERARD, D. L., & SIEGEL, J. Family Background Interview and Rating Scales

Avail: 1950 Ref.

Variables Measured: Parenting style, agreement between parents, family interaction styles, and issues related to adjustment of parents to family life

Instrument Description: Parents are questioned during an unstructured three-hour interview about their attitudes and behaviors on 19 categories, ranging from their relationship to the adjustment of their children. A minimum of direct questioning is used. Ratings are made on all categories following the interview.

Reference:

Gerard, D. L., & Siegel, J. (1950). The family background of schizophrenia. *Psychiat Q, 24,* 47–73.

I-4/IV-2/a
1068. GOODRICH, D. W., & BOOMER, D. S. Color-Matching Technique

Avail: NAPS-1

Variables Measured: Conflict resolution, activity level, communication, ability to agree, dominance-submission, and maintenance of esteem

Instrument Description: Husband and wife independently see and identify color matches. They attempt to agree on which shade is represented. Half the colors seen by partners are identical. Half are different. Conflict resolution where differences occur is the focus.

Reference:

Goodrich, D. W., & Boomer, D. S. (1963). Experimental assessment of modes of conflict resolution. *Fam Process, 2,* 15–24.

I-4/c
1069. GUTTMAN, H. A. A Unit Method of Coding Unfamiliar Interaction

Avail: 1972 Ref.

Variables Measured: Interaction of family members

Instrument Description: Tape recordings of interactions between mother, father, and child are time-sampled for relevant content. All activity, including silences, is coded every five seconds.

Reference:

Guttman, H. A. (1972). A time-unit method of coding intrafamilial interaction from the audiotape. *Psychother, 9,* 267–268.

I-4/c
1070. HALEY, J. Family Interaction Patterns

Avail: 1964 Ref.

Variables Measured: Family oral interactional patterns; areas of organization or patterning in family interactions

Instrument Description: A specially built machine, the Family Interaction Analyzer, analyzes verbal input by each member of a family triad while they discuss items and stories that are presented. Frequency of interactions between each combination of mother, father, and child are determined and compared.

Reference:

Haley, J. (1964). Research on family patterns: An instrument measurement. *Fam Process, 3,* 41–65.

I-4/b/C
1071. HARTUP, W. W. Parental Imitation Interview

Avail: ADI Doc. 7745

Variables Measured: Child's choice of same-sex versus opposite-sex parent as a model when making decisions involving setting of goals and values

Instrument Description: Child is presented with 18 situations in which he or she manipulates a child doll while the mother and father dolls are manipulated by the experimenter.

Reference:

Hartup, W. W. (1962). Some correlates of parental imitation in young children. *Child Dev, 33,* 85–96.

I-4/c/C
1072. HAWORTH, M. R. Rock-a-Bye Baby (Projective Film for Children)

Avail: 1959 Ref.

Variables Measured: Identification, jealousy, aggression toward parents, guilt, anxiety, and obsessive trends

Instrument Description: Children are shown a film about a boy puppet and his baby-sitter. The film is stopped early and subjects are asked to provide endings. Following completion, subjects are queried as to their impressions of the boy puppet.

Reference:

Haworth, M. R., & Woltmann, A. G. (1959). *Rock-a-Bye Baby: A group projective test for children* [Manual and film]. University Park, PA: Psychological Cinema Register.

I-4/c
1073. HAYWARD, R. S. Family Inventory

Avail: 1935 Ref.

Variables Measured: Adjustment of child and parents, attitudes toward child adjustment, compatibility of husband and wife, and compatibility of other family members

Instrument Description: This instrument, designed for children ages 9 and over and adults, measures the variables listed above. The long form contains 319 items. The short form contains 80 items.

Reference:

Hayward, R. S. (1935). The child's report of psychological factors in the family. *Arch Psychol, New York, 189,* 75.

I-4/b/C
1074. HEILBRUN, A. B., Jr. Parent-Child Identification Measures

Avail: 1965 Ref.

Variables Measured: Primary identification of child with mother versus father

Instrument Description: This is a 3-part, 300-item, adjective checklist on which the child indicates items where there is identification with parent.

Reference:

Heilbrun, A. B., Jr. (1965). The measurement of identification. *Child Dev, 36,* 111–127.

I-4/c/C
1075. HESTON, J. C. Heston Personal Adjustment Inventory

Avail: 1949 Ref.

Variables Measured: Child's satisfaction with home life

Instrument Description: A total of 270 questions, each answered *yes-no* and meant to be administered to children, deal with various aspects of home life satisfaction for children.

Reference:

Heston, J. C. (1949). *Heston Personal Adjustment Inventory.* Yonkers, NY: World Book.

I-4/b/C
1076. HETHERINGTON, E. M., & FRANKIE, G. Parent-Imitation Task

Avail: 1967 Ref.

Variables Measured: Child's imitation of mother versus father during free play

Instrument Description: Child watches mother and father play, then enters the playroom without parents present. Observations are made concerned with which parent is imitated.

Reference:

Hetherington, E. M., & Frankie, G. (1967). Effects of parental dominance, warmth, and conflict on imitation in children. *J Pers Soc Psy, 6,* 119–125.

I-4/a
1077. HILL, R. L. Husband-Wife Interaction Index

Avail: 1970 Ref.

Variables Measured: Husband and wife roles in marital communication strategies

Instrument Description: Interviewer rates husband and wife as they attempt to come to agreement regarding the answers to six questions designed to generate discussion. Ratings are according to a structured code.

Reference:

Hill, R. L. (1970). *Family development in three generations*. Cambridge MA: Schenkman.

I-4/a
1078. HILL, R. L., STYCOS, J. M., & BACK, K. W. Spousal Communication Scale

Avail: 1959 Ref.

Variables Measured: Husband's and wife's views on issues related to religion, discipline of children, future plans, sexual relations, birth control, and ideal family size

Instrument Description: Husbands are asked 4 items and wives are asked 5 items related to their communication on various topics.

Reference:

Hill, R. L., Stycos, J. M., & Back, K. W. (1959). *The family and population control: A Puerto Rican experiment in social change*. Chapel Hill: University of North Carolina Press.

I-4/V-2/a
1079. HUNTINGTON, R. M. The Marital Projection Series

Avail: NAPS-1

Variables Measured: Ability of the husband and wife to agree and compromise

Instrument Description: Husband and wife are each separately presented with 10 pictures. When later brought together, they are asked to jointly come up with a story about each. Responses may be analyzed using any of three techniques provided.

Reference:

Huntington, R. M. (1958). The personality-interaction approach to study of the marital relationship. *Mar Fam Living, 20,* 43–46.

I-4/c/C
1080. JACKSON, L. A Test of Family Attitudes

Avail: 1950 Ref.

Variables Measured: Child's maternal and sibling dependency, jealousy, guilt, and fears

Instrument Description: This is a projective technique in which subjects view each of six cards and tell stories related to each card. Scoring procedures are provided.

Reference:

Jackson, L. (1950). Emotional attitudes towards the family of normal, neurotic, and delinquent children. *Br J Psycho, 41,* 35–51 (part 1), 173–185 (part 2).

I-4/b/C
1081. JOHNSON, M. H., & MEADOW, A. Measure of Parental Identification

Avail: 1966 Ref.

Variables Measured: Child's identification with mother versus father

Instrument Description: This is a 70-item list of adjectives and short phrases to be Q-sorted into seven categories. Five separate sorts are conducted: two self-sorts, an ideal sort, and father and mother sorts. The two self-sorts serve as a reliability check.

Reference:

Johnson, M. H., & Meadow, A. (1966). Parental identification among male schizophrenics. *J Personal, 34,* 300–309.

I-4/a
1082. KEELER, R. Marriage Readiness Rating Scale (MRRS)

Avail: 1962 Ref.

Variables Measured: Degree of readiness for marriage of high school girls

Instrument Description: Three descriptive statements under a 7-point graphic rating scale are used for each of 41 items. The scale, designed for use by school counselors, assesses maturity, interpersonal skills, and homemaking abilities.

Reference:

Keeler, R. (1962). The development of a marriage readiness rating scale. *University of Nebraska Agricultural Experiment Station Bulletin* [Lincoln], no. 204.

I-4/IV-2/a
1083. KERCKHOFF, A. C. Dimensions of Husband-Wife Interaction

Avail: 1972 Ref.

Variables Measured: Leadership, assertion, cooperation, and dependence in the marital relationship

Instrument Description: Conversations between husband and wife are transcribed and coded along dimensions of dominance-submission and integration-division. Scores are summed to arrive at combinations and categories.

Reference:

Kerckhoff, A. C. (1972). Two dimensions of husband-wife interaction. *Sociol Q, 13,* 49–60.

I-4/II-5/c
1084. KLAPP, O. E. Family Solidarity Index

Avail: 1959 Ref.

Variables Measured: Family cohesiveness

Instrument Description: This is a three-part questionnaire with a total of 21 items asking whether statements apply to the respondent and his or her family.

Reference:

Klapp, O. E. (1959). Ritual and family solidarity. *Social Forc, 37,* 212–214.

I-4/IV-2/c
1085. LEVINGER, G., & GUNNER, J. Interpersonal Grid

Avail: 1967 Ref.

Variables Measured: Family love-hate and dominance-submission dimensions

Instrument Description: Subjects place pairs of silhouetted human and rectangular figures onto a neutral background. Horizontal closeness indicates love or hate. Relative vertical position indicates power relationship.

Reference:

Levinger, G., & Gunner, J. (1967). The interpersonal grid: 1. Felt and tape techniques for the measurement of social relationships. *Psychonom Sci, 8,* 173–174.

I-4/b/a
1086. LEWIN, M. Family Relations Scales

Avail: NAPS-2

Variables Measured: Marital authority structure, parental expectations, control, and tolerance for children's ideas and behaviors

Instrument Description: This questionnaire consists of seven scales with 68 multiple-choice items. The primary form emphasizes attitudes related to adolescent children. An alternate husband/wife form is available for some variables.

Reference:

Papanek, M. L. (1969). Authority and sex roles in the family. *J Mar Fam, 31,* 88–96.

I-4/c
1087. MacFARLANE, J. W. Scales for Rating Family Situations

Avail: 1938 Ref.

Variables Measured: Aspects of family life including adjustment issues, personalities of family members, status, cooperation, and use of leisure time

Instrument Description: Ratings are based on structured, quasi-conversational interviews. Two scales are scored: (1) scale for rating family background data and (2) code sheet on the family situation.

Reference:

MacFarlane, J. W. (1938). Studies in child guidance: I. Methodology of data collection and organization. *Mon S Res C, 3.*

I-4/c
1088. MARTIN, B. Three-Way Family Interaction Task

Avail: 1967 Ref.

Variables Measured: Family interaction and blaming patterns

Instrument Description: Three family members seated around a table are instructed to communicate with each other about various topics. A small movable panel is controlled by the speaker and serves to keep each interaction between two of the three participants. Interactions are rated on several criteria.

Reference:

Martin, B. (1967). Family interaction associated with child disturbance: Assessment and modification. *Psychother, 4,* 30–35.

I-4/c
1089. MISHLER, E. G., & WAXLER, N. Mishler and Waxler Interaction Codes

Avail: 1968 Ref.

Variables Measured: Specific aspects of family interaction, each of which is measured by an independent code

Instrument Description: A questionnaire is used to generate discussions among three family members. The interaction is both observed and tape-recorded. Ratings are made on the basis of observations and transcripts of the interaction.

Reference:

Mishler, E. G., & Waxler, N. E. (1968). *Interaction in families.* New York: John Wiley.

I-4/a
1090. MITCHELL, R. E. Mitchell Family Relationship Indexes

Avail: 1972 Ref.

Variables Measured: Interactional styles of parents during typical conversations as well as in solving family and marital disputes

Instrument Description: Questions covering eight categories are asked during an interview with the marital couple.

Reference:

Mitchell, R. E. (1972). Husband-wife relations and family-planning practices in urban Hong Kong. *J Mar Fam, 34,* 139–146.

I-4/II-5/c
1091. MOXLEY, R. L. Family Solidarity Scale

Avail: 1973 Ref.

Variables Measured: Extent to which family attempts to project an image of unity

Instrument Description: Examiner scores family on 11 criteria designed to measure the projection of unity following a brief interview.

Reference:

Moxley, R. L. (1973). Family solidarity and quality of life in an agricultural Peruvian community. *J Mar Fam, 35,* 497–504.

I-4/c
1092. MURRELL, S. A., & STACHOWIAK, J. G. Family Interaction Tasks

Avail: 1967 Ref.

Variables Measured: Family structural stability and interactional style

Instrument Description: Mother, father, and one child are observed during the completion of three tasks (write answers to questions about family, list adjectives about the family, and answer situation choice questionnaire). Criteria are established for categorizing response patterns and specific answers.

Reference:

Murrell, S. A., & Stachowiak, J. G. (1967). Consistency, rigidity, and power in the interaction patterns of clinic and nonclinic families. *J Abn Psych, 72,* 265–272.

I-4/c/C
1093. MYERS, T. R. Intra-Family Relationships Questionnaire

Avail: 1935 Ref.

Variables Measured: Relationships between parents, parent and children, and children as well as parental supervision and discipline

Instrument Description: Questionnaire with 113 items answered by children is used to examine the above-listed variables.

Reference:

Myers, T. R. (1935). Intra-family relationships and pupil adjustment. *Teachers College Contribution to Education,* no. 651.

I-4/c/C
1094. NEUGARTEN, B. L., & GUTMANN, D. L. Adult Family Scene

Avail: 1958 Ref.

Variables Measured: Intergenerational relationships between young adults and their parents as well as age and sex-role characteristics of adult children

Instrument Description: Subject is asked to tell a story in response to a thematic apperception picture showing a young man and woman and an older man and woman in a group arrangement. Stories are analyzed in several dynamic ways.

Reference:

Neugarten, B. L., & Gutmann, D. L. (1958). Age-sex roles and personality in middle age: A thematic apperception study. *Psychol Mono, 72* (Whole No. 470).

I-4/c/C
1095. NYE, F. I. Nye Family Relationships Scale

Avail: 1958 Ref.

Variables Measured: Children's attitudes toward parents and toward parental involvement in aspects of their lives

Instrument Description: From 5 to 11 items on each of 18 instruments assess acceptance of family interactional styles.

Reference:

Nye, F. I. (1958). *Family relationships and delinquent behavior.* New York: John Wiley.

I-4/b/C
1096. OLINER, M. Measure of Parental Identification

Avail: NAPS-2

Variables Measured: Relative similarity of child to mother and father

Instrument Description: Child responds to 44 items in terms of own interests and those of idealized self, mother, and father.

Reference:

Singer, J. L., & Schonbar, R. A. (1961). Correlates of day dreaming: A dimension of self-awareness. *J Cons Psych, 25,* 1–6.

I-4/c
1097. REISS, D. Hypothesis Testing Task

Avail: 1970 Ref.

Variables Measured: Family styles in terms of risk-taking behavior, cooperation between members, imitation, and reliance on feedback in investigating their environment

Instrument Description: This measure consists of a complex task in which family members simultaneously attempt to solve letter codes on adjacent but connected computers. Strategies and cooperative behaviors are noted. Total task requires approximately two hours.

Reference:

Reiss, D., & Sheriff, W. H., Jr. (1970). A computer-automated procedure for testing some experience of family membership. *Behav Sci, 15,* 431–443.

I-4/I-1/c
1098. ROSEN, B. C. Family Interaction Observation System

Avail: 1973 Ref.

Variables Measured: Level of communication, degree of reciprocity, flow of affect, power, achievement behavior, and aspiration level

Instrument Description: Father, mother, son (aged 10–12) triad is observed and rated during an hour-and-a-half, semistructured activity in their home. Ratings are made during brick stacking, tinker toy construction, and pick up sticks activities.

Reference:

Rosen, B. C. (1973). Social change, migration and family interaction in Brazil. *Am Sociol R, 38,* 198–212.

I-4/c/C
1099. ROSENBERG, S. Stein Family Attitudes Sentence Completion Test

Avail: 1947 Ref.

Variables Measured: Positive versus negative affect toward family members

Instrument Description: One hundred sentence stems are presented, many of which are related to feelings about the subject's mother or father. Responses are scored as positive, negative, or evasive.

Reference:

Stein, M. I. (1947). The use of a sentence completion for the diagnosis of personality. *J Clin Psyc, 3,* 47–56.

I-4/V-2/a
1100. SAFILIOS-ROTHSCHILD, C. Level of Communication Measure

Avail: 1969 Ref.

Variables Measured: Quality and frequency of communication between the husband and wife

Instrument Description: Subject is interviewed and asked about eight areas of communication with his or her spouse. Responses indicate the level of communication and openness present in the marital relationship.

Reference:

Safilios-Rothschild, C. (1969). Attitudes of Greek spouses toward marital infidelity. In G. Neubeck (Ed.), *Extramarital relations* (pp. 77–93). Englewood Cliffs, NJ: Prentice-Hall.

I-4/a
1101. SCHULMAN, M. L. Empathy Test for Idealization in Engaged Couples

Avail: NAPS-2

Variables Measured: Agreements and disagreements between partners in areas covering religion, sexual relations, roles, economics, parents, and politics

Instrument Description: Couples are individually presented with a 37-item *true/false* questionnaire. They are also asked how many times they expect to disagree with their partner and how many times their partner will expect to disagree with them.

Reference:

Schulman, M. L. (1974). Idealization in engaged couples. *J Mar Fam, 36,* 139–147.

I-4/IV-2/c/C
1102. SEARS, R. R., PINTLER, M. H., & SEARS, P. S. Doll Play Family Aggression Measure

Avail: 1946 Ref.

Variables Measured: Children's aggressive play with dolls designed to represent family members

Instrument Description: Free play is allowed with dolls for two 20-minute sessions. Aggressive behaviors are noted and scored.

Reference:

Sears, R. R., Pintler, M. H., & Sears, P. S. (1946). Effect of father separation on preschool children's doll play aggression. *Child Dev, 17,* 219–243.

I-4/IV-2/b/C
1103. SEVERY, L. J. Value Parent Scale

Avail: NAPS-2

Variables Measured: Child's behaviors toward parents

Instrument Description: Eleven *true-false* and multiple-choice items ask the frequency of various behaviors of child toward parent.

Reference:

Severy, L. J. (1973). Exposure to deviance committed by valued peer group and family members. *J Res Crime, 10,* 35–46.

I-4/a
1104. SHOSTROM, E., & KAVANAUGH, J. Abridged Love Attraction Inventory

Avail: 1971 Ref.

Variables Measured: Similarity of love relationship to each of seven categories: mother/son, daddy/doll, bitch/nice-guy, master/servant, hawk, dove, and rhythmic

Instrument Description: A total of 112 *true/false* items assess how close the relationship is to each of the seven categories.

Reference:

Shostrom, E., & Kavanaugh, J. (1971). *Between man and woman.* Los Angeles: Nash.

I-4/c
1105. SIGAL, J. J., RAKOFF, V., & EPSTEIN, N. B. Family Interaction Score

Avail: 1967 Ref.

Variables Measured: Therapist's view of family participation in therapeutic work

Instrument Description: Therapist responds to the statement: "The family cooperates with the therapist. Describe briefly the patterns of collaboration." Reports of interactions between each other, as well as with the therapist, are coded on a scale ranging from *resistant family* unit to *active engagement.* A formula is then used to compute the family interaction score.

Reference:

Sigal, J. J., Rakoff, V., & Epstein, N. B. (1967). Indicators of therapeutic outcome in conjoint family therapy. *Fam Process, 6,* 215–226.

I-4/g
1106. SPORAKOWSKI, M. J. Marital Preparedness Instrument

Avail: 1968 Ref.

Variables Measured: Self-perceptions of marital readiness

Instrument Description: Subject responds to 31 5-point items indicating how well prepared for marriage he or she is in each area. Questionnaire was designed for use in counseling and educational settings.

Reference:

Sporakowski, M. J. (1968). Marital preparedness, prediction, and adjustment. *Fam Coord,* *17,* 155–161.

I-4/b/g/C
1107. STEIMEL, R. J., & SUZIEDELIS, A. Perceived Parental Influence Scale

Avail: 1963 Ref.

Variables Measured: Adults' perception of their mothers' versus fathers' influence during their childhoods

Instrument Description: Subjects respond to 10 items indicating mother's influence and 10 for father's influence during childhood.

Reference:

Steimel, R. J., & Suziedelis, A. (1963). Perceived parental influence and inventoried interests. *J Coun Psyc, 10,* 289–295.

I-4/c/C
1108. SUNDBERG, N., SHARMA, V., WODTLI, T., & ROHILA, P. Family Cohesiveness Score

Avail: NAPS-2

Variables Measured: Adolescents' attitudes toward joint family activities

Instrument Description: A total of 25 questions examine joint activities, to which subjects respond either *yes* or *no.*

Reference:

Sundberg, N., Sharma, V., Wodtli, T., & Rohila, P. (1969). Family cohesiveness and autonomy of adolescents in India and the United States. *J Mar Fam, 31,* 403–407.

I-4/b/C
1109. TEEVAN, J. J., Jr. Parent Orientation Index

Avail: 1972 Ref.

Variables Measured: Extent to which parents serve as the primary reference group for adolescents

Instrument Description: Three questions are asked regarding similarity between subject and each parent.

Reference:

Teevan, J. J., Jr. (1972). Reference groups and premarital sexual behavior. *J Mar Fam, 34,* 283–291.

I-4/g

1110. TERMAN, L. M. Terman Marital Prediction Test

Avail: 1938 Ref.

Variables Measured: Social background and personality factors predictive of marital success

Instrument Description: Subjects answer a 140-item general personality inventory and 29 items related to experiences within the family of origin. Responses are evaluated to determine predictions of marital success.

Reference:

Terman, L. M., assisted by Buttenweiser, P., Ferguson, L. W., Johnson, W. B., & Wilson, D. P. (1938). *Psychological factors in marital happiness.* New York: McGraw-Hill.

I-4/c

1111. TERRILL, J. M., & TERRILL, R. E. Family Communication Method (Interpersonal System)

Avail: 1965 Ref.

Variables Measured: Interpersonal aspects of communication within the family in terms of 8 variables

Instrument Description: The family is given 5 to 8 minutes to "plan something you can do as a family." The interaction is taped and transcribed. The discussion is then coded and rated according to a modified version of the Leary Interpersonal Check List categories.

Reference:

Terrill, J. M., & Terrill, R. E. (1965). A method for studying family communication. *Fam Process, 4,* 259–290.

I-4/b/e/C

1112. UTECH, D. A., & HOVING, K. L. Parent Conformity Measure

Avail: NAPS-2

Variables Measured: Influence of peers versus parents on children's behaviors

Instrument Description: The measure contains 10 items in which a child is forced to choose between behaviors approved of by his or her friends or parents. The scale is given twice, 10–13 days apart.

Reference:

Utech, D. A., & Hoving, K. L. (1969). Parents and peers as competing influences in the decision of children of differing ages. *J Soc Psych, 78,* 267–274.

I-4/c/C
1113. VENEZIA, P. S. Family Information Test (FIT)

Avail: 1968 Ref.

Variables Measured: Factual knowledge about siblings and parents

Instrument Description: This is a 32-item questionnaire, given in interview format, that examines a person's knowledge about his or her siblings and parents.

Reference:

Venezia, P. S. (1968). Delinquency as a function of intrafamily relations. *J Res Crime, 5,* 148–173.

I-4/c
1114. WEINSTEIN, E. A., & GEISEL, P. N. Home Environment Rating Scales

Avail: 1963 Ref.

Variables Measured: Physical and psychological aspects of the home, primarily dealing with types of interactions between family members

Instrument Description: Ratings are made based on an extensive interview with the mother. A large number of rating scales are used, of which 12 are detailed in the reference.

Reference:

Witmer, H. L., Herzog, E., Weinstein, E. A., & Sullivan, M. E. (1963). *Independent adoptions.* New York: Russell Sage.

I-4/III-2/b/e/C
1115. WON, G. Y. M., YAMAMURA, D. S., & IKEDA, K. Parental and Peer Guidance Index

Avail: 1969 Ref.

Variables Measured: Relative frequency of seeking parental versus peer guidance

Instrument Description: Adolescents check those items out of the total of 17 items that they believe to be important to them and indicate whom they would seek out for advice in those areas.

Reference:

Won, G. Y. M., Yamamura, D. S., & Ikeda, K. (1969). The relation of communication with parents and peers to deviant behavior of youth. *J Mar Fam, 31,* 43–47.

II-1/I-3/c
1116. ADAMEK, R. J., & YOST, E. D. Conventionality Index

Avail: NAPS-2

Variables Measured: Attitudes toward communal living, group marriage, living together without marriage, marital roles, premarital sex, abortion, and homosexuality

Instrument Description: This questionnaire, designed for either oral or written administration, examines communal living and group marriage attitudes by summing three items for each of these variables. Other variables are each measured by single items.

Reference:

Yost, E. D., & Adamek, R. J. (1974). Parent-child interaction and changing family values: A multivariate analysis. *J Mar Fam, 36,* 115–121.

II-1/c
1117. BARNETT, L. D. General Familism Index and Religious Familism Index

Avail: 1969 Ref.

Variables Measured: Importance of cohesive family unit and participation in family activities

Instrument Description: This 8-item questionnaire covers the two factors listed above. Item scores within each factor are summed.

Reference:

Barnett, L. D. (1969). Women's attitudes toward family life and U.S. population growth. *Pac Sociol Rev, 12,* 95–100.

II-1/g/a
1118. CAVAN, R. S. A Dating-Marriage Scale of Religious Social Distance

Avail: 1971 Ref.

Variables Measured: Acceptability of persons from various religions when selecting a marriage partner

Instrument Description: Six items are asked about persons belonging to each religion being examined. Items investigate the respondent's willingness to date and marry someone from each religion as well as their willingness to become involved in the religion of their partner.

Reference:

Cavan, R. S. (1971). A dating-marriage scale of religious social distance. *J Sci Study of Relig, 10,* 93–100.

II-1/II-4/g/a/e
1119. CUBER, J. F., & PELL, B. Family Moral Judgments Technique

Avail: 1941 Ref.

Variables Measured: Moral conformity in sexually ambiguous situations

Instrument Description: Twelve paragraphs each depicting a different situation are presented. Respondents indicate the correct moral decision for each situation.

Reference:

Cuber, J. F., & Pell, B. (1941). A method for studying moral judgments relating to the family. *Am J Sociol, 47,* 12–23.

II-1/g
1120. HILL, R. L., STYCOS, J. M., & BACK, K. W. Family Size Preference Index

Avail: 1959 Ref.

Variables Measured: Choice of family size

Instrument Description: Four questions are asked about the size of family desired by the subject.

Reference:

Hill, R. L., Stycos, J. M., & Back, K. W. (1959). *The family and population control: A Puerto Rican experiment in social change.* Chapel Hill: University of North Carolina Press.

II-1/c
1121. MIDDENDORP, C. P., BRINKMAN, W., & KOOMEN, W. Family Liberalism-Conservatism Attitude Index

Avail: 1970 Ref.

Variables Measured: Approval of various behaviors regarding courting, marriage, and family norms

Instrument Description: Six dichotomous or trichotomous items examine liberal versus conservative perspectives on the above variables. The questionnaire was shortened by correlation analysis from an original pool of 30 items. Scores range from 0 to 12.

Reference:

Middendorp, C. P., Brinkman, W., & Koomen, W. (1970). Determinants of premarital sexual permissiveness: A secondary analysis. *J Mar Fam, 32,* 369–379.

II-1/g
1122. MILLER, K. A., & INKELES, A. Acceptance of Family Limitation Scale

Avail: 1974 Ref.

Variables Measured: Acceptance of family size limitation, contraception, and government campaigns to promote limitation of family size

Instrument Description: Three forced-choice items related to family size limitation are asked, one for each of the above-named variables.

Reference:

Miller, K. A., & Inkeles, A. (1974). Modernity and acceptance of family limitation in four developing countries. *J Soc Issue, 30,* 167–188.

II-1/g/a
1123. OLSON, D. H. L. Premarital Attitude Scale

Avail: 1968 Ref.

Variables Measured: Attitudes toward aspects of marital behavior, mate selection, early adjustment, role expectations, sex information, conflict resolution, and failing relationships

Instrument Description: This instrument was designed to be used in marriage and family living courses. A total of 48 items can be given in Q-sort or questionnaire format and can be used to assess knowledge at, or prior to, a discussion or to evaluate change following the discussion.

Reference:

Olson, D. H. L., & Gravatt, A. E. (1968). Attitude change in a functional marriage course. *Fam Coord, 17,* 99–104.

II-1/c
1124. PETRICH, B. A. Traditional-Emerging Beliefs About Families

Avail: NAPS-2

Variables Measured: Importance of the family, parent-child interaction, and family unity

Instrument Description: This 54-item Likert-style questionnaire, with subscales determined by factor analysis, is designed to be used with children, adolescents, and adults to measure the above-listed variables.

Reference:

Petrich, B. A. (1969). Family beliefs of junior high school pupils. *Fam Coord, 18,* 374–378.

II-1/c
1125. RAMIREZ, M., III. Mexican-American Family Attitude Scale

Avail: NAPS-2

Variables Measured: Differentiation between traditional Mexican American family attitudes and values and those of non-Mexican Americans

Instrument Description: A total of 29 items examine attitudes such as separation of sex roles, strictness of child rearing, importance of extended family, father's authority, and self-abnegation of the mother.

Reference:

Ramirez, M., III (1961). Identification with Mexican-American values and psychological adjustment in Mexican-American adolescents. *Int J Soc Psychiat, 15,* 151–156.

II-1/I-2/g/c

1126. SAMENFINK, J. A. Catholic Sexual and Family Ideology Test

Avail: NAPS-1

Variables Measured: Beliefs of Catholics on family life, sexuality, and church dogma

Instrument Description: This test has 58 items that examine closeness of views to traditional Catholic perspective.

Reference:

Samenfink, J. A. (1958). A study of some aspects of marital behavior as related to religious control. *Mar Fam Living, 20,* 163–169.

II-1/a/g/e

1127. STINNETT, N., & MONTGOMERY, J. E. Perception of Older Marriages Scale (POM)

Avail: 1968 Ref.

Variables Measured: Views toward elderly marriages

Instrument Description: Six items examine views on whether the elderly should marry.

Reference:

Stinnett, N., & Montgomery, J. E. (1968). Youth's perceptions of marriage of older persons. *J Mar Fam, 30,* 392–396.

II-1/c/C

1128. TURNER, J. H. Familism-Individualism Scale

Avail: 1972 Ref.

Variables Measured: Adolescent independence from family

Instrument Description: Adolescents are asked whether they agree or disagree with each of five statements dealing with independent behavior.

Reference:

Turner, J. H. (1972). Structural conditions of achievement in the rural South. *Social Prob, 19,* 496–508.

II-1/I-3/d

1129. WILKENING, E. A. Familism Index

Avail: 1954 Ref.

Variables Measured: Familial dependency and support among farming families

Instrument Description: Fifteen items asked in interview format seek to establish the extent of family dependence for care and decision making.

Reference:

Wilkening, E. A. (1954). Change in farm technology as related to familism, family decision making, and family integration. *Am Sociol R, 19,* 29–36.

II-2/IV-1/a
1130. BLAZIER, D. C., & GOOSMAN, E. T. A Marriage Analysis

Contact: Family Life Pub, P.O. Box 427, Saluda, NC 28773

Variables Measured: Attitudes, feelings, and satisfaction with roles and behaviors within marriage

Instrument Description: This is a forced-choice questionnaire with 113 items and seven factors, which was designed to be administered separately to husbands and wives. Items are intended more to reveal attitudes and feelings than behaviors.

Reference:

Araoz, D. L. (1972). Thematic Apperception Test in marital therapy. *J Cont Psych, 5,* 41.

II-2/a/W
1131. BLOOD, R. O., Jr., & WOLFE, D. M. Marital Satisfaction Index

Avail: NAPS-2

Variables Measured: Marital satisfaction of the wife

Instrument Description: This is a 4-item Likert-type scale examining standard of living, spousal understanding, love and affection, and companionship. Possible responses for each item range from *disappointed* to *enthusiastic.*

Reference:

Blood, R. O., Jr., & Wolfe, D. M. (1960). *Husbands and wives: The dynamics of married living.* New York: Free Press.

II-2/a
1132. BOWERMAN, C. E. Bowerman Marital Adjustment Scales

Avail: NAPS-1

Variables Measured: Family spending, recreation, relations with in-laws and friends, religious practices, sex, homemaking activities, philosophy of life, child rearing

Instrument Description: Each area is measured along several dimensions, and items are combined to form three groups: (1) family activities and values, (2) personal centered, (3) and external family relations.

Reference:

Bowerman, C. E. (1957). Adjustment in marriage: Overall and in specific areas. *Sociol Soc Res, 41,* 257–263.

II-2/c
1133. BOWERMAN, C. E., & KINCH, J. W. Family Adjustment Index

Avail: 1959 Ref.

Variables Measured: Satisfaction with family relations

Instrument Description: Four questions examine comfort with familial interactions.

Reference:

Bowerman, C. E., & Kinch, J. W. (1959). Changes in family and peer orientation of children between the fourth and tenth grades. *Social Forc, 37,* 206–211.

II-2/a
1134. BURGESS, E. W., COTTRELL, L. S., & WALLIN, P. Burgess-Cottrell-Wallin Marital Adjustment Scale

Avail: 1953 Refs.

Variables Measured: Marital satisfaction and adjustment; success of the marriage

Instrument Description: This scale asks for multiple-choice self-ratings in three areas: (1) marital satisfaction, including areas such as affection, confiding, loneliness; (2) disagreements over family life matters; (3) and a checklist of items indicating sources of marital unhappiness.

Reference:

Burgess, E. W., & Wallin, P. (1953). *Engagement and marriage.* New York: Lippincott.

II-2/a
1135. BURR, W. R. Marital Satisfaction Indexes

Avail: NAPS-2

Variables Measured: Handling of finances, social activities, household tasks, companionship, sex, and relationships with children

Instrument Description: There are six indexes, one for each of the above areas, and 3 items for each index. Respondent indicates degree of satisfaction for each item. No data are provided where an overall score was obtained, although direct summation is possible.

Reference:

Burr, W. R. (1970). Satisfaction with various aspects of marriage over the life cycle: A random middle-class sample. *J Mar Fam, 32,* 29–37.

II-2/I-4/a/W
1136. DYER, E. D. Marital Agreement and Adjustment Measures

Avail: 1970 Ref.

Variables Measured: Wife's perception of the level of husband-wife agreement and marital adjustment

Instrument Description: Eleven items ask wife's perception of husband-wife agreement in various areas, plus one each on family problem solving and wife's marital happiness. Items are combined into a marital adjustment rating from *excellent* to *very poor.*

Reference:

Dyer, E. D. (1970). Upward social mobility and nuclear family integration as perceived by the wife in Swedish urban families. *J Mar Fam, 32,* 341–350.

II-2/a
1137. ESHLEMAN, J. R. Marital Integration Mean

Avail: 1965 Ref.

Variables Measured: The extent to which attitudes, services, and goods expected from the marital relation are received

Instrument Description: Ten items ask each partner questions about needs that should be, and are, filled by his or her spouse. Responses are rated for fulfillment. A composite index is derived.

Reference:

Eshleman, J. R. (1965). Mental health and marital integration in young marriages. *J Mar Fam, 27,* 255–262.

II-2/a
1138. FINK, S. L., SKIPPER, J. K., Jr., & HALLENBECK, P. N. Marital Satisfaction Scale

Avail: NAPS-2

Variables Measured: Marital satisfaction subdivided by companionship, social status, power, understanding, affection, esteem, and sex

Instrument Description: This 26-item questionnaire is used to interview subjects. Judges listen to tape-recorded interviews and rate subjects on each item according to their perceptions of subject's levels of satisfaction.

Reference:

Fink, S. L., Skipper, J. K., Jr., & Hallenbeck, P. N. (1968). Marital Satisfaction Scale. *J Mar Fam, 30,* 64–73.

II-2/a
1139. HAMILTON, G. V. Marital Adjustment Test

Avail: 1929 Ref.

Variables Measured: Marital satisfaction

Instrument Description: Interviewer asks 13 open-ended questions. Responses are recorded verbatim. Responses are later compared with those from an answer key in order to determine the level of marital satisfaction evidenced.

Reference:

Hamilton, G. V. (1929). *A research in marriage.* New York: Boni.

II-2/a
1140. HAWKINS, J. L. Marital Companionship Scale

Avail: NAPS-2

Variables Measured: Marital companionship on an expressive level as measured by affective behavior, self-revealing communication, and mutual recreational activities

Instrument Description: A questionnaire with 43 items focusing on behavior during the previous four weeks is discussed and filled out by the couple in the presence of the interviewer. Couples are instructed to arrive at a joint decision for each item.

Reference:

Hawkins, J. L. (1968). Associations between companionship, hostility and marital satisfaction. *J Mar Fam, 30,* 647–650.

II-2/a
1141. HAWKINS, J. L., & JOHNSEN, K. P. Current Marital Satisfaction Test

Avail: 1969 Ref.

Variables Measured: Current and recent marital satisfaction

Instrument Description: There are 4 items examining areas of marital satisfaction, each with seven possible responses ranging from *completely dissatisfied* to *completely satisfied.*

Reference:

Hawkins, J. L., & Johnsen, K. P. (1969). Perception of behavioral conformity, imputation of consensus, and marital satisfaction. *J Mar Fam, 31,* 507–511.

II-2/III-1/a/P
1142. HEATH, L. L., ROPER, B. S., & KING, C. D. Contribution of Children to Marital Stability Index

Avail: 1974 Ref.

Variables Measured: Belief that having children adds to the stability of a marriage

Instrument Description: Five multiple-choice questions ask about the influence of children on marriages.

Reference:

Heath, L. L., Roper, B. S., & King, C. D. (1974). A research note on children viewed as contributors to marital stability: The relationship to birth control use, ideal and expected family size. *J Mar Fam, 36,* 304–306.

II-2/a/W
1143. HILL, R. L. Adjustment of Family to Separation Scale

Avail: 1949 Ref.

Variables Measured: Wife's adjustment to having a husband who is away from home due to active duty in the armed services

Instrument Description: This scale contains a list of 48 sentences detailing the adjustment made by the wife of an active duty serviceman. The wife checks those that apply to her.

Reference:

Hill, R. L. (1949). *Families under stress: Adjustment to the crises of war separation and reunion.* New York: Harper.

II-2/a
1144. INSELBERG, R. M. Marital Satisfaction Sentence Completions

Avail: 1961 Ref.

Variables Measured: Marital satisfaction—subject's fears, wishes, and feelings

Instrument Description: Ratings are made of subject's responses to each of 13 sentence-completion items. Sentences are scored on a 4-point scale according to level of marital satisfaction indicated.

Reference:

Inselberg, R. M. (1961). Social and psychological factors associated with high school marriages. *J Home Ec, 53,* 766–772.

II-2/I-4/a
1145. KIEREN, D., & TALLMAN, I. Spousal Adaptability Index

Avail: NAPS-2

Variables Measured: Flexibility, empathy, and motivation related to marital adaptability

Instrument Description: Subject is presented with 18 problem-solving situations. Verbal responses are rated along the three dimensions for adaptability.

Reference:

Kieren, D., & Tallman, I. (1972). Spousal adaptability: An assessment of marital competence. *J Mar Fam, 34,* 247–256.

II-2/a
1146. KIRKPATRICK, C. Family Interests Scale

Avail: 1937 Ref.

Variables Measured: Shared family interests and marital adjustment

Instrument Description: Subjects are asked to respond to each of six items that indicate whether they enjoy activities both by themselves and in their spouses' company.

Reference:

Kirkpatrick, C. (1937). Community of interest and the measurement of marriage adjustment. *Fam, 18,* 133–137.

II-2/a
1147. LOCKE, H. J. Marital Adjustment Test

Avail: 1951 Ref.

Variables Measured: Marital adjustment

Instrument Description: There are 29 multiple-choice items related to marital adjustment, all of which were taken directly from tests constructed by other researchers.

Reference:

Locke, H. J. (1951). *Predicting adjustment in marriage: A comparison of a divorced and happily married group.* New York: Holt.

II-2/a
1148. LOCKE, H. J., & WILLIAMSON, R. C. Marital Adjustment Scale

Avail: 1958 Ref.

Variables Measured: Companionship or couple sufficiency, agreement, affectional intimacy, wife accommodation, and euphoria

Instrument Description: The 20 items in this multiple-choice questionnaire are related to the variables above. Factors are provided for easier interpretation.

Reference:

Locke, H. J., & Williamson, R. C. (1958). Marital adjustment: A factor analysis study. *Am Sociol R, 23,* 562–569.

II-2 / IV-2 / a
1149. NYE, F. I., & MacDOUGALL, E. Spousal Argument Scale

Avail: 1959 Ref.

Variables Measured: Husband-wife arguments related to money, children, recreation, and use of house, furniture, television, and radio

Instrument Description: There are 6 items related to common reasons for arguments between partners and 5 response options for each item.

Reference:

Nye, F. I., & MacDougall, E. (1959). The dependent variable in marital research. *Pac Sociol R, 2,* 67–70.

II-2/a
1150. NYE, F. I., & MacDOUGALL, E. Nye-MacDougall Marital Adjustment Scale

Avail: 1959 Ref.

Variables Measured: Marital adjustment as defined by happiness; satisfaction; quarreling; divorce consideration; postargument behavior; and arguments on house, furniture, recreation, money, and children

Instrument Description: This scale is a 9-item questionnaire examining the above-listed variables. Answers may range from *never* to *very often.*

Reference:

Nye, F. I., & MacDougall, E. (1959). The dependent variable in marital research. *Pac Sociol R, 2,* 67–70.

II-2/IV-1/a
1151. ORT, R. S. Marital Role Conflict Score

Avail: ADI Doc. 2908

Variables Measured: Role conflict and marital happiness

Instrument Description: This measure is an interview with 22 questions, each presented in terms of the following: (1) role expectations, (2) roles played, (3) mate role expectations, and (4) mate roles played.

Reference:

Ort, R. S. (1950). A study of role conflicts as related to happiness in marriage. *J Abn Soc Psy, 45,* 691–699.

II-2/a
1152. SAFILIOS-ROTHSCHILD, C. Marital Satisfaction of Couples with Mentally Ill Partner

Avail: 1968 Ref.

Variables Measured: Satisfaction with the marital relationship where the spouse suffers from mental illness

Instrument Description: Spouses whose partners are mentally ill are asked to rate 10 areas of marital relations for degree of satisfaction.

Reference:

Safilios-Rothschild, C. (1968). Deviance and mental illness in the Greek family. *Fam Process, 7,* 100–117.

II-2/a/W
1153. SAFILIOS-ROTHSCHILD, C. Marital Satisfaction Index

Avail: 1967 Ref.

Variables Measured: Wife's marital satisfaction

Instrument Description: Marital satisfaction is rated along eight general and varying dimensions. Items are scored on a 5-point scale from *very satisfied* to *disappointed.*

Reference:

Safilios-Rothschild, C. (1967). A comparison of power structure and marital satisfaction in urban Greek and French families. *J Mar Fam, 29,* 345–352.

II-2/a
1154. SCANZONI, J. Perceived Hostility Score

Avail: 1970 Ref.

Variables Measured: Hostility between partners

Instrument Description: Subjects are asked to respond to each of four items indicating hostility between them on a scale of 0–7; 0 = *never* and 7 = *very often.*

Reference:

Scanzoni, J. (1970). *Opportunity and the family.* New York: Free Press.

II-2/a
1155. SHEINBEIN, M. L. Marital Satisfaction Direct-Report

Avail: NAPS-2

Variables Measured: General marital satisfaction

Instrument Description: Couples independently rate marital satisfaction. They then each write a short paragraph about areas of satisfaction-dissatisfaction in their marriage. The interviewer also rates the couple according to the same dimensions. The couple's score is the average of the three ratings.

Reference:

Sheinbein, M. L. (1974). Multiplicity of marital adjustment ratings: A suggestion. *J Fam Couns, 2,* 49–52.

II-2/a
1156. STINNETT, N., COLLINS, J., & MONTGOMERY, J. E. Marital Need Satisfaction Scale

Avail: 1970 Ref.

Variables Measured: Satisfaction with marital relationship and fulfillment of needs of older couples

Instrument Description: A total of 24 items, representing six areas of satisfaction and need fulfillment, are scored on a 5-point scale from *very satisfactory* to *very unsatisfactory.*

Reference:

Stinnett, N., Collins, J., & Montgomery, J. E. (1970). Marital need satisfaction of older husbands and wives. *J Mar Fam, 32,* 428–434.

II-2/a
1157. TERMAN, L. M. Marital Happiness Index

Avail: 1938 Ref.

Variables Measured: Marital happiness

Instrument Description: Nineteen categories of marital satisfaction are measured by use of an 80-item questionnaire. Items cover several general areas considered to contribute to marital happiness.

Reference:

Terman, L. M. (1938). *Psychological factors in marital happiness.* New York: McGraw-Hill.

II-2/II-1/a
1158. WILKENING, E. A., & BHARADWAJ, L. K. Husband and Wife Aspirations Indexes

Avail: 1967 Ref.

Variables Measured: Striving with respect to home and farm improvement, community participation, and child development

Instrument Description: This measure consists of questionnaires administered separately to husband and wife with 19 items covering the above areas.

Reference:

Wilkening, E. A., & Bharadwaj, L. K. (1967). Dimensions of aspirations, work roles and decision-making of farm husbands and wives in Wisconsin. *J Mar Fam, 29,* 701–706.

II-3/IV-2/b/C
1159. BACH, G. R. Father-Fantasy Categories for Doll-Play Scoring

Avail: 1946 Ref.

Variables Measured: Aggression, affection, directions, and mood swings, both directed toward and received by the father

Instrument Description: Sixteen scoring categories are used in interpreting doll play by the subject. All behavior is time-sampled every 15 seconds during three 20-minute observational sessions.

Reference:

Bach, G. R. (1946). Father-fantasies and father-typing in father-separated children. *Child Dev, 17,* 63–69.

II-3/a
1160. BAUM, M. Goals in Marriage Scale

Avail: NAPS-2

Variables Measured: Romantic and companionate love

Instrument Description: This scale is a combination of three measures requiring (1) ratings of 15 marital goal statements on a 7-point scale; (2) ratings of 15 items of situations in which people should not marry, using a 4-point scale; (3) rankings of 10 descriptions of possible marital partners in order of desirability.

Reference:

Baum, M. (1971). Love, marriage, and the division of labor. *Sociol Inq, 41,* 107–116.

II-3/g/b/C
1161. BOWERMAN, C. E., & BAHR, S. J. Parental Identification Scale

Avail: 1973 Ref.

Variables Measured: Feelings of respect, admiration, and affection for parents and acceptance of parental values

Instrument Description: Eight multiple-choice statements, dealing with the above-listed variables, are presented to adolescents.

Reference:

Bowerman, C. E., & Bahr, S. J. (1973). Conjugal power and adolescent identification with parents. *Sociometry, 36,* 366–377.

II-3/a
1162. DRISCOLL, R., DAVIS, K. E., & LIPETZ, M. E. Feelings Questionnaire

Avail: NAPS-2

Variables Measured: Love, trust, and the extent to which couples are critical of each other

Instrument Description: Each member of the couple rates the other person and him- or herself on 14 items. Each item concerns an area of their relationship related to the above-listed variables.

Reference:

Driscoll, R., Davis, K. E., & Lipetz, M. E. (1973). Parental interference and romantic love: The Romeo and Juliet effect. *J Pers Soc Psy, 24,* 1–10.

II-3/I-4/a/d
1163. DRISCOLL, R., DAVIS, K. E., & LIPETZ, M. E. Parental Inter-ference Scale

Avail: NAPS-2

Variables Measured: Husband-wife concern about parental interference

Instrument Description: This 6-item scale is designed to expose in-law problems (primarily for use in counseling situations).

Reference:

Driscoll, R., Davis, K. E., & Lipetz, M. E. (1973). Parental interference and romantic love: The Romeo and Juliet effect. *J Pers Soc Psy, 24,* 1–10.

II-3/III-2/b
1164. GREENSTEIN, J. M. Father-Closeness Rating

Avail: 1966 Ref.

Variables Measured: Closeness of father-son relationship

Instrument Description: Father and son are interviewed together; afterward, the inter-viewer fills out a 7-item questionnaire rating their relationship.

Reference:

Greenstein, J. M. (1966). Father characteristics and sex typing. *J Pers Soc Psy, 3,* 271–277.

II-3/b/e/C
1165. LEIDERMAN, P. H., & LEIDERMAN, G. F. Attachment Index

Avail: 1974 Ref.

Variables Measured: Infant's response to mother, caretaker, and stranger

Instrument Description: Infant is approached by a stranger while only in the company of the mother, and then, a caretaker. Mother then leaves for two minutes. Responses of the infant are noted and rated.

Reference:

Leiderman, P. H., & Leiderman, G. F. (1974). Affective and cognitive consequences of polymatric infant care in the East African highlands. In A. D. Pick (Ed.), *Minnesota symposia on child psychology* (Vol. 8). Minneapolis: University of Minnesota Press.

II-3/b/C
1166. McKINLEY, D. Source of Emotional Support Measure

Avail: 1964 Ref.

Variables Measured: Child's preference (mother versus father) for support and affection

Instrument Description: Children are asked four questions concerning their relationship with their parents. For each question they indicate with which parent they would prefer to interact.

Reference:

McKinley, D. (1964). *Social class and family life.* New York: Free Press.

II-3/b/C
1167. MILLER, B. B. Perceived Closeness-to-the-Mother Scale

Avail: 1940 Ref.

Variables Measured: Closeness and emotional support given to a child by his or her mother

Instrument Description: This measure is an 11-item multiple-choice scale for use with junior high school youth that examines various ways in which a child might depend upon his or her mother.

Reference:

Anderson, J. P. (1940). *A study of the relationship between certain aspects of parental behavior and attitudes and the behavior of junior high school pupils.* New York: Teachers College, Columbia University, Bureau of Publications.

II-3/a
1168. PETERMAN, D. J., RIDLEY, C. A., & ANDERSON, S. M. Relationship Quality Index

Avail: 1974 Ref.

Variables Measured: Quality of a heterosexual relationship according to closeness to ideal partner, openness, need satisfaction, sexual attractiveness, and sexual satisfaction

Instrument Description: Five items concerning the areas listed above are used to evaluate the quality of a current heterosexual relationship. Each response is scored from 1 to 5, allowing for a total quality of relationship score of 5 to 25.

Reference:

Peterman, D. J., Ridley, C. A., & Anderson, S. M. (1974). A comparison of cohabiting and non-cohabitating college students. *J Mar Fam, 36,* 344–354.

II-3/IV-2/b/C
1169. PURCELL, K., & CLIFFORD, E. Story Completion Test

Avail: 1966 Ref.

Variables Measured: Children's perceived power, nurturance, and punitiveness of parents

Instrument Description: Child completes 12 stories that are then subjectively scored for nurturance and punitiveness, and a summation score is derived.

Reference:

Purcell, K., & Clifford, E. (1966). Binocular rivalry and the study of identification in asthmatic and nonasthmatic boys. *J Cons Psych, 30,* 388–394.

II-3/b/C
1170. ROBERTSON, L. S., & DOTSON, L. E. Parental Expressivity Scale

Avail: 1969 Ref.

Variables Measured: Adolescent's rating of parental warmth, rejection, indulgence, concern, and love

Instrument Description: Adolescents rate each parent on an 8-item questionnaire reflecting the above-named variables.

Reference:

Robertson, L. S., & Dotson, L. E. (1969). Perceived parental expressivity, reaction to stress, and affiliation. *J Pers Soc Psy, 12,* 229–234.

II-3/b/C
1171. SEATON, J. K. Incomplete Story Test

Avail: 1949 Ref.

Variables Measured: Parental acceptance or rejection

Instrument Description: Subject is presented with a series of 15 incomplete stories and is offered a multiple-choice assortment of possible outcomes or responses. Responses are scored as indicating acceptance or rejection of parents.

Reference:

Seaton, J. K. (1949). A projective experiment using incomplete stories with multiple-choice endings. *Genetic Psy Mono, 40,* 149–228.

II-3/a
1172. SMITH, J. R. Perception of Interpersonal Hostility Scale and Perception of Marital Interaction Scale

Avail: NAPS-2

Variables Measured: Interpersonal relations and hostility within the marriage

Instrument Description: Each partner responds to a 20-item scale of potentially hostile situations from both his or her own and the spouse's perspective. The man's perception score is subtracted from that of the woman in order to form a composite score.

Reference:

Smith, J. R. (1967). Suggested scales for prediction of client movement and the duration of marriage counseling. *Sociol Soc, 52,* 63–71.

II-3/b/C
1173. STRYKER, S. Married Offspring-Parent Adjustment Checklist

Avail: NAPS-1

Variables Measured: Married child-parent affection, intimacy, tension, sympathy, and dependency

Instrument Description: This checklist contains 50 statements dealing with the parent-child relationship. Married child indicates which statements are *true* or *false* of the relationship.

Reference:

Stryker, S. (1955). The adjustment of married offspring to their parents. *Am Sociol R, 20,* 149–154.

II-3/c/C
1174. UTTON, A. C. Childhood Experience Rating Scales

Avail: 1949 Ref.

Variables Measured: Childhood home environment, acceptance, criticism, child-centeredness, rapport, and affection

Instrument Description: The Utton version is a modification of Baldwin et al. (1949). There are 30 items that range from depicting a warm to a cold family environment. Subject indicates how accurate each statement is for his or her family.

Reference:

Baldwin, A. L., Kalhorn, J. C., & Breese, F. H. (1949). The appraisal of parent behavior. *Psychol Mono, 63* (Whole No. 299).

II-3/b/C
1175. WEINSTEIN, L. Parental Acceptance Measure

Avail: NAPS-2

Variables Measured: Child's perception of parental acceptance

Instrument Description: This measure consists of a 12-item questionnaire from which the child is read a statement and asked to indicate how much like the character in the story he or she is and how much each parent would like the subject to be like the story child.

Reference:

Weinstein, L. (1967). Social experience and social schemata. *J Pers Soc Psy, 6,* 429–434.

II-4/IV-1/b/e
1176. LIBBY, R. W. Sex Education Liberalism Scale (SELS)

Avail: NAPS-2

Variables Measured: Desired role of educational institutions and parents in providing sex education

Instrument Description: This is a 9-item questionnaire assessing liberal versus conservative attitude toward sex education in schools.

Reference:

Libby, R. W. (1971). Parental attitudes toward high school sex education programs: Liberalism-traditionalism and demographic correlates. *Fam Coord, 20,* 127–136.

II-4/II-5/g/c/H
1177. ROBERTO, E. I. Belief About Vasectomy Index

Avail: 1974 Ref.

Variables Measured: Relationship of vasectomy to self-actualization, family, contraception, and sexual pleasure

Instrument Description: Each of the 19 items in this series is presented three times to measure expectancies, values, and attitudes related to vasectomies.

Reference:

Roberto, E. L. (1974). Marital and family planning expectancies of men regarding vasectomy. *J Mar Fam, 36,* 698–706.

II-5/b/C
1178. AHSEN, A. Eidetic Parents Test

Contact: Brandon House, 555 Riverdale Station, New York, NY 10471

Variables Measured: Images and emotions evoked by descriptions of parents under painful, pleasurable, or conflictual situations

Instrument Description: Subjects are asked to visualize each of 30 different settings involving parents. They are then asked particulars about the images of their parents in those situations.

Reference:

Ahsen, A. (1965). *Eidetic psychotherapy: A short introduction.* New York: Brandon House, Inc.

II-5/b
1179. ALEXANDER, T. Adult-Child Interaction Test (ACI Test)

Avail: 1952 Ref.

Variables Measured: Adults' and children's perceptions of each other on several dimensions; also, subject's motivation and adult's acceptance of aspects of children's personalities

Instrument Description: In this projective technique, subjects are successively shown eight cards depicting children and adults and are then asked to tell stories about each card.

Reference:

Alexander, T. (1952). The adult-child interaction test: A projective test for use in research. *Mon S Res C, 17,*(2, No. 55).

II-5/b/P
1180. BACH, G. R. Father-Typing Rating Scales

Avail: 1946 Ref.

Variables Measured: View of father given by mother to children

Instrument Description: This scale consists of a home interview and observational ratings of mother's attitudes toward father that are conveyed to children.

Reference:

Bach, G. R. (1946). Father-fantasies and father-typing in father-separated children. *Child Dev, 17,* 63–79.

II-5/b/C
1181. COOPER, J. B., & BLAIR, M. A. Parent Evaluation Scale

Avail: 1966 Ref.

Variables Measured: Child's evaluation of parent's positive or negative perceptions of child

Instrument Description: Child checks which of 50 statements are *true* of his or her relationship with parents.

Reference:

Cooper, J. B. (1966). Two scales for parent evaluation. *J Genet Psy, 108,* 49–53.

II-5/II-2/g/a
1182. DENTLER, R. A., & PINEO, P. Personal Growth in Marriage Index

Avail: 1960 Ref.

Variables Measured: Personal growth

Instrument Description: The question is asked: "What have you gained from the marriage?" Subject checks each of the nine items that applies.

Reference:

Dentler, R. A., & Pineo, P. (1960). Sexual adjustment, marital adjustment and personal growth of husbands: A panel analysis. *Mar Fam Living, 22,* 45–48.

II-5/c
1183. FERREIRA, A. J. Color Flag Test

Avail: 1964 Ref.

Variables Measured: Acceptance or rejection of family members

Instrument Description: Each family member colors flags and then indicates acceptance or rejection of others' drawings. Acceptance or rejection of flag presumably indicates acceptance or rejection of the family member who colored the flag.

Reference:

Ferreira, A. J. (1964). Interpersonal perceptivity among family members. *Am J Orthop, 34,* 64–70.

II-5/a
1184. GOODMAN, N., & OFSHE, R. Empathy Test

Avail: 1968 Ref.

Variables Measured: Empathic accuracy when assessing spouse's reactions

Instrument Description: Partners individually rate each of 12 words according to how they perceive the word. They then indicate how they believe their partner rated the word.

Reference:

Goodman, N., & Ofshe, R. (1968). Empathy, communication efficiency, and marital status. *J Mar Fam, 30,* 597–603.

II-5/IV-1/c
1185. HALEY, J. Family Coalition Experiment

Avail: 1962 Ref.

Variables Measured: Forming of coalitions among family members

Instrument Description: Three family members seated at a table separated by partitions signal each other in attempts to form coalitions. Formation of coalitions is evaluated.

Reference:

Haley, J. (1962). Family experiments: A new type of experimentation. *Fam Process, 1,* 265–293.

II-5/II-2/a
1186. KARLSSON, G. Adaptability Indexes

Avail: 1951 Ref.

Variables Measured: General adaptability both within and outside marriage situations

Instrument Description: Adaptability is examined through a 24-item questionnaire.

Reference:

Karlsson, G. (1951). *Adaptability and communication in marriage: A Swedish predictive study of marital satisfaction.* Uppsala: Almquist and Wiksells.

II-5/a
1187. LAING, R. D., PHILLIPSON, H., & LEE, A. R. Interpersonal Perception Method (IPM)

Avail: 1966 Ref.

Variables Measured: Husband's and wife's interpersonal perceptions of each other

Instrument Description: This hour-long test involving 720 items examines various aspects of perception of spouse.

Reference:

Laing, R. D., Phillipson, H., & Lee, A. R. (1966). *Interpersonal perception.* New York: Springer.

II-5/a/b
1188. LEARY, T. F. Leary Interpersonal Check List

Avail: 1957 Ref.

Variables Measured: Husband-wife or parent-child similarity with respect to dominance, submission, affection, and hostility as well as eight personality dimensions reflected by these factors

Instrument Description: The subject is asked which of 64 items apply to him- or herself and to the other family member with whom he or she is being compared. Ratings can also be done by observers.

Reference:

Leary, T. F. (1957). *Interpersonal diagnosis of personality*. New York: Ronald.

II-5/c
1189. NIEMI, R. Bias in Perception of Family Relations Measure

Avail: 1974 Ref.

Variables Measured: Extent of agreement between family members regarding participation in joint activities

Instrument Description: Children and parents are individually asked 10 items related to their activities with other family members. Three-point scales are used for responses.

Reference:

Niemi, R. (1974). *How family members perceive each other*. New Haven, CT: Yale University Press.

II-5/b/C
1190. SIMMONS, R. G., ROSENBERG, F., & ROSENBERG, M. Perceived Opinion of Parents Scale

Avail: 1973 Ref.

Variables Measured: Children's perceptions of parent's opinion of them

Instrument Description: Child is asked three questions, one of which is open-ended, in order to determine what the child believes the parent's view of him or her is.

Reference:

Simmons, R. G., Rosenberg, F., & Rosenberg, M. (1973). Disturbance in the self-image at adolescence. *Am Sociol R, 38,* 553–568.

II-5/I-4/c/C
1191. SLOCUM, W. L., & STONE, C. L. Family Image Scales

Avail: 1959 Ref.

Variables Measured: Family affection, cooperation, democracy, and disciplinary fairness

Instrument Description: This measure is a 21-item scale for use with teenagers.

Reference:

Slocum, W. L., & Stone, C. L. (1959). A method for measuring family images held by teenagers. *Mar Fam Living, 21,* 245–250.

II-5/IV-2/b/g

1192. STEWART, L. H. Q-Sort for Mother-Son Identification

Avail: 1959 Ref.

Variables Measured: Mother's and son's satisfaction with themselves and the mother's satisfaction with the son

Instrument Description: Subject sorts 76 statements, going from *most* to *least like* the concept being tested. Ranking is done three times by sons and twice by mothers.

Reference:

Stewart, L. H. (1959). Mother-son identification and vocational interest. *Genet Psych Mono, 60,* 31–63.

II-5/b/P

1193. STOGDILL, R. M. Attitudes Toward Child Behavior Scale

Avail: NAPS-1

Variables Measured: Parental approval of introverted versus extroverted child

Instrument Description: Parent rates how he or she feels about each of 99 statements related to social adjustment and introversion-extroversion of the child.

Reference:

Stogdill, R. M. (1936). The measurement of attitudes toward parental control and the social adjustments of children. *J Appl Psyc, 20,* 359–367.

II-5/IV-1/c

1194. WATZLAWICK, P., BEAVIN, J., SIKORSKI, L., & MECIA, B. Structured Family Interview

Avail: 1970 Ref.

Variables Measured: Tendency of family members both to falsely accuse and to protect other family members from accusations of wrongdoing

Instrument Description: Family members write down what they believe to be the greatest faults each other, with each person assigned to write about one other family member. Interviewer adds two general faults, then announces each fault. Family members each indicate the person about whom that fault was written.

Reference:

Watzlawick, P., Beavin, J., Sikorski, L., & Mecia, B. (1970). Protection and scapegoating in pathological families. *Fam Process, 9,* 27–39.

II-5/IV-1/c

1195. WELLS, C. F., & RABINER, E. L. Family Index of Tension (FIT)

Avail: NAPS-2

Variables Measured: Relationship between identified patient and remainder of family regarding patient and family expectations, frustration of patient by family, and family disagreement regarding patient

Instrument Description: Ratings on 15 criteria about the identified patient's relationship with his or her family are based on observations of the family during a 90-minute clinical interview of the family.

Reference:

Wells, C. F., & Rabiner, E. L. (1973). The conjoint family diagnostic interview and the family index of tension. *Fam Process, 12,* 127–144.

III-1/c
1196. CVETKOVICH, G. T., & LONNER, W. J. Hypothetical Family Questionnaire (HYFAM)

Avail: NAPS-2

Variables Measured: Importance of situational variables in planning to have children

Instrument Description: This is a series of 40 case studies detailing different family circumstances. For each case, subjects indicate whether they believe the family should have a (or another) child.

Reference:

Cvetkovich, G. T., & Lonner, W. J. (1973). A transnational comparison of individual birth planning decisions for hypothetical families. *J Cross-Cul, 4,* 470–480.

III-1/c/P
1197. DYER, E. D. Parenthood Crisis Scale

Avail: 1963 Ref.

Variables Measured: Family crises resulting from birth of first child

Instrument Description: There are 6 items, administered separately to husband and wife, that consist of questions about redefinitions of roles upon the birth of the first child.

Reference:

Dyer, E. D. (1963). Parenthood as crisis: A re-study. *Mar Fam Living, 25,* 196–201.

III-1/g
1198. FISCHER, E. H. Birth Planning Attitudes

Avail: 1972 Ref.

Variables Measured: Concern over population growth and expected family size

Instrument Description: This measure is a 26-item questionnaire examining views about birth planning.

Reference:

Fischer, E. H. (1972). Birth planning of youth: Concern about overpopulation and intention to limit family size. *Am Psychol, 27,* 951–958.

III-1/b/P
1199. GREENBERG, M. Greenberg First-Father Engrossment Survey

Avail: 1974 Ref.

Variables Measured: Father's feelings of involvement with newborn child as evidenced by planning for conception, participation during labor, and experiences surrounding birth

Instrument Description: This 50-item questionnaire examines several aspects of paternal involvement in the process of bringing a newborn child into the family, with father's experiences and feelings highlighted.

Reference:

Greenberg, M., & Morris, N. (1974). Engrossment: The newborn's impact upon the father. *Am J Orthop, 44,* 520–539.

III-1/g
1200. HILL, R. L., STYCOS, J. M., & BACK, K. W. Contraceptive Information Index

Avail: 1959 Ref.

Variables Measured: Knowledge of contraceptive techniques

Instrument Description: Three questions are asked during the course of an extended interview dealing with contraceptive awareness.

Reference:

Hill, R. L., Stycos, J. M., & Back, K. W. (1959). *The family and population control: A Puerto Rican experiment in social change.* Chapel Hill: University of North Carolina Press.

III-1/c
1201. MAXWELL, J. W., & MONTGOMERY, J. E. Timing of Parenthood Scale (ATOP)

Avail: 1969 Ref.

Variables Measured: Beliefs regarding having children during first two married years

Instrument Description: Ten items ask questions of young married couples regarding having children during the first two years of marriage.

Reference:

Maxwell, J. W., & Montgomery, J. E. (1969). Societal pressure toward early parenthood. *Fam Coord, 18,* 340–344.

III-1/e/H
1202. PAIGE, K. E., & PAIGE, J. M. Husband Involvement During Pregnancy Scale

Avail: 1973 Ref.

Variables Measured: Societal requirements for changes in men's behavior during pregnancy

Instrument Description: Ethnographic sources are used to determine societal customs regarding changes in husband's behavior during the pregnancy of his wife.

Reference:

Paige, K. E., & Paige, J. M. (1973). The politics of birth practices: A strategic analysis. *Am Sociol R, 38,* 663–677.

III-1/e/W
1203. PAIGE, K. E., & PAIGE, J. M. Maternal Restrictions During Pregnancy Scale

Avail: 1973 Ref.

Variables Measured: Societal restriction of women's behavior during pregnancy

Instrument Description: Ethnographic sources are used to determine societal customs regarding close monitoring and restrictions of behavior during pregnancy.

Reference:

Paige, K. E., & Paige, J. M. (1973). The politics of birth practices: A strategic analysis. *Am Sociol R, 38,* 663–677.

III-1/W
1204. SCHNAIBERG, A. Child-Years-of-Dependency Measure (CYD)

Avail: 1973 Ref.

Variables Measured: Spacing and number of children

Instrument Description: This measure examines circumstantial variables, such as number of years the woman has had a husband, that contribute to ability to conceive.

Reference:

Schnaiberg, A. (1973). The concept and measurement of child dependency: An approach to family formation analysis. *Pop Stud, 27,* 69–84.

III-1/I-4/g
1205. STOLKA, S. M., & BARNETT, L. D. Childbearing Motivation Scales

Avail: 1969 Ref.

Variables Measured: Marital happiness, role expectations, religious duty, and prestige associated with having children

Instrument Description: Subject indicates agreement or disagreement with each of 11 items dealing with the above-listed variables.

Reference:

Stolka, S. M., & Barnett, L. D. (1969). Education and religion as factors in women's attitudes motivating childbearing. *J Mar Fam, 31,* 740–750.

III-1/g/P
1206. VEROFF, J., & FELD, S. Parental Negative Orientation Index (PNOI)

Avail: 1970 Ref.

Variables Measured: Satisfying versus frustrating nature of changes brought on by parenthood

Instrument Description: Ratings of parental satisfaction are made based on responses to interview questions.

Reference:

Veroff, J., & Feld, S. (1970). *Marriage and work in America.* New York: Van Nostrand Reinhold.

III-1/g/P
1207. VEROFF, J., & FELD, S. Parental Restrictiveness Index (PRI)

Avail: 1970 Ref.

Variables Measured: Restrictions and burdens associated with parenthood

Instrument Description: Ratings of parental perceptions are made based on responses to interview questions.

Reference:

Veroff, J., & Feld, S. (1970). *Marriage and work in America.* New York: Van Nostrand Reinhold.

III-1/II-1/g
1208. WANT, C. K. A., & THURSTONE, L. L. Attitude Toward Birth Control Scale

Avail: 1931 Ref.

Variables Measured: Acceptance of birth control

Instrument Description: There are two forms with 20 items each asking subjects to mark how strongly they *agree* or *disagree* with each statement.

Reference:

Thurstone, L. L. (1931). *The measurement of social attitudes*. Chicago: University of Chicago
   Press.

III-1/g
1209. WILLIAMSON, J. B. Favorability Toward Birth Control Index

Avail: 1970 Ref.

Variables Measured: Favorability toward birth control

Instrument Description: Three items are summed to obtain a favorability score.

Reference:

Williamson, J. B. (1970). Subjective efficacy and ideal family size as predictors of favorability
   toward birth control. *Demography, 7*, 329–339.

III-2/IV-2/b
1210. ACKERLEY, L. A. Ackerley Parental Attitude Scales

Avail: 1967 Ref.

Variables Measured: Using fear to control children, attitude toward providing sex information, and disapproval of older children's telling lies

Instrument Description: There are three scales, with 32, 33, and 9 items, respectively.
Parents check those statements with which they agree.

Reference:

Shaw, M. E., & Wright, J. M. (1967). *Scales for the measurement of attitudes*. New York:
   McGraw-Hill.

III-2/I-1/b/P
1211. ANANDAM, K., & HIGHBERGER, R. Communication Congruence Measure

Avail: 1972 Ref.

Variables Measured: Verbal and nonverbal congruence of messages from mother to child;
encouraging versus discouraging and positive versus negative communication

Instrument Description: Mother's behavior is observed and coded during two 30-minute,
semistructured sessions between mother and child. A method for coding both verbal and
nonverbal behavior is provided.

Reference:

Anandam, K., & Highberger, R. (1972). Child compliance and congruity between verbal and
   nonverbal maternal communication—a methodological note. *Fam Process, 11*, 219–
   226.

III-2/b/C

1212. AUSUBEL, D. P., BALTHAZAR, E. E., ROSENTHAL, I., BLACKMAN, L. S., SCHPOONT, S. H., & WELKOWITZ, J. Disagreement with Perceived Parent Opinion Test

Avail: NAPS-1

Variables Measured: Child's perception of divergence of opinions with parents

Instrument Description: Subject answers 41 questions as he or she believes they would be answered by his or her parents. One week later the subject answers the same questions for self. Responses are compared in order to come up with the divergence score.

Reference:

Ausubel, D. P., Balthazar, E. E., Rosenthal, I., Blackman, L. S., Schpoont, S. H., & Welkowitz, J. (1954). Perceived parent attitudes as determinants of children's ego structure. *Child Dev, 25,* 173–183.

III-2/b/C

1213. AUSUBEL, D. P., BALTHAZAR, E. E., ROSENTHAL, I., BLACKMAN, L. S., SCHPOONT, S. H., & WELKOWITZ, J. Perceived Parent Attitude Rating

Avail: NAPS-1

Variables Measured: Child's perception of parental acceptance or rejection, and intrinsic or extrinsic valuation of the child

Instrument Description: There are 36 items in which child rates his or her parents' attitudes and behaviors.

Reference:

Ausubel, D. P., Balthazar, E. E., Rosenthal, I., Blackman, L. S., Schpoont, S. H., & Welkowitz, J. (1954). Perceived parent attitudes as determinants of children's ego structure. *Child Dev, 25,* 173–183.

III-2/II-3/IV-2/b/C

1214. BACHMAN, J. G., MEDNICK, M. T., DAVIDSON, T. N., & JOHNSTON, L. D. Composite Measure of Family Relations

Avail: 1970 Ref.

Variables Measured: Closeness between adults and their parents and parental punitiveness

Instrument Description: Adults answer 21 multiple-choice items indicating the closeness they felt with their parents while they were growing up.

Reference:

Bachman, J. G. (1970). *Youth in transition: Vol. 2. The impact of family background and intelligence on tenth-grade boys.* Ann Arbor: Institute for Social Research, Survey Research Center.

III-2/b/P
1215. BALDWIN, A. L., KALHORN, J. C., & BREESE, F. H. Fels Parent Behavior Rating Scales

Avail: 1949 Ref.

Variables Measured: Warmth, objectivity, and control styles of parents

Instrument Description: Following four hours of interviews, ratings are made of parent's style on each of 30 categories.

Reference:

Baldwin, A. L., Kalhorn, J. C., & Breese, F. H. (1949). The appraisal of parent behavior. *Psychol Mono, 63* (Whole No. 299).

III-2/IV-1/b/P
1216. BEHRENS, M. L. Maternal Character Rating Scales

Avail: 1954 Ref.

Variables Measured: Mother's personality, behaviors, and ability to integrate character traits to meet maternal role requirements

Instrument Description: Mothers are rated across 20 criteria on the basis of interviews with all family members, psychological tests, and therapy sessions. Scores are summed in order to examine the above-listed variables.

Reference:

Behrens, M. L. (1954). Child rearing and the character structure of the mother. *Child Dev, 25,* 225–238.

III-2/IV-2/b/P
1217. BISHOP, B. M. Mother-Child Interaction Observation Categories

Avail: 1951 Ref.

Variables Measured: Interactions and control of behaviors of child by mother

Instrument Description: A time-sampling technique is used to gather data on mother-child interactions. Interactions are coded and ratings of mother's controlling techniques are made.

Reference:

Bishop, B. M. (1951). Mother-child interaction and the social behavior of children. *Psych Mono, 65* (Whole No. 328).

III-2/V-2/b/C
1218. BLOCK, V. L. Conflicts with Mother Checklist

Avail: 1937 Ref.

Variables Measured: Adolescent's perception of conflict areas with mother

Instrument Description: This checklist contains 50 statements on which adolescent indicates those areas that represent current problems with his or her mother.

Reference:

Block, V. L. (1937). Conflicts of adolescents with their mothers. *J Abn Soc Psy, 32,* 193–206.

III-2/b
1219. BOLLES, M., METZGER, H. F., & PITTS, M. W. Home Background Scale

Avail: 1941 Ref.

Variables Measured: Favorableness of home background for mental health

Instrument Description: Parent-child relationships are classified on 18 items using a 4-point scale. Ratings indicate how favorable or unfavorable the home environment is for the development of good mental health.

Reference:

Bolles, M., Metzger, H. F., & Pitts, M. W. (1941). Early home background and personality adjustment. *Am J Orthop, 11,* 530–534.

III-2/IV-2/b/P
1220. BORDIN, E. S. Parents Questionnaire

Avail: 1970 Ref.

Variables Measured: Control versus freedom allowed a teenage child by parents

Instrument Description: Parents indicate the amount of freedom allowed their teenage child in each of 29 areas such as clothes, dating, and drinking.

Reference:

Bordin, E. S., Shaevitz, M. H., & Lacher, M. (1970). Entering college student's preparation for self-regulation. *J Coun Psyc, 17,* 291–298.

III-2/b/P
1221. BRIM, O. G., Jr., GLASS, D. C., & LAVIN, D. E. Parental Concern Test

Avail: 1962 Ref.

Variables Measured: Parents' child-rearing practices regarding obedience, sex, hygiene, honesty, peer relations, religion, work habits, sibling relations, and economic behavior

Instrument Description: Parent responds (from *strongly agree* to *strongly disagree*) to 5 items related to each of 10 concepts.

Reference:

Brim, O. G., Jr., Glass, D. C., & Lavin, D. E. (1962). *Personality and decision processes: Studies in the social psychology of thinking.* Stanford, CA: Stanford University Press.

III-2/b/P
1222. BRODY, G. F. Maternal Behavior Observation Categories

Avail: ADI Doc. 8464

Variables Measured: Maternal interaction styles with child

Instrument Description: Counts of each of 15 behaviors typical of interaction styles are kept during 30 minutes of observing mother-child interactions.

Reference:

Brody, G. F. (1965). Relationship between maternal attitudes and behavior. *J Pers Soc Psy, 2,* 317–323.

III-2/c/C
1223. BROWN, A. W., MORRISON, J., & COUCH, G. B. Affectional Family Relationships Questionnaire

Avail: 1949 Ref.

Variables Measured: Children's perceptions of various aspects of the family environment related to the communication of affect

Instrument Description: This measure is designed for grades 4–12 and subjects answer a series of questions related to family interactions.

Reference:

Brown, A. W., Morrison, J., & Duddman, J. M. (1949). Methods of studying affectional family relationships. In R. J. Havighurst & H. Taba (Eds.), *Adolescent characters and personality* (pp. 233–242). New York: John Wiley.

III-2/IV-2/b/e
1224. BRUCE, J. A. Maternal Involvement in the Courtship of Daughters Scale

Avail: NAPS-2

Variables Measured: Mother's attempts to promote courtship of daughter by suitors

Instrument Description: Daughter indicates which of 12 behaviors are exhibited by mother.

Reference:

Bruce, J. A. (1974). The role of mothers in the social placement of daughters: Marriage or work? *J Mar Fam, 36,* 492–497.

III-2/II-3/b/C
1225. BRUNKAN, R. J., & CRITES, J. O. Family Relations Inventory (FRI)

Avail: NAPS-1

Variables Measured: Parental acceptance, avoidance, and concentration regarding their children

Instrument Description: Children rate their parents' behaviors on 202 items detailing the above-listed variables.

Reference:

Brunkan, R. J., & Crites, J. O. (1964). An inventory to measure the parental attitude variable in Roe's theory of vocational choice. *J Coun Psyc, 11,* 3–11.

III-2 / b
1226. CALONICO, J. M., & THOMAS, D. L. Role-Taking Scale

Avail: NAPS-2

Variables Measured: Ability of child and parent to correctly guess decisions the other would make

Instrument Description: Parents and children are asked for their responses and the likely responses of the other person to each of 10 situations. Each situation depicts a behavioral dilemma with two possible responses.

Reference:

Calonico, J. M., & Thomas, D. L. (1973). Role-taking as a function of value similarity and affect in the nuclear family. *J Mar Fam, 35,* 655–665.

III-2/b
1227. CASS, L. K. Parent-Child Relationship Questionnaire

Avail: ADI Doc. 3498

Variables Measured: Mother's ability to correctly predict child's responses, similarity of beliefs between mother and child, and mother's incorrect beliefs about child's perspective

Instrument Description: Mothers and their adolescent children check items from a list that relate to the children's personal preferences, vocational ambitions, fears, and self-description. Extent of agreement between mother and child is of primary interest.

Reference:

Cass, L. K. (1952). Parent-child relationships and delinquency. *J Abn Soc Psyc, 47,* 101–104.

III-2/IV-2/b
1228. CICCHETTI, D. V. The Child Rearing Attitude Scale (CRAS)

Avail: NAPS-2

Variables Measured: Dominance, overprotection, and rejection of adult by his or her parents during the adolescent years

Instrument Description: Subjects are individually presented with 63 statements. For each statement, they are instructed to indicate whether their parents each would have agreed with that statement when the adult child was an adolescent.

Reference:

Cicchetti, D. V., & Ornston, P. S. (1968). Reliability of reported parent-child relationships among neuropsychiatric patients. *J Abn Psych, 73,* 15.

III-2/b/g/C
1229. CLIFFORD, E. Reward and Punishment Preferences Evaluation

Avail: 1959 Ref.

Variables Measured: Child's preferred rewards and punishments from parents

Instrument Description: Child is read a story following which he or she indicates preferences for punishments and rewards from 28 forced-choice sets.

Reference:

Clifford, E. (1959). Ordering of phenomenon in a paired comparisons procedure. *Child Dev, 30,* 381–388.

III-2/II-1/b
1230. COUNT-VanMANEN, G. Intrafamily Identification Measures

Avail: 1973 Ref.

Variables Measured: Similarity between parent and child in values and behaviors

Instrument Description: Children indicate the similarity between themselves and each parent on a series of items related to personality and values.

Reference:

Count-VanManen, G. (1973). The validity of parent-child socialization measures: A comparison of the use of assumed and real parent-child similarity with criterion variables. *Genet Psych Mon, 88,* 201–227.

III-2/c/C
1231. COX, F. N., & LEAPER, P. M. Parent Behavior Question Schedule

Avail: 1963 Ref.

Variables Measured: Parental love, restrictions, and family cohesion

Instrument Description: This measure is designed to be used with 11- to 12-year-old children. Subjects choose from a list of acceptable answers an answer to each of 74 items related to the above-listed variables.

Reference:

Cox, F. N. (1963). A second study of four family variables. *Child Dev, 34,* 619–630.

III-2/IV-2/b
1232. CRANDALL, V. J., ORLEANS, S., PRESTON, A., & RABSON, A. Rating Scales for Child-to-Parent Compliance

Contact: Fels Research Institute, Yellow Springs, OH 45387

Variables Measured: Child compliance with maternal commands, rewards, and punishments

Instrument Description: Behaviors of mother and child are rated based on home observations.

Reference:

Crandall, V. J., Orleans, S., Preston, A., & Rabson, A. (1958). The development of social compliance in young children. *Child Dev, 29,* 429–443.

III-2/II-3/b/P
1233. CRANDALL, V. J., PRESTON, A., & RABSON, A. Rating Scales for Home Observations of Mother-Child Interaction

Contact: Fels Research Institute, Yellow Springs, OH 45387

Variables Measured: Maternal affection and rewarding of child's effort and approval-seeking, help-seeking, and emotional-support-seeking behaviors

Instrument Description: Ratings are made based on observations of interactions between mother and child in the home.

Reference:

Crandall, V. J., Preston, A., & Rabson, A. (1960). Maternal reactions and the development of independence and achievement behavior in young children. *Child Dev, 31,* 243–251.

III-2/IV-2/b/P
1234. CROSS, H. J. Assessment of Parental Training Conditions Interview

Avail: 1966 Ref.

Variables Measured: Parents' allowance of feedback from children in decision making

Instrument Description: Mothers and fathers are interviewed separately. Responses to six questions are rated to determine amount of control exercised versus feedback allowed.

Reference:

Cross, H. J. (1966). The relation of parental training conditions to conceptual level in adolescent boys. *J Personal, 34,* 348–365.

III-2/IV-2/b/P
1235. DANZIGER, K. Autonomy in Decision-Making Index

Avail: 1971 Ref.

Variables Measured: Children's autonomy allowed over decisions related to their own activities

Instrument Description: Children indicate who usually makes each of 12 decisions regarding their activities.

Reference:

Danziger, K. (1971). *The socialization of immigrant children.* Toronto: York Institute of Behavioral Research.

III-2/b/C
1236. DANZIGER, K. Parental Expectations of Child's Task Involvement

Avail: 1974 Ref.

Variables Measured: Child's perceptions of parental expectations

Instrument Description: Child responds to each of 4 items on a 5-point scale indicating parental expectations for specific behaviors.

Reference:

Danziger, K. (1974). The acculturation of Italian immigrant girls in Canada. *Int J Psycho, 9,* 129–137.

III-2/V-2/b/C
1237. DENTLER, R. A., & MONROE, L. J. Interpersonal Relations Scale

Avail: 1961 Ref.

Variables Measured: Strain in parent-child relations

Instrument Description: Nine dichotomized items are designed to yield a subjective index of parent-child relations.

Reference:

Dentler, R. A., & Monroe, L. J. (1961). The family and early adolescent conformity and deviance. *J Mar Fam, 23,* 241–247.

III-2/b/P
1238. DYK, R. B., & WITKIN, H. A. Mother's Differentiation Fostering Behavior Index

Avail: 1965 Ref.

Variables Measured: Mother-child interactions that facilitate or interfere with the child's developing an independent sense of self

Instrument Description: Long open-ended interview with mother when child is not at home serves as the basis for ratings on nine criteria.

Reference:

Dyk, R. B., & Witkin, H. A. (1965). Family experiences related to the development of differentiation in children. *Child Dev, 36,* 21–55.

III-2/V-2/b
1239. EDWARDS, J. N., & BRAUBURGER, M. B. Parent-Youth Conflict Scale

Avail: NAPS-2

Variables Measured: Types of arguments between adolescents and their parents

Instrument Description: This 9-item questionnaire asks adolescents the frequency and types of arguments between themselves and their parents.

Reference:

Edwards, J. N., & Brauburger, M. B. (1973). Exchange and parent-youth conflict. *J Mar Fam, 35,* 101–107.

III-2/IV-2/b/C
1240. ELDER, G. H., Jr. Independence Training Index

Avail: NAPS-2

Variables Measured: Fostering of and preparation for independence in the child by the parents

Instrument Description: Adolescents indicate the amount of control exercised by each parent in each of five areas.

Reference:

Evans, F. B., & Anderson, J. G. (1973). The psychocultural origins of achievement and achievement motivation: The Mexican-American family. *Sociol Educ, 46,* 396–416.

III-2/b/C
1241. EMMERICH, W. A. Child Nurturance-Control Scale

Avail: 1959 Ref.

Variables Measured: Young child's identification with parents

Instrument Description: This measure is for use only with preschool children and uses dolls and play situations to assess child's understanding of parental attitudes.

Reference:

Emmerich, W. A. (1959). Parent identification in young children. *Genet Psych Mon, 60,* 257–308.

III-2/IV-2/b/C
1242. EMMERICH, W. A. Parent and Child Role Conception Pictures

Avail: 1959 Ref.

Variables Measured: Child's perception of own and parental power and goal facilitation

Instrument Description: Subject is presented with each of four cards 12 times, and each time a different question is asked regarding power situations between parent and child.

Reference:

Emmerich, W. A. (1959). Parent identification in young children. *Genet Psych Mon, 60,* 257–308.

III-2/b/P
1243. EMMERICH, W. A. Parental Nurturance-Control Attitude Scale

Avail: 1959 Ref.

Variables Measured: Parent's attitudes toward nurturing and controlling children; child's identification with the parent

Instrument Description: Parent is asked a series of eight questions similar to those examined with the child in the Child Nurturance-Control Scale.

Reference:

Emmerich, W. A. (1959). Parent identification in young children. *Genet Psych Mon, 60,* 257–308.

III-2/b/P
1244. EMMERICH, W. A. Parental Role Perceptions Questionnaire

Avail: 1962 Ref.

Variables Measured: Parental nurturing and restrictive behaviors toward children

Instrument Description: This measure is a 32-item questionnaire concerning reactions to hypothetical child behaviors by parents.

Reference:

Emmerich, W. A. (1962). Variations in the parent role as a function of the parent's sex and the child's sex and age. *Merrill-Pal, 8,* 3–11.

III-2/b/P
1245. EMMERICH, W. A. Parental Role Questionnaire (PRQ)

Avail: 1969 Ref.

Variables Measured: Parents' goals, values, and beliefs as to whether the means justify the ends

Instrument Description: Parents answer a 151-item questionnaire indicating their behavioral choices in varying circumstances.

Reference:

Emmerich, W. A. (1969). A parental role and functional-cognitive approach. *Mon S Res C, 34,* 1–71.

III-2/IV-2/b
1246. ERON, L. D., BANTA, T. J., WALDER, L. O., & LAULICHT, J. H. Aggression Scales for Child in Home

Avail: ADI Doc. 7660

Variables Measured: Forms of aggression in the family

Instrument Description: Sixty questions covering 22 areas of family aggression are asked during an hour-and-a-half individual interview with each parent.

Reference:

Eron, L. D., Banta, T. J., Walder, L. O., & Laulicht, J. H. (1961). Comparison of data obtained from mothers and fathers on childrearing practices and their relation to child aggression. *Child Dev, 32,* 457–472.

III-2/IV-2/b
1247. ERON, L. D., WALDER, L. O., & LEFKOWITZ, M. M. Approval of Home Aggression Scale

Avail: 1971 Ref.

Variables Measured: Parental approval of different levels of child's aggressive behavior

Instrument Description: Parents indicate their level of acceptance of aggressive behavior by their child under 13 sets of widely varying circumstances.

Reference:

Eron, L. D., Walder, L. O., & Lefkowitz, M. M. (1971). *Learning of aggression in children.* Boston: Little, Brown.

III-2/IV-2/b

1248. ERON, L. D., WALDER, L. O., & LEFKOWITZ, M. M. Dependency Conflict Scales (Parts A and B)

Avail: 1971 Ref.

Variables Measured: Rewards and punishments resulting from the child's asking for help, and willingness or unwillingness of child to ask for help

Instrument Description: Ratings are made on 10 items following open-ended interviews with the child's parents.

Reference:

Eron, L. D., Walder, L. O., & Lefkowitz, M. M. (1971). *Learning of aggression in children.* Boston: Little, Brown.

III-2/b/g/P

1249. ERON, L. D., WALDER, L. O., & LEFKOWITZ, M. M. Judgement of Punishment Scale (JUP)

Avail: 1971 Ref.

Variables Measured: Harshness of punishment by parents

Instrument Description: Parents rate the harshness of 40 punishments.

Reference:

Eron, L. D., Walder, L. O., & Lefkowitz, M. M. (1971). *Learning of aggression in children.* Boston: Little, Brown.

III-2/II-3/b

1250. ERON, L. D., WALDER, L. O., & LEFKOWITZ, M. M. Nurturance Scales

Avail: 1971 Ref.

Variables Measured: Nurturant and punishing parental behavior

Instrument Description: Parents are interviewed and asked how they would respond to their children under a variety of circumstance. Responses are coded by judges.

Reference:

Eron, L. D., Walder, L. O., & Lefkowitz, M. M. (1971). *Learning of aggression in children.* Boston: Little, Brown.

III-2/II-3/b/P

1251. ERON, L. D., WALDER, L. O., & LEFKOWITZ, M. M. Parental Rejection Scale

Avail: 1971 Ref.

Variables Measured: Acceptance versus rejection of the child's behavior by the parent

Instrument Description: Parents answer 10 questions about their child's behavior on a 0–2 scale (*Yes—Sometimes* or *Don't Know—No*). Answers indicate relative acceptance or rejection of the child's behavior.

Reference:

Eron, L. D., Walder, L. O., & Lefkowitz, M. M. (1971). *Learning of aggression in children.* Boston: Little, Brown.

III-2/IV-2/b/P
1252. ERON, L. D., WALDER, L. O., & LEFKOWITZ, M. M. Sanctions for Aggression Scale

Avail: 1971 Ref.

Variables Measured: Rewards and punishments given by parents for aggressive behavior in children

Instrument Description: Parents are asked 11 questions about their responses to their children's aggressive behavior. Responses are coded by judges on a scale from 1 to 7 according to the rewards and punishments handed out by parents in response to aggression by the child.

Reference:

Eron, L. D., Walder, L. O., & Lefkowitz, M. M. (1971). *Learning of aggression in children.* Boston: Little, Brown.

III-2/IV-2/b/P
1253. ERON, L. D., WALDER, L. O., & LEFKOWITZ, M. M. Shaming Index

Avail: 1971 Ref.

Variables Measured: Willingness to punish children in public

Instrument Description: Parents are asked if they would use specific punishments in 20 situations in various public environments where their child might become embarrassed.

Reference:

Eron, L. D., Walder, L. O., & Lefkowitz, M. M. (1971). *Learning of aggression in children.* Boston: Little, Brown.

III-2/IV-2/b/P
1254. ERON, L. D., WALDER, L. O., TOIGO, R., & LEFKOWITZ, M. M. Punishment Indexes

Avail: 1963 Ref.

Variables Measured: Physical versus psychological punishment for child's aggression

Instrument Description: Parents are asked which of 24 punishments they would use to control their child's aggression depending on whether the target of the child's aggression was one of the parents or another child.

Reference:

Eron, L. D., Walder, L. O., Toigo, R., & Lefkowitz, M. M. (1963). Social class, parental punishment for aggression, and child aggression. *Child Dev, 34,* 849–868.

III-2/II-5/b/g
1255. FARBER, B., & JENNE, W. C. Parent-Child Relationship Indexes

Avail: 1963 Ref.

Variables Measured: Parent-child communication, parental criticism and dissatisfaction, and child's perception of parental dissatisfaction

Instrument Description: Parents and children indicate their choices on 50 questionnaire items for each of the four indexes listed above.

Reference:

Farber, B., & Jenne, W. C. (1963). Family organization and parent-child communications. *Mon S Res C, 28* (Whole No. 7).

III-2/II-1/b/C
1256. FARBER, B., & JENNE, W. C. Scale of Parental Dissatisfaction with Instrumental Behavior

Avail: 1963 Ref.

Variables Measured: Child's meeting of parents' behavioral expectations

Instrument Description: Fourteen questions examine parents' and child's views as to whether child's behavior conforms to social norms as perceived by parents.

Reference:

Farber, B., & Jenne, W. C. (1963). Family organization and parent-child communications. *Mono S Res C, 28* (Whole No. 7).

III-2/g/b/P
1257. FEINMAN, S. Measure of Disapproval of Cross-Sex Behavior

Avail: 1976 Ref.

Variables Measured: Approval or disapproval of cross-gender behaviors exhibited by 3- to 8-year-old children

Instrument Description: Ten sentences are presented to adolescent or adult subjects. Subjects indicate their approval or disapproval, on a 7-point scale, of behaviors described by each sentence.

Reference:

Feinman, S. (1976). Measure of Disapproval of Cross-Sex Behavior. In O. G. Johnson (Eds.), *Tests and measurements in child development: Handbook* (Vol. 2, pp. 817–818). San Francisco: Jossey-Bass.

III-2/c/e/C
1258. FLOYD, H. H., Jr., & SOUTH, D. R. Parent-Peer Need Satisfaction Scale

Avail: NAPS-2

Variables Measured: Children's need satisfaction within the family, and the extent to which parents, as opposed to friends, meet these needs

Instrument Description: Child indicates the importance of each of 12 needs as well as whether each need is primarily met by peers or parents.

Reference:

Floyd, H. H., Jr., & South, D. R. (1972). Dilemma of youth: A choice of parents or peers as a source of orientation. *J Mar Fam, 34,* 627–634.

III-2/b/C
1259. FUNKENSTEIN, D. H., KING, S. H., & DROLETTE, M. E. Measure of Perception of Parental Roles

Avail: 1957 Ref.

Variables Measured: Authority of, identification with, and affection from each parent

Instrument Description: Subjects are asked 12 questions concerning their parents. Responses are scored according to which parent is perceived to be the primary authority and primary source of affection, and with which one the child primarily identifies.

Reference:

Funkenstein, D. H., King, S. H., & Drolette, M. E. (1957). *Mastery of stress.* Cambridge, MA: Harvard University Press.

III-2/b/g/P
1260. GLIDEWELL, J. C., GILDEA, M. C.-L., KANTOR, M. B., MENSH, I. N., DOMKE, H. R., & BUCHMUELLER, A. D. Maternal Attitude Scale

Avail: 1961 Ref.

Variables Measured: Certainty of own child-rearing practices, control, and protection of the child

Instrument Description: This scale is a 17-item questionnaire filled out by parent indicating attitudes and behaviors related to the above-listed variables.

Reference:

Gildea, M. C.-L., Glidewell, J. C., & Kantor, M. B. (1961). Maternal attitudes and general adjustment in school children. In J. C. Glidewell (Ed.), *Research on parental attitudes and child behavior* (pp. 42–89). Springfield, IL: Charles C Thomas.

III-2/c
1261. GLUECK, S., & GLUECK, E. T. Social Prediction Table

Avail: 1950 Ref.

Variables Measured: Family characteristics indicative of likely juvenile delinquency

Instrument Description: Families are rated on 5 items based on a detailed reading of a case history and a two- to three-hour home interview.

Reference:

Glueck, S., & Glueck, E. T. (1950). *Unraveling juvenile delinquency.* Cambridge, MA: Harvard University Press.

III-2/b/P
1262. GORDON, T. Parental Authority Index

Avail: 1970 Ref.

Variables Measured: Types of punishments and rewards used by parents

Instrument Description: Parents indicate how likely they are to use each of 40 punishments and rewards with their children.

Reference:

Gordon, T. (1970). *Parent effectiveness training.* New York: Peter H. Wyden.

III-2/IV-2/b/C
1263. GRACE, H. A., & LOHMANN, J. J. Parent-Child Conflict Stories

Avail: 1952 Ref.

Variables Measured: Child's emotional, constructive, active oppositional, and simple compliant reactions to stories of parent-child conflict situations

Instrument Description: Child, aged 5–9, is presented with 10 stories depicting various conflict situations between a child and parent. Child is asked to complete the story, with responses scored along the four dimensions listed above.

Reference:

Grace, H. A., & Lohmann, J. J. (1952). Children's reactions to stories depicting parent-child conflict situations. *Child Dev, 23,* 61–74.

III-2/b/P
1264. GUERNEY, B. G., Jr., STOVER, L., & O'CONNELL, M. Behavioral Measure of Empathy

Avail: 1971 Ref.

Variables Measured: Acceptance of child's views and self-directed behaviors by adults

Instrument Description: Adult-child interactions are observed and time-sampled for ratings of parental communication of acceptance, allowing of child's self-direction, and involvement in the interaction with the child.

Reference:

Stover, L., Guerney, B. G., Jr., & O'Connell, M. (1971). Measurements of acceptance allowing self-direction, involvement and empathy in adult-child interactions. *J Psychol, 77,* 261–269.

III-2/b/P
1265. GUINAGH, B. J., & JESTER, R. E. Parent as Reader Scale

Avail: 1972 Ref.

Variables Measured: Types of interactions involved in having a parent read a book to a very young child

Instrument Description: This is a 10-item observational scale used in rating the behavior of parents while they are reading to their 1- to 5-year-old child. Parent behaviors, both verbal and nonverbal, are observed and rated.

Reference:

Guinagh, B. J. (1972). How parents read to children. *Theory into Practice, 11,* 171–177.

III-2/b/P
1266. HARRIS, I. D., & HOWARD, K. I. Child Responsibility and Independence Indexes

Avail: 1968 Ref.

Variables Measured: Age at which children should have varying levels of responsibility and independence

Instrument Description: Subjects answer 14 items concerned with the proper age for the initiation of various types of responsibility and independence.

Reference:

Harris, I. D., & Howard, K. I. (1968). Birth order and responsibility. *J Mar Fam, 30,* 427–432.

III-2/II-3/b/P
1267. HART, I. Child Disciplining Practices Score

Avail: NAPS-1

Variables Measured: Love-oriented versus non-love-oriented discipline by parents

Instrument Description: A combination of structured interview (35 items) with mother and projective questions are used to determine extent of love-oriented discipline.

Reference:

Hart, I. (1957). Maternal child-rearing practices and authoritarian ideology. *J Abn Soc Psych, 55*, 232–237.

III-2/b
1268. HATTWICK, B. W. Home Factors Rating Scales

Avail: 1936 Ref.

Variables Measured: Maternal overattentiveness to children, general maternal disposition, and child's behavioral tendencies

Instrument Description: Ratings on the above variables are made on the basis of home observations.

Reference:

Hattwick, B. W. (1936). Interrelations between the preschool child's behavior and certain factors in the home. *Child Dev, 7*, 200–227.

III-2/IV-2/b/C
1269. HAWKES, G. R., & LEWIS, D. B. Hawkes-Lewis Family Control Scale

Avail: NAPS-1

Variables Measured: Children's perceptions of control parents exercise in deciding family matters

Instrument Description: Children are asked 59 questions regarding how much control their parents exercise versus how much input children are allowed in family decisions.

Reference:

Hawkes, G. R., Burchinal, L. G., & Gardner, B. (1957). Measurement of pre-adolescents' views of family control of behavior. *Child Dev, 28*, 387–392.

III-2/f/b/C
1270. HELSON, R. Sibling Differences Questionnaire

Avail: NAPS-2

Variables Measured: Differences in siblings as children

Instrument Description: Sixty items are asked of adult siblings about their relationships with each other and differences in how they were treated by their parents.

Reference:

Helson, R. (1968). Effects of sibling characteristics and parental values on creative interest and achievement. *J Personal, 36,* 589–605.

III-2/II-3/IV-2/b/P

1271. HETHERINGTON, E. M. Family Interaction Task

Avail: 1967 Ref.

Variables Measured: Parental warmth, hostility, conflict, and dominance

Instrument Description: Parents are interviewed individually and in groups. In both situations they are asked how seven hypothetical situations would be handled.

Reference:

Hetherington, E. M., & Frankie, G. (1967). Effects of parental dominance, warmth, and conflict on imitation in children. *J Pers Soc Psy, 6,* 119–125.

III-2/b/P

1272. HILL, R. L., STYCOS, J. M., & BACK, K. W. Parental Traditional-ism Index

Avail: 1959 Ref.

Variables Measured: Mother's traditional versus modern perspective regarding attitudes possessed by her child

Instrument Description: The index contains 4 items where mother is asked to choose between two opposing behaviors of her child.

Reference:

Hill, R. L., Stycos, J. M., & Back, K. W. (1959). *The family and population control: A Puerto Rican experiment in social change.* Chapel Hill: University of North Carolina Press.

III-2/b

1273. HILTON, I. R. Observation Schedule for Mother-Child Interaction

Avail: ADI Doc. 9554

Variables Measured: Child's independence and mother's nonproductive involvement in child's activities

Instrument Description: Ratings are made based on two periods during which mother and child are observed.

Reference:

Hilton, I. R. (1967). Differences in the behavior of mothers towards first and later born children. *J Pers Soc Psy, 7,* 282–290.

III-2/IV-2/b
1274. HOEFLIN, R., & KELL, L. Kell-Hoeflin Incomplete Sentence Blank: Youth-Parent Relations

Avail: 1959 Ref.

Variables Measured: Democratic versus autocratic family environment

Instrument Description: There are two forms, one for parent and one for adolescent, and each one contains 20 sentence stems to be finished by the subject. Responses are scored by judges as being in one of eight categories.

Reference:

Hoeflin, R., & Kell, L. (1959). The Kell-Hoeflin Incomplete Sentence Blank: Youth-parent relations. *Mon S Res C, 24* (Whole No. 72).

III-2/IV-2/b
1275. HOFFMAN, L. W., ROSEN, S., & LIPPITT, R. Parental Coerciveness and Child Autonomy Questionnaire

Avail: 1960 Ref.

Variables Measured: Parental coerciveness and child autonomy

Instrument Description: This is a two-part questionnaire assessing likely coercive behaviors by the parent and how often the child is allowed by the parent to behave in a certain manner.

Reference:

Hoffman, L. W., Rosen, S., & Lippitt, R. (1960). Parental coerciveness, child autonomy, and child's role at school. *Sociometry, 23,* 15–22.

III-2/IV-2/b/P
1276. HOFFMAN, M. L. Parental Influence Techniques

Avail: 1963 Ref.

Variables Measured: Mother's acceptance of her child's behavior as well as whether discipline is other-oriented or consequence-oriented

Instrument Description: This is a method of categorizing responses based on a detailed interview protocol. Parent's responses are coded according to the above-listed variables.

Reference:

Hoffman, M. L. (1963). Parent discipline and the child's consideration for others. *Child Dev, 34,* 573–587.

III-2/IV-2/b
1277. HOFFMAN, M. L. Unqualified Power Assertion Index (UPA)

Avail: 1957 Ref.

Variables Measured: Parents' attempts to explain to the child their attempts to control his or her behavior

Instrument Description: Extensive interviews are conducted with each parent. Recordings and transcriptions are studied in order to determine disciplinary styles.

Reference:

Hoffman, M. L. (1957). An interview method for obtaining descriptions of parent child interaction. *Merrill-Pal, 4,* 76–83.

III-2/IV-2/b
1278. HURLEY, J. R. Manifest Rejection Index (MRI)

Avail: ADI Doc. 8146

Variables Measured: Disciplinary policy of parents toward their children

Instrument Description: Thirty questions are asked concerning disciplinary issues and actions taken by the parents. Parents are asked whether they agree or disagree with each statement.

Reference:

Hurley, J. R. (1965). Parental acceptance-rejection and children's intelligence. *Merrill-Pal, 11,* 19–31.

III-2/IV-2/b
1279. JACKSON, P. W. Child-Rearing Situation Questionnaire

Avail: 1956 Ref.

Variables Measured: Acceptance of children versus creation of fear by parents

Instrument Description: Parents are asked to indicate their responses to each of 11 situations. Responses are given along a 17-level continuum.

Reference:

Jackson, P. W. (1956). Verbal solutions to parent-child problems. *Child Dev, 27,* 339–349.

III-2/II-3/IV-2/b/P
1280. JOHNSON, S. M., & LOBITZ, G. K. Parental Negativeness Measure

Avail: 1974 Ref.

Variables Measured: Parental negativeness toward the child

Instrument Description: Communications by the parent to the child are coded according to various criteria indicating negativeness during a semistructured 45-minute observation of the family in their home.

Reference:

Johnson, S. M., & Lobitz, G. K. (1974). The personal and marital adjustment of parents as related to observed child deviance and parenting behaviors. *J Abn C Psy, 2,* 193–207.

III-2/IV-2/b/P
1281. JURKOVIC, G. J., & PRENTICE, N. M. Mother-Son Interaction Ratings

Avail: 1974 Ref.

Variables Measured: Maternal dominance, hostility, complexity, encouragement, and warmth with her son

Instrument Description: Mother-son pairs are presented with a series of three moral dilemmas and instructed to come to an agreement. Their interactions are observed and rated.

Reference:

Jurkovic, G. J., & Prentice, N. M. (1974). Dimensions of moral interaction and moral judgment in delinquent and nondelinquent families. *J Cons Clin, 42,* 256–262.

III-2/b
1282. KAFFMAN, M. Parent-Child Relationship Categories (PARC)

Avail: NAPS-2

Variables Measured: Parental acceptance, autonomy of the child, frustration tolerance, protectiveness, consistency, parental assertiveness, and adequacy of stimulation by parent in kibbutzim

Instrument Description: Each parent and an educator fill out questionnaires. These, together with results from a family interview, are used in assessing families.

Reference:

Kaffman, M. (1965). Family diagnosis and therapy in child emotional pathology. *Fam Process, 4,* 241–258.

III-2/b/C
1283. KAGAN, J., & LEMKIN, J. Parental Attributes Technique

Avail: 1960 Ref.

Variables Measured: Child's perceptions of parents as nurturant, punitive, competent, and a source of fear

Instrument Description: In addition to answering direct questions, child indicates which drawings (father, mother, boy, girl) and pictures possess various characteristics.

Reference:

Kagan, J., & Lemkin, J. (1960). The child's differential perception of parental attributes. *J Abn Soc Psy, 61,* 440–447.

III-2/b/P

1284. KATKOVSKY, W., PRESTON, A., & CRANDALL, V. J. Parent Reaction Questionnaire

Avail: NAPS-2

Variables Measured: Parents' positive, negative, and total reactions to their children's achievements

Instrument Description: Parents indicate how they would be likely to respond to each of 48 situations where their child achieves in either intellectual, mechanical, artistic, or physical areas.

Reference:

Katkovsky, W., Preston, A., & Crandall, V. J. (1964). Parent's achievement attitudes and their behavior with their children in achievement situations. *J Genet Psy, 104,* 105–121.

III-2/b

1285. KING, D. L. Contact Comfort Ratings

Avail: 1973 Ref.

Variables Measured: Physical contact of a comforting nature initiated by the mother

Instrument Description: This test consists of two paragraphs. Subject is presented with one of 16 possible combinations of these paragraphs and is asked his or her rating of the contact between mother and child.

Reference:

King, D. L. (1973). Expectations of behaviors of mothers preceding initiation of contact comfort with their children. *Psychol Rep, 33,* 131–137.

III-2/b/P

1286. KLATSKIN, E. H., JACKSON, E. B., & WILKIN, L. C. Scales for Rating Flexibility of Maternal and Child Behavior

Avail: 1955 Ref.

Variables Measured: Maternal flexibility in feeding, sleeping, toileting, and socialization of children

Instrument Description: Ratings on the above-listed variables are made on the basis of interviews with mother when her child is 1, 2, and 3 years old.

Reference:

Klatskin, E. H., & Jackson, E. B. (1955). Methodology of the Yale rooming-in project on parent-child relationship. *Am J Orthop, 25,* 81–108.

III-2/IV-2/b
1287. KLEIN, M. M., PLUTCHIK, R., & CONTE, H. R. Parental Patterns Inventory

Avail: 1973 Ref.

Variables Measured: Passivity and dominance of parents

Instrument Description: Therapist rates each parent on 22 items related to passivity and dominance following a clinical interview.

Reference:

Klein, M. M., Plutchik, R., & Conte, H. R. (1973). Parental dominance-passivity and behavior problems of children. *J Cons Clin, 40,* 416–419.

III-2/IV-2/b/P
1288. KOCH, H. L., DENTLER, M., DYSART, B., & STREIT, H. Attitude Towards Children's Freedom Scale

Avail: 1934 Ref.

Variables Measured: Adult attitudes toward control of children's environments versus allowing the children to pursue actions independently

Instrument Description: Two forms are provided, each containing 33 items. Subject answers either *agree, disagree,* or *undecided* to each item.

Reference:

Koch, H. L., Dentler, M., Dysart, B., & Streit, H. (1934). A scale for measuring attitude toward the question of children's freedom. *Child Dev, 5,* 253–266.

III-2/g/b/P
1289. LANSKY, L. Sex-Role Attitude Test (SRAT)

Avail: NAPS-2

Variables Measured: Parents' attitudes regarding gender-role rigidity with respect to their children

Instrument Description: Parents answer a series of 50 questions about the appropriateness of various activities for boys and girls.

Reference:

Lansky, L. (1967). The family structure also affects the model: Sex-role attitudes in parents of preschool children. *Merrill-Pal, 13,* 139–150.

III-2/b
1290. LEON, G. R. Parent-Child Interaction Scores

Avail: NAPS-2

Variables Measured: Child's aggression, restlessness, complaints, and noncompliance; mother's reactions to child's behaviors

Instrument Description: Behavior of child is time-sampled during observations. Child also responds to projective pictures, with responses being rated for above characteristics.

Reference:

Leon, G. R. (1971). Case report: The use of a structured mother-child interaction and projective material in studying parent influence on child behavior problems. *J Clin Psyc, 27,* 413–416.

III-2/b/P
1291. LESLIE, G. R., & JOHNSEN, K. P. Maternal Role Concept and Performance Scales

Avail: NAPS-1

Variables Measured: Maternal behaviors with children regarding sex and modesty training, aggression toward the mother, and encouragement of self-direction

Instrument Description: Mothers indicate their likely responses to 33 situations concerning their children.

Reference:

Leslie, G. R., & Johnsen, K. P. (1963). Changed perceptions of the maternal role. *Am Sociol R, 28,* 919–928.

III-2/b/g/P
1292. LETON, D. A. Parental Attitude Inventory (PAI)

Avail: NAPS-2

Variables Measured: Attitudes toward children in a variety of areas

Instrument Description: Subjects respond to 120 items revised from the Minnesota Teacher Attitude Inventory.

Reference:

Leton, D. A. (1958). A study of the validity of parent attitude measurement. *Child Dev, 29,* 515–520.

III-2/IV-2/b
1293. LI, A. K.-F. Parental Attitude Scale in Chinese

Avail: NAPS-2

Variables Measured: Chinese child-rearing attitudes regarding dominance, obedience, and communication

Instrument Description: This measure is available in both Chinese and English. Subjects are asked the extent of their agreement with 18 items.

Reference:

Li, A. K.-F. (1973). A parental attitude scale in Chinese. *Psychologia, 16,* 174–176.

III-2/b
1294. LINDEN, E., & HACKLER, J. Family Closeness Index

Avail: NAPS-2

Variables Measured: Several variables related to communication and the relationship between adolescents and their parents

Instrument Description: A total of 25 questions, answered *yes-no,* ask adolescents about various parent-child communication and relationship issues.

Reference:

Linden, E., & Hackler, J. (1973). Affective ties and delinquency. *Pac Sociol Rev, 16,* 27–46.

III-2/b/C
1295. LOSCIUTO, L. A., & KARLIN, R. M. Child-Parent Dissidence Scale

Avail: 1972 Ref.

Variables Measured: Adolescent's perceived agreement with parents

Instrument Description: Adolescent rates extent of expected agreement with parents on 15 items covering various social issues assumed to be relevant to adolescents.

Reference:

Losciuto, L. A., & Karlin, R. M. (1972). Correlates of the generation gap. *J Psychol, 81,* 253–262.

III-2/b/C
1296. LYNN, D. B., & DePALMA-CROSS, A. Parent-Preference Play Situations

Avail: 1974 Ref.

Variables Measured: Parent favored by child for play activities

Instrument Description: Child is successively presented with each of seven different play situations while parents wait in another room. Following each presentation, the child is asked which parent he or she would like to play with. Parent receiving four nominations is considered to be favored.

Reference:

Lynn, D. B., & DePalma-Cross, A. (1974). Parent preference of preschool children. *J Mar Fam, 36*, 555–559.

III-2/IV-2/b/P
1297. LYTTON, H. Mother (Father) Rating Scales and Child Rating Scales

Avail: NAPS-2

Variables Measured: Parents' punishments and rewards for 2- to 3-year-old child's compliant, dependent, and independent behaviors

Instrument Description: Interview with mother, maternal 24-hour diary, and observations of the child serve as the bases for ratings.

Reference:

Lytton, H. (1973). Three approaches to the study of parent-child interaction: Ethological, interview and experimental. *J Child Psychol Psychi, 14*, 1–17.

III-2/II-1/b
1298. MAPSTONE, J. R. Familism Index

Avail: 1970 Ref.

Variables Measured: Parental role in adult children's lives

Instrument Description: Solidity of family system is determined to be a positive function of involvement of parents in their adult children's lives, as assessed by an 11-item questionnaire.

Reference:

Mapstone, J. R. (1970). Familistic determinants of property acquisition. *J Mar Fam, 32*, 143–150.

III-2/b
1299. MARK, J. C. Mark Attitude Survey

Avail: ADI Doc. 3672

Variables Measured: Parental control, intellectual objectivity, and warmth of relationship with child

Instrument Description: Parents indicate level of agreement with 139 statements covering the above-listed variables.

Reference:

Mark, J. C. (1953). The attitudes of the mothers of male schizophrenics toward child behavior. *J Abn Soc Psych, 48*, 185–189.

III-2/IV-1/b
1300. MAXWELL, P. H., CONNOR, R., & WALTERS, J. Perception of Parent Role Performance Questionnaire

Avail: 1961 Ref.

Variables Measured: Adolescent's and parents' perceptions of parents' behaviors toward the child

Instrument Description: This questionnaire consists of parallel mother-child and father-child forms, each containing 17 items concerning the parent-adolescent relationship. Score is determined by extent of agreement between parent and child.

Reference:

Maxwell, P. H., Connor, R., & Walters, J. (1961). Family member perception of parent role performance. *Merrill-Pal, 7,* 31–37.

III-2/II-3/ b
1301. McKINLEY, D. Father's Hostility Measure

Avail: 1964 Ref.

Variables Measured: Child's perception of father's hostility toward him or her

Instrument Description: Subjects are presented with four situations and are asked how similarly to the hypothetical father their own father would react.

Reference:

McKinley, D. (1964). *Social class and family life.* New York: Free Press.

III-2/IV-2/b/C
1302. McKINLEY, D. Severity of Socialization Scale

Avail: 1964 Ref.

Variables Measured: Perceptions of punishments used when subject was 10–12 years old

Instrument Description: Subject is asked to indicate which three of ten listed punishments each of his or her parents were most likely to use.

Reference:

McKinley, D. (1964). *Social class and family life.* New York: Free Press.

III-2/I-1/b
1303. McLEOD, J. M. Family Communications Patterns

Avail: NAPS-2

Variables Measured: Parents' encouragement of children to express their ideas and to challenge others versus encouragement in maintaining harmonious relationships

Instrument Description: Both parents and children answer 10 questions regarding familial communication strategies.

Reference:

Chaffee, S. H., McLeod, J. M., & Atkin, C. K. (1971). Parental influences on adolescent media use. *Am Behav Sc, 14,* 323–340.

III-2/b
1304. MEADOW, K. P., & SCHLESINGER, H. S. Interaction Rating Scale for Mothers and Deaf Children

Avail: NAPS-2 & 1972 Ref.

Variables Measured: In all, 28 aspects of mother-child interactions, including control intrusiveness, creativity, anxiety, rigidity, enjoyment of other, irritability, and mutual understanding in families where the child is deaf

Instrument Description: Videotaped interactions between mother and child serve as the basis for ratings on 28 scales.

Reference:

Schlesinger, H. S., & Meadow, K. P. (1972). *Sound and sign: Childhood deafness and mental health.* Berkeley: University of California Press.

III-2/b
1305. MEYER, M. M., & TOLMAN, R. S. Parent Image Checklist

Avail: 1955 Ref.

Variables Measured: Attitudes of parents toward children on 12 criteria dealing primarily with attachment and dependency issues, and child's ratings of parents in five general categories

Instrument Description: Parental assessment is a result of TAT interviews. Children are assessed based on interviews. Response categories are provided.

Reference:

Myer, M. M., & Tolman, R. S. (1955). Correspondence between attitudes and images of parental figures in TAT stories and in therapeutic interviews. *J Cons Psych, 19,* 79–82.

III-2/IV-2/b
1306. MORGAN, P. K., & GAIER, E. L. Punishment Situation Index (PSI)

Avail: NAPS-1

Variables Measured: Punishments used by mothers with their children

Instrument Description: This is a projective technique using 10 scenes set up like comic strips. Children are asked seven questions about each picture. Responses are coded and scored.

Reference:

Morgan, P. K., & Gaier, E. L. (1956). The direction of aggression in the mother-child punishment situation. *Child Dev, 27,* 447–457.

III-2/IV-2/b
1307. MOULTON, R. W., BURNSTEIN, E., LIBERTY, P. G., Jr., & ALTUCHER, N. Measure of Parental Dominance in Discipline

Avail: 1966 Ref.

Variables Measured: Mother versus father dominance in use of discipline

Instrument Description: Subject is asked 5 items concerned with which parent disciplines in various situations.

Reference:

Moulton, R. W., Burnstein, E., Liberty, P. G., Jr., & Altucher, N. (1966). Patterning of parental affection and disciplinary dominance as a determinant of guilt and sex typing. *J Pers Soc Psy, 4,* 356–363.

III-2/b
1308. MOUSTAKAS, C. E., SIGEL, I. E., & SCHALOCK, H. D. Adult-Child Interaction Schedule

Avail: 1956 Ref.

Variables Measured: In all, 89 adult and 82 child categories of behavior

Instrument Description: The incidence of 171 verbal behaviors during a parent-child interaction is recorded every 5 seconds for 16 minutes.

Reference:

Moustakas, C. E., Sigel, I. E., & Schalock, H. D. (1956). An objective method for the measurement and analysis of child-adult interaction. *Child Dev, 27,* 109–134.

III-2/a/P
1309. MURSTEIN, B. I. Attitude of Mother of Hospitalized Child Toward Husband

Avail: 1958 Ref.

Variables Measured: Perceptions of husbands by mothers of hospitalized children

Instrument Description: This measure consists of 20 statements concerning wife's sentiments toward husband when a child is ill.

Reference:

Murstein, B. I. (1958). Attitudes of parents of hospitalized children toward doctors, nurses, and husbands: The construction of three scales. *J Clin Psyc, 14,* 184–186.

III-2/II-5/b/C
1310. MUSSEN, P. H., & DISTLER, L. Child's Perception of Parental Behavior

Avail: 1959 Ref.

Variables Measured: Child's perception of parents as nurturant, rewarding, punitive, and threatening

Instrument Description: Child is told nine incomplete family situations. Stories are completed by the child by use of a doll and a play situation. Objective rating criteria are provided.

Reference:

Mussen, P. H., & Distler, L. (1959). Masculinity, identification, and father-son relationships. *J Abn Soc Psy, 59,* 350–356.

III-2/b
1311. NAKAMURA, C. Y., & ROGERS, M. M. Parents' Expectations Inventory

Avail: NAPS-2

Variables Measured: Parents' expectations for children's practical and assertive independent behaviors as well as for independence demonstrated by the child

Instrument Description: Parents indicate behavioral expectations and frequency of each of 20 independent behaviors in their children.

Reference:

Nakamura, C. Y., & Rogers, M. M. (1969). Parents' expectations of autonomous behavior and children's autonomy. *Devel Psych, 1,* 613–617.

III-2/b/P
1312. OJEMANN, R. H. Self-Reliance Test

Avail: 1934 Ref.

Variables Measured: Age at which parent believes various independent behaviors are appropriate for children

Instrument Description: Test has separate forms for parents of preschool-, elementary-, and high school-aged children. Parent indicates appropriate age for the introduction of various independent behaviors.

Reference:

Ojemann, R. H. (1934). Measurement of self-reliance. *U of Iowa Studies in Child Welfare, 10,* 103–111.

III-2/b/P
1313. OLSEN, N. J. Independence Training Measure

Avail: 1973 Ref.

Variables Measured: Parental attitudes toward independent behavior in young children

Instrument Description: Parent is asked four questions concerning children's independence.

Reference:

Olsen, N. J. (1973). Family structure and independence training in a Taiwanese village. *J Mar Fam, 35,* 512–519.

III-2/g/P
1314. OPPENHEIM, A. N. Parent Attitude Inventory

Avail: NAPS-2

Variables Measured: Overprotection, democracy, autocracy, acceptance, rejection, strictness, and objectivity

Instrument Description: Parent indicates degree of agreement with 52 statements dealing with the above-listed variables.

Reference:

Pitfield, M., & Oppenheim, A. N. (1964). Child rearing attitudes of mothers of psychotic children. *J Child Psychol Psychi, 5,* 51–57.

III-2/g/P
1315. PEARLIN, L. I. Parental Aspirations

Avail: 1971 Ref.

Variables Measured: Parents' expectations for children's educations and occupations

Instrument Description: Parents are asked seven open-ended questions concerning their hopes for their children's educations and occupations.

Reference:

Pearlin, L. I. (1971). *Class context and family relations.* Boston: Little, Brown.

III-2/IV-2/b/P
1316. PEARLIN, L. I., YARROW, M. R., & SCARR, H. A. Parental Pressure for Success Scale

Avail: 1967 Ref.

Variables Measured: Parental pressure for doing well

Instrument Description: Ratings based on observation of child and each parent when child is given tasks to complete and the importance of doing well is stressed.

Reference:

Pearlin, L. I., Yarrow, M. R., & Scarr, H. A. (1967). Unintended effects of parental aspirations: A case of children's cheating. *Am J Sociol, 73,* 73–83.

III-2/b/P
1317. PERDUE, O. R., & SPIELBERGER, C. D. Disapproval of Childhood Behavior Index

Avail: 1966 Ref.

Variables Measured: Parental disapproval of typically punished childhood behaviors

Instrument Description: Parents rate each of 10 behaviors in terms of their disapproval of that behavior.

Reference:

Perdue, O. R., & Spielberger, C. D. (1966). Anxiety and the perception of punishment. *Mental Hygiene, 50,* 390–397.

III-2/IV-2/b/C
1318. PETERSON, E. T. Maternal Interest and Control Index

Avail: 1961 Ref.

Variables Measured: Daughter's perception of mother's interest in and control over her

Instrument Description: Subjects indicate the degree of maternal interest in six activities and problem areas dealing with the adolescent, and the extent to which mothers would be upset at six behaviors were they to be exhibited by the adolescent.

Reference:

Peterson, E. T. (1961). The impact of maternal employment on the mother-daughter relationship. *Mar Fam Living, 23,* 355–361.

III-2/IV-2/b/C
1319. PIKAS, A. Rational and Inhibiting Parental Authority Inventories

Avail: NAPS-1

Variables Measured: Child's reaction to parental authority that is inhibiting, rational, restrictive, altruistic, or authoritarian

Instrument Description: This measure is a 90-minute, 324-item questionnaire filled out by parents, including *yes-no* and sentence-completion items.

Reference:

Pikas, A. (1961). Children's attitudes toward rational versus inhibiting parental authority. *J Abn Soc Psych, 62,* 315–321.

III-2/b/C
1320. RABIN, A. I. Sentence Completion Test of Children's Views of Parents

Avail: 1959 Ref.

Variables Measured: Adjustment of child to family, mother, and father

Instrument Description: Child is given a series of 12 sentences to complete. Two judges rate the responses as *positive* or *other.*

Reference:

Rabin, A. I. (1959). Attitudes of kibbutz children to family and parents. *Am J Orthop, 29,* 172–179.

III-2/b/P
1321. RADIN, N., & WEIKART, P. Cognitive Home Environment Scale

Avail: NAPS-2

Variables Measured: Educational environment of the home

Instrument Description: Mothers of preschool children are asked 25 questions about educational activities and supplies in the home during a semistructured interview.

Reference:

Radin, N. (1969). The impact of a kindergarten home counseling program. *Except Chil, 36,* 251–256.

III-2/c/C
1322. RADKE, M. J. Doll Play

Avail: 1946 Ref.

Variables Measured: Relations of child with mother, father, and siblings

Instrument Description: Child's free play with four dolls for 20 minutes (mother, father, boy, and girl doll) is observed and rated by unseen judges on several specific criteria.

Reference:

Radke, M. J. (1946). The relation of parental authority to children's behavior and attitudes. *University of MN Child Welfare Monographs, 22.*

III-2/IV-2/b/P
1323. RADKE, M. J. Parent's Inventory

Avail: 1946 Ref.

Variables Measured: Several variables related to parental discipline

Instrument Description: This measure is a multiple-choice questionnaire composed of 127 items to be filled out by parents.

Reference:

Radke, M. J. (1946). The relation of parental authority to children's behavior and attitudes. *U of MN Child Welfare Monographs, 22.*

III-2/g/b/P
1324. REMMERS, H. H., & STEDMAN, L. A. Bringing Up Children—An Inventory of Attitudes

Avail: 1966 Ref.

Variables Measured: Knowledge of social and emotional development of children

Instrument Description: This measure is a 45-item questionnaire used in evaluating subjects' knowledge of child development issues.

Reference:

Stedman, L. A. (1966). An investigation of knowledge and attitudes toward child behavior. In *Studies in Higher Education* (No. 62). Lafayette, IN: Purdue University, Division of Educational Reference.

III-2/b/P
1325. RHEINGOLD, H. L. Maternal Care Checklist

Avail: 1960 Ref.

Variables Measured: Mother's activities in caring for her infant

Instrument Description: A total of 42 items are time-sampled over a period of two days, based on four hours of observation each day.

Reference:

Rheingold, H. L. (1960). The measurement of maternal care. *Child Dev, 31,* 565–575.

III-2/b/P
1326. ROSENBERG, M. Parental Interest Index

Avail: 1965 Ref.

Variables Measured: Parental interest in child's friends, interests, and report cards

Instrument Description: Children are asked to rate their parents' interest in seven areas.

Reference:

Rosenberg, M. (1965). *Society and the adolescent self-image.* Princeton, NJ: Princeton University Press.

III-2/b
1327. ROSENBERG, M. Relationship with Father Score

Avail: 1965 Ref.

Variables Measured: Quality of child-father relationship

Instrument Description: Child is asked six questions about his or her child-father relationship. A multiple-choice answer format is provided.

Reference:

Rosenberg, M. (1965). *Society and the adolescent self-image.* Princeton, NJ: Princeton University Press.

III-2/g/b/P
1328. ROTHBART, M. K., & MACCOBY, E. E. Parental Attitudes About Sex Differences Questionnaire

Avail: NAPS-2

Variables Measured: Differences parents feel do and should exist between boys and girls

Instrument Description: Parents indicate which of 40 characteristics differentiate boys from girls and the importance of their sons and daughters having those characteristics.

Reference:

Rothbart, M. K., & Maccoby, E. E. (1966). Parents differential reactions to sons and daughters. *J Pers Soc Psy, 4,* 237–243.

III-2/b/P
1329. RUBENSTEIN, J. L. Maternal Attentiveness Scale

Avail: 1967 Ref.

Variables Measured: Mother's attempts to provide her infant with stimulation

Instrument Description: Mother's behavior with the infant is time-sampled during a three-hour visit in the home. Touching, looking, and holding behaviors are noted.

Reference:

Rubenstein, J. L. (1967). Maternal attentiveness and subsequent exploratory behavior in the infant. *Child Dev, 38,* 1089–1100.

III-2/b/P
1330. SANDLER, H. M., & BARBRACK, C. R. Maternal Teaching Style Instrument (MTSI)

Avail: 1971 Ref.

Variables Measured: Strategies used by mothers in teaching their preschool-aged children a structured task

Instrument Description: Mothers are instructed to assist their children in forming patterns using blocks varying in size, color, and shape. Activities of mother and child are videotaped and analyzed later using exact scoring criteria.

Reference:

Sandler, H. M., Stewart, L. T., & Barbrack, C. R. (1971). Toward the development of a maternal teaching style instrument. *DARCEE Papers and Reports, 5.*

III-2/II-3/IV-2/b/C
1331. SCANZONI, J. Parental Nurture and Control Scales

Avail: 1967 Ref.

Variables Measured: Children's perceptions of parent's warmth toward and control of them

Instrument Description: Multiple-choice responses are given to 27 questions asked of the child, either in interview or questionnaire format. Factor analyses have led to the development of scoring categories for responses.

Reference:

Scanzoni, J. (1967). Socialization, N achievement, and achievement values. *Am Sociol R, 32,* 449–456.

III-2/b/P
1332. SCHAEFER, E. S., BELL, R. Q., & BAYLEY, N. Maternal Behavior Research Instrument

Avail: 1959 Ref.

Variables Measured: A series of more than 20 mostly negative maternal behaviors and attitudes

Instrument Description: Mothers are periodically observed during the first three years of the infant's life. Ratings are made based on a combination of observations and interviews.

Reference:

Schaefer, E. S., Bell, R. Q., & Bayley, N. (1959). Development of a maternal behavior research instrument. *J Genet Psy, 95,* 83–104.

III-2/IV-2/b/P
1333. SCHMITT, D. R., & MARWELL, G. Child-Rearing Technique Measure

Avail: 1967 Ref.

Variables Measured: Love- versus punishment-oriented child-rearing techniques

Instrument Description: Four situations are presented. For each situation, parent rank orders the appropriateness of 16 possible actions designed to gain compliance of his or her child.

Reference:

Marwell, G., & Schmitt, D. R. (1967). Attitudes toward parental use of promised rewards to control adolescent behavior. *J Mar Fam, 29,* 500–504.

III-2/b/C
1334. SCHWARZWELLER, H. K., & LYSON, T. A. Perceived Parental Interest Scale (PPI)

Avail: NAPS-2

Variables Measured: Child's perception of parental responsiveness to needs and interests

Instrument Description: This 5-item self-administered questionnaire examines the child's perception of his or her parent's responsiveness.

Reference:

Schwarzweller, H. K., & Lyson, T. A. (1974). Social class, parental interest and the educational plans of American and Norwegian rural youth. *Sociol Educ, 47,* 443–465.

III-2/IV-2/b/P
1335. SEARS, R. R. Mother Attitude Scales for Sex and Aggression

Avail: ADI Doc. 8381

Variables Measured: Parental attitudes and punishment for nudity, masturbation, social sex play, and aggression toward parents of young children

Instrument Description: This measure contains 79 items, each receiving a rating on one of four levels for each situation, depending on the severity of punishment the parent believes is necessary.

Reference:

Sears, R. R. (1965). Comparison of interviews with questionnaires for measuring mothers' attitudes toward sex and aggression. *J Pers Soc Psy, 2,* 37–44.

III-2/b
1336. SEARS, R. R., WHITING, J. W. M., NOWLIS, V., & SEARS, P. S. Child-Rearing Procedures Rating Scales

Avail: 1953 Ref.

Variables Measured: Infant frustration, maternal nurturance, punitiveness, and responsiveness

Instrument Description: This interview covers two and one-half to four hours, with 15 general topics and many specific questions within each topic.

Reference:

Sears, R. R., Whiting, J. W. M., Nowlis, V., & Sears, P. S. (1953). Some child-rearing antecedents of aggression and dependency in young children. *Genet Psych Mono, 47,* 135–236.

III-2/e
1337. SEIDL, F. W., & PILLITTERI, A. Parent Participation Attitude Scale

Avail: NAPS-2

Variables Measured: Attitudes of nursing personnel toward parental involvement in hospital pediatric programs

Instrument Description: This scale is a 24-item questionnaire filled out by nursing personnel.

Reference:

Seidl, F. W., & Pillitteri, A. (1967). Development of an attitude scale toward parent participation. *Nurs Res, 16.*

III-2/g/b/P
1338. SHAPIRO, M. B. Parental Opinion Inventory

Avail: 1952 Ref.

Variables Measured: Parental restrictiveness

Instrument Description: Parent indicates level of agreement with each of 40 statements on restriction of child's actions.

Reference:

Shapiro, M. B. (1952). Some correlates of opinions on the upbringing of children. *Br J Psycho, 43,* 141–149.

III-2/II-3/II-5/b
1339. SHAW, M. E. Parental Childrearing Attitude Measure

Avail: 1965 Ref.

Variables Measured: Child's and parent's perceptions and acceptance of the child

Instrument Description: Parents and children indicate how often the child can be described by each of a list of adjectives and how much they like or dislike each trait.

Reference:

Wyer, R. S., Jr. (1965). Self-acceptance, discrepancy between parents' perceptions of their children, and goal-seeking effectiveness. *J Pers Soc Psy, 2,* 311–316.

III-2/IV-1/b/C
1340. SHERMAN, A. W., Jr. Sherman Emancipation Questionnaire

Avail: 1946 Ref.

Variables Measured: Social and emotional independence of college students from their parents

Instrument Description: This is a 60-item questionnaire asking college students whether they depend on their parents in various decisions and behaviors.

Reference:

Sherman, A. W., Jr. (1946). Emancipation status of college students. *J Genet Psy, 68,* 171–180.

III-2/g/b/P
1341. SHOBEN, E. J., Jr. Parent Attitude Survey

Avail: 1949 Ref.

Variables Measured: Parental dominant, possessive, and ignoring attitudes toward their problem children

Instrument Description: Parent indicates level of agreement with 85 statements regarding actions to be taken with their problem children.

Reference:

Shoben, E. J., Jr. (1949). The assessment of parental attitudes in relation to child adjustment. *Genet Psych Mono, 39,* 101–148.

III-2/b/P

1342. SMITH, H. T. Maternal Behavior Interview Rating Scales

Avail: ADI Doc. 5635

Variables Measured: Mother's handling of dependency behaviors by young children

Instrument Description: Ratings are made based on an interview consisting of 36 open-ended questions. Ratings are made according to mother's feelings for the child and restrictions placed on the child by the mother.

Reference:

Smith, H. T. (1958). A comparison of interview and observation measures of mother behavior. *J Abn Soc Psy, 57,* 278–282.

III-2/b

1343. SMITH, H. T. Observation Scales for Maternal and Child Behavior

Avail: ADI Doc. 5635

Variables Measured: Mother's handling of child's dependency behaviors; child's behaviors designed to evoke maternal attention

Instrument Description: Mother and child are observed during 45 minutes together in a playroom. Ratings of mother's behaviors are made on 16 categories.

Reference:

Smith, H. T. (1958). A comparison of interview and observation measures of mother behavior. *J Abn Soc Psy, 57,* 278–282.

III-2/IV-2/b/C

1344. SPECTOR, S. I. Home Discipline Patterns

Avail: 1962 Ref.

Variables Measured: Child's view of home discipline as firm or permissive

Instrument Description: Child answers *yes* or *no* to each of 10 questions about parental disciplinary techniques.

Reference:

Spector, S. I. (1962). A study of firm and permissive home discipline. *J Educ Soc, 36,* 115–123.

III-2/IV-2/b/C

1345. STOGDILL, R. M. Attitudes Toward Parental Control of Children

Avail: NAPS-1

Variables Measured: Parental approval of children's freedom from authority

Instrument Description: Child indicates level of agreement with 70 statements detailing areas in which he or she may be free from controls.

Reference:

Stogdill, R. M. (1936). The measurement of attitudes toward parental control and the social adjustments of children. *J Appl Psyc, 20,* 359–367.

III-2/IV-2/b/C
1346. STONE, C. L., & LANDIS, P. H. Family Authority Pattern Scale

Avail: 1953 Ref.

Variables Measured: Democratic versus authoritarian parental control of teenage children

Instrument Description: Child answers six items concerning degree of control exercised by his or her parents.

Reference:

Stone, C. L., & Landis, P. H. (1953). An approach to authority pattern in parent-teenage relationships. *Rural Socio, 18,* 233–242.

III-2/IV-2/b/P
1347. STOTT, L. H. Parental Control Attitude Scale

Avail: 1940 Ref.

Variables Measured: Parents' attitudes toward controlling children's activities

Instrument Description: Parent rates 30 items on control issues according to their level of agreement with each.

Reference:

Stott, L. H. (1940). Parental attitudes of farm, town and city parents in relation to certain personality adjustments of their children. *J Soc Psych, 11,* 325–339.

III-2/IV-2/c
1348. STRODTBECK, F. L., HUTCHINSON, J. G., & RAY, M. P. Family Consensus Score (FCS) and Adolescent Autonomy Scale (AAS)

Avail: NAPS-2

Variables Measured: Family consensus in parent and adolescent problem situations

Instrument Description: Each member of the family is administered a 76-item questionnaire with *yes-no* responses. Answers are evaluated to locate areas of common agreement.

Reference:

Dentler, R. A., & Hutchinson, J. G. (1961). Socioeconomic versus family membership status as sources of family attitude consensus. *Child Dev, 32,* 249–254.

III-2/IV-2/b/e/C
1349. SUNDBERG, N., SHARMA, V., WODTLI, T., & ROHILA, P. Adolescent Autonomy Index

Avail: NAPS-2

Variables Measured: Adolescents' independence from their parents

Instrument Description: This measure consists of a two-part questionnaire with *10 yes-no* items and 40 items asking who typically makes various decisions for the adolescent.

Reference:

Sundberg, N., Sharma, V., Wodtli, T., & Rohila, P. (1969). Family cohesiveness and autonomy of adolescents in India and the United States. *J Mar Fam, 31,* 403–407.

III-2/IV-2/II-3/b/C
1350. SWITZER, D. K. Parental Attitude Scale

Avail: NAPS-2

Variables Measured: Child's perceptions of parental overdemanding and rejecting behavior

Instrument Description: Subjects indicate agreement or disagreement with each of 50 items in terms of how their mothers, fathers, and they themselves would respond.

Reference:

Switzer, D. K., Grigg, A. E., Miller, J. S., & Young, R. K. (1962). Early experiences and occupational choice: A test of Roe's hypothesis. *J Coun Psyc, 9,* 1.

III-2/b/P
1351. TALLMAN, I. Parental Adaptability Instrument

Avail: ADI Doc. 6838

Variables Measured: Parental motivation, affective involvement, empathy, and flexibility

Instrument Description: Subjects are presented with 24 situations dealing with the above-listed variables during an interview. Following the interview, ratings are made on the basis of their responses to each situation.

Reference:

Tallman, I. (1961). Adaptability: A problem-solving approach to assessing child-rearing practices. *Child Dev, 32,* 651–668.

III-2/IV-2/b/C
1352. TALLMAN, I., MAROTZ-BADEN, R., STRAUS, M. A., & WILSON, L. R. Simulated Career Choice Game (SIMCAR)

Avail: NAPS-2 & 1974 Ref.

Variables Measured: Parent-adolescent issues related to life-styles, power and support, and economic success or failure

Instrument Description: This is a board game patterned after the game *Career.* In the game, the adolescent starts out with money and time available. Decisions are made regarding careers, money earned, and occupational level achieved.

Reference:

Tallman, I., Wilson, L. R., & Straus, M. A. (1974). SIMCAR: A game simulation method for cross-cultural family research. *Social Science Info, 13,* 121–144.

III-2/IV-2/b/C
1353. TEC, N. Parental Pressure for Educational Achievement Index

Avail: 1973 Ref.

Variables Measured: Parental pressure for educational achievement by children

Instrument Description: Child is asked three questions regarding pressures placed on them by their parents regarding educational achievement.

Reference:

Tec, N. (1973). Parental educational pressure, adolescent educational conformity, and marijuana use. *Youth Soc, 4,* 291–312.

III-2/b/C
1354. TIFFANY, D. W. Picture Q. Technique (PQT)

Avail: ADI Doc. 7316

Variables Measured: Child versus adult control with male and female parent figures

Instrument Description: Child is presented with a deck of 48 pictures and is asked to sort the cards into piles according to how satisfactorily they answer each of several questions about parent-child interactions.

Reference:

Tiffany, D. W., & Shontz, F. C. (1962). The measurement of experienced control in preadolescents. *J Cons Psych, 26,* 491–497.

III-2/IV-2/b/P
1355. TROST, J. Child-Rearing Scale

Avail: 1967 Ref.

Variables Measured: Attitudes regarding physical versus nonphysical punishment of children

Instrument Description: Adult subjects indicate their agreement or disagreement with each of four attitude statements regarding punishment of children.

Reference:

Trost, J. (1967). Some data on mate selection: Homogomy and perceived homogomy. *J Mar Fam, 29,* 739–755.

III-2/b/P
1356. TULKIN, S. R., & KAGAN, J. Maternal Behavior Measures

Avail: 1972 Ref.

Variables Measured: Mother's reactions to and interactions with her infant

Instrument Description: Mother-infant interactions are observed for two hours over two days during which time maternal behaviors are coded every five seconds on nine criteria.

Reference:

Tulkin, S. R., & Kagan, J. (1972). Mother-child interaction in the first year of life. *Child Dev, 43,* 31–41.

III-2/b
1357. TYLER, F. B., TYLER, B. B., & RAFFERTY, J. E. Parent-Child Need Assessment

Avail: NAPS-1

Variables Measured: Recognition, status, protection, dependency, dominance, independence, love, and affection

Instrument Description: Ratings on the above-listed variables are made based on a parental interview and observations of the child.

Reference:

Tyler, F. B., Tyler, B. B., & Rafferty, J. E. (1961). Need value and expectancy interrelations as assessed from motivational patterns of parents and their children. *J Cons Psy, 25,* 304–311.

III-2/g/b/P
1358. VEROFF, J., & FELD, S. Parental Inadequacy Index (PII)

Avail: 1970 Ref.

Variables Measured: Parental feelings of inadequacy regarding tolerance and time spent with their children

Instrument Description: Parental responses, during interviews based on two open-ended questions, are rated.

Reference:

Veroff, J., & Feld, S. (1970). *Marriage and work in America.* New York: Von Nostrand Reinhold.

III-2/b/P
1359. WALTERS, J., IRELAND, F., STROMBERG, F. I., & LONIAN, G. Children's Responsibility Inventory

Avail: 1957 Ref.

Variables Measured: Parents' beliefs regarding responsibilities of young children

Instrument Description: Parents indicate how early children should assume responsibility for each of 50 behaviors or activities.

Reference:

Walters, J., Stromberg, F. I., & Lonian, G. (1957). Perceptions concerning development of responsibility in young children. *Elem Sch J, 57,* 209–216.

III-2/b/P
1360. WEATHERLY, D. Mother's Responses to Childhood Aggression

Avail: NAPS-2

Variables Measured: Permissive versus punitive actions of mother toward aggressive child

Instrument Description: This measure is a 3-item questionnaire given to mothers.

Reference:

Weatherly, D. (1963). Maternal response to childhood aggression and subsequent anti-Semitism. *J Abn Soc Psych, 66,* 183–185.

III-2/b/C
1361. WECHSLER, H., & FUNKENSTEIN, D. H. Perceptions of Family Questionnaire

Avail: 1957 Ref.

Variables Measured: Children's perceptions of parental authority and affection

Instrument Description: This is a series of questions, taking up to four hours to administer, in which a child alternately answers for him- or herself, mother, and father.

Reference:

Funkenstein, D. H., King, S. H., & Drolette, M. E. (1957). *Mastery of stress.* Cambridge, MA: Harvard University Press.

III-2/IV-2/b/P
1362. WHITING, J. W. M., CHILD, I. L., & LAMBERT, W. W. Child Socialization Techniques Scales

Avail: 1966 Ref.

Variables Measured: Mother's use of rules, warmth, hostility, praise, and so on in communicating and enforcing rules

Instrument Description: Mother's use of various socialization techniques is evaluated based on several causal observations of mother-child interactions.

Reference:

Whiting, J. W. M., Child, I. L., & Lambert, W. W. (1966). *Field guide for a study of socialization.* New York: John Wiley.

III-2/b/P
1363. WHITING, J. W. M., CHILD, I. L., & LAMBERT, W. W. Maternal Behavior Factor Indexes

Avail: 1966 Ref.

Variables Measured: Maternal warmth, instability, responsibility, and use of and response to aggression

Instrument Description: A total of 28 rating scales are used in evaluating mother-child interactions following administration of 84 open-ended questions.

Reference:

Whiting, J. W. M., Child, I. L., & Lambert, W. W. (1966). *Field guide for a study of socialization.* New York: John Wiley.

III-2/IV-2/b/P
1364. WILLIAMS, J. R., & SCOTT, R. B. Child Care Rating Scales

Avail: 1953 Ref.

Variables Measured: Mother's rigidity in early raising and training of her child

Instrument Description: Ratings of mother's maternal style are made on 15 items following a one-hour interview.

Reference:

Williams, J. R., & Scott, R. B. (1953). Growth and development of Negro infants. IV. Motor development and its relationship to child rearing practices in two groups of Negro infants. *Child Dev, 24,* 103–121.

III-2/b/C

1365. WILLIAMS, W. C. Parental Authority-Love Statements (PALS Test and PEN PALS Test)

Avail: NAPS-1

Variables Measured: Parental authority, exploitiveness, and general parenting style

Instrument Description: PALS is a set of 64 items, 32 to be answered by children as they relate to each parent. PEN PALS is a set of 16 cartoons responded to by the child.

Reference:

Williams, W. C. (1958). The PALS tests: A technique for children to evaluate both parents. *J Cons Psych, 22,* 487–495.

III-2/IV-2/b/C

1366. WILLIS, R. H. Authoritarian Upbringing Test (UPB)

Avail: ADI Doc. 4838

Variables Measured: Authoritarian upbringing of subjects who are currently parents

Instrument Description: Subjects are interviewed regarding their freedom of activities and the voice they had in parent-child relations while growing up. Responses to each of 12 questions are rated by the interviewer.

Reference:

Willis, R. H. (1956). Political and child-rearing attitudes in Sweden. *J Abn Soc Psych, 53,* 74–77.

III-2/IV-2/b/P

1367. WILLIS, R. H. Demands for Obedience Test (DFO)

Avail: ADI Doc. 4838

Variables Measured: Parents' views on punishment, child obedience, and belief that parents know best

Instrument Description: Subjects are asked 13 questions during the course of an interview. Interviewer rates each response on a two- or three-point scale.

Reference:

Willis, R. H. (1956). Political and child-rearing attitudes in Sweden. *J Abn Soc Psych, 53,* 74–77.

III-2/b/P
1368. WINDER, C. L., & RAU, L. Stanford Parent Questionnaire

Avail: ADI Doc. 7091

Variables Measured: Parental ambivalence, strictness, aggression and punitiveness, adjustment, models, and mastery

Instrument Description: Fathers are asked 518 and mothers are asked 491 questions covering 27 (mothers') or 28 (fathers') areas during interviews lasting 90 minutes.

Reference:

Winder, C. L., & Rau, L. (1962). Parental attitudes associated with social deviance in preadolescent boys. *J Abn Soc Psych, 64,* 418–424.

III-2/IV-2/b/P
1369. WINTERBOTTOM, M. R. Independence and Achievement Training Scales

Avail: 1958 Ref.

Variables Measured: Parental standards for achievement and rewards or punishments for achievement or lack of achievement

Instrument Description: Parents are presented with 40 statements regarding achievement, reward, and punishment of activities engaged in by their children. They are asked to check those that apply to themselves.

Reference:

Winterbottom, M. R. (1958). The relation of need for achievement to learning experiences in independence and mastery. In G. W. Atkinson (Ed.), *Motives in fantasy, action, and society* (pp. 453–478). New York: Van Nostrand.

III-2/b
1370. WITTENBORN, J. R. Social Reaction Interview

Avail: 1956 Ref., Appendix A

Variables Measured: Mothers' child-rearing practices and behavioral reactions to their children, and the reactions of older versus younger children to those practices

Instrument Description: Interviews are conducted with children and their mothers. General child-rearing practices are discussed with the mother, and 53 questions are posed to children dealing with their mothers' behaviors toward them.

Reference:

Wittenborn, J. R. (1956). A study of adoptive children. I. Interviews as a source of scores for children and their homes. *Psychol Mon, 70*(1).

III-2/g/b/P
1371. WOLFENSBERGER, W., & KURTZ, R. A. Parent Realism Assessment Technique (PRAT) and Parental Expectations of Child Development Technique (PECDT)

Contact: Microfiche Publications, 305 E. 46th St., New York, NY 10017, Doc. 01183

Variables Measured: Parents' perceptions of possibly retarded child's developmental level as well as parents' perceptions of likely level of achievement of the child as an adult

Instrument Description: Parent is asked to indicate the age level at which child is currently functioning and that at which he or she is likely to function as an adult according to each of eight behavioral areas.

Reference:

Wolfensberger, W., & Kurtz, R. A. (1971). Measurement of parent's perception of their children's development. *Genet Psych Mono, 83,* 3.

III-2/II-5/b/P
1372. WYER, R. S., Jr. Parental Differences Score

Avail: NAPS-2

Variables Measured: Parental attitudes and behaviors toward their children; parents' perceptions of how their children view them

Instrument Description: This measure is a 117-item questionnaire, with each item rated on a 6-point scale. Differences between parents' general attitude, behaviors toward the child, and interpretations of the child's responses are assessed.

Reference:

Wyer, R. S., Jr. (1965). Effects of child-rearing attitudes and behavior on children's responses to hypothetical social situations. *J Pers Soc Psy, 2,* 480–486.

III-2/b
1373. YARROW, M. R., CAMPBELL, J. D., & BURTON, R. V. Child Questionnaire for Early Childhood Behavior and Relationships, and Mother Interview of Child Behavior and Relationships

Avail: 1970 Ref.

Variables Measured: Mother's and child's memories of infant characteristics, early care, infant development, family environment, and preschool personality

Instrument Description: Mother is asked 50 open-ended questions and child is asked 50 parallel questions related to the above-listed variables. Even though the questions are open-ended, the response format is structured.

Reference:

Yarrow, M. R., Campbell, J. D., & Burton, R. V. (1970). Recollection of childhood: A study of the retrospective method. *Mon S Res C, 35.*

III-2/g/b/P

1374. ZUK, G. H., MILLER, R. L., BARTRAN, J. B., & KLING, F.
Maternal Acceptance of Retarded Children Questionnaire

Avail: NAPS-1

Variables Measured: Retarded children's mothers' attitudes and beliefs regarding maternal fulfillment, overprotection, discipline and diagnostic acceptance

Instrument Description: Mothers indicate extent of agreement with each of 50 statements related to their feelings about their retarded children.

Reference:

Zuk, G. H., Miller, R. L., Bartran, J. B., & Kling, F. (1961). Maternal acceptance of retarded children: A questionnaire study of attitudes and religious background. *Child Dev, 32,* 525–540.

III-2/b/P

1375. ZUNICH, M. Mother-Child Interaction Test

Avail: 1962 Ref.

Variables Measured: Mother's interactions with her child

Instrument Description: This test consists of a series of 17 categories for observing interactions between mothers and their children. The primary focus is on the mother's behavior toward her child. A 12-category adaptation of this system, titled *Observational Technique for Adult-Child Interaction*, was developed by Schlieper (1975).

References:

Schlieper, A. (1975). Mother-child interaction observed at home. *Am J Orthop, 45,* 468–472. Reprinted in S. Chess & A. Thomas (Eds.). (1977). *Annual progress in child psychiatry and child development.* New York: Brunner/Mazel.
Zunich, M. (1962). Relationship from maternal behavior and attitudes toward children. *J Genet Psych, 100,* 155–165.

IV-1/c

1376. ALDOUS, J. Household Task Performance Index

Avail: 1969 Ref.

Variables Measured: Spouse typically responsible for various family chores

Instrument Description: Division of labor for 10 typical household responsibilities is discussed during a semistructured interview.

Reference:

Aldous, J. (1969). Wives' employment status and lower-class men as husband-fathers: Support for the Moynihan thesis. *J Mar Fam, 31,* 469–476.

IV-1/a
1377. ALDOUS, J., & STRAUS, M. A. Task Differentiation Index

Avail: NAPS-2

Variables Measured: Division of gender-role-oriented household tasks

Instrument Description: Subjects indicate who generally performs each of 16 tasks, some traditionally male-oriented and some traditionally female-oriented.

Reference:

Aldous, J., & Straus, M. A. (1966). Social networks and conjugal roles: A test of Bott's hypothesis. *Social Forc, 44,* 576–580.

IV-1/a/W
1378. ARNOTT, C. C. Homemaking Comparison Level of Alternatives

Avail: 1970 Ref.

Variables Measured: Satisfaction with full-time homemaker role and other roles that combine homemaker with other outside interests

Instrument Description: This measure contains 14 items, each with three questions. Issues examined include profit, both financial and emotional, in full-time homemaker and other roles, dual-role profit, and saliency of each role for the individual homemaker.

Reference:

Arnott, C. C. (1970). Married women and the pursuit of profit: An exchange theory perspective. *J Mar Fam, 34,* 495–507.

IV-1/a/W
1379. ARNOTT, C. C. Marital Role Comparison Level Index

Avail: 1972 Ref.

Variables Measured: Extent to which female experiences a sense of marital role fulfillment in areas such as housekeeping, children, husband, and friends

Instrument Description: This measure has 9 three-part items. Each item refers to a role. The three parts (expectations, role performance, and role saliency) combine to produce the index.

Reference:

Arnott, C. C. (1972). Married women and the pursuit of profit: An exchange theory perspective. *J Mar Fam, 34,* 122–131.

IV-1/a
1380. BALLWEG, J. Household Task Performance Index

Avail: 1967 Ref.

Variables Measured: Division of household tasks

Instrument Description: Subjects indicate extent to which each performs 12 selected tasks. The responses also allow for the possibility of having household tasks performed by hired help.

Reference:

Ballweg, J. (1967). Resolution of conjugal role adjustment after retirement. *J Mar Fam, 29,* 277–281.

IV-1/a
1381. BLOOD, R. O., Jr. Division of Labor Index

Avail: 1958 Ref.

Variables Measured: Division of household tasks

Instrument Description: Subjects are asked which partner generally performs a series of eight household tasks.

Reference:

Blood, R. O., Jr. (1958). The division of labor in city and farm families. *Mar Fam Living, 20,* 170–174.

IV-1/c
1382. BLOOD, R. O., Jr. Traditional-Developmental Family Role Concepts Scale

Avail: NAPS-1 & 1958 Ref.

Variables Measured: Traditional versus developmental conceptions of behaviors consistent with being a good mother, father, or child

Instrument Description: This is a 30-item questionnaire with five traditional and five developmental roles for each of mother, father, and child. Subject picks which 5 of the 10 items on each scale (mother, father, child) is most important.

Reference:

Conner, R., Greene, H., & Walters, J. (1958). Agreement of family member conceptions of "good" parent and child roles. *Social Forc, 36,* 354–358.

IV-1/a
1383. BLOOD, R. O., Jr., & HAMBLIN, R. L. Household Task Performance Index

Avail: NAPS-2

Variables Measured: Division of household tasks.

Instrument Description: In this measure, each partner indicates hours per week spent performing a series of 12 household activities

Reference:

Blood, R. O., Jr., & Hamblin, R. L. (1958). The effect of the wife's employment on the family power structure. *Social Forc, 36,* 347–352.

IV-1/II-2/a
1384. BUERKLE, J. V., & BADGLEY, R. F. Yale Marital Interaction Battery

Avail: NAPS-1

Variables Measured: Viewing the situation from the spouse's perspective, sympathy for spouse's expectations, conforming own role to spouse's desires, and altruism

Instrument Description: For a series of 40 behavioral sequences involving role conflict, subject selects one of four possible solutions to each sequence.

Reference:

Buerkle, J. V., & Badgley, R. F. (1959). Couple role taking: The Yale marital interaction battery. *J Mar Fam, 21,* 53–58.

IV-1/II-5/a/g
1385. BURNS, M. S. A. Women's Life Style Attitude Scale

Avail: 1974 Ref.

Variables Measured: Career versus motherhood orientation of women

Instrument Description: Females answer 20 items according to their current beliefs. Males answer as they would prefer their future wives to answer.

Reference:

Burns, M. S. A. (1974). Life styles for women, an attitude scale. *Psychol Rep, 35,* 227–230.

IV-1/a
1386. BURR, W. R. Marital Role Discrepancy Index

Avail: NAPS-2

Variables Measured: Congruence between role expectations for spouse and spousal behavior

Instrument Description: This 65-item questionnaire is completed twice. Subjects are directed first to answer the questionnaire with respect to the extent to which they would be bothered by each behavior, and then with regard to actual spousal behaviors.

Reference:

Burr, W. R. (1971). An expansion and test of a role theory of marital satisfaction. *J Mar Fam, 33,* 368–372.

IV-1/a
1387. BUXBAUM, J. Marital Roles Questionnaire

Avail: NAPS-2

Variables Measured: Role changes in couples where husband becomes disabled

Instrument Description: Role changes due to disability and acceptance of new role structure are examined through a series of 15 questions, each asked four different times.

Reference:

Buxbaum, J. (1967). Effect of nurturance of wives' appraisals of their marital satisfaction and the degree of their husbands' aphasia. *J Cons Psych, 31,* 240–243.

IV-1/a/g/W
1388. CAMERON, C. Autonomy for Women Attitude Inventory

Avail: 1972 Ref.

Variables Measured: Women's self- versus other-orientation related to socialization, maternal and husband-wife relationships, vocational choice, sexuality, and legal matters

Instrument Description: Ten items covering various areas of autonomy for women are asked of female subjects. Results are interpreted in terms of the woman's general orientation.

Reference:

Arnott, C. C. (1972). Husbands' attitude and wives' commitment to employment. *J Mar Fam, 34,* 673–684.

IV-1/III-2/c/C
1389. COUCH, A. S. Authoritarian Child Attitudes Scale

Avail: ADI Doc. 7860

Variables Measured: Authoritarian parental attitudes

Instrument Description: Subjects respond to each of three statements regarding child rearing.

Reference:

Nuttall, R. L. (1964). Some correlates of high need for achievement among northern Negroes. *J Abn Soc Psych, 68,* 593–600.

IV-1/c
1390. COUCH, C. J. Family Role Specialization Questionnaire

Avail: NAPS-1

Variables Measured: Role assignments within families

Instrument Description: Subject indicates division of labor within families for each of 17 items.

Reference:

Couch, C. J. (1962). Family role specialization and self-attitudes in children. *Sociol Q, 3,* 115–121.

IV-1/a
1391. COUCH, C. J. Role Concept Questionnaire

Avail: 1958 Ref.

Variables Measured: Role performance and husband-wife consensus in role prescription

Instrument Description: Partners individually answer an open-ended questionnaire asking what the five most important obligations are of both the husband and the wife as well as their partner's likely response.

Reference:

Couch, C. J. (1958). The use of the concept "role" and its derivatives in a study of marriage. *Mar Fam Living, 20,* 353–357.

IV-1/c
1392. DANZIGER, K. Household Sex Role Specialization Index

Avail: 1974 Ref.

Variables Measured: Division of household tasks according to gender

Instrument Description: Subject is asked the frequency of six behaviors by males and females within the household.

Reference:

Danziger, K. (1974). The acculturation of Italian immigrant girls in Canada. *Int J Psyco, 9,* 129–137.

IV-1/c
1393. DOWDALL, J. A. Attitudes Toward Married Women's Employment Scale

Avail: 1974 Ref.

Variables Measured: Attitudes toward employment of wife under varying circumstances

Instrument Description: This scale consists of a series of 5 items examining acceptance of wife's working outside the home under various conditions related to presence of children and financial need.

Reference:

Dowdall, J. A. (1974). Women's attitudes toward employment and family roles. *Sociol Anal, 35,* 251–262.

IV-1/V-2/a
1394. FARBER, B. Role Tension Index

Avail: 1956 Ref.

Variables Measured: Role tension ratings by husband and wife of themselves and each other

Instrument Description: Partners rate themselves and each other on 10 traits indicative of role tension. Ratings are scored and compared.

Reference:

Farber, B., & Blackman, L. S. (1956). Marital role tensions and number and sex of children. *Am Sociol R, 21,* 596–601.

IV-1/c
1395. FENGLER, A. P. Marital Ideology Scales

Avail: 1973 Ref.

Variables Measured: Marital commitment and economic security, companionship, and parental responsibility

Instrument Description: This measure contains 20 items examining views on commitment issues within marriage.

Reference:

Fengler, A. P. (1973). The effects of age and education on marital ideology. *J Mar Fam, 35,* 264–271.

IV-1/IV-2/c
1396. HAAVIO-MANNILA, E. Equality of the Sexes in the Family Scale

Avail: 1972 Ref.

Variables Measured: Equality in household chore assignments and decision making

Instrument Description: This 4-item interview questionnaire concerns attitudes about male and female roles within families. Reliability and validity data are provided.

Reference:

Haavio-Mannila, E. (1972). Cross-national differences in adoption of new ideologies and practices in family life. *J Mar Fam, 34,* 525–537.

IV-1/c/C
1397. HARRIS, D. B., CLARK, K. E., ROSE, A. M., & VALASEK, F.
What Are My Jobs?

Avail: 1954 Ref. & NAPS-1

Variables Measured: Home chores engaged in by children

Instrument Description: Subjects indicate which chores out of a list of 24 they engage in and which they enjoy.

Reference:

Harris, D. B., Clark, K. E., Rose, A. M., & Valasek, F. (1954). The relationship of children's home duties to an attitude of responsibility. *Child Dev, 25,* 2933.

IV-1/a
1398. HAWKINS, J. L., & JOHNSEN, K. P. Perceived Role Discrepancy (PRO) and Imputed Role Consensus (IRC) Scores

Avail: NAPS-2

Variables Measured: Role performance versus role expectation and spousal role performance versus own expectations for spouse

Instrument Description: Subjects are asked to relate the acceptability of alternative behaviors in 48 situations. Comparisons between levels of acceptability and actual performance for themselves and their spouses are computed.

Reference:

Hawkins, J. L., & Johnsen, K. P. (1969). Perception of behavioral conformity, imputation of consensus, and marital satisfaction. *J Mar Fam, 31,* 507–511.

IV-1/c/W
1399. HECKSCHER, B. T. Mother's Housework Score

Avail: NAPS-2

Variables Measured: Wife's degree of involvement in housework

Instrument Description: This measure contains a series of 14 household tasks presented to wife. The score equals the number of tasks performed exclusively by her.

Reference:

Heckscher, B. T. (1967). Household structure and achievement orientation in lower class Barbadian families. *J Mar Fam, 29,* 521–526.

IV-1/IV-2/c
1400. HILL, R. L. Family Control Type Classification

Avail: 1949 Ref.

Variables Measured: Relative positions of power in the family held by the husband and wife

Instrument Description: This is a 4-item questionnaire about how husbands and wives handle and share specific responsibilities within the family.

Reference:

Hill, R. L. (1949). *Families under stress: Adjustment to the crises of war separation and reunion.* New York: Harper.

IV-1/IV-2/c
1401. HILL, R. L., STYCOS, J. M., & BACK, K. W. Familism Typology

Avail: 1959 Ref.

Variables Measured: Eight types of family organization based on dominant partner, wife working or at home, and prohibited activities for wife

Instrument Description: Eight items with forced-choice responses are asked during an interview with the wife. The results are used in categorizing the family into one of eight family organizational types.

Reference:

Hill, R. L., Stycos, J. M., & Back, K. W. (1959). *The family and population control: A Puerto Rican experiment in social change.* Chapel Hill: University of North Carolina Press.

IV-1/IV-2/a
1402. HOFFMAN, L. W. Male-Dominance Ideology

Avail: 1960 Ref.

Variables Measured: Traditional male dominance versus equal rights in relationships

Instrument Description: Four items examining the traditional view of male dominance are asked of both male and female subjects. Response to each item is indicated in terms of agreement or disagreement on a 4-point scale.

Reference:

Hoffman, L. W. (1960). Effects of the employment of mothers on parental power relations and the division of household tasks. *Mar Fam Living, 22,* 27–35.

IV-1/IV-2/a
1403. HOFFMAN, L. W. Marital Power and Task Participation Measures

Avail: 1960 Ref.

Variables Measured: Sharing of household responsibilities, power of husband versus wife

Instrument Description: There are 33 paired items that ask which partner does routine household tasks.

Reference:

Hoffman, L. W. (1960). Effects of the employment of mothers on parental power relations and the division of household tasks. *Mar Fam Living, 22,* 27–35.

IV-1/IV-2/c
1404. HURVITZ, N. Control Roles Attitude Scale

Avail: 1959 Ref.

Variables Measured: Family leadership, attitudes toward a wife who works outside the home, decisions regarding children, relationships between men and women

Instrument Description: The scale has 19 items covering the above-mentioned six subscales. Subjects indicate the intensity of their agreement or disagreement with each item.

Reference:

Hurvitz, N. (1959). A scale for the measurement of superordinate-subordinate roles in marriage. *Am Cath Sociol R, 20,* 234–241.

IV-1/a
1405. HURVITZ, N. Marital Roles Inventory

Avail: 1960 Ref.

Variables Measured: Role expectations and performance of husband and wife for him- or herself and spouse; strain put on the marital relationship related to role expectations and performance

Instrument Description: Eleven roles are ranked according to how the subject's and spouse's roles are perceived within the family.

Reference:

Hurvitz, N. (1960). The marital roles inventory and the measurement of marital adjustment. *J Clin Psych, 16,* 377–380.

IV-1/g/e/H
1406. HUTTER, M. Husband Role Attitude Index and Father Role Attitude Index

Avail: 1974 Ref.

Variables Measured: Married college students' views of father and husband roles

Instrument Description: Subjects are asked if they believe others should pursue the same roles and activities as themselves.

Reference:

Hutter, M. (1974). Significant others and married student role attitudes. *J Mar Fam, 36,* 31–36.

IV-1/I-4/a

1407. LEVINGER, G. Task and Social-Emotional Marriage Behaviors (Instrumental and Expressive Marital Behaviors)

Avail: 1964 Ref.

Variables Measured: Communication, sexual relationship, supportiveness

Instrument Description: This measure contains 16 questions regarding the husband's and wife's behaviors and attitudes toward each other on the above-listed variables.

Reference:

Levinger, G. (1964). Task and social behavior in marriage. *Sociometry, 27,* 433–448.

IV-1/g/W

1408. KATELMAN, D. K., & BARNETT, L. D. Favorableness to Wife Working Index

Avail: 1968 Ref.

Variables Measured: Traditional versus modern orientation toward women working

Instrument Description: There are 11 items examining views on women working outside the home.

Reference:

Katelman, D. K., & Barnett, L. D. (1968). Work orientations of urban, middle-class, married women. *J Mar Fam, 30,* 80–88.

IV-1/g/W

1409. KELLAR, B. Attitude Toward Any Homemaking Activity

Avail: 1967 Ref.

Variables Measured: Enjoyment of various homemaking activities

Instrument Description: Two forms of a 45-item questionnaire ask the extent to which the woman enjoys performing a series of homemaking activities (originally published in 1934).

Reference:

Shaw, M. E., & Wright, J. M. (1967). *Scales for the measurement of attitudes.* New York: McGraw-Hill.

IV-1/V-2/c

1410. KING, K., McINTYRE, J., & AXELSON, L. J. Adolescent Perception of Maternal Employment Scale

Avail: 1968 Ref.

Variables Measured: Adolescents' perceptions of a mother's employment as a threat to the success of her marriage

Instrument Description: This 5-item scale rates the threat posed by maternal employment.

Reference:

King, K., McIntyre, J., & Axelson, L. J. (1968). Adolescents' views of maternal employment as a threat to the marital relationship. *J Mar Fam, 30,* 633–637.

IV-1/I-4/a
1411. KIRKPATRICK, C., & HOBART, C. W. Family Opinion Survey

Avail: NAPS-1

Variables Measured: Role prescriptions for husbands and wives

Instrument Description: This 81-item questionnaire covering 14 subject areas is used in assessing role prescriptions for marital partners.

Reference:

Kirkpatrick, C., & Hobart, C. W. (1954). Disagreement, disagreement estimate, and non-empathetic imputations for intimacy groups varying from favorite date to married. *Am Sociol R, 19,* 10–19.

IV-1/c/g/W
1412. LAKIN, M. Female Role Attitudes Test

Avail: 1957 Ref.

Variables Measured: Attitudes toward parental relationships, role acceptance, adequacy, psychosexual adjustment, and motherliness

Instrument Description: Ten cards with pictures depicting various role activities are used to elicit female role attitudes. Each story given in response to a picture is scored according to affective content.

Reference:

Lakin, M. (1957). Assessment of significant role attitudes in primiparous mothers by means of a modification of the TAT. *Psychos Med, 19,* 50–60.

IV-1/a
1413. LAMOUSE, A. Family Division of Labor Scale

Avail: 1969 Ref.

Variables Measured: Gender roles and tasks performed by husbands and wives

Instrument Description: Fourteen tasks are listed. Subjects indicate which member of their family performs each task.

Reference:

Lamouse, A. (1969). Family roles of women: A German example. *J Mar Fam, 31,* 145–152.

IV-1/IV-2/a
1414. LAUMANN, E. O. Traditional Marital Role Relations Index

Avail: 1973 Ref.

Variables Measured: Traditionalism of marital gender roles

Instrument Description: Subject indicates level of agreement with three statements covering various marital roles.

Reference:

Laumann, E. O. (1973). *Bonds of pluralism.* New York: Wiley-Interscience.

IV-1/c/W
1415. LOEVINGER, J., & SWEET, B. Family Problems Scale

Avail: NAPS-1

Variables Measured: Authoritarianism, anxiety, orderliness, rejection of women's biological role, masochism

Instrument Description: A total of 86 forced-choice questions examine personalities of women with respect to their family role opinions. Items included represent role identities typical of various parts of the day and life span.

Reference:

Loevinger, J., & Sweet, B. (1961). Construction of a test of mothers' attitudes. In J. C. Glidewell (Ed.), *Parental attitudes and child behavior* (pp. 110–123). Springfield, IL: Charles C Thomas.

IV-1/III-2/b/C
1416. McCLEERY, R. L. McCleery Scale of Adolescent Development

Avail: 1955 Ref.

Variables Measured: Adjustment of adolescent to current and likely future roles

Instrument Description: There are 150 statements, 16 of which are contained within a family life scale, with the adolescent indicating a subjective level of importance for each.

Reference:

McCleery, R. L. (1955). *McCleery Scale of Adolescent Development.* Lincoln: University of Nebraska Press.

IV-1/a
1417. McDONALD, A. P., Jr. Social-Domestic Work Factor of the Sex Role Survey (SRS)

Avail: 1974 Ref.

Variables Measured: Equality of household division of labor

Instrument Description: This survey contains a subscale of 11 items from the original 53-item Sex Role Survey. Subjects indicate agreement or disagreement with statements on a scale from +3 to -3.

Reference:

McDonald, A. P., Jr. (1974). Identification and measurement of multidimensional attitudes toward equality between the sexes. *J Homosexual, 1,* 165–182.

IV-1/g/a/e
1418. MOTZ, A. B. Role Conception Inventory

Avail: 1952 Ref.

Variables Measured: Marital role conformity for self and spouse

Instrument Description: Each partner is presented with 24 items and is asked to check those that apply to him- or herself and to the general public.

Reference:

Motz, A. B. (1952). The Role Conception Inventory: A tool for research in social psychology. *Am Sociol R, 17,* 465–471.

IV-1/a/W
1419. NELSON, H. Y. Wife Works Scale

Avail: NAPS-2

Variables Measured: Favorability toward wife working at varying stages of the family life cycle

Instrument Description: Nine statements address the issue of the wife working during each of three periods of the marital life cycle. Subject indicates a *yes, no,* or *undecided* response to each item.

Reference:

Nelson, H. Y., & Goldman, P. R. (1969). Attitudes of high school students and young adults toward the gainful employment of married women. *Fam Coord, 18,* 251–255.

IV-1/V-2/c/W

1420. NEVILL, D., & DAMICO, S. Role Conflict Questionnaire for Women

Avail: NAPS-2

Variables Measured: Time management, husband relationship, household management, finances, child care, expectations, and guilt

Instrument Description: This 8-item questionnaire examines areas of conflict and stresses present in the woman's life. Seven possible responses per item.

Reference:

Nevill, D., & Damico, S. (1974). Development of a role conflict questionnaire for women: Some preliminary findings. *J Cons Clin, 42,* 743.

IV-1/c

1421. OLSEN, M. E. Household Division of Labor Schedule

Avail: 1960 Ref.

Variables Measured: Division of labor within the family

Instrument Description: Subject is asked which family member is typically responsible for each of 100 household duties.

Reference:

Olsen, M. E. (1960). Distribution of family responsibilities and social stratification. *Mar Fam Living, 22,* 60–65.

IV-1/g/a/H

1422. PARKER, S., & KLEINER, R. J. Husbands' Marital Role Discrepancy Index

Avail: 1969 Ref.

Variables Measured: Husband's perception of his real versus ideal marital role performance

Instrument Description: This 4-item scale is given twice during the course of an extended interview. The initial time it is administered, the questions relate to the ideal role; the second time, they relate to actual roles.

Reference:

Parker, S., & Kleiner, R. J. (1969). Social and psychological dimensions of the family role performance of the Negro male. *J Mar Fam, 31,* 500–506.

IV-1/c
1423. PODELL, L. Familial Role Expectation Scale

Avail: 1967 Ref.

Variables Measured: Specificity versus diffuseness and neutrality versus affectivity in family role expectations

Instrument Description: Subjects are asked if they agree or disagree with each of 9 items.

Reference:

Podell, L. (1967). Occupational and familial role-expectations. *J Mar Fam, 29,* 492–493.

IV-1/c
1424. PODELL, L. Familial-Occupational Exclusion-Inclusion Scale

Avail: 1966 Ref.

Variables Measured: Attitudes concerning the direct involvement of family members in the husband's occupational life

Instrument Description: Four statements, each responded to with *agree/disagree,* examine attitudes regarding including family members in occupational roles and activities.

Reference:

Podell, L. (1966). Sex and role conflict. *J Mar Fam, 28,* 163–165.

IV-1/IV-2/a
1425. POLGAR, S., & ROTHSTEIN, F. Conjugal Role Index

Avail: NAPS-2

Variables Measured: Marital role separation with regard to task participation, decision-making power, and social participation

Instrument Description: This 15-item questionnaire examines joint versus separate roles of the marital relationship.

Reference:

Polgar, S., & Rothstein, F. (1970). Family planning and conjugal roles in New York City poverty areas. *Social Sci Med, 4,* 135–139.

IV-1/c
1426. PROPPER, A. M. Household Chores Scale

Avail: NAPS-2

Variables Measured: Frequency of performing various household tasks

Instrument Description: Subjects indicate how frequently they perform each of 23 household chores.

Reference:

Propper, A. M. (1972). The relationship of maternal employment to adolescent roles, activities, and parental relationships. *J Mar Fam, 34,* 417–421.

IV-1/a
1427. SCHNAIBERG, A. Nuclear Family Role Structure Index

Avail: 1970 Ref.

Variables Measured: Husband and wife acceptance of traditional marital roles

Instrument Description: The wife is asked 19 questions dealing with her acceptance of a male-dominated relationship and behavioral freedoms she maintains within the relationship.

Reference:

Schnaiberg, A. (1970). Measuring modernism: Theoretical and empirical explorations. *Am J Sociol, 76,* 399–425.

IV-1/a
1428. STOKES, C. S. Family Role Structure

Avail: NAPS-2

Variables Measured: Joint versus segregated role relations and decision-making processes

Instrument Description: Either or both partners are given a 17-item questionnaire dealing with family activities and decisions. Subjects indicate which of them is most likely to be actively involved in various decisions.

Reference:

Stokes, C. S. (1973). Family structure and socio-economic differentials in fertility. *Pop Stud, 27,* 295–304.

IV-1/g/a
1429. THEODORSON, G. A. Romanticism Index

Avail: 1965 Ref.

Variables Measured: Romantic versus contractual view toward marriage

Instrument Description: Five multiple-choice items examine the extent to which the subject views marriage as a romantic undertaking versus a contractual arrangement between the partners.

Reference:

Theodorson, G. A. (1965). Romanticism and motivation to marry in the U.S., Singapore, Burma, and India. *Social Forc, 44,* 17–27.

IV-1/III-2/b/C
1430. THOMES, M. M. Children's Concept of Parental Characteristics

Avail: NAPS-2

Variables Measured: Children's perceptions of their mothers' versus fathers' role-related activities within the family

Instrument Description: This measure is an interview in which children, aged 9 to 11, are asked which parent performs each of 15 functions in families where both the mother and the father are present.

Reference:

Thomes, M. M. (1968). Children with absent fathers. *J Mar Fam, 30,* 89–96.

IV-1/c
1431. TOOMEY, D. M. Domestic Tasks Performance Index

Avail: 1971 Ref.

Variables Measured: Husband's performance of traditionally female household tasks

Instrument Description: Husband and wife are each asked questions about the husband's performance of traditionally female household tasks. The husband is asked 6 items, while the wife is asked 3 items.

Reference:

Toomey, D. M. (1971). Conjugal roles and social networks in an urban working class sample. *Human Relat, 24,* 417–431.

IV-1/a
1432. UDRY, J. R., & HALL, M. Role Segregation Index

Avail: 1965 Ref.

Variables Measured: Husband and wife marital roles

Instrument Description: Each partner is asked a series of 25 items examining which of them performs various functions and tasks within the family.

Reference:

Udry, J. R., & Hall, M. (1965). Marital role segregation and social networks in middle-class, middle-aged couples. *J Mar Fam, 27,* 392–395.

IV-1/III-2/b/P
1433. VEROFF, J., & FELD, S. Parental Distancing Index

Avail: 1970 Ref.

Variables Measured: Active involvement in parental role

Instrument Description: Parent is asked open-ended questions, with responses coded for active involvement in the parental role.

Reference:

Veroff, J., & Feld, S. (1970). *Marriage and work in America.* New York: Van Nostrand Reinhold.

IV-1/II-5/c/W

1434. WHITING, J. W. M., CHILD, I. L., & LAMBERT, W. W. Family Structure Scales

Avail: 1966 Ref.

Variables Measured: Mother's responsibility for child training and caretaking, esteem of parents for each other, and mother's authority in family affairs

Instrument Description: Ratings are made of family interactions as they relate to each of the above areas. Repeated observations made over an unspecified period of time are used.

Reference:

Whiting, J. W. M., Child, I. L., & Lambert, W. W. (1966). *Field guide for a study of socialization.* New York: John Wiley.

IV-1/a

1435. WILKENING, E. A., & BHARADWAJ, L. K. Husband-Wife Task Involvement Indexes

Avail: 1967 Ref.

Variables Measured: Rural husband and wife marital roles and responsibilities

Instrument Description: The wife is asked how tasks are actually divided. The husband is asked how he believes they should be divided. Fifteen items are asked of each partner.

Reference:

Wilkening, E. A., & Bharadwaj, L. K. (1967). Dimensions of aspirations, work roles, and decision-making of farm husbands and wives in Wisconsin. *J Mar Fam, 29,* 701–706.

IV-2/II-5/b/C

1436. ALDOUS, J. Adult Role Perception Index

Avail: 1972 Ref.

Variables Measured: Child's perception of his or her father as a powerful leader, authority, disciplinarian, expressive leader, and responsible earner

Instrument Description: This measure was designed for 4- to 5-year-old children. The child responds to 55 items with respect to which member, first of a pretend family and then of his or her real family, best fits the item.

Reference:

Aldous, J. (1972). Children's perceptions of adult role assignment: Father-absence, class, race and sex influences. *J Mar Fam, 34,* 55–65.

IV-2/c
1437. ALKIRE, A. A., GOLDSTEIN, M. J., & WEST, K. L. UCLA Family Project Social Influence and Counterinfluence Coding System

Avail: NAPS-2

Variables Measured: Verbal styles used by family members in attempts to influence each other and counterinfluence strategies used to guard against such pressures

Instrument Description: Family members are instructed to react to simulated interactions as if the other person were present. Other family members react after hearing the initial responses.

Reference:

Alkire, A. A., Goldstein, M. J., Rodnick, E. H., & Judd, L. L. (1971). Social influence and counterinfluence within families of four types of disturbed adolescents. *J Abn Psych, 77,* 32–41.

IV-2/a/C
1438. BAHR, S. J., BOWERMAN, C. E., & GECAS, V. Adolescent Perception of Conjugal Power Index

Avail: 1974 Ref.

Variables Measured: Adolescents' perceptions of which parent rules when there are disagreements and which exerts the primary influence when parents agree

Instrument Description: This index is an 8-item questionnaire with seven possible responses to each item. Responses indicate which parent is dominant in the stated situation.

Reference:

Bahr, S. J., Bowerman, C. E., & Gecas, V. (1974). Adolescent perceptions of conjugal power. *Social Forc, 52,* 357–367.

IV-2/c
1439. BARDIS, P. D. Family Violence Scale

Avail: NAPS-2 & 1973 Ref.

Variables Measured: Extent of violent threats and behaviors within the family

Instrument Description: This scale contains 25 questions regarding the extent of violence within the family.

Reference:

Bardis, P. D. (1973). Violence: Theory and quantification. *J Polit Mil, 1,* 121–146.

IV-2/c/C
1440. BILLER, H. B. Father Dominance Index

Avail: NAPS-2

Variables Measured: Kindergarten children's perceptions of their fathers' versus mothers' dominance in family decision making

Instrument Description: There are 5 items in each of four areas: decision making, competence, nurturance, and limit setting. Child indicates which parent has the primary say in making decisions in each area.

Reference:

Biller, H. B. (1969). Father dominance and sex-role development in kindergarten-age boys. *Devel Psych, 1,* 87–94.

IV-2/a/P
1441. BILLER, H. B. Paternal Dominance and Conflict Situational Task

Avail: NAPS-2

Variables Measured: Father dominance in mother-father interactions

Instrument Description: Interviews, first individually and then together, are conducted with both the mother and the father in which each indicates how they would respond to hypothetical situations. The individual answering first, last, and most frequently is noted.

Reference:

Biller, H. B. (1969). Father dominance and sex-role development in kindergarten-age boys. *Devel Psych, 1,* 87–94.

IV-2/III-2/b/P
1442. ERON, L. D., WALDER, L. O., & LEFKOWITZ, M. M. Parental Restrictiveness Scale

Avail: 1971 Ref.

Variables Measured: Parental control of children's behaviors

Instrument Description: Parents are asked eight questions regarding the amount of control they typically exercise over various children's behaviors.

Reference:

Eron, L. D., Walder, L. O., & Lefkowitz, M. M. (1971). *Learning of aggression in children.* Boston: Little, Brown.

IV-2/a/H
1443. FOX, G. L. Power Index

Avail: 1973 Ref.

Variables Measured: Husband's marital power

Instrument Description: This index has two parts: (1) concerning husband's power in making the final decision in various situations and (2) concerning the extent to which the husband forbids certain behaviors by the wife. A total of 13 items are asked.

Reference:

Fox, G. L. (1973). Another look at the comparative resources model: Assessing the balance of power in Turkish marriages. *J Mar Fam, 35,* 718–730.

IV-2/a
1444. GREENSTEIN, J. M. Father Dominance Rating

Avail: 1966 Ref.

Variables Measured: Husband-wife decision-making dominance

Instrument Description: This is a subjective rating on the part of the interviewer, based on a clinical interview, of comparative dominance of husband versus wife. Interviewer uses a 6-point scale to rate the couple's decision-making process on seven criteria.

Reference:

Greenstein, J. M. (1966). Father characteristics and sex typing. *J Pers Soc Psy, 3,* 271–277.

IV-2/III-2/c/C
1445. KOHN, M. L., & CLAUSEN, J. A. Parental Authority Behavior Checklist

Avail: NAPS-1

Variables Measured: Child's perception of which parent makes decisions and exercises authority for the family

Instrument Description: The child indicates which of 25 traits related to decision-making behavior describe each parent.

Reference:

Kohn, M. L., & Clausen, J. A. (1956). Parental authority behavior and schizophrenia. *Am J Orthop, 26,* 297–313.

IV-2/a
1446. LUPRI, E. Farm Husband Power Questionnaire

Avail: 1969 Ref.

Variables Measured: Husband and wife decision-making power for rural couples

Instrument Description: The wife indicates the extent to which she or her husband typically makes various decisions regarding the running of the farm. Responses are on a 5-point scale, ranging from *husband always decides* to *wife always decides.*

Reference:

Lupri, E. (1969). Contemporary authority patterns in the West German family: A study in cross-national validation. *J Mar Fam, 31,* 134–144.

IV-2/a
1447. LUPRI, E. Urban Husband Authority Questionnaire

Avail: 1969 Ref.

Variables Measured: Husband and wife decision-making power for urban couples

Instrument Description: Wife is interviewed about her relative power in four decision-making situations. Six response categories are allowed for each of four items.

Reference:

Lupri, E. (1969). Contemporary authority patterns in the West German family: A study in cross-national validation. *J Mar Fam, 31,* 134–144.

IV-2/III-2/g/b/C
1448. LYLE, W. H., Jr., & LEVITT, E. E. Problem Situation Test

Avail: NAPS-1

Variables Measured: Child's willingness to punish others

Instrument Description: Children are presented with either of two forms containing 32 open-ended or 14 multiple-choice questions. The child evaluates behaviors of others in a hypothetical situation and decides on an appropriate punishment. Children's behaviors are scored by judges.

Reference:

Lyle, W. H., Jr., & Levitt, E. E. (1955). Punitiveness, authoritarianism, and parental discipline of grade school children. *J Abn Soc Psych, 51,* 42–46.

IV-2/IV-1/c/C
1449. McKINLEY, D. Source of Authority Measure

Avail: 1964 Ref.

Variables Measured: Child's perception of mother's versus father's authority, discipline, and decision-making power within the family

Instrument Description: Three questions are asked, one about each variable. Item scores are summed to come up with an overall index of authority.

Reference:

McKinley, D. (1964). *Social class and family life.* New York: Free Press.

IV-2/a
1450. RYDER, R. G. Problem Inventory

Avail: NAPS-2

Variables Measured: Reactions to marital disputes; ability to reconcile differences

Instrument Description: Subject is presented with two disputes from each of seven problem areas. Options available are to agree with a hypothetical response, modify the response, or to disagree with the response.

Reference:

Ryder, R. G. (1964). Profile factor analysis and variable factor analysis. *Psychol Rep, 15,* 119–127.

IV-2/III-2/c/P
1451. SCHULMAN, R. E., SHOEMAKER, D. J., & MOELIS, I. Laboratory Measurement of Parental Frustration and Model Behavior

Avail: 1962 Ref.

Variables Measured: Parental direction, rejection, hostility, and dominance, both with the child and with the other parent

Instrument Description: Time-sampling of family interactions during 45 minutes of parent-child activities is used as the basis for ratings along the above-listed variables.

Reference:

Schulman, R. E., Shoemaker, D. J., & Moelis, I. (1962). Laboratory measurement of parental behavior. *J Cons Psych, 26,* 109–114.

IV-2/III-2/b/C
1452. SCHWARTZ, A. J. Independence from Family Authority Scale

Avail: 1971 Ref.

Variables Measured: Adolescents' willingness to assume independent behaviors and their attitudes toward parental authority

Instrument Description: Subjects respond to each of 4 items regarding parental authority. Scale was normed on ninth- and twelfth-grade students.

Reference:

Schwartz, A. J. (1971). A comparative study of values and achievement: Mexican-American and Anglo youth. *Sociol Educ, 44,* 438–462.

IV-2/I-4/a

1453. SPEER, D. C. Prisoner's Dilemma Game as a Measure of Marital Interaction

Avail: 1972 Ref.

Variables Measured: Forgiveness, repentance, trust, seduction or set up, retaliation, exploitation, revenge, and distrust as they apply to marital interactions

Instrument Description: This measure is an experimental situation in which husband and wife are seated back-to-back and each can score points only at the expense of the other, but the exact nature of the game is not explained to them. The game is designed such that cooperative behavior is self-defeating.

Reference:

Speer, D. C. (1972). Variations of prisoner's dilemma game as measures of marital interaction: Sequential dyadic measures. *J Abn Psych, 80,* 287–293.

IV-2/II-3/c

1454. STRAUS, M. A., & CYTRYNBAUM, S. Family Power and Support Score System

Avail: NAPS-2

Variables Measured: Personal support and power of family members for each dyadic family relationship

Instrument Description: This is a method for scoring the TAT. Protocols are evaluated for instances of family members' attempting to influence each other or to provide or seek affective support.

Reference:

Straus, M. A., & Cytrynbaum, S. (1962). Support and power structure in Sinhalese, Tamil, and Burgher student families. *Int J Comp, 3,* 138–153.

IV-2/a

1455. TOOMEY, D. M. Marital Power and Decision-Making Index

Avail: 1971 Ref.

Variables Measured: Marital power in singular and joint decision making

Instrument Description: This measure contains 3 items in which responses of partners are compared to determine whether decisions are jointly made.

Reference:

Toomey, D. M. (1971). Conjugal roles and social networks in an urban working class sample. *Human Relat, 24,* 417–431.

IV-2/c/P
1456. WILKENING, E. A. Father-Centered Decision-Making Index

Avail: 1954 Ref.

Variables Measured: Father control for family decisions

Instrument Description: This index has a total of 12 questions, some asked of each partner separately and some of the marital couple while they are together, examining the father's influence in various family decisions.

Reference:

Wilkening, E. A. (1954). Change in farm technology as related to familism, family decision-making, and family integration. *Am Sociol R, 19,* 29–36.

IV-2/a
1457. WILKENING, E. A., & BHARADWAJ, L. K. Husband-Wife-Decision-Making Indexes

Avail: 1967 Ref.

Variables Measured: Decision-making power of husband versus wife in primarily rural settings

Instrument Description: This questionnaire was designed for rural families. A series of 18 questions regarding family decision-making processes are utilized.

Reference:

Wilkening, E. A., & Bharadwaj, L. K. (1967). Dimensions of aspirations, work roles and decision-making of farm husbands and wives in Wisconsin. *J Mar Fam, 29,* 701–706.

IV-2/a
1458. WOLFE, D. M. Marital Authority Index

Avail: 1959 Ref.

Variables Measured: Marital authority, authority types, and shared authority in family situations

Instrument Description: Subjects are asked who makes the final decision in eight family areas. Responses are used to determine the relative authority of husbands and wives as well as the extent to which authority is shared in the marriage.

Reference:

Wolfe, D. M. (1959). Power and authority in the family. In D. Cartwright (Ed.), *Studies in social power* (pp. 99–117). Ann Arbor, MI: Institute of Social Research.

V-1/e
1459. BLOCH, D. A., & BEHRENS, M. L. Multiproblem Family Index

Avail: 1960 Ref.

Variables Measured: Areas of family pathology

Instrument Description: An interview conducted with a social worker familiar with the family serves as the basis for conclusions about several areas of family pathology.

Reference:

Wagner, N. (1960). Developmental aspects of impulse control. *J Cons Psych, 24,* 537–540.

V-1/c
1460. DENTLER, R. A., & MONROE, L. J. Life Chance Scale

Avail: 1961 Ref.

Variables Measured: Quality of the home environment

Instrument Description: Children are asked six questions from which conclusions are drawn regarding the quality of their home environments.

Reference:

Dentler, R. A., & Monroe, L. J. (1961). The family and early adolescent conformity and deviance. *J Mar Fam, 23,* 241–247.

V-1/e
1461. GEISMAR, L. L., LASORTE, M. A., & AYRES, B. St. Paul Scale of Family Functioning

Avail: 1971 Ref.

Variables Measured: Family functioning on each of nine categories and 26 subcategories

Instrument Description: Caseworkers review records of families and judge their functional level on each category and subcategory.

Reference:

Geismar, L. L. (1971). *Family and community functioning: A manual of measurement for social work practice and policy.* Metuchen, NJ: Scarecrow.

V-1/c
1462. GREENBERG, I. M. Family Interaction Questionnaire

Contact: Educational Testing Service, Princeton, NJ

Variables Measured: Family social, emotional, and physical health

Instrument Description: This is a two-hour interview focusing on 13 areas of family health, broadly defined.

Reference:

Greenberg, I. M. (1969). Developmental and clinical correlates of cerebral dysrhythmia. *Arch G Psyc, 21,* 595–601.

V-1/V-2/c
1463. HILL, R. L. Adjustment to Reunion Score

Avail: 1949 Ref.

Variables Measured: Conflicts and readjustment related to husband and wife relations, division of labor, roles, and father-child relations for families with the father returning from war

Instrument Description: The husband or wife indicates the level of adjustment to each of 20 items.

Reference:

Hill, R. L. (1949). *Families under stress: Adjustment to the crises of war separation and reunion.* New York: Harper.

V-1/II-2/g/a/b
1464. HOBART, C. W. Criticism of Parents' Marriage Score

Avail: NAPS-1

Variables Measured: Evaluation of parents' marriage

Instrument Description: This is a 10-item checklist of areas where respondents would like to see their marriages differ from that of their parents.

Reference:

Hobart, C. W. (1958). Emancipation from parents and courtship in adolescents. *Pac Sociol R, 1,* 25–29.

V-1/c
1465. JANSEN, L. T., Jr. Family Solidarity Scales

Avail: NAPS-1

Variables Measured: Family solidarity as indicated by husband-wife agreement, cooperation, concern for others, enjoyment of interpersonal associations, affection, esteem, interest in each other, and confidence or trust

Instrument Description: Five multiple-choice questions are asked for each dimension. All scores are combined to yield the total index.

Reference:

Jansen, L. T., Jr. (1952). Measuring family solidarity. *Am Sociol R, 17,* 727–733.

V-1/c
1466. POULSON, J., WARREN, R., & KENKEL, W. F. Goal Agreement Score

Avail: 1966 Ref.

Variables Measured: Family goals, agreement, agreement of spouse regarding goals, and change in agreement of spouses regarding goals

Instrument Description: The 5 most important from among 15 possible goals are independently selected by each member of the couple. Choices are compared for husbands and wives. One open-ended question is also used.

Reference:

Poulson, J., Warren, R., & Kenkel, W. F. (1966). The measurement of goal agreement between husbands and wives. *Sociol Q, 7,* 480–488.

V-1/c/C
1467. SPREITZER, E. A., & RILEY, L. E. Family of Orientation Pathology Index

Avail: NAPS-2

Variables Measured: Stability versus pathology in family of origin

Instrument Description: Information gathered during a life-history interview is summarized in order to evaluate the extent of pathology present in the subject's family of origin.

Reference:

Spreitzer, E. A., & Riley, L. E. (1974). Factors associated with singlehood. *J Mar Fam, 36,* 533–542.

V-1/I-4/c/C
1468. WAXLER, N. E. Artificial Family Technique

Avail: 1974 Ref.

Variables Measured: Whether family processes cause or are caused by deviant behavior of the child

Instrument Description: Artificial triads are formed from normal or deviant parents and normal or deviant children. Parents and children, both as a family and as separate units, perform a series of 20 tasks.

Reference:

Waxler, N. E. (1974). Parent and child effects on cognitive performance: An experimental approach to the etiological and responsive theories of schizophrenia. *Fam Process, 13,* 1–22.

V-2/I-4/a/g
1469. CLEMENTS, W. H. Interspouse Sensitivity Rating Scale

Avail: 1967 Ref.

Variables Measured: The participant's awareness of the effects of his or her behavior on the spouse in both stable and unstable marriages

Instrument Description: Couples individually rank-order 24 behaviors according to how upsetting they are to themselves and to their spouses.

Reference:

Clements, W. H. (1967). Marital interaction and marital stability: A point of view and a descriptive comparison of stable and unstable marriages. *J Mar Fam, 29,* 697–702.

V-2/III-2/b/P
1470. FARBER, B. Maternal Involvement with Retarded Child Scale

Avail: 1959 Ref.

Variables Measured: The impact of a retarded child on the mother's behaviors

Instrument Description: Four items ask the mother for some of the negative effects of caring for a retarded child.

Reference:

Farber, B. (1959). Effects of a severely retarded child on family integration. *Mon S Res C, 24*(2).

V-2/I-1/a/g
1471. MICHEL, A. Husband-Wife Communication Index

Avail: 1970 Ref.

Variables Measured: Communication about worries and other issues of importance to the wife

Instrument Description: Five-item questionnaire, probably given orally, examines whether the husband asks his wife about various problems or personal issues. It also examines the wife's worries and emotional state.

Reference:

Michel, A. (1970). Wife's satisfaction with husband's understanding in Parisian urban families. *J Mar Fam, 32,* 351–359.

V-3/a/g
1472. THURSTONE, L. L. Attitude Toward Divorce Scale

Avail: 1931 Ref.

Variables Measured: Views on divorce

Instrument Description: Subjects indicate their agreement or disagreement with 22 statements about when divorcing is appropriate.

Reference:

Thurstone, L. L. (1931). *The measurement of social attitudes.* Chicago: University of Chicago Press.

Author Index

Note: Numbers in parentheses refer to abstracts.

721

LEIGH, G. K. (132, Marital Satisfaction), (376, Role Enactment), (377, Role Consensus).

BALDWIN, A. L., KALHORN, J. C., & BREESE, F. H. (1215).

BALDWIN, L. M., see EPSTEIN, N. B. (440).

BALLWEG, J. (1380).

BALSWICK, J. (1014); also see DAVIDSON, B. (181).

BALTHAZAR, E. E., see AUSUBEL, D. P. (1212), (1213).

BANTA, T. J., see ERON, L. D. (1246).

BARANOWSKI, T., RASSIN, D. K., RICHARDSON, C. J., BROWN, J. P., & BEE, D. E. (258).

BARBER, B. K., & THOMAS, D. L. (259).

BARBRACK, C. R., see SANDLER, H. M. (1330).

BARDIS, P. D. (119, Familism), (175, Borromean), (1439, Family Violence).

BARLOW, D. H., BECKER, R., LEITENBERG, H., & AGRAS, W. S. (214).

BARNES, H., & OLSON, D. H. (3).

BARNETT, L. D. (1117); also see KATELMAN, D. K. (1408); STOLKA, S. M. (1205).

BARRETT-LENNARD, G. T. (176).

BARRY, W. A., see RAUSH, H. L. (160).

BARTON, K., see DIELMAN, T. E. (284).

BARTRAN, J. B., see ZUK, G. H. (1374).

BASCOM, H. L., see MICHAELSON, R. (83).

BAUM, M. (1160).

BAUMAN, K. E., see SCHAEFER, E. S. (351).

BAVOLEK, S. J. (260).

BAYLEY, N., see SCHAEFER, E. S. (1332).

BEARD, D. (41).

BEAVERS, W. R., GOSSETT, J., & KELSEY-SMITH, M. (438).

BEAVERS, W. R., HAMPSON, R. B., & HULGUS, Y. F. (42).

BEAVIN, J., see WATZLAWICK, P. (1194).

BECKER, H. J., see EPSTEIN, J. L. (291).

BECKER, R., see BARLOW, D. H. (214).

BECKMAN, L. J. (120).

BEE, D. E., see BARANOWSKI, T. (258).

BEHRENS, M. L. (1216).

BEHRENS, M. L., MEYERS, D. I., GOLDFARB, W., GOLDFARB, N., & FIELDSTEEL, N. D. (1046); also see BLOCH, D. A. (1459).

BEIER, E. G., & STERNBERG, D. P. (133).

BELL, D. C., BELL, L. G., & CORNWELL, C. (4).

BELL, D. C., see BELL, L. G. (44).

BELL, L. G. (43); also see BELL, D. C. (4).

BELL, L. G., CORNWELL, C. S., & BELL, D. C. (44).

BELL, R. Q., see SCHAEFER, E. S. (347), (1332).

BELLAK, L., & BELLAK, S. S. (45).

BELLAK, S. S., see BELLAK, L. (45).

BENE, E., & ANTHONY, J. (46).

BENGTSON, V., see GILFORD, R. (139).

BENGTSON, V. L. (47, Interaction), (177, Positive Affect).

BENNETT, S. M., & DICKINSON, W. B. (215).

BENNUN, I., see RUST, J. (163).

BERARDO, F. M. (1031).

BERDIE, R., see LOEFFLER, D. (1012).

BERG, B., & KURDEK, L. A. (486).

BERG, I. (1047).

BERGAN, J. R., see HENDERSON, R. W. (25).

BERMAN, W. H. (487).

BHARADWAJ, L. K., see WILKENING, E. A. (1158), (1435), (1457).

BIENVENU, M. J., Sr. (5, Marital Communication), (6, Premarital Communication), (7, Parent-Adolescent), (8, Sexual Communication).

BIGNER, J. J. (261, Attitudes Fathering), (262, Father-Child Activity).

BILLER, H. B. (1440, Father Dominance), (1441, Paternal Dominance).

BIRCHLER, G. R., see WEISS, R. L. (113), (116).

BIRD, G. A., see BIRD, G. W. (378).

BIRD, G. W., & BIRD, G. A. (378).

BISHOP, B. M. (1217).

BISHOP, D. S., see EPSTEIN, N. B. (440).

BJORKQUIST, P. A. (379).

BLACKMAN, L. S., see AUSUBEL, D. P. (1212), (1213).

BLAIR, M. A., see COOPER, J. B. (1181).

DENTLER, M., see KOCH, H. L. (1288).
DENTLER, R. A., & MONROE, L. J. (1015, Home Activities), (1237, Interpersonal Relations), (1460, Life Chance).
DENTLER, R. A., & PINEO, P. (1182).
DePALMA-CROSS, A., see LYNN, D. B. (1296).
DEROGATIS, L. R. (223).
DeSALVO, F. J., Jr., & ZURCHER, L. A. (283).
DESKIN, J., see GILBERT, R. (64).
DeTURCK, M. A., & MILLER, G. A. (12).
DEVEREUX, E. C., Jr., see BRONFENBRENNER, U. (266), (267).
DIBBLE, E., see COHEN, D. J. (278).
DICKINSON, W. B., see BENNETT, S. M. (215).
DIELMAN, T. E., & BARTON, K. (284).
DISTLER, L., see MUSSEN, P. H. (1310).
DOMKE, H. R., see GLIDEWELL, J. C. (1260).
DOTSON, L. E., see ROBERTSON, L. S. (1170).
DOWDALL, J. A. (1393).
DREGER, R. M. (285).
DRISCOLL, R., DAVIS, K. E., & LIPETZ, M. E. (1162, Feelings Questionnaire), (1163, Parental Interference).
DROLETTE, M. E., see FUNKENSTEIN, D. H. (1259).
DRUCKMAN, J. M., see OLSON, D. H. (157).
DUBERMAN, L. (488).
DUKES, J., see BLECHMAN, E. A. (9); MADANES, C. (421).
DUNN, M. S. (383).
DYER, E. D. (1016, Democratic Companionship), (1017, Leisure Time), (1136, Marital Agreement), (1197, Parenthood Crisis).
DYK, R. B., & WITKIN, H. A. (1238).
DYSART, B., see KOCH, H. L. (1288).

EASTERBROOKS, M. A., & GOLDBERG, W. A. (286).
EASTON, M., see HATFIELD, E. (183).
EDGERTON, M., see SCHAEFER, E. S. (348), (349), (427).

EDMONDS, V. H. (138).
EDWARDS, J. N., see BOOTH, A. (134); JOHNSON, D. R. (144), (145); WHITE, L. (117), (173).
EDWARDS, J. N., & BRAUBURGER, M. B. (1239).
EGAN, K. J., see LINEHAN, M. M. (320).
EGGEMAN, K., see SCHUMM, W. R. (101).
EGINTON, R., see KELSO, J. (146).
EIDELSON, R. J., & EPSTEIN, N. (182).
ELDER, G. H. (287).
ELDER, G. H., Jr. (1006, Maternal Explanations), (1240, Independence Training).
ELIAS, G. (288).
EMERY, R. E. (289, Children's Perception), (489, Acrimony Scale).
EMMERICH, W. A. (1241, Child Nurturance-Control), (1242, Role Conception), (1243, Parental Nurturance-Control), (1244, Role Perceptions), (1245, Parental Role).
ENGLUND, C. L. (248).
EPSTEIN, A. S. (290).
EPSTEIN, J. L., & BECKER, H. J. (291).
EPSTEIN, J. L., & McPARTLAND, J. M. (292, Decision-Making), (293, Rules).
EPSTEIN, N., see EIDELSON, R. J. (182); PRETZER, J. (456).
EPSTEIN, N. B., BALDWIN, L. M., & BISHOP, D. S. (440).
EPSTEIN, N. B., see SIGAL, J. J. (1105).
ERICSON, P. M., & ROGERS, L. E. (412).
ERON, L. D., BANTA, T. J., WALDER, L. O., & LAULICHT, J. H. (1246).
ERON, L. D., WALDER, L. O., & LEFKOWITZ, M. M. (1063, Parental Disharmony), (1247, Home Aggression), (1248, Dependency Conflict), (1249, Punishment), (1250, Nurturance), (1251, Rejection), (1252, Sanctions for Aggression), (1253, Shaming), (1442, Restrictiveness).
ERON, L. D., WALDER, L. O., TOIGO, R., & LEFKOWITZ, M. M. (1254).
ESHLEMAN, J. R. (1137).
EVANS, R. B. (1064).
EYBERG, S. M., & ROBINSON, E. A. (294).

GIDDINGS, C. W., see ANDERSON, S. A. (236).

GILBERT, L. A., & HANSON, G. R. (300).

GILBERT, R., SALTAR, K., DESKIN, J., KARAGOZIAN, A., SEVERANCE, G., & CHRISTENSEN, A. (64).

GILDEA, M. C.-L., see GLIDEWELL, J. C. (1260).

GILFORD, R., & BENGTSON, V. (139).

GILNER, F., see SWENSEN, C. H. (207).

GINSBERG, B., see STOVER, L. (205), (244).

GJERDE, P. F., BLOCK, J., & BLOCK, J. H. (301).

GLASGOW, R. E., see CHRISTENSEN, A. (274), (275), (276).

GLASS, D. C., see BRIM, O. G., Jr. (1003), (1221).

GLEZER, H. (125, Family Values), (302, Living at Home).

GLIDEWELL, J. C., GILDEA, M. C.-L., KANTOR, M. B., MENSH, I. N., DOMKE, H. R., & BUCHMUELLER, A. D. (1260).

GLUECK, E. T., see GLUECK, S. (1261).

GLUECK, S., & GLUECK, E. T. (1261).

GNEZDA, T., see HOCK, E. (468).

GOETTING, A. (491).

GOLDBERG, W. A. (384); also see EAS-TERBROOKS, M. A. (286); GREEN-BERGER, E. (303).

GOLDFARB, N., see BEHRENS, M. L. (1046).

GOLDFARB, W., see BEHRENS, M. L. (1046).

GOLDSMITH, J., see AHRONS, C. R. (1), (483), (484), (485).

GOLDSTEIN, M. J., see ALKIRE, A. A. (1437).

GOLOMBOK, S., see RUST, J. (163), (233).

GONYEA, J. G., see MONTGOMERY, R. J. V. (476).

GOODMAN, N., & OFSHE, R. (1007, Communication Efficiency), (1184, Empathy).

GOODRICH, D. W., & BOOMER, D. S. (1068).

GOOSMAN, E. T., see BLAZIER, D. C. (1130).

GORDON, T. (1008, Listening for Feelings), (1262, Parental Authority).

GOSSETT, J., see BEAVERS, W. R. (438).

GOTTMAN, J. M., see LEVENSON, R. W. (75).

GOTTMAN, J. M., NOTARIUS, C. I., & MARKMAN, H. J. (65).

GRACE, H. A., & LOHMANN, J. J. (1263).

GRAYSON, M., see SAUNDERS, D. G. (99).

GRAZIANO, W., see RICKARD, K. (337).

GREBSTGEIN, L. C., see TAVITIAN, M. L. (461).

GREEN, L. A., see TAVITIAN, M. L. (461).

GREEN, L. W., see CARLAN, R. W. (1054).

GREEN, R. G. (140), (492); also see KOLEVZON, M. S. (448).

GREEN, V. P. (493).

GREENBERG, I. M. (1462).

GREENBERG, J., see BOSS, P. (34).

GREENBERG, M. (1199).

GREENBERG, M. T., see ARMSDEN, G. C. (40); FRIEDRICH, W. N. (467).

GREENBERGER, E., GOLDBERG, W. A., & CRAWFORD, T. J. (303).

GREENE, R. J., see RABIN, A. I. (254).

GREENE, W. M., see HAUSER, S. T. (306).

GREENGLASS, E. R., see DANZIGER, K. (1005).

GREENSTEIN, J. M. (1164, Father Closeness), (1444, Father Dominance).

GREENWOOD, P., see GEER, J. H. (225).

GREER, S. A., see WINCH, R. F. (1044).

GRIEST, D. L., see FOREHAND, R. L. (299).

GROAT, H. T., see NEAL, A. G. (154).

GROTEVANT, H. D., see CONDON, S. M. (57).

GRUNEBAUM, H., see COHLER, B. J. (279).

GUERNEY, B. G., Jr. (443, Family Life); also see SCHLEIN, S. (100), (200); STOVER, L. (205), (244).

GUERNEY, B. G., Jr., & CAVANAUGH, J. (66).

GUERNEY, B. G., Jr., STOVER, L., & O'CONNELL, M. (1264).

GUIDUBALDI, J., & CLEMINSHAW, H. K. (304).

KIRKPATRICK, C. (1146, Family Interests), (1411, Family Opinion).
KITSON, G. C. (497).
KLAPP, O. E. (1021, Family Ritual), (1084, Family Solidarity).
KLATSKIN, E. H., JACKSON, E. B., & WILKIN, L. C. (1286).
KLEIN, D. M., see JORGENSEN, S. R. (27).
KLEIN, M. M., PLUTCHIK, R., & CONTE, H. R. (1287).
KLEINER, R. J., see PARKER, S. (1422).
KLING, F., see ZUK, G. H. (1374).
KNAUB, P. K., & HANNA, S. L. (498, Remarried Family), (499, Remarried Family/Children).
KNOX, D. (186).
KOCH, A. (471).
KOCH, H. L., DENTLER, M., DYSART, B., & STREIT, H. (1288).
KOHLI, G., see HAHLWEG, K. (15).
KOHN, M. L. (316).
KOHN, M. L., & CLAUSEN, J. A. (1445).
KOLEVZON, M. S., & GREEN, R. G. (448).
KOOMEN, W., see MIDDENDORP, C. P. (1121).
KOVAL, J., see JOANNING, H. (16).
KUETHE, J. L. (187).
KURDEK, L. A., see BERG, B. (486).
KURTZ, R. A., see WOLFENSBERGER, W. (1371).
KVEBAEK, D., see CROMWELL, R. (58).

LaFORGE, R., & SUCZEK, R. S. (242).
LAING, R. D., PHILLIPSON, H., & LEE, A. R. (1187).
LAKIN, M. (1412).
LAMBERT, W. W., see WHITING, J. W. M. (1362), (1363), (1434).
LAMOUSE, A. (1413).
LANDIS, P. H., see STONE, C. L. (1346).
LANER, M. R. (419).
LANGE, S., see WORELL, J. (213).
LANSKY, L. (1289).
LARSEN, A. S., see McCUBBIN, H. I. (473),; OLSON, D. H. (452).
LARZELERE, R. E., & HUSTON, T. L. (188).
LASORTE, M. A., see GEISMAR, L. L. (1461).

LAULICHT, J. H., see ERON, L. D. (1246).
LAUMANN, E. O. (1414).
LAVEE, Y., see OLSON, D. H. (453).
LAVIN, D. E., see BRIM, O. G., Jr. (1003), (1221).
LAWTON, J. T., COLEMAN, M., BOGER, R., GALEJS, I., PEASE, D., PORESKY, R., & LOONEY, E. (317).
LAZARUS, R. S., see KANNER, A. D. (470).
LEAPER, P. M., see COX, F. N. (1231).
LEARY, T. F. (1188).
LeCOMTE, G. K., see LeCOMTE, W. F. (1022).
LeCOMTE, W. F., & LeCOMTE, G. K. (1022).
LEDERHAUS, M. A. (420).
LEE, A. R., see LAING, R. D. (1187).
LEFCOURT, H. M., see MILLER, P. C. (85).
LEFCOURT, H. M., see MILLER, R. S. (194).
LEFKOWITZ, M. M., see ERON, L. D. (1063), (1247), (1248), (1249), (1250), (1251), (1252), (1253), (1254), (1442).
LEIDERMAN, G. F., see LEIDERMAN, P. H. (1165).
LEIDERMAN, P. H., & LEIDERMAN, G. F. (1165).
LEIGH, G. K., see BAHR, S. J. (132), (376), (377).
LEITENBERG, H., see BARLOW, D. H. (214).
LEMKIN, J., see KAGAN, J. (1283).
LEON, G. R. (1290).
LERNER, A., see MANSON, M. P. (150), (1149).
LESLIE, G. R., & JOHNSEN, K. P. (1291).
LESLIE, L. A. (318, Parental Influence Dating), (319, Parental Reaction Dating).
LESSER, G. S., see KANDEL, D. B. (1033).
LETON, D. A. (1292).
LEVENSON, R. W., & GOTTMAN, J. M. (75).
LEVIN, D. M., see TURNER, R. J. (39).
LEVIN, H., see SEARS, R. R. (354).
LEVINGER, G. (1407).
LEVINGER, G., & GUNNER, J. (1085).

MARTIN, M., see MARTIN, D. V. (78).

MARWELL, G., see SCHMITT, D. R. (1333).

MASCHHOFF, T. A., FANSHIER, W. E., & HANSEN, D. J. (229).

MASH, E. J., TERDAL, L. G., & ANDERSON, K. A. (324).

MATHES, E. W. (193).

MAXWELL, J. W., & MONTGOMERY, J. E. (1201).

MAXWELL, P. H., CONNOR, R., & WALTERS, J. (1300).

McARTHUR, D. S., see ROBERTS, G. E. (96).

McBRIDE, S., see HOCK, E. (468).

McCLEERY, R. L. (1416).

McCUBBIN, H. I. (472); also see McCUBBIN, M. A. (450); OLSON, D. H. (452); SKINNER, D. A. (458).

McCUBBIN, H. I., & COMEAU, J. K. (449).

McCUBBIN, H. I., McCUBBIN, M. A., & THOMPSON, A. I. (28).

McCUBBIN, H. I., OLSON, D. H., & LARSEN, A. S. (473).

McCUBBIN, H. I., & PATTERSON, J. M. (390, A-FILE), (474, FILE).

McCUBBIN, H. I., & THOMPSON, A. I. (79, Celebrations), (80, Traditions).

McCUBBIN, M. A. (475); also see McCUBBIN, H. I. (28).

McCUBBIN, M. A., McCUBBIN, H. I., & THOMPSON, A. I. (450).

McDONALD, A. P., Jr. (1417).

McENROE, M. J. (81); also see BLECHMAN, E. A. (9).

McHUGH, G. (82, Courtship), (230, Sex Knowledge).

McINTYRE, J., see KING, K. (1410).

McKINLEY, D. (1166, Emotional Support), (1301, Father's Hostility), (1302, Socialization), (1449, Source of Authority).

McLEOD, J. M. (1303).

McMAHON, R. J., see FOREHAND, R. L. (299).

McPARTLAND, J. M., see EPSTEIN, J. L. (292), (293).

MEADOW, A., see JOHNSON, M. H. (1081).

MEADOW, K. P., & SCHLESINGER, H. S. (1304).

MECIA, B., see WATZLAWICK, P. (1194).

MEDNICK, M. T., see BACHMAN, J. G. (1214).

MEHRABIAN, A., see FALENDER, C. A. (295).

MELTON, W. (391).

MENSH, I. N., see GLIDEWELL, J. C. (1260).

MERCIER, J. M. (127).

METZGER, H. F., see BOLLES, M. (1219).

MEYER, M. M., & TOLMAN, R. S. (1305).

MEYERS, C. E., MINK, I. T., & NIHIRA, K. (325).

MEYERS, D. I., see BEHRENS, M. L. (1046).

MICHAELSON, R., & BASCOM, H. L. (83).

MICHEL, A. (1471).

MIDDENDORP, C. P., BRINKMAN, W., & KOOMEN, W. (1121).

MIDDLETON, M. R., see ROELOFSE, R. (457).

MILLER, B. B. (1167).

MILLER, B. C. (84, Companionate Activities), (151, Marital Satisfaction), (392, Role Socialization), (393, Role Transitions).

MILLER, G. A., see DeTURCK, M. A. (12).

MILLER, K. A., & INKELES, A. (1122).

MILLER, K. A., see INKELES, A. (1020).

MILLER, L., see KINSTON, W. (447).

MILLER, P. C., LEFCOURT, H. M., & WARE, E. E. (85).

MILLER, R. L., see ZUK, G. H. (1374).

MILLER, R. S., & LEFCOURT, H. M. (194).

MILNER, J. S. (423).

MINDEL, C. H. (394).

MINDEL, C. H., & WRIGHT, R., Jr. (29).

MINK, I. T., see MEYERS, C. E. (325).

MISHLER, E. G., & WAXLER, N. (1089).

MITCHELL, R. E. (1090).

MOELIS, I., see SCHULMAN, R. E. (1451).

MOERK, E. L. (326).

MONROE, L. J., see DENTLER, R. A. (1015), (1237), (1460).

MONTGOMERY, J. E., see MAXWELL, J. W. (1201); STINNETT, N. (1127), (1156).

PARKER, G., TUPLING, H., & BROWN, L. (327).
PARKER, S., & KLEINER, R. J. (1422).
PARKS, P. L., & SMERIGLIO, V. L. (328).
PARRY, G., & WARR, P. (396).
PATE, L. E., see GARRISON, J. P. (415).
PATTERSON, G. R. (454); also see WEISS, R. L. (114).
PATTERSON, G. R., RAY, R. S., SHAW, D. A., & COBB, J. A. (91).
PATTERSON, J. M., see McCUBBIN, H. I. (390), (474).
PAUL, E., see LINEHAN, M. M. (320).
PEARCE-McCALL, D., see BOSS, P. (34).
PEARLIN, L. I. (329, Parental Stress), (1315, Parental Aspirations).
PEARLIN, L. I., YARROW, M. R., & SCARR, H. A. (1316).
PEASE, D., see CRASE, S. J. (281); LAWTON, J. T. (317).
PEED, S., see FOREHAND, R. L. (299).
PELL, B., see CUBER, J. F. (1119).
PENDLETON, B. F., POLOMA, M. M., & GARLAND, T. N. (397).
PERDUE, O. R., & SPIELBERGER, C. D. (1317).
PEROSA, L. M., & PEROSA, S. L. (92).
PEROSA, S. L., see PEROSA, L. M. (92).
PERRIS, C., JACOBSSON, L., LINDSTROM, H., VON KNORRING, L., & PERRIS, H. (330).
PERRIS, H., see PERRIS, C. (330).
PERSHING, B. (93).
PETERMAN, D. J., RIDLEY, C. A., & ANDERSON, S. M. (1168).
PETERSON, D. R. (477).
PETERSON, E. T. (1318).
PETRICH, B. A. (1124).
PHILLIPS, S. B., see CHRISTENSEN, A. (274), (275), (276).
PHILLIPSON, H., see LAING, R. D. (1187).
PIERCY, F. P., see HOVESTADT, A. J. (446).
PIKAS, A. (1319).
PILLITTERI, A., see SEIDL, F. W. (1337).
PINEO, P., see DENTLER, R. A. (1182).
PINO, C. J., SIMONS, N., & SLAWINOWSKI, M. J. (455).
PINTLER, M. H., see SEARS, R. R. (1102).

PITTS, M. W., see BOLLES, M. (1219).
PLESS, I. B., & SATTERWHITE, B. (159).
PLOMIN, R., see DANIELS, D. (240).
PLUTCHIK, R., see KLEIN, M. M. (1287).
PODELL, L. (1423, Role Expectation), (1424, Familial-Occupational).
POLGAR, S., & ROTHSTEIN, F. (1425).
POLOMA, M. M., see PENDLETON, B. F. (397).
PORESKY, R., see LAWTON, J. T. (317).
PORESKY, R. H. (331).
PORTER, B. (332); also see O'LEARY, K. D. (424).
PORTNER, J., see OLSON, D. H. (453).
POTKAY, C. R., see ALLEN, B. P. (235).
POULSON, J., WARREN, R., & KENKEL, W. F. (1466).
POWER, T. G., see SLATER, M. A. (358).
POWERS, S. I., see HAUSER, S. T. (306).
POWERS, W. G., & HUTCHINSON, K. (18).
PRATT, L. (398).
PRENTICE, N. M., see JURKOVIC, G. J. (1281).
PRENTICE-DUNN, S., see CAMPIS, L. K. (273).
PRESTON, A., see CRANDALL, V. J. (1232), (1233); KATKOVSKY, W. (1284).
PRETZER, J., EPSTEIN, N., & FLEMING, B. (456).
PRICE, S. J. (425).
PRINZ, R. J. (94, Conflict Behavior), (333, Home Report), (334, Interaction Behavior), (335, Issues).
PROCIDANO, M. E., & HELLER, K. (38).
PROPPER, A. M. (1426).
PUMROY, D. K. (336).
PURCELL, K., & CLIFFORD, E. (1169).

RABIN, A. I. (1320).
RABIN, A. I., & GREENE, R. J. (254).
RABINER, E. L., see WELLS, C. F. (1195).
RABSON, A., see CRANDALL, V. J. (1232), (1233).
RADIN, N., & WEIKART, P. (1321).
RADKE, M. J. (1322, Doll Play), (1323, Parent's Inventory).

ROTHBART, M. K., & MACCOBY, E. E. (1328).

ROTHBAUM, F., & SCHNEIDER-ROSEN, K. (345).

ROTHSTEIN, F., see POLGAR, S. (1425).

RUBENSTEIN, J. L. (1329).

RUBIN, Z. (197).

RUFF, M., see BLECHMAN, E. A. (9).

RUST, J., BENNUN, I., CROWE, M., & GOLOMBOK, S. (163).

RUST, J., & GOLOMBOK, S. (233).

RYDER, R. G. (198, Lovesickness), (1450, Problem Inventory).

SABAGH, G., see LOCKE, H. J. (17).

SABATELLI, R. M. (164).

SAFILIOS-ROTHSCHILD, C. (1100, Communication), (1152, Satisfaction/Mentally Ill), (1153, Marital Satisfaction).

SALTAR, K., see GILBERT, R. (64).

SAMENFINK, J. A. (1126).

SANDER, J., see SIGEL, I. E. (357).

SANDLER, H. M., & BARBRACK, C. R. (1330).

SANDLER, I. N., WOLCHIK, S. A., BRAVER, S. L., & FOGAS, B. S. (502).

SANFORD, D. G. (426).

SANTA-BARBARA, J., see SKINNER, H. A. (459).

SANTROCK, J. W., & WARSHAK, R. A. (98).

SATTERWHITE, B., see PLESS, I. B. (159).

SAUNDERS, D. G., LYNCH, A. B., GRAYSON, M., & LINZ, D. (99).

SAUNDERS, M. M., see SCHAEFER, E. S. (351).

SCANZONI, J. (403, Roles), (1154, Perceived Hostility), (1331, Nurture and Control); also see MORGAN, M. Y. (152).

SCARR, H. A., see PEARLIN, L. I. (1316).

SCHAEFER, C., see KANNER, A. D. (470).

SCHAEFER, E. S. (346).

SCHAEFER, E. S., & BELL, R. Q. (347).

SCHAEFER, E. S., BELL, R. Q., & BAYLEY, N. (1332).

SCHAEFER, E. S., & EDGERTON, M.

(348, Parental Values), (349, Parental Modernity), (427, Autonomy & Relatedness).

SCHAEFER, E. S., & FINKELSTEIN, N. W. (350).

SCHAEFER, E. S., INGRAM, D. D., BAUMAN, K. E., SIEGEL, E., & SAUNDERS, M. M. (351).

SCHAEFER, E. S., & MANHEIMER, H. (479).

SCHAEFER, M. T., & OLSON, D. H. (199).

SCHALOCK, H. D., see MOUSTAKAS, C. E. (1308).

SCHECK, D. C. (352, Inconsistent Discipline), (428, Parental Expectations).

SCHIESSL, D., see YOURGLICH, A. (1045).

SCHINDLER, L., see HAHLWEG, K. (15).

SCHLEIN, S., & GUERNEY, B. G., Jr. (100).

SCHLEIN, S., GUERNEY, B. G., Jr., & STOVER, L. (200).

SCHLEIN, S., see STOVER, L. (205), (244).

SCHLESINGER, H. S., see MEADOW, K. P. (1304).

SCHMITT, D. R., & MARWELL, G. (1333).

SCHNAIBERG, A. (1038, Extended Family Ties), (1204, Child Dependency), (1427, Family Roles).

SCHNEIDER, C., see HELFER, R. E. (309).

SCHNEIDER-ROSEN, K., see ROTHBAUM, F. (345).

SCHPOONT, S. H., see AUSUBEL, D. P. (1212), (1213).

SCHRODER, H. M., see CROUSE, B. (1061).

SCHULMAN, M. L. (1101).

SCHULMAN, R. E., SHOEMAKER, D. J., & MOELIS, I. (1451).

SCHULTZ, K. V. (31).

SCHUMM, W. R. (353, Parental Satisfaction), (429, Marital Conflict).

SCHUMM, W. R., EGGEMAN, K., & MOXLEY, V. (101).

SCHUMM, W. R., JURICH, A. P., & BOLLMAN, S. R. (165, Family Satisfaction), (166, Marital Satisfaction).

WALKER, A. J., & THOMPSON, L. (211).

WALKER, A. J., see THOMPSON, L. (209).

WALLACE, K. M., see LOCKE, H. J. (149).

WALLIN, P., see BURGESS, E. W. (1053), (1134).

WALSTER, E., UTNE, M. K., & TRAUPMANN, J. (111).

WALTER, C. L., see BORKIN, J. (10).

WALTERS, J., IRELAND, F., STROM-BERG, F. I., & LONIAN, G. (1359).

WALTERS, J., see MAXWELL, P. H. (1300).

WAMPLER, K. S., & HALVERSON, C. F., Jr. (463).

WANT, C. K. A., & THURSTONE, L. L. (1208).

WARE, E. E., see MILLER, P. C. (85).

WARR, P., see PARRY, G. (396).

WARREN, R., see POULSON, J. (1466).

WARSHAK, R. A., see SANTROCK, J. W. (98).

WASIK, B. H., & BRYANT, D. (371).

WATZLAWICK, P., BEAVIN, J., SIKORSKI, L., & MECIA, B. (1194).

WAXLER, N., see MISHLER, E. G. (1089).

WAXLER, N. E. (1468).

WEATHERLY, D. (1360).

WECHSLER, H., & FUNKENSTEIN, D. H. (1361).

WEIKART, P., see RADIN, N. (1321).

WEINRAUB, M., see WOLF, B. (372).

WEINSTEIN, E. A., & GEISEL, P. N. (1114).

WEINSTEIN, L. (1175).

WEIS, D. L. (112, Marital Exclusivity), (234, Sex-Love-Marriage).

WEISS, J. L., see COHLER, B. J. (279).

WEISS, R. L., & BIRCHLER, G. R. (113).

WEISS, R. L., & CERRETO, M. C. (172).

WEISS, R. L., PATTERSON, G. R., HOPS, H., & WILLS, T. A. (114).

WEISS, R. L., SUMMERS, K. J., & FENN, D. (115).

WEISS, R. L., VINCENT, J. P., & BIRCHLER, G. R. (116).

WEISS-PERRY, B., see HAUSER, S. T. (306).

WELKOWITZ, J., see AUSUBEL, D. P. (1212), (1213).

WELLS, C. F., & RABINER, E. L. (1195).

WENTE, A. S., & CROCKENBERG, S. B. (256).

WEST, K. L., see ALKIRE, A. A. (1437).

WHITE, J. G. (212).

WHITE, L., BOOTH, A., JOHNSON, D. R., & EDWARDS, J. N. (173).

WHITE, L., see BOOTH, A. (134); JOHN-SON, D. R. (144), (145).

WHITE, L., JOHNSON, D. R., BOOTH, A., & EDWARDS, J. N. (117).

WHITING, J. W. M., CHILD, I. L., & LAMBERT, W. W. (1362, Socialization Techniques), (1363, Maternal Behavior), (1434, Family Structure).

WHITING, J. W. M., see SEARS, R. R. (1336).

WILKENING, E. A. (1129, Familism), (1456, Father-Centered).

WILKENING, E. A., & BHARADWAJ, L. K. (1158, Aspirations), (1435, Task Involvement), (1457, Decision-Making).

WILKIN, L. C., see KLATSKIN, E. H. (1286).

WILLIAMS, A. M. (174).

WILLIAMS, J. R., & SCOTT, R. B. (1364).

WILLIAMS, W. C. (1365).

WILLIAMSON, J. B. (1209).

WILLIAMSON, R. C., see LOCKE, H. J. (1148).

WILLIS, R. H. (1366, Authoritarian Upbringing), (1367, Obedience).

WILLS, T. A., see WEISS, R. L. (114).

WILSON, L. R., see TALLMAN, I. (1352).

WINCH, R. F., & GREER, S. A. (1044).

WINDER, C. L., & RAU, L. (1368).

WINTERBOTTOM, M. R. (1369).

WITKIN, H. A., see DYK, R. B. (1238).

WITTEMAN, H., see FITZPATRICK, M. A. (413).

WITTENBORN, J. R. (1370).

WODTLI, T., see SUNDBERG, N. (1108), (1349).

WOLCHIK, S. A., see SANDLER, I. N. (502).

WOLF, B., WEINRAUB, M., & HAIMO, S. (372).

Title Index

Anticipatory Role Socialization Measure [MILLER, B. C.] (392).

APPROACH: A Procedure for Patterning the Responses of Adults and Children [CALDWELL, B. M., & HONIG, A. S.] (270).

Approval of Home Aggression Scale [ERON, L. D., WALDER, L. O., & LEFKOWITZ, M. M.] (1247).

Areas of Change Questionnaire (AC) [WEISS, R. L., & BIRCHLER, G. R.] (113).

Artificial Family Technique [WAXLER, N. E.] (1468).

Assessment of Parental Training Conditions Interview [CROSS, H. J.] (1234).

Attachment Index [LEIDERMAN, P. H., & LEIDERMAN, G. F.] (1165).

Attachment Inventory [SCHAEFER, E. S., INGRAM, D. D., BAUMAN, K. E., SIEGEL, E., & SAUNDERS, M. M.] (351).

Attachment Scale [THOMPSON, L., & WALKER, A. J.] (209).

Attachment to Family of Orientation Index [CRAWFORD, C. O.] (1060).

Attempt to Influence Parental Reaction to Dating Relationship Scale (AIPRDR) [LESLIE, L. A.] (318).

Attitude of Mother of Hospitalized Child Toward Husband [MURSTEIN, B. I.] (1309).

Attitude Toward Any Homemaking Activity [KELLAR, B.] (1409).

Attitude Toward Birth Control Scale [WANT, C. K. A., & THURSTONE, L. L.] (1208).

Attitude Toward Divorce Scale [THUR-STONE, L. L.] (1472).

Attitude Towards Children's Freedom Scale [KOCH, H. L., DENTLER, M., DY-SART, B., & STREIT, H.] (1288).

Attitudes and Beliefs about Breastfeeding [BARANOWSKI, T., RASSIN, D. K., RICHARDSON, C. J., BROWN, J. P., & BEE, D. E.] (258).

Attitudes to Having Children [CALLAN, V. J.] (271).

Attitudes Toward Child Behavior Scale [STOGDILL, R. M.] (1193).

Attitudes Toward Childlessness [BLAKE, J.] (246).

Attitudes Toward Divorce Scale

[KINNAIRD, K. L., & GERRARD, M.] (496).

Attitudes Toward Fathering Scale [BIGNER, J. J.] (261).

Attitudes Toward Marital Exclusivity Scale [WEIS, D. L.] (112).

Attitudes Toward Marriage Scale [KINNAIRD, K. L., & GERRARD, M.] (147).

Attitudes Toward Married Women's Employment Scale [DOWDALL, J. A.] (1393).

Attitudes Toward Multigenerational Households [MINDEL, C. H.] (394).

Attitudes Toward Parental Control of Children [STOGDILL, R. M.] (1345).

Attitudes Towards Family Planning Education Scale [MERCIER, J. M.] (127).

Attributions Regarding Conflict [MAD-DEN, M. E., & JANOFF-BULMAN, R.] (422).

Authoritarian Child Attitudes Scale [COUCH, A. S.] (1389).

Authoritarian Upbringing Test (UPB) [WIL-LIS, R. H.] (1366).

Autonomy and Relatedness Inventory (ARI) [SCHAEFER, E. S., & EDGERTON, M.] (427).

The Autonomy-Control Scale (A-C Scale) [DE MAN, A. F.] (282).

Autonomy for Women Attitude Inventory [CAMERON, C.] (1388).

Autonomy in Decision-Making Index [DAN-ZIGER, K.] (1235).

The (Barrett-Lennard) Relationship Inventory [BARRETT-LENNARD, G. T.] (176).

Beavers Interactional Scales [BEAVERS, W. R., GOSSETT, J., & KELSEY-SMITH, M.] (438).

Behavioral Coding System [FOREHAND, R. L., PEED, S., ROBERTS, M., McMAHON, R. J., GRIEST, D. L., & HUMPHREYS, L.] (299).

Behavioral Measure of Empathy [GUERNEY, B. G., Jr., STOVER, L., & O'CONNELL, M.] (1264).

Beier-Sternberg Discord Questionnaire (DQ) [BEIER, E. G., & STERN-BERG, D. P.] (133).

Belief About Vasectomy Index [RO-BERTO, E. I.] (1177).

Beliefs About the Consequences of Mater-

Children's Perception Questionnaire (CPQ) [EMERY, R. E.] (289).

Children's Responsibility Inventory [WALTERS, J., IRELAND, F., STROMBERG, F. I., & LONIAN, G.] (1359).

Children's Version Family Environment Scale (CFES) [PINO, C. J., SIMONS, N., & SLAWINOWSKI, M. J.] (455).

Child Responsibility and Independence Indexes [HARRIS, I. D., & HOWARD, K. I.] (1266).

Child Socialization Techniques Scales [WHITING, J. W. M., CHILD, I. L., & LAMBERT, W. W.] (1362).

Child's Non-Adherence to Parental Advice Scale [SMALL, S. A.] (360).

Child's Perception of Parental Behavior [MUSSEN, P. H., & DISTLER, L.] (1310).

Child's Report of Parental Behavior Inventory (CRPBI) [SCHAEFER, E. S.] (346).

The Child Study Inventory (CSI) [RABIN, A. I., & GREENE, R. J.] (254).

Child-Years-of-Dependency Measure (CYD) [SCHNAIBERG, A.] (1204).

Cleminshaw Guidubaldi Parent Satisfaction Scale [GUIDUBALDI, J., & CLEMINSHAW, H. K.] (304).

Clinical Assessment System (CAS) [HUDSON, W. W.] (71).

Clinical Rating Scale (CRS) for the Circumplex Model of Marital and Family Systems [OLSON, D. H.] (90).

Closeness to Parent [BOWERMAN, C. E., & IRISH, D. P.] (264).

A Coding Scheme for Interpersonal Conflict (CSIC) [RAUSH, H. L., BARRY, W. A., HERTEL, R. K., & SWAIN, M. A.] (160).

Cognitive Home Environment Scale [RADIN, N., & WEIKART, P.] (1321).

Color Flag Test [FERREIRA, A. J.] (1183).

Color-Matching Technique [GOODRICH, D. W., & BOOMER, D. S.] (1068).

Commitment Attitude Questionnaire [MURSTEIN, B. I., & MacDONALD, M. G.] (153).

Communication Congruence Measure [ANANDAM, K., & HIGHBERGER, R.] (1211).

Communication Efficiency Test [GOODMAN, N., & OFSHE, R.] (1007).

Communication Patterns Questionnaire [CHRISTENSEN, A., & SULLAWAY, M.] (11).

The Communication Rapid Assessment Scale (CRAS) [JOANNING, H., BREWSTER, J., & KOVAL, J.] (16).

Communication Scale [SWEETSER, D. A.] (1042).

Communication Skills Test (CST) [FLOYD, F. J., & MARKMAN, H. J.] (14).

Communication Style Q-Set (CSQS) [STEPHEN, T. D., & HARRISON, T. M.] (20).

Companionate Activities Measure [MILLER, B. C.] (84).

Comparative Family Modernism-1 Scale [INKELES, A., & MILLER, K. A.] (1020).

Competitiveness Scale [LANER, M. R.] (419).

Composite Measure of Family Relations [BACHMAN, J. G., MEDNICK, M. T., DAVIDSON, T. N., & JOHNSTON, L. D.] (1214).

Concern for Pressures and Sanctions That Accompany Nonparenthood [HOUSEKNECHT, S. K.] (253).

The Conflict Behavior Questionnaire (CBQ) [PRINZ, R. J.] (94).

Conflict Tactics Scales (CTS) [STRAUS, M. A.] (435).

Conflicts with Mother Checklist [BLOCK, V. L.] (1218).

Conforming Family Life-Style Scale [STROUP, A. L., & ROBINS, L. N.] (1024).

Conjugal Organization Index [PRATT, L.] (398).

Conjugal Role Index [POLGAR, S., & ROTHSTEIN, F.] (1425).

Conjugal Understanding Measure [DeTURCK, M. A., & MILLER, G. A.] (12).

Contact Comfort Ratings [KING, D. L.] (1285).

Content of Coparental Interaction [AHRONS, C. R., & GOLDSMITH, J.] (483).

Contraceptive Information Index [HILL,

dex [UDRY, J. R., & HALL, M.] (1043).

Intergenerational Continuity Index [AL-DOUS, J.] (1030).

Intergeneration Communication Questionnaire [LOEFFLER, D., BERDIE, R., & ROTH, J.] (1012).

Interpersonal Checklist (ICL) [LaFORGE, R., & SUCZEK, R. S.] (242).

Interpersonal Grid [LEVINGER, G., & GUNNER, J.] (1085).

Interpersonal Perception Method (IPM) [LAING, R. D., PHILLIPSON, H., & LEE, A. R.] (1187).

The Interpersonal Relationship Scale (IRS) [SCHLEIN, S., GUERNEY, B. G., Jr., & STOVER, L.] (200).

Interpersonal Relations Scale [DENTLER, R. A., & MONROE, L. J.] (1237).

Interspousal Agreement Index [CARLAN, R. W., REYNOLDS, R., GREEN, L. W., & KHAN, N. I.] (1054).

Interspouse Sensitivity Rating Scale [CLEMENTS, W. H.] (1469).

Intimacy and Disputing Styles [ALFORD, R. D.] (409).

Intimacy Scale [WALKER, A. J., & THOMPSON, L.] (211).

Intimacy Status Interview and Rating Manual [ORLOFSKY, J. L., & LEVITZ-JONES, E. M.] (196).

The Intimate Negotiation Coding System (INCS) [TING-TOOMEY, S.] (109).

Intimate Relationship Scale [HETHERINGTON, S. E.] (251).

Intradyad Purchasing Agreement Scale [LEDERHAUS, M. A.] (420).

Intra-Family Attitude Scales [ITKIN, W.] (314).

Intrafamily Identification Measures [COUNT-VanMANEN, G.] (1230).

Intra-Family Relationships Questionnaire [MYERS, T. R.] (1093).

Inventories of Pre-Marital, Marital, Parent-Child, and Parent-Adolescent Conflict [OLSON, D. H.] (89).

Inventory of Alternative Attractions (IAA) [GREEN, R. G.] (140).

Inventory of Beliefs About Wife Beating (IBWB) [SAUNDERS, D. G., LYNCH, A. B., GRAYSON, M., & LINZ, D.] (99).

Inventory of External Pressures to Remain Married (IEP) [GREEN, R. G.] (492).

Inventory of Family Feelings (IFF) [LOWMAN, J.] (191).

Inventory of Parent-Adolescent Communication [BARNES, H., & OLSON, D. H.] (3).

Inventory of Parent and Peer Attachment (IPPA) [ARMSDEN, G. C., & GREENBERG, M. T.] (40).

Inventory of Rewarding Activities (IRA) [WEISS, R. L., VINCENT, J. P., & BIRCHLER, G. R.] (116).

Inventory of Sexual Decision-Making Factors [CHRISTOPHER, F. S., & CATE, R. M.] (221).

The Iowa Parent Behavior Inventory (IPBI) [CRASE, S. J., CLARK, S. G., & PEASE, D.] (281).

Issues Checklist (IC) [PRINZ, R. J.] (335).

Job-Family Role Strain Scale [BOHEN, H. H., & VIVEROS-LONG, A.] (465).

Judgement of Punishment Scale (JUP) [ERON, L. D., WALDER, L. O., & LEFKOWITZ, M. M.] (1249).

The Juvenile Love Scale (JLS) (A Child's Version of the Passionate Love Scale) [HATFIELD, E., & EASTON, M.] (183).

Kansas Family Life Satisfaction Scale [SCHUMM, W. R., JURICH, A. P., & BOLLMAN, S. R.] (165).

Kansas Marital Conflict Scales [SCHUMM, W. R.] (429).

Kansas Marital Goals Orientation Scale [SCHUMM, W. R., EGGEMAN, K., MOXLEY, V.] (101).

Kansas Marital Satisfaction Scale [SCHUMM, W. R., JURICH, A. P., & BOLLMAN, S. R.] (166).

Kansas Parental Satisfaction Scale [SCHUMM, W. R.] (353).

Kategoriensystem fur Partnerschaftliche Interaktion (KPI) [HAHLWEG, K., REISNER, L., KOHLI, G., VOLLMER, M., SCHINDLER, L., & REVENSTORF, D.] (15).

Kell-Hoeflin Incomplete Sentence Blank: Youth-Parent Relations [HOEFLIN, R., & KELL, L.] (1274).

[SCHWARZWELLER, H. K., & LYSON, T. A.] (1334).

Perceived Parent Attitude Rating [AUSUBEL, D. P., BALTHAZAR, E. E., ROSENTHAL, I., BLACKMAN, L. S., SCHPOONT, S. H., & WELKOWITZ, J.] (1213).

Perceived Role Discrepancy (PRO) and Imputed Role Consensus (IRC) Scores [HAWKINS, J. L., & JOHNSEN, K. P.] (1398).

Perceived Social Support—Family (PSS-Fa) [PROCIDANO, M. E., & HELLER, K.] (38).

Perception of Older Marriages Scale (POM) [STINNETT, N., & MONTGOMERY, J. E.] (1127).

Perception of Parent Role Performance Questionnaire [MAXWELL, P. H., CONNOR, R., & WALTERS, J.] (1300).

Perceptions of Appropriate and/or Expected Grandparent Behavior [ROBERTSON, J. F.] (401).

Perceptions of Family Questionnaire [WECHSLER, H., & FUNKENSTEIN, D. H.] (1361).

Perception of Interpersonal Hostility Scale and Perception of Marital Interaction Scale [SMITH, J. R.] (1172).

Perceptions of Parental Role Scales (PPRS) [GILBERT, L. A., & HANSON, G. R.] (300).

Perceptual Indicators of Family Well-Being: Resource Exchange Theory [RETTIG, K. D., & BUBOLZ, M. M.] (399).

Perinatal Anxieties and Attitudes Scale (PAAS) [FIELD, T.] (249).

Personal Assessment of Intimacy in Relationships (PAIR) Inventory [SCHAEFER, M. T., & OLSON, D. H.] (199).

Personal Growth in Marriage Index [DENTLER, R. A., & PINEO, P.] (1182).

Personal Network Inventory [OLIVERI, M. E., & REISS, D.] (37).

Personal Report of Spouse Communication Apprehension (PRSCA) [POWERS, W. G., & HUTCHINSON, K.] (18).

Pervasiveness of Kinship Organization Index [ABRAHAMSON, M.] (1029).

Picture Q. Technique (PQT) [TIFFANY, D. W.] (1354).

The Pie [COWAN, C. P., & COWAN, P. A.] (239).

Porter Parental Behavior and Feelings Inventory [PORTER, B.] (332).

Positive Affect Index: Subjective Solidarity Between Parents and Children [BENGTSON, V. L.] (177).

Positive Attitudes Toward Living at Home [GLEZER, H.] (302).

Positive Feelings Questionnaire (PFQ) [O'LEARY, K. D., FINCHAM, F., & TURKEWITZ, H.] (195).

Postdivorce Problems and Stress Scale (PPSS) [RASCHKE, H. J.] (501).

Power Index [FOX, G. L.] (1443).

Premarital Attitude Scale [OLSON, D. H. L.] (1123).

A Premarital Communication Inventory (PCI) [BIENVENU, M. J., Sr.] (6).

Price Decision-Making Scale [PRICE, S. J.] (425).

Primary Communication Inventory (PCI) [LOCKE, H. J., SABAGH, G., & THOMES, M. M.] (17).

Prisoner's Dilemma Game as a Measure of Marital Interaction [SPEER, D. C.] (1453).

Problem Inventory [RYDER, R. G.] (1450).

The Problem Situations Scale [CHRISTENSEN, A., PHILLIPS, S. B., GLASGOW, R. E., & JOHNSON, S. M.] (275).

Problem Situation Test [LYLE, W. H., Jr., & LEVITT, E. E.] (1448).

A Procedure for Analyzing Family Interaction from Video Tapes [BORKE, H.] (1049).

Provision of Social Relations (PSR) [TURNER, R. J., FRANKEL, B. G., & LEVIN, D. M.] (39).

Psycholinguistic Classification System for Analyzing Mother-Child Interactions [MOERK, E. L.] (326).

Psychophysiological Measures of Female Sexual Arousal [GEER, J. H., MOROKOFF, P., & GREENWOOD, P.] (225).

Psychophysiological Measures of Male Sexual Arousal [BARLOW, D. H.,

(T-JTA) [TAYLOR, R. M., & MORRISON, L. P.] (245).

Taylor's Affiliation Inventory [TAYLOR, J.] (108).

Taylor's Control Inventory [TAYLOR, J.] (437).

Teacher Attitude Toward Divorce and the Role of the School [GREEN, V. P.] (493).

Terman Marital Prediction Test [TERMAN, L. M.] (1110).

A Test of Family Attitudes [JACKSON, L.] (1080).

Thematic Apperception Test (TAT) [MURRAY, H. A.] (86).

Three-Way Family Interaction Task [MARTIN, B.] (1088).

Timing of Parenthood Scale (ATOP) [MAXWELL, J. W., & MONTGOMERY, J. E.] (1201).

Traditional-Developmental Family Role Concepts Scale [BLOOD, R. O., Jr.] (1382).

Traditional-Emerging Beliefs About Families [PETRICH, B. A.] (1124).

Traditional Family Ideology Scale (TFI) [LEVINSON, D. J., & HUFFMAN, P. E.] (126).

Traditional Family Values [GLEZER, H.] (125).

Traditional Marital Role Relations Index [LAUMANN, E. O.] (1414).

Transition Difficulty [STEFFENSMEIER, R. H.] (255).

Turning Point Code I [SURRA, C. A.] (206).

Two-Factor Marital Satisfaction Scale [GILFORD, R., & BENGTSON, V.] (139).

UCLA Family Project Social Influence and Counterinfluence Coding System [ALKIRE, A. A., GOLDSTEIN, M. J., & WEST, K. L.] (1437).

A Unit Method of Coding Unfamiliar Interaction [GUTTMAN, H. A.] (1069).

Unqualified Power Assertion Index (UPA) [HOFFMAN, M. L.] (1277).

Upsetting Behavior Questionnaire [CHRISTENSEN, A., PHILLIPS, S. B., GLASGOW, R. E., & JOHNSON, S. M.] (276).

Urban Husband Authority Questionnaire [LUPRI, E.] (1447).

Value of Children (VOC) [FAWCETT, J. T.] (123).

Value Parent Scale [SEVERY, L. J.] (1103).

Verbal Exchange Analysis [DANZIGER, K., & GREENGLASS, E. R.] (1005).

Verbal Interaction Compliance-Gaining Coding Scheme (VICS) [FITZPATRICK, M. A., & WITTEMAN, H.] (413).

The View Sharing Inventory (VSI) [GUERNEY, B. G., Jr., & CAVANAUGH, J.] (66).

The Washington Family Role Inventory [NYE, F. I., & GECAS, V.] (395).

What Are My Jobs? [HARRIS, D. B., CLARK, K. E., ROSE, A. M., & VALASEK, F.] (1397).

The "Who Does What?" [COWAN, C. P., & COWAN, P. A.] (382).

Wife's Self-Sufficiency Score [HILL, R. L.] (1019).

Wife Works Scale [NELSON, H. Y.] (1419).

Women's Life Style Attitude Scale [BURNS, M. S. A.] (1385).

Yale Marital Interaction Battery [BUERKLE, J. V., & BADGLEY, R. F.] (1384).

Youth Information and Opinion Form [SMITH, T. E.] (364).

Classification Index

Note: The initial numbers in parentheses refer to abstracts; the following numbers denote classification.

I-1/a—Communication (husband-wife)

KOVAL, J. The Communication Rapid Assessment Scale (CRAS) (16: I-1/a).

KAHN, M. Marital Communication Scale (1010: I-1/a).

KARLSSON, G. Spousal Communication Indexes (1011: I-1/a).

LOCKE, H. J., SABAGH, G., & THOMES, M. M. Primary Communication Inventory (PCI) (17: I-1/a).

POWERS, W. G., & HUTCHINSON, K. Personal Report of Spouse Communication Apprehension (PRSCA) (18: I-1/a).

STEPHEN, T. D., & HARRISON, T. M. Communication Style Q-Set (CSQS) (20: I-1/a).

VINCENT, J. P., COOK, N. I., & BRADY, C. P. Marital Coding System (MCS) (22: I-1/III-1/a).

I-1/b—Communication (parent-child)

BARNES, H., & OLSON, D. H. Inventory of Parent-Adolescent Communication (3: I-1/b).

BIENVENU, M. J., Sr. Parent-Adolescent Communication Inventory (PACI) (7: I-1/b/C).

BRIM, O. G., Jr., GLASS, D. C., & LAVIN, D. E. Parent Decision Process Test (1003: I-1/III-2/b).

BUGENTAL, D. B. Measure of Conflicting Communication (1004: I-1/b).

DANZIGER, K., & GREENGLASS, E. R. Verbal Exchange Analysis (1005: I-1/b).

ELDER, G. H., Jr. Index of Maternal Explanations (1006: I-1/III-2/b/C).

GORDON, T. Listening for Feelings of Children (1008: P/I-1/III-2/b).

LOEFFLER, D., BERDIE, R., & ROTH, J. Intergeneration Communication Questionnaire (1012: I-1/III-2/b).

I-1/c—Communication (nuclear family)

ALEXANDER, J. F. Defensive and Supportive Communication Interaction System (2: I-1/c).

ALKIRE, A. A. Parent-Child Communication Assessment (1002: I-1/c).

BELL, D. C., BELL, L. G., & CORN-WELL, C. Interaction Process Coding Scheme (IPCS) (4: I-1/c).

BLECHMAN, E. A., McENROE, M. J., RUFF, M., CARR, R., ACHATZKES, A., SHEIBER, F., & DUMAS, J. Blechman Interaction Scoring System (BLISS) (9: I-1/c).

REISS, D. Lattice Language Communication Task (1013: I-1/c).

REISS, D. Pattern Recognition Card Sort for Families (19: I-1/c).

TITTLER, B. I., FRIEDMAN, S., & SEEMAN, L. The Tailored Family Interaction Measurement Method (21: I-1/c).

I-2/a—Life-Style (husband-wife)

BALSWICK, J. Spouse Participation Support Scale (1014: I-2/a).

ORTHNER, D. K. Leisure Activity-Interaction Index (LAII) (30: I-2/a).

SCHULTZ, K. V. The Lifestyle Profile Series (31: I-2/a).

SCHWARZ, J. C. Schwarz Inter-Parental Conflict Scale (IPC) (430: I-2/a).

SEKARAN, U. Integration (33: I-2/I-4/a).

I-2/b—Life-Style (parent-child)

HENDERSON, R. W., BERGAN, J. R., & HURT, M., Jr. Henderson Environmental Learning Process Scale (HELPS) (25: I-2/III-2/b/C).

LeCOMTE, W. F., & LeCOMTE, G. K. Family Traditionalism Scales (1022: I-2/I-4/b/g/C).

I-2/c—Life-Style (nuclear family)

BOHEN, H. H., & VIVEROS-LONG, A. Family Management Scale (23: I-2/IV-1/c/e).

CALDWELL, B. M., & BRADLEY, R. H. Home Observation for Measurement of the Environment (HOME) (24: I-2/III-2/c/P).

DENTLER, R. A., & MONROE, L. J. Home Centered Activity Scale (1015: I-2/c/e/C).

DYER, E. D. Democratic Companionship Conception of the Family (1016: I-2/II-2/c).

BELL, D. C. Global Coding Scheme (44: I-4/c).

BELLAK, L., & BELLAK, S. S. Children's Apperception Test (CAT) (45: I-4/c/C).

BENE, E., & ANTHONY, J. Family Relations Test (46: I-4/c).

BLINN, L. M. Family Photo Assessment Process (FPAP) (48: I-4/c).

BORKE, H. A Method for Systematically Observing Family Interaction (1048: I-4/c).

BORKE, H. A Procedure for Analyzing Family Interaction from Video Tapes (1049: I-4/c).

BOWERMAN, C. E., & KINCH, J. W. Family-Peer Group Orientation Questionnaire (1050: I-4/c/e/C).

BRIM, O. G., Jr., FAIRCHILD, R. W., & BORGATTA, E. F. Family Problems Index (1051: I-4/c).

BURNS, R. C., & KAUFMAN, S. H. Kinetic Family Drawing (K-F-D) (52: I-4/c/C).

CATTELL, R. B., & CABOT, P. S. Family Attitude Scales (1055: I-4/c).

CAVAN, R. Rating Scales for Family Integration and Adaptability (1056: I-4/c).

CHANCE, E. Family Interaction Scoring System (1057: I-4/IV-2/c).

COBB, H. V. Sentence-Completion Wish Test (1058: I-4/c/C).

CONDON, S. M., COOPER, C. R., & GROTEVANT, H. D. Family Discourse Code (57: I-4/c/C).

COUGHENOUR, M. C. Family Functions of Activities in Food Consumption (1059: I-4/c/W).

CRAWFORD, C. O. Attachment to Family of Orientation Index (1060: I-4/c).

CROMWELL, R., FOURNIER, D., & KVEBAEK, D. The Kvebaek Family Sculpture Technique (KFST) (58: I-4/c).

ERON, L. D., WALDER, L. O., & LEFKOWITZ, M. M. Parental Disharmony Scale (1063: I-4/c).

EVANS, R. B. Family Background Questionnaire (1064: I-4/II-4/c/C).

FERDINAND, T. N., & LUCHTERHAND, E. G. Family Background Scores (1066: I-4/c/g/C).

GEHRING, T. M. Family System Test (FAST) (62: I-4/IV-2/c).

GERARD, D. L., & SIEGEL, J. Family Background Interview and Rating Scales (1067: I-4/c).

GERBER, G. L., & KASWAN, J. W. Family Distance Doll Placement Technique (63: I-4/c).

GILBERT, R., SALTAR, K., DESKIN, J., KARAGOZIAN, A., SEVERANCE, G., & CHRISTENSEN, A. The Family Alliances Coding System (FACS) (64: I-4/c).

GUTTMAN, H. A. A Unit Method of Coding Unfamiliar Interaction (1069: I-4/c).

HALEY, J. Family Interaction Patterns (1070: I-4/c).

HANNUM, J. W., & CASALNUOVO, J. Family Interaction Coding System (FICS) (67: I-4/c).

HAWORTH, M. R. Rock-a-Bye Baby (Projective Film for Children) (1072: I-4/c/C).

HAYWARD, R. S. Family Inventory (1073: I-4/c).

HESTON, J. C. Heston Personal Adjustment Inventory (1075: I-4/c/C).

HOWELLS, J. G., & LICKORISH, J. R. Family Relations Indicator (FRI) (70: I-4/c).

JACKSON, L. A Test of Family Attitudes (1080: I-4/c/C).

KINSTON, W., LOADER, P., & STRATFORD, J. Current Family State Assessment (CFSA) (74: I-4/c).

KLAPP, O. E. Family Solidarity Index (1084: I-4/II-5/c).

LEVINGER, G., & GUNNER, J. Interpersonal Grid (1085: I-4/IV-2/c).

MacFARLANE, J. W. Scales for Rating Family Situations (1087: I-4/c).

MARTIN, B. Three-Way Family Interaction Task (1088: I-4/c).

McCUBBIN, H. I., & THOMPSON, A. I. Family Celebrations Index (FCELEBI) (79: I-4/c).

McCUBBIN, H. I., & THOMPSON, A. I. Family Traditions Scale (FTS) (80: I-4/II-1/c).

McENROE, M. J. Evaluation of the Process and Impact of Communication (EPIC) (81: I-4/c).

MICHAELSON, R., & BASCOM, H. L.

WARE, E. E. Marital Locus of Control Scale (85: I-4/II-2/IV-2/g/a).

SPORAKOWSKI, M. J. Marital Preparedness Instrument (1106: I-4/g).

TERMAN, L. M. Terman Marital Prediction Test (1110: I-4/g).

ZARIT, S. H., REEVER, K. E., & BACH-PETERSON, J. Caregiver Burden Scale (118: I-4/V-2/g/a).

II-1/a—Family Values (husband-wife)

STINNETT, N., & MONTGOMERY, J. E. Perception of Older Marriages Scale (POM) (1127: II-1/a/g/e).

II-1/b—Family Values (parent-child)

FAWCETT, J. T. Value of Children (VOC) (123: II-1/III-1/b/P).

II-1/c—Family Values (nuclear family)

ADAMEK, R. J., & YOST, E. D. Conventionality Index (1116: II-1/I-3/c).

BARNETT, L. D. General Familism Index and Religious Familism Index (1117: II-1/c).

FARBER, B. Index of Consensus (121: II-1/c).

FAVER, C. A. Family Values Scale (122: II-1/c).

LEVINSON, D. J., & HUFFMAN, P. E. Traditional Family Ideology Scale (TFI) (126: II-1/IV-1/c).

MERCIER, J. M. Attitudes Towards Family Planning Education Scale (127: II-1/II-4/c).

MIDDENDORP, C. P., BRINKMAN, W., & KOOMEN, W. Family Liberalism-Conservatism Attitude Index (1121: II-1/c).

PETRICH, B. A. Traditional-Emerging Beliefs About Families (1124: II-1/c).

RAMIREZ, M. III. Mexican-American Family Attitude Scale (1125: II-1/c).

SOURANI, T., & ANTONOVSKY, A. Family Sense of Coherence Scale (FSOC) (130: II-1/c).

TURNER, J. H. Familism-Individualism Scale (1128: II-1/c/C).

II-1/d—Family Values (extended family)

BARDIS, P. D. Familism Scale (119: II-1/d).

GALLAGHER, B. J., III. The Generationalism Scale (124: II-1/d/b).

ROBERTSON, J. F. Meaning of Grandparenthood (129: II-1/d).

WILKENING, E. A. Familism Index (1129: II-1/I-3/d).

II-1/g—Family Values (intrapsychic processes)

BECKMAN, L. J. The Motivations for Children and Work Questionnaire (120: II-1/IV-1/g/W).

CAVAN, R. S. A Dating-Marriage Scale of Religious Social Distance (1118: II-1/g/a).

CUBER, J. F., & PELL, B. Family Moral Judgments Technique (1119: II-1/II-4/g/a/e).

GLEZER, H. Traditional Family Values (125: II-1/g).

HILL, R. L., STYCOS, J. M., & BACK, K. W. Family Size Preference Index (1120: II-1/g).

MILLER, K. A., & INKELES, A. Acceptance of Family Limitation Scale (1122: II-1/g).

O'BRYANT, S. L. Subjective Value of Home Scale (128: II-1/g).

OLSON, D. H. L. Premarital Attitude Scale (1123: II-1/g/a).

SAMENFINK, J. A. Catholic Sexual and Family Ideology Test (1126: II-1/I-2/g/c).

II-2/a—Marital and Family Adjustment (husband-wife)

AZRIN, N. H., NASTER, B. J., & JONES, R. Marital Happiness Scale (131: II-2/a).

BAHR, S. J., CHAPPELL, C. B., & LEIGH, G. K. Marital Satisfaction (132: II-2/a).

BEIER, E. G., & STERNBERG, D. P. Beier-Sternberg Discord Questionnaire (DQ) (133: II-2/a).

MacDougall Marital Adjustment Scale (1150: II-2/a).

NYE, F. I., & MacDOUGALL, E. Spousal Argument Scale (1149: II-2/IV-2/a).

OLSON, D. H., FOURNIER, D. G., & DRUCKMAN, J. M. Enriching and Nurturing Relationship Issues, Communication and Happiness (ENRICH), and Premarital Personal Relationship Evaluation (157: II-2/I-1/a).

ORDEN, S. R., & BRADBURN, N. M. Marriage Adjustment Balance Scale (MABS) (158: II-2/a).

ORT, R. S. Marital Role Conflict Score (1151: II-2/IV-1/a).

RAUSH, H. L., BARRY, W. A., HERTEL, R. K., & SWAIN, M. A. A Coding Scheme for Interpersonal Conflict (CSIC) (160: II-2/IV-2/a).

ROACH, A. J. Marital Satisfaction Scale (MSS): Form B (161: II-2/a).

ROFE, Y. Marital Happiness Scale (162: II-2/a).

RUST, J., BENNUN, I., CROWE, M., & GOLOMBOK, S. The Golombok Rust Inventory of Marital State (GRIMS) (163: II-2/a).

SABATELLI, R. M. The Marital Comparison Level Index (MCLI) (164: II-2/a).

SAFILIOS-ROTHSCHILD, C. Marital Satisfaction Index (1153: II-2/a/W).

SAFILIOS-ROTHSCHILD, C. Marital Satisfaction of Couples with Mentally Ill Partner (1152: II-2/a).

SCANZONI, J. Perceived Hostility Score (1154: II-2/a).

SCHUMM, W. R., JURICH, A. P., & BOLLMAN, S. R. Kansas Marital Satisfaction Scale (166: II-2/a).

SHEINBEIN, M. L. Marital Satisfaction Direct-Report (1155: II-2/a).

SNYDER, D. K. Marital Satisfaction Inventory (MSI) (167: II-2/a).

SPANIER, G. B. Dyadic Adjustment Scale (DAS) (168: II-2/a).

STARR, S., & MANN, J. Marriage Satisfaction Survey (169: II-2/a).

STINNETT, N., COLLINS, J., & MONTGOMERY, J. E. Marital Need Satisfaction Scale (1156: II-2/a).

SWENSEN, C. H., & FIORE, A. Scale of Marriage Problems (170: II-2/a).

TERMAN, L. M. Marital Happiness Index (1157: II-2/a).

UDRY, J. R. Marital Alternatives Scale (171: II-2/a).

WEISS, R. L., & CERRETO, M. C. The Marital Status Inventory (MSI) (172: II-2/a).

WHITE, L., BOOTH, A., JOHNSON, D. R., & EDWARDS, J. N. Nebraska Scale of Marital Disagreement (173:II-2/a).

WILKENING, E. A., & BHARADWAJ, L. K. Husband and Wife Aspirations Indexes (1158: II-2/II-1/a).

WILLIAMS, A. M. Marital Satisfaction Time Lines (MSTL) (174: II-2/a).

II-2/c—Marital & Family Adjustment (nuclear family)

BOWERMAN, C. E., & KINCH, J. W. Family Adjustment Index (1133: II-2/c).

KINNAIRD, K. L., & GERRARD, M. Family Atmosphere Questionnaire (148: II-2/c).

PLESS, I. B., & SATTERWHITE, B. Family Functioning Index (FFI) (159: II-2/c).

SCHUMM, W. R., JURICH, A. P., & BOLLMAN, S. R. Kansas Family Life Satisfaction Scale (165: II-2/c).

II-3/a—Love, Liking, Affection, & Trust (husband-wife)

BARRETT-LENNARD, G. T. The (Barrett-Lennard) Relationship Inventory (176: II-3/a).

BAUM, M. Goals in Marriage Scale (1160: II-3/a).

BRAIKER, H. B., & KELLEY, H. H. Development of Intimate Relationships (178: II-3/a).

CHRISTENSEN, A., & KING, C. E. The Relationship Events Scale (179: II-3/a).

DAVIDSON, B., & BALSWICK, J. The Affective Self-Disclosure Scale for Couples (ASDC) (181: II-3/a).

DRISCOLL, R., DAVIS, K. E., & LIPETZ, M. E. Feelings Questionnaire (1162: II-3/a).

DRISCOLL, R., DAVIS, K. E., &

II-3/b—Love, Liking, Affection, & Trust (parent-child)

II-3/c—Love, Liking, Affection, & Trust (nuclear family)

CONGER, R. D. Social Interaction Scoring System (SISS) (180: II-3/IV-2/c).

KUETHE, J. L. Kuethe's Symbolic Figure Placement Technique (SFPT) (187: II-3/c).

LOWMAN, J. Inventory of Family Feelings (IFF) (191: II-3/c).

STOVER, L., GUERNEY, B. G., Jr., GINSBERG, B., & SCHLEIN, S. The Acceptance of Other Scale (AOS) (205: II-3/c).

UTTON, A. C. Childhood Experience Rating Scales (1174: II-3/c/C).

VAUX, A. Social Support Appraisals Scale (SS-A) (210: II-3/II-5/c/e).

II-3/e—Love, Liking, Affection, & Trust (others outside the family)

HATFIELD, E., & EASTON, M. The Juvenile Love Scale (JLS) (A Child's Version of the Passionate Love Scale) (183: II-3/e/C).

II-3/g—Love, Liking, Affection, & Trust (intrapsychic processes)

BOWERMAN, C. E., & BAHR, S. J. Parental Identification Scale (1161: II-3/g/b/C).

SURRA, C. A. Turning Point Code I (206: II-3/g).

II-4/a—Sex (husband-wife)

BUUNK, B. Actual Sexual Jealousy Scale (218: II-4/II-3/a).

BUUNK, B. Anticipated Sexual Jealousy Scale (219: II-4/II-3/a).

DAVIDSON, J. K., Sr., & DARLING, C. A. Desired Changes in Sex Life Checklist (222: II-4/a).

DEROGATIS, L. R. Derogatis Sexual Functioning Inventory (DSFI) (223: II-4/I-4/a).

HUDSON, W. W. The Index of Sexual Satisfaction (ISS) (227: II-4/a).

LoPICCOLO, J., & STEGER, J. C. The Sexual Interaction Inventory (SII) (228: II-4/a).

MASCHHOFF, T. A., FANSHIER, W. E., & HANSEN, D. J. Sexual and Marital

Impact of Vasectomy (229: II-4/I-4/a/H).

REISS, I. L. Reiss Extramarital Sexual Permissiveness Scales (231: II-4/a/e).

RUST, J., & GOLOMBOK, S. Golombok Rust Inventory of Sexual Satisfaction (GRISS) (233: II-4/a).

WEIS, D. L. The Sex-Love-Marriage Association (SLM) Scale (234: II-4/II-3/a).

II-4/b—Sex (parent-child)

BENNETT, S. M., & DICKINSON, W. B. Sex Education Inventory (SEI) (215: II-4/III-2/b/C).

LIBBY, R. W. Sex Education Liberalism Scale (SELS) (1176: II-4/IV-1/b/e).

II-4/e—Sex (others outside the family)

BRUCE, K. E. M. Herpes Attitudes Scale (HAS) (216: II-4/e).

BRUCE, K. E. M. Herpes Knowledge Scale (HKS) (217: II-4/e).

BUUNK B. Extramarital Behavioral Intentions Scale (220: II-4/e).

CHRISTOPHER, F. S., & CATE, R. M. Inventory of Sexual Decision-Making Factors (221: II-4/e).

REISS, I. L. Reiss Male and Female Premarital Sexual Permissiveness Scales (232: II-4/e).

II-4/g—Sex (intrapsychic processes)

BARLOW, D. H., BECKER, R., LEITENBERG, H., & AGRAS, W. S. Psychophysiological Measures of Male Sexual Arousal (214: II-4/g/H).

FINLAY, B. Scale of Favorability Toward Abortion (224: II-4/g).

GEER, J. H., MOROKOFF, P., & GREENWOOD, P. Psychophysiological Measures of Female Sexual Arousal (225: II-4/g/W).

HENDRICK, S. S., & HENDRICK, C. Sexual Attitudes Scale (226: II-4/g).

McHUGH, G. Sex Knowledge Inventory (230: II-4/g).

ROBERTO, E. I. Belief About Vasectomy Index (1177: II-4/II-5/g/c/H).

III-1/b—Pregnancy, Childbearing, & Transition to Parenthood (parent-child)

GREENBERG, M. Greenberg First-Father Engrossment Survey (1199: III-1/b/P).

III-1/c—Pregnancy, Childbearing, & Transition to Parenthood (nuclear family)

CVETKOVICH, G. T., & LONNER, W. J. Hypothetical Family Questionnaire (HYFAM) (1196: III-1/c).

DYER, E. D. Parenthood Crisis Scale (1197: III-1/c/P).

MAXWELL, J. W., & MONTGOMERY, J. E. Timing of Parenthood Scale (ATOP) (1201: III-1/c).

WENTE, A. S., & CROCKENBERG, S. B. Changes in Routine (256: III-1/c/P).

III-1/e—Pregnancy, Childbearing, & Transition to Parenthood (others outside the family)

HARRIMAN, L. C. Parenthood Adjustment Questionnaire (250: III-1/e/a/P).

HOUSEKNECHT, S. K. Concern for Pressures and Sanctions That Accompany Nonparenthood (253: III-1/e/P).

PAIGE, K. E., & PAIGE, J. M. Husband Involvement During Pregnancy Scale (1202: III-1/e/H).

PAIGE, K. E., & PAIGE, J. M. Maternal Restrictions During Pregnancy Scale (1203: III-1/e/W).

III-1/g—Pregnancy, Childbearing, & Transition to Parenthood (intrapsychic processes)

BLAKE, J. Attitudes Toward Childlessness (246: III-1/g/P).

BRODZINSKY, D. M., SINGER, L. M., & BRAFF, A. M. Adoption Motivation Q-Sort (247: III-1/g/P).

ENGLUND, C. L. Perceived Importance of Children (248: III-1/g/P).

FIELD, T. Perinatal Anxieties and Attitudes Scale (PAAS) (249: III-1/V-2/g/P).

FISCHER, E. H. Birth Planning Attitudes (1198: III-1/g).

HILL, R. L., STYCOS, J. M., & BACK, K. W. Contraceptive Information Index (1200: III-1/g).

HOBBS, D. F., Jr. Difficulty Index for First-Time Parents (252: III-1/g/c/e/d/P).

RABIN, A. I., & GREENE, R. J. The Child Study Inventory (CSI) (254: III-1/g/P).

STEFFENSMEIER, R. H. Transition Difficulty (255: III-1/g/P).

STOLKA, S. M., & BARNETT, L. D. Childbearing Motivation Scales (1205: III-1/I-4/g).

VEROFF, J., & FELD, S. Parental Negative Orientation Index (PNOI) (1206: III-1/g/P).

VEROFF, J., & FELD, S. Parental Restrictiveness Index (PRI) (1207: III-1/g/P).

WANT, C. K. A., & THURSTONE, L. L. Attitude Toward Birth Control Scale (1208: III-1/II-1/g).

WILLIAMSON, J. B. Favorability Toward Birth Control Index (1209: III-1/g).

III-2/a—Parenting (husband-wife)

CALLAN, V. J. Attitudes to Having Children (271: III-2/II-1/a/P).

HEMING, G, COWAN, P. A., & COWAN, C. P. Ideas About Parenting (310: III-2/II-5/a/P).

MURSTEIN, B. I. Attitude of Mother of Hospitalized Child Toward Husband (1309: III-2/a/P).

III-2/b—Parenting (husband-wife)

ABELMAN, R. Parental Disciplinary Orientations (257: III-2/IV-2/b/P).

ACKERLEY, L. A. Ackerley Parental Attitude Scales (1210: III-2/IV-2/b).

ANANDAM, K., & HIGHBERGER, R. Communication Congruence Measure (1211: III-2/I-1/b/P).

AUSUBEL, D. P., BALTHAZAR, E. E., ROSENTHAL, I., BLACKMAN, L. S., SCHPOONT, S. H., & WELKOWITZ, J. Disagreement with Perceived Parent Opinion Test (1212: III-2/b/C).

ing Profile of Parenting (MSPP) (309: III-2/d/e/P).

III-2/e—Parenting (others outside the family)

CONE, J. D., WOLFE, V. V., & DeLAWYER, D. D. Parent/Family Involvement Index (P/FII) (280: III-2/e/b/P).

EPSTEIN, J. L., & BECKER, H. J. Hopkins Surveys of School and Family Connections (291: III-2/e/b/C).

HARRELL, J. E., & RIDLEY, C. A. Parent Satisfaction with Child Care Scale (305: III-2/e/P).

SEIDL, F. W., & PILLITTERI, A. Parent Participation Attitude Scale (1337: III-2/e).

WOLF, B., WEINRAUB, M., & HAIMO, S. Social Network Form (SNF) (372: III-2/I-3/e).

III-2/f—Parenting (siblings)

HELSON, R. Sibling Differences Questionnaire (1270: III-2/f/b/C).

III-2/g—Parenting (intrapsychic processes)

FEINMAN, S. Measure of Disapproval of Cross-Sex Behavior (1257: III-2/g/b/P).

LANSKY, L. Sex-Role Attitude Test (SRAT) (1289: III-2/g/b/P).

OPPENHEIM, A. N. Parent Attitude Inventory (1314: III-2/g/P).

PEARLIN, L. I. Parental Aspirations (1315: III-2/g/P).

PEARLIN, L. I. Parental Stress (329: III-2/V-2/g/P).

REMMERS, H. H., & STEDMAN, L. A. Bringing up Children—An Inventory of Attitudes (1324: III-2/g/b/P).

ROTHBART, M. K., & MACCOBY, E. E. Parental Attitudes About Sex Differences Questionnaire (1328: III-2/g/b/P).

SHAPIRO, M. B. Parental Opinion Inventory (1338: III-2/g/b/P).

SHOBEN, E. J., Jr. Parent Attitude Survey (1341: III-2/g/b/P).

VEROFF, J., & FELD, S. Parental Inadequacy Index (PII) (1358: III-2/g/b/P).

WOLFENSBERGER, W., & KURTZ, R.

A. Parent Realism Assessment Technique (PRAT), and Parental Expectations of Child Development Technique (PECDT) (1371: III-2/g/b/P).

ZUK, G. H., MILLER, R. L., BARTRAN, J. B., & KLING, F. Maternal Acceptance of Retarded Children Questionnaire (1374: III-2/g/b/P).

IV-1/a—Roles (husband-wife)

ALDOUS, J., & STRAUS, M. A. Task Differentiation Index (1377: IV-1/a).

AMATEA, E., & CROSS, G. Life Role Salience Scale (LRSS) (375: IV-1/a).

ARNOTT, C. C. Homemaking Comparison Level of Alternatives (1378: IV-1/a/W).

ARNOTT, C. C. Marital Role Comparison Level Index (1379: IV-1/a/W).

BAHR, S. J., CHAPPELL, C. B., & LEIGH, G. K. Quality of Role Enactment (376: IV-1/a).

BAHR, S. J., CHAPPELL, C. B., & LEIGH, G. K. Role Consensus (377: IV-1/a).

BALLWEG, J. Household Task Performance Index (1380: IV-1/a).

BIRD, G. W., & BIRD, G. A. Family Task Sharing Scale (378: IV-1/a).

BJORKQUIST, P. A. Family Responsibility Index (FRI) (379: IV-1/a).

BLOOD, R. O., Jr. Division of Labor Index (1381: IV-1/a).

BLOOD, R. O., Jr., & HAMBLIN, R. L. Household Task Performance Index (1383: IV-1/a).

BLOOD, R. O., Jr., & WOLFE, D. M. Task Participation Index and Role Specialization Index (380: IV-1/a).

BUERKLE, J. V., & BADGLEY, R. F. Yale Marital Interaction Battery (1384: IV-1/II-2/a).

BURNS, M. S. A. Women's Life Style Attitude Scale (1385: IV-1/II-5/a/g).

BURR, W. R. Marital Role Discrepancy Index (1386: IV-1/a).

BUXBAUM, J. Marital Roles Questionnaire (1387: IV-1/a).

CAMERON, C. Autonomy for Women Attitude Inventory (1388: IV-1/a/g/W).

COUCH, C. J. Role Concept Questionnaire (1391: IV-1/a).

Questionnaire (FRQ) (416: IV-2/II-3/c).

HERBST, P. G. Day at Home (417: IV-2/c).

KOHN, M. L., & CLAUSEN, J. A. Parental Authority Behavior Checklist (1445: IV-2/III-2/c/C).

MADANES, C., DUKES, J., & HARBIN, H. T. Family Hierarchy Test (FHT) (421: IV-2/I-4/c).

McKINLEY, D. Source of Authority Measure (1449: IV-2/IV-1/c/C).

SCHULMAN, R. E., SHOEMAKER, D. J., & MOELIS, I. Laboratory Measurement of Parental Frustration and Model Behavior (1451: IV-2/III-2/c/P).

STANLEY, S. F. Family Decision-Making Attitude Scale (FDMAS) (434: IV-2/c).

STRAUS, M. A. Conflict Tactics Scales (CTS) (435: IV-2/c).

STRAUS, M. A., & CYTRYNBAUM, S. Family Power and Support Score System (1454: IV-2/II-3/c).

STRAUS, M. A., & TALLMAN, I. Simulated Family Activity Measurement (SIMFAM) (436: IV-2/I-4/c).

TAYLOR, J. Taylor's Control Inventory (437: IV-2/c).

WILKENING, E. A. Father-Centered Decision-Making Index (1456: IV-2/c/P).

IV-2/f—Power (siblings)

FURMAN, W., & BUHRMESTER, D. Sibling Relationship Questionnaire (SRQ) (414: IV-2/II-3/f/C).

IV-2/g—Power (intrapsychic processes)

LYLE, W. H., Jr., & LEVITT, E. E. Problem Situation Test (1448: IV-2/III-2/g/b/C).

V-1/a—Overall Family Functioning & Adjustment (husband-wife)

PRETZER, J., EPSTEIN, N., & FLEMING, B. Marital Attitude Survey (MAS). (456: V-1/a).

V-1/c—Overall Family Functioning & Adjustment (nuclear family)

BEAVERS, W. R., GOSSETT, J., & KELSEY-SMITH, M. Beavers Interactional Scales (438: V-1/c).

CALDWELL, S. M. Family Well-Being Assessment (FWA) (439: V-1/V-2/c).

DENTLER, R. A., & MONROE, L. J. Life Chance Scale (1460: V-1/c).

EPSTEIN, N. B., BALDWIN, L. M., & BISHOP, D. S. McMaster Family Assessment Device (FAD) (440: V-1/c).

FRISTAD, M. A. Family Assessment Scale (FAS) (442: V-1/c).

GREENBERG, I. M. Family Interaction Questionnaire (1462: V-1/c).

GUERNEY, B. G., Jr. The Family Life Questionnaire (FLQ) (443: V-1/c).

HILL, R. L. Adjustment to Reunion Score (1463: V-1/V-2/c).

HOVESTADT, A. J., ANDERSON, W. T., PIERCY, F. P., COCHRAN, S. W., & FINE, M. Family of Origin Scale (FOS) (446: V-1/c/d).

JANSEN, L. T., Jr. Family Solidarity Scales (1465: V-1/c).

KINSTON, W., LOADER, P., & MILLER, L. The Family Health Scale (FHS) (447: V-1/c).

KOLEVZON, M. S., & GREEN, R. G. Family Awareness Scales (FAS) (448: V-1/c).

McCUBBIN, H. I., & COMEAU, J. K. Family Inventory of Resources for Management (FIRM) (449: V-1/c).

McCUBBIN, M. A., McCUBBIN, H. I., & THOMPSON, A. I. Family Hardiness Index (FHI) (450: V-1/c).

MOOS, R. H., & MOOS, B. S. Family Environment Scale (FES) (451: V-1/c).

OLSON, D. H., LARSEN, A. S., & McCUBBIN, H. I. Family Strengths Scale (452: V-1/c).

OLSON, D. H., PORTNER, J., & LAVEE, Y. FACES III (Family Adaptability and Cohesion Evaluation Scales) (453: V-1/c).

PATTERSON, G. R. Oregon Social Learning Center (OSLC) Family Crisis List (454: V-1/V-2/c/e).

PINO, C. J., SIMONS, N., &

tated Personal Evaluation Scales (F-COPES) (473: V-2/I-3/c/e).

McCUBBIN, H. I., & PATTERSON, J. M. Family Inventory of Life Events and Changes (FILE) (474: V-2/V-1/c/e).

V-2/d—Stress (extended family)

HOLROYD, J. Questionnaire on Resources and Stress for Families with Chronically Ill or Handicapped Members (QRS) (469: V-2/d).

ROBINSON, B. C. Caregiver Strain Index (CSI) (478: V-2/d).

ZIMMERMAN, S. L. Adult Day Care: Its Coping Effects for Families of Primary Caregivers of Elderly Disabled Persons (482: V-2/d).

V-2/e—Stress (others outside the family)

CALVERT, J. D., MOORE, D., & JENSEN, B. J. Dating Anxiety Survey (DAS) (466: V-2/I-4/e).

V-2/g—Stress (intrapsychic processes)

HOCK, E., GNEZDA, T., & McBRIDE, S. The Maternal Separation Anxiety Scale (MSAS) (468: V-2/III-2/g/P).

MONTGOMERY, R. J. V., GONYEA, J. G., & HOOYMAN, N. R. Measurement of Burden (476: V-2/g/d).

VAN METER, M. J. S. Role Strain Scale (481: V-2/IV-1/g/W).

V-3/a—Divorce, Separation, & Remarriage (husband-wife)

AHRONS, C. R., & GOLDSMITH, J. Feelings and Attitudes Toward Former Spouse (484: V-3/a).

BERMAN, W. H. Ex-Spouse Preoccupation Scale (487: V-3/a).

EMERY, R. E. Acrimony Scale (AS) (489: V-3/a/P).

FISHER, B. F. Fisher Divorce Adjustment Scale (FDAS) (490: V-3/a).

GOETTING, A. Divorce Chain Questionnaire (491: V-3/a).

GREEN, R. G. Inventory of External Pressures to Remain Married (IEP) (492: V-3/V-2/a).

HARDY, K. R. Hardy Divorce Scale (494: V-3/II-1/a).

KINNAIRD, K. L., & GERRARD, M. Attitudes Toward Divorce Scale (496: V-3/II-1/a).

KITSON, G. C. Dimensions of Attachment to the Spouse in Divorce (497: V-3/II-3/a).

THOMPSON, L., & SPANIER, G. B. Acceptance of Marital Termination: The Thompson and Spanier Revision of Kitson's Dimensions of Attachment to the Spouse in Divorce (504: V-3/II-3/a).

THURSTONE, L. L. Attitude Toward Divorce Scale (1472: V-3/a/g).

V-3/b—Divorce, Separation, & Remarriage (parent-child)

AHRONS, C. R., & GOLDSMITH, J. Content of Coparental Interaction (483: V-3/III-2/b/P).

AHRONS, C. R., & GOLDSMITH, J. Nonresidential Parent-Child Involvement Scale (485: V-3/III-2/b/P).

BERG, B., & KURDEK, L. A. Children's Beliefs About Parental Divorce Scales (486: V-3/b/C).

HOBART, C. Semantic Index of Relationships (SIR) (495: V-3/b).

SANDLER, I. N., WOLCHIK, S. A., BRAVER, S. L., & FOGAS, B. S. Divorce Events Schedule for Children (DES-C) (502: V-3/V-2/b/g/C).

SHILLER, V. M. Loyalty Conflict Assessment Test (503: V-3/b/C).

V-3/c—Divorce, Separation, & Remarriage (nuclear family)

DUBERMAN, L. Reconstituted Family Integration Scale (488: V-3/I-1/c).

KNAUB, P. K., & HANNA, S. L. Remarried Family Inventory (498: V-3/I-4/c).

KNAUB, P. K., & HANNA, S. L. Remarried Family Inventory for Children (499: V-3/I-4/c/C).

LOWERY, C. R. Custody Decision Form (CDF) (500: V-3/III-2/c/P).